PEARSON ALWAYS LEARNING

Introduction to Computers and Software Applications with Microsoft® Office 2013

Second Custom Edition for Ocean County College

Taken from:
Technology in Action, Introductory, Thirteenth Edition
by Alan Evans, Kendall Martin, and Mary Anne Poatsy

GO! With Office 2013, Volume 1, First Edition
by Shelley Gaskin, Alicia Vargas, and Carolyn McLellan

Cover Art: Courtesy of Photodisc/Getty Images

Taken from:

Technology in Action, Introductory, Thirteenth Edition
by Alan Evans, Kendall Martin, and Mary Anne Poatsy

New York, NY 10013

GO! With Office 2013, Volume 1, First Edition
by Shelley Gaskin, Alicia Vargas, and Carolyn McLellan

New York, NY 10013

This special edition published in cooperation with Pearson Education, Inc.

Pearson Education, Inc., 330 Hudson Street, New York, New York 10013
A Pearson Education Company
www.pearsoned.com

Printed in the United States of America

1 16

000200010272045132

ES

PEARSON

ISBN 10: 1-323-45578-7
ISBN 13: 978-1-323-45578-4

Contents at a Glance

Chapters 1-3, 5, 7, 9, taken from *Technology in Action, Introductory*, Thirteenth Edition by Alan Evans, Kendall Martin, and Mary Anne Poatsy

Word Chapters 1-3, Excel Chapters 1-3, Access Chapters 1-3, Powerpoint Chapters 1-3, taken from *GO! With Office 2013, Volume 1*, First Edition by Shelley Gaskin, Alicia Vargas, and Carolyn McLellan

Word

Excel

Access

PowerPoint

Technology in Action, Introductory, Thirteenth Edition
by Alan Evans, Kendall Martin, and Mary Anne Poatsy

Chapters 1-3, 5, 7, 9

Contents

Chapter 3

Chapter 5

1 Using Technology to Change the World

Make This: MAKE: A Virtual Assistant on **page 11**

All media accompanying this chapter can be found in MyITLab.

For an overview of the chapter, watch the **Preview Video**.

(John Lund/Blend Images/Getty Images, Carlos Castilla/Shutterstock, Winui/Shutterstock, Sergey Nivens/Shutterstock)

HOW COOL IS THIS?

Want to **make a difference with technology**? The good news is that it has never been easier. Technology is allowing more and more of us to become **agents of change in our communities** and in the world. In London, over 20,000 school-age children are joining **Apps for Good**, a program that links students, educators, and local experts to guide students in designing and building apps to help solve problems they see around them. The **Verizon Innovative App Challenge** led students to develop apps to customize texts for students with dyslexia and apps to help connect people with causes they wanted to support with volunteer time. Civic hacking events, like one called **Random Hacks of Kindness**, are helping people create apps to track lobbyists in government, to map the location of murals in a city, and to help organize people to dig out fire hydrants after snowstorms. What kind of good can you do with technology? *(Aleciccotelli/Fotolia)*

How Will You Put Technology in Action?

Learning Outcome 1.1 You will be able to discuss the impact of technology on global and national issues.

Ask yourself: Why are you in this class? Maybe it's a requirement for your degree, or maybe you want to improve your computer skills. But let's step back and look at the bigger picture.

Technology today is not just a means for career advancement or merely a skill set needed to survive in society. It's a tool that enables us all to make an impact beyond our own lives. We've all seen movies that dangle the dream in front of us of being the girl or guy who saves the world—and gets to drive a nice car while doing it! Whether it's *The Avengers* or *Big Hero 6*, we are drawn to heroes because we want our lives and our work to mean something and to benefit others.

Technology can be your ticket to doing just that, to influencing and participating in projects that will change the world. We'd like to ask you to think about how your talents and skills in technology will let you contribute on a larger scale, beyond the benefits they will bring to you personally.

technology on the WORLD STAGE

Recent political and global issues are showing that technology is accelerating change around the world and galvanizing groups of people in new ways. Let's look at a few examples.

FIGURE 1.1 The Irish referendum on marriage equality meant many Irish living abroad traveled home just to vote, documenting their trips using #HomeToVote. *(Brian Lawless/AP Images)*

Political Issues

Objective 1.1 *Recognize how becoming proficient with technology can help you understand and participate in political issues in the world at large.*

Social Media

Social media tools enable the gathering of groups of people to connect and exchange ideas, and they have brought together people facing repression and censorship in many countries. In fact, in 2014, uprisings in the Ukraine were organized using Facebook pages. Managing control of the media is no longer simple for regimes.

Politicians worldwide have also begun to incorporate social media as part of their political strategy. In the United States, politicians like Barack Obama have Twitter and Facebook accounts that they use to communicate with their constituents. In Italy, Beppe Grillo drew the largest vote in a recent election for a single party using mainly Facebook and Twitter in place of television and newspaper ads, and in the United Kingdom politicians post over two million social media updates a year.

Social media has proven to be a very effective way of motivating people to vote. Ireland has a socially conservative heritage, decriminalizing homosexuality as recently as 1993. In the recent vote on same-sex marriage equality, Irish nationals living abroad—many young and with liberal views—were not allowed to mail in a ballot. Thousands traveled back to Ireland to cast a "yes" vote in support of same-sex marriage, encouraging each other with a Twitter feed #HomeToVote (see Figure 1.1). Facebook posts for the "Yes Equality" page topped 1.6 million. With a large voter turnout, Ireland became the first country to legalize gay marriage through a popular vote.

Social media tools are providing a level of instant connection and information distribution that is reshaping the world. What can you do with social media tools that will change the future of your community?

Crisis-Mapping Tool

Another example of the interaction of technology and society is the software tool Ushahidi. Following a disputed election in

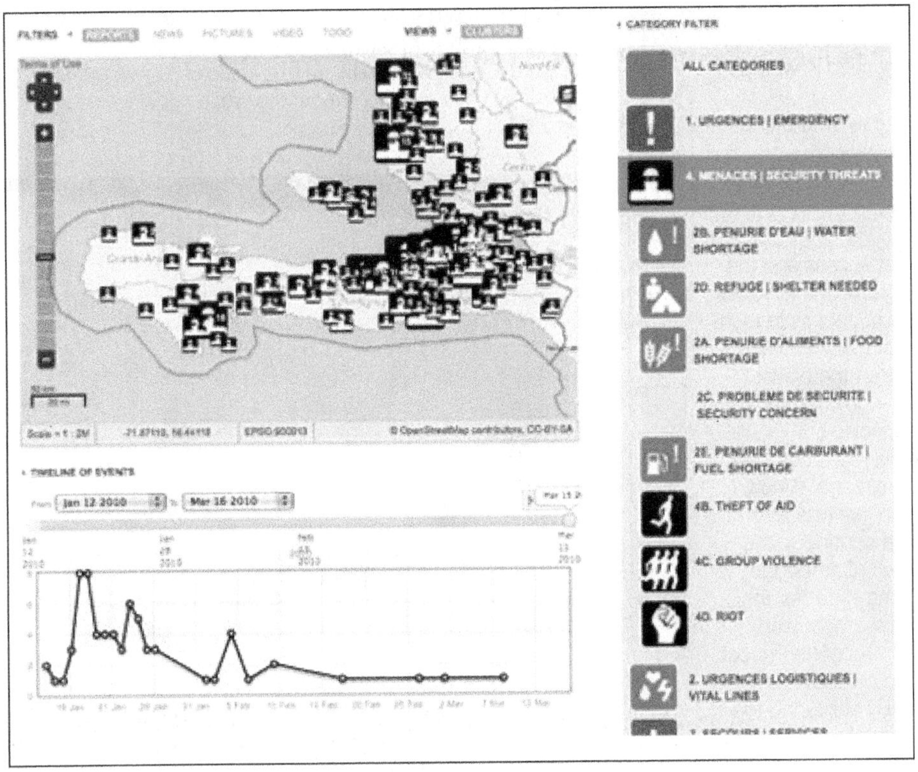

FIGURE 1.2 During a natural disaster in Haiti, Ushahidi crisis-mapping software helped identify areas of violence, helped people locate food and water, and directed rescuers to those in need. *(Reprinted with permission of Ushahidi, Inc. www.ushahidi.com)*

Kenya, violence broke out all over the country. Nairobi lawyer Ory Okolloh tried to get word of the violence out to the world through her blog, but she couldn't keep up with the volume of reports. But two programmers saw her request for help and in a few days created Ushahidi (Swahili for "testimony"). It is a **crisis-mapping tool** that collects information from e-mails, text messages, blog posts, and Twitter tweets and then maps them, instantly making the information publicly available. The developers then made Ushahidi a free platform anyone in the world can use (see Figure 1.2). So when earthquakes rocked Haiti, Ushahidi instantly told rescuers where injured people were located. When a tsunami brought Japan to the brink of a nuclear catastrophe, Ushahidi let anyone with a mobile phone find locations with clean water and food. Chile, Syria, Somalia, and the Democratic Republic of the Congo have all used this crisis-mapping software to save lives in times of political upheaval. In what other ways could technology help us face times of crisis?

Other Global Issues

Objective 1.2 *Describe how technology affects social issues in different societies.*

Political crises are not the only arena in which technology is enabling global change. Technology is impacting social issues in different countries around the world.

Health Care

Infectious diseases account for about one-fifth of all deaths worldwide. Researchers say the odds of a flu pandemic occurring in the next century are nearly 100%. Could technology help us develop and deliver vaccines in a way that saves lives? With newer scientific visualization tools, scientists are developing antibodies for flu viruses and even HIV, viruses that are difficult to target because they continually change shape. Computationally intense modeling software is helping researchers increase the pace of vaccine production, saving lives.

Retinal prosthetics are another example of global health concerns being addressed with technology. Macular degeneration and retinitis pigmentosa are two diseases that destroy the retina; they account for the majority of blindness in developing nations. Sheila Nirenberg of Cornell University is working on a microchip that can replace the function of the retina, translating incoming light into the electrical pulses the brain needs for vision. These biomedical chips could restore quality vision to the blind.

The Environment

What if every cell phone in the world had built-in atmospheric sensors? Then millions of points of air and water quality data from around the world could be constantly acquired. Tagged with geographical information, the data could alert scientists to new trends in our environment. Ideas like these are being explored by Mark Nieuwenhuijsen of the Center for Research in Environmental Epidemiology in Barcelona, Spain.

Smart Internet-connected water sprinklers are another technology that is saving water in California and other dry areas of the country. The sprinkler system checks the weather forecasts so it won't use water when rain is coming the next day. It can adjust the watering schedule based on the season and can adjust the times of watering to encourage root growth. The system is showing a 30% reduction in water usage.

Can you think of other ways you could use mobile and wearable technology to improve society?

The Digital Divide

There is a great gap in the levels of Internet access and the availability of technical tools in different regions of the world. The term coined for this difference in ease of access to technology is the **digital divide**. One danger of a digital divide is that it prevents us from using all the minds on the planet to solve the planet's problems. But this challenge created by technology is also being answered by technology.

The Next Einstein Initiative (NEI) is a plan to focus resources on the talented mathematical minds of Africa (see Figure 1.3). By expanding the African Institute for Mathematical Sciences (AIMS) across the continent, the future of Africa can be profoundly changed. Cambridge professor Neil Turok founded AIMS to bring together the brightest young minds across Africa with the best lecturers in the world. The NEI has won funding from Google's Project 10^{100}, an initiative to award $10 million to a set of five projects selected by open public voting. By capturing the enthusiasm of the world with presentations distributed through TED (**ted.com**) and Project 10^{100}, there is now a push to create 15 additional AIMS centers across Africa.

Figure 1.4 shows additional examples of people putting technology into action to impact the world. How will you join them? ■

FIGURE 1.3 The Next Einstein Initiative (NEI) is rallying the support of the world to identify mathematical genius.
(African Institute for Mathematical Sciences Next Einstein Initiative (AIMS-NEI))

FIGURE 1.4

Technology in Action: Taking on Global Problems

PERSON/ ORGANIZATION	GLOBAL PROBLEM	TECHNOLOGY USED	ACTION	FIND OUT MORE ...
Peter Gabriel/ The Witness Project	Human rights abuses	Video cameras	Provide video documentation of human rights abuses; the project contributed to the arrest of warlords in the.Democratic Republic of the Congo for the recruitment of child soldiers	The Witness Project: **witness.org**
SolaRoad/ Netherlands	The need for a renewable, nonpolluting energy resource	Solar cells	Solar cells are integrated into the asphalt roadway. They collect solar energy and distribute electricity all day	Netherlands' SolaRoad: **solaroad.nl**
United Nations World Food Programme (WFP)	One in seven people in the world do not get enough food to eat	GIS (geographical information systems) and mobile devices	The WFP can analyze the location and need for food, positioning food where it will help the most	World Food Programme: **wfp.org**
e-Nable	Need for inexpensive, easily maintained prosthetic hands	3D printing	This group of engineers, parents, and artists work to print and assemble hands for people they may never meet	e-Nable: **enablingthefuture.org**

technology and OUR SOCIETY

Technology is also allowing us to redefine very fundamental parts of our social makeup—how we think, how we connect with each other, and how we purchase and consume products.

Technology Impacts How We Think

Objective 1.3 *Describe how technology is changing our cognitive processes.*

What We Think About

What do you think about in your free time? In the late twentieth century, a common trend was to think about what to buy next—or perhaps what to watch or listen to next. Information and products were being served up at an amazing rate, and the pattern of consumption became a habit. As more and more web applications began to appear that allowed each individual to become a "creator" of the web, a new kind of Internet came into being. It was nicknamed **Web 2.0**, and it had a set of new features and functionality that allowed users to contribute content easily and to be easily connected to each other. Now everyone could collaborate internationally at the click of a mouse.

Web 2.0 has fostered a dramatic shift across the world from simply consuming to having the ability to volunteer and collaborate on projects. In his book *Cognitive Surplus: Creativity and Generosity in a Connected Age*, author Clay Shirky created the term **cognitive surplus** to mean the combination of leisure time and the tools to be creative. The world's population has an estimated one trillion hours a year of free time. When coupled with the available media tools and the easy connectivity of Web 2.0, and with generosity and a need to share, projects like Ushahidi and the Witness Project (see Figure 1.4) emerge.

But why would anyone bother to work on projects like these in their free time? Modern theories of motivation show that what pushes people to apply their free time in altruistic causes, for no money, is the excitement of autonomy, mastery, and purpose (see Figure 1.5):

- **Autonomy:** the freedom to work without constant direction and control.
- **Mastery:** the feeling of confidence and excitement from seeing your own skills progress.
- **Purpose:** the understanding that you are working for something larger than yourself.

Together, these three factors play into how we are fundamentally wired and can produce incredibly motivated behavior. The combination of motivation, technology, and a cognitive surplus is leading to powerful projects that are changing the world.

FIGURE 1.5 Our understanding of human motivation can play a role in our use of technology to impact society. *(Bonninturina/Fotolia, lzf/Fotolia, Vadymvdrobot/Fotolia)*

Technology Impacts How We Connect

Objective 1.4 *Explain how technology is expanding the ways we can collaborate.*

Connecting Through Music

In many societies, people connect intimately by creating and sharing music. Blend (**blend.io**) (see Figure 1.6) is a site that allows people to exchange the songs they have written as well as the electronic data and settings they used to create the song. People can explore different musical styles and techniques on the site and immediately download the components that made a song and begin to modify it. There is also a Blend blogging community that trades musical ideas among its readers. In addition, Blend is a publishing house, distributing and selling its users' digital music for them through all major outlets like iTunes,

FIGURE 1.6 Blend (**blend.io**) is an example of a community that lets musicians exchange not only songs but the electronic settings and data used to create the songs. *(Stuart Hughes/Corbis)*

Spotify, and Google Play. If you can get 100 likes from the community for your song, it is qualified for release on the Blend label!

Connecting Through Business

One of the most profound ways we can connect with each other is to support other people's dreams. Kickstarter (**kickstarter.com**) helps us connect in this way by allowing people to post their ideas for community projects, games, and inventions and to ask for funding directly. Donors are given rewards for different levels of pledges, such as a signed edition of a book or a special color of a product. This style of generating capital to start a business is known as **crowdfunding**, asking for small donations from a large number of people, often using the Internet. Successful Kickstarter projects have included ice chests with integrated blenders, DNA analysis machines that could inexpensively diagnose disease, and many entertainment projects. In total, almost $2 billion of funding for businesses has been raised using Kickstarter.

Technology Impacts How We Consume

Objective 1.5 *Summarize how technology has impacted the way we choose and consume products and services.*

Technology is changing all aspects of how we decide what we'll purchase and how we actually buy goods and services—from strategies for convincing you to purchase a certain product to the mechanics of how you buy and own things.

Marketing

New strategies in marketing are counting on the fact that most people have a cell phone with a camera and Internet access. **QR (quick response) codes** like the one shown here let any piece of print host a link to online information and video content. And studies show 82% of shoppers use their cell phone to go on the Internet before they make a purchase. They are often using so-called location-aware price comparison tools. Apps like ShopSavvy and RedLaser scan the bar code of the item and then compare prices with those of nearby stores and with the best prices available online. Techy shoppers can then get "mobile coupons" (or *mobi coupons*) delivered to their cell phones, thanks to sites like SnipSnap and Coupon Sherpa. The future promises specialized coupons created just for you based on your location and past buying preferences.

Marketers also have to be aware of the phenomenon of **crowdsourcing**—checking in with the voice of the crowd. Consumers are using apps like ScanLife to check people's verdicts on the quality of items. Forward-thinking companies are using this input to improve their products and services. AT&T, for example, has an app that lets customers report locations of coverage gaps.

Access Versus Ownership

Even the idea of ownership is evolving, thanks to new technologies. Items like cars and bikes can become "subscriptions" instead of large one-time purchases. For example, Zipcar allows hundreds of thousands of people to use shared cars. With Zipcar, a phone call or online reservation activates your personal Zipcar. This card allows you to automatically open the door of the car you have reserved, and away you drive. GPS technology is used to track where the car is, whether it has been dropped off at the right location, and how far it has been driven. Call a Bike is a bike-sharing program in Germany. Racks of Call a Bikes are located at major street corners in large cities in the country. Simply call the phone number printed on the bike and it texts you a code to unlock the bike. When you're done riding the bike, simply relock it and you're billed automatically. The New York City version of this program, Citi Bike, has already seen riders take over seven million trips (see Figure 1.7).

FIGURE 1.7 New York City's Citi Bike program uses digital technology to change our lifestyle from one of ownership to one of subscription. Riders are now taking over one million trips per month. *(Tim Clayton/Corbis)*

These subscription-style business models are spreading now to smaller goods. **Swap.com** helps people trade books, clothes, and video games with one another using the power of peer-to-peer connections—for example, to find those who want to swap used roller blades for a baby crib.

Rachel Botsman and Roo Rogers make the case in their book *What's Mine Is Yours: The Rise of Collaborative Consumption* that the real fuel beneath these services is a shift in our acceptance of sharing. **Collaborative consumption** implies that we are joining together as a group to use a specific product more efficiently. We are so constantly connected with each other that we have again found the power of community. There are increasing opportunities to redistribute the things we have purchased and to share the services a product provides instead of owning it outright. Add in the pressure of mounting environmental concerns and global financial pressures, and we are migrating toward collaborative consumption. ■

Before moving on to Part 2:

1. **Watch Replay Video 1.1.**
2. **Then check your understanding of what you've learned so far.**

check your understanding // review & practice

For a quick review to see what you've learned so far, answer the following questions.

multiple choice

1. Which is NOT a technology that has been used to deliver assistance during times of crisis?
   - **a.** Ushahidi
   - **b.** blend.io
   - **c.** social media
   - **d.** e-mail
2. Cognitive surplus means that we now find many people with
   - **a.** more money than free time.
   - **b.** limited access to the Internet.
   - **c.** excess time and free tools for collaboration.
   - **d.** mobile devices.
3. Collaborative consumption is when people get together to
   - **a.** find the best prices on products.
   - **b.** exchange reviews on services and goods they have purchased.
   - **c.** fight diseases of the respiratory tract.
   - **d.** increase the use of a single product by sharing access to it.
4. Crowdfunding helps start-up businesses by
   - **a.** selling stock more easily.
   - **b.** gathering financial contributions from supporters.
   - **c.** using QR codes to advertise and market products.
   - **d.** replacing Web 2.0 technology.
5. Social media has been used to
   - **a.** increase voter turnout in elections.
   - **b.** increase communication between elected officials and their constituents.
   - **c.** replace television and radio advertising in political elections.
   - **d.** all of the above

MyITLab Go to **MyITLab** to take an autograded version of the *Check Your Understanding* review and to find all media resources for the chapter.

TECHBYTES WEEKLY

Stay current with the TechBytes Weekly Newsletter.

Continue

TRY THIS Skyping Around the World

Understanding what your computer can do to improve your life is one of the benefits of being computer literate. In this exercise, we'll show you how to make a free phone call over the Internet using the desktop version of Skype, a popular Voice over Internet Protocol (VoIP) service. (Note: These instructions are for the desktop version of Skype. The interface when using Skype on a mobile device may be different.)

What You Need

WIRED INTERNET CONNECTION OR WIFI SIGNAL	A DEVICE (COMPUTER, SMARTPHONE, TABLET, SKYPE-READY TELEVISION)	A FRIEND

(Gst/Shutterstock, Dvougao/Digital Vision Vectors/Getty Images, Filo/DigitalVision Vectors/Getty Images)

Step 1 Set Up an Account. Go to Skype (**skype.com**), click on the **Get Skype button**, and create an account. Download the proper version for your device and install. You'll be able to call anyone with Skype and talk with just audio, with audio and video, or with free instant messaging. *(STANCA SANDA/Alamy Stock Photo)*

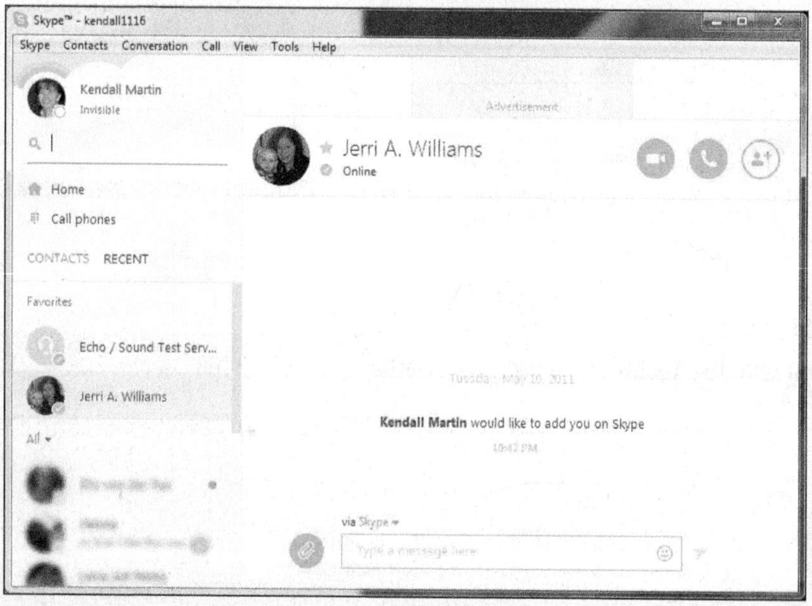

Step 2 Build Your Contact List. To build your list of contacts, you can add friends one at a time by clicking **Contacts**, **Add Contact**, then **Search Skype Directory** (as shown here). You can search for people using their name, their Skype name, or their e-mail address. *(Screenshot of Skype, part of Microsoft)*

(You only need to add a phone number if you plan on using Skype to call people on their *phone*, which, unlike computer-to-computer calls, is not a free service.)

For people you call frequently, drag their name up into the Favorites section.

Step 3 **Make a Call.** Now we're ready to call someone! Let's start by calling the people at Skype and making sure everything is hooked up properly. Under your Contacts list, click the **Echo/Sound Test Service**. Then call in by clicking the **Call button**. The Skype service will answer your call, record a short message from you, and play it back to you. You'll know everything is set to go, and you can begin calling the world for free! *(Screenshots of Skype, part of Microsoft)*

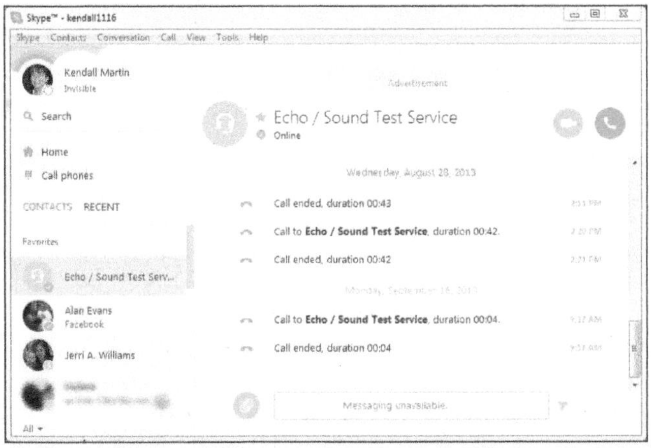

Make This TOOL: IFTTT/.com (If This Then That)

MAKE: A Virtual Assistant

If This Then That (**IFTTT.com**) is an Internet-based tool that helps you get things done automatically. By using "recipes" within this web-based tool, you can automate tasks you do during the day, such as:

- Automatically silencing your phone when you go into class
- Automatically texting your manager when you're on your way to work
- Notifying you when the president signs a new law

In this exercise, you'll explore using IFTTT to create recipes like these. *(IFTTT, Inc)*

Make the Internet work for you by knowing this one programming statement: IF THIS THEN THAT.

For the instructions for this exercise, go to MyITLab.

How Will Technology Improve Your Life?

Learning Outcome 1.2 You will be able to discuss personal impacts technology can have on your life and your career.

Technology is creating huge changes in the world as well as in how we behave socially, but it is also important to you on a more personal level. Being computer literate means being familiar enough with computers that you understand their capabilities and limitations and that you know how to use them safely and efficiently. As we discuss here, the more you understand technology, the more productive and protected you'll be at home, and the better prepared you'll be for any career.

technology at HOME

Everywhere you go, you see ads like the one in Figure 1.8 for computers and other devices. Do you know what all the words in the ad mean? What is RAM? What is a GPU? What are MB, GB, GHz, and cache? How fast do you need your computer to be, and how much memory should it have? If you're computer literate, you'll be a more informed consumer when it comes time to buy computers, peripherals, and technology services. Understanding computer terminology and keeping current with technology will help you better determine which computers and devices you need.

Computer Literacy

Objective 1.6 *Characterize computer literacy, and list some of its benefits.*

Let's look at a few examples of what it means to be a savvy computer user and consumer—in other words, **computer literate** (see Figure 1.9).

If you're not a savvy user now, don't worry—the following topics and more are covered in detail in the remaining chapters.

- **Avoiding hackers and viruses.** Do you know what hackers and viruses are? Both can threaten a computer's security. Being aware of how hackers and viruses operate and knowing the damage they can do to your computer can help you avoid falling prey to them.
- **Protecting your privacy.** You've probably heard of identity theft—you see and hear news stories all the time about people whose "identities" are stolen and whose credit ratings are ruined by "identity thieves." But do you

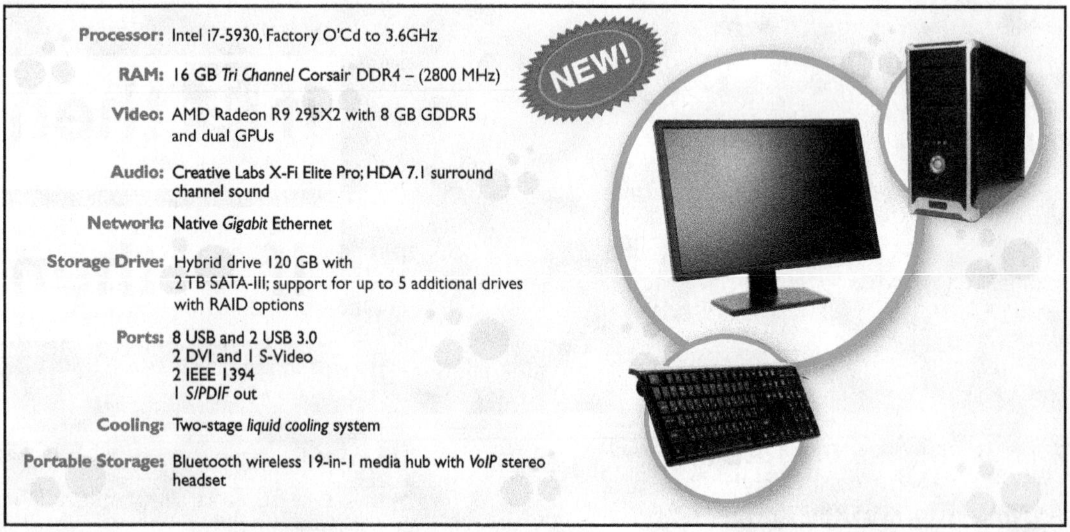

FIGURE 1.8 Do you know what all the words in a computer ad mean? Can you tell whether the ad includes all the information necessary to make a purchasing decision?

FIGURE 1.9

What Does It Mean to Be Computer Literate?

You can **avoid falling prey to hackers and viruses** because you are aware of how they operate.

You know how to **protect yourself from identity theft**.

You can **separate the real privacy and security risks from things you don't have to worry about**.

You know how to find information and **use the web effectively**.

You can **avoid being overwhelmed by spam, adware, and spyware**.

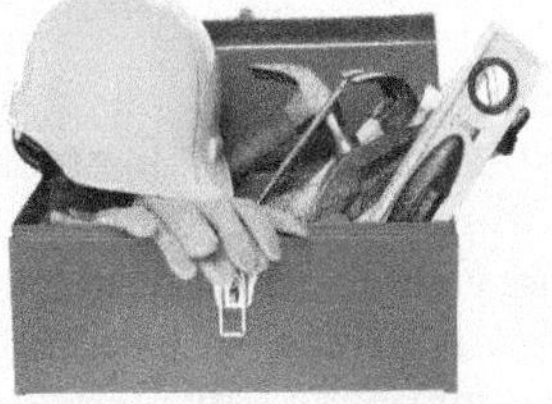

You know how to **diagnose and fix problems** with your hardware and software.

(Pn_photo/Fotolia, Danil Melekhin/E+/Getty Images, Zakai/DigitalVision Vectors/Getty Images, Sergey Nivens/Shutterstock, D. Hurst/Alamy, Ivanastar/E+/Getty Images)

know how to protect yourself from identity theft when you're online?

- **Understanding the real risks.** Part of being computer literate means being able to separate the real privacy and security risks from things you don't have to worry about. For example, do you know what a *cookie* is? Do you know whether it poses a privacy risk for you when you're on the Internet? What about a *firewall*? Do you know what one is? Do you really need a firewall to protect your computer?
- **Using the web wisely.** Anyone who has ever searched the web can attest that finding information and finding *good* information are two different things. People who are computer literate know how to find the information they want effectively. How effective are your searches?
- **Avoiding online annoyances.** If you have an e-mail account, chances are you've received electronic junk mail, or **spam**. How can you avoid spam? What about adware and spyware—do you know what they are? Do you know the difference between those and viruses, worms, and Trojan horses? Do you know which **software** programs—the instructions that tell the computer what to do—you should install on your computer to avoid online annoyances?
- **Being able to maintain, upgrade, and troubleshoot your computer.** Learning how to care for and maintain your computer and knowing how to diagnose and fix certain problems can save you a lot of time and hassle. Do you know how to upgrade your computer if you want more memory, for example? Do you know which software and computer settings can keep your computer in top shape?

Finally, becoming computer literate means knowing which technologies are on the horizon and how to integrate them into your own life. Can you connect your television to your wireless network? What is a media server, and do you need one? Can a USB 3.0 flash drive be plugged into a USB 2.0 port? Knowing the answers to these and other questions will help you make better purchasing decisions.

This book will help you become computer literate. In Chapter 3, you'll find out how to get the most from the web while staying free from the spam and clutter Internet surfing can leave behind on your computer. Chapter 6 shows you how to determine if your hardware is limiting your computer's performance and how to upgrade or shop for a new system. Chapter 9 covers how to keep your computer and your digital life secure. You'll be able to save money, time, and endless frustration by understanding the basics of how computers and computer systems operate. ■

> **SOUND BYTE**
> **Questions to Ask Before You Buy a Computer**
> This Sound Byte will help you consider important questions to ask before you buy a computer.

ethics in IT — Ethics and Technology

Should there be rules for conduct in a virtual world? If so, what should they be? What does plagiarism mean in a world where people can easily copy, paste, and upload content of all kinds? Should workplaces be allowed to monitor their employees' computing activities without their knowledge? Should websites be allowed to capture data related to what visitors do on their sites and analyze and sell that data? Should programmers be responsible if their software malfunctions and leads to personal injury or financial loss? Should Internet access be provided for free by communities to their citizens who cannot afford it? Are implantable devices that track the whereabouts of children and vulnerable adults a good thing, or a slippery slope to breaches of privacy? These are the sorts of ethical questions and challenges that technology poses—questions that did not even exist just a few years ago.

As the reach of technology continues to spread, these are questions that more and more societies must face and develop their own answers to. And because different societies and cultures have different ideas of what it means to behave ethically, there will be many different solutions to ethical questions and interpretations of ethical issues. How we navigate the different cultural responses to ethical challenges therefore becomes more and more important as the pace of technology quickens. For example, how should U.S. companies respond to censorship of their websites in countries such as China? A state in the United States can declare that online gambling is illegal, but what does that mean when its citizens have access to foreign websites hosting gambling (see Figure 1.10)?

Answering challenging ethical questions related to technology is part of being an informed citizen. This course will help you to understand technology and the ethical issues it poses. Taking the time to think deeply about the connection between technology and ethics is one step in being a more knowledgeable and thoughtful global citizen.

FIGURE 1.10 How do we enforce ethical standards in our global, Internet-enabled environment? *(John Lamb/Photodisc/Getty Images)*

technology and YOUR CAREER

Information technology (IT) is a field of study focused on the management and processing of information and the automatic retrieval of information. IT careers include working with computers, telecommunications, and software deployment. Career opportunities in IT are on the rise, but no matter what career you choose, new technology in the workplace is creating a demand for new skill levels in technology from employees. A study from the National Research Council concludes that by the year 2030, computers will displace humans in 60% of current occupations. Having advanced skills is becoming more critical every year.

Impact of Computer Literacy on Your Career

Objective 1.7 *Characterize the impact computer literacy has on a variety of careers.*

One of the benefits of being computer literate is that you will undoubtedly be able to perform your job more effectively. It also will make you more desirable as an employee and more likely to earn more and to advance in your career. In fact, your understanding of key concepts in technology can "future-proof" you, letting you easily and quickly react to the next round of new technologies.

Before we begin looking at a computer's parts and how a computer operates in Chapter 2, let's look at a whole range of industries and examine how computers are a part of getting work done.

Retail

The amount of data generated each minute of the day is staggering (see Figure 1.11). **Big Data** is the term for this new easy accessibility to extremely large data sets. But how do businesses make sense of it? They use a technique known as **data mining**, the process of searching huge amounts of data with the hope of finding a pattern. For example, retailers often study the data gathered from register terminals to determine which products are selling on a given day and in a specific location. In addition to inventory control systems, which help managers figure out how much merchandise they need to order to replace stock that is sold, managers can use mined data to determine that if they want a certain product to sell well, they

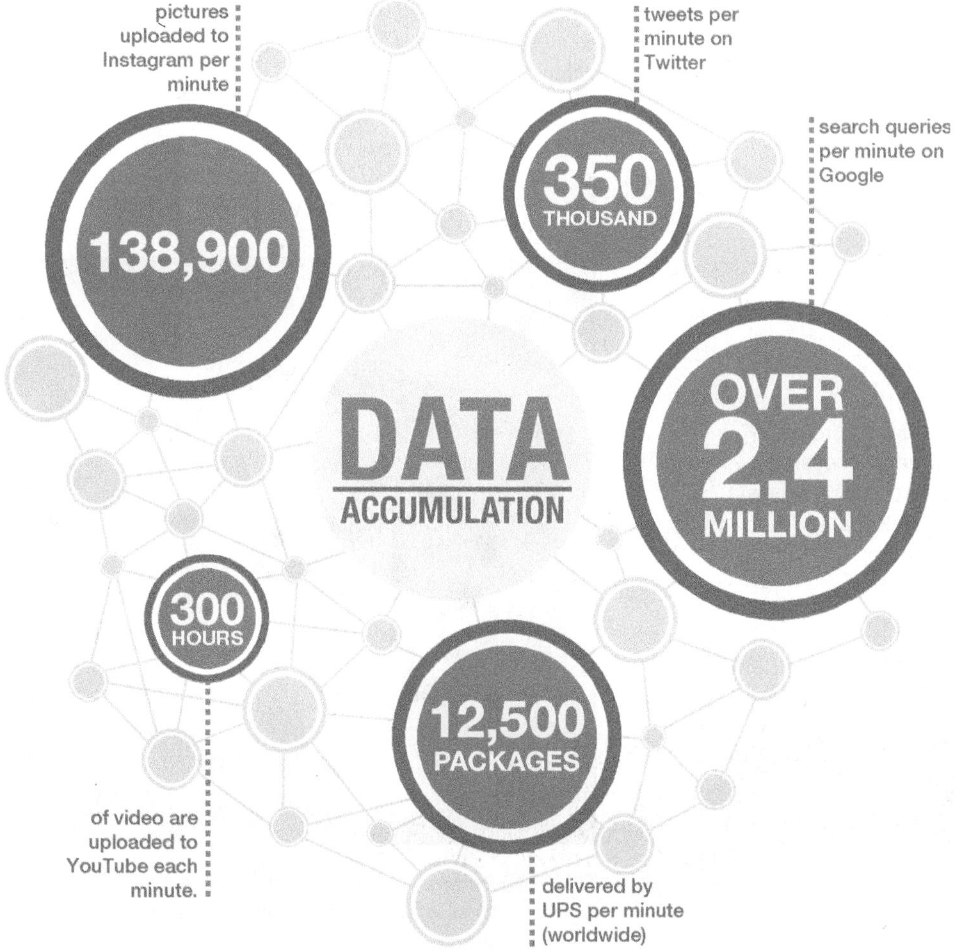

FIGURE 1.11 Enormous amounts of data are produced every minute. Data mining is the art of translating that huge volume of raw data into useful information.

must lower its price—especially if they cut the price at one store and see sales increase, for example. Data mining thus allows retailers to respond to consumer buying patterns.

Have you ever wondered how Amazon or Netflix suggest items that fit your taste? Data mining can keep track of the purchases customers make, along with their geographic data, past buying history, and lists of items they looked at but did not purchase. These data can be translated into marketing that is customized to your shopping. This is the motivation behind the discount cards grocery stores and drugstores offer. In exchange for tracking your buying habits, they offer you special pricing. In the age of Big Data, you may be using data mining in a number of careers.

Arts

Some design students think that because they're studying art, there's no reason for them to study computers. Of course, not all artwork is created using traditional materials such as paint and canvas. Many artists today work exclusively with computers. Mastery of software such as Adobe Illustrator, Adobe Photoshop, and Corel Painter is essential to creating digital art. Eventually, you'll want to sell your work, and you'll need to showcase your designs and artistic creations to employers and customers. Wouldn't it be helpful if you knew how to create and manage a website?

Using computers in the arts and entertainment fields goes far beyond just producing web pages, though. Dance and music programs like the ones at the Atlanta Ballet and the Juilliard School use computers to create new performances for audiences. A live dancer can be wired with sensors connected to a computer that captures the dancer's movements. Based on the data it collects, the computer generates a virtual dancer on a screen. The computer operator can easily manipulate this virtual dancer, as well as change the dancer's costume and other aspects of the dancer's appearance, with the click of a mouse. This allows artists to create new experiences for the audience.

And what if you see yourself working in an art museum? Today, museums are using technology to enhance visitors' experiences (see Figure 1.12). New York's Museum of Modern Art (MoMA), for example, offers a full range of options for tech-savvy visitors: old-fashioned museum audio guides, podcasts that visitors can listen to with their smartphones, and multimedia tours that visitors download through MoMA WiFi (**moma.org**) to their own mobile device. These multimedia guides even enable visitors to listen to music the artist listened to when he or she was creating a particular work or to look at other works that reflect similar techniques or themes as those they're viewing. Developing these solutions for museums is a great career for someone with an artistic education and knowledge of technology.

Education

The education industry uses computer technology in numerous ways. Electronic textbooks are simpler to search and provide great media supports. Courses are designed around course management software such as Blackboard or Moodle so that students can communicate outside of class, take quizzes online, and find their class materials easily. The Internet has obvious advantages in the classroom as a research tool for students, and effective use of the Internet allows teachers to expose students to places students otherwise couldn't access. There are simulations and instructional software programs on the web that are incredible learning tools. For example, teachers can employ these products to give

BITS&BYTES

Computational Art

Generative design is a revolutionary new method of creating artwork, models, and animations from sets of rules, or algorithms. Artists use simple programming languages, like the free product Processing, to produce designs and animations. Try this new-age tool for self-expression! Download Processing from **processing.org** and generate your own artistic works like the one shown here.

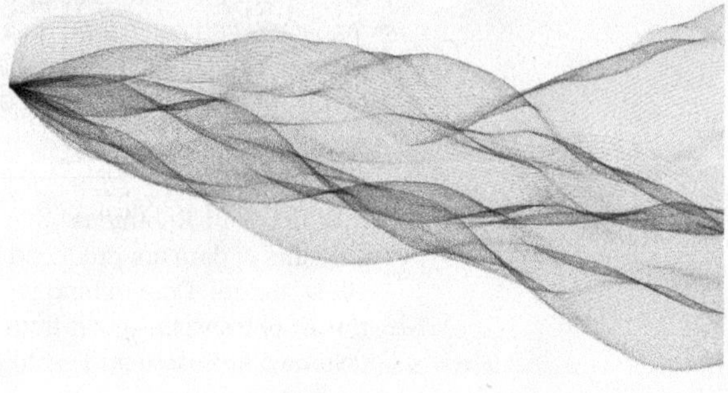

FIGURE 1.12 Multimedia tours using mobile devices and wireless technology are commonplace in museums and galleries. *(Paul Quayle/Alamy)*

students a taste of running a global business using SimVenture (**simventure.co.uk**) or experience an amazing tour of the human body (see Figure 1.13) through the Time Machine from Carnegie Mellon University (**timemachine.cmucreatelab.org**).

Want to take your students to a museum in another state or country? Many museums offer virtual tours on their websites that allow students to examine the museum collections. Another resource, the Art Project, is a collaboration of several museums that allows online visitors to explore over a thousand pieces of art using the same technology employed in Google Street View (see Figure 1.14). A custom viewer allows visitors to zoom in on the artwork itself at incredibly high resolution. The information panel takes you to related videos and other related websites. So, even if you teach in Topeka, Kansas, you can take your students on a virtual tour of the Tate Britain in London.

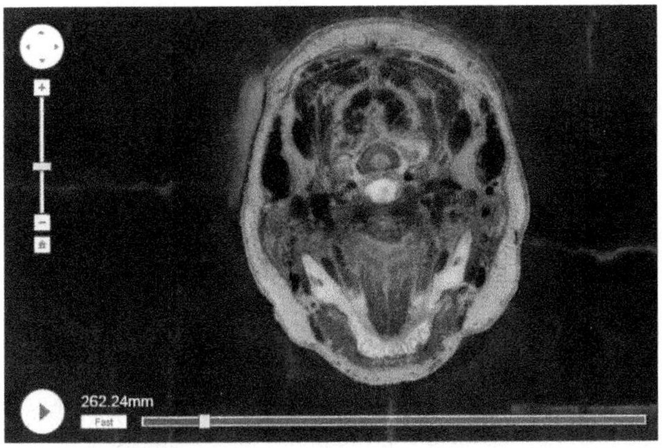

FIGURE 1.13 The Internet supports sophisticated learning resources. The Time Machine from Carnegie Mellon University shows time-lapse views of many phenomenon, from building a sculpture to a tour of the human body. *(Reprinted courtesy of Carnegie Mellon University and the Visible Human Project®)*

FIGURE 1.14 The Google Art Project (**googleartproject.com**) uses a custom camera on a moving trolley to generate a high-resolution experience of art museums located in more than 40 different countries. *(Richard Bord/Getty Images)*

Computerized education in the classroom may prove to be the tool that helps teachers reach greater success, despite increasing class sizes and tightening financial constraints. The Khan Academy (**khanacademy.org**) is a terrific example of a technological tool for education. Salman Khan was an investment analyst in Boston who began to post videos to YouTube so that he could teach algebra to his young cousins in New Orleans. Today, his nonprofit Khan Academy contains over 6,500 videos, and several million students a month use the site.

A classroom teacher can also follow what is happening in the classroom by using the *dashboard*, a screen that shows which topics each student has mastered, which ones they are making progress with, and which ones have them spinning their wheels. Now a teacher can approach a student already knowing exactly what is frustrating them and can avoid the dreaded question, "Oh, what don't you understand?"

As an educator, being computer literate will help you constructively integrate computer technologies like those discussed here into lesson plans and interactions for your students.

Law Enforcement

Today, wearing out shoe leather to solve crimes is far from the only method available to you if you want to pursue a career in law enforcement. Computers are being used in police cars and crime labs to solve an increasing number of crimes. For example, facial reconstruction systems like the one shown in Figure 1.15 can turn a skull into a finished digital image of a face, allowing investigators to proceed far more quickly with identification than before.

One technique used by modern detectives to solve crimes uses the vast number of databases on the Internet. Proprietary law enforcement databases such as the National Center for the Analysis of Violent Crime database enable detectives to analyze a wealth of information for similarities between crimes in an attempt to detect patterns that may reveal serial crimes. In fact, a law enforcement specialty called computer forensics is growing in importance in order to fight modern crime. **Computer forensics** analyzes computer systems with specific techniques to gather potential legal evidence. For example, Steven Zirko was convicted for two Chicago-area murders based on computer forensics work. Computer forensics examiners trained by the FBI scoured Zirko's computer and located searches for terms like *hire a hitman*. In many cases, files, videos, and

FIGURE 1.15 Tissue-rendering programs add layers of muscles, fat, and skin to create faces that can be used to identify victims. *(Pixologicsstudio/Science Photo Library/Glow Images)*

conversations conducted using a computer can be recovered by forensics specialists and can be used as evidence of criminal activity.

Medicine

A career in medicine will connect you to new ways of using technology to better people's lives. Earlier we mentioned how biomedical chips may one day restore sight to the blind. Modern biomedical research is providing technological solutions to physical problems in other ways as well.

There has already been experimentation on implanting chips in humans as a means of verifying a person's identity. Called VeriMed, this personal identification chip is about the size of a grain of rice and is implanted under the skin. When exposed to radio waves from a scanning device, the chip transmits its serial number to the scanner. The scanner then connects to a database that contains the name, address, and medical conditions of the person in whom the chip has been implanted. In the course of a nursing career, you may be using a device like VeriMed to help keep Alzheimer's patients safe, for example.

The design and construction of prosthetic devices is another area of medicine impacted by modern technology. MIT's Biomechatronics lab has developed software that uses an array of pressure sensors to gauge the softness or stiffness of a patient's remaining tissue to create a better fit for a prosthetic to the limb. Meanwhile, 3D printing is allowing more inexpensive designs for prosthetic arms and legs, and more stylish artificial limbs as well (see Figure 1.16).

Digital medication has arrived with the Food and Drug Administration (FDA) approval of digestible microchips (see Figure 1.17). Looking like regular pills, these medications have embedded sensors that transmit information to the doctor. The sensor itself is the size of a grain of sand. As it is digested, a small voltage is generated and detected by a patch worn on the patient's skin. The patch then transmits to the physician that the pill was taken; it also monitors the patient's heart rate, respiration, and temperature.

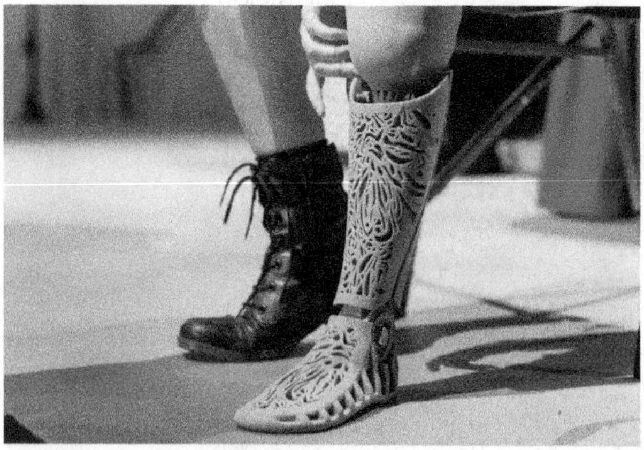

FIGURE 1.16 3D printing has become a tool for developing more inexpensive, and more stylish, prosthetic devices. *(Photographer Eliot Wright. Reprinted with permission of Thinking Robot Studios.)*

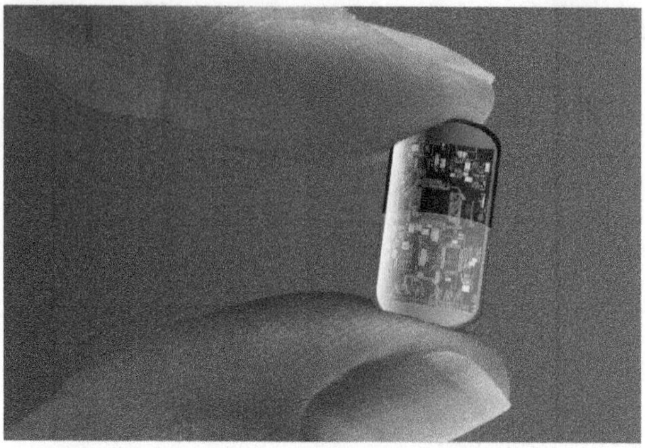

FIGURE 1.17 Digital medications are able to report information back to physicians about how the patient is responding to the medicine. *(ImageBROKER/SuperStock)*

Science

Thanks to a partnership between the National Severe Storms Lab and the National Center for Supercomputing Applications, tornado forecasting is becoming increasingly accurate. Scientists have been able to create a model so detailed that it takes nine days for a supercomputer to generate it, even though the computer is executing four trillion operations a second. Simulations also can model the structure of solar magnetic flares, which can interfere with broadcasts on Earth. With a career in meteorology, you will be studying the data produced by these simulations, hoping to improve predictions about weather phenomena.

Other technological applications in the sciences are being used on some of the oldest sites on Earth (see Figure 1.18). For example, the Galassi Tomb, located in the ancient Italian city of Caere, was originally designed in 650 B.C. and was rich with ornamentation and jewelry. These treasures were taken to the Vatican State collection in the 1800s when

FIGURE 1.18 Archeologists use computer-aided design (CAD) systems to build virtual reconstructions of ancient sites like this one. *(O. Louis Mazzatenta/Getty Images)*

DIG DEEPER Augmentative and Virtual Realities

Reality is reality, right? So what is *augmentative reality*? And how is it different from *virtual reality*?

Augmentative reality (AR) is the addition of digital information directly into our reality, either to add more detail or at times to remove unwanted visual effects. How does this happen?

AR combines our normal sense of the world around us with an additional layer of digital information. The extra information can be displayed on a separate device, such as in augmented reality apps for smartphones. Displays in stores can augment your image with the clothing you're interested in, creating a virtual fitting room (see Figure 1.19). Microsoft has announced a product named the HoloLens that will let you manipulate holographic images as part of your reality (see Figure 1.20).

Meanwhile, researcher Stephen Mann at the University of Toronto is working with wearable computers that use "point of eye" (PoE) cameras as AR devices. A PoE camera is designed so that the camera is positioned directly in front of the eye itself. The ultimate PoE camera would be one that is implanted within the eye or eye socket. Mann's research group is exploring this as a way to assist partially sighted or blind people.

Instead of adding information to the reality you perceive, **virtual reality (VR)** replaces it with a different world. Virtual reality creates an artificial environment that is immersive and interactive. VR environments can be as simple as a pair of goggles or as elaborate as entire "caves" that you walk into (see Figure 1.21). One "cave" (cave automatic

FIGURE 1.19 This high-tech fitting room uses augmented reality technology to allow shoppers to try on clothes virtually. *(Yoshikazu Tsuno/AFP/Getty Images)*

FIGURE 1.20 The Microsoft HoloLens augments your reality by adding holographic images you can manipulate. *(CALVETTI/Science Photo Library/Corbis)*

visual environment) is being used at Temple University to study balance in stroke victims.

VR is also coming to the consumer gaming market with the introduction of VR goggles, like Sony's Project Morpheus and the Rift by Oculus (see Figure 1.22). These goggles have high pixel count displays that wrap your full field of view.

So reality may be a bit less absolute than it once seemed. Whether it is being augmented with additional information or replaced by new virtual realms, technology is expanding our sense of what is real.

FIGURE 1.21 Virtual reality "caves" replace our ordinary reality with a new, immersive environment. *(Reprinted with permission of photographer Khairi Reda. University of Illinois at Chicago.)*

FIGURE 1.22 VR goggles like these wrap around your full field of view, creating a totally immersive environment. *(Edgar Su/Reuters/Corbis)*

the tomb was discovered. Today, scientists are using 3D scanners and imaging software to re-create the experience of seeing the tomb and the artifacts together as they once were. This virtual re-creation is so lifelike that archaeologists can study the ruins on-screen instead of at the actual site. Will you be using these tools someday to make records of other decaying sites?

Psychology

Fear of speaking in public is common, but for people with autism spectrum disorders, making proper eye contact and reacting to social cues is so difficult it can severely limit their opportunities for jobs and relationships. Researchers at the MIT Media Lab have developed a system to help improve interpersonal skills for people who have autism.

MACH (My Automated Conversation CoacH) is a computer system that generates an on-screen person that can, for example, conduct a job interview or appear ready for a first date. The computerized person (see Figure 1.23) nods and smiles in response to the user's speech and movement. This is an example of **affective computing**, developing systems that can recognize and simulate human emotions. MACH users can practice as many times as they wish in a safe environment. They receive an analysis that shows how well they modulated their voices, maintained eye contact, smiled, and how often they lapsed into "umms" and "uhhhs." The software runs on an ordinary laptop, using a webcam and microphone.

While engineers work to create computers that can process data faster and faster, psychologists and computer scientists are also working to evolve systems toward a more complete understanding of human behavior. With a career that blends computer science and psychology, you could find yourself at the heart of developing a new kind of relationship between man and machine. ■

FIGURE 1.23 My Automated Conversation CoacH (MACH) generates an on-screen interviewer you can practice with over and over. *(Cultura Limited/SuperStock)*

Before moving on to the Chapter Review:

1. **Watch Replay Video 1.2.**
2. **Then check your understanding of what you've learned so far.**

check your understanding // review & practice

For a quick review to see what you've learned so far, answer the following questions.

multiple choice

1. Analyzing computer systems to gather legal evidence is known as the field of
   - **a.** crowdsourcing.
   - **b.** information technology.
   - **c.** computer forensics.
   - **d.** simulation theory.
2. The MACH project shows that
   - **a.** there is a digital divide limiting access to computer systems.
   - **b.** sports performance can be recorded and analyzed by software.
   - **c.** there are some things computers cannot teach.
   - **d.** computers can help people with interpersonal skills development.
3. Which of the following allows retailers to respond to consumer buying patterns?
   - **a.** outsourcing
   - **b.** data mining
   - **c.** smart labels
   - **d.** Bluetooth technology
4. Computer technology is used in the arts by
   - **a.** integrating it into new works of performance art.
   - **b.** creating web pages to advertise and sell art.
   - **c.** creating multimedia museum tours.
   - **d.** all of the above
5. IT is the abbreviation for
   - **a.** information training.
   - **b.** Internet training.
   - **c.** Internet technology.
   - **d.** information technology.

MyITLab Go to **MyITLab** to take an autograded version of the *Check Your Understanding* review and to find all media resources for the chapter.

TECHBYTES WEEKLY

Stay current with the TechBytes Weekly Newsletter.

Continue

1 Chapter Review

summary //

How Will You Put Technology in Action?

Learning Outcome 1.1 **You will be able to discuss the impact of technology on global and national issues.**

Technology on the World Stage

Objective 1.1 *Recognize how becoming proficient with technology can help you understand and participate in political issues in the world at large.*

- Technology can be the means by which you find your voice in the world and impact others in meaningful ways.
- Social media is impacting elections worldwide.
- Crisis-mapping tools are an example of technology helping in different kinds of global conflicts and disasters.

Objective 1.2 *Describe how technology affects social issues in different societies.*

- Global health care issues, like the spread of disease, require international cooperation and technological solutions.
- Environmental issues are global in nature and will require technology to address.
- The digital divide, an uneven distribution of access to computer technology, will make it difficult for us to solve global problems.

Technology and Our Society

Objective 1.3 *Describe how technology is changing our cognitive processes.*

- Web 2.0 is a set of features and functionality that allows Internet users to contribute content easily and to be easily connected to each other.
- Cognitive surplus is the combination of leisure time and access to tools to work on problems and be creative.

Objective 1.4 *Explain how technology is expanding the ways we collaborate.*

- New collaborative tools available on the Internet allow us to work together on projects with much larger groups.
- Crowdfunding is a group of people connecting through the Internet to fund projects by strangers.

Objective 1.5 *Summarize how technology has impacted how commerce is conducted.*

- Marketing is changing because most consumers now shop with Internet access on their phones and can therefore check competing prices and online review.
- The idea of ownership is changing because technology is allowing subscription services for products like cars and bikes to be available. Such collaborative consumption means that we are joining together as a group to use specific products more efficiently.

How Will Technology Improve Your Life?

Learning Outcome 1.2 You will be able to discuss personal impacts technology can have on your life and your career.

Technology at Home

Objective 1.6 *Characterize computer literacy, and list some of its benefits.*

- If you're computer literate, you understand the capabilities and limitations of computers and know how to use them wisely.
- By understanding how a computer is constructed and how its various parts function, you'll be able to get the most out of your computer.
- You'll be able to avoid hackers, viruses, and Internet headaches; protect your privacy; and separate the real risks of privacy and security from things you don't have to worry about.
- You'll also be better able to maintain, upgrade, and troubleshoot your computer; make good purchasing decisions; and incorporate the latest technologies into your existing equipment.
- Being computer literate also enables you to understand the many ethical, legal, and societal implications of technology today.

Technology and Your Career

Objective 1.7 *Characterize the impact computer literacy has on a variety of careers.*

- Computer literacy impacts the full range of careers, from arts and psychology to science and≈medicine.
- Understanding how to use software, how to use and maintain computer hardware, and how to take advantage of Internet resources will help you be a more productive and valuable employee, no matter which profession you choose.

MyITLab

Be sure to check out **MyITLab** for additional materials to help you review and learn. And don't forget the Replay Videos.

key terms //

chapter quiz // assessment

For a quick review to see what you've learned, answer the following questions. Submit the quiz as requested by your instructor. If you are using **MyITLab**, the quiz is also available there.

multiple choice

1. Social media

- **a.** prevents two-way dialog between people.
- **b.** is incorporated as part of a political strategy by many politicians.
- **c.** cannot be immediate enough to react to quickly developing issues.
- **d.** only is useful for personal friendships.

2. Web 2.0 has led to a shift from just consuming content toward

- **a.** spending all our time on leisure activities.
- **b.** less sharing of the work we produce.
- **c.** new standards for HTML.
- **d.** producing content.

3. Examples of crowdfunding and crowdsourcing include

- **a.** Kickstarter and MobileVoice.
- **b.** Bing and Google.
- **c.** Call a Bike and Zipcar.
- **d.** Ushahidi and Kiva.

4. Being computer literate includes being able to

- **a.** avoid spam, adware, and spyware.
- **b.** use the web effectively.
- **c.** diagnose and fix hardware and software problems.
- **d.** all of the above

5. Computer forensics

- **a.** tests computers for hardware malfunction.
- **b.** analyzes computer systems to gather potential legal evidence.
- **c.** analyzes the design of a computer system.
- **d.** is used to create three-dimensional art.

6. Data mining is

- **a.** important now because it is so easy to gather enormous data sets.
- **b.** the study of data using algorithms to detect patterns.
- **c.** the translation of Big Data sets into meaningful information.
- **d.** all of the above

true/false

_____ **1.** The move toward access instead of ownership is a sign of collaborative consumption.

_____ **2.** The Next Einstein Initiative uses the power of supercomputing to enhance mathematical education.

_____ **3.** Virtual reality is the addition of infographics to your visual field.

_____ **4.** Web-based databases are being used to help investigators solve criminal cases.

critical thinking

1. What Occupies Your Mind?

What we think about is influenced by the information fed to our mind all day long. Web 2.0 has created numerous channels for people to offer their own work for free—open source software, free music, books, and artwork. How has this affected your thinking? Have you created things to share freely with the online world? Has it changed the value you put on music, books, and art?

2. Career and Computers

This chapter lists many ways in which becoming computer literate is beneficial. Think about what your life will be like once you're started in your career. What areas of computing will be most important for you to understand? How would an understanding of computer hardware and software help you in working from home, working with groups in other countries, and contributing your talents?

team time //

A Culture of Sharing

Problem

As more and more peer-to-peer music-sharing services appeared, like BitTorrent and LimeWire, many felt a culture of theft was developing. Some argued there was a mind-set that property rights for intellectual works need not be respected and that people should be able to download, for free, any music, movies, or other digital content they wanted.

But there is another view of the phenomenon. Some are suggesting that the amount of constant access to other people—through texting, e-mail, blogging, and the easy exchange of digital content—has created a culture of trust and sharing. This Team Time will explore both sides of this debate as it affects three different parts of our lives—finance, travel, and consumerism.

Task

Each of three groups will select a different area to examine—finance, travel, or consumerism. The groups will find evidence to support or refute the idea that a culture of sharing is developing. The finance group will want to explore projects like Kickstarter (**kickstarter.com**) and Kiva (**kiva.org**). The travel group should examine what is happening with Couchsurfing (**couchsurfing.com**) to start their research. The team investigating consumerism will want to look at goods-exchange programs like Freecycle (**freecycle.org**).

Process

1. Divide the class into three teams.
2. Discuss the different views of a "culture of sharing." With the other members of your team, use the Internet to research up-and-coming technologies and projects that would support your position. People use social media tools to connect into groups to exchange ideas. Does that promote trust? Does easy access to digital content promote theft, or has the value of content changed? Are there other forces like the economy and the environmental state of the world that play a role in promoting a culture of sharing? What evidence can you find to support your ideas?
3. Present your group's findings to the class for debate and discussion.
4. Write a strategy paper that summarizes your position and outlines your predictions for the future. Will the pace of technology promote a change in the future from the position you are describing?

Conclusion

The future of technology is unknown, but we do know that it will impact the way our society progresses. To be part of the developments that technology will bring will take good planning and attention, no matter what area of the culture you're examining. Begin now—learn how to stay on top of technology.

ethics project //

Can Big Data Predict Your Grade?

Problem

As you move through your academic career, you leave an enormous swath of data: which courses you chose to register for, which ones you looked at but didn't pick, and how you did on each homework assignment, test, and project. Could this massive amount of data be analyzed to predict your grade in a course? To suggest which courses you should take next? Should those predictions be public to your instructor? To you? To financial aid officers?

Research Topics to Consider

- Course Signals
- Degree Compass, Austin Peay State University

Process

1. Divide the class into teams. Each team will select a web-based tool that allows access to information.
2. Team members should each think of a situation where a person would benefit from the type of results data mining of Big Data can bring to a campus and a situation where it might be undesirable.
3. Team members should select the most powerful and best-constructed arguments and develop a summary conclusion.
4. Team members should present their findings to the class or submit a PowerPoint presentation for review by the rest of the class, along with the summary conclusion they developed.

Conclusion

As technology becomes ever more prevalent and integrated into our lives, ethical dilemmas will present themselves to an increasing extent. Being able to understand and evaluate both sides of the argument, while responding in a personally or socially ethical manner, will be an important skill.

Solve This

MyITLab® grader

How Technology Is Used on the World Stage and in My Personal Life

In this activity, you'll use Microsoft Word to reflect on how technology is affecting the world as well as you, personally and professionally. Reflect on the content in Chapter 1 as you work through this exercise.

You will use the following skills as you complete this activity:

• Open and Modify a Document Template	• Insert Text
• Apply Styles and Advanced Font Formats	• Apply Themes
• Use Format Painter	• Create a Header and Footer

Instructions

1. Start Microsoft Word 2016 and open the Facet design (blank) template. Save the document as **TIA_Ch1_LastFirst**, using your own Last and First names.
2. Double-click the **Title placeholder** and type **Technology**, then double-click the **Heading placeholder** and type **Introduction**. Replace the remaining placeholder text with the following: **Political and global issues are showing that technology is accelerating change around the world and galvanizing groups of people in new ways. Technology allows us to refine how we connect with each other, and it also impacts our daily personal and professional experiences.** Press **Enter**.
3. Type **How Technology Impacts Society**, press **Enter**, and then type a few sentences that describe how technology is impacting global events such as political revolutions, health care, the environment, and the digital divide. In addition, address how businesses are using social media. Press Enter.
4. Type **How Technology Impacts Me Personally and Professionally**, press **Enter**, and then type a few sentences that describe how technology is impacting your personal life. You should address the importance of being computer literate. You should also address the kinds of technology being used in the industry of your current or desired career.
5. Click anywhere in the heading *Introduction*, then using **Format Painter**, apply the **Heading 1** format to the paragraph headers: *How Technology Impacts Society* and *How Technology Impacts Me Personally and Professionally*.
   a. Hint: Format Painter is in the Clipboard group on the Home tab.
6. Change the Document Theme style to the **Slice Theme**.
   a. Hint: Document Themes are found on the Design tab, in the Document Formatting group.
7. Select the title *Technology*, then format the font as **Small Caps**. **Center align** the title.
   a. Hint: Click the dialog box launcher in the Font group on the Home tab to access the Small caps font effects.
8. Apply the **Whisp header style** to the document. Click to add Today's date in the Date header and delete the Document title header. Add a **File Path** to the document footer. Select the footer text and change the font size to **8**. Close the Header and Footer.
   a. Hint: Headers are found on the Insert tab in the Header & Footer group. File Path is found in Document Info in the Insert group on the Header & Footer Tools Design tab.
9. Save the document and submit based on your instructor's directions.

2 Looking at Computers: Understanding the Parts

Make This: MAKE: A Mobile App on **page 49**

All media accompanying this chapter can be found in MyITLab.

For an overview of the chapter, watch the **Preview Video**.

HOW COOL IS THIS?

Now that we are used to the **touch experience** with our devices, where do we go next? How about **no touch**! The Ring ZERO from Logbar Inc. is a wearable device that **senses the movements of the finger** on which it is worn and transmits those gestures to compatible devices (iOS and Android). You can type text, control home appliances, or make payments all by **making gestures with one finger**. The device has preprogrammed gestures, but you can also customize them (or create your own) with the **companion app**. So controlling your devices may soon only require a small wave of your finger! *(Logbar)*

Understanding Digital Components

Learning Outcome 2.1 You will be able to describe the devices that make up a computer system.

After reading Chapter 1, you can see why becoming computer literate is important. But where do you start? You've no doubt gleaned some knowledge about computers just from being a member of society. However, even if you have used a computer before, do you really understand how it works, what all its parts are, and what those parts do?

understanding your COMPUTER

Let's start our look at computers by discussing what a computer does and how its functions make it such a useful machine.

Computers Are Data Processing Devices

Objective 2.1 *Describe the four main functions of a computer system and how they interact with data and information.*

What exactly does a computer do? Strictly defined, a **computer** is a data processing device that performs four major functions:

1. **Input:** It gathers data or allows users to enter data.
2. **Process:** It manipulates, calculates, or organizes that data into information.
3. **Output:** It displays data and information in a form suitable for the user.
4. **Storage:** It saves data and information for later use.

What's the difference between data and information? People often use the terms *data* and *information* interchangeably. Although they may mean the same thing in a simple conversation, the distinction between data and information is an important one.

In computer terms, **data** is a representation of a fact, a figure, or an idea. Data can be a number, a word, a picture, or even a recording of sound. For example, the number 7135553297 and the names Zoe and Richardson are pieces of data. Alone, these pieces of data probably mean little to you. **Information** is data that has been organized or presented in a meaningful fashion. When your computer provides you with a contact listing that indicates that Zoe Richardson can be reached at (713) 555-3297, the data becomes useful—that is, it becomes information.

How do computers interact with data and information? Computers are excellent at **processing** (manipulating, calculating, or organizing) data into information. When you first arrived on campus, you probably were directed to a place where you could get an ID card. You most likely provided a clerk with personal data that was entered into a computer. The clerk then took your picture with a digital camera (collecting more data). All of the data was then processed appropriately so that it could be printed on your ID card (see Figure 2.1). This organized output of data on your ID card is useful information.

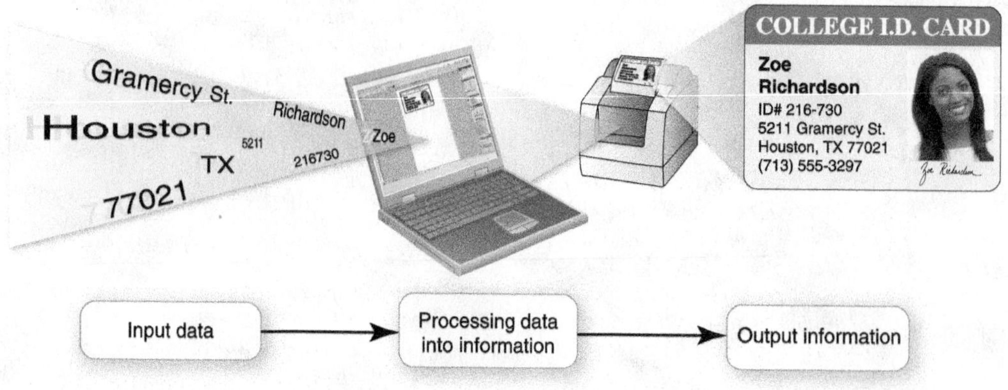

FIGURE 2.1 Computers process data into information. *(mocker_bat/Fotolia)*

SOUND BYTE
Binary Numbers Interactive

This Sound Byte helps remove the mystery surrounding binary numbers. You'll learn about base conversion between decimal, binary, and hexadecimal numbers using colors, sounds, and images.

ACTIVE HELPDESK
Understanding Bits and Bytes

In this Active Helpdesk, you'll play the role of a helpdesk staffer, fielding questions about the difference between data and information, what bits and bytes are, and how bytes are measured.

Bits and Bytes: The Language of Computers

Objective 2.2 *Define bits and bytes, and describe how they are measured, used, and processed.*

How do computers process data into information? Unlike humans, computers work exclusively with numbers (not words). To process data into information, computers need to work in a language they understand. This language, called **binary language**, consists of just two digits: 0 and 1. Everything a computer does, such as processing data, printing a report, or editing a photo, is broken down into a series of 0s and 1s. Each 0 and 1 is a **binary digit**, or **bit** for short. Eight binary digits (or bits) combine to create one **byte**. In computers, each letter of the alphabet, each number, and each special character (such as @, pronounced "at") consists of a unique combination of eight bits, or a string of eight 0s and 1s. So, for example, in binary language, the letter *K* is represented as 01001011. This is eight bits or one byte.

What else can bits and bytes be used for? Bits and bytes not only are used as the language that tells the computer what to do, they are also used to represent the *quantity* of data and information that the computer inputs and outputs. Word processing files, digital pictures, and even software are represented inside computing devices as a series of bits and bytes. These files and applications can be quite large, containing millions or billions of bytes.

To make it easier to measure the size of such files, we need units of measure larger than a byte. Kilobytes, megabytes, and gigabytes are therefore simply larger amounts of bytes. As shown in Figure 2.2, a **kilobyte (KB)** is approximately 1,000 bytes, a **megabyte (MB)** is about 1 million bytes, and a **gigabyte (GB)** is around 1 billion bytes. Today, personal computers are capable of storing **terabytes (TB)** of data (around 1 trillion bytes), and many business computers can store up to a **petabyte (PB)** (1,000 terabytes) of data. The Google search engine processes more than 1 PB of user-generated data per *hour*!

How does your computer process bits and bytes? Your computer uses hardware and software to process data into information that lets you complete tasks such as writing a letter or playing a game. **Hardware** is any part of the computer you can physically touch. However, a computer needs more than just hardware to work. **Software** is the set of computer programs that enables the hardware to perform different tasks.

There are two broad categories of software: *application software* and *system software*. **Application software** is the set of programs you use on a computer to help you carry out tasks such as writing a research paper. If you've ever typed a document, created a spreadsheet, or edited a digital photo, for example, you've used application software.

System software is the set of programs that enables your computer's hardware devices and application software to work together. The most common type of system software is the **operating system (OS)**—the program that controls how your computer system functions. It manages the hardware, such as the monitor and printer, and provides a means by which users can interact with the computer. Most likely, the computer you own or use at school runs a version of Windows as the system software. However, if you're working on an Apple computer, you're probably running OS X.

Types of Computers

Objective 2.3 *List common types of computers, and discuss their main features.*

What types of computers are popular for personal use? There are two basic designs of computers: portable and stationary. For portable computers, a number of options exist:

- A **tablet computer**, such as the iPad or Microsoft Surface, is a portable computer integrated into a flat multitouch-sensitive screen. It uses an on-screen virtual keyboard, but you can connect separate keyboards to it via Bluetooth or wires.
- A **laptop** or **notebook computer** is a portable computer that has a keyboard, monitor, and other devices integrated into a single compact case.
- An **ultrabook** is a full-featured but lightweight laptop computer designed to compete with the MacBook Air. Ultrabooks feature low-power processors and solid-state drives and try to reduce their size and weight to extend battery life without sacrificing performance.
- A **2-in-1 PC** is similar to a laptop computer, but the monitor swivels and folds flat (see Figure 2.3a). This allows it to function both as a conventional laptop and as a tablet computer using its touchscreen.
- A **Chromebook** is a special breed of laptop that uses the Google Chrome OS and is designed to be connected to the Internet at all times. Documents and apps are stored primarily in the cloud as opposed to on the local hard drive.

A **desktop computer** is intended for use at a single location, so it's stationary. Most desktop computers consist of a separate case or tower (called the **system unit**) that houses the main components of the computer plus peripheral devices. A **peripheral device** is a component, such as a monitor or keyboard, that connects to the computer. An

FIGURE 2.2

How Much Is a Byte?

NAME	NUMBER OF BYTES	RELATIVE SIZE
Byte (B)	1 byte	One character of data (8 bits or binary digits)
Kilobyte (KB)	1,024 bytes (2^{10} bytes)	1,024 characters or about 1 page of plain text
Megabyte (MB)	1,048,576 bytes (2^{20} bytes)	 About 4 books (200 pages, 240,000 characters)
Gigabyte (GB)	1,073,741,824 bytes (2^{30} bytes)	 About 4,500 books or over twice the size of Sir Isaac Newton's library (considered very large for the time)
Terabyte (TB)	1,099,511,627,776 bytes (2^{40} bytes)	About 4.6 million books or about the number of volumes in the Rutgers University Library
Petabyte (PB)	1,125,899,906,842,624 bytes (2^{50} bytes)	 About 4.7 billion books, which would fill the Library of Congress (the United States' largest library) 140 times!
Exabyte (EB)	1,152,921,504,606,846,976 bytes (2^{60} bytes)	About 4.8 trillion books, which, if stored as they are in the Library of Congress, would occupy about 11,000 square miles or an area almost the size of the state of Maryland
Zettabyte (ZB)	1,180,591,620,717,411,303,424 bytes (2^{70} bytes)	 The library required to house the 4.9 quadrillion books equal to a ZB of data would occupy about 11.3 million square miles or an area about 1 million square miles larger than all of North America

(Ninice64/Fotolia, Georgios Kollidas/Fotolia, Daniel/Fotolia, Flavijus Piliponis/Fotolia)

FIGURE 2.3 (a) A 2-in-1 PC has a monitor that swivels (or folds) to become a touch-sensitive input device. (b) An all-in-one computer does not need a separate tower. *(Julie Jacobson/AP Images, best pixels/Shutterstock)*

all-in-one computer, such as the Apple iMac (Figure 2.3b), eliminates the need for a separate tower because these computers house the computer's processor and memory in the monitor. Many all-in-one models also incorporate touch-screen technology.

Are there other types of computers? Although you may never come into direct contact with the following types of computers, they are still very important and do a lot of work behind the scenes of daily life:

- A **mainframe** is a large, expensive computer that supports many users simultaneously. Mainframes are often used in businesses that manage large amounts of data, such as insurance companies, where many people are working at the same time on similar operations, such as claims processing. Mainframes excel at executing many computer programs at the same time.
- A **supercomputer** is a specially designed computer that can perform complex calculations extremely rapidly. Supercomputers are used when complex models requiring intensive mathematical calculations are needed (such as weather forecasting or atomic energy research). Supercomputers are designed to execute a few programs as quickly as possible, whereas mainframes are designed to handle many programs running at the same time but at a slower pace.
- An **embedded computer** is a specially designed computer chip that resides in another device, such as your car or the electronic thermostat in your home. Embedded computers are self-contained computer devices that have their own programming and that typically don't receive input from you or interact with other systems (see Figure 2.4).

FIGURE 2.4 Quadcopters and drones contain embedded computers. *(Kletr/Fotolia)*

Even your smartphone is a computer. Today's **smartphones** offer many features you probably use day to day, including a wide assortment of apps, media players, high-quality cameras, and web connectivity. And just like your laptop, your smartphone has a CPU, memory, and storage.

Each part of your computer has a specific purpose that coordinates with one of the functions of the computer—input, processing, output, or storage (see Figure 2.5). Additional devices, such as WiFi adapters and routers, help a computer communicate with the Internet and other computers to facilitate the sharing of documents and other resources. Let's begin our exploration of hardware by looking at your computer's input devices. ■

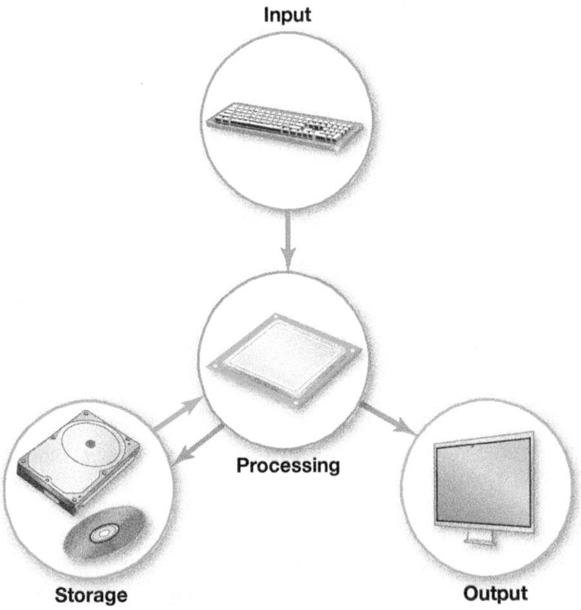

FIGURE 2.5 Each part of the computer serves a special function.

input DEVICES

An **input device** lets you enter data (text, images, and sounds) and instructions (user responses and commands) into your computer. Let's look at some of the most popular input devices used today.

Keyboards and Touch Screens

Objective 2.4 *Identify the main types of keyboards and touch screens.*

What is the most common way to input data and commands? A **keyboard** is an input device you use to enter typed data and commands. However, most computing devices, such as smartphones and tablets, now respond to touch. **Touch screens** are display screens that respond to commands initiated by touching them with your finger or a **stylus**—an input device that looks like a pen and that you use to tap commands or draw on a screen. Touch-screen devices use a virtual keyboard (see Figure 2.6) that displays on screen when text input is required. These keyboards show basic keyboard configurations but allow you to switch to numeric, punctuation, and other special keys.

FIGURE 2.6 Virtual keyboards are found on tablets and other touch-screen devices. *(Nathan Alliard/Glow Images)*

Are all keyboards the same? Whether on-screen touch keyboards or physical keyboards, the most common keyboard layout is a standard **QWERTY keyboard**. This keyboard layout gets its name from the first six letters in the top-left row of alphabetic keys and is the standard English-language keyboard layout. The QWERTY layout was originally designed for typewriters and was meant to slow typists and prevent typewriter keys from jamming. Although the QWERTY layout is considered inefficient because it slows typing speeds, efforts to change to more efficient layouts, such as that of the Dvorak keyboard (see Figure 2.7), have not been met with much public interest.

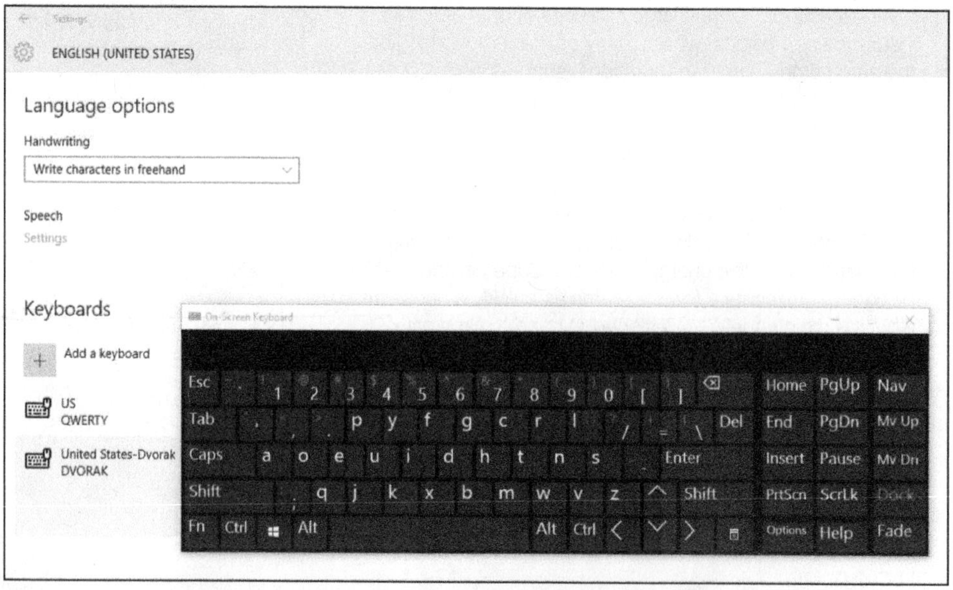

FIGURE 2.7 The Dvorak keyboard is an alternative keyboard layout that puts the most commonly used letters in the English language on "home keys"—the keys in the middle row of the keyboard. The Dvorak keyboard's design reduces the distance your fingers travel for most keystrokes, increasing typing speed. You can customize the layout of your keyboard using the Windows operating system. *(Windows 10, Microsoft Corporation)*

>To change your keyboard layout in Windows 10, click ***Settings*** *from the Start menu, click* ***Time & language****, then click* ***Region & language****. Select* ***Windows display language****, select* ***Options****, click* ***Add a keyboard****, and then select* ***United-States-Dvorak****.*

What alternatives are there to an onscreen touch keyboard? Touch-screen keyboards are not always convenient when a great deal of typing is required. Most computing devices can accept physical keyboards as an add-on accessory. Wired keyboards plug into a data port on the computing device. Wireless keyboards send data to the computer using a form of wireless technology that uses *radio frequency (RF)*. A radio transmitter in the keyboard sends out signals that are received either by a receiving device plugged into a port on the device or by a Bluetooth receiving device located in the device. You've probably heard of **Bluetooth technology** if you use a headset or earpiece with your cell phone. Bluetooth is a wireless transmission standard that lets you connect devices such as smartphones, tablets, and laptops to peripheral devices such as keyboards and headsets. Often, wireless keyboards for tablets are integrated with a case to protect your tablet (see Figure 2.8a).

a

b

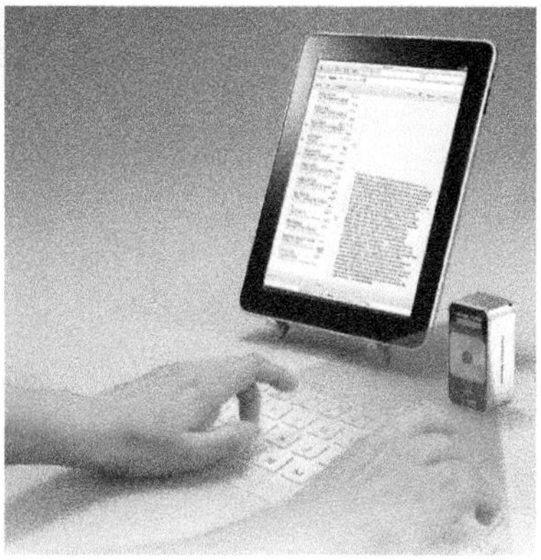

FIGURE 2.8 (a) Cases with integrated physical keyboards make tablets more typing-friendly. (b) Virtual keyboard devices project the image of a QWERTY keyboard on any surface. Sensors detect typing motions, and data is transmitted to your device via Bluetooth technology. *(Logitech, Inc.; Splash News/Hammacher Schlemmer/Newscom)*

Flexible keyboards are a terrific alternative if you want a full-sized keyboard for your laptop or tablet. You can roll one up, fit it in your backpack, and plug it into a USB port when you need it. Another compact keyboard alternative is a *virtual keyboard* (see Figure 2.8b), which is about the size of a matchbox. They project an image of a keyboard onto any flat surface, and sensors detect the motion of your fingers as you "type." Data is transmitted to the device via Bluetooth. These keyboards work with the latest iPhones, iPads, and Android devices.

BITS&BYTES

Distributed Computing: Putting Your Computer to Work While You Sleep

Complex scientific research, such as processing data from radio telescopes, requires vast computing power. Software has been developed to tie individual computing devices (including tablets and smartphones) into a grid to enable them to work together. This is known as **distributed** or **grid computing**. This effectively creates a cheap supercomputer that many not-for-profit research organizations use to research problems that will benefit the greater good—and your computer can help. Visit theSkyNet (**theskynet.org**) and download its software. Once installed, it allows your device to process astronomical data during the many times when your CPU is idle (or at least not working to its full potential). With theSkyNet, your computing device can help astronomers explore the heavens (see Figure 2.9).

FIGURE 2.9 Help astronomers process data by having your computer join theSkyNet. *(James Thew/Fotolia)*

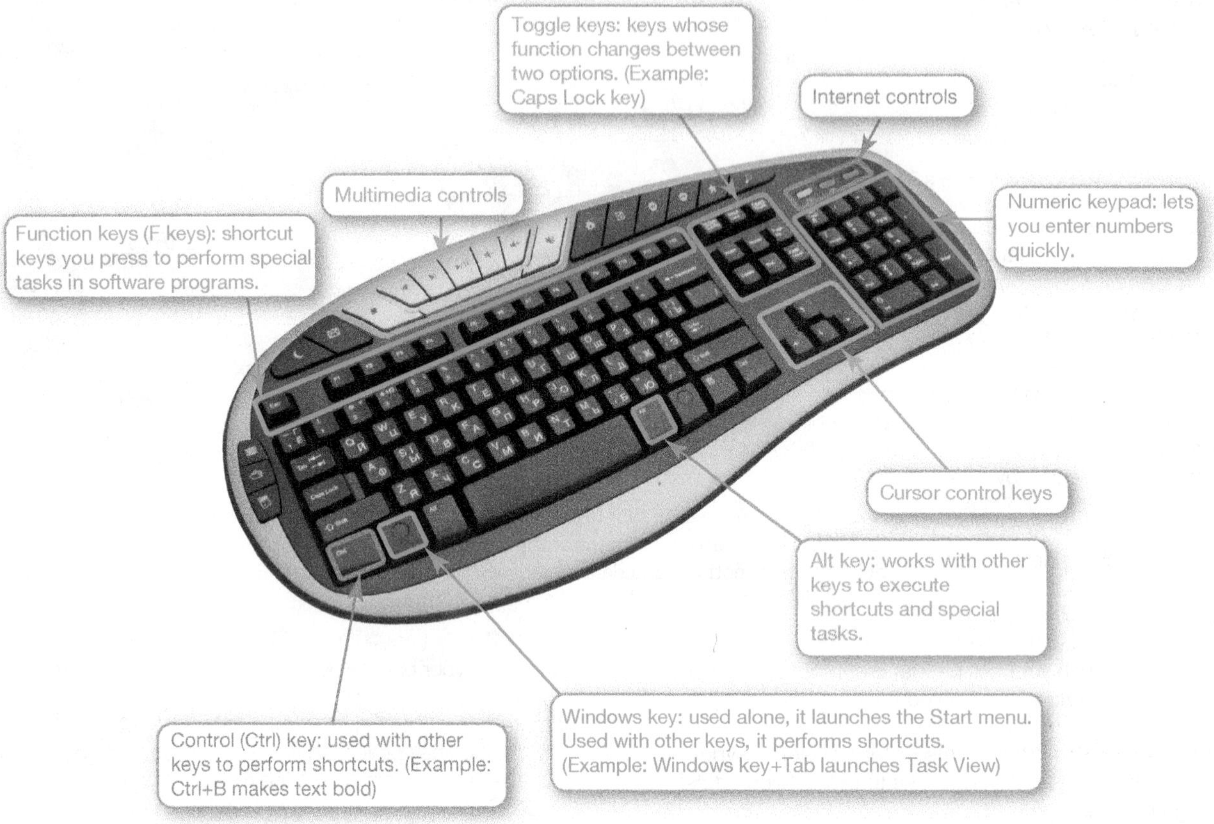

FIGURE 2.10 Keyboards have a variety of keys that help you work more efficiently. (Note that on Macs, function keys are slightly different: The Control function is the Apple key or Command key, and the Alt function is the Option key.)

How can I use my keyboard most efficiently? All keyboards have the standard set of alphabetic and numeric keys that you regularly use when typing. As shown in Figure 2.10, many keyboards for laptop and desktop computers have additional keys that perform special functions. Knowing how to use the special keys shown in Figure 2.10 will help you improve your efficiency.

Mice and Other Pointing Devices

Objective 2.5 *Describe the main types of mice and pointing devices.*

What kinds of mice are there? A **mouse** is an input device used to enter user responses and commands. The mouse type you're probably most familiar with is the **optical mouse**. An optical mouse uses an internal sensor or laser to detect the mouse's movement. The sensor sends signals to the computer, telling it where to move the pointer on the screen. Optical mice don't require a mouse pad, though you can use one to enhance the movement of the mouse on an uneven surface or to protect your work surface from being scratched.

If you have special ergonomic needs or want to customize the functionality of your mouse, there are plenty of options (see Figure 2.11). Most mice have two or three buttons that let you execute commands and open shortcut menus. (Mice for Macs sometimes have only one button.) Many customizable mice have additional programmable buttons and wheels

FIGURE 2.11 Customizable mice offer programmable buttons and adjustable fittings to meet most any need. *(kirill87/Fotolia)*

that let you quickly maneuver through web pages or games. These mice are also customizable to fit any size hand and grip style by allowing for length and width adjustments. Aside from gamers, many people use customizable mice to reduce susceptibility to repetitive strain injuries or if they suffer from physical limitations that prevent them from using standard mice.

How do wireless mice work? Wireless mice usually connect the same way that wireless keyboards do—either through Bluetooth or a receiver that plugs into a USB port. Wireless mice have receivers that often clip into the bottom of the mouse for easy storage when not in use.

Why would I want to use a mouse with a touch-screen device? If you're using a conventional keyboard with your touch-screen device, it's often easier to perform actions with a mouse rather than taking your hands off the keyboard and reaching to touch the screen. In addition, there are new kinds of mice, called *touch mice*, that are designed with touch-screen computers in mind. Unlike older mice, there are no specifically defined buttons. The top surface of a touch mouse is the button. You use one, two, or three fingers to perform touch-screen tasks such as scrolling, switching through open apps, and zooming. Touch mice also allow you to perform traditional mouse tasks, such as moving the cursor when you move the mouse.

What input devices do laptops use? Most laptops have an integrated pointing device, such as a **touch pad** (or **trackpad**)—a small, touch-sensitive area at the base of the keyboard. Mac laptops include multitouch trackpads, which don't have buttons but are controlled by various one-, two-, three-, and four-finger actions. For example, scrolling is controlled by brushing two fingers along the trackpad in any direction. Most touch pads are sensitive to taps, interpreting them as mouse clicks. Most laptops also have buttons under or near the pad to record mouse clicks.

What input devices are used with games? Game controllers such as joysticks, game pads, and steering wheels are also considered input devices because they send data to computing devices. Game controllers, which are similar to the devices used on gaming consoles such as the Xbox One and the PlayStation, are also available for use with computers. They have buttons and miniature pointing devices that provide input to the computer. Most game controllers, such as those for Rock Band and the Wii U, are wireless to provide extra mobility.

Image and Sound Input

Objective 2.6 *Explain how images and sounds are input into computing devices.*

What are popular input devices for images? Digital cameras, camcorders, and cell phones are common devices for capturing pictures and video and are all

BITS&BYTES

Keystroke Shortcuts

Did you know that you can combine certain keystrokes to take shortcuts within an application, such as Microsoft Word, or within the operating system itself? The following are a few of the most helpful Windows-based shortcuts. For more, visit **support.microsoft.com**. For a list of shortcuts for Macs, see **apple.com/support**.

TEXT FORMATTING	FILE MANAGEMENT	CUT/COPY/PASTE	WINDOWS CONTROLS
Ctrl+B applies (or removes) **bold** formatting to/from selected text.	**Ctrl+O** opens the Open dialog box.	**Ctrl+X** cuts (removes) selected text and stores it in the Clipboard.	**Windows key+Arrow key** snaps active windows to corner or side.
Ctrl+I applies (or removes) *italic* formatting to/from selected text.	**Ctrl+N** opens a new document.	**Ctrl+C** copies selected text to the Clipboard.	**Alt+Tab** switches between apps and windows using Task view.
Ctrl+U applies (or removes) underlining to/from selected text.	**Ctrl+S** saves a document.	**Ctrl+V** pastes selected text (previously cut or copied) from the Clipboard.	**Windows key+Ctrl+D** creates a new virtual desktop.
	Ctrl+P opens the Print page (backstage view) in Office 2016.		**Windows key+Ctrl+F4** closes the current virtual desktop.

DIG DEEPER How Touch Screens Work

Touch-screen technology was developed in 1971 and used primarily with ATMs and fast-food order displays. The technology for monitors and other displays was made popular by the iPod Touch in 2007 and is now in smartphones, tablets, and laptop and desktop monitors. But how do touch-screen monitors know where you're touching? How do they know what you want them to do?

The basic idea behind touch screens is pretty straightforward—when you place your finger or stylus on a screen, it changes the physical state of the screen and registers your touch. The location of your touch is then translated into a command. Three basic systems are used to recognize a person's touch: *resistive*, *capacitive*, and *surface acoustic wave*. All of these systems require the basic components of a touch-responsive glass panel, controller, and software driver, combined with a display and computer processor.

The *resistive system* maps the exact location of the pressure point created when a user touches the screen. The *capacitive system* (see Figure 2.12) uses the change in the electrical charge on the glass panel of the monitor, which is created by the user's touch, to generate a location. The third technology, *surface acoustic wave system*, uses two transducers (electrical devices that convert energy from one form to another) that are placed along the x and y axes of the monitor's glass plate. Reflectors, which are also placed on the glass, are used to reflect an electric signal sent from the sending transducer to the receiving transducer. The receiving transducer determines whether the signal has been disturbed by a touch event and locates the touch instantly. With all three systems, the display's software driver then translates the touch into something the operating system can understand, similar to how a mouse driver translates a mouse's movements into a click or drag.

Because the resistive system uses pressure to register a touch, it doesn't matter if the touch is created by a finger or another device. On the other hand, a capacitive system must have conductive input, so generally a finger is required. The surface acoustic wave system allows touches by any object.

The iPhone introduced another complexity to the touch-screen system—a multitouch user interface. In addition to just pressing the screen in one location, multitouch technology can process multiple simultaneous touches on the screen. For example, pinching or spreading out your thumb and finger together makes the display zoom out and in, respectively. The features of each touch, such as size, shape, and location, are also determined.

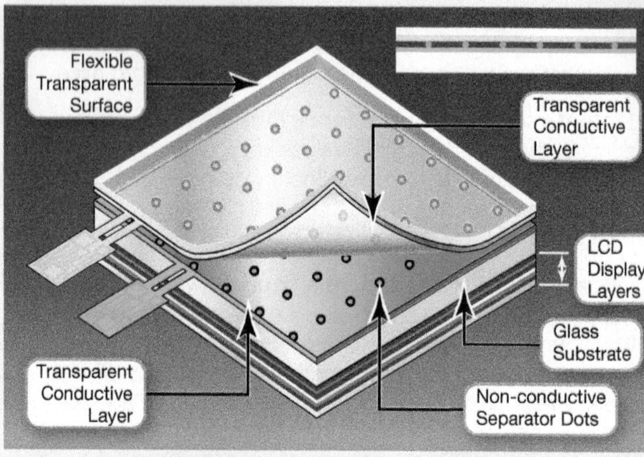

FIGURE 2.12 Some basic touch screens use a capacitive system to detect touches and translate them into meaningful commands that are understood by the computer's operating system.

A touch-sensitive screen, like the one used with the iPhone and iPad and with many other smartphones and tablets, arranges the capacitors in a coordinate system so the circuitry can sense changes at each point along the grid (see Figure 2.13).

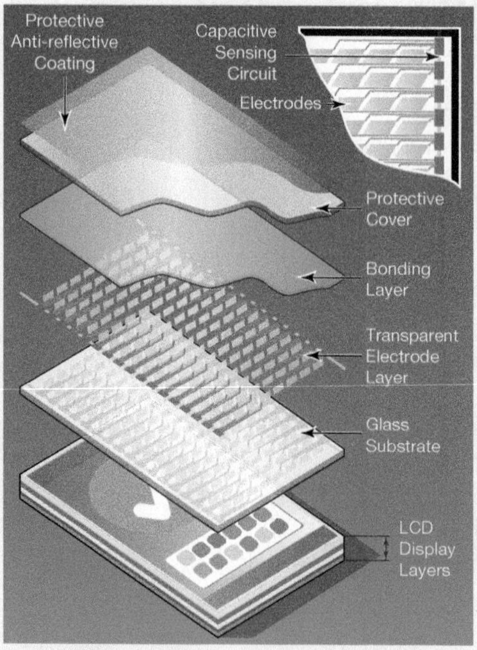

FIGURE 2.13 Multitouch screens use a coordinate-based grid to arrange the capacitors so the circuitry can detect and respond to multiple touches occurring at the same time.

Consequently, every point on the grid generates its own signal when touched and can do so even as another signal is being generated simultaneously. The signals are then relayed to the device's processor. This allows the device to determine the location and movement of simultaneous touches in multiple locations.

After detecting the position and type of touch occurring on the display, the device's processor combines this information with the information it has about the application in use and what was being done in the application when the touch occurred. The processor relays that information to the program in use, and the command is executed. All this happens seemingly instantaneously.

considered input devices. These devices can connect to your computer with a cable, transmit data wirelessly, or transfer data automatically through the Internet. **Scanners** can also input images. They work similarly to a photocopy machine; however, instead of generating the image on paper, they create a digital image, which you can then print, save, or e-mail.

How do I capture live video from my computing device? A **webcam** is a front-facing camera that attaches to a desktop computer or is built into a laptop, tablet, smartphone, or desktop monitor. Although webcams are able to capture still images, they're used mostly for capturing and transmitting live video. Videoconferencing software lets a person using a device equipped with a webcam and a microphone transmit video and audio across the Internet. Video apps such as Skype (see the Try This in Chapter 1, pages 11–12) and ooVoo make it easy to videoconference with multiple people (see Figure 2.14). With many apps, you can also exchange files, swap control of computers, and text message during calls.

How do my computing devices benefit from accepting sound input? In addition to letting others hear you in a videoconference, equipping your device to accept sound input opens up a variety of possibilities. You can conduct audio conferences with work colleagues, chat with friends or family over the Internet, record podcasts, and even control computing devices with your voice. Inputting sound to your computer requires using a **microphone (**or **mic)**—a device that lets you capture sound waves (such as your voice) and transfer them to digital format on your computer. Laptops, tablets, and smartphones come with built-in microphones.

FIGURE 2.14 Videoconferencing relies on two input devices: a *webcam* and a *microphone*. *(Rocketclips/Shutterstock)*

How can I use my voice to control my computing device? Voice recognition software allows you to control your computing devices by speaking into the device's microphone instead of using a keyboard or mouse. Apps like Dragon Naturally Speaking are available as stand-alone apps but voice recognition features are built into the Windows and OS X operating systems as well.

Popular extensions of voice recognition software are **intelligent personal assistants** such as Apple's Siri and Microsoft's Cortana (see Figure 2.15). These

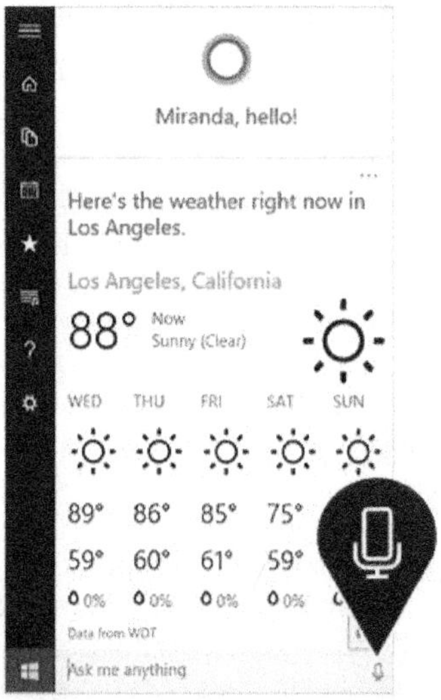

FIGURE 2.15 Just tap the microphone icon and ask Microsoft's intelligent personal assistant Cortana a question. She communicates using natural language processing techniques. *(Microsoft Cortana, Windows 10, Microsoft Corporation)*

so-called *software agents* respond to voice commands and then use your input, access to the Internet, and location-aware services to perform various tasks, such as finding the closest pizza parlor to your present location.

What types of add-on microphones are available? For specialized situations, built-in microphones don't always provide the best performance. You may want to consider adding other types of microphones, such as those shown in Figure 2.16, to your system for the best results. ■

FIGURE 2.16

Types of Microphones

MICROPHONE TYPE	ATTRIBUTES	BEST USED FOR
Close Talk 	• Attached to a headset (allows for listening) • Leaves hands free	• Video conferencing • Phone calls • Speech recognition software
Omnidirectional 	• Picks up sounds equally well from all directions	• Conference calls in meeting rooms
Unidirectional 	• Picks up sounds from only one direction	• Recordings with one voice (podcasts)
Clip-On (Lavalier) 	• Clips to clothing • Available as wireless	• Presentations requiring freedom of movement • Leaves hands free for writing on whiteboards

(Fotolia, Joseph Branston/PC Format Magazine/Future/Getty Images, Sumnersgraphicsinc/Fotolia, Feliks Gurevich/Shutterstock)

BITS&BYTES

Near Field Communication (NFC): Now Pay (or Get Paid) Anywhere with Your Phone

Paid for anything in a retail store with your phone lately? To accomplish this, your phone (and other devices) use a set of communication protocols called **near field communication (NFC)**. Devices equipped with NFC can communicate with each other when they are held in close proximity. When paying with your phone, NFC enables the input of payment information (your credit/debit card number) into a merchant's computer system.

But how can an artist selling his or her work at an art show in a park, for example, accept mobile payments? Now companies like Square are deploying readers (see Figure 2.17) that connect wirelessly to Apple and Android devices (like phones or tablets) and allow customers to pay using NFC-enabled devices. Now you can sell your products and services anywhere and still accept all the latest payment technologies!

FIGURE 2.17 Portable NFC communication devices for accepting payments are now available. *(Mika Images/Alamy)*

output DEVICES

An **output device** lets you send processed data out of your computer in the form of text, pictures (graphics), sounds (audio), or video. Let's look at some popular output devices you'll encounter at school and in the workplace.

Monitors

Objective 2.7 *Name common types of monitors, and identify important aspects of their quality.*

What are the different types of monitors? The most common output device is a **monitor** (sometimes referred to as a **display screen**), which displays text, graphics, and videos as soft copies (copies you can see only on screen). The most common type of monitor is a **liquid crystal display (LCD)**. An LCD monitor, also called a flat-panel monitor, is light and energy efficient. Some newer monitors use **light-emitting diode (LED)** technology, which is more energy efficient and may have better color accuracy and thinner panels than LCD monitors. LCD flat-panel monitors have replaced cathode ray tube (CRT) monitors. CRT monitors are considered **legacy technology**, or computing devices that use techniques, parts, and methods that are no longer popular. Although legacy technology may still be functional, it has been replaced by newer technological advances.

Organic light-emitting diode (OLED) displays use organic compounds that produce light when exposed to an electric current. Unlike LCDs and LEDs, OLEDs do not require a backlight to function and therefore draw less power and have a much thinner display, sometimes as thin as 3 mm. They are also brighter and more environmentally friendly than LCDs. Because of their lower power needs, OLED displays run longer on a single battery charge than do LEDs, which is why OLED technology is probably the technology used in your cell phone, iPod, and digital camera.

Companies like LG are now working on transparent and flexible OLED display screens (see Figure 2.18). These screens allow you to see what is behind the screen while still being able to display information on the screen. These types of screens present interesting possibilities for augmented reality. *Augmentative reality (AR)* is a view of a real-world environment whose elements are *augmented* (or supplemented) by some type of computer-generated sensory input such as video, graphics, or GPS data (see Chapter 1, pages 20–21). For instance, if you had a transparent screen on your smartphone and held it up to view street signs that were in English, you could possibly have your phone display the signs in another language. Currently, applications like this exist but require the use of a camera as well as your screen. But transparent screens will eliminate the need for the camera.

How do LCD monitors work? Monitor screens are grids made up of millions of tiny dots, called **pixels**. When these pixels are illuminated by the light waves generated by a fluorescent panel at the back of your screen, they create the images you see on the screen or monitor. Each pixel on the newest 4K resolution TVs and monitors is actually made up of four yellow, red, blue, and green subpixels. (Older devices don't have yellow subpixels.) Some newer TVs further split the subpixels into upper and lower, which can brighten and darken independently. LCD monitors are made of two or more sheets of material filled with a liquid crystal solution (see Figure 2.19). A fluorescent panel at the back of the LCD monitor generates light waves. When electric current passes through the liquid crystal solution, the crystals move around and either block the fluorescent light or let the light shine through. This blocking or passing of light by the crystals causes images to form on the screen. The various combinations of yellow, red, blue, and green make up the components of color we see on our monitors.

FIGURE 2.18 Because they don't need a backlight, OLED displays can be made transparent and flexible. *(Yonhap/EPA/Newscom)*

What factors affect the quality of an LCD monitor? When choosing an LCD monitor, the most important factors to consider are aspect ratio and resolution. The **aspect ratio** is the width-to-height proportion of a monitor. Traditionally, aspect ratios have been 4:3, but newer monitors are available with an aspect ratio of 16:9 to accommodate HD format video. The screen **resolution**, or the clearness or sharpness of the image, reflects the number of pixels on the screen. An LCD monitor may have a native (or maximum) resolution of 1600 × 1200, meaning it contains 1600 vertical

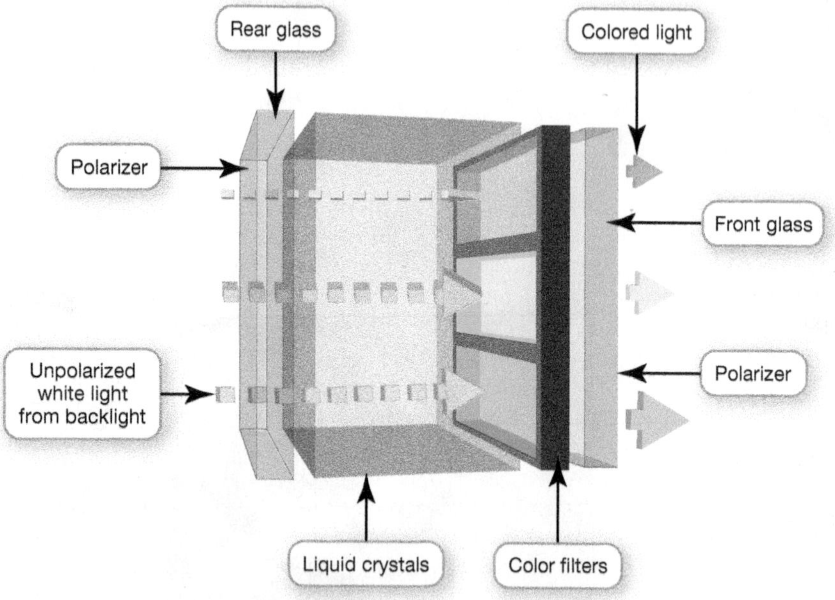

FIGURE 2.19 A magnification of a single pixel in a conventional LCD monitor. (The newest 4K resolution TVs and monitors also have a yellow subpixel.)

columns with 1200 pixels in each column. The higher the resolution, the sharper and clearer the image will be, but generally, the resolution of an LCD monitor is dictated by the screen size and aspect ratio. Although you can change the resolution of an LCD monitor beyond its native resolution, the images will become distorted. Generally, you should buy a monitor with the highest resolution available for the screen size (measured in inches). Figure 2.20 lists these and other factors to consider when judging the quality of an LCD monitor.

Is a bigger screen size always better? The bigger the monitor, the more you can display, and depending on what you want to display, size may matter. In general, the larger the panel, the larger number of pixels it can display. For example, a 27-inch monitor can display 2560 × 1440 pixels, whereas a 21.5-inch monitor may only be able to display 1680 × 1050 pixels. However, most new monitors have at least the 1920 × 1080 resolution required to display Blu-ray movies.

Larger screens can also allow you to view multiple documents or web pages at the same time, creating the effect of using two separate monitors side by side. However, buying two smaller monitors might be cheaper than buying one large monitor. For either option—a big screen or two separate screens—check that your computer has the appropriate video hardware to support these display devices.

What other features should I look for in an LCD monitor? Some monitors, especially those on laptop computers, come with built-in features such as speakers,

FIGURE 2.20

Factors to Consider When Shopping for a Monitor

FACTOR	POSSIBLE PROBLEMS	LOOK FOR
Aspect Ratio: Width-to-height proportion of a screen	• An odd aspect ratio may make images look distorted	• Ratios of 4:3 or 16:9 (HDTV)
Screen Resolution: Number of pixels displayed on the screen	• Low screen resolution = unclear image • High resolution on a small size monitor results in image being too small	• Highest resolution monitor is capable of displaying (make sure you are comfortable viewing that size image)
Contrast Ratio: Difference in light intensity between brightest white and darkest black a monitor can produce	• Ratio too low results in colors fading when adjusting brightness	• Ratios between 400:1 and 1,000:1
Viewing Angle: Distance in degrees from which you can move to the side of (or above or below) a monitor before the image degrades	• Angle too low means people not sitting directly in front of the monitor will see a poor image	• 150 degrees or more is preferable
Brightness: Greatest amount of light showing when the monitor is displaying pure white (measured in candelas per square meter [cd/m^2] or *nits*)	• Image will be hard to see in bright rooms if brightness level is too low	• 300 cd/m^2 or greater
Response Time: Time it takes for a pixel to change color (in milliseconds)	• High response time results in images appearing jerky	• Seek lowest possible response time if viewing live action sports

BITS&BYTES

Forget HDTV—Here Comes Ultra HD!

Now that everyone loves their HDTVs, what can manufacturers do next? Ultra HD (otherwise known as 4K) TV is the emerging standard. HDTVs feature a resolution of 1920 × 1080 pixels (height and width, respectively). Ultra HD TVs, on the other hand, boast 3840 × 2160 resolution, which provides screens with four times as many pixels as HDTV devices. More pixels generally provide a sharper picture on a large screen, so screen sizes of 50 inches and up should have a noticeable difference in picture quality.

So should you throw away your HDTV and replace it with an Ultra HD TV? Probably not yet. Ultra HD TVs are expensive, and there is not much programming available yet in the Ultra HD format. But as more programming becomes available and prices of Ultra HD TVs fall, it may soon make sense to consider a higher resolution TV.

Or, you may just hang on and wait for 8K TVs (7680 × 4320 resolution), which may be available on the consumer market within three years. The technology to record 8K already exists—in fact, the BBC recorded much of the 2012 Summer Olympics in 8K format. Whatever happens, expect your TV picture to just keep getting better!

webcams, and microphones. A built-in multiformat memory card reader is convenient for displaying images directly on the monitor or for downloading pictures quickly from a camera memory card to your PC. Another nice feature to look for in a desktop LCD monitor is built-in USB ports. This feature lets you connect extra peripherals easily without reaching around the back of the PC.

How do I show output to a large group of people? A **projector** lets you project images from your computing device onto a wall or viewing screen. Projectors are commonly used in business and education settings such as conference rooms and classrooms. Many projectors are small and lightweight and some are small enough to fit in the palm of your hand. These portable projectors are ideal for businesspeople who have to make presentations at client locations. *Entertainment projectors* include stereo speakers and an array of multimedia connectors, making them a good option for use in the home to display TV programs, DVDs, digital images, or video games in a large format. If your computing device is equipped with an HDMI port, you can also choose to connect your computer directly to an HDTV using an HDMI cable. The most common HDMI connector types are shown in Figure 2.21. Full size (or type A) connectors are found on most TVs and laptops. Tablets and phones are more likely to have a mini (type C) or micro (type D) HDMI port.

FIGURE 2.21 Cables with the appropriate connectors are available to facilitate connection of your mobile devices to your HDTV for enhanced viewing. *(Tether Tools)*

Printers

Objective 2.8 *Describe various types of printers, and explain when you would use them.*

What are the different types of printers? In addition to monitors, another common output device is the **printer**, which creates hard copies (copies you can touch) of text and graphics. There are two primary categories of printers: inkjet and laser, both of which are considered nonimpact printers.

A **nonimpact printer** such as an inkjet printer sprays ink or uses laser beams to transfer marks onto the paper. An **impact printer** has tiny hammer-like keys that strike the paper through an inked ribbon to make marks on the paper. For most users, impact printers are legacy technology.

What are the advantages of inkjet printers? An **inkjet printer** (see Figure 2.22) is the type of printer found in many homes. These printers are popular because they're affordable and produce high-quality printouts quickly and quietly. Inkjet printers work by spraying tiny drops of ink onto

ACTIVE HELPDESK

Using Output Devices

In this Active Helpdesk, you'll play the role of a helpdesk staffer, fielding questions about different output devices.

paper and are great for printing black-and-white text as well as color images. In fact, when loaded with the right paper, higher-end inkjet printers can print images that look like professional-quality photos. One thing to consider when buying an inkjet printer is the type and cost of the ink cartridges the printer needs. Some printers use two cartridges: black and color. Others use four or more cartridges: typically, cyan, magenta, yellow, and black. The four-color printing process many inkjets use is known as **CMYK** (this acronym stands for cyan, magenta, yellow, and key, which is usually represented by black). The inks are layered onto a lighter (usually white) surface to partially or entirely mask different colors. The layering reduces the brightness of the white so this process is known as a *subtractive color model*.

Why would I want a laser printer? A **laser printer** uses laser beams and static electricity to deliver toner (similar to ink) onto the correct areas of the page (see Figure 2.23). Heat is used to fuse the toner to the page, making the image permanent. Laser printers are often used in office or classroom settings because they print faster than inkjet printers and produce higher-quality printouts. Black-and-white laser printers have also been common in homes for a decade. Over the past few years, the price of color laser printers has fallen dramatically, making them price competitive with high-end inkjet printers. Thus, color laser printers are a viable option for the home. If you print a high volume of pages, consider a laser printer. When you include the price of ink or toner in the overall cost, color laser printers can be more economical than inkjets.

FIGURE 2.23 Laser printers print quickly and offer high-quality printouts. *(Xerox Corporation)*

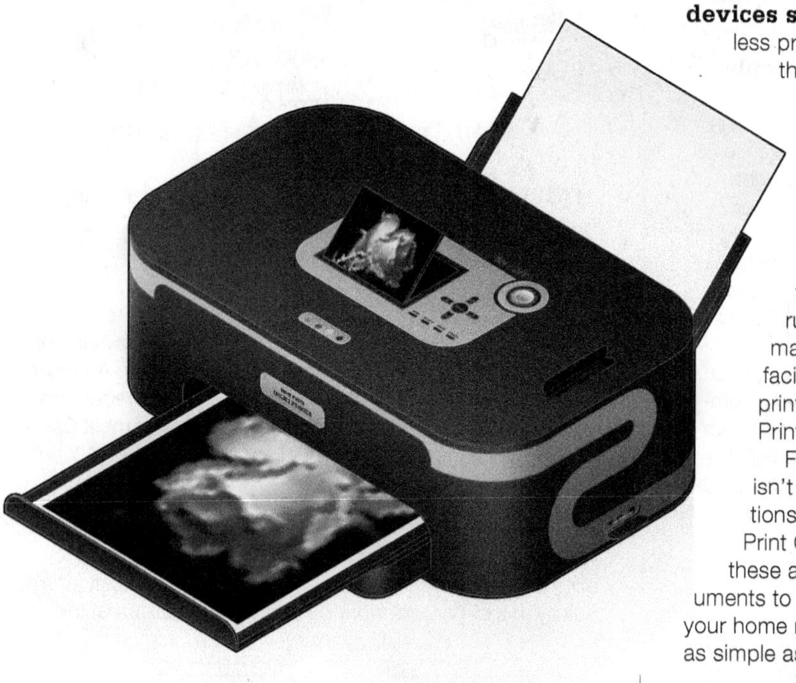

FIGURE 2.22 Inkjet printers are popular among home users, especially with the rise of digital photography. Many inkjet printers are optimized for printing photos from digital cameras. *(TheVectorminator/Shutterstock)*

What's the best way to print from portable devices such as tablets and smartphones? Wireless printers are a good option for home networks as they let several people print to the same printer from different devices and any location in the home. There are two types of wireless printers: WiFi and Bluetooth. Both WiFi and Bluetooth printers have a range of up to approximately 300 feet. WiFi, however, sends data more quickly than Bluetooth.

Wireless printers are also great for printing from portable devices. If you're using a device running Apple's iOS (such as an iPhone), AirPrint makes printing easy. AirPrint is a feature of iOS that facilitates printing to AirPrint-compatible wireless printers, and many printers produced today are AirPrint compatible.

For non-Apple mobile devices (or if your printer isn't compatible with AirPrint), you can try other solutions, such as Presto by Collobos Software and ThinPrint Cloud Printer by Cortado. Once you install one of these apps on your portable device, you can send documents to printers that are connected to PCs and Macs on your home network. It makes printing from mobile devices as simple as hitting print on your laptop.

Can I carry my printer with me? Although some inkjet printers are small enough to be considered portable, you may want to consider a printer designed for portability. These compact printers can connect to your computer, tablet, or smartphone via Bluetooth technology or through a USB port. Portable printers are often compact enough to fit in a briefcase

a

b

c

FIGURE 2.24 Specialty printers: (a) all-in-one printer, (b) large format printer, (c) thermal printer. *(Image reprinted courtesy of Epson America, Inc.; Image reprinted courtesy of Epson America, Inc.; Vetkit/Fotolia)*

or backpack, are lightweight, and can run on batteries as well as AC power.

Are there any other types of specialty printers? Although you'll probably use laser or inkjet printers most often, you might also encounter several other types of printers (shown in Figure 2.24):

- An **all-in-one printer** combines the functions of a printer, scanner, copier, and fax into one machine. Popular for their space-saving convenience, all-in-one printers may use either inkjet or laser technology.
- A **large format printer** generates oversize images such as professional graphics, high resolution photographs, banners, posters, and infographics that require more sophisticated color detail. Some of these printers use up to 12 different inks to achieve high-quality realistic color images.
- A **thermal printer** works either by melting wax-based ink onto ordinary paper (a process called *thermal wax transfer printing*) or by burning dots onto specially coated paper (a process called *direct thermal printing*). Thermal printers are used in stores to print receipts and in airports for electronic ticketing, and many models feature wireless technology. Thermal printers are also popular for mobile printing in conjunction with smartphones and tablets.

How do I choose the best printer? Your first step is to decide what your primary printing need is. If you're planning to print color photos and graphics, an inkjet printer or color laser printer is a must, even though the cost per page will be higher. If you'll be printing mostly black-and-white text-based documents or will be sharing your printer with others, a black-and-white laser printer is best because of its speed and overall economy for volume printing. It's also important to determine whether you want just a printer or a device that prints and scans, copies, or faxes (an all-in-one). In addition, you should decide whether you need to print from mobile devices.

Once you have narrowed down the *type* of printer you want, you can use the criteria listed in Figure 2.25 to help you determine the best model to meet your needs.

Sound Output

Objective 2.9 *Discuss options for outputting sound from your computing devices.*

What are the output devices for sound? Most computers include inexpensive **speakers**, which are the output devices for sound. These speakers are sufficient to play the standard audio clips you find on the web and usually for letting you participate in videoconferencing or phone calls over the Internet. However, if you plan to digitally edit audio files or are particular about how your music sounds, you may want a more sophisticated speaker system, such as one that includes subwoofers (special speakers that produce only low bass sounds) and surround-sound speakers. A **surround-sound system** is a set of speakers and audio processing that envelops the listener in a 360-degree field of sound. In addition, wireless speaker systems are available to help you avoid cluttering up your rooms with speaker wires.

If you work in close proximity to other employees or travel with a laptop, you may need to use headphones or earbuds to avoid distracting other people. Both devices plug into the same jack on your computing device to which speakers connect. Studies of users of portable media players have shown that hearing might be damaged by excessive volume, especially when using earbuds because they fit into the ear canals. Exercise caution when using these devices. ■

BITS&BYTES

Does It Matter What Paper I Print On?

The quality of your printer is only part of what controls the quality of a printed image. The paper you use and the printer settings that control the amount of ink used are equally important.

- If you're printing text-only documents for personal use, using low-cost paper is fine. You also may want to consider selecting draft mode in your printer settings to conserve ink. However, if you're printing more formal documents, such as business correspondence, you may want to choose a higher-quality paper (determined by the paper's weight, whiteness, and brightness) and adjust your print setting to "normal" or "best."
- The weight of paper is measured in pounds, with 20 pounds being standard. A heavier paper may be best for projects such as brochures, but be sure to check that your printer can handle the added thickness of the paper.
- The degree of paper whiteness is a matter of personal preference. Generally, the whiter the paper, the brighter the printed color. However, for documents that are more formal, you may want to use a creamier color.
- The brightness of paper usually varies from 85 to 94. The higher the number, the brighter the paper, and the easier it is to read printed text.
- Opacity, or the "show through" of ink from one side of the paper to the other, is especially important if you're printing on both sides of the paper.

If you're printing photos, paper quality can have a big impact on your results. Photo paper is more expensive than regular paper and comes in a variety of textures ranging from matte to high gloss. For a photo-lab look, high-gloss paper is the best choice. Semigloss (often referred to as satin) is good for formal portraits, while a matte surface is often used for black-and-white photo printing.

FIGURE 2.25

Major Printer Attributes

ATTRIBUTE	CONSIDERATIONS
Speed	• Print speed is measured in *pages per minute (PPM)*. • Black-and-white documents print faster than color documents. • Laser printers often print faster than inkjets.

Resolution	• Resolution refers to a printer's image clarity.
	• Resolution is measured in *dots per inch (dpi)*.
	• Higher dpi = greater level of detail and clarity.
	• Recommended dpi:
	  • Black-and-white text: 300
	  • General purpose images: 1200
	  • Photos: 4800

Color Output	• Printers with separate cartridges for each color produce the best quality output. • Inkjet and laser color printers generally have four cartridges (black, cyan, magenta, and yellow). • Higher-quality printers have six cartridges (the four above plus light cyan and light magenta). • With separate cartridges, you only need to replace the empty one.
Cost of Consumables	• Consumables are printer cartridges and paper. • Printer cartridges can exceed the cost of some printers. • Consumer magazines such as *Consumer Reports* can help you research costs.

(Freshidea/Fotolia, Michael Nivelet/Fotolia, Thomas Amby/Fotolia, Tomislav Forgo/Fotolia)

Before moving on to Part 2:

1. **Watch Replay Video 2.1.**
2. **Then check your understanding of what you've learned so far.**

check your understanding // review & practice

For a quick review to see what you've learned so far, answer the following questions.

multiple choice

1. Which of the following is NOT one of the four major functions of a computer?
   - **a.** input
   - **b.** processing
   - **c.** indexing
   - **d.** storage
2. Which of the following can be both an input and an output device?
   - **a.** mouse
   - **b.** keyboard
   - **c.** monitor
   - **d.** laser printer
3. Which of the following display screens does not require a backlight to function?
   - **a.** organic light-emitting diode (OLED) display
   - **b.** liquid crystal display (LCD)
   - **c.** light-emitting diode (LED) display
   - **d.** cathode ray tube (CRT)
4. What type of printer sprays tiny drops of ink onto paper?
   - **a.** inkjet
   - **b.** impact
   - **c.** thermal
   - **d.** laser
5. When buying a monitor, which factor is NOT important to consider?
   - **a.** screen resolution
   - **b.** viewing angle
   - **c.** color depth
   - **d.** aspect ratio

MyITLab

Go to **MyITLab** to take an autograded version of the *Check Your Understanding* review and to find all media resources for the chapter.

TECHBYTES WEEKLY

Stay current with the TechBytes Weekly Newsletter.

Continue

TRY THIS What's Inside My Computer?

Understanding what capabilities your current computer has is one of the first steps toward computer literacy. In this exercise, you'll learn how to explore the components of your Windows computer.

Step 1 To gather information about the storage devices on our computer, click **File Explorer** from the Taskbar or from the Start menu. Then in the navigation pane, click **This PC** to display information about your computer's devices. *(Windows 10, Microsoft Corporation)*

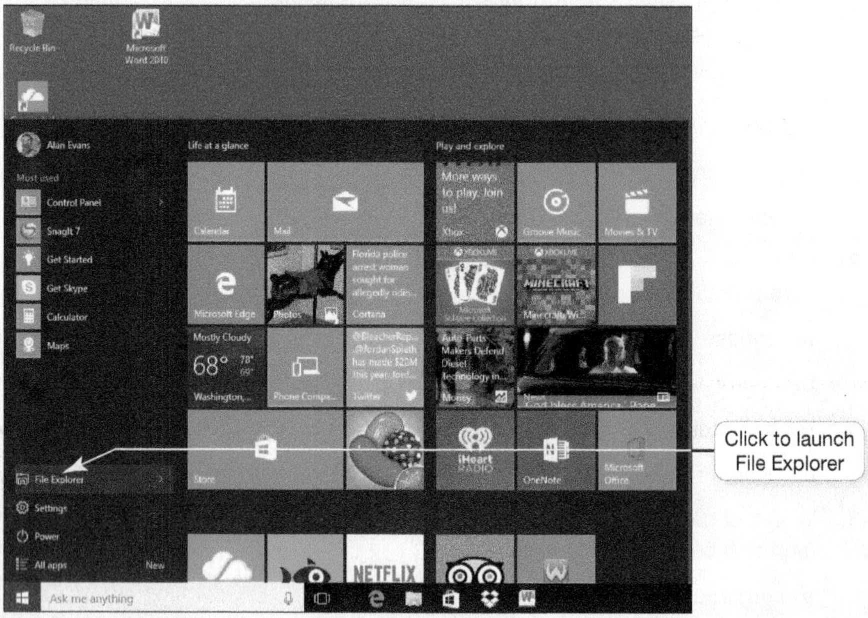

Step 2 The File Explorer This PC screen displays information about internal storage devices (such as internal hard drives), optical storage devices (such as DVD drives), and portable storage devices (such as flash drives and external hard drives). To display the System screen, click the **Computer tab** on the File Explorer ribbon, and then the **System properties button**. *(Windows 10, Microsoft Corporation)*

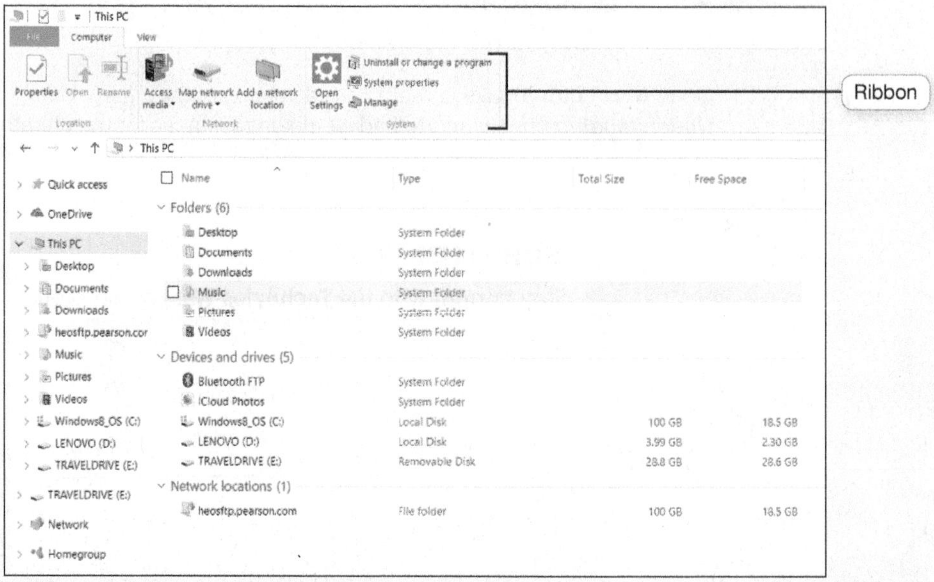

Step 3 You can gather quite a bit of information from the System screen, such as:

- Version of Windows
- Type of processor
- Speed of the processor
- Amount of RAM installed
- System type (32-bit or 64-bit) *(Windows 10, Microsoft Corporation)*

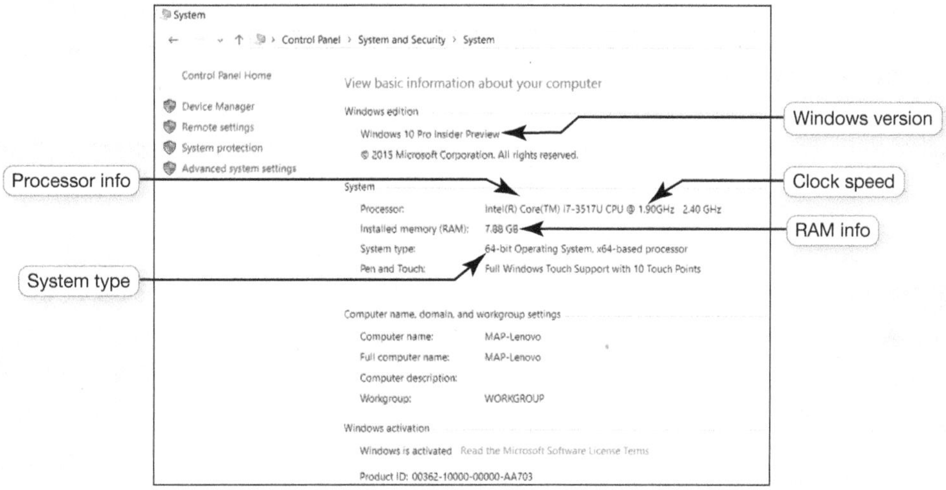

Make This TOOL: App Inventor 2

MAKE: A Mobile App

Want to build your own Android app from scratch? You can, with a simple tool called **App Inventor**. To get started, have ready:

1. A computer connected to a WiFi network
2. The Chrome browser
3. A Google account
4. The MIT AI2 Companion app
5. [optional] An Android device connected to the same WiFI network

In this exercise, you'll explore the **App Inventor** tool and begin working with your first simple app. As you'll see, making your device work for you is as easy as drag and drop with **App Inventor**. *(MIT App Inventor 2, Massachusetts Institute of Technology. Creative Commons Attribution-ShareAlike 3.0 Unported License)*

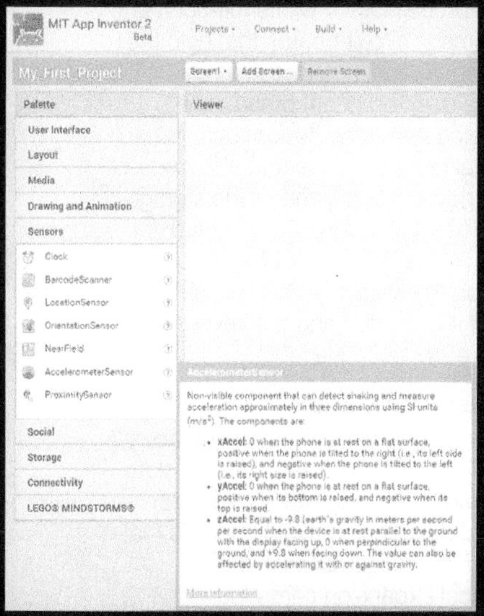

App Inventor is a programming platform used to create apps for Android devices. Using App Inventor, you can easily drag and drop components to design your App's interface and its behavior.

For the instructions for this exercise, go to MyITLab.

Processing, Storage, and Connectivity

Learning Outcome 2.2 You will be able to describe how computers process and store data and how devices connect to a computer system.

So far, we have explored the components of your computer that you use to input and output data. But where does the processing take place, and where is the data stored? And how does your computer connect with peripherals and other computers?

processing and memory on the MOTHERBOARD

The main processing functions of your computer take place in the CPU and memory, both of which reside on your computer's motherboard. In the following sections, we'll explore the components of the motherboard and how memory helps your computer process data.

The Motherboard and Memory

Objective 2.10 *Define motherboard and RAM.*

What exactly is a motherboard? The **motherboard** is the main circuit board that contains the central electronic components of the computer, including the computer's processor (CPU), its memory, and the many circuit boards that help the computer function (see Figure 2.26). On a desktop, the motherboard is located inside the system unit, the metal or plastic case that also houses the power source and all the storage devices (CD/DVD drive and hard drive). In a laptop or all-in-one computer, the system unit is combined with the monitor and the keyboard into a single package.

What's on the motherboard besides the CPU and memory? The motherboard also includes slots for **expansion cards (**or **adapter cards)**, which are circuit boards that provide additional functionality. Typical expansion cards found in the system unit are sound and video cards. A **sound card** provides a connection for the speakers and microphone, whereas a **video card** provides a connection for the monitor. Laptops and tablets have video and sound capabilities integrated into their motherboards. High-end desktops use expansion cards to provide video and sound capabilities.

Other expansion cards provide a means for network and Internet connections. A **network interface card (NIC)**, which enables your computer to connect with other computers or to a cable modem to facilitate a high-speed Internet connection, is often integrated into the motherboard. Lastly, some expansion cards provide additional USB and Thunderbolt ports.

FIGURE 2.26 A motherboard contains the socket for the computer's processor (CPU), slots for memory (RAM) modules, ports, and slots for expansion cards. *(GIGA-BYTE Technology Co., Ltd.)*

What exactly is RAM? Random access memory (RAM) is the place in a computer where the programs and data that the computer is currently using, are stored. RAM is much faster to read from and write to than the hard drive and other forms of storage. The processor can request the RAM's contents, which can be located, opened, and delivered to the CPU for processing in a few nanoseconds (billionths of a second). If you look at a motherboard, you'll see RAM as a series of small cards (called *memory cards* or *memory modules*) plugged into slots on the motherboard.

Because the entire contents of RAM are erased when you turn off the computer, RAM is a temporary or **volatile storage** location. To save data permanently, you need to save it to your hard drive or to another permanent storage location such as a flash drive or cloud storage.

Does the motherboard contain any other kinds of memory besides RAM? In addition to RAM, the motherboard contains a form of memory called **read-only memory (ROM)**. ROM holds all the instructions the computer needs to start up when it's powered on. Unlike data stored in RAM, which is volatile storage, the instructions stored in ROM are permanent, making ROM a **nonvolatile storage** location, which means the data isn't erased when the power is turned off.

Processing

Objective 2.11 *Explain the main functions of the CPU.*

What is the CPU? The **central processing unit (CPU or processor)** is sometimes referred to as the "brains" of the computer because it controls all the functions performed by the computer's other components and processes all the commands issued to it by software instructions. Modern CPUs can perform as many as tens of billions of tasks per second without error, making them extremely powerful components.

How is processor speed measured? Processor speed is measured in units of hertz (Hz). *Hertz* is a measurement of machine cycles per second. A *machine cycle* is the process of the CPU getting the data or instructions from RAM and decoding the instructions into something the computer can understand. Once the CPU has decoded the instructions, it executes them and stores the result back in system memory. Current systems run at speeds measured in **gigahertz (GHz)** or billions of machine cycles per second. Therefore, a 3.8 GHz processor performs work at a rate of 3.8 billion machine cycles per second. It's important to realize, however, that CPU processor speed alone doesn't determine the performance of the CPU.

What else determines processor performance? Although speed is an important consideration when determining processor performance, CPU performance is also affected by other factors. One factor is the number of *cores*, or processing paths, a processor has. Initially, processors could handle only one instruction at a time. Now, processors have been designed so that they can have two, four, or even ten different paths, allowing them to process more than one instruction at a time (see Figure 2.27). Applications such as virus protection software and the operating system, which are always running behind the scenes, can have their own processor paths, freeing up the other paths to run other applications such as a web browser, Word, or iTunes more efficiently.

Besides the number of cores, what other factors determine processing power? The "best" processor will depend on your particular needs and is not always the processor with the highest processor speed and the greatest number of cores. Intel, one of the leading manufacturers of computer processor chips, has created a pictorial rating system for CPU chips. Intel provides a website (**ark.intel.com**) that assists in comparing the performance of different models of CPUs. ■

> **SOUND BYTE**
> **Virtual Computer Tour**
> In this Sound Byte, you'll take a video tour of the inside of a desktop system unit. From opening the cover to locating the power supply, CPU, and memory, you'll become more familiar with what's inside your computer.

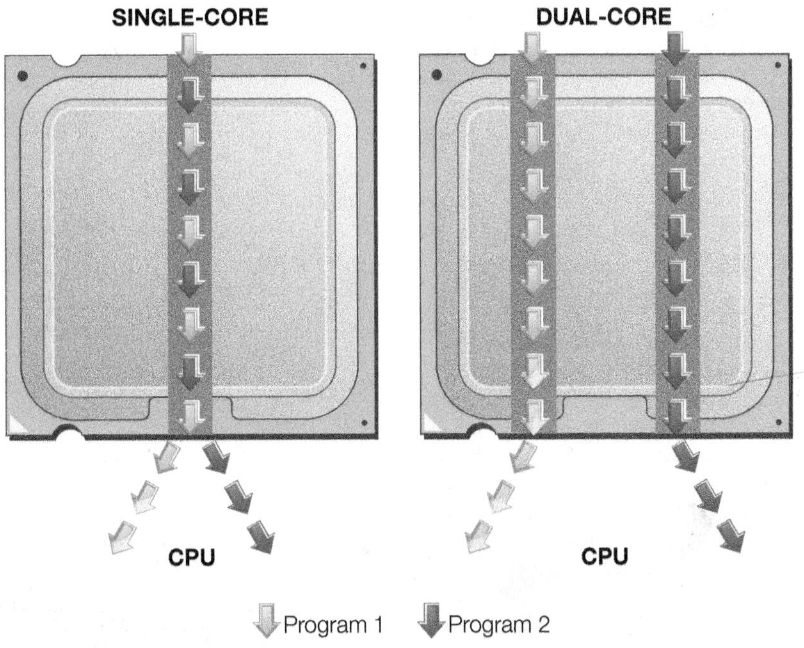

FIGURE 2.27 With multi-core processors, CPUs can work in parallel, processing two or more separate programs at the same time instead of switching back and forth between them.

storing data and INFORMATION

Because RAM is volatile storage, it can't be used to store information indefinitely. To save your data and information permanently, you need to save it to a nonvolatile storage device, such as a hard drive, cloud storage location, DVD, or flash drive.

Hard Drives

Objective 2.12 *List the various types of hard drives.*

Are there different kinds of hard drives? The **hard disk drive (HDD, or hard drive)** is your computer's primary device for permanent storage of software and documents. The hard drive is a nonvolatile storage device. An **internal hard drive** resides within the system unit and usually holds all permanently stored programs and data. Today's internal hard drives (see Figure 2.28) have capacities of as much as 8 TB or more. **External hard drives** offer similar storage capacities but reside outside the system unit and connect to the computer via a port.

The most common type of hard drive has moveable parts—spinning platters and a moving arm with a read/write head—that can fail and lead to devastating disk failure. However, the **solid-state drive (SSD)** has recently become a popular option for ultrabooks and laptop storage. SSDs have no moving parts, so they're more efficient, run with no noise, emit little heat, and require little power. In addition, they're less likely to fail after being bumped or dropped.

Permanent storage devices are located in your desktop or laptop computer in a space called a **drive bay**. There are two kinds of drive bays:

1. *Internal drive bays* cannot be seen or accessed from outside the system unit. Generally, internal drive bays are reserved for internal hard drives.
2. *External drive bays* can be seen and accessed from outside the system unit. External drive bays house DVD and Blu-ray drives, for example. On desktop computers, sometimes there are empty external drive bays that can be used to install additional drives. These extra spaces are covered by a faceplate on the front panel. Laptop computers generally do not give you the ability to add additional drives. Such expansion is done by attaching an external drive to the computer through a USB port.

FIGURE 2.28 Internal hard drives (shown here open—normally, they are sealed) are a computer's primary nonvolatile storage. *(Mbongo/Fotolia)*

Cloud Storage

Objective 2.13 *Define cloud storage, and explain how to use it.*

How can I easily access my files if I constantly switch between devices? You may find yourself using multiple devices, such as a smartphone, laptop, and a tablet, at different times during the day. Invariably, you'll find you need access to a current version of a file that is stored on a device other than the one you're using. If your devices are connected to the Internet, cloud storage provides a convenient option.

Cloud storage refers to using a service that keeps your files on the Internet (in the "cloud") rather than storing your files solely on a local device. Using a cloud storage service requires that you install software or an app on your device. A popular web-based application for storing files on the cloud is Dropbox. Dropbox supports computers running Windows, OS X, and Linux as well as many smartphones and tablets. After installing the Dropbox software on your devices, any files you save in the Dropbox folder are accessible by all your other devices via the Internet. You can also share folders in Dropbox with other Dropbox users, making it ideal for group projects.

For example, when you save a history term paper to Dropbox on your laptop, the Dropbox software also copies the paper onto a computer attached to the web. Now when you grab your smartphone and head off to class, you can access the paper created on your laptop through the Internet connection on your smartphone and make changes to it if necessary.

Dropbox storage capacity is limited to between 2 GB and 18 GB for free accounts. Other cloud storage alternatives include Microsoft OneDrive and Google Drive, each of which provide 15 GB of free space, and Apple iCloud, which offers 5 GB of free storage.

Portable and Optical Storage Options

Objective 2.14 *Describe the various portable and optical storage options.*

How can I take my files with me without relying on cloud storage? For large portable storage needs, there are portable external hard drives, which are small enough to fit into your pocket and have storage capacities of 4 TB

ethics in IT

What Is Ethical Computing?

You've probably heard news stories about people using computers to unleash viruses or commit identity theft. You may also have read about students who were prosecuted for illegally sharing copyrighted material, such as songs and videos. These are both examples of *unethical* behavior while using a computer. However, what constitutes *ethical* behavior while using a computer?

Loosely defined, *ethics* is a system of moral principles, rules, and accepted standards of conduct (see Figure 2.29). So what are the accepted standards of conduct when using computers? The Computer Ethics Institute has developed the Ten Commandments of Computer Ethics, which is widely cited as a benchmark for companies developing computer usage and compliance policies for employees. These guidelines are applicable for schools and students, as well. The following ethical computing guidelines are based on the Computer Ethics Institute's work:

FIGURE 2.29 There are different ways to define ethics, but they all apply to a common code of behavior for groups or individuals. *(Marek/Fotolia)*

Ethical Computing Guidelines

1. Avoid causing harm to others when using computers.
2. Do not interfere with other people's efforts at accomplishing work with computers.
3. Resist the temptation to snoop in other people's computer files.
4. Do not use computers to commit theft.
5. Agree not to use computers to promote lies.
6. Do not use software (or make illegal copies for others) without paying the creator for it.
7. Avoid using other people's computer resources without appropriate authorization or proper compensation.
8. Do not claim other people's intellectual output as your own.
9. Consider the social consequences of the products of your computer labor.
10. Only use computers in ways that show consideration and respect for others.

The United States has enacted laws that support some of these guidelines, such as Guideline 6, the breaking of which would violate copyright laws, and Guideline 4, which is enforceable under numerous federal and state larceny laws. Other guidelines, however, require more subtle interpretation as to what behavior is unethical because there are no laws designed to enforce them.

Consider Guideline 7, which covers unauthorized use of resources. The school you attend probably provides computer resources for you to use for coursework. But if your school gives you access to computers and the Internet, is it ethical for you to use those resources to run an online business on the weekends? Although it might not be technically illegal, you're tying up computer resources that other students could use for their intended purpose: learning and completing coursework. (This behavior also violates Guidelines 2 and 10.)

Throughout the chapters in this book, we touch on many topics related to these guidelines. So keep them in mind as you study, and think about how they relate to the actions you take as you use computers in your life.

FIGURE 2.30 Smaller, portable external hard drives enable you to take a significant amount of data and programs on the road with you. *(Inga Nielsen/Shutterstock)*

(or larger). These devices are lightweight and enclosed in a protective case. They attach to your computer via a USB port (see Figure 2.30).

A **flash drive** (sometimes referred to as a **jump drive, USB drive,** or **thumb drive**) uses solid-state flash memory, storing information on an internal memory chip. When you plug a flash drive into your computer's USB port, it appears in the operating system as another disk drive. You can write data to it or read data from it as you would a hard drive. Because a flash drive contains no moving parts, it's quite durable. It's also tiny enough to fit in your pocket (see Figure 2.31). Despite their size, flash drives can have significant storage capacity—currently as much as 1 TB. Often, flash drives are combined with other devices such as pens or keychains for added convenience.

Wireless flash drives are available that make transferring files from portable devices easier. Although they look like normal flash drives, these wireless drives can connect to your portable devices via WiFi after installing the appropriate app. Up to eight devices can be connected to the flash drive at once, and the drive can even stream media to three devices simultaneously. So your friend could be watching a movie stored on the flash drive while you're uploading pictures from your phone.

Another convenient means of portable storage is a **flash memory card**, such as an SD card. Like the flash drive, memory cards use solid-state flash memory. Most desktops and laptops include slots for flash memory cards, but if your computer is not equipped, there are memory card readers that you can plug into a USB port. Flash memory cards let you transfer digital data between your computer and devices such as digital cameras, smartphones, tablets, video cameras, and printers. Although incredibly small—some are even smaller than the size of a postage stamp—these memory cards have capacities that exceed the capacity of a DVD. Figure 2.32 compares the storage capacities of hard drives and flash drives.

What other kinds of storage devices are available? Most desktop and all-in-one computers come with at least one **optical drive** that can read from and maybe even write to CDs, DVDs, or Blu-ray discs. As we have moved toward streaming media services and cloud-based delivery of software, optical drives have not been included in laptops and ultrabooks to save weight and space. However, if you still have the need (or desire) to use optical drives, inexpensive portable drives that attach via USB ports are readily available.

Data is saved to optical discs as tiny pits that are burned into the disc by a high-speed laser. **Compact discs (CDs)** were initially created to store audio files. **Digital video (**or

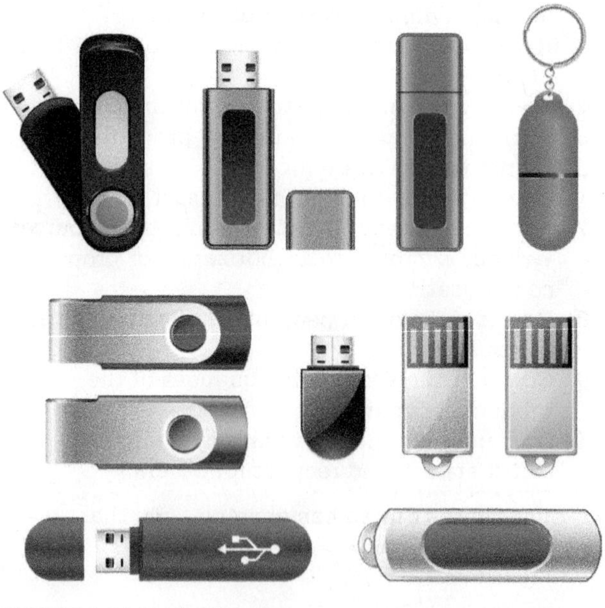

FIGURE 2.31 Flash drives are a convenient means of portable storage and come in many different shapes and sizes. *(Ekler/Shutterstock)*

FIGURE 2.32

Hard Drive and Flash Drive Storage Capacity

DRIVE TYPE	IMAGE	TYPICAL CAPACITY	DRIVE TYPE	IMAGE	TYPICAL CAPACITY
Solid-state drive (SSD)		1 TB or more	Flash drive	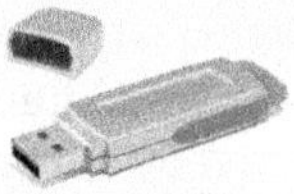	256 GB or more
External portable hard drive		4 TB or more	Flash memory card		128 GB or more
Mechanical internal hard drive		8 TB or more			

(Oleksiy Mark/Shutterstock, Julia Ivantsova/Shutterstock, D. Hurst/Alamy, Cphoto/Fotolia, ZUMA Press, Inc/Alamy)

versatile) discs (DVDs) are the same size and shape as CDs but can store up to 14 times more data than CDs.

What if you want even more storage capacity? Blu-ray is the latest incarnation of optical storage. **Blu-ray discs (BDs)**, which are similar in size and shape to CDs and DVDs, can hold as much as 50 GB of data—enough to hold approximately 4.5 hours of movies in high-definition (HD) digital format. Many desktop systems are now available with BD-ROM drives and Blu-ray burners. External BD drives are another inexpensive way to add HD storage capacity to your system. Figure 2.33 shows the storage capacities of the various optical storage media. ■

FIGURE 2.33

Optical Storage Media Capacities

MEDIUM TYPE	TYPICAL CAPACITY
Blu-ray (dual layer)	50 GB
Blu-ray	25 GB
DVD DL (dual layer)	8.5 GB
DVD	4.7 GB
CD	700 MB

connecting peripherals to the COMPUTER

Throughout this chapter, we have discussed peripheral devices that input, store, and output data and information. We will now look at how these types of devices are connected to computers so they can exchange data.

Computer Ports

Objective 2.15 *List the common types of ports used today.*

What is a port? A **port** is a place through which a peripheral device attaches to the computer so that data can be exchanged between it and the operating system. Although peripherals may connect to devices wirelessly, ports are still often used for connections.

What is the fastest data transfer port available on today's computing devices? Thunderbolt is the newest input/output technology on the market. It was developed by Intel using fiber optic technology and Thunderbolt 2 ports can achieve

trends in IT

Green Computing (Green IT)

"Going green" is a goal for many modern businesses. **Green computing** (or **green IT**) is a movement to encourage environmentally sustainable computing. The main goal is to reduce the overall carbon footprint of a company through the strategic use of computing resources and environmentally friendly computing devices. A business's *carbon footprint* is the total amount of greenhouse gases produced directly and indirectly to support the activities of the business. Carbon footprints are expressed in equivalent tons of carbon dioxide (CO_2). CO_2 is the main greenhouse gas that is contributing to global warming. Reduction of greenhouse gas emissions is critical to sustaining a healthy environment.

The main goals of green computing are

1. Reducing the use of hazardous processes or materials in the production of computing equipment
2. Promoting the use of recyclable or biodegradable materials to facilitate safe disposal of products
3. Buying products that use energy efficiently
4. Using technology to reduce employee travel

(Weerapat1003/Fotolia)

5. Reducing the use of energy and consumption of materials through shared computing resources

Sharing computing resources can make a vast difference in the consumption of resources and electricity. This is one of the reasons cloud storage is becoming so popular. Rather than having 20 individual companies each maintaining a large group of computers to hold data, savings can be achieved by having one company maintain computer resources that are able to serve the 20 other companies. However, it's not all up to businesses to practice green computing. Figure 2.34 lists a few ways you can participate:

FIGURE 2.34

Green Computing Problems and Solutions

ISSUE	ELECTRICITY	COMMUTING	USE TECHNOLOGY LONGER
	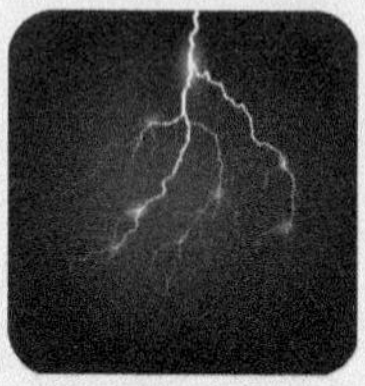		
Problems	• Electricity is often generated using fossil fuels, which produce greenhouse gas emissions • Devices are not energy efficient	• Cars generate greenhouse gases • Many people commute to work alone	• Items are replaced before their useful life is over • Old items are discarded instead of continuing to be used • Technology is not disposed of or recycled properly
Solutions	• Buy energy efficient computing equipment with high Energy Star ratings • Turn off computing devices when not in use • Use appropriate power management settings to use less power when operating devices	• Use technology to telecommute to your job • Use public transportation to commute, which uses energy more efficiently than cars • Use a green vehicle (bicycle, electric car) for your commute	• Only upgrade your technology when absolutely necessary • Donate your old technology to someone who will continue to use it (friends, family, charitable organization) • Only dispose of electronic devices at approved e-waste recycling facilities

(kovalto1/Fotolia, Berc/Fotolia, Marek/Fotolia)

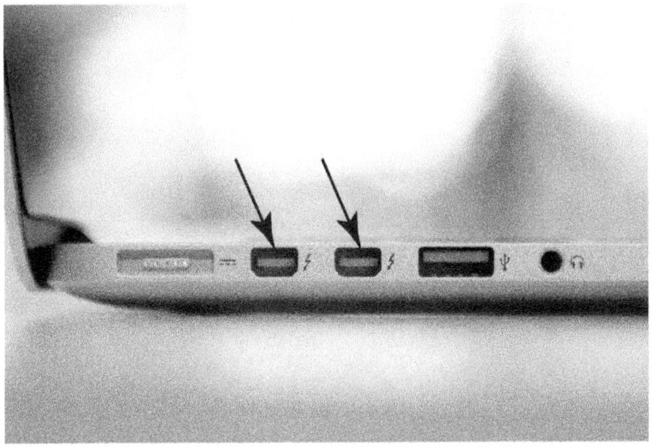

FIGURE 2.35 Thunderbolt ports are slim and speedy, making them popular on today's ultrabooks and laptops. *(David Paul Morris/Bloomberg/Getty Images)*

blazingly fast transfer speeds of up to 20 Gb/s (the upcoming Thunderbolt 3 protocol should double this to 40 Gb/s). **Thunderbolt ports** (see Figure 2.35) are very useful for laptops and ultrabooks because one Thunderbolt port can allow you to connect up to six different peripherals to your computer. Apple was the first computer maker to integrate the ports into their hardware although other manufacturers are now following suit.

What is the most common port on digital devices? A **universal serial bus (USB) port** is the port type most commonly used to connect input and output devices to the computer. This is mainly because of the ready availability of USB-compatible peripherals. USB ports can connect a wide variety of peripherals to computing devices, including keyboards, printers, mice, smartphones, external hard drives, flash drives, and digital cameras. The new USB 3.1 standard provides transfer speeds of 10 Gbps and charges devices faster than previous USB ports. USB ports come in variety of standard and proprietary configurations (see Figure 2.36), plus the new Type-C connector (and port), which is expected to supplant older connections as USB 3.1 continues to roll out (see Figure 2.37).

Which ports help me connect with other computers and the Internet? Another set of ports on your computer helps you communicate with other computers. A **connectivity port** can give you access to networks and the Internet. To find a connectivity port, look for a port that resembles a standard phone jack but is slightly larger. This port is called an **Ethernet port**. Ethernet ports transfer data at speeds up to 10,000 Mbps. You can use an Ethernet port to connect your computer to either a cable modem or a network.

How do I connect monitors and multimedia devices? Other ports on the back and sides of the computer include audio and video ports. Audio ports are where you connect headphones, microphones, and speakers to the computer. Whether you're attaching a monitor to a desktop computer, or adding a second, larger display to a laptop computer, you'll use a video port. HDMI ports are now the most common video port on computing devices.

A **high-definition multimedia interface (HDMI) port** is a compact audio–video interface that allows both HD video and uncompressed digital audio to be carried on one cable. Because HDMI can transmit uncompressed audio and video, there's no need to convert the signal, which could ultimately reduce the quality of the sound or picture. All currently available monitors, DVD players, televisions, and game consoles have at least one HDMI port (see Figure 2.38).

What ports might I encounter on older computers and peripherals? The **video graphics array (VGA) port** and the **digital video interface (DVI) port** are two ports to which older LCD monitors and televisions connect (see

FIGURE 2.36 USB connectors come in a wide variety of styles. *(TaraPatta/Shutterstock)*

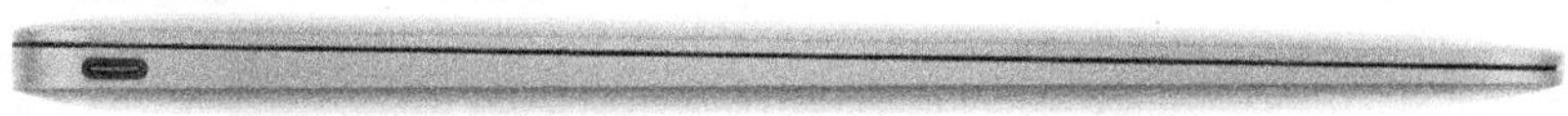

FIGURE 2.37 Some Apple computers now feature the new USB-C port that supports data transfer, video output, and charging all in a single port. *(EPA/Alamy)*

FIGURE 2.38 HDMI is the latest digital connector type for HD monitors, televisions, and home theater equipment. *(Feng Yu/Shutterstock)*

Figure 2.39). Older Apple computers feature a Mini DisplayPort for connection of video peripherals. Adapters are available for the Mini DisplayPort that allow the connection of older DVI and VGA devices.

Adding Ports: Expansion Cards and Hubs

Objective 2.16 *List the options for adding ports to your device.*

What if I don't have all the ports I need? If you're looking to add the newest ports to an older desktop computer or to expand the number of ports on it, you can install special

FIGURE 2.39 DVI (left) and VGA (right) cables are used to connect older LCD monitors and televisions to computing devices. *(Marek Kosmal/Fotolia)*

expansion cards (see Figure 2.40) into an open expansion slot on the motherboard to provide additional ports.

Another alternative is adding an expansion hub (shown in Figure 2.41). An expansion hub is a device that connects to one port, such as a USB port, to provide additional ports. It works like the multiplug extension cords used with electrical appliances. ■

FIGURE 2.40 Expansion cards fit into slots on the motherboard in a desktop computer. *(Andrew Kitching/Alamy)*

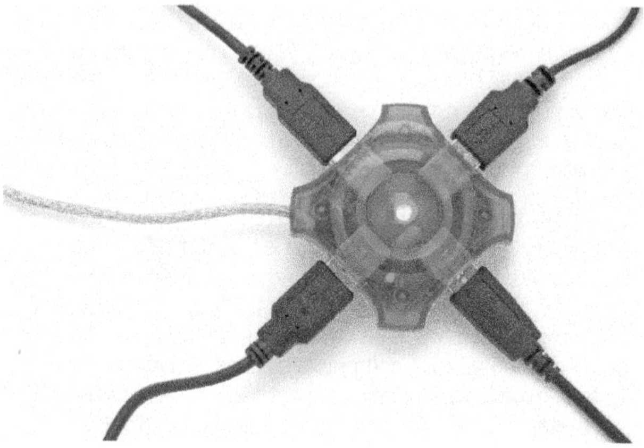

FIGURE 2.41 If you don't have enough USB ports to support your USB devices, consider getting an expansion hub, which can add four or more USB ports to your system. *(Norman Chan/Fotolia)*

ACTIVE HELPDESK

Exploring Storage Devices and Ports

In this Active Helpdesk, you'll play the role of a helpdesk staffer, fielding questions about the computer's main storage devices and how to connect various peripheral devices to the computer.

SOUND BYTE

Port Tour: How Do I Hook It Up?

In this Sound Byte, you'll take a tour of both a desktop system and a laptop system to compare the number and variety of available ports. You'll also learn about the different types of ports and compare their speed and expandability.

power controls and ERGONOMICS

Conserving energy and setting up workspaces so they are comfortable for employees are goals of many businesses. However, these are also excellent goals to strive for at your house. In the next two sections, we will explore optimizing the power consumption of computing devices as well as the proper workspace setup to minimize injuries.

Power Controls

Objective 2.17 *Describe how to manage power consumption on your computing devices.*

What's the best way to turn my computer on and off? The **power supply**, which is housed inside the system unit, transforms the wall voltage to the voltages required by computer chips. Powering on your computer from a completely turned off state, such as when you start your computer in the morning, is called a **cold boot**. In Windows 10, you can turn your computer off by displaying the Start menu, selecting Power, and then choosing the Shut down option.

Should I turn off my computer every time I'm done using it? Some people say you should leave your computer on at all times. They argue that turning your computer on and off throughout the day subjects its components to stress because the heating and cooling process forces the components to expand and contract repeatedly. Other people say you should shut down your computer when you're not using it. They claim that it's not as environmentally friendly and that you'll end up wasting money on electricity from the computer running all the time.

Modern operating systems include power-management settings that allow the most power-hungry components of the system (the hard drive and monitor) to shut down after a short idle period. With the power-management options of Windows 10, for example, you only need to shut down your computer completely when you need to repair or install hardware in the system unit or move it to another location. However, if you use your computer only for a little while each day, it would be best to power it off completely after each daily use.

Can I "rest" my computer without turning it off completely? In Windows 10, the main method of power management is Sleep. When your computer enters **Sleep mode**, all of the documents, applications, and data you were using remain in RAM (memory), where they're quickly accessible when you restart your computer.

In Sleep mode, the computer enters a state of greatly reduced power consumption, which saves energy. To put your computer into Sleep mode in Windows 10, display the Start menu, select Power, then select the Sleep option. To wake up your computer, press a key or the physical power button. In a few seconds, the computer will resume with exactly the same programs running and documents displayed as when you put it to sleep.

If you don't ever want to completely turn off your computer, you can change what happens when you press the power button or close the lid on your laptop. By accessing the Power Options System Settings window (see Figure 2.42), you can decide if you want your computer to Sleep, Hibernate, or Shut down when you press the power button. The **Hibernate** option is similar to Sleep except that your data is stored on your hard drive instead of in RAM and your computer is powered off. This uses much less battery power than Sleep and is a good choice if you won't be using your laptop for a long time and won't have the opportunity to charge it. However, Sleep is still a good option to choose if you just won't be using your computer for a short time. You may want to set your computer so it sleeps when you close the lid but hibernates when you press the power button, giving you quick access to either option.

What's the Restart option in Windows for? If you're using Windows 10, you have the option to restart the computer when you access the Power option on the Start menu (see Figure 2.43). Restarting the system while it's powered on is called a **warm boot**. You might need to perform a warm boot if the operating system or other software application stops responding or if you've installed new programs. It takes less time to perform a warm boot than to power down completely and then restart all your hardware.

Setting It All Up: Ergonomics

Objective 2.18 *Define ergonomics, and discuss the ideal physical setup for using computing devices.*

What is ergonomics? It's important that you understand not only your computer's components and how they work together but also how to set up these components safely. **Ergonomics** is the science that deals with the design and location of machines and furniture so that the people using them aren't subjected to an uncomfortable or unsafe experience. In terms of computing, ergonomics refers to how you set up your computer and other equipment to minimize your risk of injury or discomfort.

Why is ergonomics important? Studies suggest that teenagers, on average, spend 7.5 hours per day using computing devices. When you factor in other computer uses such as playing video games, there is great potential for injury. The repetitive nature of long-term computing activities can place too much stress on joints and pull at the tendons and muscles, causing repetitive stress injuries such as carpal tunnel syndrome and tendonitis. These injuries can take months or years to develop to a point where they become painful, and by the time you notice the symptoms, the damage has already taken

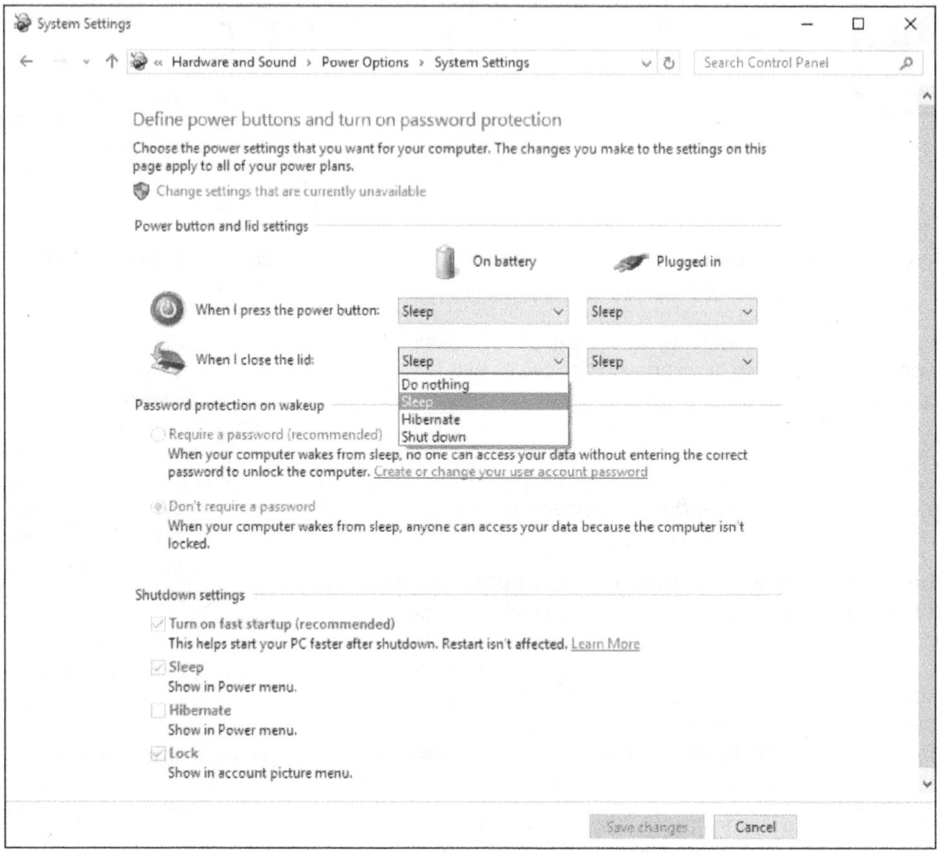

FIGURE 2.42 You can determine what happens when you click the power button on your computer or close the lid through the Power Options System Settings screen. *(Windows 10, Microsoft Corporation)* >*To access Power Options System Settings, from the Start Menu, select* ***Settings****, select* ***System****, select* ***Power & sleep****, click the* ***Additional power settings link****, then select* ***Choose what the power button does****.*

place. If you take precautionary measures now, you may prevent years of unnecessary pain later.

How can I avoid injuries when I'm working at my computer? As Figure 2.44 illustrates, it's important to arrange your monitor, chair, body, and keyboard in ways that will help you avoid injury, discomfort, and eyestrain. The following additional guidelines can help keep you comfortable and productive:

- **Position your monitor correctly.** Studies suggest it's best to place your monitor at least 25 inches from your eyes. Experts recommend that you position your monitor either at eye level or at an angle 15–20 degrees below your line of sight.
- **Purchase an adjustable chair.** Adjust the height of your chair so that your feet touch the floor (or use a footrest to get the right position). The back support needs to be adjustable so that you can position it to support your lumbar (lower back) region. You should also be able to move the seat or adjust the back so that you can sit without exerting pressure on your knees. If your chair doesn't adjust, place a pillow behind your back to provide support.
- **Assume a proper position while typing.** Improperly positioned keyboards are one of the leading causes of repetitive stress

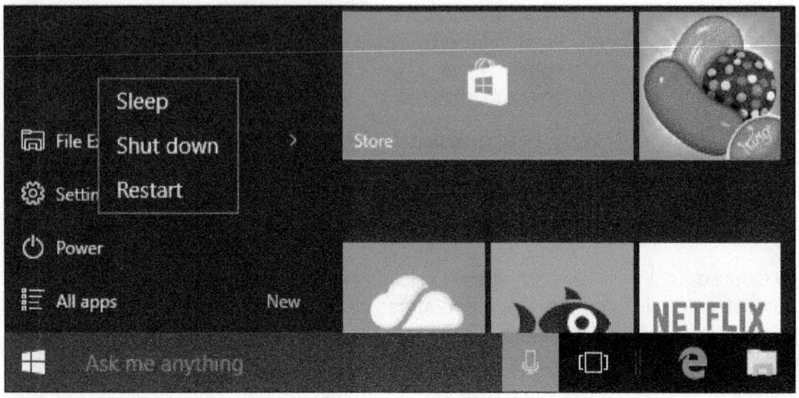

FIGURE 2.43 The Power option on the Windows 10 Start menu presents several power options. *(Windows 10, Microsoft Corporation)* >*For a warm boot, choose* ***Restart****. To power down the computer completely, choose* ***Shut down****. To put your computer into a lower power mode, select* ***Sleep****.*

FIGURE 2.44 Using proper equipment that is adjusted correctly helps prevent repetitive strain injuries while working at a computer.

injuries in computer users. Your wrists should be flat (not bent) with respect to the keyboard, and your forearms should be parallel to the floor. Additionally, your wrists should not be resting on the keyboard while typing. You can adjust the height of your chair or install a height-adjustable keyboard tray to ensure a proper position. Specially designed ergonomic keyboards such as the one shown in Figure 2.46 can help you achieve the proper wrist position.

- **Take breaks.** Remaining in the same position for long periods of time increases stress on your body. Shift your position in your chair and stretch your hands and fingers periodically. Likewise, staring at the screen for long periods can lead to eyestrain, so rest your eyes by periodically taking them off the screen and focusing them on an object at least 8 feet away.
- **Ensure the lighting is adequate.** Ensuring that you have proper lighting in your work area minimizes eyestrain. Eliminate sources of direct glare (light shining directly into your eyes) or reflected glare (light shining off the computer screen) and ensure there is enough light to read comfortably. If you still can't eliminate glare from your computer screen, you can buy an antiglare screen to place over your monitor.

Is ergonomics important when using mobile devices? Working with mobile computing devices presents interesting challenges when it comes to injury prevention. For example, many users work with laptops resting on their laps, placing the monitor outside of the optimal line of sight and thereby increasing neck strain. Figure 2.47 provides guidelines on preventing injuries when computing on the go.

So, whether you're computing at your desk or on the road, consider the ergonomics of your work environment. Doing so will help you avoid injury and discomfort.

BITS&BYTES

Save Power and Avoid Eyestrain: Use Blackle

Your computer uses less energy when it displays black as opposed to white (or other lighter colors). Also, bright colors such as white tend to increase eyestrain when viewing a computer screen (see Figure 2.45). For a quick fix, try using an alternative search engine called Blackle (**blackle.com**). Powered by Google, this customized search engine displays a predominantly black screen instead of white. Since most modern monitors don't backlight the black parts of a display, you save a little bit of energy when using this alternative search engine. Yes, it's a small amount of energy—but every little bit helps!

FIGURE 2.45 Want to save energy while reducing eyestrain? Using apps or websites that use less white and more black helps. *(Grgroup/Fotolia)*

FIGURE 2.46 Ergonomic keyboards have curved keyboards and wrist rests to help you maintain the proper hand position while typing to reduce the risk of repetitive strain injuries.
(Dmitriy Melnikov/Fotolia)

What devices are available for people with disabilities? People who have physical challenges sometimes need special devices to access computers. **Assistive** (or **adaptive**) **technology** are products, devices, equipment, or software that are used to maintain, increase, or improve the functional capabilities of individuals with disabilities. For visually impaired users and individuals who can't type with their hand, voice recognition is a common input option. For those users whose visual limitations are less severe, keyboards with larger keys are available.

People with motor control issues may have difficulty with pointing devices. To aid such users, special trackballs are available that can be easily manipulated with one finger and can be attached to almost any surface, including a wheelchair. When arm motion is severely restrained, head-mounted pointing devices can be used. Generally, these involve a camera mounted on the computer monitor and a device attached to the head (often installed in a hat). When the user moves his or her head, the camera detects the movement and moves the cursor. In this case, mouse clicks are controlled by a switch that can be manipulated by the user's hands or feet or even by using an instrument that fits into the mouth and senses the user blowing into it. ■

> **SOUND BYTE**
> **Healthy Computing**
> In this Sound Byte, you'll see how to set up your workspace in an ergonomically correct way. You'll learn the proper location of the monitor, keyboard, and mouse, as well as ergonomic features to look for when choosing the most appropriate chair.

FIGURE 2.47

Preventing Injuries While on the Go

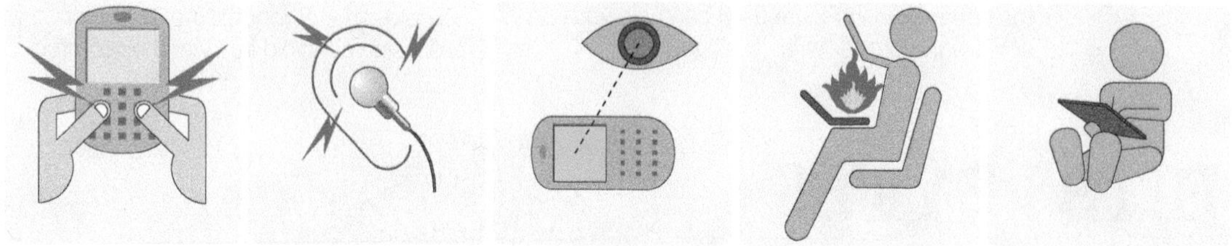

	SMARTPHONE REPETITIVE STRAIN INJURIES	PORTABLE MEDIA PLAYER HEARING DAMAGE	SMALL-SCREEN VISION ISSUES	LAP INJURIES	TABLET REPETITIVE STRAIN INJURIES
Malady	Repetitive strain injuries (such as DeQuervain's tendonitis) from constant typing of instant messages	Hearing loss from high-decibel sound levels in earbuds	Blurriness and dryness caused by squinting to view tiny screens on mobile devices	Burns on legs from heat generated by laptop	Pain caused from using tablets for prolonged periods in uncomfortable positions
Preventative Measures	Restrict length and frequency of messages, take breaks, and perform other motions with your thumbs and fingers during breaks to relieve tension.	Turn down volume (you should be able to hear external noises, such as people talking), use software that limits sound levels (not to exceed 60 decibels), and use external, over-ear style headphones instead of earbuds.	Blink frequently or use eye drops to maintain moisture in eyes, after 10 minutes take a break and focus on something at least 8 feet away for 5 minutes, use adequate amount of light, and increase the size of fonts.	Place a book, magazine, or laptop cooling pad between your legs and laptop.	Restrict the length of time you work at a tablet, especially typing or gaming. Use the same ergonomic position you would use for a laptop when using a tablet.

trends in IT

Innovations in Printing

With the advent of the computer, many speculated that ours would become a paperless society. Instead of saving printed documents and other output as was done prior to the PC, information would be saved in a digital state: hard drives replacing filing cabinets, online photo buckets replacing photo albums and scrapbooks, and e-books replacing our favorite texts. Hard drive capacities do enable us to save more content, and online storage systems enable us to save pictures and other files to the "cloud." Additionally, e-book readers have increased in popularity. But has this push toward digital content begun to make the printer obsolete? Surprisingly, no. People still have a deep-rooted need to see, feel, mark, share, or use their digital images or information in a physical form. New technologies that push the boundaries of printing, such as printing from the cloud and 3-D printing, are being developed and refined.

Cloud Printing

To print a document from a desktop or laptop computer, you must have a printer associated with your computer. Usually, this is not a problem because at home, at school, or in the office, there is generally one printer, and all the PCs connected to it have the software and cables or wireless capabilities needed to use it. But what happens if you want to print something from your smartphone or tablet? Common solutions have been to e-mail the document to yourself or transfer the document to a web-based storage service such as Dropbox so that a printer-connected computer could access it. Another solution is Google Cloud Print, a service that lets you configure your printers so you can access them from mobile devices.

Google Cloud Print uses cloud-ready printers (see Figure 2.48) that are now available from manufacturers such as HP, Kodak, and Epson. These printers connect directly to the Internet and register themselves with Google Cloud Print without needing to be connected to a computer. Once a printer is registered with Cloud Print, printing jobs can be sent to it from mobile devices (such as tablets and smartphones) using the Internet. Conventional printers that you already own can also be registered with Cloud Print, although they require connection to the Internet through a computer.

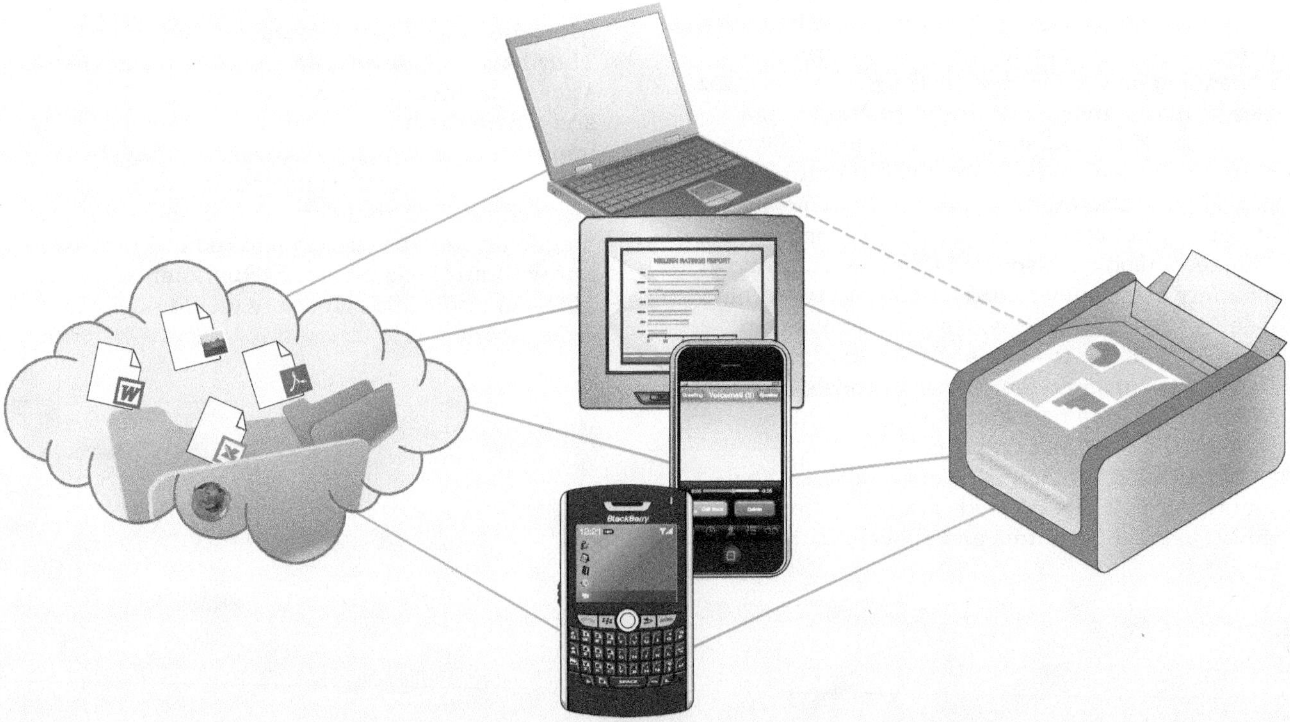

FIGURE 2.48 Cloud-ready printers only need an Internet connection to be accessed from any mobile device.

FIGURE 2.49 3-D printing is being used to fabricate parts for all sorts of devices on demand. (Hopsalka/Fotolia)

3-D Printing

Printing a 3-D model of a proposed building or new prototype is common for architects and engineers. The process builds a model one layer at a time from the bottom up. The procedure begins by spreading a layer of powder on a platform. Then, depending on the technology, the printer uses nozzles similar to those in an inkjet printer to spray tiny drops of glue at specific places to solidify the powder, or the powder is solidified through a melting process. The printer repeats solidifying layers of powder until the model is built to specifications. This technology has spurred the manufacturing of a variety of consumer goods, from toys to clothing (see Figure 2.49). Shapeways (**shapeways.com**) uses 3-D printing to enable anyone to turn his or her 3-D designs into real physical models. Then, those models can be personalized, bought, or sold through Shapeways's online community.

3-D printing is being used in the medical community as well. Hearing aids are now being produced using 3-D printers and allow manufacturers to not only offer a custom fit but individual skin color matching as well (to make the devices less visible). And researchers at Wake Forest Institute for Regenerative Medicine have developed a way to use similar inkjet technologies to build heart, bone, and blood vessel tissues in the lab. They have also developed a way to "print" restorative cells directly into a soldier's wound at the site where the injury occurred, thus significantly improving the soldier's chances of survival.

Taking traditional technologies, such as inkjet printing, and applying them to solve current human struggles is a long and tedious process, but without these pioneers experimenting with different applications, society would advance a lot more slowly.

Before moving on to the Chapter Review:

1. Watch Replay Video 2.2.
2. Then check your understanding of what you've learned so far.

check your understanding // review & practice

For a quick review to see what you've learned so far, answer the following questions.

multiple choice

1. Which of the following is NOT found on a motherboard?

- **a.** RAM
- **b.** CPU
- **c.** sound card
- **d.** hard drive

2. Which of these is an example of optical storage media?

- **a.** DVD
- **b.** SSD
- **c.** thumb drive
- **d.** a flash memory card

3. Which of the following is the fastest data transfer port?

- **a.** HDMI
- **b.** VGA
- **c.** USB 3.1
- **d.** Thunderbolt

4. Which of these is considered volatile storage?

- **a.** SSD
- **b.** ROM
- **c.** RAM
- **d.** thumb drive

5. Which power control option performs a warm boot?

- **a.** Restart
- **b.** Sleep
- **c.** Log off
- **d.** Shut down

MyITLab Go to **MyITLab** to take an autograded version of the *Check Your Understanding* review and to find all media resources for the chapter.

TECHBYTES WEEKLY

Stay current with the TechBytes Weekly Newsletter.

Continue »

2 Chapter Review

summary //

Understanding Digital Components

Learning Outcome 2.1 You will be able to describe the devices that make up a computer system.

Understanding Your Computer

Objective 2.1 *Describe the four main functions of a computer system and how they interact with data and information.*

- The computer's four major functions are: (1) input: gather data or allow users to enter data; (2) process: manipulate, calculate, or organize that data; (3) output: display data and information in a form suitable for the user; and (4) storage: save data and information for later use.
- Data is a representation of a fact or idea. The number 3 and the words *televisions* and *Sony* are pieces of data.
- Information is data that has been organized or presented in a meaningful fashion. An inventory list that indicates that 3 Sony televisions are in stock is processed information. It allows a retail clerk to answer a customer query about the availability of merchandise. Information is more powerful than raw data.

Objective 2.2 *Define bits and bytes, and describe how they are measured, used, and processed.*

- To process data into information, computers need to work in a language they understand. This language, called *binary language*, consists of two numbers: 0 and 1. Each 0 and each 1 is a binary digit or bit. Eight bits create one byte.
- In computers, each letter of the alphabet, each number, and each special character consists of a unique combination of eight bits (one byte)—a string of eight 0s and 1s.
- For describing large amounts of storage capacity, the terms *megabyte* (approximately 1 million bytes), *gigabyte* (approximately 1 billion bytes), *terabyte* (approximately 1 trillion bytes), and *petabyte* (1,000 terabytes) are used.

Objective 2.3 *List common types of computers, and discuss their main features.*

- A tablet computer is a portable computer integrated into a flat multitouch-sensitive screen.
- A laptop or notebook computer is a portable computer that has a keyboard, monitor, and other devices integrated into a single compact case.
- An ultrabook is a lightweight laptop computer featuring low-power processors and solid-state drives.
- Chromebook computers use the Google Chrome OS. Documents and apps are stored primarily in the cloud.
- Desktop computers consist of a separate case (called the system unit) that houses the main components of the computer plus peripheral devices.

Input Devices

Objective 2.4 *Identify the main types of keyboards and touch screens.*

- You use keyboards to enter typed data and commands. Most keyboards use the QWERTY layout.
- Touch screens are display screens that respond to commands initiated by a touch with a finger or a stylus.
- Wireless keyboards mainly use Bluetooth connectivity and provide alternatives to on-screen keyboards.

Objective 2.5 *Describe the main types of mice and pointing devices.*

- Mice are used to enter user responses and commands.
- Optical mice use a laser to detect mouse movement.
- Some mice can be adjusted to provide better ergonomics for users.
- Laptops have integrated pointing devices called touch pads (trackpads).

Objective 2.6 *Explain how images and sounds are input into computing devices.*

- Images are input into the computer with scanners, digital cameras, camcorders, and smartphones.
- Live video is captured with webcams and digital video recorders.
- Microphones capture sounds. There are many different types of microphones, including desktop, headset, and clip-on models.

Output Devices

Objective 2.7 *Name common types of monitors, and identify important aspects of their quality.*

- Monitors display soft copies of text, graphics, and video.
- Liquid crystal display (LCD) and light-emitting diode (LED) are the most common types of computer monitors.
- OLED displays use organic compounds to produce light and don't require a backlight, which saves energy.
- Aspect ratio, screen resolution, contrast ratio, viewing angle, brightness, and response time are key aspects to consider when choosing a monitor.

Objective 2.8 *Describe various types of printers, and explain when you would use them.*

- Printers create hard copies of text and graphics.
- There are two primary categories of printers: inkjet and laser. Laser printers usually print faster and deliver higher-quality output than inkjet printers. However, inkjet printers can be more economical for casual printing needs.
- Specialty printers are also available such as all-in-one printers, large format printers, and thermal printers.
- When choosing a printer, you should be aware of factors such as speed, resolution, color output, and cost of consumables.

Objective 2.9 *Discuss options for outputting sound from your computing devices.*

- Speakers are the output devices for sound. Most computers include basic speakers.
- More sophisticated systems include subwoofers and surround sound.
- Headphone or earbuds are useful to avoid disturbing others.

Processing, Storage, and Connectivity

Learning Outcome 2.2 **You will be able to describe how computers process and store data and how devices connect to a computer system.**

Processing and Memory on the Motherboard

Objective 2.10 *Define motherboard and RAM.*

- The motherboard, the main circuit board of the system, contains a computer's CPU, which coordinates the functions of all other devices on the computer.
- The motherboard also houses slots for expansion cards, which have specific functions that augment the computer's basic functions. Typical expansion cards are sound and video cards.
- RAM, the computer's volatile memory, is also located on the motherboard. RAM is where all the data and instructions are held while the computer is running.

Objective 2.11 *Explain the main functions of the CPU.*

- The CPU controls all the functions performed by the computer's other components. The CPU also processes all commands issued to it by software instructions.
- The performance of a CPU is affected by the speed of the processor (measured in GHz), the amount of cache memory, and the number of processing cores.

Storing Data and Information

Objective 2.12 *List the various types of hard drives.*

- The internal hard drive is your computer's primary device for permanent storage of software and files. The hard drive is a nonvolatile storage device, meaning it holds the data and instructions your computer needs permanently, even after the computer is turned off.

- SSD drives have no moving parts so they are more energy efficient and less susceptible to damage.
- External hard drives are essentially internal hard drives that have been made portable by enclosing them in a protective case and making them small and lightweight.

Objective 2.13 *Define cloud storage, and explain how to use it.*

- Cloud storage refers to nonvolatile storage locations that are maintained on the Internet (in the "cloud"). Examples are OneDrive, Google Drive, and Dropbox.
- Storing your data in the cloud allows you to access it from almost any computing device that is connected to the Internet.

Objective 2.14 *Describe the various portable and optical storage options.*

- Optical drives that can read from and write to CD, DVD, or Blu-ray discs are another means of permanent, portable storage. Data is saved to CDs, DVDs, and Blu-ray discs as pits that are burned into the disc by a laser.
- Flash drives are another portable means of storing data. Flash drives plug into USB ports.
- Flash memory cards let you transfer digital data between your computer and devices such as digital cameras, smartphones, video cameras, and printers.

Connecting Peripherals to the Computer

Objective 2.15 *List the common types of ports used today.*

- The fastest type of port used to connect devices to a computer is the Thunderbolt port.
- The most common type of port used to connect devices to a computer is the USB port.
- Connectivity ports, such as Ethernet ports, give you access to networks and the Internet.
- HDMI ports are the most common multimedia port. They are used to connect monitors, TVs, and gaming consoles to computing devices and handle both audio and video data.
- Audio ports are used to connect headphones, microphones, and speakers to computing devices.

Objective 2.16 *List the options for adding ports to your device.*

- Expansion cards can be plugged into the motherboard on desktop computers to add ports.
- Expansion hubs can be plugged into existing ports to provide additional ports of the same type.

Power Controls and Ergonomics

Objective 2.17 *Describe how to manage power consumption on your computing devices.*

- Turning off your computer when you won't be using it for long periods of time saves energy. In Windows 10, you can turn your computer off by accessing the Power option on the Start menu, then selecting Shut down.
- If you are not using your computer for short periods of time, selecting the Sleep option will help your computer save energy but allows it to be quickly "awakened" for use.

Objective 2.18 *Define ergonomics, and discuss the ideal physical setup for using computing devices.*

- Ergonomics refers to how you arrange your computer and equipment to minimize your risk of injury or discomfort.
- Achieving proper ergonomics includes positioning your monitor correctly, buying an adjustable chair, assuming a proper position while typing, making sure the lighting is adequate, and not looking at the screen for long periods. Other good practices include taking frequent breaks and using specially designed equipment such as ergonomic keyboards.
- Ergonomics is also important to consider when using mobile devices.

MyITLab

Be sure to check out **MyITLab** for additional materials to help you review and learn. And don't forget the Replay Videos.

key terms //

chapter quiz // assessment

For a quick review to see what you've learned, answer the following questions. Submit the quiz as requested by your instructor. If you are using **MyITLab**, the quiz is also available there.

multiple choice

1. What is a gigabyte?

- **a.** one billion bytes
- **b.** one trillion bytes
- **c.** one billion bits
- **d.** one million bits

2. Which of the following is NOT an output device?

- **a.** touch-screen monitor
- **b.** optical mouse
- **c.** speakers
- **d.** laser printer

3. Monitor screens are made up of millions of tiny dots known as

- **a.** bytes.
- **b.** resolution points.
- **c.** pixels.
- **d.** bits.

4. Which of these is located on the motherboard?

- **a.** SSD drive
- **b.** RAM
- **c.** Hard drive
- **d.** DVD drive

5. Which of these is an optical storage device?

- **a.** flash drive
- **b.** SSD drive
- **c.** External hard drive
- **d.** Blu-ray drive

6. Ergonomics is an important consideration

- **a.** only for desktop computers.
- **b.** only for laptop computers.
- **c.** only for laptop and desktop computers, but never for mobile devices.
- **d.** for all computing devices.

true/false

1. Data and information are interchangeable terms.

2. Microsoft Word is a type of application software.

3. The fastest data transfer port is an HDMI port.

4. A typical CPU can complete billions of machine cycles in one second.

critical thinking

1. Computers of the Future

Embedded computers keep turning up in new places. They can be found in cars, household appliances, smoke detectors, and thermostats too, enabling us to interact with even more of these "smart" devices every day. What common objects do you think might benefit from an embedded computer? What capabilities can you envision?

2. New Display Features

The display screen of the future may be paper-thin, flexible, and transparent. Companies like Samsung and LG are already working on it. What uses can you envision for this new technology? What advantages and disadvantages do you foresee? Do you have any suggestions for the manufacturers to help make this successful?

team time //

Data Storage Options

Problem

You've joined a small business that's beginning to evaluate its technology setup. Because of the addition of several new sales representatives and other administrative employees, the company needs to reconsider the various ways its data is stored. You've been asked to evaluate options for on-site and off-site data storage.

Task

Split your class into teams of three and assign the following tasks:

- Member A explores the benefits and downfalls of cloud storage.
- Member B explores the benefits and downfalls of external hard drives.
- Member C explores the benefits and downfalls of portable storage devices.

Process

1. Think about what the storage needs are for the company and what information and resources you will need to tackle this project.
2. Research and then discuss the components of each method you're recommending. Are any of these options better suited for the particular needs of certain types of employees (sales representatives versus administrative staff)? Consider the types of data to be stored. Is some data confidential? How long should it be retained?
3. Consider the different types of employees in the company. Would a combination of methods be better than a single solution? If so, what kinds of employees would use which type of storage?
4. As a team, write a summary position paper. Support your recommendation for the company. Each team member should include why his or her data storage option will or will not be part of the solution.

Conclusion

There are advantages and disadvantages to any data storage option. Being aware of the pros and cons and knowing which method is best for a particular scenario or employee will help you to become a better consumer as well as a better computer user.

ethics project //

Green Computing

Ethical conduct is a stream of decisions you make all day long. In this exercise, you'll research and then role-play a complicated ethical situation. The role you play may or may not match your own personal beliefs, but your research and use of logic will enable you to represent whichever view is assigned. An arbitrator will watch and comment on both sides of the arguments, and together, the team will agree on an ethical solution.

Background

Green computing—conducting computing needs with the least possible amount of power and impact on the environment—is on everyone's minds. Although it's hard to argue with an environmentally conscious agenda, the pinch to our pocketbooks and the loss of some comforts sometimes make green computing difficult. Businesses, including colleges, need to consider a variety of issues and concerns before jumping into a complete green overhaul.

Research Areas to Consider

End-of-life management: e-waste and recycling

- Energy-efficient devices
- Renewable resources used in computer manufacturing
- Costs of green computing
- Government funding and incentives

Process

1. Divide the class into teams.
2. Research the areas cited above and devise a scenario in which your college is considering modifying its current technology setup to a more green information technology (IT) strategy.
3. Team members should write a summary that provides background information for their character—for example, environmentalist, college IT administrator, or arbitrator—and that details their character's behaviors to set the stage for the role-playing event. Then, team members should create an outline to use during the role-playing event.
4. Team members should arrange a mutually convenient time to meet, using a virtual meeting tool or by meeting in person.
5. Team members should present their case to the class or submit a PowerPoint presentation for review by the rest of the class, along with the summary and resolution they developed.

Conclusion

As technology becomes ever more prevalent and integrated into our lives, more and more ethical dilemmas will present themselves. Being able to understand and evaluate both sides of the argument, while responding in a personally or socially ethical manner, will be an important skill.

Solve This

MyITLab® grader

Technology Wish List

You are in need of a significant technology upgrade, and your parents have told you they will help you finance your purchases by loaning you the money. You will need to repay them with a modest 2.5% interest rate over two years. The only catch is that they want you to create a list of all the new devices that you need, note the cost, and provide a website for each device where they can find more information. Then, they want you to calculate how much you will need to give them each month to pay them back.

You will use the following skills as you complete this activity:

- Merge and Center
- Modify Workbook Themes
- Apply Number Formats
- Use the SUM, PMT, and COUNTA Functions
- Modify Column Widths
- Insert a Hyperlink
- Create a Formula
- Wrap Text

Instructions:

1. Open *TIA_Ch2_Start* and save as **TIA_Ch2_LastFirst**.
2. Format the title in cell A1 with the **Title Cell Style**, and format the column headers in cells A3:F3 with the **Heading 3 Cell Style**.
   a. Hint: To format cell styles, on the Home tab, in the Styles group, click **Cell Styles**.
3. **Merge and Center** cell A1 across columns A through F, and **Center align** the column headers in cells A3:F3.
   a. Hint: To Merge and Center text, on the Home tab, in the Alignment group, click **Merge & Center**.
4. Modify column widths so that Column A is **25** and Column D is **45**.
   a. Hint: To modify column widths, on the Home tab, in the Cells group, click **Format**, and then select **Column Width**.
5. In cells B4:F9, fill in the table with the Brand and Model of the six devices that you would like to purchase. The device type is filled out for you. In the *Reason* column, write a brief note as to why this device will help you. (You'll format the text so it all displays later.) Enter the cost of the device in the Cost column. Don't include tax and/or shipping.
6. Change the Workbook Theme to **Integral**.
   a. Hint: To apply the Theme, on the Page Layout tab, in the Themes group, click **Themes**.
7. In cells F4:F9, create a **Hyperlink** to a webpage that features each respective product so your grandparents can have access to more information if they need it. Ensure that each hyperlink includes the URL to the exact webpage for the device in the Address, but displays the Make/Model of the device in the worksheet.
   a. Hint: To insert a hyperlink, on the Insert tab, in the Links group, click **Hyperlink**. In the Insert Hyperlink dialog box, enter the URL in the Address: box and enter the Make/Model in the Text to display box.
8. Wrap the text in cells C4:C9, D4:D9, and F4:F9 so all text displays.
   a. Hint: To wrap text, on the Home tab, in the Alignment group, click **Wrap Text**.
9. Format the values in cells E4:E9 with the **Accounting Number format with two decimals**.
10. In cell A10, type **Subtotal**, then in cell E10, use a **SUM function** to calculate the total cost of all devices. Format the results in the **Accounting Number format with two decimals**.
11. In cell A11, type **Estimated Tax**, then in cell E11, create a formula that references the subtotal in cell E10 and multiplies it by a tax of 6%. Format the results in the **Accounting Number format with two decimals**.
12. In cell A12, type **Estimated Shipping**, then in cell E12, create a formula to calculate the shipping charge by using the **COUNTA function** to determine the number of devices being purchased and then multiplying that by a $10 shipping charge. Format the results in **Accounting Number Format with two decimals**.
13. In cell A13, type **Total Cost**, then in cell E13, use the **SUM function** to create a formula that adds up the *Subtotal, Estimated Tax*, and *Estimated Shipping costs*. Format the results in **Accounting Number Format with two decimals**. Format the cells A13:E13 with the **Total Cell Style**.
14. **Right align** cells A10:A13.
15. In cell D14, type **Estimated Monthly Payment**, and then in cell E14, use the **PMT function** to calculate the monthly payment owed to your parents to pay back the total purchase amount in two years at a 2.5% annual interest rate.
16. Save the workbook and submit based on your instructor's directions.

3 Using the Internet: Making the Most of the Web's Resources

Working and Playing on the Web

Learning Outcome 3.1 **You will be able to explain how the Internet works and how it is used for collaboration, communication, commerce, and entertainment purposes.**

The Internet and How It Works 76

Objective 3.1 *Describe how the Internet got its start.*

Objective 3.2 *Explain how data travels on the Internet.*

Collaborating and Communicating on the Web 79

Objective 3.3 *Discuss the tools and technologies used to collaborate and communicate on the web.*

Sound Byte: Blogging

Objective 3.4 *Summarize how e-mail and instant messaging are used to communicate over the web.*

Business and Entertainment on the Web 85

Objective 3.5 *Describe the different types of e-commerce.*

Objective 3.6 *Summarize precautions you should take when doing business online.*

Active Helpdesk: Doing Business Online

Objective 3.7 *Describe the types of multimedia files found on the web.*

Using the Web Effectively

Learning Outcome 3.2 **You will be able to describe the tools and techniques required to navigate and search the web.**

Accessing and Moving Around the Web 92

Objective 3.8 *Explain what web browsers are, and describe their common features.*

Sound Byte: Welcome to the Web

Objective 3.9 *Explain what a URL is, and discuss its main parts.*

Objective 3.10 *Describe tools used to navigate the web.*

Objective 3.11 *Describe tools used to mark websites for future use.*

Active Helpdesk: Getting Around the Web

Searching the Web Effectively 98

Objective 3.12 *Describe the types of tools used to search the web, and summarize strategies used to refine search results.*

Sound Byte: Finding Information on the Web

Objective 3.13 *Describe how to evaluate a website to ensure it is appropriate to use for research purposes.*

Active Helpdesk: Evaluating Websites

Using the Web Ethically 102

Objective 3.14 *Demonstrate an understanding of intellectual property and cyberbullying.*

Objective 3.15 *Demonstrate an understanding of the ethical issues regarding privacy and geolocation.*

Make This: MAKE: A Web-Capable App on **page 91**

All media accompanying this chapter can be found in MyITLab.

For an overview of the chapter, watch the **Preview Video.**

(Dny3d/Fotolia, Marish/Shutterstock, Gheatza/Fotolia, Maksym Yemelyanov/Fotolia, HaywireMedia/Fotolia, Totallypic/Fotolia)

HOW COOL IS THIS?

Have you ever wanted to **share your computer screen** with someone but couldn't because you didn't know how or didn't have the right software? Now you can share your computer screen **with anyone on any device via the web** with one click, hassle-free, with **Screenleap (screenleap.com)**.

All you need to do is **click a link that generates a code**, then send the code to whomever you want to share your screen with; they will be able to view your screen immediately from their web browser on their smartphone, tablet, or PC. You can share your screen publically or privately to only a select few. There is also an extension to initiate sharing directly from your Gmail account. Using this technology may help you **better communicate** with classmates or your professors when seeking or offering help. **A free account** will give you two hours of sharing time per day. So, share your screen with someone today with Screenleap! (By-studio/Fotolia)

Working and Playing on the Web

Learning Outcome 3.1 You will be able to explain how the Internet works and how it is used for collaboration, communication, commerce, and entertainment purposes.

You most likely know at least a little bit about how to use the web's resources to communicate and collaborate with others, how to work with multimedia files, and how business is conducted over the web. In this section, we'll explore these and other topics. But first, let's start with a brief lesson on the history of the Internet.

the internet and how IT WORKS

It's hard to imagine life without the Internet. The Internet is actually a network of networks that connects billions of computer users globally, but its beginnings were much more modest.

The Origin of the Internet

Objective 3.1 *Describe how the Internet got its start.*

Why was the Internet created? The concept of the **Internet**—the largest computer network in the world—was developed in the late 1950s while the United States was in the midst of the Cold War with the Soviet Union (see Figure 3.1). At that time, the U.S. Department of Defense needed a computer network that wouldn't be disrupted easily in the event of an attack.

FIGURE 3.1 How the Internet Began

1958 — The **Advanced Research Projects Agency (ARPA)** is established for the U.S. Department of Defense. This agency creates the ARPANET—the beginnings of the Internet.

ASCII Code - Character to Binary

0	0011 0000	I	0100 1001	b	0110 0010	v	0111 0110
1	0011 0001	J	0100 1010	c	0110 0011	w	0111 0111
2	0011 0010	K	0100 1011	d	0110 0100	x	0111 1000
3	0011 0011	L	0100 1100	e	0110 0101	y	0111 1001
4	0011 0100	M	0100 1101	f	0110 0110	z	0111 1010
				g	0110 0110		

1963 — **ASCII code** is developed as the standard for computers from different manufacturers to exchange data.

1964 — A **new network scheme** is developed with multiple paths so if one communication path was destroyed (from a potential Soviet Union attack), the rest of the network would still be able to communicate.

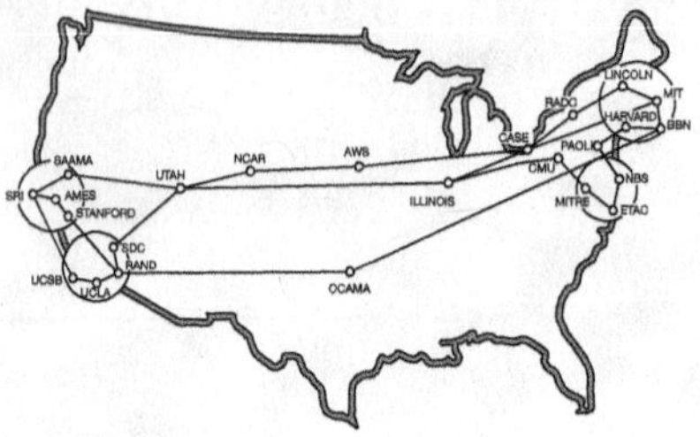

1969 — Researchers at UCLA **send the first message via a networked computer system** to researchers at Stanford University.

(Cristi180884/Shutterstock)

At the same time, researchers for the Department of Defense were trying to get different computers to work with each other using a common communications method that all computers could use. The Internet was created to respond to these two concerns: establishing a *secure* form of communications and creating a means by which *all* computers could communicate.

Who invented the Internet? The modern Internet evolved from an early U.S. government-funded "internetworking" project called the Advanced Research Projects Agency Network (ARPANET). ARPANET began as a four-node network involving UCLA, Stanford Research Institute, the University of California at Santa Barbara, and the University of Utah in Salt Lake City. The first real communication occurred in 1969 between the computer at Stanford and the computer at UCLA. Although the system crashed after the third letter of "Login" was transmitted, it was the beginning of a revolution. Many people participated in the creation of the ARPANET, but two men, Vinton Cerf and Robert Kahn, are generally acknowledged as the "fathers of the Internet." These men earned this honor because in the 1970s, they were primarily responsible for developing the communications protocols (standards) still in use on the Internet today.

So are the web and the Internet the same thing? Because the **World Wide Web** (**WWW** or the **web**) is what we use the most, we sometimes think of the Internet and the web as being interchangeable. However, the web is only a subset of the Internet, dedicated to broadcasting HTML pages; it is the means by which we access information over the Internet. The web is based on the Hypertext Transfer Protocol (HTTP), which is why you see an *http://* at the beginning of web addresses. What distinguishes the web from the rest of the Internet is its use of the following:

- Common communications protocols that enable computers to talk to each other and display information in compatible formats
- Special links that enable users to navigate from one place to another on the web

Who created the web? The web began in 1991. It was based on a protocol developed by Tim Berners-Lee, a physicist at the European Organization for Nuclear Research (CERN), who wanted a method for linking his research documents so that other researchers could access them. In conjunction with Robert Cailliau, Berners-Lee developed the basic architecture of the web and created the first *web browser*, software that lets you display and interact with text and other media on the web. The original browser could handle only text. Then, in 1993, the Mosaic browser, which could display graphics as well as text, was released. The once-popular Netscape Navigator browser evolved from Mosaic and heralded the beginning of the web's monumental growth.

How the Internet Works

Objective 3.2 *Explain how data travels on the Internet.*

How does the Internet work? All computers and other devices such as tablets and smartphones that are connected

1973

Vincent Cerf and Robert develop a set of communication rules–the **TCP/IP protocol**–that allow different types of computers to communicate.

1991

Tim Berners-Lee developed and made public **HTTP protocol and the World Wide Web**. WWW is a subset of the Internet that is connected via hypertext (text containing hyperlinks to other documents and media).

1972

Ray Tomlinson writes a program to send **e-mail** over the ARPANET and develops the "user@host" convention.

1978

By 1978, there were 111 Internet domains on ARPANET.

1997

By 1997, there were over 1 million Internet domains on ARPANET.

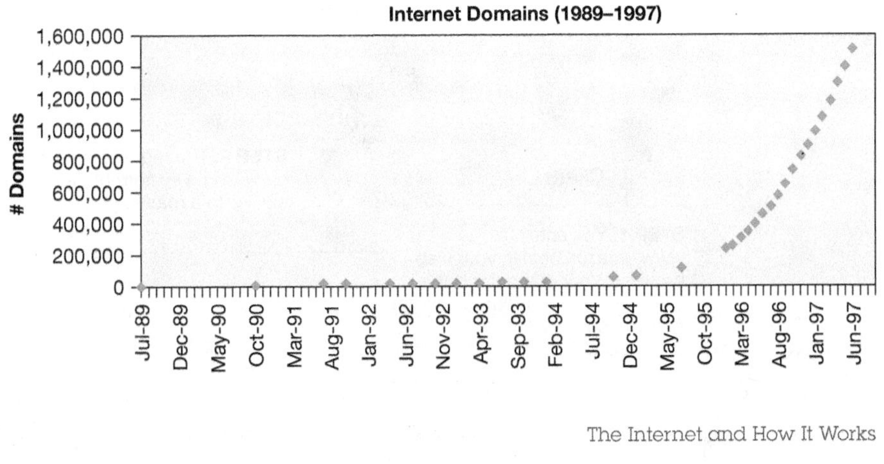

(Beboy/Shutterstock, Matthias Pahl/Shutterstock, LvNL/Shutterstock)

BITS&BYTES

Ever Heard of Internet2?

Although Internet2 may sound like a new and separate network meant to replace the Internet, this is not the case. Internet2 is actually a consortium of U.S. leaders in education, research, industry, and government that seeks to expand the possibilities of the existing Internet by developing new technologies and applications and then deploying them to the public. These experimental technologies require a faster and more efficient Internet, so the researchers use separate data lines that support extremely high-speed communications—up to 8.8 terabits per second (Tbps). In fact, many of the Internet's current technologies are possible because of the research done by the Internet2 consortium.

to the Internet create a network of networks. These Internet-connected devices communicate with each other in turns, just as we do when we ask a question or reply with an answer. Thus, a computer (or other device) connected to the Internet acts in one of two ways: Either it's a **client**, a computer that asks for data, or it's a **server**, a computer that receives the request and returns the data to the client. Because the Internet uses clients and servers, it's referred to as a **client/server network**.

When a client computer puts out a request for information from the server computer, the request travels along transmission lines. These transmission lines are similar to our highway system of roads, with some roads having different speed limits. The transmission lines with the fastest speeds are referred to as **Internet backbones**.

How do computers talk to each other? Suppose you want to order something from Amazon.com. Figure 3.2 illustrates what happens when you type **www.amazon.com** into your web browser and when Amazon's home page displays on your computer monitor. As you can see, the data request from your computer (the client computer) is sent via Internet communication pathways to a server computer. The server computer (in this case, Amazon's server) processes the request and returns the requested data to your client computer via Internet communication pathways. The data reply most likely takes a different route than did the data request. The web browser on your client computer interprets the data and displays it on its monitor.

How does the data get sent to the correct computer? Each time you connect to the Internet, your computer is assigned a unique identification number. This number, called an **Internet Protocol (IP) address**, is a set of four groups of numbers separated by periods, such as 123.45.245.91, and is commonly referred to as a *dotted quad* or *dotted decimal*. IP addresses are the means by which computers connected to the Internet identify each other. Similarly, each website is assigned a unique IP address. However, because the numbers that make up IP addresses are difficult for people to remember, websites are given text versions of their IP addresses. So, Amazon's website has an IP address of 72.21.211.176 and a name of **www.amazon.com**. When you type **"www.amazon.com"** into your browser, your computer (with its unique IP address) looks for Amazon's IP address (72.21.211.176). Data is exchanged between Amazon's server computer and your computer using these unique IP addresses. ■

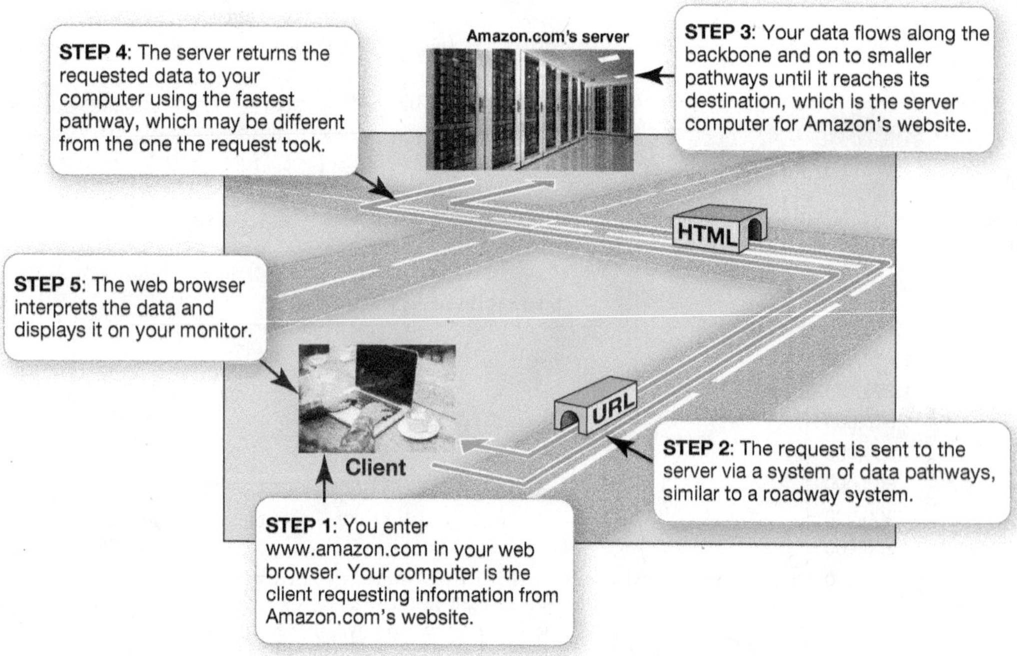

FIGURE 3.2 How the Internet's Client/Server Model Works
(Sashkin/Fotolia, peshkov/Fotolia)

collaborating and communicating ON THE WEB

In this section, we'll explore some popular means of collaborating and communicating on the web.

Collaborating with Web 2.0 Tools

Objective 3.3 *Discuss the tools and technologies used to collaborate and communicate on the web.*

How do we collaborate and communicate on the web? Over time, our use of the web has evolved from passively browsing web pages that were created for us, to actively creating our own web content and sharing and collaborating on it with others. This new collaborative, user-created web, sometimes classified as the *social web*, in which the user is also a participant, is possible due to the advancement of **Web 2.0** technologies. Web 2.0 technologies enable us to collaborate with others through web applications such as Google Drive, to rate and recommend products or services with Yelp, to tag a friend on social networks such as Facebook, and to share a video on YouTube or a favorite image on Pinterest. These means of Web 2.0 communication are collectively called **social media** and include social networking, wikis, blogs, podcasts, and webcasts.

Social Networking

Is there more to social networking than Facebook? As you probably know, **social networking** refers to using the web to communicate and share information among your friends and others. Professional, business-oriented online networks such as LinkedIn are helpful for members seeking potential clients, business opportunities, jobs, or job candidates. Like a true business network, these sites can help you meet other professionals through the people you already know. In addition, businesses use social networking for marketing and communicating directly with their customers. For example, companies may post special deals and offers on their Facebook page or solicit responses from followers that may help with product development or future marketing campaigns.

Figure 3.3 shows various sites that are considered Web 2.0 social networking sites. As you can see, there is more to social networking than just Facebook and Twitter.

What are some dos and don'ts of social networking? When social networking sites first became popular, there was concern over privacy issues, especially for school-aged children who put personal information on their pages without considering the possibility of that information being misused by a stalker or identity thief. Although those concerns still exist, many of the most popular social networking sites have improved their privacy policies, thereby reducing, but not eliminating, such concerns. Still, users must be cautious about the type of content they post on these sites. Consider these precautions as you use social networking sites:

- Keep your personal information personal. The year you were born, your physical address, and the routines of your life (sports games, practices, work schedules) should not be broadcast to the general public.
- Know who your friends are, and know who can see the information you post. Review your privacy settings periodically, as sites change and update their privacy practices frequently.
- Do not post information such as your favorite teacher or your first pet's name because these are often used as security questions to verify your identity.
- Use caution when posting images, and know what images others are posting of you. Although privacy settings may offer some comfort, some images may be available for viewing through search engines and may not require site registration to be seen. Online images may become public property and subject to reproduction, and you might not want some—or any—of those images to be distributed.

Many employers and colleges use social networks as a means of gaining information about potential applicants before granting an interview or extending admission or a job offer. In fact, there have been instances of people being fired from their jobs and being expelled from school for using social media, such as Facebook, Twitter, and blogs, in a questionable way. Generally, questionable content on social media includes negative discussion about the poster's job, employer, or colleagues or inappropriate content about the poster. The responsibility for your content rests with you. Even though you may have strong privacy settings, you can't control what those who you allow to see your content do with it. Therefore, treat all information posted on the web as public, and avoid posting damaging words and pictures. Bottom line: Make sure your profile, images, and site content project an image that positively and accurately represents you.

Wikis and Project Collaboration Tools

What is a wiki? Rather than needing to pass documents back and forth via e-mail and possibly losing track of which version is the most recent, wikis are a great alternative. A **wiki** is a web application that allows users to add, remove, or edit its content. Wiki content is created collaboratively by multiple users, resulting in an emergent "common" opinion rather than the opinion of an individual writer. Wikis allow all who have

FIGURE 3.3

Types of Social Networking Sites

	DESCRIPTION	SUGGESTED URLS
Social Exchange Networks	Allow users to connect with others, provide status updates	**facebook.com** **twitter.com**
Create Your Own Social Networks	Allow users to create their own social network around a common topic; groups can be public or private	**ning.com**
Business-Related Social Networks	Allow users to seek potential clients, business opportunities, jobs, or job candidates	**linkedin.com**
Media Sharing Networks	Allow users to share pictures and videos	**youtube.com** **instagram.com** **pinterest.com**
Information Sharing Networks	Allow users to share information	**delicious.com** **wikipedia.org** **slideshare.net**
Information Recommendations and Filtering (Bookmarking) Networks	Allow users to post their opinion of a product, service, news, or web item for others to see and use	**reddit.com** **digg.com**

(Kevin Britland/Alamy, M4OS Photos/Alamy, Anil Kumar/Alamy, Kristoffer Tripplaar/Alamy, PhotoEdit/Alamy, TP/Alamy, Web Pix/Alamy, PhotoEdit/Alamy, Shutterstock, M4OS Photos/Alamy, NetPics/Alamy)

access to the wiki page to post their ideas and modify the content of the current version of a single document. Wikis provide the extra benefit of users being able to access, review, and even revert to past versions at any time.

Wikipedia (**wikipedia.org**), the popular collaborative online encyclopedia, is one example of a wiki. Wiki content such as that found on Wikipedia is created collaboratively by multiple users. Because of wiki technology, Wikipedia's content can be updated continually. The Wikimedia Foundation, which hosts Wikipedia, also hosts other collaborative projects, such as Wikibooks (textbooks), Wikiversity (learning tools), and Wikisource (a document library). These wiki-type collaborative efforts apply to a variety of other useful applications. For example, wikiHow (**wikihow.com**) is an online project that uses both wikis and the collaborative process to build a large, online how-to manual.

Note that some web-based document products, such as Google Drive (**drive.google.com**), have wiki-like features to promote similar online collaboration, and specific wiki software, such as Wikispaces (**wikispaces.com**) and MediaWiki (**mediawiki.org**), is available that you can download for free.

What other web tools are used to help with project collaborations? In addition to using wikis and wiki-like documents, other tools such as videoconferencing, screen sharing, and project management tools are used to facilitate collaboration. There are full-featured business enterprise solutions, but for smaller collaborative projects, such as those you might encounter in a group project for school or in a small business environment, there are a wide variety of web-based options to choose from, many of which are free. **Project management tools** incorporate tasks and calendars so the individual components as well as the entire project can stay on schedule. Trello, for example, is a free project management

BITS&BYTES

Why Isn't Wikipedia Good to Use as a Source for a Research Paper?

The idea behind content that is managed and edited by many users, such as that found on Wikipedia and other large public wikis, is that the group will keep the content current and valid. However, because wikis are publicly editable, they can't be trusted completely. If a user adds erroneous content, the community of users can catch and correct it, but if you used Wikipedia as a source, you may have referenced erroneous content before it was corrected. To help address these concerns, Wikipedia has implemented tighter access controls, requiring users who want editing privileges to register with the site, but the risks still remain. Citizendium (**citizendium.org**), another open wiki encyclopedia, requires contributors to provide real names and sign an ethics pledge, and all postings are monitored.

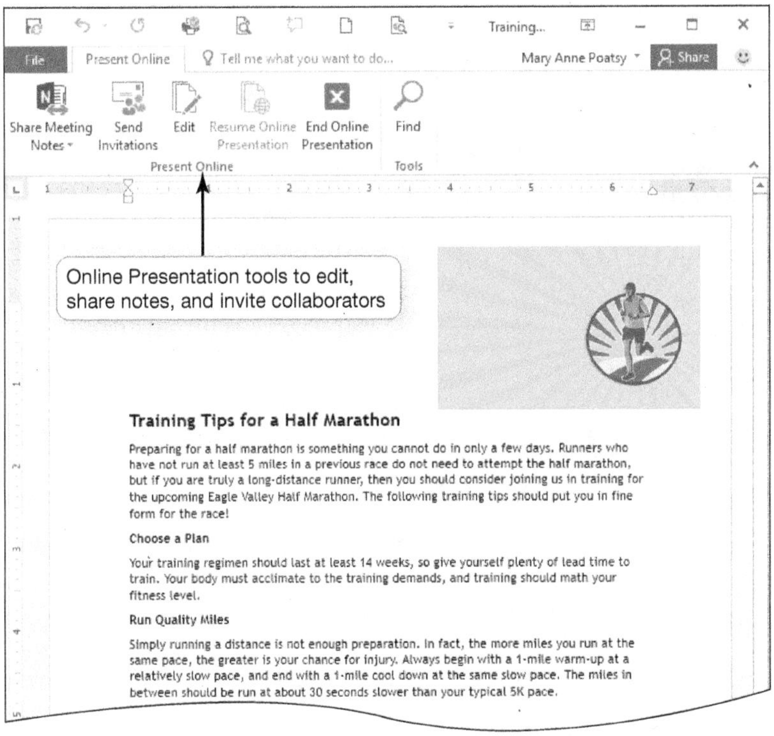

FIGURE 3.4 You can present a Word document or PowerPoint presentation to an online audience using built-in technology in Microsoft Office. *(Microsoft Word 2016, Windows 10, Microsoft Corporation; Patrimonio designs/Fotolia)*

tool that organizes projects onto boards and specific tasks onto cards. Cards can contain checklists, images, labels, discussion notes, and the like. All cards are searchable, shareable, and can have reminders.

When working with a group whose members are not in the same location, screen sharing or videoconferencing software can be helpful. Products such as Join.me and Screenleap (see the How Cool Is This? feature on page 75) offer free screen-sharing solutions. In addition, built into the latest versions of Microsoft Word and PowerPoint is the capability to present online (see Figure 3.4). When you initiate Present Online, a link is generated that you share with the desired recipients, and then anyone who uses the link can see the slide show or document while you are presenting online. Skype and Google Hangouts are also handy solutions for videoconferencing.

Blogs

Why do people write blogs? A **blog** (short for **weblog**) is a personal log or journal posted on the web. Anyone can create a blog, and there are millions of blogs available to read, follow, and comment on. Blogs are generally written by a single author and are arranged as a listing of entries on a single page, with the most recent blog entry appearing at the top of the list. In addition, blogs are public and readers can post comments on your blog, often creating an engaging, interactive experience. Blogs have searchable and organized content, making them user friendly. They're accessible from anywhere using a web browser.

Many people use blogs as a sort of personal scrapbook. Whenever the urge strikes, they report on their daily activities. Many other blogs focus on a particular topic (see Figure 3.5). For example, the Movie Blog (**themovieblog.com**) contains reviews and opinions about movies, and Engadget (**engadget.com**) is a blog devoted to discussing technogadgets. Many corporations, such as Walmart and Best Buy, have blogs written by employees. BlogCatalog (**blogcatalog.com**) is a blog directory that can help you find blogs that fit your interests.

Are all blogs text-based? The traditional form of a blog is primarily text-based but may also include images and audio. A **video log** (**vlog** or **video blog**) is a blog that uses video as the primary content (although it can also contain text, images, and audio). Vlogs are a popular means of personal expression, and many can be found by searching YouTube (**youtube.com**).

SOUND BYTE
Blogging

In this Sound Byte, you'll see why blogs are one of today's most popular publishing mediums. You'll also learn how to create and publish your own blog.

How do I create a blog? Many websites provide the tools you need to create your own blog. Two sites that offer free blog hosting are Blogger (**blogger.com**) and WordPress (**wordpress.com**). Such tools also let you add features like pictures or subpages to your blog. You can also choose to host your blog yourself so that the URL reflects your name or the name of your business. If you choose this option, you'll need your own website and a URL so people can access it.

Are there any problems with blogs? The popularity of blogs has brought about a new problem—*spam blogs* (*splogs*)—which are artificially created blog sites filled with fake articles or stolen text (a tactic known as *blog scraping*). Splogs, which contain links to other sites associated with the splog's creator, have the intention of either increasing traffic to, or increasing search engine rankings for, these usually disreputable or useless websites. Although not really harmful, splogs are another unwanted form of content that continues to grow like weeds on the web.

Are Twitter and Tumblr considered blogs? Twitter and Tumblr are examples of *microblogs*, where users post short text with usually frequent updates. With Twitter, the posts are limited to 140 characters. Tumblr allows users to post multimedia and other content. Posts can be public or restricted to a certain audience.

FIGURE 3.5 Many online news and radio sites offer podcasts of their programs.
(DWD-Media/Alamy Stock Photo)

Podcasts and Webcasts

How can I distribute audio or video files over the Internet to a wide audience? A **podcast** is a form of digital media comprised of a series of audio or video files that are distributed over the Internet. There are podcasts for radio shows, audiobooks, magazines, and even educational programs, which you can download to any device that can play audio files. What makes podcasts different from other audio files found on the web is that podcasts deliver their content using **Really Simple Syndication (RSS)**. RSS is a format that sends the latest content of the podcast series automatically to an **aggregator** such as iTunes or Feedspot. An aggregator locates all the RSS series to which you've subscribed and automatically downloads only the new content to your computer or media player. If you have several favorite websites or podcasts, rather than checking each site for updated content, aggregators collect all the site updates in one place. These updates or changes to the content are then delivered automatically if you subscribe to the podcast, instead of you having to search for the latest content and download it manually.

Where can I find podcasts? Most online news and radio sites offer podcasts of their programs. Although many podcasts are news related, others offer entertaining and educational content. For example, you can access lessons on yoga, foreign language classes, or DIY tips. Many schools supply students with course content updates through podcasts, and instructors sometimes create podcasts of their lectures. Figure 3.6 lists some websites where you can find podcasts.

Can I create my own podcast? It's simple to create a podcast. To record the audio content all you need is a computer with a microphone, and if you want to make a video podcast, you also need a webcam or video camera. Although high-end equipment will produce more sophisticated output, you certainly can use whatever equipment you might own. You may also need additional software to edit the audio and video content, depending on how professional you wish the podcast to be. After you've recorded and edited the podcast content, you need to export it to MP3 format. The free program Audacity (**audacity.sourceforge.net**) lets you both edit audio files and export them to MP3 format. All that's left for you is to create an RSS feed (tricky, but doable) and then upload the content to a site that hosts podcasts, such as iTunes, Podfeed, or Stitcher.

What is a webcast? A **webcast** is the (usually live) broadcast of audio or video content over the Internet. Unlike podcasts, which are prerecorded and made available for download, most webcasts are distributed in "real time," meaning that they're live or one-time events. Some webcasts are archived so they can be viewed at a later date. Webcasts are not updated automatically like podcasts.

Webcasts use continuous audio and video feeds, which let you view and download large audio and video files. Webcasts can include noninteractive content such as a simultaneous broadcast of a radio or television program, but some webcasts invite interactive responses from the viewing or listening audience. For example, ORLive (**orlive.com**) provides surgical webcasts that demonstrate the latest surgical innovations and techniques. Webcasts also are used in the corporate world to broadcast annual meetings and in the educational arena to transmit seminars.

Figure 3.7 lists the popular methods of online collaboration and communication that we've discussed.

FIGURE 3.6

Podcast Directories and Aggregators

iTunes (itunes.com)
- Software makes it easy to play, manage, and share your favorite podcasts

Podfeed (podfeed.net)
- Broad collection of podcasts

Stitcher (stitcher.com)
- Customize podcast playlists

YouTube (youtube.com)
- Good source for video blogs (vlogs)

FIGURE 3.7

Methods of Online Collaboration and Communication

SOCIAL NETWORKING

- Web 2.0 technology
- Lets you build an online network of friends
- Lets you share media content

WIKIS

- Great collaborative tool
- Content updated by many users
- Historical content kept so you can revert to past versions

PROJECT COLLABORATION

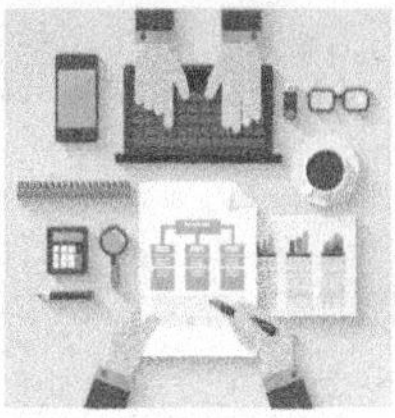

- Screen sharing
- Project management
- Videoconferencing

BLOGS

- Written by a single author
- Chronologic entries
- Searchable content
- May include images, audio, and video

PODCASTS

- Audio/video files delivered via RSS
- New RSS content collected with aggregator
- Can download and view content on portable media player

WEBCASTS

- Most often live, streamed broadcasts

E-MAIL

- Most common form of online communication
- Asynchronous (not having to be done at the same time)

INSTANT MESSAGING

- Real-time exchange
- Can be used with multiple persons simultaneously
- Video/audio chats available

(Lowe Standards/Fotolia, Michael D Brown/Shutterstock, Maglara/Shutterstock, Ayzek/Shutterstock, www.3drenderedlogos com/Shutterstock, Batshevs/Shutterstock, Beboy/Fotolia, LiveStock/Shutterstock)

Communicating over the Web

Objective 3.4 *Summarize how e-mail and instant messaging are used to communicate over the web.*

Why do I still need e-mail? Despite the popularity of social media, **e-mail** (short for **electronic mail**)—a written message sent or received over the Internet—still remains the most widely used form of communication on the Internet. E-mail is the primary method of electronic communication worldwide because it's fast and convenient. And because it's *asynchronous*, users do not need to be communicating at the same time. They can send and respond to messages at their own convenience. E-mail is also convenient for exchanging and collaborating on documents via attachments.

How private is e-mail? Although e-mail is a more private exchange of information than public social networking sites, e-mails are not really private. Consider the following:

- Because e-mails can be printed or forwarded to others, you never know who may read your e-mail.
- Most e-mail content is not protected, so you should never use e-mail to send personal or sensitive information such as bank account or Social Security numbers. Doing so could lead to identity theft.
- Employers have access to e-mail sent from the workplace, so use caution when putting negative or controversial content in e-mail.
- Even after you've deleted a message, it doesn't really vanish. Many Internet service providers and companies archive e-mail, which can be accessed or subpoenaed in the event of a lawsuit or investigation.

What are some tips on e-mail etiquette? When you write a casual e-mail to friends, you obviously don't need to follow any specific e-mail guidelines (except to remember that your e-mail may be forwarded). But when you send e-mail for professional reasons, you should use proper e-mail etiquette. The following are a few guidelines (also see Figure 3.8):

- Be concise and to the point.
- Use the spell-checker and proofread your e-mail before sending it.

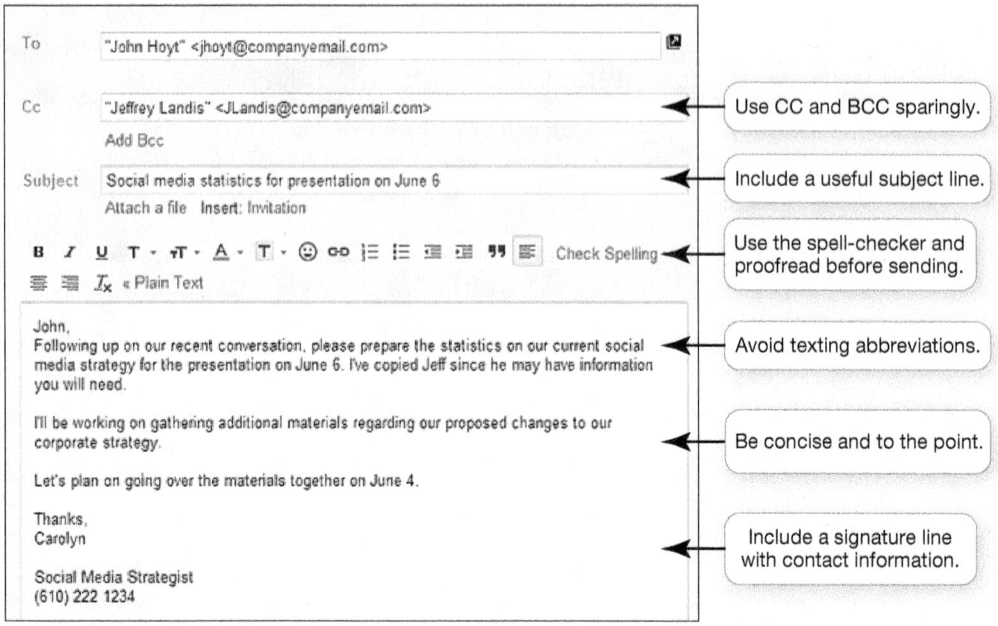

FIGURE 3.8 Using simple guidelines of e-mail etiquette can promote a professional image and make your message more effective. *(Microsoft Outlook, Windows 8.1, Microsoft Corporation)*

- Avoid using abbreviations such as *u*, *r*, *LOL*, and *BTW*.
- Include a meaningful subject line to help recipients prioritize and organize e-mails.
- Add a signature line that includes your contact information.
- Include only those people on the e-mail who truly need to receive it.

Following such guidelines maintains professionalism, increases efficiency, and might even help protect a company from lawsuits.

Are there different types of e-mail systems? There are two different types of e-mail systems:

1. **Web-based e-mail**, such as Yahoo! Mail or Gmail, is managed with your web browser and allows you to access your e-mail from the web.
2. An **e-mail client** requires a program, such as Microsoft Outlook, to be installed on your computer. When you open the program, your e-mail is downloaded to your computer.

The primary difference between the two is access. Web-based e-mail allows you to access e-mail from any Internet-connected device, but you can't use your e-mail when you're offline. With an e-mail client, you view your e-mail on the computer on which the e-mail client software has been installed, but you can then view and manage your e-mail while you're offline. Both systems can be used together for the "best of both worlds." You can have a Gmail account, for example, so that you can read your e-mail from any computer connected to the Internet, and you can also have Outlook installed on your primary computer and set up the program to display your Gmail account (see Figure 3.9).

Who uses instant messaging? Instant messaging (IM), a way of communicating in real time over the Internet, was a primary means of chatting with friends in real time. But with the proliferation of texting and social networking, instant messaging has begun to lose its attraction as a social tool. However, instant messaging still is an important means of quick and efficient communication in the business world.

Some IM systems provide mechanisms to hold conversations with more than one person, either through simultaneous individual conversations or with group chats. And some programs even let you conduct video chats using a webcam. Other advantages of using IM for business communications is that you can monitor who is allowed to contact you, and people can only communicate with you if they know your exact e-mail or IM address.

Google+ and Hangouts, Skype, and Yahoo! Messenger are proprietary IM services, meaning you can IM or chat only with those who share the same IM service and are on your contact or buddy list. Another option is to chat with those you've "friended" on Facebook through Facebook's chat option. There are also universal chat services such as Trillian and Digsby that you install on your computer and that allow you to chat with users of all popular IMs, regardless of the service they use. There are some IM services that have been developed primarily for business use such as Cisco Jabber and Oracle Beehive.

How is instant messaging different from texting? Although both IM and texting provide means to chat, there are differences. Instant messaging is synchronous: both parties need to be participating at the same time, whereas texting is asynchronous in that you do not need to immediately respond to a text once it is received. Texting uses the Short Message Service (SMS) to send short messages between mobile devices. Some texting services that use Multimedia Message Service (MMS) can include images or videos. Snapchat is a popular app that allows users to send brief videos or images. A differentiating aspect to Snapchat is that once a message is opened, the video or image is only available to be viewed for a brief amount of time and is generally not able to be saved.

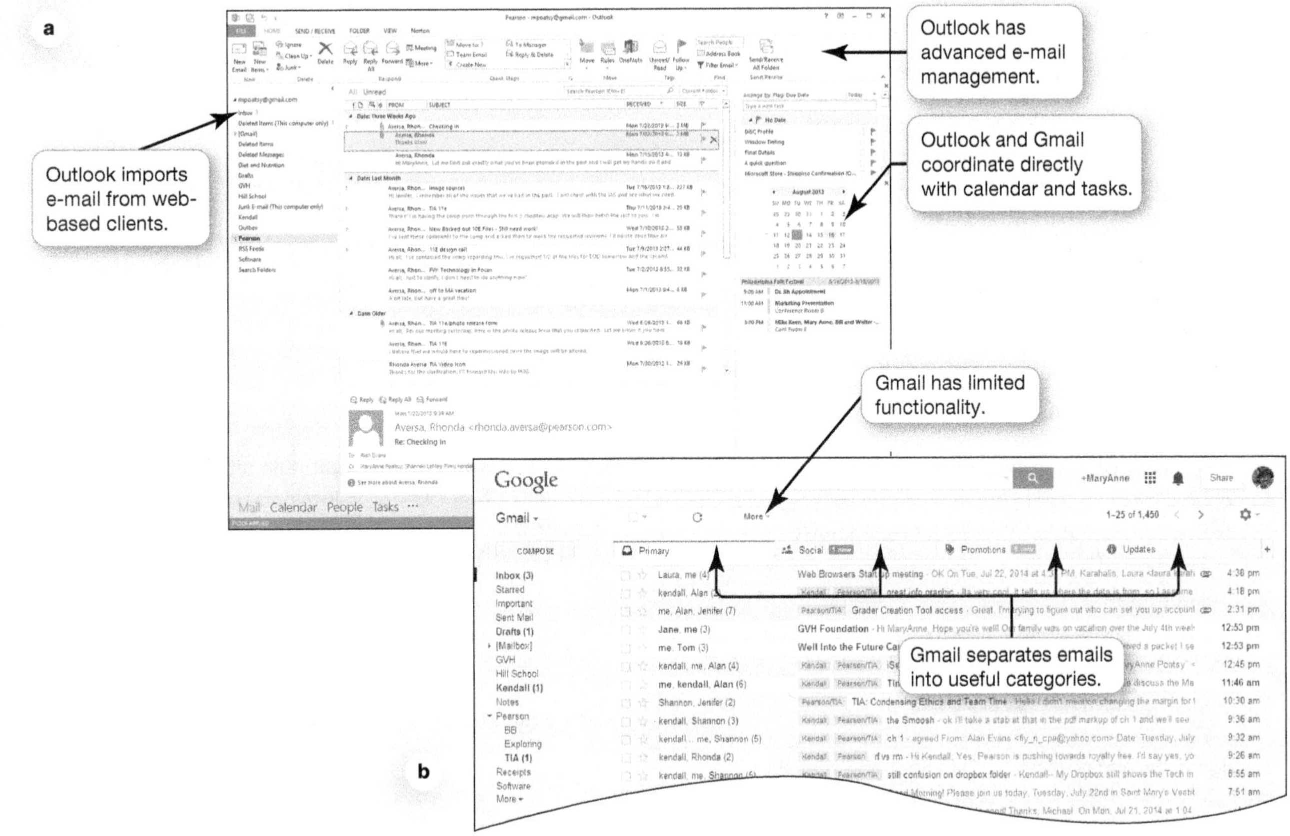

FIGURE 3.9 (a) Client-Based and (b) Web-Based E-Mail Systems *(Microsoft Outlook, Windows 8.1, Microsoft Corporation; © 2015 Google Inc, used with permission. Google and the Google logo are registered trademarks of Google Inc.)*

Can I make phone calls over the Internet? Using apps such as Skype, FaceTime, or Google Hangouts, users can communicate using audio (voice) and video. These services use VoIP (Voice over IP) that allows calls to be transmitted over the Internet rather than over traditional phone lines or cellular networks. The advantage of VoIP is that as long as you have an Internet connection, you can make a call. In instances when Internet access is free, making long-distance or international connections with VoIP is a much more affordable option to keep in touch with friends and family far away. ■

business and entertainment ON THE WEB

It's hard to believe that only a few years ago, many people were scared to buy things online. Today, there is little hesitation, and you can buy nearly anything on the web, including big-ticket items such as homes and cars. Similarly, the types and accessibility of multimedia on the web have become much more plentiful. In this section, we'll take a look at e-commerce and web entertainment.

Types of E-Commerce

Objective 3.5 *Describe the different types of e-commerce.*

What are the different types of e-commerce? **E-commerce**—short for **electronic commerce**—is the process of conducting business online. There are three types of e-commerce business models:

1. **Business-to-consumer (B2C)** transactions take place between businesses and consumers. Such transactions include those between customers and completely online businesses (such as **Amazon.com**) and those between customers and stores that have both an online and a physical presence, such as Target (**target.com**). Such businesses are referred to as *click-and-brick* businesses. Some click-and-bricks allow online purchases and in-store pickups and returns.
2. **Business-to-business (B2B)** transactions occur when businesses buy and sell goods and services to other businesses. An example is Omaha Paper Company (**omahapaper.com**), which distributes paper products to other companies.
3. **Consumer-to-consumer (C2C)** transactions occur when consumers sell to each other through sites such as eBay (**ebay.com**), Craigslist (**craigslist.org**), and Etsy (**etsy.com**).

Social commerce is a subset of e-commerce that uses social networks to assist in marketing and purchasing products. If you're on Facebook, you've no doubt noticed the many businesses that have Facebook pages asking you to "Like" them. Consumers are voicing their opinions on Facebook and other sites about products and services by providing ratings and reviews, and studies show that such peer recommendations have a major influence on buying behavior. When you see your friend on Facebook recommend a product or service, you're more likely to click through to that retailer and check out the product.

Other peer-influenced e-commerce trends include group-buying and individual customization. Groupon and LivingSocial are two popular deal-of-the-day group purchase websites that require a certain number of people to buy the discounted deal before the deal can go through. CafePress and Zazzle sell T-shirts and other items that are customized with your own graphic designs.

But e-commerce encompasses more than just shopping opportunities. Many people use online services to check their bank account balances, pay bills online, and check stock and mutual fund performance. Credit card companies allow you to view, schedule, and pay your credit card bill; brokerage houses allow you to conduct investment activities online.

E-Commerce Safeguards

Objective3.6 *Summarize precautions you should take when doing business online.*

Just how safe are online transactions? When you buy something online, you may use a credit card; therefore, money is exchanged directly between your credit card company and the online merchant's bank. Because online shopping eliminates a salesclerk or other human intermediary from the transaction, it can actually be safer than traditional retail shopping.

What precautions should I take when shopping online? In addition to using some basic common computing sense such as having a firewall and up-to-date antivirus software on your computer, and using strong passwords for all your online accounts, there are several important guidelines to follow to ensure your online shopping experience is a safe one (see Figure 3.10):

- **Look for visual indicators that the website is secure.** Check that the beginning of the URL changes from "http://" to "https://"—with the *s* standing for secure, indicating that the **secure sockets layer** protocol has been applied to manage the security of the website. Also, look for a small icon of a closed padlock in the toolbar (in both Microsoft Edge and Firefox) and a green-colored address bar—indications that the site may be secure. (However, note that even if a site has these indicators, it still might not be safe. Consider the validity of the site before making a purchase.)
- **Shop at well-known, reputable sites.** If you aren't familiar with a site, investigate it with the Better Business Bureau (**bbb.org**) or at Bizrate (**bizrate.com**). Make sure the company has a phone number and street address in addition to a website. You can also look for third-party verification such as that from TRUSTe or the Better Business Bureau. But let common sense prevail. Online deals that seem too good to be true are generally just that—and may be pirated software or illegal distributions.
- **Pay by credit card, not debit card.** Federal laws protect credit card users, but debit card users don't have the same level of protection. If possible, reserve one credit card for Internet purchases only; even better, use a prepaid credit card that has a small credit limit. For an extra layer of security, find out if your credit card company has a service that confirms your identity with an extra password or code that only you know to use when making an online transaction or that offers a one-time-use credit card number. Also, consider using a third-party payment processor such as PayPal or Apple Pay. PayPal also offers a security key that provides additional security to your PayPal account.
- **When you place an order, check the return policy, save a copy of the order, and make sure you receive a confirmation number.** Make sure you read and understand the fine print on warranties, return policies, and the retailer's privacy statements. If the site disappears overnight, this information may help you in filing a dispute or reporting a problem to a site such as the Better Business Bureau.
- **Avoid making online transactions when using public computers.** Public computers may have *spyware* installed, which are programs that track and log your keystrokes and can retrieve your private information. Similarly, unless you have specific protection on your own mobile device, avoid making wireless transactions on public hotspots.

Whether you're doing business, playing games, or communicating with friends or colleagues, the Internet makes these activities more accessible. The Internet can potentially make these experiences and activities more enriched as well, although you must take precautions for the safest of experiences.

FIGURE 3.10

Online Shopping Precautions

When shopping at home, use a firewall and antivirus software for general computer protection.

Don't shop on public WiFi networks, as they may contain spyware.

Check for visual indicators such as https:// in the URL, a closed padlock icon, and a green address bar.

Look for third-party verification from TRUSTe or the Better Business Bureau symbol.

Use a credit card, not a debit card, to protect transactions, or use a third-party payer such as PayPal or Google Wallet.

Create a strong password for all online accounts (one that includes numbers and other symbols such as @).

Deals that are too good to be true are usually just that.

Read and understand the fine print on warranties, return policies, and the retailer's privacy statements.

(Shutterstock, Roy Wylam/Alamy, Photoinnovation/Shutterstock, Newscom, Maxx-Studio/ Shutterstock, Isak55/Shutterstock, Alhovik/Shutterstock, Shutterstock)

Web Entertainment

Objective 3.7 *Describe the types of multimedia files found on the web.*

How can I use the web for entertainment? When you think of how you use the Internet for entertainment purposes, what comes to mind? Streaming audio and video, Internet radio, and social media sharing are all favorite responses. What makes all these forms of web entertainment so popular is their multimedia content. **Multimedia** is anything that involves one or more forms of media in addition to text. It includes the following:

- *Graphics* such as drawings, charts, and photos (the most basic form of multimedia)
- *Audio files* such as the clips you hear when you visit websites, MP3 files you download, podcasts and webcasts, and live broadcasts you can listen to through Internet radio
- *Video files* ranging from simple, short video clips on sites such as YouTube (**youtube.com**) to movies and television shows on sites such as Hulu (**hulu.com**)

ACTIVE HELPDESK

Doing Business Online

In this Active Helpdesk, you'll play the role of a helpdesk staffer, fielding questions about e-commerce and e-commerce safeguards.

What is streaming media? Streaming media is multimedia (audio and video) that is continuously fed to your browser so you avoid having to wait for the entire file to download completely before listening to or watching it. Without streaming media, you wouldn't be able to watch movies on Netflix or on demand from your cable provider, listen to live audio broadcasting, or even play some online games. Internet radio also uses streaming media to present a continuous stream of audio to its listeners.

Where can I share music, pictures, and videos on the web? Social media sharing sites such as Flickr, Instagram, YouTube, and SoundCloud enable anyone to create and share multimedia. Flickr was created to store and share photos online. Although not as "social" as some other sites, Flickr enables users to tag not only their images but others' images, thus providing a strong search capability to quickly locate images with similar tags. Instagram is primarily a mobile app that allows users to take photos on their cell phones or tablets, add a caption, and then instantly upload them. SoundCloud is both a distribution platform and a music streaming service. Fledgling musicians can upload original music to share, and music enthusiasts can track and follow new and favorite artists. SoundCloud has a strong online community of followers. YouTube enables users to upload videos offering a variety of content from educational pieces to cute or funny videos. Many YouTube videos become so popular and are shared or recommended to be seen by so many that they go "viral."

BITS&BYTES

Making Safe Online Payments

When people first began making online purchases, many were not comfortable because the sites required them to give personal financial information such as credit card numbers in a web form. It was unknown who had access to that information. PayPal (**paypal.com**) resolved that issue by serving as a payment intermediary that allows anyone to pay with credit cards and bank accounts without sharing their financial information. PayPal is now a standard means of payment for many online merchants and offers buyer protection and dispute resolution services. Figure 3.11 shows how PayPal works. Similarly, for in-person retail exchanges, Apple Pay uses security features that shield your credit card information from merchants (and Apple!).

Another level of protection for securing online accounts that is becoming more popular is the use of mobile biometrics. Biometrics is the process of authenticating users by physiological or behavioral traits such as signatures, fingerprints, and even irises. Apple introduced Touch ID with a fingerprint scanner on the iPhone 5S. Many mobile apps, especially those for financial services companies, have integrated Touch ID as part of the login procedure. Touch ID systems are being built into other devices, such as Samsung smartphones, and PayPal and other companies are also incorporating the feature.

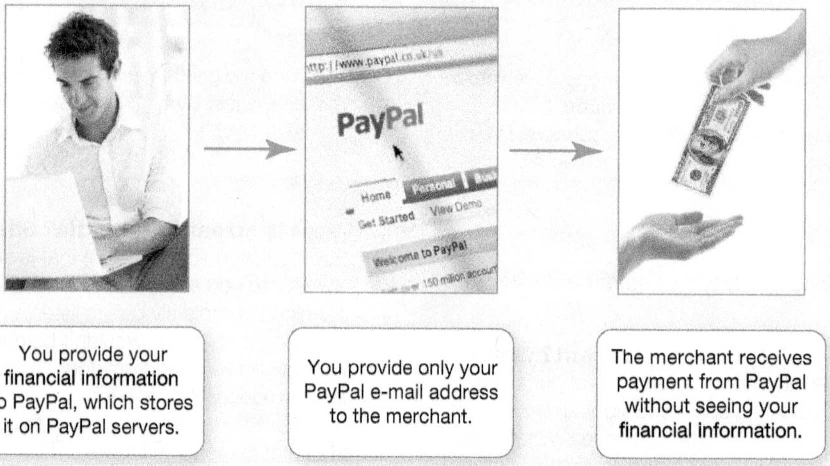

FIGURE 3.11 How PayPal Works *(Shutterstock, AKP Photos/Alamy, Happydancing/Shutterstock)*

Is there any way to get multimedia web content to load faster? When you're on the Internet, your browser keeps track of the sites you've visited so that it can load them faster the next time you visit them. This *cache* (temporary storage place) of the text pages, images, and video files from recently visited websites can make your web surfing more efficient, but it can also slow down your hard drive. Additionally, if you don't have your cache settings configured to check for updates to the web page, your browser may not load the most recent content. To keep your system running efficiently, consider doing the following:

- Delete your temporary Internet cache every month or so, depending on your usage.
- To ensure the most recent website content is displayed, click Refresh or press the F5 key if you revisit a site in the same browsing session.
- Clear your Internet cache manually or adjust the setting in your web browser so that it clears the cache automatically every time you exit the browser. ■

Before moving on to Part 2:

1. **Watch Replay Video 3.1.**
2. **Then check your understanding of what you've learned so far.**

check your understanding // review & practice

For a quick review to see what you've learned so far, answer the following questions.

multiple choice

1. Which is NOT an event associated with the beginning of the Internet?

- **a.** The U.S. Department of Defense creates ARPA.
- **b.** TCP/IP protocol was developed that allowed different computers to communicate with each other.
- **c.** Amazon.com was one of the first websites on the Internet.
- **d.** The first e-mail program was written by Ray Tomlinson.

2. What do you need if you want to read, send, and organize e-mail from *any* computer connected to the Internet?

- **a.** e-mail client program
- **b.** e-mail server
- **c.** e-mail aggregator
- **d.** web-based e-mail account

3. Which of the following would be best for *synchronous* text-based communication?

- **a.** e-mail
- **b.** texting
- **c.** blogging
- **d.** instant messaging

4. Which technology is being used in creating a document on Google Drive?

- **a.** blog
- **b.** wiki
- **c.** microblog
- **d.** e-mail

5. Which of the following would be an example of a C2C business?

- **a.** BestBuy
- **b.** Target
- **c.** Etsy
- **d.** Google

MyITLab Go to **MyITLab** to take an autograded version of the *Check Your Understanding* review and to find all media resources for the chapter.

TECHBYTES WEEKLY
Stay current with the TechBytes Weekly Newsletter.

Continue

TRY THIS

Create a OneDrive Account to Store and Share Your Files in the Cloud

You probably have your favorite ways of moving your files around. Perhaps you have a USB drive or you e-mail files to yourself, or maybe you have a portable external hard drive. With any of these solutions, there can be confusion as to which is the most current version of the file if you have worked on it on multiple devices at different times. You also run the risk of losing your USB drive or deleting the e-mail attachment by mistake. These methods also make exchanging files difficult if you want to share your files or collaborate with a group.

A simpler solution is to use a web-based or cloud storage and sharing service such as OneDrive or Dropbox. OneDrive is part of Microsoft's Office Online. With 15 GB of free storage space for new users, you can store thousands of files and get to them anytime you're online.

Step 1 Sign in to OneDrive: Go to **onedrive.com**. Sign in to your Microsoft account. If you don't have a Microsoft account, creating one is easy. A Microsoft account will give you access to services such as OneDrive, Xbox LIVE, and **Outlook.com**. *(Microsoft One Drive, Windows 10, Microsoft Corporation)*

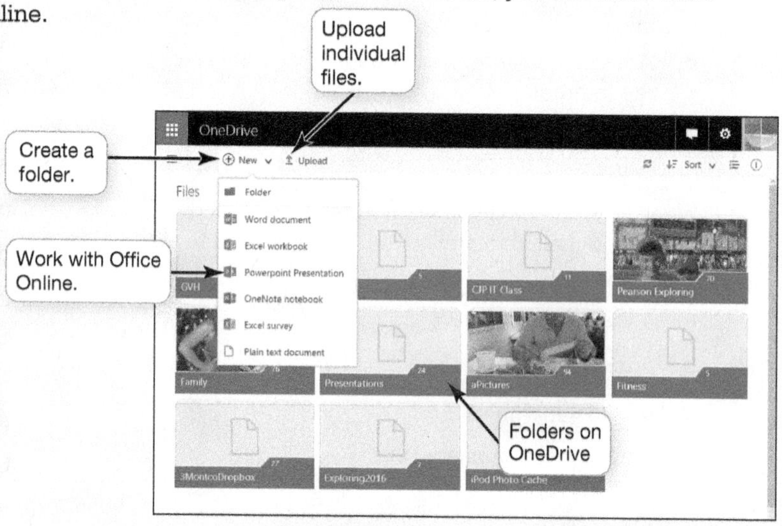

Step 2 Create a Folder and Add Files: Once you're in OneDrive, you can create a folder and then begin to add files.

- To create a folder: Click **New** at the top of the page, click **Folder**, and then give your new folder a name. Click the new folder to open it.
- To add a file: Click **Upload** at the top of the page, select **Files**, then locate the file and click **Open**. To upload more than one file, press and hold **Ctrl** while you select each file. *(Microsoft One Drive, Windows 10, Microsoft Corporation)*

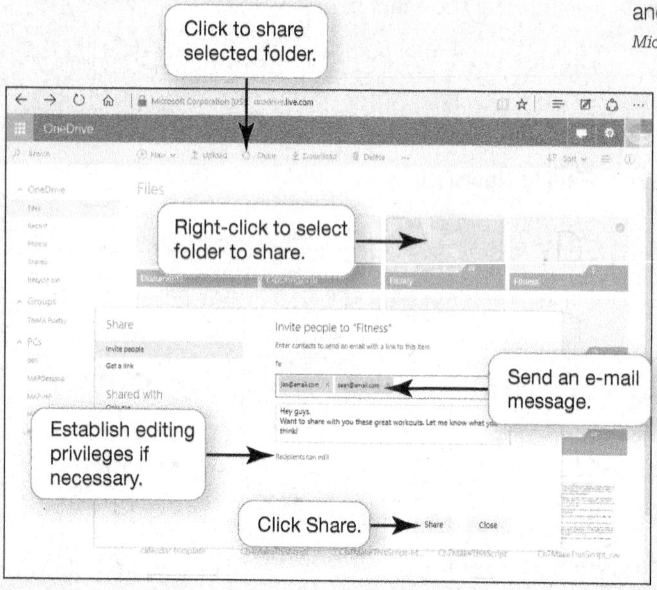

Step 3 Share a File or Folder: To share a file or folder, complete the following steps:

1. Right-click the file or folder that you want to share and click **Share**, or click **Share** in the top menu after selecting the desired file or folder.
2. Ensure *Invite people* is highlighted in the Share pane, then enter e-mail addresses in the To box. You can add a note if you would like.
3. Editing privileges are established by default, so if you want to restrict editing privileges, click **Recipients can edit**, then choose **Recipients can only view**.
4. If you are unsure whether the recipients have a Microsoft account, you can select **Recipients don't need a Microsoft account**.
5. Click **Share**.
6. To see what files that have been shared with you, click **Shared** in the left menu. *(Microsoft One Drive, Windows 10, Microsoft Corporation)*

Step 4 Sync Selective Folders: By default, all the files and folders on OneDrive are synced with the devices that have OneDrive installed. To save space on those devices with small hard drives, you can select only the folders you want to be synced. For all non-synced folders, you could still access the content from the OneDrive Online. To select specific folders to sync, complete the following steps:

1. Right-click the **OneDrive icon** from the Notification area on the taskbar.
2. Click **Settings**, then click the **Choose folders tab**.
3. Click **Choose folders**. From the dialog box, uncheck the folders you don't want to sync. Any check boxes with checks will be synced to your computer. When you're done, click **OK**. If you have OneDrive installed on several devices, you would need to repeat this process on each device, as needed. *(Microsoft One Drive, Windows 10, Microsoft Corporation)*

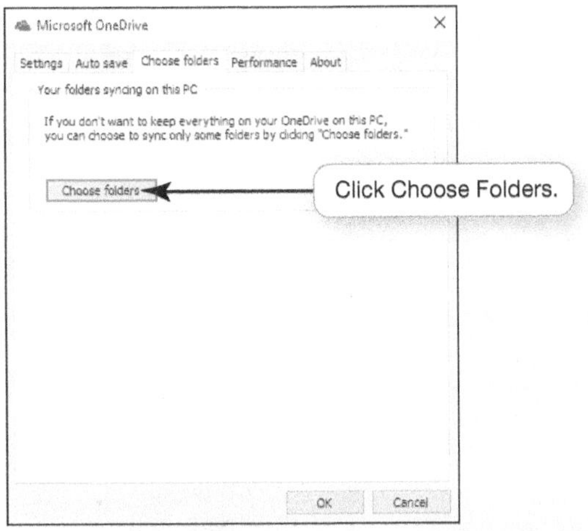

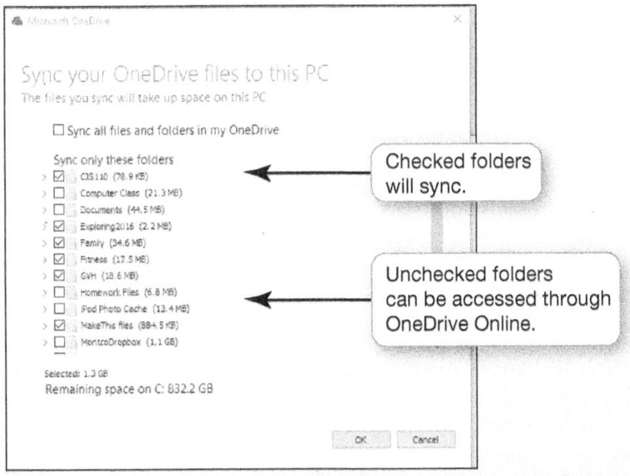

Make This TOOL: App Inventor 2

MAKE: A Web-Capable App

Want your app to be able to display a web page?

In this exercise, you'll continue your mobile app development by adding a new power to your apps: web browsing.

It's as easy as using the WebViewer component in **App Inventor**. Drag a WebViewer component onto your Designer screen, then control it with the Blocks for WebViewer. These allow you to go back, forward, to the home page, or to any specific URL. *(MIT App Inventor 2, Massachusetts Institute of Technology. Creative Commons Attribution-ShareAlike 3.0 Unported License)*

The WebViewer component allows you to control a live browser inside your mobile app.

For the instructions for this exercise, go to MyITLab.

Using the Web Effectively

Learning Outcome 3.2 You will be able to describe the tools and techniques required to navigate and search the web.

You no doubt know how to use the web—to buy products, send e-mail, visit Facebook, and use Google—but do you know how to use it effectively? In this section, we'll look at ways to make your online experience more enjoyable, more productive, and more efficient.

accessing and moving AROUND THE WEB

None of the activities for which we use the web could happen without an important software application: a web browser.

Web Browsers

Objective 3.8 *Explain what web browsers are, and describe their common features.*

What is a web browser exactly? A **web browser** is a software that lets you locate, view, and navigate the web. Most browsers today are *graphical* browsers, meaning they can display pictures (graphics) in addition to text and other forms of multimedia such as sound and video. The most common browsers are displayed in Figure 3.12. Notice that a new browser, Microsoft Edge, has replaced Internet Explorer. This transition happened with the introduction of Windows 10, the latest version of Microsoft's operating system. Although Internet Explorer will still be around for businesses, individual users will only have access to Microsoft Edge. (See the Bits&Bytes box about the new features of Microsoft Edge.)

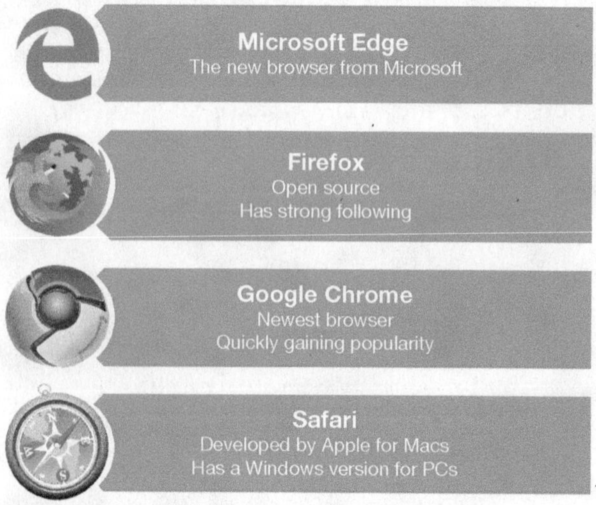

FIGURE 3.12 Common Web Browsers *(Microsoft Corporation, Lucia Lanpur/Alamy, Tommy (Louth)/Alamy, 2020WEB/Alamy)*

BITS&BYTES

New Browser: Microsoft Edge

When Microsoft released the latest version of its operating system, Windows 10, it said good-bye to its long-standing browser Internet Explorer and introduced Microsoft Edge, a new browser, built from scratch, intended to give users a browser that works with how they use the Internet today. In addition to the features you are most likely familiar with already, such as tabs, InPrivate Browsing, and the like, Microsoft Edge adds other features to enrich your browsing experience. For example, with Microsoft Edge, you can make "Webnotes" by annotating a web page and then share them to OneNote or Evernote or save them for later use. Microsoft Edge is also integrated with Microsoft's personal assistant Cortana, which will share web content with you based on your indicated preferences and interests. Finally, you can save online content to read later, and if the "noise" of a web page is distracting to you, you can use Reading View for a cleaner, simpler layout.

What features do web browsers offer? Most popular browsers share similar features that make the user experience more efficient (see Figure 3.13). For example, most browsers include a combined search and address bar so you can both type a website URL or search the web from the address bar. Other features include the following:

- *Tabbed browsing*: Web pages are loaded in "tabs" within the same browser window. Rather than having to switch among web pages in several open windows, you can flip between the tabs in one window. You may also save a group of tabs as a Favorites group if there are several tabs you often open at the same time.

FIGURE 3.13 Tabbed and privacy browsing and an address bar that doubles as a search bar are common features in today's browsers. (Internal Revenue Service, NASA)

- *Pinned tabs*: You can "pin" tabs to the Start menu in Microsoft Edge or minimize and save them permanently with Google Chrome and Firefox for easier navigation of your favorite sites.
- *Tear-off tabs*: An opened tab can be dragged or moved away from its current window so it's then opened in a new window.
- *Thumbnail previews*: Another convenient navigation tool that most browsers share is providing thumbnail previews of all web pages in open tabs.
- *Tab isolation*: With this feature, tabs are independent of each other, so if one crashes, it does not affect the other tabs.
- *SmartScreen filter*: Most browsers offer built-in protection against phishing, malware, and other web-based threats.
- *Privacy browsing*: Privacy features (such as InPrivate Browsing in Microsoft Edge or Incognito in Chrome) let you browse the web without retaining a history trail, temporary Internet files, cookies, or usernames and passwords. These features are especially helpful when you use public computers at school or the public library, for example.
- *Add-ons and extensions*: *Add-ons* (also known as *extensions*) are small programs that customize and increase the functionality of the browser. Examples include Video DownloadHelper, which converts web videos like those found on YouTube to files you can save, as well as a Facebook toolbar that integrates Facebook functionality into your browser.
- *Session Restore*: Brings back all your active web pages if the browser or system shuts down unexpectedly.

SOUND BYTE

Welcome to the Web

In this Sound Byte, you'll visit the web in a series of guided tours of useful websites. This tour serves as an introductory guide for web newcomers but is also a great resource for more experienced users.

URLs, Protocols, and Domain Names

Objective 3.9 *Explain what a URL is, and discuss its main parts.*

What do all the parts of a URL mean? You gain initial access to a particular website by typing its unique address, or **Uniform Resource Locator (URL**, pronounced "you-are-ell"), in your browser. A website is comprised of many different web pages, each of which is a separate document with its own unique URL. Like a regular street address, a URL is comprised of several parts that help identify the web document it stands for (see Figure 3.14):

- the *protocol* (set of rules) used to retrieve the document;
- the **domain name**; and
- the *path* or subdirectory.

Although every part of a URL is important information that ensures the web page you requested actually displays in your browser, you don't have to type in every part in the location or address bar of the browser. Most current browsers no longer require you to enter the http:// protocol or the "www," and most don't even require the domain if it's a .com—the browser will enter those automatically.

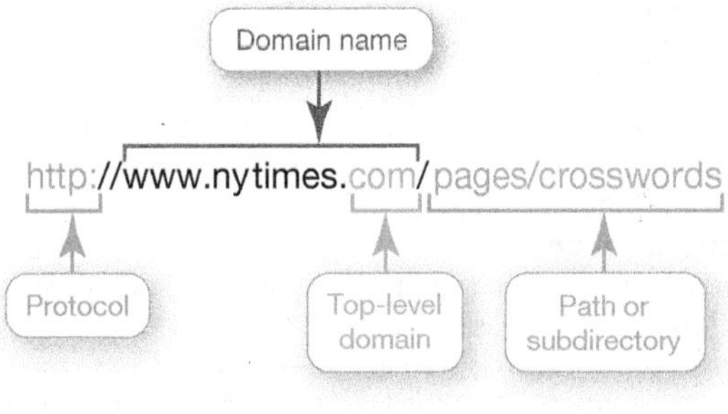

FIGURE 3.14 The Parts of a URL

FIGURE 3.15

Common Top-Level Domains and Their Authorized Users

DOMAIN NAME	WHO CAN USE IT
.biz	Businesses
.com	Originally for commercial sites, but now can be used by anyone
.edu	Degree-granting institutions
.gov	Local, state, and federal U.S. governments
.info	Information service providers
.mil	U.S. military
.net	Originally for networking organizations, but no longer restricted
.org	Organizations (often not-for-profits)

What's the protocol? You're probably most familiar with URLs that begin with *http*, which is short for **Hypertext Transfer Protocol (HTTP)**. HTTP is the protocol that allows files to be transferred from a **web server**—a computer that hosts the website you're requesting—so that you can see it on your computer. The HTTP protocol is what the web is based on.

Is HTTP the only protocol I need to use? HTTP is the most common protocol, but it's not the only one. HTTP is part of the Internet protocol suite, a group of protocols that govern how information is exchanged on a network. Another protocol in that group is the **File Transfer Protocol (FTP)**. As its name implies, FTP was originally designed to transfer files from a computer to a web server. Today, FTP is often used when you have large files to upload or download. To connect to most FTP servers, you need a user ID and password. To upload and download files from FTP sites, you can use a browser or file transfer software such as CuteFTP, Fetch, or FileZilla.

BitTorrent, like FTP, is a protocol used to transfer files, though it's not part of the Internet protocol suite. To use BitTorrent, you install a software client program. It uses a *peer-to-peer networking system* so that sharing occurs between connected computers that also have the BitTorrent client installed. BitTorrent was developed in 2001 and is popular especially among users who want to share music, movies, and games. Use caution, however, when accessing BitTorrent content. Because it is a peer-to-peer system, it's possible for copyrighted material to be shared illegally.

What's in a domain name? The domain name identifies the site's **host**, the location that maintains the computers that store the website files. For example, **www.berkeley.edu** is the domain name for the University of California at Berkeley website. The suffix in the domain name after the dot (such as "com" or "edu") is called the **top-level domain**. This suffix indicates the kind of organization to which the host belongs. Figure 3.15 lists the most frequently used top-level domains.

Each country has its own top-level domain. These are two-letter designations such as .za for South Africa and .us for the United States. A sampling of country codes is shown in Figure 3.16. Within a country-specific domain, further subdivisions can be made for regions or states. For instance, the .us domain contains subdomains for each state, using the two-letter abbreviation of the state. For example, the URL for Pennsylvania's website is **www.state.pa.us.**

What's the information after the domain name that I sometimes see? When the URL is the domain name, such as **www.nytimes.com**, you're requesting a site's home page. However, sometimes a forward slash and additional text follow the domain name, such as in **www.nytimes.com/pages/crosswords**. The information after each slash indicates a particular file or **path** (or **subdirectory**) within the website. In Figure 3.14, you would connect to the crossword page on the *New York Times* site.

Navigating the Web

Objective 3.10 *Describe tools used to navigate the web.*

What's the best way to get around in a website? As its name implies, the web is a series of interconnected paths, or links. You've no doubt moved around the web by clicking on **hyperlinks**, specially coded elements that let you jump from one web page to another within the same website or to another site altogether (see Figure 3.17). Generally, text that operates as a hyperlink appears in a different color (often blue) and is usually underlined, but sometimes images also act as hyperlinks. When you hover your cursor over a hyperlink, the cursor changes to a hand with a finger pointing upward.

FIGURE 3.16

Examples of Country Codes

COUNTRY CODE	COUNTRY
.au	Australia
.ca	Canada
.jp	Japan
.uk	United Kingdom

Note: For a full listing of country codes, refer to **iana.org/domains/root/db/**.

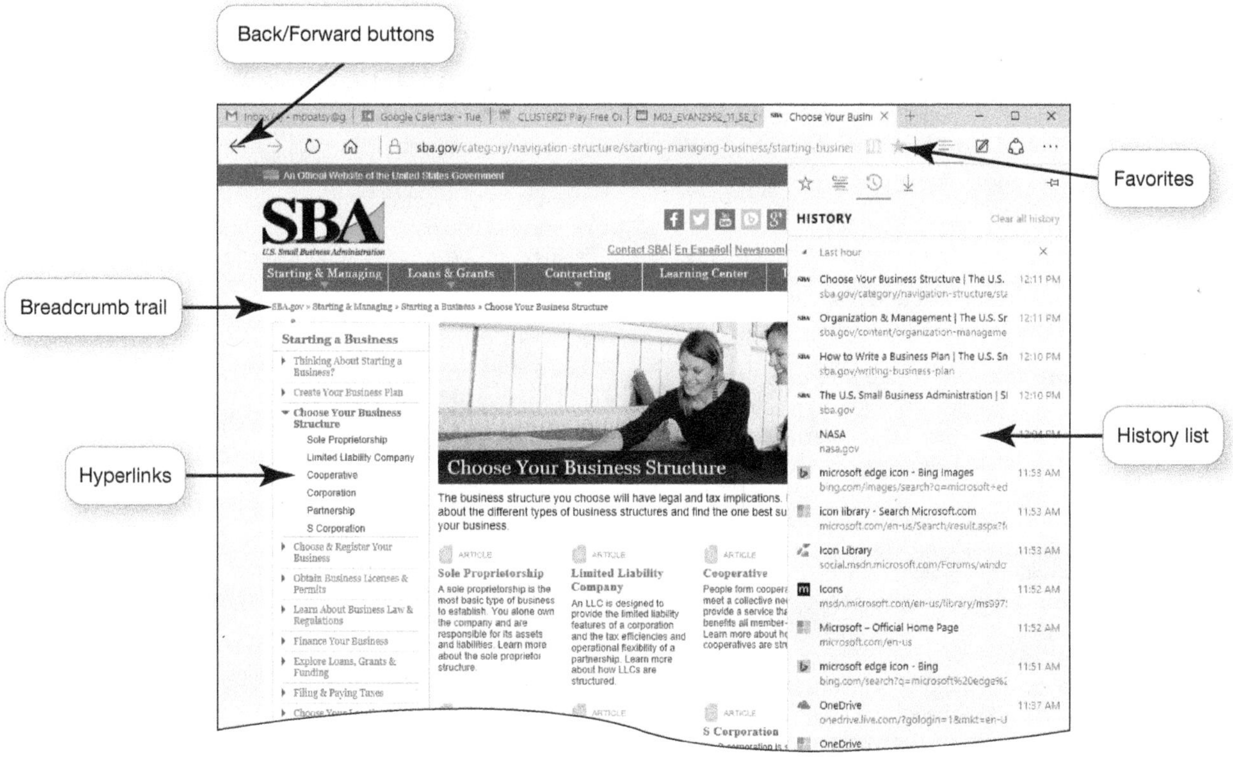

FIGURE 3.17 Navigating a Web Page *(U.S. Small Business Administration)*

What other tools can I use to navigate a website? To move back or forward one page at a time, you can use the browser's Back and Forward buttons (see Figure 3.17).

To help navigate more quickly through a website, some sites provide a **breadcrumb trail**—a navigation aid that shows users the path they have taken to get to a web page, or where the page is located within the website. It usually appears at the top of a page. Figure 3.17 shows an example of a breadcrumb trail. "Breadcrumbs" get their name from the fairy tale "Hansel and Gretel," in which the characters drop breadcrumbs on the trail to find their way out of a forest. By clicking on earlier links in a breadcrumb trail, you can go directly to a previously visited web page without having to use the Back button to navigate back through the website.

Most browsers offer *carat browsing*, which lets you use your keyboard to grab text instead of swiping across with a mouse. To activate carat browsing, press F7 on your keyboard while you have the browser open. You might have to add an extension (Google Chrome) or enable a preference (Firefox) before you can activate the feature. Then, you can use your mouse pointer as an insertion pointer (similar to working in Word) and the arrow keys to move around. Press Shift and an arrow key to select text. Press F7 again to turn off carat browsing. This method offers more precise text selection and is very handy when you frequently copy and paste text from web pages.

The History list on your browser's toolbar is also a handy feature. The History list shows all the websites and pages

BITS&BYTES

Maintain Your Privacy While Searching the Web

Privacy is important to many people, but creating a private online experience is not always an easy task. Although you can use the privacy or incognito mode in some web browsers, these only disable your browsing history and web cache so that data generated from your searches cannot be retrieved later. DuckDuckGo (**duckduckgo.com**) is different—this search engine doesn't collect your personal browsing information to share with third parties for marketing purposes. And although most search engines sell your search term information to third parties, which then use that information to generate display ads and recommendations on pages you visit, DuckDuckGo doesn't sell your search terms to other sites. Moreover, DuckDuckGo doesn't save your search history. Using DuckDuckGo eliminates third-party sharing of your personal information.

you've visited over a certain period of time. These sites are organized according to date and can go back as far as three weeks, depending on your browsing activity. To access the History list in Microsoft Edge, click Hub (the three horizontal lines next to the star in the upper right-hand corner of the browser window) and then click the History icon.

Favorites, Live Bookmarks, and Tagging

Objective 3.11 *Describe tools used to mark sites for future use.*

What's the best way to mark a site so I can return to it later? If you want an easy way to return to a specific web page, you can use your browser's **Bookmarks** feature (Microsoft Edge calls this feature **Favorites**). This feature places a marker of the site's URL in an easily retrievable list in your browser's toolbar. To organize the sites into categories, most browsers offer tools to create folders.

Favorites and Bookmarks are great for quickly locating those sites you use most, but they're accessible to you only when you're on your own computer. Although most browsers provide features that let you export the list of bookmarks to a file you can import to another computer or another browser, another way to access your Bookmarks and Favorites from any computer is to use MyBookmarks (**mybookmarks.com**)—a free Internet service that stores your Bookmarks and Favorites online.

What are live bookmarks? Because the web is constantly changing, the site you bookmarked last week may subsequently change and add new content. Traditionally, you would notice the change only the next time you visited the site. **Live bookmarks** deliver content updates to you as soon as they become available using RSS, the same technology that updates blogs and podcasts that we described earlier in the chapter. Live bookmarks and RSS feeds are useful if you're interested in the most up-to-date news stories, sports scores, or stock prices. Firefox, Safari, and Microsoft Edge have built-in RSS readers, while Chrome requires that you add on an extension.

What is tagging? Tagging, also known as **social bookmarking**, is like bookmarking your favorite website, but instead of saving it to your browser for only you to see, you're saving it to a social bookmarking site so that you can share it with others. A social bookmark or tag is a term that you assign to a web page, digital image, or video. A tag can be something you create to describe the digital content, or it can be a suggested term provided by the website. For example, if you came across a web page with a great article on inexpensive places to go for spring break, you might tag the article with the term *vacations*. Others on the same social bookmarking site who are looking for websites about vacations may use *vacations* as the search term and find the article you tagged.

Delicious (**delicious.com**) is one of the original social bookmarking sites. Delicious lets you group related links and organize them into "bundles." So if you've collected several links to websites about different places to go to over spring break, you can collect all those links into one bundle about vacations. Or if you want to see what links others may have found about interesting vacations, you could search Delicious with the term *vacations* to see other vacation-related bundles.

Other social bookmarking sites include Reddit, StumbleUpon, and Pinterest. Reddit encourages its community to vote on links and stories, so the most popular rise to the top. StumbleUpon offers a Stumble! button that, when clicked, provides new web content that you can like or dislike, which eventually contours the Stumble results more to your interests. Unlike other social bookmarking sites, Pinterest enables you to share only images. You can post images that you find online or that you directly upload. You do not need a Pinterest account to look at other's pins and boards. ■

ACTIVE HELPDESK

Getting Around the Web

In this Active Helpdesk, you'll play the role of a helpdesk staffer, fielding questions about web browsers, URLs, and how to use hyperlinks and other tools to get around the web.

DIG DEEPER Discovering the Semantic Web

Think about all the types of data on the web that you access manually, such as appointment times, transportation and entertainment schedules, and store locations and hours. It would seem that computers would be helpful in plugging through all this web data, but oddly, that is not the case. Web pages are designed for people to read, not for computers to manipulate. As yet, no reliable way exists for computers to process the meaning of data on a web page so that it can be used to see relationships or make decisions.

The **semantic web** (or **Web 3.0**) is an evolving extension of the web in which data is defined in such a way to make it more easily processed by computers. Right now, search engines function by recognizing keywords such as *office hours* and *dentist*, but they can't determine, for example, in which office and on what days Dr. Smith works and what his available appointment times are. By using a so-called "agent," the semantic web would enable computers to find that type of information, coordinate it with your other schedules and preferences, and then make the appointment for you.

The semantic web would also assist you in comparing products, prices, and shipping options by finding the best product option based on specified criteria and then placing the order for you. Additionally, the agent would record the financial transaction into your personal bookkeeping software and arrange for a technician to help install the software, if needed.

For the semantic web to work, businesses, services, and software would all use the same categorization structures so that similar information would share the same attributes, ensuring consistency of metadata throughout the web. The semantic web would build on this type of capability so that each website would have text and pictures (for people to read) and metadata (for computers to read) describing the information on the web (see Figure 3.18).

Although some of the semantic web's functionalities are beginning to emerge in technologies such as the digital assistants Siri, Google Now, and Cortana, the majority of its functionality and implementation are still in development. The greatest challenge is recoding all the information currently available on the web into the type of metadata that computers can recognize. The very grandeur of that task means that we will not see a fully functional semantic web until sometime in the distant future. In the meantime, we can continue to benefit from each small step toward that goal.

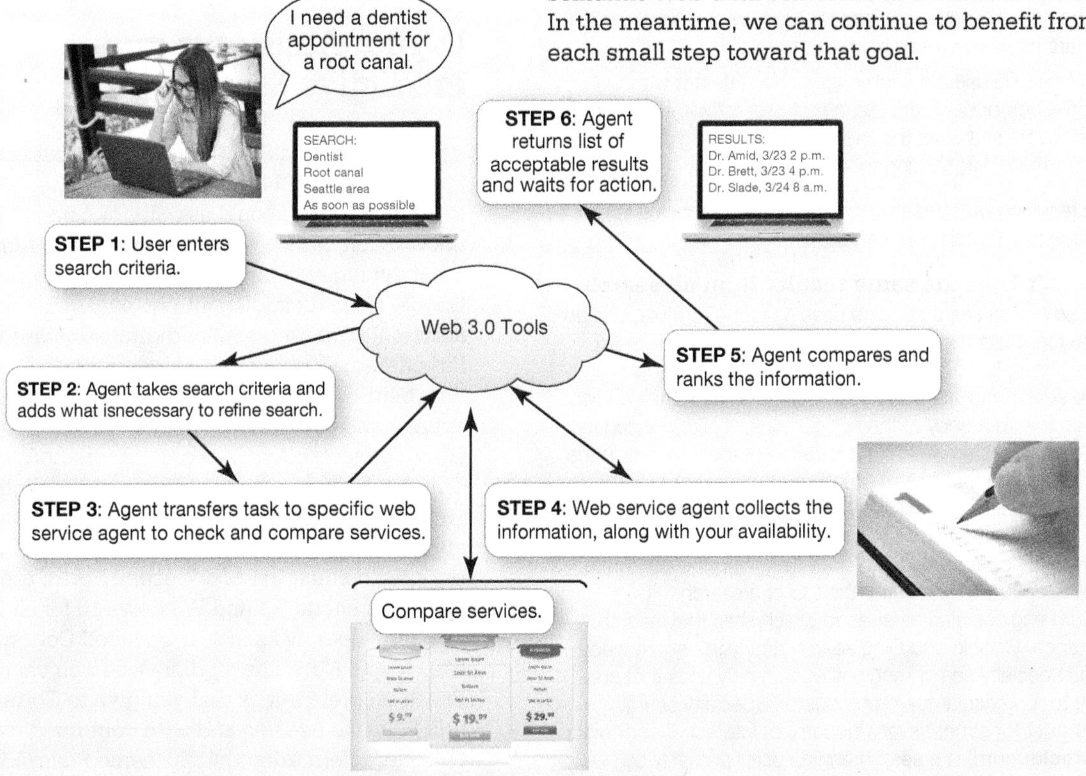

FIGURE 3.18 The Semantic Web *(jpkirakun/Fotolia, SergeyIT/Shutterstock, mileswork/Shutterstock)*

searching the web EFFECTIVELY

You've most likely "Googled" something today, and if you did, your search is one of over five billion daily searches. Let's take a look at how to search the web effectively.

Using Search Engines

Objective 3.12 *Describe the types of tools used to search the web, and summarize strategies used to refine search results.*

How do search engines work? Google is the world's most popular **search engine**—a set of programs that searches the web for **keywords** (specific words you wish to look for or *query*) and then returns a list of the sites on which those keywords are found. Search engines have three components:

1. The first component is a program called a *spider*, which constantly collects data on the web, following links in websites and reading web pages. Spiders get their name because they crawl over the web using multiple "legs" to visit many sites simultaneously.
2. As the spider collects data, the second component of the search engine, an *indexer program*, organizes the data into a large database.
3. When you use a search engine, you interact with the third component: the *search engine software*. This software searches the indexed data, pulling out relevant information according to your search.

The resulting list appears in your web browser as a list of hits—sites that match your search.

Why don't I get the same results from all search engines? Each search engine uses a unique formula, or *algorithm*, to formulate the search and create the resulting index of related sites. In addition, search engines differ in how they rank the search results. Most search engines rank their results based on the frequency of the appearance of your queried keywords in websites as well as the location of those words in the sites. This means that sites that include the keywords in their URL or site name will most likely appear at the top of the results list. An important part of a company's marketing strategy is search engine optimization, which is designing the corporate website to ensure it ranks near the top of a search.

Search engines also differ as to which sites they search. For instance, Google and Bing search nearly the entire web, whereas specialty search engines search only sites that are relevant to a particular topic or industry. Specialty search engines exist for almost every industry or interest. DailyStocks (**dailystocks.com**) is a search engine used primarily by investors that searches for corporate information. Search Engine Watch (**searchenginewatch.com**) has a list of many specialty search engines, organized by industry.

If you can't decide which search engine is best, you may want to try a metasearch engine. **Metasearch engines**, such as Dogpile (**dogpile.com**), search other search engines rather than individual websites.

Can I use a search engine to search just for images and videos? With the increasing popularity of multimedia, search engines such as Google, Bing, and Yahoo! let you search the web for digital images and audio and video files. After putting in your search term, select Video from Google's top menu to display only the search results that are videos. You can further narrow down the video selection by using the filtering tools. Blinkx (**blinkx.com**) is a video search engine that helps you sift through all the video posted on the web.

BITS&BYTES

Digital Assistants and Predictive Search

Apple introduced Siri, the personal digital assistant for iPhones, in 2011. Using Siri's voice recognition technology, users could ask Siri for help in finding information, getting directions, creating reminders, and other everyday tasks. One year later, Google introduced Google Now, its intelligent personal assistant. In addition to offering similar digital assistant tasks that Siri offered, Google Now added predictive search capabilities: Google Now recognizes a user's repeated actions and searches and, using Google's Knowledge Graph project, offers relevant and predictive information. This might include delays in upcoming flights, news stories relevant to your interests, travel time to your next appointment, and perhaps which friend might have a birthday coming up. Most recently, with the release of Windows Phone 8.1 and Windows 10 for all Windows-based devices, Microsoft introduced Cortana. Cortana, like Google Now, has predictive search capabilities. Based on preferences that you give to Cortana when you first begin to use her, and with continued use, Cortana will offer information that is deemed relevant to you.

How can I refine my searches for better results? You've probably searched for something on Google and gotten back a list of hits that includes thousands—even millions—of web pages that have no relevance to the topic you're interested in. Initially, Boolean operators were needed to help refine a search. **Boolean operators** are words such as *AND*, *NOT*, and *OR* that describe the relationships between keywords in a search. With the simple addition of a few words or constraints, you can narrow your search results to a more manageable and more meaningful list.

Are there other helpful search strategies? Other strategies can help refine your searches when entering your search keywords:

- **Search for a phrase.** To search for an exact phrase, place quotation marks around your keywords. The search engine will look for only those websites that contain the words in *that exact order*. For example, if you want information on the movie *The Green Hornet* and you type these words without quotation marks, your search results will contain pages that include either of the words *Green* and *Hornet*, although not necessarily in that order. Typing *"The Green Hornet"* in quotation marks guarantees that search results will include this exact phrase.
- **Search within a specific website.** To search just a specific website, you can use the search keyword, then *site*: followed by the website's URL. For example, searching with *processor site*—**www.wired.com**—returns results about processors from the **Wired.com** website. The same method works for entire classes of sites in a given top-level domain or country code.
- **Use a wild card.** The asterisk ("*") is a wild card, or placeholder, feature that is helpful when you need to search with unknown terms. Another way to think about the wild card search feature is as a "fill in the blank." For example, searching with *Congress voted * on the * bill* might bring up an article about the members of Congress who voted *no* on the *healthcare* bill or a different article about the members of Congress who voted *yes* on the *energy* bill.

How else can I customize my searches? Many other specialty search strategies and services are available. By clicking on Search tools in Google's menu at the top of a Google search, you can restrict search results by time, location, and even reading level (see Figure 3.19). You can also click on the Apps button in Google's main page, then click the More and Even more from Google options for all the specialized search products Google offers (see Figure 3.20):

- *Custom Search* lets you create a customized search engine to search only a selected set of sites tailored to your needs. You can add this specialized search engine to a website or blog or design it for a specific organization.

BITS&BYTES

Searching to Do Good

Wouldn't it be great to benefit others just by searching the web? Now there's an easy way to "do good" with every search. Goodsearch (**goodsearch.com**) is a Yahoo!-powered search engine that donates half of its revenues (approximately a penny per search) to approved U.S. charities and schools that users designate. The money Goodsearch donates comes from the site's advertisers. More than 100,000 charitable organizations are being helped by Goodsearch, but if the organization you're interested in isn't on the list, as long as it's a registered U.S. not-for-profit organization, you can apply to have it added. Goodsearch has expanded its program to online shopping and dining out.

You can also contribute to your favorite charity by shopping online through Goodshop (**goodshop.com**). Instead of going directly to your favorite online store, go to Goodshop first, find and click through to the store of your choice, and start shopping. Participating stores donate up to 30% of the purchased amount. Similarly, through the GoodDining program, dine at a participating restaurant and a percentage of your bill will go to your cause. So, search, shop, and eat—and do some good!

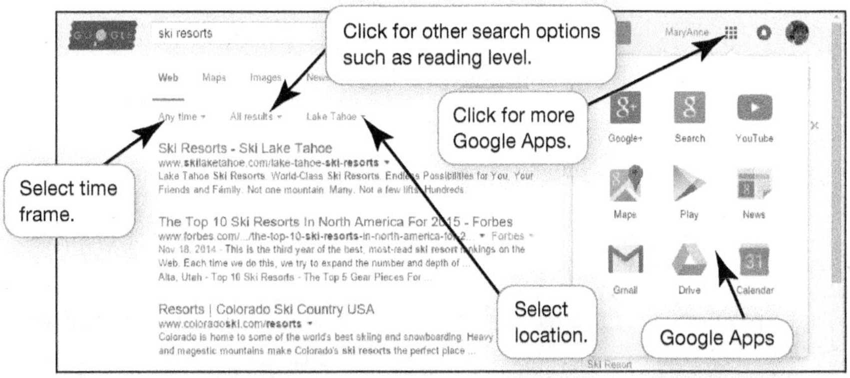

FIGURE 3.19 Using Google's Search Tools to Restrict the Time Frame, the Location, and Even the Reading Level of Your Search Results *(© 2015 Google Inc, used with permission. Google and the Google logo are registered trademarks of Google Inc.)*

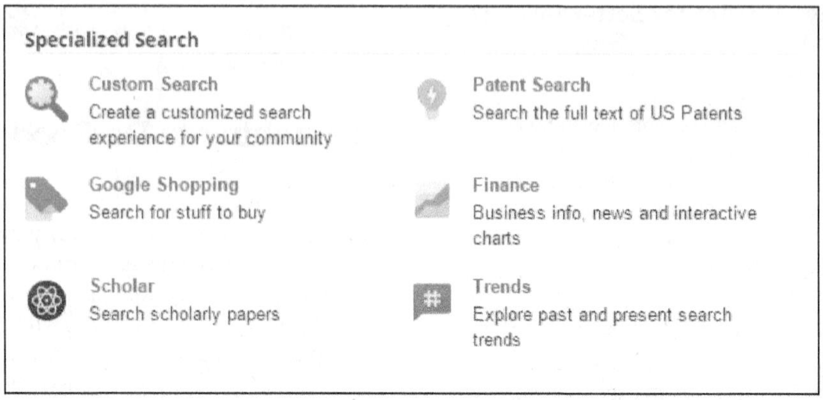

FIGURE 3.20 Google's Specialized Search Tools *(© 2015 Google Inc, used with permission. Google and the Google logo are registered trademarks of Google Inc.)*

- *Google Shopping* lets you search by product rather than by company. So if you're interested in buying a digital camera, Google Shopping lists cameras by popularity and provides information on the stores that carry the cameras, along with the average price.
- *Scholar* searches scholarly literature such as peer-reviewed papers, theses, and publications from academic organizations. Each search result contains bibliographic information as well.
- *Patent Search* provides access to patents from the United States Patent and Trademark Office, the European Patent Office, and the World Intellectual Property Organization.
- *Finance* gives you access to real-time stock quotes and charts as well as financial news. You can also track your portfolio holdings.
- *Trends* features trending stories in real-time, organized by category and location.

Evaluating Websites

Objective 3.13 *Describe how to evaluate a website to ensure it is appropriate to use for research purposes.*

How can I make sure a website is appropriate to use for research? When you're using the Internet for research, you shouldn't assume that everything you find is accurate and appropriate to use. The following is a list of questions to consider before you use an Internet resource; the answers to these questions will help you decide whether you should consider a website to be a good source of information:

- **Authority:** Who is the author of the article or the sponsor of the site? If the author is well known or the site is published by a reputable news source (such as *The New York Times*), then you can feel more confident using it as a source than if you are unable to locate such information. *Note*: Some sites include a page with information about the author or the site's sponsor.
- **Bias:** Is the site biased? The purpose of many websites is to sell products or services or to persuade rather than inform. These sites, though useful in some situations, present a biased point of view. Look for sites that offer several sets of facts or consider opinions from several sources.
- **Relevance:** Is the information on the site current? Material can last a long time on the web. Some research projects (such as historical accounts) depend on older records. However, if you're writing about cutting-edge technologies, you need to look for the most recent sources. Therefore, look for a date on information to make sure it is current.
- **Audience:** For what audience is the site intended? Ensure that the content, tone, and style of the site match your needs. You probably wouldn't want to use information from a site geared toward teens if you're writing for adults, nor would you use a site that has a casual style and tone for serious research.
- **Links:** Are the links available and appropriate? Check out the links provided on the site to determine whether they're still working and appropriate for your needs. Don't assume that the links provided are the only additional sources of information. Investigate other sites on your topic, as well. You should also be able to find the same information on at least three different websites to help verify the information is accurate. ■

SOUND BYTE
Finding Information on the Web

In this Sound Byte, you'll learn how and when to use search engines and subject directories. Through guided tours, you'll learn effective search techniques, including how to use Boolean operators and metasearch engines.

ACTIVE HELPDESK
Evaluating Websites

In this Active Helpdesk, you'll play the role of a helpdesk staffer, fielding questions about how websites can be evaluated as appropriate to use for research.

trends in IT

Doing Business on a Shoestring—Thanks to the Internet

Let's say you think that flip-flops in school colors would be a popular product. Your school's bookstore carries everything else with the school's colors and logo, but not flip-flops. You've asked your friends and several classmates, and most of them say they would buy flip-flops in the school's colors. So what do you do next? How do you move from product concept to selling a physical product?

Before the Internet, it would have been much more difficult and expensive to get your product produced and distributed. Today, however, the Internet brings the power of the global economy right to your door (see Figure 3.21). For product design and manufacturing, you can visit a site like Alibaba (**alibaba.com**), which helps entrepreneurs locate manufacturers of all sorts of products. Many manufacturers are happy to work with small business owners to custom-design products.

To sell your product, you might be able to find a retailer or you can set up a website to sell them yourself. Although there are several websites that offer great templates and tools you can use to build your own website, you might want to use a freelance professional to help by using sites such as Guru (**guru.com**) or Elance (**elance.com**). You simply create a description of the job you need done, post it on the site, and invite freelancers to bid on your job. You then contact the freelancers who look promising, review samples of their work, and decide on someone who can help you—and at a competitive price. After your website is up and running, you can place your business on social networking sites, such as Facebook, to help potential customers discover your product and spread the word about your great flip-flops. You might also want to use crowdfunding sites such as Kickstarter and Indiegogo to raise some capital to help finance your new venture.

Another hurdle is determining where you'll store your product and who will package and ship it to customers. If your parents' basement isn't large enough, you can outsource warehousing and order fulfillment to **Amazon.com**. Amazon will (for a fee) warehouse your inventory and then package and ship it when customer orders are received. Orders don't have to come through Amazon's site (although that is an option); you can provide ordering information collected on your site to Amazon, and Amazon will take care of the rest.

Although there is always a cost to starting up a business, up-front costs are much lower when you take advantage of the global marketplace and the Internet. So, take that brilliant idea you have and turn it into a business today!

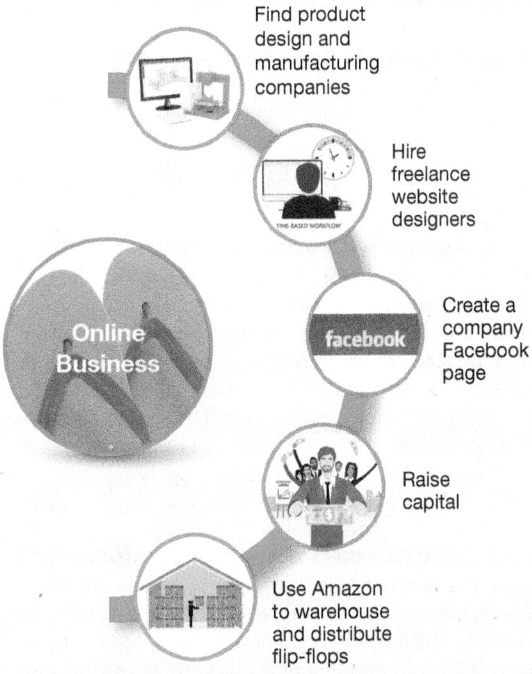

FIGURE 3.21 By using the services of a few websites, you can create and distribute products, such as your own line of flip-flops. *(Pixindy/Fotolia, lucadp/Fotolia, WaD/Fotolia, Kevin Britland/Alamy, ProStockStudio/Shutterstock, Gstudio Group/Fotolia)*

using the web ETHICALLY

As you've read in this chapter, the web offers a vast array of opportunities for business, communication, collaboration, and entertainment. It also poses some temptations for inappropriate behavior, often to seek gain at another's expense. In this section, we'll explore several ethical issues that are challenging how we use the web.

Intellectual Property and Cyberbullying

Objective 3.14 *Demonstrate an understanding of intellectual property and cyberbullying.*

What is intellectual property and what issues does it pose? Intellectual property is the result of someone's creativity and knowledge, such as music, writing, and software, which is protected by copyright law and documented by copyrights, patents, and trademarks. Anti-piracy efforts by various organizations and governments aim to protect intellectual property rights—an issue that has been an ongoing and important one, especially in the technology industry.

One of the challenges of anti-piracy efforts is the economic and trading ramifications that occur when countries refuse to enforce copyright laws. For example, countries such as China and the Philippines have been known for their high use of pirated software. Businesses and individuals in those countries and elsewhere that use illegal copies of operating and productivity software potentially gain an advantage in the international marketplace. Microsoft has taken several measures to combat illegal piracy but still hasn't managed to effectively reduce the number of pirated copies of its operating system.

The music and film industries also struggle with piracy issues. Although efforts to increase digital sales of music and film is helping, piracy challenges have placed significant pressures on existing business models for the creative arts industries, both at home and in the global marketplace. Time will tell whether copyright laws will need to be revised to adapt to the predominant digital culture, whether regulatory agencies will need to improve the methods of controlling piracy, or whether the industries themselves will need to change their business models.

What are the effects of cyberbullying? Cyberbullying involves the use of digital technologies such as the Internet, cell phones, or video to bully another (see Figure 3.22). Cyberbullying can include actions such as bombarding a victim with harassing instant messages or text messages, spreading rumors or lies on social networking sites, posting embarrassing photos or videos of a victim on the web, or infecting the victim's computer with malware, usually to spy on that person.

The effects of cyberbullying can be devastating. Infamous cases include Hannah Smith, the English girl who at 14 committed suicide after being repeatedly taunted on social networking sites, and Tyler Clementi, a Rutgers freshman who committed suicide after his roommate showed fellow students videos of him having sex.

FIGURE 3.22 Cyberbullying involves the use of digital technologies both to bully and to disseminate acts of bullying. *(Rawdon Wyatt/Alamy)*

There is currently no federal law prohibiting cyberbullying, but a recently passed law against cyberstalking may cover this area. According to the Cyberbullying Research Center (**cyberbullying.us**), as of July 2015, all states had anti-bullying laws or policies on the books. However, only 48 state laws cover electronic harassment, and a mere 22 state laws cover cyberbullying. Many legislatures are reluctant to pass laws that instruct parents on how to raise their children because this tends to raise issues about personal freedom. Therefore, anti-cyberbullying laws tend to place the burden of detection on the schools. For instance, the Massachusetts law requires schools to provide age-appropriate education on bullying to students, to train school employees in detection and prevention of bullying, and to have plans developed for detecting and reporting bullying.

Privacy and Geolocation

Objective 3.15 *Demonstrate an understanding of the ethical issues regarding online privacy and geolocation.*

What, exactly, is privacy? The idea of privacy is often associated with hiding something (a behavior, a relationship, or a secret). However, privacy really means not being required to reveal your behavior to others. Social media sites such as Facebook are inherently about sharing information with others. Does this mean there is no such thing as personal privacy on social media sites (see Figure 3.23)?

What are the ethical issues regarding privacy online? Facebook and other social media allow you to set privacy filters on your personal information. You can choose to share information publically, share it just with your friends, or keep it totally private. Employers now routinely check social media sites to gather publically shared information on prospective employees. However, recently, many government agencies, such as police departments and some private employers, have been asking job seekers for access to their *private* Facebook information.

Although the Password Protection Act still has not been passed into law, over a dozen states, including Maryland, New Jersey, and California, have enacted similar legislation. Employers in those states are currently prohibited from asking prospective employees for passwords to social networking sites in an effort to garner information related to their gender, race, religion, age, and sexual orientation. Regardless, this information is often found in social media site profiles, and employers are finding more subtle methods, such as encouraging prospective employees to "friend" them on Facebook, which gives the company more access to a candidate's public profile. The control and privacy of information will continue to be a fine balancing act for the foreseeable future, with employers trying to gather intelligence while appeasing the concerns of privacy advocates.

FIGURE 3.24 Geolocation applications help you find cool places and businesses. But who do you want to find you? *(Cseke Timea/Fotolia)*

Leaving a trail of electronic breadcrumbs is, to a certain extent, inevitable. But cleaning up or hiding your "trail" is still important to many users, not because they're trying to hide something but because they value their basic right to privacy.

What is geolocation and what privacy risks does it pose? "Where are you?" is the burning social networking question these days, and your smartphone probably has the answer. The technology is called **geolocation** (see Figure 3.24), and most mobile devices have a GPS chip that can calculate your exact position. Starbucks, Snapchat, and Uber are just a handful of apps that have the capacity to track your location, with your permission. Why is this an issue? User location data is often shared with third-party advertising networks and even with law enforcement agencies. While you can modify or turn off the location aspects in most mobile apps, these measures cannot guarantee that data will not be shared with third parties since the location data is "leaked" in other ways. Even with app location tracking turned off, your location can be captured just when your device is turned on. This feature has been useful to pinpoint users in emergency situations, but the data, if placed in the wrong hands, or for the wrong purposes, can be a violation of your privacy. Retrospectively, historical location data can be discerned from service provider records, and additionally, WiFi hotspots can be used to track mobile devices. Moreover, other features of a smartphone, such as the camera and phone, can capture a user's geolocation data. Therefore, the privacy implications still remain. Although legislation has been initiated, no specific law has been passed to address the privacy concerns of location-tracking devices and applications. Although most mobile device users are aware of location data collection practices, they are not aware of what was being collected and how it is, and can be, used. ■

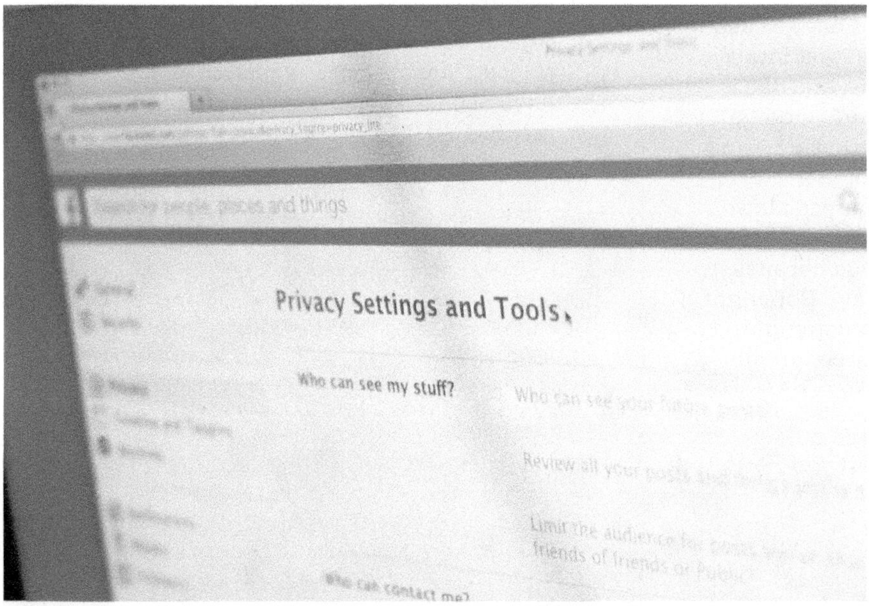

FIGURE 3.23 What information are you sharing on Facebook and with whom? *(Dolphfyn/Alamy)*

ethics in IT Plagiarism and Copyright Violation: What Can You Borrow from the Internet?

Using information from the web without receiving proper permissions is not only wrong but can also be illegal. So what can you borrow from the web and what must you seek permission to use? Consider these scenarios:

1. You copy a political cartoon into your PowerPoint presentation for your civics class.
2. For children's books that you write and later sell online, you sometimes borrow story ideas from other children's books, just changing a few characters or situations. You do not obtain permission from the originators of the story ideas you borrow.
3. You copy information from an obscure website into your research paper without documenting the source.
4. You download a song from the Internet and incorporate it into a PowerPoint presentation for a school project. Because you assume everyone knows the song, you don't credit it in your sources.

Which of the preceding scenarios represent copyright violations? Which represent plagiarism? The distinctions between these scenarios are narrow in some cases, but it's important to understand the differences.

Plagiarism occurs when you use someone else's ideas or words and represent them as your own. In today's computer society, it's easy to use information from the Internet and paste it into a Word document, change a few words, and call it your own. To avoid plagiarism, properly credit all information you obtain from the Internet by using quotation marks around all words you borrow directly, and credit your sources for any ideas you paraphrase or borrow.

Copyright violation is more serious because it, unlike plagiarism, is punishable by law. Copyright law assumes that all original work is copyrighted even if the work does not display the copyright symbol (©). Copyright violation occurs when you use another person's material for your own personal economic benefit or when you take away from the economic benefit of the originator. In most cases, citing the source is not sufficient; you need to seek and receive written permission from the copyright holder.

There are exceptions to this rule. There is no copyright on government documents, so you can download and reproduce material from any government website. Teachers and students receive special consideration that falls under a provision called *academic fair use*. As long as the material is being used for educational purposes only, limited copying and distribution is allowed.

So, do you now know which of the four scenarios above are plagiarism or copyright violations? Let's review them.

1. You are not in violation because the use of the cartoon is for educational purposes and falls under the academic fair use provision. You must still credit the source, however.
2. You are in violation of copyright laws because you are presenting others' ideas for children's stories as your own and receiving personal economic benefit from them.
3. You are guilty of plagiarism because you copied content from another source and implied it was your own work.
4. Again, because your copying is for a school project, you are not in violation of copyright laws because of the academic fair use provision. However, it's always important to document your sources.

Before moving on to the Chapter Review:

1. **Watch Replay Video 3.2.**
2. **Then check your understanding of what you've learned so far.**

check your understanding // review & practice

For a quick review to see what you've learned so far, answer the following questions.

multiple choice

1. What is the navigation aid that shows users the path they have taken to get to a web page located within a website?

a. Favorites
b. Breadcrumb trail
c. Bookmarks
d. Social bookmarks

2. Which search strategy should you use to search for a specific phrase?

a. Use quotation marks around the phrase.
b. Use asterisks around the phrase.
c. Include Boolean operators in the phrase.
d. Use a wild card around the phrase.

3. When using the Internet for research, you

a. can assume that everything you find is accurate and appropriate.
b. should evaluate sites for bias and relevance.
c. can assume if there is no author listed, the site is not appropriate for research.
d. should look for sites with many links to other resources.

4. Which of the following is not an Internet protocol?

a. ARPANET
b. HTTP
c. FTP
d. BitTorrent

5. Which type of website would StumbleUpon be classified as?

a. Crowdfunding site
b. Live bookmarking site
c. Metasearch site
d. Social bookmarking site

MyITLab — Go to **MyITLab** to take an autograded version of the *Check Your Understanding* review and to find all media resources for the chapter.

TECHBYTES WEEKLY
Stay current with the TechBytes Weekly Newsletter.

Continue

3 Chapter Review

summary //

Working and Playing on the Web

Learning Outcome 3.1 **You will be able to explain how the Internet works and how it is used for collaboration, communication, commerce, and entertainment purposes.**

The Internet and How It Works

Objective 3.1 *Describe how the Internet got its start.*

- The Internet is the largest computer network in the world, connecting millions of computers.
- Government and military officials developed the early Internet as a reliable way to communicate in the event of war. Eventually, scientists and educators used the Internet to exchange research.
- Today, we use the Internet and the web (which is a part of the Internet) to shop, research, communicate, and entertain ourselves.

Objective 3.2 *Explain how data travels on the Internet.*

- A computer (or other device) connected to the Internet acts as either a client (a computer that asks for information) or a server (a computer that receives the request and returns the information to the client).
- Data travels between clients and servers along a system of communication lines or pathways. The largest and fastest of these pathways form the Internet backbone.
- To ensure that data is sent to the correct computer along the pathways, IP addresses (unique ID numbers) are assigned to all computers connected to the Internet.

Collaborating and Communicating on the Web

Objective 3.3 *Discuss the tools and technologies used to collaborate and communicate on the web.*

- Web 2.0 can be described as the social web, in which the user is also a participant. Examples of Web 2.0 technologies include social networking, blogs, wikis, podcasts, and webcasts.
- Social networking enables you to communicate and share information with friends as well as meet and connect with others.
- Blogs are journal entries posted to the web that are generally organized by a topic or area of interest and are publically available.
- Video logs are personal journals that use video as the primary content in addition to text, images, and audio.
- A wiki is a type of website that allows users to collaborate on content—adding, removing, or editing it.
- Some web tools that are useful for group collaboration online are screen sharing, project management, and videoconferencing applications.
- Podcasts are audio or video content available over the Internet. Users subscribe to receive updates to podcasts.
- Webcasts are broadcasts of audio or video content over the Internet.

Objective 3.4 *Summarize how e-mail and instant messaging are used to communicate over the web.*

- E-mail allows users to communicate electronically without the parties involved being available at the same time.
- Instant-messaging services are programs that enable you to communicate in real time with others who are online.

Business and Entertainment on the Web

Objective 3.5 *Describe the different types of e-commerce.*

- E-commerce is the business of conducting business online.
- E-commerce includes transactions between businesses (B2B), between consumers (C2C), and between businesses and consumers (B2C).

Objective 3.6 *Summarize precautions you should take when doing business online.*

- Because more business than ever before is conducted online, numerous safeguards have been put in place to ensure that transactions are protected.

Objective 3.7 *Describe the types of multimedia files found on the web.*

- Multimedia is anything that involves one or more forms of media in addition to text, such as graphics, audio, and video clips.

Using the Web Effectively

Learning Outcome 3.2 You will be able to describe the tools and techniques required to navigate and search the web.

Accessing and Moving Around the Web

Objective 3.8 *Explain what web browsers are, and describe their common features.*

- Once you're connected to the Internet, in order to locate, navigate to, and view web pages, you need software called web browser.
- The most common web browsers are Microsoft Edge, Firefox, Google Chrome, and Safari.

Objective 3.9 *Explain what a URL is, and discuss its main parts.*

- You gain access to a website by typing in its address, called a Uniform Resource Locator (URL).
- A URL is comprised of several parts, including the protocol, the domain, the top-level domain, and paths (or subdirectories).

Objective 3.10 *Describe tools used to navigate the web.*

- One unique aspect of the web is that you can jump from place to place by clicking on specially formatted pieces of text or images called hyperlinks.
- You can also use the Back and Forward buttons, History lists, and breadcrumb trails to navigate the web.

Objective 3.11: *Describe tools used to mark websites for future use.*

- Favorites, live bookmarks, and social bookmarking help you return to specific web pages without having to type in the URL and help you organize the web content that is most important to you.

Searching the Web Effectively

Objective 3.12 *Describe the types of tools used to search the web and summarize strategies used to refine search results.*

- A search engine is a set of programs that searches the web using specific keywords you wish to query and then returns a list of the websites on which those keywords are found.
- Search engines can be used to search for images, podcasts, and videos in addition to traditional text-based web content.
- Metasearch engines search other search engines.

Objective 3.13 *Describe how to evaluate a website to ensure it is appropriate to use for research purposes.*

- To evaluate whether it is appropriate to use a website as a resource, determine whether the author of the site is reputable, whether the site is intended for your particular needs, that the site content is not biased, that the information on the site is current, and that all the links on the site are available and appropriate.

Using the Web Ethically

Objective 3.14 *Demonstrate an understanding of intellectual property and cyberbullying.*

- Intellectual property is the result of someone's creativity and knowledge.
- There have been significant issues with piracy of software, music, and other online content that have placed burdens on the creative arts industries, technology industries, and regulators.
- Cyberbullying is bullying with digital technologies. It is not clear who should bear the responsibility for monitoring against cyberbullying.

Objective 3.15 *Demonstrate an understanding of the ethical issues regarding privacy and geolocation.*

- Privacy is the right to be left alone, but it is often difficult to achieve with social media.
- Apps with geolocation technology garner much information about your location. Users should be aware of why companies need to track a user's location, and what the companies will do with that location data.

MyITLab Be sure to check out **MyITLab** for additional materials to help you review and learn.

key terms //

aggregator **82**
blog (weblog) **81**
Bookmarks **96**
Boolean operators **99**
breadcrumb trail **95**
business-to-business (B2B) **86**
business-to-consumer (B2C) **86**
client **78**
client/server network **78**
consumer-to-consumer (C2C) **86**
cyberbullying **102**
domain name **93**
e-commerce (electronic commerce) **85**
e-mail (electronic mail) **83**
e-mail client **84**
Favorites **96**
File Transfer Protocol (FTP) **94**
geolocation **103**
host **94**
hyperlink **94**
Hypertext Transfer Protocol (HTTP) **94**
instant messaging (IM) **84**
Internet **76**
Internet backbone **78**
Internet Protocol (IP) address **78**
intellectual property **102**
keyword **98**
live bookmark **96**
metasearch engine **98**
multimedia **87**
path (subdirectory) **94**
podcast **82**
project management tools **80**
Really Simple Syndication (RSS) **82**
search engine **98**
secure sockets layer **86**
semantic web (Web 3.0) **97**
server **78**
social commerce **86**
social media **79**
social networking **79**
streaming media **87**
tagging (social bookmarking) **96**
top-level domain **94**
Uniform Resource Locator (URL) **93**
video log (vlog or video blog) **81**
Web 2.0 **79**
web-based e-mail **84**
web browser **92**
webcast **82**
web server **94**
wiki **79**
World Wide Web (WWW or the web) **77**

chapter quiz // assessment

For a quick review to see what you've learned, answer the following questions. Submit the quiz as requested by your instructor. If you are using **MyITLab**, the quiz is also available there.

multiple choice

1. The Internet was created to provide

- **a.** a secure form of communications.
- **b.** a common communication means for all computers.
- **c.** both a and b
- **d.** neither a nor b

2. Which of the following describes an IP address?

- **a.** It is referred to as a dotted quad.
- **b.** It identifies any computer connecting to the Internet.
- **c.** It identifies a website.
- **d.** all of the above

3. Which of the following browsers was introduced with Windows 10?

- **a.** Chrome
- **b.** Firefox
- **c.** Microsoft Edge
- **d.** Internet Explorer

4. What web browser feature would be particularly useful when using public computers?

- **a.** Pinned tabs
- **b.** Session restore
- **c.** Privacy browsing
- **d.** all of the above

5. In the URL http://www.whitehouse.gov/blog, which part is considered the protocol?

- **a.** http
- **b.** .gov
- **c.** www.whitehouse.gov
- **d.** /blog

6. Search engines that search other search engines are called

- **a.** megasearch engines.
- **b.** betasearch engines.
- **c.** gigasearch engines.
- **d.** metasearch engines.

true/false

_____ **1.** Google Docs, a part of Google Drive, uses wiki technology.

_____ **2.** Webcasts are only delivered as prerecorded audio and video content.

_____ **3.** The "s" in HTTPS stands for secure and indicates that the secure sockets layer protocol has been applied to the website.

_____ **4.** Paraphrasing content from a website into your research paper without documenting the source is considered plagiarism.

critical thinking

1. The Power of Google

Google is the largest and most popular search engine on the Internet today. Because of its size and popularity, some people claim that Google has enormous power to influence a web user's search experience solely by its website-ranking processes. What do you think about this potential power? How could it be used in negative or harmful ways?

- **a.** Some websites pay search engines to list them near the top of the results pages. These sponsors, therefore, get priority placement. What do you think of this policy?
- **b.** What effect (if any) do you think that Google has on website development? For example, do you think website developers intentionally include frequently searched words in their pages so that they will appear in more hit lists?

2. Mobile E-Commerce Safety

The text lists several ways to ensure your online transactions are secure and to reduce the risk of things going awry as you shop and sell online. However, surveys indicate that many feel that shopping from a mobile device, such as a smartphone, presents additional risks. Do you agree there are additional risks when conducting e-commerce from a mobile device? Why or why not?

team time //

Collaborating with Technology

Problem

Collaborating on projects with team members is a regular part of business and academia. Many great tools are available that facilitate online collaboration, and it's important to be familiar with them. In this Team Time, each team will create a group report on a specific topic, using online collaboration tools, and compare and rate the tools and the collaboration process.

Process

Split your group into teams. To appreciate fully the benefits of online collaboration, each team should have at least five or six members. Each group will create a team report on a topic that is approved by your instructor. As part of the report, one group member should record the process the group took to create the report, including a review of the tools used and reflections on the difficulties encountered by the group.

1. Conduct a virtual meeting. Agree on an online meeting and video collaboration tool such as Skype, Google+ Hangouts, or Apple FaceTime and conduct a group chat. In this phase, outline your group project strategy and delegate work responsibilities.
2. Share documents and collaborate online. Your group must create one document that is accessible to every member at all times. Explore document-sharing sites such as Google Drive, Evernote, OneDrive, or Dropbox and collaboratively create your group document. All members are responsible for reviewing the entire document.

Conclusion

After all the team group reports have been completed and shared, discuss the following with your class: What is the benefit of using online collaboration technology to create group projects? How did collaboration technologies help or hinder the team process?

ethics project //

Plagiarism

In this exercise, you'll research and then role-play a complicated ethical situation. The role you play may or may not match your own personal beliefs, but your research and use of logic will enable you to represent whichever view is assigned. An arbitrator will watch and comment on both sides of the arguments, and together the team will agree on an ethical solution.

Problem

Plagiarism, or portraying another's work as your own, has been around for a long time and extends well beyond the classroom. For example, Nick Simmons, the son of Gene Simmons (from KISS) and a member of A&E's *Family Jewels* reality series, created a comic book series, *Incarnate*. Radical Publishing picked up the series but quickly stopped publication when Internet messages accused the author of copying from other similar series. Similarly, the Australian band Men at Work was cited for copying a melody from *Kookaburra Sits in the Old Gum Tree* for its 1980s hit *Down Under* and owes the owner years of royalties.

Research Areas to Consider

- Plagiarism violations
- Comic book series *Incarnate*
- Australian band Men at Work
- Plagiarism consequences

Process

1. Divide the class into teams. Research the areas cited above and devise a scenario in which someone has violated plagiarism rules.
2. Team members should write a summary that provides background information for their character—for example, author, publisher, or arbitrator—and that details their character's behaviors to set the stage for the role-playing event. Then team members should create an outline to use during the role-playing event.
3. Team members should arrange a mutually convenient time to meet for the exchange, using a virtual meeting tool or by meeting in person.
4. Team members should present their case to the class or submit a PowerPoint presentation for review by the rest of the class, along with the summary and resolution they developed.

Conclusion

As technology becomes ever more prevalent and integrated into our lives, more and more ethical dilemmas will present themselves. Being able to understand and evaluate both sides of an argument, while responding in a personally or socially ethical manner, will be an important skill.

Solve This

MyITLab® grader

Create a Report: Conducting Research on the Web

You and a partner have been asked to write a report on alternatives to using the Google search engine, as well as how to evaluate a website for a research paper. The paper needs to cite references within the body of the text, and include a list of your works cited at the end of the report. Your partner has begun the report. You are going to modify what has been started.

You will use the following skills as you complete this activity:

- Use Find and Replace
- Format Bulleted Lists
- Insert SmartArt
- Insert a Hyperlink
- Add Sources
- Insert Citations and Bibliography

Instructions:

1. Start Word. Open *TIACh03_Start.docx* and save it as **TIACh03_LastFirst.docx**, using your last and first names.
2. Using Find and Replace, find all instances of *metasearch* and replace them with **meta-search**.
3. At the blank paragraph after the end of the second paragraph of text under *Alternative Search Engines*, insert a **Vertical Box List SmartArt graphic**. Open the text pane, if necessary. With the cursor active in the first bullet, type **Google Scholar**. (Do not include the period.) Press **Enter**, press **Tab**, and then type **Searches scholarly literature**. (Do not include the period.)

   Repeat these steps to add the following information for the next two bullets:

   Dogpile

   Meta-search engine that searches Google, Yahoo!, and Bing

   Specialty Search Engines

   Search only sites that are relevant to a topic or industry

   a. Hint: To insert a SmartArt graphic, on the Insert tab, in the Illustrations group, click **SmartArt**.
4. Change the SmartArt graphic colors to **Colorful—Accent Colors**. Move the Google Scholar box and bullet point to the bottom of the SmartArt. Change the SmartArt Style to **Intense Effect**.

   a. Hint: To change the colors, on the SmartArt Tools Design tab, in the SmartArt Styles group, click **Colors**. To move the box and bullet point, select the content, then in the Create Graphic group, click **Move Down**. To change the style, in the SmartArt Styles group, click the **More button** for Styles.
5. In the second to last sentence of the first paragraph in the *Alternative Search Engines* section, select the text **specialty search engines**. Then, create a hyperlink to the web page **bestonlineuniversities.com/2011/20-useful-specialty-search-engines-for-college-students/**.
6. At the end of the first paragraph in the *Evaluating Websites* section, immediately to the left of the period, insert a citation to a new website. Before entering information, click the check box for **Show All Bibliography Fields**. Use the following information:

   Author: **Kapoun, Jim**

   Name of Web Page: **Five criteria for evaluating web pages**

   Name of Website: **Olin & Uris Libraries, Cornell University**

   Year: **2010**

   Month: **May**

   Day: **10**

   URL: **olinuris.library.cornell.edu/ref/research/webcrit.html.**
7. In the *Evaluating Websites* section, create a bulleted list with the five points beginning with *Authority, Bias or Objectivity, Relevance, Audience, and Coverage*. Use a checkmark as the bullet point.
8. Press **Ctrl+End** to go to the end of the document, press **Enter** twice, and then insert a Works Cited Bibliography. Change the citation style to **APA Sixth Edition**.
9. Save the document, and then close Word.
10. Submit the document as directed.

Technology in Focus

The History of the Personal Computer

Learning Outcome 3B.1 You will be able to describe the history of personal computer hardware and software development.

Ever wonder how big the first personal computer was or how much the first laptop weighed? Computers are such an integral part of our lives that we don't often stop to think about how far they've come or where they got their start. In just over 40 years, computers have evolved from expensive, huge machines that only corporations could own to small, powerful devices that almost anyone can have. In this Technology in Focus feature, we look at the history of the personal computer.

FIGURE 1 Timeline of Early Personal Computer Development

1975 — The Altair 8800

- Only 256 bytes of memory
- No keyboard or monitor
- Switches on front used to enter data in machine code (1s and 0s)
- Lights on front indicated results of a program

1976

Apple I

Steve Jobs and Steve Wozniak form Apple Computer

June 1977

Apple II

- Featured color monitor, sound, and game paddles
- 4 KB of RAM
- Operating system stored in ROM
- Optional floppy disk to load programs (mostly games)

October 1977 — Commodore PET

- Featured in *Popular Science* magazine
- Popular in business settings in Europe

(B Christopher/Alamy Stock Photo, Jerry Mason/Science Source, SSPL/The Image Works, Marilyn K. Yee/Getty Images, Steve Castillo/AP Images, Science & Society Picture Library/Getty Images)

Early Personal Computers

Our journey through the history of the personal computer starts in 1975. At that time, most people weren't familiar with the mainframes and supercomputers that large corporations and the government owned. With price tags exceeding the cost of buildings, and with few (if any) practical home uses, these monster machines weren't appealing to or attainable by average Americans.

The First Personal Computer: The Altair

Objective 3B.1 *Describe the earliest personal computer ever designed.*

However, in 1975, the first personal computer, the **Altair 8800** (see Figure 1), was born. At $395 for a do-it-yourself kit or $498 for a fully assembled unit (about $2,253 in today's dollars), the price was reasonable enough that computer fanatics could finally own their own computers.

The Altair was primitive by today's standards—no keyboard, no monitor, and completely not user friendly. Despite its limitations, computer enthusiasts flocked to the machine. Many who bought it had been taught to program, but until that point, they had access only to big, clumsy computers at their jobs. With the Altair, they could create their own programs. Within 3 months, 4,000 orders were placed for the machine.

The release of the Altair marked the start of the personal computer boom. In fact, two men whose names you might have heard were among the first Altair owners—Bill Gates and Paul Allen were so enamored by the "minicomputer" that they wrote a compiling program (a program that translates user commands into commands the computer can understand) for it. The two later convinced the Altair's developer to buy their program, marking the start of a company called Microsoft. We'll get to that story later. First, let's see what their rivals were up to.

The Apple I and II

Objective 3B.2 *Describe the distinguishing features of the Apple I and Apple II.*

Around the time the Altair was released, **Steve Wozniak**, an employee at Hewlett-Packard, was dabbling with his own computer design. **Steve Jobs**, who was working for computer game manufacturer Atari at the time, liked Wozniak's prototypes and made a few suggestions. Together, the two built a personal computer, the **Apple I**, in Wozniak's garage (see Figure 1) and formed the Apple Computer Company in 1976.

November 1977

TRS-80

- Introduced by Radio Shack
- Monochrome display
- 4 KB of RAM
- Circuitry hidden under keyboard
- Wildly popular with consumers—sold 10,000 units in the first month

April 1981

Osbourne

- First "portable" computer
- Weighed 24.5 pounds
- 5-inch screen
- 64 kilobytes of RAM
- Two floppy disk drives
- Preinstalled with spreadsheet and word processing software

August 1981

IBM PC (5150)

- Marketed to businesses and consumers
- 64 KB to 256 KB of RAM
- Floppy disk drives optional
- Hard disks not supported in early models

(Interfoto/History/Alamy, Science & Society Picture Library/Getty Images, Interfoto/History/Alamy)

BITS&BYTES

Why Is It Called "Apple"?

Steve Jobs wanted Apple Computer to be the "perfect" computer company. Having recently worked at an apple orchard, Jobs thought of the apple as the perfect fruit because it was high in nutrients, came in a nice package, and was not easily damaged. Thus, he and Wozniak decided to name their computer company Apple. *(Frommenwiler Peter/Prisma Bildagentur AG/Alamy)*

One year later, in 1977, the **Apple II** was born (see Figure 1). The Apple II included a color monitor, sound, and game paddles. Priced around $1,300 (about $5,245 in today's dollars), one of its biggest innovations was that the operating system was stored in read-only memory (ROM). Previously, the operating system had to be rewritten every time the computer was turned on. The friendly features of the Apple II operating system encouraged less technically oriented computer enthusiasts to write their own programs.

An instant success, the Apple II would eventually include a spreadsheet program, a word processor, and desktop publishing software. These programs gave personal computers like the Apple functions beyond gaming and special programming and led to their popularity.

Enter the Competition

Around the time Apple was experiencing success with its computers, a number of competitors entered the market. The largest among them were Commodore, Radio Shack, Osborne, and IBM. The **Commodore PET** (see Figure 1) was aimed at the business market and did well in Europe, while Radio Shack's **TRS-80** (see Figure 1) was clearly aimed at the U.S. consumer market. Just 1 month after its release in 1977, it had sold about 10,000 units.

The Osborne: The Birth of Portable Computing

Objective 3B.3 *Describe the first portable computer.*

The Osborne Company introduced the first portable computer, the **Osborne**, in 1981 (see Figure 1). Although portable, the computer weighed 24.5 pounds. It featured a minuscule 5-inch screen and carried a price tag of $1,795 (about $4,884 today). The Osborne was an overnight success, and its sales quickly reached 10,000 units per month. However, despite the computer's popularity, the Osborne Company eventually closed. Compaq bought the Osborne design and in 1983 produced its own portable computer.

IBM PCs

Objective 3B.4 *Describe the development of the IBM PC.*

Until 1980, IBM primarily made mainframe computers, which it sold to large corporations, and hadn't taken the personal computer seriously. In 1981, however, IBM released its first personal computer, the **IBM PC** (see Figure 1). Because many companies were familiar with IBM mainframes, they adopted the IBM PC. The term *PC* soon became the term used to describe all personal computers.

IBM marketed its PC through retail outlets such as Sears to reach home users, and it quickly dominated that market. In January 1983, *Time* magazine, playing on its annual person of the year issue, named the computer "1982 Machine of the Year."

Other Important Advancements

It wasn't just personal computer hardware that was changing. At the same time, advances in programming languages and operating systems and the influx of application software were leading to more useful and powerful machines.

The Importance of BASIC

Objective 3B.5 *Explain why BASIC was an important step in revolutionizing the software industry.*

The software industry began in the 1950s with programming languages such as FORTRAN, ALGOL, and COBOL. These languages were used mainly by businesses to create financial, statistical, and engineering programs. However, the 1964 introduction of **Beginners All-Purpose Symbolic Instruction Code (BASIC)** revolutionized the software industry. BASIC was a language that beginning programming students could easily learn. It thus became enormously popular—and the key language of the PC. In fact, **Bill Gates** and **Paul Allen** (see Figure 2) used BASIC to write their program for the Altair.

FIGURE 2 Bill Gates and Paul Allen are the founders of Microsoft. *(Doug Wilson/Corbis)*

As we noted earlier, this program led to the creation of Microsoft, a company that produced computer software.

The Advent of Operating Systems

Objective 3B.6 *Explain why the development of the operating system was an important step in PC development.*

Because data on the earliest personal computers was stored on audiocassettes, many programs weren't saved or reused. This meant that programs had to be rewritten whenever they were needed. In 1978, Steve Wozniak designed a 5.25-inch floppy disk drive so that programs could be saved easily and operating systems developed.

Operating systems are written to coordinate with the specific processor chip that controls the computer. At that time, Apples ran on a Motorola chip, whereas PCs (IBMs and so on) ran on an Intel chip. **Disk Operating System (DOS)**, developed by Wozniak and introduced in 1977, was the OS that controlled the first Apple computers. The **Control Program for Microcomputers (CP/M)**, developed by Gary Kildall, was the OS designed for the Intel 8080 chip (the processor for PCs).

In 1980, when IBM was entering the personal computer market, it approached Bill Gates at Microsoft to write an OS program for the IBM PC. Gates recommended that IBM investigate the CP/M OS, but IBM couldn't arrange a meeting with the founder, Gary Kildall. Microsoft reconsidered the opportunity to write an OS program and developed **MS-DOS** for IBM computers. Eventually, virtually all PCs running on the Intel chip used MS-DOS as their OS (see Figure 3). Microsoft's reign as one of the dominant players in the personal computer landscape had begun.

The Software Application Explosion: VisiCalc and Beyond

Objective 3B.7 *List early application software that was developed for the PC.*

Because the floppy disk was a convenient way to distribute software, its inclusion in personal computers set off an application software explosion. In 1978, Harvard Business School student Dan Bricklin recognized the potential for a personal computer spreadsheet program. He and his friend Bob Frankston created the program **VisiCalc**, which became an instant success. Finally, ordinary home users could see the benefit of owning a personal computer. More than 100,000 copies of VisiCalc were sold in its first year.

After VisiCalc, other electronic spreadsheet programs entered the market. **Lotus 1-2-3** came on the market in 1983, and **Microsoft Excel** entered the scene in 1985. These products became so popular that they eventually put VisiCalc out of business.

Meanwhile, word processing software was also gaining a foothold in the industry. Until then, there were separate, dedicated word processing machines; personal computers, it was believed, were for computation and data management only. However, once **WordStar**, the first word processing application, became available for personal computers in 1979, word processing became another important use for the personal computer. Competitors such as **Word for MS-DOS** (the precursor to Microsoft Word) and **WordPerfect** soon entered the market. Figure 4 lists some of the important dates in application software development.

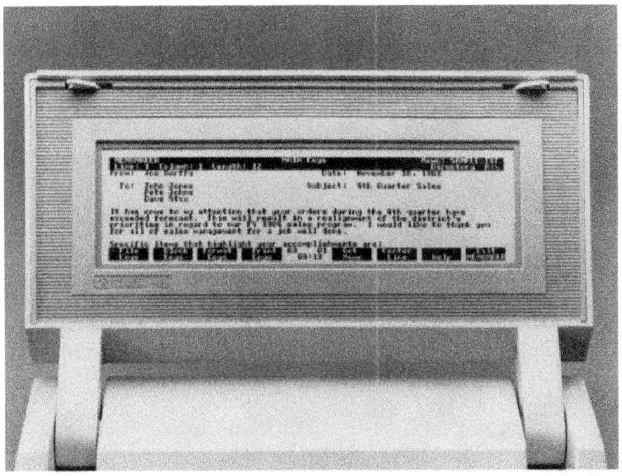

FIGURE 3 This 1983 Hewlett-Packard computer used an early version of the MS-DOS operating system as well as the Lotus 1-2-3 spreadsheet program. *(Everett Collection/SuperStock)*

The Graphical User Interface and the Internet Boom

Other important advancements related to personal computers came in the form of the graphical user interface and the Internet.

Xerox and Apple's Lisa and Macintosh

Objective 3B.8 *Describe the features of the Lisa and Macintosh computers and their predecessor, the Xerox Alto.*

A **graphical user interface (GUI)**, which uses icons to represent programs and actions, allowed users to interact

FIGURE 4

Application Software Development

YEAR	APPLICATION
1978	**VisiCalc:** First electronic spreadsheet application **WordStar:** First word processing application
1980	**WordPerfect:** Best DOS-based word processor, was eventually sold to Novell and later acquired by Corel
1983	**Lotus 1-2-3:** Added integrated charting, plotting, and database capabilities to spreadsheet software **Word for MS-DOS:** Introduced in the pages of *PC World* magazine on the first magazine-inserted demo disk
1985	**Excel:** One of the first spreadsheets to use a graphical user interface **PageMaker:** The first desktop publishing software

FIGURE 5 The Alto was the first computer to use a GUI, and it provided the basis for the GUI that Apple used. However, because of marketing problems, the Alto never was sold. *(Josie Lepe/MCT/Newscom)*

FIGURE 6 The Lisa was the first computer to introduce a GUI to the market. Priced too high, it never gained the popularity it deserved. *(SSPL/The Image Works)*

with the computer more easily. Until that time, users had to use complicated command- or menu-driven interfaces. Apple was the first company to take full commercial advantage of the GUI, but the GUI was not invented by a computer company.

In 1972, a few years before Apple launched its first personal computer, photocopier manufacturer **Xerox** was designing a personal computer of its own. Named the **Alto** (see Figure 5), the computer included a word processor, based on the What You See Is What You Get (WYSIWYG) principle, that incorporated a file management system with directories and folders. It also had a mouse and could connect to a network. None of the other personal computers of the time had these features. For a variety of reasons, Xerox never sold the Alto commercially. Several years later, it developed the Star Office System, which was based on the Alto. Despite its convenient features, the Star never became popular because no one was willing to pay the $17,000 asking price.

Xerox's ideas were ahead of their time, but many of the ideas present in the Alto and Star would soon catch on. In 1983, Apple introduced the **Lisa**—the first successful personal computer brought to market that used a GUI (see Figure 6). Legend has it that Jobs had seen the Alto during a visit to Xerox in 1979 and was influenced by its GUI. He therefore incorporated a similar user interface into the Lisa, providing features such as windows, drop-down menus, icons, a file system with folders and files, and a point-and-click device called a mouse. The only problem with the Lisa was its price. At $9,995 (about $24,047 in today's dollars), few buyers were willing to take the plunge.

One year later, in 1984, Apple introduced the **Macintosh**, shown in Figure 7. The Macintosh was everything the Lisa was and then some, at about a third of the cost. The Macintosh was also the first personal computer to utilize 3.5-inch floppy disks with a hard cover, which were smaller and sturdier than the previous 5.25-inch floppies.

The Internet Boom

Objective 3B.9 *List the first successful web browsers.*

The GUI made it easier for users to work on the computer. The Internet provided another reason for people to buy computers. Now people could conduct research and communicate in a new way. In 1993, the web browser **Mosaic** was introduced. This browser allowed users to view multimedia on the web, causing Internet traffic to increase by nearly 350%.

FIGURE 7 The Macintosh became one of Apple's best-selling computers, incorporating a GUI along with other innovations such as the 3.5-inch floppy disk drive. *(Corbis)*

Meanwhile, companies discovered the Internet as a means to do business, and computer sales took off. IBM-compatible PCs became the computer system of choice when, in 1995, Microsoft introduced **Internet Explorer**, a browser that integrated web functionality into Microsoft Office applications, and **Windows 95**, the first Microsoft OS designed to be principally a GUI OS.

About one year earlier, in 1994, a team of developers launched the **Netscape** web browser, which soon became a predominant player in browser software. However, pressures from Microsoft became too strong, and in 1998, Netscape announced it would no longer charge for the product and would make the code available to the public.

Making the Personal Computer Possible: Early Computers

Billions of personal computers have been sold over the past four decades. But the computer is a compilation of parts, each of which is the result of individual inventions. Let's look at some early machines that helped to create the personal computer we know today.

The Pascalene Calculator and the Jacquard Loom

Objective 3B.10 *Discuss the features of the Pascalene calculator and the Jacquard loom that inspired modern computer elements.*

From the earliest days of humankind, we have been looking for a more systematic way to count and calculate. Thus, the evolution of counting machines led to the development of the computer we know today. The **Pascalene** was the first accurate mechanical calculator. This machine, created by the French mathematician **Blaise Pascal** in 1642, used revolutions of gears, like odometers in cars, to count by tens. The Pascalene could be used to add, subtract, multiply, and divide. The basic design of the Pascalene was so sound that it lived on in mechanical calculators for more than 300 years.

Nearly 200 years later, **Joseph Jacquard** revolutionized the fabric industry by creating a machine that automated the weaving of complex patterns. Although not a counting or calculating machine, the **Jacquard loom** (shown in Figure 8) was significant because it relied on stiff cards with punched holes to automate the weaving process. Much later, this punch-card process would be adopted as a means for computers to record and read data.

FIGURE 8 The Jacquard loom used holes punched in stiff cards to make complex designs. This technique would later be used in punch cards that controlled the input and output of data in computers. *(Janek Skarzynski/Newscom)*

Babbage's Engines and the Hollerith Tabulating Machine

Objective 3B.11 *Discuss the contributions of Babbage's engines and the Hollerith Tabulating Machine to modern computing.*

In 1834, **Charles Babbage** designed the first automatic calculator, called the **Analytical Engine** (see Figure 9). The machine was actually based on another machine called the **Difference Engine**, which was a huge steam-powered mechanical calculator that Babbage designed to print astronomical tables. Although the Analytical Engine was never developed, Babbage's detailed drawings and descriptions of the machine include components similar to those found in today's computers, including the store (akin to RAM) and the mill (a central processing unit) as well as input and output devices. This invention gave Charles Babbage the title of the "father of computing."

Meanwhile, Ada Lovelace, who was the daughter of poet Lord Byron and a student of mathematics (which was unusual for women of the time), was fascinated with Babbage's engines. She translated an Italian paper on Babbage's machine and, at the request of Babbage, added her own extensive notes. Her efforts are thought to be the best description of Babbage's engines.

In 1890, **Herman Hollerith**, while working for the U.S. Census Bureau, was the first to take Jacquard's punch-card concept and apply it to computing with his **Hollerith Tabulating Machine**. Until that time, census data had been tabulated manually in a long, laborious process. Hollerith's tabulating machine automatically read data that had been punched onto small punch cards, speeding up the tabulation process. Hollerith's machine became so successful that he left

FIGURE 9 The Analytical Engine, designed by Charles Babbage, was never fully developed but included components similar to those found in today's computers. *(Chris Howes/Wild Places Photography)*

the Census Bureau in 1896 to start the Tabulating Machine Company. His company later changed its name to International Business Machines, or IBM.

The Z1, the Atanasoff–Berry Computer, and the Harvard Mark I

Objective 3B.12 *Discuss the features of the Z1, the Atansoff–Berry Computer, and the Mark I.*

German inventor **Konrad Zuse** is credited with a number of computing inventions. His first, in 1936, was a mechanical calculator called the **Z1**. The Z1 is thought to be the first computer to include certain features integral to today's systems, such as a control unit and separate memory functions.

In 1939, John Atanasoff, a professor at Iowa State University, and his student Clifford Berry built the first electrically powered digital computer, called the **Atanasoff–Berry Computer (ABC)**, shown in Figure 10. The computer was the first to use vacuum tubes, instead of the mechanical switches used in older computers, to store data. Although revolutionary at the time, the machine weighed 700 pounds, contained a mile of wire, and took about 15 seconds for each calculation. (In comparison, today's personal computers can perform billions of calculations in 15 seconds.) Most importantly, the ABC was the first computer to use the binary system and to have memory that repowered itself upon booting. The design of the ABC would be central to that of future computers.

From the late 1930s to the early 1950s, **Howard Aiken** and **Grace Hopper** designed the Mark series of computers used by the U.S. Navy for ballistic and gunnery calculations. Aiken, an electrical engineer and physicist, designed the computer, while Hopper did the programming. The **Harvard Mark I**, finished in 1944, could add, subtract, multiply, and divide.

However, many believe Hopper's greatest contribution to computing was the invention of the **compiler**—a program that translates English-language instructions into computer language. The team was also responsible for a common computer-related expression. Hopper was the first to "debug" a computer when she removed a moth that had flown into the Harvard Mark I and had caused the computer to break down (see Figure 11). After that, problems that caused a computer not to run were called bugs.

The Turing Machine, the ENIAC, and the UNIVAC

Objective 3B.13 *Discuss the major features of the Turing Machine, the ENIAC and the UNIVAC.*

Meanwhile, in 1936, British mathematician **Alan Turing** created an abstract computer model that could perform logical operations. The **Turing Machine** was not a real

FIGURE 10 The Atanasoff–Berry Computer laid the design groundwork for many computers to come. *(Frederick News Post/AP Images)*

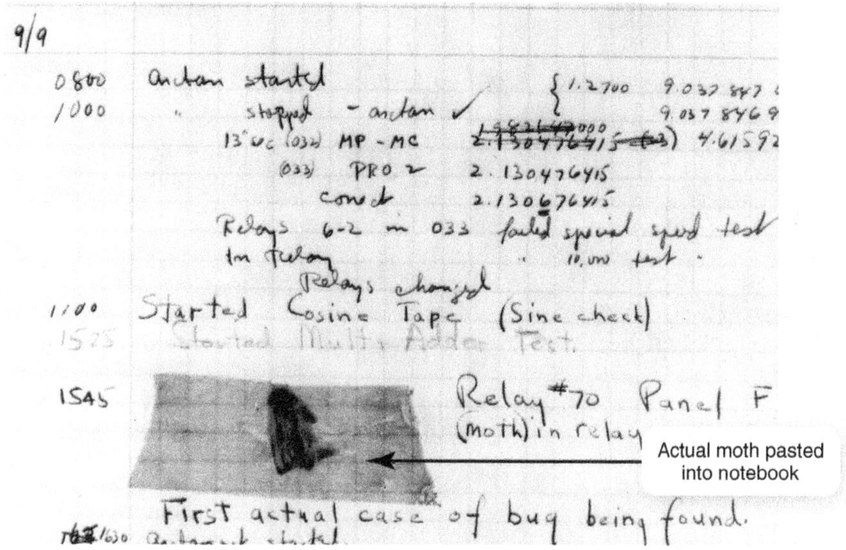

FIGURE 11 Grace Hopper coined the term *computer bug* when a moth flew into the Harvard Mark I, causing it to break down. *(Naval History & Heritage Command)*

machine but rather a hypothetical model that mathematically defined a mechanical procedure (or algorithm). Additionally, Turing's concept described a process by which the machine could read, write, or erase symbols written on squares of an infinite paper tape. This concept of an infinite tape that could be read, written to, and erased was the precursor to today's RAM.

The **Electronic Numerical Integrator and Computer (ENIAC)**, shown in Figure 12, was another U.S. government–sponsored machine developed to calculate the settings used for weapons. Created by **John W. Mauchly** and **J. Presper Eckert** at the University of Pennsylvania, it was put into operation in 1944. Although the ENIAC is generally thought of as the first successful high-speed electronic digital computer, it was big and clumsy. The ENIAC used nearly 18,000 vacuum tubes and filled approximately 1,800 square feet of floor space. Although inconvenient, the ENIAC served its purpose and remained in use until 1955.

The **Universal Automatic Computer**, or **UNIVAC**, was the first commercially successful electronic digital computer. Completed in 1951, the UNIVAC operated on magnetic tape (see Figure 13), setting it apart from its competitors, which ran on punch cards. The UNIVAC gained notoriety when, in a 1951 publicity stunt, it was used to predict the outcome of the Stevenson–Eisenhower presidential race. After analyzing only 5% of the popular vote, the UNIVAC correctly identified Dwight D. Eisenhower as the victor. After that, UNIVAC soon became a household word. The UNIVAC and computers like it were considered **first-generation computers** and were the last to use vacuum tubes to store data.

Transistors and Beyond

Objective 3B.14 *Describe the milestones that led to each "generation" of computers.*

Only one year after the ENIAC was completed, scientists at the Bell Telephone Laboratories in New Jersey invented the

FIGURE 12 The ENIAC took up an entire room and required several people to manipulate it. *(Interfoto/Alamy Stock Photo)*

FIGURE 13 UNIVACs were the first computers to use magnetic tape for data storage. *(CBS/Landov)*

transistor—another means to store data (see Figure 14). The transistor replaced the bulky vacuum tubes of earlier computers and was smaller and more powerful than tubes. It was used in almost everything, from radios to phones. Computers that used transistors were referred to as **second-generation computers**. Still, transistors were limited as to how small they could be made.

A few years later, in 1958, **Jack Kilby**, while working at Texas Instruments, invented the world's first **integrated circuit**—a small chip capable of containing thousands of transistors. This consolidation in design enabled computers to become smaller and lighter. The computers in this early integrated-circuit generation were considered **third-generation computers**.

Other innovations in the computer industry further refined the computer's speed, accuracy, and efficiency. However, none was as significant as the 1971 introduction by the Intel Corporation of the **microprocessor chip**—a small chip containing millions of transistors (see Figure 15). The microprocessor functions as the CPU, or brains, of the computer. Computers that use a microprocessor chip are called **fourth-generation computers**. Over time, Intel and Motorola became the leading manufacturers of microprocessors. Today, the Intel Core i7 is one of Intel's most powerful processors.

As you can see, personal computers have come a long way since the Altair and have a number of inventions and people to thank for their amazing popularity. What will the future bring? ■

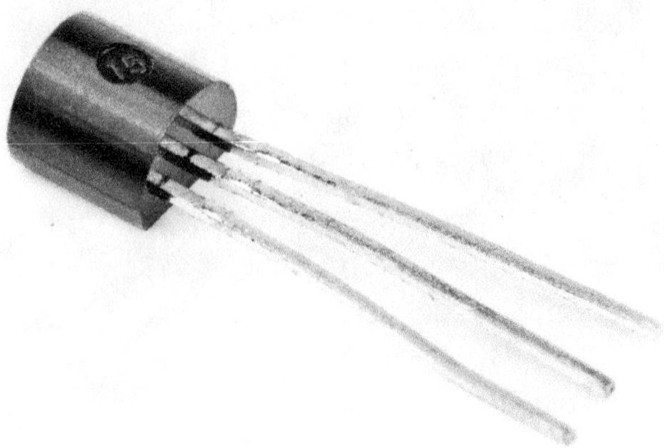

FIGURE 14 Transistors were one-tenth the size of vacuum tubes, faster, and produced much less heat. *(Borissos/Fotolia)*

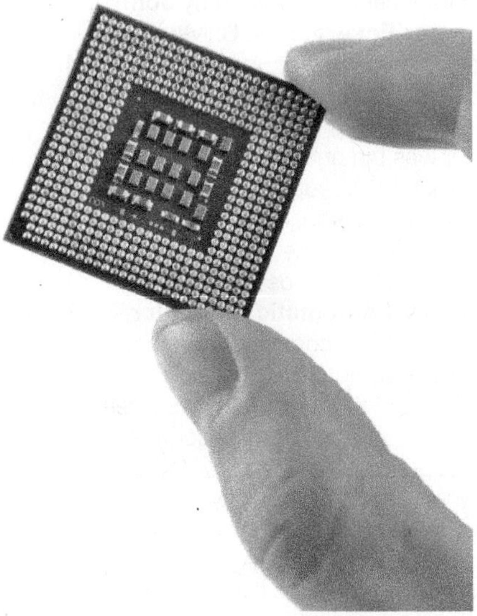

FIGURE 15 Today's microprocessors can contain billions of transistors. *(Tudor Voinea/Shutterstock)*

check your understanding // review & practice

For a quick review of what you've learned, answer the following questions.

multiple choice

1. What was the name of the first web browser?

- **a.** Mosaic
- **b.** Internet Explorer
- **c.** Netscape
- **d.** Firefox

2. Which operating system was specifically developed for the first IBM PC?

- **a.** CP/M
- **b.** COBOL
- **c.** MS-DOS
- **d.** VisiCalc

3. Which invention replaced vacuum tubes in computers?

- **a.** the integrated circuit
- **b.** the transistor
- **c.** the microprocessor chip
- **d.** magnetic tape

4. Which computer was touted as the first personal computer?

- **a.** Altair
- **b.** Commodore PET
- **c.** Lisa
- **d.** Osborne

5. What was the importance of the Turing machine to today's computers?

- **a.** It described a system that was a precursor to today's notebook computer.
- **b.** It was the first electronic calculator and a precursor to the computer.
- **c.** It was the first computer to have a monitor.
- **d.** It described a process to read, write, and erase symbols on a tape and was the precursor to today's RAM.

6. Which computer first stored its operating system in ROM?

- **a.** Apple I
- **b.** Apple II
- **c.** Lisa
- **d.** Macintosh

7. What was the first word processing application?

- **a.** Word for MS-DOS
- **b.** WordPerfect
- **c.** WordStar
- **d.** Alto

8. Which components are a characteristic of second-generation computers?

- **a.** transistors
- **b.** vacuum tubes
- **c.** integrated circuits
- **d.** microprocessor chips

9. For what is the Atanasoft–Berry Computer best known?

- **a.** It was the first computer to use vacuum tubes instead of mechanical switches.
- **b.** It was the first computer to use the binary system.
- **c.** It was the first computer to incorporate a magnetic tape system.
- **d.** It was the first computer used as a mechanical calculator.

10. Who were the founders of Microsoft?

- **a.** Paul Allen and Bill Gates
- **b.** Steve Jobs and Steve Wozniak
- **c.** Steve Jobs and Bill Gates
- **d.** Bill Gates and Steve Wozniak

MyITLab Go to **MyITLab** to take an autograded version of the *Check Your Understanding* review and to find all media resources for the chapter.

5

System Software: The Operating System, Utility Programs, and File Management

Understanding System Software

Learning Outcome 5.1 You will be able to explain the types and functions of an operating system and explain the steps in the boot process.

Operating System Fundamentals 162

Objective 5.1 *Discuss the functions of the operating system.*

Objective 5.2 *Explain the different kinds of operating systems for machines, networks, and business.*

Objective 5.3 *Explain the most common operating systems for personal use.*

Sound Byte: Customizing Windows

What the Operating System Does 167

Objective 5.4 *Explain how the operating system provides a means for users to interact with the computer.*

Objective 5.5 *Explain how the operating system helps manage hardware such as the processor, memory, storage, and peripheral devices.*

Objective 5.6 *Explain how the operating system interacts with application software.*

Starting Your Computer 172

Objective 5.7 *Discuss the process the operating system uses to start up the computer and how errors in the boot process are handled.*

Active Helpdesk: Starting the Computer: The Boot Process

Using System Software

Learning Outcome 5.2 You will be able to describe how system software is used, including managing the user interface, file management, and utility programs.

The Windows Interface 178

Objective 5.8 *Describe the main features of the Windows interface.*

File Management 181

Objective 5.9 *Summarize how the operating system helps keep your computer organized.*

Sound Byte: File Management

Objective 5.10 *Summarize how to view, sort, name, and manage files and folders.*

Active Helpdesk: Organizing Your Computer: File Management

Objective 5.11 *Summarize how file compression works.*

Sound Byte: File Compression

Utility Programs 189

Active Helpdesk: Using Utility Programs

Objective 5.12 *Outline the tools used to enhance system productivity.*

Sound Byte: Letting Your Computer Clean Up After Itself

Objective 5.13 *Summarize the utilities used to backup and restore files and the computer system.*

Sound Byte: Hard Disk Anatomy

Objective 5.14 *Describe the assistive technology utilities used to make using the computer system easier.*

Make This: MAKE: A Notification Alert on **page 177**

All media accompanying this chapter can be found in MyITLab.

For an overview of the chapter, watch the **Preview Video.**

(Dizain/Fotolia; Artender/Fotolia; Revers/Shutterstock; Windows 8.1, Microsoft Corporation; Stanislav Popov/Shutterstock; Reji/Fotolia)

HOW COOL IS THIS?

Tony Stark built the Iron Man suit using a **hologram**. Princess Leia delivered her message to Obi-Wan Kenobi as a hologram. Now, thanks to Microsoft, you might be able to use holograms in your own home. What's a hologram? Holograms are **three-dimensional photographic images** that appear to be **freestanding images**. They are created using two two-dimensional images of the same object taken from different angles and superimposed to display what appears to the brain to be one image. Microsoft is incorporating this holographic technology with **HoloLens**. HoloLens are wireless lenses that will enable you to **interact freely with holograms**. What can you do with holograms? The possibilities are still being explored, but think of how you might interact with a touch-screen device, and then remove the need to physically touch the device. Instead, you'll interact with a holographic image. It might not be long before you're using holographic technology for your next project. *(Corbis)*

Understanding System Software

Learning Outcome 5.1 You will be able to explain the types and functions of an operating system and explain the steps in the boot process.

As discussed in the previous chapter, your computer uses two basic types of software: application software and system software. *Application software* is the software you use to do everyday tasks at home and at work. *System software* is the set of programs that helps run the computer and coordinates instructions between application software and the computer's hardware devices. From the moment you turn on your computer to the time you shut it down, you're interacting with system software.

OPERATING SYSTEM operating system FUNDAMENTALS

Every computer, from the smallest laptop to the largest supercomputer, has an operating system. Even cell phones, game consoles, cars, and some appliances have operating systems. The role of the operating system is critical; a computer can't operate without it.

Operating System Basics

Objective 5.1 *Discuss the functions of the operating system.*

What does the operating system do? System software consists of two primary types of programs: the *operating system* and *utility programs*. The **operating system (OS)** is a group of programs that controls how your computer functions. The operating system has three primary functions:

- It manages the computer's hardware, including the processor, memory, and storage devices, as well as peripheral devices such as the printer.
- It provides a consistent means for application software to work with the central processing unit (CPU).
- It is responsible for the management, scheduling, and coordination of tasks.

You interact with your OS through the **user interface**—the *desktop*, *icons*, and *menus* that let you communicate with your computer.

A **utility program** is a small program that performs many of the general housekeeping tasks for your computer, such as system maintenance and file compression. A set of utility programs is bundled with each OS, but you can also buy standalone utility programs that often provide more features. We'll discuss utility programs in more detail later in the chapter.

Are all operating systems alike? You're probably familiar with Microsoft Windows, Apple OS X, and perhaps the Android operating system if it's on your phone, but many other operating systems exist. Laptops, tablet computers, and smartphones all need specific operating systems designed to take advantage of their unique characteristics. However, as devices begin to converge in terms of functionality, and operating systems continue to become more powerful, developers such as Microsoft and Apple are making operating systems that have similar functionality (such as OS X and iOS) or single operating systems (such as Windows 10) that can run on a variety of devices. Figure 5.1 lists a number of common operating systems.

FIGURE 5.1

Common Operating Systems

OS NAME	DEVELOPED BY	AVAILABLE ON
Windows 	Microsoft	Laptops, tablets, desktops, all-in-ones, cell phones
OS X 	Apple	Laptops, desktops, all-in-ones
iOS 	Apple	Tablets, iPhones, iPod touches
Android 	Google	Cell phones, tablets
Linux 	Open source	Laptops, desktops, tablets

(Top Photo Group/Alamy, Aleksey Boldin/Alamy, David Paul Morris/Bloomberg/Getty Images, YAY Media AS/Alamy, Tibbbb/Fotolia)

When operating systems were originally developed, they were designed for a single user performing one task at a time (that is, they were *single-user, single-task operating systems*). However, modern operating systems allow a single user to **multitask**—to perform more than one process at a time. And operating systems such as Windows and OS X provide networking capabilities as well, essentially making them *multiuser, multitasking operating systems*.

Operating systems can be categorized by the type of device in which they're installed, such as robots and specialized equipment with built-in computers, mainframes and network computers, mobile devices, and personal computers. Next, we'll look at these different types of operating systems.

Operating Systems for Machinery, Networks, and Business

Objective 5.2 *Explain the different kinds of operating systems for machines, networks, and business.*

Why do machines with built-in computers need an OS? Machinery that performs a repetitive series of specific tasks in an exact amount of time requires a **real-time operating system (RTOS)**. Also referred to as *embedded systems*, RTOSs require minimal user interaction. This type of OS is a program with a specific purpose, and it must guarantee certain response times for particular computing tasks; otherwise, the machine is useless. The programs are written specifically for the needs of the devices and their functions. Therefore, there are no commercially available standard RTOS software programs. Devices that must perform regimented tasks or record precise results—such as measurement instruments found in the scientific, defense, and aerospace industries—require RTOSs. Examples include digital storage oscilloscopes and the Mars Reconnaissance Orbiter.

You also encounter RTOSs every day in devices such as fuel-injection systems in car engines, automobile "infotainment" systems, and some common appliances. RTOSs are also found in many types of robotic equipment. Television stations use robotic cameras with RTOSs that glide across a suspended cable system to record sports events from many angles (see Figure 5.2).

What kind of operating systems do networks use? A **multiuser operating system** (or **network operating system**) lets more than one user access the computer system at a time by handling and prioritizing requests from multiple users. Networks (groups of computers connected to each other so that they can communicate and share resources) need a multiuser OS because many users simultaneously access the server (the computer that manages network resources such as printing and communications). The latest versions of Windows and OS X can be considered network operating systems: They enable users to set up basic networks in their homes and small businesses.

In larger networks, a more robust network OS is installed on servers and manages all user requests. For example, on a network where users share a printer, the network OS ensures that the printer prints only one document at a time in the order the requests were made. Examples of network operating systems include Windows Server, Linux, and UNIX.

What is UNIX? UNIX is a multiuser, multitasking OS that is used as a network OS, although it can also be found on PCs. Developed in 1969 by Ken Thompson and Dennis Ritchie of AT&T's Bell Labs, the UNIX code was initially not proprietary—in other words, no company owned it. Rather, any programmer was allowed to use the code and modify it to meet his or her needs. UNIX is now a brand that belongs to the company The Open Group, but any vendor that meets the testing requirements and pays a fee can use the UNIX name. Individual vendors then modify the UNIX code to run specifically on their hardware.

What other kinds of computers require a multiuser OS? Mainframes and supercomputers also require multiuser operating systems. Mainframes routinely support hundreds

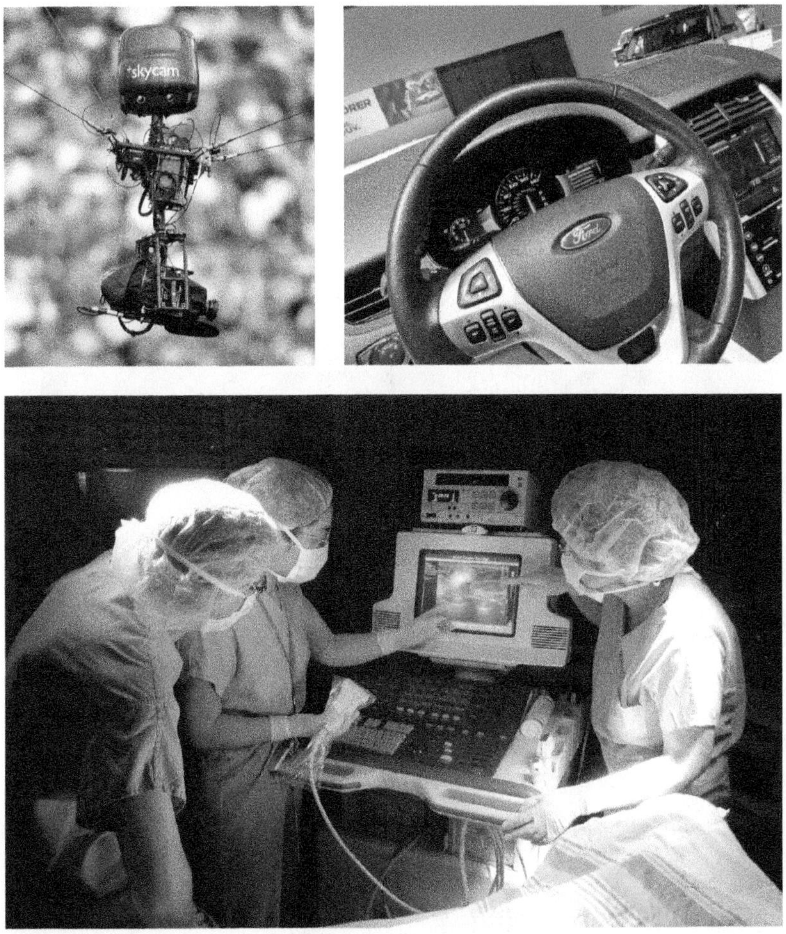

FIGURE 5.2 Devices such as TV sky cameras, cars, and medical equipment use RTOSs. *(John Pyle/Cal Sport Media/Newscom, Mark Gail/The Washington Post via Getty Images, Elfstrom/Getty Images)*

or thousands of users at time, and supercomputers are often accessed by multiple people working on complex calculations. Examples of mainframe operating systems include UNIX, Linux on System z, and IBM's z/OS, whereas the vast majority of supercomputers use Linux.

Operating Systems for Personal Use

Objective 5.3 *Explain the most common operating systems for personal use.*

What kind of OS does a smartphone use? Figure 5.3 shows the market share for the most common operating systems found on smartphones. The two major players in this arena are Android and Apple with its iOS operating system. Microsoft, with its newest cross-platform operating system, is gaining market share, leaving Blackberry, once the leader in the field, and others such as Symbian to barely have an impact on the market. Today's smartphone operating systems offer personal assistants with predictive search capabilities, the ability to use a wide variety of apps, a search engine, a camera, and of course a phone, as well as texting and e-mail capabilities. Some even enable note taking on their touch-screen displays. Most smartphones support Bluetooth and WiFi as standard, and some are introducing near field communication (NFC) for wireless transfers and mobile payments.

What OS do tablets use? Popular tablet operating systems include iOS, Android, and Windows. iPads use iOS, whereas a number of different tablets (such as the Samsung Galaxy Tab and the Google Nexus) use versions of Android. The Kindle Fire also runs a customized version of Android. Until the release of Windows 8 in 2012, Microsoft didn't have a popular tablet OS, but the company is expected to have a 10% market share by 2017. Such growth was spurred on by the introduction of Windows 8, which was optimized for tablet devices like Microsoft's Surface tablet, as well as by the latest release of Windows 10.

Do gaming consoles and iPods use an OS? Gaming systems such as Microsoft's Xbox 360, the Nintendo Wii, and the Sony PlayStation, as well as personal media players such as the iPod, all require system software developed specifically for the particular device. The system software controls the physical aspects of the device (such as game controllers) as well as other application programs that come with the device. For example, the operating systems on gaming consoles control web browsing and file storage of media and photos as well as playing of DVDs and games.

What are the most popular operating systems for personal computers? Microsoft Windows, Apple OS X, and Linux (an open source OS) are the top three operating systems for personal computers. Although they share similar features, each is unique.

What's special about Windows? Microsoft **Windows** is an operating environment that incorporates a user-friendly, visual interface like the one that was first introduced with Apple's OS. Over time, improvements in Windows have

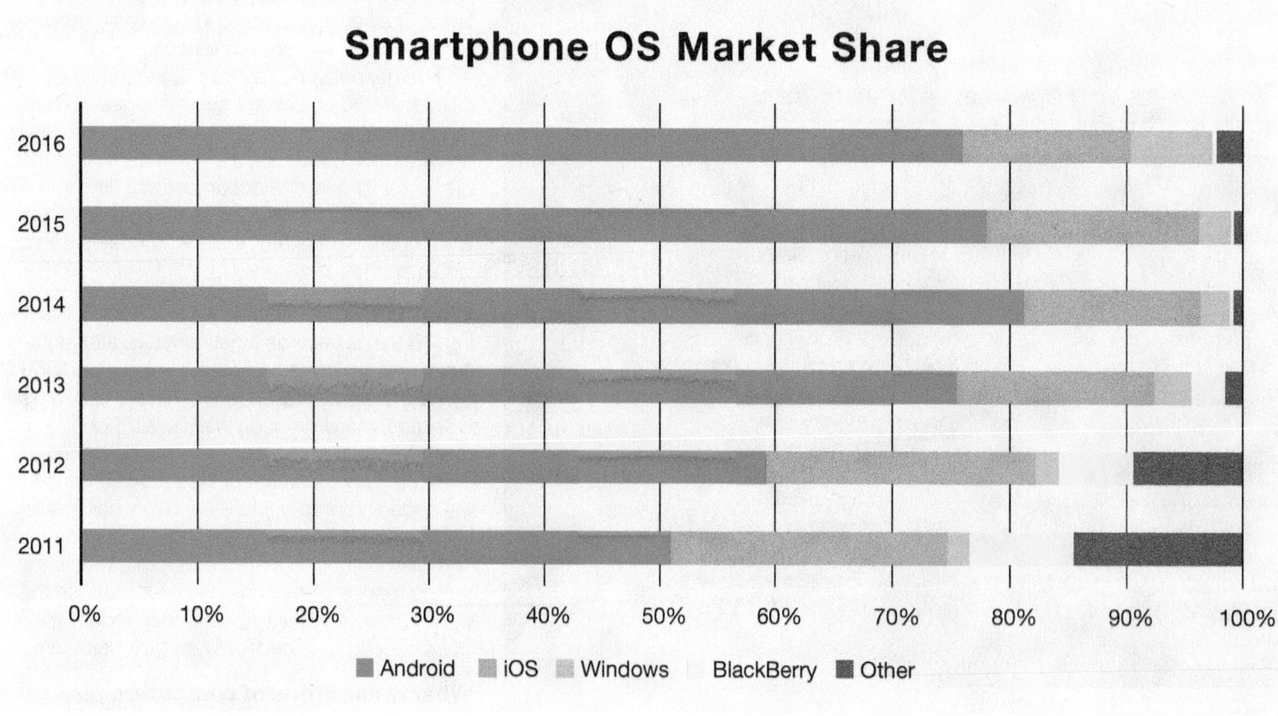

FIGURE 5.3 Popular Smartphone Operating Systems *(Data from Smartphone OS Market Share, 2015 Q2, IDC Corporate USA - available at http://www.idc.com/prodserv/smartphone-os-market-share.jsp)*

concentrated on increasing user functionality and friendliness, improving Internet capabilities, supporting home networks, and enhancing file privacy and security. Microsoft's newest OS, **Windows 10**, provides an interface optimized for touch-screen devices and is designed to run across all devices: phones, tablets, laptops, and desktops.

What's special about the Mac OS? In 1984, **Mac OS** became the first commercially available OS to incorporate the ability to interact with the computer with user-friendly point-and-click technology. With the release of the Mountain Lion version, Apple added many of the popular and innovative features loved by iOS users, such as messages, reminders, notes, and a notification center. The latest version, El Capitan, released in the fall of 2015, offers new features such as Split View (similar to Snap in Windows), touch-screen functionality, and natural language capabilities to Spotlight, OS X's search feature. OS X uses the same desktop metaphors as Windows, including icons for folders and a Trash Can (similar to a Recycle Bin) for deleted files. OS X also includes a window-based interface like the one in Windows.

OS X is based on the UNIX operating system, which is exceptionally stable and reliable. However, just as with any other OS, you still need to install updates as they become available and protect yourself from viruses, spyware, and other malicious software.

What is Linux? Linux is an open source OS designed for use on personal computers and as a network OS. Open source software is freely available for anyone to use or modify as he or she wishes. Linux began in 1991 as a part-time project of Finnish university student Linus Torvalds. It has since been tweaked by scores of programmers as part of the Free Software Foundation GNU Project (**gnu.org**).

Linux has a reputation as a stable OS that is not subject to crashes or failures. Because the code is open and available to anyone, Linux can be modified or updated quickly by hundreds of programmers around the world.

Where can I get Linux? Linux is available for download in various packages known as **distributions** or **distros**. Distros include the underlying Linux kernel (the code that provides Linux's basic functionality) and special modifications to the OS, and may also include additional open source software (such as OpenOffice). A good place to start researching distros is **distrowatch.com**. This site tracks Linux distros and provides helpful tips for beginners on choosing one.

Does it matter what OS is on my computer? An OS is designed to run on specific CPUs. CPUs have different designs, which can require modifying the OS software to allow it to communicate properly with each CPU. The combination of an OS and a specific processor is referred to as a computer's **platform**.

For user convenience, computers and other devices usually come with an OS already installed. Windows and Linux can run on most of the hardware being sold today. Your choice of an OS in this case is mostly a matter of price and personal preference. However, Apple equipment—computers, iPhones, iPads, and iPod touches—can only work with the Apple operating system made for that device. iOS is the operating system for mobile devices, and OS X is the operating system for desktop and laptop computers.

Also, most *application software* is OS dependent. You need to make sure you get the correct version of the application software for your OS. For example, you would need Microsoft Office 2016 for Mac for Apple devices and Microsoft Office 2016 for Windows for Windows devices.

BITS&BYTES

Upgrading Your Operating System

Every couple of years or so, Apple and Windows announce plans to upgrade their operating systems. For Apple OS X users, the most recent upgrades have been delivered via a download. For Windows users, upgrades have been released on new devices and were subsequently offered for purchase to install on your current device, should you decide to do so. The decision to upgrade to the newest version of Windows depended on several factors, such as whether Microsoft would still be supporting the OS you were using, whether there were significantly different or enticing features in the new version that you wanted, whether your hardware could support the new version of the OS, or whether your application software was compatible with the new OS.

With the release of Windows 10, Microsoft is changing all of that. The company has claimed that this will be "the last version of Windows." Windows 10 was offered free of charge for the first year to anyone running Windows 7 or 8 (or 8.1). From now on, Microsoft's "Windows as a Service" model will deliver automatic OS updates, including new features, apps, and patches, as necessary, without any additional notice. That is, we shouldn't expect there to be a Windows 11, 12, or anything else. The days of deciding whether to upgrade your operating system may be over.

SOUND BYTE

Customizing Windows

In this Sound Byte, you'll find out how to customize your desktop. You'll learn how to configure the desktop, set up a screen saver, change pointer options, customize the Start menu, and manage user accounts.

Can I have more than one OS on my computer? Many people run more than one OS on their computers because different operating systems offer different features. For example, Windows and Linux both run well on Apple computers. A standard utility included in OS X called Boot Camp lets you boot into either Windows or OS X. And if you want to run both OS X and Windows at the same time, you can create "virtual drives" using virtualization software such as Parallels or VMware Fusion.

In Windows, you can create a separate section of your hard drive (called a *partition*) and install another OS on it while leaving your original Windows installation untouched. After installing the second OS, when your computer starts, you're offered a choice of which OS to use.

How do operating systems use the "cloud"? Now that broadband Internet access and providing computer resources via the Internet (so-called cloud computing) are becoming more commonplace, operating systems have features that are tied to cloud computing. Here are a few examples:

- Windows 10 features tighter integration with the cloud. Using your *Microsoft account*, Windows 10 stores your settings and keeps track of applications you've purchased from the Windows store online. You can easily access and store files online in your *OneDrive account*. You can also log into your Windows account from any Windows-based machine and be able to see your familiar desktop and applications.
- Similarly, OS X allows you to sign in with your *Apple ID*, which provides access to Apple's *iCloud* system. iCloud stores your content online and automatically pushes it out to all your Apple devices.
- Google has launched the *Google Chrome OS* (see Figure 5.4), which is a web-based OS. With the Chrome OS, virtually no files are installed on your computing device. Rather, the main functionality of the OS is provided by accessing the web through a web browser. Chrome OS is only available on certain hardware from Google's manufacturing partners, and these devices are called *Chromebooks*. The Chrome OS should not be confused with the *Google Chrome browser*. The browser is application software that can run in many different operating systems.

FIGURE 5.4 The Google Chrome OS has a very minimalist look. *(© 2015 Google Inc. All rights reserved. Google and the Google Logo are registered trademarks of Google Inc.)*

BITS&BYTES

OS Market Share Battle

So who is winning the OS market share war? It depends on the type of device. For conventional desktop and laptop computers, hands down the winner is still various versions of Windows, with 90.7% of the market (see Figure 5.5). But as of July 2015, Windows only had a 2.5% market share on mobile devices versus Android's 51%. Apple comes in second in both races with 7.6% market share of desktop operating systems and 41.5% market share of mobile operating systems.

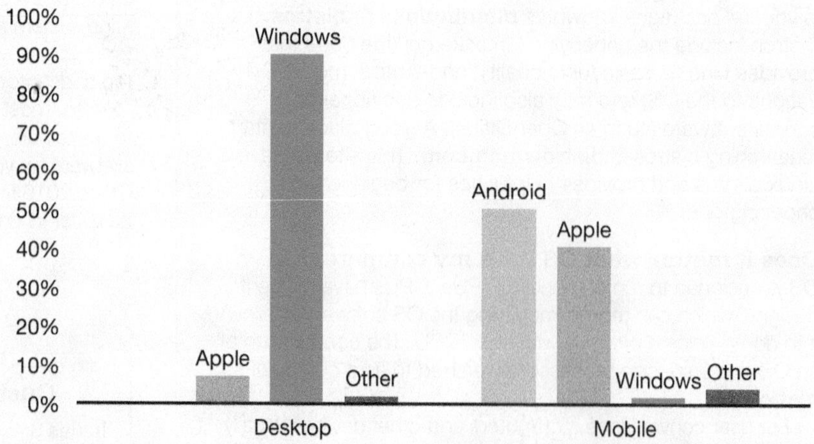

FIGURE 5.5 Operating System Market Share *(Data from Market Share Reports, NetMarketShare - available at http://www.netmarketshare.com/)*

what the operating SYSTEM DOES

As shown in Figure 5.6, the OS is like an orchestra's conductor. It coordinates and directs the flow of data and information through the computer system. In this section, we explore the operations of the OS in detail.

The User Interface

Objective 5.4 *Explain how the operating system provides a means for users to interact with the computer.*

How does the OS control how I interact with my computer? The OS provides a user interface that lets you interact with the computer. The first personal computers used *Microsoft Disk Operating System* (*MS-DOS* or just *DOS*), which had a command-driven interface, as shown in Figure 5.7a. A **command-driven interface** is one in which you enter commands to communicate with the computer system. The DOS commands were not always easy to understand; as a result, the interface proved to be too complicated for the average user. Therefore, PCs were used primarily in business and by professional computer operators.

The command-driven interface was later improved by incorporating a menu-driven interface, as shown in Figure 5.7b. A **menu-driven interface** is one in which you choose commands from menus displayed on the screen. Menu-driven interfaces eliminated the need for users to know every command because they could select most of the commonly used commands from a menu. However, they were still not easy enough for most people to use.

What kind of interface do operating systems use today? Current computer and mobile operating systems such as Microsoft Windows and OS X use a **graphical user interface** or **GUI** (pronounced "gooey"). Unlike command- and menu-driven interfaces, GUIs display graphics and use the point-and-click technology of the mouse and cursor (or human finger), making them much more user-friendly.

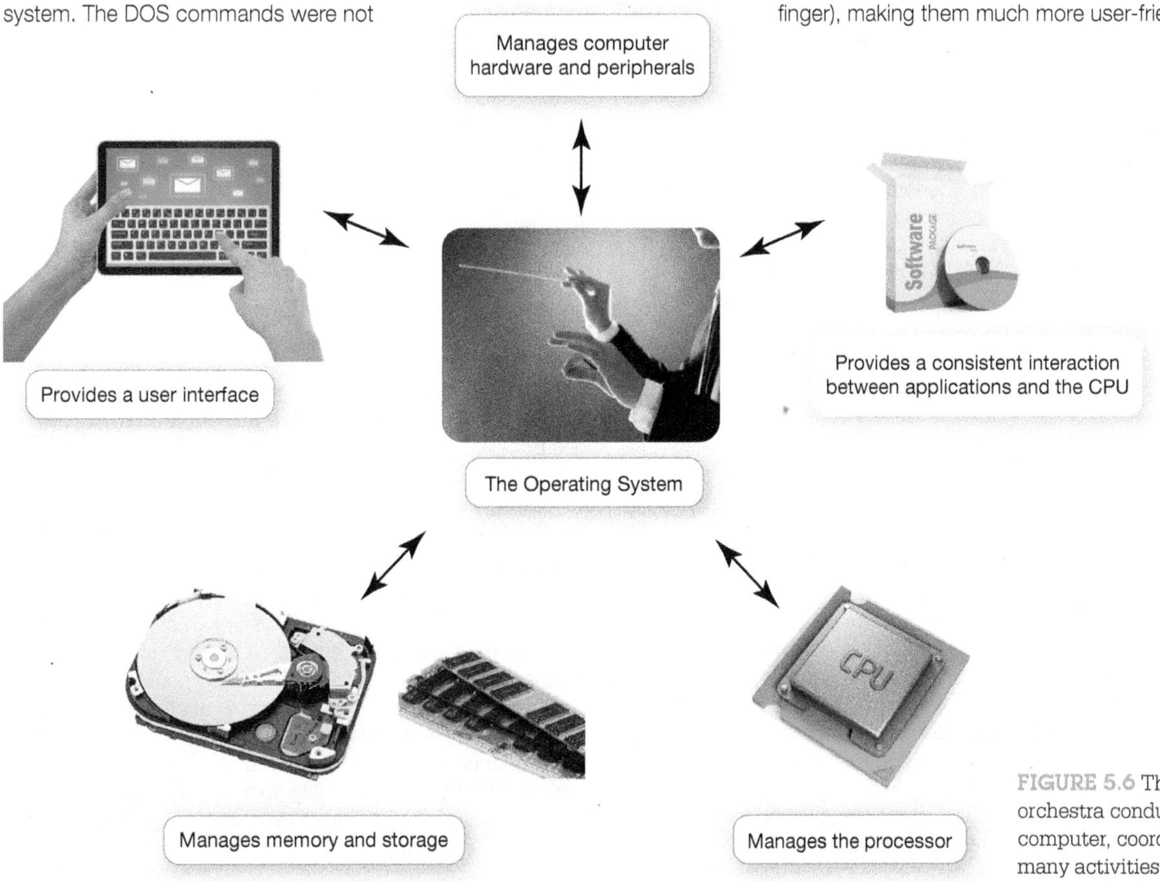

(StockPhotosArt/Shutterstock, Ra2studio/Shutterstock, Ragnarock/Shutterstock, Arno van Dulmen/Shutterstock, Shcherbakov Roman/Shutterstock)

FIGURE 5.6 The OS is the orchestra conductor of your computer, coordinating its many activities and devices.

a

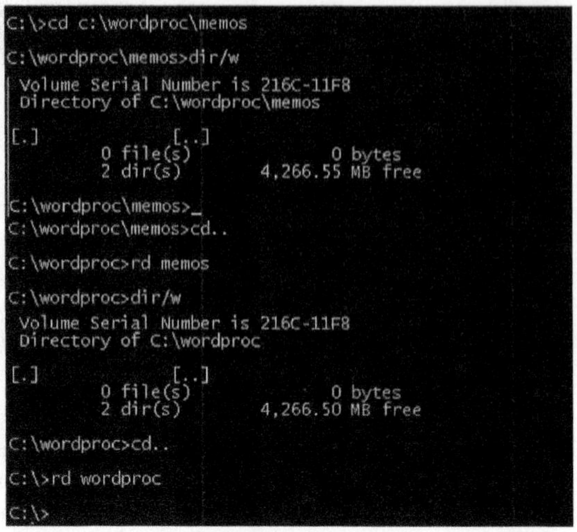

b

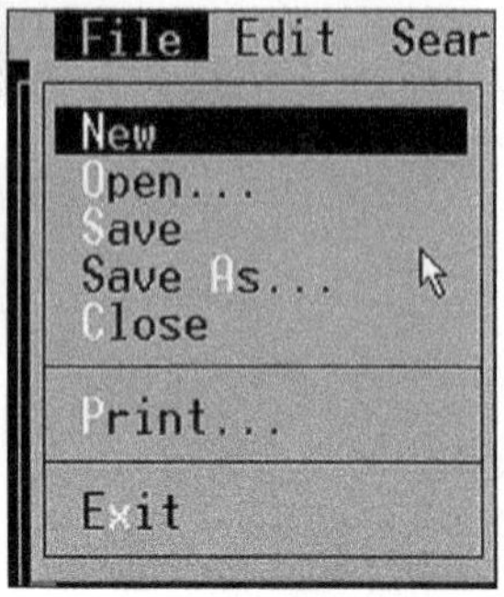

FIGURE 5.7 (a) A command-driven interface. (b) A menu-driven interface. *(Windows 8.1, Microsoft Corporation)*

Linux-based operating systems do not have a single default GUI interface. Instead, users are free to choose among many commercially available and free interfaces, such as GNOME and KDE, each of which provides a different look and feel.

Hardware Coordination

Objective 5.5 *Explain how the operating system helps manage hardware such as the processor, memory, storage, and peripheral devices.*

Why does the OS need to manage the processor? When you use your computer, you're usually asking the processor (also called the CPU) to perform several tasks at once. For example, you might be printing a Word document, chatting with your friends on Facebook, and watching a movie using the Blu-ray drive—all at the same time, or at least what appears to be at the same time. Although the CPU is powerful, it still needs the OS to arrange the execution of all these activities in a systematic way.

To do so, the OS assigns a slice of its time to each activity that requires the processor's attention. The OS must then switch among different processes billions of times a second to make it appear that everything is happening seamlessly. Otherwise, you wouldn't be able to watch a movie and print at the same time without experiencing delays in the process.

How exactly does the OS coordinate all the activities? When you create and print a document in Word while also watching a Blu-ray movie, for example, many different devices in the computer are involved, including your keyboard, mouse, Blu-ray drive, and printer. Every keystroke, every mouse click (or touch on the screen), and each signal to the printer and from the Blu-ray drive creates an action, or **event**, in the respective device (keyboard, mouse, Blu-ray drive, or printer) to which the OS responds.

Sometimes these events occur sequentially (such as when you type characters one at a time), but other events involve two or more devices working concurrently (such as the printer printing while you type and watch a movie). Although it looks as though all the devices are working at the same time, the OS in fact switches back and forth among processes, controlling the timing of events on which the processor works.

For example, assume you're typing and want to print a document. When you tell your computer to print your document, the printer generates a unique signal called an **interrupt** that tells the OS that it's in need of immediate attention. Every device has its own type of interrupt, which is associated with an **interrupt handler**, a special numerical code that prioritizes the requests. These requests are placed in the interrupt table in the computer's primary memory (RAM). The OS processes the task assigned a higher priority before processing a task assigned a lower priority. This is called **preemptive multitasking**.

In our example, when the OS receives the interrupt from the printer, it suspends the CPU's typing activity and Blu-ray activity and puts a "memo" in a special location in RAM called a *stack*. The memo is a reminder of what the CPU was doing before it started to work on the printer request. The CPU then retrieves the printer request from the interrupt table and begins to process it. On completion of the printer request, the CPU goes back to the stack, retrieves the memo it placed about the keystroke or Blu-ray activity, and returns to that task until it is interrupted again, in a very quick and seamless fashion, as shown in Figure 5.8.

What happens if more than one document is waiting to be printed? The OS also coordinates multiple activities for peripheral devices such as printers. When the processor receives a request to send information to the printer, it first checks with the OS to ensure that the printer is not already in use. If it is, the OS puts the request in another temporary storage area in RAM, called the *buffer*. The request then waits in the buffer until the **spooler**, a program that helps coordinate all print jobs currently being sent to the printer, indicates the printer is available. If more than one print job is waiting, a line (or *queue*) is formed so that the printer can process the requests in order.

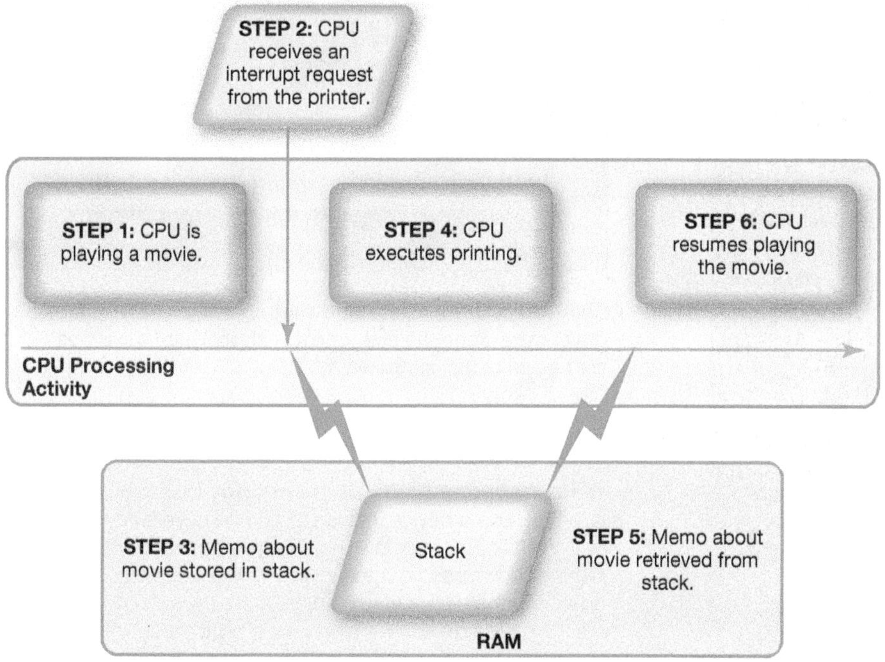

FIGURE 5.8 How Preemptive Multitasking Works

Memory and Storage Management

Why does the OS have to manage the computer's memory? As the OS coordinates the activities of the processor, it uses RAM as a temporary storage area for instructions and data the processor needs. The processor then accesses these instructions and data from RAM when it's ready to process them. The OS is, therefore, responsible for coordinating the space allocations in RAM to ensure there is enough space for all the pending instructions and data. The OS then clears the items from RAM when the processor no longer needs them.

Can my computer ever run out of RAM? RAM has limited capacity. Like most users, you will add new software and peripherals to your computer over time. Most computers sold for home use have between 4 and 16 GB of RAM. As you add and upgrade software and increase your usage of the computer system, you might find that the amount of RAM you have is no longer sufficient for your needs. If you have an older computer system with less RAM, it might be time to consider buying a new computer or adding more RAM.

What happens if my computer runs out of RAM? When there isn't enough RAM for the OS to store the required data and instructions, the OS borrows from the more spacious hard drive. This process of optimizing RAM storage by borrowing hard drive space is called **virtual memory**. As shown in Figure 5.9, when more RAM is needed, the OS swaps out from RAM the data or instructions that haven't recently been used and moves them to a temporary storage area on the hard drive called the **swap file** (or **page file**). If the data or instructions in the swap file are needed later, the OS swaps them back into active RAM and replaces them in the hard drive's swap file with less active data or instructions. This process of swapping is known as **paging**.

Can I ever run out of virtual memory? Only a portion of the hard drive is allocated to virtual memory. You can manually change this setting to increase the amount of hard drive space allocated, but eventually your computer will become sluggish as it is forced to page more often. This condition of excessive paging is called **thrashing**. The solution to this

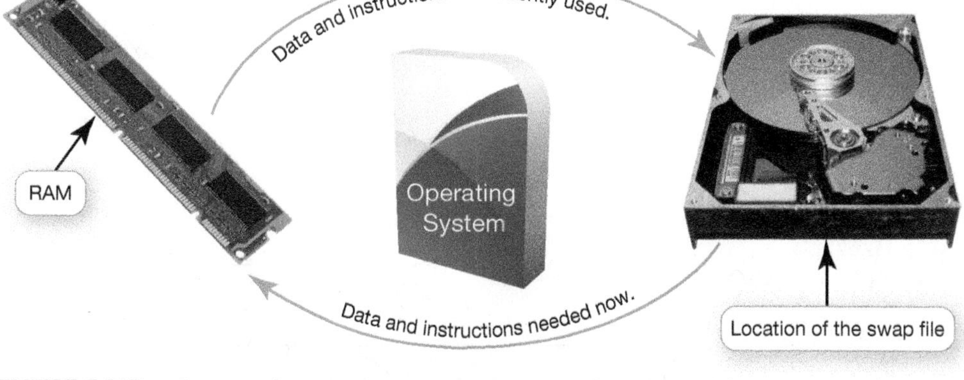

FIGURE 5.9 Virtual memory borrows excess storage capacity from the hard drive when there isn't enough capacity in RAM. *(Arno van Dulmen/Shutterstock, Ragnarock/Shutterstock)*

problem is to increase the amount of RAM in your computer, if there is excess capacity available, so that it won't be necessary for it to send data and instructions to virtual memory. If you cannot add additional RAM to your computer, then it may be time to get a new device.

How does the OS manage storage? If it weren't for the OS, the files and applications you save to the hard drive and other storage locations would be an unorganized mess. Fortunately, the OS has a file-management system that keeps track of the name and location of each file you save and the programs you install. We'll talk more about file management later in this chapter.

Hardware and Peripheral Device Management

How does the OS manage the hardware and peripheral devices? Each device attached to your computer comes with a special program called a **device driver** that facilitates communication between the device and the OS. Because the OS must be able to communicate with every device in the computer system, the device driver translates the device's specialized commands into commands the OS can understand, and vice versa. Devices wouldn't function without the proper device drivers because the OS wouldn't know how to communicate with them.

Do I always need to install drivers? Today, most devices, such as flash drives, mice, keyboards, and digital cameras, come with the driver already installed in Windows. The devices whose drivers are included in Windows are called Plug and Play devices. **Plug and Play (PnP)** is a software and hardware standard designed to facilitate the installation of new hardware in PCs by including in the OS the drivers these devices need in order to run. Because the OS includes this software, incorporating a new device into your computer system seems automatic. PnP lets you plug a new device

FIGURE 5.10 A Windows message showing a successful driver installation the first time an external hard drive was connected to the computer. *(Windows 8.1, Microsoft Corporation)*

into your computer, turn it on, and immediately play (use) the device (see Figure 5.10).

What happens if the device is not PnP? Sometimes you may have a device that is so new the drivers aren't yet available automatically in Windows. You'll then be prompted to install or download from the Internet the driver that was provided with the device. If you obtain a device secondhand without the device driver, or if you're required to update the device driver, you can often download the necessary driver from the manufacturer's website. You can also go to websites such as DriverZone (**driverzone.com**) to locate drivers.

Can I damage my system by installing a device driver? Occasionally, when you install a driver, your system may become unstable (that is, programs may stop responding, certain actions may cause a crash, or the device or the entire system may stop working). Although this is uncommon, it can happen. Fortunately, to remedy the problem, Windows has a Roll Back Driver feature that removes a newly installed driver and replaces it with the last one that worked (see Figure 5.11).

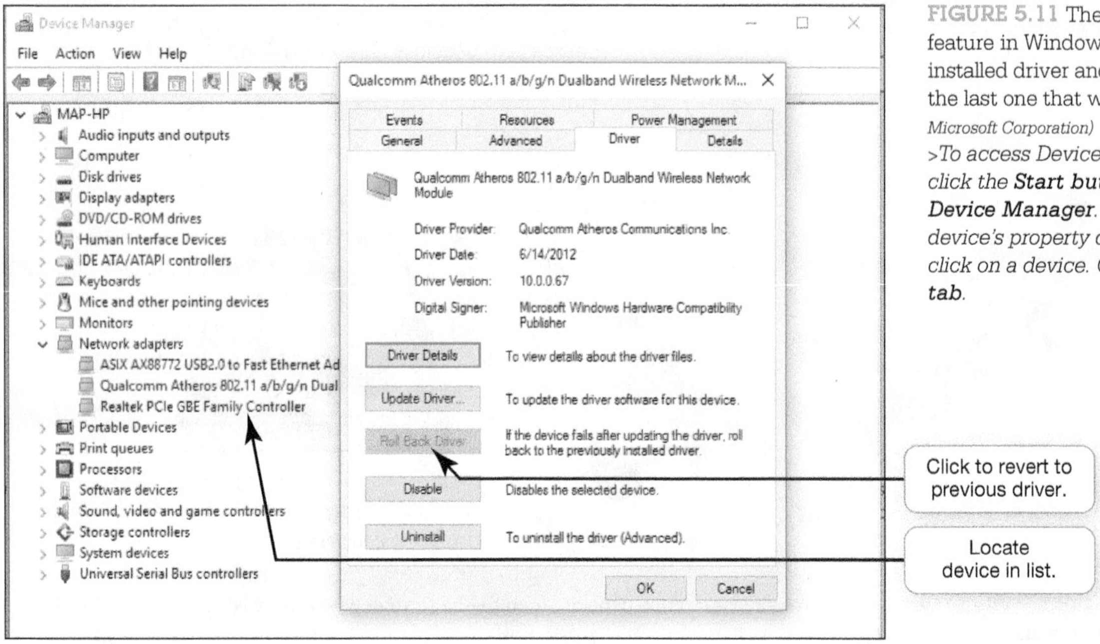

FIGURE 5.11 The Roll Back Driver feature in Windows removes a newly installed driver and replaces it with the last one that worked. *(Windows 8.1, Microsoft Corporation)*

*>To access Device Manager, right-click the **Start button** and select **Device Manager**. To display the device's property dialog box, double-click on a device. Click the **Driver tab**.*

ethics in IT

The Great Debate: Is Mac OS X Safer Than Windows?

Many Mac users feel they are impervious to viruses and malware (software that can disable or interfere with the use of a computing device) because those are "just Windows problems." This means that Mac users often run their computers with only the basic protection provided by Apple in its operating system software. Are Mac users wild risk takers, or are they actually safe from hackers? As with many issues, it's a little bit of both.

Threats Are Out There

Windows users have been bombarded by malware and virus attacks for decades. When you bought your last Windows device, it invariably came with a trial version of third-party antivirus/anti-malware software. Running a Windows computer without antivirus/anti-malware software is just asking for trouble.

However, over the past several years, the attacks against Macs have also increased. Why weren't Macs attacked frequently in the past? Most malware is designed to steal sensitive information such as credit card numbers. When thieves expend the time, money, and effort to develop malware, they want to ensure that it targets the largest population of potential victims. As OS X gains market share, Mac users are becoming a larger group of potential targets. In fact, in many affluent nations, Mac ownership has reached 20% of the market. And since Macs tend to cost more than Windows machines, it can be argued that Mac users may have more disposable income than other computer buyers. And wealthy people always make attractive targets for thieves.

But Isn't OS X Just Safer Than Windows by Design?

To a certain extent, this is true. OS X does have certain design features that tend to prevent the installation and spread of malware. Apple has also designed current versions of iOS and OS X to prevent the installation of unapproved software (i.e., software not available on Apple's approved online outlets like the App Store). In addition, apps sold on the App Store are required to be designed using the access control technology known as *App Sandbox*.

When most software programs or apps are running, they have broad latitude to interact with the OS. Usually, they have all the rights that the user has over the OS. So if hackers can design an exploit that takes advantage of a security flaw in an app, they can potentially gain extensive control over the computer using the access that the user has to the OS. As noted, Apple requires all approved apps to be "sandboxed." When an app is sandboxed, the developer defines what the app needs to do in order to interact with the OS. The OS then grants only those specific rights and privileges to the app and nothing else. By doing this, it severely limits what hackers can do in an OS if they breach the security of an app. It's like being in a high-walled sandbox (or playpen) as a child. You can play within the confines of your space, but you can't make mischief outside certain limits.

So I'll Buy a Mac and Be Safe Forever, Right?

Alas, it's not that simple. Although it's more difficult to design exploits for OS X and iOS, it's not impossible. And a great deal of cybercrime relies on social engineering techniques like those used in scareware scams. *Scareware* is software designed to make it seem as if there is something wrong with your computer. The author of the scareware program then "persuades" you to buy a solution to the problem, acquiring your credit card number in the process. Scareware victims can be both Mac and PC users, so even if you own a Mac, you need to be aware of such scams and avoid falling prey to them (see Chapter 9).

The Solution: Extra Security Precautions

The current versions of OS X, iOS, and Windows all include some level of security tools and precautions. But there are a few things you should do to protect yourself:

1. **Make sure your software is set to download and install updates automatically.** As OS developers discover holes in their software's security, they provide updates to repair these problems.
2. **Use third-party antivirus/anti-malware software (even on a Mac).** Although no product will detect 100% of malware, detecting some is better than detecting none.
3. **Be aware of social engineering techniques.** Use vigilance when surfing the Internet so you don't fall prey to scams.

So, no OS is 100% safe. But if you're informed and proceed with caution, you can avoid a lot of schemes perpetrated by hackers and thieves.

Software Application Coordination

Objective 5.6 Explain how the operating system interacts with application software.

How does the OS help application software run on the computer? Every computer program, no matter what its type or manufacturer, needs to interact with the CPU using computer code. For programs to work with the CPU, they must contain code the CPU recognizes. Rather than having the same blocks of code for similar procedures in each program, the OS includes the blocks of code—each called an **application programming interface (API)**—that application software needs in order to interact with the CPU. Microsoft DirectX, for example, is a group of multimedia APIs built into the Windows OS that improves graphics and sounds when you're playing games or watching videos on your PC.

What are the advantages of using APIs? To create applications that can communicate with the OS, software programmers need only refer to the API code blocks when they write an application. They don't need to include the entire code sequence. APIs not only prevent redundancies in software code, they make it easier for software developers to respond to changes in the OS. Software companies also take advantage of APIs to make applications in software suites (such as Microsoft Office) that have a similar interface and functionality. And since these applications share common APIs, data exchange is facilitated between two programs, such as inserting a chart from Excel into a Word document. ■

starting YOUR COMPUTER

Many things happen quickly between the time you turn on your computer and the time it's ready for you to start using it. As we discussed earlier, all data and instructions, including the OS, are stored in RAM while your computer is on. When you turn off your computer, RAM is wiped clean of all its data, including the OS. How does the computer know what to do when you turn it on if there is nothing in RAM? It runs through a special start-up process to load the OS into RAM.

The Boot Process

Objective 5.7 *Discuss the process the operating system uses to start up the computer and how errors in the boot process are handled.*

What are the steps involved in the boot process? As illustrated in Figure 5.12, the **boot process** consists of four basic steps. The term *boot*, from *bootstrap loader* (a small program used to start a larger program), alludes to the straps of leather, called *bootstraps*, that people used to use to help them pull on their boots. This is also the source of the expression "pull yourself up by your bootstraps." Let's look at each step of the boot process in detail.

Step 1: Activating BIOS

What's the first thing that happens after I turn on my computer? In the first step of the boot process, the CPU activates the **basic input/output system (BIOS)**. BIOS is a program that manages the exchange of data between the OS and all the input and output devices attached to the system. BIOS is also responsible for loading the OS into RAM from its permanent location on the hard drive. BIOS itself is stored on a read-only memory (ROM) chip on the motherboard. Unlike data stored in RAM, data stored in ROM is permanent and is not erased when the power is turned off.

Step 2: Performing the Power-On Self-Test

How does the computer determine whether the hardware is working properly? The first job BIOS performs is to ensure that essential peripheral devices are attached and operational—a process called the **power-on self-test (POST)**. The BIOS compares the results of the POST with the various hardware configurations permanently stored in CMOS (pronounced "see-moss"). CMOS, which stands for *complementary metal-oxide semiconductor*, is a special kind of memory that uses almost no power. A small battery provides enough power so that the CMOS contents won't be lost after the computer is turned off. CMOS contains information about the system's memory, types of disk drives, and other essential input and output hardware components. If the results of the POST compare favorably with the hardware configurations stored in CMOS, the boot process continues.

Step 3: Loading the OS

How does the OS get loaded into RAM? Next, BIOS goes through a preconfigured list of devices in its search for the drive that contains the **system files**, the main files of the OS. When it is located, the OS loads into RAM from its permanent storage location on the hard drive.

Once the system files are loaded into RAM, the **kernel** (or **supervisor program**) is loaded. The kernel is the essential component of the OS. It's responsible for managing the processor and all other components of the computer system. Because it stays in RAM the entire time your computer is powered on, the kernel is said to be *memory resident*. Other,

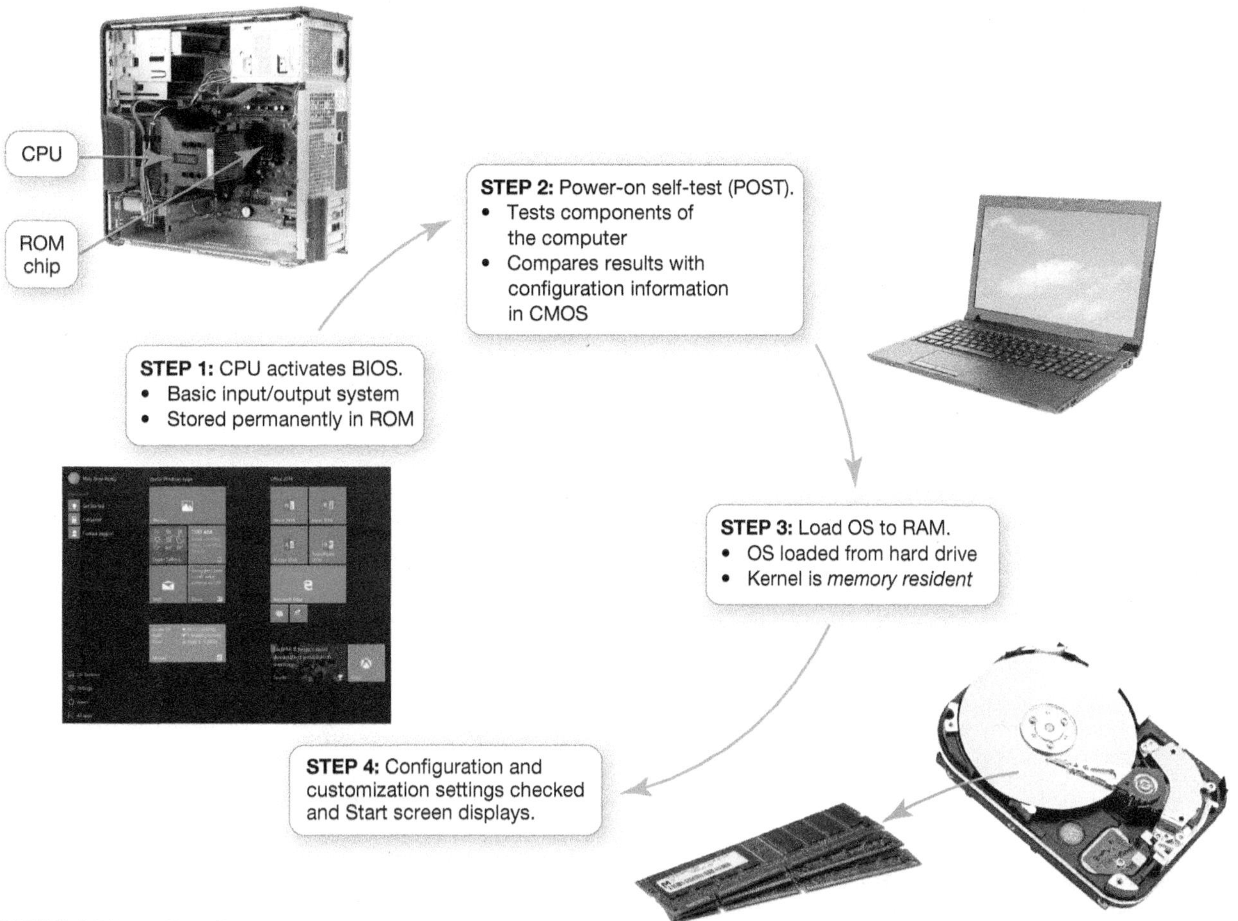

FIGURE 5.12 The Boot Process *(Arno van Dulmen/Shutterstock, Ragnarock/Shutterstock)*

less critical, parts of the OS stay on the hard drive and are copied over to RAM on an as-needed basis so that RAM is managed more efficiently. These programs are referred to as *nonresident*. Once the kernel is loaded, the OS takes over control of the computer's functions.

Step 4: Checking Further Configurations and Customizations

Is that it? Finally, the OS checks the registry for the configuration of other system components. The **registry** contains all the different configurations (settings) used by the OS and by other applications. It contains the customized settings you put into place, such as mouse speed, as well as instructions as to which programs should be loaded first.

Why do I sometimes need to enter a login name and password at the end of the boot process? The verification of your login name and password is called **authentication**. The authentication process blocks unauthorized users from entering the system. You may have your home computer set up for authentication, especially if you have multiple users accessing it. All large networked environments, like your college, require user authentication for access.

On a Windows 10 computer, after your computer has completely booted up, you are brought to the Lock Screen where you are to log into your **Microsoft account**. Your Microsoft account is a combination of an e-mail address and a password. Because configuration settings are stored online and associated with a particular Microsoft account, it is easy for multiple people to share any Windows 10 computer and have access to their individual settings and preferences.

How do I know if the boot process is successful? The entire boot process takes only a few minutes to complete. If the entire system is checked out and loaded properly, the

> **ACTIVE HELPDESK**
> **Starting the Computer: The Boot Process**
>
> In this Active Helpdesk, you'll play the role of a helpdesk staffer, fielding questions about how the operating system helps the computer start up.

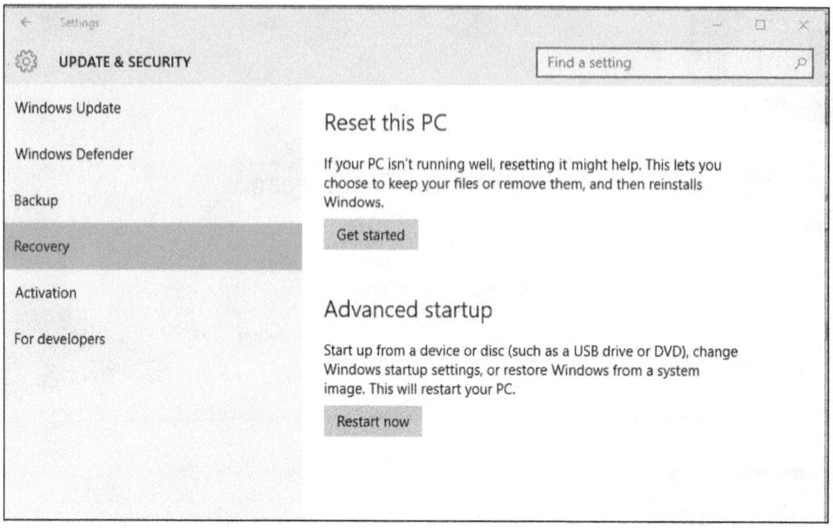

FIGURE 5.13 The recovery control in Windows 10 provides access to Reset this PC option.
(Windows 10, Microsoft Corporation)
>*To access the Recovery control, from the Start menu, click* ***Settings****, then click* ***Update & security****. On the Update & security screen, select* ***Recovery****.*

process completes by displaying the lock screen. After logging in, the computer system is now ready to accept your first command.

Handling Errors in the Boot Process

What should I do if my computer doesn't boot properly? Sometimes problems occur during the boot process. Here are some suggestions for solving a boot problem:

- If you've recently installed new software or hardware, try uninstalling it. (Make sure you uninstall through *Apps & features* in System Settings to remove the software.) If the problem no longer occurs when rebooting, you can reinstall the device or software.
- Try accessing the Windows Advanced Options Menu (accessible by pressing the F8 key during the boot process). If Windows detects a problem in the boot process, it will add Last Known Good Configuration to the Windows Advanced Options Menu. Every time your computer boots successfully, a configuration of the boot process is saved. When you choose to boot with the Last Known Good Configuration, the OS starts your computer by using the registry information that was saved during the last shut down.
- Try resetting your computer (in Update & Security Settings).

What happens when a PC is "reset"? Sometimes Windows does not boot properly or the system does not respond properly. You may even see messages related to "fatal exceptions." **Reset this PC** is a utility program in Windows 10 that attempts to diagnose and fix errors in your Windows system files that are causing your computer to behave improperly (see Figure 5.13). When a PC is reset, the following occurs:

- Your data files (documents, music, videos, etc.) and personalization settings are not removed or changed.
- Apps that you have downloaded from the Windows Store are kept intact.
- Apps that you have downloaded from the Internet or installed from DVDs will be removed from your PC. Therefore, you'll need to reinstall them after the reset.

It's recommended that you back up your PC prior to resetting it as a precautionary measure. Finally, if all other attempts to fix your computer fail, try *Go back to an earlier build* to revert to a past configuration. System Recovery is covered in more detail later in this chapter.

What should I do if my keyboard or another device doesn't work after I boot my computer? Sometimes during the boot process, BIOS skips a device (such as a keyboard) or improperly identifies it. Your only indication that this problem has occurred is that the device won't respond after the system has been booted. When that happens, try restarting the computer. If the problem persists, check the OS's website for any patches (or software fixes) that may resolve the issue. If there are no patches or the problem persists, you may want to try to update the device driver or get technical assistance. ■

Before moving on to Part 2:

1. **Watch Replay Video 5.1.**
2. **Then check your understanding of what you've learned so far.**

check your understanding // review & practice

For a quick review to see what you've learned so far, answer the following questions.

multiple choice

1. Which is NOT an example of a mobile operating system?
   - **a.** iOS
   - **b.** OS X
   - **c.** Android
   - **d.** Windows 10
2. You are most likely to find an RTOS
   - **a.** in a robotic camera.
   - **b.** on a supercomputer.
   - **c.** on a mainframe.
   - **d.** on an iPad.
3. The blocks of code that application software needs to interact with the CPU is called
   - **a.** Automatic Programming Interface.
   - **b.** Automatic Program Instruction.
   - **c.** Application Programming Interface.
   - **d.** Application Program Instruction.
4. Operating systems that have windows and icons have what type of user interface?
   - **a.** command-driven
   - **b.** graphical user
   - **c.** menu-driven
   - **d.** magnetic tape–based
5. The OS can optimize RAM storage by using
   - **a.** thrashing.
   - **b.** virtual memory.
   - **c.** an interrupt handler.
   - **d.** a spooler.

MyITLab Go to **MyITLab** to take an autograded version of the *Check Your Understanding* review and to find all media resources for the chapter.

TECHBYTES WEEKLY
Stay current with the TechBytes Weekly Newsletter.

Continue

TRY THIS Using Virtual Desktops in Windows 10

Virtual desktops are a great way to organize your working space into different displays when you're multitasking between projects, job and school, or just work and entertainment. This exercise will walk you through the process of organizing your files into virtual desktops.

Step 1 Click **Task View** on the Task bar to bring up the Task View interface. This interface consists of a display area that shows large thumbnails of all the open windows running on your system. If you haven't created any virtual desktops, this is all you'll see. Task View is also a way to switch between open windows: You can make active any window by clicking on the desired thumbnail. This is similar to what you would see if you used Alt+Tab to cycle through all open windows. *(Windows 10, Microsoft Corporation)*

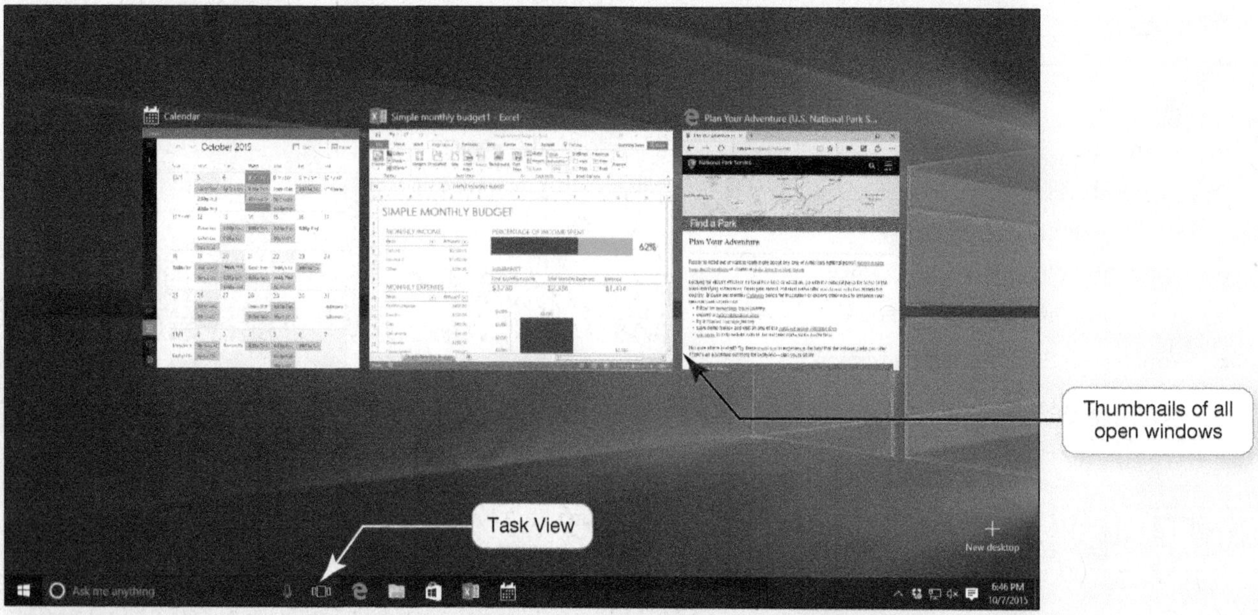

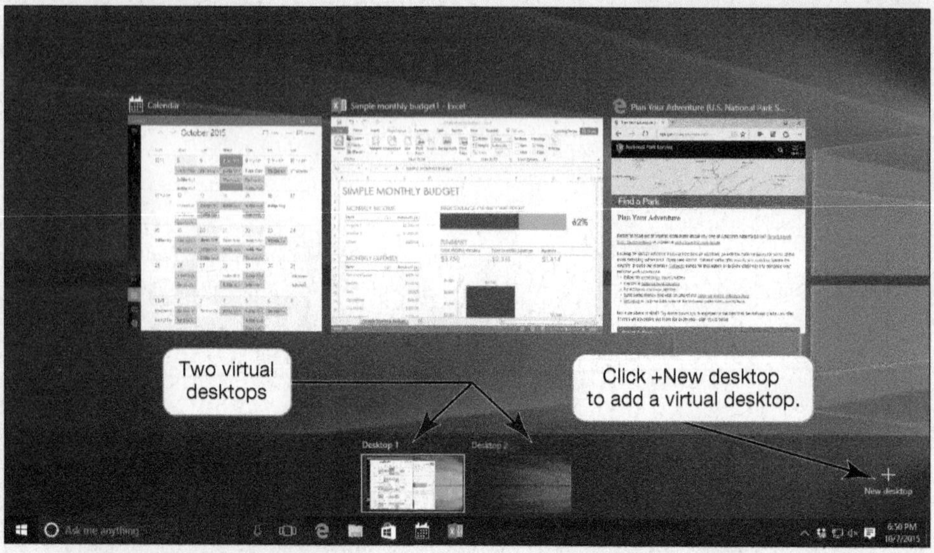

Step 2 In order to organize your open windows into specific groups, you need to create virtual desktops. To create virtual desktops, while in Task View, click **+New desktop** in the lower right corner. This adds another virtual desktop, Desktop 2. When you click **Task View** again, all your open windows display in Desktop 1, and Desktop 2 is empty. *(Windows 10, Microsoft Corporation)*

Step 3 To move programs from Desktop 1 to the newly created Desktop 2, click **Task View**, then click and drag the window you want to move to Desktop 2. Alternatively, you can right-click the window you want to move, select **Move to**, and then select **Desktop 2**. While in Task View, when you hover the mouse over the desktop thumbnail, all open windows in that desktop display. *(Windows 10, Microsoft Corporation)*

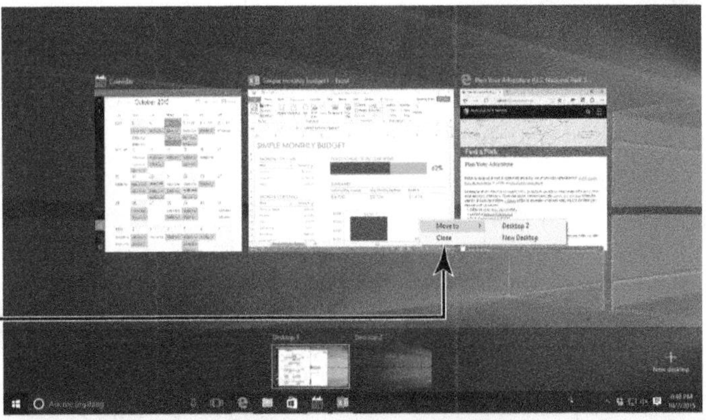

Step 4 To move between desktops, press the **Windows key+Tab**, or open Task View and click on the desired desktop to switch. To delete desktops, click **Task View**, point to the thumbnail of the desktop you want to delete, and then click the **(X)** that displays above the desktop thumbnail. *(Windows 10, Microsoft Corporation)*

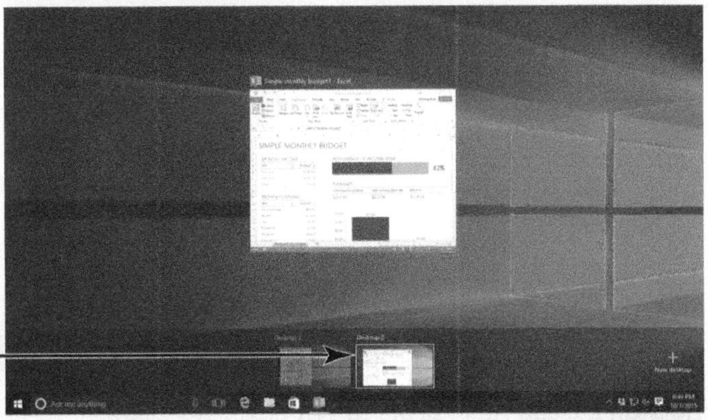

Make This TOOL: App Inventor 2

MAKE: A Notification Alert

Does your app need to communicate with or provide feedback to the user? With the Notifier component of **App Inventor**, you can make your program generate message boxes or ask for a response from the user.

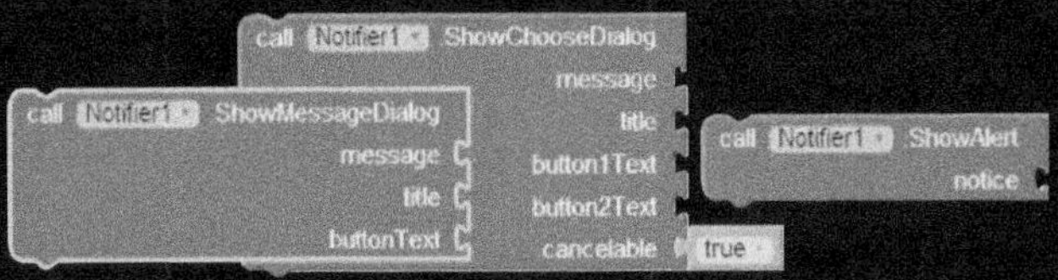

In this exercise, you'll use the Notifier component of **App Inventor** to show a message box, post a user choice with two buttons for response, or post an alert. Your apps can now use more of the features of the Android operating system to communicate! *(MIT App Inventor 2, Massachusetts Institute of Technology. Creative Commons Attribution-ShareAlike 3.0 Unported License)*

The Notifier component allows you to communicate with alerts, message boxes, and text choice popups within your mobile app.

For the instructions for this exercise, go to MyITLab.

Using System Software

Learning Outcome 5.2 You will be able to describe how system software is used, including managing the user interface, file management, and utility programs.

Now that you know how system software works, let's explore how specific operating systems and their tools function.

the windows INTERFACE

As noted earlier, one of the functions of the operating system is to provide a *user interface* that lets you communicate with your computer. As was explained earlier, today's operating systems use a graphical user interface. We describe the Windows 10 user interface in this section, but it is very similar to the user interfaces for the OS X and Linus operating systems.

Using Windows 10

Objective 5.8 *Describe the main features of the Windows interface.*

How do I accomplish tasks in Windows 10? Starting with Windows 8, and now with Windows 10, the Windows operating system is designed to run on multiple devices: desktops, laptops, tablets, and phones, including those devices with touch screens. To enable Windows 10 to function on all types of devices and displays, there are often three different ways to accomplish tasks:

1. Using a mouse
2. Touching the screen (on touch-enabled devices)
3. Using keystrokes

Which method you use depends on the type of device you're using and, to a large extent, on your personal preferences.

What are the main features of the Windows 10 desktop? After logging into your Microsoft account by entering or confirming your e-mail address and entering a password, you're brought to the primary working area: the **desktop**. The Windows 10 desktop still has features like the **taskbar**, which displays open and favorite applications for easy access. You can point to an icon to preview windows of open files or programs, or move your mouse over a thumbnail to preview a full-screen image. You can also right-click an icon to view a Jump List—the most recently or commonly used files or commands for that application.

Opening into the desktop is a modification from the Windows 8 experience, in which you were initially brought into the Start screen and then had to switch to the desktop. In Windows 10, you display the **Start menu** by clicking the Windows icon (or Start button) on the lower left corner of the screen or by pressing the Windows key on the keyboard. The Windows 10 Start menu provides you with access to all your applications in one convenient screen. We'll discuss personalizing the Start menu later in this section.

What are the main features of the Windows 10 Start menu? The Start menu is divided into two sections (see Figure 5.14a). The right side has the block tiles introduced with Windows 8. The tiles represent installed

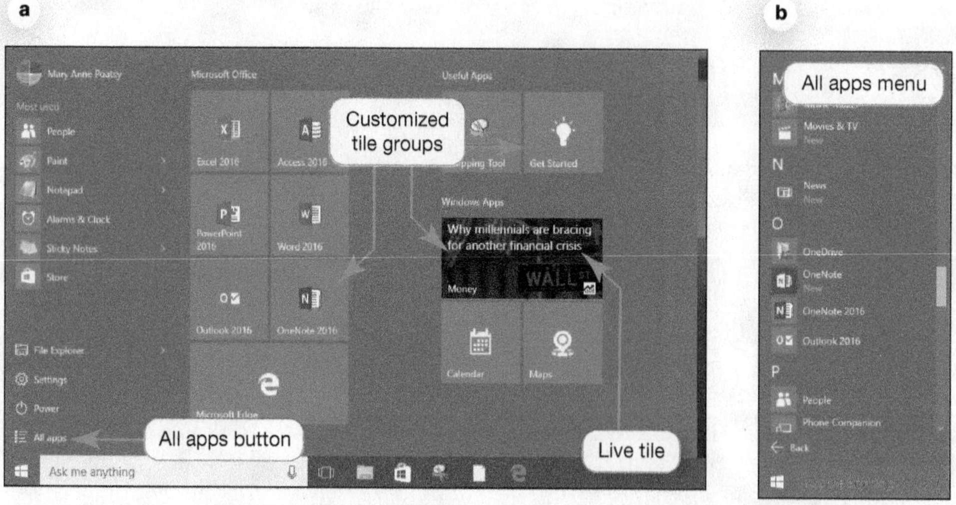

FIGURE 5.14 (a) The Windows 10 Start menu provides access to your most used programs and apps. (b) Click All apps to display an alphabetical listing of all installed programs and apps.
(Windows 10, Microsoft Corporation)

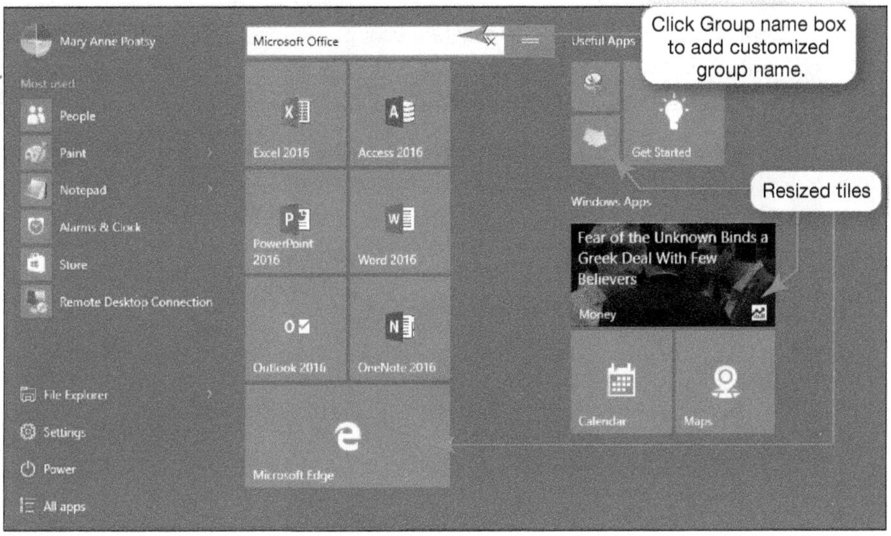

FIGURE 5.15 You can customize the Windows 10 Start menu by adding, resizing, and grouping tiles of your favorite programs and apps.
(Windows 10, Microsoft Corporation)

software and Windows apps (such as Weather, Skype, and Money). In addition to programs, tiles can represent files and folders. If there are more tiles on the Start menu than displayed, a scroll bar becomes available. The left side of the Start menu provides access to *Most used* programs as well as to File Explorer, Settings, Power, and All apps. When you click All apps, the left side changes to display a list of all the installed apps and programs on your computer (see Figure 5.14b).

How can I add programs to the Start menu? The most useful feature of the Start menu is that it lets you customize it to meet your needs (see Figure 5.15). It is easy to add, remove, resize, move, and group application tiles on the Start menu. You can choose which applications are visible on the Start menu through a process called **pinning**. Just right-click any application in the All apps list or in the Most Used list, and chose Pin to Start.

Once on the Start menu, a tile can be resized by right-clicking the tile, pointing to Resize, and then selecting the desired size. Most apps can be sized to Small, Medium, Wide, and Large, although some are limited to only Small or Medium. You can rearrange apps on the Start menu by dragging them. You can also arrange several tiles near each other to create a group. Point to the top of the group to display a name box where you can type a group name. If there is a tile on the Start menu you don't need, just right-click it (or touch and hold), and select Unpin from Start.

Because of the potential for customization, the Start menu on your computer may be different from the Start menu on your friend's computer. And because your Windows 10 settings and preferences are saved in your Microsoft account, when you log on to any Windows 10 computer, you'll see your own personal settings, preferences, and applications reflected on the Start menu.

How can I change the appearance of my Start menu and desktop? You can personalize the desktop, Start menu, and lock screen (the screen where you enter a password to resume using your computer) to suit your tastes. You'll find Personalization settings in Settings. For example, you can choose to have a picture, a slide show, or a single color display on the desktop and lock screen. You can also determine whether you'd like other information to display on the lock screen, such as the weather, time, or your e-mail or calendar. Choosing a theme sets a color and font scheme for your entire system. You can also determine which folders display on the left side of the Start menu. The default is File Explorer and Settings, but there are others to choose from, including Music, Pictures, or Documents.

How can I see more than one window on my screen at a time? Windows 7 introduced "snapping" windows: fixing open programs into place on either the left or right

BITS&BYTES

The Snipping Tool

The Snipping Tool is a Windows tool found in the Windows Accessories Folder in All apps that enables you to capture, or snip, a screen display so that you can save, annotate, or share it. You can capture screen elements as a rectangular, free-form window or as a full-screen snip. You can also draw on or annotate the screen capture, save it, or send it to others. In Windows 10, a new feature to the Snipping Tool is a delay timer so you can pause the capturing process for up to five seconds to set up screenshots of dialog boxes, menus, or other features that don't stay displayed when you initiate the Snipping Tool.

side of the screen, to easily display two apps at the same time. Windows 10 goes a bit further with more snapping options. Once you snap a window into place, thumbnails of all the other windows display. Clicking any thumbnail will snap that window into place. You can also snap windows to the corners, thus having up to four windows displayed at the same time.

How can I see open windows and quickly move between them? A new feature on the Windows 10 taskbar is Task View, which allows you to view all the tasks you're working on in one glance. For example, you might have a Word document, a web browser, and a PowerPoint presentation all open as you pull together a presentation that is required from a research paper you wrote for your business class, and a Word document and an Excel spreadsheet for a project you're working on for your job. To see all documents at once, click Task View on the taskbar.

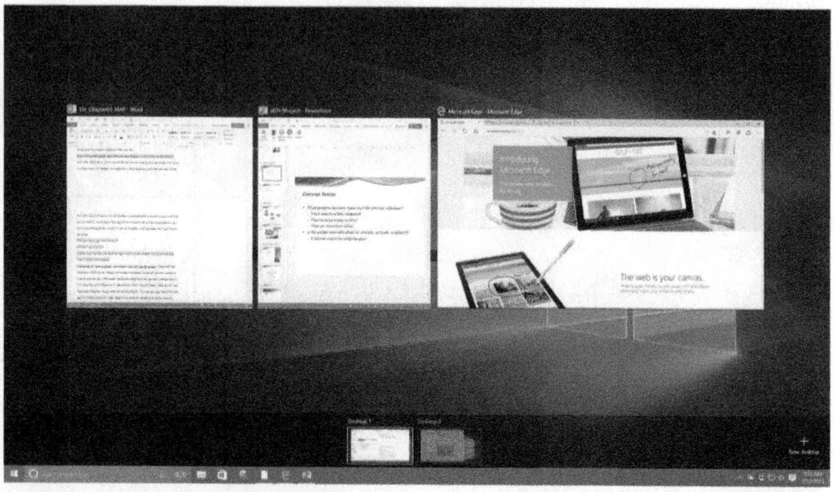

FIGURE 5.16 Virtual Desktops enable you to organize your open files into separate working spaces. *(Windows 10, Microsoft Corporation)*

Can I group my open programs and windows into task-specific groups? When faced with situations in which you're working with multiple documents for multiple projects, it might be easier to group the sets of documents together for each project and just switch between projects. You can do that now in Windows 10 with a feature called **virtual desktops**, which allow you to organize groups of windows into different displays (see Figure 5.16). There is no limit as to the number of desktops you can create. You can see all virtual desktops by clicking Task View. For more information on how to work with virtual desktops in Windows 10, see the Try This on pp. 176–177.

Mac and Linux User Interfaces

How does the Mac user interface compare with Windows 10? Although the OS X and the Windows operating systems aren't compatible, they're extremely similar in terms of functionality. For example, as is the case with Windows, OS X programs appear in resizable windows and use menus and icons. However, instead of the Start menu, OS X features a Dock with icons on the bottom for your most popular programs (see Figure 5.17). Although Windows 10 will be deployed on all types of devices, as noted earlier, Apple runs two separate operating systems: OS X for desktops and laptops and iOS for the iPhone and iPad. However, the latest version of OS X, El Capitan, and its predecessor Yosemite, feature tight integration between OS X and portable devices running iOS. Apple wants to

FIGURE 5.17 OS X El Capitan is Apple's latest operating system for desktop and laptop computers. *(Aleksey Boldin/Alamy)*

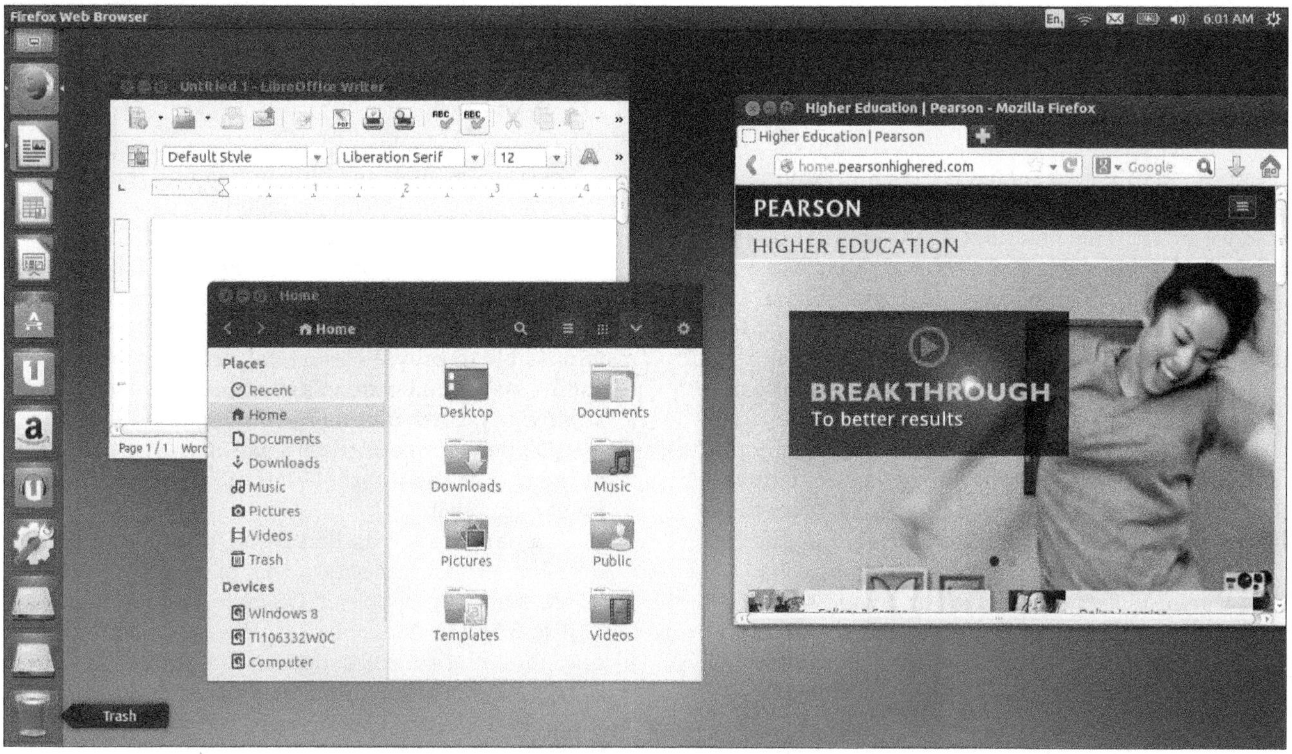

FIGURE 5.18 The Ubuntu Linux user interface resembles the Windows desktop. *(Ubuntu is a trademark of Canonical Limited and is used with the permission of Canonical Limited. Pearson is not endorsed by or affiliated with Canonical Limited or the Ubuntu project.)*

make transferring data and tasks from one device to another seamless.

Is a Linux user interface similar to OS X and Windows? Different distros of Linux feature different user interfaces. But most of them, like Ubuntu (see Figure 5.18), are based on familiar Windows and OS X paradigms, such as using icons to launch programs and having apps run in a window environment. ■

file MANAGEMENT

So far we've discussed how the OS manages the processor, memory, storage, and devices, and how it provides a way for applications and users to interact with the computer. An additional function of the OS is to enable **file management**, which provides an organizational structure to your computer's contents. In this section, we discuss how you can use this organizational structure to make your computer more organized and efficient.

Organizing Your Files

Objective 5.9 *Summarize how the operating system helps keep your computer organized.*

How does the OS organize files? Windows organizes the contents of your computer in a hierarchical **directory** structure composed of *drives*, *libraries*, *folders*, *subfolders*, and *files*. The hard drive, represented as the C: drive, is where

trends in IT

Open Source Software: Why Isn't Everyone Using Linux?

Proprietary software such as Microsoft Windows and Apple's OS X is developed by corporations and sold for profit. This means that the source code, the actual lines of instructional code that make the program work, is not accessible to the general public. Without being able to access the source code, it's difficult for a user to modify the software or see exactly how the program author constructed various parts of the OS.

Restricting access to the source code protects companies from having their programming ideas stolen, and it prevents customers from using modified versions of the software. However, in the late 1980s, computer specialists became concerned that the large software companies were controlling a large portion of market share and driving out competitors. They also felt that proprietary software was too expensive and contained too many bugs.

These people felt that software should be developed without a profit motive and distributed with its source code free for all to see. The theory was that if many computer specialists examined, improved, and changed the source code, a more full-featured, bug-free product would result. Hence, the open source movement was born, and Linux evolved as an open source operating system.

So, if an OS such as Linux is free and relatively bug-free, why does Windows, which users must pay for, have such a huge market share? One reason is that corporations and individuals have grown accustomed to one thing that proprietary software makers can provide: technical support. It's almost impossible to provide technical support for open source software because anyone can freely modify it. Similarly, corporations have been reluctant to install open source software extensively because of the cost of the internal staff of programmers that must support it.

Companies such as Red Hat, Ubuntu, and Xandros have been combating this problem. Red Hat offers a free, open source OS called Fedora (see Figure 5.19). In addition, Red Hat has modified the original Linux source code and markets a version, Red Hat Enterprise Linux, as a proprietary program. Fedora is the testing ground for what eventually goes into this proprietary program. Red Hat Enterprise Linux comes in versions for servers and desktops. Purchasers of Red Hat Enterprise Linux receive a warranty and technical support. Packaging open source software in this manner has made its use much more attractive to businesses. As a result, many web servers are hosted on computers running Linux.

FIGURE 5.19 Companies like Red Hat provide free or low-cost Linux software, such as Fedora, but technical support is often not available (or not free).
(AP Images)

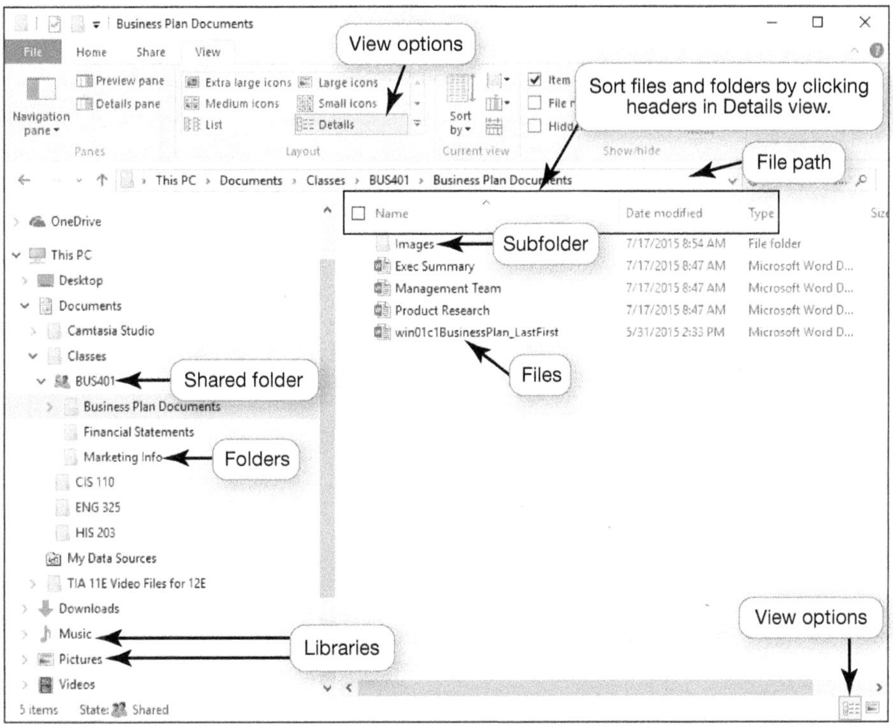

FIGURE 5.20 File Explorer lets you see the contents of your computer.
(Windows 10, Microsoft Corporation)
>*Click* ***File Explorer*** *from the Start menu or from the taskbar.*

contents of your computer. It shows the location and contents of every drive, folder, and file. As illustrated in Figure 5.20, File Explorer is divided into two panes or sections:

1. The *Navigation pane* on the left shows the contents of your computer. It displays commonly accessed areas, organized by Favorites and Libraries (Documents, Music, Pictures, and Videos).
2. When you select a folder, drive, or library from the Navigation pane, the contents of that particular area are displayed in the *File list* on the right.

For those folders that have been shared with others using an online storage system such as OneDrive or Dropbox, there is a new feature in Windows 10 that displays a shared icon instead of the traditional yellow folder icon.

When you save a file for the first time, you give the file a name and designate where you want to save it. For easy reference, the OS includes libraries where files are saved unless you specify otherwise. In Windows, the default libraries are Documents for files, Music for audio files, Pictures for graphics files, and Videos for video files.

You can determine the location of a file by its **file path**. The file path starts with the drive in which the file is located and includes all folders, subfolders (if any), the file name, and the extension. For example, if you were saving a picture of Andrew Carnegie for a term paper for a U.S. History course, the file path might be C:\Documents\HIS182\Term Paper\Illustrations\ACarnegie.jpg.

As shown in Figure 5.21, "C:" is the drive on which the file is stored (in this case, the hard drive), and "Documents" is the file's primary folder. "HIS182," "Term Paper," and "Illustrations" are successive subfolders within the "Documents" main folder. Last comes the file name, "ACarnegie," separated from the file extension (in this case, "jpg") by a period. The backslash character (\), used by Windows, is referred to as a **path separator**. OS X files use a colon (:), whereas UNIX and Linux files use the forward slash (/) as the path separator.

you permanently store most of your files. Each additional storage drive, such as optical drive, flash drive, or external hard drive, is given a unique letter (*D*, *E*, *F*, and so on). The C: drive is like a large filing cabinet in which all files are stored. As such, the C: drive is the top of the filing structure of your computer and is referred to as the **root directory**. All other folders and files are organized within the root directory. There are areas in the root directory that the OS has filled with files and folders holding special OS files. The programs within these files help run the computer and generally shouldn't be accessed. Sometimes the manufacturer will store files used to reinstate your computer back to the original factory state. Those files should not be accessed unless necessary.

What exactly are files, folders, and libraries? In an OS, a **file** is a collection of program instructions or data that is stored and treated as a single unit. Files can be generated from an application such as a Word document or an Excel workbook. In addition, files can represent an entire application, a web page, a set of sounds, an image, or a video. Files can be stored on the hard drive, a flash drive, online, or on any other permanent storage medium. As the number of files you save increases, it becomes more important to keep them organized in folders and libraries. A **folder** is a collection of files.

How can I easily locate and see the contents of my computer? In Windows, **File Explorer** is the main tool for finding, viewing, and managing the

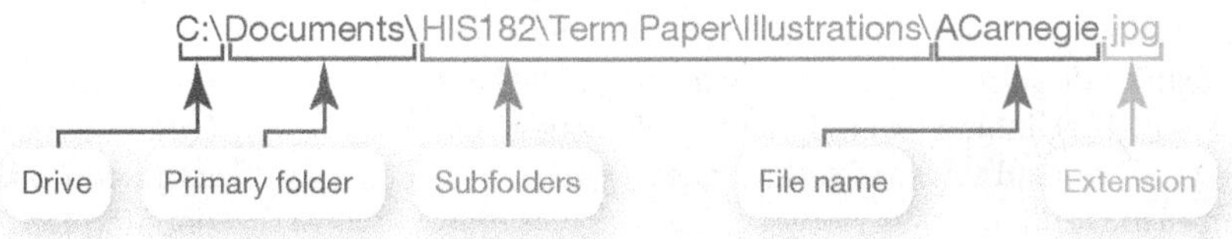

FIGURE 5.21 Understanding File Paths

Working with Files and Folders

Objective 5.10 *Summarize how to view, sort, name, and manage files and folders.*

Are there different ways I can view and sort my files and folders? Clicking on the View tab in File Explorer offers you different ways to view the folders and files.

1. *Details view:* This is the most interactive view. As shown in Figure 5.20 on the previous page, files and folders are displayed in list form, and the additional file information is displayed in columns alongside the name of the file. You can sort and display the contents of the folder by any of the column headings, so you can sort the contents alphabetically by name or type or hierarchically by date last modified or file size. Right-click the column heading area to modify the display of columns.
2. *Icons view:* There are a number of icon views that display files and folders in sizes ranging from small to extra-large. In most icon views, the folders are displayed as *Live Icons*. Live Icons allow you to preview the actual contents of a specific folder without opening the folder. As shown in Figure 5.22, Large Icons view is the best view to use if your folder contains picture files because you can see a bit of the actual images peeking out of the folder. It's also good to use if your folder contains PowerPoint presentations because the title slide of the presentation will display, making it easier for you to distinguish among presentations.

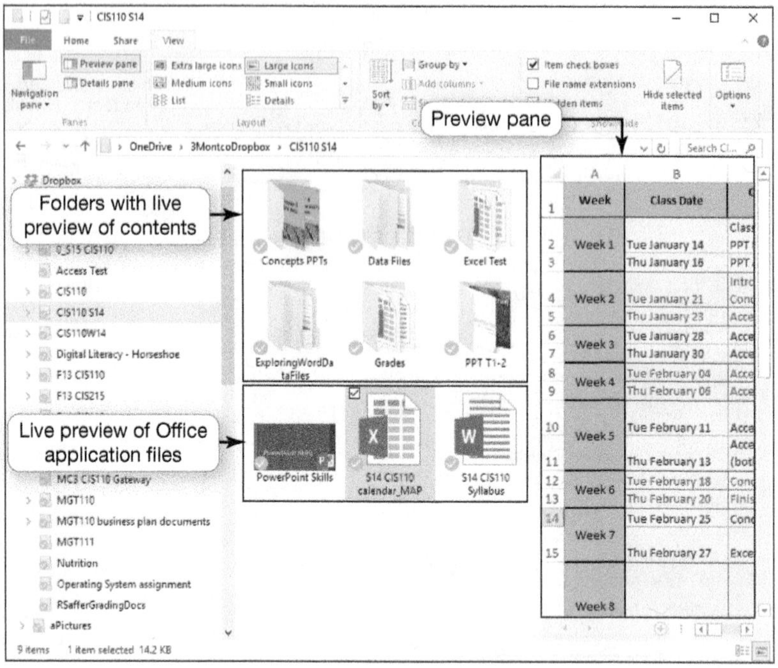

FIGURE 5.22 The Large Icons view is a good way to display the contents of files and folders. The Preview pane on the right lets you see the first page of your document without first opening it. *(Windows 10, Microsoft Corporation)*
>To access Large Icons view, click the ***View tab*** *in File Explorer, and then select* ***Large Icons*** *in the Layout group. To display the* ***Preview pane***, *click Preview pane in the Panes group on the File Explorer View tab.*

You can change the views from the Layout group on the View tab, or by clicking between Details view and Large Icon view from the bottom right corner of File Explorer. The View

SOUND BYTE
File Management

In this Sound Byte, you'll examine the features of file management and maintenance. You'll learn the various methods of creating folders, how to turn a group of unorganized files into an organized system of folders with related files, and how to maintain your file system.

BITS&BYTES

Tips for Organizing Your Files

Creating folders is the key to organizing files because folders keep related documents together. For example, you might create one folder called "Classes" to hold your class work. Inside the "Classes" folder, you could create subfolders for each of your classes (such as ENG 325 and BUS 401). Inside each of those subfolders, you could create further subfolders for each class's assignments, homework, and so on.

Grouping related files into folders makes it easier for you to identify and find files. Which would be easier—going to the BUS 401 folder to find a file or searching through the hundreds of individual files in the Documents library hoping to find the right one? Grouping files in a folder also allows you to move files more efficiently, so you can quickly transfer critical files needing frequent backup, for instance.

BITS&BYTES

Save Files in the Cloud Right from Your Apps

When you sign up for a Windows account, you automatically get free storage on OneDrive, Microsoft's cloud storage site. Taking advantage of this free storage space helps ensure that you have files available to you whenever you need them and have access to the Internet.

Fortunately, it's easy to save files to OneDrive in Windows 10. When you use the Save As command in an application, OneDrive shows up as a location (see Figure 5.23) to which you can save files. So instead of saving your research paper to your C: drive, save it to a folder on OneDrive. Other cloud services like Dropbox and Google Drive work in the same manner. Using cloud storage will ensure the availability of your files when you need them.

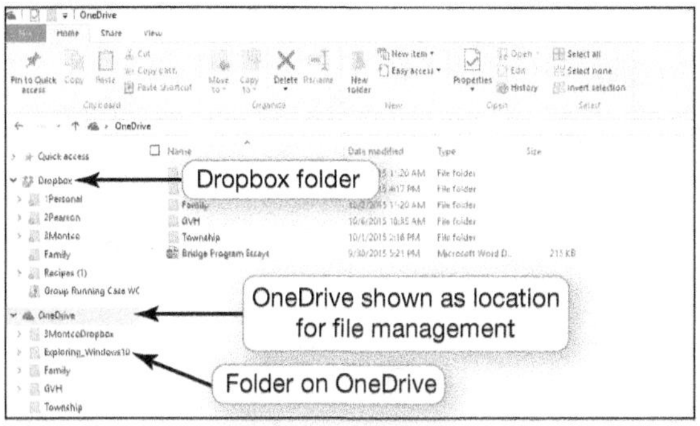

FIGURE 5.23 OneDrive displays as a location in which you can create folders and save files. *(Windows 10, Microsoft Corporation)*

tab also enables you to display a Preview pane or a Details pane. The Preview pane displays the first page of the selected document, and the Details pane displays the file or folder's properties.

Naming Files

Are there special rules I have to follow when I name files? The first part of a file, or the **file name**, is generally the name you assign to the file when you save it. For example, "bioreport" may be the name you assign a report you have completed for a biology class.

In a Windows application, an **extension** or **file type**, follows the file name and a period or dot (.). Like a last name, this extension identifies what kind of family of files the file belongs to, or which application should be used to read the file. For example, if "bioreport" is a spreadsheet created in Microsoft Excel 2016, it has an .xlsx extension and its name is "bioreport.xlsx." You can choose to display file extensions by checking or unchecking the File name extensions box in the Show/hide group on the View tab in File Explorer.

Figure 5.24 lists some common file extensions and the types of documents they indicate.

Why is it important to know the file extension? When you save a file created in most applications running under the Windows OS, you don't need to add the extension to

FIGURE 5.24

Common File Name Extensions

EXTENSION	TYPE OF DOCUMENT	APPLICATION
.docx	Word processing document	Microsoft Word 2007 and later
.xlsx	Workbook	Microsoft Excel 2007 and later
.accdb	Database	Microsoft Access 2007 and later
.pptx	Presentation	Microsoft PowerPoint 2007 and later
.pdf	Portable Document Format	Adobe Acrobat or Adobe Reader
.rtf	Text (Rich Text Format)	Any program that can read text documents
.txt	Text	Any program that can read text documents
.htm or .html	HyperText Markup Language (HTML) for a web page	Any program that can read HTML
.jpg	Joint Photographic Experts Group (JPEG) image	Most programs capable of displaying images
.zip	Compressed file	Various file compression programs

FIGURE 5.25

File-Naming Conventions

	OS X	WINDOWS
File and folder name length	As many as 255 characters*	As many as 255 characters
Case sensitive?	Yes	No
Forbidden characters	Colon (:)	" / \ * ? < > | :
File extensions needed?	No	Yes

*Although OS X supports file names with as many as 255 characters, many applications running on OS X still support only file names with a maximum of 31 characters.

the file name; it is added automatically for you. Mac and Linux operating systems don't require file extensions. This is because the information as to the type of application the computer should use to open the file is stored inside the file itself. However, if you're using the Mac or Linux OS and will be sending files to Windows users, you should add an extension to your file name so that Windows can more easily open your files.

Have you ever been sent a file by e-mail and couldn't open it? Most likely, that was because your computer didn't have the program needed to open the file. Sometimes, similar programs that you already have installed can be used to open the file, so it's helpful to know what the file extension is. Sites such as FILExt (**filext.com**) can help you identify the source program.

Are there things I shouldn't do when naming my files? Each OS has its own naming conventions, or rules, which are listed in Figure 5.25. Beyond those conventions, it's important that you name your files so that you can easily identify them. File names can have as many as 255 characters, so don't be afraid to use as many characters as you need. A file name such as "BIO 101 Research Paper First Draft.docx" makes it very clear what that file contains.

Keep in mind, however, that all files must be uniquely identified, unless you save them in different folders or in different locations. Therefore, although files may share the same file name (such as "bioreport.docx" or "bioreport.xlsx") or share the same extension ("bioreport.xlsx" or "budget.xlsx"), no two files stored in the same folder can share *both* the same filename and the same file extension.

Copying, Moving, and Deleting Files

How can I move and copy files? Once you've located your file with File Explorer, you can perform many other file management actions such as opening, copying, moving, renaming, and deleting files. You open a file by double-clicking the file from its storage location. You can copy a file to another location using the Copy command. To move a file from one location to another, use the Cut command. You can access both of these commands easily by right-clicking on a file's name, which displays a shortcut menu.

ACTIVE HELPDESK
Organizing Your Computer: File Management

In this Active Helpdesk, you'll play the role of a helpdesk staffer, fielding questions about the desktop, window features, and how the OS helps keep the computer organized.

BITS&BYTES

Use Cortana to Find Your Files

Microsoft's personal assistant, Cortana, was originally a part of Windows Phone but is now incorporated into the Windows 10 operating system deployed across all devices. In Windows 10, Cortana lives on the taskbar, to the right of the Start button. Click on the microphone icon to initiate voice-activated commands, or type your queries in the text box. You can ask Cortana to set reminders, create appointments, as well as tell you the weather or the current scores of your favorite teams. In addition, you can use Cortana to find files and folders. Cortana understands natural language, so she could respond to a query such as *Show me files relating to the fundraiser* or you could type *Fundraiser* into the Search box. Click MyStuff for Cortana to search File Explorer and OneDrive, or click Web for Cortana to offer related contents on the web.

Where do deleted files go? The **Recycle Bin** is a folder on the desktop, represented by an icon that looks like a recycling bin, where files deleted from the hard drive reside until you permanently purge them from your system. Unfortunately, files deleted from other drives don't go to the Recycle Bin but are deleted from the system immediately. In addition, files stored in the cloud are not cycled through the Recycle Bin. When you delete a file from a thumb drive or a network drive, consider it gone forever!

Mac systems have something similar to the Recycle Bin, called Trash, which is represented by a wastebasket icon. To delete files on a Mac, drag the files to the Trash icon.

How do I permanently delete files from my system? Files placed in the Recycle Bin or the Trash remain in the system until they're permanently deleted. To delete files from the Recycle Bin permanently, select Empty Recycle Bin after right-clicking the desktop icon. On Macs, select Empty Trash from the Finder menu in OS X.

What happens if I need to recover a deleted file? Getting a file back after the Recycle Bin has been emptied still may be possible using one of two methods:

- File History is a Windows 10 utility that automatically backs up files and saves previous versions of files to a designated drive (such as an external hard drive). If you're using File

History, you can restore previously deleted files or even previous versions of files you've changed. (We'll discuss File History in more detail later in the chapter.)

- When the Recycle Bin is emptied, only the reference to the file is deleted permanently, so the OS has no easy way to find the file. The file data actually remains on the hard drive until it's written over by another file. You may be able to use a program such as FarStone's RestoreIT or Norton Online Backup to try to retrieve files you think you've permanently deleted. These programs reveal files that are still intact on the hard drive and help you recover them. This is how they do it on *CSI*!

File Compression

Objective 5.11 *Summarize how file compression works.*

Why would I want to compress a file? File compression makes a large file more compact, making it easier and faster for you to send large attachments by e-mail, upload them to the web, or save them onto a flash drive or other storage medium. As shown in Figure 5.26, Windows has a built-in

> **SOUND BYTE**
> **File Compression**
> In this Sound Byte, you'll learn about the advantages of file compression and how to use Windows to compress and decompress files. This Sound Byte also teaches you how to find and install file compression shareware programs.

file compression utility that takes out redundancies in a file (zips it) to reduce the file size. You can also obtain several stand-alone freeware and shareware programs, such as WinZip (for Windows) and StuffIt (for Windows or Mac), to compress your files.

How does file compression work? Most compression programs look for repeated patterns of letters and replace these patterns with a shorter placeholder. The repeated patterns and the associated placeholder are cataloged and stored temporarily in a separate file called the *dictionary*.

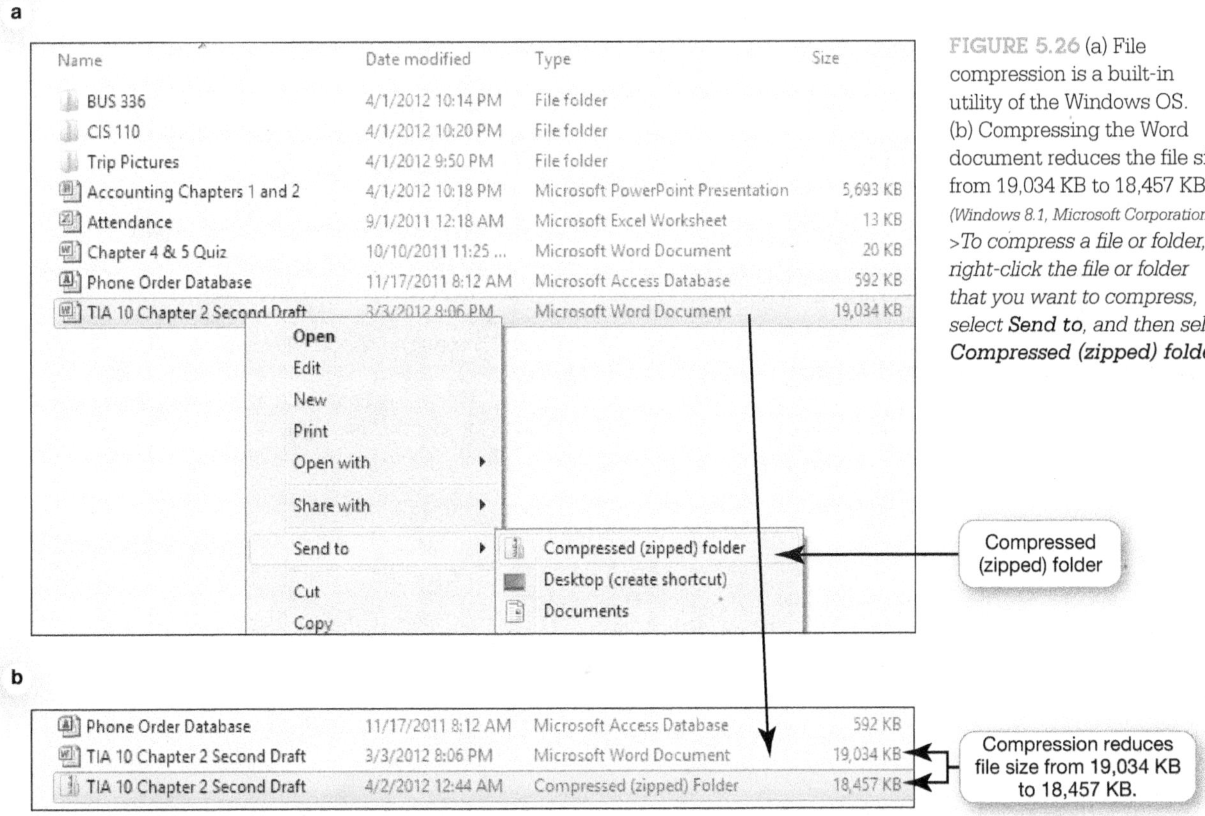

FIGURE 5.26 (a) File compression is a built-in utility of the Windows OS. (b) Compressing the Word document reduces the file size from 19,034 KB to 18,457 KB. *(Windows 8.1, Microsoft Corporation)*
>*To compress a file or folder, right-click the file or folder that you want to compress, select **Send to**, and then select **Compressed (zipped) folder**.*

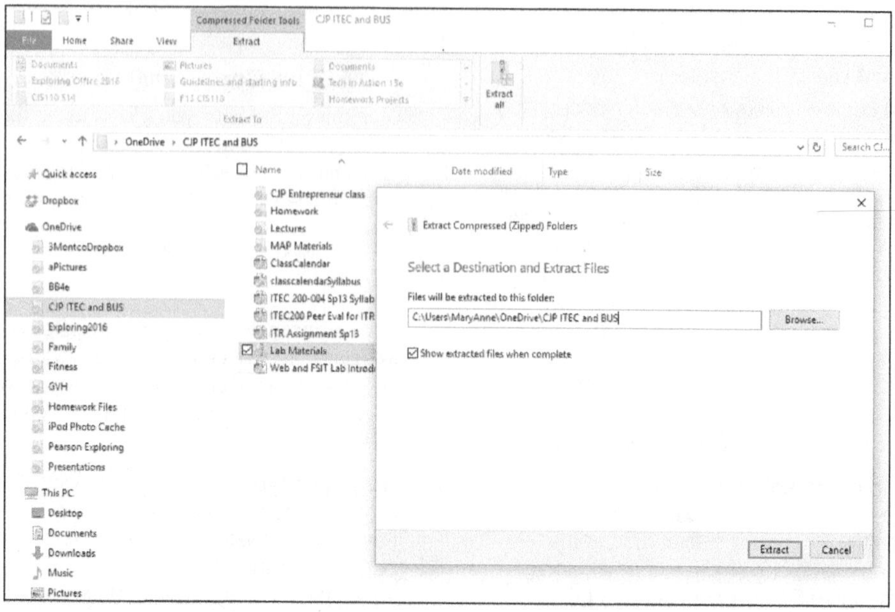

FIGURE 5.27 Extracting files from a zipped folder is simply done through the Extract all feature in File Explorer. *(Windows 10, Microsoft Corporation)*

For example, in the following sentence, you can easily see the repeated patterns of letters.

The rain in Spain falls mainly on the plain.

Although this example contains obvious repeated patterns (ain and the), in a large document, the repeated patterns may be more complex. The compression program's algorithm (a set of instructions designed to complete a solution in a step-by-step manner), therefore, runs through the file several times to determine the optimal repeated patterns needed to obtain the greatest compression.

How effective are file compression programs? Current compression programs can reduce text files by 50% or more, depending on the file. However, some files, such as PDF files, already contain a form of compression, so they don't need to be compressed further. Image files such as JPEG, GIF, and PNG files discard small variations in color that the human eye might not pick up. Likewise, MP3 files permanently discard sounds that the human ear can't hear. These graphic and audio files don't need further compression.

How do I decompress a file I've compressed? When you want to restore the file to its original state, you need to *decompress* the file. In File Explorer, when you click on a Compressed (or zipped) folder, the Compressed Folders Tools tab displays (see Figure 5.27). Click Extract all to open the Extract Compressed (Zipped) Folders dialog box. Browse to locate where you want to save the extracted files, or just click Extract to accept the default location (which is generally the location of the zipped folder). ■

utility PROGRAMS

The main component of system software is the OS. However, *utility programs*—small applications that perform special functions on the computer—are also an essential part of system software. Utility programs come in three flavors:

1. Those that are included with the OS (such as System Restore)
2. Those sold as stand-alone programs (such as Norton antivirus)
3. Those offered as freeware (such as anti-malware software like Ad-Aware from Lavasoft)

Figure 5.28 lists some of the various types of utility programs available within the Windows OS as well as some alternatives available as stand-alone programs. In general, the basic utilities designed to manage and tune your computer hardware are incorporated into the OS. The stand-alone utility programs typically offer more features or an easier user interface for backup, security, diagnostic, or recovery functions. For some Windows programs, like Task Manager and Resource Monitor, no good stand-alone alternatives exist.

Windows Administrative Utilities

Objective 5.12 *Outline the tools used to enhance system productivity.*

What utilities can make my system work faster? Disk Cleanup is a Windows utility that removes unnecessary files from your hard drive. These include files that have accumulated in the Recycle Bin as well as temporary files—files created by Windows to store data temporarily while a program is running. Windows usually deletes these temporary files when you exit the program, but sometimes it forgets to do this or doesn't have time because your system freezes or incurs a problem that prevents you from properly exiting a program.

Disk Cleanup also removes temporary Internet files (web pages stored on your hard drive for quick viewing) as well as offline web pages (pages stored on your computer so you can view them without being connected to the Internet). If not deleted periodically, these unnecessary files can slow down your computer.

How can I control which files Disk Cleanup deletes? When you run Disk Cleanup, the program scans your hard drive to determine which folders have files that can be deleted and calculates the amount of hard drive space that will be

ACTIVE HELPDESK
Using Utility Programs

In this Active Helpdesk, you'll play the role of a helpdesk staffer, fielding questions about the utility programs included in system software and what these programs do.

FIGURE 5.28

Utility Programs Available Within Windows and as Stand-Alone Programs

WINDOWS UTILITY PROGRAM	STAND-ALONE ALTERNATIVES	WHAT IT DOES
Disk Cleanup	McAfee Total Protection	Removes unnecessary files from your hard drive
Disk Defragmenter	Norton Utilities, iDefrag	Rearranges files on your hard drive to allow for faster access of files
Task Manager and Resource Monitor	Process Explorer	Displays performance measures for processes; provides information on programs and processes running on your computer
File History, File Recovery	Acronis True Image, Norton Online Backup	Backs up important files, makes a complete mirror image of your current computer setup
System Restore	FarStone RestoreIT, Acronis True Image	Restores your system to a previous, stable state

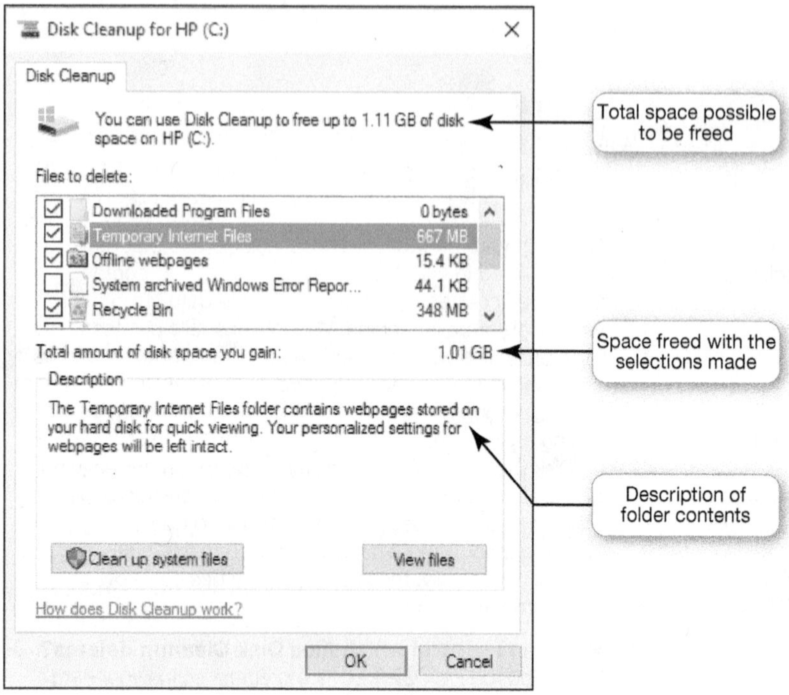

FIGURE 5.29 Using Disk Cleanup will help free space on your hard drive.
(Windows 10, Microsoft Corporation)
>*To access Disk Cleanup, click **All apps** on the Start menu, scroll to Windows Administrative Tools, click **Disk Cleanup**.*

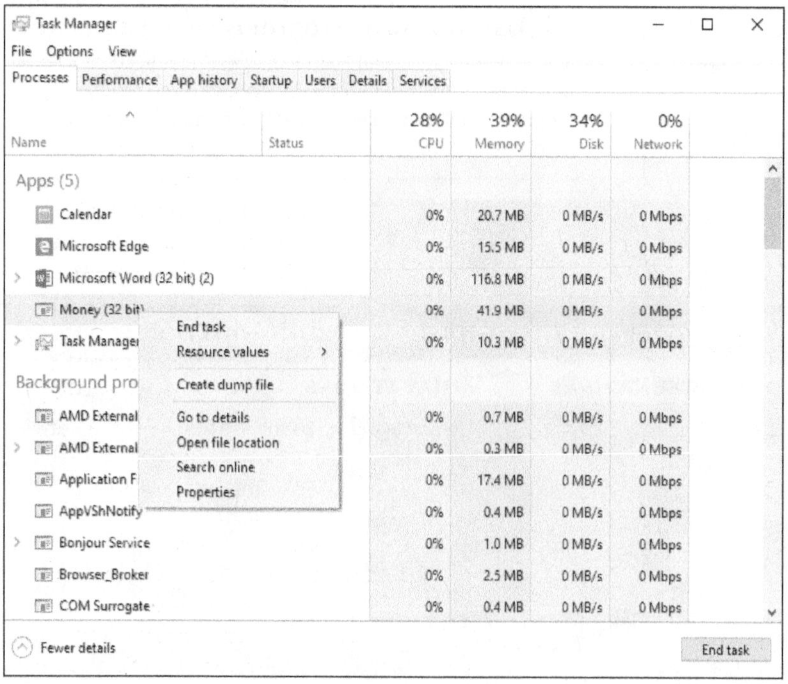

FIGURE 5.30 You can use Task Manager to close nonresponsive programs.
(Windows 10, Microsoft Corporation)
>*To access Task Manager, click **All apps** on the Start menu, scroll to Windows System, click **Task Manager**.*

freed up by doing so. You check off which type of files you would like to delete, as shown in Figure 5.29.

How can I check on a program that's stopped running? If a program has stopped working, you can use the Windows **Task Manager** utility (see Figure 5.30) to check on the program or to exit the nonresponsive program. The Processes tab of Task Manager lists all the programs you're using and indicates their status. "Not responding" will be shown next to a program that stopped improperly. If the status section is blank (Figure 5.30), then the program is working normally. You can terminate programs that aren't responding by right-clicking the app name and selecting End Task from the shortcut menu.

How can I improve my computer's performance? After you have used your computer for a while, uploading, creating, changing, and deleting content, the hard drive becomes fragmented: parts of files get scattered (fragmented) around the hard disk making the hard disk do extra work which can slow down your computer. **Disk defragmentation** rearranges fragmented data so that related file pieces are unified. The Disk Defragmenter utility is found in the Windows Administrative Tools folder in All apps. Before you defragment your hard drive, you should first determine if the disk needs to be defragmented by selecting Analyze disk. If your disk is more than 10% fragmented, you should run the disk defragmenter utility. See the Dig Deeper, *How Disk Defragmenter Utilities Work* for more information.

SOUND BYTE

Letting Your Computer Clean Up After Itself

In this Sound Byte, you'll learn how to use the various maintenance utilities within the OS. You'll also learn why maintenance tasks should be done on a routine basis to make your system more efficient.

DIG DEEPER How Disk Defragmenter Utilities Work

Disk defragmenting programs group together related pieces of files on the hard drive, allowing the OS to work more efficiently. To understand how disk defragmenter utilities work, you first need to understand the basics of how a hard disk drive stores files. A hard disk drive is composed of several platters, or round, thin plates of metal, covered with a special magnetic coating that records the data. The platters are about 3.5 inches in diameter and are stacked onto a spindle. There are usually two or three platters in any hard disk drive, with data stored on one or both sides. Data is recorded on hard disks in concentric circles called **tracks**. Each track is further broken down into pie-shaped wedges, each called a **sector** (see Figure 5.31). The data is further identified by **clusters**, which are the smallest segments within the sectors.

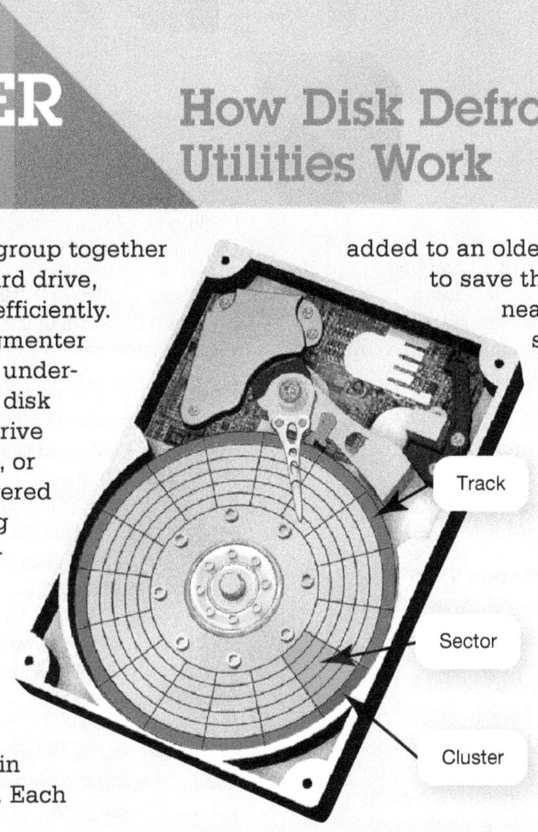

FIGURE 5.31 On a hard disk platter, data is recorded onto tracks, which are further divided into sectors and clusters.

When you want to save (or write) a file, the bits that make up your file are recorded onto one or more clusters of the drive. To keep track of which clusters hold which files, the drive also stores an index of all sector numbers in a table. To save a file, the computer looks in the table for clusters that aren't already being used. It then records the file information on those clusters. When you open (or read) a file, the computer searches through the table for the clusters that hold the desired file and reads that file. Similarly, when you delete a file, you're actually not deleting the file itself but rather the reference in the table to the file.

So, how does a disk become fragmented? When only part of an older file is deleted, the deleted section of the file creates a gap in the sector of the disk where the data was originally stored. In the same way, when new information is added to an older file, there may not be space to save the new information sequentially near where the file was originally saved. In that case, the system writes the added part of the file to the next available location on the disk, and a reference is made in the table as to the location of this file fragment. Over time, as files are saved, deleted, and modified, the bits of information for various files fall out of order and the disk becomes fragmented.

Disk fragmentation is a problem because the OS isn't as efficient when a disk is fragmented. It takes longer to locate a whole file because more of the disk must be searched for the various pieces, slowing down your computer.

Defragmenting tools take the hard drive through a defragmentation process in which pieces of files scattered over the disk are placed together and arranged sequentially on it. Also, any unused portions of clusters that were too small to save data in before are grouped, increasing the available storage space on the disk. Figure 5.32 shows before and after shots of a fragmented disk that has gone through the defragmentation process.

The disk defragmentation utility in Windows 10 is set by default to automatically defragment the hard drive on a regular basis. Macs don't have a defragmentation utility built into the system. Those users who feel the need to defragment their Mac can use iDefrag, an external program from Coriolis Systems.

For more about hard disks and defragmenting, check out the Sound Byte "Hard Disk Anatomy."

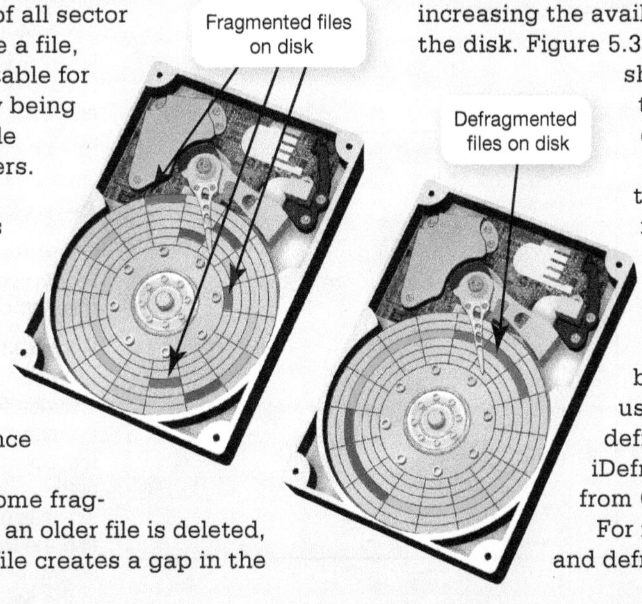

FIGURE 5.32 Defragmenting the hard drive arranges file fragments so that they are located next to each other. This makes the hard drive run more efficiently.

> **SOUND BYTE**
> **Hard Disk Anatomy**
> In this Sound Byte, you'll watch a series of animations that show various aspects of a hard drive, including the anatomy of a hard drive, how a computer reads and writes data to a hard drive, and the fragmenting and defragmenting of a hard drive.

File and System Backup Utilities

Objective 5.13 *Summarize the utilities used to backup and restore files and the computer system.*

How can I protect my data in the event something malfunctions in my system? As noted earlier, when you use the **File History** utility, you can have Windows automatically create a duplicate of your libraries, desktop, contacts, and favorites and copy it to another storage device, such as an external hard drive (see Figure 5.33). A backup copy protects your data in the event your hard drive fails or files are accidentally erased. File History also keeps copies of different versions of your files. This means that if you need to go back to the second draft of your history term paper, even though you are now on your fifth draft, File History should allow you to recover it. File History needs to be turned on by the user and requires an external hard drive (or network drive) that is always connected to the computer to function. You can choose to backup all folders on the C: drive, or select certain ones that you use most often or contain the most sensitive files to backup.

Windows 10 also includes recovery tools that allow you to complete backups of your entire system (system image) that you can later restore in the event of a major hard drive crash.

How can I recover my entire system? Suppose you've just installed a new software program and your computer freezes. After rebooting the computer, when you try to start the application, the system freezes once again. You uninstall the new program, but your computer continues to freeze after rebooting. What can you do now?

Windows has a utility called **System Restore** that lets you roll your system settings back to a specific date when everything was working properly. A **system restore point**, which is a snapshot of your entire system's settings, is generated prior to certain events, such as installing or updating software, or automatically once a week if no other restore points were created in that time. You also can create a restore point manually at any time.

Should problems occur, if the computer was running just fine before you installed new software or a hardware device, you could restore your computer to the settings that were in effect before the software or hardware installation (see Figure 5.34). System Restore doesn't affect your personal data files (such as Word documents or e-mail), so you won't lose changes made to these files.

OS X includes a backup utility called Time Machine that automatically backs up your files to a specified location. Apple also offers backup hardware called Time Capsules, which are hard disk drives with wireless connectivity, designed to work with Time Machine and record your backup data. Because Time Machine makes a complete image copy of your system, it can also be used to recover your system in the case of a fatal error. (For more information on backing up your files, see Chapter 9.)

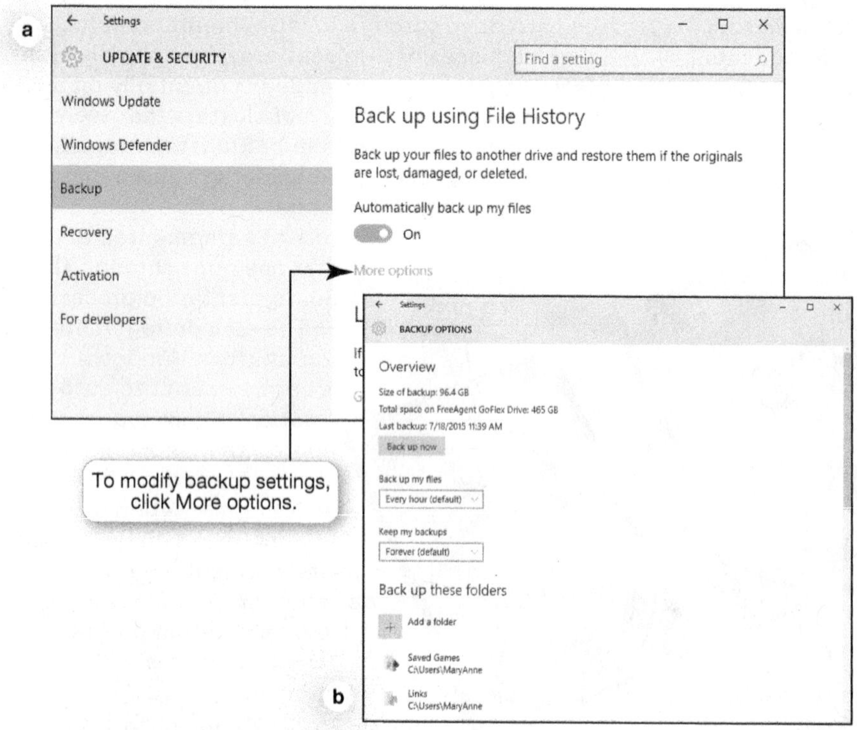

FIGURE 5.33 File History backs up files to an external hard drive. *(Windows 10, Microsoft Corporation)*
>*To turn on File History, choose* ***Settings****, select* ***Update & security****, and then select* ***Backup****. To modify File History and Backup settings, click* ***More options****.*

Accessibility Utilities

Objective 5.14 *Describe the assistive technology utilities used to make using the computer system easier.*

What utilities are designed for users with special needs? Microsoft Windows includes an Ease of Access Center, which is a centralized location for assistive technology and tools to adjust accessibility settings. In the Ease of Access Center, which is accessible from Settings, you can find the tools to help users with disabilities, shown in Figure 5.35. The tools shown in the figure are just a sampling of the available tools. If you're not sure where to start or what settings might help, a questionnaire asks you about routine

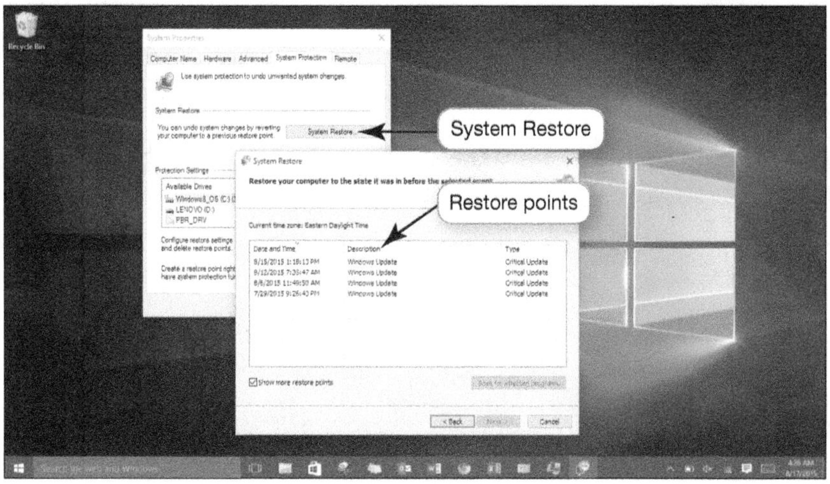

FIGURE 5.34 This System Restore Wizard shows restore points set manually by a user and automatically by Windows when updates were installed. Setting a restore point is good practice before installing any hardware or software. *(Windows 10, Microsoft Corporation)*

>To access System Restore, right-click the ***Start button****, choose* ***System****, select* ***System Protection****, and then click* ***System Restore****. The System Restore Wizard displays, with the restore points shown on the second page of the Wizard.*

tasks and provides a personalized recommendation for settings that will help you better use your computer.

Whether you use Windows, OS X, Linux, or another operating system, a fully featured OS is available to meet your needs. As long as you keep the operating system updated and regularly use the available utilities to fine-tune your system, you should experience little trouble from your OS. ■

Before moving on to the Chapter Review:

1. **Watch Replay Video 5.2.**
2. **Then check your understanding of what you've learned so far.**

FIGURE 5.35

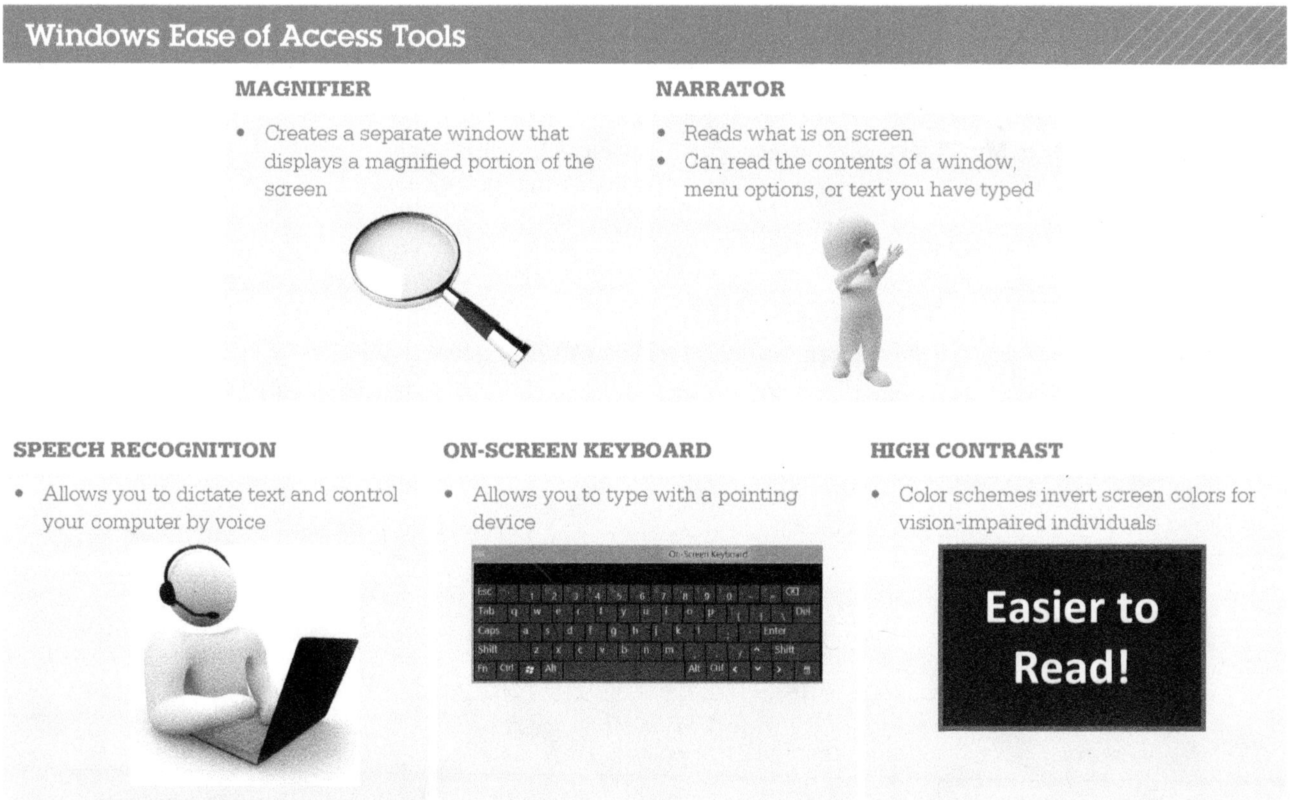

(Imagery Majestic/Fotolia, Anatoly Maslennikov/Fotolia, iqoncept/123RF, Pockgallery/Shutterstock)

>To access Ease of Access, click ***Settings****, then select* ***Ease of Access****.*

check your understanding // review & practice

For a quick review to see what you've learned so far, answer the following questions.

multiple choice

1. What is used to reduce the file size of a file or folder?
   - **a.** defragmenter
   - **b.** compression
   - **c.** extraction
   - **d.** shrinker
2. The process of adding a Windows 10 app to the Start menu is known as
   - **a.** clipping.
   - **b.** visualizing.
   - **c.** pinning.
   - **d.** screening.
3. The Windows app used for locating files and folders is
   - **a.** Disk Manager.
   - **b.** Finder.
   - **c.** File Explorer.
   - **d.** Library Explorer.
4. Which of the following is NOT a common file name extension?
   - **a.** .docx
   - **b.** .jpg
   - **c.** .pptx
   - **d.** .zipped
5. Which utility is used to exit out of a nonresponsive program?
   - **a.** Task Manager
   - **b.** Disk Cleanup
   - **c.** System Refresh
   - **d.** File Explorer

MyITLab Go to **MyITLab** to take an autograded version of the *Check Your Understanding* review and to find all media resources for the chapter.

TECHBYTES WEEKLY
Stay current with the TechBytes Weekly Newsletter.

Continue

5 Chapter Review

summary //

Understanding System Software

Learning Outcome 5.1 **You will be able to explain the types and functions of an operating system and explain the steps in the boot process.**

Operating System Fundamentals

Objective 5.1 *Discuss the functions of the operating system.*

- System software is the set of software programs that helps run the computer and coordinates instructions between application software and hardware devices. It consists of the operating system (OS) and utility programs.
- The OS controls how your computer system functions. It manages the computer's hardware, provides a means for application software to work with the CPU, and is responsible for the management, scheduling, and coordination of tasks.
- Utility programs are programs that perform general housekeeping tasks for the computer, such as system maintenance and file compression.
- Modern operating systems allow for multitasking—to perform more than one process at a time.

Objective 5.2 *Explain the different kinds of operating systems for machines, networks, and business.*

- Real-time operating systems (RTOSs) require no user intervention.
- A multiuser operating system (network operating system) provides access to a computer system by more than one user at a time.
- UNIX is a multiuser, multitasking OS that is used as a network OS, though it can be used on PCs.
- Mainframes and supercomputers are specialty computers that require mainframe operating systems.

Objective 5.3 *Explain the most common operating systems for personal use.*

- Smartphones have their own specific operating systems, which allow the user to multitask.
- Some operating systems allow interaction with touch-screen interfaces.
- Gaming consoles use operating systems developed specifically for those particular devices.
- Microsoft Windows is the most popular OS. The most recent release is Windows 10. The Mac OS, which is designed to work on Apple computers, and Linux is an open source OS based on UNIX and designed primarily for use on personal computers.
- An OS is designed to run on specific CPUs. The combination of an OS and a CPU is a computer's platform. Application software is OS dependent.
- All personal operating systems incorporate elements to share and store on the Internet.

What the Operating System Does

Objective 5.4 *Explain how the operating system provides a means for users to interact with the computer.*

- The OS provides a user interface that enables users to interact with the computer.
- Most OSs today use a graphical user interface (GUI). Common features of GUIs include windows, menus, and icons.

Objective 5.5 *Explain how the operating system helps manage hardware such as the processor, memory, storage, and peripheral devices.*

- When the OS allows you to perform more than one task at a time, it is multitasking. To provide for seamless multitasking, the OS controls the timing of the events on which the processor works.
- As the OS coordinates the activities of the processor, it uses RAM as a temporary storage area for instructions and data the processor needs. The OS coordinates the space allocations in RAM to ensure that there is enough space for the waiting instructions and data. If there isn't sufficient space in RAM for all the data and instructions, then the OS allocates the least necessary files to temporary storage on the hard drive, called *virtual memory*.

- The OS manages storage by providing a file management system that keeps track of the names and locations of files and programs.
- Programs called *device drivers* facilitate communication between devices attached to the computer and the OS.

Objective 5.6 *Explain how the operating system interacts with application software.*

- All software applications need to interact with the CPU. For programs to work with the CPU, they must contain code that the CPU recognizes.
- Rather than having the same blocks of code appear in each application, the OS includes the blocks of code to which software applications refer. These blocks of code are called *application programming interfaces* (APIs).

Starting Your Computer

Objective 5.7 *Discuss the process the operating system uses to start up the computer, and how errors in the boot process are handled.*

- When you start your computer, it runs through a special process called the *boot process*.
- The boot process consists of four basic steps: (1) The basic input/output system (BIOS) is activated when the user powers on the CPU. (2) In the POST check, the BIOS verifies that all attached devices are in place. (3) The OS is loaded into RAM. (4) Configuration and customization settings are checked.
- An authentication process occurs at the end of the boot process to ensure an authorized user is entering the system.
- Sometimes errors occur in the boot process, or otherwise. Try rebooting the computer or resetting the computer if the problem persists.

Using System Software

Learning Outcome 5.2 You will be able to describe how system software is used, including managing the user interface, file management, and utility programs.

The Windows Interface

Using Windows 10

Objective 5.8 *Describe the main features of the Windows interface.*

- In Windows 10, the Start menu provides access to your computer's apps, tools, and commonly used programs and the desktop is the main working area.
- You can customize the Start menu by pinning and resizing tiles and organizing tiles into groups.
- Virtual desktops are used to organize open programs into different working areas.

File Management

Objective 5.9 *Summarize how the operating system helps keep your computer organized.*

- Files and folders are organized in a hierarchical directory structure composed of drives, libraries, folders, subfolders, and files.
- The C: drive represents the hard drive and is where most programs and files are stored.
- File Explorer is the main tool for finding, viewing, and managing the contents of your computer.

Objective 5.10 *Summarize how to view, sort, name, and manage files and folders.*

- File Explorer helps you manage your files and folders by showing the location and contents of every drive, folder, and file on your computer.
- There are specific rules to follow when naming files.
- The Recycle Bin is the temporary storage location for deleted files from the hard drive.

Objective 5.11 *Summarize how file compression works.*

- File compression reduces the size of a file by temporarily storing components of a file and then when the file is extracted (uncompressed) the removed components are brought back into the file.

Utility Programs

Objective 5.12 *Outline the tools used to enhance system productivity.*

- Task Manager is used to exit nonresponsive programs.
- Disk Cleanup removes unnecessary files from your hard drive. If not deleted periodically, these unnecessary files can slow down your computer.

- Disk Defragmentation rearranges fragmented data so that related file pieces are unified. When a disk is fragmented, it can slow down your computer.

Objective 5.13 *Summarize the utilities used to backup and restore files and the computer system.*

- File History automatically creates a duplicate of your hard drive (or parts of your hard drive) and copies it to another storage device, such as an external hard drive. You can use File History to recover deleted or corrupted files.
- System Restore lets you roll your system settings back to a specific date (restore point) when everything was working properly.

Objective 5.14 *Describe the assistive technology utilities used to make using the computer system easier.*

- Windows Ease of Access Center includes tools that help adjust computer settings for those users with disabilities.

MyITLab Be sure to check out **MyITLab** for additional materials to help you review and learn. And don't forget the Replay Videos.

key terms //

application programming interface (API) **172**
authentication **173**
basic input/output system (BIOS) **172**
boot process **172**
cluster **191**
command-driven interface **167**
desktop **178**
device driver **170**
directory **181**
Disk Cleanup **189**
Disk defragmentation **190**
distributions (distros) **165**
event **168**
extension (file type) **185**
file **183**
file compression utility **187**
File Explorer **183**
File History **192**
file management **181**
file name **185**
file path **183**
folder **183**
graphical user interface (GUI) **167**
interrupt **168**
interrupt handler **168**
kernel (supervisor program) **172**
Linux **165**
Mac OS **165**
menu-driven interface **167**
Microsoft account **173**
multitask **163**
multiuser operating system (network operating system) **163**
operating system (OS) **162**
paging **169**
path separator **183**
pinning **178**
platform **165**
Plug and Play (PnP) **170**
power-on self-test (POST) **172**
preemptive multitasking **168**
real-time operating system (RTOS) **163**
Recycle Bin **186**
Reset this PC **174**
registry **173**
root directory **183**
sector **191**
spooler **168**
Start menu **178**
swap file (page file) **169**
system files **172**
System Restore **192**
system restore point **193**
taskbar **178**
Task Manager **190**
thrashing **169**
track **191**
UNIX **163**
user interface **162**
utility program **162**
virtual desktops **180**
virtual memory **169**
Windows **164**
Windows 10 **165**

chapter quiz // assessment

For a quick review to see what you've learned, answer the following questions. Submit the quiz as requested by your instructor. If you are using MyITLab, the quiz is also available there.

multiple choice

1. Which of the following would you not see on a Windows 10 Start menu?
   - **a.** tiles
   - **b.** power
   - **c.** All apps
   - **d.** Task View
2. When an OS processes tasks in a priority order, it is known as
   - **a.** preemptive interrupting.
   - **b.** interruptive multitasking.
   - **c.** preemptive multitasking.
   - **d.** multitasking handling.
3. An example of an open source OS is
   - **a.** Windows.
   - **b.** OS X.
   - **c.** Linux.
   - **d.** DOS.
4. Which of the following is not considered an accessibility utility?
   - **a.** System Restore
   - **b.** Magnifier
   - **c.** Narrator
   - **d.** Speech Recognition
5. Special programs that facilitate communication between a device and the OS are called
   - **a.** APIs.
   - **b.** device drivers.
   - **c.** utility programs.
   - **d.** hardware player.
6. A new feature in Windows 10 that is used to organize open windows into task-specific groups is called
   - **a.** Program Manager.
   - **b.** Virtual Desktops.
   - **c.** Snap Assist.
   - **d.** Task View.

true/false

_____ **1.** Different versions of Linux are known as distros.

_____ **2.** The power-on self-test (POST) ensures all peripheral devices are attached an operational.

_____ **3.** System restore points can only be created by Windows automatically on a regular schedule.

_____ **4.** Files deleted from a flash drive are sent to the Recycle Bin and could be recovered, if necessary.

critical thinking

1. **Protecting Embedded Systems**

   As more devices and appliances make use of RTOSs, the necessity of protecting them from hackers becomes increasingly critical. Developers are working to improve the security of the software and to safeguard communications between such devices. How concerned are you about the security of RTOSs in cars, smart homes, and wearable technology? Is enough being done to ensure the safety of these devices? What else can be done?

2. **Ease of Access**

   Windows and Mac OS X both include a number of features and utilities designed for users with special needs. Compare the offerings of each OS. Are there options offered by one OS that are not available in the other? Which OS do you think has the best selection? Can you think of any areas that have not been addressed by this assistive technology? Research software from third-party developers to see if there are other tools that would also be useful. Should these tools be included in the OS? Why or why not?

team time //

Choosing the Best OS

Problem

You're the owner of a technology consulting firm. Your current assignments include advising start-up clients on their technology requirements. The companies include a nonprofit social service organization, a small interior design firm, and a social media advertising agency. Obviously, one of the critical decisions for each company is the choice of OS.

Task

Recommend the appropriate OS for each company.

Process

1. Break up into teams that represent the three primary operating systems: Windows, Mac, or Linux.
2. As a team, research the pros and cons of your OS. What features does it have that would benefit each company? What features does it not have that each company would need? Discuss why your OS would be the appropriate (or inappropriate) choice for each company?
3. Develop a presentation that states your position with regard to your OS. Your presentation should have a recommendation and include facts to back it up.
4. As a class, decide which OS would be the best choice for each company.

Conclusion

Because the OS is the most critical piece of software in the computer system, the selection should not be taken lightly. The OS that is best for a nonprofit social service organization may not be best for an interior design firm. A social media advertising agency may have different needs altogether. It is important to make sure you consider all aspects of the work environment and the type of work being done to ensure a good fit.

ethics project //

Upgrade Your World

In this exercise, you'll research and then role-play a complicated ethical situation. The role you play may or may not match your own personal beliefs, but your research and use of logic will enable you to represent whichever view is assigned. An arbitrator will watch and comment on both sides of the arguments, and together, the team will agree on an ethical solution.

Problem

With the release of Windows 10, Microsoft began the "Upgrade your World" program, to work with 10 global nonprofit groups and 100 local nonprofits (10 in 10 countries). Microsoft has identified nine organizations around the world and will determine the 10th global nonprofit, as well as the 100 local nonprofits through crowdsourcing. Each local nonprofit will receive $50,000 cash investment plus technology from Microsoft.

Research Areas to Consider

- Windows 10 features
- Upgrade Your World Project
- The nine global Upgrade Your World nonprofits (Care, Code.org, Keep a Child Alive, Malala Fund, Pencils of Promise, Save the Children, Special Olympics, The Global Poverty Project, and The Nature Conservancy)

Process

1. Divide the class into teams. Each team member will play a different character. Each character has an individual perspective toward the decision at hand.
2. Research the areas cited above and determine a local nonprofit that you think would be deserving of an Upgrade Your World grant.
3. Team members should write a summary that provides background information for their character—for example, representative of Microsoft, nonprofit executive, local small business executive who thinks his business is worthier to receive the grant, a local community member, and arbitrator—and that details their character's behaviors to set the stage for the role-playing event. Then, team members should create an outline to use during the role-playing event.
4. Team members should determine the pros and cons of awarding the local nonprofit nominee the Upgrade Your World grant, and reach an agreeable conclusion. The team will present their case to the class or submit a PowerPoint presentation for review by the rest of the class, along with the summary and resolution they developed.

Conclusion

As deserving as most nonprofits seem to be, some may benefit more than others, and ultimately serve the community better than others, after receiving a substantial grant such as Upgrade Your World. Being able to understand and evaluate a decision, while responding in a personally or socially ethical manner, will be an important skill.

Solve This

MyITLab® grader

Mobile Operating Systems: Changing Market Share

Using Excel 2016, you will display the market share statistics of both mobile and desktop operating systems using line, column, and pie charts.

You will use the following skills as you complete this activity:

- Create a Line Chart
- Create and Format a Pie Chart
- Create and Format a Column Chart
- Add Shape to Chart
- Insert Sparklines

Instructions:

1. Open *TIA_Ch5_Start* and save as **TIA_Ch5_LastFirst**.
2. Create a 2-D Line chart from the range A3:F8. Modify the chart as follows:
   a. Add a title: **Change in Mobile OS Market Share 2011–2015**. *2011–2015* should be on a separate line. Change the font size of *2011–2015* to **10**.
   b. Move the chart to a separate worksheet. Rename the new worksheet **Line Chart**, and place after the Data worksheet.
   c. Filter out the *Symbian* and *Others* data so only *Android*, *iOS*, and *Windows* data displays.
   d. Add a **Line Callout 1 shape** to the chart with the line pointing where the Android and the iOS lines intersect. Add text to the callout: **2014: When Android surpassed iOS**.
   Hint: Line Callout 1 is in the Callouts section in the Insert Shape group on the Format Chart Tools tab.
3. Create a 2-D Pie chart from the ranges A3:A8 and F3:F8.
   Hint: Press the **Ctrl key** while selecting nonadjacent ranges. Modify the chart as follows:
   a. Add a title: **2015 Mobile OS Market Share**
   b. Use **Quick Layout 1** to add data % and Series data labels to each data point.
   c. Resize the chart so it fits in the range A14:H30.
4. Create a Clustered Column chart that compares just Android and iOS data for 2011–2015. Modify the chart as follows:
   a. Add a title: **Android versus iOS Market Share**
   b. Format the chart with **Style 8**.
   c. Move the chart to a separate worksheet. Rename the new worksheet **Column Chart**, and place it after the *Line Chart* worksheet.
5. On the Data worksheet, add a **Line Sparkline** to cell G4 using the data in range B4:F4. Using the **Fill Handle**, copy the Sparkline to range G5:G8. Add a **High Point** to each Sparkline.
6. Save the document and submit based on your instructor's directions.

Technology in Focus

Information Technology Ethics

Learning Outcome 5B.1 You will be able to define ethics, describe different types of ethical systems, and explain how personal ethics develop.

The ethical choices we make have a far-reaching impact on our lives. In this Technology in Focus feature, we examine how technology and ethics affect each other. We'll discuss several key issues related to technology and ethics, including the following:

- Social justice
- Intellectual property
- Privacy
- Property rights
- Electronic information access
- Computer abuse

We'll discuss both personal ethics as well as how our technology affects our personal ethics. Then we'll consider what your personal ethics are and how you make ethical choices.

Ethics

Let's get started by asking an important question: What is ethics?

Defining Ethics and Examining Ethical Systems

Objective 5B.1 *Define ethics, and describe the five major ethical systems.*

Ethics is the study of the general nature of morals and of the specific moral choices individuals make. Morals involve conforming to established or accepted ideas of right and wrong (as generally dictated by society) and are usually viewed as being black or white. Ethical issues often involve subtle distinctions, such as the difference between fairness and equity. Ethical principles are the guidelines you use to make decisions each day.

For example, say you stop to use a photocopier on campus. You discover a copy of the upcoming final exam for your psychology course that your teacher left behind. Do you give it back to your professor without looking at the questions? Do you share it with your friends so you can all get good grades on the final? Do you give a copy to your friend who really needs to pass the course in order to prevent losing his or her financial aid?

Doesn't everyone have the same basic ethics? There are many systems of ethical conduct. Figure 1 lists the five major ethical systems.

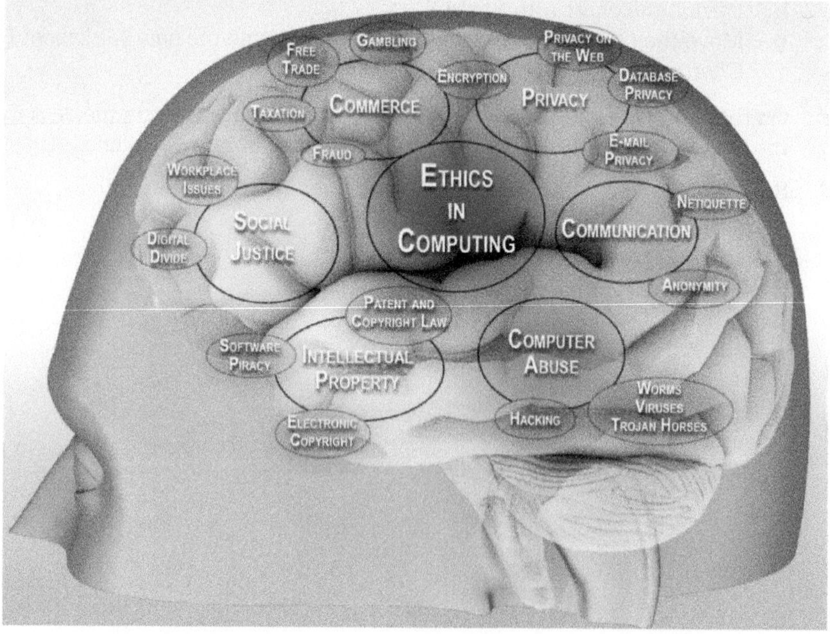

FIGURE 1

Systems of Ethics

ETHICAL SYSTEM	BASIC TENETS	EXAMPLES
Relativism 	• No universal moral truth • Moral principles dictated by cultural tastes and customs	Topless bathing is prevalent in Europe but generally banned on public beaches in the United States
Divine Command Theory 	• God is all-knowing and sets moral standards • Conforming to God's law is right; breaking it is wrong	Christians believe in rules such as the Ten Commandments
Utilitarianism 	• Actions are judged solely by consequences • Actions that generate greater happiness are judged to be better than actions that lead to unhappiness • Individual happiness is not important—consider the greater good	Using weapons of mass destruction ends a war sooner and therefore saves lives otherwise destroyed by conventional fighting
Virtue Ethics 	• Morals are internal • Strive to be a person who behaves well spontaneously	A supervisor views the person who volunteered to clean up a park as a better person than the workers who are there because of court-ordered community service
Deontology (Duty-Based) 	• Focus on adherence to moral duties and rights • Morals should apply to everyone equally	Human rights (like freedom of religion) should be respected for all people because human rights should be applied universally

(Solomin Andrey/Fotolia, Olga Galushko/Fotolia, Kentoh/Fotolia, Alexmillos/Fotolia, Oleksiy Mark/Fotolia)

Aren't laws meant to guide people's ethical actions? Laws are formal, written standards designed to apply to everyone. Laws are enforced by government agencies and interpreted by the courts. However, it's impossible to pass laws that cover every possible behavior in which humans can engage. Therefore, ethics provide a general set of unwritten guidelines for people to follow.

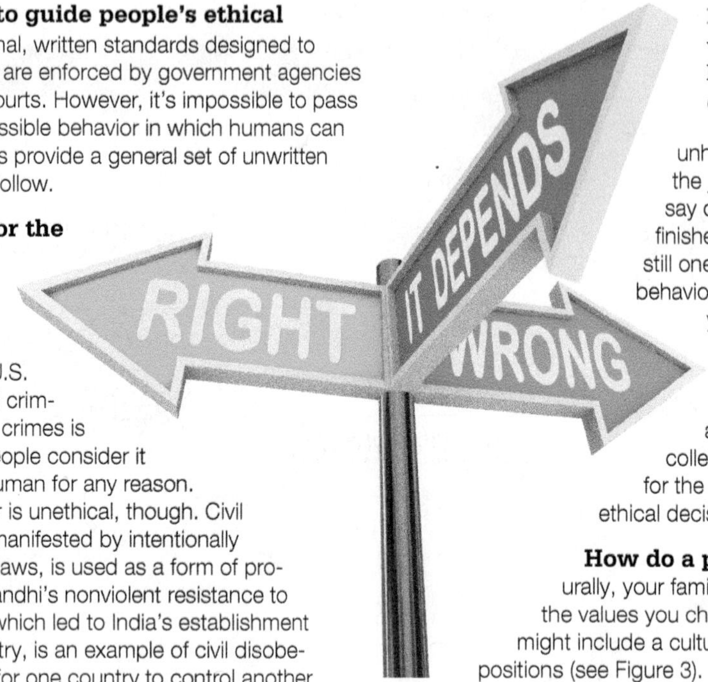

FIGURE 2 It would be nice if there were signposts to ethical conduct, but the issues are complex. *(iQoncept/Shutterstock)*

Is unethical behavior the same as illegal behavior? Unethical behavior isn't necessarily illegal. Take the death penalty. In many U.S. states, putting convicted criminals to death for certain crimes is legal. However, many people consider it unethical to execute a human for any reason.

Not all illegal behavior is unethical, though. Civil disobedience, which is manifested by intentionally refusing to obey certain laws, is used as a form of protest to effect change. Gandhi's nonviolent resistance to the British rule of India, which led to India's establishment as an independent country, is an example of civil disobedience. Is it ever ethical for one country to control another country's people?

Note that there is also a difference between *unethical* behavior and *amoral* behavior:

- *Unethical behavior* can be defined as not conforming to a set of approved standards of behavior. For instance, using your phone to text message a test answer to your friend during an exam is unethical.
- *Amoral behavior* occurs when a person has no sense of right and wrong and no interest in the moral consequences of his or her actions, such as when a murderer shows no remorse for his or her crime.

Which system of ethics works best? There is no universal agreement on which is the best system of ethics. Most societies use a blend of different systems. Regardless of the ethical system of the society in which you live, all ethical decisions are greatly influenced by personal ethics.

Personal Ethics

Objective 5B.2: *Define personal ethics, and describe influences on the development of personal ethics.*

What are personal ethics? Every day you say and do certain things, and each time, you're making decisions. As you choose your words and actions, you're following a set of **personal ethics**—a set of formal or informal ethical principles you use to make decisions in your life. Some people have a clear, well-defined set of principles they follow. Others' ethics are inconsistent or are applied differently in different situations.

It can be challenging to adhere to your own ethical principles if the consequences of your decisions might lead to an unhappy result. For example, to get the job of your dreams, should you say on your résumé that you've already finished your degree, even though you're still one credit short? Is this lying? Is such behavior justified in this setting? After all, you do intend to finish that last credit, and you would work really hard for this company if you were hired. If you tell the truth and state that you haven't finished college yet, you might be passed over for the position. Making this choice is an ethical decision (see Figure 2).

How do a person's ethics develop? Naturally, your family plays a major role in establishing the values you cherish in your own life, and these might include a cultural bias toward certain ethical positions (see Figure 3). Your religious affiliation is another major influence on your ethics because most religions have established codes of ethical conduct. How these sets of ethics interact with the values of the larger culture is often challenging. Issues such as abortion, the death penalty, and war often create conflict between personal ethical systems and the larger society's established legal–ethical system.

As you mature, your life experiences also affect your personal ethics. Does the behavior you see around you make sense within the ethical principles that your family, your church, or your first-grade teacher taught you? Has your experience led you to abandon some ethical rules and adopt others? Have you modified how and when you apply these laws of conduct depending on what's at stake?

Define Your Own Personal Values

Objective 5B.3: *Define your personal values that form your ethics.*

What if I'm not sure what my personal ethics are? When you have a clear idea of what values are important to you, it may be easier to handle situations in your life that demand ethical action. Follow these steps to help define a list of personal values:

1. **Describe yourself.** Write down words that describe who you are, based on how others view you. Would a friend describe you as honest, or helpful, or kind? These keywords will give you a hint as to the values and behaviors that are important to you.
2. **List the key principles you believe in.** Make a list of the key principles that influence your decisions. For example, would you be comfortable working in a lab that used animals for medical research? If not, is it because you

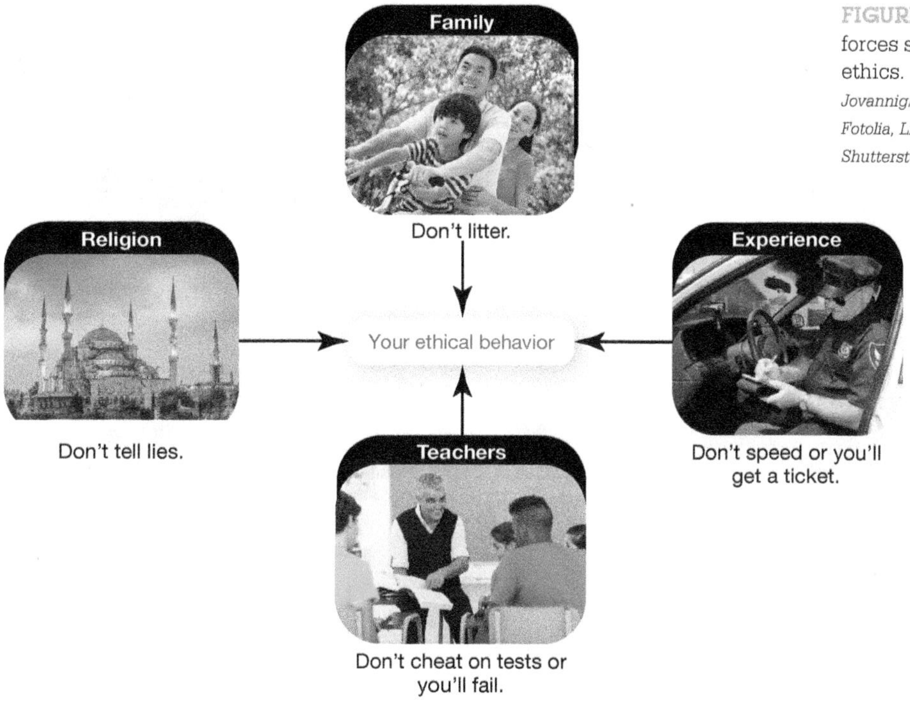

FIGURE 3 Many different forces shape your personal ethics. *(imtmphoto/Fotolia, Jovannig/Fotolia, Michaeljung/Fotolia, Lisa F. Young/Shutterstock)*

value protecting any living being? How important is it to you that you never tell a lie? Or do you feel it is kind to lie in some situations? List the key ideas you believe to be important in conducting your life. Do you always behave this way, or are you flexible? Are there situations in which your answers might change (say, if the medical research was to cure cancer or the lie was to protect someone's feelings)?

3. **Identify external influences.** Where did your key principles come from—your parents? Your friends? Spiritual advisors? Television and movies? You may want to question some of your beliefs once you actually identify where they came from.
4. **Consider why.** After writing down your beliefs, think about *why* you believe them. Have you accepted them without investigation? Do they stand up in the context of your real-world experiences?
5. **Prepare a statement of values.** Distill what you have written into a short statement. By having a well-defined statement of the values you hold most important in your own life, which you can refer to in times of challenge, it will be easier for you to make ethical decisions.

Benefits to Ethical Living

Objective 5B.4: *Describe the benefits of ethical living.*

What are the benefits of ethical living? Society has established its own set of rules of conduct in the form of laws. Ignoring or being inconsistent in following these rules can have an immediate impact. And more and more research is showing the health benefits of ethical living. When your day-to-day decisions are in conflict with your ethical principles, you often develop stress and anger.

Perhaps even happiness itself is a result of living ethically (see Figure 4). **Positive psychology** is a new focus in the field of psychology. Pioneered by Dr. Martin Seligman of the University of Pennsylvania, this field works to discover the *causes* of happiness instead of addressing the treatment of mental dysfunctions. Dr. Seligman's research has shown that by identifying your personal strengths and values and then aligning your life so that you can apply them every day, you can be happier (and suffer less depression)—an effect equivalent to that of antidepressant medication and therapy. Thus, finding a way to identify and then apply your ethics and values to your daily life can impact your health and happiness.

Personal Ethics and Your Work Life

Objective 5B.5: *Describe the interaction between a person's work life and his or her personal ethics.*

How do employers affect personal ethics? You may have a set of personal ethics that guide your behavior, but do your ethics change when you go to work? Of course, your employer expects you to follow the rules of conduct established for the business. However, this doesn't mean you need to blindly follow corporate practices that you feel are unethical or detrimental to society (see Figure 5).

FIGURE 4 The field of positive psychology shows that living and working ethically affects your happiness. *(Holbox/Shutterstock, Michaeljung/Shutterstock)*

If you spot unethical behavior at your company, what do you do? Whistle-blowers are people who report businesses to regulatory agencies for committing illegal acts, or who expose unethical (but still legal) acts committed by their employers by publicizing unethical behavior through various media outlets. The Sarbanes–Oxley Act of 2002 requires companies to provide mechanisms for employees and third parties to report complaints, including ethics violations, anonymously. In addition, many businesses are using their websites to allow whistle-blowers to report wrongdoing anonymously, replacing previously used e-mail and telephone hotline systems, which did not shield employees from being identified. With an online system, it's easier for a company to sort and classify complaints and designate them for appropriate action.

Should your employer have control over your conduct outside of the office? Do behavior, integrity, and honesty off the job relate to job performance? They might. But even if they don't, from your employer's perspective, your actions could reflect poorly on your employer. Consider the day-care employee in Texas who was fired because of a comment on Facebook before she even started her job. The management of the day-care company didn't appreciate her post about starting a new job but *hating working in a day-care center*. The day-care owners probably assumed customers wouldn't want an employee with these feelings taking care of their children. Therefore, although your ethics might dictate one mode of behavior, you need to consider how your employer might view your actions.

How does making ethical choices in a business setting differ from making personal ethical choices? Most personal ethical decisions involve few people. However, before making an ethical choice for a business, you need to consider the effect your choice will have on all of the business's stakeholders. **Stakeholders** are those people or entities who are affected by the operations of a business. Typical business stakeholders include

FIGURE 5 How should you respond if you see people in authority at work behaving unethically? *(Kritchanut/Shutterstock)*

customers, suppliers, employees, investors (shareholders), financial lenders, and society at large.

For instance, suppose you decide to cut costs in your restaurant by hiring workers "off the books" by paying them in cash. Although doing so might boost profits in the short term, the long-term impact on stakeholders can be severe. If you're caught avoiding paying payroll taxes by paying workers in cash, fines will be levied against your business, which may cause investors to lose money and may affect the company's ability to repay lenders. The negative publicity from being caught doing something illegal may cause a downturn in business, which, in turn, might force layoffs of employees or even closure of the business. Your simple decision on cutting costs isn't as simple as it may seem.

In summary, in a business environment, your behavior is guided by the ethical principles defined by the business owner or management, but you're ultimately guided by your own personal ethics.

Technology and Ethics: How One Affects the Other

Because technology moves faster than rules can be formulated to govern it, how technology is used is often left up to the individual and the guidance of his or her personal ethics. In the rest of this Technology in Focus feature, we explore situations in which ethics and technology affect each other: social justice (robotic ethics), intellectual property (3D printers), privacy (implanted data chips), property rights (ownership of outer space), electronic information access (business and free speech), and computer abuse (hacking).

Ethical considerations are never clear-cut. They're complex, and reasonable people can have different, yet equally valid, views. We present alternative viewpoints in each setting for you to consider and discuss. Figure 6 summarizes the issues we'll be discussing.

FIGURE 6

Ethics in Computing

TOPIC	ETHICAL DISCUSSION	DEBATE ISSUE
Social Justice	Should the ethics of robotic systems be programmable by individuals?	Should manufacturers, the government, or individuals set the ethical parameters of robotic systems?
Intellectual Property	Who is responsible when 3D printers are misused?	Can we impose regulations effectively on 3D printers?
Privacy	Do human-implanted data chips benefit society or violate personal privacy?	Should personal privacy be protected at all costs?
Property Rights	Should any country, company, or individual own outer space?	Should we develop laws governing ownership of outer space?
Electronic Information Access	When does big business limit free speech?	Should companies allow the Chinese government to dictate when to curtail free speech?
Computer Abuse	Is hacktivism civil disobedience or terrorism?	Is hacking a natural extension of civil disobedience or a crime?

SOCIAL JUSTICE

Who Sets the Ethics for Robots?

Summary of the Issue

The rise of the Internet of Things means that more embedded computers and robotics are being included in devices every year. Personal robots in households are not far off. But who controls the ethical constraints by which robotic machinery operates?

Automobiles now contain sophisticated robotic systems to exercise control over the vehicle and respond faster than humans can. Using radar, accident-avoidance systems can apply the brakes and even change lanes to help drivers avoid accidents. In the coming years, these systems may exercise even more control of your vehicle, such as the self-driving cars that are under development by Google.

Consider this scenario: You come up over the crest of a hill. A school bus is disabled in your lane and you're traveling too fast to brake in time to avoid hitting it. To the left is a lane of oncoming traffic. To the right is a large grove of trees. A robotic system controlling your car has three options: (1) Apply the brakes to slow the vehicle. You will hit the school bus, but at a lower speed. You will survive, but some occupants of the bus may be killed. (2) Swerve to the left into oncoming traffic to avoid hitting the school bus. You may hit another car, but the risk of loss of human life is limited to just the occupants of two vehicles. (3) Swerve to the right into the trees. Only you are at risk of being killed if your car hits a tree. So which scenario does the robotic system controlling your car choose?

At this point, automobile manufacturers program robotic devices when they build the cars. But should owners have a choice of overriding the programming in their vehicles and adjust the ethical parameters of the robotic systems? If an owner was selfless, he or she could program the car to always make decisions that resulted in less harm to others (option 3 above). Alternatively, he or she could program the car to choose option 1, which minimizes his or her chance of injury.

And what would you as a manufacturer do until laws are passed regarding robotic ethics? If you program the car to protect the driver's life at all costs and the accident described above results in children on the bus dying, you could be sued by the families of the bus occupants. On the other hand, if you program the car to minimize harm to others, you could be sued by the driver's family when the car swerves into the woods and crashes into a tree killing the driver.

Meanwhile, researchers at Harvard University are experimenting with *robot swarms*—groups of robots that are programmed to work together to perform tasks without human intervention. But what happens if something goes wrong? Say a swarm of robots is assembling a building and they malfunction, causing a section of the building to collapse and injuring several bystanders. Who is responsible? Should it be the company who manufactured the robots or the human foreman who was supposedly supervising the job site?

What is best for society as a whole? The answer is not very clear-cut but is one we will need to wrestle with in the coming years.

Questions to Think About and Research

1. Who should be responsible for controlling the ethics of robotic systems? Why?
2. If a collision avoidance system in an automobile takes control of the vehicle to avoid an accident and a death results, who is responsible—human or machine?
3. When do the benefits of robotic controls outweigh the risks of the technology taking ethical decisions out of the hands of human beings?
4. Does relying on robots to make ethical decisions make us less human?

POINT

Individuals Should Have the Right to Set Ethics for Robotic Systems They Own

Advocates of individual choice over robotic ethics feel that just as individuals are free to make choices in their own lives, these choices should be extended to robots that they own.

1. Society dictates what is legal and illegal by passing laws. As long as choices over robotic ethics don't violate laws, they should be in the hands of individual owners.
2. Individuals should have the right to set ethical parameters for their robots because they may wish to be even more selfless than society dictates (i.e., by having the robots protect other people's lives, even at the cost of their own life).
3. When devices such as automobiles don't have robotic systems, individuals make ethical decisions in times of crisis. Robotic systems should be an extension of the individual's ethical values.

COUNTERPOINT

Robotic Ethics Should Be Controlled by the Government or Manufacturers

Critics maintain that individuals cannot be trusted to make decisions on robotic ethics that will benefit society as a whole. The greater good is served by making universal ethics programming decisions at the point of manufacture.

1. If robots do not contain ethical constraints that prevent harm to human beings, human lives may be lost.
2. Robots must have ethical programming that allows them to make decisions regarding the best possible outcomes in life and death situations.
3. Allowing individuals to adjust the ethics of robotic devices exposes society to risks from careless, thoughtless, or psychotic individuals.

FIGURE 7 Who should set the ethics for robotic systems? Individuals? Manufacturers? The government? *(Magictorch/Alamy)*

3D Printing: Who Is Responsible When Things Go Awry?

Summary of the Issue

3D printing is potentially going to revolutionize the way items are manufactured. With the cost of 3D printers falling, it may soon be practical and cost effective to produce a wide variety of products at home instead of buying them from a retail outlet or a manufacturer. However, this shift will potentially cause a range of issues involving intellectual property rights and liability.

In traditional manufacturing, it is relatively easy to enforce safety laws. Consider the manufacture of bicycle safety helmets. Traditional manufacturers are held accountable for delivering safely designed products free from defects in workmanship. Products are subjected to safety testing prior to being sold to the public and must conform to legal safety guidelines. If you buy a helmet and are injured while riding your bike because of a defect in the design of or materials used in the helmet, you would sue the manufacturer for damages. Manufacturers protect their designs (intellectual property) by obtaining patents.

3D printers produce objects from design plans generated with various types of software. Anyone that is reasonably proficient with design software can generate a design for an object to be printed. However, a person could also use a 3D scanner to scan an existing object (say a helmet designed and sold by a traditional manufacturer) and use design software to create their own plan for how to print it. If the object is patented, this would be a violation of the law. But it certainly makes it easier to steal someone's intellectual property.

Design plans for objects are often shared online. Even if the same design is used, the product quality can be vastly different depending on the type of 3D printer used and the raw materials (usually plastics) selected to be used when printing.

So you buy a 3D printer and raw materials. You download a design for a bicycle helmet from the Internet. You print out a helmet on your printer and give it to your neighbor. While riding his bicycle your neighbor is injured because the design of the helmet was flawed and the materials you used to make it were substandard. Who is responsible for the injuries? The manufacturer of the printer? The owner of the printer (i.e., you)? The manufacturer of the raw materials used to make the helmet? The creator of the flawed design plans? The person who decided to produce and distribute an untested product (again, you)? The person who decided to use an untested product (i.e., your neighbor)? What if the design you used was created from a patented product? You could be sued by the company that owns the patent for illegally producing its product design.

Questions to Think About and Research

1. Should individuals be allowed to distribute (or sell) products they make at home on 3D printers, or should the output be limited to personal use?
2. What regulations should the government put in place to regulate the safety and efficacy of product designs distributed for use on 3D printers? Are there any existing laws in the United States covering 3D printing technology?
3. How can we enforce intellectual property laws against the owners of 3D printers?

POINT

Regulating 3D Printing Protects Designers and the Public

Those arguing that 3D printing must be regulated contend the following:

1. Manufacturers depend on the integrity of the protection of intellectual property to make a fair profit on their work. The general public expects products to be produced that are free from design and material defects. If governments do not regulate 3D printing materials and designs, the public is placed in unnecessary peril.
2. Because designs of existing products are easy to produce, there is an increased chance of intellectual property theft.
3. Users of 3D printers need to understand the risks, responsibilities, and liabilities of producing products on demand for their use and for resale.

COUNTERPOINT

Unregulated 3D Printing Encourages Creativity

3D printing enthusiasts who believe that 3D printing should not be regulated argue the following:

1. The existing laws on intellectual property have worked to serve the interests of manufacturers. Manufacturers can seek legal remedies for violation of designs under existing laws.
2. Heavily regulating 3D printing will stifle creativity and ingenuity in the design and production of new products.
3. Consumers should be aware of the principle of "caveat emptor" (let the buyer beware) when using untested or unproven products. People should use untested products wisely and cautiously.

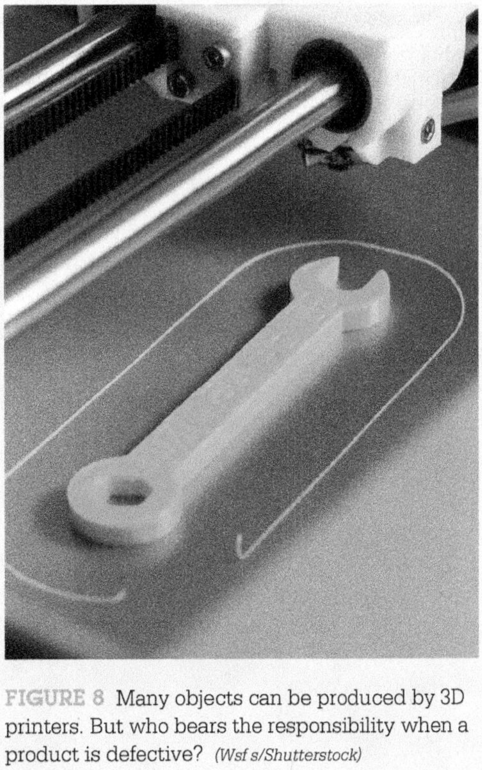

FIGURE 8 Many objects can be produced by 3D printers. But who bears the responsibility when a product is defective? *(Wsf s/Shutterstock)*

PRIVACY

Human-Implanted Data Chips: Protection or Orwellian Nightmare?

Summary of the Issue

Like respect and dignity, many people perceive privacy as a basic human right. However, many of us give up quite a bit of our privacy voluntarily via the devices we carry and the apps we use. Our smartphones include GPS chips that track our location, allowing us to check in on social media to let our friends know where we are. Activity trackers such as the Fitbit and even more sophisticated wireless medical devices can monitor our health. Even our smartphones use biometric data such as fingerprints to identify their owners. So why does the thought of implanting a data chip inside the human body cause so much uproar and dissent?

Human-implantable microchips have been available in the United States since 2004, when the FDA approved the VeriChip (now PositiveID). The basic advantages of implanted chips are that they can receive and transmit information and are extremely difficult to counterfeit. An implanted chip could positively identify you when you make a retail transaction, virtually eliminating fraud. Your chip could provide instant access to your medical records when you arrive in the emergency room unconscious after a car accident. Parents (and law enforcement) could potentially use the chips to locate lost or missing children. Alzheimer's patients could be tracked down if they go missing. And law enforcement could track the movement of convicted criminals out on parole. Sounds like a utopia, doesn't it?

Not at all, say a great deal of people. In fact, the idea of having a tracking chip or information-gathering chip implanted in the body makes many people extremely uncomfortable. It seems to go even one step further than the society in George Orwell's classic novel *1984* where everyone was monitored via cameras in public and at home. Despite the benefits, people see great potential for privacy infringement and potential misuse of data. Would you want your parents (or the government) to know where you are at any time? Would someone be able to read the medical information in your chip without your permission and use it against you? In fact, there is so much resistance from the public to implants that some states such as Wisconsin, California, Georgia, and North Dakota have already enacted legislation to prohibit mandatory data chips implants in the future, even though it is not being considered now.

The debate will most likely rage on as technologies continue to be developed that will allow implanted chips to gather and provide even more data. Whether the public embraces this technology remains to be seen.

Questions to Think About and Research

1. Would you ever be willing to have a data chip implanted in your body? Why or why not?
2. What data do you think would be useful to have on an implanted chip? What precautions should be taken to ensure that the data is not misused or collected without your knowledge?
3. Are there groups of people that you feel should be required to have chips implanted in them for the public good? If yes, list the groups and explain your rationale. If no, justify your answer.
4. In which states are mandatory chip implants currently illegal? Is there any federal legislation pending regarding chip implants?

POINT

Chip Implants Would Benefit Society

Advocates for personal chip implants feel the advantages of such implants outweigh the potential loss of privacy. They argue the following:

1. Data from implants can be used responsibly given adequate laws and safeguards to prevent misuse of data.
2. The benefits gained from monitoring criminals, vulnerable adults, and children outweigh the likelihood that individuals will be harmed by a loss of privacy.
3. In the digital age, loss of a certain amount of privacy is inevitable.

COUNTERPOINT

Chip Implants Would Lead to an Erosion of Personal Privacy

Advocates of protecting privacy in the United States contend that privacy concerns should outweigh the needs of governments, individuals, or businesses to have unrestricted access to personal information. They argue the following:

1. If businesses or government entities screen personal information contained in the implants, they might misuse or lose control of the data.
2. People should be able to choose not to share sensitive information, but implants take away individual control.
3. Being monitored without your explicit consent, via a mandatory implant, violates the basic human right to privacy.

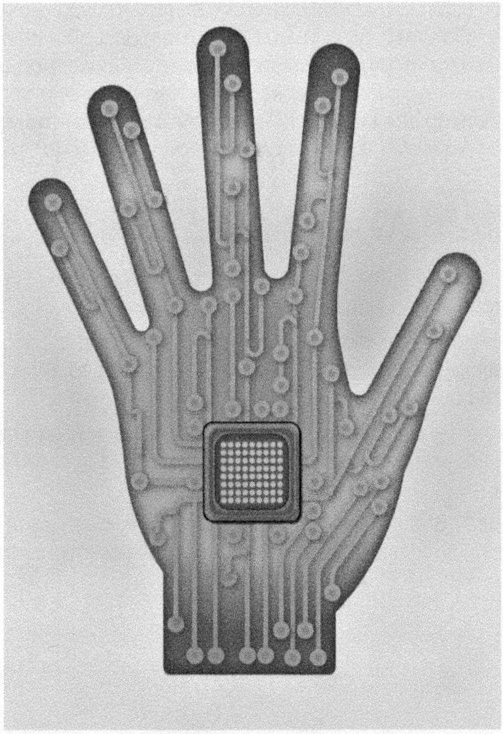

FIGURE 9 Data chip implants could provide physicians with faster access to medical records—but at what cost to our privacy? *(Juan Pablo Rada/ Shutterstock)*

PROPERTY RIGHTS

Mining an Asteroid: Who Owns Outer Space?

Summary of the Issue

Development of technology hardware requires lots of rare metals. Metals are mainly obtained from Earth via mining (although some metals could potentially be recovered from seawater). Whoever owns a piece of land usually owns the mineral rights to it as well and can mine it for its wealth. But there are places beyond Earth, like asteroids and planets, which appear to contain a wealth of minerals and metals. It's pretty clear who owns real estate on Earth (except for Antarctica, which isn't owned by any sovereign nation). But who owns the moon? Or Pluto? Or the asteroids in the asteroid belt between Mars and Jupiter?

Real property (or real estate) is either land or something built on land (like a building) considered immovable. Personal property items, such as cars and smartphones, are generally moveable from place to place. For personal property, possession usually presumes ownership. (You wouldn't have your neighbor's TV in your home, would you?) Real estate property ownership is usually proven by registered title or deed to avoid possession disputes. You may want to own land but not live on it, so to prove you own it and keep squatters from claiming it, you have a legal document proving ownership. So how do you get a deed to the moon?

The major law governing ownership of extraterrestrial territory (currently ratified by all spacefaring nations) is the 1967 Outer Space Treaty (OST). This treaty was mainly the result of the Cold War space race to the moon between the United States and the Soviet Union. Neither country wanted the other claiming the moon as their territory and building missile bases on it. The OST states that "outer space, including the moon and other celestial bodies, is not subject to national appropriation by claim of sovereignty, by means of use or occupation, or by any other means." So this means that the United States was unable to claim the moon as part of U.S. territory when it became the first country to land men on the moon. However, the OST language is vague on whether territory in outer space can be claimed by private parties for commercial purposes such as mining. With current advances in technology, it may soon be economically feasible to mine planets or asteroids.

So say your company identifies an asteroid that is rich in platinum. How do you gain ownership? That is currently unclear. Space mining rights are a bit like the Wild West at this point. Small asteroids, unlike planets or moons, are movable. If you find an asteroid and tow it back to Earth's orbit for mining, is it personal property? Possession might then signify ownership. But what about mining on the moon? On Earth, mining companies like to establish ownership to mineral rights before beginning operations through deeds or licenses. But because no one technically "owns" the moon, how do you protect the rights to your lunar mine? What if another company takes over your lunar mine by force? Who do you go to for resolution of the dispute?

Questions to Think About and Research

1. The moon is defined as a "celestial body" in the OST. Does the term *celestial body* in the OST include asteroids? If not, can a country claim ownership to asteroids because they are movable?
2. What would constitute laying claim to an asteroid? Would sending a probe to an asteroid to assess mineral content and leaving a radio transponder constitute ownership? Or would the asteroid need to be occupied by people? Would towing the asteroid into Earth's orbit constitute ownership?
3. Currently, if a meteor falls from space and destroys personal property, no one is to blame. What if while mining an asteroid a chunk (now a meteor) falls to Earth and destroys a building? Who should bear the risks of parking and mining asteroids in Earth's orbit?
4. Should the OST treaty be rescinded? Should governments be allowed to claim parts of outer space as their sovereign territory? Would being able to claim territory in space head off disputes that might otherwise arise?

POINT

Outer Space Belongs to the Human Race

The advocates of sharing outer space resources feel that no one country has the right to claim them, and all mankind should benefit from exploration and exploitation. They argue the following:

1. Cost of exploration can be controlled by consortiums of nations providing funding and offsetting costs incurred before distributing excess wealth recovered.
2. Space is large and there are plenty of resources for everyone to share.
3. Once a country claimed a territory, it would only recognize the rights of its sovereign citizens to that territory and that the country would actively defend its citizens' claims from incursions by other nations. Society must avoid such unproductive conflicts over ownership of outer space territory.

COUNTERPOINT

Outer Space Can Be Claimed by Private Companies

The advocates for private ownership of outer space generally feel that those who "discover" a territory and hold it (usually by occupation of citizens and a standing army) should have claim to it and the available resources. They argue the following:

1. The high cost of outer space exploration and mining deserves to be offset by the exploitation of resources recovered. Exploration will be limited if there is no incentive for profit.
2. Laws and regulations will need to be created to create ownership records (deeds and titles) to outer space properties claimed. Mining rights need to be protected in outer space so that claims are not "jumped" by unlawful individuals.
3. Competition for limited resources spurs innovation.

FIGURE 10 Asteroids are rich in rare metals. But who owns an asteroid? *(Johan Swanepoel/Fotolia)*

Should Everyone Have Free Access to Uncensored Information?

Summary of the Issue

In the United States, we expect free and uncensored access to the Internet. However, people in other parts of the globe do not always enjoy these same freedoms. For instance, India's IT Act Rule 12 states that websites can be blocked if it is "necessary or expedient so to do in the interest of sovereignty and integrity of India, defense of India, security of the State, friendly relations with foreign states or public order or for preventing incitement to the commission of any cognizable offence relating to above." Citing this rule, India banned and blocked over 800 pornographic sites in August 2015. The ban sparked a huge debate among the populace about free speech and personal freedom. The ban was partially lifted in a few days with only sites deemed to be promoting child pornography still blocked. Blocking child pornography is obviously a laudable goal, but other countries block many different types of websites.

In early 2006, when Google launched its search engine services in China, it conceded to the Chinese government's demands that it self-censor its search engine, restricting search results for sensitive information such as the details of the Tiananmen Square protests and of human rights groups. This decision prompted much discussion, with some condemning Google's decision for putting business profits over what they saw as basic human rights (see Figure 11). Google justified its actions by stating that a company must operate within the rules of the market in which it operates and that the benefits of increased access to information for people in China "outweighed our discomfort in agreeing to censor some results." And, compared with search results from **Baidu.com**, the leading Chinese search engine, Google was not censoring all information.

However, in 2010, Google announced that it was no longer willing to censor search results and moved the site to Hong Kong, where it hoped there would be less censorship. The departure was a reaction to a sophisticated, targeted cyberattack that Google believes was done to gather information on Chinese human rights activists. At that time, Google had about a 35% market share.

Microsoft had only a 1% share of the market, so it decided to partner with **Baidu.com** to provide English-language search results for China's largest search engine. Microsoft stated it would agree to abide by Chinese censorship laws (so search terms like *freedom* and *democracy* deliver filtered results), thereby respecting the laws of the countries where it operates. However, before honoring any censor requests, Microsoft insisted that Chinese authorities made legally binding requests in writing.

So how did it all work out? As of the end of 2014, Google's market share had dropped to 12.04% in China, whereas **Baidu.com** has increased its market share to 79.45%. Microsoft's decision to keep censoring its searches appears to have paid off—at least from a monetary perspective. But is the financial result more important than the social implications of its behavior?

Questions to Think About and Research

1. Is there anything else that Google could have done that would have a major impact on China's censorship laws?
2. Has Microsoft's compliance with censorship laws furthered the Chinese government's cooperation in combating software piracy in China? Are Microsoft's financial incentives even deeper than just Internet market share?
3. Can the U.S. government compel technology companies to take a firmer stance on free speech in China and elsewhere by instituting criminal charges if U.S. companies do not take reasonable steps to protect human rights?

POINT

U.S. Companies Should Comply with Local Laws in Foreign Countries

Those in favor of Microsoft's actions to remain in China feel that if a company chooses to operate in a foreign country, it knows the local laws and should be prepared to work within those laws as it does business. They argue the following:

1. It is not the place of a company to try to change laws of foreign countries. Reform must come from within.
2. Working in China does not mean a company supports all of China's policies.
3. Microsoft's presence continues to advance the progress the Chinese government is making toward democracy. U.S. companies can ethically stay in China if they make an effort to improve human rights there. U.S. companies operating in China should agree on guidelines that respect human rights.

COUNTERPOINT

U.S. Companies Should Put What Is Right Ahead of What Is Financially Expedient

Those in favor of Google's actions believe that international corporations should begin to take a firm stance against governments that do not promote basic human rights. They argue the following:

1. China will never change unless there are financial and political incentives to do so. Google's departure helps pressure the Chinese government.
2. Google's withdrawal from China threatens the viability of many advertising resellers in China.
3. Google's decision to leave helps put pressure on China's government to play by global standards. China cannot expect to compete in the global marketplace while refusing to have a global exchange of ideas.

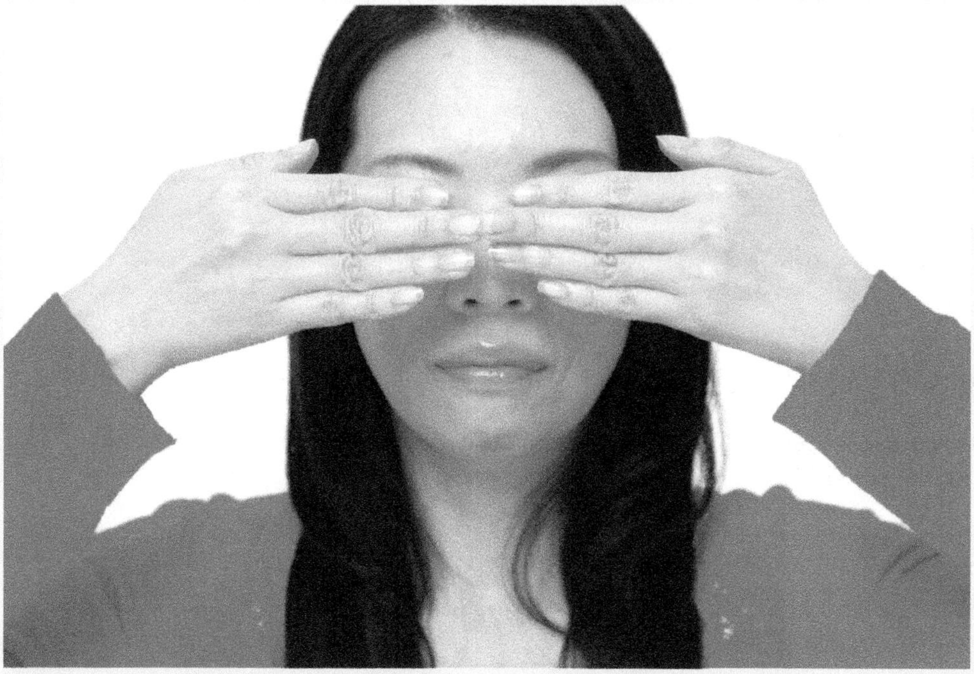

FIGURE 11 Is free access to content attainable in countries (such as China and India) where information availability can be restricted by law? *(Deeepblue/Shutterstock)*

Hacktivism: Civil Disobedience or Terrorism?

Summary of the Issue

Civil disobedience and the right to assemble and protest are basic liberties to which many Americans feel entitled. After all, this type of activism is part of what helped create America. Remember that little protest in 1773 that became known as the Boston Tea Party or that little document called the *Declaration of Independence*? Those are both shining examples of civil disobedience.

With the rise of e-commerce, it might be difficult to stage an event such as the Boston Tea Party. For instance, suppose you felt Amazon was treating some segment of their customers unfairly. Where would you go to protest when Amazon doesn't have any physical stores? This type of problem has given rise to acts of hacktivism.

Hacktivism (derived from *hack* and *activism*) involves using computers and computer networks in a subversive way to promote an agenda usually related to causes such as free speech, human rights, or freedom of information. Essentially, it's using computer hacking to affect some sort of social change. As computer security has grown more sophisticated, attacks today are usually carried out by groups of hackers (such as Anonymous or LulzSec) or groups of computer scientists funded by nation states for the specific purpose of hacking.

Hacktivism often takes the form of denial-of-service attacks in which websites are bombarded with requests for information until they are overwhelmed and legitimate users can't access the site. Other times, they take the form of cyberterrorism, where the objective is to embarrass or harass a company by penetrating its computer networks and stealing (and often publishing) sensitive information. Certain countries (like China) are rumored to maintain cadres of computer scientists whose main goal is to spy on other countries by hacking into their computer networks.

One of the most famous instances of hacktivism revolved around the scheduled release of the movie ***The Interview*** by Sony Entertainment Pictures in late 2014. With a plot revolving around two television personalities who are recruited by the CIA to assassinate leader of North Korea Kim Jong Un, the movie was controversial as soon as its preview was released and sparked protests from the North Korean government. In late November 2014, a hacktivist group penetrated Sony's computer networks and stole a tremendous amount of confidential data. It then posted four unreleased movies to pirate websites and threatened to publish additional data unless the release of ***The Interview*** was canceled. In addition, the group totally trashed Sony's internal networks, making them unusable. Eventually, over 38 million files of confidential data were leaked, including personal finance information and e-mails of Sony employees.

Many saw the Sony incident as an example of terrorism given the viciousness of the attack. But other attacks that change the content of websites to promote agendas might seem less harmful. Regardless of the intent of the hacktivists, hacking into computer systems is illegal in almost every part of the globe. However, civil disobedience does involve breaking the law to bring to light social injustice. So is hacking a computer network any different than tossing tea overboard in the Boston Harbor? Or is it just civil disobedience 21st-century style?

Questions to Think About and Research

1. Can you think of any instances where hacking a computer system is morally justified? For your examples, what other types of protest strategies could be used other than hacking?
2. There are federal laws that make hacking a crime. Are there instances where these laws should be ignored, such as if public opinion is overwhelmingly on the side of an issue?
3. What responsibility does the government have to combat hacktivism attacks on private companies such as Sony Pictures? Should security of digital information be a constitutional right?

POINT

Hacking Is a Natural Extension of Civil Disobedience

Proponents of hacktivism generally feel that the ends justify the means. They argue the following:

1. Society as a whole benefits when injustices are exposed.
2. Civil disobedience is an inalienable right upon which the United States was born.
3. Methods of civil disobedience need to keep pace with modern technology in order to have the greatest impact possible.

COUNTERPOINT

Hacktivism Is Illegal and Therefore Wrong

Opponents of hacktivism usually cite the fact that there are laws preventing the unauthorized penetration of computer systems. They argue the following:

1. Computer technology provides many opportunities for reaching a wide audience with a message without resorting to illegal activities such as hacking.
2. Personal data of individuals needs to be protected as a basic right of privacy.
3. Hacking into computer systems for alleged acts of "civil disobedience" are often hard to distinguish from acts of cyberterrorism.

FIGURE 12 Is hacktivism civil disobedience or terrorism? It can be difficult to tell the difference. *(Frank Peters/Shutterstock)*

Using Computers to Support Ethical Conduct

Although there are many opportunities to use computers and the Internet unethically, we can also use technology to support ethical conduct. For example, many charitable organizations use the Internet and other technology tools for fundraising. When a severe earthquake swept through Nepal in April 2015, the Red Cross and other charities received many pledges via their websites.

Google Crisis Response is a project sponsored by Google that helps disseminate information before and after a crisis to coordinate relief efforts and provide updates to the public (see Figure 13). Google Person Finder, part of Google Crisis Response, helps individuals and organizations to provide information and updates on persons missing (or located) after a disaster.

Computing devices and the Internet provide many opportunities for you to start or get involved in ethical initiatives. Consider the Empty Bowls movement that was started by students at Wichita State University. Local potters, students, and educators worked to create bowls and then guests were invited to consume a simple meal of bread and soup from them. For a donation to help local organizations feed the hungry, donors were encouraged to keep the bowls as a reminder of all the empty bowls in the world. This movement is now spreading across the United States through the website **emptybowls.net**. What can you and your fellow students do in your community?

Throughout your life, you'll encounter many ethical challenges relating to information technology. Your personal ethics—combined with the ethical guidelines your company provides and the general ethical environment of society—will guide your decisions.

For further information on ethics, check out the following websites:

- Ethics in Computing (**ethics.csc.ncsu.edu**)
- The Center for Ethics in Science and Technology (**ethicscenter.net**)
- Business Ethics: The Magazine of Corporate Responsibility (**business-ethics.com**)
- Council for Ethical Leadership at Capital University (**businessethics.org**)
- John J. Reilly Center at University of Notre Dame (**reilly.nd.edu**)

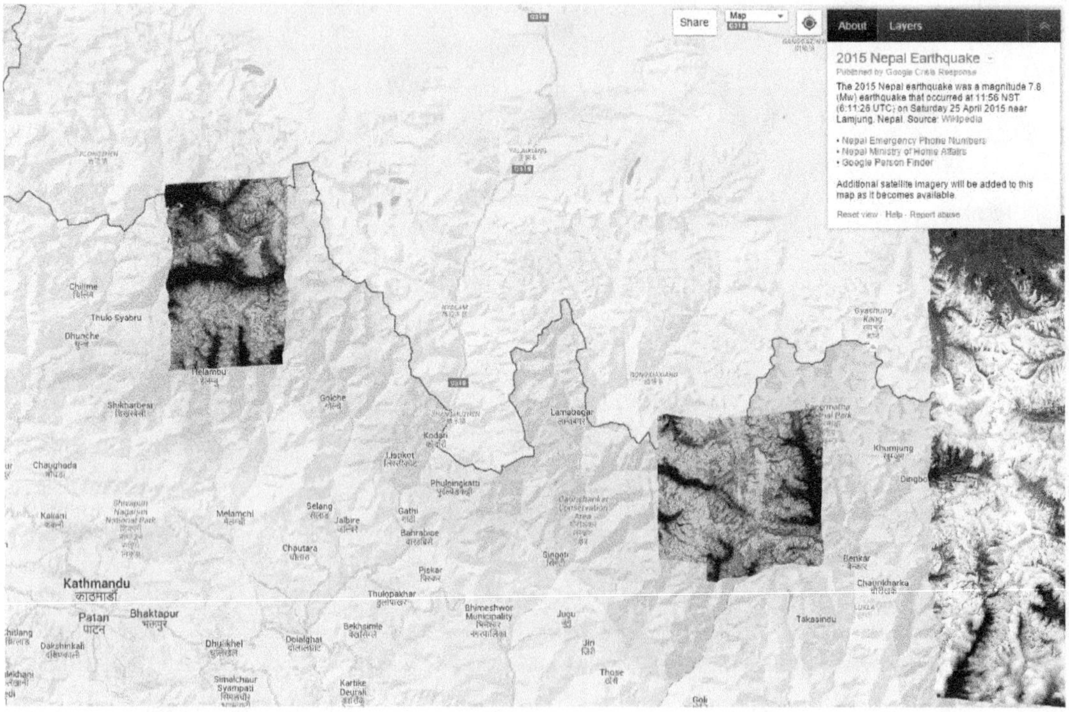

FIGURE 13 Tools provided by Google Crisis Response help disseminate information and locate lost individuals after a disaster such as the earthquake in Nepal in 2015. *(© 2015 Google Inc. All rights reserved. Google and the Google Logo are registered trademarks of Google Inc.)*

check your understanding // review & practice

For a quick review of what you've learned, answer the following questions.

multiple choice

1. Which ethical theory focuses on adherence to moral duties and rights?

- **a.** deontology
- **b.** divine command theory
- **c.** utilitarianism
- **d.** relativism

2. The ethical theory that states that deities are all-knowing and set moral truth is

- **a.** utilitarianism.
- **b.** virtue ethics.
- **c.** deontology.
- **d.** divine command theory.

3. Which ethical philosophy states that morals are internal?

- **a.** deontology
- **b.** virtue ethics
- **c.** relativism
- **d.** divine command theory

4. Which of the following statements is *false*?

- **a.** Individuals who have no sense of right or wrong exhibit amoral behavior.
- **b.** Ethical decisions are usually influenced by personal ethics.
- **c.** Unethical behavior is always illegal.
- **d.** Life experience affects an individual's personal ethics.

5. Unethical behavior is

- **a.** the same as illegal behavior.
- **b.** based on civil disobedience.
- **c.** different from illegal behavior.
- **d.** governed by specific laws passed by legislative bodies.

6. The field of psychology that theorizes that happiness results from ethical living is known as

- **a.** principled psychology.
- **b.** positive psychology.
- **c.** moral psychology.
- **d.** affirmative psychology.

7. Which system of ethics states there is no universal moral truth?

- **a.** utilitarianism
- **b.** relativism
- **c.** virtue ethics
- **d.** There is no universally agreed-on best system.

8. What should you do if you spot unethical behavior at your workplace?

- **a.** Nothing, as long as the behavior is legal.
- **b.** Report it to the police immediately.
- **c.** Follow company procedures for reporting unethical behavior.
- **d.** Start looking for a new job.

9. Which of the following actions would NOT help to identify your personal ethics?

- **a.** Describe yourself.
- **b.** Identify the influences of your work environment.
- **c.** Conduct a genealogic study of your extended family.
- **d.** Prepare a list of values that are most important to you.

10. Ethical decisions in business affect which of the following?

- **a.** employees
- **b.** business's clients and customers
- **c.** suppliers and financial lenders
- **d.** all stakeholders

MyITLab Go to **MyITLab** to take an autograded version of the *Check Your Understanding* review and to find all media resources for the chapter.

7 Networking: Connecting Computing Devices

How Networks Function

Learning Outcome 7.1 You will be able to explain the basics of networking, including the components needed to create networks, and describe the different ways you can connect networks to the Internet.

Networking Fundamentals 260

Objective 7.1 *Explain what a network is and the pros and cons of having one.*

Active Helpdesk: Understanding Networking

Network Architectures 262

Objective 7.2 *Discuss how networks are defined by distance.*

Objective 7.3 *Discuss how networks are classified by levels of administration.*

Objective 7.4 *Describe the Ethernet protocols for wired and wireless networks.*

Network Components 265

Objective 7.5 *Describe the types of transmission media used in networks.*

Objective 7.6 *Describe the basic devices necessary for networks.*

Objective 7.7 *Describe the type of software necessary for networks.*

Connecting to the Internet 269

Objective 7.8 *Compare and contrast the broadband options available to access the Internet.*

Sound Byte: Connecting to the Internet

Objective 7.9 *Explain how to access the Internet wirelessly.*

Active Helpdesk: Connecting to the Internet

Objective 7.10 *Summarize the pros and cons of dial-up connections.*

Your Home Network

Learning Outcome 7.2 You will be able to describe what you need to install and configure a home network and how to manage and secure a wireless network.

Installing and Configuring Home Networks 276

Objective 7.11 *Explain steps you should take before creating a home network.*

Objective 7.12 *Describe what you need in order to connect devices to a network.*

Sound Byte: Installing a Home Computer Network

Objective 7.13 *Describe specialized devices you can add to a home network.*

Objective 7.14 *Summarize how to configure home network software.*

Managing and Securing Wireless Networks 285

Objective 7.15 *Describe the potential problems with wireless networks and how to avoid them.*

Objective 7.16 *Describe how to secure a wireless home network.*

Sound Byte: Securing Wireless Networks

Make This: MAKE: Networked Devices on **page 275**

All media accompanying this chapter can be found in MyITLab.

For an overview of the chapter, watch the **Preview Video**.

(Sergey Nivens/Fotolia, Nicotombo/Fotolia, AKS/Fotolia, Vlad Kochelaevskiy/123RF, Hywards/Fotolia, Mipan/Fotolia)

HOW COOL IS THIS?

Many of us have multiple wireless devices but often **no access to WiFi**, or we're too near the limit on our mobile device data plan to do what we want without costing a small fortune. Now, using **Karma WiFi**, you can travel with your own **personal hotspot**, and you can share the connection while **earning more data** as you do. All you need to do is buy a Karma device and set up an account. You get 1 GB of data, which is enough to watch a two-hour movie or listen to eight hours of music. When you've used that up, you can purchase more—no subscription needed. And you can stretch how often you need to buy more data by **sharing your connection**. As others connect to your Karma hotspot, you each earn a free 100 MB. You only share the connection—not your data—so the more you share, the more free bandwidth you accumulate. The benefits of social networking have come to WiFi! *(Mathisworks/Getty Images)*

How Networks Function

Learning Outcome 7.1 You will be able to explain the basics of networking, including the components needed to create networks, and describe the different ways you can connect networks to the Internet.

You access wired and wireless networks all the time—when you use an ATM, print out a document, or use the Internet (the world's largest network). It's important to understand the fundamentals of networking, such as how networks are set up, what devices are necessary to establish a network, and how you can access a network so that you can share, collaborate, and exchange information among your friends, family, and colleagues.

networking FUNDAMENTALS

Many of today's homes have more than one computing device capable of connecting to the Internet. A typical family engages in many activities that involve sharing and accessing files over and from the Internet and using a variety of Internet-connected devices (see Figure 7.1). What makes all this technology transfer and sharing possible? A computer network!

Understanding Networks

Objective 7.1 *Explain what a network is and the pros and cons of having one.*

What exactly is a network? A computer **network** is simply two or more computers that are connected via software and hardware so they can communicate with each other. Each device connected to a network is referred to as a **node**. A node can be a computer, a peripheral such as a printer or a game console, or a network device such as a router (see Figure 7.2).

What are the benefits of networks? There are several benefits to having computers networked:

- **Sharing an Internet connection:** A network lets you share the high-speed Internet connection coming into your home.
- **Sharing printers and other peripherals:** Networks let you share printers and other peripheral devices. For

FIGURE 7.1 With a home network, all family members can connect their computing devices whenever and wherever they want.

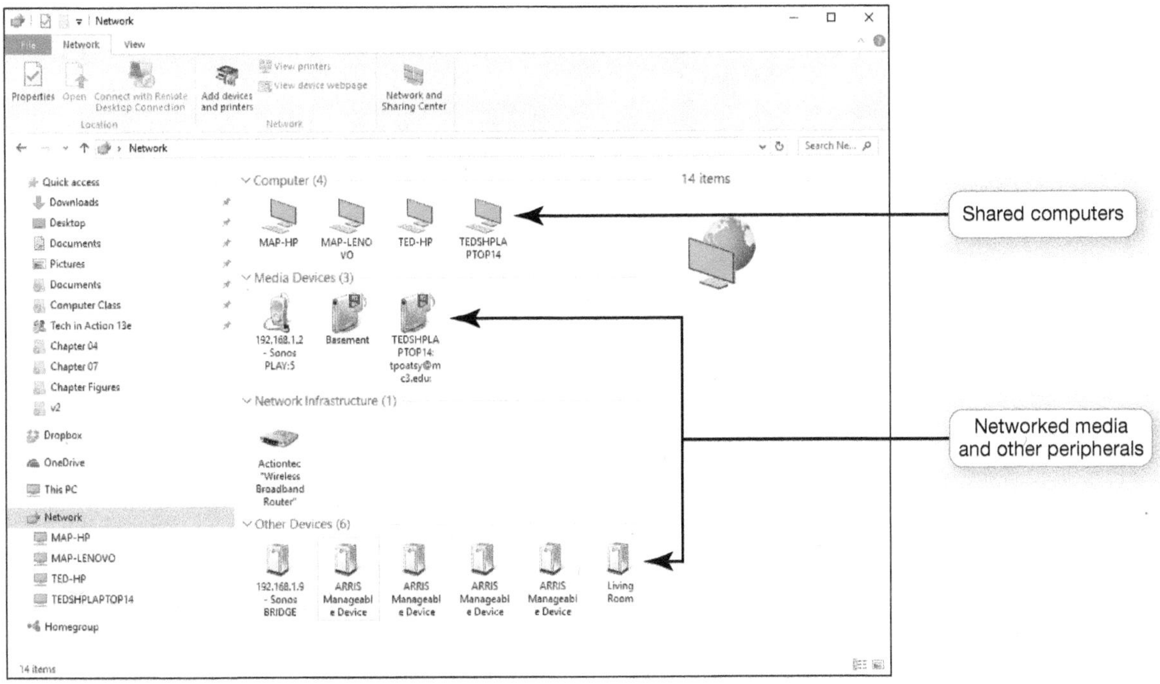

FIGURE 7.2 File Explorer shows computers, media, and other devices (such as set-top boxes) that are networked for sharing. *(Windows 10, Microsoft Corporation)*

example, say you have a laptop that isn't connected to a printer. To print a document from your laptop without a network, you would need to transfer the file using a flash drive or other device to another computer that's connected to the printer or carry your laptop to the printer and connect your laptop to it. With a network, you can print directly from your device even if it's not physically connected to the printer.

- **Sharing files:** You can share files between networked computers without having to use portable storage devices such as flash drives to transfer the files. In addition, you can set sharing options in Windows or OS X that let the user of each computer on the network access files stored on any other computer on the network.
- **Common communications:** Computers running different operating systems can communicate on the same network.

Are there disadvantages to setting up networks? Fortunately, after most home networks have been set up, there isn't much else that needs to be done to maintain or administer the network; therefore, the benefits of using a home network outweigh the disadvantages. However, large networks involve an initial purchase of equipment to set them up. They also need to be administered, which can be costly and time consuming. **Network administration** involves tasks such as:

- Installing new computers and devices,
- Monitoring the network to ensure it is performing efficiently,
- Updating and installing new software on the network, and
- Configuring, or setting up, proper security for a network.

How fast does data move through networks? Data transfer rate (also called **bandwidth**) is the maximum speed at which data can be transmitted between two nodes on a network. **Throughput** is the actual speed of data transfer that is achieved. Throughput is always less than or equal to the data transfer rate. Data transfer rate and throughput are usually measured in *megabits per second (Mbps)*. A megabit is one million bits. One of the main factors that determines how fast data moves is the type of network, which we'll discuss later in this chapter. ■

ACTIVE HELPDESK
Understanding Networking

In this Active Helpdesk, you'll play the role of a helpdesk staffer, fielding questions about home networks—their advantages, their main components, and the most common types—as well as about wireless networks and how they are created.

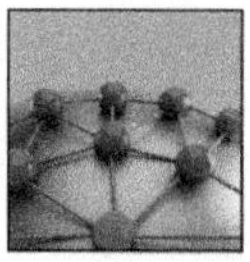

network ARCHITECTURES

The network you have in your home differs greatly in terms of its size, structure, and cost from the one on your college campus. This difference is based in part on how the networks are designed or configured. Networks are classified according to:

- The distance between nodes
- The way in which the network is managed (or administered)
- The set of rules (or *protocol*) used to exchange data between network nodes

In this section, we'll look at these network classifications.

Network Architectures Defined by Distance

Objective 7.2 *Discuss how networks are defined by distance.*

How does the distance between nodes define a network? The distance between nodes on a network is one type of **network architecture** or network design. Networks can range from the smallest network of just one person with multiple connected devices to the largest network that spans between cities and even the world. The following are common types of networks (see Figure 7.3):

- A **personal area network (PAN)** is a network used for communication among devices close to one person, such as smartphones and tablets using wireless technologies such as Bluetooth and WiFi.
- A **local area network (LAN)** is a network in which the nodes are located within a small geographic area. Examples include a network in a computer lab at school or at a fast-food restaurant.
- A **home area network (HAN)** is a specific type of LAN located in a home. HANs are used to connect all of a home's digital devices, such as computers, peripherals, phones, gaming devices, digital video recorders (DVRs), and televisions.
- A **metropolitan area network (MAN)** is a large network designed to provide access to a specific geographic area, such as an entire city. Many U.S. cities are now deploying MANs to provide Internet access to residents and tourists. Some MANs employ WiMAX wireless technology that extends local WiFi networks across greater distances.
- A **wide area network (WAN)** spans a large physical distance. The Internet is the largest WAN, covering the globe. A WAN is also a networked collection of LANs. If a school has multiple campuses located in different towns, each with its own LAN, connecting the LANs of each campus by telecommunications lines allows the users of the LANs to communicate. All the connected LANs would be described as a single WAN.

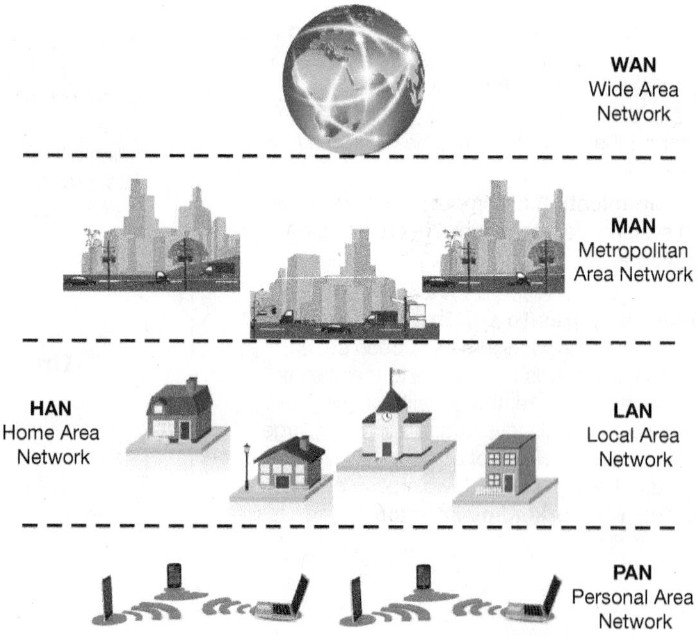

FIGURE 7.3 Networks can be classified by the distance between their nodes.
(SiuWing/Shutterstock)

Network Architectures Defined by Levels of Administration

Objective 7.3 *Discuss how networks are classified by levels of administration.*

How does the level of administration define a network? A network can be administered, or managed, in two main ways—centrally or locally (see Figure 7.4):

- *Central administration*: In a centrally administered network, tasks performed from one computer can affect the other computers on the network. A **client/server network** is an example. In a client/server network, a *client* is a computer on which users accomplish tasks and make requests, whereas the *server* is the computer that provides information or resources to the client computers as well as central administration for network functions such as printing. Most networks that have 10 or more nodes are client/server networks.
- *Local administration*: In a locally administered network, the configuration and maintenance of the network must be performed on each individual computer attached to the network. A **peer-to-peer (P2P) network** is an example. In a P2P network, each node connected on the network can communicate directly with every other node on the network. Thus, all nodes on this type of network are peers (equals). When printing, for example, a computer on a P2P network doesn't have to go through the computer that's connected to the printer. Instead, it can communicate directly with the printer. Because they're simple to set up, cost less than client/server networks, and are easier to configure and maintain, P2P networks are the most common type of home network. Very small schools and offices may also use P2P networks.

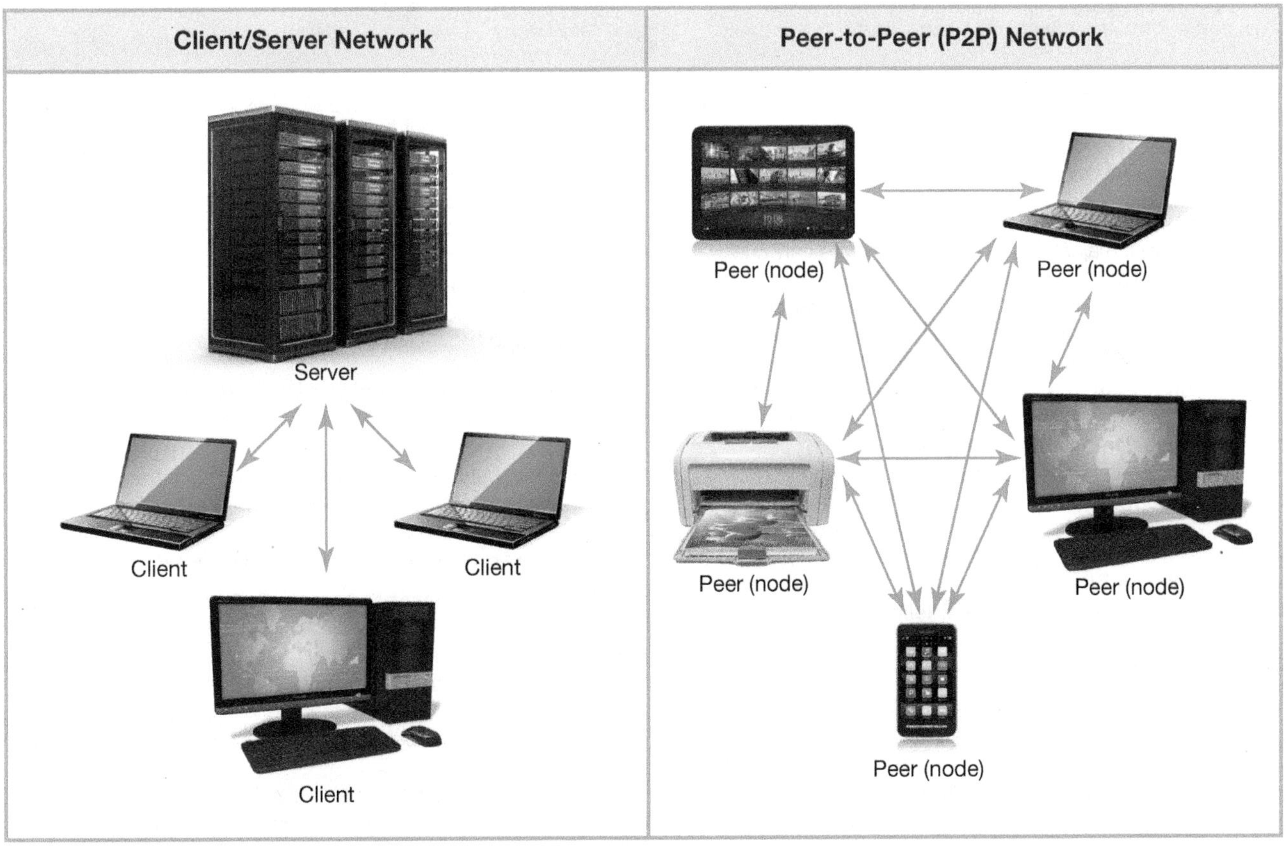

FIGURE 7.4 Client/Server and P2P Networks *(Oleksiy Mark/Fotolia, Oleksiy Mark/Fotolia, Sashkin/Fotolia, Maksym Dykha/Fotolia, Oleksiy Mark/Fotolia, Tuulijumala/Fotolia)*

BITS&BYTES

The Rise of Wearable Technology

Wearable technology is, as its name indicates, technology incorporated into things you wear. The devices become a part of your personal area network as they transfer data via Bluetooth to a mobile app or your computer. Popular wearable devices include fitness trackers, such as those from Jawbone and Fitbit, and interactive digital fabrics such as Athos Gear, which have built-in sensors that monitor specific activity as well as your heart rate while you're working out. In addition to health and fitness monitoring, smartwatches such as Apple's iWatch let you connect to your e-mail and calendar, among other personal productivity tools (see Figure 7.5). The medical industry is also implementing wearable devices, such as those to monitor cardiac patients for heart rate and blood pressure. Nearly 50% of American adults already own some form of a wearable device, and the trend is increasing at a remarkable rate. Do you have any wearable technology as a part of your PAN?

FIGURE 7.5 Smartwatches are a form of wearable technology that can monitor your activity and let you connect to personal productivity tools like your e-mail and calendar. *(Guido Mieth/Taxi/Getty Images)*

Ethernet Protocols

Objective 7.4 *Describe the Ethernet protocols for wired and wireless networks.*

What network standard is used in my home network? The vast majority of home and corporate networks are Ethernet networks. An **Ethernet network** is so named because it uses the Ethernet protocol as the means (or standard) by which the nodes on the network communicate.

The Ethernet protocol was developed by the Institute of Electrical and Electronics Engineers (IEEE), which develops many standard specifications for electronic data transmission that are adopted throughout the world. Establishing standards for networking is important so that devices from different manufacturers will work well together.

There are different standards for wired and wireless networks. The standard for wired Ethernet networks is 802.3, also known as **gigabit Ethernet**. The standard for wireless Ethernet networks, also known as **wireless fidelity (WiFi)**, is 802.11. The current version of wireless Ethernet is 802.11ac. Previous versions included 802.11n, 802.11g, 802.11b, and 802.11a.

How is the 802.11ac version different from the previous versions? The newer wireless Ethernet standard, 802.11ac, is faster and has a better signal range than the 802.11n standard. The 802.11n standard, often referred to as *dual band*, operates at either a 2.4 GHz or a 5 GHz frequency. Prior standards operated only at the 2.4 GHz frequency that many other wireless devices (such as wireless landline phones) run on. The 802.11ac standard operates at a 5 GHz frequency. This means the 802.11ac standard is more resistant to signal interference from other wireless devices in the home.

Are there emerging standards? 802.11ad, also known as WiGig, is an upcoming wireless option. WiGig is expected to deliver speeds up to 7 gigabits per second (Gbps) at 60 GHz frequencies but for short distances. It's anticipated that 802.11ac and 802.11ad will work in tandem: 802.11ad providing very fast transmission speeds for a room-sized area—perfect for delivering streaming media or quick data transfers between devices—and 802.11ac for all other wireless transmissions. Two other standards, 802.11af (Super WiFi or White-Fi) and 802.11ah (Low Power WiFi), are being developed to help accommodate the anticipated continued dependence on wireless devices.

Will devices using older WiFi standards still work on a newer network? Devices using older standards, such as 802.11n, will still work with newer 802.11ac networks, but they'll operate with slower data transfer rates and may run into some frequency interference. The ability of current devices to use earlier standards in addition to the current standard is known as **backward compatibility**.

Are there different standards for wired Ethernet? Just as there are different WiFi standards, there are different wired Ethernet standards. The most commonly used wired Ethernet standard for home networks is the gigabit Ethernet standard. A data transfer rate of up to 1 Gbps is possible using this standard. Computers generally ship with gigabit Ethernet cards installed in them.

For even faster data transfer speeds, 10, 40, and even 100 gigabit Ethernet is available, providing maximum data transfer rates of 10, 40, and 100 Gbps, respectively. However, these networks are not currently meant for home use. The 10 and 40 gigabit Ethernet (GbE) are intended for businesses, whereas 100 GbE is used for the major transmission lines of the Internet known as the *Internet backbone*. Cable Internet provider Comcast has begun to test trial markets of 10 gigabit Ethernet for home use. As promising as this may sound, the monthly charge is estimated to be $300, putting it out of reach for many home users. ■

network COMPONENTS

To function, all networks must include:

- A means of connecting the nodes on the network (cables or wireless technology)
- Special hardware devices that allow the nodes to communicate with each other and to send data
- Software that allows the network to run (see Figure 7.6)

Transmission Media

Objective 7.5 *Describe the types of transmission media used in networks.*

How do nodes connect to each other? All network nodes are connected to each other and to the network by transmission media. **Transmission media** can be either wired or wireless; they establish a communications channel between the nodes on a network. The media used depend on the requirements of a network and its users.

What transmission media is used on a wired network? Wired networks use various types of cable (wire) to connect nodes (see Figure 7.7). The type of network and the distance between nodes determines the type of cable used:

- **Twisted-pair cable** is made up of copper wires that are twisted around each other and surrounded by a plastic jacket. Normal telephone cable is a type of twisted-pair cable, although phone cable won't work for connecting a LAN or HAN. A slightly different type of twisted-pair cable, called **unshielded twisted-pair (UTP) cable**, is used for networks. UTP is composed of four pairs of wires twisted around each other to reduce electrical interference.
- **Coaxial cable** consists of a single copper wire surrounded by layers of plastic. If you have cable TV, the cable running into your TV or cable box is most likely coaxial cable.
- **Fiber-optic cable** is made up of plastic or glass fibers that transmit data at extremely fast speeds.

What type of cable is used in most wired home networks? The most popular transmission media option for wired Ethernet networks is UTP cable. You can buy UTP cable in varying lengths with Ethernet connectors (called RJ-45

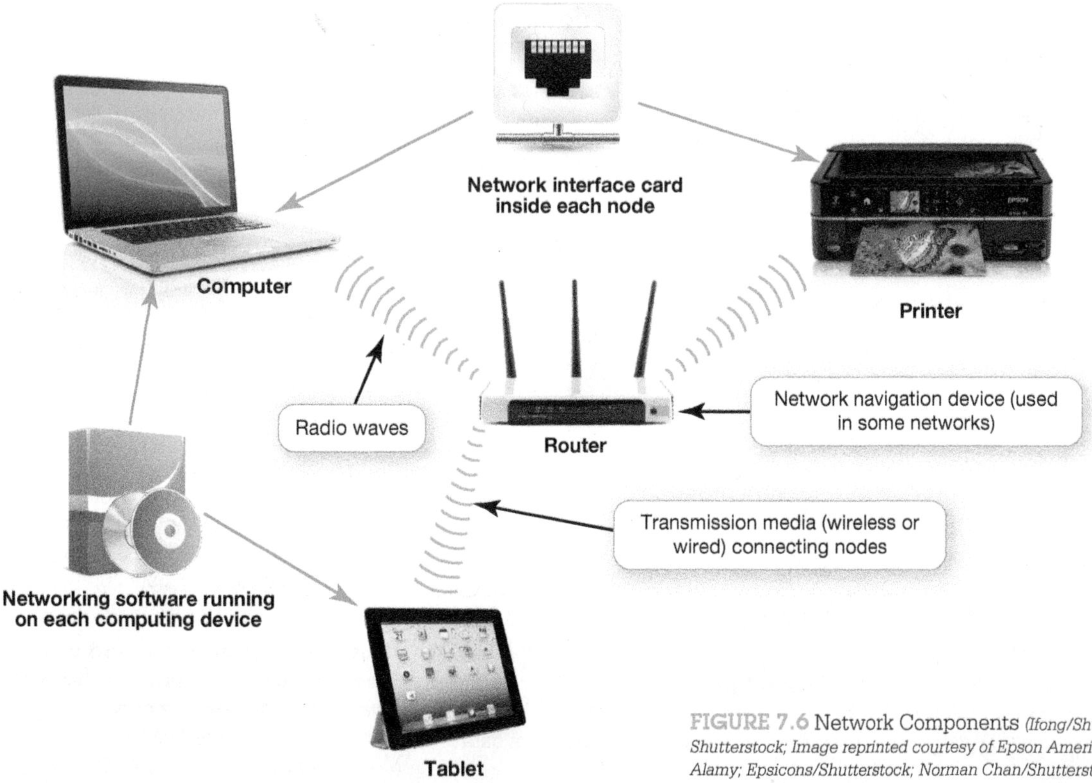

FIGURE 7.6 Network Components *(Ifong/Shutterstock; Sergii Korolko/Shutterstock; Image reprinted courtesy of Epson America, Inc.; Adrian Lyon/Alamy; Epsicons/Shutterstock; Norman Chan/Shutterstock)*

FIGURE 7.7

Wired Transmission Media

(Deepspacedave/Shutterstock, Zwola Fasola/Shutterstock, Zentilia/Shutterstock)

connectors) already attached. Ethernet connectors resemble standard phone connectors (called RJ-11 connectors) but are slightly larger and have contacts for eight wires (four pairs) instead of four wires.

Do all wired Ethernet networks use the same kind of UTP cable? The three main types of UTP cable you would consider using in wired Ethernet home networks and their data transfer rates are as follows (also see Figure 7.8):

1. *Cat 5E*: Although Cat 5E cable is the cheapest of the three types and is sufficient for many home networking tasks, it was designed for 100 Mbps–wired Ethernet networks that were popular before gigabit Ethernet networks became the standard. Therefore, you should probably not install Cat 5E cable, even though it's still available in stores.
2. *Cat 6*: Because **Cat 6 cable** is designed to achieve data transfer rates that support a gigabit Ethernet network, it's probably the best choice for home networking cable, though it's more expensive and more difficult to work with than Cat 5E cable.
3. *Cat 6a*: Cat 6a cable is designed for ultrafast Ethernet networks that run at speeds as fast as 10 Gbps. Installing a 10 gigabit Ethernet network in the home is probably unnecessary because today's home applications (even gaming and streaming media) don't require this rate of data transfer.

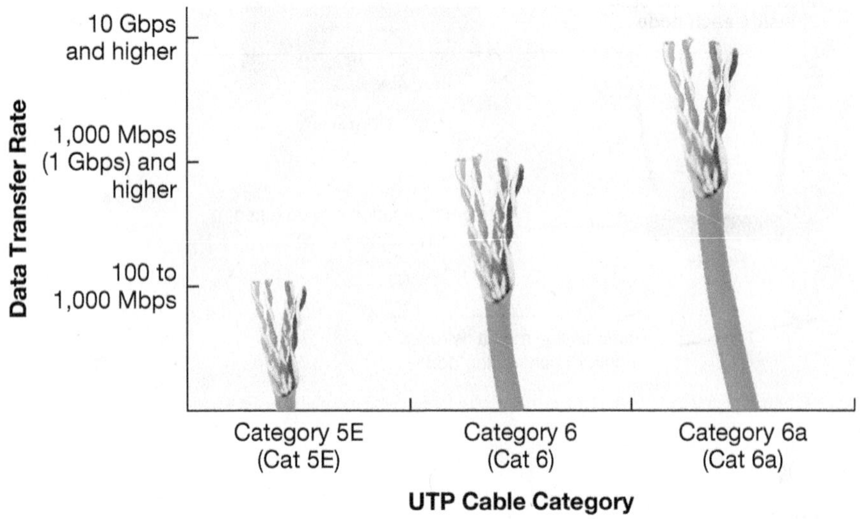

FIGURE 7.8 The three main UTP cable types used in home networks have different data transfer rates *(Emran/Shutterstock)*

What transmission media is used to connect nodes on a wireless network? As noted earlier, *WiFi* is a standard for wireless transmissions using radio waves to connect computing devices to wireless networks and the Internet. With so many portable devices being connected to networks, a network with wireless connectivity is used in businesses as well as in most homes. However, note that wireless networks generally have decreased throughput compared with that of wired networks.

Why are wireless networks slower than wired networks? The following are some common reasons why wireless signals may have decreased throughput:

- Wireless signals are more susceptible to interference from magnetic and electrical sources.
- Other wireless networks (such as your neighbor's network) can interfere with the signals on your network.
- Certain building materials (such as concrete and cinderblock) and metal (such as a refrigerator) can decrease throughput.
- Throughput varies depending on the distance between your networking equipment.
- Wireless networks usually use specially coded signals to protect their data, whereas wired connections don't protect their signals. This process of coding signals can slightly decrease throughput, although once coded, data travels at usual speeds.

Can I have both wired and wireless nodes on the same network? One network can support nodes with both wireless and wired connections. Most people use wireless connections for portable devices such as laptops. However, many of the devices connected to a network, such as printers and TVs, usually stay in one location. Although these devices probably feature wireless connectivity, hooking them up to wired connections lets you take advantage of the faster throughput achieved by wired connectivity. In situations where you want to achieve the highest possible throughput on your portable device, you may want to use a wired connection temporarily.

Basic Network Hardware

Objective 7.6 *Describe the basic devices necessary for networks.*

What hardware is needed for different nodes on the network to communicate? For the different nodes on a network to communicate with each other and access the network, each node needs a **network adapter**. All desktop and laptop computers as well as smartphones, tablets, and many peripherals sold today contain network adapters installed *inside* the device. This type of integrated network adapter is referred to as a **network interface card (NIC)**. Different NICs are designed to use different types of transmission media. Most NICs included in computing devices today are built to use wireless media, but many can use wired media as well.

What equipment do I need in order to connect to broadband? A broadband Internet connection requires a **modem**. A modem connects your network to the Internet. Depending on the type of broadband service you have, you'll have either a cable modem or a DSL modem. Often, your Internet service provider will rent the appropriate modem to you or specify what type of modem you have to buy to work properly with the Internet service provider's technology.

What hardware is necessary to share data through a network? Data is sent through a network in bundles called **packets**. For computers to communicate, these packets of data must be able to flow between network nodes. **Network navigation devices**, such as a router or a switch, facilitate and control the flow of data through a network:

- A **router** transfers packets of data between two or more networks. On a home network, you need a router to transfer data between your home network and the Internet, which is considered a separate network. To add WiFi to your home network, you need a router that features wireless capabilities.
- A **switch** acts like a traffic signal on a network (see Figure 7.9). All routers sold for home use have integrated switches. Switches receive data packets and send them to their intended nodes on the same network (not between different networks). During the transmission process, data packets can suffer collisions; subsequently, the data in them is damaged or lost and the network doesn't function efficiently. The switch keeps track of the data packets and, in conjunction with NICs, helps the data packets find their destinations without running into each other. The switch also keeps track of all the nodes on the network and sends the data packets directly to the node for which they're headed. This keeps the network running efficiently.

Where should you place the router on your network? Most modems today have integrated routers, so only one device is needed (see Figure 7.10). The modem/router

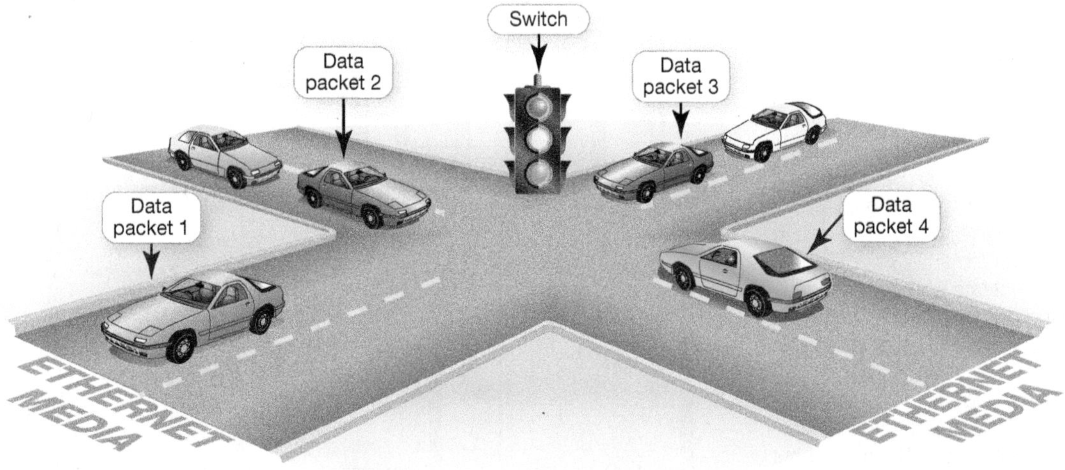

FIGURE 7.9 A simplified explanation of the function of switches is that, together with NICs, they act like traffic signals or traffic cops. They enforce the rules of the data road on an Ethernet network and help prevent data packets from crashing into each other

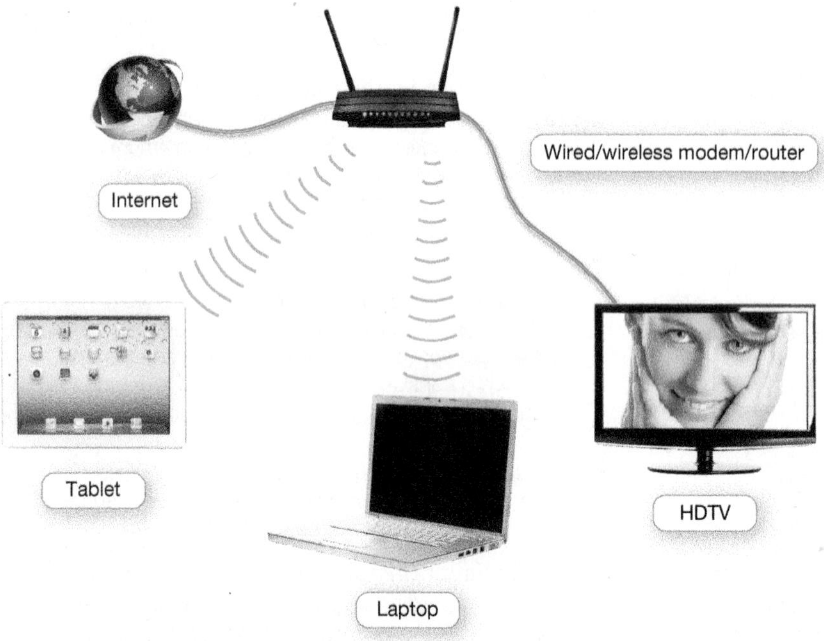

FIGURE 7.10 A Small Network with a Wired/Wireless Modem/Router Attached
(Beboy/Shutterstock, Laurentiu Iordache/Fotolia, Iko/Shutterstock, Sergey Peterman/Shutterstock, Oleksiy Maksymenko/Alamy)

should connect directly to the Ethernet cable, and all computer devices—such as laptops, tablets, smartphones, HDTVs, gaming consoles, and printers—are connected to the modem/router via a wired or wireless connection.

Besides computers, what can be connected to a network? The short answer: almost anything. Have you ever heard of the **Internet of Things (IoT)**? It's not a new concept—it has been around since the new millennium. The IoT is defined as the interconnection of uniquely identifiable embedded computing devices that transfer data over a network without requiring human-to-human or human-to-computer interaction (see Figure 7.11). "Things" can be anything—machines, appliances, buildings, vehicles, even animals, people, plants, and soil. In addition to all the "smart" TVs, refrigerators, and thermostats we hear so much about, a thing can be a heart monitor implant that can warn of an oncoming problem or a device in an automobile that monitors driving behaviors so insurance companies can better assess risk. Ultimately, the Internet of Things is about connecting companies, people, and technology in real time via an extension of the Internet into the physical world. By the year 2020, there will be an estimated 50 billion connected devices.

Network Software

Objective 7.7 *Describe the type of software necessary for networks.*

What network software do home networks require? Because home networks are P2P networks, they need operating system software that supports P2P networking. Windows, OS X, and Linux all support P2P networking. You can connect computers running any of these operating systems to the same home network.

Is the same network software used in client/server networks? As opposed to P2P networks, the nodes on a client/server network don't communicate directly with each other; rather, they communicate through a centralized server. Communicating through a server is more efficient in a network with a large number of nodes, but it requires more complex software than is necessary for P2P networks. Therefore, the servers on client/server networks have specialized **network operating system (NOS)** software installed. This software handles requests for information, Internet access, and the use of peripherals for the rest of the network nodes. Examples of NOS software include Windows Server and SUSE Linux Enterprise Server. ■

FIGURE 7.11 The Internet of Things has resulted in devices—like smoke detectors, dishwashers, and pacemakers—using the Internet more than people do. *(Fotographic1980/Shutterstock)*

ethics in IT — Ethical Challenges of the Internet of Things

We interact with the Internet of Things (IoT)—knowingly and sometimes unknowingly—on a daily basis in both our professional and personal lives. As we become more connected to the Internet through our vast array of devices, we also become part of the information infrastructure, each of us essentially acting as nodes on the Internet of Things. Although the interconnectivity of the IoT brings with it many benefits, it also poses ethical concerns, including those related to privacy and equal access.

Let's consider privacy issues. As we use our Internet-connected devices, we generate huge amounts of data. Many organizations are acquiring and using that data to help with decision-making, resource allocation, and operations. Although we may be used to having Internet advertisers take our search data and send us targeted advertising, how would you feel about companies using information gleaned from an IoT-connected device? For example, say you wear a fitness tracker, such as a Fitbit or iWatch. The sensors in these activity monitors are connected wirelessly to smartphones and to the Internet to enable users to track their workout activities. How would you feel if the data collected by your Fitbit or iWatch was then shared by your mobile phone carrier with a third-party marketer? How would you feel if you received text messages while you were in a restaurant or grocery store offering discounts or coupons for low-calorie offerings from those third-party marketers, simply because your behavior implied that weight loss is one of your goals? Although some might welcome these opportunities, others might consider the offerings an invasion of their privacy.

The Internet of Things also adds to the ethical dilemma of the digital divide—the technological gap between those who can and cannot afford to own these devices. At the very core of the dilemma is the ability for users to access the Internet at all. Significant work has been done to provide developing countries with access to the Internet. But now, the IoT adds new considerations, not only discriminating against certain groups of people that do not have access to the Internet but also those who cannot afford IoT devices. There have been discussions about providing free nationwide wireless Internet access to bridge this gap, but the creation and delivery of that type of service is complicated and fraught with political and corporate debate, preventing any type of public access anytime soon.

As the Internet of Things continues to grow, we will continue to be faced with not only these issues but certainly others as well. Can you think of other ethical issues the Internet of Things might create?

connecting TO THE INTERNET

One of the main reasons for setting up a network is to share an Internet connection. Broadband is the preferred way to access the Internet, but in some situations, cellular or dial-up access may be necessary.

Wired Broadband Internet Connections

Objective 7.8 *Compare and contrast the broadband options available to access the Internet.*

What exactly is broadband Internet access? Broadband, often referred to as high-speed Internet, refers to a type of connection that offers a means to connect to the Internet with faster throughput. Broadband has a data transmission rate that ranges from 1 to 500 Mbps. This high rate of access is in contrast to dial-up Internet access, which has a maximum transmission speed of 56 Kbps (kilobits per second). Some businesses and large organizations have a dedicated connection to the Internet, but other businesses and homeowners purchase Internet access from **Internet service providers (ISPs)**. ISPs may

FIGURE 7.12

Comparing Common Wired Broadband Internet Connection Options

BROADBAND TYPE	TRANSMISSION MEDIUM	SPEED CONSIDERATIONS	AVERAGE AND MAXIMUM DOWNLOAD SPEEDS
Cable	Coaxial cable, similar to cable TV wire	Cable connections are shared, so speed can drop during high-usage periods	Average speed of 10 Mbps, with maximum of 30 Mbps
DSL (Digital Subscriber Line)	Copper wire phone line	Speed drops as distance from the main signal source increases	Average speed of 3.7 Mbps, with maximum of 15 Mbps
Fiber-Optic	Strands of optically pure glass or plastic	Transmits data via light signals, which do not degrade over long distances	Average speed of 50 Mbps, with maximum of 500 Mbps

be specialized providers, like Juno, or companies like Comcast that provide additional services, such as phone and cable TV.

What types of broadband are available? As shown in Figure 7.12, the standard wired broadband technologies in most areas are *cable*, *DSL* (*digital subscriber line*), and *fiber-optic service*. *Satellite broadband* is used mostly in rural or mountain areas where DSL, cable, or fiber-optic service is unavailable or very costly.

There are also wireless broadband options. *Mobile broadband* is offered through many cell-phone service providers through 3G and 4G networks. *Wireless Internet* is also available via WiFi radio waves. We'll discuss these options later in the chapter.

How does cable Internet work? Cable Internet is a broadband service that transmits data over the coaxial cables that also transmit cable television signals; however, cable TV and cable Internet are separate services. Cable TV is a one-way service in which the cable company feeds programming signals to your television. To bring two-way Internet connections to homes, cable companies had to upgrade their networks with two-way data-transmission capabilities.

How does DSL work? DSL (digital subscriber line) uses twisted-pair cable, the same as that used for regular telephones, to connect your computer to the Internet. The bandwidth of the wires is split into three sections, like a three-lane highway. One lane is used to carry voice data. DSL uses the remaining two lanes to send and receive data separately at much higher frequencies than voice data. Although DSL uses a standard phone line, having a traditional phone line in your house doesn't mean you have access to DSL service. Your local phone company must have special DSL technology to offer you the service.

> **SOUND BYTE**
> **Connecting to the Internet**
> In this Sound Byte, you'll learn the basics of connecting to the Internet from home, including useful information on the various types of Internet connections and selecting the right ISP.

How does fiber-optic service work? Fiber-optic service uses fiber-optic lines, which are strands of optically pure glass or plastic that are as thin as a human hair. They're arranged in bundles called *optical cables* and transmit data via light signals over long distances. Because light travels so quickly, this technology can transmit an enormous amount of data at superfast speeds. When the data reaches your house, it's converted to electrical pulses that transmit digital signals your computer can "read." Note that fiber-optic cable is not usually run *inside* the home. On a fiber-optic network, twisted-pair or coaxial cable is still used inside the home to transport the network signals.

How does satellite Internet work? To take advantage of **satellite Internet**, you need a satellite dish which is placed outside your home and connected to your computer with coaxial cable, the same type of cable used for cable TV. Data from your computer is transmitted between your personal satellite dish and the satellite company's receiving satellite dish by a satellite that sits in geosynchronous orbit thousands of miles above the Earth (see Figure 7.13).

How do I choose which broadband connection option is best for me? Depending on where you live, you might not have a choice of the broadband connection available. Check with your local cable TV provider, phone company, and satellite TV provider(s) to determine what broadband options are available and what the transfer rates are in your area.

Often, the most difficult decision is choosing between high-speed plans offered by the same company. For instance, at the time of printing, Verizon offered several fiber-optic plans that featured download speeds from 25 to 500 Mbps. Although 25 Mbps is fine for everyday browsing, e-mail, and shopping, it may not be fast enough for streaming HD movies or satisfying the needs of multiple devices on the Internet at the same time. Finally, you may also need to consider what other services you want bundled into your payment, such as phone or TV. Consulting with friends and neighbors about the plan they have and whether it's meeting their needs can help you decide on the right plan for you.

FIGURE 7.13 Internet data is transmitted between your personal satellite dish and the satellite company's receiving satellite dish by a satellite that sits in geosynchronous orbit thousands of miles above Earth. *(Rendeeplumia/Fotolia)*

Wireless Internet Access

Objective 7.9 *Explain how to access the Internet wirelessly.*

How can I access the Internet wirelessly at home? To access the Internet wirelessly at home without relying on your cellular network, you need to establish WiFi on your home network by using a router that features wireless capabilities. You also need the right equipment on your mobile device. Virtually all laptops, smartphones, game systems, and personal media players sold today are WiFi enabled and come with wireless capability built in.

How can I access WiFi when I'm away from home? When you're away from home, you need to find a WiFi hotspot. Many public places, such as libraries, hotels, airports, and fast-food and coffee shops, offer WiFi access. Most locations are free, though a few still charge or require a special password to access the connection. Websites like Wi-Fi-FreeSpot (**wififreespot.com**) or apps such as WiFiGet help you locate a free hotspot wherever you're planning to go. When you have to buy WiFi access, you can pay for a single session or a monthly membership through services such as Boingo (**boingo.com**). Boingo has over 1 million hotspots worldwide, including airports, hotels, and restaurants. Even wireless in-flight Internet service is available. Gogo (**gogoair.com**) is a wireless broadband network that provides coverage on participating airlines across the continental United States.

How can I access the Internet when WiFi isn't available? When you're not in a WiFi hotspot but still need to access the Internet, you may want to consider mobile broadband. **Mobile broadband** connects you to the Internet through the same cellular network that cell phones use to get 3G or 4G Internet access.

3G and 4G can be thought of as "WiFi everywhere" in that they provide Internet access to your mobile devices in the same way they provide voice service to your mobile phone. *3G* and *4G* refer to the third and fourth generations, respectively, of cell-phone networks. **4G** is the latest service standard and offers the fastest data-access speeds over cell-phone networks. To utilize the 3G or 4G capabilities of a mobile device, you need to sign up for an access plan with a mobile data provider such as Verizon or AT&T.

BITS&BYTES

Net Neutrality

If you posted a blog on the Internet or created a new web-based business, it would have the same opportunity of being accessed as a new on-demand movie from Verizon or an online sale at Target. This is because data on the Internet is treated equally. There has been no differentiation by the type of user, the content that is being uploaded, or by the mode of communication. This is the concept of *net neutrality*.

However, big Internet service providers, such as Comcast, Verizon, and Time Warner Cable, would like to change that. In their perfect world, the Internet would be transformed into a tiered structure in which large users that "hog" the Internet, such as Netflix, Google, and Facebook, would have to pay for priority and faster access, whereas smaller users, for whom paying for priority access would be difficult or impossible, would have less priority and slower access. The Internet service providers claim that this type of tiered priority system would promote competition and innovation. Companies like Netflix and Google claim that having to pay for faster access would put small start-ups at a disadvantage and ultimately stifle innovation. In February 2015, the U.S. Federal Communications Commission (FCC) voted in favor of maintaining net neutrality, keeping the Internet open and free—at least for now.

How does mobile broadband Internet compare with wired Internet access? 3G performs similarly to a standard DSL connection (roughly 3 Mbps). According to the standards set for 4G, the data transfer rate you would get while in a moving vehicle is approximately 100 Mbps; from a fixed location, you can expect up to a 1 Gbps data transfer rate. Some of the early 4G systems released in the market support less than the required 1 Gbps rate and are not fully compliant with the 4G standards and so are being tagged as 4G LTE. They are still faster than 3G, however.

How can I get 3G/4G service if my device doesn't have the right equipment? Many devices, such as the iPad, Kindle Fire, Chromebook, and some laptops, are available with built-in 3G or 4G capabilities. If your device doesn't have built-in 3G or 4G equipment, you can connect to the Internet using a **mobile hotspot**. Mobile hotspots let you connect more than one device to the Internet but require access to a data plan. Although you can buy a separate mobile hotspot device, most smartphones have built-in functionality, enabling you to turn your smartphone into a mobile hotspot (see Figure 7.14). If you have several mobile devices that need wireless Internet access, this may be the most economical and functional way to access the Internet while on the road when you can't access free WiFi.

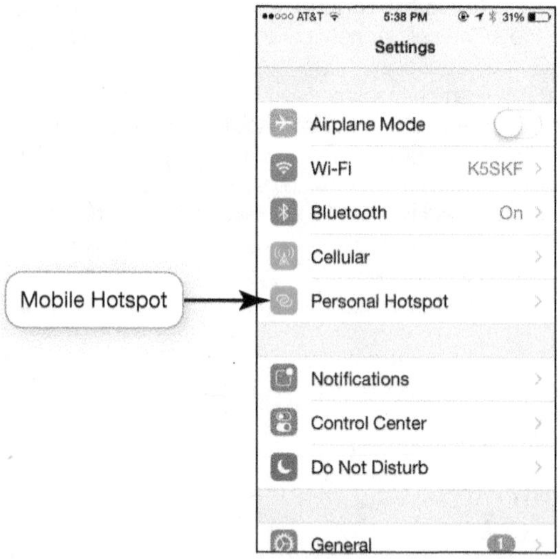

FIGURE 7.14 You can turn your smartphone into a mobile hotspot. On an iPhone, the feature is in Settings. *(Screen shot(s) reprinted with permission from Apple, Inc.)*

ACTIVE HELPDESK
Connecting to the Internet

In this Active Helpdesk, you'll play the role of a helpdesk staffer fielding questions about various options for connecting to the Internet.

Dial-Up Connections

Objective 7.10 *Summarize the pros and cons of dial-up connections.*

Why would I ever want to consider a dial-up connection to the Internet? Although about 90% of Internet users in the United States use high-speed Internet connections such as DSL, cable, or fiber-optic, there are still some areas (usually rural) where broadband service isn't available. A dial-up connection needs only a standard phone line and a modem to access the Internet. Therefore, some people choose to use a dial-up connection when there's no high-speed service in their area. Additionally, a dial-up connection is the least costly way to connect to the Internet, so for those who don't use the Internet frequently, the extra cost of broadband may be unnecessary.

What are the disadvantages of dial-up? The major downside to dial-up is speed. Dial-up modems transfer data about 600 times slower than a fiber-optic broadband connection. Also, dial-up uses a traditional phone line to connect to the Internet; therefore, unless you have a separate phone line just for your dial-up connection, when you're using dial-up, you tie up your phone line. ■

Before moving on to Part 2:
1. Watch Replay Video 7.1.
2. Then check your understanding of what you've learned so far.

check your understanding // review & practice

For a quick review to see what you've learned so far, answer the following questions.

multiple choice

1. An emerging standard of wireless Ethernet, also known as 802.11ad, is

- **a.** WiGig.
- **b.** Low Power WiFi.
- **c.** White-Fi.
- **d.** Super WiFi.

2. The type of network used for communication among a laptop and smartphone using Bluetooth is a

- **a.** WAN.
- **b.** PAN.
- **c.** LAN.
- **d.** MAN.

3. The fastest broadband Internet service is usually

- **a.** fiber-optic.
- **b.** DSL.
- **c.** cable.
- **d.** satellite.

4. Which of the following allows you to connect to the Internet wirelessly?

- **a.** WiFi
- **b.** 4G LTE
- **c.** mobile hotspot
- **d.** all of the above

5. The device used to connect a network to the Internet is called a

- **a.** gateway.
- **b.** switch.
- **c.** modem.
- **d.** router.

MyITLab Go to **MyITLab** to take an autograded version of the *Check Your Understanding* review and to find all media resources for the chapter.

TECHBYTES WEEKLY

Stay current with the TechBytes Weekly Newsletter.

Continue

TRY THIS Testing Your Internet Connection Speed

Your ISP may have promised you certain downloading and uploading data speeds. How can you tell if you're getting what was promised? Numerous sites on the Internet, such as SpeedOf.Me and speedtest.net, test the speed of your Internet connection. You can see how your results compare with others, as well as determine whether you're getting the results promised by your ISP.

Step 1 Type **SpeedOf.Me** in any browser. SpeedOf.Me is an HTML5 Internet speed test, so it will work on PCs, Macs, and Android devices. *(SpeedOf.Me)*

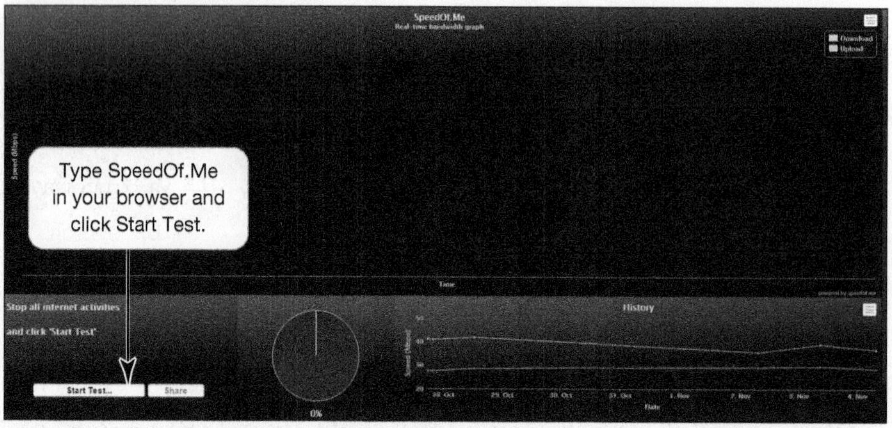

Step 2 SpeedOf.Me tests upload and download speeds using sample files of varying sizes, starting with a 128 KB sample until it reaches a sample size that takes more than 8 seconds to upload or download (with the largest possible sample size being 128 MB). The results are based on the last sample file. As the test runs, graphics illustrate the process, with the final results displaying when the test is finished. *(SpeedOf.Me)*

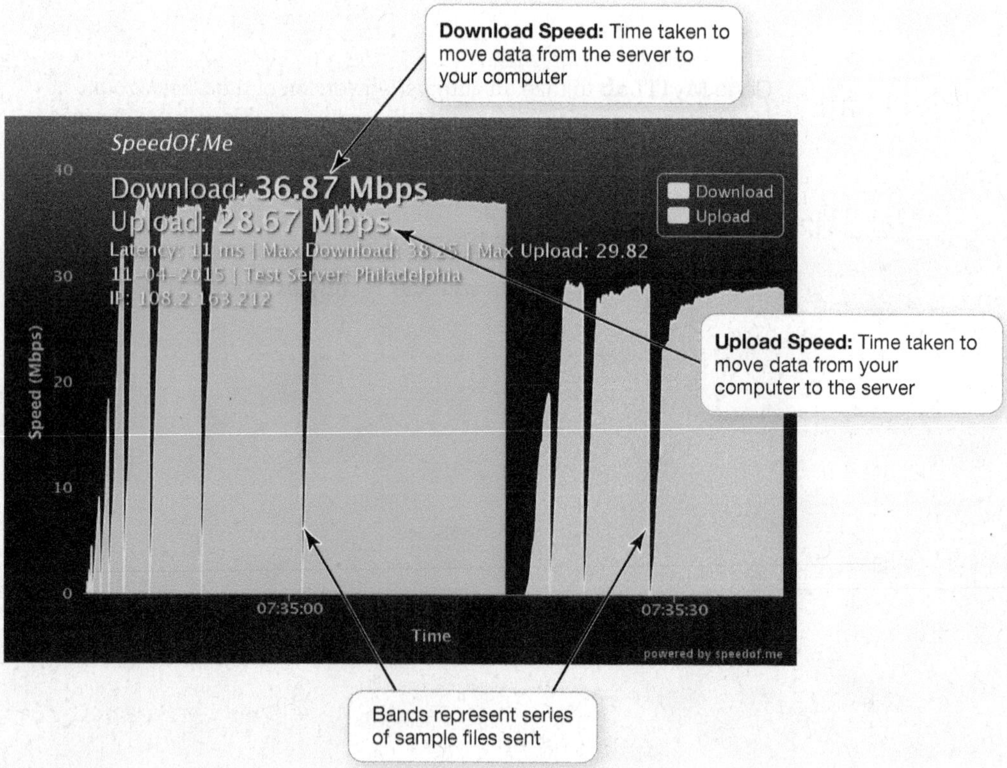

Step 3 A history chart displays at the bottom of the screen, showing the results of any tests you have run on that particular device over time. If you want to share your results, you can use the Share button to post them to your favorite social media site or by e-mail.

(SpeedOf.Me)

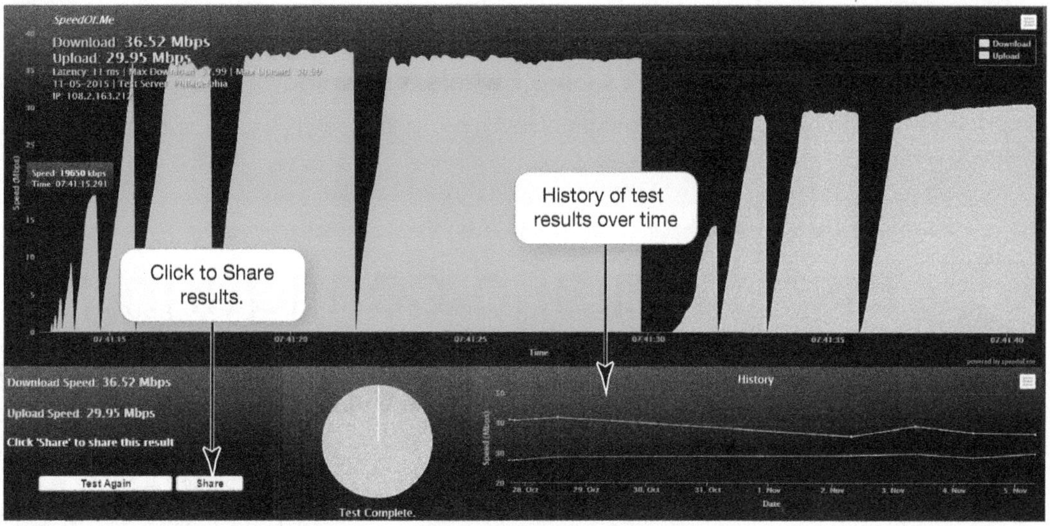

Make This TOOL: Ping and Telnet

MAKE: Networked Devices

One of the nice features of programming in **App Inventor** is that you can instantly see changes on your target device as you work. The two devices connect using WiFi. But what is going on behind the scenes to allow this?

In this exercise, you'll explore how the AI Companion software works with the AI program to connect your systems. You'll see how useful networking utilities like Ping and Telnet are to investigate how network firewalls are set up.

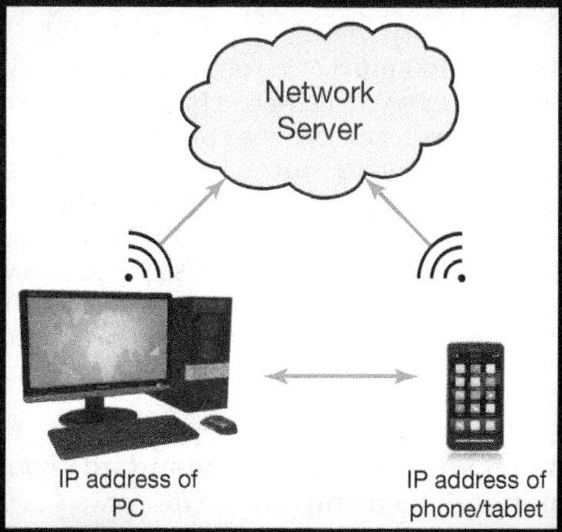

The App Inventor Companion app and program communicate across WiFi to make your programming easier.

For the instructions for this exercise, go to MyITLab.

Your Home Network

Learning Outcome 7.2 You will be able to describe what you need to install and configure a home network and how to manage and secure a wireless network.

You know what a network is and the advantages of having one. In this section, we look at installing or updating a home network and keeping it safe.

installing and configuring HOME NETWORKS

Now that you understand the basic components of a network and your Internet connection options, you're ready to install a network in your home. If you already have a network in your home, it's useful to examine your network settings and configuration to make sure they're still meeting your needs, especially if you've added new devices.

Only a few years ago, most home networks included just a few computers and a printer. However, a network that can manage those devices is often very different from one that can support the smartphones, gaming consoles, tablets, and smart TVs many homes have added to their networks since. If you're using any of these additional devices and you haven't updated your network equipment or setup in a while, it may be time to do so.

Planning Your Home Network

Objective 7.11 *Explain steps you should take before creating a home network.*

Where do I start? One of the first things you should do to evaluate your network is list all the devices you're using. Consider not only the obvious devices such as computers, laptops, tablets, and printers, but also include smartphones, DVR boxes, smart TVs, wireless stereo equipment, and any other appliance that connects to the Internet wirelessly. You might be surprised at how many devices you list. Then include any devices you think you may add in the near future. Once you have a complete list, determine whether your network is sufficiently up to date to support all your devices.

What wireless Ethernet standard should my network be using? For a home network to run most efficiently and to provide the fastest experience, it's best that all network nodes—computers, network adapters (NICs), routers, and so on—use the latest Ethernet standard. Devices that support the 802.11n standard have been around for a while, so if you've bought a laptop or other portable device in the past few years, it most likely has an 802.11n NIC. Your router may also be supporting the 802.11n standard.

However, many newer devices support the 802.11ac standard. If you have the fastest 802.11ac NIC in your laptop but the router is the slower 802.11n standard, then data will be sent at the speeds supported by the lower standard. If you haven't updated your router in a while, you may want to consider getting an 802.11ac router (see Figure 7.15) to get the fastest connection speeds.

Additionally, the newer standard gives your wireless signal more range, so if you feel that some of your devices aren't connecting properly to the Internet from certain parts of your home, you may want to upgrade to the newer standard.

How can I tell what wireless standard my router supports? You may be able to tell whether your router is supporting the faster 802.11ac standard just by looking at it. Many routers have the wireless standard indicated on the device. If you're still not sure, you can search for more information on your router by entering the model number into a search engine. If your router is provided by your ISP and it's an older standard, you should consider having your ISP provide you with a new router.

FIGURE 7.15 802.11ac wireless routers offer the fastest connection speeds and a greater wireless signal range. *(Photo courtesy of Linksys)*

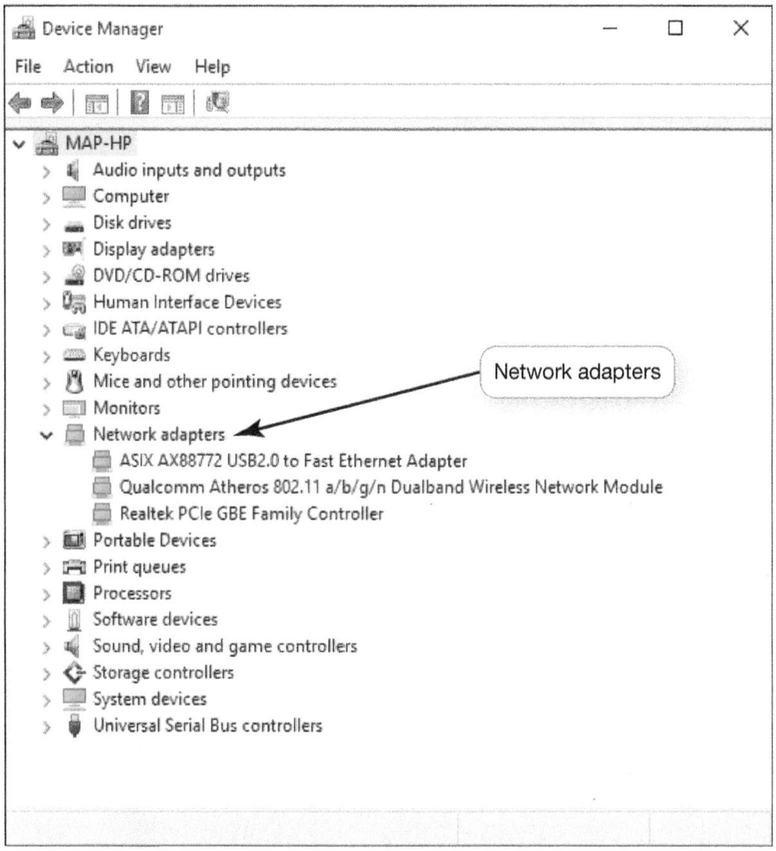

FIGURE 7.16 The Windows Device Manager shows the wireless and wired network adapters installed on a computer. *(Windows 10, Microsoft Corporation)*
>*To access the Device Manager, click* ***Settings*** *from the Start menu, click* ***Devices****, and then select* ***Device manager*** *at the bottom of the screen.*

How can I tell what network adapters are installed in my computer? To see which network adapters are installed in your Windows computer, use the Device Manager utility (see Figure 7.16), which lists all the adapters. If you can't tell which wireless standard the adapter supports from the list, search the Internet for information on your specific adapter to determine its capability. The Device Manager can also alert you if there's a problem with the adapter.

Connecting Devices to a Network

Objective 7.12 *Describe what you need in order to connect devices to a network.*

How can I directly connect multiple devices to my router? Most home routers have three or four Ethernet ports on the back to support wired connections. This is usually sufficient for the general house that has at least one computer, maybe a printer, and perhaps some entertainment devices that are connected directly to the router.

Occasionally, you also may want to connect a laptop with a wired connection to increase the bandwidth. If you need additional ports for plugging in wired connections to your network, you can buy a stand-alone switch and plug it into one of the ports on your router (see Figure 7.17). This will give you additional ports for making wired connections. However, don't mistakenly buy another router with an embedded switch and try adding that to your network. The two routers will cause conflicts as they fight for control over network navigation.

How many wireless devices can connect to a router in a home network? Most home wireless routers can support up to 253 wireless connections at the same time, although most home networks have far fewer. Regardless of how many devices your home network has, they all share bandwidth when they're connected to a router. Therefore, the more devices actively transmitting data that you connect to a single router, the smaller the portion of the router's bandwidth each device receives.

To look at this another way, say you have a pizza that represents your router's bandwidth. You can cut the pizza into six or eight pieces (that is, you can connect either six or eight devices to the network). If you cut the pizza into eight pieces, each person who gets a slice receives a smaller portion than if you had cut the pizza into six pieces. Similarly, when you connect eight devices to the network, each device has less bandwidth than it would if only six devices were connected to the network.

Are wireless routers for Windows and OS X networks different? All routers that support the 802.11n standard and the newer 802.11ac standard should work with computers running the more recent versions of Windows or OS X. However, Apple has designed routers

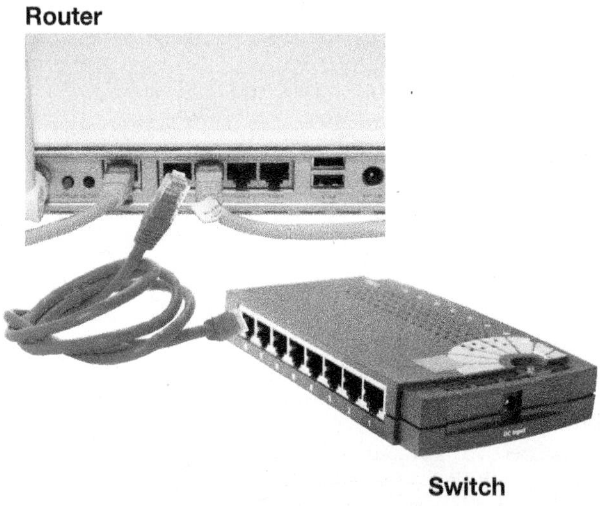

FIGURE 7.17 You can add ports to your network by connecting a switch to your router. *(Alarich/Shutterstock, Lexan/Shutterstock)*

that are optimized for working with Apple computers. So if you're connecting Apple computers to your network, you may want to use the Apple AirPort Extreme router for larger home networks or the AirPort Express for smaller networks. Windows devices can also connect to an AirPort router, so it's a great choice for households with both Apples and PCs. The AirPort Extreme uses the newest 802.11ac technology for the fastest data transfers. In addition, it offers the option of creating a guest network, which can use a different password or no password at all, keeping all your networked devices and files secure.

How do I know what's connected to my router? To determine what's connected to your router, you need to log in to an account associated with your router's IP address. You can find your router's IP address on the router manufacturer's website. Once you know it, type it into a web browser. You may need to enter a user name and password, but eventually you'll get to a configuration page that lists what wired and wireless devices are in your network. You may be surprised at all the various devices associated with your network.

Figure 7.18 shows a router network listing with wired (desktop computer) and wireless (DVR, laptop, iPhone, and iPad) devices connected in a home network. You'll notice that each device also has an IP address. You can think of your network as an apartment building. The router's IP address is the building's street address, while the IP addresses of the individual devices connected to the router are the apartment numbers. Each device needs an IP address so the router knows to which device to send information.

SOUND BYTE

Installing a Home Computer Network

Installing a network is relatively easy if you watch someone else do it. In this Sound Byte, you'll learn how to install the hardware and to configure Windows for a wired or wireless home network.

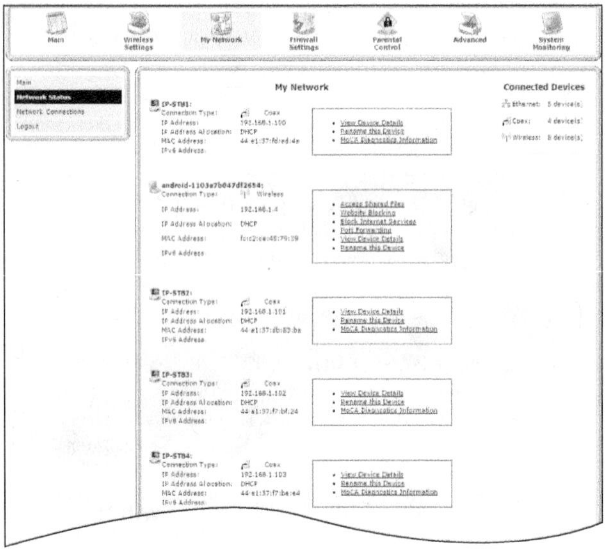

FIGURE 7.18 Wired and wireless connections can use the same router. *(Mary Anne Poatsy)*

Specialized Home Networking Devices

Objective 7.13 *Describe specialized devices you can add to a home network.*

What can I attach to my network to facilitate file sharing and backup of data? Network-attached storage (NAS) devices are specialized devices designed to store and manage all network data. Although data can always be stored on individual hard drives in computers on a network, NAS devices provide for centralized data storage and access.

Popular for years on business networks, NAS devices are now being widely marketed for home networks (see Figure 7.19). You can think of them as specialized external hard drives (many of them actually resemble external hard drives). NAS devices connect directly to the network through a router or switch. Specialized software is installed on computers attached to the network to ensure that all data saved to an individual computer is also stored on the NAS device as a backup.

For Apple computers, the AirPort Time Capsule is a wireless router combined with a hard drive that facilitates the backup of all computers connected to the network. The AirPort Time Capsule looks very similar to the AirPort router, and it works in conjunction with the Time Machine backup feature of OS X. If you buy an AirPort Time Capsule, you won't need to buy an AirPort router (or other router) because the AirPort Time Capsule also fulfills this function on your network. When the AirPort Time Capsule is installed on your network, Macs connected to the network will ask the user if they want to use the AirPort Time Capsule as their source for Time Machine backups. The AirPort Time Capsule is another type of NAS device.

FIGURE 7.19 A network-attached storage device provides centralized data storage and access. *(Alamy)*

BITS&BYTES

Mesh Networks: An Emerging Alternative

Have you ever heard of a *mesh network*? This emerging technology uses small radio transmitters instead of wireless routers as its network nodes. What is so great about mesh networks is that only one node needs to physically connect to a network connection, and then all other nodes can share wirelessly with each other. This connection sharing between nodes can extend almost endlessly, since one wired node can share its Internet connection wirelessly with other nearby nodes, and then those nodes can share their connection wirelessly with nodes closest to them—thus creating a "mesh" of connectivity. The truly wireless aspect of mesh networks poses several advantages to the wireless networks that are in place today: they are easier to install because fewer wires need to be run; they can accommodate more nodes; and they enable wireless networks to be created in outdoor and unstructured venues.

In developing nations as well as in some areas in the United States, mesh networks have helped provide access to the Internet in a more timely and inexpensive manner than waiting for the physical connections to be established. Mesh networks can also help promote cellular communications during times of disasters when traditional communications are halted. And if you have an Android mobile phone, you can participate in the Serval Mesh, which allows users to send and receive information without depending on established cellular networks.

Besides external hard drives, are there other NAS devices I could use on my network? A more sophisticated type of NAS device is a home network server. **Home network servers** are specialized devices designed to store files, share files across the network, and back up files on computers connected to the network. All computers connected to the network can access the server.

Home network servers often look like oversized external hard drives. They are configured with operating systems like Windows Server and connect directly as a node on your network. Home servers have more sophisticated functionality than NAS devices and often handle the following tasks:

- Automatically back up all computers connected to the network
- Act as a repository for files to be shared across the network
- Function as an access gateway to allow any computer on the network to be accessed from a remote location via the Internet (see Figure 7.20)

Note that even though these devices are servers, they don't convert a home P2P network into a client/server network because these servers don't perform all the functions performed on client/server networks. Also note that you can access the media stored on your Windows Server computer through your Xbox One as long as the Xbox is also connected to your home network.

What kinds of digital entertainment devices can connect directly to the network? A **network-ready device** (or Internet-ready device) can be connected directly to a network, either through a wired or wireless connection. Most game consoles, Blu-ray players, and DVRs, as well as many televisions (smart TVs) and home theater systems, are network ready. A device that is not network ready requires that the device be connected directly to another computer via a cable on the network.

Why should I connect digital entertainment devices to my network? One reason for connecting entertainment devices to your network is to access and share digital content between devices on your network. Connecting these devices to your network also connects them to the Internet so you can access a lot of entertainment content, including movies, videos, and music available online.

You can also use gaming devices to play multiplayer games with players in the next room or all over the world. The content you access is either downloaded or streamed to your devices. Newer smart TVs and other smart devices (such as Blu-ray players, game consoles, and home theater systems) are continually adding apps and video services so that you can play games, view on-demand and online videos, listen to Internet radio, and access social networking sites (see Figure 7.21). Some smart devices also feature an integrated web browser that lets you access the web directly, without the use of apps.

What if I don't have a smart TV? You can get the same services on your existing television by using a Blu-ray player that features integrated wireless connectivity to receive streaming media from various ISPs. For best video viewing, look for a Blu-ray player that has high-definition resolution and the capability to display 3D video. Some set-top boxes also provide the same types of connectivity as a Blu-ray player. Alternatively, you can use devices such as Apple TV or Google Chromecast that enable you to send Internet-based media to your traditional TV.

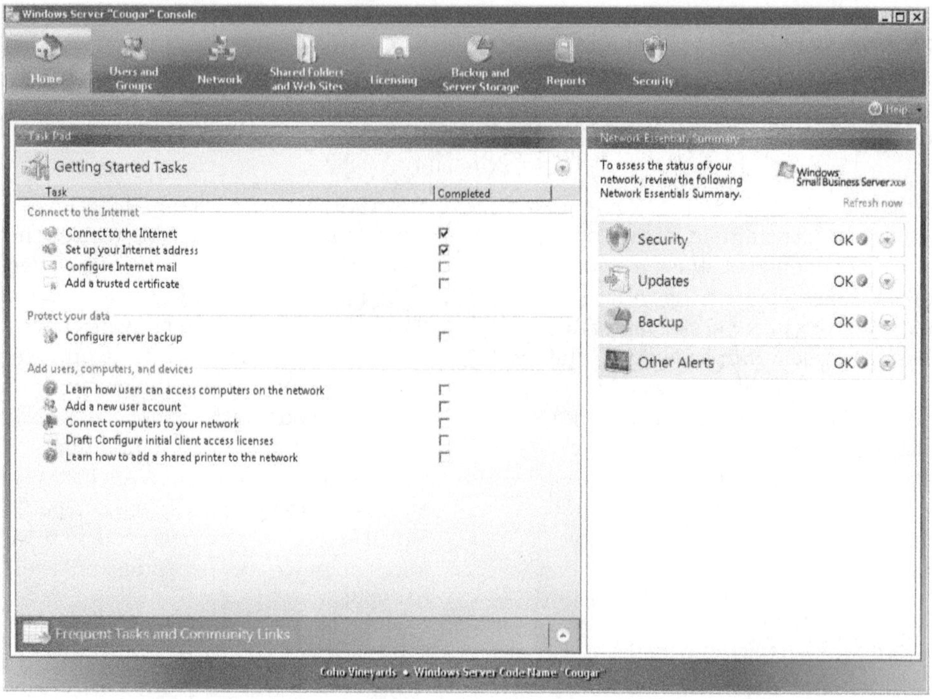

FIGURE 7.20 Home network servers are often configured with software such as Windows Server. *(Windows 8.1, Microsoft Corporation)*

Why should I connect my gaming consoles to my home network? Current gaming systems, like the Play-Station 4 (PS4), can function as a total entertainment platform when connected to the Internet through your network. The PS4 has a built-in Blu-ray drive and can play Blu-ray discs, DVDs, and music files. You can download movies, games, and videos from the Internet directly to the PS4. You can also use it to share media across your network and to import photos or video from cameras and phones.

If you have a PS Vita, you can use an application called Remote Play (see Figure 7.22) to access features of your
PS4 from your Vita. You can use the Vita to turn your PS4 on and off; access photos, music, and video files; play games; and browse the Internet. Media is transmitted from your PS4 and displayed on the Vita screen.

How can I use my home network to enhance my home security? Monitoring cameras, both for indoor and outdoor use, are now available for the home that feature wireless connectivity so you can keep track of your home while you're away. You can connect these cameras to your network and monitor them in real time through software and portable devices such as an iPhone or Android phone (see Figure 7.23).

The software can be configured to alert you via e-mail or text message when the cameras detect movement, such as a vehicle entering your driveway. Some systems also allow you to receive alerts when there is a lack of movement. This can be useful for monitoring an aging relative or for monitoring the arrival of children coming home from school.

As time goes on, many more types of entertainment devices and home gadgets will be connected to be part of your smart home.

FIGURE 7.21 Smart TVs have their own apps and let you directly access the web. *(Robert Daly/Getty Images)*

FIGURE 7.22 The Remote Play feature of the PS Vita lets you access PS4 features directly from your Vita. *(Kyodo/AP Images)*

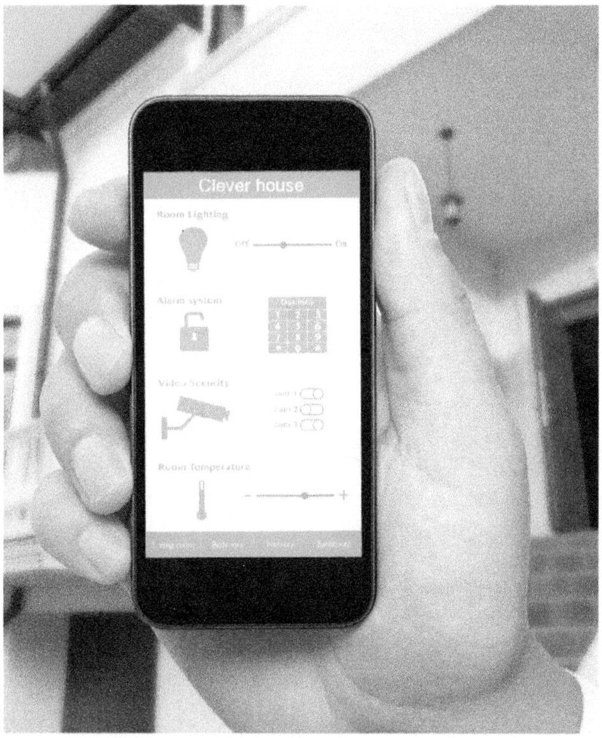

FIGURE 7.23 Many security systems can help you monitor your home's security from your mobile devices. *(Denys Prykhodov/Fotolia)*

Configuring Software for Your Home Network

Objective 7.14 *Summarize how to configure home network software.*

How do I set up a Windows home network for the first time? In Windows, the process of setting up a network is fairly automated, especially if you're using the same version of Windows on all your computers. The Windows examples in this section assume all computers are running Windows 10. Before configuring the computers to the network, do the following:

1. Make sure there are network adapters on each node.
2. For any wired connections, plug all the cables into the router, nodes, and so on.
3. Make sure your broadband modem is connected to your router and that the modem is connected to the Internet.
4. Turn on your equipment in the following order (allowing the modem and the router about one minute each to power up) and configure:

   a. Your broadband modem
   b. Your router
   c. All computers and peripherals (printers, scanners, and so on)

You can add other devices, such as TVs, Blu-ray players, and gaming consoles, to the network after you configure the computers.

After you've completed the previous steps, launch the Windows network setup wizards from the Network and Sharing Center, which you access via the Network & Internet group in Settings (see Figure 7.24):

- If your computer has a wired connection to the network, you should automatically be connected. You should give the network the same secured name you give to your router (see the *Troubleshooting Wireless Network Problems* section in this chapter).
- If you're connecting wirelessly, ensure that your WiFi is turned on by selecting Wi-Fi in the Network & Internet group in Settings. Then, from the Notification area on the taskbar, click Internet access. A panel opens, displaying the wired and wireless connection options. You will need to enter your security passphrase to connect to your wireless network initially.

How do I share files with other computers on my network? For ease of file and peripheral sharing, Windows has the *HomeGroup* feature. The HomeGroup is a software device that makes it easier to allow computers on a Windows network to share peripherals and information. To create a homegroup after connecting your first Windows computer to your network, complete the steps outlined in Figure 7.25.

What if I don't have the same version of Windows on all my computers? Computers with various versions of Windows can coexist on the same network. Always set up the computers running the newest version of Windows first. Then consult the Microsoft website for guidance on how to configure computers with previous versions of Windows.

How do I connect a mobile device to a wireless network? Connecting a mobile device, regardless of its operating system, to a wireless network is an easy process

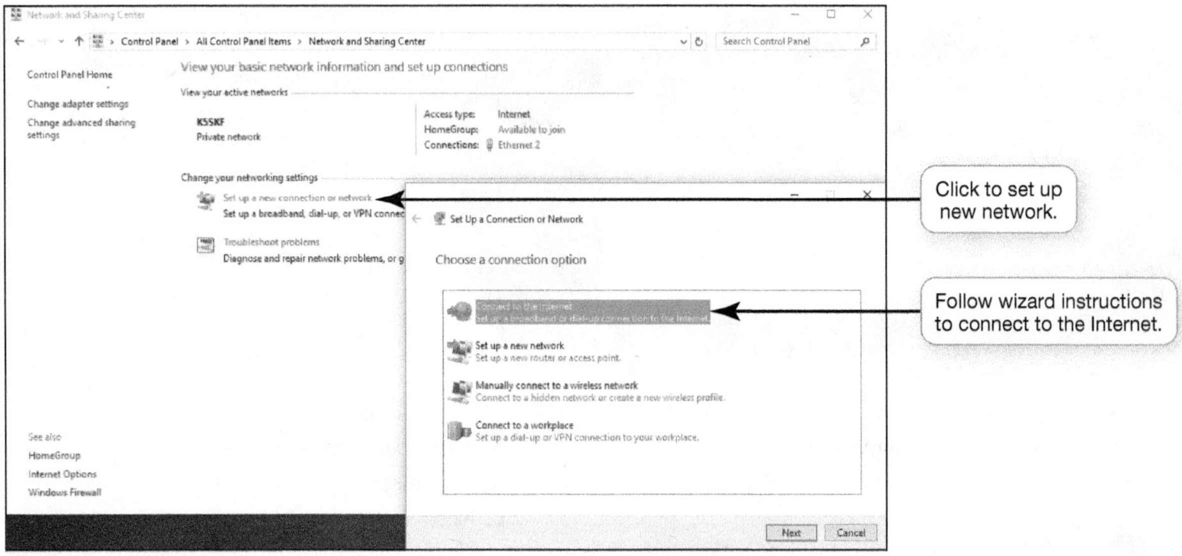

FIGURE 7.24 Connecting a Windows 10 computer to a network for the first time is fairly automated.
(Windows 10, Microsoft Corporation)

these days. When you boot up your device, your device will display a list of available networks that the NIC in your device detects. On Macs, the list pops up in the network login screen. On Windows devices, you can click on the Internet access icon in the system tray to display available networks. If there is a padlock icon next to the network name, this means that the network is secure and will require a password. Enter the password for the network in the password box, and click the Join button. For unsecure networks, you don't need a password. Checking the "Remember this network" check box will make any network a preferred network, enabling the computer to connect to the network automatically when that network is available. You can have multiple preferred networks, such as your home, school, work, and local coffee shop networks. ■

BITS&BYTES

Analyzing Network Problems

If you have areas in your home where you have little or no WiFi coverage, try using a WiFi analyzer to gather information before embarking on ways to improve your coverage. There are free apps such as WiFi Analyzer (Android) or Wi-Fi Inspector (Windows) that provide signal strength and other details that will be helpful in remedying the problem.

FIGURE 7.25

Creating a HomeGroup in Windows

Step 1: Open Network & Internet from Settings, then click Home-Group. In the HomeGroup dialog box, click Create a homegroup.

Step 2: Choose the sharing options for computers that belong to the homegroup. You can choose to share pictures, music, videos, documents, and printers and other devices with other Windows computers that belong to the homegroup. Although these are global settings for every computer in the homegroup, you can change these settings on individual computers if you wish.

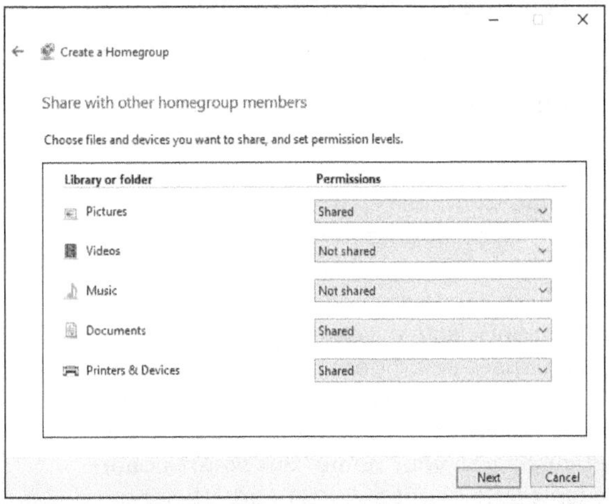

Step 3: Windows generates a password. All other computers added to the network will need this password to join the homegroup. Once you've created the homegroup on the first computer, it will belong to that homegroup. You can then begin connecting other Windows computers to the network and join them to the homegroup you created.

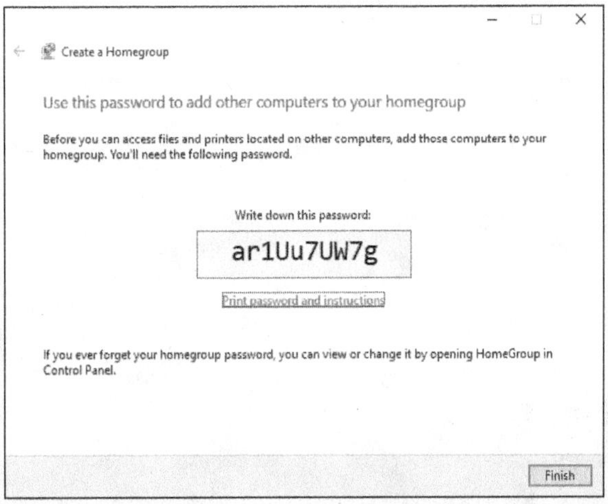

(Windows 10, Microsoft Corporation)

trends in IT

How Smart Is Your Home?

Although once thought of as a futuristic way of life, the automated home depicted in the Jetsons TV show and science fiction movies is emerging and may soon become the new normal (see Figure 7.26). The concept of a **smart home**—where devices and appliances are automated or controlled by apps installed on your smartphone or tablet—is in full play today, thanks (in part) to the power and availability of strong wireless networks and other forms of connectivity.

How do smart homes work? With smart home automation, you can dictate how and when a device should engage or respond. For some devices and appliances, all you need to do is set a schedule and the rest is automated. Other devices and appliances work using some type of sensor and react to changes in their surrounding environment, such as motion, light, or temperature. For example, some smart home thermostats learn your habits (such as waking and sleeping patterns) and heating and cooling preferences over time and create automatic settings. Some smart home draperies and blinds open and close in reaction to the timing of sunrise and sunset using geolocation settings.

Smart home automation can also alert you to unpredictable events such as water leaks and unexpected visitors to your home. But smart home technology isn't only about security and efficiency. It's also used to help control your entertainment devices as well. Altogether, smart home devices are intended to provide convenience, control, money savings, and an overall smarter home.

At the heart of many smart homes are hubs that are used to control a variety of devices from different manufacturers. A good hub, like a UN translator, receives the different wireless signals from smart devices and then translates those into one WiFi signal that your router can understand. In addition, the hub consolidates the controls required by each device and provides one single app for you to interact with, thus simplifying your experience. Other hubs, such as the Belkin WeMo, have smaller ambitions. Plug a device (e.g., a lamp or coffee maker) into the WeMo and you can control it from your phone or tablet. An alternative to a hub is getting a single home automation platform such as those offered by Google, Microsoft, Lowe's, and AT&T.

If you're really into controlling things yourself, you can use the IFTTT (If This Then That) app (**IFTTT.com**). All you need is the right device (such as a WeMo motion detector, Nest thermostat, or Philips lightbulb) and you can create your own Do Recipe, such as setting the temperature of your home at the press of a button on your phone.

Although smart homes offer numerous benefits, as of yet, no single standard has been adopted for home automation. Some devices work on WiFi, others work on Bluetooth. Some smart devices interact with apps on mobile devices, whereas others interact with each other directly. There have been some attempts at single platforms, such as Google's Android@Home platform and Microsoft's Home 2.0 program, but neither of these programs, nor anything else, has yet to take off. Also, while costs have come down significantly on many smart home devices, the overall cost is not completely affordable to most, especially as a complete smart home solution.

Still, the smart home technology industry is estimated to increase to $44 billion by 2017. Most likely the smart home is here to stay.

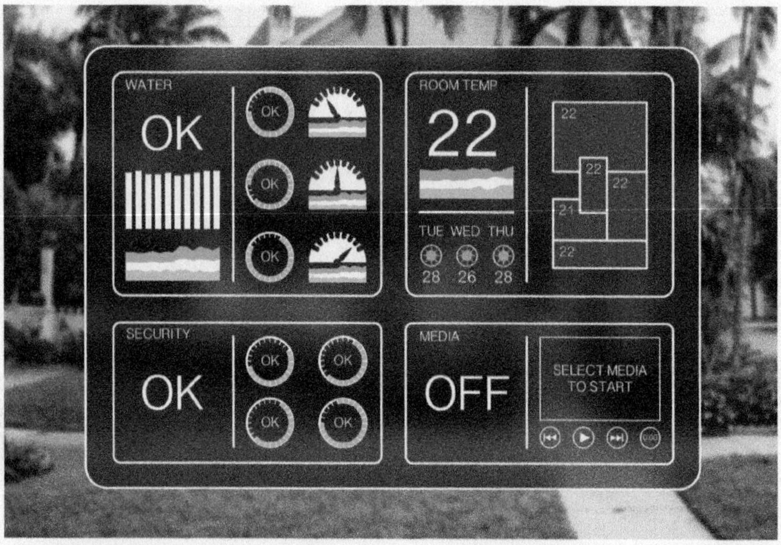

FIGURE 7.26 You can remotely monitor your home with smart home technology. *(A-image/Shutterstock)*

managing and securing WIRELESS NETWORKS

All networks require some maintenance and management, but there are some situations that are particular to wireless networks. In addition, wireless networks require additional security measures. In this section, we'll look at how to troubleshoot typical wireless network problems and how to protect wireless networks from common security threats.

Troubleshooting Wireless Network Problems

Objective 7.15 *Describe the potential problems with wireless networks and how to avoid them.*

What types of problems can I run into when installing wireless networks? The maximum range of 802.11n or 802.11ac wireless devices is about 350 feet. But as you go farther away from your router, the throughput you achieve decreases. Obstacles between wireless nodes also decrease throughput. Walls, floors, and large metal objects (such as refrigerators) are the most common sources of interference with wireless signals.

What if a node on the network seems slow? Repositioning the node within the same room (sometimes even just a few inches from the original position) can affect communication between nodes. If this doesn't work, move the device closer to the router or to another room in your house. If these solutions don't work, consider upgrading to an ac router or adding a wireless range extender to your network.

What's a wireless range extender? A **wireless range extender** is a device that amplifies your wireless signal to extend to parts of your home that are experiencing poor connectivity. For example, as shown in Figure 7.27, Laptop C on the back porch can't connect to the wireless network, even though Computer B in the den can. By placing a range extender in the den, where there is still good connectivity to the wireless network, the wireless signal is amplified and beamed farther out to the back porch. This allows Laptop C to make a good connection to the network.

Securing Wireless Networks

Objective 7.16 *Describe how to secure a wireless home network.*

Why is a wireless network more vulnerable than a wired network? All computers that connect to the Internet, whether or not they're on a network, need to be secured from intruders. This is usually accomplished by using a firewall, which is a hardware or software solution that helps shield your network from prying eyes. (We discuss firewalls at length in Chapter 9.) Wireless networks present special vulnerabilities; therefore, you should take additional steps to keep your wireless network safe.

With a wired network, it's fairly easy to tell if a hacker, someone who breaks into computer systems to create mischief or steal information, is using your network. However, the newer wireless 802.11 networks have wide ranges that may

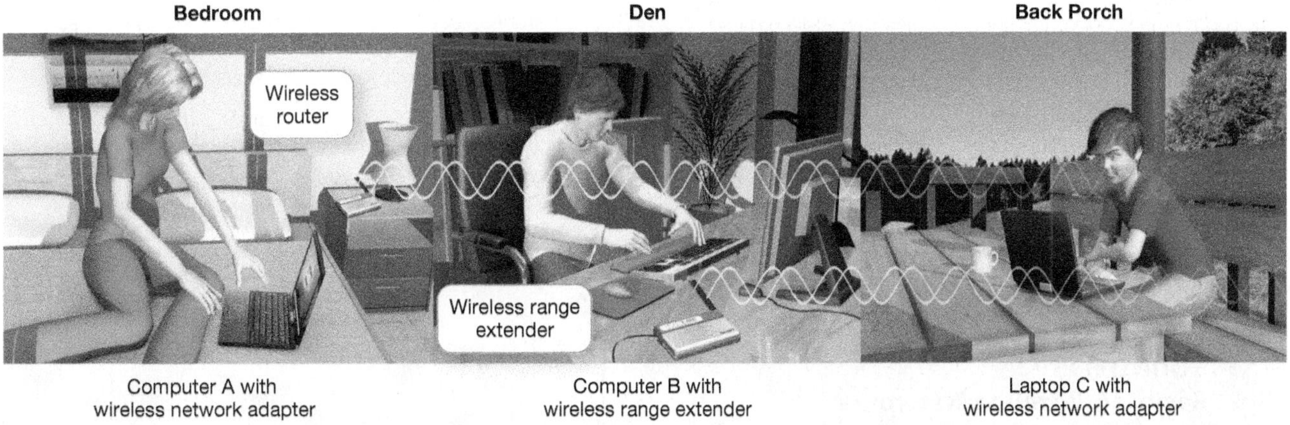

FIGURE 7.27 Because a wireless range extender is installed in the den, Laptop C on the back porch can now connect to the wireless network.

extend outside your house. This makes it possible for a hacker to access your network without your knowledge.

Also, in some areas where residences are close together, wireless signals can reach a neighbor's residence. Most wireless network adapters are set up to access the strongest wireless network signal detected. **Piggybacking** is connecting to a wireless network without the permission of the owner. This practice is illegal in many jurisdictions but often happens inadvertently between neighbors.

Why should I be worried about someone logging onto my wireless network without my permission? If your neighbor is using your network connection, his or her usage could be slowing down your connection speed. Some neighbors might even be computer savvy enough to penetrate your unprotected wireless network and steal personal information, just as any other hacker would. And any cyberattack or illegal behavior a hacker initiates from your wireless network could get you in trouble with the authorities.

How is my wireless network vulnerable? Packets of information on a wireless network are broadcast through the airwaves. Savvy hackers can intercept and decode information from your transmissions that may allow them to bypass standard protections, such as a firewall, that you have set up on your network. Therefore, to secure a wireless network, take the additional precautions described in the Sound Byte "Securing Wireless Networks" and summarized as follows:

1. **Change your network name (SSID).** Each wireless network has its own name to identify it, known as the **service set identifier (SSID)**. Unless you change this name when you set up your router, the router uses a default network name that all routers from that manufacturer use (such as "Wireless" or "Netgear"). Hackers know the default names and access codes for routers. If you haven't changed the SSID, it's advertising the fact that you probably haven't changed any of the other default settings for your router either.
2. **Disable SSID broadcast.** Most routers are set up to broadcast their SSIDs so that other wireless devices can find them. If your router supports disabling SSID broadcasting, turn it off. This makes it more difficult for a hacker to detect your network and nearly impossible for a neighbor to inadvertently connect to your network.
3. **Change the default password on your router.** Routers have default user names and passwords. Hackers can use these to access your router and break into your network. Change the password on your router to something hard to guess. Use at least twelve characters that are a combination of letters, symbols, and numbers.
4. **Turn on security protocols.** Most routers ship with security protocols such as Wired Equivalent Privacy (WEP) or Wi-Fi Protected Access (WPA). Both use encryption (a method of translating your data into code) to protect data in your wireless transmissions. WPA is a much stronger protocol than WEP, so enable WPA if you have it; enable WEP if you don't.
5. **Create a passphrase.** When you enable these protocols, you're forced to create a security encryption key (passphrase). When you attempt to connect a node to a security-enabled network for the first time, you're required to enter the security key. The security key or passphrase (see Figure 7.28) is the code that computers on your network need to decrypt (decode) data transmissions. Without this key, it's extremely difficult, if not impossible, to decrypt the data transmissions from your network. The Windows 10 Networks panel shows all wireless networks within range. Moving your cursor over the network name will reveal details about the network such as whether it's a secured network. Clicking on a network name allows you to connect to it or prompts you for more information such as the SSID name and security key.
6. **Implement media access control.** Each network adapter on your network has a unique number (like a serial number) assigned to it by the manufacturer. This is called a media access control (MAC) address, and it's a number printed right on the network adapter. Many routers allow you to restrict access to the network to only certain MAC addresses. This helps ensure that only authorized devices can connect to your network.
7. **Limit your signal range.** Many routers allow you to adjust the transmitting power to low, medium, or high. Cutting down the power to low or medium could prevent your signal from reaching too far away from your home, making it tougher for interlopers to poach your signal.
8. **Apply firmware upgrades.** Your router has read-only memory that has software written to it. This software is known as **firmware**. As bugs are found in the firmware (which hackers might exploit), manufacturers issue patches, just as the makers of operating system software do. Periodically check the manufacturer's website and apply any necessary upgrades to your firmware.

If you follow these steps, you'll greatly improve the security of your wireless network. In Chapter 9, we'll explore many other ways to keep your computer safe from malicious individuals on the Internet and ensure that your digital information is secure. ■

SOUND BYTE

Securing Wireless Networks

In this Sound Byte, you'll learn some simple steps to secure your wireless network against intruders.

Before moving on to the Chapter Review:

1. Watch Replay Video 7.2.
2. Then check your understanding of what you've learned so far.

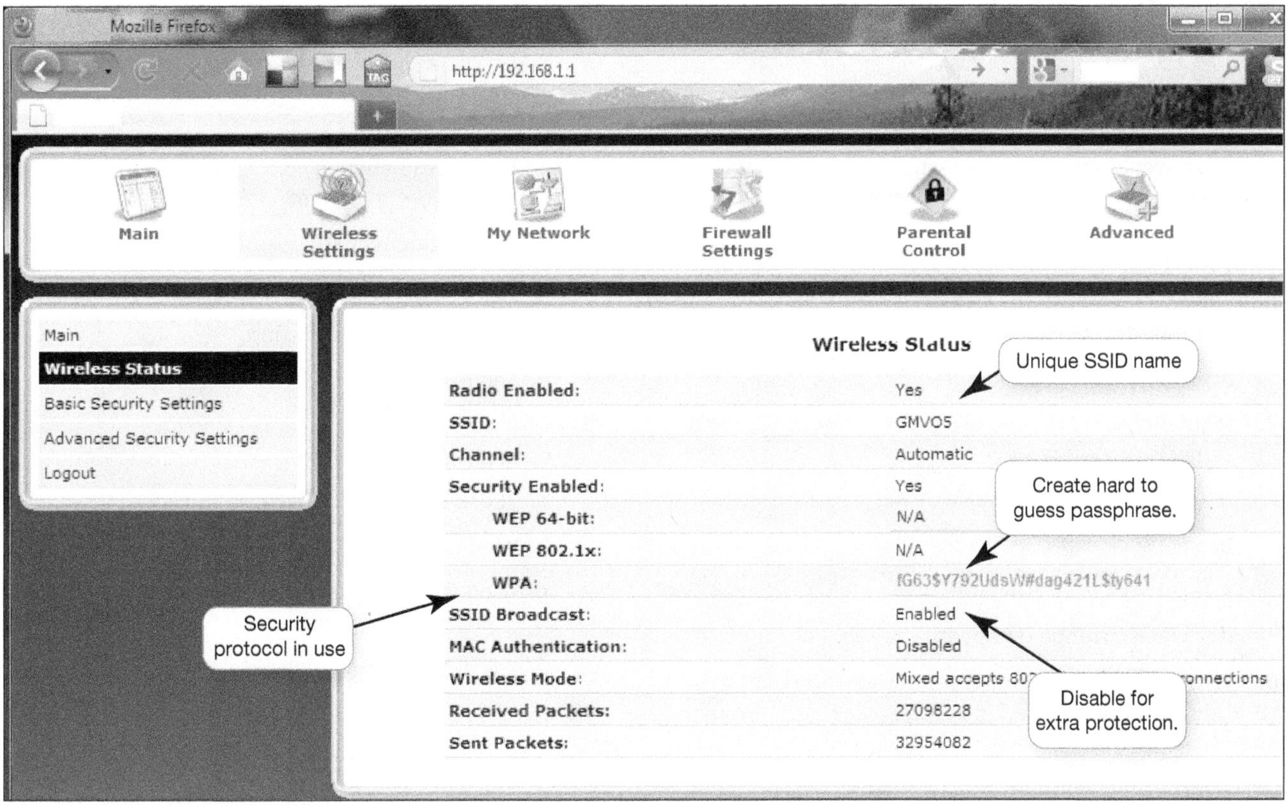

FIGURE 7.28 By accessing your router, you can configure the security protocols available on your router and change the SSID.
(Firefox logo® is a registered trademark of the Mozilla Foundation)

check your understanding // review & practice

For a quick review to see what you've learned so far, answer the following questions.

multiple choice

1. What would you use to see what network adapters are installed in your Windows computer?
   - **a.** Device Manager utility
   - **b.** Programs and Utilities manager
   - **c.** Ethernet Manager utility
   - **d.** Home Network manager
2. What device would you use to amplify your wireless signal?
   - **a.** dual-band N router
   - **b.** network extender device
   - **c.** network access switch
   - **d.** wireless range extender
3. Why would you want to disable SSID broadcast?
   - **a.** to make it more difficult for hackers to detect your network
   - **b.** to make it difficult for a neighbor to connect to your network
   - **c.** both A and B
   - **d.** neither A or B
4. To share files between computers on a Windows home network, you must
   - **a.** enable groupsharing.
   - **b.** create a homegroup.
   - **c.** enable Windows sharing.
   - **d.** none of the above
5. How can you tell what wireless devices are connected to your router?
   - **a.** Look at the router itself.
   - **b.** Look at the device's wireless settings.
   - **c.** Log in to the router's IP address and check the configuration page.
   - **d.** all of the above

MyITLab Go to **MyITLab** to take an autograded version of the *Check Your Understanding* review and to find all media resources for the chapter.

TECHBYTES WEEKLY

Stay current with the TechBytes Weekly Newsletter.

Continue

7 Chapter Review

summary //

How Networks Function

Learning Outcome 7.1 **You will be able to explain the basics of networking, including components needed to create a network, and describe the different ways a network can connect to the Internet.**

Networking Fundamentals

Objective 7.1 *Explain what a network is and the pros and cons of networks.*

- A computer network is simply two or more computers that are connected using software and hardware so they can communicate.
- Advantages of networks include allowing users to share an Internet connection, share printers and other peripheral devices, share files, and communicate with computers regardless of their operating system.
- Disadvantages for larger networks are that they require administration and that they may require costly equipment.

Network Architectures

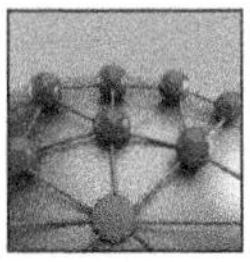

Objective 7.2 *Discuss how networks are defined by distance.*

- Networks can be defined by the distance between nodes:
- A personal area network (PAN) is used for communication among personal mobile devices using Bluetooth or WiFi wireless technologies.
- A local area network (LAN) connects nodes that are located in a small geographic area.
- A home area network (HAN) is a specific type of LAN located in a home.
- A metropolitan area network (MAN) is a large network in a specific geographic area.
- A wide area network (WAN) spans a large physical distance.

Objective 7.3 *Discuss how networks are classified by levels of administration.*

- *Central*: A client/server network contains two types of computers: a client computer on which users perform specific tasks and a server computer that provides resources to the clients and central control for the network. Most networks that have 10 or more nodes are client/server networks.
- *Local*: Peer-to-peer (P2P) networks enable each node connected to the network to communicate directly with every other node. Most home networks are P2P networks.

Objective 7.4 *Describe the Ethernet protocols for wired and wireless networks.*

- Ethernet networks are the most common networks used in home networking.
- Most Ethernet networks use a combination of wired and wireless connections, depending on the data throughput required. Wired connections usually achieve higher throughput than wireless connections.
- Wired Ethernet home networks use the gigabit Ethernet standard.
- Wireless Ethernet networks are identified by a protocol standard: 802.11a/b/g/n/ac. 802.11ac is the newest standard. WiGig (802.11ad) is a new wireless link between devices. WiGig is similar to but faster than Bluetooth.

Network Components

Objective 7.5 *Describe the types of transmission media used in networks.*

- Wired networks use various types of cable to connect nodes, including twisted-pair cable, coaxial cable, and fiber-optic cable. The type of network and the distance between the nodes determines the type of cable used.
- Wireless networks use radio waves.

Objective 7.6 *Describe the basic devices necessary for networks.*

- All devices must have a network adapter. All devices sold today contain an integrated network interface card.
- Network navigation devices, such as routers and switches, are necessary for computers to communicate in a network.

Objective 7.7 *Describe the type of software necessary for networks.*

- Home networks need operating system software that supports peer-to-peer networking. Windows, OS X, and Linux all support P2P networking.
- Servers on client/server networks use network operating systems (NOS).

Connecting to the Internet

Objective 7.8 *Summarize the broadband options available to access the Internet.*

- Broadband connections include the following types:
- Cable transmits data over coaxial cable, which is also used for cable television.
- DSL uses twisted-pair wire, similar to that used for telephones.
- Fiber-optic cable uses glass or plastic strands to transmit data via light signals.
- Satellite is a connection option for those who do not have access to faster broadband technologies. Data is transmitted between a satellite dish and a satellite that is in a geosynchronous orbit.

Objective 7.9 *Summarize how to access the Internet wirelessly.*

- WiFi allows users to connect to the Internet wirelessly but is not as fast as a wired connection.
- Mobile broadband is a 3G or 4G service delivered by cell-phone networks.

Objective 7.10 *Summarize the pros and cons of dial-up connections.*

- Dial-up is the cheapest means of accessing the Internet, but it is also the slowest.

Your Home Network

Learning Outcome 7.2 **You will be able to describe what is necessary to install and configure a home network, and how to manage and secure a wireless network.**

Installing and Configuring Home Networks

Objective 7.11 *Explain what should be considered before creating a home network.*

- Most home network routers should support both wireless and wired access to the Internet.
- For a home network to run efficiently, all nodes such as NICs and routers should use the same Ethernet standard.
- The Device Manager utility in Windows lists all adapters installed on your computer.

Objective 7.12 *Describe what is necessary to connect devices to a network.*

- All devices are connected to your router, either wirelessly or with a wired connection. Wired connections deliver better throughput than wireless.
- To add additional ports to your network, you can connect a switch to your router.

Objective 7.13 *Describe some specialized devices that can be added to a home network.*

- Network-attached storage (NAS) devices let you store and share data files such as movies and music, as well as provide a central place for file backups.
- Home network servers can be used instead of an NAS device if your needs require more sophisticated functionality than NAS devices.
- Devices such as gaming consoles each have their own setup procedures for connecting to wireless networks but usually require the same information as that needed for connecting a computer to a secured wireless network.

Objective 7.14 *Summarize how to configure home network software.*

- The latest versions of Windows make it easy to set up wired and wireless networks.

Managing and Securing Wireless Networks

Objective 7.15 *Describe the potential problems with wireless networks and means to avoid them.*

- You may not get the throughput you need through a wireless connection. Therefore, you may need to consider a wired connection for certain devices.
- Distance from the router, as well as walls, floors, and large metal objects between a device and the router, can interfere with wireless connectivity.

- To solve connectivity problems, dual-band N routers allow for simultaneous support for devices running on both the 2.4 and 5 GHz frequency bands for 802.11n and earlier standards. Wireless range extenders can amplify signals to improve connectivity in areas of poor signal strength.

Objective 7.16 *Describe how to secure wireless home networks.*

- Wireless networks are even more susceptible to hacking than wired networks because the signals of most wireless networks extend beyond the walls of your home.
- Neighbors may unintentionally (or intentionally) connect to the Internet through your wireless connection, and hackers may try to access it.
- To prevent unwanted intrusions into your network, you should change the default password on your router to make it tougher for hackers to gain access, use a hard-to-guess SSID (network name), disable SSID broadcasting to make it harder for outsiders to detect your network, enable security protocols such as WPA or WEP, create a network passphrase, implement media access control, limit your signal range, and apply firmware upgrades.

MyITLab Be sure to check out **MyITLab** for additional materials to help you review and learn. And don't forget the Replay Videos.

key terms //

4G **271**
backward compatibility **264**
bandwidth **261**
broadband **269**
cable Internet **270**
Cat 6 cable **266**
client/server network **263**
coaxial cable **265**
data transfer rate **261**
digital subscriber line (DSL) **270**
Ethernet network **264**
fiber-optic cable **265**
fiber-optic service **270**
firmware **286**
gigabit Ethernet **264**
home area network (HAN) **262**
home network server **279**
Internet of Things (IoT) **268**
Internet service provider (ISP) **269**
local area network (LAN) **262**
metropolitan area network (MAN) **262**
mobile broadband **271**
mobile hotspot **272**
modem **267**
network **260**
network adapter **267**
network administration **261**
network architecture **262**
network-attached storage (NAS) device **278**
network interface card (NIC) **267**
network navigation device **267**
network operating system (NOS) **268**
network-ready device **279**
node **256**
packet **267**
peer-to-peer (P2P) network **263**
personal area network (PAN) **262**
piggybacking **286**
router **267**
satellite Internet **270**
service set identifier (SSID) **286**
smart home **284**
switch **267**
throughput **261**
transmission media **265**
twisted-pair cable **265**
unshielded twisted-pair (UTP) cable **266**
wide area network (WAN) **262**
wireless fidelity (WiFi) **264**
wireless range extender **285**

chapter quiz // assessment

For a quick review to see what you've learned, answer the following questions. Submit the quiz as requested by your instructor. If you are using MyITLab, the quiz is also available there.

multiple choice

1. Which of the following would NOT be a benefit of networking computers?
   - **a.** sharing an Internet connection
   - **b.** sharing printers and other peripherals
   - **c.** sharing software licenses
   - **d.** sharing files
2. Bethany is in her home, watching a video she took on vacation, while her brother is playing FIFA Soccer on his Xbox, and her dad is checking stock quotes on his iPad. What kind of network does this family have?
   - **a.** P2P network
   - **b.** Client/server network
   - **c.** both a and b
   - **d.** neither a and b
3. What two devices are often combined into one device in a small network to connect the home network to the Internet and to share the connection between devices on the network?
   - **a.** router hub and switch
   - **b.** switch and router
   - **c.** modem and router
   - **d.** modem and switch
4. Which of the following is used to access the Internet when WiFi is not available?
   - **a.** mobile hotspot
   - **b.** 4G LTE Internet access
   - **c.** 3G Internet access
   - **d.** all of the above
5. Which of the following should you NOT do to secure a wireless network?
   - **a.** Implement media access control.
   - **b.** Keep the default network name and router password.
   - **c.** Create a security encryption passphrase.
   - **d.** Disable SSID broadcasting.
6. Which of the following might cause interference or poor connectivity between nodes on a wireless network?
   - **a.** concrete walls
   - **b.** nodes that are too far apart
   - **c.** some appliances
   - **d.** all of the above

true/false

_____ **1.** 802.11ac is the current wireless Ethernet standard.

_____ **2.** 4G is the latest WiFi standard.

_____ **3.** Actual data throughput is usually higher on wireless networks than on wired networks.

_____ **4.** Data is sent through the network in bundles called packages.

critical thinking

1. **Using Online Storage**

   Sneakernet is jargon for physically transporting files from one location to another, as in using a flash drive. Think about the advantages and disadvantages of using flash drives versus online storage systems, such as Dropbox, Google Drive, and OneDrive. Defend your preferred method of storing and sharing files.
2. **Internet of Things**

   Think about the term "Internet of Things" in which things (objects, animals, and people) are connected to the Internet and can automatically transfer data over a network. Our society is already filled with many examples of "smart nodes"—such as cars, appliances, and entertainment devices—that are connected to the Internet. What are the advantages and disadvantages of developing a more robust Internet of Things and continuing to add more smart nodes?

team time //

Providing Wireless Internet Access to the Needy

Problem

Not everyone can afford wireless Internet access, and this can put families, especially ones with school-aged children, at a disadvantage.

Task

You're volunteering for a charity that wants to install wireless networks in the homes of needy families. The project is funded by charitable grants with the objective of providing basic broadband Internet access and networking capabilities at no cost to the recipients.

Process

Break the class into three teams. Each team will be responsible for investigating one of the following issues:

1. **Internet service providers:** Research ISPs that serve the town where your school is located. Compare maximum upload and download speeds as well as costs. Be sure to consider the cost of the modems—whether they're purchased or rented. Select what your group considers the best deal.
2. **Networking equipment and network-ready peripherals:** Each home needs to be provided with an 802.11ac-capable wireless router and a network-ready all-in-one printer. Research three options for these devices, considering price as well as functionality.
3. **Security:** Work in conjunction with the group researching routers to determine the best router to purchase since it needs to support a security protocol such as WPA. Consider other types of protection needed, such as antivirus software and firewalls.

Present your findings to your class and come to a consensus about the solution you would propose for the charity.

Conclusion

Providing technology to underserved populations on a cost-effective basis will go a long way toward closing the digital divide.

ethics project //

Firing Employees for Expressing Views on Social Media Sites

In this exercise, you'll research and then role-play a complicated ethical situation. The role you play may or may not match your own personal beliefs; regardless, your research and use of logic will enable you to represent the view assigned. An arbitrator will watch and comment on both sides of the arguments, and together the team will agree on an ethical solution.

Problem

Employers often are intolerant of employees who express negative opinions or expose inside information about their employers on social media sites. Given that most jurisdictions in the United States use the doctrine of employment at will (employees can be fired at any time for any reason), many employers are quick to discipline or terminate employees who express opinions with which the company disagrees. When such cases come to court, the courts often find in favor of the employers.

Research Areas to Consider

- Ellen Simonetti and Delta Airlines
- Fired for blogging about work
- Free speech
- Joyce Park or Michael Tunison

Process

1. Divide the class into teams. Research the areas above and devise a scenario in which someone has complained about an employee blogging about an issue such as cleanliness at a food manufacturing facility.
2. Team members should write a summary that provides background information for their character—for example, employee, human resources manager, or arbitrator—and that details their character's behaviors to set the stage for the role-playing event. Then, team members should create an outline to use during the role-playing event.
3. Team members should present their case to the class or submit a PowerPoint presentation for review, along with the summary and resolution they developed.

Conclusion

As technology becomes ever more prevalent and integrated into our lives, more and more ethical dilemmas will present themselves. Being able to understand and evaluate both sides of the argument, while responding in a personally or socially ethical manner, will be an important skill.

Solve This

MyITLab® grader

Home Networking Guide

You write a newsletter, **The Everyday Technologist**, which specializes in technology tips and tricks for the casual everyday technology user. Your current newsletter is a guide to home networks. The basic document has been created, and now using Word 2016 you need to add formatting and images to make the guide more visually appealing.

You will use the following skills as you complete this activity:

- Apply Text Effects
- Insert WordArt
- Insert Columns
- Insert Section Breaks
- Insert Column Break
- Insert Images
- Apply Text Wrapping
- Use Custom Margins

Instructions:

1. Open *TIA_Ch7_Start.docx* and save as **TIA_Ch7_LastFirst.docx**.
2. Select the title **Home Networking Guide**, and convert the text to a WordArt Object using **Gradient Fill—Blue, Accent 1, Reflection**.
3. With the WordArt object still selected, click **Layout Options**, and select **Top and Bottom**. Then, click **See more...** at the bottom of the Layout Options window, and in the Layout dialog box, in the *Horizontal* section, select the **Alignment option**, and then choose **Centered** from the dropdown box.
4. Apply the **Fill—Orange, Accent 2, Outline—Accent 2 Text Effect** to the three headings: *Hardware*, *Wireless versus Wired*, and *Powerline Adapters*. Increase the font size of each heading to 18.
5. Create custom margins so all margins are 0.7".
6. Position the cursor before the heading *Hardware*. Insert a **Section Break (Continuous)**, and then apply **Two Column** formatting.
7. Place the cursor at the end of the second bullet point paragraph in the *Hardware* section. Insert the image TIA_Ch7_Modem Router. Change the Layout Option of the image to **Square**. Resize the image so the height is **0.9"** and the width is **1.2"**, and then move the image so that the two top lines of the Router paragraph display above the image, and the left side of the image is flush with the left margin.
8. Place the cursor at the beginning of the Powerline Adapters paragraph. Insert the image TIA_Ch7_Powerline. Change the Layout Option to **Tight**. Change the height of the image to **1"**, and then move the image so the right side is flush with the right margin of the document and centered vertically in the Powerline Adapter paragraph.
9. Place the cursor at the beginning of *Current Wireless (Wi-Fi) Standards*. Insert a column break. Format the text with bold and italics.
10. Save and submit for grading.

9 Securing Your System: Protecting Your Digital Data and Devices

Make This: MAKE: A Password Generator on **page 365**

All media accompanying this chapter can be found in MyITLab.

For an overview of the chapter, watch the **Preview Video**.

(Robert Mizerek/Fotolia, Wk1003mike/Shutterstock, Carlos Amarillo/Shutterstock, James Thew/Fotolia, Ymgerman/Fotolia, Graja/Shutterstock)

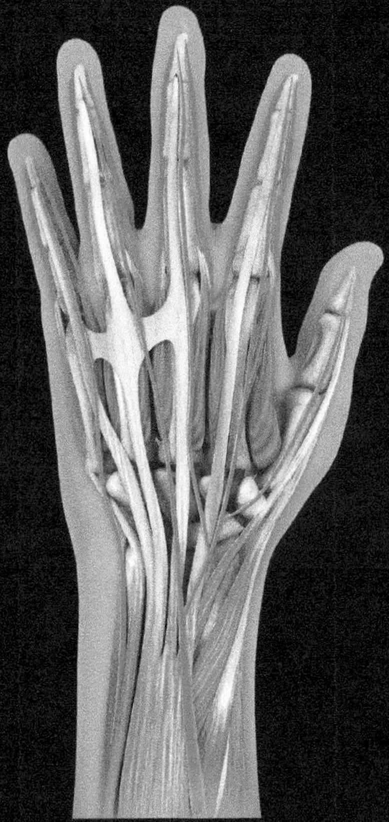

HOW COOL IS THIS?

Biometrics authentication for bank customers has gotten a major upgrade. Banks now use scanners that utilize **finger vein authentication technology**. The scanners read the unique vein patterns inside your finger to **verify your identity**. How does this improve upon fingerprint scans? Fingerprint scanning technology has flaws—impressions of your fingerprints can be left on scanner surfaces and can be duplicated to fool security devices. However, because your veins are inside your body, **they don't leave residue on scanners**. Perhaps your bank will offer this more secure technology soon! *(Nerthuz/Fotolia)*

Threats to Your Digital Assets

Learning Outcome 9.1 You will be able to describe hackers, viruses, and other online annoyances and the threats they pose to your digital security.

The media is full of stories about malicious computer programs damaging computers, criminals stealing people's identities online, and attacks on corporate websites bringing major corporations to a standstill. These are examples of *cybercrime*—any criminal action perpetrated primarily through the use of a computer. *Cybercriminals* are individuals who use computers, networks, and the Internet to perpetrate crime. Anyone with a computer and the wherewithal to arm himself or herself with the appropriate knowledge can be a cybercriminal. In this part of the chapter, we'll discuss the most serious types of cybercrime you need to worry about as well as some online annoyances to avoid.

identity theft and HACKERS

Every year, the Internet Crime Complaint Center (IC3)—a partnership between the FBI and the National White Collar Crime Center—receives hundreds of thousands of complaints related to Internet crime. Figure 9.1 shows four common categories of complaints the IC3 receives. Government impersonation scams involve people pretending to represent official organizations, such as the FBI, the IRS, or Homeland Security, to defraud. Nonauction/non-delivery scams involve running auctions (or sales) of merchandise that does not really exist, wherein the perpetrators just collect funds and disappear without delivering the promised goods. Advance fee fraud involves convincing individuals to send money as a "good faith" gesture to enable them to receive larger payments in return. The scammers then disappear with the advance fees. Identity

FIGURE 9.1

Common Types of Cybercrimes Reported to the IC3

(Peter Kim/Fotolia, Snyfer/Fotolia, Viperagp/Fotolia, Mikeledray/Shutterstock)

theft involves the stealing of someone's personal information for financial gain. Although these complaints relate to some type of fraud, other complaints received involve equally serious matters such as computer intrusions (hacking), extortion, and blackmail. In this section, we'll look at both identity theft and hacking in more detail.

Identity Theft

Objective 9.1 *Describe how identity theft is committed and the types of scams identity thieves perpetrate.*

What is the most financially damaging cybercrime plaguing individuals? Theft of personal data such as bank account numbers and credit/debit card numbers is of most concern to individuals because this information is usually used for fraudulent purposes. As noted above, **identity theft** occurs when a thief steals personal information such as your name, address, Social Security number, birth date, bank account number, and credit card information and runs up debts in your name. Many victims of identity theft spend months, or even years, trying to repair their credit and eliminate fraudulent debts.

What types of scams do identity thieves perpetrate? The nefarious acts cover a wide range:

- Counterfeiting your existing credit and debit cards
- Requesting changes of address on your bank and credit card statements, which makes detecting fraudulent charges take longer
- Opening new credit cards and bank accounts in your name and then writing bad checks and not paying off the credit card balances (ruining your credit rating in the process)
- Obtaining medical services under your name, potentially causing you to later lose coverage if the thief's treatment exceeds the limits of your policy's covered services
- Buying a home with a mortgage in your name, then reselling the house and absconding with the money (leaving you with the debt)

Many people believe that the only way your identity can be stolen is by a computer. However, the Federal Trade Commission (**ftc.gov**) has identified other methods thieves use to obtain others' personal information:

- Stealing purses and wallets, in which people often keep personal information such as their ATM PIN codes
- Stealing mail or looking through trash for bank statements and credit card bills
- Posing as bank or credit card company representatives and tricking people into revealing sensitive information over the phone
- Installing skimming devices on ATM machines that record information, such as account numbers and passcodes

Although foolproof protection methods don't exist, there are precautions that will help you minimize your risk, which we'll discuss later in this chapter.

With all the news coverage about identity theft and other cybercrimes, aren't people being more cautious? Although most people are aware of spam, a survey by the Messaging, Malware and Mobile Anti-Abuse Working Group (M3AAWG) found that half of e-mail users in North America and Europe have opened spam, some of which are designed to trick you into divulging sensitive information. The M3AAWG also discovered that 46% of people who opened spam did so intentionally—out of idle curiosity, to follow links to unsubscribe to unwanted e-mails (which only brings more spam), or because they are interested in the product being offered.

Hacking

Objective 9.2 *List and describe the different types of hackers.*

What exactly defines a hacker? Although there's a great deal of disagreement as to what a hacker actually is, especially among hackers themselves, a **hacker** is most commonly defined as anyone who unlawfully breaks into a computer system—either an individual computer or a network (see Figure 9.2).

Are there different kinds of hackers? Some hackers are offended by being labeled as criminals and therefore attempt to classify different types of hackers as follows:

- **White-hat hackers** (or **ethical hackers**) break in to systems for nonmalicious reasons, such as to test system security vulnerabilities or to expose undisclosed weaknesses.

FIGURE 9.2 Hacking humor. Hackers are a real problem in many instances, but don't let your fears overwhelm you! *(© Andy Singer www.andysinger.com)*

They believe in making security vulnerabilities known either to the company that owns the system or software or to the general public, often to embarrass a company into fixing a problem.

- **Black-hat hackers** break into systems to destroy information or for illegal gain. The terms *white hat* and *black hat* are references to old Western movies in which the heroes wore white hats and the outlaws wore black hats.
- **Grey-hat hackers** are a bit of a cross between black and white—they often illegally break into systems merely to flaunt their expertise to the administrator of the system they penetrated or to attempt to sell their services in repairing security breaches.

Regardless of the hackers' opinions, the laws in the United States and in many other countries consider *any* unauthorized access to computer systems a crime.

Hacking Tools and Attack Types

Objective 9.3 *Describe the various tools hackers use and the types of attacks they might launch against computers.*

Could a hacker steal my debit card or bank account number? Hackers often try to break in to computers or websites that contain credit card information. If you perform financial transactions online, such as banking or buying goods and services, you probably do so using a credit or debit card. Credit card and bank account information can thus reside on your hard drive or an online business's hard drive and may be detectable by a hacker.

Aside from your home computer, you have personal data stored on various websites. For example, many sites require that you provide a login ID and password to gain access. Even if this data isn't stored on your computer, a hacker may be able to capture it when you're online by using a *packet analyzer (sniffer)* or a *keylogger* (a program that captures all keystrokes made on a computer).

What's a packet analyzer? Data travels through the Internet in small pieces called *packets*. The packets are identified with an IP address, in part to help identify the computer to which they are being sent. Once the packets reach their destination, they're reassembled into cohesive messages. A **packet analyzer (sniffer)** is a program deployed by hackers that looks at (or sniffs) each packet as it travels on the Internet—not just those addressed to a particular computer, but all packets coming across a particular network. For example, a hacker might sit in a coffee shop and run a packet sniffer to capture sensitive data (such as debit/credit card numbers) from patrons using the coffee shop's free wireless network. Wireless networks such as these can be particularly vulnerable to this type of exploitation if encryption of data isn't enabled when the networks are set up. (This topic was covered in more detail in Chapter 7.)

What do hackers do with the information they "sniff"? Once a hacker has your debit/credit card information, he or she can use it to purchase items illegally or can sell the number to someone who will. If a hacker steals the login ID and password to an account where you have your bank card information stored (such as eBay or Amazon), he or she can also use your account to buy items and have them shipped to him- or herself instead of to you. If hackers can gather enough information in conjunction with your credit card information, they may be able to commit identity theft.

Although this sounds scary, you can easily protect yourself from packet sniffing by installing a firewall (which we discuss later in this chapter) and using data encryption on a wireless network (which was covered in Chapter 7).

Trojan Horses and Rootkits

Besides stealing information, what other problems can hackers cause if they break into my computer? Hackers often use individuals' computers as a staging area for mischief. To commit widespread computer attacks, for example, hackers need to control many computers at the same time. To this end, hackers often use Trojan horses to install other programs on computers. A **Trojan horse** is a program that appears to be something useful or desirable, like a game or a screen saver, but while it runs it does something malicious in the background without your knowledge (see Figure 9.3).

What damage can Trojan horses do? Often, the malicious activity perpetrated by a Trojan horse program is the installation of a backdoor program or a rootkit. **Backdoor programs** and **rootkits** are programs (or sets of programs) that allow hackers to gain access to your computer and take almost complete control of it without your knowledge. Using a backdoor program, hackers can access and delete all the files on your computer, send e-mail, run programs, and do just about anything else you can do with your computer. A computer that a hacker controls in this manner is referred to as a **zombie**. Zombies are often used to launch *denial-of-service attacks* on other computers.

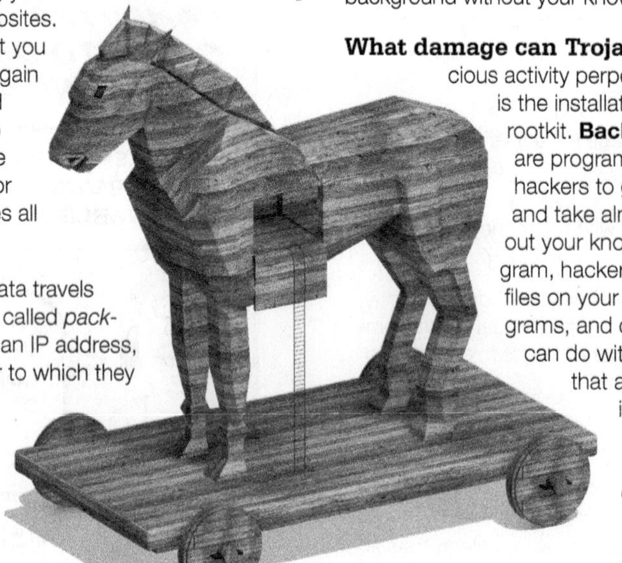

FIGURE 9.3 The term *Trojan horse* derives from Greek mythology and refers to the wooden horse that the Greeks used to sneak into the city of Troy and conquer it. Therefore, computer programs that contain a hidden, and usually dreadful, "surprise" are referred to as Trojan horses.
(Ralf Kraft/Fotolia)

Denial-of-Service Attacks

What are denial-of-service attacks? In a **denial-of-service (DoS) attack**, legitimate users are denied access to a computer system because a hacker

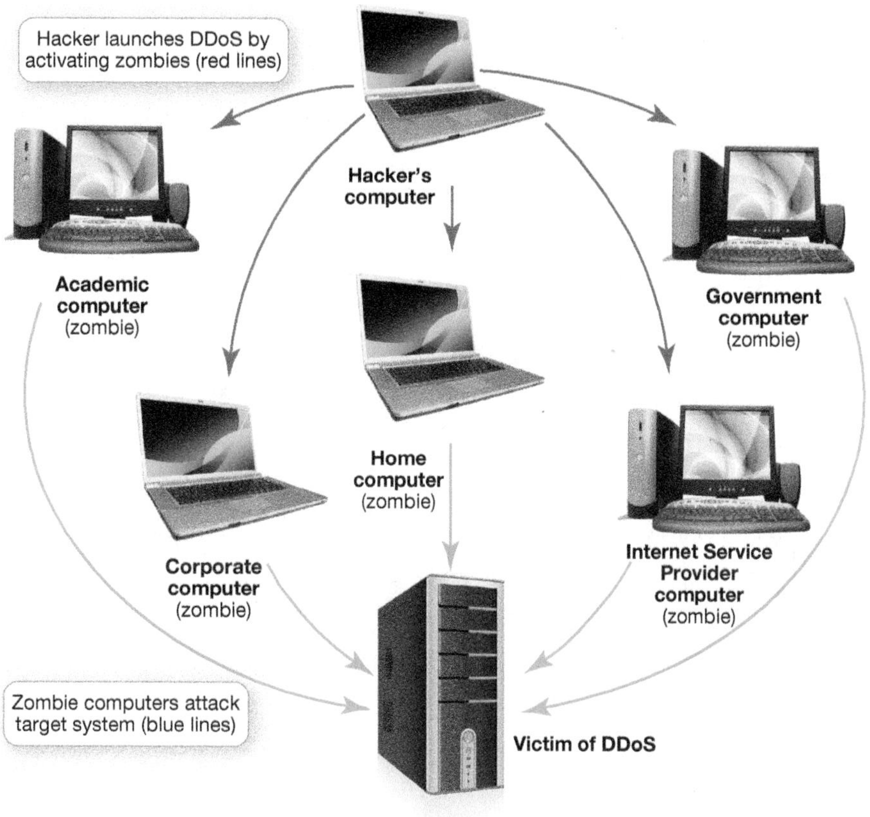

FIGURE 9.4 Zombie computers are used to facilitate a DDoS attack. *(Vovan/Shutterstock, Nicholas Monu/E+/Getty)*

is repeatedly making requests of that computer system through a computer he or she has taken over as a zombie. A computer system can handle only a certain number of requests for information at one time. When it is flooded with requests in a DoS attack, it shuts down and refuses to answer any requests for information, even if the requests are from a legitimate user. Thus, the computer is so busy responding to the bogus requests for information that authorized users can't gain access.

Couldn't a DoS attack be traced back to the computer that launched it? Launching a DoS attack on a computer system from a single computer is easy to trace. Therefore, most savvy hackers use a **distributed denial-of-service (DDoS) attack**, which launches DoS attacks from more than one zombie (sometimes thousands of zombies) at the same time.

Figure 9.4 illustrates how a DDoS attack works. A hacker creates many zombies and coordinates them so that they begin sending bogus requests to the same computer at the same time. Administrators of the victim computer often have a great deal of difficulty stopping the attack because it comes from so many computers. Often, the attacks are coordinated automatically by botnets. A **botnet** is a large group of software programs (called *robots* or *bots*) that runs autonomously on zombie computers. Some botnets have been known to span millions of computers.

Because many commercial websites receive revenue from users, either directly (such as via subscriptions to online games) or indirectly (such as when web surfers click on advertisements), DDoS attacks can be financially distressing for the owners of the affected websites.

How Hackers Gain Computer Access

How exactly does a hacker gain access to a computer? Hackers can gain access to computers directly or indirectly. Direct access involves sitting down at a computer and installing hacking software. It's unlikely that such an attack would occur in your home, but it's always a wise precaution to set up your computer so that it requires a password for a user to gain access.

Indirect access involves subtler methods. Many professional hackers use exploit kits. **Exploit kits** are software programs that run on servers and search for vulnerabilities of computers that visit the server. Exploit kits look for security holes in browsers and operating systems that haven't yet been patched by the users. When they detect a vulnerability,

FIGURE 9.5 Open logical ports are an invitation to hackers.

they can deliver spyware, bots, backdoor programs, or other malicious software to your computer. Fortunately, most exploit kits take advantage of known vulnerabilities, so if your antivirus software and operating system is up to date, you should be secure. We'll discuss both of these topics later in the chapter.

Hackers also can access a computer indirectly through its Internet connection. Many people forget that their Internet connection is a two-way street. Not only can you access the Internet, but people on the Internet can access your computer. Think of your computer as a house. Common sense tells you to lock your home's doors and windows to deter theft when you aren't there. Hooking your computer up to the Internet without protection is like leaving the front door to your house wide open. Your computer obviously doesn't have doors and windows like a house, but it does have logical ports.

What are logical ports? Logical ports are virtual—that is, not physical—communications gateways or paths that allow a computer to organize requests for information, such as web page downloads or e-mail routing, from other networks or computers. Unlike physical ports, such as USB ports, you can't see or touch a logical port; it's part of a computer's internal organization.

Logical ports are numbered and assigned to specific services. For instance, logical port 80 is designated for hypertext transfer protocol (HTTP), the main communications protocol for the web. Thus, all requests for information from your browser to the web flow through logical port 80. Open logical ports, like open windows in a home, invite intruders, as illustrated in Figure 9.5. Unless you take precautions to restrict access to your logical ports, other people on the Internet may be able to access your computer through them. Fortunately, you can thwart most hacking problems by installing a firewall, which we discuss later in the chapter. ■

BITS&BYTES

Are Your Photos Helping Criminals Target You?

All cell phones today contain GPS chips. The cameras in phones often use information gathered from the GPS chips to encode information onto photos in the form of geotags. A **geotag** is a piece of data attached to a photo that indicates your latitude and longitude when you took the photo. Geotagging is useful for applications that can take advantage of this information, but problems arise when you share geotagged photos on the web.

If you post a lot of photos, cybercriminals and cyberstalkers can use the information from the geotags on your photos to figure out the patterns of your movements. They may be able to ascertain when you're at work or that you're currently on vacation, which leads them to determine prime times for burglarizing your home. Some sites such as Facebook and Twitter have measures in place to limit the amount of geotagged information that can be seen in photos in order to prevent their users from unwittingly revealing personal information. However, many photo-sharing sites don't have such protections in place.

The safest thing to do is not tag your photos with geotags in the first place. It's usually easy to disable location tracking on your smartphone in the settings. So stop geotagging your photos, and make it tougher for the cybercriminals to figure out your movements. For photos that already have geotags, you can remove them using software such as BatchPurifier LITE or Pixelgarde. .

computer VIRUSES

Creating and disseminating computer viruses is one of the most widespread types of cybercrimes. Some viruses cause only minor annoyances, whereas others cause destruction or theft of data. Many viruses are designed to gather sensitive information such as credit card numbers.

Virus Basics

Objective 9.4 *Explain what a computer virus is, why they are a threat to your security, how a computing device catches a virus, and the symptoms it might display.*

What is a computer virus? A computer **virus** is a computer program that attaches itself to another computer program (known as the *host* program) and attempts to spread to other computers when files are exchanged.

Why are viruses such a threat to my security? Computer viruses are threatening because they are engineered to evade detection. Viruses normally attempt to hide within the code of a host program to avoid detection. And viruses are not just limited to computers. Smartphones, tablet computers, and other devices can be infected with viruses. Viruses such as SpyEye Mobile Banking are used to trick users into downloading an infected file to their phones, which then steals their online banking information.

I have an Apple computer, so I don't need to worry about viruses, do I? This is a popular misconception! Everyone, even Apple users, needs to worry about viruses. As the OS X and iOS operating systems have gained market share, the number of virus attacks against Apple operating systems is on the rise.

What do computer viruses do? A computer virus's main purpose is to replicate itself and copy its code into as many other host files as possible. This gives the virus a greater chance of being copied to another computer system so that it can spread its infection. However, computer viruses require human interaction to spread. Although there might be a virus in a file on your computer, a virus normally can't infect your computer until the infected file is opened or executed.

Although virus replication can slow down networks, it's not usually the main threat. The majority of viruses have secondary objectives or side effects, ranging from displaying annoying messages on the computer screen to destroying files or the contents of entire hard drives.

How does my computer catch a virus? If your computer is exposed to a file infected with a virus, the virus will try to copy itself and infect a file on your computer.

Downloading infected audio and video files from peer-to-peer file-sharing sites is a major source of virus infections. Shared flash drives are also a common source of virus infection, as is e-mail. Just opening an e-mail message usually won't infect your computer with a virus, although some new viruses are launched when viewed in the preview pane of your e-mail software. Downloading and running (executing) a file that's attached to the e-mail are common ways that your computer becomes infected. Thus, be extremely wary of e-mail attachments, especially if you don't know the sender. Figure 9.6 illustrates the steps by which computer viruses are often passed from one computer to the next:

1. An individual writes a virus program, attaches it to a music file, and posts the file to a file-sharing site.
2. Unsuspecting Bill downloads the "music file" and infects his computer when he listens to the song.
3. Bill sends his cousin Fred an e-mail with the infected "music file" and contaminates Fred's tablet.
4. Fred syncs his phone with his tablet and infects his phone when he plays the music file.
5. Fred e-mails the file from his phone to Susan, one of his colleagues at work. Everyone who copies files from Susan's infected work computer, or whose computer is networked to Susan's computer, risks spreading the virus.

How can I tell if my computer is infected with a virus? Sometimes it can be difficult to definitively tell whether your computer is infected with a virus. However, if your computer displays any of the following symptoms, it may be infected with a virus:

1. Existing program icons or files suddenly disappear. Viruses often delete specific file types or programs.
2. You start your browser and it takes you to an unusual home page (i.e., one you didn't set) or it has new toolbars.
3. Odd messages, pop-ups, or images are displayed on the screen, or strange music or sounds play.
4. Data files become corrupt. (However, note that files can become corrupt for reasons other than a virus infection.)
5. Programs stop working properly, which could be caused by either a corrupted file or a virus.
6. Your system shuts down unexpectedly, slows down, or takes a long time to boot up.

Types of Viruses

Objective 9.5: *List the different categories of computer viruses, and describe their behaviors.*

What types of viruses exist? Although thousands of computer viruses and variants exist, they can be grouped into

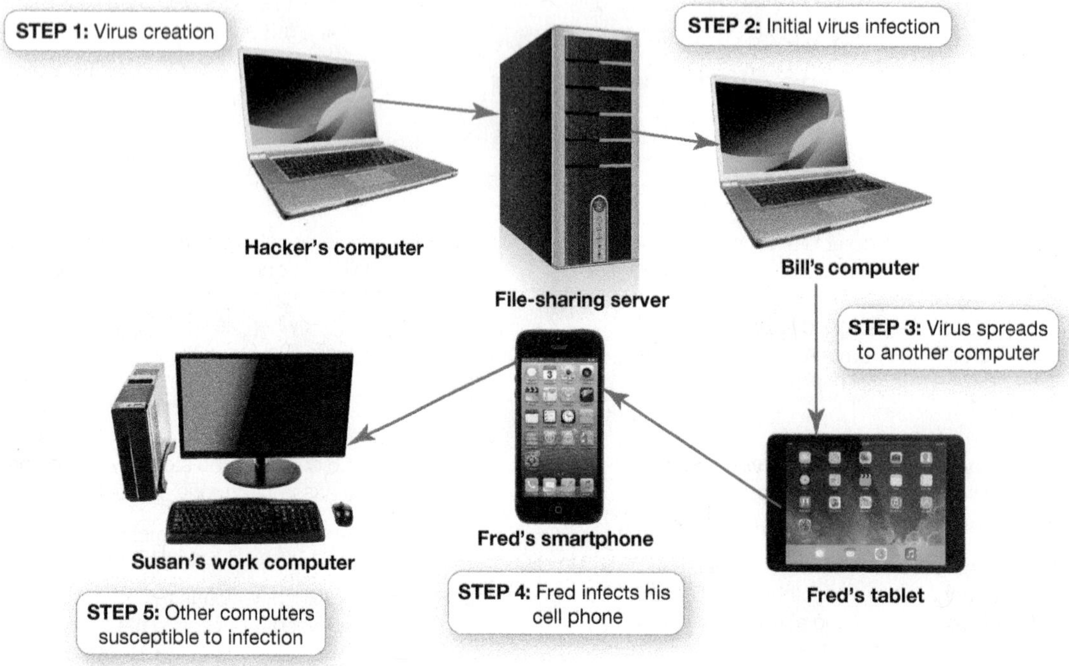

FIGURE 9.6 Computer viruses are passed from one unsuspecting user to the next. *(Vovan/Shutterstock, Juffin/DigitalVision Vectors/Getty Images, Denis Rozhnovsky/Alamy, Ian Dagnall/Alamy, Stanca Sanda/Alamy)*

six broad categories based on their behavior and method of transmission.

Boot-Sector Viruses

What are boot-sector viruses? A **boot-sector virus** replicates itself onto a hard drive's master boot record. The **master boot record** is a program that executes whenever a computer boots up, ensuring that the virus will be loaded into memory immediately, even before some virus protection programs can load. Boot-sector viruses are often transmitted by a flash drive left in a USB port. When the computer boots up with the flash drive connected, the computer tries to launch a master boot record from the flash drive, which is usually the trigger for the virus to infect the hard drive.

Logic Bombs and Time Bombs

What are logic bombs and time bombs? A **logic bomb** is a virus that is triggered when certain logical conditions are met, such as opening a file or starting a program a certain number of times. A **time bomb** is a virus that is triggered by the passage of time or on a certain date. For example, the Michelangelo virus was a famous time bomb that was set to trigger every year on March 6, Michelangelo's birthday. The effects of logic bombs and time bombs range from the display of annoying messages on the screen to the reformatting of the hard drive, which causes complete data loss.

Worms

What is a worm? Although often called a virus, a **worm** is subtly different. Viruses require human interaction to spread, whereas worms take advantage of file transport methods, such as e-mail or network connections, to spread on their own. A virus infects a host file and waits until that file is executed to replicate and infect a computer system. A worm, however, works independently of host file execution and is much more active in spreading itself. Recently developed worms, like The Moon, even attack peripheral devices such as routers. Worms can generate a lot of data traffic when trying to spread, which can slow down the Internet.

Script and Macro Viruses

What are script and macro viruses? Some viruses are hidden on websites in the form of scripts. A **script** is a series of commands—actually, a miniprogram—that is executed without your knowledge. Scripts are often used to perform useful, legitimate functions on websites, such as collecting name and address information from customers. However, some scripts are malicious. For example, you might click a link to display a video on a website, which causes a script to run that infects your computer with a virus.

A **macro virus** is a virus that attaches itself to a document that uses macros. A *macro* is a short series of commands that usually automates repetitive tasks. However, macro languages are now so sophisticated that viruses can be written with them. In 1999, the Melissa virus became the first major macro virus to cause problems worldwide.

E-Mail Viruses

What is an e-mail virus? In addition to being a macro virus, the Melissa virus was the first practical example of an

FIGURE 9.7

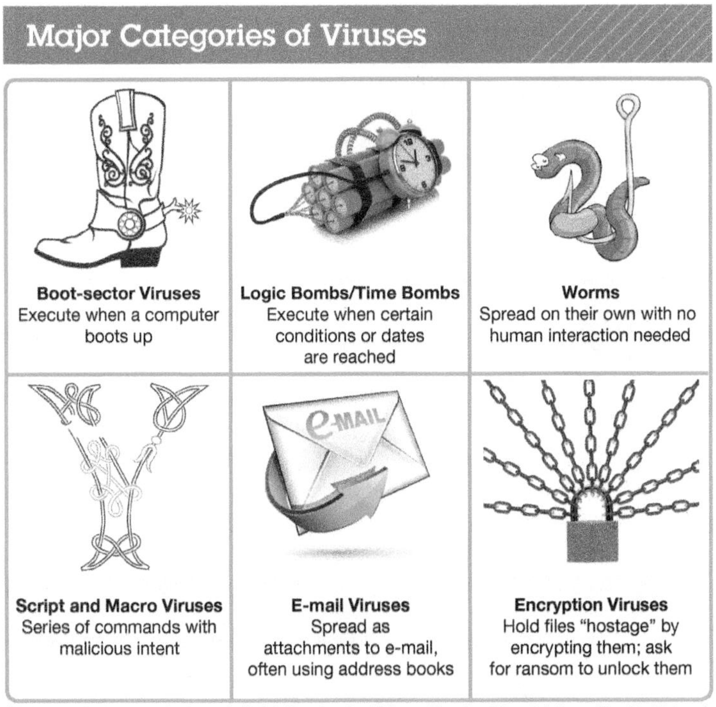

(Tribalium81/Fotolia, Oleksandr Delyk/Fotolia, DedMazay/Fotolia, Theo Malings/Fotolia, Beboy/Fotolia, Lukas Gojda/Fotolia)

e-mail virus. **E-mail viruses** use the address book in the victim's e-mail system to distribute the virus. In the case of the Melissa virus, anyone opening an infected document triggered the virus, which infected other documents on the victim's computer. Once triggered, the Melissa virus sent itself to the first 50 people in the e-mail address book on the infected computer.

Encryption Viruses

What are encryption viruses? When **encryption viruses** (also known as *ransomware*) infect your computer, they run a program that searches for common types of data files, such as Microsoft Word files, and compresses them using a complex encryption key that renders your files unusable. You then receive a message that asks you to send payment to an account if you want to receive the program to decrypt your files. The flaw with this type of virus, which keeps it from being widespread, is that law enforcement officials can trace the payments to an account and may possibly be able to catch the perpetrators. Figure 9.7 summarizes the major categories of viruses.

Additional Virus Classifications

How else are viruses classified? Viruses can also be classified by the methods they take to avoid detection by antivirus software:

- A **polymorphic virus** changes its own code or periodically rewrites itself to avoid detection. Most polymorphic viruses infect a particular type of file such as .EXE files, for example.
- A **multipartite virus** is designed to infect multiple file types in an effort to fool the antivirus software that is looking for it.
- **Stealth viruses** temporarily erase their code from the files where they reside and then hide in the active memory of the computer. This helps them avoid detection if only the hard drive is being searched for viruses. Fortunately, current antivirus software scans memory as well as the hard drive. ■

online annoyances and SOCIAL ENGINEERING

Surfing the web, using social networks, and sending and receiving e-mail have become common parts of most of our lives. Unfortunately, the web has become fertile ground for people who want to advertise their products, track our browsing behaviors, or even con people into revealing personal information. In this section, we'll look at ways in which you can manage, if not avoid, these and other online headaches.

Malware: Adware and Spyware

Objective 9.6 *Explain what malware is, and list the common types of malware.*

What is malware? Malware is software that has a malicious intent (hence the prefix *mal*). There are three primary forms of malware: adware, spyware, and viruses. Adware and spyware are not physically destructive like viruses and worms, which can destroy data. Known collectively as *grayware*, most malware are intrusive, annoying, or objectionable online programs that are downloaded to your computer when you install or use other online content such as a free program, game, or utility.

What is adware? Adware is software that displays sponsored advertisements in a section of your browser window or as a pop-up box. It's considered a legitimate, though sometimes annoying, means of generating revenue for those developers who do not charge for their software or information. Fortunately, because web browsers such as Firefox, Chrome, and Edge have built-in pop-up blockers, the occurrence of annoying pop-ups has been greatly reduced.

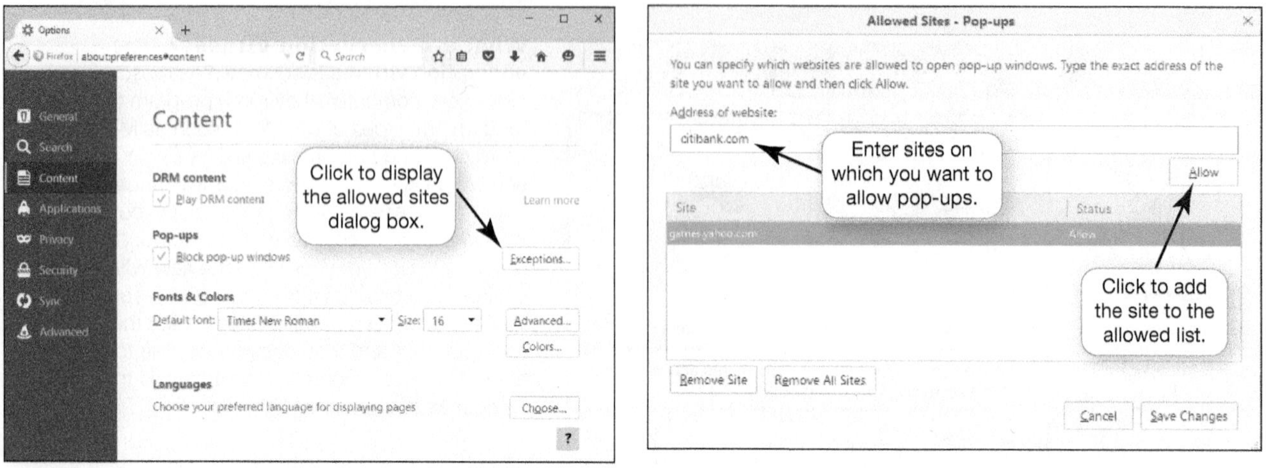

FIGURE 9.8 Firefox's Allowed Sites - Pop-ups dialog box lets you control which sites you'll allow to display pop-ups. *(Firefox logo® is a registered trademark of the Mozilla Foundation)*
>*To display the pop-up blocker in Firefox, click the* **Open Menu button**, *select* **Options**, *and then select the* **Content option**.

Some pop-ups, however, are legitimate and increase the functionality of the originating site. For example, your account balance may pop up on your bank's website. To control which sites to allow pop-ups on, you can access the pop-up blocker settings in your browser (see Figure 9.8) and add websites for which you allow pop-ups. Whenever a pop-up is blocked, the browser displays an information bar or plays a sound to alert you. If you feel the pop-up is legitimate, you can choose to accept it.

What is spyware? Spyware is an unwanted piggyback program that usually downloads with other software you install from the Internet and that runs in the background of your system. Without your knowledge, spyware transmits information about you, such as your Internet-surfing habits, to the owner of the program so that the information can be used for marketing purposes. Many spyware programs use tracking cookies (small text files stored on your computer) to collect information. One type of spyware program known as a **keystroke logger (key logger)** monitors keystrokes with the intent of stealing passwords, login IDs, or credit card information.

Can I prevent spyware from spying on me? Anti-spyware software detects unwanted programs and allows you to delete the offending software easily. Most Internet security suites now include anti-spyware software. You can also obtain stand-alone anti-spyware software and run it on your computer to delete unwanted spyware. Because so many variants of spyware exist, your Internet security software may not detect all types that attempt to install themselves on your computer. Therefore, it's a good idea to install one or two additional stand-alone anti-spyware programs on your computer.

Because new spyware is created all the time, you should update and run your anti-spyware software regularly. Windows comes with a program called Windows Defender, which scans your system for spyware and other potentially unwanted software. Malwarebytes Anti-Malware, Ad-Aware, and Spybot–Search & Destroy (all available from **download.com**) are other anti-spyware programs that are easy to install and update. Figure 9.9 shows an example of Windows Defender in action.

Spam

Objective 9.7 *Define spam, and describe strategies to combat it.*

How can I best avoid spam? Companies that send out **spam**—unwanted or junk e-mail—find your e-mail address either from a list they purchase or with software that looks for e-mail addresses on the Internet. Unsolicited instant messages are also a form of spam, called *spim*. If you've used your e-mail address to purchase anything online, open an online account, or participate in a social network such as Facebook, your e-mail address eventually will appear on one of the lists that spammers get.

One way to avoid spam in your primary account is to create a free e-mail address that you use only when you fill out forms or buy items on the web. For example, both Outlook.com and Yahoo! let you set up free e-mail accounts. If your free e-mail account is saturated with spam, you can abandon that account with little inconvenience. It's much less convenient to abandon your primary e-mail address.

Another way to avoid spam is to filter it. A **spam filter** is an option you can select in your e-mail account that places known or suspected spam messages into a special folder (called "Spam" or "Junk Mail"). Most web-based e-mail services, such as Gmail and Yahoo!, offer spam filters (see Figure 9.10). Microsoft Outlook also features a spam filter.

You can also buy third-party programs that provide some control over spam, including SPAMfighter, which you can download at download.com.

How do spam filters work? Spam filters and filtering software can catch as much as 95% of spam by checking incoming e-mail subject headers and senders' addresses against databases of known spam. Spam filters also check

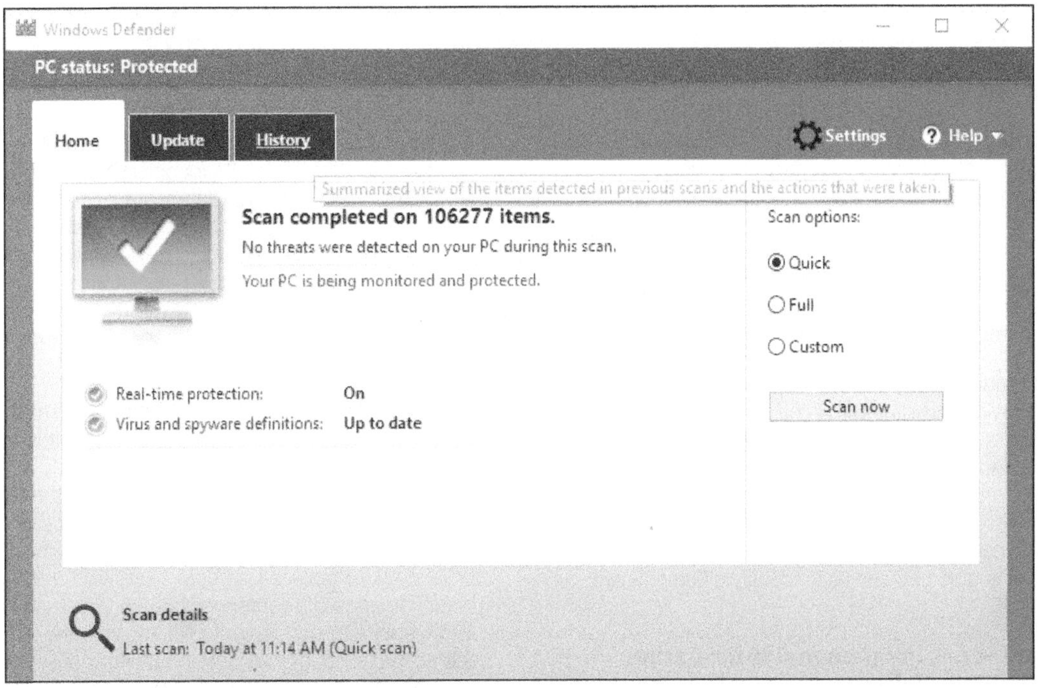

FIGURE 9.9 Routine scans of a computer by Windows Defender will detect and eliminate spyware and other unwanted types of software. *(Microsoft Windows Defender, Microsoft Corporation)*

your e-mail for frequently used spam patterns and keywords, such as "for free" and "over 21." Spam filters aren't perfect, and you should check the spam folder before deleting its contents because legitimate e-mail might end up there by mistake. Most programs let you reclassify e-mails that have been misidentified as spam (see Figure 9.10).

How else can I prevent spam? Here are a few other ways you can prevent spam:

1. Before registering on a website, read its privacy policy to see how it uses your e-mail address. Don't give the site permission to pass on your e-mail address to third parties.
2. Don't reply to spam to remove yourself from the spam list. By replying, you're confirming that your e-mail address is active. Instead of stopping spam, you may receive more.
3. Subscribe to an e-mail forwarding service such as VersaForward (versaforward.com) or Sneakemail (sneakemail.com). These services screen your e-mail messages, forwarding only those messages you designate as being okay to accept.

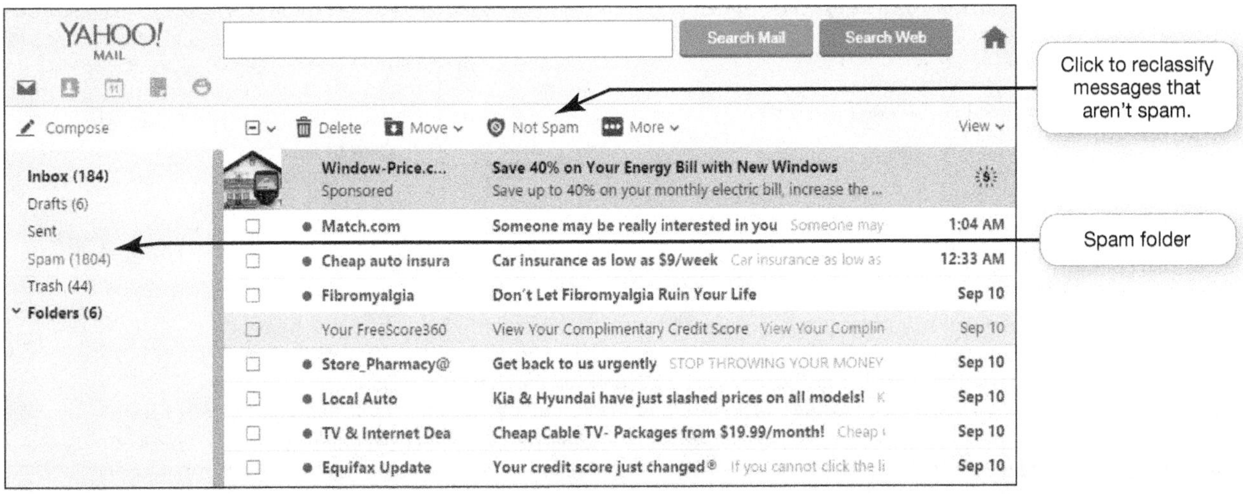

FIGURE 9.10 In Yahoo! Mail, messages identified as spam are directed into a folder called "Spam" for review and deletion. *(Reproduced with permission of Yahoo. ©2015 Yahoo. YAHOO! and the YAHOO! logo are registered trademarks of Yahoo.)*

Cookies

Objective 9.8 *Explain what cookies are and whether they pose a security threat.*

What are cookies? Cookies are small text files that some websites automatically store on your hard drive when you visit them. When you log on to a website that uses cookies, a cookie file assigns an ID number to your computer. The unique ID is intended to make your return visit to a website more efficient and better geared to your interests. The next time you log on to that site, the site marks your visit and keeps track of it in its database.

What do websites do with cookie information? Cookies can provide websites with information about your browsing habits, such as the ads you've opened, the products you've looked at, and the time and duration of your visits. Companies use this information to determine the traffic flowing through their website and the effectiveness of their marketing strategy and placement on websites. By tracking such information, cookies enable companies to identify different users' preferences.

Can companies get my personal information when I visit their sites? Cookies do not go through your hard drive in search of personal information such as passwords or financial data. The only personal information a cookie obtains is the information you supply when you fill out forms online.

Do privacy risks exist with cookies? Some sites sell the personal information their cookies collect to web advertisers who are building huge databases of consumer preferences and habits, collecting personal and business information such as phone numbers, credit reports, and the like. The main concern is that advertisers will use this information indiscriminately, thus invading your privacy. And you may feel your privacy is being violated by cookies that monitor where you go on a website.

Should I delete cookies from my hard drive? Cookies pose no *security* threat because it is virtually impossible to hide a virus or malicious software program in a cookie. Because they take up little room on your hard drive, and offer you small conveniences on return visits to websites, there is no great reason to delete them. Deleting your cookie files could actually cause you the inconvenience of reentering data you have already entered into website forms. However, if you're uncomfortable with the accessibility of your personal information, you can periodically delete cookies (as shown in Figure 9.11) or

FIGURE 9.11 Tools are available, either through your browser (Firefox is shown here) or as separate programs, to distinguish between cookies you want to keep and cookies you don't want on your system. *(Firefox logo® is a registered trademark of the Mozilla Foundation)*
>*On the Firefox menu toolbar, click the* ***Open Menu button****, click* ***Options****, choose the* ***Privacy option****, choose* ***Use custom settings for history****, and then click the* ***Show Cookies button*** *to display the Cookies dialog box.*

ethics in IT — You're Being Watched … But Are You Aware You're Being Watched?

Think you aren't being closely watched by your employer? Think again! A recent survey of employers by the American Management Association and the ePolicy Institute revealed that, of the employers surveyed:

- 73% monitored e-mail messages
- 66% monitored web surfing
- 48% monitored activities using video surveillance
- 45% monitored keystrokes and keyboard time
- 43% monitored computer files in some other fashion

FIGURE 9.12 George Orwell was right—Big Brother is watching you at work! It's legal for employers to monitor your computer usage. *(Beatriz Gascon J/Shutterstock)*

As you can see, there is a high probability that you're being monitored while you work and when you access the Internet via your employer's Internet connection.

The two most frequently cited reasons for employee monitoring are to prevent theft and to measure productivity. Monitoring for theft isn't new—monitoring cameras have been around for years, and productivity monitoring has been used for assembly line workers for decades. However, the Internet has led to a new type of productivity drain of concern to employers. **Cyberloafing** (or *cyberslacking*) means using your computer for nonwork activities while you're being paid to do your job. Examples of cyberloafing activities include playing games and using social networks. Some employees even do multiple nonwork tasks at the same time, which is known as *multishirking*. Estimates of business productivity losses due to cyberloafing top $50 billion annually.

Do you have a right to privacy in the workplace? Laws such as the 1986 Electronic Communications Privacy Act (ECPA), which prohibits unauthorized monitoring of electronic communications, have been interpreted by the courts in favor of employers. The bottom line is that employers who pay for equipment and software have the *legal* right to monitor their usage (see Figure 9.12).

So, is it *ethical* for employers to monitor their employees? Certainly, it seems fair that employers ensure they're not the victims of theft and that they're getting a fair day's work from their employees, just as employees have an obligation to provide a fair effort for a fair wage. The ethical issue is whether employees are adequately informed of monitoring policies. Employers have an ethical responsibility (and a legal one as well, depending on the jurisdiction) not to place monitoring devices in sensitive locations such as bathrooms and dressing areas. However, in many states, the employer does not legally need to inform employees in advance that they're being monitored. Conscientious employers include monitoring disclosures in published employee policies to avoid confusion and conflict.

The bottom line? Because employers may have a legal right to monitor you in the workplace, operate under the assumption that everything you do on your work computer is subject to scrutiny and behave accordingly. Do your online shopping at home!

BITS&BYTES

I Received a Data Breach Letter ... Now What?

Data breaches are becoming more common, and companies that are the subject of data breaches now routinely notify customers of data breaches—usually by physical letter, but sometimes via e-mail. Here's what you should do if you receive such a letter:

1. Take it seriously. 22.5% of recipients of these letters become the victim of identity theft per a study by Javelin Strategy and Research.
2. Contact one of the three big credit bureaus (Equifax, Experian, and TransUnion) and have a fraud alert put on your credit report. This alerts people accessing your credit report that your identity information has been stolen and that the person who is applying for credit in your name might be an imposter.
3. For even better security, contact all three credit bureaus and have a credit freeze put on your credit reports. This prevents anyone (even you) from getting credit in your name. You can always unfreeze your accounts later if you need to apply for credit yourself.
4. Review your credit reports regularly. You are entitled to one free credit report per year from each of the three big agencies. Go to **annualcreditreport.com** and request a report from one of the agencies. Repeat the process every four months from a different agency. Review the reports for any suspicious activity.

configure your browser to block certain types of cookies. Software such as Powerful Cookies (available at **download.com**) also can help you monitor cookies.

Social Engineering

Objective 9.9 *Describe social engineering techniques, and explain strategies to avoid falling prey to them.*

What is social engineering? Social engineering is any technique that uses social skills to generate human interaction that entices individuals to reveal sensitive information. Social engineering often doesn't involve the use of a computer or face-to-face interaction. For example, telephone scams are a common form of social engineering because it is often easier to manipulate someone when you don't have to look at them.

How does social engineering work? Most social engineering schemes use a pretext to lure their victims. **Pretexting** involves creating a scenario that sounds legitimate enough that someone will trust you. For example, you might receive a phone call during which the caller says he is from your bank and that someone tried to use your account without authorization. The caller then tells you he needs to confirm a few personal details such as your birth date, Social Security number, bank account number, and whatever other information he can get out of you. The information he obtains can then be used to empty your bank account or commit some other form of fraud. The most common form of pretexting in cyberspace is *phishing*.

Phishing and Pharming

How are phishing schemes conducted? Phishing (pronounced "fishing") lures Internet users to reveal personal information such as credit card numbers, Social Security numbers, or other sensitive information that could lead to identity theft. The scammers send e-mail messages that look like they're from a legitimate business such as an online bank. The e-mail usually states that the recipient needs to update or confirm his or her account information. When the recipient clicks on the provided link, he or she goes to a website. The site looks like a legitimate site but is really a fraudulent copy that the scammer has created. Once the e-mail recipient enters his or her personal information, the scammers capture it and can begin using it.

Is pharming a type of phishing scam? Pharming is much more insidious than phishing. Phishing requires a positive action by the person being scammed, such as going to a website mentioned in an e-mail and typing in personal information. **Pharming** occurs when malicious code is planted on your computer, either by viruses or by your visiting malicious websites, which then alters your browser's ability to find web addresses. Users are directed to bogus websites even when they enter the correct address of the real website. You end up at a fake website that looks legitimate but is expressly set up for the purpose of gathering information.

How can I avoid being caught by phishing and pharming scams? Follow these guidelines to avoid falling prey to such schemes:

- Never reply directly to any e-mail asking you for personal information.
- Don't click on a link in an e-mail to go to a website. Instead, type the website address in the browser.
- Check with the company asking for the information and only give the information if you're certain it's needed.
- Never give personal information over the Internet unless you know the site is secure. Look for the closed padlock, *https*, or a certification seal such as Norton Secured to help reassure you that the site is secure.
- Use phishing filters. The latest versions of Firefox, Chrome, and Edge have phishing filters built in, so each time you

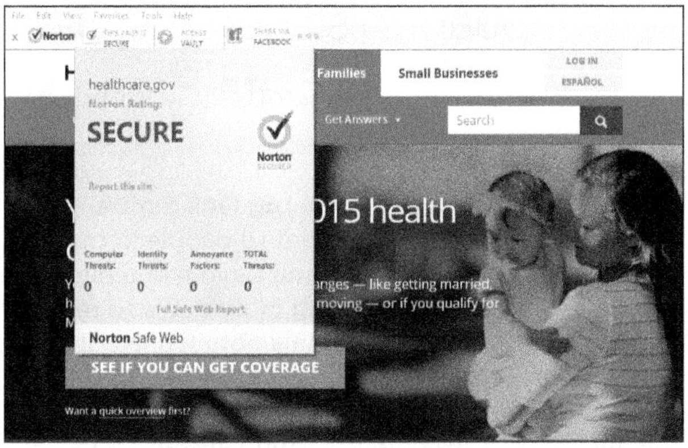

FIGURE 9.13 Not sure whether you're on the Healthcare.gov website or a cleverly disguised phishing site? Norton Safe Web reassures you that all is well. *(U.S. Centers for Medicare & Medicaid Services, www.healthcare.gov)*

access a website, the phishing filter checks for the site's legitimacy and warns you of possible web forgeries.

- Use Internet security software on your computer that's constantly being updated.

Most Internet security packages can detect and prevent pharming attacks. The major Internet security packages—for example, McAfee and Norton (see Figure 9.13)—also offer phishing-protection tools. When you have the Norton Toolbar displayed in your browser, you're constantly informed about the legitimacy of the site you are visiting.

Scareware

What is scareware? **Scareware** is a type of malware that downloads onto your computer and tries to convince you that your computer is infected with a virus (see Figure 9.14) or other type of malware. Pop-ups, banners, or other annoying types of messages will flash on your screen saying frightening things like, "Your computer is infected with a virus . . . immediate removal is required." You're then directed to a website where you can buy fake removal or antivirus tools that provide little or no value. Panda Security estimates that scareware scams generate in excess of $34 million a month for cybercriminals. Some scareware even goes so far as to encrypt your files and then demand that you pay to have them unencrypted, which is essentially extortion.

Scareware is a social engineering technique because it uses people's fear of computer viruses to convince them to part with their money. Scareware is often designed to be extremely difficult to remove from your computer and to interfere with the operation of legitimate security software. Scareware is usually downloaded onto your computer from infected websites or Trojan horse files.

How do I protect myself against scareware? Most Internet security suites, antivirus, and anti-malware software packages now detect and prevent the installation of scareware. But make sure you never click on website banners or pop-up boxes that say "Your computer might be infected, click here to scan your files" because these are often the starting points for installing malicious scareware files on your computer.

> **Before moving on to Part 2:**
> 1. Watch Replay Video 9.1.
> 2. Then check your understanding of what you've learned so far.

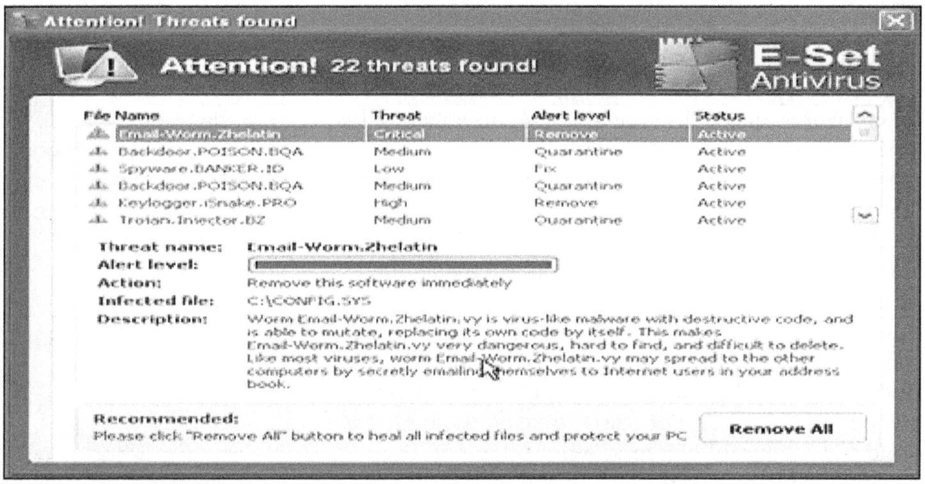

FIGURE 9.14 Preying on people's fears, scareware attempts to convince you that your computer is infected with a virus and you need to purchase a "solution." *(Reprinted courtesy of McAfee, Inc.)*

trends in IT

Computers in Society: Spear Phishing: The Bane of Data Breaches

Most people have vast amounts of personal data residing in the databases of the various companies with which they conduct business. Amazon.com has your credit card and address information. Your bank has your Social Security number, birth date, and financial records. Your local supermarket probably has your e-mail address from when you joined its loyalty club to receive grocery discounts. All this data in various places puts you at risk when companies responsible for keeping your data confidential suffer a data breach.

A **data breach** occurs when sensitive or confidential information is copied, transmitted, or viewed by an individual who isn't authorized to handle the data. Data breaches can be intentional or unintentional. Intentional data breaches occur when hackers break into digital systems to steal sensitive data. Unintentional data breaches occur when companies controlling data inadvertently allow it to be seen by unauthorized parties, usually due to some breakdown in security procedures or precautions.

Unfortunately, data breaches appear to be quite common, as there always seems to be another one in the news. The Identity Theft Resource Center, a nonprofit organization that monitors data breaches, reported 5,541 data breaches for U.S. companies in the first eight months of 2015. At least 140.1 million records were exposed, although this data is not available for all the breaches. These breaches pose serious risks to the individuals whose data has been compromised, even if financial data is not involved. The data thieves now have the basis with which to launch targeted social engineering attacks even if they just have contact information, such as e-mail addresses.

With regular phishing techniques, cybercriminals just send out e-mails to a wide list of e-mail addresses, whether they have a relationship with the company or not. For example, a criminal might send out a general phishing e-mail claiming that a person's Citibank checking account had been breached. People who receive this e-mail that don't have any accounts at Citibank should immediately realize this is a phishing attack and ignore the instructions to divulge sensitive data.

But when cybercriminals obtain data on individuals that includes information about which companies those individuals have a relationship with, they can engage in much more targeted attacks known as **spear phishing** (see Figure 9.15). Spear phishing e-mails are sent to people known to be customers of a company and have a much greater chance of successfully getting individuals to reveal sensitive data. If cybercriminals obtain a list of e-mail addresses of customers from Barclays Bank, for example, they can ensure that the spear phishing e-mails purport to come from Barclays and will include the customer's full name. This type of attack is much more likely to succeed in fooling people than just random e-mails sent out to thousands of people who might not have a relationship with the company mentioned in the phishing letter.

So how can you protect yourself after a data breach? You need to be extra suspicious of any e-mail correspondence from companies involved in the data breach. Companies usually never contact you by e-mail or phone asking you to reveal sensitive information or reactivate your online account by entering confidential information. Usually, these requests come via regular snail mail.

So, if you receive any e-mails or phone calls from companies you deal with purporting to have problems with your accounts, your best course of action is to delete the e-mail or hang up the phone. Then contact the company that supposedly has the problem by a phone number that you look up yourself either in legitimate correspondence from the company (say, the toll-free number on your credit card statement) or in the phone book. The representatives from your company can quickly tell if a real problem exists or if you were about to be the victim of a scam.

FIGURE 9.15 Not that kind of fishing! Spear phishing is a targeted type of social engineering. *(Ehrlif/Shutterstock)*

check your understanding // review & practice

For a quick review to see what you've learned so far, answer the following questions.

multiple choice

1. When a hacker steals personal information with the intent of impersonating another individual to commit fraud, it is known as

- **a.** impersonation theft.
- **b.** scareware theft.
- **c.** identity theft.
- **d.** malware theft.

2. An attack that renders a computer unable to respond to legitimate users because it is being bombarded with data requests is known as a ______________ attack.

- **a.** stealth
- **b.** backdoor
- **c.** scareware
- **d.** denial-of-service

3. A series of commands that are executed without your knowledge is a typical attribute of a ______________ virus.

- **a.** boot-sector
- **b.** script
- **c.** time bomb
- **d.** encryption

4. Software that pretends your computer is infected with a virus to entice you into spending money on a solution is known as

- **a.** scareware.
- **b.** spyware.
- **c.** adware.
- **d.** trackingware.

5. A technique that uses illegally obtained information about individuals to perform targeted attacks in the hopes of getting them to reveal sensitive information is known as

- **a.** spear phishing.
- **b.** pretexting.
- **c.** keystroke logging.
- **d.** logic bombing.

MyITLab — Go to **MyITLab** to take an autograded version of the *Check Your Understanding* review and to find all media resources for the chapter.

TECHBYTES WEEKLY
Stay current with TechBytes Weekly Newsletter.

Continue

TRY THIS Testing Your Network Security

A properly installed firewall should keep you relatively safe from wily hackers. But how do you know if your computer system is safe? Many websites help test your security. In this exercise, we'll use tools provided by Gibson Research Corporation (**grc.com**) to test the strength of your protection.

Step 1 Open a web browser and navigate to **grc.com**. From the pull-down Services menu at the top of the screen, select **ShieldsUP!** On the ShieldsUP! welcome screen, click the **Proceed button**. *(Reprinted courtesy of Gibson Research Corporation)*

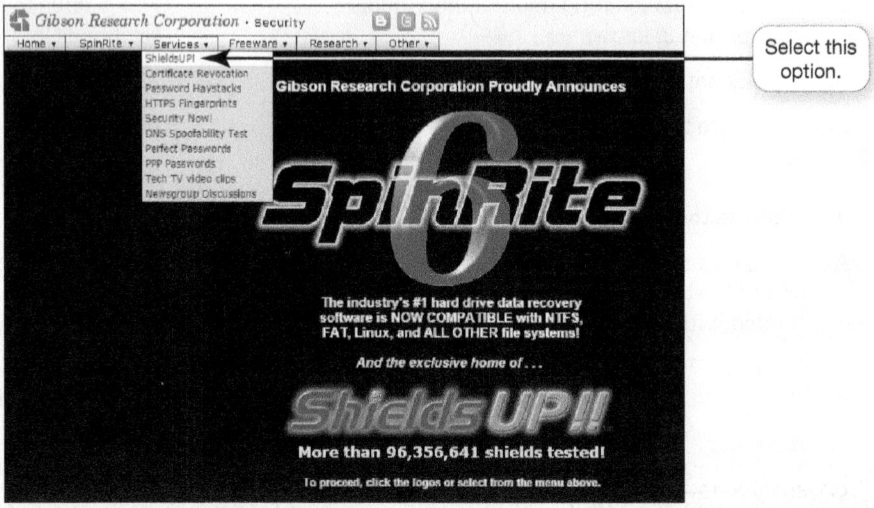

Step 2 Click the **Common Ports link** to begin the security test. It will take a few moments for the results to appear, depending on the speed of your Internet connection. *(Reprinted courtesy of Gibson Research Corporation)*

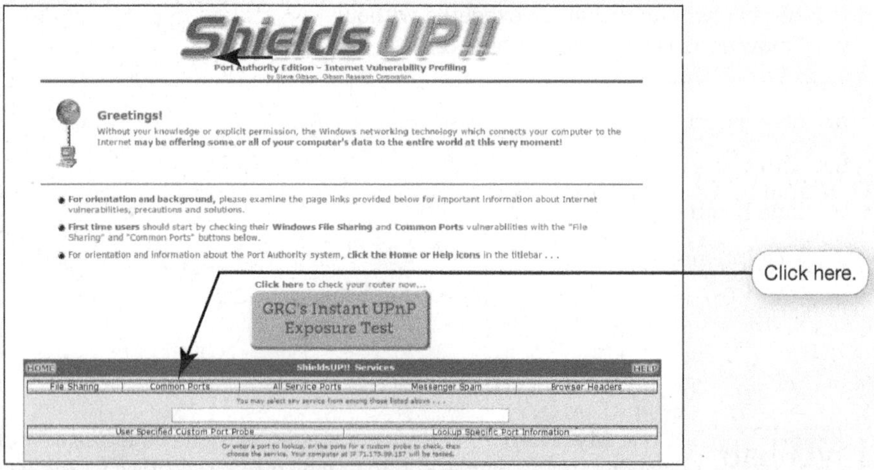

Step 3 Hopefully, you'll see a report indicating that your computer has passed the TruStealth analysis test. This means that your computer is very safe from attack. However, don't panic if your results say **failed for true stealth analysis**. Consider these common issues:

- Ports that only report as being closed will result in a TruStealth analysis failure. As long as all common ports are reporting as stealth or closed, you are well protected. However, if any ports report as being open, this means your computer could be exposed to hackers. Consult your firewall documentation to resolve the problem.

- Another common failure on the TruStealth test is ping reply. This means GRC attempted to contact your computer using a method called ping and it replied to the GRC computer. This is not a serious problem. It just means it's a little easier for a hacker to tell your computer network is there, but that doesn't mean that a hacker can break in. Often, your ISP has your home modem configured to reply to ping requests to facilitate remote diagnostics if there is ever a problem with your modem. As long as your ports are closed (or stealthed), your system should still be secure. *(Reprinted courtesy of Gibson Research Corporation)*

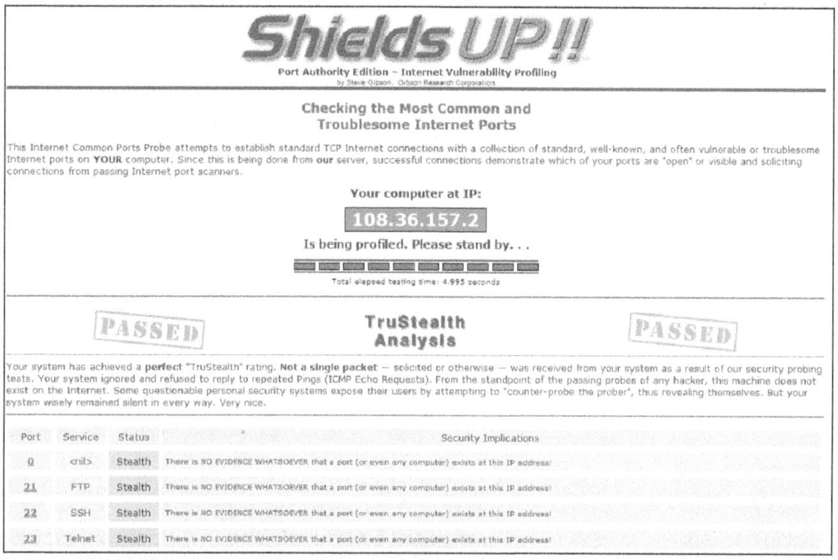

Make This TOOL: AI TinyDB

MAKE: A Password Generator

Want to make sure your passwords are randomly selected so they are more secure, but afraid you'll forget what you chose?

In this exercise, you'll continue your mobile app development by using the TinyDB component in **App Inventor** to store information on your phone so it can be recalled by your application the next time it runs. This is called data persistence and as you'll see, it is very easy to do! *(MIT App Inventor 2, Massachusetts Institute of Technology. Creative Commons Attribution-ShareAlike 3.0 Unported License)*

The TinyDB component allows you to store data on your device to use the next time the app opens.

For the instructions for this exercise, go to MyITLab.

Protecting Your Digital Property

Learning Outcome 9.2 **Describe various ways to protect your digital property and data from theft and corruption.**

Often, we can be our own worst enemies when using computing devices. If you're not careful, you might be taken in by thieves or scam artists who want to steal your digital and physical assets. As we'll discuss in this section, protecting yourself is key, and there are many relatively easy measures you can take to increase your level of security.

restricting access to your DIGITAL ASSETS

Keeping hackers and viruses at bay is often just a matter of keeping them out. You can achieve this by:

- Preventing hackers from accessing your computer (usually through your Internet connection)
- Using techniques to prevent virus infections from reaching your computer
- Protecting your digital information in such a way that it can't be accessed (by using passwords, for example)
- Hiding your activities from prying eyes

In this section, we explore strategies for protecting access to your digital assets and keeping your Internet-surfing activities from being seen by the wrong people.

Firewalls

Objective 9.10 *Explain what a firewall is and how a firewall protects your computer from hackers.*

What is a firewall? A **firewall** is a software program or hardware device designed to protect computers from hackers. It's named after a housing construction feature that slows the spread of fires from house to house. A firewall specifically designed for home networks is called a **personal firewall**. By using a personal firewall, you can close open logical ports (communications pathways) to invaders and potentially make your computer invisible to other computers on the Internet.

Which is better, a software firewall or a hardware firewall? Both hardware and software firewalls will protect you from hackers. One type isn't better than the other. Although installing either a software or a hardware firewall on your home network is probably sufficient, you should consider installing both for maximum protection. This will provide you with additional safety, just as wearing multiple layers of clothing helps keep you warmer in the winter than a single layer.

Types of Firewalls

What software firewalls are there? Both Windows and OS X include reliable firewalls. The Windows Action Center is a good source of information about the security status of your computer. The status of your Windows Firewall is shown in the Windows Firewall dialog box (see Figure 9.16). Security suites such as Norton Security, McAfee Internet Security, and Trend Micro Internet Security Suite also include firewall software. Although the firewalls that come with Windows and OS X will protect your computer, firewalls included in security suites often come with additional features such as monitoring systems that alert you if your computer is under attack.

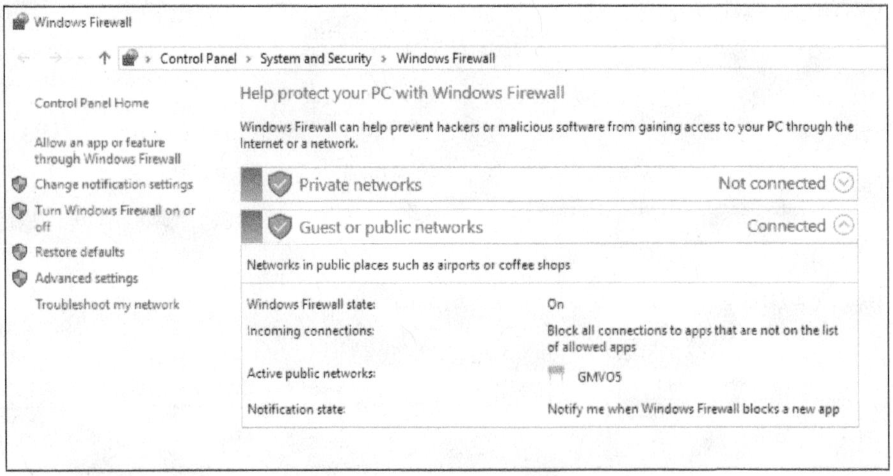

FIGURE 9.16 The Windows Firewall dialog box provides the status of your firewall. *(Windows 10, Microsoft Corporation)*

>*To view the Windows Firewall dialog box, access* ***Settings****, select* ***Network & Internet****, select* ***Wi-Fi****, and then click the* ***Windows Firewall link****.*

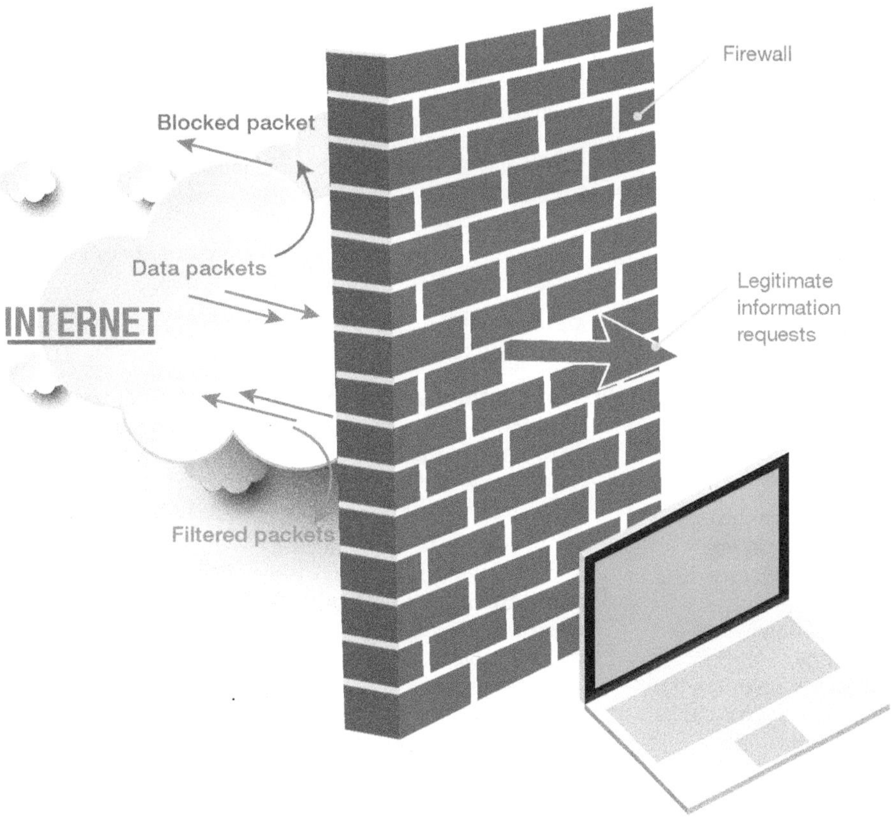

FIGURE 9.17 Firewalls use filtering and blocking to keep out unwanted data and keep your network safe.

If you're using a security suite that includes a firewall, the suite should disable the firewall that came with your OS. Two firewalls running at the same time can conflict with each other and cause your computer to slow down or freeze up.

What are hardware firewalls? You can also buy and configure hardware firewall devices. Many routers sold for home networks include firewall protection. Just like software firewalls, the setup for hardware firewalls is designed for novices, and the default configuration on most routers keeps unused logical ports closed. Documentation accompanying routers can assist more-experienced users in adjusting the settings to allow access to specific ports if needed.

How Firewalls Work

How do firewalls protect you from hackers? Firewalls are designed to restrict access to a network and its computers. Firewalls protect you in two major ways:

1. By blocking access to logical ports
2. By keeping your computer's network address secure

How do firewalls block access to your logical ports? As you'll recall, logical ports are virtual communications gateways or paths that allow a computer to organize requests for information from other networks or computers. Certain logical ports are very popular in hacker attacks. To block access to logical ports, firewalls examine data packets that your computer sends and receives. Data packets contain information such as the address of the sending and receiving computers and the logical port that the packet will use. Firewalls can be configured so that they filter out packets sent to specific logical ports in a process known as **packet filtering**. Firewalls are also often configured to ignore requests that originate from the Internet asking for access to certain ports. This process is referred to as **logical port blocking**. By using filtering and blocking, firewalls keep hackers from accessing your computer (Figure 9.17).

How do firewalls keep your network address secure? Every computer connected to the Internet has a unique address called an *Internet Protocol address (IP address)*. Data is routed to the correct computer on the Internet based on the IP address. This is similar to how a letter finds its way to your mailbox. You have a unique postal address for your home. If a hacker finds out the IP address of your computer, he or she can locate it on the Internet and try to break into it. This is similar to how a conventional thief might target your home after finding out you collect antique cars by using your street address to locate your house.

Your IP address for your home network is assigned to your router by your Internet service provider (ISP), but each device on your home network also has an IP address. Firewalls use a process called **network address translation (NAT)** to assign internal IP addresses on a network. The internal IP addresses are used only on the internal network and therefore can't be detected by hackers. For hackers to access your computer, they must know your computer's internal IP address. With a NAT-capable router/firewall installed on your network, hackers are unable to access the internal IP address assigned to your computer, so your computer is safe. You can use NAT in your home by purchasing a hardware firewall with NAT capabilities. Many routers sold for home use are also configured as firewalls, and many feature NAT.

ACTIVE HELPDESK
Understanding Firewalls

In this Active Helpdesk, you'll play the role of a helpdesk staffer, fielding questions about how hackers can attack networks and what harm they can cause as well as what a firewall does to keep a computer safe from hackers.

FIGURE 9.18

Common Logical Ports

PORT NUMBER	PROTOCOL USING THE PORT
21	FTP (File Transfer Protocol) control
23	Telnet (unencrypted text communications)
25	SMTP (Simple Mail Transfer Protocol)
53	DNS (domain name system)
80	HTTP (Hypertext Transfer Protocol)
443	HTTPS (HTTP with Transport Layer Security [TLS] encryption)

Knowing Your Computer Is Secure

How can I tell if my firewall is protecting my computer? For peace of mind, you can visit websites that offer free services that test your computer's vulnerability. One popular site is Gibson Research Corporation (**grc.com**). The company's ShieldsUP and LeakTest programs are free and easy to run and can pinpoint security vulnerabilities in a system connected to the Internet. If you get a clean report from these programs, your system is probably not vulnerable to attack. See the Try This section in this chapter (page 00–00) for instructions on how to test your system.

What if I don't get a clean report from the testing program? If the testing program detects potential vulnerabilities and you don't have a firewall, you should install one as soon as possible. If the firewall is already configured and common ports (such as those shown in Figure 9.18) are identified as being vulnerable, consult your firewall documentation for instructions on how to close or restrict access to those ports.

> **SOUND BYTE**
> **Installing a Personal Firewall**
> Firewalls provide excellent protection against hackers on a home network. In this Sound Byte, you'll learn how to install and configure software firewalls to protect your computer.

Preventing Virus Infections

Objective 9.11 *Explain how to protect your computer from virus infection.*

What is the best way to protect my devices from viruses? Earlier in the chapter, we discussed the various viruses that hackers may unleash on your system. There are two main ways to protect your computer from viruses: by installing antivirus software and by keeping your software up to date.

Antivirus Software

What antivirus software do I need? Antivirus software is specifically designed to detect viruses and protect your computer and files from harm. Symantec, Kaspersky, Trend Micro, and McAfee are among the companies that offer highly rated antivirus software packages. Antivirus protection is also included in comprehensive Internet security packages such as Norton Security, Trend Micro Internet Security, and McAfee Total Protection. These software packages also help protect you from threats other than computer viruses. For example, Windows 10 includes Windows Defender, which defends against malware as well as viruses.

How often do I need to run antivirus software? Although antivirus software is designed to detect suspicious activity on your computer at all times, you should run an active virus scan on your entire system at least once a week. By doing so, all files on your computer will be checked for undetected viruses.

Current antivirus programs run scans in the background when your CPU is not being heavily utilized. But you can also configure the software to run scans at times when you aren't using your system—for example, when you're asleep (see Figure 9.19). (However, it's important to note that your computer has to be on and not in sleep mode for these virus scans to take place.) Alternatively, if you suspect a problem, you can launch a scan and have it run immediately.

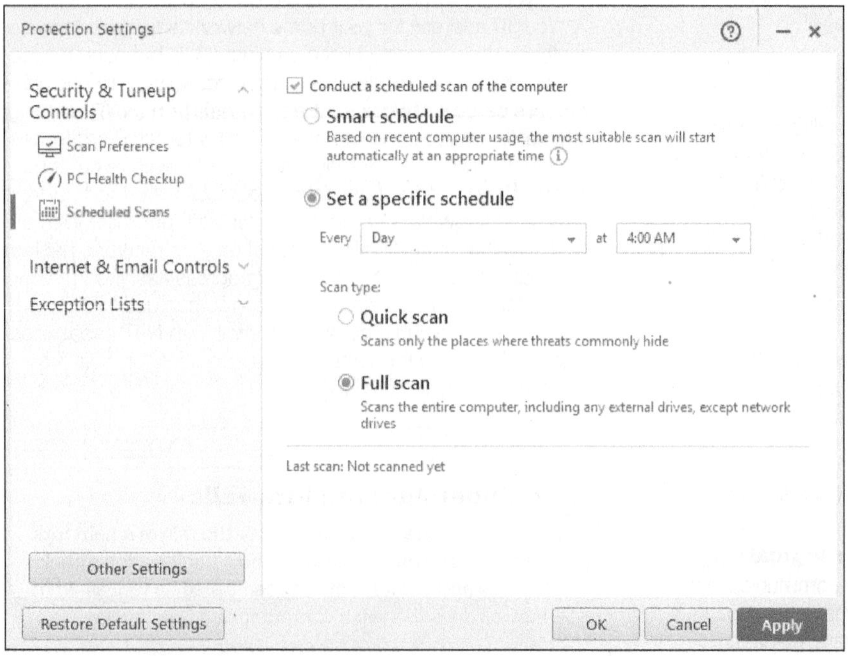

FIGURE 9.19 In Trend Micro Internet Security, you can set up virus scans to run automatically. This computer will be scanned every day at 4 a.m. *(Reprinted courtesy of Trend Micro Incorporated. All rights reserved.)*

How does antivirus software work? The main functions of antivirus software are as follows:

- *Detection*: Antivirus software looks for virus signatures in files. A **virus signature** is a portion of the virus code that's unique to a particular computer virus. Antivirus software scans files for these signatures when they're opened or executed and identifies infected files and the type of virus infecting them.
- *Stopping virus execution*: If the antivirus software detects a virus signature or suspicious activity, such as the launch of an unknown macro, it stops the execution of the file and virus and notifies you that it has detected a virus. It also places the virus in a secure area on your hard drive so that it won't spread to other files; this procedure is known as **quarantining**. Usually, the antivirus software then gives you the choice of deleting or repairing the infected file. Unfortunately, antivirus programs can't always fix infected files to make them usable again. You should keep backup copies of critical files so that you can restore them in case a virus damages them irreparably.
- *Prevention of future infection*: Most antivirus software will also attempt to prevent infection by inoculating key files on your computer. In **inoculation**, the antivirus software records key attributes about your computer files, such as file size and date created, and keeps these statistics in a safe place on your hard drive. When scanning for viruses, the antivirus software compares the attributes of the files with the attributes it previously recorded to help detect attempts by virus programs to modify your files.

FIGURE 9.20 Many protection packages, such as Trend Micro Internet Security, offer other types of security features besides basic malware protection. *(Reprinted courtesy of Trend Micro Incorporated. All rights reserved.)*

Does antivirus software always stop viruses? Antivirus software catches *known* viruses effectively. However, new viruses are written all the time. To combat unknown viruses, modern antivirus programs search for suspicious virus-like activities as well as virus signatures. To minimize your risk, you should keep your antivirus software up to date.

My new computer came with antivirus software installed, so shouldn't I already be protected? Most new computers do come with antivirus software preinstalled. However, these are usually trial versions of the software that only provide updates to the software for a limited period of time, usually 90 or 180 days. After that, you have to buy a full version of the software to ensure you remain protected from new viruses. If you have Windows 10 and there is no third-party antivirus software installed, Windows Defender will be active by default so you should have some protection.

How do I make sure my antivirus software is up to date? Most antivirus programs have an automatic update feature that downloads updates for virus signature files every time you go online. Also, the antivirus software usually shows the status of your update subscription so that you can see how much time you have remaining until you need to buy another version of your software. Many Internet security packages offer bonus features such as cloud storage scanners and password managers (see Figure 9.20) to provide you with extra protection.

What should I do if I think my computer is infected with a virus? Boot up your computer using the antivirus installation disc. This should prevent most virus programs from loading and will allow you to run the antivirus software directly from your disk drive. (*Note*: If you download your antivirus software from the Internet, copy the files to a DVD in case you have problems in the future.) If the software does detect viruses, you may want to research them further to determine whether your antivirus software will eradicate them completely or whether you'll need to take additional manual steps to eliminate the viruses. Most antivirus company websites, such as the Symantec site (**symantec.com**), contain archives of information on viruses and provide step-by-step solutions for removing them.

How do I protect my phone from viruses? Because smartphones and other mobile devices run operating systems and contain files, they are susceptible to infection by viruses. Cybercriminals are now hiding viruses in legitimate-looking apps for download to mobile devices. Most antivirus software companies now offer antivirus software specifically designed for mobile devices. The Google Play store even offers very effective free products to protect your Android devices such

ACTIVE HELPDESK
Avoiding Computer Viruses

In this Active Helpdesk, you'll play the role of a helpdesk staffer, fielding questions about different types of viruses and what users should do to protect their computer from them.

as 360 Security and Avast! Mobile Security. In addition to providing protection from malware, these apps also provide other useful features such as the ability to wipe your phone's contents if it is lost or stolen.

Software Updates

Why does updating my operating system (OS) software help protect me from viruses? Many viruses exploit weaknesses in operating systems. Malicious websites can be set up to attack your computer by downloading harmful software onto your computer. According to research conducted by Google, this type of attack, known as a **drive-by download**, affects almost 1 in 1,000 web pages. To combat these threats, make sure your OS is up to date and contains the latest security patches.

Do OS updates only happen automatically? Prior to the release of Windows 10, you updated your Windows OS with an automatic update utility called Windows Update. You had the ability to decide when to download updates and when to install them. However, with Windows 10, you no longer have as many choices. Updates are now downloaded automatically whenever they are provided by Microsoft. You do have the choice to allow Windows to automatically schedule a restart of your computer to apply the updates or pick a more convenient restart time manually (see Figure 9.21). Mac OS X has a similar utility for gathering updates.

The Advanced Options screen for Windows Update provides a few other options (see Figure 9.22). The most notable is the ability to receive updates for other Microsoft products (like MS Office). (Note that the ability to defer upgrades is not available on the Windows 10 Home edition—you must install updates as they are delivered by Microsoft).

Authentication: Passwords and Biometrics

Objective 9.12 *Describe how passwords and biometric characteristics can be used for user authentication on computer systems.*

How can I best use passwords to protect my computer? You no doubt have many passwords you need to remember to access your digital life. However, creating strong passwords—ones that are difficult for hackers to guess—is an essential piece of security that people sometimes overlook. Password-cracking programs have become more sophisticated. In fact, some commonly available programs can test more than one million password combinations per second! Creating a secure password is therefore more important than ever.

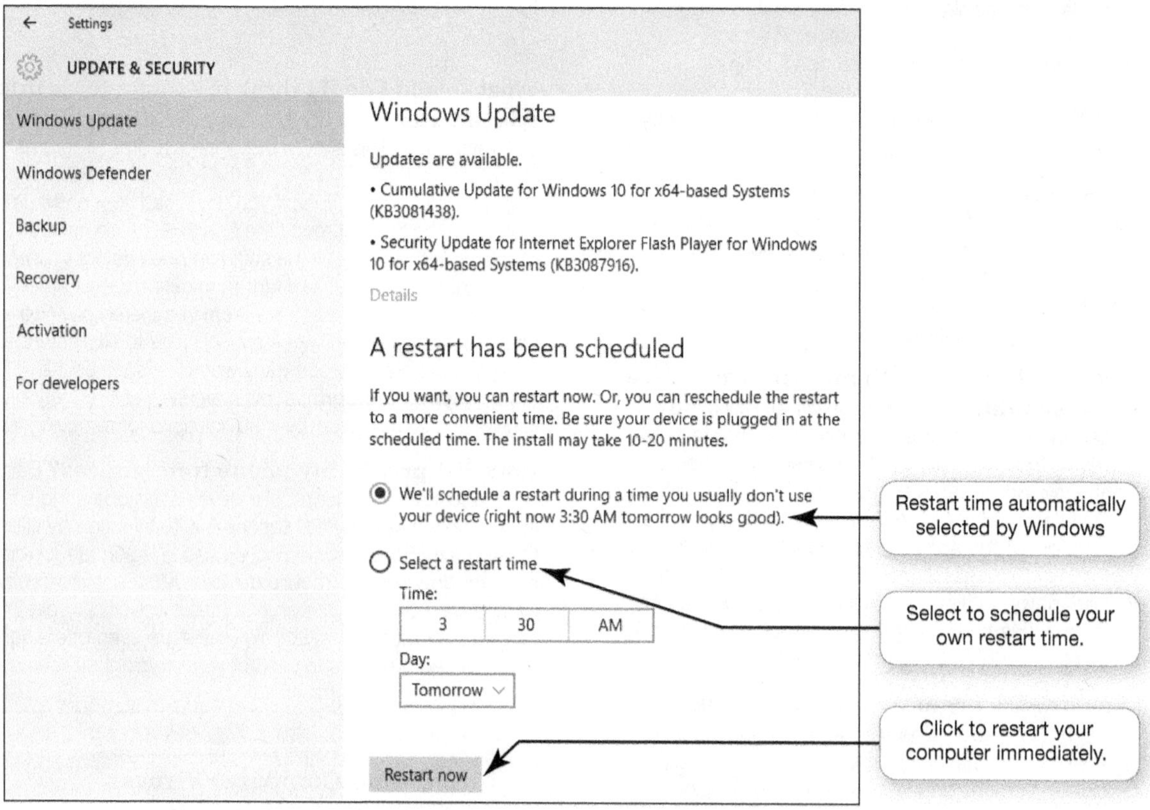

FIGURE 9.21 The Windows Update screen makes it easy for users to stay abreast of software updates and manage restarts.
(Windows 10, Microsoft Corporation)
>*To access the Windows Update screen, from the Start menu, select* ***Settings****, select* ***Update & security****, then select* ***Windows Update****.*

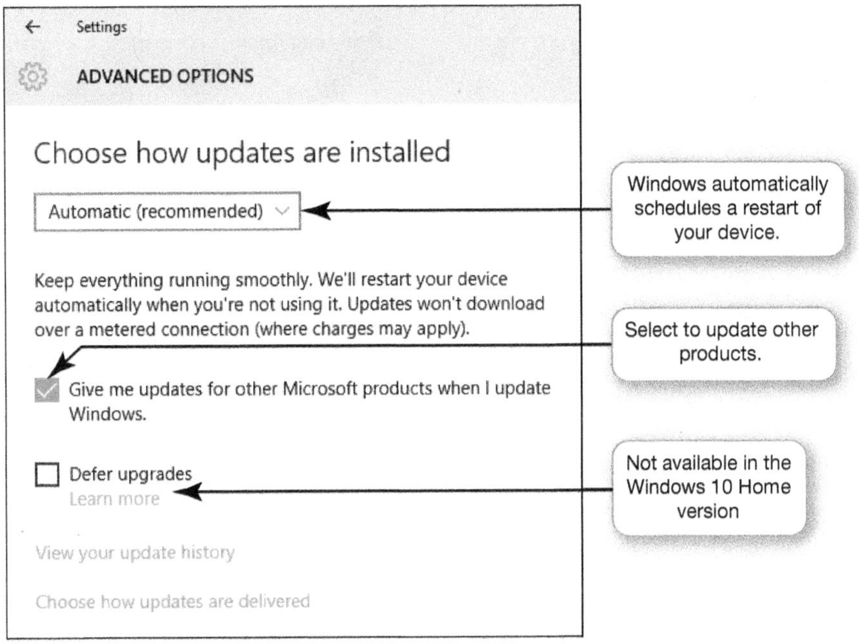

FIGURE 9.22 The Windows Update Advanced Options screen provides a few more user controlled update options. *(Windows 10, Microsoft Corporation)*
>To access the Windows Update Advanced Options screen, scroll to the bottom of the Windows Update screen (Figure 9.21) and click the ***Advanced options link****.*

SOUND BYTE
Protecting Your Computer
In this Sound Byte, you'll learn how to use a variety of tools to protect your computer, including antivirus software and Windows utilities.

Many people use extremely weak passwords. The Imperva Application Defense Center, a computer-security research organization, conducted a review of 32 million passwords that were used at the website **rockyou.com**. More than 345,000 people were using "12345," "123456," or "123456789" as their password. And almost 62,000 people were using "password"! Passwords such as these are easy for hackers to crack.

Websites that need to be very secure, such as those for financial institutions, usually have strong defenses to prevent hackers from cracking passwords. But sites that need less security, such as casual gaming or social networking sites, might have less protection. Hackers attack poorly defended sites for passwords because many people use the same password for every site they use. So if a hacker can get your password from a poorly secured gaming site, they might be able to access your bank account with the same password.

Creating Strong Passwords

What constitutes a strong password? Strong passwords are difficult for someone to guess. Follow these guidelines to create strong passwords (see Figure 9.23):

- Don't use easily deduced components related to your life, such as parts of your name, your pet's name, your street address, or the name of the website or institution for which you are creating the password (i.e., don't use "Citibank" for your online banking password).
- Use a password that is at least 14 characters long. Longer passwords are more difficult to deduce. Consider using a passphrase that is even longer (see the Bits & Bytes on page 375).
- Don't use words found in the dictionary.
- Use a mix of upper- and lowercase letters and symbols (such as # or %).
- Never tell anyone your password or write it down in a place where others might see it, like in your wallet or a sticky note on your computer screen!
- Change your passwords on a regular basis, such as monthly or quarterly. Your school or your employer probably requires you to change your password regularly. This is also a good idea for your personal passwords.
- Don't use the same password for every account you have.

FIGURE 9.23

Strong and Weak Password Candidates

PASSWORD	RATING	GOOD POINTS	BAD POINTS
Joysmithl022	Poor	• Contains upper- and lowercase letters • Contains letters and numbers	• Less than 14 characters • Contains name and birth date
test44drive6car	Mediocre	• 15 characters in length	• Contains three words found in the dictionary • Numbers repeated consecutively
8$RanT%5ydTTtt&	Better	• Good length • Contains upper- and lowercase letters • Contains symbols	• Upper- and lowercase letters repeated consecutively • Still contains one dictionary word (rant)
7R3m3mB3R$5%y38	Best	• All good points from above • Dictionary word (remember) has 3s instead of Es	• None

BITS&BYTES

CAPTCHA: Keeping Websites Safe from Bots

Automated programs called *bots* (or web robots) are used to make tasks easier on the Internet. For example, search engines use bots to search and index web pages. Unfortunately, bots can also be used for malicious or illegal purposes because they can perform some computing tasks faster than humans. For example, bots can be used on ticket-ordering sites to buy large blocks of high-demand concert tickets. They are also often used to post spam in the comment sections of blogs. Fortunately, website owners can deploy CAPTCHA software to prevent such bot activities.

CAPTCHA (Completely Automated Public Turing Test to Tell Computers and Humans Apart) programs used to generate distorted text and require that it be typed into a box. Newer programs, like Google's reCAPTCHA, monitor users' website behavior to determine if you are a human or a bot. reCAPTCHA merely asks you to click a check box (Figure 9.24a) and if it displays a green check (Figure 9.24b), you have passed the bot test. If the app isn't sure if you are a human, it may ask you to type in some distorted text (Figure 9.24c) just like older versions of the program did. If you want to try integrating a CAPTCHA program into your website (to protect your e-mail address), go to **google.com/recaptcha**, which offers free CAPTCHA tools to help you protect your data.

FIGURE 9.24 CAPTCHA programs like reCAPTCHA monitor a user's website behavior and can often determine if a user is human just by having the user check a box. If a green check mark appears, you are human! If the app isn't sure if you're a bot, you may be asked to enter some text. *(Metrue/Shutterstock)*

FIGURE 9.25 Drawing three gestures (a swipe and two circles) on this image (and repeating them once) sets your picture password options in Windows. *(Windows 10, Microsoft Corporation)*

If you have trouble thinking of secure passwords, there are many password generators available for free, such as the Strong Password Generator (**strongpasswordgenerator.com**).

How can I check the strength of my passwords? You can use online password strength testers, such as the Password Meter (**passwordmeter.com**), to evaluate your passwords. The Password Meter provides guidelines for good passwords and shows you how integrating various elements, such as symbols, affects the strength score of your password.

How do I restrict access to my computer? Windows, OS X, and most other operating systems have built-in password (or passcode) protection for files as well as the entire desktop. After a certain period of idle time, your computer is automatically password locked, and your password (or PIN) must be entered to gain access to the computer. This provides excellent protection from casual snooping if you need to walk away from your computer for a period of time. If someone attempts to log on to your computer without your password, that person won't be able to gain access. It's an especially good idea to use passwords on laptop computers, smartphones, and tablets because this provides additional protection of your data if your device is lost or stolen.

Windows allows you to use picture passwords. You select a picture and then draw three gestures on it—either straight lines, circles, or taps. This picture then works as an additional method for accessing your computer. You just unlock your computer by repeating the gestures (see Figure 9.25). But if you forget your gestures, you can always access your computer via the conventional password.

Managing Your Passwords

How can I remember all of my complex passwords? Good security practices suggest that you have different passwords for all the different websites that you access and that you change your passwords frequently. The problem with well-constructed passwords is that they can be hard to remember. Fortunately, password-management tools are now available. They take the worry out of forgetting passwords because the password-management software does the remembering for you.

Where can I obtain password-management software? Most current Internet security suites and web browsers make it easy to keep track of passwords by providing password-management tools. For example, Microsoft Edge will remember passwords for you. When you go to a website that requires a login, Microsoft Edge will display a dialog box prompting you to have Microsoft Edge remember the password for the site (see Figure 9.26). Then, when you return to the site and type in your user name, Microsoft Edge will fill in the password information for you using a process known as *auto complete*. However, there are some passwords that you shouldn't have your browser remember, such as your online banking password. So be selective when using this feature.

Biometric Authentication Devices

Besides passwords, how else can I restrict the use of my computer? A **biometric authentication device** is a device that reads a unique personal characteristic such as a fingerprint or the iris pattern in your eye and converts its pattern to a digital code. When you use the device, your pattern is read and compared to the one stored on the computer. Only users having an exact fingerprint or iris pattern match are allowed to access the computer.

Because no two people have the same biometric characteristics (fingerprints and iris patterns are unique), these devices provide a high level of security. They also eliminate the human error that can occur in password protection. You might forget your password, but you won't forget to bring your fingerprints

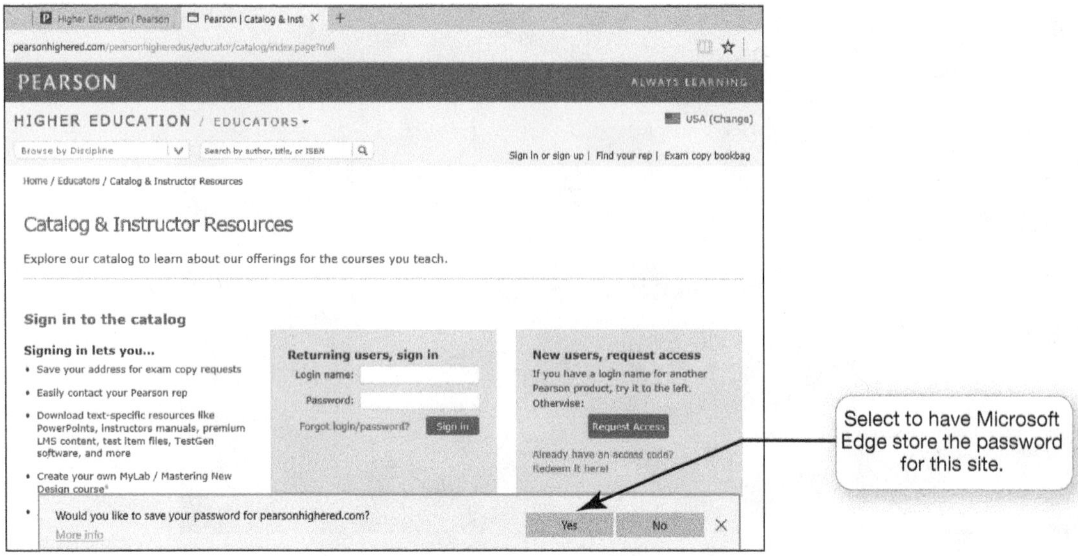

FIGURE 9.26 The password dialog box in Microsoft Edge displays whenever you type in a password for a website for which Microsoft Edge hasn't yet stored the password. *(Screenshot of Pearson Higher Education website, Pearson Education, Inc.)*

when you're working on your computer! Some smartphones, such as the iPhone, now include fingerprint readers. But since Touch ID (the Apple software for fingerprint identification) has already been hacked, you might be safer using a regular password. Other biometric devices, including voice authentication and facial recognition systems, are now widely offered in laptops (see Figure 9.27), tablets, and smartphones (such as the Samsung Galaxy phones).

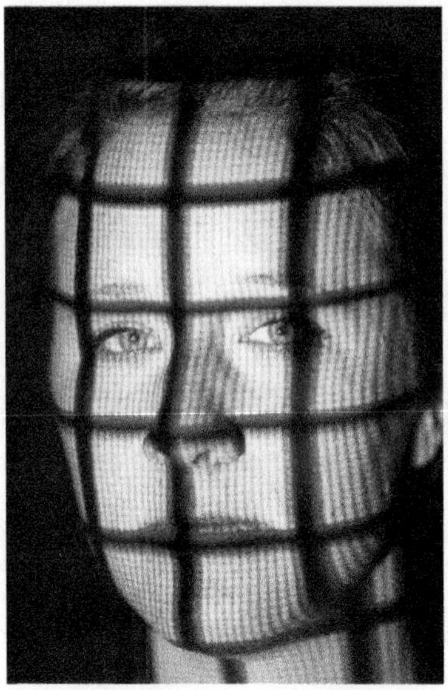

FIGURE 9.27 Face recognition software is now available on laptops. You might forget your password, but you won't forget to bring your face! *(Jochen Tack/Alamy)*

Anonymous Web Surfing: Hiding from Prying Eyes

Objective 9.13 *Describe ways to surf the web anonymously.*

Should I be concerned about surfing the Internet on shared, public, or work computers? If you use shared computers in public places such as libraries, coffee shops, or student unions, you never know what nefarious tools have been installed by hackers on a public computer. When you browse the Internet, traces of your activity are left behind on that computer, often as temporary files. A wily hacker can glean sensitive information long after you've finished your surfing session. In addition, many employers routinely review the Internet browsing history of employees to ensure workers are spending their time on the Internet productively.

What tools can I use to keep my browsing activities private when surfing the Internet? The current versions of Mozilla Firefox, Microsoft Edge, and Google Chrome include privacy tools (called Private Browsing, InPrivate, and Incognito, respectively) that help you surf the web anonymously (see Figure 9.28). When you choose to surf anonymously, all three browsers open special versions of their browser windows that are enhanced for privacy. When surfing in these windows, records of websites you visit and files you download don't appear in the web browser's history files. Furthermore, any temporary files generated in that browsing session are deleted when you exit the special window.

Are there any other tools I could use to protect my privacy? Portable privacy devices, such as the Ironkey Personal Flash Drives (**ironkey.com**), provide an even higher level of surfing privacy. Simply plug the device into an available

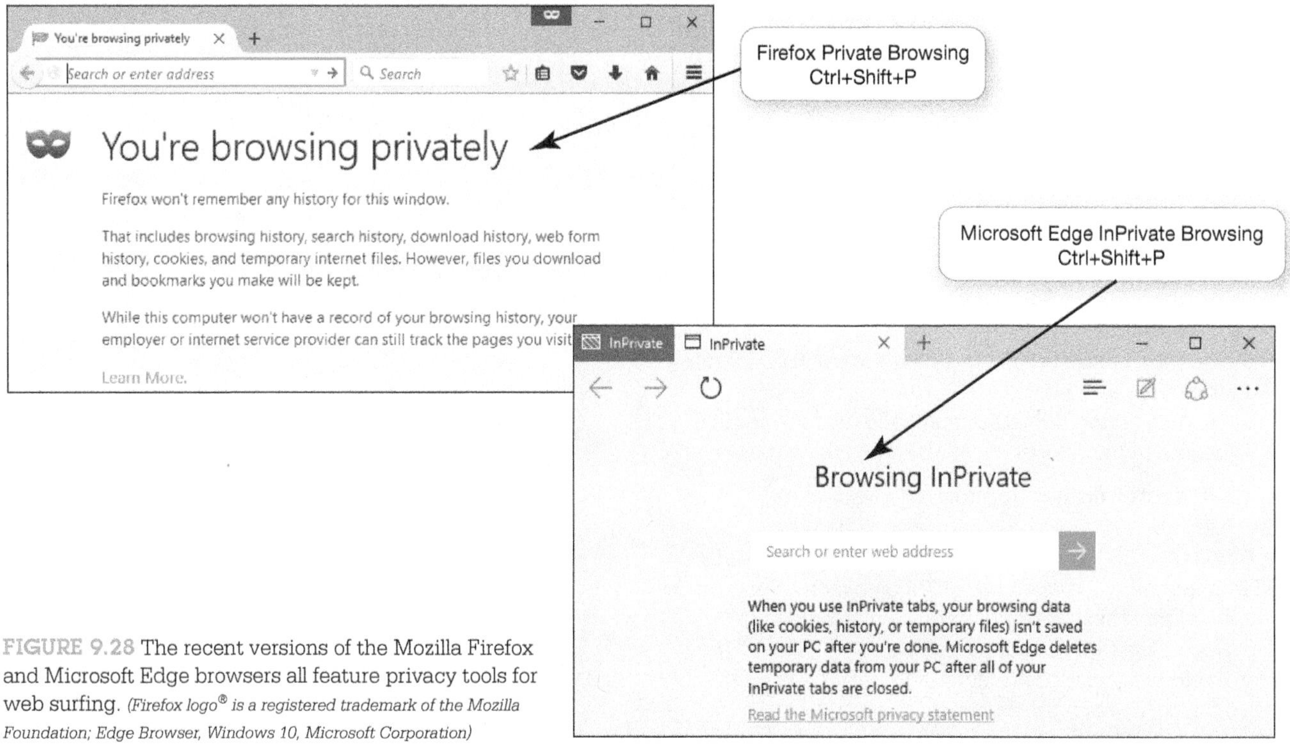

FIGURE 9.28 The recent versions of the Mozilla Firefox and Microsoft Edge browsers all feature privacy tools for web surfing. *(Firefox logo® is a registered trademark of the Mozilla Foundation; Edge Browser, Windows 10, Microsoft Corporation)*

USB port on the machine on which you'll be working. All sensitive Internet files, such as cookies, passwords, Internet history, and browser caches, will be stored on the privacy device, not on the computer you're using. Privacy devices such as these often come preloaded with software designed to shield your IP address from prying eyes, making it difficult (if not impossible) for hackers to tell where you're surfing on the Internet. These privacy devices also have password-management tools that store all of your login information and encrypt it so it will be safe if your privacy device falls into someone else's hands.

Is there anything else I can do to keep my data safe on shared computers? Another free practical solution is to take the Linux OS with you on a flash drive and avoid using the public or work computer's OS. The interfaces of many Linux distros look almost exactly like Windows and are easy to use. There are several advantages to using a Linux-based OS on a public or work computer:

- Your risk of picking up viruses and other malicious programs is significantly reduced because booting a computer from a flash drive completely eliminates any interaction with the computer's OS. This, in turn, significantly reduces the chance that your flash drive will become infected by any malware running on the computer.
- Virus and hacking attacks against Linux are far less likely than attacks against Windows. Because Windows has about 90% of the OS market, people who write malware tend to target Windows systems.
- When you run software from your own storage medium, such as a flash drive, you avoid reading and writing to the hard disk of the computer. This significantly enhances your privacy because you don't leave traces of your activity behind.

Pendrivelinux (**pendrivelinux.com**) is an excellent resource that offers many different versions of Linux for download and includes step-by-step instructions on how to install them on your flash drive. If you're a Mac user, the Elementary OS Luna distro of Linux provides a close approximation of OS X, so you can feel right at home.

How can I protect sensitive data transmissions if I have to use a public wireless network? Virtual private networks (VPNs) are secure networks that are established using the public Internet infrastructure. Using specialized software, servers and data transmission protocols, VPNs are used to send information on the public Internet in a such a manner that the data is as secure as sending it on a private network. VPNs used to be only used by businesses. But with public concerns about information security on the rise, many VPN software providers (such as Private Internet Access and Nord VPN) are marketing affordable solutions to individuals. So if you routinely transmit sensitive information, you should consider a personal VPN solution.

Make sure to use some (or all) of these methods to keep your activities from prying eyes and to restrict access to your digital information. ■

BITS&BYTES

Multi-Factor Authentication: Don't Rely Solely on Passwords!

Computer system security depends on authentication—proving the user is who they say they are. There are three independent authentication factors:

- Knowledge factor: Something the user knows (password, PIN)
- Possession factor: Something the user has (ATM card, mobile phone)
- Inherence factor: Something only the user is (biometric characteristics, such as fingerprints)

Multi-factor authentication requires two of the three above factors be demonstrated before authorization is granted (see Figure 9.30). At the bank's ATM machine, you present an ATM card (something you have) and then use a PIN code (something you know) to access your account.

For online access, multi-factor authentication often relies on the use of mobile phones. For instance, when you register a Google account, you supply your mobile phone number. If you then want to make changes to your account, you supply the password (something you know). The second step of authentication is Google sending an SMS message with a unique code to your mobile phone. Retrieving the code and entering it online proves you have the phone (something the user has) and serves as the second authentication step.

Multi-factor authentication is much safer than single-factor authentication. So make use of it when it is offered to you to enhance your account security.

FIGURE 9.30

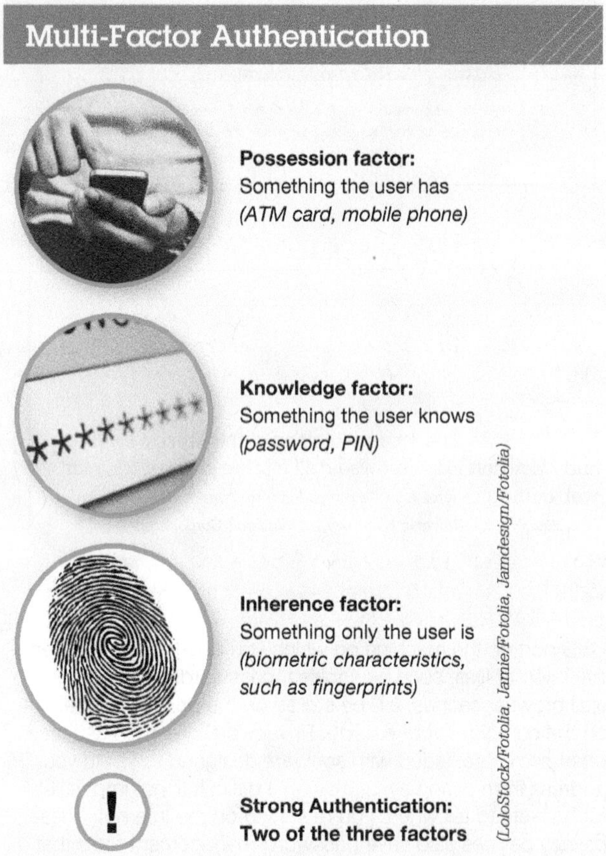

(LoloStock/Fotolia, Jamie/Fotolia, Jamdesign/Fotolia)

keeping your DATA SAFE

People are often too trusting or just plain careless when it comes to protecting private information about themselves or their digital data. In this section, we discuss ways to keep your data safe from damage, either accidental or intentional.

Protecting Your Personal Information

Objective 9.14 *Describe the types of information you should never share online.*

If a complete stranger walked up to you on the street and asked you for your address and phone number, would you give it to him or her? Of course you wouldn't! But many people are much less careful when it comes to sharing sensitive information online. And often people inadvertently share information that they really only intended to share with their friends. With cybercrimes like identify theft rampant, you need to take steps to protect your personal information.

What information should I never share on websites? A good rule of thumb is to reveal as little information as possible, especially if the information would be available to everyone. Figure 9.31 gives you some good guidelines.

Your Social Security number, phone number, date of birth, and street address are four key pieces of information that identity thieves need to steal an identity. This information should never be shared in a public area on any website.

How can I tell who can see my information on a social network? Social networking sites like Facebook make privacy settings available in your profile settings. If you've never changed your default privacy settings in Facebook, you're probably sharing information more widely than you should.

How can I protect my information on Facebook? To begin, you need to change your privacy settings in your profile from some of the default options. In general, it's a bad idea to make personal information available to the public, although this is a default setting for some items in Facebook. It's a good idea to set most of the options in your profile's Basic Information section to Friends or to Only Me because, presumably, these are personal details you should wish to share only with friends.

In the Contact Information section, restricting this information only to friends or to yourself is imperative. You don't want scammers contacting you via e-mail or snail mail and trying to trick you into revealing sensitive information.

Backing Up Your Data

Objective 9.15 *List the various types of backups you can perform on your computing devices, and explain the various places you can store backup files.*

How might I damage the data on my computer? The data on your computer faces three major threats:

1. Unauthorized access
2. Tampering
3. Destruction

FIGURE 9.31

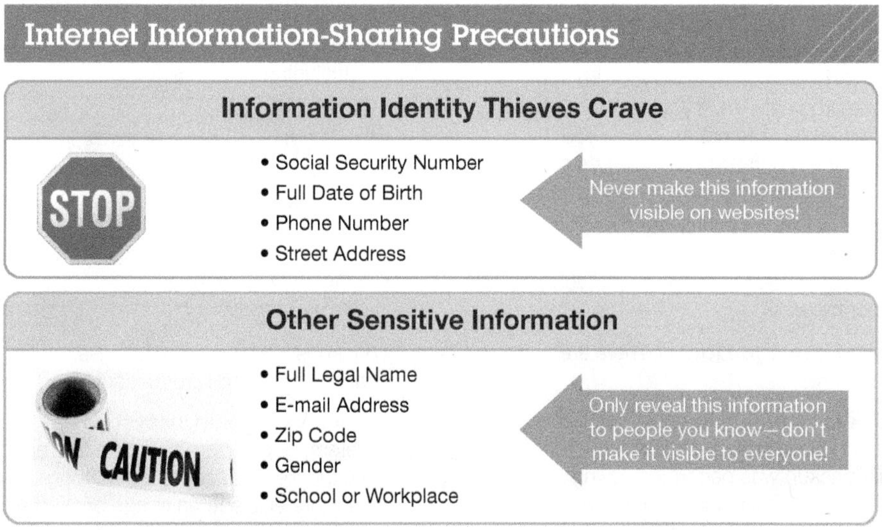

(Mograph/Fotolia, Kevin Largent/Fotolia)

BITS&BYTES

Social Networking: Looking Beyond Facebook

Are the posts you see on Facebook too general for your liking? Do you wish you could participate in a social networking community with more people who share your specific interests or passions? Facebook is the largest social networking site, but it isn't the only option out there. Many social networking sites exist that cater to specific types of users or interests.

Are you a graduate student that needs to monitor progress in a specific field of research? Try **Academia.edu**, which is a site specifically designed to promote the sharing of research papers in the academic community. If cooking is your passion, start your own food blog on **cucumbertown.com** and gain followers who like your recipes. People who love clubbing can meet at **dontstayin.com** and find out about events at clubs in a specific area. Trying to learn English as a second language? **Englishbaby.com** is a community of ESL students and teachers dedicated to helping members learn conversational English and slang. Free English lessons are posted every day! The Experience Project (**experienceproject.com**) encourages members to post personal experiences and form groups based on people with similar experiences or interests.

So no matter where your interests lie, there is probably a social network that caters to you. If you can't find one that suits you, then use **ning.com** and create your own specialized social network!

As noted earlier, a hacker can gain access to your computer and steal or alter your data. However, a more likely scenario is that you'll lose your data unintentionally. You may accidentally delete files. You may drop your laptop on the ground, causing the hard drive to break and resulting in complete data loss. A virus from an e-mail attachment you opened may destroy your original file. Your house may catch fire and destroy your computer. Because many of these possibilities are beyond your control, you should have a strategy for backing up your files (see Figure 9.32). **Backups** are copies of files that you can use to replace the originals if they're lost or damaged.

What types of files do I need to back up? Two types of files need backups:

1. **Program files** include files used to install software, usually found on DVDs or downloaded from the Internet. As long as you have the DVDs in a safe place, you shouldn't need to back up these program files. If you've downloaded a program file from the Internet, however, you should make a copy of the program installation files on a removable storage device as a backup.
2. **Data files** include files you've created or purchased, such as research papers, spreadsheets, music and photo files, contact lists, address books, e-mail archives, and your Favorites list from your browser.

What types of backups can I perform? There are two main options for backing up files:

1. An **incremental backup** (or **partial backup**) involves backing up only files that have changed or have been created since the last backup was performed. Using backup software that has an option for incremental backups will save time because backing up files that haven't changed is redundant.
2. An **image backup** (or **system backup**) means that all system, application, and data files are backed up, not just the files that changed. Although incremental backups are more efficient, an image backup ensures you capture

FIGURE 9.32

An Effective Backup Strategy

Files to Back Up

- **Program files:** Installation files for productivity software (i.e., Microsoft Office)
- **Data files:** Files you create (term papers, spreadsheets, etc.)

Types of Backups

- **Incremental (partial):** Only backs up files that have changed
- **Image (system):** Snapshot of your entire computer, including system software

Where to Store Backup Files

- Online (in the cloud)
- External hard drives
- Network-attached storage devices or home servers

changes to application files, such as automatic software updates, that an incremental backup might not capture. The idea of imaging is to make an exact copy of the setup of your computer so that in the event of a total hard drive failure you could copy the image to a new hard drive and have your computer configured exactly the way it was before the crash.

Where should I store my backups? To be truly secure, backups must be stored away from where your computer is located and should be stored in at least two different places. You wouldn't want a fire or a flood destroying the backups along with the original data. You have three main choices for where to back up your files (see Figure 9.33):

1. *Online (in the cloud)*: The beauty of online storage is that you don't need to be at your home computer or lug around your external hard drive to access your data. More importantly, because the information is stored online, it's in a secure, remote location, so data is much less vulnerable to the disasters that could harm data stored in your computer or external hard drive. Free storage options include Microsoft OneDrive (**onedrive.com**) and ADrive (**adrive.com**). However, image backups probably won't fit within the storage limits offered by free providers. For a fee, companies such as Carbonite (**carbonite.com**) and IBackup (**ibackup.com**) provide larger storage capacity.
2. *External hard drives*: External hard drives, or even large-capacity flash drives, are popular backup options that are usually connected to a single computer. Although convenient and inexpensive, using external hard drives for backups still presents the dilemma of keeping the hard drive in a safe location. Also, external hard drives can fail, possibly leading to loss of your backed-up data. Therefore, using an external hard drive for backups is best done in conjunction with an online backup strategy for added safety.
3. *Network-attached storage (NAS) devices and home servers*: NAS devices are essentially large hard drives connected to a network of computers instead of one computer, and they can be used to back up multiple computers simultaneously. Home servers also act as high-capacity NAS devices for automatically backing up data and sharing files.

How often should I back up my data files? You should back up your data files every time you make changes to them, which can be difficult to remember to do. Fortunately, most backup software can be configured to do backups

FIGURE 9.33

A Comparison of Typical Data Backup Locations

BACKUP LOCATION	PROS	CONS
Online (in the Cloud) 	• Files stored at a secure, remote location • Files/backups accessible anywhere through a browser	• Most free storage sites don't provide enough space for image backups
External Hard Drive 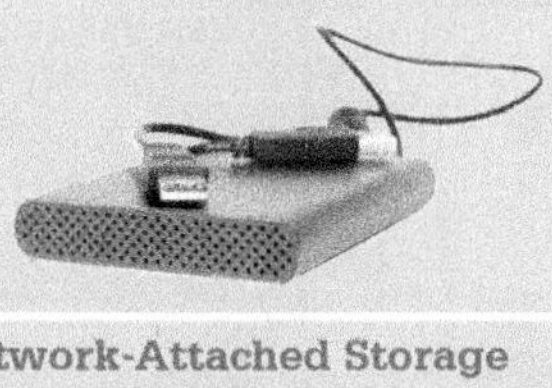	• Inexpensive, one-time cost • Fast backups with USB 3.0 devices connected directly to your computer	• Could be destroyed in one event (fire/flood) with your computer • Can be stolen • Slightly more difficult to back up multiple computers with one device
Network-Attached Storage (NAS) Device and Home Server 	• Makes backups much easier for multiple computing devices	• More expensive than a stand-alone external hard drive • Could be destroyed in one event (fire/flood) with your computer • Can be stolen

(Mipan/Fotolia, Prapass Wannapinij/Fotolia, Darkdesigns/Fotolia)

automatically so you don't forget to perform them. For example, with the Windows File History utility, you can have Windows automatically save your data files from your libraries, desktop, contacts, and favorites to an external hard drive or NAS device. The default setting for File History saves files you changed every hour to the backup location you specify. File History even keeps previous versions of the file on the backup drive so you can revert to a previous version of the file if you need to do so.

To set up File History, you first need to connect an external hard drive to your computer or a NAS device (or home server) to your network. You can then access File History through the Control Panel (in the System and Security group) and set it up (see Figure 9.35). Once configured, your data files will be backed up as often as you indicate. You can also restore files that you've backed up from the File History utility.

How often should I create an image backup? Because your program and OS files don't change as often as your data files, you can perform image backups on a less frequent basis. You might consider scheduling an image backup of your entire system on a weekly basis, but you should definitely perform one after installing new software.

How do I perform an image backup? Windows includes the System Image Backup utility, which provides a quick and easy way to perform image backups. You can access this utility from the System Image Backup link on the File History screen (see Figure 9.34), which launches the Backup and Restore (Windows 7) screen (see Figure 9.35a). Before starting this utility, make sure your external hard drive or NAS device is connected to your computer or network and is powered on. To set it up, follow these steps:

1. Click the Create a system image link. Select the location (drive) for your backup files and click Next to proceed.
2. On the second screen (see Figure 9.35b), you can select the drives/partitions from your computer to be backed up. Notice that all the drives/partitions that are required for Windows to run are preselected for you. Windows will back up all data files and system files on all selected drives/partitions. Click Next to proceed.
3. On the third screen, click Start backup to start your system image.

After the system image backup runs for the first time, you will see the results of the last backup and the date of the next scheduled backup on the Backup and Restore (Windows 7) screen (see Figure 9.35a). If the scheduled backup time is not convenient for you, click the Change settings link to select an alternative time.

From the Backup and Restore screen, you can also create a system repair disc. A system repair disc contains files that can be used to boot your computer in case of a serious Windows error.

What about backing up Apple computers? For OS X users, backups are very easy to configure. The Time Machine feature in OS X detects when an external hard drive is connected to the computer or a NAS device is connected to your network. You're then asked if you want this to be your backup drive. If you answer yes, all of your files (including OS files) are automatically backed up to the external drive or NAS device.

Should I back up my files that are stored on my school's network? Most likely, if you're allowed to store files on your school's network, these files are backed up

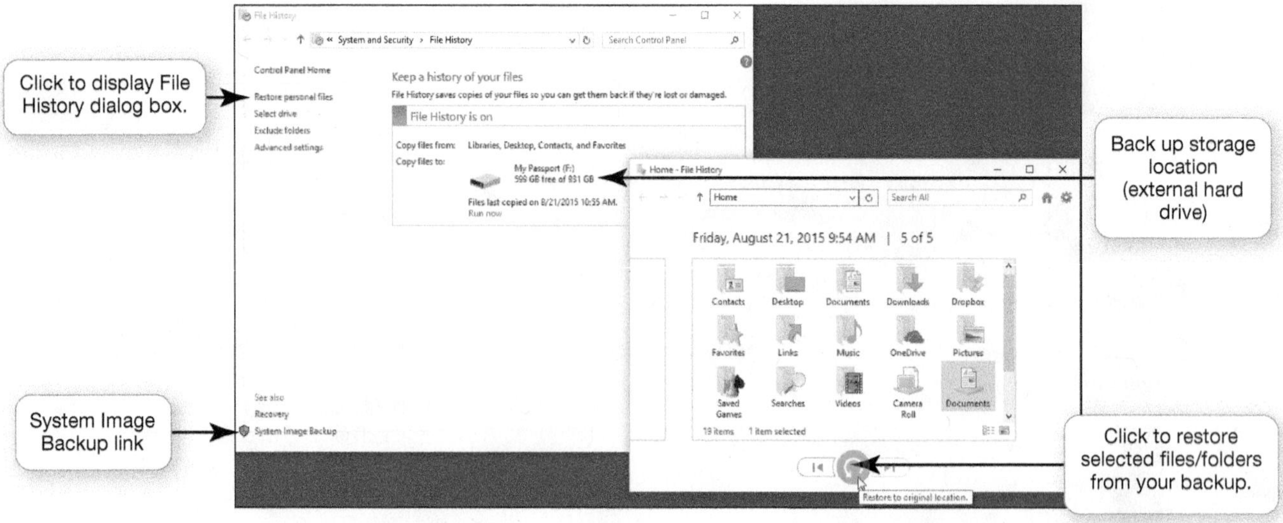

FIGURE 9.34 You can use the Windows File History utility to back up files and restore files from a previous backup. *(Windows 10, Microsoft Corporation)*
*>Right-click **Start**, select **Control Panel**, select **System and Security**, and then click the **File History link**.*

regularly. You should check with your school's network administrators to determine how often they're backed up and how you would request that files be restored from the backup if they're damaged or deleted. But don't rely on these network backups to bail you out if your data files are lost or damaged. It may take days for the network administrators to restore your files. It's better to keep backups of your data files yourself, especially homework and project files, so that you can immediately restore them. ■

> **SOUND BYTE**
> ### Managing Computer Security with Windows Tools
> In this Sound Byte, you'll learn how to monitor and control your computer security using features built into the Windows OS.

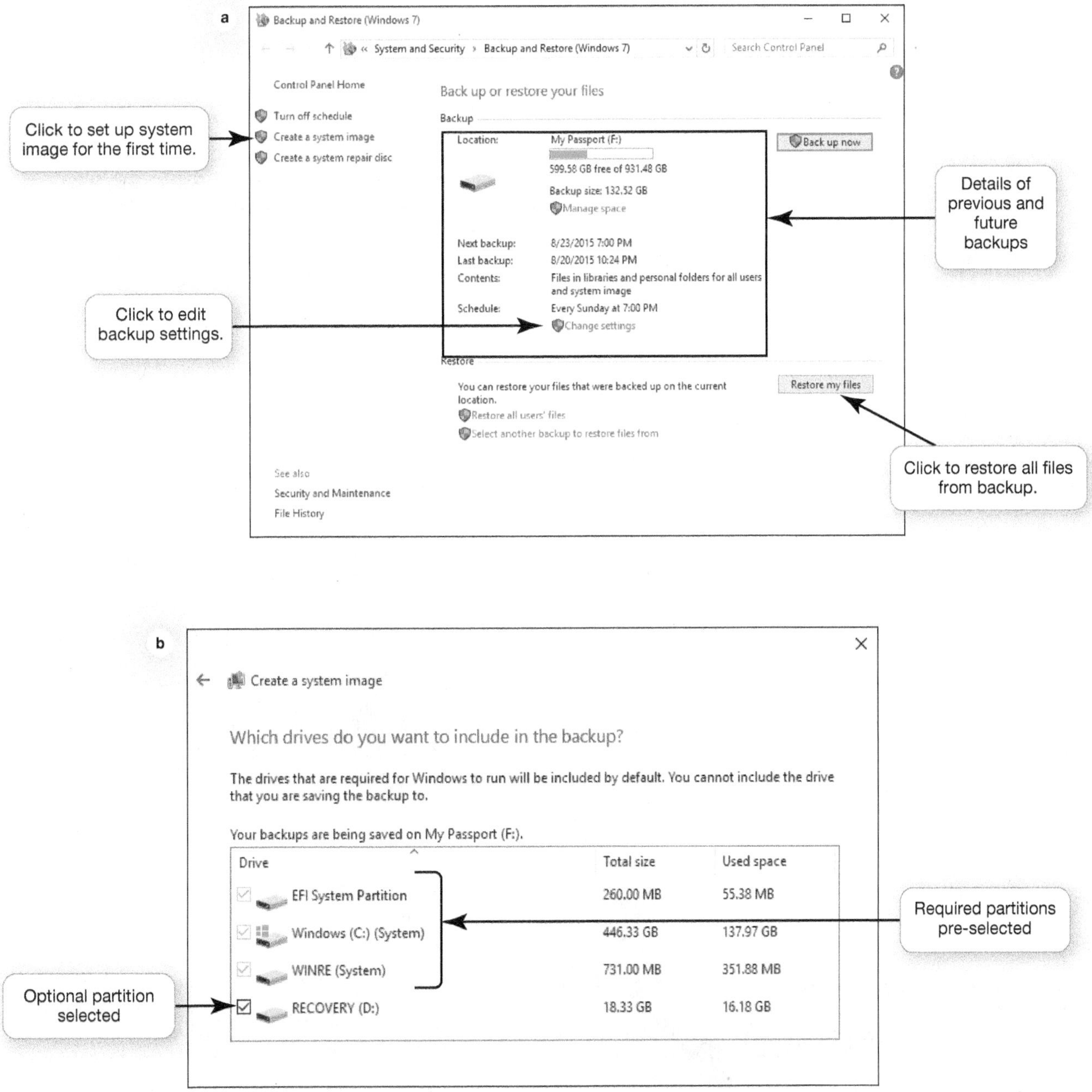

FIGURE 9.35 (a) The Backup and Restore utility allows you to perform an image backup and restore from one. (b) Select partitions to be included in the system image backup. *(Windows 10, Microsoft Corporation)*

protecting your physical COMPUTING ASSETS

Your computer, tablet, and phone aren't useful to you if they're damaged. Therefore, it's essential to select and ensure a safe environment for these devices. This includes protecting them from environmental factors, power surges, power outages, and theft.

Environmental Factors and Power Surges

Objective 9.16 *Explain the negative effects environment and power surges can have on computing devices.*

Why is the environment critical to the operation of my computer equipment? Computers are delicate devices and can be damaged by the adverse effects of abuse or a poor environment. Sudden movements, such as a fall, can damage your computing device's internal components. You should make sure that your computer sits on a flat, level surface, and if it's a laptop or a tablet, you should carry it in a protective case.

Electronic components don't like excessive heat or excessive cold. Don't leave computing devices and phones in a car during especially hot or cold weather because components can be damaged by extreme temperatures. Unfortunately, computers generate a lot of heat, which is why they have fans to cool their internal components. Chill mats that contain cooling fans and sit underneath laptop computers are useful accessories for dissipating heat. Make sure that you place your desktop computer where the fan's intake vents, usually found on the rear of the system unit, are unblocked so air can flow inside.

Naturally, a fan drawing air into a computer also draws in dust and other particles, which can wreak havoc on your system. Therefore, keep the room in which your computer is located as clean as possible. Finally, because food crumbs and liquid can damage keyboards and other computer components, consume food and beverages away from your computer.

What is a power surge? Power surges occur when electrical current is supplied in excess of normal voltage. Old or faulty wiring, downed power lines, malfunctions at electric company substations, and lightning strikes can all cause power surges. A **surge protector** is a device that protects your computer against power surges (see Figure 9.36).

Note that you should replace your surge protectors every two to three years. Also, after a major surge, the surge protector will no longer function and must be replaced. And it's wise to buy a surge protector that includes indicator lights, which illuminate when the surge protector is no longer functioning properly. Don't be fooled by old surge protectors—although they can still function as multiple-outlet power strips, they deliver power to your equipment without protecting it.

Besides my computer, what other devices need to be connected to a surge protector? All electronic devices in the home that have solid-state components, such as TVs, stereos, printers, and smartphones (when charging), should be connected to a surge protector. However, it can be inconvenient to use individual surge protectors on everything. A more practical method is to install a **whole-house surge protector** (see Figure 9.37). Whole-house surge protectors function

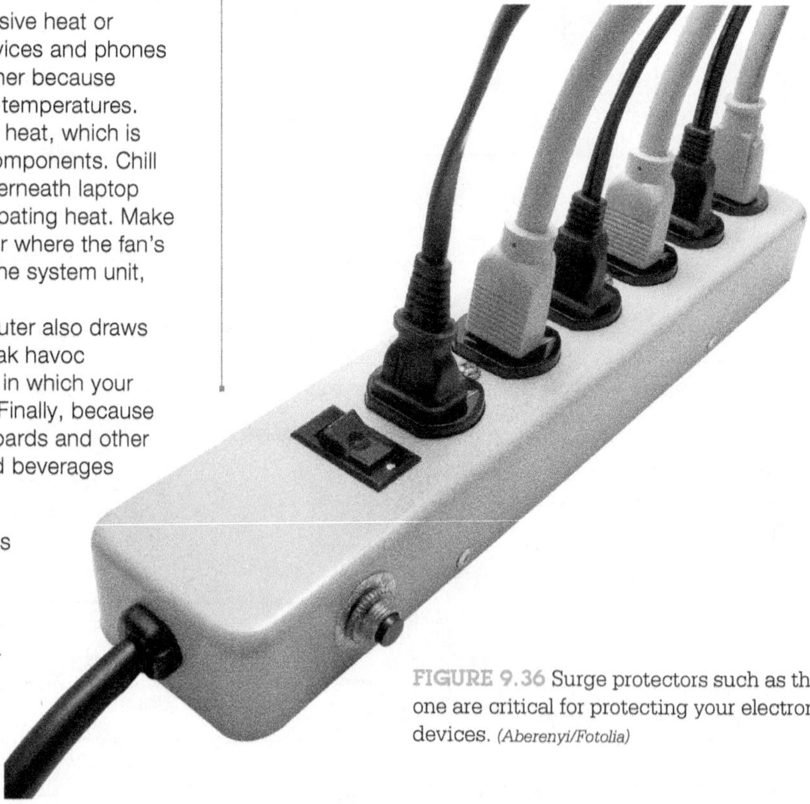

FIGURE 9.36 Surge protectors such as this one are critical for protecting your electronic devices. *(Aberenyi/Fotolia)*

FIGURE 9.37 A whole-house surge protector is usually installed at the breaker panel or near the electric meter.

> **SOUND BYTE**
> **Surge Protectors**
> In this Sound Byte, you'll learn about the major features of surge protectors and how they work. You'll also learn about the key factors you need to consider before buying a surge protector, and you'll see how easy it is to install one.

like other surge protectors, but they protect *all* electrical devices in the house. Typically, you'll need an electrician to install a whole-house surge protector, which will cost $300 to $500 (installed).

Is my equipment 100% safe when plugged into a surge protector? Lightning strikes can generate such high voltages that they can overwhelm a surge protector. As tedious as it sounds, unplugging electronic devices during an electrical storm is the only way to achieve absolute protection.

Preventing and Handling Theft

Objective 9.17 *Describe the major concerns when a device is stolen and strategies for solving the problems.*

What do I need to worry about if my computing device is stolen? Although theft of computer equipment is not classified as a cybercrime (it is considered larceny), the theft of tablets, smartphones, notebook computers, and other portable computing devices is on the rise. The resale value for used electronic equipment is high, and the equipment can be easily sold online. And because they're portable, laptops, tablets, and phones are easy targets for thieves. You have four main security concerns with mobile devices:

1. Keeping them from being stolen
2. Keeping data secure in case they are stolen
3. Finding a device if it is stolen
4. Remotely recovering and wiping data off a stolen device

Keep Them Safe: Alarms

What type of alarm can I install on my mobile device? Motion alarm software is a good, inexpensive theft deterrent. Free software such as LAlarm (**lalarm.com**) is effective for laptops. Apps such as Motion Alarm and Alarmomatic help secure your iPad or iPhone. Alarm software either detects motion, like your device being picked up, or sounds near your device and then sets off an ear-piercing alarm until you enter the disable code. Thieves normally don't like it when attention is drawn to their activities, so alarms can be a very effective theft deterrent.

Keeping Mobile Device Data Secure

How can I secure the data on my mobile devices? Encrypting the data on your mobile device can make it extremely difficult, if not impossible, for thieves to obtain sensitive data from your stolen equipment. *Encryption* involves transforming your data using an algorithm that can only be unlocked by a secure code (or key). Encrypted data is impossible to read unless it's decrypted, which requires a secure password, hopefully known only to you.

Safe is an app that provides 256-bit encryption, which is very hard to crack, for data and images on your iPhone and iPad. If your password is not entered, no one can access the data and images on your iPhone or iPad. Mobile StrongBox is a similar app for Android devices. SensiGuard and SafeHouse are available for laptop computers to provide encryption for files or even entire hard drives.

Software Alerts and Data Wipes

How can my computer help me recover it when it is stolen? You've probably heard of LoJack, the theft-tracking device used in cars. Similar systems now exist for computers. Tracking software such as Absolut LoJack (**lojack.absolute.com/en**), PC PhoneHome, and Mac PhoneHome (**brigadoonsoftware.com**) enables your computer to alert authorities to the computer's location if it is stolen. A similar tracking app for Android and iOS devices is iHound.

To enable your mobile device to help with its own recovery, you install the tracking software on your device. The software contacts a server at the software manufacturer's website each time the device connects to the Internet. If your device is stolen, you notify the software manufacturer. The software manufacturer instructs your device to transmit tracking information, such as an IP address, WiFi hotspot, or cell tower location, that will assist authorities in locating and retrieving the mobile device.

What if the thieves find the tracking software and delete it? The files and directories holding the software aren't visible to thieves looking for such software, so they probably won't know the software is there. Furthermore, the tracking software is written in such a way that even if the thieves tried to reformat the hard drive, it would detect the reformat and hide the software code in a safe place in memory or on the hard drive. This works because some sectors of a hard drive are not rewritten during most reformatting. That way, the tracking software can reinstall itself after the reformatting is complete.

What if my device can't be recovered by the authorities? In the event that your laptop can't be recovered, software packages are available that provide for remote recovery and deletion of files. Absolute LoJack has these features and allows you to lock your device to keep the thieves from accessing it or to remotely wipe its contents by deleting all your data from your laptop.

For all iOS devices, Apple offers the Find My iPhone service, which is now part of iCloud. Enabling this service on your device provides you with numerous tools that can assist you in recovering and protecting your mobile devices. Did you forget where you left your iPad? Just sign in with your Apple ID at the iCloud website to see a map showing the location of your iPad (see Figure 9.38). You can send a message to your device, remotely password lock the device, or wipe all data from the device to completely protect your privacy. For Android devices, Where is My Droid? offers similar features, such as texting your device and having it reply with its location. You can even capture images with the front and rear cameras to see what your device is looking at (such as the thief)!

FIGURE 9.38 The Find My iPhone app can really help if your iOS device goes astray. You can play a sound to help you find it (if it's misplaced where you are), display a message on the device (Lost Mode), or erase all data on the device. *(LearningStockImages/Alamy)*

How can I ensure that I've covered all aspects of protecting my digital devices? Figure 9.39 provides a guide to ensure you haven't missed critical aspects of security. If you've addressed all of these issues, you can feel reasonably confident that your data and devices are secure. ■

FIGURE 9.39

Computer Security Checklist

Firewall

- Do all your computers and tablets have firewall software installed and activated before connecting to the Internet?
- Is your router also able to function as a hardware firewall?
- Have you tested your firewall security by using the free software available at grc.com?

Virus and Spyware Protection

- Is antivirus and anti-spyware software installed on all your devices?
- Is the antivirus and anti-spyware software configured to update itself automatically and regularly?
- Is the software set to scan your device on a regular basis (at least weekly) for viruses and spyware?

Software Updates

- Have you configured your operating systems (Windows, OS X, iOS) to install new software patches and updates automatically?
- Is other software installed on your device, such as Microsoft Office or productivity apps, configured for automatic updates?
- Is the web browser you're using the latest version?

Protecting Your Devices

- Are all computing devices protected from electrical surges?
- Do your mobile devices have alarms or tracking software installed on them?

Before moving on to the Chapter Review:

1. Watch Replay Video 9.2.
2. Then check your understanding of what you've learned so far.

DIG DEEPER Computer Forensics: How It Works

On law enforcement TV shows, you often see computer technicians working on suspects' computers to assist detectives in solving crimes. It may look simple, but the science of computer forensics is a complex, step-by-step process that ensures evidence is collected within the confines of the law.

Forensic means that something is suitable for use in a court of law. There are many branches of forensic science. For example, forensic pathologists provide evidence about the nature and manner of death in court cases involving deceased individuals. **Computer forensics** involves identifying, extracting, preserving, and documenting computer evidence. Computer forensics is performed by individuals known as *computer forensic scientists*, who rely primarily on specialized software to collect their evidence.

Phase 1: Obtaining and Securing Computer Devices

The first step in a computer forensics investigation is to seize the computer equipment that law enforcement officials believe contains pertinent evidence. Police are required to obtain a warrant to search an individual's home or place of business. Warrants must be very specific by spelling out exactly where detectives can search for evidence and exactly what type of evidence they're seeking. If a warrant indicates that the police may search an individual's home for his laptop computer, they can't then confiscate a tablet computer they notice in his car. It is important to specify in the warrant all types of storage devices where potential evidence might be stored, such as external hard drives, flash drives, and servers.

Once permission to collect the computers and devices containing possible evidence has been obtained, law enforcement officials must exercise great care when collecting the equipment. They need to ensure that no unauthorized persons are able to access or alter the computers or storage devices. The police must make sure the data and equipment are safe; if the equipment is connected to the Internet, the connection must be severed without data loss or damage. It's also important for law enforcement officials to understand that they may not want to power off equipment because potential evidence contained in RAM may be lost. After the devices are collected and secured, the computer forensic scientists take over the next phase of the investigation.

Phase 2: Cataloging and Analyzing the Data

It's critical to preserve the data exactly as it was found, or attorneys may argue that the computer evidence was subject to tampering or altering. Because just opening a file can alter it, the first task is to make a copy of all computer systems and storage devices collected (see Figure 9.40). The investigators then work from the copies to ensure that the original data always remains preserved exactly as it was when it was collected.

After obtaining a copy to work from, forensics professionals attempt to find every file on the system, including deleted files. Files on a computer aren't actually deleted, even if you empty the Recycle Bin, until the section of the hard disk they're stored on is overwritten with new data. Therefore, using special forensic software tools such as SIFT, EnCase, and FTK, the forensic scientists catalog all files found on the system or storage medium and recover as much information from deleted files as they can. Forensic software like FTK can readily detect hidden files and perform procedures to crack encrypted files or access protected files and reveal their contents.

The most important part of the process is documenting every step. Forensic scientists must clearly log every procedure performed because they may be required to provide proof in court that their investigations did not alter or damage information contained on the systems they examined. Detailed reports should list all files found, how the files were laid out on the system, which files were protected or encrypted, and the contents of each file. Finally, computer forensic professionals are often called on to present testimony in court during a trial.

Criminals are getting more sophisticated and are now employing anti-forensics techniques to foil computer forensic investigators. Although techniques for hiding or encrypting data are popular, the most insidious anti-forensics techniques

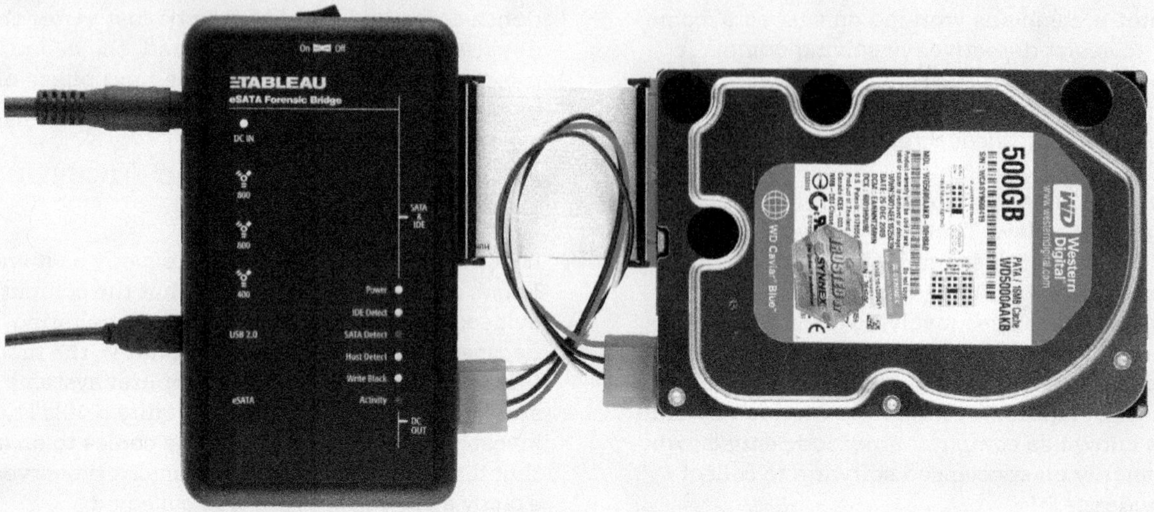

FIGURE 9.40 Portable computer forensic devices make it easy to copy storage devices at crime scenes. *(Lance Mueller/Alamy)*

are programs designed to erase data if unauthorized persons (i.e., not the criminal) access a computer system or if the system detects forensics software in use. When computer forensic investigators detect these countermeasures, they must often use creative methods and custom-designed software programs to retrieve and preserve the data.

Computer forensics is an invaluable tool to law enforcement in many criminal investigations, but only if the correct procedures are followed and the appropriate documentation is prepared.

check your understanding // review & practice

For a quick review to see what you've learned so far, answer the following questions.

multiple choice

1. Firewalls work by closing _____ in your computer.
   a. logical ports
   b. software gaps
   c. logical doors
   d. backdoors
2. _____ involve using a physical attribute such as a fingerprint for authentication.
   a. Backdoors
   b. Rootkits
   c. Biometrics
   d. Trojan horses
3. A backup of only the files on your computing device that have been created (or changed) since the last backup is known as a(n)
   a. total backup.
   b. incremental backup.
   c. image backup.
   d. global backup.
4. Antivirus software looks for _____ to detect viruses in files.
   a. virus artifacts
   b. virus signatures
   c. virus bots
   d. virus VPNs
5. Updating your operating software on a regular basis helps prevent system corruption from _____, which are malicious websites downloading harmful software to your computer.
   a. CAPTCHA
   b. pharming
   c. phishing
   d. drive-by-downloads

MyITLab Go to **MyITLab** to take an autograded version of the *Check Your Understanding* review and to find all media resources for the chapter.

TECHBYTES WEEKLY

Stay current with TechBytes Weekly Newsletter.

Continue

9 Chapter Review

summary //

Major Threats to Your Digital Assets

Learning Outcome 9.1 **You will be able to describe hackers, viruses, and other online annoyances and the threats they pose to your digital security.**

Identity Theft and Hackers

Objective 9.1 *Describe how identity theft is committed and the types of scams identity thieves perpetrate.*

- Identity theft occurs when a thief steals personal information about you and runs up debts in your name. Identify thieves can obtain information by stealing mail, searching through trash, or tricking people into revealing information over the phone or via e-mail. Identity thieves counterfeit existing credit cards, opening new credit card and bank accounts, change your address on financial statements, obtain medical services, and buy homes with a mortgage in the victim's name.

Objective 9.2 *List and describe the different types of hackers.*

- White-hat hackers break into systems for nonmalicious reasons such as testing security to expose weaknesses. Black-hat hackers break into systems to destroy information or for illegal gain. Grey-hat hackers often break into systems just for the thrill or to demonstrate their prowess.

Objective 9.3 *Describe the various tools hackers use and the types of attacks they might launch against computers.*

- Packet analyzers (sniffers) are programs used to intercept and read data packets and they travel across a network. Trojan horses are programs that appear to be something else but are really a tool for hackers to access your computer. Backdoor programs and rootkits are tools used by hackers to gain access to and take total control of a computer system. Denial-of-service attacks overwhelm computer systems with so many requests for data that legitimate users can't access the system.

Computer Viruses

Objective 9.4 *Explain what a computer virus is, why they are a threat to your security, and how a computing device catches a virus, and the symptoms it might display.*

- A computer virus is a computer program that attaches itself to another computer program and attempts to spread to other computers when files are exchanged. Computer viruses can display annoying messages, destroy your information, corrupt your files, or gather information about you. Computers catch viruses when exposed to infected files. This can occur from downloading infected files, downloading and running infected e-mail attachments, or sharing flash drives that contain infected files. Symptoms of virus infection include: (1) files or app icons disappear, (2) browser is reset to an unusual home page, (3) odd messages, pop-ups, or images are displayed, (4) data files become corrupt, and (5) Programs stop working properly

Objective 9.5 *List the different categories of computer viruses, and describe their behaviors.*

- Boot-sector viruses copy themselves onto the master boot record of a computer and execute when the computer is started. Logic bombs and time bombs are viruses triggered by the completion of certain events or by the passage of time. Worms can spread on their own without human intervention, unlike conventional viruses. Macro viruses lurk in documents that use macros (short series of commands that automate repetitive tasks). E-mail viruses access the address book of a victim to spread to the victim's contacts. Encryption viruses render files unusable by compressing them with complex encryption keys. Polymorphic viruses periodically rewrite themselves to avoid detection. Stealth viruses temporarily erase their code and hide in the active memory of the computer.

Online Annoyances and Social Engineering

Objective 9.6 *Explain what malware is, and list the common types of malware*

- Malware is software that has a malicious intent. Adware is software that displays sponsored advertisements in a section of your browser window or as a pop-up box. Spyware collects information about you, without your knowledge, and transmit it to the owner of the program.

Objective 9.7 *Define spam, and describe strategies to combat it.*

- Spam is unwanted or junk e-mail. Spim is unsolicited instant messages, which is also a form of spam. Spam filters in e-mail systems forward junk mail to their own folder. Never reply to spam or click on unsubscribe links as this usually just generates more spam.

Objective 9.8 *Explain what cookies are and whether they pose a security threat.*

- Cookies are small text files that some websites automatically store on your hard drive when you visit them. Cookies are usually used to keep track of users and personalize their browsing experience. Cookies do not pose a security threat although some individuals view them as privacy violations.

Objective 9.9 *Describe social engineering techniques, and explain strategies to avoid falling prey to them*

- Social engineering is any technique that uses social skills to generate human interaction that entices individuals to reveal sensitive information. Phishing lures people into revealing personal information via bogus e-mails that appear to be from legitimate sources and direct people to scammer's websites. Pharming occurs when malicious code is planted on your computer, either by viruses or by your visiting malicious websites, which then alters your browser's ability to find web addresses. Scareware attempts to convince you that your computer is infected with a virus and then tries to sell you a "solution." Most Internet security software packages have scareware, phishing and pharming protection built-in.

Protecting Your Digital Property

Learning Outcome 9.2 **Describe various ways to protect your digital property and data from theft and corruption.**

Restricting Access to Your Digital Assets

Objective 9.10 *Explain what a firewall is and how a firewall protects your computer from hackers.*

- A FIREWALL is a software program or hardware device designed to protect computers from hackers. Firewalls block access to your computer's logical ports and help keep your computer's network address secure. Firewalls use PACKET FILTERING to identify packets sent to specific logical ports and discard them. Firewalls use network address translation to assign internal IP addresses on networks. The internal IP addresses are much more difficult for hackers to detect.

Objective 9.11 *Explain how to protect your computer from virus infection.*

- ANTIVIRUS SOFTWARE is specifically designed to detect viruses and protect your computer and files from harm. Antivirus software detects viruses by looking for VIRUS SIGNATURES: code that specifically identifies a virus. Antivirus software stops viruses from executing and quarantines INfected files in a secure area on the hard drive. Virus software must be constantly updated to remain effective.

Objective 9.12 *Describe how passwords and biometric characteristics can be used for user authentication on computer systems.*

- Secure passwords contain a mixture of upper- and lowercase letters, numbers, and symbols and are at least 14 characters long. Passwords should not contain words that are in the dictionary or easy-to-guess personal information. Utilities built into web browsers and Internet security software can be used to manage your passwords.
- A biometric authentication device is a device that reads a unique personal characteristic to identify an authorized user. Fingerprint readers, iris scanners and facial recognition software are common examples of biometric security devices.

Objective 9.13 *Describe ways to surf the web anonymously.*

- Privacy tools built into web browsers help your surf anonymously by not recording your actions in the history files. USB devices containing privacy tools are available that prevent the computer you are using from storing any information about you on the computer. Virtual private networks (VPNs) are secure networks that can be used to send information securely across the public Internet.

Keeping Your Data Safe

Objective 9.14 *Describe the types of information you should never share online.*

- Reveal as little information as possible about yourself. Your Social Security number, phone number, date of birth, and street address are four key pieces of information that identity thieves need to steal an identity.

Objective 9.15 *List the various types of backups you can perform on your computing devices, and explain the various places you can store backup files.*

- An INCREMENTAL BACKUP involves backing up only files that have changed or have been created since the last backup was performed. An IMAGE BACKUP (or SYSTEM BACKUP) means that all system, application, and data files are backed up, not just the files that changed. You can store backups online (in the cloud), on external hard drives, or on network-attached storage (NAS) devices.

Protecting Your Physical Computing Assets

Objective 9.16 *Explain the negative effects environment and power surges can have on computing devices.*

- Computing devices should be kept in clean environments free from dust and other particulates and should not be exposed to extreme temperatures (either hot or cold). You should protect all electronic devices from power surges by hooking them up through surge protectors, which will protect them from most electrical surges that could damage the devices.

Objective 9.17 *Describe the major concerns when a device is stolen and strategies for solving the problems.*

- The four main security concerns regarding computing devices are (1) keeping them from being stolen, (2) keeping data secure in case they are stolen, (3) finding a device if it is stolen, and (4) remotely recovering and wiping data off a stolen device.
- Software is available for installation on devices that will (1) set off an alarm if the device is moved, (2) help recover the device, if stolen, by reporting the computer's whereabouts when it is connected to the Internet, and (3) allow you to lock or wipe the contents of the device remotely.

MyITLab

Be sure to check out **MyITLab** for additional materials to help you review and learn. And don't forget the Replay Videos.

key terms //

adware **355**
antivirus software **368**
backdoor program **350**
backup **378**
biometric authentication device **373**
black-hat hacker **350**
boot-sector virus **354**
botnet **351**
computer forensics **385**
cookie **358**
cyberloafing **359**
data breach **362**
data file **378**
denial-of-service (DoS) attack **350**
distributed denial-of-service (DDoS) attack **351**
drive-by download **370**
e-mail virus **355**
encryption virus **355**
exploit kits **351**
firewall **366**
geotag **352**
grey-hat hacker **350**
hacker **349**
identity theft **349**
image backup (system backup) **378**
incremental backup (partial backup) **378**
inoculation **369**
keystroke logger (keylogger) **356**
logical port **352**
logical port blocking **367**
logic bomb **354**
macro virus **354**
malware **355**
master boot record **354**
multi-factor authentication **376**
multipartite virus **355**
network address translation (NAT) **367**
packet analyzer (sniffer) **350**
packet filtering **367**
personal firewall **366**
pharming **360**
phishing **360**
polymorphic virus **355**
pretexting **360**
program file **378**
quarantining **369**
rootkit **350**
scareware **361**
script **354**
social engineering **360**
spam **356**
spam filter **356**
spear phishing **362**
spyware **356**
stealth virus **355**
surge protector **382**
time bomb **354**
Trojan horse **350**
virtual private network (VPN) **375**
virus **353**
virus signature **369**
white-hat hacker (ethical hacker) **349**
whole-house surge protector **382**
worm **354**
zombie **350**

chapter quiz // assessment

For a quick review to see what you've learned, answer the following questions. Submit the quiz as requested by your instructor. If you are using **MyITLab**, the quiz is also available there.

multiple choice

1. Which of the following is NOT a major type of cybercrime reported to the IC3?
   - **a.** Government impersonation scams
   - **b.** identity theft
   - **c.** malware fraud
   - **d.** advance fee fraud
2. Viruses that load from USB drives left connected to computers when computers are turned on are known as
   - **a.** boot-sector viruses.
   - **b.** script viruses.
   - **c.** polymorphic viruses.
   - **d.** encryption viruses.
3. Software designed to close logical ports in your computer is known as a(n)
   - **a.** firewall.
   - **b.** packet filter.
   - **c.** anti-malware blocker.
   - **d.** network address translator.
4. Which is NOT a tool hackers use to gain access to and take control of your computer?
   - **a.** Trojan horse
   - **b.** backdoor programs
   - **c.** rootkits
   - **d.** phishing software
5. A computer that a hacker has gained control of in order to launch DoS attacks is known as a ________ computer.
   - **a.** rootkit
   - **b.** compromised
   - **c.** zombie
   - **d.** breached
6. A backup of all the files on your computer, which essentially creates a "snapshot" of what your computer looks like at that point in time, is known as a(n)
   - **a.** total backup.
   - **b.** incremental backup.
   - **c.** image backup.
   - **d.** modification backup.

true/false

______ **1.** Password strength is solely determined by the length of the password.

______ **2.** One of the best and simplest ways to keep hackers out of your computer is to use a firewall.

______ **3.** Sending e-mails to lure people into revealing personal information is a technique known as phishing.

______ **4.** Encrypting data is not an appropriate measure for protecting mobile devices such as smartphones.

critical thinking

1. **Protecting Your Data from Data Breaches**

   You most likely have provided personal information to many websites and companies. What information have you provided to companies that you wish you had never disclosed? What types of information have companies asked you to provide that you believe was unnecessary? List specific companies and examples of the extraneous information.

2. **Phishing**

   Have you or anyone you know ever been a victim of a phishing scam? What sorts of scams have you heard about? Research and discuss at least three types of common scams.

team time //

Protecting a Network

Problem

Along with easy access to the web comes the danger of theft of digital assets.

Task

A school alumnus is in charge of the county government computer department. The network contains computers running Windows 10, Windows 8, Windows 7, and OS X. He asked your instructor for help in ensuring that his computers and network are protected from viruses, malware, and hackers. He is hoping that there may be free software available that can protect his employees' computers.

Process

1. Break the class into three teams. Each team will be responsible for investigating one of the following issues:
   a. **Antivirus software:** Research alternatives that protect computers from viruses. Find three alternatives and support your recommendations with reviews that evaluate free packages.
   b. **Anti-malware software:** Research three free malware alternatives and determine whether the software can be updated automatically. You may want to recommend that the county purchase software to ensure that a minimum of employee intervention is needed to keep it up to date.
   c. **Firewalls:** Determine if the firewall software provided with Windows 10, Windows 8, Windows 7, and OS X is reliable. If it is, prepare documentation (for all three OSs) for county employees to determine if their firewalls are properly configured. If additional firewall software is needed, research free firewall software and locate three options that can be deployed by the county.
   d. Present your findings to the class and provide your instructor with a report suitable for eventual presentation to the manager of the county office network.

Conclusion

With the proliferation of viruses and malware, it is essential to protect computers and networks. Free alternatives might work, but you should research the best protection solution for your situation.

ethics project //

Content Control: Censorship to Protect Children

In this exercise, you'll research and then role-play a complicated ethical situation. The role you play might or might not match your own personal beliefs; in either case, your research and use of logic will enable you to represent the view assigned. An arbitrator will watch and comment on both sides of the arguments, and together, the team will agree on an ethical solution.

Problem

Many parents use web-filtering software (content-control software) to protect their children from objectionable Internet content. In 2000, the U.S. federal government began requiring libraries to use content-control software as a condition to receiving federal funds under the provisions of the Children's Internet Protection Act (CIPA). Some states, such as Virginia, have passed laws requiring libraries to install filtering software even if they did not receive federal funds. Upon installation of the software, it's up to the library administrators to decide what content is restricted. Therefore, content restriction can vary widely from library to library.

Research Areas to Consider

- U.S. Supreme Court case *United States v. American Library Association* (2003)
- Content-control software and First Amendment rights
- Violation of children's free speech rights
- Children's Internet Protection Act (CIPA)

Process

1. Divide the class into teams. Research the areas above and devise a scenario in which someone has complained about innocuous content that was blocked.
2. Team members should write a summary that provides background information for their character—for example, library patron, library administrator, or arbitrator—and that details their character's behaviors to set the stage for the role-playing event. Then, team members should create an outline to use during the role-playing event.
3. Team members should present their case to the class or submit a PowerPoint presentation for review by the class, along with the summary and resolution they developed.

Conclusion

As technology becomes ever more prevalent and integrated into our lives, more and more ethical dilemmas will present themselves. Being able to understand and evaluate both sides of the argument, while responding in a personally or socially ethical manner, will be an important skill.

Solve This

MyITLab® grader

Computer Security

You have been asked to prepare a report on computer security using Word 2016. You have written the majority of the report, but you have to make some final modifications and refinements such as adding the results of some research of good antivirus software, adding a cover page, and generating a table of contents.

You will use the following skills as you complete this activity:

- Create and Modify Tables
- Insert Tab Stops
- Add Watermark
- Insert Cover Page
- Create and Update Table of Contents
- Add Footnote
- Use Find and Replace

Instructions:

1. Open *TIA_Ch9_Start* and save as **TIA_Ch9_LastFirst**.
2. Find all instances of *e-mail* and replace with **e-mail**.
   a. Hint: Click **Replace** in the Editing group on the Home tab, type **e-mail** in the Find what box, and type **e-mail** in the Replace with box. Click **Replace All**.
3. Find the first instance of malware. Place the cursor after the word *malware* (before the period) and insert the footnote: **Malware is defined as software that is intended to gain access to, or damage or disable, computer systems for the purposes of theft or fraud.** Close the Navigation pane.
   a. Hint: Use Find in the Editing group on the Home tab to locate malware.
   b. Hint: Click **Insert Footnote** in the Footnotes group on the References tab to insert a footnote.
4. In the section, *Types of Viruses*, highlight the six lines of text that outline the categories of computer viruses and variants. Add a Right Align Tab Stop at 1½" and a Left Align Tab Stop at 2".
   a. Hint: To set tab stop, display ruler, select tab stop style from Select tab box to the left of the ruler, click at the desired position on the ruler.
5. Place cursor at the end of the paragraph in the Antivirus Software section. Press **Enter**, then insert a **3×4 Table**. Type **Product Name, Description/Review**, and **Cost** in the top three cells. Adjust the width of the Description/Review column to **3.5"** and the width of the Cost column to **1"**.
   a. Hint: Click **Table** in the Tables group on the Insert tab, and drag to select the desired grid.
6. Add a row at the top of the table, **Merge Cells**, type **Antivirus Software Reviews**, and **Align Center** the contents. Format the table with **Grid Table 4—Accent 1 style**.
   a. Hint: Click **Insert** above in the Rows & Columns group on the Table Tools Layout tab.
7. Open a browser, and go to **www.pcmag.com/reviews/antivirus**. Research four antivirus software programs and place the software name, review, and cost of the software in the respective columns in the table.
   a. Hint: Press **tab** at the end of the third row to add an additional line to the table to accommodate a fourth review.
8. Press **Ctrl+Home**, then insert the **Banded Cover Page**. Ensure *Computer Security* displays as the title and *your name* displays as the Author. Delete the Company and Address placeholders.
9. Insert **Page Numbers** at the bottom of the page using the **Plain Number 3 format**. Ensure Different First Page is checked. Close Header and Footer.
10. On the page 2 of the document, insert a **Page Break** before the report title, Computer Security.
11. Place the cursor at the top of the new blank page, and insert a **Table of Contents** using the Contents format.
    a. Hint: Click **Table of Contents** in the Table of Contents group on the References tab.
12. Press **Ctrl+End**, scroll up and change the heading style of *Firewalls* to **Heading 2**, change the heading style of *Software Firewalls* and *Hardware Firewalls* to **Heading 3**.
13. Update the Table of Contents to reflect the changes in headings, ensure you update the entire table.
    a. Hint: Click anywhere in the Table of Contents, and click **Update Table**, and then click **Update entire table**.
14. Add a **Draft 1 Watermark** to the report.
    a. Hint: Click **Watermark** in the Page Backgroup group on the Design tab.
15. Save the document and submit based on your instructor's directions.

EDITION 13 thirteenth

Glossary

3-D sound card An expansion card that enables a computer to produce omnidirectional or three-dimensional sounds.

4G The latest mobile communication standard with faster data transfer rates than 3G.

A

access time The time it takes a storage device to locate its stored data.

accounting software An application program that helps business owners manage their finances more efficiently by providing tools for tracking accounting transactions such as sales, accounts receivable, inventory purchases, and accounts payable.

adware A program that downloads on your computer when a user installs a freeware program, game, or utility. Generally, adware enables sponsored advertisements to appear in a section of a browser window or as a pop-up ad.

affective computing A type of computing that relates to emotion or that deliberately tries to influence emotion.

aggregator A software program that finds and retrieves the latest update of web material (usually podcasts) according to your specifications.

all-in-one computer A desktop system unit that houses the computer's processor, memory, and monitor in a single unit.

all-in-one printer A device that combines the functions of a printer, scanner, copier, and fax.

analog Waves that illustrate the loudness of a sound or the brightness of the colors in an image at a given moment in time.

analog-to-digital converter chip A chip that converts analog signals into digital signals.

antivirus software Software specifically designed to detect viruses and protect a computer and files from harm.

app marketplace (app store) Online software stores, such as Google Play, where users can purchase and download apps.

application programming interface (API) A set of software routines that allows one software system to work with another.

application software The set of programs on a computer that helps a user carry out tasks such as word processing, sending e-mail, balancing a budget, creating presentations, editing photos, taking an online course, and playing games.

aspect ratio The width-to-height proportion of a monitor.

assistive (adaptive) technology Any device, software feature, or app that is designed to improve the functional capabilities of individuals with disabilities.

audio MIDI interface Interface technology that allows a user to connect guitars and microphones to their computer.

audio-editing software Programs that perform basic editing tasks on audio files such as cutting dead air space from the beginning or end of a song or cutting a portion from the middle.

augmentative reality/augmented reality A combination of our normal sense of the objects around us with an overlay of information displayed.

authentication The process of identifying a computer user, based on a login or username and password. The computer system determines whether the computer user is authorized and what level of access is to be granted on the network.

B

backdoor program A program that enables a hacker to take complete control of a computer without the legitimate user's knowledge or permission.

backup A copy of a computer file that can be used to replace the original if it's lost or damaged.

backward compatibility The accommodation of current devices being able to use previously issued software standards in addition to the current standards.

bandwidth The maximum speed at which data can be transmitted between two nodes on a network; usually measured in megabits per second (Mbps). See also *data transfer rate*.

base transceiver station A large communications tower with antennas, amplifiers, and receivers/transmitters.

basic input/output system (BIOS) A program that manages the data between a computer's operating system and all the input and output devices attached to the computer; also responsible for loading the operating system (OS) from its permanent location on the hard drive to random access memory (RAM).

beta version A version of the software that's still under development. Many beta versions are available for a limited trial period and are used to help the developers correct any errors before they launch the software on the market.

Big Data Very large data sets that are analyzed to reveal patterns, trends, and associations.

binary digit (bit) A digit that corresponds to the on and off states of a computer's switches. A bit contains a value of either 0 or 1.

binary language The language computers use to process data into information, consisting of only the values 0 and 1.

biometric authentication device A device that uses some unique characteristic of human biology to identify authorized users.

black-hat hacker A hacker who uses his or her knowledge to destroy information or for illegal gain.

blog (weblog) A personal log or journal posted on the web; short for *web log*.

Bluetooth technology A type of wireless technology that uses radio waves to transmit data over short distances (approximately 3–300 feet depending on power); often used to connect peripherals such as printers and keyboards to computers or headsets to cell phones.

Blu-ray disc (BD) A method of optical storage for digital data, developed for storing high-definition media. It has the largest storage capacity of all optical storage options.

Bookmarks Features in some browsers that place markers of websites' Uniform Resource Locators (URLs) in an easily retrievable list.

Boolean operators A word used to refine logical searches. For Internet searches, the words AND, NOT, and OR describe the relationships between keywords in the search.

boot process The process for loading the operating system (OS) into random access memory (RAM) when the computer is turned on.

boot-sector virus A virus that replicates itself into the master boot record of a flash drive or hard drive.

botnet A large group of software applications (called *robots* or *bots*) that run without user intervention on a large number of computers.

breadcrumb trail A navigation aid that shows users the path they have taken to get to a web page or where the page is located within the website; it usually appears at the top of a page.

broadband A high-speed Internet connection such as cable, satellite, or digital subscriber line (DSL).

business-to-business (B2B) E-commerce transactions between businesses.

business-to-consumer (B2C) E-commerce transactions between businesses and consumers.

byte Eight binary digits (bits).

C

cable Internet A broadband service that transmits data over coaxial cables.

cache memory Small blocks of memory, located directly on and next to the central processing unit (CPU) chip, that act as holding places for recently or frequently used instructions or data that the CPU accesses the most. When these instructions or data are stored in cache memory, the CPU can more quickly retrieve them than if it had to access the instructions or data from random access memory (RAM).

Cat 6 cable A UTP cable type that provides more than 1 Gb/s of throughput.

cellular (cell) phone A telephone that operates over a mobile network. Cell phones can also offer Internet access, text messaging, personal information management (PIM) features, and more.

central processing unit (CPU or **processor)** The part of the system unit of a computer that is responsible for data processing; it is the largest and most important chip in the computer. The CPU controls all the functions performed by the computer's other components and processes all the commands issued to it by software instructions.

Chromebook Any laptop or tablet running the Chrome OS as its operating system.

client A computer that requests information from a server in a client/server network (such as your computer when you are connected to the Internet).

client/server network A type of network that uses servers to deliver services to computers that are requesting them (clients).

clock speed The steady and constant pace at which a computer goes through machine cycles, measured in hertz (Hz).

cloud computing The process of storing data, files, and applications on the web, which allows access to and manipulation of these files and applications from any Internet-connected device.

cloud storage A service that keeps files on the Internet (in the "cloud") rather than storing files solely on a local device.

cluster The smallest increment in which data is stored on hard disks; hard disks are divided into *tracks*, then *wedges*, then *sectors*, then clusters.

CMYK A color model in which all colors are described as a mixture of four base colors (cyan, magenta, yellow, and black).

coaxial cable A single copper wire surrounded by layers of plastic insulation, metal sheathing, and a plastic jacket; used mainly in cable television and cable Internet service.

codec A rule, implemented in either software or hardware, which squeezes a given amount of audio and video information into less space.

cognitive surplus The combination of leisure time and the tools needed to be creative.

cold boot The process of starting a computer from a powered-down or off state.

collaborative consumption Joining together as a group to use a specific product more efficiently.

command-driven interface Interface between user and computer in which the user enters commands to communicate with the computer system.

compact disc (CD) A method of optical storage for digital data; originally developed for storing digital audio.

computer A data-processing device that gathers, processes, outputs, and stores data and information.

computer forensics The application of computer systems and techniques to gather potential legal evidence; a law enforcement specialty used to fight high-tech crime.

computer literate Being familiar enough with computers that a user knows how to use them and understands their capabilities and limitations.

computer-aided design (CAD) A 3-D modeling program used to create automated designs, technical drawings, and model visualizations.

connectivity port A port that enables a computing device to be connected to other devices or systems such as networks, modems, and the Internet.

consumer-to-consumer (C2C) E-commerce transactions between consumers through online sites such as eBay.

cookie A small text file that some websites automatically store on a client computer's hard drive when a user visits the site.

copyleft A simplified licensing scheme that enables copyright holders to grant certain rights to a work while retaining other rights.

core A complete processing section from a central processing unit, embedded into one physical chip.

course management software A program that provides traditional classroom tools, such as calendars and grade books, over the Internet, as well as areas for students to exchange ideas and information in chat rooms, discussion forums, and e-mail.

CPU benchmarks Measurements used to compare performance between processors.

CPU usage The percentage of time the central processing unit (CPU) is working.

CPU usage graph Records central processing unit (CPU) usage for several seconds.

crisis-mapping tool A tool that collects information from e-mails, text messages, blog posts, and Twitter tweets and maps them, making the information instantly publicly available.

crowdfunding Asking for small donations from a large number of people, often using the Internet; a style of generating capital to start a business through social media.

crowdsourcing The phenomenon of consumers checking in with the voice of the crowd before making purchases.

custom installation The process of installing only those features of a software program that a user wants on the hard drive.

cyberbullying Using technology to harass or intimidate another individual.

cybercrime Any criminal action perpetrated primarily through the use of a computer.

cybercriminal An individual who uses computers, networks, and the Internet to perpetrate crime.

cyberloafing Doing anything with a computer that's unrelated to a job (such as playing video games) while one's supposed to be working. Also called *cyberslacking*.

D

data Numbers, words, pictures, or sounds that represent facts, figures, or ideas; the raw input that users have at the start of a job.

data breach When sensitive or confidential information is copied, transmitted, or viewed by an individual who is not authorized to handle the data.

data file A file that contains stored data.

data mining The process by which great amounts of data are analyzed and investigated. The objective is to spot significant patterns or trends within the data that would otherwise not be obvious.

data plan A connectivity plan or text messaging plan in which data charges are separate from cell phone calling charges and are provided at rates different from those for voice calls.

data transfer rate The maximum speed at which data can be transmitted between two nodes on a network; measured in megabits per second (Mbps) or gigabits per second (Gbps).

database administrator (database designer) An information technology professional responsible for designing, constructing, and maintaining databases.

database software An electronic filing system best used for larger and more complicated groups of data that require more than one table and the ability to group, sort, and retrieve data and generate reports.

denial-of-service (DoS) attack An attack that occurs when legitimate users are denied access to a computer system because a hacker is repeatedly making requests of that computer system that tie up its resources and deny legitimate users access.

desktop computer A computer that is intended for use at a single location. A desktop computer consists of a case that houses the main components of the computer, plus peripheral devices.

desktop publishing (DTP) software Programs for incorporating and arranging graphics and text to produce creative documents.

device driver Software that facilitates the communication between a device and its operating system or between a network adapter and a server's operating system and the operating system of the computer in which the adapter is installed.

digital convergence The use of a single unifying device to handle media, Internet, entertainment, and telephony needs; expressed in the range of devices now on the market.

digital divide The discrepancy between those who have access to the opportunities and knowledge that computers and the Internet offer and those who do not.

digital rights management (DRM) A system of access control that allows only limited use of material that has been legally purchased.

digital signal processor A specialized chip that processes digital information and transmits signals very quickly.

digital subscriber line (DSL) A type of connection that uses telephone lines to connect to the Internet and that allows both phone and data transmissions to share the same line.

digital video (or **versatile) disc (DVD)** A method of optical storage for digital data that has greater storage capacity than compact discs.

digital video interface (DVI) port: Video interface technology that newer LCD monitors, as well as other multimedia devices such as televisions, DVD players, and projectors, use to connect to a PC.

digital video-editing software A program for editing digital video.

directory A hierarchical structure that include files, folders, and drives used to create a more organized and efficient computer.

Disk Cleanup A Windows utility that removes unnecessary files from the hard drive.

disk defragmentation The process of regrouping related pieces of files on the hard drive, enabling faster retrieval of the data.

distributed (grid) computing A software system in which components located on networked computers interact to achieve a common goal.

distributed denial-of-service (DDoS) attack An automated attack that's launched from more than one zombie computer at the same time.

distributions (distros) Linux download packages.

domain name A part of a Uniform Resource Locator (URL). Domain names consist of two parts: the site's host and a suffix that indicates the type of organization (example: popsci.com, where *popsci* is the domain name and *com* is the suffix).

drawing software (illustration software) Programs for creating or editing two-dimensional line-based drawings.

drive bay A special shelf inside a computer that is designed to hold storage devices.

drive-by download The use of malicious software to attack a computer by downloading harmful programs onto a computer, without the user's knowledge, while they are surfing a website.

E

e-commerce (electronic commerce) The process of conducting business online for purposes ranging from fund-raising to advertising to selling products.

electronic ink (E Ink) A very crisp, sharp grayscale representation of text achieved by using millions of microcapsules with white and black particles in a clear fluid.

electronic text (e-text) Textual information stored as digital information so that it can be stored, manipulated, and transmitted by electronic devices.

e-mail (electronic mail) Internet-based communication in which senders and recipients correspond.

e-mail client A software program that runs on a computer and is used to send and receive e-mail through an Internet service provider's server.

e-mail virus A virus transmitted by e-mail that often uses the address book in the victim's e-mail system to distribute itself.

embedded computer A specially designed computer chip that resides inside another device, such as a car. These selfcontained computer devices have their own programming and typically neither receive input from users nor interact with other systems.

encryption virus A malicious program that searches for common data files and compresses them into a file using a complex encryption key, thereby rendering the files unusable.

End User License Agreement (EULA) An agreement between the user and the software developer that must be accepted before installing the software on a computer.

e-reader A device that can display e-text and that has supporting tools, like note taking, bookmarks, and integrated dictionaries.

ergonomics How a user sets up his or her computer and other equipment to minimize risk of injury or discomfort.

Ethernet network A network that uses the Ethernet protocol as the means (or standard) by which the nodes on the network communicate.

Ethernet port A port that's slightly larger than a standard phone jack and that transfers data at speeds of up to 10,000 Mbps; used to connect a computer to a DSL or cable modem or to a network.

ethics The study of the general nature of morals and the choices individuals make.

event The result of an action, such as a keystroke, mouse click, or signal to the printer, in the respective device (keyboard, mouse, or printer) to which the operating system responds.

expansion cards (or adapter cards) A circuit board with specific functions that augment the computer's basic functions and provide connections to other devices; examples include the sound card and the video card.

exploit kits A software toolkit used to take advantage of security weaknesses found in apps or operating systems, usually to deploy malware.

extension (file type) In a file name, the three letters that follow the user-supplied file name after the dot (.); the extension identifies what kind of family of files the file belongs to, or which application should be used to read the file.

external hard drive A hard drive that is enclosed in a protective case to make it portable; the drive is connected to the computer with a data transfer cable and is often used to back up data.

F

Favorites A feature in Microsoft Internet Explorer that places a marker of a website's Uniform Resource Locator (URL) in an easily retrievable list in the browser's toolbar. (Called Bookmarks in some browsers.)

feature phone Inexpensive cell phones with modest processors, simple interfaces, and, often, no touch screens.

fiber-optic cable A cable that transmits data at close to the speed of light along glass or plastic fibers.

fiber-optic service Internet access that is enabled by transmitting data at the speed of light through glass or plastic fibers.

file A collection of related pieces of information stored together for easy reference.

file compression utility A program that takes out redundancies in a file in order to reduce the file size.

File Explorer The main tool for finding, viewing, and managing the contents of your computer by showing the location and contents of every drive, folder, and file; called Windows Explorer prior to Windows 8.

File History A Windows utility that automatically creates a duplicate of your libraries, desktop, contacts, and favorites and copies it to another storage device, such as an external hard drive.

file management The process by which humans or computer software provide organizational structure to a computer's contents.

file name The first part of the label applied to a file; generally the name a user assigns to the file when saving it.

file path The exact location of a file, starting with the drive in which the file is located and including all folders, subfolders (if any), the file name, and the extension (example: C:\ Users\ username\Documents\Illustrations\ EBronte.jpg).

File Transfer Protocol (FTP) A protocol used to upload and download files from one computer to another over the Internet.

financial planning software Programs for managing finances, such as Intuit's Quicken, which include electronic checkbook registers and automatic bill-payment tools.

firewall A software program or hardware device designed to prevent unauthorized access to computers or networks.

firmware System software that controls hardware devices.

flash drive (jump drive, USB drive, or **thumb drive)** A drive that plugs into a universal serial bus (USB) port on a computer and that stores data digitally. Also called a USB drive, jump drive, or thumb drive.

flash memory card A form of portable storage; this removable memory card is often used in digital cameras, smartphones, video cameras, and printers.

folder A collection of files stored on a computer.

freeware Any copyrighted software that can be used for free.

full installation The process of installing all the files and programs from the distribution media to the computer's hard drive.

G

geolocation The method of identifying the geographical location of a person or device, usually by utilizing information processed through the Internet.

geotag Data attached to a photograph that indicates the latitude and longitude where you were standing when you took the photo.

gigabit Ethernet The most commonly used wired Ethernet standard deployed in devices designed for home networks; provides bandwidth of up to 1 Gbps.

gigabyte (GB) About a billion bytes.

gigahertz (GHz) One billion hertz.

global positioning system (GPS) A system of 21 satellites (plus 3 working spares), built and operated by the U.S. military, that constantly orbit the earth. The satellites provide information to GPS-capable devices to pinpoint locations on the earth.

graphical user interface (GUI) Unlike the command- and menu-driven interfaces used in earlier software, GUIs display graphics and use the point-and-click technology of the mouse and cursor, making them much more user friendly.

graphics double data rate 5 (GDDR5) A standard of video memory.

graphics processing unit (GPU) A specialized logic chip that's dedicated to quickly displaying and calculating visual data such as shadows, textures, and luminosity.

green computing (green IT) A movement that encourages environmentally sustainable computing (or IT).

grey-hat hacker A cross between black and white—a hacker who will often illegally break into systems merely to flaunt his or her expertise to the administrator of the system he or she penetrated or to attempt to sell his or her services in repairing security breaches.

H

hacker Anyone who unlawfully breaks into a computer system (whether an individual computer or a network).

hacktivism Using computers and computer networks in a subversive way to promote an agenda.

hard disk drive (HDD, or hard drive) The computer's nonvolatile, primary storage device for permanent storage of software and documents.

hardware Any part of a computer or computer system you can physically touch.

head crash Impact of the read/write head against the magnetic platter of the hard drive; often results in data loss.

Hibernate A power-management mode that saves the current state of the current system to the computer's hard drive.

high definition A standard of digital TV signal that guarantees a specific level of resolution and a specific *aspect ratio*, which is the rectangular shape of the image.

high-definition multimedia interface (HDMI) port A compact audio–video interface standard that carries both high-definition video and uncompressed digital audio.

home area network (HAN) A network located in a home that's used to connect all of its digital devices.

home network server A device designed to store media, share media across the network, and back up files on computers connected to a home network.

host The portion of a domain name that identifies who maintains a given website. For example, berkeley.edu is the domain name for the University of California at Berkeley, which maintains that site.

hyperlink A type of specially coded text that, when clicked, enables a user to jump from one location, or web page, to another within a website or to another website altogether.

Hypertext Transfer Protocol (HTTP) The protocol that allows files to be transferred from a web server so that you can see them on your computer by using a browser.

hyperthreading A technology that permits quicker processing of information by enabling a new set of instructions to start executing before the previous set has finished.

I

identity theft The process by which someone uses personal information about someone else (such as the victim's name, address, and Social Security number) to assume the victim's identity for the purpose of defrauding another.

image backup (system backup) A copy of an entire computer system, created for restoration purposes.

image-editing software Programs for editing photographs and other images.

impact printer A printer that has tiny hammer-like keys that strike the paper through an inked ribbon, thus making a mark on the paper. The most common impact printer is the dot-matrix printer.

incremental backup (partial backup) A type of backup that only backs up files that have changed since the last time files were backed up.

information Data that has been organized or presented in a meaningful fashion; the result, or output that users require at the end of a job.

information technology (IT) The set of techniques used in processing and retrieving information.

inkjet printer A nonimpact printer that sprays tiny drops of ink onto paper.

inoculation A process used by antivirus software; compares old and current qualities of files to detect viral activity.

input device: A hardware device used to enter, or input, data (text, images, and sounds) and instructions (user responses and commands) into a computer. Some input devices are keyboards and mice.

instant messaging (IM) A program that enables users to communicate online in real time with others who are also online.

intellectual property Refers to products derived from the mind, such as works of art and literature, inventions, and software code.

intelligent personal assistant Software designed to perform tasks or services for individuals.

internal hard drive A hard drive that resides within the computer's system unit and that usually holds all permanently stored programs and data.

Internet A network of networks that's the largest network in the world, connecting billions of computers globally.

Internet backbone The main pathway of high-speed communications lines over which all Internet traffic flows.

Internet of Things (IoT) The interconnection of uniquely identifiable embedded computing devices that transfer data over a network without requiring human-to-human or human-to-computer interaction.

Internet Protocol (IP) address The means by which all computers connected to the Internet identify each other. It consists of a unique set of four numbers separated by dots, such as 123.45.178.91.

Internet service provider (ISP) A company that specializes in providing Internet access. ISPs may be specialized providers, like Juno, or companies that provide other services in addition to Internet access (such as phone and cable television).

interrupt A signal that tells the operating system that it's in need of immediate attention.

interrupt handler A special numerical code that prioritizes requests from various devices. These requests then are placed in the interrupt table in the computer's primary memory.

K

kernel (supervisor program) The essential component of the operating system that's responsible for managing the processor and all other components of the computer system. Because it stays in random access memory (RAM) the entire time the computer is powered on, the kernel is called memory resident.

keyboard A hardware device used to enter typed data and commands into a computer.

keystroke logger (keylogger) A type of spyware program that monitors keystrokes with the intent of stealing passwords, login IDs, or credit card information.

keyword (1) A specific word a user wishes to query (or look for) in an Internet search. (2) A specific word that has a predefined meaning in a particular programming language.

kilobyte (KB) A unit of computer storage equal to approximately 1,000 bytes.

L

laptop (or notebook) computer A portable computer with a keyboard, a monitor, and other devices integrated into a single compact case.

large format printer A printer that prints on oversized paper. Often used for creating banners and signs.

laser printer A nonimpact printer known for quick and quiet production and high-quality printouts.

latency The process that occurs after the read/write head of the hard drive locates the correct track and then waits for the correct sector to spin to the read/write head.

legacy technology Comprises computing devices, software, or peripherals that use techniques, parts, and methods from an earlier time that are no longer popular.

light-emitting diode (LED) A newer, more energy-efficient technology used in monitors. It may result in better color accuracy and thinner panels than traditional LCD monitors.

Linux An open-source operating system based on UNIX. Because of the stable nature of this operating system, it's often used on web servers.

liquid crystal display (LCD) The technology used in flat-panel computer monitors.

live bookmark A bookmark that delivers updates as soon as they become available, using Really Simple Syndication (RSS).

local apps Apps installed on your computing device that usually do not require an Internet connection to function.

local area network (LAN) A network in which the nodes are located within a small geographic area.

logic bomb A computer virus that runs when a certain set of conditions is met, such as when a program is launched a specific number of times.

logical port A virtual communications gateway or path that enables a computer to organize requests for information (such as web page downloads and e-mail routing) from other networks or computers.

logical port blocking A condition in which a firewall is configured to ignore all incoming packets that request access to a certain port so that no unwanted requests will get through to the computer.

M

Mac OS The first commercially available operating system to incorporate a graphical user interface (GUI) with user-friendly pointand- click technology.

machine cycle The series of steps a central processing unit goes through when it performs a program instruction.

macro virus A virus that's distributed by hiding it inside a macro.

macro A small program that groups a series of commands to run as a single command.

mainframe A large, expensive computer that supports hundreds or thousands of users simultaneously and executes many different programs at the same time.

malware Software that's intended to render a system temporarily or permanently useless or to penetrate a computer system completely for purposes of information gathering. Examples include spyware, viruses, worms, and Trojan horses.

master boot record A small program that runs whenever a computer boots up.

megabyte (MB) A unit of computer storage equal to approximately 1 million bytes.

memory module (memory card) A small circuit board that holds a series of random access memory (RAM) chips.

menu-driven interface A user interface in which the user chooses a command from menus displayed on the screen.

metasearch engine A search engine, such as Dogpile, that searches other search engines rather than individual websites.

metropolitan area network (MAN) A wide area network (WAN) that links users in a specific geographic area (such as within a city or county).

microphone (mic) A device that allows you to capture sound waves, such as those created by your voice, and to transfer them to digital format on your computer.

Microsoft account Registered user profile with specific user id and password to log into Windows account from any machine and access familiar desktop and applications.

mobile apps Apps installed on mobile computing devices (such as tablets or phones). Usually these apps require an Internet connection to provide full functionality.

mobile broadband Connection to the Internet through the same cellular network that cell phones use to get 3G or 4G Internet access.

mobile hotspot Devices that enable you to connect more than one device to the Internet; they require access to a data plan. Most smartphones have this capability built-in.

mobile switching center A central location that receives cell phone requests for service from a base station.

modem A device that connects a network to the Internet.

monitor (display screen) A common output device that displays text, graphics, and video as soft copies (copies that can be seen only on screen).

Moore's Law A prediction, named after Gordon Moore, the co-founder of Intel; states that the number of transistors on a central processing unit chip will double every two years.

motherboard A special circuit board in the system unit that contains the central processing unit, the memory (RAM) chips, and the slots available for expansion cards; all of the other boards (video cards, sound cards, and so on) connect to it to receive power and to communicate.

mouse A hardware device used to enter user responses and commands into a computer.

multi-factor authentication A process that requires two of the three assigned factors be demonstrated before authentication is granted.

multimedia Anything that involves one or more forms of media plus text.

multimedia message service (MMS) A service that allows users to send messages that include text, sound, images, and video clips to other phones or e-mail addresses.

multimedia software Programs that include image-, video-, and audio-editing software, animation software, and other specialty software required to produce computer games, animations, and movies.

multipartite virus Literally meaning "multipart" virus; a type of computer virus that attempts to infect computers using more than one method.

multitask The ability of an operating system to perform more than one process at a time.

multiuser operating system (network operating system) An operating system that enables more than one user to access the computer system at one time by efficiently juggling all the requests from multiple users.

N

near field communication (NFC) A set of communication protocols that enable devices to communicate with each other when they are held in close proximity. NFC is commonly used for mobile payments.

network A group of two or more computers (or nodes) that are configured to share information and resources such as printers, files, and databases.

network adapter A device that enables the computer (or peripheral) to communicate with the network using a common data communication language, or protocol.

network address translation (NAT) A process that firewalls use to assign internal Internet protocol addresses on a network.

network administration Involves tasks such as (1) installing new computers and devices, (2) monitoring the network to ensure it's performing efficiently, (3) updating and installing new software on the network, and (4) configuring, or setting up, proper security for a network.

network architecture The design of a computer network; includes both physical and logical design.

network interface card (NIC) An expansion card that enables a computer to connect other computers or to a cable modem to facilitate a high-speed Internet connection.

network navigation device A device on a network such as a router or switch that moves data signals around the network.

network operating system (NOS) Software that handles requests for information, Internet access, and the use of peripherals for the rest of the network node, providing the services necessary for the computers on the network to communicate.

network-attached storage (NAS) device A specialized computing device designed to store and manage network data.

network-ready device A device (such as a printer or an external hard drive) that can be attached directly to a network instead of needing to attach to a computer on the network.

node A device connected to a network such as a computer, a peripheral (such as a printer), or a communications device (such as a modem).

nonimpact printer A printer that sprays ink or uses laser beams to make marks on the paper. The most common nonimpact printers are inkjet and laser printers.

nonvolatile storage Permanent storage, as in read-only memory (ROM).

O

offshoring When outsourcing is done by a company located in a country other than the one in which the firm procuring the services is physically located.

open source software Program code made publicly available for free; it can be copied, distributed, or changed without the stringent copyright protections of proprietary software products.

operating system (OS) The system software that controls the way in which a computer system functions, including the management of hardware, peripherals, and software.

optical drive A hardware device that uses lasers or light to read from, and even write to, CDs, DVDs, or Blu-ray discs.

optical media Portable storage devices, such as CDs, DVDs, and Blu-ray discs, that use a laser to read and write data.

optical mouse A mouse that uses an internal sensor or laser to control the mouse's movement. The sensor sends signals to the computer, telling it where to move the pointer on the screen.

organic light-emitting diode (OLED) displays Displays that use organic compounds to produce light when exposed to an electric current. Unlike LCDs, OLEDs do not require a backlight to function and therefore draw less power and have a much thinner display, sometimes as thin as 3 mm.

output device A device that sends processed data and information out of a computer in the form of text, pictures (graphics), sounds (audio), or video.

outsourcing A process whereby a business hires a third-party firm to provide business services that were previously handled by in-house employees.

overclocking Running the central processing unit at a speed faster than the manufacturer recommends.

P

packet A small segment of data that's bundled for sending over transmission media. Each packet contains the address of the computer or peripheral device to which it's being sent.

packet analyzer (sniffer) A computer hardware device or software program designed to detect and record digital information being transmitted over a network.

packet filtering A process in which firewalls are configured so that they filter out packets sent to specific logical ports.

paging The process of swapping data or instructions that have been placed in the swap file for later use back into active random access memory (RAM). The contents of the hard drive's swap file then become less active data or instructions.

path (subdirectory) The information after the slash that indicates a particular file or path (or subdirectory) within the website.

path separator The backslash mark (\)used by Microsoft Windows and DOS in file names. Mac files use a colon (:), and UNIX and Linux use the forward slash (/) as the path separator.

peer-to-peer (P2P) network A network in which each node connected to the network can communicate directly with every other node on the network.

peer-to-peer (P2P) sharing The process of users transferring files between computers.

peripheral device A device such as a monitor, printer, or keyboard that connects to the system unit through a data port.

personal area network (PAN) A network used for communication among devices close to one person, such as smartphones, laptops, and tablets, using wireless technologies such as Bluetooth.

personal ethics The set of formal or informal ethical principles that an individual uses to guide their ethical decisions.

personal firewall A firewall specifically designed for home networks.

personal information manager (PIM) software Programs such as Microsoft Outlook or Lotus Organizer that strive to replace the various management tools found on a traditional desk such as a calendar, address book, notepad, and to-do lists.

petabyte 10^{15} bytes of digital information.

pharming Planting malicious code on a computer that alters the browser's ability to find web addresses and that directs users to bogus websites.

phishing The process of sending e-mail messages to lure Internet users into revealing personal information such as credit card or Social Security numbers or other sensitive information that could lead to identity theft.

physical memory The amount of random access memory (RAM) that's installed in a computer.

piggybacking The process of connecting to a wireless network without the permission of the owner of the network.

pinning The process through which you choose which applications are visible on the Windows Start screen.

pixel A single point that creates the images on a computer monitor. Pixels are illuminated by an electron beam that passes rapidly back and forth across the back of the screen so that the pixels appear to glow continuously.

platform The combination of a computer's operating system and processor. The two most common platform types are the PC and the Apple.

platter A thin, round, metallic storage plate stacked onto the hard drive spindle.

Plug and Play (PnP) The technology that enables the operating system, once it is booted up, to recognize automatically any new peripherals and to configure them to work with the system.

podcast A clip of audio or video content that's broadcast over the Internet using compressed audio or video files in formats such as MP3.

polymorphic virus A virus that changes its virus signature (the binary pattern that makes the virus identifiable) every time it infects a new file. This makes it more difficult for antivirus programs to detect the virus.

port An interface through which external devices are connected to the computer.

positive psychology A field that attempts to discover the causes of happiness rather than to address the treatment of mental dysfunctions.

power supply A power supply regulates the wall voltage to the voltages required by computer chips; it's housed inside the system unit.

power-on self-test (POST) The first job the basic input/output system (BIOS) performs, ensuring that essential peripheral devices are attached and operational. This process consists of a test on the video card and video memory, a BIOS identification process (during which the BIOS version, manufacturer, and data are displayed on the monitor), and a memory test to ensure memory chips are working properly.

preemptive multitasking When the operating system processes the task assigned a higher priority before processing a task that has been assigned a lower priority.

presentation software An application program for creating dynamic slide shows, such as Microsoft PowerPoint or Apple Keynote.

pretexting The act of creating an invented scenario (the pretext) to convince someone to divulge information.

printer A common output device that creates tangible or hard copies of text and graphics.

processing Manipulating or organizing data into information.

productivity software Programs that enable a user to perform various tasks generally required in home, school, and business. Examples include word processing, spreadsheet, presentation, personal information management, and database programs.

program A series of instructions to be followed by a computer to accomplish a task.

program file Files that are used in the running of software programs and that do not store data.

project management tools Software designed to help assess the progress of a project as it moves towards completion.

projector A device that can project images from your computer onto a wall or viewing screen.

proprietary (commercial) software Custom software application that's owned and controlled by the company that created it.

Q

quarantining The placement (by antivirus software) of a computer virus in a secure area on the hard drive so that it won't spread infection to other files.

quick response (QR) code Technology that lets any piece of print in the real world host a live link to online information and video content.

QWERTY keyboard A keyboard that gets its name from the first six letters on the top-left row of alphabetic keys on the keyboard.

R

RAID 0 The strategy of running two hard drives in one system, cutting in half the time it takes to write a file.

RAID 1 The strategy of mirroring all the data written on one hard drive to a second hard drive, providing an instant backup of all data.

random access memory (RAM) The computer's temporary storage space or shortterm memory. It's located in a set of chips on the system unit's motherboard, and its capacity is measured in megabytes or gigabytes.

read/write head The mechanism that retrieves (reads) and records (writes) the magnetic data to and from a data disk.

read-only memory (ROM) A set of memory chips, located on the motherboard, which stores data and instructions that cannot be changed or erased; it holds all the instructions the computer needs to start up.

Really Simple Syndication (RSS) An XML–based format that allows frequent updates of content on the World Wide Web.

real-time operating system (RTOS) A program with a specific purpose that must guarantee certain response times for particular computing tasks or else the machine's application is useless. Real-time operating systems are found in many types of robotic equipment.

Recycle Bin A folder on a Windows desktop in which deleted files from the hard drive are held until permanently purged from the system.

redundant array of independent disks (RAID) A set of strategies for using more than one drive in a system.

registry A portion of the hard drive containing all the different configurations (settings) used by the Windows operating system as well as by other applications.

Reset this PC A utility program in Windows 10 that attempts to diagnose and fix errors in Windows system files that are causing a computer to behave improperly.

resolution The clearness or sharpness of an image, which is controlled by the number of pixels displayed on the screen.

root directory The top level of the filing structure in a computer system. In Windows computers, the root directory of the hard drive is represented as C:\.

rootkit Programs that allow hackers to gain access to your computer and take almost complete control of it without your knowledge. These programs are designed to subvert normal login procedures to a computer and to hide their operations from normal detection methods.

rotational delay The process that occurs after the read/write head of the hard drive locates the correct track and then waits for the correct sector to spin to the read/write head.

router A device that routes packets of data between two or more networks.

S

sampling rate The number of times per second a signal is measured and converted to a digital value. Sampling rates are measured in kilobits per second.

satellite Internet A way to connect to the Internet using a small satellite dish, which is placed outside the home and is connected to a computer with coaxial cable. The satellite company then sends the data to a satellite orbiting the Earth. The satellite, in turn, sends the data back to the satellite dish and to the computer.

scanner A type of input device that inputs images into computers.

scareware A type of malware that's downloaded onto your computer and that tries to convince you that your computer is infected with a virus or other type of malware.

script A list of commands (mini-programs or macros) that can be executed on a computer without user interaction.

search engine A set of programs that searches the web for specific words (or keywords) you wish to query (or look for) and that then returns a list of the websites on which those keywords are found.

sector A section of a hard drive platter, wedge-shaped from the center of the platter to the edge.

secure sockets layer A network security protocol that provides for the encryption of data transmitted using the Internet. The current versions of all major web browsers support SSL.

seek time The time it takes for the hard drive's read/write heads to move over the surface of the disk to the correct track.

semantic web (Web 3.0) An evolving extension of the World Wide Web in which information is defined in such a way as to make it more easily readable by computers.

server A computer that provides resources to other computers on a network.

service set identifier (SSID) A network name that wireless routers use to identify themselves.

short message service (SMS) Technology that enables short text messages (up to 160 characters) to be sent over mobile networks.

simulation programs Software, often used for training purposes, which allows the user to experience or control an event as if it's reality.

Sleep mode A low-power mode for electronic devices such as computers that saves electric power consumption and saves the last-used settings. When the device is "woken up," work is resumed more quickly than when cold booting the computer.

smart home A house in which devices and appliances are automated or controlled by apps.

smartphone A device with features of a computer including a wide assortment of apps, media players, high-quality cameras, and web connectivity.

social commerce A subset of e-commerce that uses social networks to assist in marketing and purchasing products.

social engineering Any technique that uses social skills to generate human interaction for the purpose of enticing individuals to reveal sensitive information.

social media Websites or apps that allow users to create and share content and/or participate in social networking with others.

social media directors People who are responsible for directing the company strategy on all social media platforms where the company has a presence.

social networking A means by which people use the Internet to communicate and share information among their immediate friends and to meet and connect with others through common interests, experiences, and friends.

software The set of computer programs or instructions that tells the computer what to do and that enables it to perform different tasks.

Software as a Service (SaaS) Software that's delivered on demand over the Internet.

software license An agreement between the user and the software developer that must be accepted before installing the software on a computer.

software piracy Violating a software license agreement by copying an application onto more computers than the license agreement permits.

software suite A collection of software programs that have been bundled together as a package.

solid-state drive (SSD) A storage device that uses the same kind of memory that flash drives use but that can reach data in only a tenth of the time a flash drive requires.

solid-state drive (SSD) A storage device that uses the same kind of memory that flash drives use but that can reach data in only a tenth of the time a flash drive requires.

solid-state hybrid drive (SSHD) A drive that is a combination of both a mechanical hard drive and an SSD into a single device.

sound card An expansion card that attaches to the motherboard inside the system unit and that enables the computer to produce sounds by providing a connection for the speakers and microphone.

spam Unwanted or junk e-mail.

spam filter An option you can select in your e-mail account that places known or suspected spam messages into a folder other than your inbox.

speakers Output devices for sound.

spear phishing A targeted phishing attack that sends e-mails to people known to be customers of a company. Such attacks have a much greater chance of successfully getting individuals to reveal sensitive data.

spooler A program that helps coordinate all print jobs being sent to the printer at the same time.

spreadsheet software An application program such as Microsoft Excel or Lotus 1-2-3 that enables a user to do calculations and numerical analyses easily.

spyware An unwanted piggyback program that downloads with the software you want to install from the Internet and then runs in the background of your system.

stakeholders People or entities who are affected by the operations of a business.

Start menu A feature in Windows 10 that provides access to all applications in one convenient screen.

stealth virus A virus that temporarily erases its code from the files where it resides and hides in the active memory of the computer.

streaming media Multimedia (audio and video) that is fed continuously fed to the browser to avoid waiting for the entire file to download completely before listening to or watching it.

stylus A pen-shaped device used to tap or write on touch-sensitive screens.

supercomputer A specially designed computer that can perform complex calculations extremely rapidly; used in situations in which complex models requiring intensive mathematical calculations are needed (such as weather forecasting or atomic energy research).

SuperFetch A memory-management technique used by Windows 7. Monitors the applications you use the most and preloads them into your system memory so that they'll be ready to go.

surge protector A device that protects computers and other electronic devices from power surges.

surround sound A type of audio processing that makes the listener experience sound as if it were coming from all directions.

surround-sound speaker A system of speakers set up in such a way that it surrounds an entire area (and the people in it) with sound.

swap file (page file) A temporary storage area on the hard drive where the operating system "swaps out" or moves the data or instructions from random access memory (RAM) that haven't recently been used. This process takes place when more RAM space is needed.

switch A device for transmitting data on a network. A switch makes decisions, based on the media access control address of the data, as to where the data is to be sent.

synchronizing (or syncing) The process of updating data on portable devices (such as a cell phone or iPod) and a computer so that they contain the same data.

system evaluation The process of looking at a computer's subsystems, what they do, and how they perform to determine whether the computer system has the right hardware components to do what the user ultimately wants it to do.

system files The main files of an operating system.

system requirements The set of minimum storage, memory capacity, and processing standards recommended by the software manufacturer to ensure proper operation of a software application.

System Restore A utility in Windows that restores system settings to a specific previous date when everything was working properly.

system restore point In Windows, a snapshot of your entire system's settings used for restoring your system to a prior point in time.

system software The set of programs that enables a computer's hardware devices and application software to work together; it includes the operating system and utility programs.

system unit The metal or plastic case that holds all the physical parts of the computer together, including the computer's processor (its brains), its memory, and the many circuit boards that help the computer function.

T

tablet (2-in-1) PC A laptop computer designed specifically to work with handwriting recognition technology.

tablet computer A mobile computer, such as the Apple iPad or Samsung Galaxy Tab, integrated into a flat multitouch-sensitive screen. It uses an onscreen virtual keyboard, but separate keyboards can be connected via Bluetooth or wires.

tagging (social bookmarking) A keyword or term that Internet users assign to a web resource such as a web page, digital image, or video.

Task Manager A Windows utility that shows programs currently running and permits you to exit nonresponsive programs when you click End Task.

taskbar In later versions of Windows operating systems, a feature that displays open and favorite applications for easy access.

tax preparation software An application program, such as Intuit's TurboTax or H&R Block's At Home, for preparing state and federal taxes. Each program offers a complete set of tax forms and instructions as well as expert advice on how to complete each form.

telephony The use of equipment to provide voice communications over a distance.

template A form included in many productivity applications that provides the basic structure for a particular kind of document, spreadsheet, or presentation.

terabyte (TB) 1,099,511,627,776 bytes or 2^{40} bytes.

tethering Approach which makes sure that as long as you have a 3G signal, your computer can access the Internet even when it tells you there are no available wireless networks. Several smartphones offer this capability.

thermal printer A printer that works either by melting wax-based ink onto ordinary paper (in a process called *thermal wax transfer printing*) or by burning dots onto specially coated paper (in a process called *direct thermal printing*).

thrashing A condition of excessive paging in which the operating system becomes sluggish.

throughput The actual speed of data transfer that's achieved. It's usually less than the data transfer rate and is measured in megabits per second (Mbps).

Thunderbolt port A high speed input/ output port; Thunderbolt 2 provides two channels of 20 Gbps capacity on one port.

time bomb A virus that's triggered by the passage of time or on a certain date.

top-level domain The suffix, often of three letters (such as .com or .edu), in the domain name that indicates the kind of organization the host is.

touch pad (trackpad) A small, touchsensitive screen at the base of a laptop keyboard that's used to direct the cursor.

touch screen A type of monitor (or display in a smartphone or tablet computer) that accepts input from a user touching the screen.

track A concentric circle that serves as a storage area on a hard drive platter.

transmission media The radio waves or the physical system (cable) that transports data on a network.

Trojan horse A computer program that appears to be something useful or desirable (such as a game or a screen saver), but at the same time does something malicious in the background without the user's knowledge.

twisted-pair cable Cables made of copper wires that are twisted around each other and are surrounded by a plastic jacket (such as traditional home phone wire).

U

ultrabook A full-featured but lightweight laptop computer that features a low-power processor and a solid-state drive; it tries to reduce its size and weight to extend battery life without sacrificing performance.

Uniform Resource Locator (URL) A website's unique address; an example is microsoft.com.

universal serial bus (USB) port A port that can connect a wide variety of peripheral devices to the computer, including keyboards, printers, mice, smartphones, external hard drives, flash drives, and digital cameras.

UNIX An operating system originally conceived in 1969 by Ken Thompson and Dennis Ritchie of AT&T's Bell Labs. In 1974, the UNIX code was rewritten in the standard programming language C. Today there are various commercial versions of UNIX.

unshielded twisted-pair (UTP) cable The most popular transmission media option for Ethernet networks. UTP cable is composed of four pairs of wires that are twisted around each other to reduce electrical interference.

user interface Part of the operating system that enables individuals to interact with the computer.

utility program A small program that performs many of the general housekeeping tasks for the computer, such as system maintenance and file compression.

V

vertical market software Software that's developed for and customized to a specific industry's needs (such as a wood inventory system for a sawmill) as opposed to software that's useful across a range of industries (such as word processing software).

video card (video adapter) An expansion card that's installed inside a system unit to translate binary data (the 1s and 0s the computer uses) into the images viewed on the monitor.

video graphics array (VGA) port: A port to which a cathode ray tube monitor connects.

video log (vlog or video blog) A personal online journal that uses video as the primary content in addition to text, images, and audio.

video memory Random access memory that's included as part of a video card.

virtual desktops A Windows 10 feature that allows you to organize groups of windows into different displays.

virtual memory The space on the hard drive where the operating system stores data if there isn't enough random access memory to hold all of the programs you're currently trying to run.

virtual private network (VPN) A network that uses the public Internet communications infrastructure to build a secure, private network among various locations.

virus A computer program that attaches itself to another computer program (known as the host program) and attempts to spread itself to other computers when files are exchanged.

virus signature A portion of the virus code that's unique to a particular computer virus and that makes it identifiable by antivirus software.

Voice over Internet Protocol (VoIP) A technology that facilitates making telephone calls across the Internet instead of using conventional telephone lines.

voice recognition software Software that allows you to control your computing devices by speaking into the microphone instead of using a keyboard or mouse.

volatile storage Temporary storage, such as in random access memory. When the power is off, the data in volatile storage is cleared out.

W

warm boot The process of restarting the system while it's powered on.

Web 2.0 Tools and web-based services that emphasize online collaboration and sharing among users.

web authoring software Programs you can use to design interactive web pages without knowing any HyperText Markup Language (HTML) code.

web browser (browser) Software installed on a computer system that allows individuals to locate, view, and navigate the web.

web server A computer running a specialized operating system that enables it to host web pages (and other information) and to provide requested web pages to clients.

web-based apps A program that is hosted on a website and that doesn't require installation on the computer.

web-based e-mail A type of e-mail system that's managed by a web browser and that allows access to e-mail from the web.

webcam A small camera that sits on top of a computer monitor (connected to the computer by a cable) or that's built into a laptop computer and is usually used to transfer live video.

webcast A location on the web.

whistle-blowers People who report businesses to regulatory agencies for committing illegal acts, or who expose unethical (but still legal) acts committed by their employers by publicizing unethical behavior.

white-hat hacker (ethical hacker) A hacker who breaks into systems just for the challenge of it (and who doesn't wish to steal or wreak havoc on the systems). Such hackers tout themselves as experts who are performing a needed service for society by helping companies realize the vulnerabilities that exist in their systems.

whole-house surge protector A surge protector that's installed on (or near) the breaker panel of a home and that protects all electronic devices in the home from power surges.

wide area network (WAN) A network made up of local area networks (LANs) connected over long distances.

wiki A type of website that allows anyone visiting the site to change its content by adding, removing, or editing the content.

Windows 10 Newest release of Microsoft's operating system that provides an interface optimized for touch-screen devices and is designed to run across all devices: phones, tablets, laptops, and desktops.

Windows Microsoft's operating system that incorporates a user-friendly, visual interface.

wireless fidelity (WiFi) The 802.11 standard for wireless data transmissions established by the Institute of Electrical and Electronics Engineers (IEEE).

wireless Internet service provider (wireless ISP): An ISP that provides service to wireless devices such as smartphones.

wireless range extender A device that amplifies your wireless signal to get it out to parts of your home that are experiencing poor connectivity.

wizard A step-by-step guide that walks a user through the necessary steps to complete a complicated task.

word processing software Programs used to create and edit written documents such as papers, letters, and résumés.

World Wide Web (WWW or the web) The part of the Internet used the most. What distinguishes the web from the rest of the Internet are (1) its use of common communication protocols (such as Transmission Control Protocol/Internet Protocol, or TCP/IP) and special languages (such as the HyperText Markup Language,or HTML) that enable different computers to talk to each other and display information in compatible formats and (2) its use of special links (called hyperlinks) that enable users to jump from one place to another in the web.

worm A program that attempts to travel between systems through network connections to spread infections. Worms can run independently of host file execution and are active in spreading themselves.

Z

zombie A computer that is controlled by a hacker who uses it to launch attacks on other computer systems.

Index

GO! With Office 2013, *Volume 1*, First Edition
by Shelley Gaskin, Alicia Vargas, and
Carolyn McLellan

Word Chapters 1-3, Excel Chapters 1-3,
Access Chapters 1-3, Powerpoint Chapters 1-3

Table of Contents

Excel Introduction to Microsoft Excel 2013 303

Chapter 2 Using Functions, Creating Tables, and Managing Large Workbooks 369

Chapter 3 Enhancing a Presentation with Animation, Video, Tables, and Charts

About the Authors

Shelley Gaskin, Series Editor, is a professor in the Business and Computer Technology Division at Pasadena City College in Pasadena, California. She holds a bachelor's degree in Business Administration from Robert Morris College (Pennsylvania), a master's degree in Business from Northern Illinois University, and a doctorate in Adult and Community Education from Ball State University (Indiana). Before joining Pasadena City College, she spent 12 years in the computer industry, where she was a systems analyst, sales representative, and director of Customer Education with Unisys Corporation. She also worked for Ernst & Young on the development of large systems applications for their clients. She has written and developed training materials for custom systems applications in both the public and private sector, and has also written and edited numerous computer application textbooks.

This book is dedicated to my students, who inspire me every day.

Alicia Vargas is a faculty member in Business Information Technology at Pasadena City College. She holds a master's and a bachelor's degree in business education from California State University, Los Angeles, and has authored several textbooks and training manuals on Microsoft Word, Microsoft Excel, and Microsoft PowerPoint.

This book is dedicated with all my love to my husband Vic, who makes everything possible; and to my children Victor, Phil, and Emmy, who are an unending source of inspiration and who make everything worthwhile.

Carolyn McLellan is the dean of the Division of Information Technology and Business at Tidewater Community College in Virginia Beach, Virginia. She has a master's degree in Secondary Education from Regent University and a bachelor's degree in Business Education from Old Dominion University. She taught for Norfolk Public Schools for 17 years in Business Education and served as a faculty member at Tidewater Community College for eight years teaching networking, where she developed over 23 new courses and earned the Microsoft Certified Trainer and Microsoft Certified System Engineer industry certifications. In addition to teaching, Carolyn loves to play volleyball, boogie board at the beach, bicycle, crochet, cook, and read.

This book is dedicated to my daughters, Megan and Mandy, who have my eternal love; to my mother, Jean, who always believes in me and encouraged me to become a teacher; to my sister Debbie, who was my first student and who inspires me with her strength in overcoming hardships; to my niece Jenna, for her bravery, composure, and beauty; to my grandsons, Jordan and Dexter, who bring me happiness and a renewed joie de vivre; and to the students and IT faculty at Tidewater Community College.

GO! with Office 2013

GO! with Office 2013 is the right solution for you and your students in today's fast-moving, mobile environment. The GO! Series content focuses on the real-world job skills students need to succeed in the workforce. They learn Office by working step-by-step through practical job-related projects that put the core functionality of Office in context. And as has always been true of the GO! Series, students learn the important concepts when they need them, and they never get lost in instruction, because the GO! Series uses Microsoft procedural syntax. Students learn how and learn why—at the teachable moment.

After completing the instructional projects, students are ready to apply the skills in a wide variety of progressively challenging projects that require them to solve problems, think critically, and create projects on their own. *GO! with Office 2013* focuses on today's mobile worker wherever, whenever, and from whatever device. Students engage in hands-on projects covering Office Online (formerly Web Apps), Office 365, collaborative tasks, and touch devices, so students are prepared to work in any environment. And, for those who want to go beyond the classroom and become certified, GO! provides clear MOS preparation guidelines so students know what is needed to ace the Core exam!

What's New

New design reflects the look of Windows 8 and Office 2013 and enhances readability.

Enhanced chapter opener now includes a deeper introduction to the A & B instructional projects and more highly-defined chapter Objectives and Learning Outcomes.

New Application Introductions provide a brief overview of the application and put the chapters in context for students.

Coverage of new features of Office 2013 ensures that students are learning the skills they need to work in today's job market.

New chapter on Windows 8 added because Windows is so integral to teaching Office.

New Office Online versions of Projects A and B and Office 365 Online Collaboration projects using Outlook, SharePoint, and Lync make it easy to teach these tools in your course and help students learn to use touchscreens as well as traditional devices so they know how to get things done from anywhere on any Windows 8 device.

New Application Capstone Projects for each application ensure that students are ready to move on to the next application. Each Application Capstone Project can be found on the Instructor Resource Center and is also a Grader project in MyITLab.

More Grader Projects based on the E, F, and G mastering-level projects, both homework and assessment versions! These projects are written by our GO! authors, who are all instructors in colleges like yours!

New Training & Assessment Simulations are now written by the authors to match the book one-to-one!

New book Capstone project that you can use as a course final, a test-out exam, or any other way you choose. This can be found on the Instructor Resource Site.

New MOS Map on the Instructor Resource Site and in the Annotated Instructor's Edition indicates clearly where each required MOS Objective is covered.

Three Types of Videos help students understand and succeed in the real world:

- ***Student Training Videos*** are broken down by Objective and created by the author—a real instructor teaching the same types of courses that you do. Real personal instruction.
- ***GO! to Work*** videos are short interviews with workers showing how they use Office in their jobs.
- ***GO! for Job Success*** videos relate to the projects in the chapter and cover important career topics such as *Dressing for Success*, *Time Management*, and *Making Ethical Choices*.

New GO! Learn it Online section at the end of the chapter indicates where various student learning activities can be found, including multiple choice and matching activities.

New styles for in-text boxed content: Another Way, Notes, More Knowledge, Alerts, and **new *By Touch* instructions** are included in line with the instruction and not in the margins so that the student is more likely to read this information.

Clearly indicated Build from Scratch projects: GO! has always had many projects that begin "from scratch," and now we have an icon to really call them out!

New Visual Summary focuses on the four key concepts to remember from each chapter.

New Review and Assessment Guide summarizes the end-of-chapter assessments for a quick overview of the different types and levels of assignments and assessments for each chapter.

New Skills and Procedures Summary chart (online at the Instructor Resource Center) summarizes all of the shortcuts and commands covered in the chapter.

New End-of-Chapter Key Term Glossary with definitions for each chapter, plus a comprehensive end-of-book glossary.

New Flipboards and Crossword Puzzles enable students to review the concepts and key terms learned in each chapter by completing online challenges.

Teach the Course You Want in Less Time

A Microsoft® Office textbook designed for student success!

GO!

- **Project-Based** – Students learn by creating projects that they will use in the real world.
- **Microsoft Procedural Syntax** – Steps are written to put students in the right place at the right time.
- **Teachable Moment** – Expository text is woven into the steps—at the moment students need to know it—not chunked together in a block of text that will go unread.
- **Sequential Pagination** – Students have actual page numbers instead of confusing letters and abbreviations.

New Feature

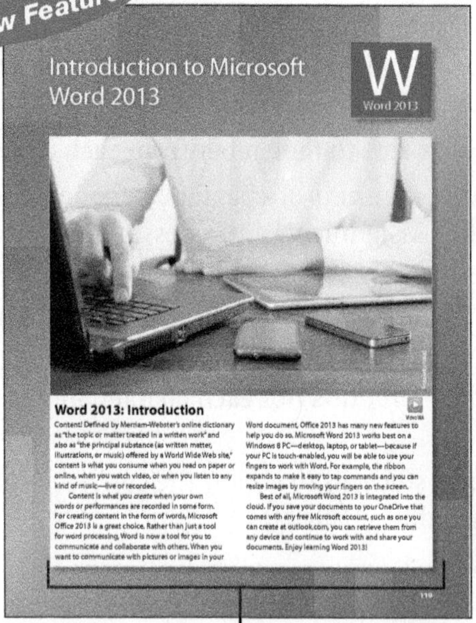

New Application Introductions – provide an overview of the application to prepare students for the upcoming chapters.

Student Outcomes and Learning Objectives – Objectives are clustered around projects that result in student outcomes.

New Design – Provides a more visually appealing and concise display of important content.

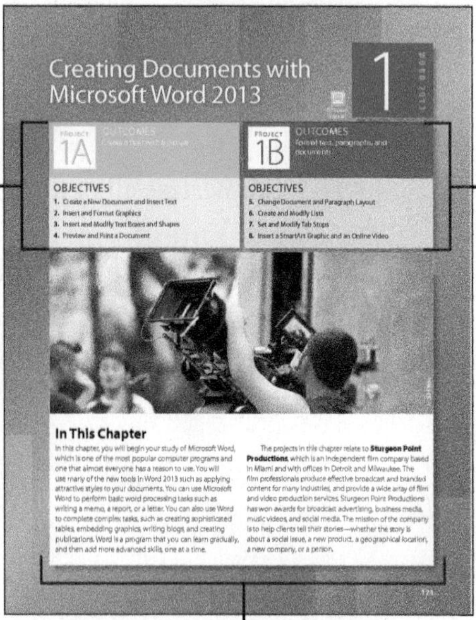

Simulation Training and Assessment – Give your students the most realistic Office 2013 experience with open, realistic, high-fidelity simulations.

Scenario – Each chapter opens with a job-related scenario that sets the stage for the projects the student will create.

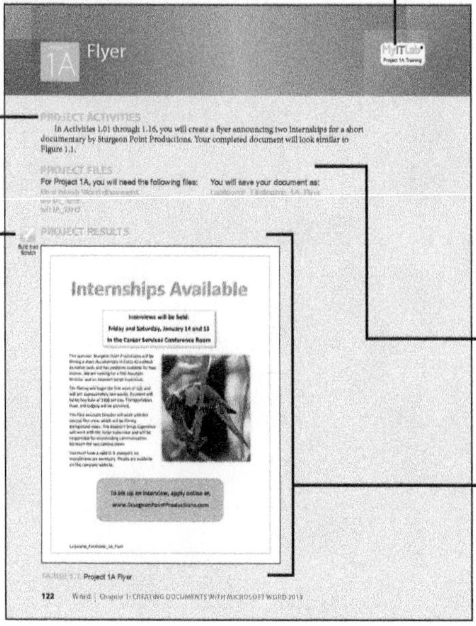

Project Activities – A project summary stated clearly and quickly.

Project Files – Clearly shows students which files are needed for the project and the names they will use to save their documents.

New Build from Scratch icons – enable you to easily see all the projects that the student builds from scratch.

Project Results – Shows students what successful completion looks like.

In-text Features

Another Way, Notes, More Knowledge, Alerts, and By Touch Instructions

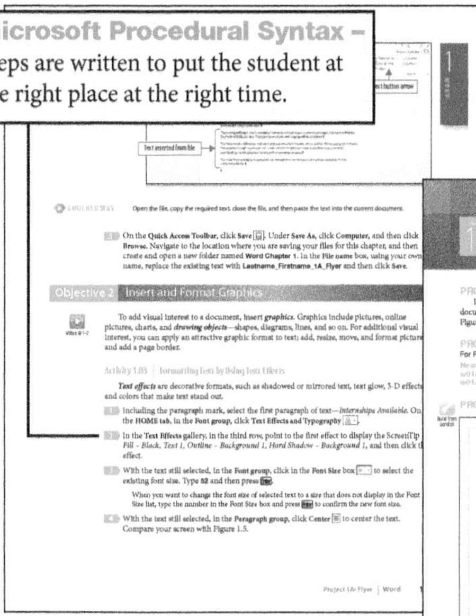

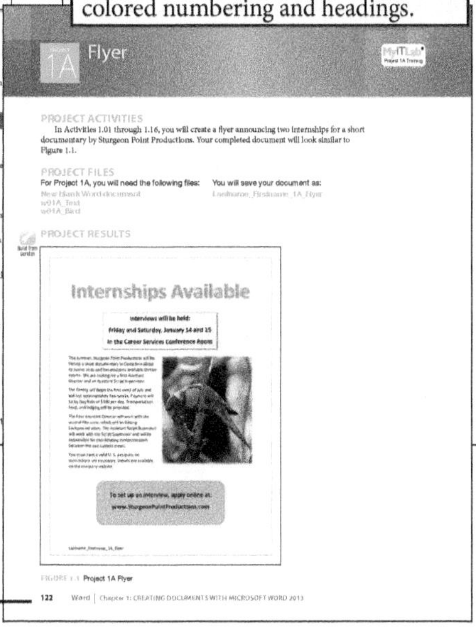

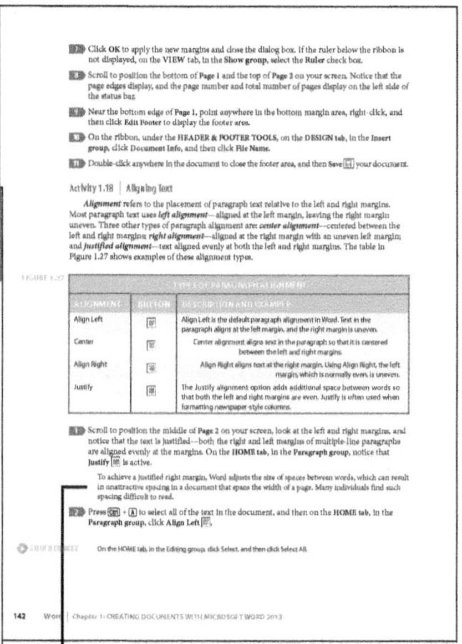

Microsoft Procedural Syntax – Steps are written to put the student at the right place at the right time.

Color Coding – Each chapter has two instructional projects, which is less overwhelming for students than one large chapter project. The two projects are differentiated by different colored numbering and headings.

Sequential Pagination – Students are given actual page numbers to navigate through the textbook instead of confusing letters and abbreviations.

Teachable Moment – Expository text is woven into the steps—at the moment students need to know it—not chunked together in a block of text that will go unread.

End-of-Chapter

Content-Based Assessments – Assessments with defined solutions.

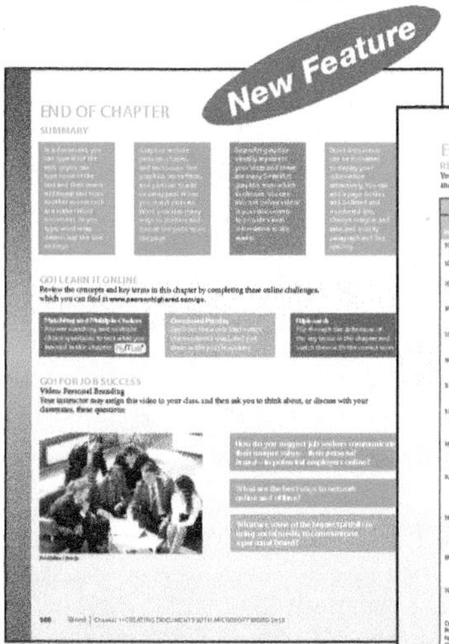

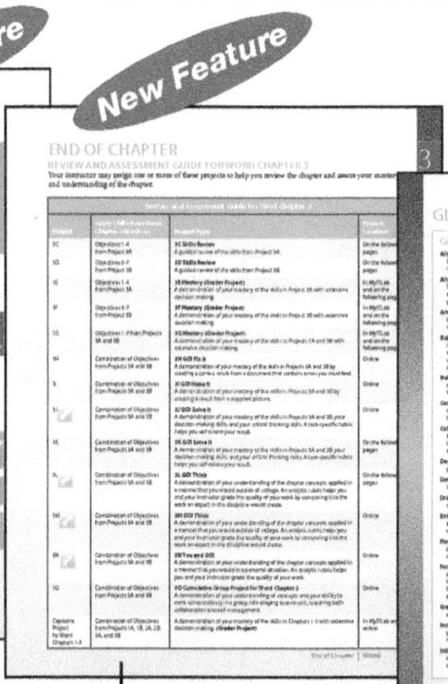

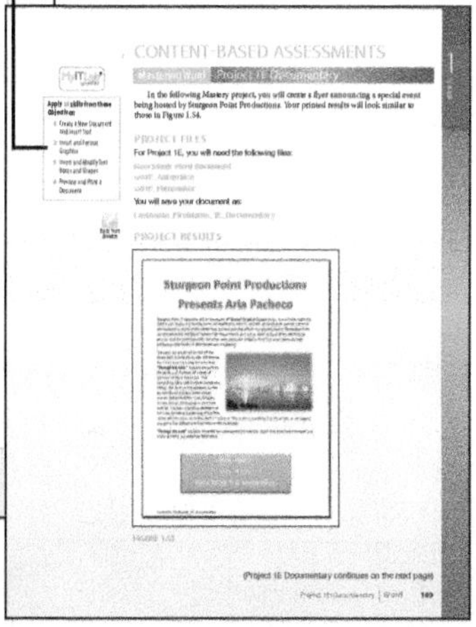

Objective List – Every end-of-chapter project includes a listing of covered objectives from Projects A and B.

Review and Assessment Chart – Displays a comprehensive list of each chapter assessment with a description and location to make planning easier.

End-of-Chapter Glossary – Gives students an easy way to review key terms.

End-of-Chapter

Content-Based Assessments – Assessments with defined solutions. (continued)

Grader projects – Each chapter has six MyITLab Grader projects—three homework and three assessment—clearly indicated by the MyITLab logo.

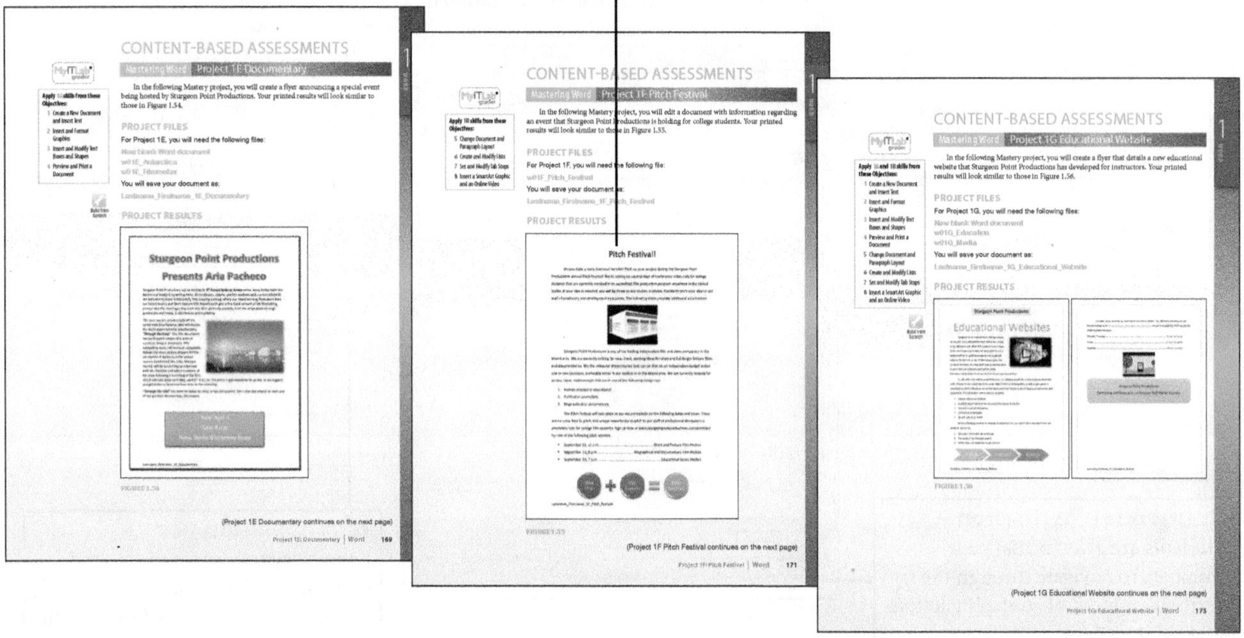

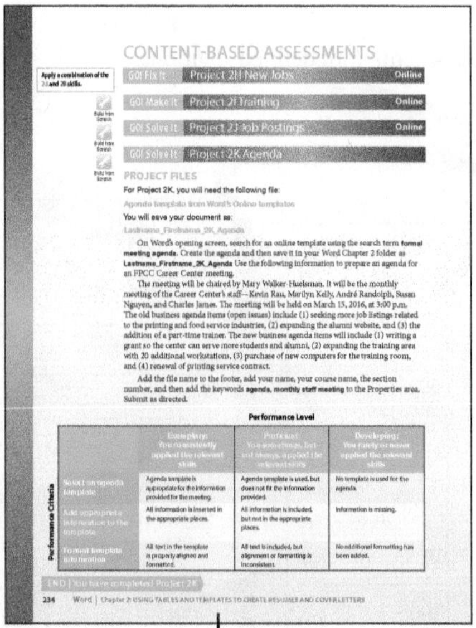

Task-Specific Rubric – A matrix specific to the GO! Solve It projects that states the criteria and standards for grading these defined-solution projects.

End-of-chapter

Outcomes-Based Assessments – Assessments with open-ended solutions.

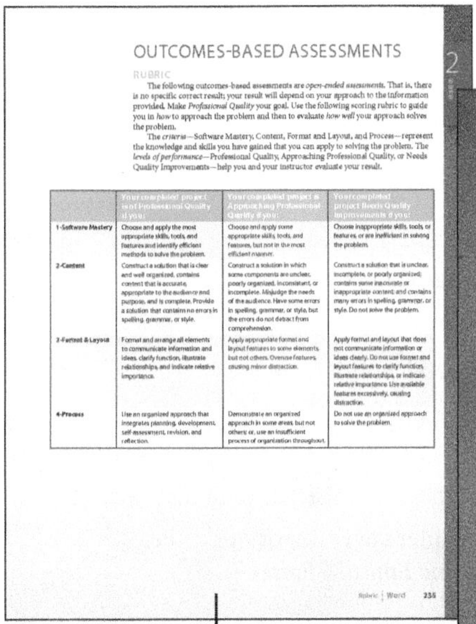

Outcomes Rubric – A matrix specific to the GO! Think projects that states the criteria and standards for grading these open-ended assessments.

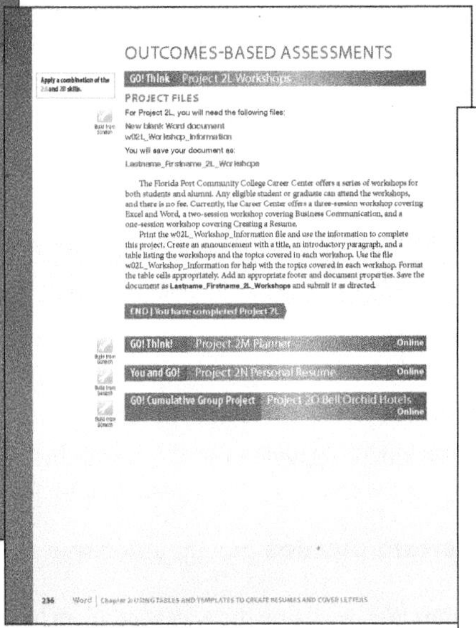

Sample Solution – Outcomes-based assessments include a sample solution so the instructor can compare student work with an example of expert work.

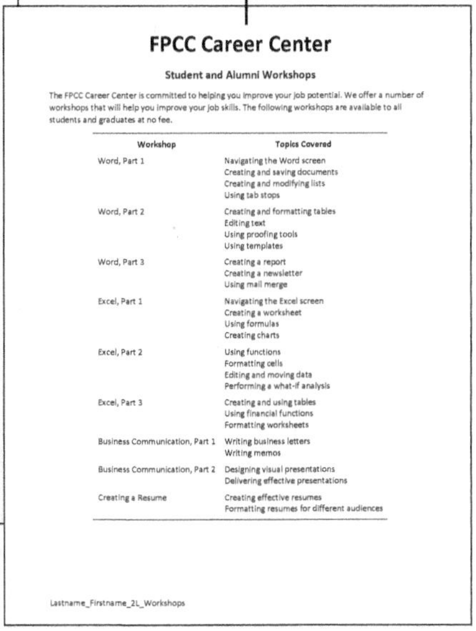

GO! with Microsoft Office 365 – A collaboration project for each chapter teaches students how to use the cloud-based tools of Office 365 to communicate and collaborate from any device, anywhere.

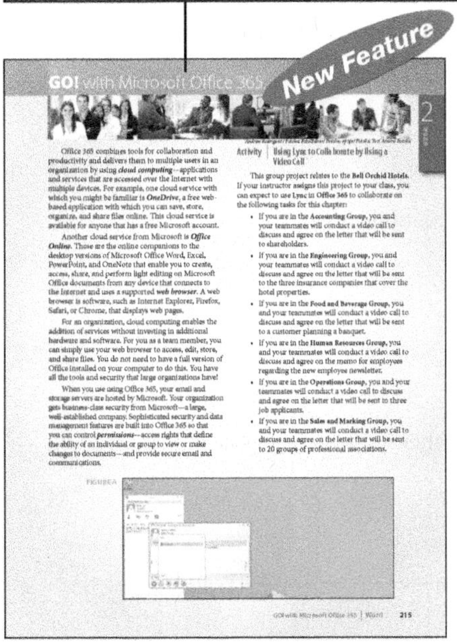

Office Online (formerly Web Apps) – For each instructional project, students can create the same or similar result in the corresponding Office Online application - 24 projects in all!

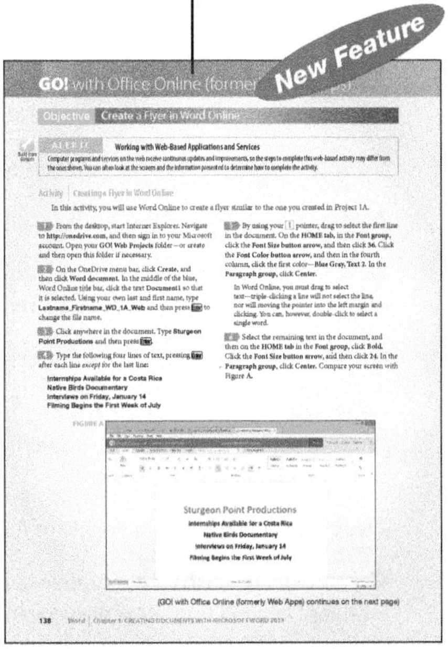

GO! with MyITLab
Gives you a completely integrated solution
Instruction ▪ Training ▪ Assessment
All of the content in the book and MyITLab is written by the authors, who are instructors, so the instruction works seamlessly with the simulation trainings and grader projects — true 1:1.
eText, Training & Assessment Simulations, and Grader Projects

Student Materials

Student Data Files – All student data files are available to all on the Companion Website: www.pearsonhighered.com/go

3 Types of Videos help students understand and succeed in the real world:

- **Student Training Videos** are by Objective and created by the author—a real instructor teaching the same types of courses that you teach.
- ***GO! to Work*** videos are short interviews with workers showing how they use Office in their job.
- ***GO! for Job Success*** videos related to the projects in the chapter cover important career topics such as *Dressing for Success*, *Time Management*, and *Making Ethical Choices*.

Flipboards and crossword puzzles provide a variety of review options for content in each chapter.
Available on the Companion Website using the access code included with your book.
pearsonhighered.com/go

All Instructor and Student materials available at pearsonhighered.com/go

Instructor Materials

Annotated Instructor Edition – An instructor tool includes a full copy of the student textbook and a guide to implementing your course in three different ways, depending on the emphasis you want to place on digital engagement. Also included are teaching tips, discussion topics, and other useful pieces for teaching each chapter.

Assignment Sheets – Lists all the assignments for the chapter. Just add the course information, due dates, and points. Providing these to students ensures they will know what is due and when.

Scripted Lectures – A script to guide your classroom lecture of each instructional project.

Annotated Solution Files – Coupled with the scorecards, these create a grading and scoring system that makes grading easy and efficient.

PowerPoint Lectures – PowerPoint presentations for each chapter.

Audio PowerPoints – Audio versions of the PowerPoint presentations for each chapter.

Scoring Rubrics – Can be used either by students to check their work or by you as a quick check-off for the items that need to be corrected.

Syllabus Templates – For 8-week, 12-week, and 16-week courses.

MOS Map provided at the Instructor Resource Center site and in the Annotated Instructor's Edition, showing where each required MOS Objective is covered either in the book or via additional instructional material provided.

Test Bank – Includes a variety of test questions for each chapter.

Companion Website – Online content such as the Online Chapter Review, Glossary, and Student Data Files are all at www.pearsonhighered.com/go.

Reviewers

GO! Focus Group Participants

Kenneth Mayer	Heald College
Carolyn Borne	Louisiana State University
Toribio Matamoros	Miami Dade College
Lynn Keane	University of South Carolina
Terri Hayes	Broward College
Michelle Carter	Paradise Valley Community College

GO! Reviewers

Abul Sheikh	Abraham Baldwin Agricultural College
John Percy	Atlantic Cape Community College
Janette Hicks	Binghamton University
Shannon Ogden	Black River Technical College
Karen May	Blinn College
Susan Fry	Boise State University
Chigurupati Rani	Borough of Manhattan Community College / CUNY
Ellen Glazer	Broward College
Kate LeGrand	Broward College
Mike Puopolo	Bunker Hill Community College
Nicole Lytle-Kosola	California State University, San Bernardino
Nisheeth Agrawal	Calhoun Community College
Pedro Diaz-Gomez	Cameron
Linda Friedel	Central Arizona College
Gregg Smith	Central Community College
Norm Cregger	Central Michigan University
Lisa LaCaria	Central Piedmont Community College
Steve Siedschlag	Chaffey College
Terri Helfand	Chaffey College
Susan Mills	Chambersburg
Mandy Reininger	Chemeketa Community College
Connie Crossley	Cincinnati State Technical and Community College
Marjorie Deutsch	City University of New York - Queensborough Community College
Mary Ann Zlotow	College of Dupage
Christine Bohnsak	College of Lake County
Gertrude Brier	College of Staten Island
Sharon Brown	College of The Albemarle
Terry Rigsby	Columbia College
Vicki Brooks	Columbia College
Donald Hames	Delgado Community College
Kristen King	Eastern Kentucky University
Kathie Richer	Edmonds Community College
Gary Smith	Elmhurst College
Wendi Kappersw	Embry-Riddle Aeronautical University
Nancy Woolridge	Fullerton College
Abigail Miller	Gateway Community & Technical College
Deep Ramanayake	Gateway Community & Technical College
Gwen White	Gateway Community & Technical College
Debbie Glinert	Gloria K School
Dana Smith	Golf Academy of America
Mary Locke	Greenville Technical College
Diane Marie Roselli	Harrisburg Area Community College
Linda Arnold	Harrisburg Area Community College - Lebanon
Daniel Schoedel	Harrisburg Area Community College - York Campus
Ken Mayer	Heald College
Xiaodong Qiao	Heald College
Donna Lamprecht	Hopkinsville Community College
Kristen Lancaster	Hopkinsville Community College
Johnny Hurley	Iowa Lakes Community College
Linda Halverson	Iowa Lakes Community College
Sarah Kilgo	Isothermal Community College
Chris DeGeare	Jefferson College
David McNair	Jefferson College
Diane Santurri	Johnson & Wales
Roland Sparks	Johnson & Wales University
Ram Raghuraman	Joliet Junior College
Eduardo Suniga	Lansing Community College
Kenneth A. Hyatt	Lonestar College - Kingwood
Glenn Gray	Lonestar College North Harris
Gene Carbonaro	Long Beach City College
Betty Pearman	Los Medanos College
Diane Kosharek	Madison College
Peter Meggison	Massasoit Community College
George Gabb	Miami Dade College
Lennie Alice Cooper	Miami Dade College
Richard Mabjish	Miami Dade College
Victor Giol	Miami Dade College
John Meir	Midlands Technical College
Greg Pauley	Moberly Area Community College
Catherine Glod	Mohawk Valley Community College
Robert Huyck	Mohawk Valley Community College
Kevin Engellant	Montana Western
Philip Lee	Nashville State Community College
Ruth Neal	Navarro College
Sharron Jordan	Navarro College
Richard Dale	New Mexico State University
Lori Townsend	Niagara County Community College
Judson Curry	North Park University
Mary Zegarski	Northampton Community College
Neal Stenlund	Northern Virginia Community Colege
Michael Goeken	Northwest Vista College
Mary Beth Tarver	Northwestern State University
Amy Rutledge	Oakland University
Marcia Braddock	Okefenokee Technical College
Richard Stocke	Oklahoma State University - OKC
Jane Stam	Onondaga Community College
Mike Michaelson	Palomar College
Kungwen (Dave) Chu	Purdue University Calumet
Wendy Ford	City University of New York - Queensborough Community College
Lewis Hall	Riverside City College
Karen Acree	San Juan College
Tim Ellis	Schoolcraft College
Dan Combellick	Scottsdale Community College
Pat Serrano	Scottsdale Community College
Rose Hendrickson	Sheridan College
Kit Carson	South Georgia College
Rebecca Futch	South Georgia State College
Brad Hagy	Southern Illinois University Carbondale
Mimi Spain	Southern Maine Community College
David Parker	Southern Oregon University
Madeline Baugher	Southwestern Oklahoma State University
Brian Holbert	St. Johns River State College
Bunny Howard	St. Johns River State College
Stephanie Cook	State College of Florida
Sharon Wavle	Tompkins Cortland Community College
George Fiori	Tri-County Technical College
Steve St. John	Tulsa Community College
Karen Thessing	University of Central Arkansas
Richard McMahon	University of Houston-Downtown
Shohreh Hashemi	University of Houston-Downtown
Donna Petty	Wallace Community College
Julia Bell	Walters State Community College
Ruby Kowaney	West Los Angeles College
Casey Thompson	Wiregrass Georgia Technical College
DeAnnia Clements	Wiregrass Georgia Technical College

Introduction to Microsoft Word 2013

W
Word 2013

Word 2013: Introduction

Video WA

Content! Defined by Merriam-Webster's online dictionary as "the topic or matter treated in a written work" and also as "the principal substance (as written matter, illustrations, or music) offered by a World Wide Web site," content is what you consume when you read on paper or online, when you watch video, or when you listen to any kind of music—live or recorded.

Content is what you *create* when your own words or performances are recorded in some form. For creating content in the form of words, Microsoft Office 2013 is a great choice. Rather than just a tool for word processing, Word is now a tool for you to communicate and collaborate with others. When you want to communicate with pictures or images in your Word document, Office 2013 has many new features to help you do so. Microsoft Word 2013 works best on a Windows 8 PC—desktop, laptop, or tablet—because if your PC is touch-enabled, you will be able to use your fingers to work with Word. For example, the ribbon expands to make it easy to tap commands and you can resize images by moving your fingers on the screen.

Best of all, Microsoft Word 2013 is integrated into the cloud. If you save your documents to your OneDrive that comes with any free Microsoft account, such as one you can create at outlook.com, you can retrieve them from any device and continue to work with and share your documents. Enjoy learning Word 2013!

Creating Documents with Microsoft Word 2013

1

WORD 2013

GO! to Work Video W1

PROJECT 1A

OUTCOMES
Create a flyer with a picture.

OBJECTIVES

1. Create a New Document and Insert Text
2. Insert and Format Graphics
3. Insert and Modify Text Boxes and Shapes
4. Preview and Print a Document

PROJECT 1B

OUTCOMES
Format text, paragraphs, and documents.

OBJECTIVES

5. Change Document and Paragraph Layout
6. Create and Modify Lists
7. Set and Modify Tab Stops
8. Insert a SmartArt Graphic and an Online Video

A_ya / Fotolia

In This Chapter

In this chapter, you will begin your study of Microsoft Word, which is one of the most popular computer programs and one that almost everyone has a reason to use. You will use many of the new tools in Word 2013 such as applying attractive styles to your documents. You can use Microsoft Word to perform basic word processing tasks such as writing a memo, a report, or a letter. You can also use Word to complete complex tasks, such as creating sophisticated tables, embedding graphics, writing blogs, and creating publications. Word is a program that you can learn gradually, and then add more advanced skills, one at a time.

The projects in this chapter relate to **Sturgeon Point Productions**, which is an independent film company based in Miami and with offices in Detroit and Milwaukee. The film professionals produce effective broadcast and branded content for many industries, and provide a wide array of film and video production services. Sturgeon Point Productions has won awards for broadcast advertising, business media, music videos, and social media. The mission of the company is to help clients tell their stories—whether the story is about a social issue, a new product, a geographical location, a new company, or a person.

PROJECT 1A Flyer

MyITLab®
Project 1A Training

PROJECT ACTIVITIES

In Activities 1.01 through 1.16, you will create a flyer announcing two internships for a short documentary by Sturgeon Point Productions. Your completed document will look similar to Figure 1.1.

PROJECT FILES

For Project 1A, you will need the following files:
New blank Word document
w01A_Text
w01A_Bird

You will save your document as:
Lastname_Firstname_1A_Flyer

PROJECT RESULTS

Build from Scratch

Internships Available

Interviews will be held:

Friday and Saturday, January 14 and 15

In the Career Services Conference Room

This summer, Sturgeon Point Productions will be filming a short documentary in Costa Rica about its native birds and has positions available for two interns. We are looking for a first Assistant Director and an Assistant Script Supervisor.

The filming will begin the first week of July and will last approximately two weeks. Payment will be by Day Rate of $100 per day. Transportation, food, and lodging will be provided.

The First Assistant Director will work with the second film crew, which will be filming background video. The Assistant Script Supervisor will work with the Script Supervisor and will be responsible for coordinating communication between the two camera crews.

You must have a valid U. S. passport; no inoculations are necessary. Details are available on the company website.

To set up an interview, apply online at:

www.SturgeonPointProductions.com

Lastname_Firstname_1A_Flyer

FIGURE 1.1 Project 1A Flyer

NOTE **If You Are Using a Touchscreen**

- Tap an item to click it.
- Press and hold for a few seconds to right-click; release when the information or commands display.
- Touch the screen with two or more fingers and then pinch together to zoom in or stretch your fingers apart to zoom out.
- Slide your finger on the screen to scroll—slide left to scroll right and slide right to scroll left.
- Slide to rearrange—similar to dragging with a mouse.
- Swipe from edge: from right to display charms; from left to expose open apps, snap apps, or close apps; from top or bottom to show commands or close an app.
- Swipe to select—slide an item a short distance with a quick movement—to select an item and bring up commands, if any.

Objective 1 Create a New Document and Insert Text

Video W1-1

When you start Word, documents you have recently opened, if any, display on the left. On the right, you can select either a blank document or a ***template***—a preformatted document that you can use as a starting point and then change to suit your needs. When you create a new document, you can type all of the text or you can type some of the text and then insert additional text from another source.

Activity 1.01 Starting a New Word Document

1. **Start** Word, and then click **Blank document**. On the **HOME tab**, in the **Paragraph group**, if necessary, click **Show/Hide** ¶ so that it is active and the formatting marks display. If the rulers do not display, click the **VIEW tab**, and then in the **Show group**, select the **Ruler** check box.

2. Type **Internships Available** and then press Enter two times. As you type the following text, press the Spacebar only one time at the end of a sentence: **This summer, Sturgeon Point Productions will be filming a short documentary in Costa Rica about its native birds and has positions available for two interns. We are looking for a First Assistant Director and an Assistant Script Supervisor.**

   As you type, the insertion point moves to the right, and when it approaches the right margin, Word determines whether the next word in the line will fit within the established right margin. If the word does not fit, Word moves the entire word down to the next line. This is ***wordwrap*** and means that you press Enter *only* when you reach the end of a paragraph—it is not necessary to press Enter at the end of each line of text.

NOTE **Spacing between Sentences**

Although you might have learned to add two spaces following end-of-sentence punctuation, the common practice now is to space only one time at the end of a sentence.

3. Press Enter. Take a moment to study the table in Figure 1.2 to become familiar with the default document settings in Microsoft Word, and then compare your screen with Figure 1.3.

   When you press Enter, Spacebar, or Tab on your keyboard, characters display in your document to represent these keystrokes. These characters do not print and are referred to as ***formatting marks*** or ***nonprinting characters***. These marks will display throughout this instruction.

FIGURE 1.2

DEFAULT DOCUMENT SETTINGS IN A NEW WORD DOCUMENT	
SETTING	**DEFAULT FORMAT**
Font and font size	The default font is Calibri and the default font size is 11 points.
Margins	The default left, right, top, and bottom page margins are 1 inch.
Line spacing	The default line spacing is 1.08, which provides slightly more space between lines than single spacing does.
Paragraph spacing	The default spacing after a paragraph is 8 points, which is slightly less than the height of one blank line of text.
View	The default view is Print Layout view, which displays the page borders and displays the document as it will appear when printed.

FIGURE 1.3

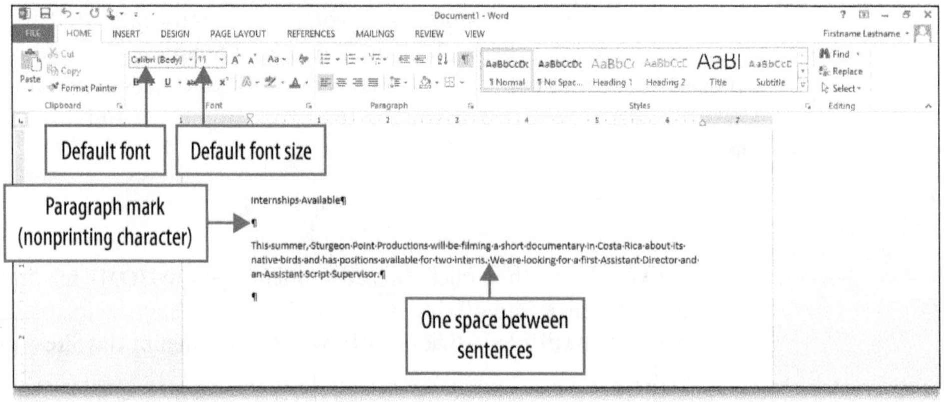

More Knowledge **Word's Default Settings Are Easier to Read Online**

Until just a few years ago, word processing programs used single spacing, an extra blank paragraph to separate paragraphs, and 12 pt Times New Roman as the default formats. Now, studies show that individuals find the Word default formats described in Figure 1.2 to be easier to read online, where many documents are now viewed and read.

Activity 1.02 | Inserting Text from Another Document

1 On the ribbon, click the **INSERT tab**. In the **Text group**, click the **Object button arrow**, and then click **Text from File**.

ALERT! **Does the Object Dialog Box Display?**

If the Object dialog box displays, you probably clicked the Object *button* instead of the Object *button arrow*. Close the Object dialog box, and then in the Text group, click the Object button arrow, as shown in Figure 1.4. Click *Text from File*, and then continue with Step 2.

2 In the **Insert File** dialog box, navigate to the student files that accompany this textbook, locate and select **w01A_Text**, and then click **Insert**. Compare your screen with Figure 1.4.

A *copy* of the text from the w01A_Text file displays at the insertion point location; the text is not removed from the original file.

FIGURE 1.4

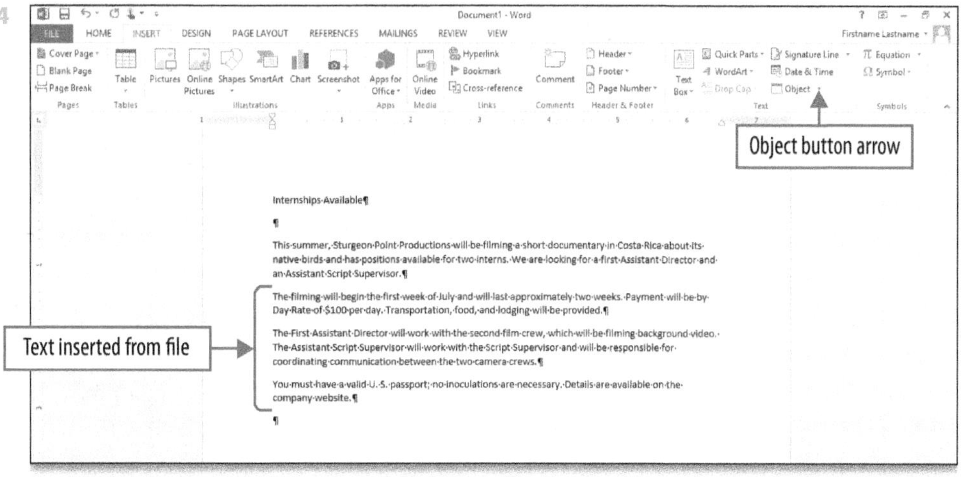

ANOTHER WAY Open the file, copy the required text, close the file, and then paste the text into the current document.

3 On the **Quick Access Toolbar**, click **Save**. Under **Save As**, click **Computer**, and then click **Browse**. Navigate to the location where you are saving your files for this chapter, and then create and open a new folder named **Word Chapter 1**. In the **File name** box, using your own name, replace the existing text with **Lastname_Firstname_1A_Flyer** and then click **Save**.

Objective 2 Insert and Format Graphics

Video W1-2

To add visual interest to a document, insert ***graphics***. Graphics include pictures, online pictures, charts, and ***drawing objects***—shapes, diagrams, lines, and so on. For additional visual interest, you can apply an attractive graphic format to text; add, resize, move, and format pictures; and add a page border.

Activity 1.03 | Formatting Text by Using Text Effects

Text effects are decorative formats, such as shadowed or mirrored text, text glow, 3-D effects, and colors that make text stand out.

1 Including the paragraph mark, select the first paragraph of text—*Internships Available*. On the **HOME tab**, in the **Font group**, click **Text Effects and Typography**.

2 In the **Text Effects** gallery, in the third row, point to the first effect to display the ScreenTip *Fill - Black, Text 1, Outline - Background 1, Hard Shadow - Background 1*, and then click this effect.

3 With the text still selected, in the **Font group**, click in the **Font Size** box 11 to select the existing font size. Type **52** and then press Enter.

When you want to change the font size of selected text to a size that does not display in the Font Size list, type the number in the Font Size box and press Enter to confirm the new font size.

4 With the text still selected, in the **Paragraph group**, click **Center** to center the text. Compare your screen with Figure 1.5.

FIGURE 1.5

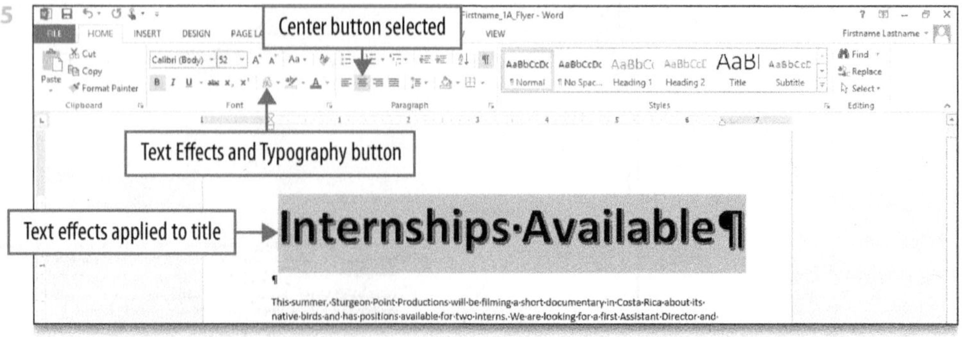

5 With the text still selected, in the **Font group**, click **Text Effects and Typography**. Point to **Shadow**, and then under **Outer**, in the second row, click the third style—**Offset Left**.

6 With the text still selected, in the **Font group**, click the **Font Color button arrow**. Under **Theme Colors**, in the sixth column, click the first color—**Orange, Accent 2**.

7 Click anywhere in the document to deselect the text, click **Save**, and then compare your screen with Figure 1.6.

FIGURE 1.6

More Knowledge **Clear Existing Formatting**

If you do not like your text effect, you can remove all formatting from any selected text. To do so, on the HOME tab, in the Font group, click Clear All Formatting.

Activity 1.04 | Inserting Pictures

1 In the paragraph that begins *This summer*, click to position the insertion point at the beginning of the paragraph.

2 On the **INSERT tab**, in the **Illustrations group**, click **Pictures**. In the **Insert Picture** dialog box, navigate to your student data files, locate and click **w01A_Bird**, and then click **Insert**.

Word inserts the picture as an ***inline object***; that is, the picture is positioned directly in the text at the insertion point, just like a character in a sentence. The Layout Options button displays to the right of the picture. You can change the ***Layout Options*** to control the manner in which text wraps around a picture or other object. Sizing handles surround the picture indicating it is selected.

3 Notice the square sizing handles around the border of the selected picture, as shown in Figure 1.7.

The corner sizing handles resize the graphic proportionally. The center sizing handles resize a graphic vertically or horizontally only; however, sizing with these will distort the graphic. A ***rotation handle***, with which you can rotate the graphic to any angle, displays above the top center sizing handle.

FIGURE 1.7

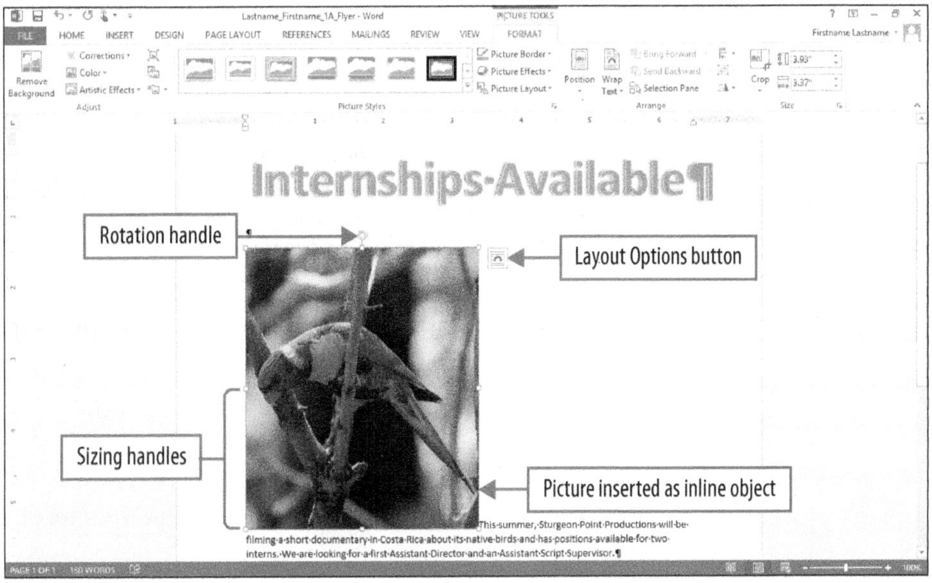

Activity 1.05 | Wrapping Text around a Picture Using Layout Options

Recall that Layout Options enable you to control ***text wrapping***—the manner in which text displays around an object.

1. Be sure the picture is selected—you know it is selected if the sizing handles display.

2. To the right of the picture, click **Layout Options** to display a gallery of text wrapping arrangements. Point to each layout option icon to view its ScreenTip.

   Each icon visually depicts how text will wrap around an object.

ANOTHER WAY On the FORMAT tab, in the Arrange group, click Wrap Text.

3. From the gallery, under **With Text Wrapping**, click the first layout—**Square**. Compare your screen with Figure 1.8.

   Select Square text wrapping when you want to wrap the text to the left or right of an image. To the left of the picture, an ***object anchor*** displays indicating that the selected object is anchored to the text at this location in the document.

FIGURE 1.8

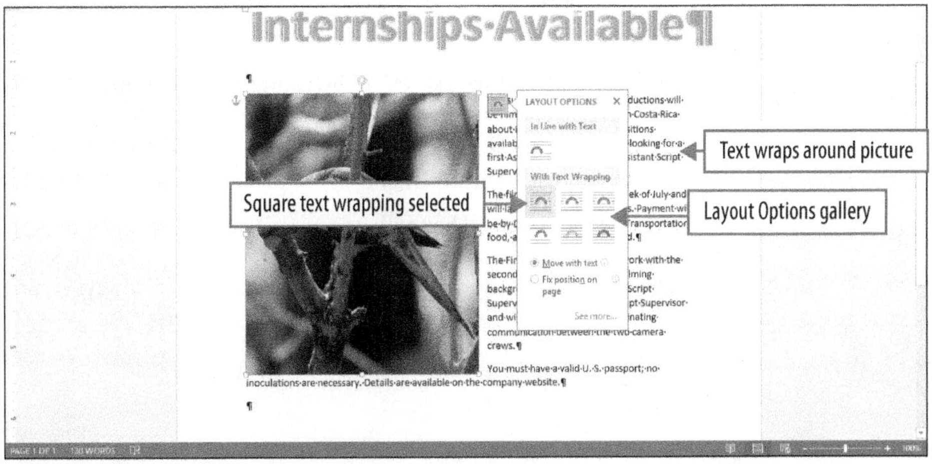

4. **Close** the **Layout Options**, and then **Save** your document.

Activity 1.06 | Resizing Pictures and Using Live Layout

When you move or size a picture, ***Live Layout*** reflows text as you move or size an object so that you can view the placement of surrounding text.

1 If necessary, scroll your document so the entire picture displays on the screen. At the lower right corner of the picture, point to the sizing handle until the pointer displays. Drag slightly upward and to the left and notice that as you drag, a green alignment guide displays at the left margin. Compare your screen with Figure 1.9.

Alignment guides display when you are moving or sizing a picture to help you with object placement, and Live Layout shows you how the document text will flow and display on the page.

FIGURE 1.9

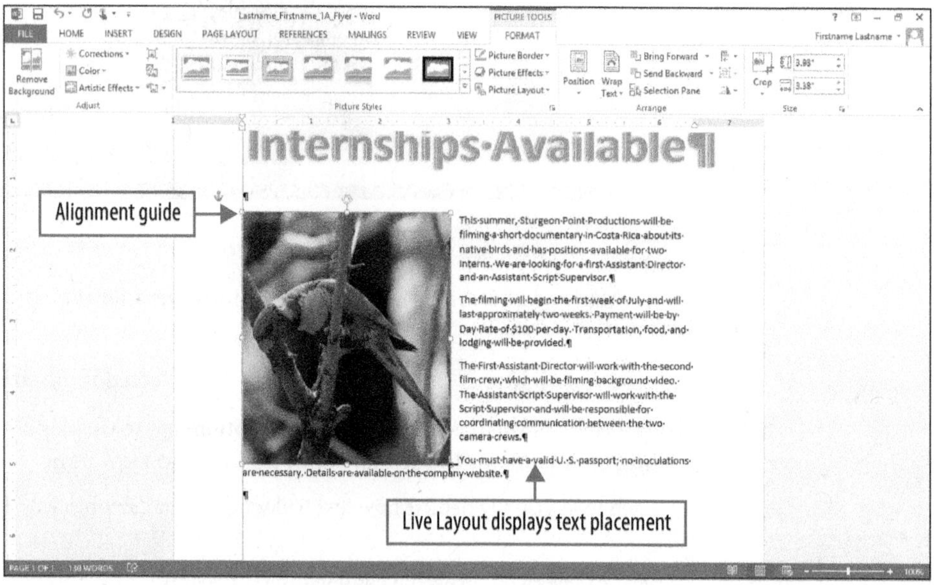

2 Continue to drag up and to the left until the bottom of the graphic is aligned at approximately **4 inches on the vertical ruler** and notice that the graphic is proportionally resized.

3 On the **Quick Access Toolbar**, click **Undo** to restore the picture to its original size.

ANOTHER WAY On the FORMAT tab, in the Adjust group, click Reset Picture.

4 On the ribbon, under **PICTURE TOOLS**, on the **FORMAT tab**, in the **Size group**, click the **Shape Height spin box arrows** Height: 0.19" as necessary to change the height of the picture to **3.8"**. If necessary, scroll down to view the entire picture on your screen, and then compare your screen with Figure 1.10.

A ***spin box*** is a small box with an upward- and downward-pointing arrow that lets you move rapidly through a set of values by clicking. When you use the Shape Height and Shape Width spin boxes to change the size of a graphic, the graphic will always resize proportionally; that is, the width adjusts as you change the height and vice versa.

FIGURE 1.10

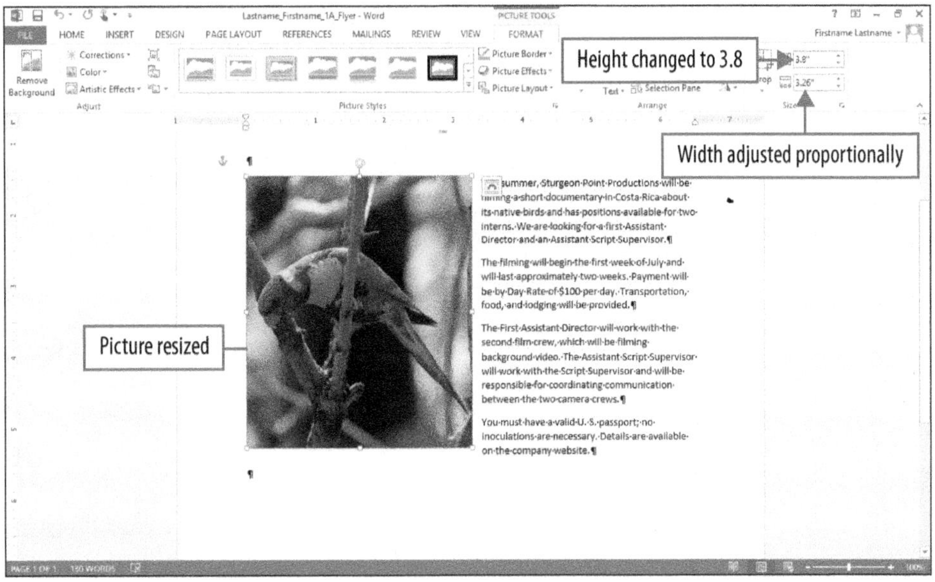

5 **Save** your document.

Activity 1.07 | Moving a Picture

There are two ways to move a picture in a document. You can point to the picture and then drag it to a new position. You can also change the picture settings in a dialog box, which gives you more precise control over the picture location.

1 Be sure the picture is selected. On the ribbon, click the **FORMAT tab**. In the **Arrange group**, click **Position**, and then click **More Layout Options**.

2 In the **Layout** dialog box, be sure the **Position tab** is selected. Under **Horizontal**, click the **Alignment** option button. To the right of **Alignment**, click the **arrow**, and then click **Right**. To the right of **relative to**, click the **arrow**, and then click **Margin**.

3 Under **Vertical**, click the **Alignment** option button. Change the **Alignment** options to **Top relative to Line**. Compare your screen with Figure 1.11.

With these alignment settings, the picture will move to the right margin of the page and the top edge will align with the top of the first line of the paragraph to which it is anchored.

FIGURE 1.11

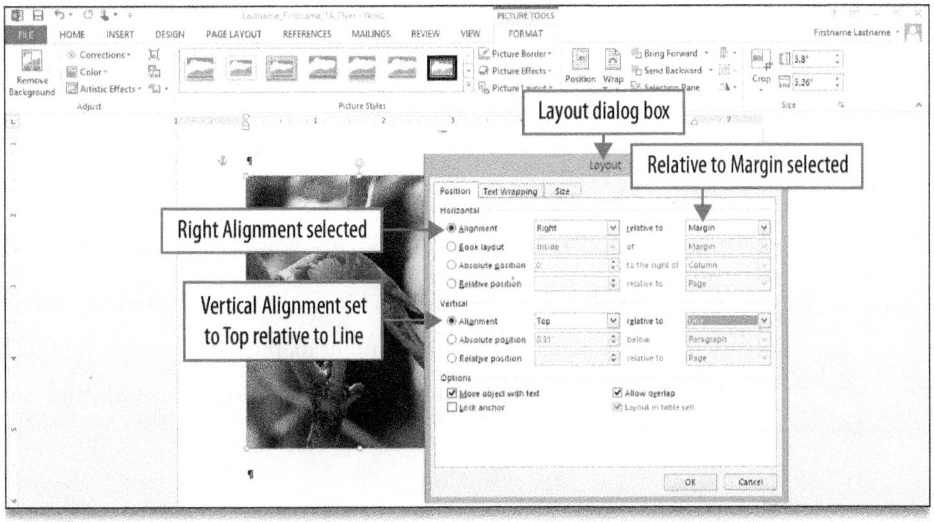

4 At the bottom of the **Layout** dialog box, click **OK**, and then on the **Quick Access Toolbar**, click **Save** [icon]. Notice that the picture moves to the right margin, and the text wraps on the left side of the picture. Compare your screen with Figure 1.12.

FIGURE 1.12

Activity 1.08 | Applying Picture Effects

Picture styles include shapes, shadows, frames, borders, and other special effects with which you can stylize an image. ***Picture Effects*** enhance a picture with effects such as shadow, glow, reflection, or 3-D rotation.

1 Be sure the picture is selected. On the **FORMAT tab**, in the **Picture Styles group**, click **Picture Effects.**

2 Point to **Soft Edges**, and then click **5 Point**.

The Soft Edges feature fades the edges of the picture. The number of points you choose determines how far the fade goes inward from the edges of the picture.

3 Compare your screen with Figure 1.13, and then **Save** [icon] your document.

FIGURE 1.13

Activity 1.09 | Applying Artistic Effects

Artistic effects are formats that make pictures look more like sketches or paintings.

1 Be sure the picture is selected. On the **FORMAT tab**, in the **Adjust group**, click **Artistic Effects.**

2 In the first row of the gallery, point to, but do not click, the third effect—**Pencil Grayscale.**

Live Preview displays the picture with the *Pencil Grayscale* effect added.

3. In the second row of the gallery, click the third effect—**Paint Brush**. **Save** your document, and then notice that the picture looks more like a painting than a photograph. Compare your screen with Figure 1.14.

FIGURE 1.14

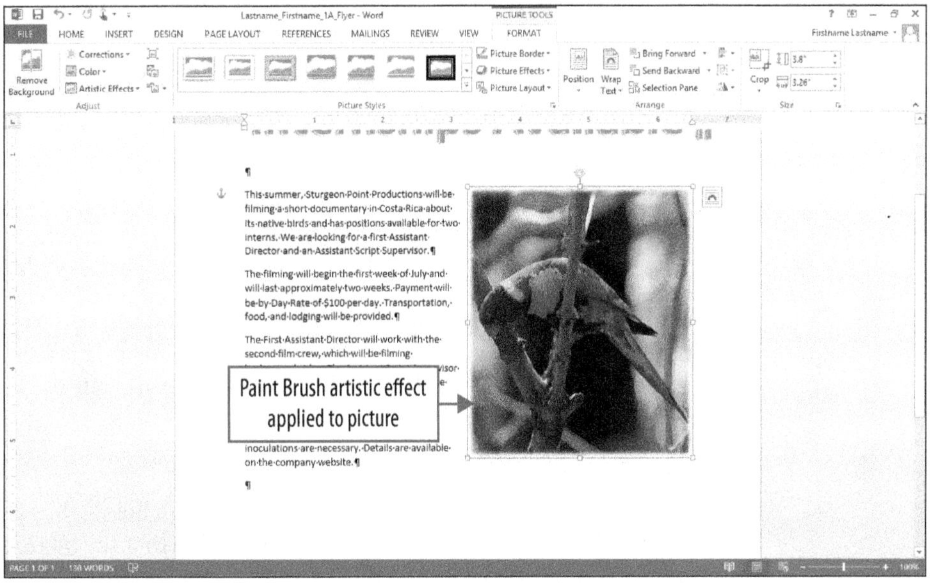

Activity 1.10 | Adding a Page Border

Page borders frame a page and help to focus the information on the page.

1. Click anywhere outside the picture to deselect it. On the **DESIGN tab**, in the **Page Background group**, click **Page Borders**.
2. In the **Borders and Shading** dialog box, on the **Page Border tab**, under **Setting**, click **Box**. Under **Style**, scroll the list and click the seventh style—double lines.
3. Click the **Color arrow**, and then in the sixth column, click the first color—**Orange, Accent 2**.
4. Under **Apply to**, be sure **Whole document** is selected, and then compare your screen with Figure 1.15.

FIGURE 1.15

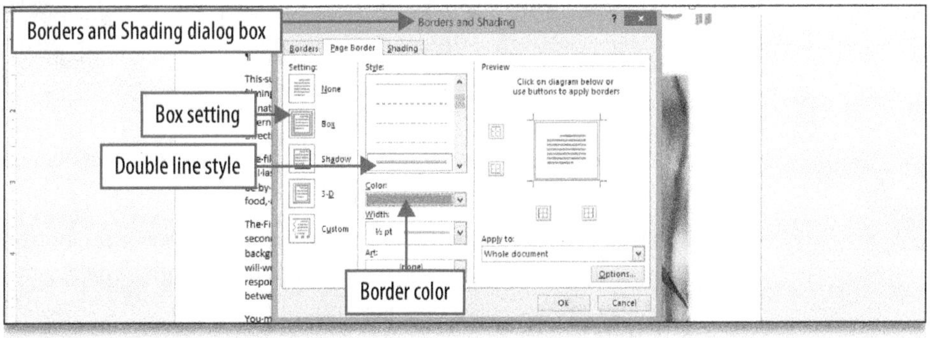

5. At the bottom of the **Borders and Shading** dialog box, click **OK**.
6. Press Ctrl + Home to move to the top of the document, click **Save**, and then compare your screen with Figure 1.16.

FIGURE 1.16

Objective 3 Insert and Modify Text Boxes and Shapes

Video W1-3

Word has predefined ***shapes*** and ***text boxes*** that you can add to your documents. A shape is an object such as a line, arrow, box, callout, or banner. A text box is a movable, resizable container for text or graphics. Use these objects to add visual interest to your document.

Activity 1.11 | Inserting, Sizing, and Positioning a Shape

1. Press ↓ one time to move to the blank paragraph below the title. Press Enter four times to create additional space for a text box, and notice that the picture anchored to the paragraph moves with the text.

2. Press Ctrl + End to move to the bottom of the document, and notice that your insertion point is positioned in the empty paragraph at the end of the document. Press Delete to remove the blank paragraph.

3. Click the **INSERT tab**, and then in the **Illustrations group**, click **Shapes** to display the gallery. Compare your screen with Figure 1.17.

FIGURE 1.17

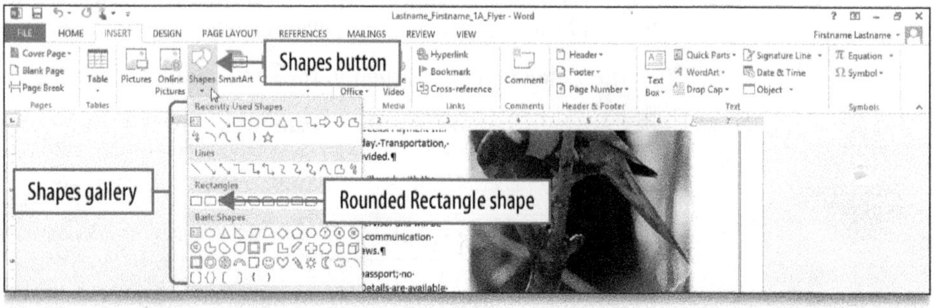

4. Under **Rectangles**, click the second shape—**Rounded Rectangle**, and then move your pointer. Notice that the + pointer displays.

5. Position the + pointer anywhere in the blank area at the bottom of the document. Click one time to insert a 1-inch by 1-inch rounded rectangle. The exact location is not important.

   A blue rectangle with rounded edges displays.

6. To the right of the rectangle object, click **Layout Options**, and then at the bottom of the gallery, click **See more** to display the **Layout** dialog box.

ANOTHER WAY On the FORMAT tab, in the Arrange group, click Position.

7 In the **Layout** dialog box, under **Horizontal**, click **Alignment**. To the right of **Alignment**, click the **arrow**, and then click **Centered**. To the right of **relative to**, click the **arrow**, and then click **Page**. Under **Vertical**, click in the **Absolute position** box to select the existing number, and then type **1** To the right of **below**, be sure that **Paragraph** displays. Click **OK**.

This action centers the rectangle on the page and positions the rectangle one inch below the last paragraph.

8 On the **FORMAT tab**, click in the **Shape Height** box [Height: 0.19"] to select the existing text. Type **1.5** and then click in the **Shape Width** box [Width: 6.49"]. Type **4.5** and then press Enter.

9 Compare your screen with Figure 1.18, and then **Save** your document.

FIGURE 1.18

Activity 1.12 Typing Text in a Shape and Formatting a Shape

1 If necessary, select the rectangle shape. Type **To set up an interview, apply online at:** and then press Enter. Type **www.SturgeonPointProductions.com**

2 Press Ctrl + A to select the text you just typed. Right-click over the selected text to display the mini toolbar, and then click **Bold** [B]. With the text still selected, click **Increase Font Size** [A] three times to increase the font size to **16 pt**.

The keyboard shortcut Ctrl + A is convenient to select all of the text in a text box.

3 With the text still selected, on the mini toolbar, click the **Font Color button arrow**. Under **Theme Colors**, click **Black, Text 1**.

4 Click outside the shape to deselect the text. Click the border of the shape to select the shape but not the text. On the **FORMAT tab**, in the **Shape Styles group**, click **Shape Fill**. In the sixth column, click the fourth color—**Orange, Accent 2, Lighter 40%**.

5 With the shape still selected, in the **Shape Styles group**, click **Shape Outline**. In the sixth column, click the first color—**Orange, Accent 2**. Compare your screen with Figure 1.19, and then **Save** your document.

FIGURE 1.19

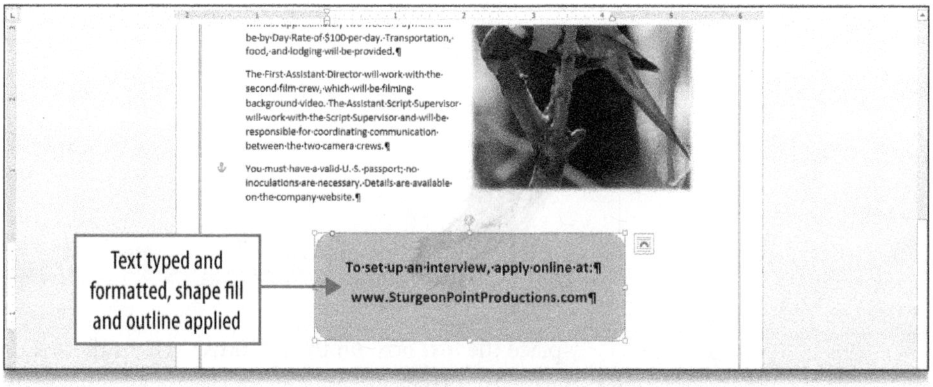

Activity 1.13 | Inserting a Text Box

A text box is useful to differentiate portions of text from other text on the page. Because it is a ***floating object***—a graphic that can be moved independently of the surrounding text characters—you can place a text box anywhere on the page.

1. Press Ctrl + Home to move to the top of the document.

2. On the **INSERT tab**, in the **Text group**, click **Text Box**. At the bottom of the gallery, click **Draw Text Box.**

3. Position the pointer over the first blank paragraph—aligned with the left margin and at approximately **1 inch on the vertical ruler**. Drag down and to the right to create a text box approximately **1.5 inches** high and **4 inches** wide—the exact size and location need not be precise.

4. With the insertion point blinking in the text box, type the following, pressing Enter after each line *except* the last line to create a new paragraph:

   Interviews will be held:

   Friday and Saturday, January 14 and 15

   In the Career Services Conference Room

5. Compare your screen with Figure 1.20, and then **Save** your document

FIGURE 1.20

Activity 1.14 | Sizing and Positioning a Text Box and Formatting a Text Box Using Shape Styles

1. Point to the text box border to display the pointer. In the space below the *Internships Available* title, by dragging, move the text box until a horizontal green alignment guide displays above the first blank paragraph mark and a vertical green alignment guide displays in the center of the page as shown in Figure 1.21.

FIGURE 1.21

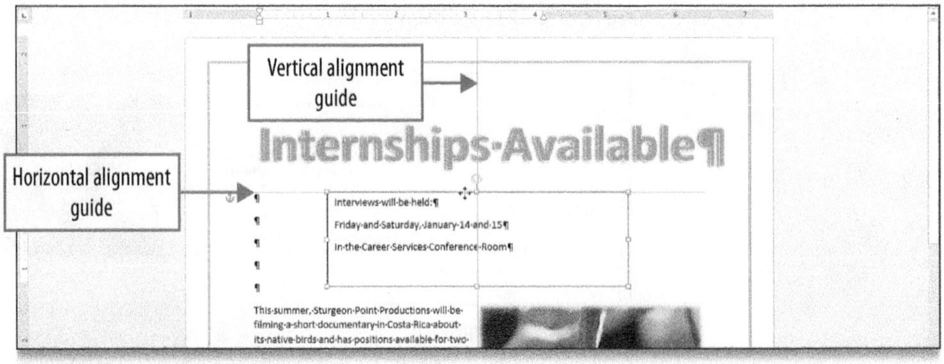

2. To precisely place the text box, on the **FORMAT tab**, in the **Arrange group**, click **Position**, and then click **More Layout Options**.

3 In the **Layout** dialog box, under **Horizontal**, click **Alignment**. To the right of **Alignment**, click the **arrow**, and then click **Centered**. To the right of **relative to**, click the **arrow**, and then click **Page**.

4 Under **Vertical**, click in the **Absolute position** box, select the existing number, and then type **1.25** To the right of **below**, click the **arrow**, and then click **Margin**.

5 In the **Layout** dialog box, click the **Size tab**. Under **Height**, select the number in the **Absolute** box. Type **1.25** and then under **Width**, select the number in the **Absolute** box. Type **4** and then click **OK**.

The text box is sized correctly, centered horizontally, and the top edge is positioned 1.25 inches below the top margin of the document.

6 Click in the text box, and then press Ctrl + A to select all of the text. Right-click over the selected text to display the mini toolbar, change the **Font Size** to **16** and apply **Bold** B. Press Ctrl + E to center the text.

Ctrl + E is the keyboard shortcut to center text in a document or object.

7 On the ribbon, under **DRAWING TOOLS**, click the **FORMAT tab**. In the **Shape Styles group**, click **More**, and then in the first row, click the third style—**Colored Outline - Orange, Accent 2.**

8 On the **FORMAT tab**, in the **Shape Styles group**, click **Shape Effects**. Point to **Shadow**, and then under **Outer**, in the first row, click the first effect—**Offset Diagonal Bottom Right.**

9 Click anywhere in the document to deselect the text box. Compare your screen with Figure 1.22, and then **Save** your document.

FIGURE 1.22

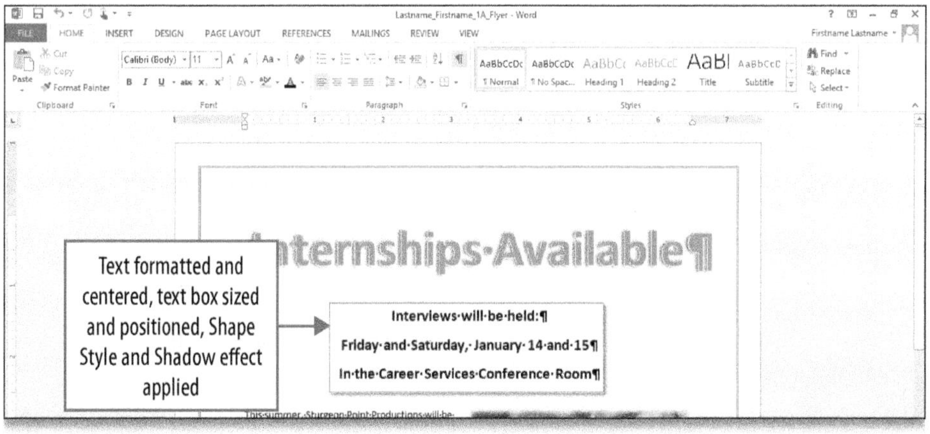

Objective 4 Preview and Print a Document

Video W1-4

While you are creating your document, it is useful to preview your document periodically to be sure that you are getting the result you want. Then, before printing, make a final preview to be sure the document layout is what you intend.

Activity 1.15 | Adding a File Name to the Footer by Inserting a Field

Information in headers and footers helps to identify a document when it is printed or displayed electronically. Recall that a header is information that prints at the top of every page; a footer is information that prints at the bottom of every page. In this textbook, you will insert the file name in the footer of every Word document.

1. Click the **INSERT tab**, and then in the **Header & Footer group**, click **Footer**.
2. At the bottom of the gallery, click **Edit Footer**.

   The footer area displays with the insertion point blinking at the left edge, and on the ribbon, the Header & Footer Tools display.

ANOTHER WAY At the bottom edge of the page, right-click, and then on the shortcut menu, click Edit Footer.

3. On the ribbon, under the **HEADER & FOOTER TOOLS**, on the **DESIGN tab**, in the **Insert group**, click **Document Info**, and then click **File Name**. Compare your screen with Figure 1.23.

FIGURE 1.23

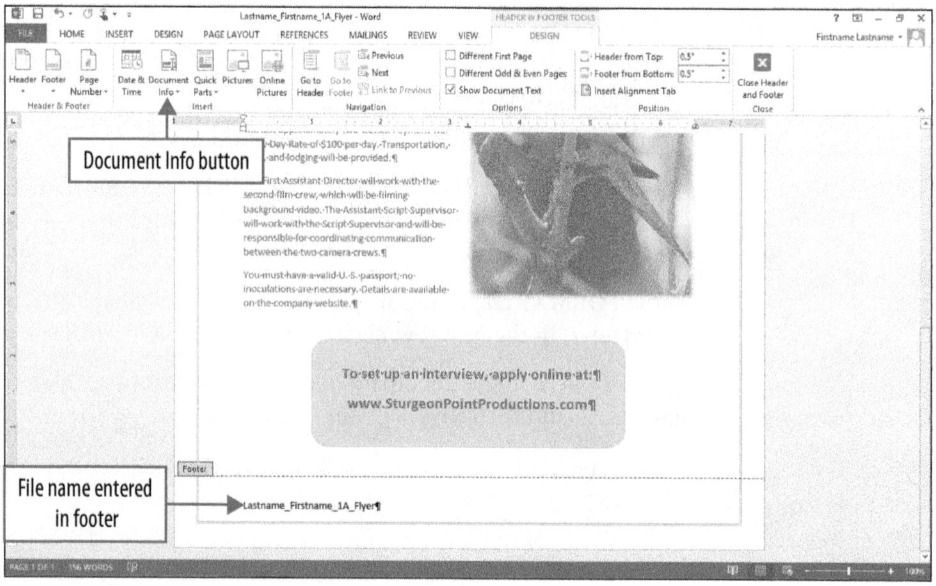

4. On the **DESIGN tab**, click **Close Header and Footer**, and then **Save** [Save] your document.

   When the body of the document is active, the footer text is dimmed—displays in gray. Conversely, when the footer area is active, the footer text is not dimmed; instead, the document text is dimmed.

ANOTHER WAY Double-click in the document outside of the footer area to close the footer and return to the document.

Activity 1.16 | Adding Document Properties and Previewing and Printing a Document

1. Press Ctrl + Home to move the insertion point to the top of the document. In the upper left corner of your screen, click the **FILE tab** to display **Backstage** view. On the right, at the bottom of the **Properties** list, click **Show All Properties**.
2. On the list of **Properties**, click to the right of **Tags** to display an empty box, and then type **internship, documentary**
3. Click to the right of **Subject** to display an empty box, and then type your course name and section number. Under **Related People**, be sure that your name displays as the author. If necessary, right-click the author name, click **Edit Property**, type your name, press Enter and click **OK**.

4 On the left, click **Print** to display the **Print Preview**. Compare your screen with Figure 1.24.

Here you can select any printer connected to your system and adjust the settings related to how you want to print. On the right, Print Preview displays your document exactly as it will print; the formatting marks do not display. At the bottom of the Print Preview area, in the center, the number of pages and arrows with which you can move among the pages in Print Preview display. On the right, Zoom settings enable you to shrink or enlarge the Print Preview.

FIGURE 1.24

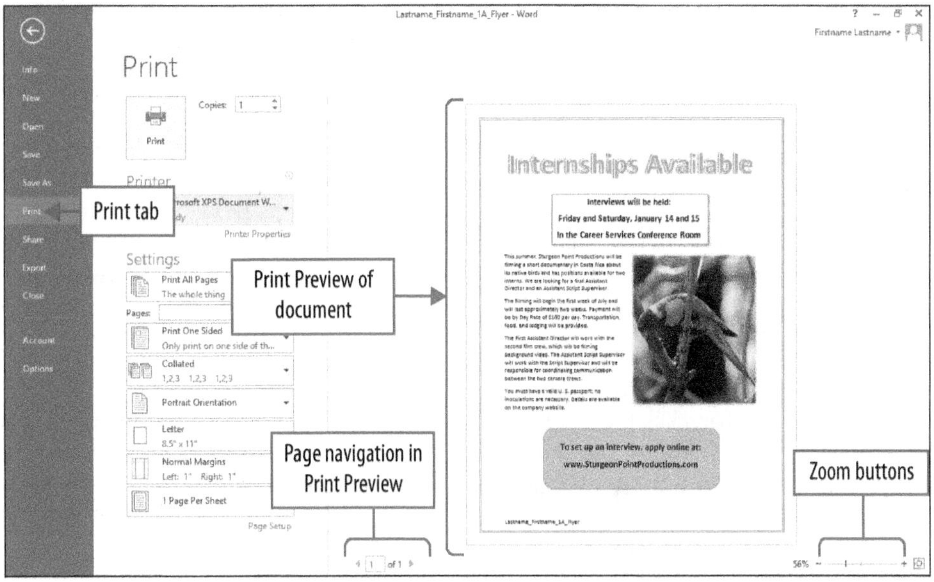

5 In the lower right corner of the window, click **Zoom In** several times to view the document at a larger size, and notice that a larger preview is easier to read. Click **Zoom to Page** to view the entire page.

6 To submit your file electronically, skip this step and move to Step 7. To print your document on paper using the default printer on your system, in the upper left portion of the screen, click **Print**.

The document will print on your default printer; if you do not have a color printer, colors will print in shades of gray. Backstage view closes and your file redisplays in the Word window.

7 To create an electronic printout, on the left, click **Export**. On the right, click **Create PDF/XPS**. In the **Publish as PDF or XPS** dialog box, navigate to your **Word Chapter 1** folder, and then click **Publish**. If your Adobe Acrobat or Adobe Reader program displays your PDF, in the upper right corner, click **Close**.

8 **Save** your document. In the upper right corner of the Word window, click **Close**. If directed by your instructor to do so, submit your paper or electronic printout or your Word file.

END | You have completed Project 1A

GO! with Office Online (formerly Web Apps)

Objective Create a Flyer in Word Online

Build from Scratch

ALERT! **Working with Web-Based Applications and Services**

Computer programs and services on the web receive continuous updates and improvements, so the steps to complete this web-based activity may differ from the ones shown. You can often look at the screens and the information presented to determine how to complete the activity.

Activity | Creating a Flyer in Word Online

In this activity, you will use Word Online to create a flyer similar to the one you created in Project 1A.

1 From the desktop, start Internet Explorer. Navigate to **http://onedrive.com**, and then sign in to your Microsoft account. Open your **GO! Web Projects** folder—or create and then open this folder if necessary.

2 On the OneDrive menu bar, click **Create**, and then click **Word document**. In the middle of the blue, Word Online title bar, click the text **Document1** so that it is selected. Using your own last and first name, type **Lastname_Firstname_WD_1A_Web** and then press Enter to change the file name.

3 Click anywhere in the document. Type **Sturgeon Point Productions** and then press Enter.

4 Type the following four lines of text, pressing Enter after each line *except* for the last line:

Internships Available for a Costa Rica
Native Birds Documentary
Interviews on Friday, January 14
Filming Begins the First Week of July

5 By using your I pointer, drag to select the first line in the document. On the **HOME tab**, in the **Font group**, click the **Font Size button arrow**, and then click **36**. Click the **Font Color button arrow**, and then in the fourth column, click the first color—**Blue Gray, Text 2**. In the **Paragraph group**, click **Center**.

In Word Online, you must drag to select text—triple-clicking a line will not select the line, nor will moving the pointer into the left margin and clicking. You can, however, double-click to select a single word.

6 Select the remaining text in the document, and then on the **HOME tab** in the **Font group**, click **Bold**. Click the **Font Size button arrow**, and then click **24**. In the **Paragraph group**, click **Center**. Compare your screen with Figure A.

FIGURE A

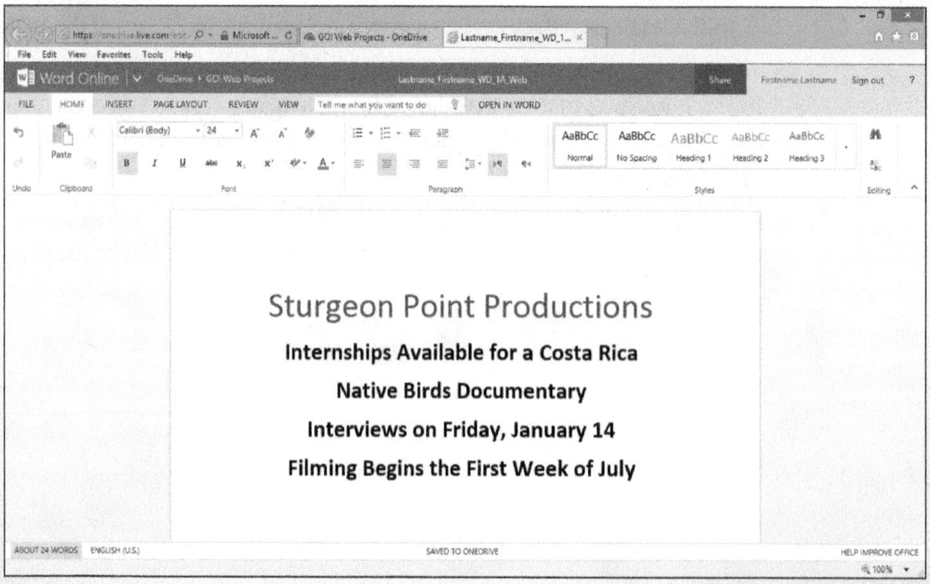

(GO! with Office Online (formerly Web Apps) continues on the next page)

7 Click at the end of the line *Interviews on Friday, January 14*, and then press Enter to insert a blank line.

8 On the **INSERT tab**, in the **Pictures group**, click **Picture**. Navigate to the location where your student data files are stored, and then click **w01A_Bird**. Click **Open**. Notice that the picture is dimmed, indicating that it is selected.

9 Under **PICTURE TOOLS**, click the **FORMAT tab**, and then in the **Image Size group**, click **Shrink** several times until the **Scale** box displays **40.48%**. If the box does not display this exact number, select the number in the **Scale** box, type **40.48%** and then press Enter.

10 With the picture still selected, on the **FORMAT tab**, in the **Picture Styles group**, click the sixth style—**Soft Edge Rectangle**.

11 Click anywhere in a blank area of the document so that the picture is not selected, and then compare your screen with Figure B.

12 Submit your file as directed by your instructor. If you are instructed to submit an electronic printout of your file, create a PDF as indicated in the Note box that follows. Sign out of your OneDrive and close Internet Explorer.

NOTE **Creating a PDF from Word Online**

Click the FILE tab, click Save As, and then click Download as PDF. In the Microsoft Word Online message box, click Click here to view the PDF of your document. In the message bar at the bottom of your screen, click the Save arrow, and then click Save as. In the Save As dialog box, navigate to your Word Chapter 1 folder, and then save the file.

FIGURE B

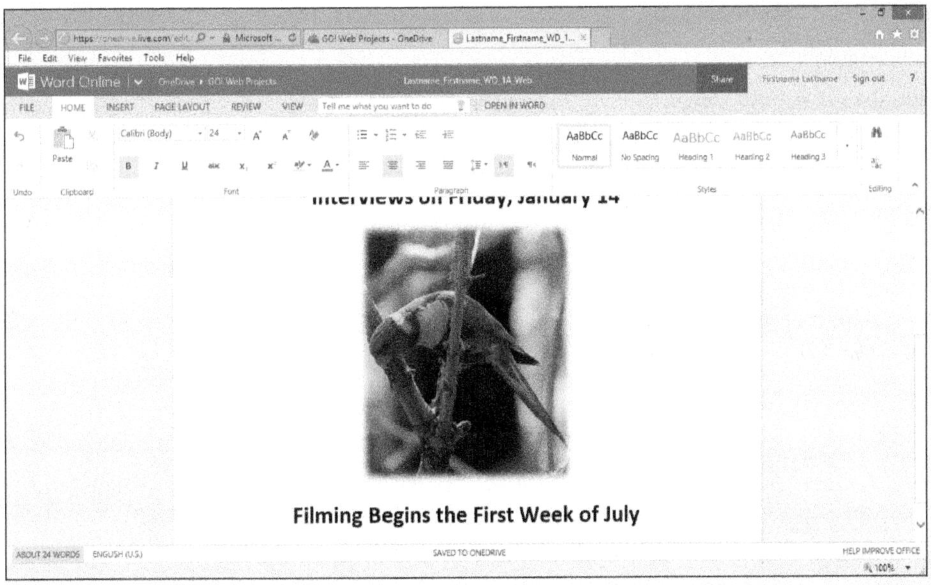

PROJECT

1B Information Handout

MyITLab®
Project 1B Training

PROJECT ACTIVITIES

In Activities 1.17 through 1.29, you will format an information handout from Sturgeon Point Productions that describes internships available to students. Your completed document will look similar to Figure 1.25.

PROJECT FILES

For Project 1B, you will need the following files:	You will save your document as:
w01B_Programs **w01B_Web**	**Lastname_Firstname_1B_Programs**

PROJECT RESULTS

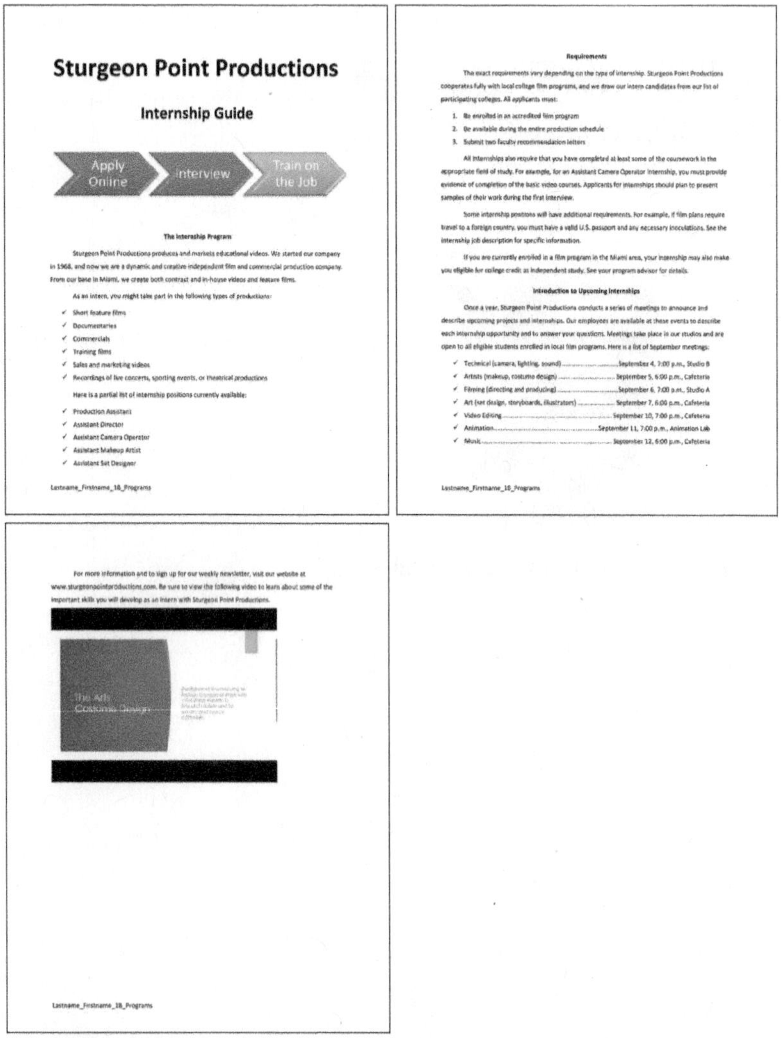

FIGURE 1.25 Project 1B Information Handout

Objective 5 Change Document and Paragraph Layout

Video W1-5

Document layout includes ***margins***—the space between the text and the top, bottom, left, and right edges of the paper. Paragraph layout includes line spacing, indents, and tabs. In Word, the information about paragraph formats is stored in the paragraph mark at the end of a paragraph. When you press Enter, the new paragraph mark contains the formatting of the previous paragraph, unless you take steps to change it.

Activity 1.17 | Setting Margins

1 Start Word, and then click **Open Other Documents.** Navigate to the student files that accompany this textbook, and then open the document **w01B_Programs.** On the **HOME tab,** in the **Paragraph group,** be sure **Show/Hide** ¶ is active so that you can view the formatting marks.

2 Click the **FILE tab,** and then click **Save As.** Navigate to your **Word Chapter 1** folder, and then using your own name, **Save** the document as **Lastname_Firstname_1B_Programs**

3 Click the **PAGE LAYOUT tab.** In the **Page Setup group,** click **Margins,** and then take a moment to study the settings in the Margins gallery.

If you have recently used custom margins settings, they will display at the top of this gallery. Other commonly used settings also display.

4 At the bottom of the **Margins** gallery, click the command followed by an ellipsis—**Custom Margins** to display the **Page Setup** dialog box.

5 In the **Page Setup** dialog box, under **Margins,** press Tab as necessary to select the value in the **Left** box, and then, with *1.25"* selected, type **1**

This action will change the left margin to 1 inch on all pages of the document. You do not need to type the inch (") mark.

6 Press Tab to select the margin in the **Right** box, and then type **1** At the bottom of the dialog box, notice that the new margins will apply to the **Whole document.** Compare your screen with Figure 1.26.

FIGURE 1.26

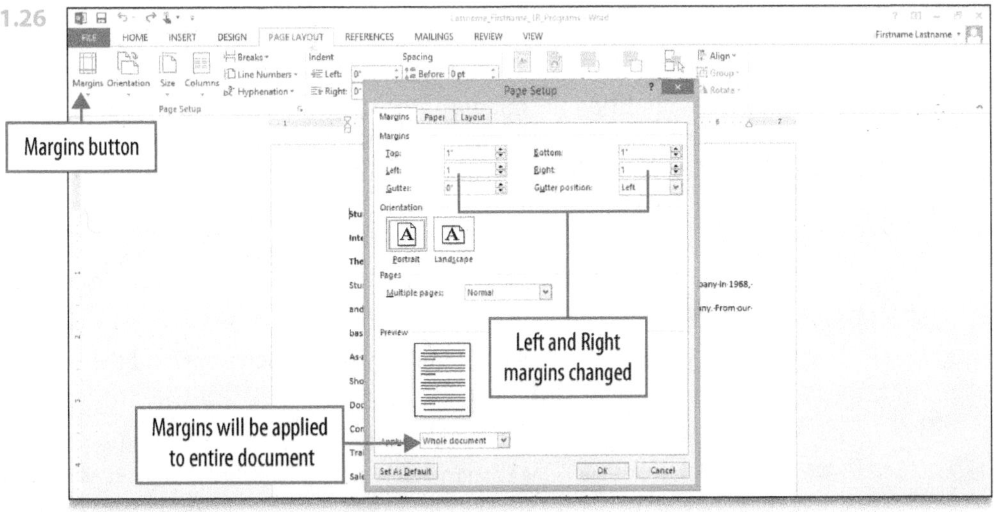

7 Click **OK** to apply the new margins and close the dialog box. If the ruler below the ribbon is not displayed, on the **VIEW** tab, in the **Show group**, select the **Ruler** check box.

8 Scroll to position the bottom of **Page 1** and the top of **Page 2** on your screen. Notice that the page edges display, and the page number and total number of pages display on the left side of the status bar.

9 Near the bottom edge of **Page 1**, point anywhere in the bottom margin area, right-click, and then click **Edit Footer** to display the footer area.

10 On the ribbon, under the **HEADER & FOOTER TOOLS**, on the **DESIGN tab**, in the **Insert group**, click **Document Info**, and then click **File Name**.

11 Double-click anywhere in the document to close the footer area, and then **Save** your document.

Activity 1.18 | Aligning Text

Alignment refers to the placement of paragraph text relative to the left and right margins. Most paragraph text uses ***left alignment***—aligned at the left margin, leaving the right margin uneven. Three other types of paragraph alignment are: ***center alignment***—centered between the left and right margins; ***right alignment***—aligned at the right margin with an uneven left margin; and ***justified alignment***—text aligned evenly at both the left and right margins. The table in Figure 1.27 shows examples of these alignment types.

FIGURE 1.27

TYPES OF PARAGRAPH ALIGNMENT		
ALIGNMENT	**BUTTON**	**DESCRIPTION AND EXAMPLE**
Align Left		Align Left is the default paragraph alignment in Word. Text in the paragraph aligns at the left margin, and the right margin is uneven.
Center		Center alignment aligns text in the paragraph so that it is centered between the left and right margins.
Align Right		Align Right aligns text at the right margin. Using Align Right, the left margin, which is normally even, is uneven.
Justify		The Justify alignment option adds additional space between words so that both the left and right margins are even. Justify is often used when formatting newspaper-style columns.

1 Scroll to position the middle of **Page 2** on your screen, look at the left and right margins, and notice that the text is justified—both the right and left margins of multiple-line paragraphs are aligned evenly at the margins. On the **HOME tab**, in the **Paragraph group**, notice that **Justify** is active.

To achieve a justified right margin, Word adjusts the size of spaces between words, which can result in unattractive spacing in a document that spans the width of a page. Many individuals find such spacing difficult to read.

2 Press Ctrl + A to select all of the text in the document, and then on the **HOME tab**, in the **Paragraph group**, click **Align Left**.

ANOTHER WAY On the HOME tab, in the Editing group, click Select, and then click Select All.

3 Press Ctrl + Home to move to the beginning of the document. In the left margin area, point to the left of the first paragraph—*Sturgeon Point Productions*—until the pointer displays, and then click one time to select the paragraph.

Use this technique to select entire lines of text.

4 On the mini toolbar, in the **Font Size** box, select the existing number, type **40** and then press Enter.

Use this technique to change the font size to a size that is not available on the Font Size list.

5 Select the second paragraph—*Internship Guide*—and then on the mini toolbar, change the **Font Size** to **26 pt**. Point to the left of the first paragraph—*Sturgeon Point Productions*—to display the pointer again, and then drag down to select the first two paragraphs, which form the title and subtitle of the document.

6 On the **HOME tab**, in the **Paragraph group**, click **Center** to center the title and subtitle between the left and right margins, and then compare your screen with Figure 1.28.

FIGURE 1.28

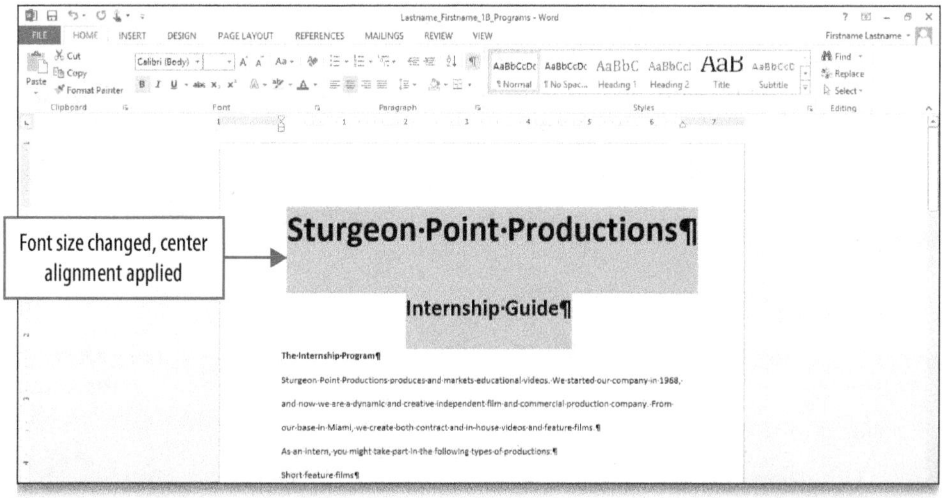

7 Near the top of **Page 1**, locate the first bold subheading—*The Internship Program*. Point to the left of the paragraph to display the pointer, and then click one time to select this text.

8 With *The Internship Program* selected, use your mouse wheel or the vertical scroll bar to bring the bottom portion of **Page 1** into view. Locate the subheading *Requirements*. Move the pointer to the left of the paragraph to display the pointer, hold down Ctrl, and then click one time. Scroll to the middle of **Page 2**, and then use the same technique to select the third subheading—*Introduction to Upcoming Internships*.

Three subheadings are selected; in Windows-based programs, you can hold down Ctrl to select multiple items.

9 Click **Center** to center all three subheadings, and then click **Save**.

Activity 1.19 | Changing Line Spacing

Line spacing is the distance between lines of text in a paragraph. Three of the most commonly used line spacing options are shown in the table in Figure 1.29.

FIGURE 1.29

LINE SPACING OPTIONS	
ALIGNMENT	**DESCRIPTION, EXAMPLE, AND INFORMATION**
Single spacing	**This text in this example uses single spacing.** Single spacing was once the most commonly used spacing in business documents. Now, because so many documents are read on a computer screen rather than on paper, single spacing is becoming less popular.
Multiple 1.08 spacing	**This text in this example uses multiple 1.08 spacing.** The default line spacing in Microsoft Word 2013 is 1.08, which is slightly more than single spacing to make the text easier to read on a computer screen. Many individuals now prefer this spacing, even on paper, because the lines of text appear less crowded.
Double spacing	**This text in this example uses double spacing.** College research papers and draft documents that need space for notes are commonly double-spaced; there is space for a full line of text between each document line.

1 Press Ctrl + Home to move to the beginning of the document. Press Ctrl + A to select all of the text in the document.

2 With all of the text in the document selected, on the **HOME tab**, in the **Paragraph group**, click **Line and Paragraph Spacing**, and notice that the text in the document is double spaced—**2.0** is checked. Compare your screen with Figure 1.30.

BY TOUCH Tap the ribbon commands.

FIGURE 1.30

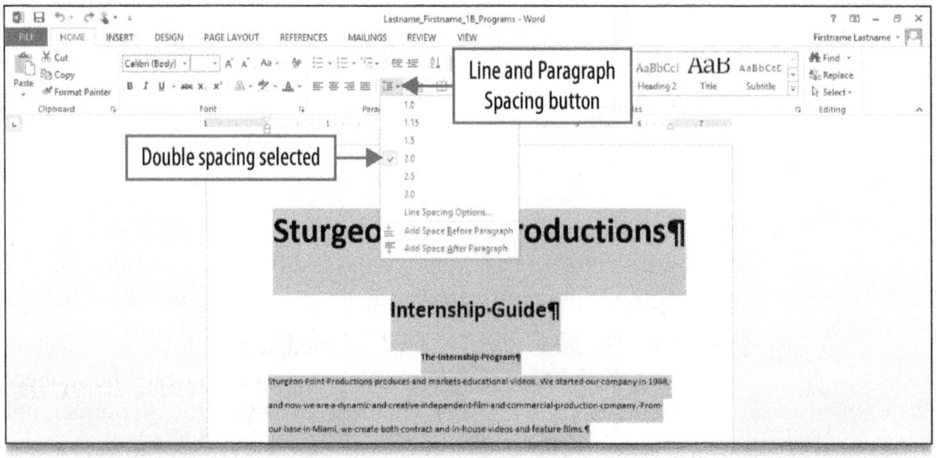

3 On the **Line Spacing** menu, click the *third* setting—**1.5**—and then click anywhere in the document to deselect the text. Compare your screen with Figure 1.31, and then **Save** your document.

FIGURE 1.31

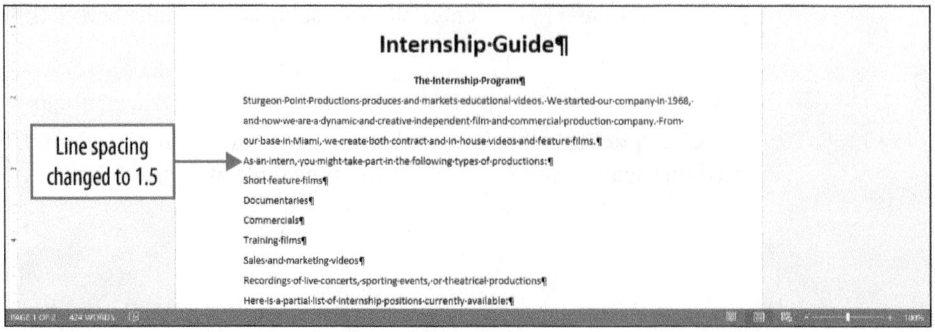

Activity 1.20 | Indenting Text

Indenting the first line of each paragraph is a common technique to distinguish paragraphs.

1. Below the title and subtitle of the document, click anywhere in the paragraph that begins *Sturgeon Point Productions produces.*

2. On the **HOME tab**, in the **Paragraph group**, click the **Dialog Box Launcher**.

3. In the **Paragraph** dialog box, on the **Indents and Spacing tab**, under **Indentation**, click the **Special arrow**, and then click **First line** to indent the first line by 0.5", which is the default indent setting. Compare your screen with Figure 1.32.

FIGURE 1.32

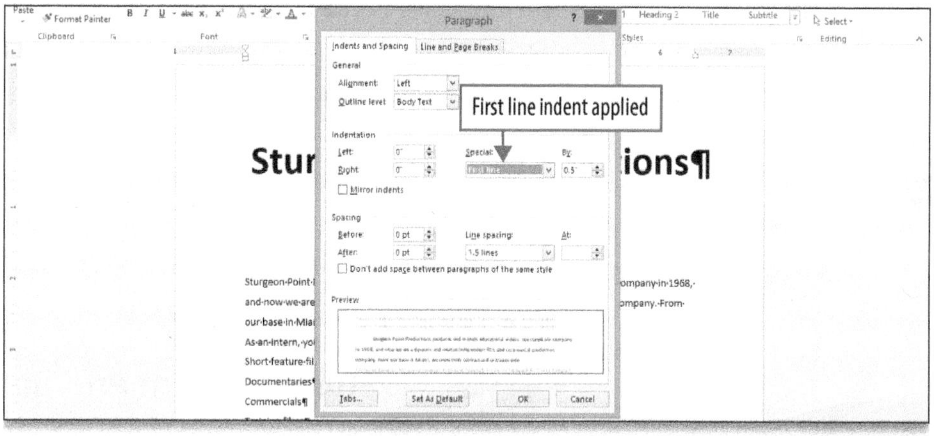

4. Click **OK**, and then click anywhere in the next paragraph, which begins *As an intern.* On the ruler under the ribbon, drag the **First Line Indent** marker to **0.5 inches on the horizontal ruler**, and then compare your screen with Figure 1.33.

FIGURE 1.33

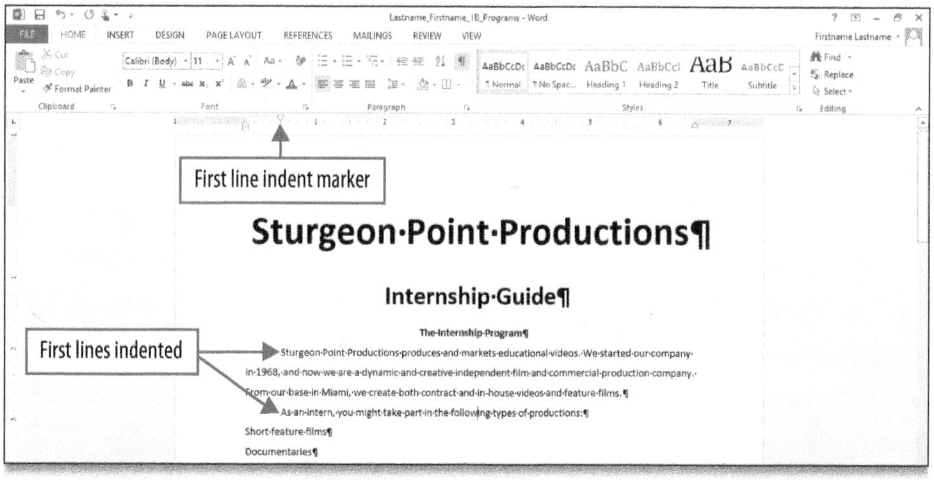

5. By using either of the techniques you just practiced, or by using the **Format Painter**, apply a first line indent of **0.5"** in the paragraph that begins *Here is a partial* to match the indent of the remaining paragraphs in the document.

6. **Save** your document.

Activity 1.21 | Adding Space Before and After Paragraphs

Adding space after each paragraph is another technique to differentiate paragraphs.

1 Press Ctrl + A to select all of the text in the document. Click the **PAGE LAYOUT tab**, and then in the **Paragraph group**, under **Spacing**, click the **After spin box up arrow** one time to change the value to **6 pt**.

To change the value in the box, you can also select the existing number, type a new number, and then press Enter. This document will use 6 pt spacing after paragraphs to add space.

ANOTHER WAY On either the HOME tab or the PAGE LAYOUT tab, display the Paragraph dialog box from the Paragraph group, and then under Spacing, click the spin box arrows as necessary.

2 Press Ctrl + Home, and then compare your screen with Figure 1.34.

FIGURE 1.34

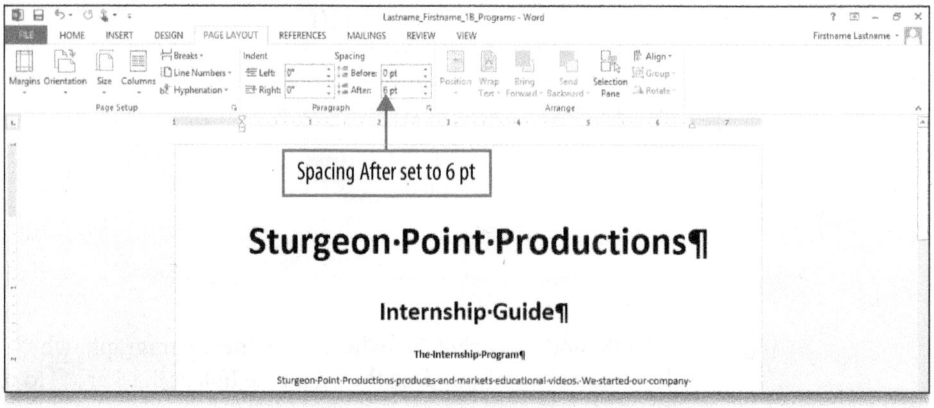

3 Near the top of **Page 1**, select the subheading *The Internship Program*, including the paragraph mark following it, scroll down, hold down Ctrl, and then select the subheadings *Requirements* and *Introduction to Upcoming Internships.*

4 With all three subheadings selected, in the **Paragraph group**, under **Spacing**, click the **Before up spin box arrow** two times to set the **Spacing Before** to **12 pt**. Compare your screen with Figure 1.35, and then **Save** your document.

This action increases the amount of space above each of the subheadings, which will make them easy to distinguish in the document. The formatting is applied only to the selected paragraphs.

FIGURE 1.35

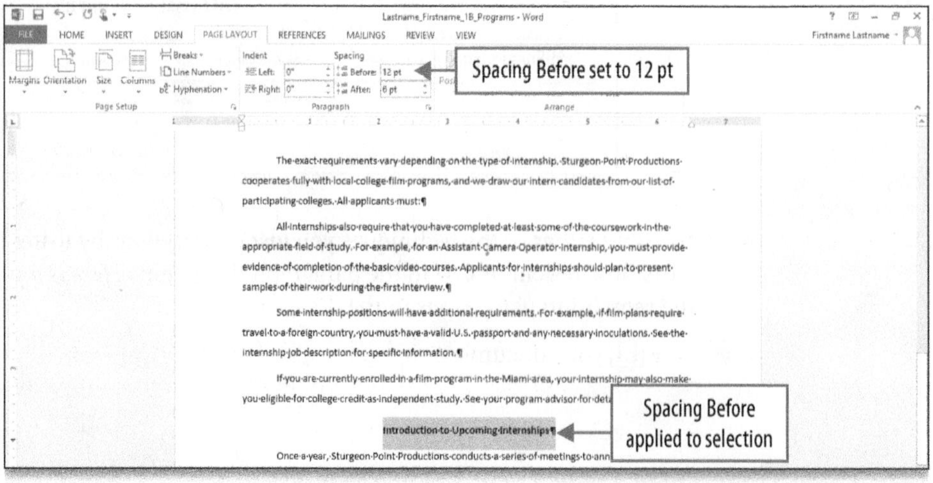

Objective 6 Create and Modify Lists

Video W1-6

To display a list of information, you can choose a ***bulleted list***, which uses ***bullets***—text symbols such as small circles or check marks—to introduce each item in a list. You can also choose a ***numbered list***, which uses consecutive numbers or letters to introduce each item in a list.

Use a bulleted list if the items in the list can be introduced in any order; use a numbered list for items that have definite steps, a sequence of actions, or are in chronological order.

Activity 1.22 | Creating a Bulleted List

1 In the upper portion of **Page 1**, locate the paragraph *Short feature films*, and then point to this paragraph from the left margin area to display the pointer. Drag down to select this paragraph and the next five paragraphs.

2 On the **HOME tab**, in the **Paragraph group**, click **Bullets** to change the selected text to a bulleted list.

The spacing between each of the bulleted points changes to the spacing between lines in a paragraph—in this instance, 1.5 line spacing. The 6 pt. spacing after each paragraph is eliminated with the exception of the last item in the list. Each bulleted item is automatically indented.

3 On the ruler, point to **First Line Indent** and read the ScreenTip, and then point to **Hanging Indent**. Compare your screen with Figure 1.36.

By default, Word formats bulleted items with a first line indent of 0.25" and adds a Hanging Indent at 0.5". The hanging indent maintains the alignment of text when a bulleted item is more than one line.

You can modify the list indentation by using Decrease Indent or Increase Indent. ***Decrease Indent*** moves your paragraph closer to the margin. ***Increase Indent*** moves your paragraph farther away from the margin.

FIGURE 1.36

4 Scroll down slightly, and then by using the pointer from the left margin area, select the five internship positions, beginning with *Production Assistant* and ending with *Assistant Set Designer*. In the **Paragraph group**, click **Bullets**.

5 Scroll down to view **Page 2**. Apply bullets to all of the paragraphs that indicate the September meetings and meeting dates, beginning with *Technical* and ending with *Music*. **Save** your document.

Activity 1.23 | Creating a Numbered List

1 Under the subheading *Requirements*, in the paragraph that begins *The exact requirements*, click to position the insertion point at the *end* of the paragraph, following the colon. Press Enter to create a blank paragraph. Notice that the paragraph is indented, because the First Line Indent from the previous paragraph carried over to the new paragraph.

2 To change the indent formatting for this paragraph, on the ruler, drag the **First Line Indent** marker to the left so that it is positioned directly above the lower button.

3 Being sure to include the period, type **1.** and press Spacebar. Compare your screen with Figure 1.37.

Word determines that this paragraph is the first item in a numbered list and formats the new paragraph accordingly, indenting the list in the same manner as the bulleted list. The space after the number changes to a tab, and the AutoCorrect Options button displays to the left of the list item. The tab is indicated by a right arrow formatting mark.

FIGURE 1.37

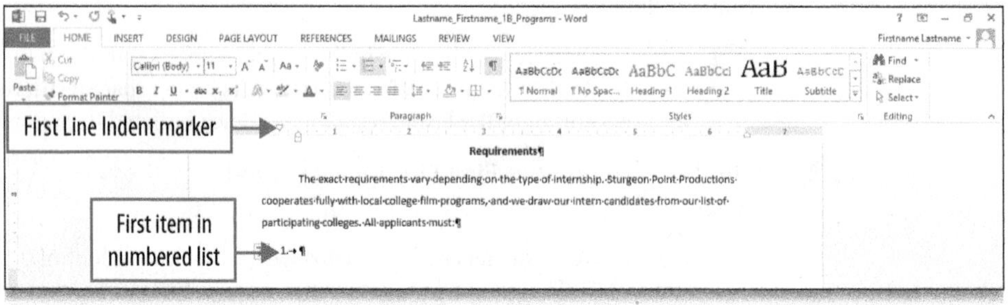

ALERT! **Activating Automatic Numbered Lists**

If a numbered list does not begin automatically, click the FILE tab, and then click the Options tab. On the left side of the Word Options dialog box, click Proofing. Under AutoCorrect options, click the AutoCorrect Options button. In the AutoCorrect dialog box, click the AutoFormat As You Type tab. Under *Apply as you type*, select the *Automatic numbered lists* check box, and then click OK two times to close both dialog boxes.

4 Click **AutoCorrect Options**, and then compare your screen with Figure 1.38.

From the displayed list, you can remove the automatic formatting here, or stop using the automatic numbered lists option in this document. You also have the option to open the AutoCorrect dialog box to *Control AutoFormat Options*.

FIGURE 1.38

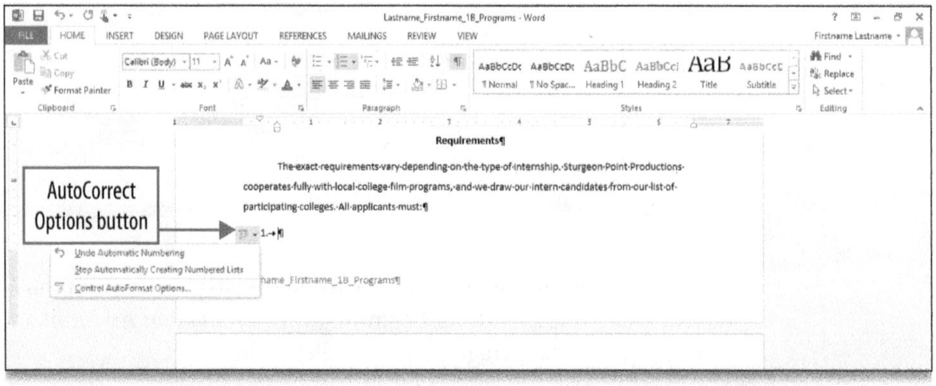

5 Click **AutoCorrect Options** again to close the menu without selecting any of the commands. Type **Be enrolled in an accredited film program** and press Enter. Notice that the second number and a tab are added to the next line.

6 Type **Be available during the entire production schedule** and press Enter. Type **Submit two faculty recommendation letters** Compare your screen with Figure 1.39, and then **Save** your document.

FIGURE 1.39

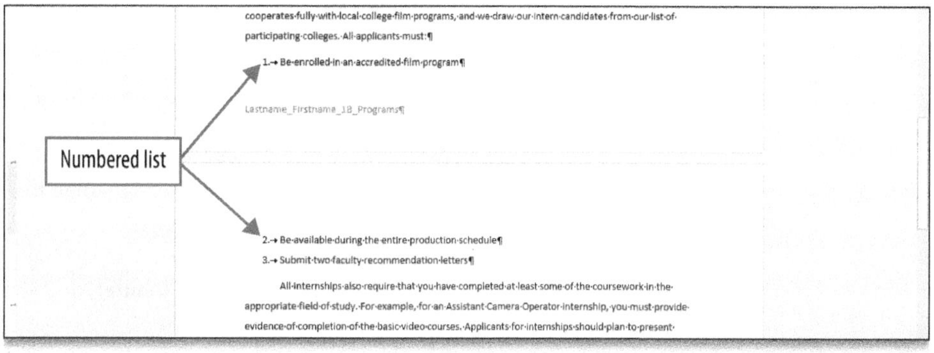

> ***More Knowledge*** **To End a List**
>
> To turn a list off, you can press Backspace, click the Numbering or Bullets button, or press Enter two times. Both list buttons—Numbering and Bullets—act as ***toggle buttons***; that is, clicking the button one time turns the feature on, and clicking the button again turns the feature off.

Activity 1.24 | Customizing Bullets

You can use any symbol from any font for your bullet characters.

1 Press Ctrl + End to move to the end of the document, and then scroll up as necessary to display the bulleted list containing the list of meetings.

2 Point to the left of the first list item to display the pointer, and then drag down to select all six meetings in the list—the bullet symbols are not highlighted.

3 On the mini toolbar, click the **Bullets button arrow** to display the **Bullet Library**, and then compare your screen with Figure 1.40.

FIGURE 1.40

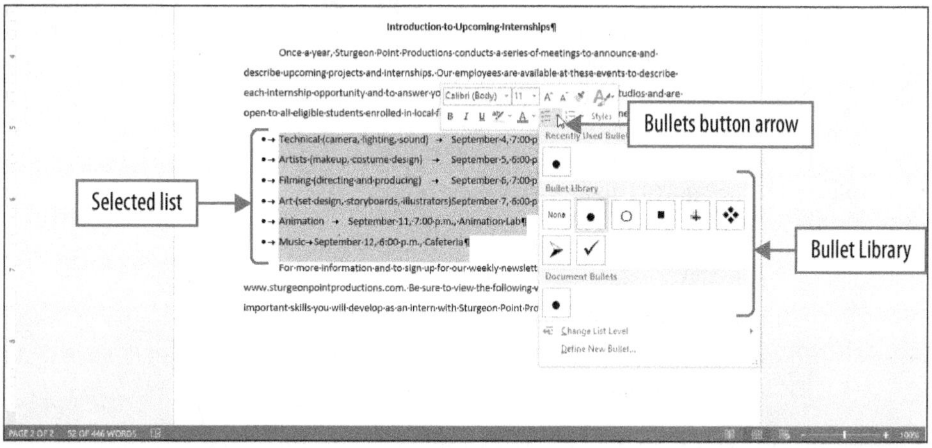

> **ALERT!** **Did Your Bullet Symbols Disappear?**
>
> If the bullet symbols no longer display, then you clicked the Bullets button. The Bullets button is a toggle button that turns the bullet symbols on and off. Click Undo to reapply the bullets, and then repeat Step 3, making sure that you click the Bullets button arrow.

4 Under **Bullet Library**, click the **check mark** symbol. If the check mark is not available, choose another bullet symbol.

5 With the bulleted list still selected, right-click over the list, and then on the mini toolbar, double-click **Format Painter** [icon].

ANOTHER WAY On the HOME tab, in the Clipboard group, click Format Painter.

6 Use the vertical scroll bar or your mouse wheel to scroll to view **Page 1**. Move the pointer to the left of the first item in the first bulleted list to display the [icon] pointer, and then drag down to select all six items in the list and to apply the format of the third bulleted list—the check mark bullets—to this list. Repeat this procedure to change the bullets in the second list to check marks. Press Esc to turn off **Format Painter**, and then **Save** [icon] your document. Compare your screen with Figure 1.41.

FIGURE 1.41

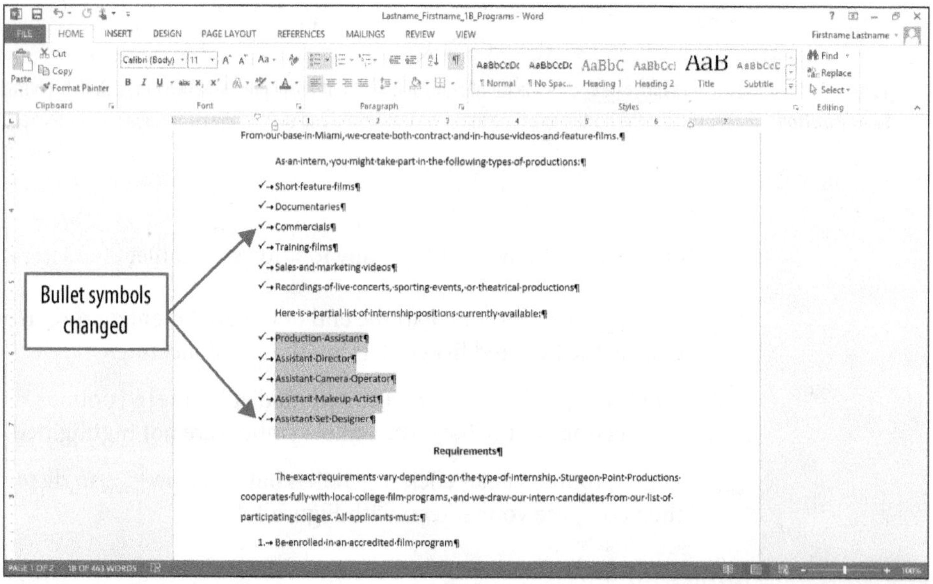

Objective 7 Set and Modify Tab Stops

Video W1-7

Tab stops mark specific locations on a line of text. Use tab stops to indent and align text, and use the Tab key to move to tab stops.

Activity 1.25 | Setting Tab Stops

1 Scroll to view **Page 2**, and then by using the [icon] pointer at the left of the first item, select all of the items in the bulleted list of meetings and dates. Notice that there is a tab mark between the name of the meeting and the date.

The arrow that indicates a tab is a nonprinting formatting mark.

2 To the left of the horizontal ruler, point to **Tab Alignment** [icon] to display the *Left Tab* ScreenTip, and then compare your screen with Figure 1.42.

FIGURE 1.42

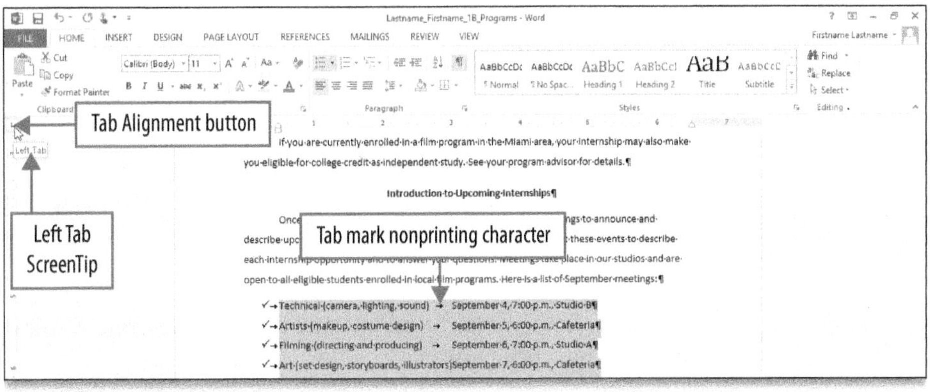

3 Click **Tab Alignment** several times to view the tab alignment options shown in the table in Figure 1.43.

FIGURE 1.43

TAB ALIGNMENT OPTIONS		
TYPE	TAB ALIGNMENT BUTTON DISPLAYS THIS MARKER	RESULT OF TAB ALIGNMENT
Left		Text is left aligned at the tab stop and extends to the right.
Center		Text is centered around the tab stop.
Right		Text is right aligned at the tab stop and extends to the left.
Decimal		The decimal point aligns at the tab stop.
Bar		A vertical bar displays at the tab stop.
First Line Indent		Text in the first line of a paragraph indents.
Hanging Indent		Text in all lines except the first line in the paragraph indents.

4 Display **Left Tab**. Along the lower edge of the horizontal ruler, point to and then click at **3.5 inches on the horizontal ruler**. Notice that all of the dates left align at the new tab stop location, and the right edge of the column is uneven.

5 Compare your screen with Figure 1.44, and then **Save** your document.

FIGURE 1.44

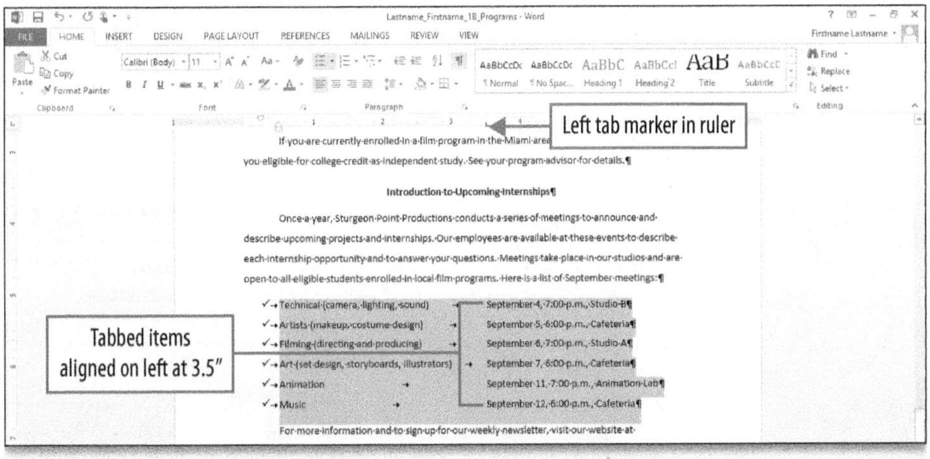

Activity 1.26 | Modifying Tab Stops

Tab stops are a form of paragraph formatting. Therefore, the information about tab stops is stored in the paragraph mark in the paragraphs to which they were applied.

1 With the bulleted list still selected, on the ruler, point to the new tab marker at **3.5 inches on the horizontal ruler**, and then when the *Left Tab* ScreenTip displays, drag the tab marker to **4 inches on the horizontal ruler**.

In all of the selected lines, the text at the tab stop left aligns at 4 inches.

2 On the ruler, point to the tab marker that you moved to display the *Left Tab* ScreenTip, and then double-click to display the **Tabs** dialog box.

ANOTHER WAY On the HOME tab, in the Paragraph group, click the Dialog Box Launcher. At the bottom of the Paragraph dialog box, click the Tabs button.

3 In the **Tabs** dialog box, under **Tab stop position**, if necessary, select *4"* and then type **6**

4 Under **Alignment**, click the **Right** option button. Under **Leader**, click the **2** option button. Near the bottom of the **Tabs** dialog box, click **Set**.

Because the Right tab will be used to align the items in the list, the tab stop at 4" is no longer necessary.

5 In the **Tabs** dialog box, in the **Tab stop position** box, click **4"** to select this tab stop, and then in the lower portion of the **Tabs** dialog box, click the **Clear** button to delete this tab stop, which is no longer necessary. Compare your screen with Figure 1.45.

FIGURE 1.45

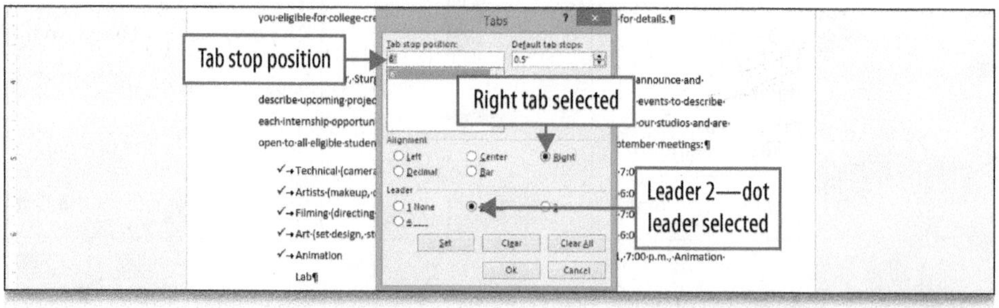

6 Click **OK**. On the ruler, notice that the left tab marker at *4"* no longer displays, a right tab marker displays at *6"*, and a series of dots—a ***dot leader***—displays between the columns of the list. Notice also that the right edge of the column is even. Compare your screen with Figure 1.46.

A ***leader character*** creates a solid, dotted, or dashed line that fills the space to the left of a tab character and draws the reader's eyes across the page from one item to the next. When the character used for the leader is a dot, it is commonly referred to as a dot leader.

FIGURE 1.46

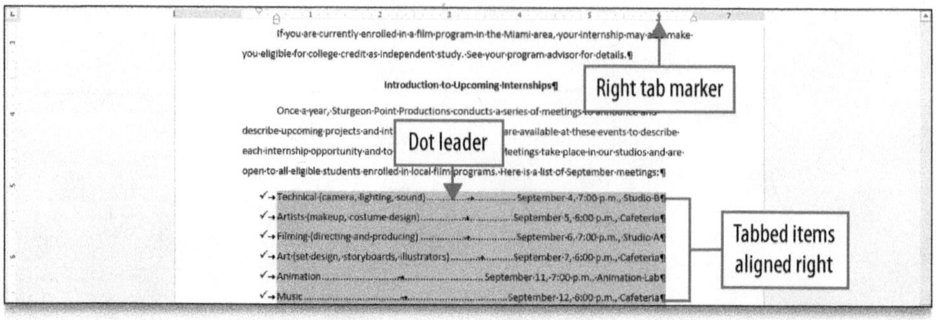

7 In the bulleted list that uses dot leaders, locate the *Art* meeting, and then click to position the insertion point at the end of that line, after the word *Cafeteria*. Press Enter to create a new blank bullet item.

8 Type **Video Editing** and press Tab. Notice that a dot leader fills the space to the tab marker location.

9 Type **September 10, 7:00 p.m., Cafeteria** and notice that the text moves to the left to maintain the right alignment of the tab stop.

10 **Save** your document.

Objective 8 Insert a SmartArt Graphic and an Online Video

Video W1-8

SmartArt graphics are designer-quality visual representations of information, and Word provides many different layouts from which you can choose. You can also insert a link to an online video from a variety of online sources, thus enabling the reader to view the video when connected to the Internet. SmartArt graphics and videos can communicate your messages or ideas more effectively than plain text and these objects add visual interest to a document or webpage.

Activity 1.27 | Inserting a SmartArt Graphic

1 Press Ctrl + Home to move to the top of the document, and then click to the right of the subtitle *Internship Guide*.

2 Click the **INSERT tab**, and then in the **Illustrations group**, point to **SmartArt** to display its ScreenTip. Read the ScreenTip, and then click **SmartArt**.

3 In the center portion of the **Choose a SmartArt Graphic** dialog box, scroll down and examine the numerous types of SmartArt graphics available.

4 On the left, click **Process**, and then by using the ScreenTips, locate and click **Basic Chevron Process**. Compare your screen with Figure 1.47.

At the right of the dialog box, a preview and description of the SmartArt displays.

FIGURE 1.47

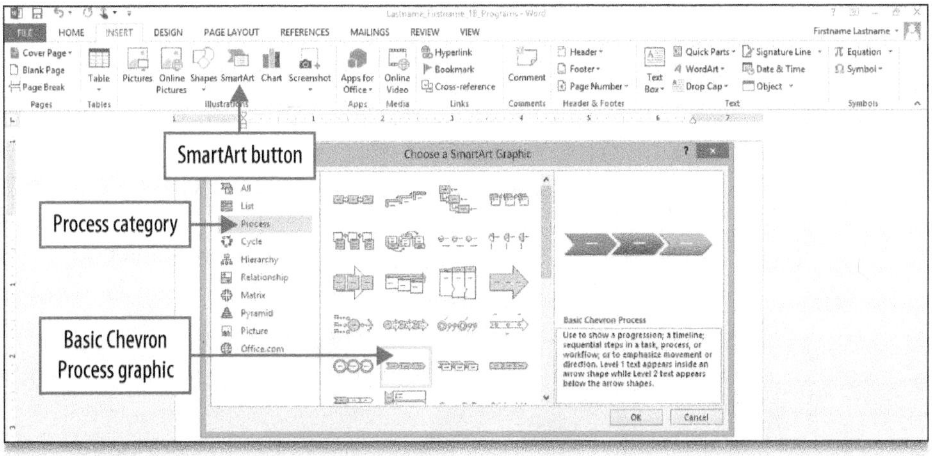

5 Click **OK** to insert the SmartArt graphic.

To the left of the inserted SmartArt graphic the text pane may display. The text pane provides one method for entering text into your SmartArt graphic. If you choose not to use the text pane to enter text, you can close it.

6 On the ribbon under **SMARTART TOOLS**, on the **DESIGN tab**, in the **Create Graphic group**, notice the **Text Pane** button. If the Text Pane button is selected, click **Text Pane** to close the pane.

7 In the SmartArt graphic, in the first blue arrow, click *[Text]*, and notice that *[Text]* is replaced by a blinking insertion point.

The word *[Text]* is called ***placeholder text***, which is non-printing text that indicates where you can type.

8 Type **Apply Online**

9 Click the placeholder text in the middle arrow. Type **Interview** and then click the placeholder text in the third arrow. Type **Train on the Job** and then compare your screen with Figure 1.48.

FIGURE 1.48

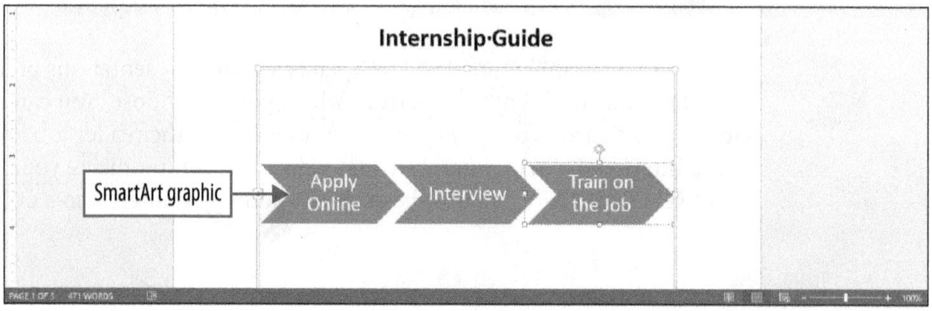

10 **Save** your document.

Activity 1.28 | Sizing and Formatting a SmartArt Graphic

1 Click the SmartArt graphic border to select it. Be sure that none of the arrows have sizing handles around their border, which would indicate the arrow was selected, not the entire graphic.

2 Click the **FORMAT tab**, and then in the **Size group**, if necessary, click **Size** to display the **Shape Height** and **Shape Width** boxes.

3 Set the **Height** to **1.75"** and the **Width** to **6.5"**, and then compare your screen with Figure 1.49.

FIGURE 1.49

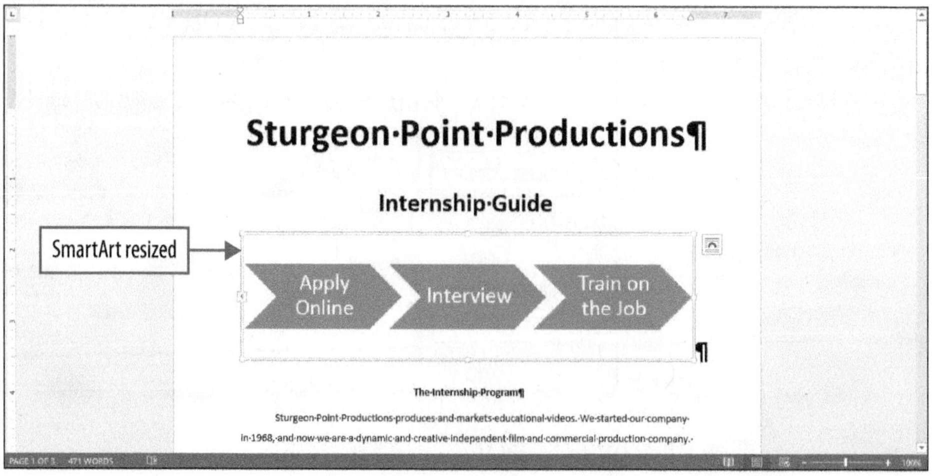

4 With the SmartArt graphic still selected, click the **SMARTART TOOLS DESIGN tab**, and then in the **SmartArt Styles group**, click **Change Colors**. Under **Colorful**, click the fourth style—**Colorful Range–Accent Colors 4 to 5**.

5 On the **SMARTART TOOLS DESIGN tab**, in the **SmartArt Styles group**, click **More** [▾]. Under **3-D**, click the second style—**Inset**. Click **Save** [💾], and then compare your screen with Figure 1.50.

FIGURE 1.50

Activity 1.29 | Inserting an Online Video

NOTE **This is an Optional Activity**

To complete this activity, you must be signed into Office 2013 with your Microsoft Account. If you are using Office 2013 in a college classroom or lab, you may need to sign in with an organizational account. Once you are signed in, verify that YouTube is available by clicking **FILE**, and then on the left click **Account**. Under Connected Services, if YouTube does not display, click **Add a Service**, point to Images & Videos, and then click **YouTube**. If you cannot activate YouTube, skip Steps 1-6 and complete Project 1B.

Microsoft's research indicates that two-thirds of people who open Word documents never edit them; they only read them. So with more and more documents being read online—and not on paper—it makes sense that you may want to include videos in your Word documents.

1 Press Ctrl + End to move to the end of the document.

2 On the **INSERT tab**, in the **Media group**, click **Online Video**. If the YouTube search box does not display, in the lower left corner of the Insert Video window, under Also insert from: click YouTube.

Here you can search the web for an online video, search YouTube, or enter an ***embed code*** to insert a link to a video from a website. An embed code is a code that creates a link to a video, picture, or other type of ***rich media*** content. Rich media, also called ***interactive media***, refers to computer interaction that responds to your actions; for example by presenting text, graphics, animation, video, audio, or games.

3 In the **Search YouTube** box, being sure to include the quotation marks, type **"Go 2013 1B Video"** and then press Enter.

4 Point to the displayed thumbnail and notice the ScreenTip. Click the **1B video**, and then click **Insert**. Compare your screen with Figure 1.51.

FIGURE 1.51

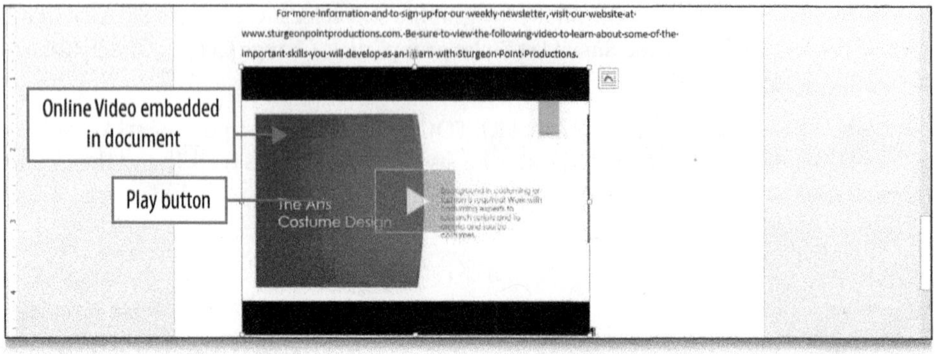

5 In the center of the video, point to the **Play** button [▶] to display the [hand] pointer, and then click. If a black screen displays, double-click one or more times until you see text on the screen, then point to the lower edge of the screen and click the Play button.

A new window opens that contains the video and a play button. You can click the play button to view the video. When you insert an online video, the embed code is stored with the document and a link is created to the online content. In this manner, you can easily share video content that is relevant to the document without increasing the file size of the document.

6 View a few seconds of the video—more if you want—and then press Esc to return to your document.

7 Click **Save** [Save], and then press Ctrl + Home to move to the top of your document.

8 Click the **FILE tab**, and then in the lower right portion of the screen, click **Show All Properties**. In the **Tags** box, type **internship** and in the **Subject** box, type your course name and section number. In the **Author** box, be sure your name displays; edit if necessary.

9 On the left, click **Print** to display **Print Preview**. At the bottom of the preview, click the **Previous Page** [◄] and **Next Page** [►] buttons to move between pages. If necessary, return to the document and make any necessary changes.

10 As directed by your instructor, print your document or submit it electronically. **Save** [Save] your document and **Close** [×] Word.

END | You have completed Project 1B

GO! with Office Online (formerly Web Apps)

Objective Create a Handout in Word Online

You can use Word Online to edit your document if you are not at a computer on which Word 2013 is installed. You can change fonts and font sizes, modify paragraph alignment, and apply bullets and numbering.

Build from Scratch

ALERT! Working with Web-Based Applications and Services

Computer programs and services on the web receive continuous updates and improvements, so the steps to complete this web-based activity may differ from the ones shown. You can often look at the screens and the information presented to determine how to complete the activity.

Activity | Creating a Handout in Word Online

In this activity, you will use Word Online to edit a flyer similar to the one you edited in Project 1B.

1 Start Word, and then below the **Recent** list, click **Open Other Documents**. Navigate to your student data files, and then open **w01_1B_Web**. If necessary, in the upper right corner, log into Office with your Microsoft account. On the **FILE tab**, click **Save As**, and then on the right, double-click the name of your OneDrive.

2 In the **Save As** dialog box, click your **GO! Web Projects** folder, and then click **Open**. In the **File name** box, type **Lastname_Firstname_WD_1B_Web** and then click **Save**.

3 Close Word, launch **Internet Explorer**, go to http://onedrive.com, sign in, open your **GO! Web Projects** folder, and then click the file you just saved there.

4 In the upper left, click **EDIT DOCUMENT**, and then click **Edit in Word Online**.

5 Press Ctrl + A to select all the text in the document. On the **HOME tab**, in the **Paragraph group**, click **Align Text Left**.

6 Drag to select the first three lines in the document. On the **HOME tab**, in the **Paragraph group**, click **Center**. Compare your screen with Figure A.

7 Click at the beginning of the paragraph that begins *Sturgeon Point Productions produces*, and then press Tab. Click at the beginning of the paragraph that begins *As an intern*, and then press Tab.

8 Scroll the document and click at the beginning of the paragraph that begins *Here is a partial*, and then press Tab.

FIGURE A

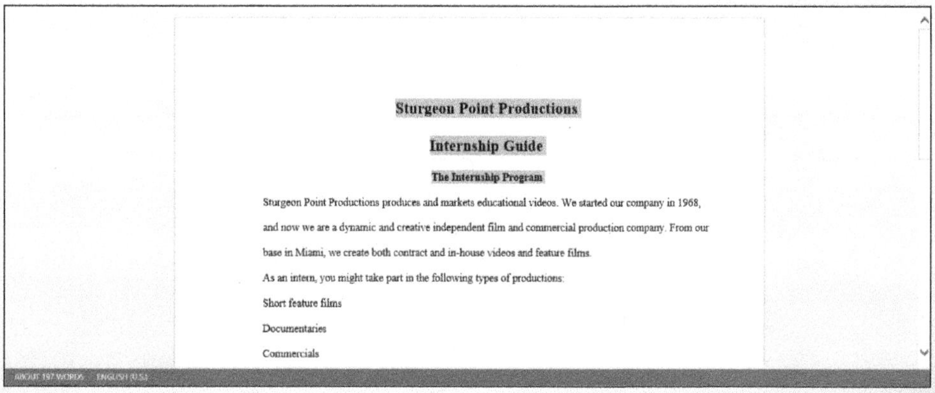

(GO! with Office Online (formerly Web Apps) continues on the next page)

9 Click anywhere in the subheading *Introduction to Upcoming Internships*, and then on the **HOME tab**, in the **Paragraph group**, click **Center** [icon]. Click at the beginning of the paragraph that begins *Once a year*, and then press Tab.

10 Select the six paragraphs that begin with *Short feature films* and that end with *Recordings of live concerts*. On the **HOME tab**, in the **Paragraph group**, click **Bullets** [icon] to apply round, filled bullets to the selection.

11 Select the list that begins with *Production Assistant* and ends with *Assistant Set Designer*, and then click **Bullets** [icon] to apply bullets to the selection.

12 Select the first list to which you applied bullets. On the **HOME tab**, in the **Paragraph group**, click the **Bullets button arrow**, and then click **Square Bullet**. Notice that the same bullet style is applied to the second list.

13 Scroll the document and then select the list that begins with *Artists* and ends with *Music*. On the **HOME tab**, in the **Paragraph group**, click **Numbering** [icon] to apply numbers to the list.

14 Press Ctrl + A to select the entire document. On the **HOME tab**, in the **Paragraph group**, click **Line Spacing** [icon], and then click **1.5** to change the line spacing for the entire document. Press Ctrl + Home to move to the top of the document and then compare your screen with Figure B.

15 Submit your file as directed by your instructor. Sign out of your OneDrive and close Internet Explorer.

FIGURE B

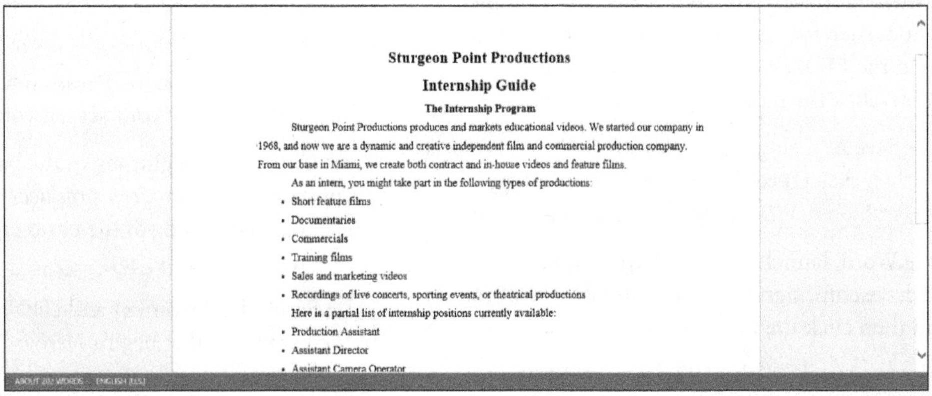

Sturgeon Point Productions

Internship Guide

The Internship Program

Sturgeon Point Productions produces and markets educational videos. We started our company in 1968, and now we are a dynamic and creative independent film and commercial production company. From our base in Miami, we create both contract and in-house videos and feature films.

As an intern, you might take part in the following types of productions:

- Short feature films
- Documentaries
- Commercials
- Training films
- Sales and marketing videos
- Recordings of live concerts, sporting events, or theatrical productions

Here is a partial list of internship positions currently available:

- Production Assistant
- Assistant Director
- Assistant Camera Operator

ABOUT 202 WORDS ENGLISH (U.S.)

GO! with Microsoft Office 365

Andrew Rodriguez / Fotolia; FotolEdhar/ Fotolia; apops/ Fotolia; Yuri Arcurs/ Fotolia

In every job, you must work and communicate with other people. A group of workers tasked with working together to solve a problem, make a decision, or create a work product is referred to as a ***team***. For a team to succeed, the team members must be able to communicate with one another easily.

If all the team members work at the same location and work the same hours, communication is easy. You schedule face-to-face meetings and exchange documents and information among yourselves. But that is a rare arrangement in today's organizations. Rather, it is more likely that the members of your team work in different locations—even different countries—and work different hours or travel extensively away from the headquarters location. Also, for specific projects, teams are frequently organized across different departments of an organization or even across different organizations entirely. Then when the project is complete, the team disbands.

Collaboration is when you work together with others as a team in an intellectual endeavor to complete a shared task or achieve a shared goal; for example, when you and one or more of your classmates work together on a class project. Collaboration involves giving feedback to and receiving feedback from others on the team, and then revising the strategies to achieve the goal or produce the work product based on the feedback.

Microsoft Office 365 is a set of secure online services that enable people in an organization to communicate and collaborate by using any Internet-connected device—a computer, a tablet, or a mobile phone. Because Office 365 offers access from anywhere to email, Web conferencing, documents, and calendars, everyone on a team can work together easily. Office 365 is intended for use by multiple users in an organization.

Activity | Using the Exchange Online Outlook Meeting Tool to Collaborate

This group project relates to the **Bell Orchid Hotels**. If your instructor assigns this project to your class, you can expect to use the **Outlook Meeting tool** in **Office 365 Exchange Online** to collaborate on the following tasks for this chapter:

- If you are in the **Accounting Group**, you and your teammates will meet virtually to compose, format, proofread, and prepare a letter to send to shareholders.
- If you are in the **Engineering Group**, you and your teammates will meet virtually to compose, format, proofread, and prepare a letter to the three insurance companies that cover the hotel properties.
- If you are in the **Food and Beverage Group**, you and your teammates will meet virtually to compose, format, proofread, and finalize a letter to a customer planning a banquet.
- If you are in the **Human Resources Group**, you and your teammates will meet virtually to compose, format, proofread, and finalize a memo for employees regarding the new employee newsletter.
- If you are in the **Operations Group**, you and your teammates will meet virtually to compose, format, proofread, and finalize letters to three job applicants.
- If you are in the **Sales and Marketing Group**, you and your teammates will meet virtually to compose, edit, and finalize a letter to 20 groups of professional associations.

FIGURE A

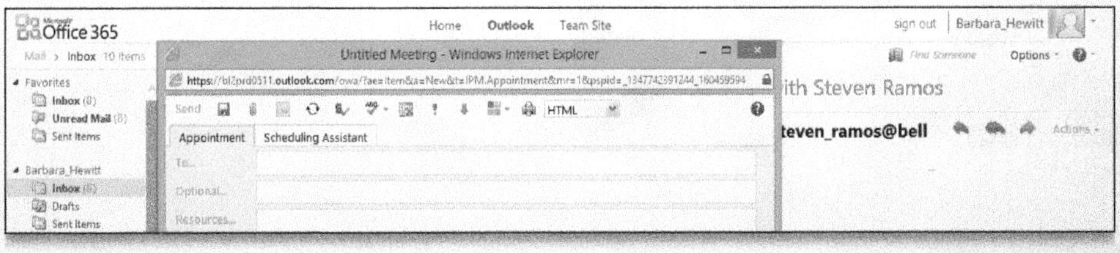

END OF CHAPTER

SUMMARY

In a document, you can type all of the text, or you can type some of the text and then insert additional text from another source such as another Word document. As you type, word wrap determines the line endings.

Graphics include pictures, shapes, and text boxes. Use graphics, text effects, and pictures to add visual appeal. When you insert pictures, Word provides many ways to position and format the pictures on the page.

SmartArt graphics visually represent your ideas and there are many SmartArt graphics from which to choose. You can also use online videos in your documents to provide visual information to the reader.

Word documents can be formatted to display your information attractively. You can add a page border, add bulleted and numbered lists, change margins and tabs, and modify paragraph and line spacing.

GO! LEARN IT ONLINE

Review the concepts and key terms in this chapter by completing these online challenges, which you can find at **www.pearsonhighered.com/go.**

Matching and Multiple Choice: Answer matching and multiple choice questions to test what you learned in this chapter. MyITLab®

Crossword Puzzle: Spell out the words that match the numbered clues, and put them in the puzzle squares.

Flipboard: Flip through the definitions of the key terms in this chapter and match them with the correct term.

GO! FOR JOB SUCCESS

Video: Personal Branding

Your instructor may assign this video to your class, and then ask you to think about, or discuss with your classmates, these questions:

FotolEdhar / Fotolia

How do you suggest job seekers communicate their unique value—their *personal brand*—to potential employers online?

What are the best ways to network online and offline?

What are some of the biggest pitfalls in using social media to communicate a personal brand?

END OF CHAPTER

REVIEW AND ASSESSMENT GUIDE FOR WORD CHAPTER 1

Your instructor may assign one or more of these projects to help you review the chapter and assess your mastery and understanding of the chapter.

Review and Assessment Guide for Word Chapter 1			
Project	**Apply Skills from These Chapter Objectives**	**Project Type**	**Project Location**
1C	Objectives 1-4 from Project 1A	**1C Skills Review** A guided review of the skills from Project 1A.	On the following pages
1D	Objectives 5-8 from Project 1B	**1D Skills Review** A guided review of the skills from Project 1B.	On the following pages
1E	Objectives 1-4 from Project 1A	**1E Mastery (Grader Project)** A demonstration of your mastery of the skills in Project 1A with extensive decision making.	In MyITLab and on the following pages
1F	Objectives 5-8 from Project 1B	**1F Mastery (Grader Project)** A demonstration of your mastery of the skills in Project 1B with extensive decision making.	In MyITLab and on the following pages
1G	Objectives 1-8 from Projects 1A and 1B	**1G Mastery (Grader Project)** A demonstration of your mastery of the skills in Projects 1A and 1B with extensive decision making.	In MyITLab and on the following pages
1H	Combination of Objectives from Projects 1A and 1B	**1H GO! Fix It** A demonstration of your mastery of the skills in Projects 1A and 1B by creating a correct result from a document that contains errors you must find.	Online
1I	Combination of Objectives from Projects 1A and 1B	**1I GO! Make It** A demonstration of your mastery of the skills in Projects 1A and 1B by creating a result from a supplied picture.	Online
1J	Combination of Objectives from Projects 1A and 1B	**1J GO! Solve It** A demonstration of your mastery of the skills in Projects 1A and 1B, your decision-making skills, and your critical thinking skills. A task-specific rubric helps you self-assess your result.	Online
1K	Combination of Objectives from Projects 1A and 1B	**1K GO! Solve It** A demonstration of your mastery of the skills in Projects 1A and 1B, your decision-making skills, and your critical thinking skills. A task-specific rubric helps you self-assess your result.	On the following pages
1L	Combination of Objectives from Projects 1A and 1B	**1L GO! Think** A demonstration of your understanding of the chapter concepts applied in a manner that you would outside of college. An analytic rubric helps you and your instructor grade the quality of your work by comparing it to the work an expert in the discipline would create.	On the following pages
1M	Combination of Objectives from Projects 1A and 1B	**1M GO! Think** A demonstration of your understanding of the chapter concepts applied in a manner that you would outside of college. An analytic rubric helps you and your instructor grade the quality of your work by comparing it to the work an expert in the discipline would create.	Online
1N	Combination of Objectives from Projects 1A and 1B	**1N You and GO!** A demonstration of your understanding of the chapter concepts applied in a manner that you would in a personal situation. An analytic rubric helps you and your instructor grade the quality of your work.	Online
1O	Combination of Objectives from Projects 1A and 1B	**1O Cumulative Group Project for Word Chapter 1** A demonstration of your understanding of concepts and your ability to work collaboratively in a group role-playing assessment, requiring both collaboration and self-management.	Online

GLOSSARY

GLOSSARY OF CHAPTER KEY TERMS

Alignment The placement of paragraph text relative to the left and right margins.

Alignment guide Green vertical or horizontal lines that display when you are moving or sizing an object to assist you with object placement.

Artistic effects Formats applied to images that make pictures resemble sketches or paintings.

Bulleted list A list of items with each item introduced by a symbol such as a small circle or check mark, and which is useful when the items in the list can be displayed in any order.

Bullets Text symbols such as small circles or check marks that precede each item in a bulleted list.

Center alignment The alignment of text or objects that is centered horizontally between the left and right margin.

Collaboration The action of working together with others as a team in an intellectual endeavor to complete a shared task or achieve a shared goal.

Decrease Indent A command that moves your paragraph closer to the margin.

Dot leader A series of dots preceding a tab that guides the eye across the line.

Drawing objects Graphic objects, such as shapes, diagrams, lines, or circles.

Embed code A code that creates a link to a video, picture, or other type of rich media content.

Floating object A graphic that can be moved independently of the surrounding text characters.

Formatting marks Characters that display on the screen, but do not print, indicating where the Enter key, the Spacebar, and the Tab key were pressed; also called nonprinting characters.

Graphics Pictures, charts, or drawing objects.

Increase Indent A command moves your paragraph farther away from the margin.

Inline Object An object or graphic inserted in a document that acts like a character in a sentence.

Interactive media Computer interaction that responds to your actions; for example by presenting text, graphics, animation, video, audio, or games. Also referred to as rich media.

Justified alignment An arrangement of text in which the text aligns evenly on both the left and right margins.

Layout Options Picture formatting options that control the manner in which text wraps around a picture or other object.

Leader character Characters that form a solid, dotted, or dashed line that fills the space preceding a tab stop.

Left alignment An arrangement of text in which the text aligns at the left margin, leaving the right margin uneven.

Line spacing The distance between lines of text in a paragraph.

Live Layout A feature that reflows text as you move or size an object so that you can view the placement of surrounding text.

Margins The space between the text and the top, bottom, left, and right edges of the paper.

Microsoft Office 365 A set of secure online services that enable people in an organization to communicate and collaborate by using any Internet-connected device—a computer, a tablet, or a mobile phone.

Nonprinting characters Characters that display on the screen, but do not print; also called formatting marks.

Numbered list A list that uses consecutive numbers or letters to introduce each item in a list.

Object anchor The symbol that indicates to which paragraph an object is attached.

Picture Effects Formatting that enhances a picture with effects such as shadow, glow, reflection, or 3-D rotation.

Picture styles Frames, shapes, shadows, borders, and other special effects that can be added to an image to create an overall visual style for the image.

Placeholder text Non-printing text that holds a place in a document where you can type.

Rich media Computer interaction that responds to your actions; for example by presenting text, graphics, animation, video, audio, or games. Also referred to as interactive media.

Right alignment An arrangement of text in which the text aligns at the right margin, leaving the left margin uneven.

Rotation handle A symbol with which you can rotate a graphic to any angle; displays above the top center sizing handle.

Shapes Lines, arrows, stars, banners, ovals, rectangles, and other basic shapes with which you can illustrate an idea, a process, or a workflow.

SmartArt A designer-quality visual representation of your information that you can create by choosing from among many different layouts to effectively communicate your message or ideas.

Spin box A small box with an upward- and downward-pointing arrow that lets you move rapidly through a set of values by clicking.

Tab stop A specific location on a line of text, marked on the Word ruler, to which you can move the insertion point by pressing the Tab key, and which is used to align and indent text.

Team A group of workers tasked with working together to solve a problem, make a decision, or create a work product.

Template A preformatted document that you can use as a starting point and then change to suit your needs.

Text box A movable resizable container for text or graphics.

Text effects Decorative formats, such as shadowed or mirrored text, text glow, 3-D effects, and colors that make text stand out.

Text wrapping The manner in which text displays around an object.

Toggle button A button that can be turned on by clicking it once, and then turned off by clicking it again.

Wordwrap The feature that moves text from the right edge of a paragraph to the beginning of the next line as necessary to fit within the margins.

CHAPTER REVIEW

Skills Review Project 1C Photography

Apply 1A skills from these Objectives:

1. Create a New Document and Insert Text
2. Insert and Format Graphics
3. Insert and Modify Text Boxes and Shapes
4. Preview and Print a Document

Build from Scratch

In the following Skills Review, you will create a flyer announcing a photography internship with Sturgeon Point Productions. Your completed document will look similar to Figure 1.52.

PROJECT FILES

For Project 1C, you will need the following files:

New blank Word document
w01C_Building
w01C_Photographer

You will save your document as:

Lastname_Firstname_1C_Photography

PROJECT RESULTS

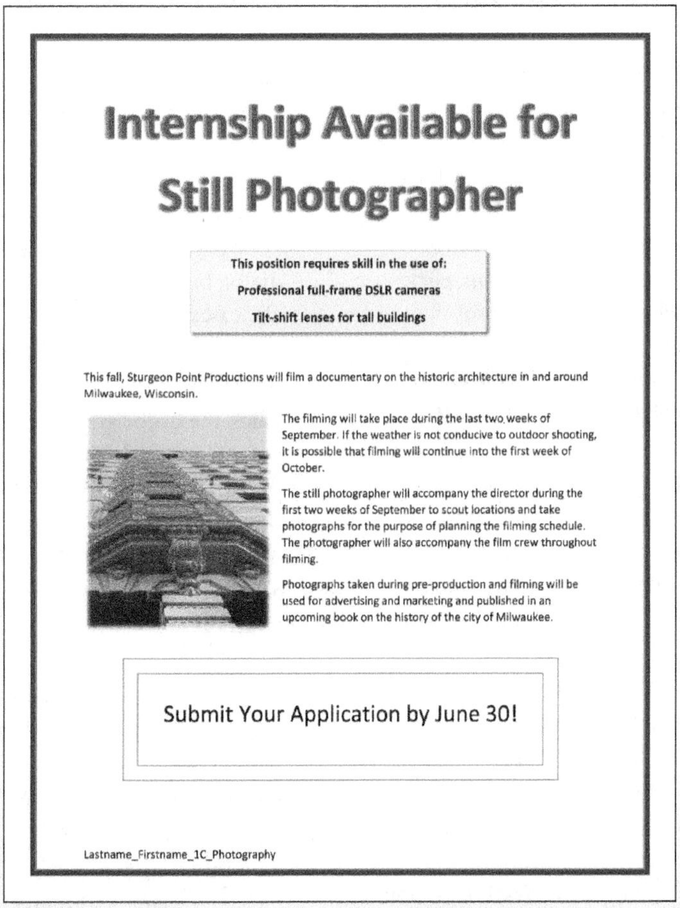

Internship Available for Still Photographer

This position requires skill in the use of:
Professional full-frame DSLR cameras
Tilt-shift lenses for tall buildings

This fall, Sturgeon Point Productions will film a documentary on the historic architecture in and around Milwaukee, Wisconsin.

The filming will take place during the last two weeks of September. If the weather is not conducive to outdoor shooting, it is possible that filming will continue into the first week of October.

The still photographer will accompany the director during the first two weeks of September to scout locations and take photographs for the purpose of planning the filming schedule. The photographer will also accompany the film crew throughout filming.

Photographs taken during pre-production and filming will be used for advertising and marketing and published in an upcoming book on the history of the city of Milwaukee.

Submit Your Application by June 30!

Lastname_Firstname_1C_Photography

FIGURE 1.52

(Project 1C Photography continues on the next page)

CHAPTER REVIEW

Skills Review Project 1C Photography (continued)

1 Start Word and then click **Blank document**. On the **HOME tab**, in the **Paragraph group**, if necessary, click **Show/Hide** to display the formatting marks. If the rulers do not display, click the **VIEW tab**, and then in the **Show group**, select the **Ruler** check box.

a. Type **Internship Available for Still Photographer** and then press Enter two times. Type the following text: **This fall, Sturgeon Point Productions will film a documentary on the historic architecture in and around Milwaukee, Wisconsin.** Press Enter.

b. On the ribbon, click the **INSERT tab**. In the **Text group**, click the **Object button arrow**, and then click **Text from File**. In the **Insert File** dialog box, navigate to the student files that accompany this textbook, locate and select **w01C_Photographer**, and then click **Insert**. Delete the blank paragraph at the end of the document.

c. Including the paragraph mark, select the first paragraph of text—*Internship Available for Still Photographer*. On the **HOME tab**, in the **Font group**, click **Text Effects and Typography**. In the **Text Effects** gallery, in the first row, click the fourth effect—**Fill - White, Outline - Accent 1, Shadow**.

d. With the text still selected, in the **Font group**, click in the **Font Size** box to select the existing font size. Type **44** and then press Enter. In the **Font group**, click the **Font Color button arrow**. Under **Theme Colors**, in the fourth column, click the first color—**Blue-Gray, Text 2**.

e. With the text still selected, in the **Font group**, click **Text Effects and Typography**. Point to **Shadow**, and then under **Outer**, in the second row, click the third style—**Offset Left**. In the **Paragraph group**, click **Center**.

f. On the **Quick Access Toolbar**, click **Save**. Under **Places**, click **Computer**, and then click **Browse**. Navigate to your **Word Chapter 1** folder. In the **File name** box, replace the existing text with **Lastname_Firstname_1C_Photography** and then click **Save**.

2 In the paragraph that begins *The filming*, click to position the insertion point at the beginning of the paragraph. On the **INSERT tab**, in the **Illustrations group**, click **Pictures**. In the **Insert Picture** dialog box, navigate to your student data files, locate and click **w01C_Building**, and then click **Insert**.

a. To the right of the selected picture, click the **Layout Options** button, and then under **With Text Wrapping**, click the first option—**Square**. **Close** the **Layout Options**.

b. On the **FORMAT tab**, in the **Size group**, click the **Shape Height spin box down arrow** as necessary to change the height of the picture to **2.7"**.

c. With the picture selected, on the **FORMAT tab**, in the **Arrange group**, click **Position**, and then click **More Layout Options**. In the **Layout** dialog box, on the **Position tab**, in the middle of the dialog box, under **Vertical**, click the **Alignment** option button. To the right of **Alignment**, click the arrow, and then click **Top**. To the right of **relative to**, click the arrow, and then click **Line**. Click **OK**.

d. On the **FORMAT tab**, in the **Picture Styles group**, click **Picture Effects**. Point to **Soft Edges**, and then click **5 Point**. On the **FORMAT tab**, in the **Adjust group**, click **Artistic Effects**. In the fourth row, click the third effect—**Crisscross Etching**.

e. Click anywhere outside the picture to deselect it. On the **DESIGN tab**, in the **Page Background group**, click **Page Borders**. In the **Borders and Shading** dialog box, on the **Page Border tab**, under **Setting**, click **Box**. Under **Style**, scroll the list and then click the third style from the bottom—a black line that fades to gray.

f. Click the **Color arrow**, and then in the next to last column, click the first color—**Blue, Accent 5**. Under **Apply to**, be sure **Whole document** is selected, and then click **OK**. Click **Save**.

3 Click the **INSERT tab**, and then in the **Illustrations group**, click **Shapes** to display the gallery. Under **Basic Shapes**, in the second row, click the fifth shape—**Frame**.

a. Position the + pointer anywhere in the blank area at the bottom of the document. Click one time to insert a 1" by 1" frame. The exact location need not be precise. To the right of the shape, click the **Layout Options** button, and at the bottom click **See more**.

b. In the **Layout** dialog box, under **Horizontal**, click the **Alignment** option button. To the right of **Alignment**, click the arrow, and then click **Centered**. To the right of **relative to**, click the arrow, and then click **Page**. Under **Vertical**, click the **Absolute position**

(Project 1C Photography continues on the next page)

option button. In the **Absolute position** box, select the existing number, and then type **1** To the right of **below**, click the arrow, and then click **Paragraph**. Click **OK**.

c. On the **FORMAT tab**, click in the **Shape Height** box. Type **1.5** and then click in the **Shape Width** box. Type **5.5** and then press Enter.

d. If necessary, select the frame shape. On the **FORMAT tab**, in the **Shape Styles group**, click **More**. In the **Shape Styles** gallery, in the first row, click the sixth style—**Colored Outline - Blue, Accent 5**. Type **Submit Your Application by June 30!** Select the text you just typed, and then on the mini toolbar, change the **Font Size** to **22**.

4 Click outside of the frame to deselect, and then press Ctrl + Home to move to the top of the document. Press ↓ two times to move to the blank paragraph below the title. Press Enter four times to make space for a text box.

a. On the **INSERT tab**, in the **Text group**, click **Text Box**. At the bottom of the gallery, click **Draw Text Box**. Position the + pointer over the first blank paragraph at the left margin. Drag down and to the right to create a text box approximately 1.5 inches high and 4 inches wide—the exact size and location need not be precise.

b. With the insertion point blinking in the text box, type the following, pressing Enter after the first two lines to create a new paragraph; do *not* press Enter after the last line:

This position requires skill in the use of:

Professional full-frame DSLR cameras

Tilt-shift lenses for tall buildings

c. To precisely place the text box, on the **FORMAT tab**, in the **Arrange group**, click **Position**, and then click **More Layout Options**. In the **Layout** dialog box, under **Horizontal**, click the **Alignment** button. To the right of **Alignment**, click the arrow, and then click **Centered**. To the right of *relative to*, click the arrow, and then click **Page**.

d. Under **Vertical**, click the **Absolute position** button. In the **Absolute position** box, select the existing number. Type **2** To the right of **below**, click the **arrow**, and then click **Margin**.

e. In the **Layout** dialog box, click the **Size tab**. Under **Height**, select the number in the **Absolute** box. Type **1** and then under **Width**, select the number in the **Absolute** box. Type **3.75** and then click **OK**.

f. In the text box, select all of the text. If necessary, right-click over the selected text to display the mini toolbar. Change the **Font Size** to **12**, apply **Bold**, and then press Ctrl + E to **Center** the text.

g. On the **FORMAT tab**, in the **Shape Styles group**, click **Shape Effects**. Point to **Shadow**, and then under **Outer**, in the first row, click the first style—**Offset Diagonal Bottom Right**.

h. In the **Shape Styles group**, click **Shape Outline**. In the fifth column, click the first color—**Blue, Accent 1** to change the color of the text box border. Click **Shape Fill**, and then in the fifth column, click the second color—**Blue, Accent 1, Lighter 80%**. Click **Save**.

5 Click the **INSERT tab**, and then in the **Header & Footer group**, click **Footer**. At the bottom of the menu, click **Edit Footer**. On the **HEADER & FOOTER TOOLS DESIGN tab**, in the **Insert group**, click **Document Info**, and then click **File Name**. Double-click in the document outside of the footer area to close the footer and return to the document.

a. Press Ctrl + Home to move the insertion point to the top of the document. In the upper left corner of your screen, click the **FILE** tab to display **Backstage** view. On the right, at the bottom of the **Properties list**, click **Show All Properties**.

b. On the list of Properties, click to the right of **Tags** to display an empty box, and then type **internship, photographer** Click to the right of **Subject** to display an empty box, and then type your course name and section #. Under **Related People**, be sure that your name displays as the author. If necessary, edit the author name.

c. **Save** your file and submit as directed by your instructor. **Close** Word.

END | You have completed Project 1C

CHAPTER REVIEW

Apply 1B skills from these Objectives:

5 Change Document and Paragraph Layout
6 Create and Modify Lists
7 Set and Modify Tab Stops
8 Insert a SmartArt Graphic and an Online Video

Skills Review Project 1D Internships

In the following Skills Review, you will edit an information handout regarding production and development internships with Sturgeon Point Productions. Your completed document will look similar to Figure 1.53.

PROJECT FILES

For Project 1D, you will need the following file:

w01D_Internship

You will save your document as:

Lastname_Firstname_1D_Internship

PROJECT RESULTS

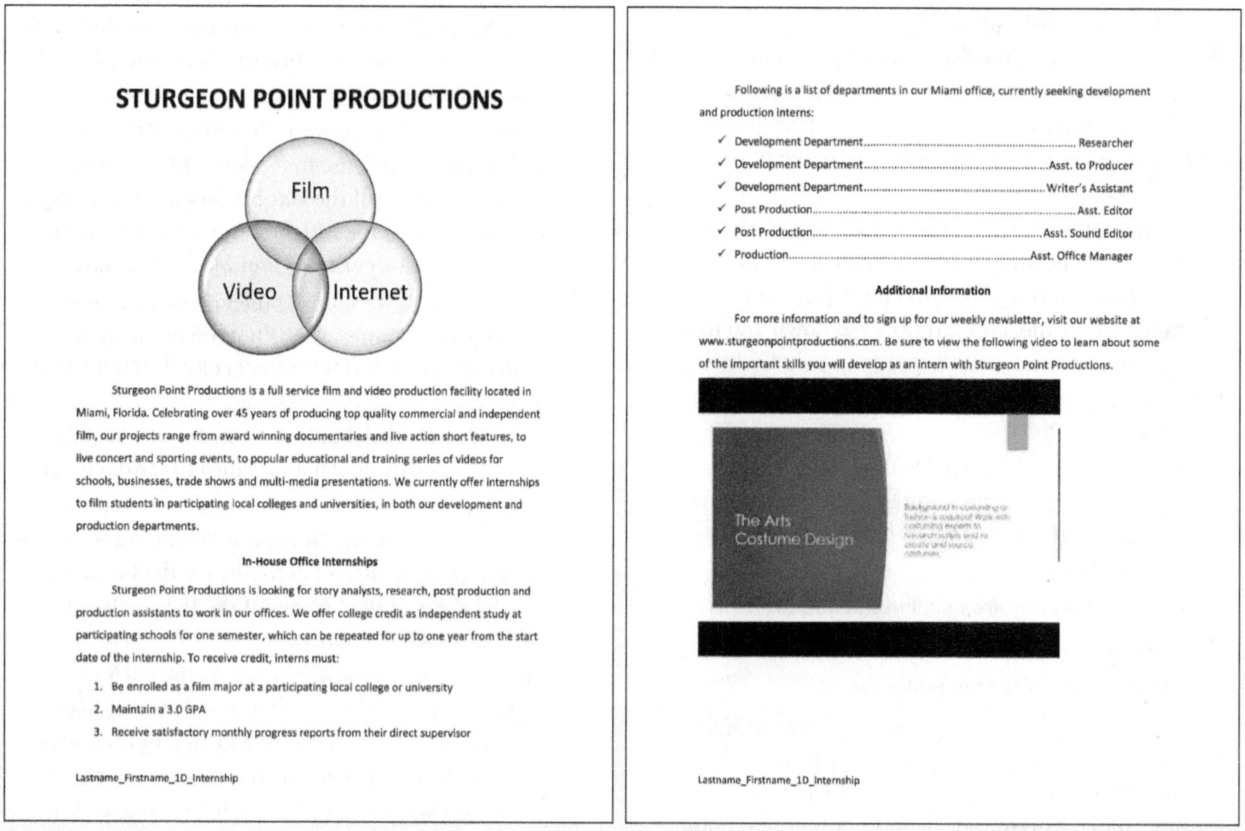

STURGEON POINT PRODUCTIONS

Sturgeon Point Productions is a full service film and video production facility located in Miami, Florida. Celebrating over 45 years of producing top quality commercial and independent film, our projects range from award winning documentaries and live action short features, to live concert and sporting events, to popular educational and training series of videos for schools, businesses, trade shows and multi-media presentations. We currently offer internships to film students in participating local colleges and universities, in both our development and production departments.

In-House Office Internships

Sturgeon Point Productions is looking for story analysts, research, post production and production assistants to work in our offices. We offer college credit as independent study at participating schools for one semester, which can be repeated for up to one year from the start date of the internship. To receive credit, interns must:

1. Be enrolled as a film major at a participating local college or university
2. Maintain a 3.0 GPA
3. Receive satisfactory monthly progress reports from their direct supervisor

Lastname_Firstname_1D_Internship

Following is a list of departments in our Miami office, currently seeking development and production interns:

- ✓ Development Department........................ Researcher
- ✓ Development Department........................Asst. to Producer
- ✓ Development Department........................Writer's Assistant
- ✓ Post Production........................Asst. Editor
- ✓ Post Production........................Asst. Sound Editor
- ✓ Production........................Asst. Office Manager

Additional Information

For more information and to sign up for our weekly newsletter, visit our website at www.sturgeonpointproductions.com. Be sure to view the following video to learn about some of the important skills you will develop as an intern with Sturgeon Point Productions.

Lastname_Firstname_1D_Internship

FIGURE 1.53

(Project 1D Internships continues on the next page)

CHAPTER REVIEW

Skills Review Project 1D Internships (continued)

1 Start Word, and then click **Open Other Documents.** Click **Computer**, and then click **Browse.** Navigate to your student files, and then open **w01D_Internship**. On the **HOME tab**, in the **Paragraph group**, be sure **Show/Hide** is active. Click the **FILE tab**, and then click **Save As.** Navigate to your **Word Chapter 1** folder, and then **Save** the document as **Lastname_Firstname_1D_Internship**

a. Click the **PAGE LAYOUT tab.** In the **Page Setup group**, click **Margins**, and then click **Custom Margins.** In the **Page Setup** dialog box, press Tab as necessary to select the value in the **Left** box. Type **1** and then press Tab to select the value in the **Right** box. Type **1** and then click **OK.**

b. Scroll down to view the bottom of **Page 1**, point anywhere in the bottom margin area, right-click, and then click **Edit Footer** to display the footer area. On the **HEADER & FOOTER TOOLS DESIGN tab**, in the **Insert group**, click **Document Info**, and then click **File Name.** Double-click anywhere in the document to close the footer area.

c. Press Ctrl + A to select all of the text in the document, and then on the **HOME tab**, in the **Paragraph group**, click **Align Left.**

d. Press Ctrl + Home. Select the document title, and then on the **HOME tab**, in the **Paragraph group**, click **Center.**

e. Locate the first bold subheading—*In-House Office Internships.* Point to the left of the paragraph to display the pointer, and then click one time to select the text. With *In-House Office Internships* selected, locate the subheading *Additional Information.* Move the pointer to the left of the paragraph to display the pointer, hold down Ctrl, and then click one time to select both paragraphs. In the **Paragraph group**, click **Center.**

f. Press Ctrl + A to select all of the text in the document. On the **HOME tab**, in the **Paragraph group**, click **Line and Paragraph Spacing**, and then click **1.5.**

2 Below the title of the document, click anywhere in the paragraph that begins *Sturgeon Point Productions is a full service.* On the **HOME tab**, in the **Paragraph group**, click the **Dialog Box Launcher**.

a. In the **Paragraph** dialog box, on the **Indents and Spacing tab**, under **Indentation**, click the **Special arrow**, and then click **First line** to indent the first line by 0.5". Click **OK**, and then click anywhere in the paragraph that begins *Sturgeon Point Productions is looking for.* On the ruler under the ribbon, drag the **First Line Indent** marker to **0.5 inches on the horizontal ruler.**

b. Press Ctrl + A to select all of the text in the document. Click the **PAGE LAYOUT tab**, and then in the **Paragraph group**, under **Spacing**, click the **After spin box up arrow** one time to change the value to **6 pt.**

c. Select the subheading *In-House Office Internships,* including the paragraph mark following it. Scroll down, hold down Ctrl, and then select the subheading *Additional Information.* With both subheadings selected, in the **Paragraph group**, under **Spacing**, click the **Before up spin box arrow** two times to set the **Spacing Before** to **12 pt. Save** your document.

3 Locate the first paragraph that begins *Development Department*, and then point to this paragraph from the left margin area to display the pointer. Drag down to select this paragraph and the next five paragraphs so that six paragraphs are selected. On the **HOME tab**, in the **Paragraph group**, click **Bullets** to change the selected text to a bulleted list.

a. Under the subheading *In-House Office Internships,* in the paragraph that begins *Sturgeon Point Productions,* click to position the insertion point at the *end* of the paragraph, following the colon. Press Enter to create a blank paragraph. On the ruler, drag the **First Line Indent** marker to the left so that it is positioned directly above the lower button. Being sure to include the period, type **1.** and then press Spacebar to create the first item in a numbered list.

b. Type **Be enrolled as a film major at a participating local college or university** and then press Enter. Type **Maintain a 3.0 GPA** and then press Enter. Type **Receive satisfactory monthly progress reports from their direct supervisor**

c. Scroll down to view the bulleted list of departments, and then select all six bulleted items in the list. On the mini toolbar, click the **Bullets button arrow**, and then under **Bullet Library**, click the **check mark** symbol. If the check mark is not available, choose another bullet symbol.

(Project 1D Internships continues on the next page)

CHAPTER REVIEW

Skills Review Project 1D Internships (continued)

4 With the list selected, move the pointer to the horizontal ruler, and then point to and click at **3.5 inches on the horizontal ruler** to insert a tab and align the job titles at the tab mark.

a. With the bulleted list still selected, on the ruler, point to the new tab marker at **3.5 inches on the horizontal ruler**, and then when the *Left Tab* ScreenTip displays, drag the tab marker to **4 inches on the horizontal ruler**.

b. On the ruler, point to the tab marker that you moved to display the *Left Tab* ScreenTip, and then double-click to display the **Tabs** dialog box.

c. In the **Tabs** dialog box, under **Tab stop position**, if necessary select *4"*, and then type **6** Under **Alignment**, click the **Right** option button. Under **Leader**, click the **2** option button. Near the bottom of the **Tabs** dialog box, click **Set**.

d. Under **Tab stop position**, select **4"**, and then click **Clear** to delete the tab stop. Click **OK**. **Save** your document.

5 Press Ctrl + Home to move to the top of the document, and then in the title, click to the right of the *S* in *PRODUCTIONS*.

a. Click the **INSERT tab**, and then in the **Illustrations group**, click **SmartArt**. On the left, click **Relationship**, and then scroll the list to the bottom. Locate and then click **Basic Venn**. Click **OK** to insert the SmartArt graphic. If necessary, close the Text Pane.

b. In the SmartArt graphic, click on *[Text]* in the top circle shape. Type **Film** and then click on the placeholder *[Text]* in the lower left shape. Type **Video** In the third circle, type **Internet**

c. Click the SmartArt graphic border to select it. Click the **FORMAT tab**, and then in the **Size group**, if necessary click **Size** to display the **Shape Height** and **Shape Width** boxes. Set the **Height** to **3"** and the **Width** to **6.5"**.

d. With the SmartArt graphic still selected, on the ribbon, under **SMARTART TOOLS**, click the **DESIGN tab**, and then in the **SmartArt Styles group**, click **Change Colors**. Under **Colorful**, click the third style—**Colorful Range–Accent Colors 3 to 4**. On the **DESIGN tab**, in the **SmartArt Styles group**, click **More** ▾. Under **3-D**, in the first row, click the third style—**Cartoon**. Click **Save**.

6 Hold down Ctrl and then press End to move to the end of the document. On the **INSERT tab**, in the **Media group**, click **Online Video**. If necessary, in the lower left corner of the Insert Video window, click YouTube. Click in the **Search YouTube** box. Including the quotation marks, type **"Go 2013 1B video"** and then press Enter. In the first row, click the first video, and then click **Insert**.

a. Click the **FILE tab**, and then on the right, click **Show All Properties**. In the **Tags** box, type **internship** and in the **Subject** box, type your course name and section number. Be sure that your name displays as the author. Click **Save**.

b. Click the **FILE tab** to display **Backstage** view. Click **Print** to display **Print Preview**. At the bottom of the preview, click the **Next Page** and **Previous Page** buttons to move between pages. If necessary, return to the document and make any necessary changes.

c. As directed by your instructor, print your document or submit it electronically. **Close** Word.

END | You have completed Project 1D

CONTENT-BASED ASSESSMENTS

MyITLab® grader

Mastering Word Project 1E Documentary

Apply 1A skills from these Objectives:

1 Create a New Document and Insert Text
2 Insert and Format Graphics
3 Insert and Modify Text Boxes and Shapes
4 Preview and Print a Document

Build from Scratch

In the following Mastery project, you will create a flyer announcing a special event being hosted by Sturgeon Point Productions. Your printed results will look similar to those in Figure 1.54.

PROJECT FILES

For Project 1E, you will need the following files:

New blank Word document
w01E_Antarctica
w01E_Filmmaker

You will save your document as:

Lastname_Firstname_1E_Documentary

PROJECT RESULTS

Sturgeon Point Productions

Presents Aria Pacheco

Sturgeon Point Productions will be hosting its ***5th Annual Script to Screen*** series, every Friday night this April in our Studio G screening room. All employees, interns, and film students with current school ID are welcome to share in this totally free, exciting evening, where our award-winning filmmakers from our Documentary and Short Feature Film Departments give a first-hand account of the filmmaking process and the challenges that went into their particular projects, from the script phase through production and finally, in distribution and marketing.

This year, we are proud to kick off the series with Aria Pacheco, who will discuss her multi-award winning documentary, **"Through the Cold."** This film documents the perils and triumphs of a team of scientists living in Antarctica. This compelling story, rich in visual complexity, follows the team as they prepare for the six months of darkness in the winter season. Celebrated film critic, Georges Harold, will be conducting an interview with Ms. Pacheco and select members of her crew following a screening of the film, which will take place on Friday, April 5th at 8 p.m. This event is guaranteed to fill up fast, so we suggest you get in line at least one hour prior to the screening.

"Through the Cold" has been heralded by critics across the country. Don't miss this chance to meet one of our greatest documentary filmmakers.

Date: April 5
Time: 8 p.m.
Place: Studio G Screening Room

Lastname_Firstname_1E_Documentary

FIGURE 1.54

(Project 1E Documentary continues on the next page)

CONTENT-BASED ASSESSMENTS

Mastering Word Project 1E Documentary (continued)

1 **Start** Word and display a **Blank document** with the ruler and formatting marks displayed. Type **Sturgeon Point Productions Presents Aria Pacheco** and then press Enter. From your student data files, insert the text file **w01E_Filmmaker**. Using your own name, **Save** the document in your **Word Chapter 1** folder as **Lastname_Firstname_1E_Documentary**

2 To the document title, apply the **Fill - White, Outline - Accent 1, Glow - Accent 1** text effect, and then change the **Font Size** to **36**. Change the **Font Color** to **Blue-Gray, Text 2**—in the fourth column, the first color. Apply an **Outer Shadow** using **Offset Left**—in the second row, the third style. **Center** the title.

3 Position the insertion point at the beginning of the paragraph that begins with *This year*, and then from your student data files, insert the picture **w01E_Antarctica**. Change the **Layout Options** to **Square** and then change the **Height** of the picture to **2.5**

4 Using the **Position** command, display the **Layout** dialog box, and then change the **Horizontal Alignment** to **Right relative to** the **Margin**. Apply a **10 Point Soft Edges** picture effect to the image, and then display the **Artistic Effects** gallery. In the third row, apply the fourth effect—**Mosaic Bubbles**.

5 Deselect the picture. Apply a **Page Border** to the document using the **Shadow** setting. Select the first style, and change the **Color** to **Blue-Gray, Text 2**. Change the **Width** to **3 pt**.

6 Below the last paragraph, draw a **Text Box** that is approximately 1.5 inches high and 4 inches wide—the exact size and location need not be precise. In the text box, type the following text:

Date: April 5

Time: 8 p.m.

Place: Studio G Screening Room

7 Change the **Height** of the text box to **1.5** and the **Width** to **4.5** and then change the font size to **18**. Apply **Bold** and **Center**. To precisely place the text box, display the **Layout** dialog box. Change the **Horizontal Alignment** to **Centered**, **relative to** the **Page**, and then change the **Vertical Absolute position** to **0.5** below the **Paragraph**.

8 Apply a **Shape Style** to the text box—in the last row, select the second style—**Intense Effect - Blue, Accent 1**. Change the **Shape Outline** to **Black, Text 1**.

9 Insert the **File Name** in the footer, and then display the document properties. As the **Tags**, type **documentary, interview** As the **Subject**, type your course and section #. Be sure your name is indicated as the **Author**. **Save** your file.

10 Display the **Print Preview** and if necessary, return to the document and make any necessary changes. As directed by your instructor, print your document or submit it electronically. **Close** Word.

END | You have completed Project 1E

CONTENT-BASED ASSESSMENTS

Mastering Word Project 1F Pitch Festival

Apply 1B skills from these Objectives:

5 Change Document and Paragraph Layout
6 Create and Modify Lists
7 Set and Modify Tab Stops
8 Insert a SmartArt Graphic and an Online Video

In the following Mastery project, you will edit a document with information regarding an event that Sturgeon Point Productions is holding for college students. Your printed results will look similar to those in Figure 1.55.

PROJECT FILES

For Project 1F, you will need the following file:

w01F_Pitch_Festival

You will save your document as:

Lastname_Firstname_1F_Pitch_Festival

PROJECT RESULTS

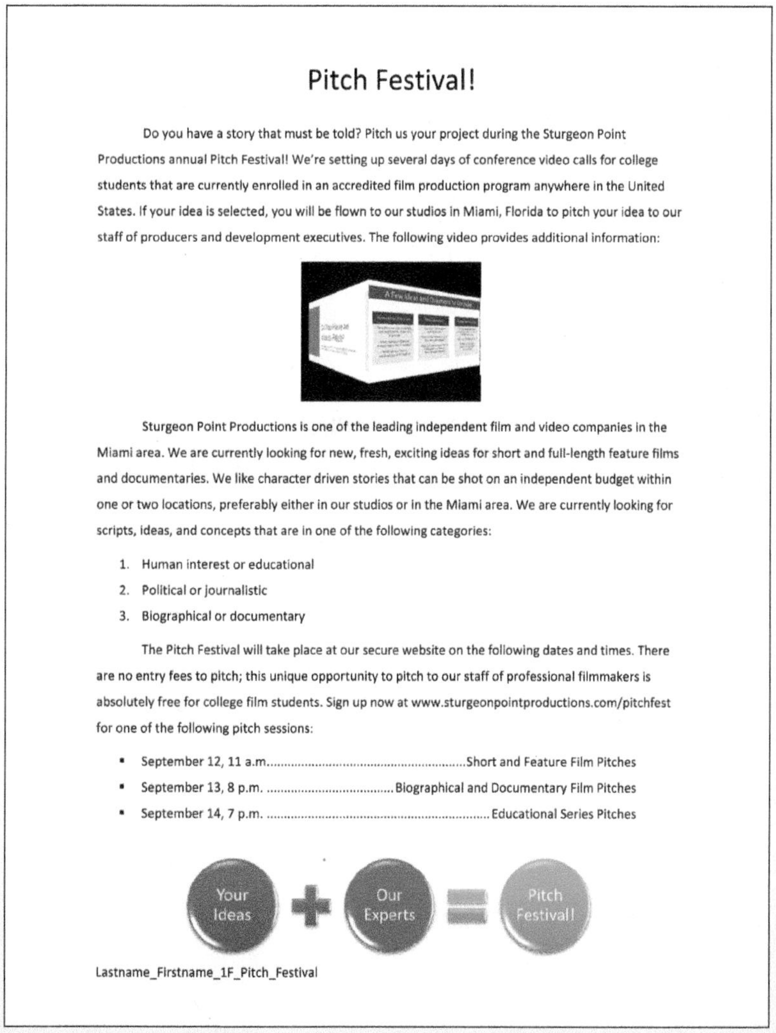

Pitch Festival!

Do you have a story that must be told? Pitch us your project during the Sturgeon Point Productions annual Pitch Festival! We're setting up several days of conference video calls for college students that are currently enrolled in an accredited film production program anywhere in the United States. If your idea is selected, you will be flown to our studios in Miami, Florida to pitch your idea to our staff of producers and development executives. The following video provides additional information:

Sturgeon Point Productions is one of the leading independent film and video companies in the Miami area. We are currently looking for new, fresh, exciting ideas for short and full-length feature films and documentaries. We like character driven stories that can be shot on an independent budget within one or two locations, preferably either in our studios or in the Miami area. We are currently looking for scripts, ideas, and concepts that are in one of the following categories:

1. Human interest or educational
2. Political or journalistic
3. Biographical or documentary

The Pitch Festival will take place at our secure website on the following dates and times. There are no entry fees to pitch; this unique opportunity to pitch to our staff of professional filmmakers is absolutely free for college film students. Sign up now at www.sturgeonpointproductions.com/pitchfest for one of the following pitch sessions:

- September 12, 11 a.m. .... Short and Feature Film Pitches
- September 13, 8 p.m. .... Biographical and Documentary Film Pitches
- September 14, 7 p.m. .... Educational Series Pitches

Lastname_Firstname_1F_Pitch_Festival

FIGURE 1.55

(Project 1F Pitch Festival continues on the next page)

CONTENT-BASED ASSESSMENTS

Mastering Word Project 1F Pitch Festival (continued)

1 Start Word, and then from your student files, open **w01F_Pitch_Festival**. Display formatting marks, and then **Save** the file in your **Word Chapter 1** folder as **Lastname_Firstname_1F_Pitch_Festival**

2 Insert the **File Name** in the footer. Select all the document text, and then change the **Line Spacing** for the entire document to **1.5**. **Center** the document title, and then change the title font size to **24**. Change the **Top** and **Bottom** margins to **0.5**

3 Select the three paragraphs below the title, and then apply a **First line** indent of 0.5". Select the entire document, and then change the **Spacing Before** to **6 pt** and the **Spacing After** to **6 pt**.

4 Select the last three paragraphs containing the dates, and then apply filled square bullets. If the bullets are not available, choose another bullet style. With the bulleted list selected, set a **Right** tab with **dot leaders** at **6"**.

5 Locate the paragraph that begins *Sturgeon Point Productions*, and then click at the end of the paragraph, after the colon. Press Enter. Create a numbered list with the following three numbered items; be sure to remove the first line indent before creating the numbered list:

Human interest or educational

Political or journalistic

Biographical or documentary

6 Position the insertion point at the end of the document after the word *Pitches*. Do *not* insert a blank line. Insert a **SmartArt** graphic from the **Process** category. Toward the bottom of the gallery, select the **Equation** SmartArt. Select the outside border of the SmartArt, and then change the **Height** of the SmartArt to **1** and the **Width** to **6.5**

7 With the SmartArt selected, change the layout to **Square**, and change the **Horizontal Alignment** to **Centered relative to** the **Page**. Change the **Vertical Alignment** to **Bottom relative to** the **Margin**.

8 In the first circle type **Your Ideas** and in the second circle type **Our Experts** In the third circle type **Pitch Festival!** Change the SmartArt color to **Colorful Range – Accent Colors 4 to 5**. Apply the **3-D Polished** style.

9 Click at the end of the paragraph below the title. Press Enter, remove the first line indent, and then center the blank line. Insert an **Online Video**. In the **Search YouTube** box, type, including the quotations marks, **"Go 2013 1F Video"** and then insert the video with the cube on a black background. Change the height of the video to **1.5**.

10 Display the document properties. In the **Tags** box, type **pitch festival** and in the **Subject** box, type your course name and section number. Be sure your name displays as the author.

11 Display the **Print Preview** and if necessary, return to the document and make any necessary changes. As directed by your instructor, print your document or submit it electronically. **Close** Word.

END | You have completed Project 1F

CONTENT-BASED ASSESSMENTS

Mastering Word Project 1G Educational Website

MyITLab® grader

Apply 1A and 1B skills from these Objectives:

1. Create a New Document and Insert Text
2. Insert and Format Graphics
3. Insert and Modify Text Boxes and Shapes
4. Preview and Print a Document
5. Change Document and Paragraph Layout
6. Create and Modify Lists
7. Set and Modify Tab Stops
8. Insert a SmartArt Graphic and an Online Video

Build from Scratch

In the following Mastery project, you will create a flyer that details a new educational website that Sturgeon Point Productions has developed for instructors. Your printed results will look similar to those in Figure 1.56.

PROJECT FILES

For Project 1G, you will need the following files:

New blank Word document
w01G_Education
w01G_Media

You will save your document as:

Lastname_Firstname_1G_Educational_Website

PROJECT RESULTS

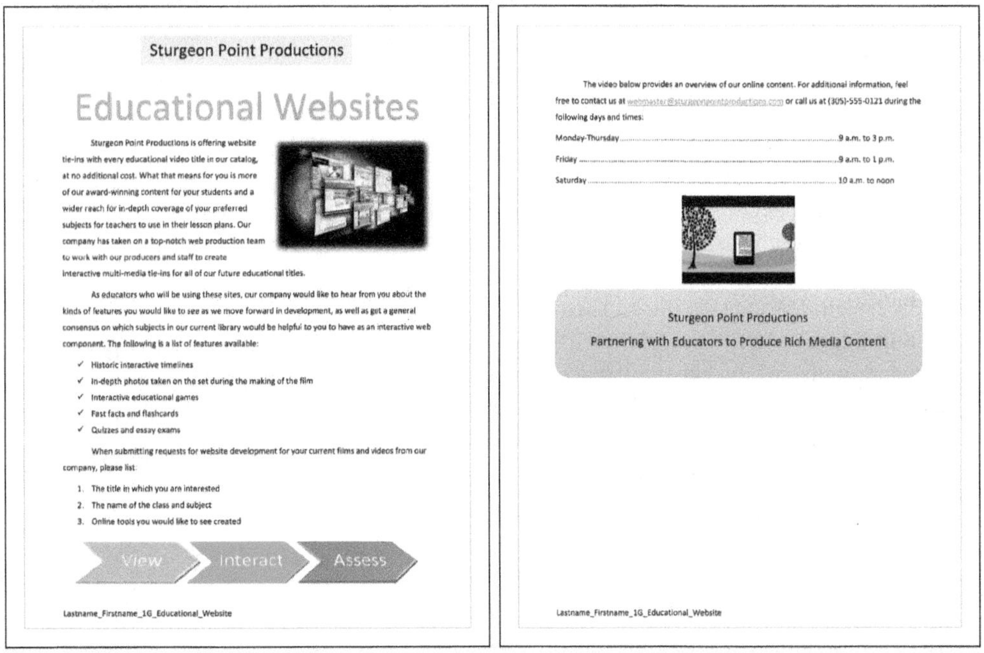

FIGURE 1.56

(Project 1G Educational Website continues on the next page)

Mastering Word | Project 1G Educational Website (continued)

1 Start Word and display a blank document. Display formatting marks and the ruler. Type **Educational Websites** and then press Enter. Type **Sturgeon Point Productions is offering website tie-ins with every educational video title in our catalog, at no additional cost.** Press Spacebar, and then **Save** the document in your **Word Chapter 1** folder as **Lastname_Firstname_1G_Educational_Website**

2 With the insertion point positioned at the end of the sentence that you typed, insert the text from your student data file **w01G_Education**. Change the **Line Spacing** for the entire document to **1.5** and the spacing **After** to **6 pt.** To each of the four paragraphs that begin *Sturgeon Point Productions*, *As educators*, *When submitting*, and *The video*, apply a **First Line** indent of **0.5"**.

3 Change the font size of the title to **50** and then display the **Text Effects and Typography** gallery. Apply the second effect to the title—**Fill - Blue, Accent 1, Shadow**, and then **Center** the title. With only the title selected, change the **Line Spacing** to **1.0**.

4 Click at the beginning of the paragraph below the title, and then from your student data files, insert the picture **w01G_Media**. Change the picture **Height** to **2** and the **Layout Options** to **Square**. Format the picture with **Soft Edges in 10 Point**, and then use the **Position** command to display the **Layout** dialog box. Change the picture position so that the **Horizontal Alignment** is **Right relative to** the **Margin**. Change the **Vertical Alignment** to **Top relative to** the **Line**.

5 Select the five paragraphs beginning with *Historic interactive timelines* and ending with *Quizzes and essay exams*, and then apply checkmark bullets. In the paragraph below the bulleted list, click after the colon. Press Enter and remove the first line indent. Type a numbered list with the following three numbered items:

The title in which you are interested

The name of the class and subject

Online tools you would like to see created

6 With the insertion point located at the end of the numbered list, insert a **SmartArt** graphic. In the **Process** category, locate and select the **Basic Chevron Process**. In the first shape type **View** In the second shape type **Interact** and in the third shape type **Assess**

7 Change the SmartArt color to **Colorful Range - Accent Colors 4 to 5**, and then apply the **3-D Flat Scene** style. Change the **Height** of the SmartArt to **1** and the **Width** to **6.5** Change the **Layout Options** to **Square**, the **Horizontal Alignment** to **Centered relative to** the **Page**, and the **Vertical Alignment** to **Bottom relative to** the **Margin**.

8 Select the days and times at the end of the document, and then set a **Right** tab with **dot leaders** at **6"**. Click in the blank line below the tabbed list, and **Center** the line. Insert an **Online Video**. In the **Search YouTube** box, type **Pearson Higher Education Learning**, and then insert the first video that displays. Change the video **Height** to **1.5**

9 In the space below the video, insert a **Rounded Rectangle** shape. The exact location need not be precise. Change the **Shape Height** to **1.5** and the **Shape Width** to **6.5** Display the **Shape Styles** gallery, and then in the fourth row, apply the second style—**Subtle Effect - Blue, Accent 1**. Use the **Position** command to display the **Layout** dialog box, and then change the position so that both the **Horizontal** and **Vertical Alignment** are **Centered relative to** the **Margin**.

10 In the rectangle, type **Sturgeon Point Productions** and then press Enter. Type **Partnering with Educators to Produce Rich Media Content** and then change the font size to **16**.

11 Move to the top of the document and insert a **Text Box** above the title. The exact location need not be precise. Change the **Height** of the text box to **0.5** and the width to **3.7** Type **Sturgeon Point Productions** and then change the font size to **22 Center** the text.

12 Use the **Position** command to display the **Layout** dialog box, and then position the text box so that the **Horizontal Alignment** is **Centered relative to** the **Page** and the **Vertical Absolute position** is **0.5 below** the **Page**.

13 With the text box selected, display the **Shape Fill** gallery, and then in the next to last column, select the second color—**Blue, Accent 5, Lighter 80%**. Change the **Shape Outline** to the same color—**Blue, Accent 5, Lighter 80%**.

14 Deselect the text box. Apply a **Page Border** to the document. Use the **Box** setting, and choose the first style. Change the **Color** to **Blue, Accent 5**. Change the **Top** margin to **1.25** and insert the **File Name** in the footer.

15 Display the document properties. As the **Tags** type **website** and as the **Subject** type your course and section #. Be sure your name displays in the **Author** box, and then **Save** your file. Submit your document as directed.

END | You have completed Project 1G

Apply a combination of the 1A and 1B skills.

CONTENT-BASED ASSESSMENTS

1

WORD

GO! Fix It | Project 1H Casting Call | Online

Build from Scratch

GO! Make It | Project 1I Development Team | Online

GO! Solve It | Project 1J Softball | Online

GO! Solve It | Project 1K Production

PROJECT FILES

For Project 1K, you will need the following files:

w01K_Production
w01K_Studio

You will save your document as:

Lastname_Firstname_1K_Production

The Marketing Director for Sturgeon Point Productions is developing marketing materials aimed at filmmakers. Use the following information to format a flyer that uses text effects, an appropriately placed picture with an artistic effect and text wrapping applied, and an appropriately formatted SmartArt graphic.

From the student files that accompany this textbook, locate and open the file w01K_Production. Format the document using techniques you learned in this chapter. From your student data files, insert the picture w01K_Studio, and then format the picture with an artistic effect. Insert a **SmartArt** graphic that illustrates two or three important points about the company. Be sure the flyer is easy to read and understand and has an attractive design. Save the file in your **Word Chapter 1** folder as **Lastname_Firstname_1K_Production** and submit it as directed.

(Project 1K Production continues on the next page)

CONTENT-BASED ASSESSMENTS

GO! Solve It Project 1K Production (continued)

Performance Level

Performance Criteria	Exemplary	Proficient	Developing
Use text effects	Text effects applied to text in an attractive and appropriate manner.	Text effects applied but do not appropriately display text.	Text effects not used.
Insert and format a picture	The picture is inserted and positioned correctly; text wrapping and an artistic effect are applied.	The picture is inserted but not formatted properly.	No picture is inserted in the document.
Insert and format SmartArt	The SmartArt is inserted and appropriately formatted.	The SmartArt is inserted but no formatting is applied.	No SmartArt is inserted in the document.

END | You have completed Project 1K

OUTCOMES-BASED ASSESSMENTS

RUBRIC

The following outcomes-based assessments are *open-ended assessments*. That is, there is no specific correct result; your result will depend on your approach to the information provided. Make *Professional Quality* your goal. Use the following scoring rubric to guide you in *how* to approach the problem and then to evaluate *how well* your approach solves the problem.

The *criteria*—Software Mastery, Content, Format and Layout, and Process—represent the knowledge and skills you have gained that you can apply to solving the problem. The *levels of performance*—Professional Quality, Approaching Professional Quality, or Needs Quality Improvements—help you and your instructor evaluate your result.

	Your completed project is of Professional Quality if you:	Your completed project is Approaching Professional Quality if you:	Your completed project Needs Quality Improvements if you:
1-Software Mastery	Choose and apply the most appropriate skills, tools, and features and identify efficient methods to solve the problem.	Choose and apply some appropriate skills, tools, and features, but not in the most efficient manner.	Choose inappropriate skills, tools, or features, or are inefficient in solving the problem.
2-Content	Construct a solution that is clear and well organized, contains content that is accurate, appropriate to the audience and purpose, and is complete. Provide a solution that contains no errors in spelling, grammar, or style.	Construct a solution in which some components are unclear, poorly organized, inconsistent, or incomplete. Misjudge the needs of the audience. Have some errors in spelling, grammar, or style, but the errors do not detract from comprehension.	Construct a solution that is unclear, incomplete, or poorly organized; contains some inaccurate or inappropriate content; and contains many errors in spelling, grammar, or style. Do not solve the problem.
3-Format & Layout	Format and arrange all elements to communicate information and ideas, clarify function, illustrate relationships, and indicate relative importance.	Apply appropriate format and layout features to some elements, but not others. Overuse features, causing minor distraction.	Apply format and layout that does not communicate information or ideas clearly. Do not use format and layout features to clarify function, illustrate relationships, or indicate relative importance. Use available features excessively, causing distraction.
4-Process	Use an organized approach that integrates planning, development, self-assessment, revision, and reflection.	Demonstrate an organized approach in some areas, but not others; or, use an insufficient process of organization throughout.	Do not use an organized approach to solve the problem.

OUTCOMES-BASED ASSESSMENTS

Apply a combination of the 1A and 1B skills.

GO! Think Project 1L Classes

PROJECT FILES

Build from Scratch

For Project 1L, you will need the following file:

New blank Word document

You will save your document as:

Lastname_Firstname_1L_Classes

The Human Resources Director at Sturgeon Point Productions needs to create a flyer to inform full-time employees of educational opportunities beginning in September. The courses are taught each year by industry professionals and are designed to improve skills in motion picture and television development and production. Employees who have been with Sturgeon Point Productions for at least two years are eligible to take the courses free of cost. The classes provide employees with opportunities to advance their careers, gain valuable skills, and achieve technical certification. All courses take place in Studio G and interested employees should contact Elana Springs in Human Resources to sign up. Information meetings are being held at 5:30 p.m. according to the following schedule: television development on June 15; motion picture production on June 17; and recording services on June 21.

Create a flyer with basic information about the courses and information meetings. Be sure the flyer is easy to read and understand and has an attractive design. Save the document as **Lastname_Firstname_1L_Classes** and submit it as directed.

END | You have completed Project 1L

Build from Scratch

GO! Think Project 1M Store Online

Build from Scratch

You and GO! Project 1N Family Flyer Online

Build from Scratch

GO! Cumulative Group Project Project 1O Bell Orchid Hotels Online

Using Tables and Templates to Create Resumes and Cover Letters

GO! to Work Video W2

2

WORD 2013

PROJECT 2A

OUTCOMES
Write a resume by using a Word table.

PROJECT 2B

OUTCOMES
Write a cover letter and use a template to create a cover sheet.

OBJECTIVES

1. Create a Table
2. Format a Table
3. Present a Word Document Online

OBJECTIVES

4. Create a Custom Word Template
5. Correct and Reorganize Text
6. Use the Proofing Options and Print an Envelope
7. Create a Document Using a Predesigned Microsoft Template

onewordphoto / Fotolia

In This Chapter

Tables are useful for organizing and presenting data. Because a table is so easy to use, many individuals prefer to arrange tabular information in a Word table rather than setting a series of tabs. For example, you can use a table when you want to present rows and columns of information or to create a format for a document such as a resume.

When using Word to write business or personal letters, use a commonly approved letter format, and always use a clear writing style. You will make a good impression on prospective employers if you use a standard business letter style when you are writing a cover letter for a resume.

The projects in this chapter relate to the **College Career Center at Florida Port Community College** in St. Petersburg, Florida, a coastal port city near the Florida High Tech Corridor. With 60 percent of Florida's high tech companies and a third of the state's manufacturing companies located in the St. Petersburg and Tampa Bay areas, the college partners with businesses to play a vital role in providing a skilled workforce. The College Career Center assists students in exploring careers, finding internships, and applying for jobs. The Center offers workshops for resume and cover letter writing and for practice interviews.

PROJECT 2A Resume

MyITLab®
Project 2A Training

PROJECT ACTIVITIES

In Activities 2.01 through 2.11, you will create a table to use as the format for a resume. The director of the Career Center, Mary Walker-Huelsman, will use this model when assisting students with building their resumes. Your completed document will look similar to Figure 2.1.

PROJECT FILES

For Project 2A, you will need the following files:
New blank Word document
w02A_Experience

You will save your document as:
Lastname_Firstname_2A_Resume

PROJECT RESULTS

Build from Scratch

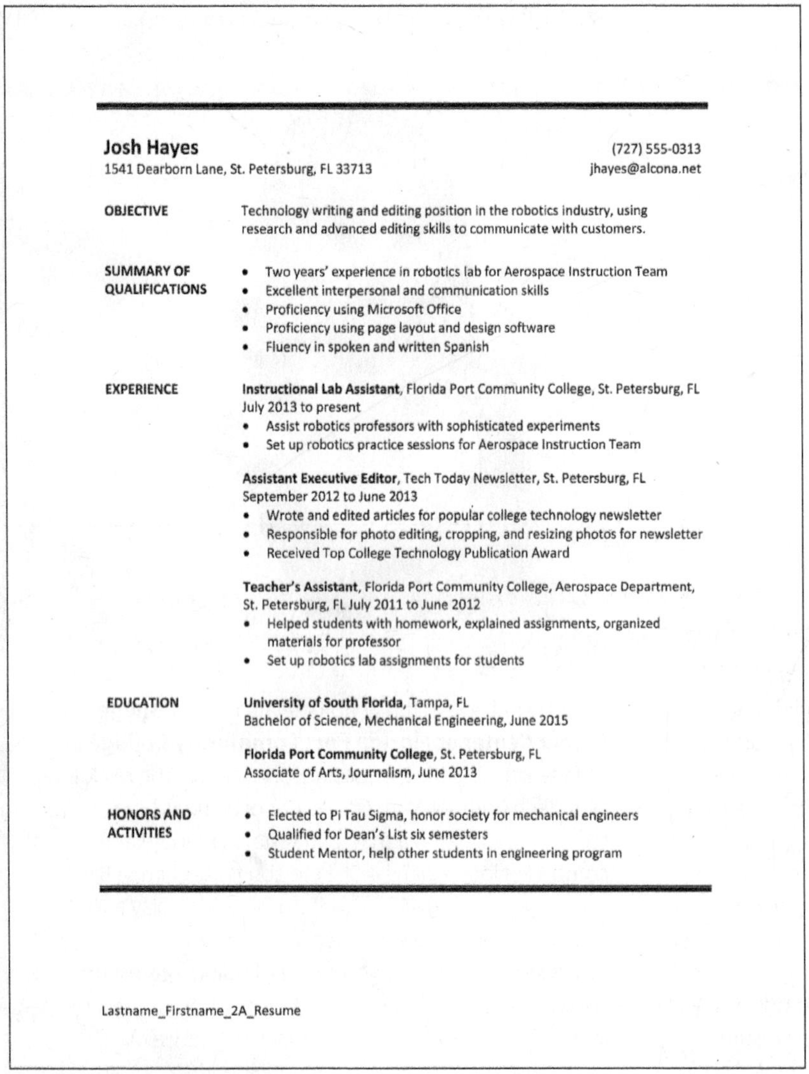

Josh Hayes (727) 555-0313
1541 Dearborn Lane, St. Petersburg, FL 33713 jhayes@alcona.net

OBJECTIVE	Technology writing and editing position in the robotics industry, using research and advanced editing skills to communicate with customers.
SUMMARY OF QUALIFICATIONS	• Two years' experience in robotics lab for Aerospace Instruction Team • Excellent interpersonal and communication skills • Proficiency using Microsoft Office • Proficiency using page layout and design software • Fluency in spoken and written Spanish
EXPERIENCE	**Instructional Lab Assistant**, Florida Port Community College, St. Petersburg, FL July 2013 to present • Assist robotics professors with sophisticated experiments • Set up robotics practice sessions for Aerospace Instruction Team **Assistant Executive Editor**, Tech Today Newsletter, St. Petersburg, FL September 2012 to June 2013 • Wrote and edited articles for popular college technology newsletter • Responsible for photo editing, cropping, and resizing photos for newsletter • Received Top College Technology Publication Award **Teacher's Assistant**, Florida Port Community College, Aerospace Department, St. Petersburg, FL July 2011 to June 2012 • Helped students with homework, explained assignments, organized materials for professor • Set up robotics lab assignments for students
EDUCATION	**University of South Florida**, Tampa, FL Bachelor of Science, Mechanical Engineering, June 2015 **Florida Port Community College**, St. Petersburg, FL Associate of Arts, Journalism, June 2013
HONORS AND ACTIVITIES	• Elected to Pi Tau Sigma, honor society for mechanical engineers • Qualified for Dean's List six semesters • Student Mentor, help other students in engineering program

Lastname_Firstname_2A_Resume

FIGURE 2.1 Project 2A Resume

Objective 1 Create a Table

Video W2-1

A ***table*** is an arrangement of information organized into rows and columns. The intersection of a row and a column in a table creates a box called a ***cell*** into which you can type. Tables are useful to present information in a logical and orderly format.

Activity 2.01 | Creating a Table by Defining Table Dimensions

1. **Start** Word and then click **Blank document.** On the **HOME tab**, in the **Paragraph group**, if necessary click **Show/Hide** to display the formatting marks. If the rulers do not display, click the **VIEW tab**, and then in the **Show group**, select the **Ruler check box.**

2. Click the **FILE tab**, and then in **Backstage** view, click **Save As.** In the **Save As** dialog box, navigate to the location where you are storing your projects for this chapter. Create a new folder named **Word Chapter 2**

3. **Save** the file in the **Word Chapter 2** folder as **Lastname_Firstname_2A_Resume**

4. On the **INSERT tab**, in the **Header & Footer group**, click **Footer**, and then at the bottom of the list, click **Edit Footer.** On the ribbon, in the **Insert group**, click **Document Info**, click **File Name**, and then at the right end of the ribbon, click **Close Header and Footer.**

5. On the **INSERT tab**, in the **Tables group**, click **Table.** In the **Insert Table** grid, in the fourth row, point to the second square, and notice that the cells are bordered in orange and *2x4 Table* displays at the top of the grid. Compare your screen with Figure 2.2.

FIGURE 2.2

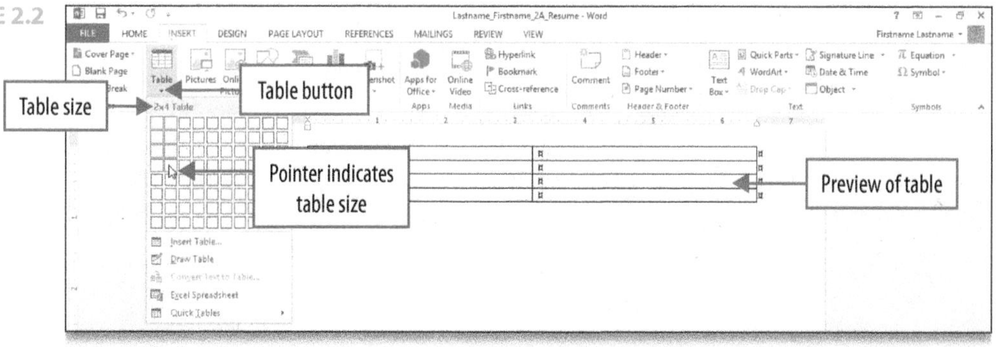

6. Click one time to create the table. Notice that formatting marks in each cell indicate the end of the contents of each cell; the mark to the right of each *row* indicates the row end. **Save** your document, and then compare your screen with Figure 2.3.

   A table with four rows and two columns displays at the insertion point location, and the insertion point displays in the upper left cell. The table fills the width of the page, from the left margin to the right margin. On the ribbon, TABLE TOOLS and two additional tabs—*DESIGN* and *LAYOUT*—display. Borders display around each cell in the table.

FIGURE 2.3

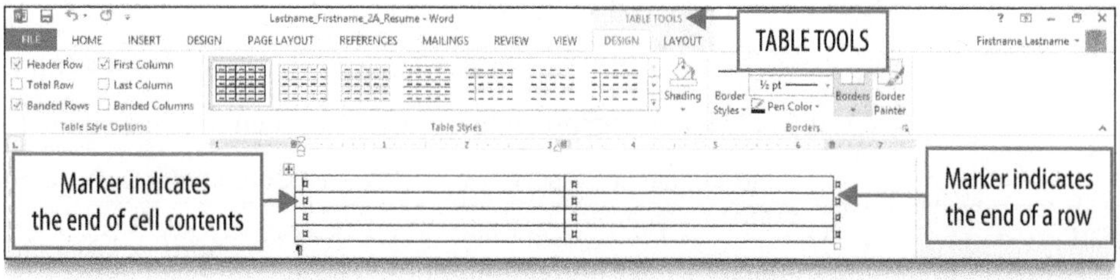

Activity 2.02 | Typing Text in a Table

In a Word table, each cell behaves similarly to a document. For example, as you type in a cell, when you reach the right border of the cell, wordwrap moves the text to the next line. When you press Enter, the insertion point moves down to a new paragraph in the same cell. You can also insert text from another document into a table cell.

There are numerous acceptable formats for resumes, many of which can be found in Business Communications textbooks. The layout used in this project is suitable for a recent college graduate and places topics in the left column and details in the right column.

1 With the insertion point blinking in the first cell in the first row, type **OBJECTIVE** and then press Tab.

Pressing Tab moves the insertion point to the next cell in the row, or, if the insertion point is already in the last cell in the row, pressing Tab moves the insertion point to the first cell in the next row.

2 Type **Technology writing and editing position in the robotics industry, using research and advanced editing skills to communicate with customers.** Notice that the text wraps in the cell and the height of the row adjusts to fit the text.

3 Press Tab to move to the first cell in the second row. Type **SUMMARY OF QUALIFICATIONS** and then press Tab. Type the following, pressing Enter at the end of each line *except* the last line:

Two years' experience in robotics lab for Aerospace Instruction Team

Excellent interpersonal and communication skills

Proficiency using Microsoft Office

Proficiency using page layout and design software

Fluency in spoken and written Spanish

The default font and font size in a table are the same as for a document—Calibri 11 pt. The default line spacing in a table is single spacing with no space before or after paragraphs, which differs from the defaults for a document.

4 **Save** your document, and then compare your screen with Figure 2.4.

FIGURE 2.4

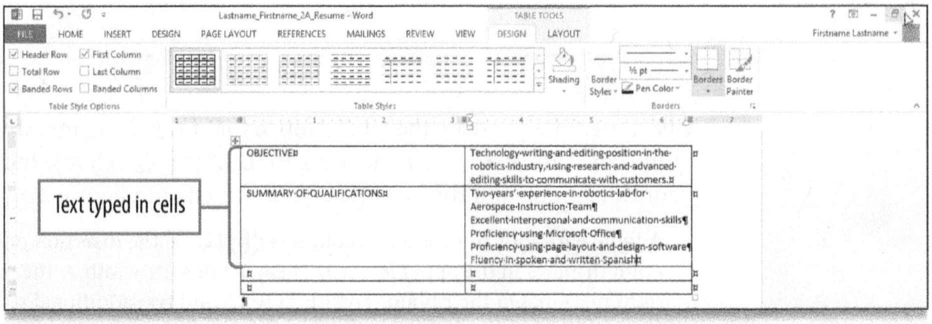

Activity 2.03 | Inserting Text from a File and Removing Blank Paragraphs

1 Press Tab to move to the first cell in the third row. Type **EXPERIENCE** and then press Tab.

2 Type the following, pressing Enter after each item, including the last item:

Instructional Lab Assistant, Florida Port Community College, St. Petersburg, FL July 2013 to present

Assist robotics professors with sophisticated experiments

Set up robotics practice sessions for Aerospace Instruction Team

3 Be sure your insertion point is positioned in the second column to the left of the cell marker below *Instruction Team*. Compare your screen with Figure 2.5.

FIGURE 2.5

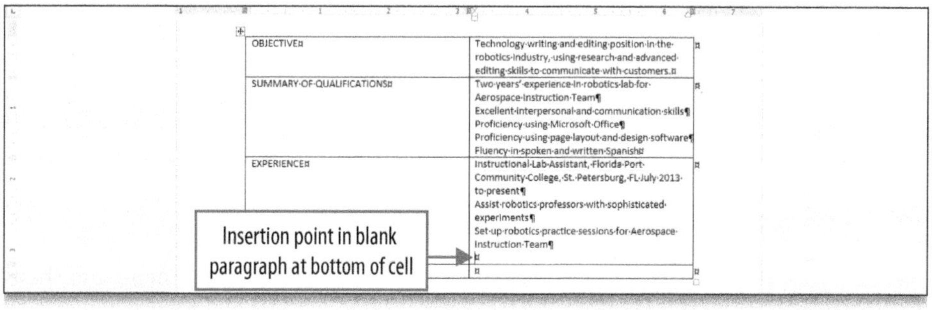

4 On the **INSERT tab**, in the **Text group**, click the **Object button arrow**, and then click **Text from File**. Navigate to your student files, select **w02A_Experience**, and then click **Insert**.

All of the text from the w02A_Experience document is added to the document at the insertion point.

ANOTHER WAY

Open the second document and select the text you want. Copy the text, and then paste at the desired location.

5 Press Backspace one time to remove the blank paragraph at the end of the inserted text, and then compare your screen with Figure 2.6.

FIGURE 2.6

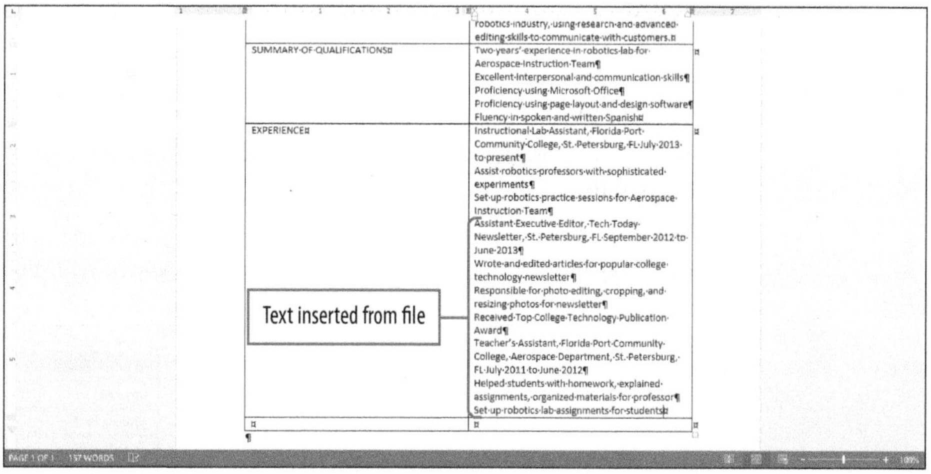

6 Press Tab to move to the first cell in the fourth row. Type **HONORS AND ACTIVITIES** and then press Tab.

7 Type the following, pressing Enter at the end of each item *except* the last one:

Elected to Pi Tau Sigma, honor society for mechanical engineers

Qualified for Dean's List, six semesters

Student Mentor, help other students in engineering program

8 **Save** your document, and then compare your screen with Figure 2.7.

FIGURE 2.7

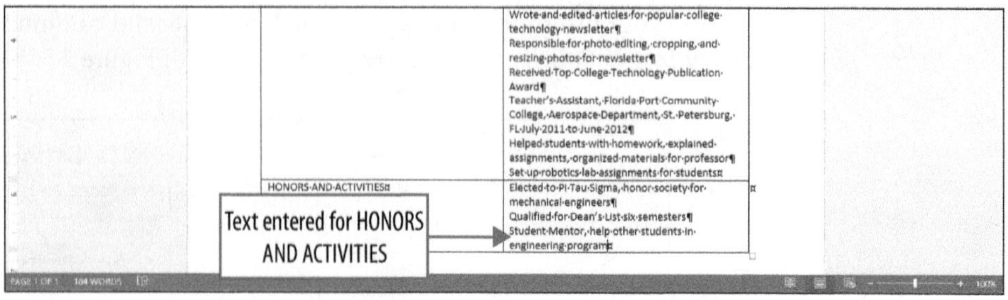

Activity 2.04 | Creating Bulleted Lists in a Table

1. Press Ctrl + Home to move to the top of your document, and then in the cell to the right of *SUMMARY OF QUALIFICATIONS*, select all of the text.

2. On the **HOME tab**, in the **Paragraph group**, click **Bullets** .

   The selected text displays as a bulleted list to make each qualification more distinctive.

3. In the **Paragraph group**, click **Decrease Indent** one time to align the bullets at the left edge of the cell.

4. Scroll as necessary so that you can view the entire *EXPERIENCE* and *HONORS AND ACTIVITIES* sections on your screen. With the bulleted text still selected, in the **Clipboard group**, double-click **Format Painter**.

5. In the cell to the right of EXPERIENCE, select the second and third paragraphs—beginning *Assist* and *Set up*—to create the same style of bulleted list as you did in the previous step.

6. In the same cell, under *Assistant Executive Editor*, select the three paragraphs that begin *Wrote* and *Responsible* and *Received* to create another bulleted list aligned at the left edge of the cell.

7. In the same cell, select the paragraphs that begin *Helped* and *Set up* to create the same type of bulleted list.

8. In the cell below, select the paragraphs that begin *Elected*, *Qualified*, and *Student* to create a bulleted list.

9. Press Esc to turn off the **Format Painter**. Click anywhere in the table to deselect the text, **Save** your document, and then compare your screen with Figure 2.8.

FIGURE 2.8

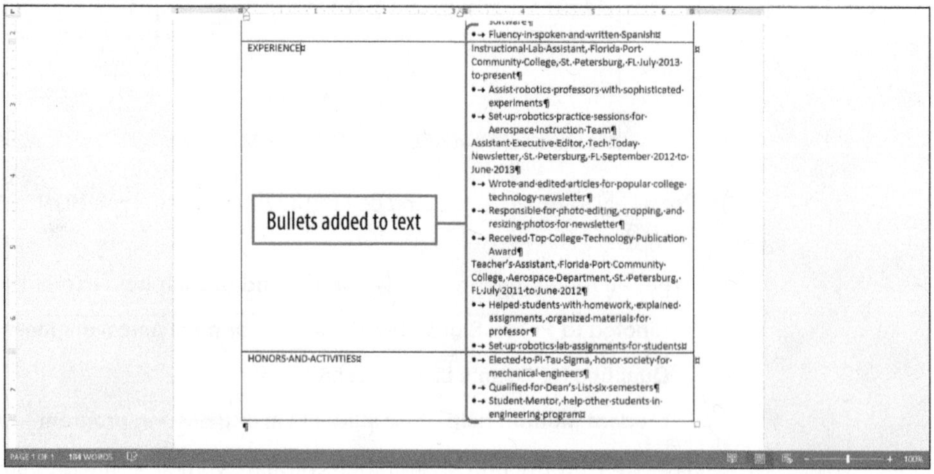

Objective 2 Format a Table

Video W2-2

Use Word's formatting tools to make your tables attractive and easy to read. Types of formatting you can add to a table include changing the row height and the column width, removing or adding borders, increasing or decreasing the paragraph or line spacing, and enhancing the text.

Activity 2.05 Changing the Width of Table Columns and Using AutoFit

When you create a table, all of the columns are of equal width. In this activity, you will change the width of the columns.

1. Press Ctrl + Home. Click anywhere in the first column, and then on the ribbon, under **TABLE TOOLS**, click the **LAYOUT tab**. In the **Cell Size group**, notice the **Width** box, which displays the width of the active column.

2. Look at the horizontal ruler and locate the **1.5-inch mark**. Then, in the table, in any row, point to the vertical border between the two columns to display the pointer.

3. Hold down the left mouse button and drag the column border to the left until the white arrow on the ruler is at approximately **1.5 inches on the horizontal ruler** and then release the left mouse button.

4. In the **Cell Size group**, click the **Width box down spin arrow** as necessary to set the column width to **1.4"** and notice that the right border of the table moves to the right.

   Adjusting column width by dragging a column border adjusts only the width of the column; adjusting column width with the Width box simultaneously adjusts the right border of the table.

5. In the **Cell Size group**, click **AutoFit**, and then click **AutoFit Window** to stretch the table across the page within the margins so that the right border of the table is at the right margin. **Save** and then compare your screen with Figure 2.9.

ANOTHER WAY You can adjust column widths by dragging the Move Table Column markers on the ruler. To maintain the right border of the table at the right margin, hold down Shift while dragging. To display measurements on the ruler, hold down Alt while dragging the marker.

FIGURE 2.9

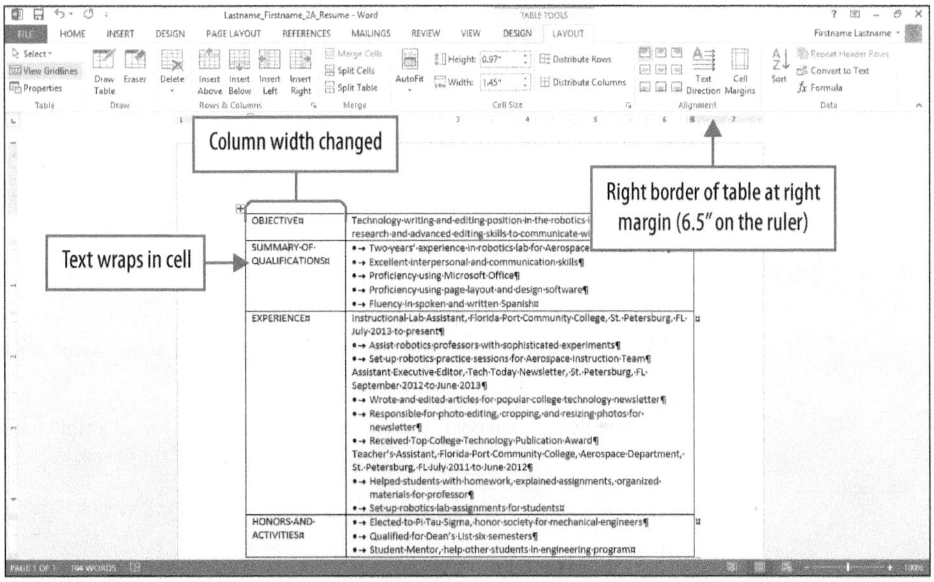

More Knowledge | **Changing Column Widths**

You will typically get the best results if you change the column widths starting at the left side of the table, especially in tables with three or more columns. Word can also calculate the best column widths for you. To do this, select the table. Then, on the LAYOUT tab, in the Cell Size group, click the AutoFit button and click AutoFit Contents.

Activity 2.06 | Using One-Click Row/Column Insertion to Modify Table Dimensions

One of the most common actions you will take in a table is adding another row or another column. By using ***One-click Row/Column Insertion*** you can do so in context by pointing to the left or top edge where you want the row or column to appear and then clicking the ⊕ button to add it.

1. Scroll to view the lower portion of the table. On the left border of the table, *point* to the upper left corner of the cell containing the text *HONORS AND ACTIVITIES* to display the **One-click Row/Column Insertion** button ⊕. Compare your screen with Figure 2.10.

FIGURE 2.10

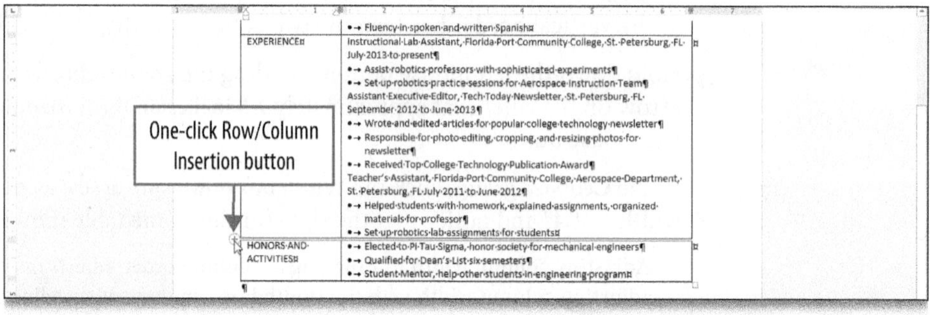

2. Click ⊕ one time to insert a new row above the HONORS AND ACTIVITIES row.
3. Click in the left cell of the new row, type **EDUCATION** and then press Tab.
4. Type the following, pressing Enter at the end of each item *except* the last one:

   University of South Florida, Tampa, FL

   Bachelor of Science, Mechanical Engineering, June 2015

   Florida Port Community College, St. Petersburg, FL

   Associate of Arts, Journalism, June 2013

5. **Save** your document, and then compare your screen with Figure 2.11.

FIGURE 2.11

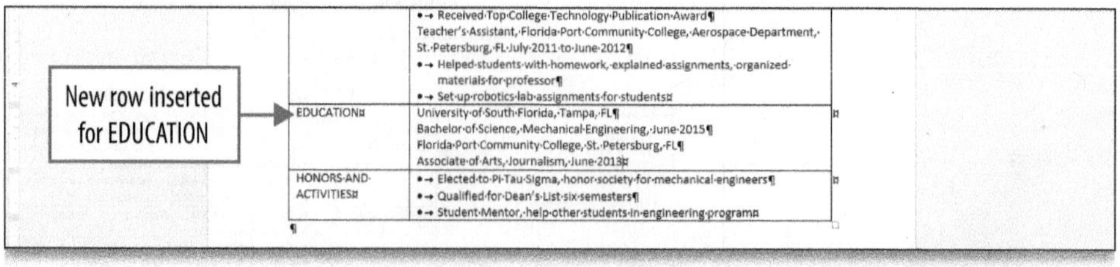

ANOTHER WAY When the insertion point is in the last cell in the bottom row of a table, you can add a row by pressing the Tab key; the insertion point will display in the first cell of the new row.

Activity 2.07 | Merging Table Cells

The title of a table typically spans all of the columns. In this activity, you will merge cells so that you can position the personal information across both columns.

1. Press Ctrl + Home to move to the top of your document, and then click anywhere in the top row of the table.
2. On the **LAYOUT tab**, in the **Rows & Columns group**, click **Insert Above**.

   A new row displays above the row that contained the insertion point, and the new row is selected. This is another method to insert rows and columns in a table; use this method to insert a new row at the top of a table.

ANOTHER WAY Right-click in the top row, point to Insert, and then click Insert Rows Above.

3. Be sure the two cells in the top row are selected; if necessary, drag across both cells to select them.
4. On the **LAYOUT tab**, in the **Merge group**, click **Merge Cells**.

   The cell border between the two cells no longer displays.

ANOTHER WAY Right-click the selected row and click Merge Cells on the shortcut menu.

Activity 2.08 | Setting Tabs in a Table

1. With the merged cell still selected, on the **HOME tab**, in the **Paragraph group**, click the **Dialog Box Launcher** to display the **Paragraph** dialog box.
2. On the **Indents and Spacing tab**, in the lower left corner, click **Tabs** to display the **Tabs** dialog box.
3. Under **Tab stop position**, type **6.5** and then under **Alignment**, click the **Right** option button. Click **Set**, and then click **OK** to close the dialog box.
4. Type **Josh Hayes** Hold down Ctrl and then press Tab. Notice that the insertion point moves to the right-aligned tab stop at 6.5".

   In a Word table, you must use Ctrl + Tab to move to a tab stop, because pressing Tab is reserved for moving the insertion point from cell to cell.

5. Type **(727) 555-0313** and then press Enter.
6. Type **1541 Dearborn Lane, St. Petersburg, FL 33713** Hold down Ctrl and then press Tab.
7. Type **jhayes@alcona.net** **Save** your document, and then compare your screen with Figure 2.12.

FIGURE 2.12

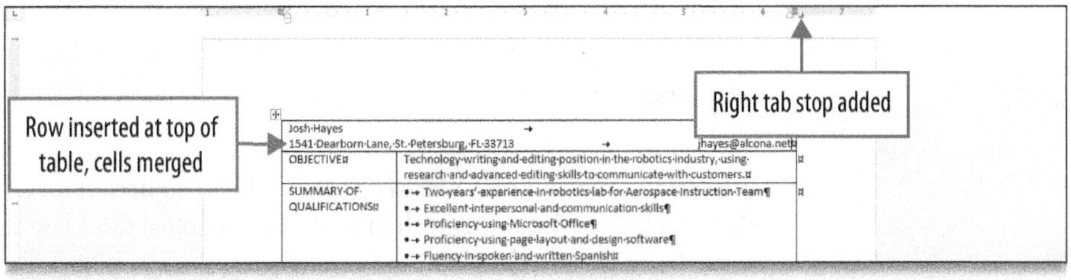

Activity 2.09 | Modifying Fonts in a Table and Using Spacing After

1. In the first row of the table, select the name *Josh Hayes*, and then on the mini toolbar, apply **Bold** [B] and change the **Font Size** to **16**.

2. Under *Josh Hayes*, click anywhere in the second line of text, which contains the address and email address.

3. On the **PAGE LAYOUT tab**, in the **Paragraph group**, click the **Spacing After up spin arrow** three times to add **18 pt** spacing between the first row of the table and the second row. Compare your screen with Figure 2.13.

   This action separates the personal information from the body of the resume and adds focus to the name.

FIGURE 2.13

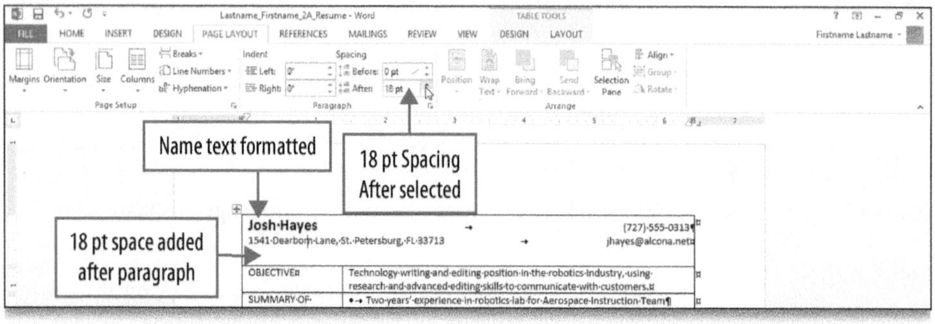

4. Using the technique you just practiced, in the second column, click in the last paragraph of *every cell* and add **18 pt Spacing After** including the last row; a border will be added to the bottom of the table, and spacing will be needed between the last row and the border.

5. In the second row, point to the word *OBJECTIVE*, hold down the left mouse button, and then drag downward in the first column to select all the headings in uppercase letters. On the mini toolbar, click **Bold** [B].

NOTE **Selecting Only One Column**

When you drag downward to select the first column, a fast mouse might also begin to select the second column when you reach the bottom. If this happens, drag upward slightly to deselect the second column and select only the first column.

6. In the cell to the right of *EXPERIENCE*, without selecting the following comma, select *Instructional Lab Assistant* and then on the mini toolbar, click **Bold** [B].

7. In the same cell, apply **Bold** [B] to the other job titles—*Assistant Executive Editor* and *Teacher's Assistant.*

8. In the cell to the right of *EDUCATION*, apply **Bold** [B] to *University of South Florida, Tampa, FL* and *Florida Port Community College, St. Petersburg, FL.*

9. In the same cell, click anywhere in the line beginning *Bachelor*. On the **PAGE LAYOUT tab,** in the **Paragraph group**, click the **Spacing After up spin arrow** two times to add **12 pt** spacing after the paragraph.

10. In the cell to the right of *EXPERIENCE*, under *Instructional Lab Assistant*, click anywhere in the second bulleted item, and then add **12 pt Spacing After** the item.

11. In the same cell, repeat this process for the last bulleted item under *Assistant Executive Editor.*

12 Scroll to view the top of your document, **Save** [icon] your document, and then compare your screen with Figure 2.14.

FIGURE 2.14

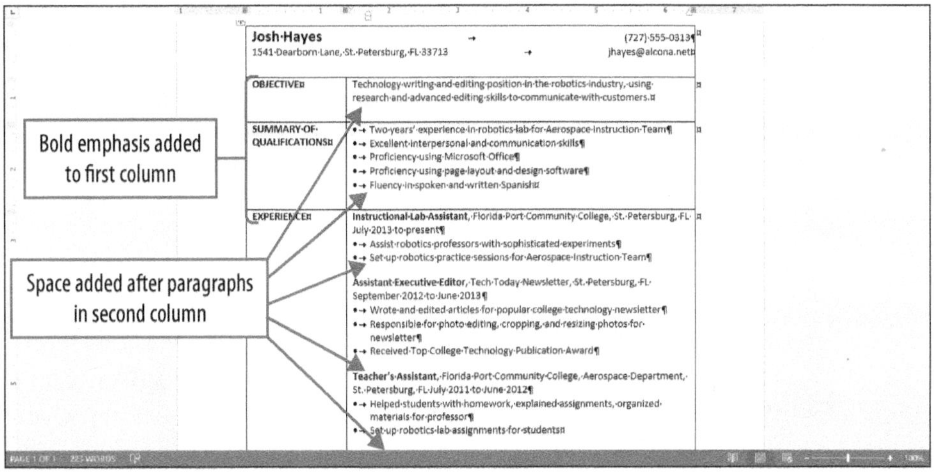

Activity 2.10 | Modifying Table Borders and Using Spacing Before

When you create a table, all of the cells have black 1/2-point, single-line, solid-line borders that print unless you remove them. Most resumes do not display any cell borders. A border at the top and bottom of the resume, however, is attractive and adds a professional look to the document.

1 Scroll as necessary to view the top margin area above the table, and then point slightly outside of the upper left corner of the table to display the **table move handle** [icon].

2 With the [icon] pointer, click one time to select the entire table, and notice that the row markers at the end of each row are also selected.

Shaded row markers indicate that the entire row is selected. Use this technique to select the entire table.

3 On the ribbon, under **TABLE TOOLS**, click the **DESIGN tab**. In the **Borders group**, click the **Borders button arrow**, and then click **No Border**.

The black borders no longer display.

4 Press Ctrl + P, which is the keyboard shortcut to view the Print Preview, and notice that no borders display in the preview. Then, press **Back** [icon] to return to your document.

5 With the table still selected, on the **DESIGN tab**, in the **Borders group**, click the **Borders button arrow**, and then at the bottom of the **Borders** gallery, click **Borders and Shading**.

6 In the **Borders and Shading** dialog box, on the **Borders tab**, under **Setting**, click **Custom**. Under **Style**, scroll down about one-third of the way, and then click the style with a **thick upper line and a thin lower line**.

7 In the **Preview** box at the right, point to the *top* border of the small preview and click one time.

ANOTHER WAY Click the top border button, which is one of the buttons that surround the Preview.

8 Under **Style**, scroll down if necessary, click the opposite style—with the **thin upper line and the thick lower line**, and then in the **Preview** box, click the *bottom* border of the preview. Compare your screen with Figure 2.15.

FIGURE 2.15

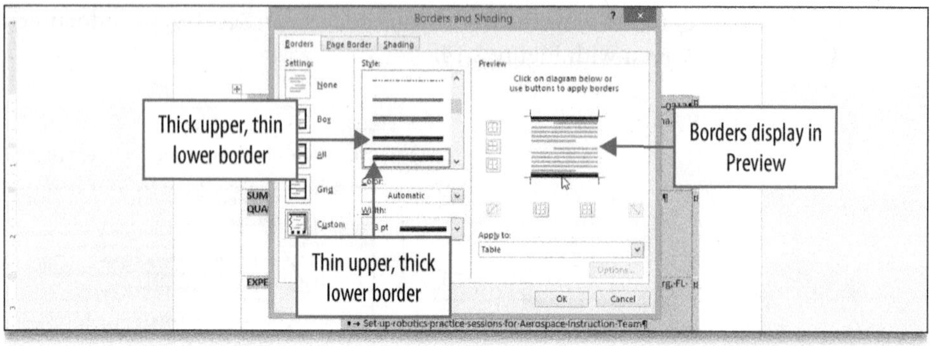

9 Click **OK**, click anywhere to cancel the selection, and then notice that there is only a small amount of space between the upper border and the first line of text.

10 Click anywhere in the text *Josh Hayes*, and then on the **PAGE LAYOUT tab**, in the **Paragraph group**, click the **Spacing Before up spin arrow** as necessary to add **18 pt** spacing before the first paragraph.

11 Press Ctrl + P to display **Print Preview**. Compare your screen with Figure 2.16.

FIGURE 2.16

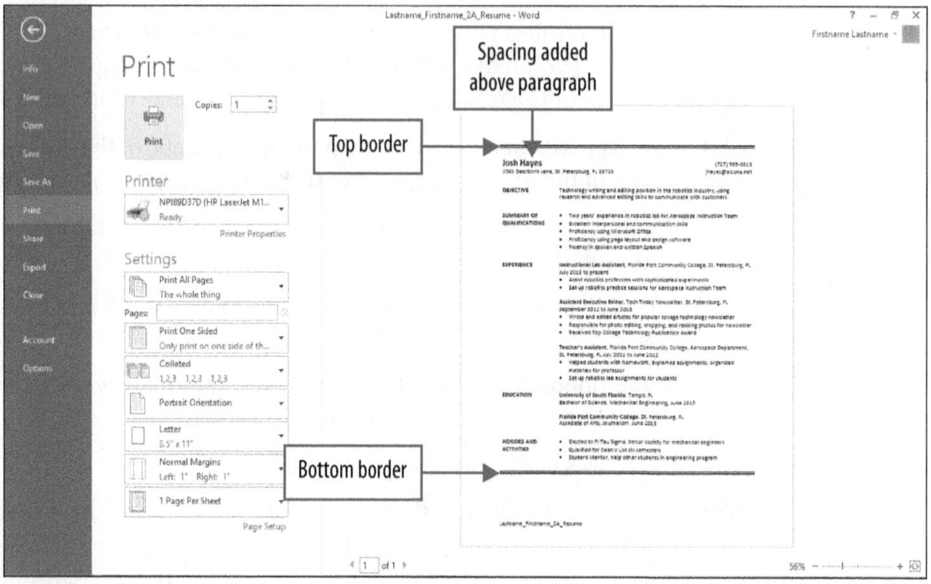

12 Press **Back** to return to your document, and then on the Quick Access Toolbar, click **Save**.

More Knowledge | **View Gridlines in a Table**

After you remove borders from a table, you can still view nonprinting gridlines, which show the cell boundaries of a table whenever the table does not have borders applied. Some people find this a useful visual aid. If you cannot see the gridlines, on the ribbon, under TABLE TOOLS, on the DESIGN tab, in the Borders group, click the Borders button arrow, and then click View Gridlines.

More Knowledge | **Convert Text to a Table**

To convert paragraphs or lists to a table, insert separator characters such as commas or tabs to show where to divide the text into columns. Then insert paragraph marks (press ENTER) to show where to begin the rows. Select the text, and then on the INSERT tab, in the Table group, click Convert Text to Table. In the Convert Text to Table dialog box, choose the options you want, and then click OK.

Objective 3 Present a Word Document Online

Video W2-3

Office Presentation Service enables you to present your Word document to others who can watch in a web browser. No preliminary setup is necessary; Word creates a link to your document that you can share with others via email or instant message. Anyone to whom you send the link can see your document while you are presenting online.

Individuals watching your presentation can navigate within the document independently of you or others in the presentation, so they can use a mouse, keyboard, or touch input to move around in the document while you are presenting it. If an individual is viewing a different portion of the document than the presenter, an alert displays on his or her screen. To return to the portion of the document that the presenter is showing, a Follow Presenter button displays.

While you are presenting, you can make minor edits to the document. If you want to share a copy of the document to the presentation attendees, you can select *Enable remote viewers to download the document* when you start the presentation. You can also share any meeting notes that you or others created in OneNote.

Activity 2.11 Presenting a Word Document Online

If you are creating your own resume, it will be valuable to get feedback from your friends, instructors, or Career Center advisors before you submit your resume for a job application. In this Activity, you will present the resume document online for others to look at.

> **NOTE** **You May Be Asked to Sign in with Your Microsoft Account**
>
> You may be asked to sign in with your Microsoft account, even if you are already signed in, to present your document online.

1. With your resume document displayed, click **Save**.
2. Click the **FILE tab**, on the left click **Share**, and then under **Share**, click **Present Online**.
3. On the right, under **Present Online**, be sure **Office Presentation Service** displays; if necessary, click the arrow on the right to select it. Click the **Present Online** button. Wait a moment for the service to connect, and then compare your screen with Figure 2.17.

   There are several methods to send your meeting invitation to others. You can click Copy Link to copy and paste the hyperlink; for example, you could copy the link into a ***Skype*** window. Skype is a Microsoft product with which you can make voice calls, make video calls, transfer files, or send messages—including instant messages and text messages—over the Internet.

   You can also select Send in Email, which will open your Outlook email window if you use Outlook as your mail client.

> **NOTE** **Other Presentation Services May Display**
>
> Under Present Online, you might have other services displayed. For example, if you are using Office 365, Microsoft Lync may display as the default presentation service.

FIGURE 2.17

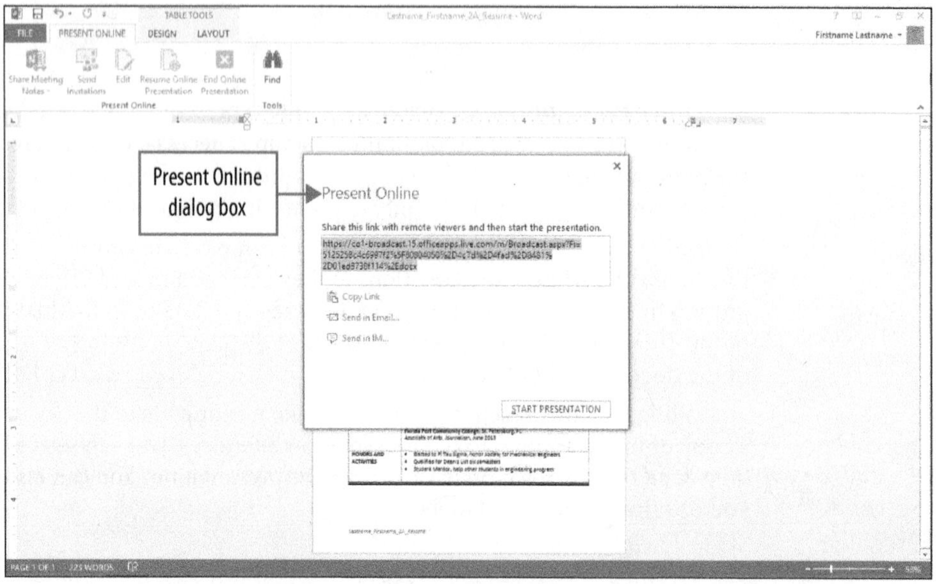

4 If you want to do so, identify a classmate or friend who is at a computer and available to view your presentation, select one of the methods to share, click **START PRESENTATION**, and when you are finished, on the ribbon, click **End Online Presentation**. Otherwise, **Close** [X] the **Present Online** dialog box.

If you present online, you will need to initiate voice communication using Skype or by simply phoning the other person.

5 Be sure you have closed the **Present Online** dialog box. On the ribbon, on the **PRESENT ONLINE tab**, click **End Online Presentation**, and then in the message, click **End Online Presentation.**

6 Press Ctrl + Home to move to the top of your document. In the lower right corner, click **Zoom In** [+] as necessary to set the Zoom level to **100%**. If necessary, on the **HOME tab**, redisplay the formatting marks by clicking **Show/Hide**.

7 Click the **FILE tab**, and then in the lower right portion of the screen, click **Show All Properties**. In the **Tags** box, type **resume, Word table** and in the **Subject** box, type your course name and section number. In the **Author** box, be sure your name is indicated and edit if necessary.

8 On the left, click **Print** to display **Print Preview**. If necessary, return to the document and make any necessary changes.

9 As directed by your instructor, print your document or submit it electronically. **Save** [save icon] your document and **Close** [x] Word.

More Knowledge **Convert a Table to Text**

To convert a table to text, select the rows or table you want to convert to paragraphs, and then on the LAYOUT tab, in the Data group, click Convert to Text. In the Convert to Text dialog box, under Separate text at, click the separator character to use in place of the column boundaries, and then click OK.

END | You have completed Project 2A

GO! with Office Online (formerly Web Apps)

Objective Edit a Resume in Word Online

You can create and edit tables in Word Online if you are not at a computer on which Word 2013 is installed.

ALERT! Working with Web-Based Applications and Services

Computer programs and services on the web receive continuous updates and improvements, so the steps to complete this web-based activity may differ from the ones shown. You can often look at the screens and the information presented to determine how to complete the activity.

Activity | Editing a Resume in Word Online

In this activity, you will use Word Online to edit a Word table containing a resume similar to the resume you created in Project 1A.

1. From the desktop, start Internet Explorer. Navigate to **http://onedrive.com** and then sign in to your Microsoft account. Click your **GO! Web Projects** folder to open it—or create and then open this folder if necessary.

2. On the OneDrive menu bar, click **Upload**. In the **Choose File to Upload** dialog box, navigate to your student data files, click **w02_2A_Web**, and then click **Open**.

3. Point to the uploaded file **w02_2A_Web**, and then right-click. On the shortcut menu, scroll down as necessary and then click **Rename**. Using your own last name and first name, type **Lastname_Firstname_WD_2A_Web** and then press Enter to rename the file.

4. Click the file that you just renamed, and then in the upper left, click **EDIT DOCUMENT**. On the list, click **Edit in Word Online**.

5. If necessary, click to place the insertion point in the cell *OBJECTIVE*. On the ribbon, under **TABLE TOOLS**, click the **LAYOUT tab**, and then in the **Insert group**, click **Insert Above**.

6. In the first cell of the new row, type **Daniela Frank** press Enter, select the text you just typed, and then on the **HOME tab**, in the **Styles group**, click the **More Styles arrow**, and then click **Title**. With the text selected, change the **Font** to **Calibri (Body)**.

7. Click in the second cell of the new row, and then type **1343 Siena Lane, Deerfield, WI 53531** and press Enter. Type **(608) 555-0588** and press Enter. Type **dfrank@alcona.net** and press Enter. Right-click the email address, and then click **Remove Link**. Select all the text in the second cell that you just typed, and then on the **HOME tab**, in the **Paragraph group**, click **Align Text Right**. Click anywhere to deselect, and then compare your screen with Figure A.

FIGURE A

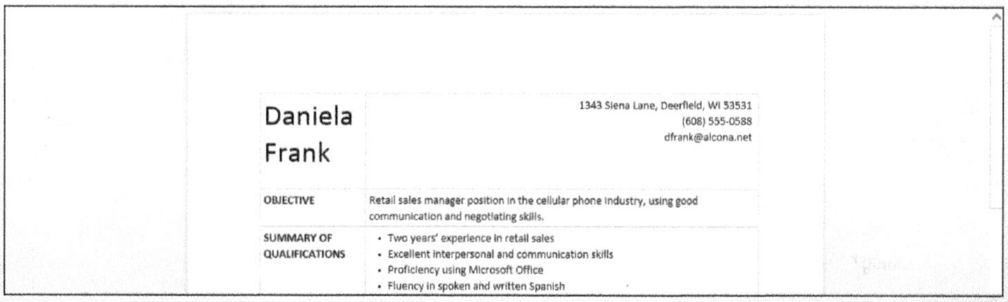

(GO! with Office Online (formerly Web Apps) continues on the next page)

8 Scroll down and click anywhere in the *EXPERIENCE* cell. On the ribbon, under **TABLE TOOLS**, click the **LAYOUT tab**, and then in the **Insert group**, click **Insert Below**. In the first cell of the new row, press Backspace one time to move the insertion point to the left edge of the cell. Type **EDUCATION** Select the text you just typed, and then if necessary, from the **HOME tab**, apply **Bold** B.

9 Press Tab to move to the second cell in the new row, press Backspace one time to move to the left edge of the cell, and then type **Madison Area Technical College, Madison, WI** and press Enter.

10 Type **Associate of Arts in Information Systems, June 2014** and press Enter. Select the line of text you just typed, and then press Ctrl + B to remove **Bold**. Click anywhere to deselect, and then compare your screen with Figure B.

11 Submit the file as directed by your instructor. Sign out of your OneDrive and close Internet Explorer.

FIGURE B

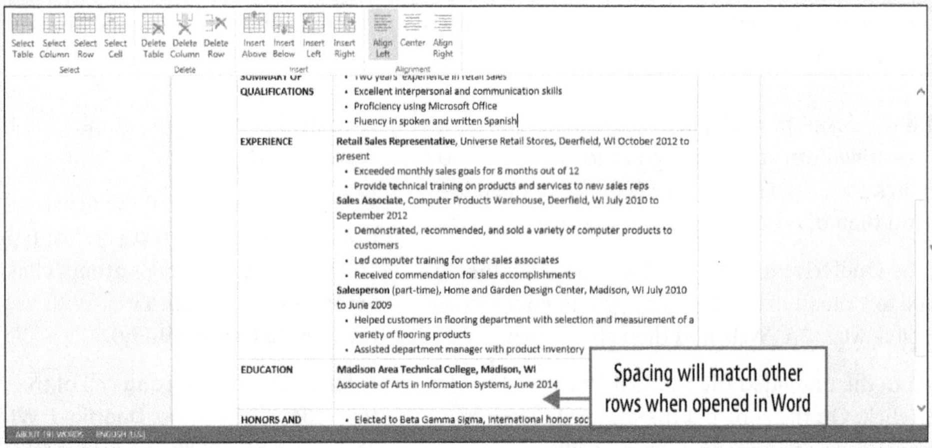

PROJECT 2B

Cover Letter, Reference List, and Envelope

MyITLab® Project 2B Training

2 WORD

PROJECT ACTIVITIES

In Activities 2.12 through 2.24, you will create a letterhead, save the letterhead as a custom Word template, and then use the letterhead to create a cover letter to accompany a resume. You will also create a list of references from a Microsoft predesigned template and, if you have an envelope and printer available, format and print an envelope. Your completed documents will look similar to Figure 2.18.

PROJECT FILES

For Project 2B, you will need the following files:	You will save your documents as:
New blank Word document	**Lastname_Firstname_2B_Cover_Letter**
w02B_Cover_Letter_Text	**Lastname_Firstname_2B_Reference_List**

PROJECT RESULTS

Build from Scratch

Jennifer Garcia

1776 Bay Cliff Drive, Tampa, FL 33602
(727) 555-0347 jgarcia@alcona.net

January 8, 2013

Ms. Mary Walker-Huelsman, Director
Florida Port Community College Career Center
2745 Oakland Avenue
St. Petersburg, FL 33713

Dear Ms. Walker-Huelsman:

I am seeking a position in which I can use my computer and communications skills. My education and experience, outlined on the enclosed resume, includes a Business Software Applications Specialist certificate from Florida Port Community College.

With a permanent position as my ultimate goal, I hope to use the Florida Port Community College Career Center to secure a temporary job. I can be available for a flexible number of hours or days and am willing to work in a variety of businesses or organizations.

As my resume illustrates, I have excellent computer skills. I am an honor student at Florida Port Community College and have outstanding references. In addition, I have part-time work experience as a software tester, where I perform the following computer activities:

Microsoft Access	Test database queries
Microsoft Excel	Enter software test data
Microsoft Word	Create and mail form letters

You can contact me by email at jgarcia@alcona.net or by telephone at (727) 555-0347. I am available for an interview at your convenience.

Sincerely,

Jennifer Garcia

Enclosure

Lastname Firstname 2B Cover Letter

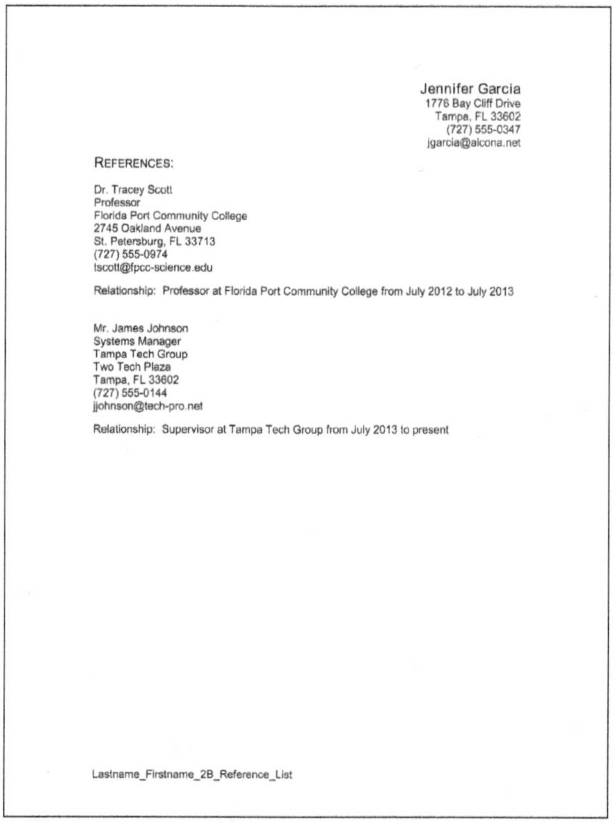

Jennifer Garcia
1776 Bay Cliff Drive
Tampa, FL 33602
(727) 555-0347
jgarcia@alcona.net

REFERENCES:

Dr. Tracey Scott
Professor
Florida Port Community College
2745 Oakland Avenue
St. Petersburg, FL 33713
(727) 555-0974
tscott@fpcc-science.edu

Relationship: Professor at Florida Port Community College from July 2012 to July 2013

Mr. James Johnson
Systems Manager
Tampa Tech Group
Two Tech Plaza
Tampa, FL 33602
(727) 555-0144
jjohnson@tech-pro.net

Relationship: Supervisor at Tampa Tech Group from July 2013 to present

Lastname_Firstname_2B_Reference_List

FIGURE 2.18 Project 2B Cover Letter and Reference List

Objective 4 Create a Custom Word Template

Video W2-4

A ***template*** is a file you use as a starting point for a *new* document. A template has a predefined document structure and defined settings, such as font, margins, and available styles. On Word's opening screen, you can select from among many different templates—or you can create your own custom template.

When you open a template as the starting point for a new document, the template file opens a copy of itself, unnamed, and then you use the structure—and possibly some content, such as headings—as the starting point for a new document.

All documents are based on a template. When you create a new blank document, it is based on Word's ***Normal template***, which serves as the starting point for all blank Word documents.

Activity 2.12 | Changing the Document Style Set for Paragraph Spacing and Applying a Bottom Border to a Paragraph

A ***letterhead*** is the personal or company information that displays at the top of a letter, and which commonly includes a name, address, and contact information. The term also refers to a piece of paper imprinted with such information at the top. In this activity, you will create a custom template for a personal letterhead.

1 Start Word and display a blank document; be sure that formatting marks and rulers display.

2 On the **DESIGN tab**, in the **Document Formatting group**, click **Paragraph Spacing**.

The Paragraph Spacing command offers various options for setting the line and paragraph spacing of your entire document. A gallery of predefined values displays; or you can create your own custom paragraph spacing.

3 On the list *point* to **Default** and notice the settings in the ScreenTip.

Recall that the default spacing for a new Word document is 0 points of blank space before a paragraph, 8 points of blank space following a paragraph, and line spacing of 1.08.

4 Point to **No Paragraph Space** and notice the settings in the ScreenTip.

The ***No Paragraph Space*** style inserts *no* extra space before or after a paragraph and uses line spacing of 1. This is the same format used for the line spacing commonly referred to as ***single spacing***.

5 Click **No Paragraph Space**.

By using the No Paragraph Space style, you will be able to follow the prescribed format of a letter, which Business Communications texts commonly describe in terms of single spacing.

ANOTHER WAY

On Word's opening screen, select the Single spaced (blank) document; or, in a blank document, select the entire document, and then on the HOME tab, in the Styles group, click No Spacing. Also, so long as you leave an appropriate amount of space between the elements of the letter, you can use Word's default spacing. Finally, you could use one of Word's predesigned templates for a cover letter and observe all spacing requirements for a letter.

6 Type **Jennifer Garcia** and then press Enter.

7 Type **1776 Bay Cliff Drive, Tampa, FL 33602** and then press Enter.

8 Type **(727) 555-0347 jgarcia@alcona.net** and then press Enter. If the web address changes to blue text, right-click the web address, and then, click **Remove Hyperlink**.

9 Select the first paragraph—*Jennifer Garcia*—and then on the mini toolbar, apply **Bold** B and change the **Font Size** to **16**.

10 Select the second and third paragraphs. On the mini toolbar, apply **Bold** [B] and change the **Font Size** to **12**.

11 With the two paragraphs still selected, on the **HOME tab**, in the **Paragraph group**, click **Align Right** [icon].

ANOTHER WAY Press Ctrl + R to align text to the right.

12 Click anywhere in the first paragraph—*Jennifer Garcia*. In the **Paragraph group**, click the **Borders button arrow** [icon], and then at the bottom, click **Borders and Shading.**

13 In the **Borders and Shading** dialog box, on the **Borders tab**, under **Style**, be sure the first style—a single solid line—is selected.

14 Click the **Width arrow**, and then click **3 pt**. To the right, under **Preview**, click the bottom border of the diagram. Under **Apply to**, be sure *Paragraph* displays. Compare your screen with Figure 2.19.

FIGURE 2.19

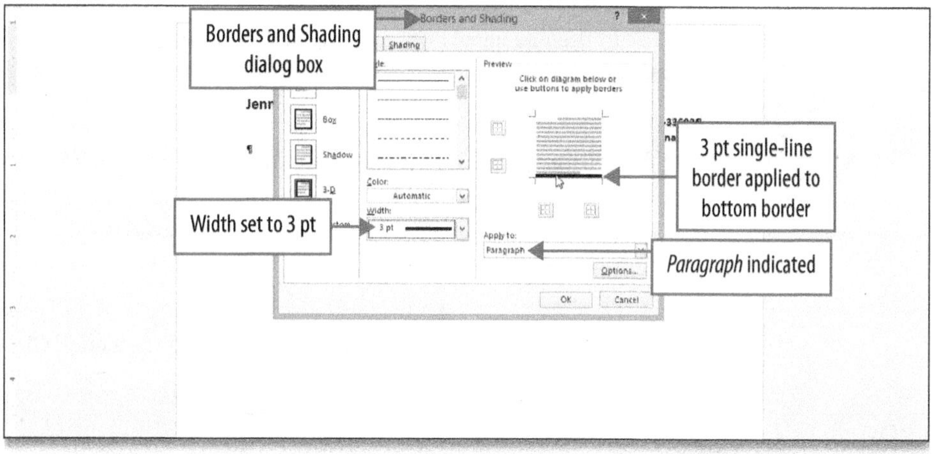

ANOTHER WAY Alternatively, under Preview, click the bottom border button [icon].

15 Click **OK** to display a 3 pt line below *Jennifer Garcia*, which extends from the left margin to the right margin.

The border is a paragraph command and uses the same margins of the paragraph to which it is applied.

Activity 2.13 | Saving a Document as a Custom Word Template

After you create a document format that you like and will use again, for example, a letterhead for personal letters during a job search, you can save it as a template and then use it as the starting point for any letter.

1 Press F12 to display the **Save As** dialog box. In the lower portion of the dialog box, in the **Save as type** box, at the right edge, click the arrow, and then click **Word Template**.

ALERT! **Are You Using a Laptop Computer?**

On some laptop computers, you might have to hold down the key labeled FN while pressing the F12 key in order to display the Save As dialog box.

2 At the top of the **Save As** dialog box, notice the path, and then compare your screen with Figure 2.20.

By default, Word stores template files on your hard drive in your user folder, in a folder named Custom Word Templates. By doing so, the template is available to you from the Word opening screen.

FIGURE 2.20

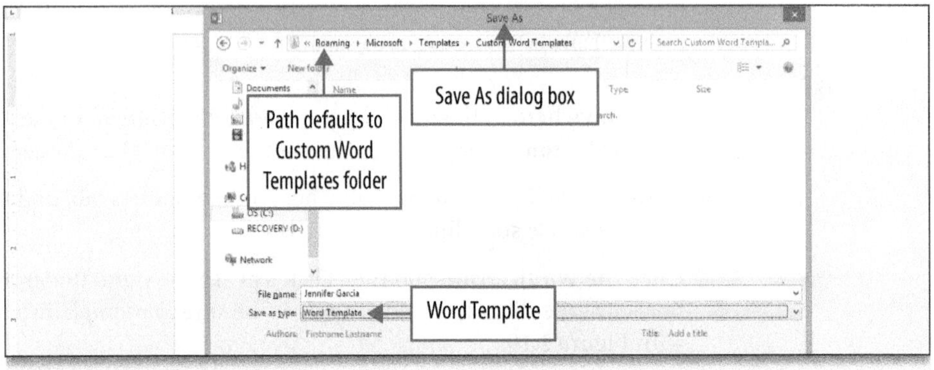

3 Click in the **File name** box, using your own name, type **Lastname_Firstname_2B_Letterhead_Template** and then click **Save**.

ALERT! **Are You Unable to Save in the Custom Word Templates Folder?**

Some college computer labs block you from saving on the hard drive. If you are unable to save your template in the Custom Word Templates folder, navigate to your Word Chapter 2 folder on your USB flash drive and save there. If you want to open a template that you stored in a location other than Word's default path, you must open the template directly from File Explorer—not from within Word—for it to open a new unnamed document based on the template.

4 Click the **FILE tab** to display **Backstage** view, and then click **Close** to close the file but leave Word open.

Activity 2.14 | Creating a Cover Letter from a Custom Word Template

A ***cover letter*** is a document that you send with your resume to provide additional information about your skills and experience. An effective cover letter includes specific information about why you are qualified for the job for which you are applying. Use the cover letter to explain your interest in the position and the organization.

ALERT! **Were You Unable to Save in the Custom Word Templates Folder?**

If you saved your template file on your USB flash drive because you were blocked from saving in the default folder on the hard drive, open your saved document, press F12 to display the Save As dialog box, and then in your storage location, save the document—using your own name—as Lastname_Firstname_2B_Cover_Letter. Then move to Activity 2.15.

1 With Word open but no documents displayed, click the **FILE tab** to display **Backstage** view, and then click **New** to display the new document options. Compare your screen with Figure 2.21.

Here you can create a new document from a blank document or from one of Word's many built-in or online templates.

FIGURE 2.21

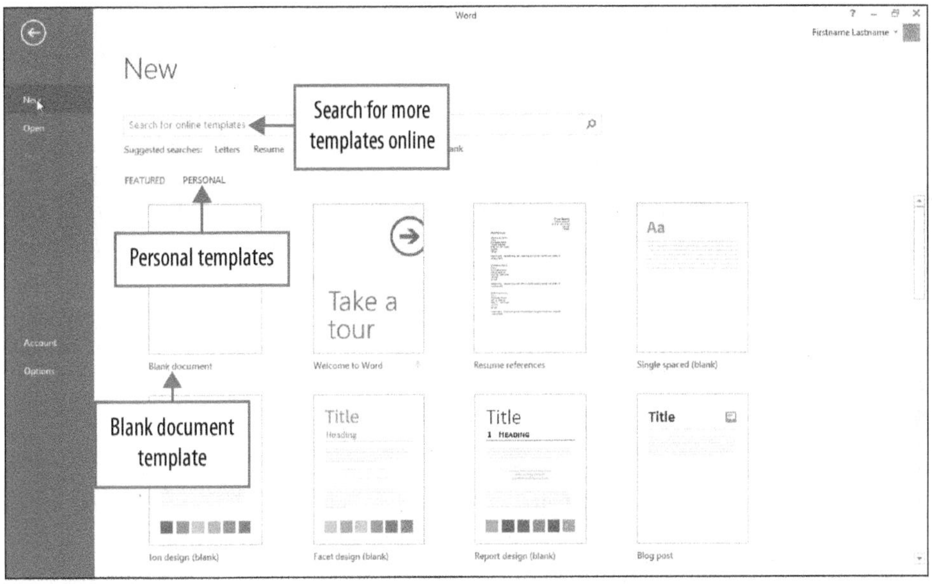

2 Under **Suggested searches**, click **PERSONAL**, *point* to the name of your letterhead template, and then compare your screen with Figure 2.22.

Custom templates that you create and that are stored in the Custom Word Templates folder on your hard drive are accessible to you here whenever you want to create a new document from your stored template.

FIGURE 2.22

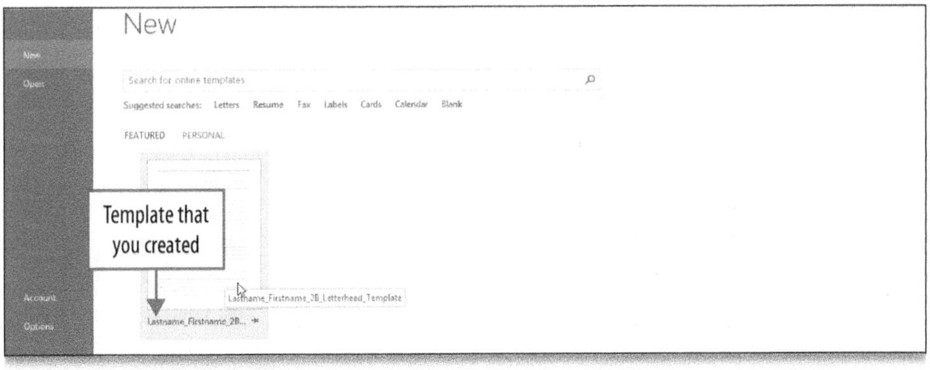

3 Click your letterhead template.

Word opens a copy of your 2B_Letterhead_Template in the form of a new Word document—the title bar indicates *Document* followed by a number. You are not opening the original template file, and changes that you make to this new document will not affect the contents of your 2B_Letterhead_Template file.

4 Press F12 to display the **Save As** dialog box, and then navigate to your **Word Chapter 2** folder. **Save** the file as **Lastname_Firstname_2B_Cover_Letter**

5 On the **INSERT tab**, in the **Header & Footer** group, click **Footer**, click **Edit Footer**, and then in the **Insert group**, click **Document Info**. Click **File Name**, and then click **Close Header and Footer**.

6 **Save** your document.

Objective 5 Correct and Reorganize Text

Video W2-5

Business letters follow a standard format and contain the following parts: the current date, referred to as the ***dateline***; the name and address of the person receiving the letter, referred to as the ***inside address***; a greeting, referred to as the ***salutation***; the text of the letter, usually referred to as the ***body*** of the letter; a closing line, referred to as the ***complimentary closing***; and the ***writer's identification***, which includes the name or job title (or both) of the writer and which is also referred to as the ***writer's signature block***.

Some letters also include the initials of the person who prepared the letter, an optional ***subject line*** that describes the purpose of the letter, or a list of ***enclosures***—documents included with the letter.

Activity 2.15 | Adding AutoCorrect Entries

Word's ***AutoCorrect*** feature corrects commonly misspelled words automatically; for example *teh* instead of *the*. If you have words that you frequently misspell, you can add them to the list for automatic correction.

1. Click the **FILE tab** to display **Backstage** view. On the left, click **Options** to display the **Word Options** dialog box.
2. On the left side of the **Word Options** dialog box, click **Proofing**, and then under **AutoCorrect options**, click the **AutoCorrect Options** button.
3. In the **AutoCorrect** dialog box, click the **AutoCorrect tab.** Under **Replace**, type **resumee** and under **With**, type **resume**

   If another student has already added this AutoCorrect entry, a Replace button will display.
4. Click **Add**. If the entry already exists, click **Replace** instead, and then click **Yes**.
5. In the **AutoCorrect** dialog box, under **Replace**, type **computr** and under **With**, type **computer** Compare your screen with Figure 2.23.

FIGURE 2.23

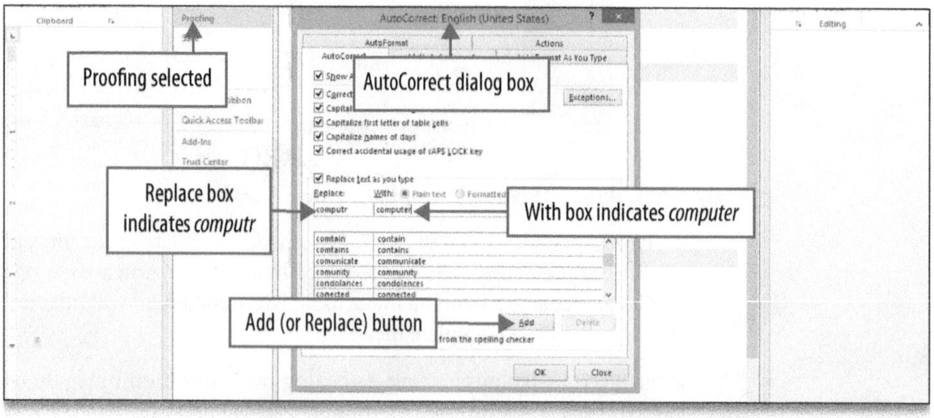

6. Click **Add** (or **Replace**) and then click **OK** two times to close the dialog boxes.

Activity 2.16 | Inserting the Current Date and Creating a Cover Letter

By using the ***Date & Time*** command, you can select from a variety of formats to insert the current date and time in a document.

For cover letters, there are a variety of accepted letter formats that you will see in reference manuals and Business Communications texts. The one used in this chapter is a block style cover letter following the style in Courtland Bovee and John Thill, *Business Communication Today*, Eleventh Edition, Pearson Prentice Hall, 2012, p. A-2.

1. Press Ctrl + End to move the insertion point to the blank line below the letterhead, and then press Enter three times.

2. On the **INSERT tab**, in the **Text group**, click **Date & Time**, and then click the third date format. Click **OK** to create the dateline.

   Most Business Communication texts recommend that the dateline be positioned at least 0.5 inch (3 blank lines) below the letterhead; or, position the dateline approximately 2 inches from the top edge of the paper.

3. Press Enter four times, which leaves three blank lines. Type the following inside address on four lines, but do *not* press Enter following the last line:

   Ms. Mary Walker-Huelsman, Director

   Florida Port Community College Career Center

   2745 Oakland Avenue

   St. Petersburg, FL 33713

   The recommended space between the dateline and inside address varies slightly among experts in Business Communication texts and office reference manuals. However, all indicate that the space can be from 1 to 10 blank lines depending on the length of your letter.

4. Press Enter two times to leave one blank line, and then compare your screen with Figure 2.24.

FIGURE 2.24

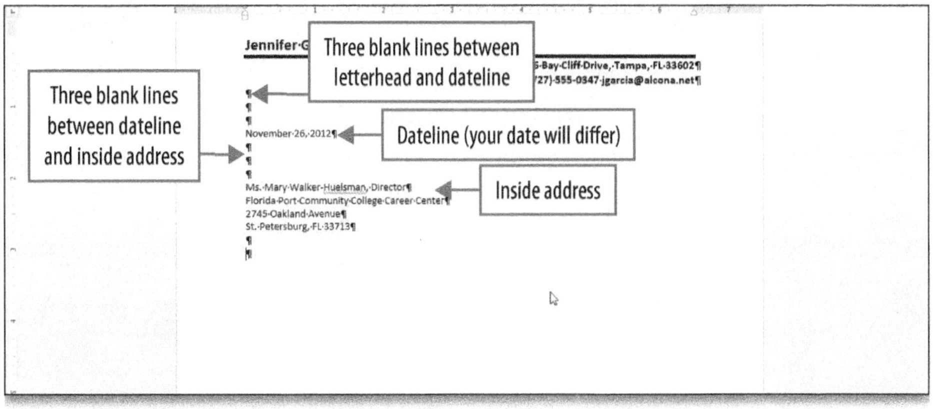

5. Type the salutation **Dear Ms. Walker-Huelsman:** and then press Enter two times.

   Always leave one blank line above and below the salutation.

6. Type, exactly as shown, the following opening paragraph that includes an intentional word usage error: **I am seeking a position in witch I can use my** and press Spacebar. Type, exactly as shown, **computr** and then watch *computr* as you press Spacebar.

   The AutoCorrect feature recognizes the misspelled word, and then changes *computr* to *computer* when you press Spacebar, Enter, or a punctuation mark.

7 Type the following, including the misspelled last word: **and communication skills. My education and experience, outlined on the enclosed resumee** and then type **,** (a comma). Notice that when you type the comma, AutoCorrect replaces *resumee* with *resume.*

8 Press Spacebar, and then complete the paragraph by typing **includes a Business Software Applications Specialist certificate from FPCC.** Compare your screen with Figure 2.25.

FIGURE 2.25

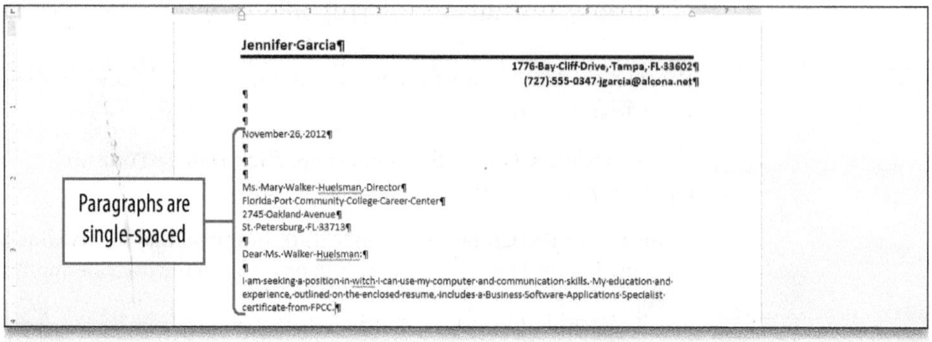

9 Press Enter two times. On the **INSERT tab**, in the **Text group**, click the **Object button arrow**, and then click **Text from File**. From your student files, locate and **Insert** the file **w02B_Cover_Letter_Text.**

Some of the words in the cover letter text display red or blue wavy underlines. These indicate potential spelling, grammar, or word usage errors, and will be addressed before the end of this project.

10 Scroll as necessary to display the lower half of the letter on your screen, and be sure your insertion point is positioned in the blank paragraph at the end of the document.

11 Press Enter one time to leave one blank line between the last paragraph of the letter and the complimentary closing.

12 Type **Sincerely,** as the complimentary closing, and then press Enter four times to leave three blank lines between the complimentary closing and the writer's identification.

13 Type **Jennifer Garcia** as the writer's identification, and then press Enter two times.

14 Type **Enclosure** to indicate that a document is included with the letter. **Save** your document, and then compare your screen with Figure 2.26.

FIGURE 2.26

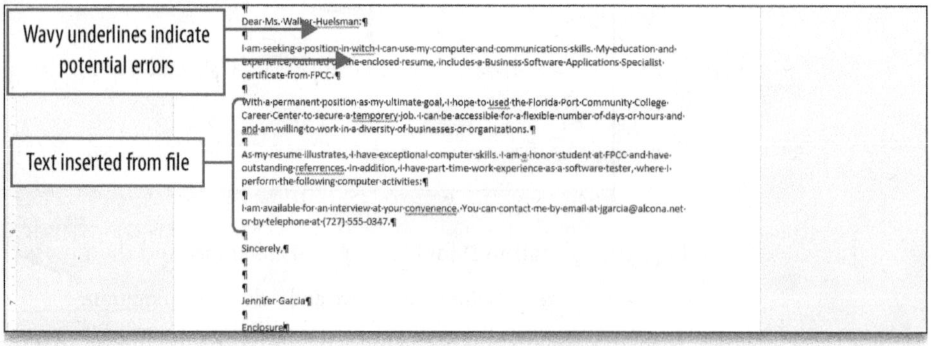

Activity 2.17 | Finding and Replacing Text

Use the Find command to locate text in a document quickly. Use the Find and Replace command to make the same change, or to make more than one change at a time, in a document.

1 Press Ctrl + Home to position the insertion point at the beginning of the document.

Because a find operation—or a find and replace operation—begins from the location of the insertion point and proceeds to the end of the document, it is good practice to position the insertion point at the beginning of the document before initiating the command.

2 On the **HOME tab**, in the **Editing group**, click **Find**.

The navigation pane displays on the left side of the screen with a search box at the top of the pane.

ANOTHER WAY Hold down Ctrl and press F.

3 In the **navigation** pane, in the search box, type **ac** If necessary, scroll down slightly in your document to view the entire body text of the letter, and then compare your screen with Figure 2.27.

In the document, the search letters *ac* are selected and highlighted in yellow for both words that begin with the letters *ac* and also for the word *contact* which contains this letter combination. In the navigation pane, the three instances are shown in context—*ac* displays in bold.

FIGURE 2.27

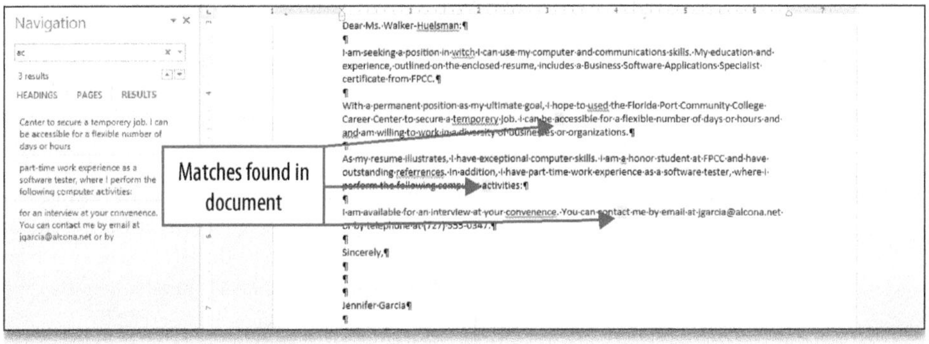

4 Click in the search box again, and type as necessary to display the word *accessible* in the search box.

One match for the search term displays in context in the navigation pane and is highlighted in the document.

5 In the document, double-click the yellow highlighted word *accessible*, and then type **available** to replace the word.

6 **Close** [x] the **navigation** pane, and then on the **HOME tab**, in the **Editing group**, click **Replace**.

7 In the **Find and Replace** dialog box, in the **Find what** box, replace the existing text by typing **FPCC** and in the **Replace with** box, type **Florida Port Community College** and then compare your screen with Figure 2.28.

FIGURE 2.28

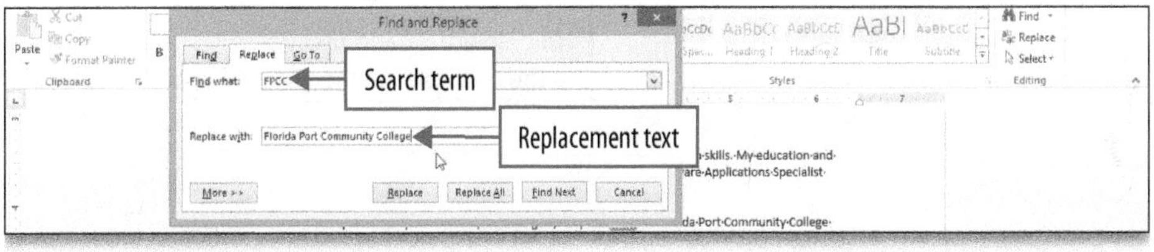

2 WORD

8 In the lower left corner of the dialog box, click **More** to expand the dialog box, and then under **Search Options**, select the **Match case** check box.

The acronym *FPCC* appears in the document two times. In a formal letter, the reader may not know what the acronym means, so you should include the full text instead of an acronym. In this instance, you must select the *Match case* check box so that the replaced text will match the case you typed in the Replace with box, and *not* display in all uppercase letters in the manner of *FPCC*.

9 In the **Find and Replace** dialog box, click **Replace All** to replace both instances of *FPCC*. Click **OK** to close the message box.

10 In the **Find and Replace** dialog box, clear the **Match case** check box, click **Less**, and then **Close** the dialog box. **Save** [Save] your document.

The Find and Replace dialog box opens with the settings used the last time it was open. Therefore, it is good practice to reset this dialog box to its default settings each time you use it.

Activity 2.18 | Selecting and Moving Text to a New Location

By using Word's ***drag-and-drop*** feature, you can use the mouse to drag selected text from one location to another. This method is most useful when the text you are moving is on the same screen as the destination location.

1 Take a moment to study the table in Figure 2.29 to become familiar with the techniques you can use to select text in a document quickly.

FIGURE 2.29

SELECTING TEXT IN A DOCUMENT	
TO SELECT THIS:	**DO THIS:**
A portion of text	Click to position the insertion point at the beginning of the text you want to select, hold down Shift, and then click at the end of the text you want to select. Alternatively, hold down the left mouse button and drag from the beginning to the end of the text you want to select.
A word	Double-click the word.
A sentence	Hold down Ctrl and click anywhere in the sentence.
A paragraph	Triple-click anywhere in the paragraph; or, move the pointer to the left of the line, into the margin area. When the [pointer] pointer displays, double-click.
A line	Point to the left of the line. When the [pointer] pointer displays, click one time.
One character at a time	Position the insertion point to the left of the first character, hold down Shift, and press ← or → as many times as desired.
A string of words	Position the insertion point to the left of the first word, hold down Shift and Ctrl, and then press ← or → as many times as desired.
Consecutive lines	Position the insertion point to the left of the first word, hold down Shift and press ↑ or ↓.
Consecutive paragraphs	Position the insertion point to the left of the first word, hold down Shift and Ctrl and press ↑ or ↓.
The entire document	Hold down Ctrl and press A. Alternatively, move the pointer to the left of any line in the document. When the [pointer] pointer displays, triple-click.

2 Be sure you can view the entire body of the letter on your screen. In the paragraph that begins *With a permanent position*, in the second line, locate and double-click *days*.

3 Point to the selected word to display the [pointer icon] pointer.

4 Drag to the right until the dotted vertical line that floats next to the pointer is positioned to the right of the word *hours* in the same line, as shown in Figure 2.30.

FIGURE 2.30

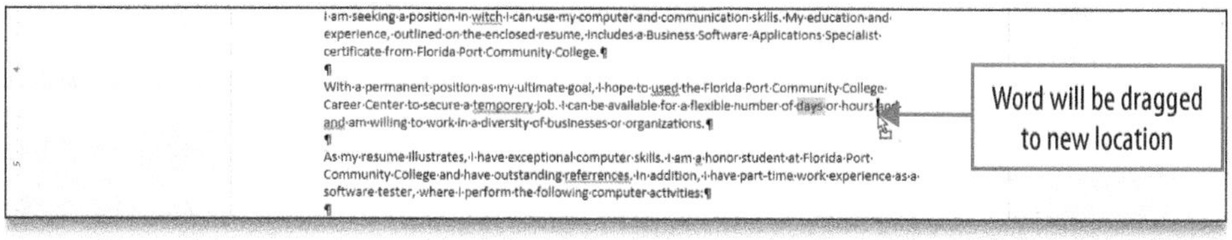

5 Release the mouse button to move the text. Select *hours* and drag it to the left of the word *or*—the previous location of the word *days*. Click anywhere to deselect the text.

6 Examine the text that you moved, and add or remove spaces as necessary.

7 Hold down Ctrl, and then in the paragraph that begins *I am available*, click anywhere in the first sentence to select the entire sentence.

8 Drag the selected sentence to the end of the paragraph by positioning the small vertical line that floats with the pointer to the left of the paragraph mark. **Save** [Save icon] your document, and then compare your screen with Figure 2.31.

FIGURE 2.31

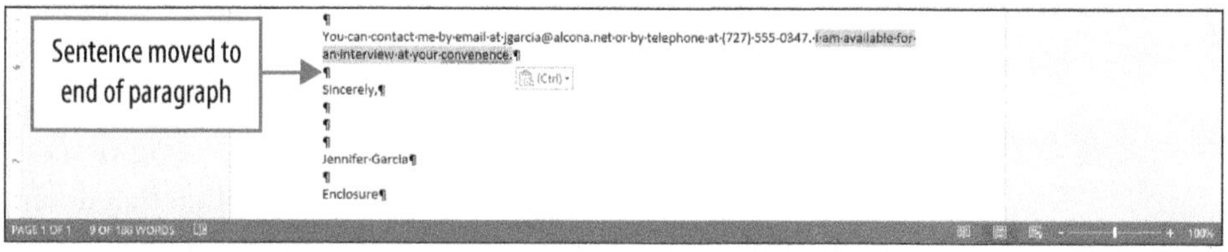

Activity 2.19 | Inserting a Table into a Document and Applying a Table Style

1 Locate the paragraph that begins *You can contact me*, and then click to position the insertion point in the blank line above that paragraph. Press Enter one time.

2 On the **INSERT tab**, in the **Tables group**, click **Table**. In the **Table** grid, in the third row, click the second square to insert a 2 × 3 table.

3 In the first cell of the table, type **Microsoft Access** and then press Tab. Type **Test database queries** and then press Tab. Complete the table using the following information:

Microsoft Excel	**Enter software test data**
Microsoft Word	**Create and mail form letters**

4 Point slightly outside of the upper left corner of the table to display the **table move handle** button [table move handle icon]. With the [move pointer icon] pointer, click one time to select the entire table.

5 On the **LAYOUT tab**, in the **Cell Size group**, click **AutoFit**, and then click **AutoFit Contents** to have Word choose the best column widths for the two columns based on the text you entered.

6 With the table still selected, on the **DESIGN tab**, in the **Table Styles group**, click **More** [icon]. Under **Plain Tables**, click the second style—**Table Grid Light**.

Use Table Styles to change the visual style of a table.

7 With the table still selected, on the **HOME tab**, in the **Paragraph group**, click **Center** [icon] to center the table between the left and right margins. Click anywhere to deselect the table.

8 **Save** [icon] and then compare your screen with Figure 2.32.

FIGURE 2.32

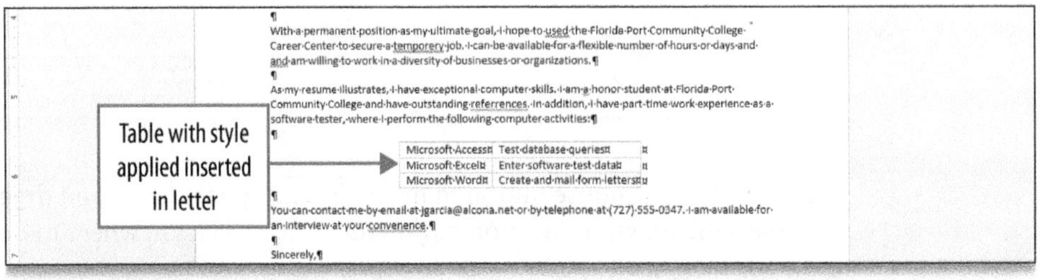

More Knowledge **Configure Cell Margins in a Table**

You can modify the margins of a cell to increase or decrease the distance between the cell border and the text in the cell. To do so, on the LAYOUT tab, in the Alignment group, click Cell Margins, and then enter the new margins.

Objective 6 Use the Proofing Options and Print an Envelope

Video W2-6

Word compares your typing to words in the Office dictionary and compares your phrases and punctuation to a list of grammar rules. This automatic proofing is set by default. Words that are not in the dictionary and words, phrases, and punctuation that differ from the grammar rules are marked with wavy underlines; for example, the misuse of *their*, *there*, and *they're*.

Word will not flag the word *sign* as misspelled even though you intended to type *sing a song* rather than *sign a song*, because both are words contained within Word's dictionary. Your own knowledge and proofreading skills are still required, even when using a sophisticated word processing program like Word.

Activity 2.20 | Checking for Spelling and Grammar Errors

There are two ways to respond to spelling and grammar errors flagged by Word. You can right-click a flagged word or phrase, and then from the shortcut menu choose a correction or action. Or, you can initiate the Spelling & Grammar command to display the Spelling and Grammar pane, which provides more options than the shortcut menus.

ALERT! **Activating Spelling and Grammar Checking**

If you do not see any wavy red or blue lines under words, the automatic spelling or grammar checking has been turned off on your system. To activate the spelling and grammar checking, display Backstage view, click Options, click Proofing, and then under *When correcting spelling in Microsoft Office programs*, select the first four check boxes. Under *When correcting spelling and grammar in Word*, select the first four check boxes, and then click the Writing Style arrow and click Grammar Only. Under *Exceptions for*, clear both check boxes. To display the flagged spelling and grammar errors, click the Recheck Document button, and then close the dialog box.

1 Position the body of the letter on your screen, and then examine the text to locate wavy underlines.

A list of grammar rules applied by a computer program like Word can never be exact, and a computer dictionary cannot contain all known words and proper names. Therefore, you will need to check any words flagged by Word with wavy underlines, and you will also need to proofread for content errors.

2 In the lower left corner of your screen, in the status bar, locate and point to the icon to display the ScreenTip *Proofing errors were found. Click to correct.* Compare your screen with Figure 2.33.

If this button displays, you know there are potential errors identified in the document.

FIGURE 2.33

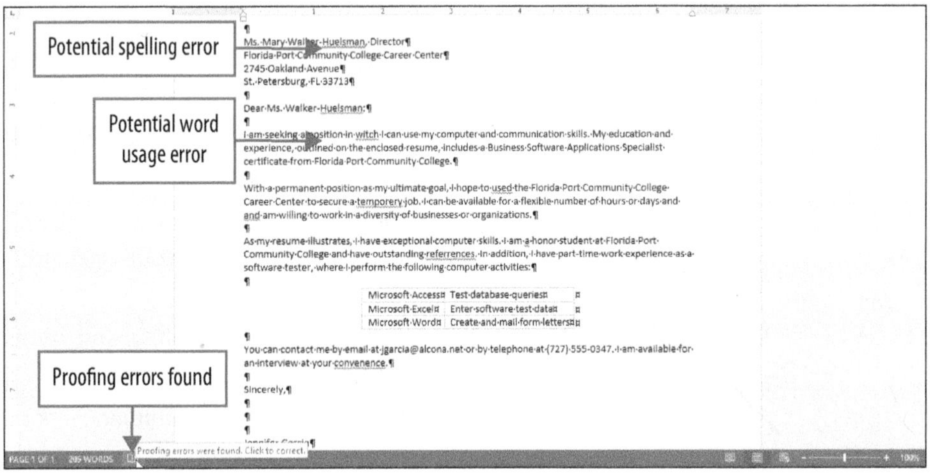

3 In the paragraph that begins *With a permanent*, in the second line, locate the word *temporery* with the wavy red underline. Point to the word and right-click, and then click **temporary** to correct the spelling error.

4 In the next line, locate the word *and* that displays with a wavy red underline, point to the word and right-click, and then on the shortcut menu, click **Delete Repeated Word** to delete the duplicate word.

5 Press Ctrl + Home to move the insertion point to the beginning of the document. Click the **REVIEW tab**, and then in the **Proofing group**, click **Spelling & Grammar** to check the spelling and grammar of the text in the document.

The Spelling pane displays on the right, and the proper name *Huelsman* is flagged. Word's dictionary contains only very common proper names—unusual names like this one will typically be flagged as a potential spelling error. If this is a name that you frequently type, consider adding it to the dictionary.

ANOTHER WAY Press F7 to start the Spelling & Grammar command.

6 In the **Spelling** pane, click **Ignore All**. Compare your screen with Figure 2.34.

The word *witch* is highlighted as a grammar error, and in the Grammar pane, *which* is suggested.

FIGURE 2.34

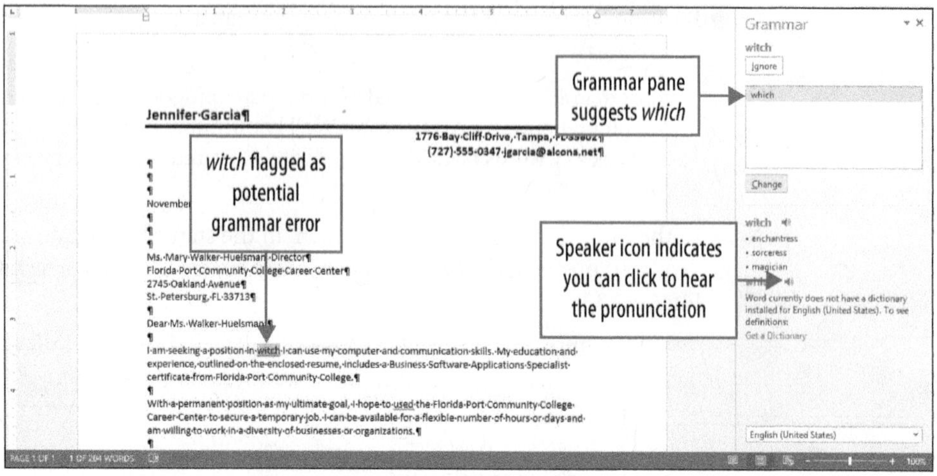

7 In the **Grammar** pane, click **Change** to change to the correct usage *which.*

The next marked word—a possible grammar error—displays.

8 Click **Change** to change *used* to *use.* Notice that the next error is a potential spelling error. In the **Spelling** pane, change *referrences* to the suggestion *references.* Notice that the next error is a possible grammar error.

9 Click **Change** to change *a* to *an.* Continue the spelling and grammar check and correct the spelling of *convenence.*

10 When Word displays the message *Spelling and grammar check complete,* click **OK.**

11 **Save** your document.

Activity 2.21 | Using the Thesaurus

A ***thesaurus*** is a research tool that lists ***synonyms***—words that have the same or similar meaning to the word you selected.

1 Scroll so that you can view the body of the letter. In the paragraph that begins *With a permanent,* double-click to select the word *diversity,* and then in the **Proofing** group, click **Thesaurus.**

The Thesaurus pane displays on the right a list of synonyms; the list will vary in length depending on the selected word.

ANOTHER WAY Right-click the word, on the shortcut menu, point to Synonyms, and then click Thesaurus.

2 In the **Thesaurus** pane, point to the word *variety,* and then click the arrow that displays. Click **Insert** to change *diversity* to *variety.*

3 In the paragraph that begins *As my resume,* double-click the word *exceptional,* and then on the ribbon, click **Thesaurus** again.

4 In the **Thesaurus** pane, point to *excellent,* click the **arrow,** and then click **Insert.** Compare your screen with Figure 2.35.

FIGURE 2.35

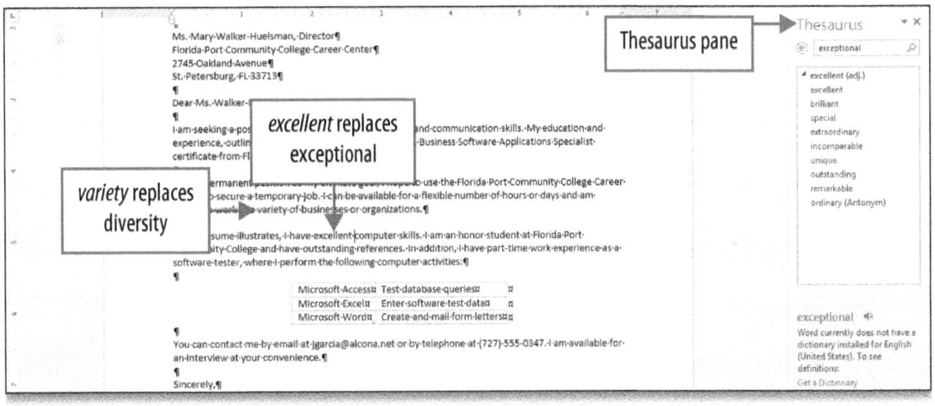

5 Close [X] the **Thesaurus** pane.

6 Click the **FILE tab** to display **Backstage** view, and then on the **Info tab**, in the lower right portion of the screen, click **Show All Properties**. If you used your template, notice that it is indicated to the right of *Template*.

7 In the **Tags** box, type **cover letter** and in the **Subject** box, type your course name and section number. In the **Author** box, be sure your name is indicated and edit if necessary.

8 On the left, click **Print** to display **Print Preview**. If necessary, return to the document and make any necessary changes.

9 As directed by your instructor, print your document or submit it electronically. **Save** your document and **Close** [X] Word.

Activity 2.22 | Addressing and Printing an Envelope

Use Word's Envelopes command on the Mailings label to format and print an envelope.

> **NOTE** **This Is an Optional Activity**
>
> This activity is optional. If you do not have an envelope and printer, or do not want to complete the activity at this time, move to Activity 2.23.

1 Display your **2B_Cover_Letter**, and then select the four lines that comprise the inside address.

2 On the **MAILINGS tab**, in the **Create group**, click **Envelopes**. Notice that the **Delivery address** contains the selected inside address.

3 Click in the **Return address** box, and then type **Jennifer Garcia** and press Enter. Type **1776 Bay Cliff Drive** and then press Enter. Type **Tampa, FL 33602**

4 In the lower portion of the **Envelopes and Labels** dialog box, click **Options**, and then compare your screen with Figure 2.36.

The default envelope size is a standard business envelope referred to as a Size 10.

FIGURE 2.36

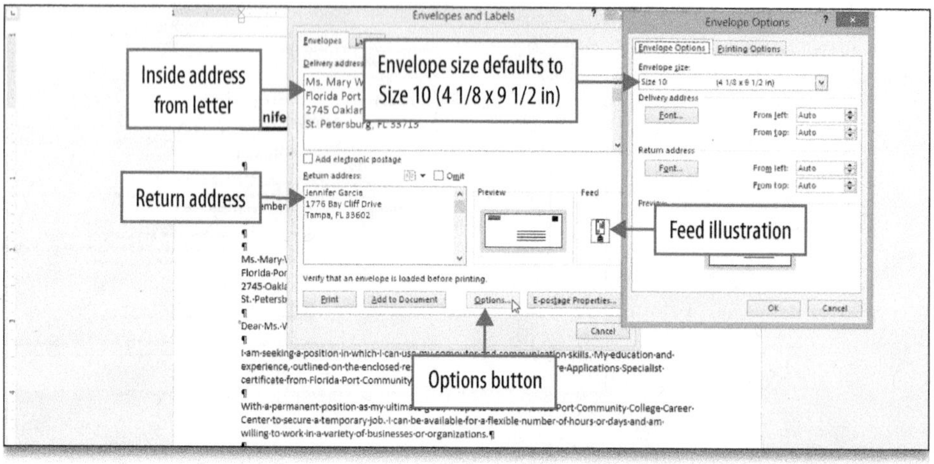

5 Click **OK** to close the **Envelope Options** dialog box. As shown under **Feed**, insert an envelope in your printer and then click **Print**.

Depending on the type and brand of printer you are using, your feed area may vary.

6 Close your **2B_Cover_Letter**, and then **Close** Word.

Objective 7 Create a Document Using a Predesigned Microsoft Template

Video W2-7

Microsoft provides predesigned templates for letters, calendars, invoices, and other types of documents. Recall that when you open a template, it opens unnamed so that you can reuse it as often as you need to do so.

Activity 2.23 | Locating and Opening a Template

In this activity, you will use a predesigned template to create a list of references to accompany a resume. References are not included on a resume, because you want to use the resume space for personal information. Most employers do not check references until after the first interview and when they have decided to consider you for a position. Be sure that you have already notified these individuals, asked their permission to use their name as a reference, and then contact them to tell them that a specific employer may be contacting them.

1 **Start** Word, and then on the opening screen, in the **Search for online templates** box, type **resume references** and press Enter.

2 Locate the reference list that contains three left-aligned reference items as shown in Figure 2.37.

FIGURE 2.37

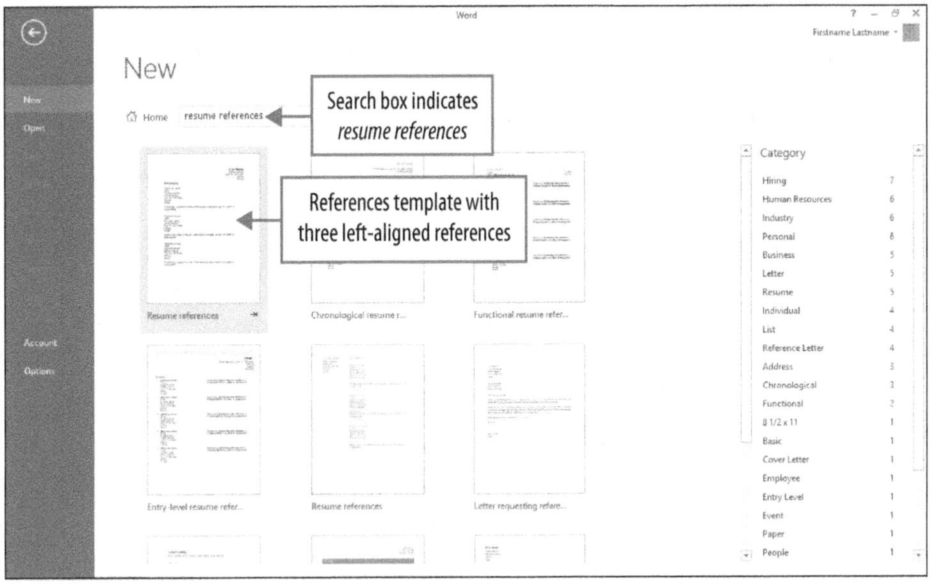

3 Click the three-item reference template, and then click **Create**. Compare your screen with Figure 2.38.

The template opens a copy of itself in the form of a new Word document—the title bar indicates *Document* followed by a number. Recall that you are not opening the template itself, and that changes you make to this new document will not affect the contents of the template file.

FIGURE 2.38

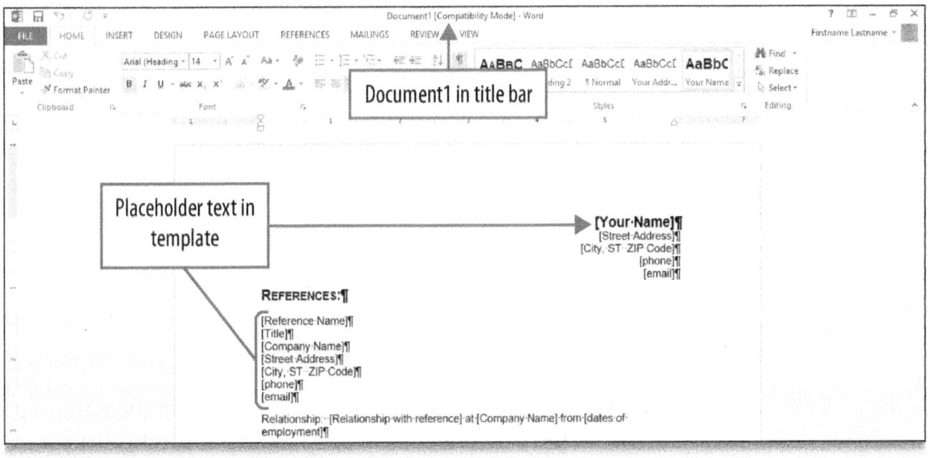

4 Press F12 to display the **Save As** dialog box. **Save** the document in your **Word Chapter 2** folder as **Lastname_Firstname_2B_Reference_List** and click **Save**. If a message indicates that you will be upgraded to the newest file format, click **OK**.

5 Add the file name to the footer, and then **Save** your document.

Activity 2.24 | Replacing Template Placeholder Text and Removing Controls

After you save the template file as a Word document, you can begin to substitute your own information in the indicated locations. ***Placeholder text*** is text that indicates the type of information to be entered. Text surrounded by brackets is called a ***content control***. There are several different types of content controls, including date, picture, and ***text controls***. All of the controls in this template are text controls.

1 In the upper right, click in the placeholder text *[Your Name]* and type **Jennifer Garcia** Click *[Street Address]* and type **1776 Bay Cliff Drive**

2 Click *[City, ST ZIP Code]* and type **Tampa, FL 33602** Click *[phone]* and type **(727) 555-0347** Click *[email]* and type **jgarcia@alcona.net**

3 Under **References,** enter two references using the following information, and then compare your screen with Figure 2.39.

TEMPLATE FIELD	REFERENCE 1	REFERENCE 2
Reference Name	**Dr. Tracey Scott**	**Mr. James Johnson**
Title	**Professor**	**Systems Manager**
Company Name	**Florida Port Community College**	**Tampa Tech Group**
Street Address	**2745 Oakland Avenue**	**Two Tech Plaza**
City, ST ZIP Code	**St. Petersburg, FL 33713**	**Tampa, FL 33602**
phone	**(727) 555-0974**	**(727) 555-0144**
email	**tscott@fpcc-science.edu**	**jjohnson@tech-pro.net**
Relationship with reference	**Professor**	**Supervisor**
Company Name	**Florida Port Community College**	**Tampa Tech Group**
dates of employment	**July 2012 to July 2013**	**July 2013 to present**

FIGURE 2.39

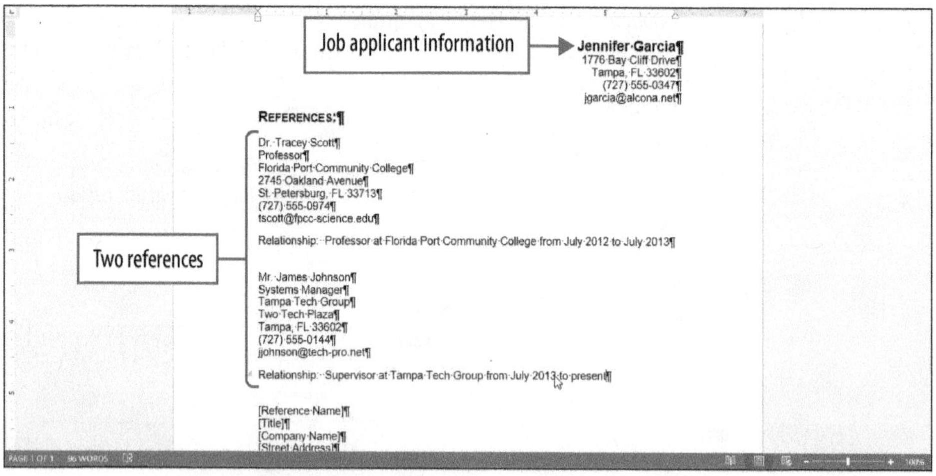

4 Scroll down to the third reference block. Select all the paragraphs of placeholder text, and then press Del to delete these unneeded controls; this list will contain only two references.

ANOTHER WAY Point to a content control, right-click, and then on the shortcut menu, click Remove Content Control.

5 Click **Save**. Click the **FILE tab**, and then in the lower right portion of the screen, click **Show All Properties**. In the **Tags** box, type **reference list** and in the **Subject** box, type your course name and section number. In the **Author** box, be sure your name is indicated and edit if necessary.

6 On the left, click **Print** to display **Print Preview**. If necessary, return to the document and make any necessary changes.

7 As directed by your instructor, print your document or submit it electronically. **Save** your document and **Close** Word.

END | You have completed Project 2B

GO! with Office Online (formerly Web Apps)

Objective Create a Table in Word Online

You can create and edit tables in Word Online if you are not at a computer on which Word 2013 is installed.

> **ALERT!** **Working with Web-Based Applications and Services**
>
> Computer programs and services on the web receive continuous updates and improvements, so the steps to complete this web-based activity may differ from the ones shown. You can often look at the screens and the information presented to determine how to complete the activity.

Activity | Creating a Table in Word Online

In this activity, you will use Word Online to create a Word table within a document similar to Project 2B.

1 From the desktop, start Internet Explorer. Navigate to **http://onedrive.com** and then sign in to your Microsoft account. Open your **GO! Web Projects** folder—or create and then open this folder if necessary.

2 On the OneDrive menu bar, click **Upload**. In the **Choose File to Upload** dialog box, navigate to your student data files, click **w02_2B_Web**, and then click **Open**.

3 Point to the uploaded file **w02_2B_Web**, and then right-click. On the shortcut menu, scroll down as necessary and then click **Rename**. Using your own last name and first name, type **Lastname_Firstname_WD_2B_Web** and then press Enter to rename the file.

4 Click the file that you just renamed, and then in the upper left, click **EDIT DOCUMENT**. On the list, click **Edit in Word Online**.

5 Press Ctrl + End to move to the end of the document, and then press Enter.

6 On the **INSERT tab**, in the **Tables group**, click **Table**, and then insert a **3×4 Table**.

7 Type **Position** and press Tab. Type **Type** and press Tab. Type **Location** and press Tab.

8 In the second row type **Paralegal** and press Tab. Type **Part-time** and press Tab. Type **Tampa** and press Tab. Compare your screen with Figure A.

FIGURE A

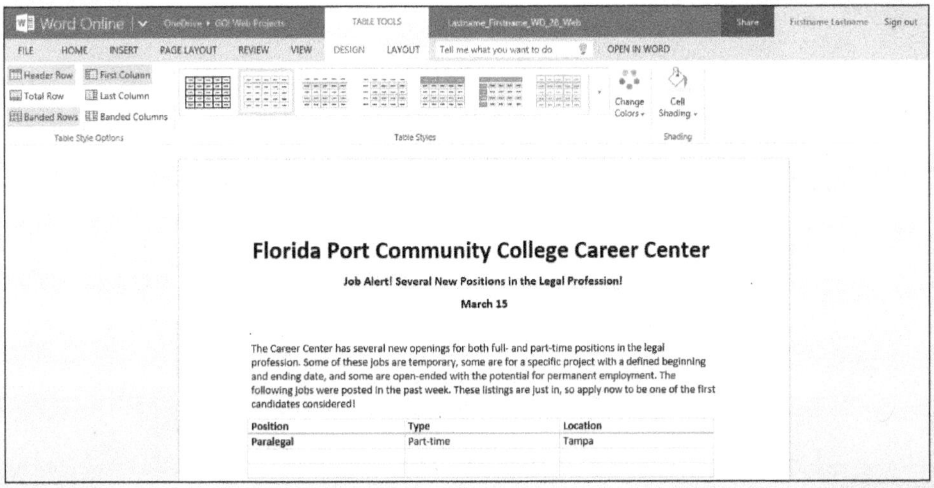

(GO! with Office Online continues on the next page)

9 Type **Legal Records Clerk** and press Tab. Type **Full-time, 2 months** and press Tab. Type **North Tampa** and press Tab.

10 On the ribbon, under **TABLE TOOLS**, click the **LAYOUT tab**, and then in the **Delete group**, click **Delete Row**.

11 Drag to select all the cells in the first row, and then on the **HOME tab**, in the **Styles group**, click **Heading 1**. With the three column titles still selected, in the **Paragraph group**, click **Center**. In the **Font group**, change the **Font Color** to **Black, Text 1**. Compare your screen with Figure B.

12 Submit the file as directed by your instructor. Sign out of your OneDrive and close Internet Explorer.

FIGURE B

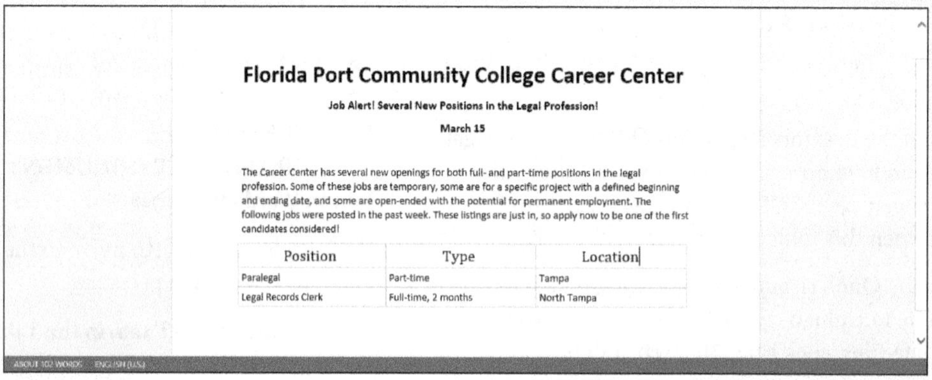
Florida Port Community College Career Center

Job Alert! Several New Positions in the Legal Profession!

March 15

The Career Center has several new openings for both full- and part-time positions in the legal profession. Some of these jobs are temporary, some are for a specific project with a defined beginning and ending date, and some are open-ended with the potential for permanent employment. The following jobs were posted in the past week. These listings are just in, so apply now to be one of the first candidates considered!

Position	Type	Location
Paralegal	Part-time	Tampa
Legal Records Clerk	Full-time, 2 months	North Tampa

GO! with Microsoft Office 365

Andrew Rodriguez / Fotolia; FotolEdhar/ Fotolia; apops/ Fotolia; Yuri Arcurs/ Fotolia

Office 365 combines tools for collaboration and productivity and delivers them to multiple users in an organization by using ***cloud computing***—applications and services that are accessed over the Internet with multiple devices. For example, one cloud service with which you might be familiar is ***OneDrive***, a free web-based application with which you can save, store, organize, and share files online. This cloud service is available for anyone that has a free Microsoft account.

Another cloud service from Microsoft is ***Office Online***. These are the online companions to the desktop versions of Microsoft Office Word, Excel, PowerPoint, and OneNote that enable you to create, access, share, and perform light editing on Microsoft Office documents from any device that connects to the Internet and uses a supported ***web browser***. A web browser is software, such as Internet Explorer, Firefox, Safari, or Chrome, that displays web pages.

For an organization, cloud computing enables the addition of services without investing in additional hardware and software. For you as a team member, you can simply use your web browser to access, edit, store, and share files. You do not need to have a full version of Office installed on your computer to do this. You have all the tools and security that large organizations have!

When you use using Office 365, your email and storage servers are hosted by Microsoft. Your organization gets business-class security from Microsoft—a large, well-established company. Sophisticated security and data management features are built into Office 365 so that you can control ***permissions***—access rights that define the ability of an individual or group to view or make changes to documents—and provide secure email and communications.

Activity | Using Lync to Collaborate by Using a Video Call

This group project relates to the **Bell Orchid Hotels**. If your instructor assigns this project to your class, you can expect to use **Lync** in **Office 365** to collaborate on the following tasks for this chapter:

- If you are in the **Accounting Group**, you and your teammates will conduct a video call to discuss and agree on the letter that will be sent to shareholders.
- If you are in the **Engineering Group**, you and your teammates will conduct a video call to discuss and agree on the letter that will be sent to the three insurance companies that cover the hotel properties.
- If you are in the **Food and Beverage Group**, you and your teammates will conduct a video call to discuss and agree on the letter that will be sent to a customer planning a banquet.
- If you are in the **Human Resources Group**, you and your teammates will conduct a video call to discuss and agree on the memo for employees regarding the new employee newsletter.
- If you are in the **Operations Group**, you and your teammates will conduct a video call to discuss and agree on the letter that will be sent to three job applicants.
- If you are in the **Sales and Marking Group**, you and your teammates will conduct a video call to discuss and agree on the letter that will be sent to 20 groups of professional associations.

FIGURE A

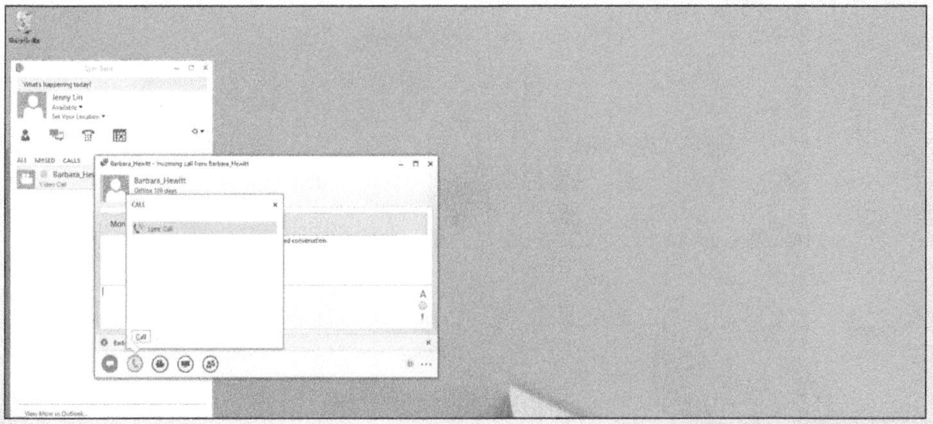

END OF CHAPTER

SUMMARY

Word tables enable you to present information in a logical and orderly format. Each cell in a Word table behaves like a document; as you type in a cell, wordwrap moves text to the next line.

A good source of information for resume formats is a business communications textbook. A simple two-column table created in Word is suitable to create an appropriate resume for a recent college graduate.

Use Word's Office Presentation Service to present a Word document to others who can watch in a web browser. Word automatically creates a link to your document that you can share with others via email.

A template is useful because it has a predefined document structure and defined settings such as font, margins, and available styles. On Word's opening screen, you can select from thousands of templates.

GO! LEARN IT ONLINE

Review the concepts and key terms in this chapter by completing these online challenges, which you can find at **www.pearsonhighered.com/go**.

Matching and Multiple Choice: Answer matching and multiple choice questions to test what you learned in this chapter. MyITLab®

Crossword Puzzle: Spell out the words that match the numbered clues, and put them in the puzzle squares.

Flipboard: Flip through the definitions of the key terms in this chapter and match them with the correct term.

GO! FOR JOB SUCCESS

Video: Cover Letter and Resume Tips

Your instructor may assign this video to your class, and then ask you to think about, or discuss with your classmates, these questions:

FotolEdhar / Fotolia

A cover letter should contain different but complimentary information than the facts on your resume and be tailored to the specific job you are applying for. Name two different things that you could mention in a cover letter.

What type of information belongs in the Career Objective portion of your resume?

When is it best to use a chronological resume layout, and when is it appropriate to use a functional resume layout?

END OF CHAPTER

REVIEW AND ASSESSMENT GUIDE FOR WORD CHAPTER 2

Your instructor may assign one or more of these projects to help you review the chapter and assess your mastery and understanding of the chapter.

Review and Assessment Guide for Word Chapter 2			
Project	**Apply Skills from These Chapter Objectives**	**Project Type**	**Project Location**
2C	Objectives 1-3 from Project 2A	**2C Skills Review** A guided review of the skills from Project 2A.	On the following pages
2D	Objectives 4-7 from Project 2B	**2D Skills Review** A guided review of the skills from Project 2B.	On the following pages
2E	Objectives 1-3 from Project 2A	**2E Mastery (Grader Project)** A demonstration of your mastery of the skills in Project 2A with extensive decision making.	In MyITLab and on the following pages
2F	Objectives 4-7 from Project 2B	**2F Mastery (Grader Project)** A demonstration of your mastery of the skills in Project 2B with extensive decision making.	In MyITLab and on the following pages
2G	Objectives 1-7 from Projects 2A and 2B	**2G Mastery (Grader Project)** A demonstration of your mastery of the skills in Projects 2A and 2B with extensive decision making.	In MyITLab and on the following pages
2H	Combination of Objectives from Projects 2A and 2B	**2H GO! Fix It** A demonstration of your mastery of the skills in Projects 2A and 2B by creating a correct result from a document that contains errors you must find.	Online
2I	Combination of Objectives from Projects 2A and 2B	**2I GO! Make It** A demonstration of your mastery of the skills in Projects 2A and 2B by creating a result from a supplied picture.	Online
2J	Combination of Objectives from Projects 2A and 2B	**2J GO! Solve It** A demonstration of your mastery of the skills in Projects 2A and 2B, your decision-making skills, and your critical thinking skills. A task-specific rubric helps you self-assess your result.	Online
2K	Combination of Objectives from Projects 2A and 2B	**2K GO! Solve It** A demonstration of your mastery of the skills in Projects 2A and 2B, your decision-making skills, and your critical thinking skills. A task-specific rubric helps you self-assess your result.	On the following pages
2L	Combination of Objectives from Projects 2A and 2B	**2L GO! Think** A demonstration of your understanding of the chapter concepts applied in a manner that you would outside of college. An analytic rubric helps you and your instructor grade the quality of your work by comparing it to the work an expert in the discipline would create.	On the following pages
2M	Combination of Objectives from Projects 2A and 2B	**2M GO! Think** A demonstration of your understanding of the chapter concepts applied in a manner that you would outside of college. An analytic rubric helps you and your instructor grade the quality of your work by comparing it to the work an expert in the discipline would create.	Online
2N	Combination of Objectives from Projects 2A and 2B	**2N You and GO!** A demonstration of your understanding of the chapter concepts applied in a manner that you would in a personal situation. An analytic rubric helps you and your instructor grade the quality of your work.	Online
2O	Combination of Objectives from Projects 2A and 2B	**2O Cumulative Group Project for Word Chapter 2** A demonstration of your understanding of concepts and your ability to work collaboratively in a group role-playing assessment, requiring both collaboration and self-management.	Online

GLOSSARY

GLOSSARY OF CHAPTER KEY TERMS

AutoCorrect A feature that corrects common typing and spelling errors as you type, for example changing *teh* to *the*.

Body The text of a letter.

Cell The box at the intersection of a row and column in a Word table.

Cloud computing Applications and services that are accessed over the Internet with multiple devices.

Complimentary closing A parting farewell in a business letter.

Content control In a template, an area indicated by placeholder text that can be used to add text, pictures, dates, or lists.

Cover letter A document that you send with your resume to provide additional information about your skills and experience.

Date & Time A command with which you can automatically insert the current date and time into a document in a variety of formats.

Dateline The first line in a business letter that contains the current date and which is positioned just below the letterhead if a letterhead is used.

Drag-and-drop A technique by which you can move, by dragging, selected text from one location in a document to another.

Enclosures Additional documents included with a business letter.

Inside address The name and address of the person receiving the letter and positioned below the date line.

Letterhead The personal or company information that displays at the top of a letter.

No Paragraph Style The built-in paragraph style—available from the Paragraph Spacing command—that inserts *no* extra space before or after a paragraph and uses line spacing of 1.

Normal template The template that serves as a basis for all Word documents.

Office Presentation Service A Word feature to present your Word document to others who can watch in a web browser.

One-click Row/Column Insertion A Word table feature with which you can insert a new row or column by pointing to the desired location and then clicking.

Placeholder text The text in a content control that indicates the type of information to be entered in a specific location.

Salutation The greeting line of a business letter.

Single spacing The common name for line spacing in which there is *no* extra space before or after a paragraph and that uses line spacing of 1.

Skype A Microsoft product with which you can make voice calls, make video calls, transfer files, or send messages—including instant message and text messages—over the Internet.

Subject line The optional line following the inside address in a business letter that states the purpose of the letter.

Synonyms Words with the same or similar meaning.

Table An arrangement of information organized into rows and columns.

Template An existing document that you use as a starting point for a new document; it opens a copy of itself, unnamed, and then you use the structure—and possibly some content, such as headings—as the starting point for a new document.

Text control A content control that accepts only a text entry.

Thesaurus A research tool that provides a list of synonyms.

Writer's identification The name and title of the author of a letter, placed near the bottom of the letter under the complimentary closing—also referred to as the *writer's signature block*.

Writer's signature block The name and title of the author of a letter, placed near the bottom of the letter, under the complimentary closing—also referred to as the *writer's identification*.

CHAPTER REVIEW

Apply 2A skills from these Objectives:

1 Create a Table
2 Format a Table
3 Present a Word Document Online

Skills Review Project 2C Student Resume

In the following Skills Review, you will use a table to create a resume for Ashley Kent. Your completed resume will look similar to the one shown in Figure 2.40.

PROJECT FILES

Build from Scratch

For Project 2C, you will need the following files:

New blank Word document
w02C_Skills
w02C_Experience

You will save your document as:

Lastname_Firstname_2C_Student_Resume

PROJECT RESULTS

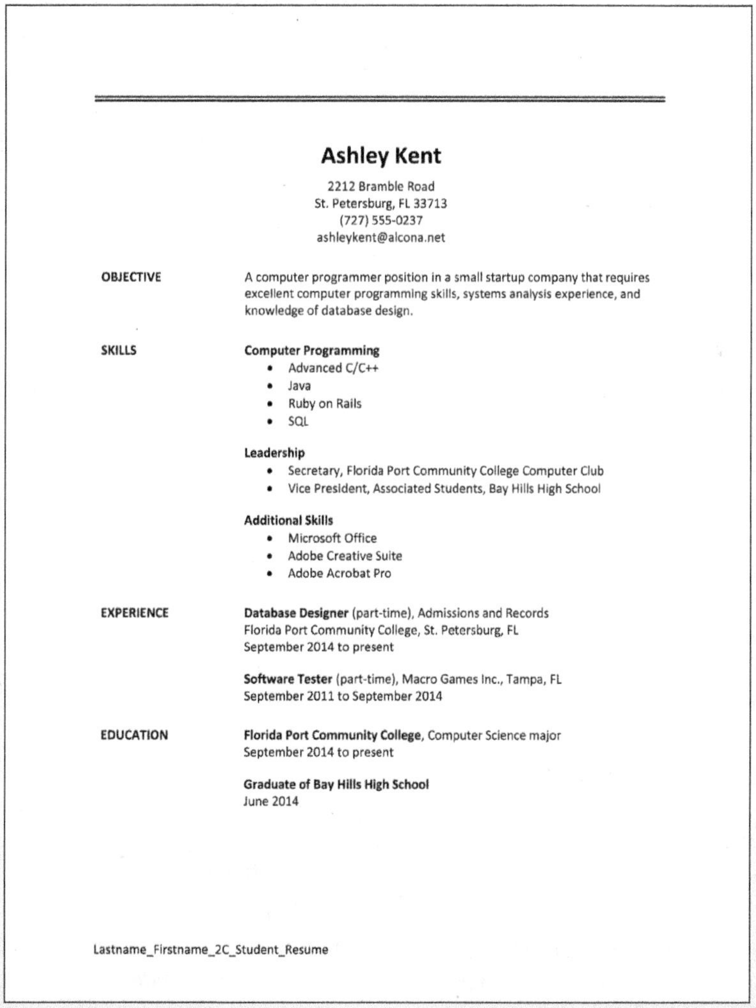

Ashley Kent

2212 Bramble Road
St. Petersburg, FL 33713
(727) 555-0237
ashleykent@alcona.net

OBJECTIVE	A computer programmer position in a small startup company that requires excellent computer programming skills, systems analysis experience, and knowledge of database design.
SKILLS	**Computer Programming** • Advanced C/C++ • Java • Ruby on Rails • SQL **Leadership** • Secretary, Florida Port Community College Computer Club • Vice President, Associated Students, Bay Hills High School **Additional Skills** • Microsoft Office • Adobe Creative Suite • Adobe Acrobat Pro
EXPERIENCE	**Database Designer** (part-time), Admissions and Records Florida Port Community College, St. Petersburg, FL September 2014 to present **Software Tester** (part-time), Macro Games Inc., Tampa, FL September 2011 to September 2014
EDUCATION	**Florida Port Community College**, Computer Science major September 2014 to present **Graduate of Bay Hills High School** June 2014

Lastname_Firstname_2C_Student_Resume

FIGURE 2.40

(Project 2C Student Resume continues on the next page)

CHAPTER REVIEW

Skills Review Project 2C Student Resume (continued)

1 **Start** Word and display a blank document. Be sure that formatting marks and rulers display. **Save** the document in your **Word Chapter 2** folder as **Lastname_Firstname_2C_Student_Resume**

a. Add the file name to the footer, and then close the footer area. Click the **INSERT tab**, and then in the **Tables group**, click **Table**. In the **Table** grid, in the fourth row, click the second square to insert a **2×4** table.

b. In the first cell of the table, type **Ashley Kent** and then press Enter. Type the following text, pressing Enter after each line *except* the last line:

2212 Bramble Road

St. Petersburg, FL 33713

(727) 555-0237

ashleykent@alcona.net

c. Press ↓ to move to the first cell in the second row. Type **SKILLS** and then press ↓ to move to the first cell in the third row.

d. Type **EXPERIENCE** and then press ↓. Type **EDUCATION**

e. In the first cell, if the email address displays in blue, right-click the email address, and then on the shortcut menu, click **Remove Hyperlink**. **Save** your document.

2 Click in the cell to the right of *SKILLS*, and then type the following, pressing Enter after each line including the last line:

Computer Programming

Advanced C/C++

Java

Ruby on Rails

SQL

a. With the insertion point in the new line at the end of the cell, click the **INSERT tab**. In the **Text group**, click the **Object button arrow**, and then click **Text from File**.

b. Navigate to your student files, select **w02C_Skills**, and then click **Insert**. Press Backspace one time to remove the blank paragraph.

c. Click in the cell to the right of *EXPERIENCE*, and then insert the file **w02C_Experience**. Press Backspace one time to remove the blank line.

d. Click in the cell to the right of *EDUCATION*, and then type the following, pressing Enter after all lines *except* the last line:

Florida Port Community College, Computer Science major

September 2014 to present

Graduate of Bay Hills High School

June 2014

3 Point to the upper left corner of the *SKILLS* cell, and then click the **Row Insertion** button. In the first cell of the new row, type **OBJECTIVE** and then press Tab.

a. Type **A computer programmer position in a small startup company that requires excellent computer programming skills, systems analysis experience, and knowledge of database design.**

b. In any row, point to the vertical border between the two columns to display the ✥ pointer. Drag the column border to the left to approximately **1.5 inches on the horizontal ruler.**

c. Under **TABLE TOOLS**, on the **LAYOUT tab**, in the **Cell Size group**, click **AutoFit**, and then click **AutoFit Window** to be sure that your table stretches across the page within the margins.

d. In the first row of the table, drag across both cells to select them. On the **LAYOUT tab**, in the **Merge group**, click **Merge Cells**. Right-click over the selected cell, and then on the mini toolbar, click **Center**.

e. In the top row, select the first paragraph of text—*Ashley Kent*. On the mini toolbar, increase the **Font Size** to **20** and apply **Bold**.

f. In the second row, point to the word *OBJECTIVE*, hold down the left mouse button, and then drag down to select the row headings in uppercase letters. On the mini toolbar, click **Bold**. **Save** your document.

4 Click in the cell to the right of *OBJECTIVE*. On the **PAGE LAYOUT tab**, in the **Paragraph group**, click the **Spacing After up spin arrow** three times to change the spacing to **18 pt**.

a. In the cell to the right of *SKILLS*, apply **Bold** to the words *Computer Programming*, *Leadership*, and *Additional Skills*. Then, under each bold heading in

(Project 2C Student Resume continues on the next page)

the cell, select the lines of text, and create a bulleted list.

b. In the first two bulleted lists, click in the last bullet item, and then on the **PAGE LAYOUT tab**, in the **Paragraph group**, set the **Spacing After** to **12 pt**.

c. In the last bulleted list, click in the last bullet item, and then set the **Spacing After** to **18 pt**.

d. In the cell to the right of *EXPERIENCE*, apply **Bold** to *Database Designer* and *Software Tester*. Click in the line *September 2014 to present* and apply **Spacing After** of **12 pt**. Click in the line *September 2011 to September 2014* and apply **Spacing After** of **18 pt**.

e. In the cell to the right of *EDUCATION*, apply **Bold** to *Florida Port Community College* and *Graduate of Bay Hills High School*.

f. In the same cell, click in the line *September 2014 to present* and apply **Spacing After** of **12 pt**.

g. In the first row, click in the last line—*ashleykent@alcona.net*—and then change the **Spacing After** to **18 pt**. Click in the first line—*Ashley Kent*—and set the **Spacing Before** to **30 pt** and the **Spacing After** to **6 pt**.

5 Point to the upper left corner of the table, and then click the **table move handle** [⊞] to select the entire table. Under **TABLE TOOLS**, on the **DESIGN tab**, in the **Table Styles group**, click the **Borders button arrow**, and then click **No Border**.

a. In the **Table Styles group**, click the **Borders button arrow** again, and then at the bottom of the gallery, click **Borders and Shading**. In the **Borders and Shading** dialog box, under **Setting**, click **Custom**. Under **Style**, scroll down slightly, and then click the style with two equal lines.

b. Click the **Width arrow**, and then click **1 1/2 pt**. Under **Preview**, click the top border of the preview box, and then click **OK**.

c. Click the **FILE tab** to display **Backstage** view, and then in the lower right portion of the screen, click **Show All Properties**. In the **Tags** box, type **resume, table** and in the **Subject** box, type your course name and section number. In the **Author** box, be sure your name is indicated and edit if necessary.

d. On the left, click **Print** to display **Print Preview**. If necessary, return to the document and make any necessary changes.

e. **Save** [💾] your document, and then if you want to do so, present your document online to a fellow classmate. Then as directed by your instructor, print your document or submit it electronically. **Close** Word.

END | You have completed Project 2C

CHAPTER REVIEW

Skills Review Project 2D Cover Letter and Reference List

Apply 2B skills from these Objectives:

4 Create a Custom Word Template
5 Correct and Reorganize Text
6 Use the Proofing Options and Print an Envelope
7 Create a Document Using a Predesigned Microsoft Template

In the following Skills Review, you will create a letterhead, save the letterhead as a custom Word template, and then use the letterhead to create a cover letter to accompany a resume. You will also create a list of references from a Microsoft predesigned template and, if you have an envelope and printer available, format and print an envelope. Your completed documents will look similar to Figure 2.41.

PROJECT FILES

Build from Scratch

For Project 2D, you will need the following files:

New blank Word document
w02D_Cover_Letter_Text

You will save your documents as:

Lastname_Firstname_2D_Cover_Letter
Lastname_Firstname_2D_Reference_List

PROJECT RESULTS

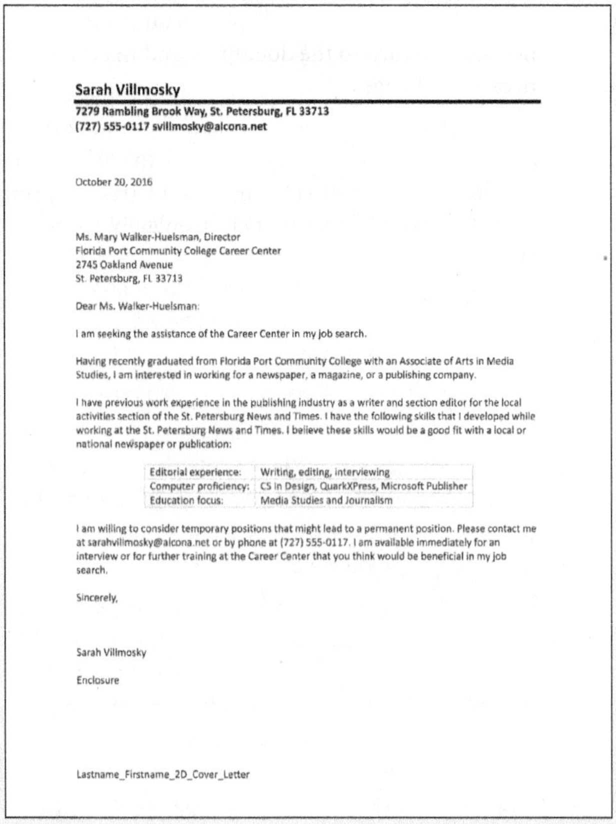

Sarah Villmosky
7279 Rambling Brook Way, St. Petersburg, FL 33713
(727) 555-0117 svillmosky@alcona.net

October 20, 2016

Ms. Mary Walker-Huelsman, Director
Florida Port Community College Career Center
2745 Oakland Avenue
St. Petersburg, FL 33713

Dear Ms. Walker-Huelsman:

I am seeking the assistance of the Career Center in my job search.

Having recently graduated from Florida Port Community College with an Associate of Arts in Media Studies, I am interested in working for a newspaper, a magazine, or a publishing company.

I have previous work experience in the publishing industry as a writer and section editor for the local activities section of the St. Petersburg News and Times. I have the following skills that I developed while working at the St. Petersburg News and Times. I believe these skills would be a good fit with a local or national newspaper or publication:

Editorial experience:	Writing, editing, interviewing
Computer proficiency:	CS In Design, QuarkXPress, Microsoft Publisher
Education focus:	Media Studies and Journalism

I am willing to consider temporary positions that might lead to a permanent position. Please contact me at sarahvilimosky@alcona.net or by phone at (727) 555-0117. I am available immediately for an interview or for further training at the Career Center that you think would be beneficial in my job search.

Sincerely,

Sarah Villmosky

Enclosure

Lastname_Firstname_2D_Cover_Letter

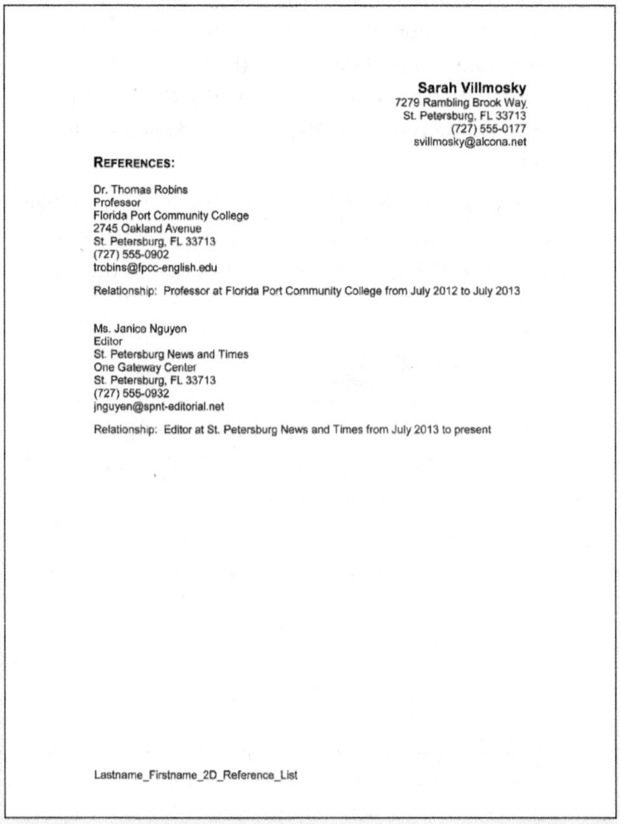

Sarah Villmosky
7279 Rambling Brook Way,
St. Petersburg, FL 33713
(727) 555-0177
svillmosky@alcona.net

REFERENCES:

Dr. Thomas Robins
Professor
Florida Port Community College
2745 Oakland Avenue
St. Petersburg, FL 33713
(727) 555-0902
trobins@fpcc-english.edu

Relationship: Professor at Florida Port Community College from July 2012 to July 2013

Ms. Janice Nguyen
Editor
St. Petersburg News and Times
One Gateway Center
St. Petersburg, FL 33713
(727) 555-0932
jnguyen@spnt-editorial.net

Relationship: Editor at St. Petersburg News and Times from July 2013 to present

Lastname_Firstname_2D_Reference_List

FIGURE 2.41

(Project 2D Cover Letter and Reference List continues on the next page)

CHAPTER REVIEW

Skills Review Project 2D Cover Letter and Reference List (continued)

1 **Start** Word and display a blank document; be sure that formatting marks and rulers display. On the **DESIGN tab**, in the **Document Formatting group**, click **Paragraph Spacing**, and then click **No Paragraph Space**.

a. Type **Sarah Villmosky** and then press Enter. Type **7279 Rambling Brook Way, St. Petersburg, FL 33713** and then press Enter.

b. Type **(727) 555-0117 svillmosky@alcona.net** and then press Enter. If the web address changes to blue text, right-click the web address, and then click **Remove Hyperlink**.

c. Select the first paragraph—*Sarah Villmosky*—and then on the mini toolbar, apply **Bold**, and change the **Font Size** to **16**.

d. Select the second and third paragraphs, and then on the mini toolbar, apply **Bold**, and change the **Font Size** to **12**.

e. Click anywhere in the first paragraph—*Sarah Villmosky*. On the **HOME tab**, in the **Paragraph group**, click the **Borders button arrow**, and then click **Borders and Shading**. Under **Style**, click the first style—a single solid line. Click the **Width arrow**, and then click **3 pt**. In the **Preview** area, click the bottom border, and then click **OK**.

f. Press F12 to display the **Save As** dialog box. In the lower portion of the dialog box, in the **Save as type** box, click the arrow, and then click **Word Template**. In the **File name** box, type **Lastname_Firstname_2D_Letterhead_Template** and then click **Save** to save the custom Word template in the default path, which is the Templates folder on the hard drive of your computer.

g. Click the **FILE tab** to display **Backstage** view, and then click **Close** to close the file but leave Word open.

h. With Word open but no documents displayed, click the **FILE tab**, and then click **New**. Under **Suggested searches**, click **PERSONAL**, and then locate and click the letterhead template that you just created.

i. Press F12 to display the **Save As** dialog box, navigate to your **Word Chapter 2** folder, and then **Save** the file as **Lastname_Firstname_2D_Cover_Letter**

j. On the **INSERT tab**, in the **Header & Footer group**, click **Footer**, click **Edit Footer**, and then in the **Insert group**, click **Document Info**. Click **File Name**, and then click **Close Header and Footer**. Click **Save**.

2 Click the **FILE tab**. On the left, click **Options**. On the left side of the **Word Options** dialog box, click **Proofing**, and then under **AutoCorrect options**, click the **AutoCorrect Options** button.

a. In the **AutoCorrect** dialog box, click the **AutoCorrect tab**. Under **Replace**, type the misspelled word **assistence** and under **With**, type **assistance** Click **Add**. If the entry already exists, click **Replace instead**, and then click **Yes**. Click **OK** two times to close the dialog boxes.

b. Press Ctrl + End, and then press Enter three times. On the **INSERT tab**, in the **Text group**, click **Date & Time**, and then click the third date format. Click **OK**.

c. Press Enter four times. Type the following inside address using four lines, but do *not* press Enter after the last line:

Ms. Mary Walker-Huelsman, Director

Florida Port Community College Career Center

2745 Oakland Avenue

St. Petersburg, FL 33713

d. Press Enter two times, type **Dear Ms. Walker-Huelsman:** and then press Enter two times. Type, exactly as shown with the intentional misspelling, and then watch *assistence* as you press Spacebar: **I am seeking the assistence**

e. Type **of the Career Center in my job search.** Press Enter two times.

f. On the **INSERT tab**, in the **Text Group**, click the **Object button arrow**, and then click **Text from File**. From your student files, locate and insert the file **w02D_Cover_Letter_Text**.

g. Scroll to view the lower portion of the page, and be sure your insertion point is in the empty paragraph mark at the end. Press Enter, type **Sincerely,** and then press Enter four times. Type **Sarah Villmosky** and press Enter two times. Type **Enclosure** and then **Save** your document.

h. Press Ctrl + Home. On the **HOME tab**, in the **Editing group**, click **Find**. In the **navigation** pane, click in the search box, and then type **journalism** In the letter,

(Project 2D Cover Letter and Reference List continues on the next page)

Skills Review Project 2D Cover Letter and Reference List (continued)

double-click the yellow highlighted word *Journalism* and type **Media Studies**

i. **Close** the **navigation** pane, and then on the **HOME tab**, in the **Editing group**, click **Replace**. In the **Find and Replace** dialog box, in the **Find what** box, replace the existing text by typing **SPNT** In the **Replace with** box, type **St. Petersburg News and Times** Click **More** to expand the dialog box, select the **Match case** check box, click **Replace All**, and then click **OK. Close** the **Find and Replace** dialog box.

j. In the paragraph that begins *I am available*, hold down Ctrl, and then click anywhere in the first sentence. Drag the selected sentence to the end of the paragraph by positioning the small vertical line that floats with the point to the left of the paragraph mark.

3 Below the paragraph that begins *I have previous*, click to position the insertion point in the blank paragraph, and then press Enter one time. On the **INSERT tab**, in the **Tables group**, click **Table**. In the **Table grid**, in the third row, click the second square to insert a 2 × 3 table. Type the following information in the table:

Editorial experience:	**Writing, editing, interviewing**
Computer proficiency:	**CS In Design, QuarkXPress, Microsoft Publisher**
Education focus:	**Media Studies and Journalism**

a. Point outside of the upper left corner of the table and click the **table move handle** button to select the entire table. On the **LAYOUT tab**, in the **Cell Size group**, click **AutoFit**, and then click **AutoFit Contents.**

b. With the table selected, on the **DESIGN tab**, in the **Table Styles group**, click **More** . Under **Plain Tables**, click the second style—**Table Grid Light.**

c. With the table still selected, on the **HOME tab**, in the **Paragraphs group**, click **Center. Save** your document.

4 Press Ctrl + Home. On the **REVIEW tab**, in the **Proofing group**, click **Spelling & Grammar**. For the spelling of *Villmosky*, in the **Spelling** pane, click **Ignore All**. For the spelling of *Huelsman*, click **Ignore All.**

a. For the grammar error *a*, click **Change**. Click **Change** to correct the misspelling of *intrested*. Click **Delete** to delete the duplicated word *for*. Change *activitys* to *activities*. Change *benificial* to *beneficial.* Click **OK** when the Spelling & Grammar check is complete.

b. In the paragraph that begins *I am willing*, in the third line, double-click the word *preparation*. In the **Proofing group**, click **Thesaurus.**

c. In the **Thesaurus** pane, point to *training*, click the arrow, and then click **Insert. Close** the **Thesaurus** pane.

d. Click **FILE tab**, and then in the lower right portion of the screen, click **Show All Properties**. In the **Tags** box, type **cover letter** and in the **Subject** box, type your course name and section number.

e. In the **Author** box, be sure your name is indicated and edit if necessary. On the left, click **Print**. If necessary, return to the document and make any necessary changes. **Save** your document, and then **Close** Word.

5 **Start** Word, and then on the opening screen, in the **Search online templates** box, type **resume references** and press Enter. Click the reference list that contains three left-aligned reference items, and then click **Create.**

a. Press F12 to display the **Save As** dialog box. **Save** the document in your **Word Chapter 2** folder as **Lastname_Firstname_2D_Reference_List** A message may indicate that the file will be upgraded to the newest file format.

b. Add the file name to the footer.

c. In the upper right, click in the placeholder text *[Your Name]* and type **Sarah Villmosky** Click *[Street Address]* and type **7279 Rambling Brook Way**

d. Click *[City, ST ZIP Code]* and type **St. Petersburg, FL 33713** Click *[phone]* and type **(727) 555-0177** Click *[email]* and type **svillmosky@alcona.net**

(Project 2D Cover Letter and Reference List continues on the next page)

CHAPTER REVIEW

Skills Review | Project 2D Cover Letter and Reference List (continued)

6 Under **References**, enter two references using the information in Table 1:

a. Delete the remaining template controls.

b. Click the **FILE tab**, click **Show All Properties**, and then in the **Tags** box, type **reference list** and in the **Subject** box type your course name and section number. In the **Author** box, be sure your name is indicated and edit if necessary.

c. On the left, click **Print**. If necessary, return to the document and make any changes. Click **Save**. As directed by your instructor, print or submit electronically the two documents that are the results of this project. **Close** Word.

TABLE 1

Template Field	Reference 1	Reference 2
Reference Name	**Dr. Thomas Robins**	**Ms. Janice Nguyen**
Title	**Professor**	**Editor**
Company Name	**Florida Port Community College**	**St. Petersburg News and Times**
Street Address	**2745 Oakland Avenue**	**One Gateway Center**
City, ST ZIP Code	**St. Petersburg, FL 33713**	**St. Petersburg, FL 33713**
phone	**(727) 555-0902**	**(727) 555-0932**
email	**trobins@fpcc-english.edu**	**jnguyen@spnt-editorial.net**
Relationship with reference	**Professor**	**Editor**
Company Name	**Florida Port Community College**	**St. Petersburg News and Times**
dates of employment	**July 2012 to July 2013**	**July 2013 to present**

Return to Step 6a

END | You have completed Project 2D

CONTENT-BASED ASSESSMENTS

MyITLab® grader

Mastering Word | Project 2E Table of Job Listings

Apply 2A skills from these Objectives:

1. Create a Table
2. Format a Table
3. Present a Word Document Online

In the following Mastering Word project, you will create an announcement for new job postings at the Career Center. Your completed document will look similar to Figure 2.42.

PROJECT FILES

Build from Scratch

For Project 2E, you will need the following files:

New blank Word document
w02E_New_Jobs

You will save your document as:

Lastname_Firstname_2E_Job_Listings

PROJECT RESULTS

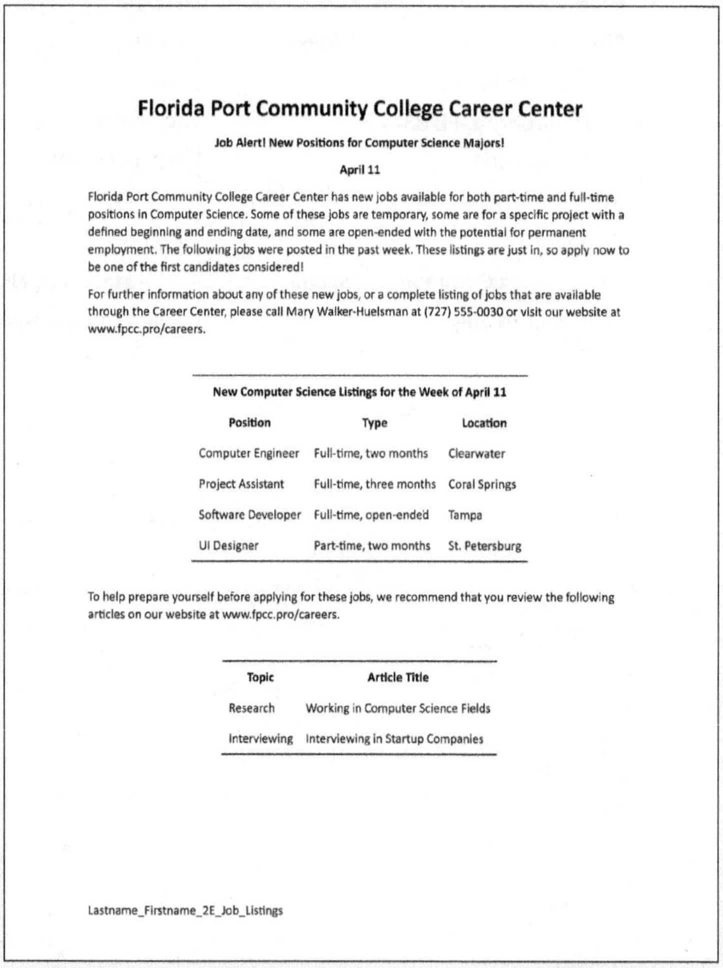

Florida Port Community College Career Center

Job Alert! New Positions for Computer Science Majors!

April 11

Florida Port Community College Career Center has new jobs available for both part-time and full-time positions in Computer Science. Some of these jobs are temporary, some are for a specific project with a defined beginning and ending date, and some are open-ended with the potential for permanent employment. The following jobs were posted in the past week. These listings are just in, so apply now to be one of the first candidates considered!

For further information about any of these new jobs, or a complete listing of jobs that are available through the Career Center, please call Mary Walker-Huelsman at (727) 555-0030 or visit our website at www.fpcc.pro/careers.

New Computer Science Listings for the Week of April 11		
Position	**Type**	**Location**
Computer Engineer	Full-time, two months	Clearwater
Project Assistant	Full-time, three months	Coral Springs
Software Developer	Full-time, open-ended	Tampa
UI Designer	Part-time, two months	St. Petersburg

To help prepare yourself before applying for these jobs, we recommend that you review the following articles on our website at www.fpcc.pro/careers.

Topic	Article Title
Research	Working in Computer Science Fields
Interviewing	Interviewing in Startup Companies

Lastname_Firstname_2E_Job_Listings

FIGURE 2.42

(Project 2E Table of Job Listings continues on the next page)

CONTENT-BASED ASSESSMENTS

Mastering Word | Project 2E Table of Job Listings (continued)

1 **Start** Word and display a blank document; display formatting marks and rulers. **Save** the document in your **Word Chapter 2** folder as **Lastname_Firstname_2E_Job_Listings** and then add the file name to the footer.

2 Type **Florida Port Community College Career Center** and press Enter. Type **Job Alert! New Positions for Computer Science Majors!** and press Enter. Type **April 11** and press Enter. **Insert** the file **w02E_New_Jobs**.

3 At the top of the document, select and **Center** the three title lines. Select the title *Florida Port Community College Career Center*, change the **Font Size** to **20 pt** and apply **Bold**. Apply **Bold** to the second and third title lines. Locate the paragraph that begins *For further*, and then below that paragraph, position the insertion point in the second blank paragraph. **Insert** a **3 × 4** table. Enter the following in the table:

Position	Type	Location
Computer Engineer	Full-time, two months	Clearwater
Software Developer	Full-time, open-ended	Tampa
UI Designer	Part-time, two months	St. Petersburg

4 In the table, point to upper left corner of the cell *Software Developer* to display the **Row Insertion** button, and then click to insert a new row. In the new row, type the following information so that the job titles remain in alphabetic order:

Project Assistant	Full-time, three months	Coral Springs

5 Select the entire table. On the **LAYOUT tab**, in the **Cell Size group**, click **AutoFit**, and then click **AutoFit Contents**. With the table still selected, on the **HOME tab**, **Center** the table. With the table still selected, on the **PAGE LAYOUT tab**, add **6 pt Spacing Before** and **6 pt Spacing After**.

6 With the table still selected, remove all table borders, and then add a **Custom 1 pt** solid line top border and bottom border. Select all three cells in the first row, apply **Bold**, and then **Center** the text. Click anywhere in the first row, and then on the **LAYOUT tab**, in the **Rows & Columns group**, insert a row above. Merge the three cells in the new top row, and then type **New Computer Science Listings for the Week of April 11** Notice that the new row keeps the formatting of the row from which it was created.

7 At the bottom of the document, **Insert** a **2 × 3** table. Enter the following:

Topic	Article Title
Research	Working in Computer Science Fields
Interviewing	Interviewing in Startup Companies

8 Select the entire table. On the **LAYOUT tab**, in the **Cell Size group**, use the **AutoFit** button to **AutoFit Contents**. On the **HOME tab**, **Center** the table. On the **PAGE LAYOUT tab**, add **6 pt Spacing Before** and **6 pt Spacing After**. With the table still selected, remove all table borders, and then add a **Custom 1 pt** solid line top border and bottom border. Select the cells in the first row, apply **Bold**, and then **Center** the text.

9 Click the **FILE tab** to display **Backstage** view, and then in the lower right portion of the screen, click **Show All Properties**. In the **Tags** box, type **new listings, computer science** and in the **Subject** box, type your course name and section number. In the **Author** box, be sure your name is indicated and edit if necessary.

10 On the left, click **Print** to display **Print Preview**. If necessary, return to the document and make any necessary changes. **Save** your document, and then if you want to do so, present your document online to a fellow classmate. Then as directed by your instructor, print your document or submit it electronically. **Close** Word.

END | You have completed Project 2E

CONTENT-BASED ASSESSMENTS

MyITLab® grader

Mastering Word | Project 2F Career Tips Memo and Fax Cover Sheet

Apply 2B skills from these Objectives:

4 Create a Custom Word Template
5 Correct and Reorganize Text
6 Use the Proofing Options and Print an Envelope
7 Create a Document Using a Predesigned Microsoft Template

In the following Mastering Word project, you will create a memo and fax cover sheet that includes job tips for students and graduates using the services of the Florida Port Community College Career Center. Your completed documents will look similar to Figure 2.43.

PROJECT FILES

For Project 2F, you will need the following files:

w02F_Memo_Template
w02F_Memo_Text
Equity Fax template from Microsoft's installed templates

You will save your documents as:

Lastname_Firstname_2F_Career_Tips
Lastname_Firstname_2F_Fax

PROJECT RESULTS

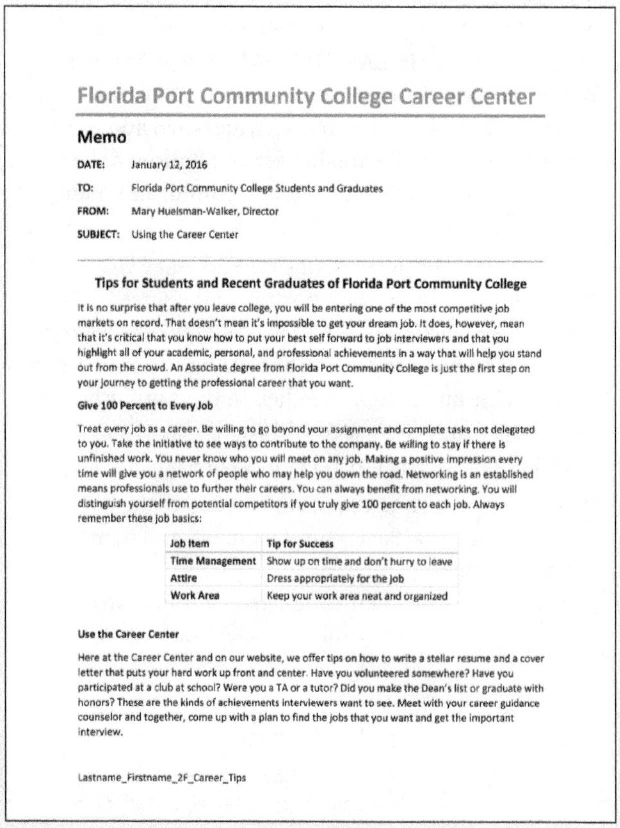

Florida Port Community College Career Center

Memo

DATE: January 12, 2016
TO: Florida Port Community College Students and Graduates
FROM: Mary Huelsman-Walker, Director
SUBJECT: Using the Career Center

Tips for Students and Recent Graduates of Florida Port Community College

It is no surprise that after you leave college, you will be entering one of the most competitive job markets on record. That doesn't mean it's impossible to get your dream job. It does, however, mean that it's critical that you know how to put your best self forward to job interviewers and that you highlight all of your academic, personal, and professional achievements in a way that will help you stand out from the crowd. An Associate degree from Florida Port Community College is just the first step on your journey to getting the professional career that you want.

Give 100 Percent to Every Job

Treat every job as a career. Be willing to go beyond your assignment and complete tasks not delegated to you. Take the initiative to see ways to contribute to the company. Be willing to stay if there is unfinished work. You never know who you will meet on any job. Making a positive impression every time will give you a network of people who may help you down the road. Networking is an established means professionals use to further their careers. You can always benefit from networking. You will distinguish yourself from potential competitors if you truly give 100 percent to each job. Always remember these job basics:

Job Item	Tip for Success
Time Management	Show up on time and don't hurry to leave
Attire	Dress appropriately for the job
Work Area	Keep your work area neat and organized

Use the Career Center

Here at the Career Center and on our website, we offer tips on how to write a stellar resume and a cover letter that puts your hard work up front and center. Have you volunteered somewhere? Have you participated at a club at school? Were you a TA or a tutor? Did you make the Dean's list or graduate with honors? These are the kinds of achievements interviewers want to see. Meet with your career guidance counselor and together, come up with a plan to find the jobs that you want and get the important interview.

Lastname_Firstname_2F_Career_Tips

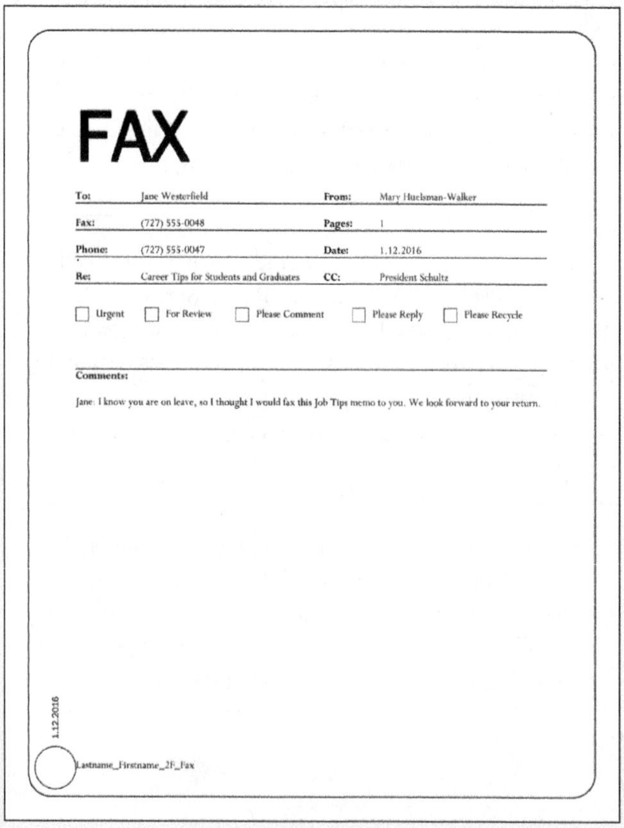

FAX

To: Jane Westerfield | From: Mary Huelsman-Walker
Fax: (727) 555-0048 | Pages: 1
Phone: (727) 555-0047 | Date: 1.12.2016
Re: Career Tips for Students and Graduates | CC: President Schultz

☐ Urgent ☐ For Review ☐ Please Comment ☐ Please Reply ☐ Please Recycle

Comments:

Jane: I know you are on leave, so I thought I would fax this Job Tips memo to you. We look forward to your return.

1.12.2016

Lastname_Firstname_2F_Fax

FIGURE 2.43

(Project 2F Career Tips Memo and Fax Cover Sheet continues on the next page)

Mastering Word Project 2F Career Tips Memo and Fax Cover Sheet (continued)

1 Be sure that Word is *closed*. On the taskbar, click **File Explorer**. Navigate to your student files and open **w02F_Memo_Template**. Notice that *Document1* displays in the title bar. (Recall that custom templates stored in a location other than the Templates folder on your hard drive must be opened directly from File Explorer in order for you to create and open a new document based on the template.)

2 Press F12. Navigate to your **Word Chapter 2** folder, and then in the **File name** box, using your own name, type **Lastname_Firstname_2F_Career_Tips**

3 Add the file name to the footer. At the top of your document, in the *DATE* paragraph, click to the right of the tab formatting mark, and then type **January 12, 2016** Use a similar technique to add the following information:

TO:	**Florida Port Community College Students and Graduates**
FROM:	**Mary Huelsman-Walker, Director**
SUBJECT:	**Using the CC**

4 Position the insertion point in the blank paragraph below the memo heading. **Insert** the file **w02F_Memo_Text**, and then press Backspace one time to remove the blank line at the end of the inserted text.

5 Select and **Center** the title *Tips for Students and Recent Graduates of Florida Port Community College*. By using either the **Spelling & Grammar** command on the **REVIEW** tab or by right-clicking words that display blue or red wavy underlines, correct or ignore words flagged as spelling, grammar, or word usage errors. Note: If you are checking an entire document, it is usually preferable to move to the top of the document, and then use the **Spelling & Grammar** command so that you do not overlook any flagged words.

6 In the paragraph that begins *Treat every job*, in the second line of the paragraph, locate and double-click *donate*. On the **REVIEW tab**, in the **Proofing group**, click **Thesaurus**, and then from the **Thesaurus** pane, change the word to *contribute*. In the last line of the same paragraph, point to *fundamentals*, right-click, point to **Synonyms**, and then click *basics*.

7 Using Match Case, replace all instances of *CC* with *Career Center*, and then in the paragraph that begins *An Associate degree*, move the first sentence to the end of the paragraph.

8 At the end of the paragraph that begins *Treat every job*, create a blank paragraph. **Insert** a **2** × **4** table, and then type the following information:

Job Item	**Tip for Success**
Time Management	**Show up on time and don't hurry to leave**
Attire	**Dress appropriately for the job**
Work Area	**Keep your work area neat and organized**

9 Select the entire table. **AutoFit Contents**, and then apply the **Grid Table 1 Light - Accent 1** table style—under **Grid Tables**, in the first row, the second style. **Center** the table.

10 Click the **FILE tab**, and then click **Show All Properties**. As the **Tags**, type **memo, job tips** and as the **Subject**, type your course name and section number. Be sure your name is indicated as the **Author**, and edit if necessary. **Save** and **Close** the document but leave Word open. Hold this file until you complete this project.

11 With Word open but no documents displayed, click the **FILE tab**, and then click **New**. In the **Search for online templates** box, type **fax (equity)** and press Enter, and then click the first **Fax (Equity theme)**template. Click **Create**. Press F12. Save the document in your **Word Chapter 2** folder, using your own name, as **Lastname_Firstname_2F_Fax** and then insert the file name in the footer. You may see a message indicating that the file will be upgraded to the newest format.

12 Use the following information to type in each control:

To:	**Jane Westerfield**
From:	**Mary Huelsman-Walker**
Fax:	**(727) 555-0048**
Pages:	**1**
Phone:	**(727) 555-0047**
Date:	**1/12/2016**
Re:	**Career Tips for Students and Graduates**
CC:	**President Schultz**
COMMENTS:	**Jane: I know you are on leave, so I thought I would fax this Job Tips memo to you. We look forward to your return.**

(Project 2F Career Tips Memo and Fax Cover Sheet continues on the next page)

CONTENT-BASED ASSESSMENTS

Mastering Word | Project 2F Career Tips Memo and Fax Cover Sheet (continued)

13 Click the **FILE tab**, and then click **Show All Properties**. As the **Tags**, type **memo, job tips** and as the **Subject**, type your course name and section number. The author will indicate *Mary Huelsman-Walker*. **Save** and **Close** the document. As directed by your instructor, print or submit electronically the two files that are the results of this project. **Close** Word.

END | You have completed Project 2F

CONTENT-BASED ASSESSMENTS

MyITLab® grader

Apply 2A and 2B skills from these Objectives:

1 Create a Table
2 Format a Table
3 Present a Word Document Online
4 Create a Custom Word Template
5 Correct and Reorganize Text
6 Use the Proofing Options and Print an Envelope
7 Create a Document Using a Predesigned Microsoft Template

Mastering Word | Project 2G Application Letter, Resume, and Fax Cover Sheet

In the following Mastering Word project, you will create a letter from a custom template, a resume, and a fax cover sheet from a Microsoft predesigned template. Your completed documents will look similar to Figure 2.44.

PROJECT FILES

For Project 2G, you will need the following files:

w02G_Letter_Text
w02G_Letterhead_Template
w02G_Resume
Equity Fax template from Microsoft's installed templates

You will save your documents as:

Lastname_Firstname_2G_Letter
Lastname_Firstname_2G_Resume
Lastname_Firstname_2G_Fax

PROJECT RESULTS

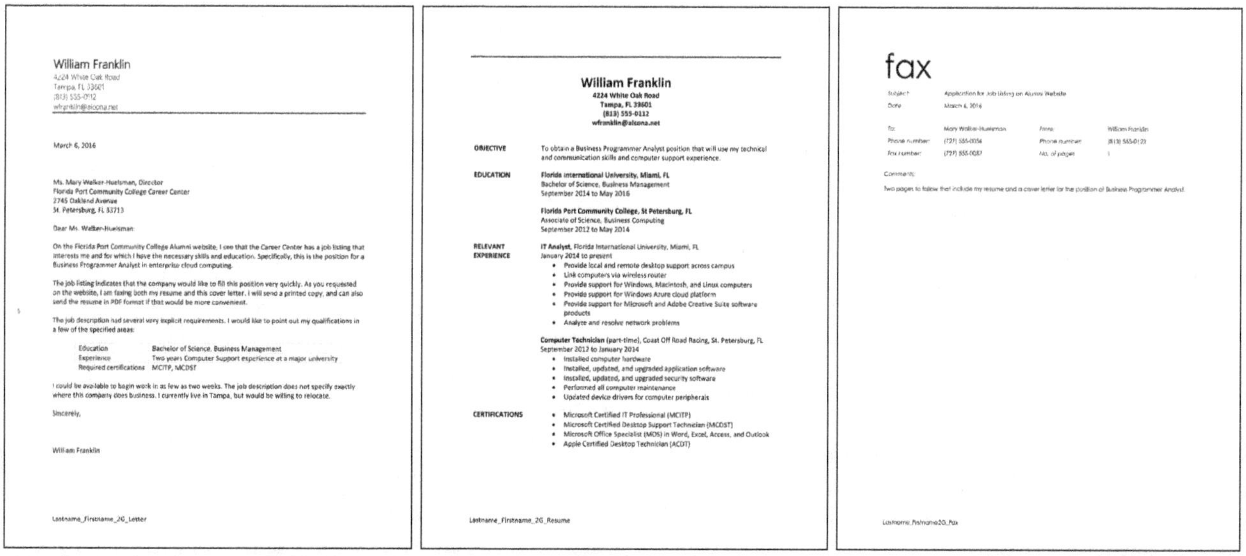

William Franklin
4224 White Oak Road
Tampa, FL 33601
(813) 555-0112
wfranklin@alcona.net

March 6, 2016

Ms. Mary Walker-Huelsman, Director
Florida Port Community College Career Center
2745 Oakland Avenue
St. Petersburg, FL 33713

Dear Ms. Walker-Huelsman:

On the Florida Port Community College Alumni website, I see that the Career Center has a job listing that interests me and for which I have the necessary skills and education. Specifically, this is the position for a Business Programmer Analyst in enterprise cloud computing.

The job listing indicates that the company would like to fill this position very quickly. As you requested on the website, I am faxing both my resume and this cover letter. I will send a printed copy, and can also send the resume in PDF format if that would be more convenient.

The job description had several very explicit requirements. I would like to point out my qualifications in a few of the specified areas:

Education	Bachelor of Science, Business Management
Experience	Two years Computer Support experience at a major university
Required certifications	MCITP, MCDST

I could be available to begin work in as few as two weeks. The job description does not specify exactly where this company does business. I currently live in Tampa, but would be willing to relocate.

Sincerely,

William Franklin

Lastname_Firstname_2G_Letter

William Franklin
4224 White Oak Road
Tampa, FL 33601
(813) 555-0112
wfranklin@alcona.net

OBJECTIVE To obtain a Business Programmer Analyst position that will use my technical and communication skills and computer support experience.

EDUCATION **Florida International University, Miami, FL**
Bachelor of Science, Business Management
September 2014 to May 2016

Florida Port Community College, St Petersburg, FL
Associate of Science, Business Computing
September 2012 to May 2014

RELEVANT EXPERIENCE **IT Analyst**, Florida International University, Miami, FL
January 2014 to present
- Provide local and remote desktop support across campus
- Link computers via wireless router
- Provide support for Windows, Macintosh, and Linux computers
- Provide support for Windows Azure cloud platform
- Provide support for Microsoft and Adobe Creative Suite software products
- Analyze and resolve network problems

Computer Technician (part-time), Coast Off Road Racing, St. Petersburg, FL
September 2012 to January 2014
- Installed computer hardware
- Installed, updated, and upgraded application software
- Installed, updated, and upgraded security software
- Performed all computer maintenance
- Updated device drivers for computer peripherals

CERTIFICATIONS
- Microsoft Certified IT Professional (MCITP)
- Microsoft Certified Desktop Support Technician (MCDST)
- Microsoft Office Specialist (MOS) in Word, Excel, Access, and Outlook
- Apple Certified Desktop Technician (ACDT)

Lastname_Firstname_2G_Resume

fax

Subject: Application for Job Listing on Alumni Website
Date: March 6, 2016

To:	Mary Walker-Huelsman	From:	William Franklin
Phone number:	(727) 555-0056	Phone number:	(813) 555-0122
Fax number:	(727) 555-0087	No. of pages:	1

Comments:

Two pages to follow that include my resume and a cover letter for the position of Business Programmer Analyst.

Lastname_Firstname2G_Fax

FIGURE 2.44

(Project 2G Application Letter, Resume, and Fax Cover Sheet continues on the next page)

Mastering Word Project 2G Application Letter, Resume, and Fax Cover Sheet (continued)

1 Be sure that Word is *closed*. On the taskbar, click **File Explorer**. Navigate to your student files and open **w02G_Letterhead_Template.** Notice that *Document1* displays in the title bar. (Recall that custom templates stored in a location other than the Templates folder on your hard drive must be opened directly from File Explorer in order for you to create and open a new document based on the template.)

2 Press F12. Navigate to your **Word Chapter 2** folder, and then in the **File name** box, using your own name, type **Lastname_Firstname_2G_Letter**

3 Add the file name to the footer. Be sure that rulers and formatting marks display. Move to the end of the document, and then press Enter three times. Use the **Date & Time** command to insert the current date using the third format, and then press Enter four times. Type the following:

Ms. Mary Walker-Huelsman, Director

Florida Port Community College Career Center

2745 Oakland Avenue

St. Petersburg, FL 33713

4 Press Enter two times, type **Dear Ms. Walker-Huelsman:** and press Enter two times. **Insert** the text from the file **w02G_Letter_Text** and press Backspace one time to remove the blank paragraph at the bottom of the selected text.

5 By using either the **Spelling & Grammar** command on the **REVIEW tab** or by right-clicking words that display blue or red wavy underlines, correct or ignore words flagged as spelling, grammar, or word usage errors. Hint: If you are checking an entire document, it is usually preferable to move to the top of the document, and then use the **Spelling & Grammar** command so that you do not overlook any flagged words.

6 Replace all instances of **posting** with **listing**. In the paragraph that begins *The job description*, use the **Thesaurus** pane or the **Synonyms** command on the shortcut menu to change *specific* to *explicit* and *credentials* to *qualifications.*

7 In the paragraph that begins *I currently live in Tampa*, select the first sentence of the paragraph and drag it to the end of the same paragraph. Click in the blank paragraph below the paragraph that begins *The job description*, and then press Enter one time. **Insert** a **2 × 3** table, and then type the text shown in Table 1.

TABLE 1

Education	**Bachelor of Science, Business Management**
Experience	**Two years Computer Support experience at a major university**
Required Certifications	**MCITP, MCDST**

8 Select the entire table. **AutoFit Contents**, and then apply the **Table Grid Light** table style—under **Plain Tables**, in the first row, the first style. **Center** the table.

9 Click the **FILE tab**, and then click **Show All Properties**. As the **Tags**, type **letter, alumni website** and as the **Subject**, type your course name and section number. Be sure your name is indicated as the **Author**, and edit if necessary. **Save** and **Close** the document but leave Word open. Hold this file until you complete this project.

10 From your student files, open **w02G_Resume**. Press F12, and then **Save** the document in your **Word Chapter 2** folder as **Lastname_Firstname_2G_Resume** Add the file name to the footer.

11 **Insert** a new second row in the table. In the first cell of the new row, type **OBJECTIVE** and then press Tab. Type **To obtain a Business Programmer Analyst position that will use my technical and communication skills and computer support experience.** In the same cell, add **12 pt Spacing After**.

12 Select the entire table. On the **LAYOUT tab**, **AutoFit Contents**. Remove the table borders, and then display the **Borders and Shading** dialog box. With the table selected, create a **Custom** single solid line **1 1/2 pt** top border.

13 In the first row of the table, select both cells and then **Merge Cells**. **Center** the five lines and apply **Bold**. In the first row, select *William Franklin* and change the **Font Size** to **20 pt** and add **24 pt Spacing Before**. In the email address at the bottom of the first row, add **24 pt Spacing After**.

14 In the first column, apply **Bold** to the four headings. In the cell to the right of *EDUCATION*, apply **Bold** to the

(Project 2G Application Letter, Resume, and Fax Cover Sheet continues on the next page)

Mastering Word | Project 2G Application Letter, Resume, and Fax Cover Sheet (continued)

name and address of the two colleges. Add **12 pt Spacing After** to the two lines that begin *September*. In the cell to the right of *RELEVANT EXPERIENCE*, apply **Bold** to the names of the two jobs—*IT Analyst* and *Computer Technician*. In the same cell, below the line that begins *January 2014*, apply bullets to the six lines that comprise the job duties. Create a similar bulleted list for the duties as a Computer Technician. Add **12 pt Spacing After** to the last line of each of the bulleted lists.

15 In the cell to the right of *CERTIFICATIONS*, select all four lines and create a bulleted list. Click the **FILE tab**, and then click **Show All Properties**. As the **Tags**, type **resume, business programmer analyst** and as the **Subject**, type your course name and section number. Be sure your name is indicated as the **Author**, and edit if necessary. **Save** and **Close** the document but leave Word open. Hold this file until you complete this project.

16 In Word's templates, search for **personal fax** and then select the second (shorter) template named **Fax cover sheet (informal)**. Click **Create**. **Save** the document in your **Word Chapter 2** folder as **Lastname_Firstname_2G_Fax** and then add the file name to the footer.

17 Type the text shown in Table 2 for the content controls.

TABLE 2

Subject:	**Application for Job Listing on Alumni Website**
Date:	**March 6, 2016**
To:	**Mary Walker-Huelsman**
From:	**William Franklin**
Phone number:	**(727) 555-0056**
Phone number:	**(813) 555-0122**
Fax number:	**(727) 555-0057**
No. of Pages	**1**
Comments:	**Two pages to follow that include my resume and a cover letter for the position of Business Programmer Analyst.**

18 Click the **FILE tab**, and then click **Show All Properties**. As the **Tags**, type **fax cover page** and as the **Subject**, type your course name and section number. Be sure your name is indicated as the **Author**, and edit if necessary. Click **Save**. As directed by your instructor, print or submit electronically the three files that are the results of this project. **Close** Word.

END | You have completed Project 2G

CONTENT-BASED ASSESSMENTS

Apply a combination of the 2A and 2B skills.

GO! Fix It | Project 2H New Jobs | Online

Build from Scratch

GO! Make It | Project 2I Training | Online

Build from Scratch

GO! Solve It | Project 2J Job Postings | Online

Build from Scratch

GO! Solve It | Project 2K Agenda

PROJECT FILES

For Project 2K, you will need the following file:

Agenda template from Word's Online templates

You will save your document as:

Lastname_Firstname_2K_Agenda

On Word's opening screen, search for an online template using the search term **formal meeting agenda.** Create the agenda and then save it in your Word Chapter 2 folder as **Lastname_Firstname_2K_Agenda** Use the following information to prepare an agenda for an FPCC Career Center meeting.

The meeting will be chaired by Mary Walker-Huelsman. It will be the monthly meeting of the Career Center's staff—Kevin Rau, Marilyn Kelly, André Randolph, Susan Nguyen, and Charles James. The meeting will be held on March 15, 2016, at 3:00 p.m. The old business agenda items (open issues) include (1) seeking more job listings related to the printing and food service industries, (2) expanding the alumni website, and (3) the addition of a part-time trainer. The new business agenda items will include (1) writing a grant so the center can serve more students and alumni, (2) expanding the training area with 20 additional workstations, (3) purchase of new computers for the training room, and (4) renewal of printing service contract.

Add the file name to the footer, add your name, your course name, the section number, and then add the keywords **agenda, monthly staff meeting** to the Properties area. Submit as directed.

Performance Level

Performance Criteria	Exemplary: You consistently applied the relevant skills	Proficient: You sometimes, but not always, applied the relevant skills	Developing: You rarely or never applied the relevant skills
Select an agenda template	Agenda template is appropriate for the information provided for the meeting.	Agenda template is used, but does not fit the information provided.	No template is used for the agenda.
Add appropriate information to the template	All information is inserted in the appropriate places.	All information is included, but not in the appropriate places.	Information is missing.
Format template information	All text in the template is properly aligned and formatted.	All text is included, but alignment or formatting is inconsistent.	No additional formatting has been added.

END | You have completed Project 2K

OUTCOMES-BASED ASSESSMENTS

RUBRIC

The following outcomes-based assessments are *open-ended assessments*. That is, there is no specific correct result; your result will depend on your approach to the information provided. Make *Professional Quality* your goal. Use the following scoring rubric to guide you in *how* to approach the problem and then to evaluate *how well* your approach solves the problem.

The *criteria*—Software Mastery, Content, Format and Layout, and Process—represent the knowledge and skills you have gained that you can apply to solving the problem. The *levels of performance*—Professional Quality, Approaching Professional Quality, or Needs Quality Improvements—help you and your instructor evaluate your result.

	Your completed project is of Professional Quality if you:	Your completed project is Approaching Professional Quality if you:	Your completed project Needs Quality Improvements if you:
1-Software Mastery	Choose and apply the most appropriate skills, tools, and features and identify efficient methods to solve the problem.	Choose and apply some appropriate skills, tools, and features, but not in the most efficient manner.	Choose inappropriate skills, tools, or features, or are inefficient in solving the problem.
2-Content	Construct a solution that is clear and well organized, contains content that is accurate, appropriate to the audience and purpose, and is complete. Provide a solution that contains no errors in spelling, grammar, or style.	Construct a solution in which some components are unclear, poorly organized, inconsistent, or incomplete. Misjudge the needs of the audience. Have some errors in spelling, grammar, or style, but the errors do not detract from comprehension.	Construct a solution that is unclear, incomplete, or poorly organized; contains some inaccurate or inappropriate content; and contains many errors in spelling, grammar, or style. Do not solve the problem.
3-Format & Layout	Format and arrange all elements to communicate information and ideas, clarify function, illustrate relationships, and indicate relative importance.	Apply appropriate format and layout features to some elements, but not others. Overuse features, causing minor distraction.	Apply format and layout that does not communicate information or ideas clearly. Do not use format and layout features to clarify function, illustrate relationships, or indicate relative importance. Use available features excessively, causing distraction.
4-Process	Use an organized approach that integrates planning, development, self-assessment, revision, and reflection.	Demonstrate an organized approach in some areas, but not others; or, use an insufficient process of organization throughout.	Do not use an organized approach to solve the problem.

OUTCOMES-BASED ASSESSMENTS

Apply a combination of the 2A and 2B skills.

GO! Think Project 2L Workshops

PROJECT FILES

Build from Scratch

For Project 2L, you will need the following files:

New blank Word document
w02L_Workshop_Information

You will save your document as:

Lastname_Firstname_2L_Workshops

The Florida Port Community College Career Center offers a series of workshops for both students and alumni. Any eligible student or graduate can attend the workshops, and there is no fee. Currently, the Career Center offers a three-session workshop covering Excel and Word, a two-session workshop covering Business Communication, and a one-session workshop covering Creating a Resume.

Print the w02L_Workshop_Information file and use the information to complete this project. Create an announcement with a title, an introductory paragraph, and a table listing the workshops and the topics covered in each workshop. Use the file w02L_Workshop_Information for help with the topics covered in each workshop. Format the table cells appropriately. Add an appropriate footer and document properties. Save the document as **Lastname_Firstname_2L_Workshops** and submit it as directed.

END | You have completed Project 2L

Build from Scratch

GO! Think! Project 2M Planner Online

Build from Scratch

You and GO! Project 2N Personal Resume Online

Build from Scratch

GO! Cumulative Group Project Project 2O Bell Orchid Hotels Online

Creating Research Papers, Newsletters, and Merged Mailing Labels

GO! to Work Video W3

3

WORD 2013

PROJECT 3A

OUTCOMES
Create a research paper that includes citations and a bibliography.

PROJECT 3B

OUTCOMES
Create a multiple-column newsletter and merged mailing labels.

OBJECTIVES

1. Create a Research Paper
2. Insert Footnotes in a Research Paper
3. Create Citations and a Bibliography in a Research Paper
4. Use Read Mode and PDF Reflow

OBJECTIVES

5. Format a Multiple-Column Newsletter
6. Use Special Character and Paragraph Formatting
7. Create Mailing Labels Using Mail Merge

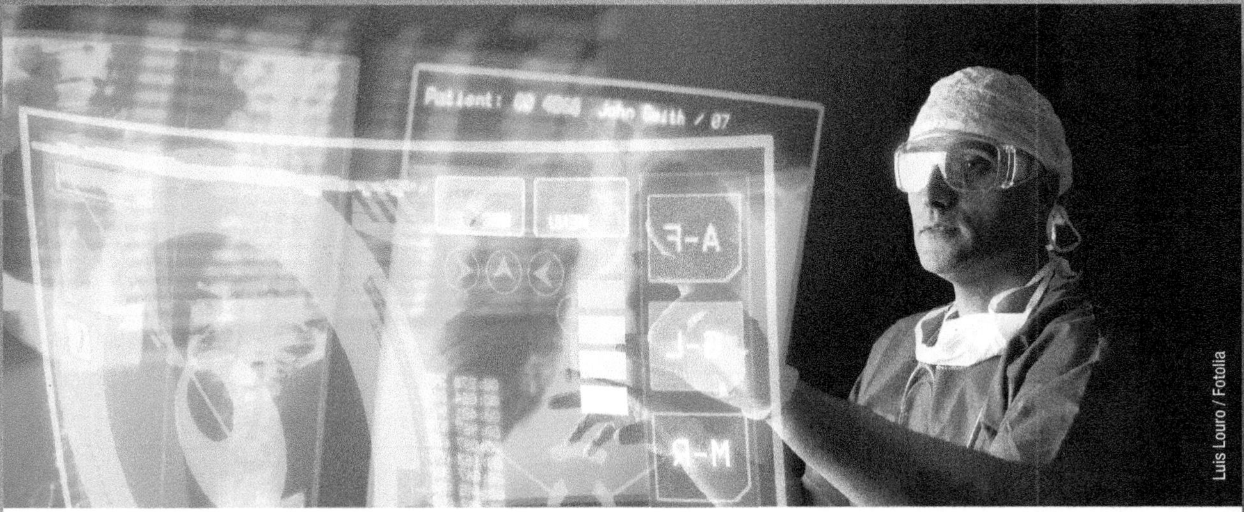

Luis Louro / Fotolia

In This Chapter

Microsoft Word provides many tools for creating complex documents. For example, Word has tools that enable you to create a research paper that includes citations, footnotes, and a bibliography. You can also create multiple-column newsletters, format the nameplate at the top of the newsletter, use special character formatting to create distinctive title text, and add borders and shading to paragraphs to highlight important information.

In this chapter, you will edit and format a research paper, create a two-column newsletter, and then create a set of mailing labels to mail the newsletter to multiple recipients.

The projects in this chapter relate to **University Medical Center**, which is a patient-care and research institution serving the metropolitan area of Memphis, Tennessee. Because of its outstanding reputation in the medical community and around the world, University Medical Center is able to attract top physicians, scientists, and researchers in all fields of medicine and achieve a level of funding that allows it to build and operate state-of-the-art facilities. A program in biomedical research was recently added. Individuals throughout the eastern United States travel to University Medical Center for diagnosis and care.

PROJECT 3A

Research Paper

MyITLab® Project 3A Training

PROJECT ACTIVITIES

In Activities 3.01 through 3.14, you will edit and format a research paper that contains an overview of a new area of study. This paper was created by Gerard Foster, a medical intern at University Medical Center, for distribution to his classmates studying various physiologic monitoring devices. Your completed document will look similar to Figure 3.1.

PROJECT FILES

For Project 3A, you will need the following file:
w03A_Quantitative_Technology

You will save your document as:
Lastname_Firstname_3A_Quantitative_Technology

PROJECT RESULTS

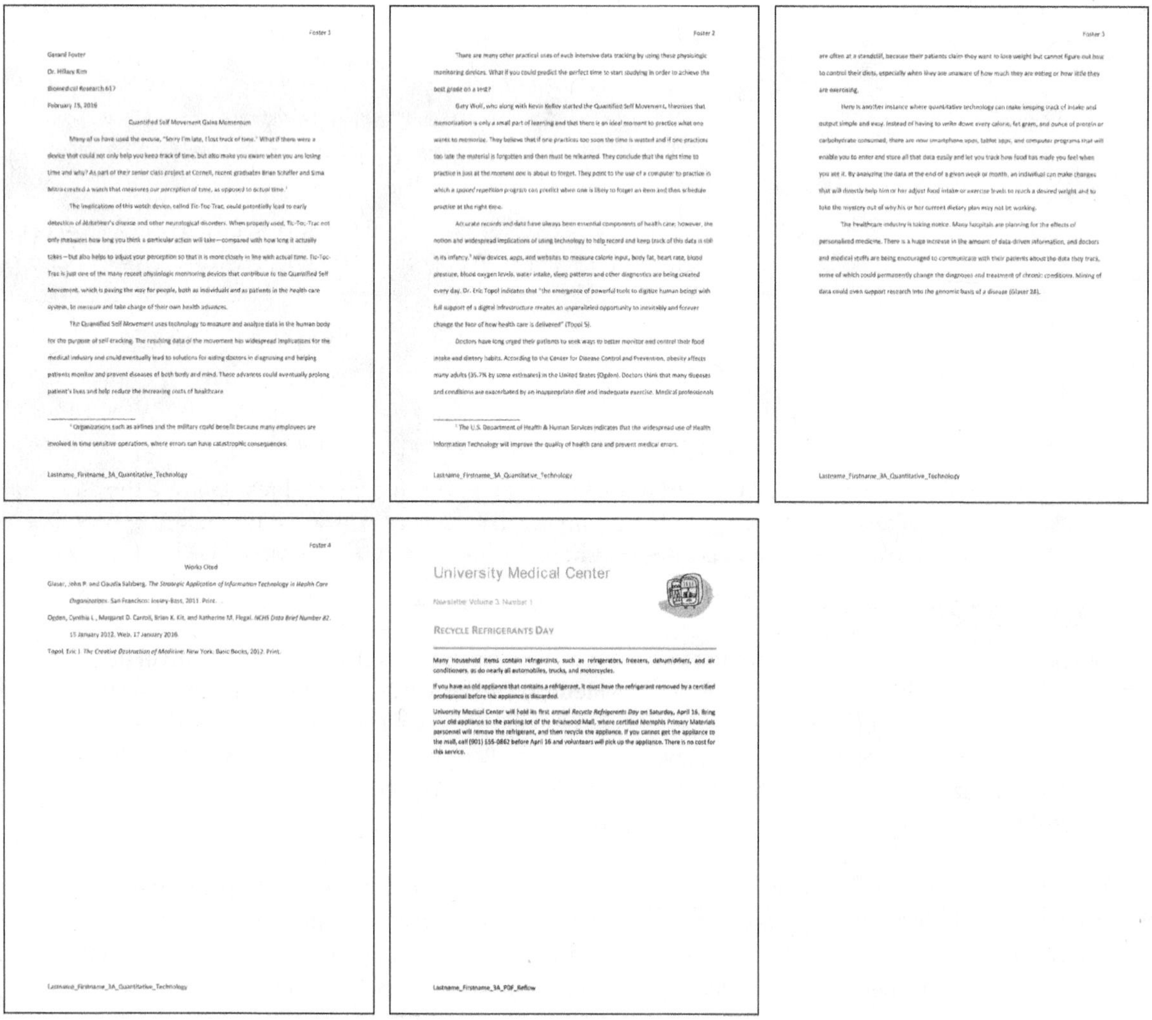

FIGURE 3.1 Project 3A Research Paper

Objective 1 Create a Research Paper

Video W3-1

When you write a research paper or a report for college or business, follow a format prescribed by one of the standard ***style guides***—a manual that contains standards for the design and writing of documents. The two most commonly used styles for research papers are those created by the ***Modern Language Association (MLA)*** and the ***American Psychological Association (APA)***; there are several others.

NOTE **If You Are Using a Touchscreen**

- Tap an item to click it.
- Press and hold for a few seconds to right-click; release when the information or commands displays.
- Touch the screen with two or more fingers and then pinch together to zoom in or stretch your fingers apart to zoom out.
- Slide your finger on the screen to scroll—slide left to scroll right and slide right to scroll left.
- Slide to rearrange—similar to dragging with a mouse.
- Swipe from edge: from right to display charms; from left to expose open apps, snap apps, or close apps; from top or bottom to show commands or close an app.
- Swipe to select—slide an item a short distance with a quick movement—to select an item and bring up commands, if any.

Activity 3.01 Formatting the Spacing and First-Page Information for a Research Paper

When formatting the text for your research paper, refer to the standards for the style guide that you have chosen. In this activity, you will create a research paper using the MLA style. The MLA style uses 1-inch margins, a 0.5" first line indent, and double spacing throughout the body of the document with no extra space above or below paragraphs.

1. Start Word. From your student files, locate and **Open** the document **w03A_Quantitative_Technology**. If necessary, display the formatting marks and rulers. In the location where you are storing your projects for this chapter, create a new folder named **Word Chapter 3** and then **Save** the file in the folder as **Lastname_Firstname_3A_Quantitative_Technology**

2. Press Ctrl + A to select the entire document. On the **HOME tab**, in the **Paragraph group**, click **Line and Paragraph Spacing**, and then change the line spacing to **2.0**. On the **PAGE LAYOUT tab**, in the **Paragraph group**, change the **Spacing After** to **0 pt**.

3. Press Ctrl + Home to deselect and move to the top of the document. Press Enter one time to create a blank line at the top of the document, and then click to position the insertion point in the blank line. Type **Gerard Foster** and press Enter.

4. Type **Dr. Hillary Kim** and press Enter. Type **Biomedical Research 617** and press Enter. Type **February 15, 2016** and press Enter.

5. Type **Quantified Self Movement Gains Momentum** and then press Ctrl + E, which is the keyboard shortcut to center a paragraph of text. Click **Save**, and then compare your screen with Figure 3.2.

***More* Knowledge** **Creating a Document Heading for a Research Paper**

On the first page of an MLA-style research paper, on the first line, type the report author. On the second line, type the person for whom the report is prepared—for example, your professor or supervisor. On the third line, type the name of the class or business. On the fourth line, type the date. On the fifth line, type the report title and center it.

FIGURE 3.2

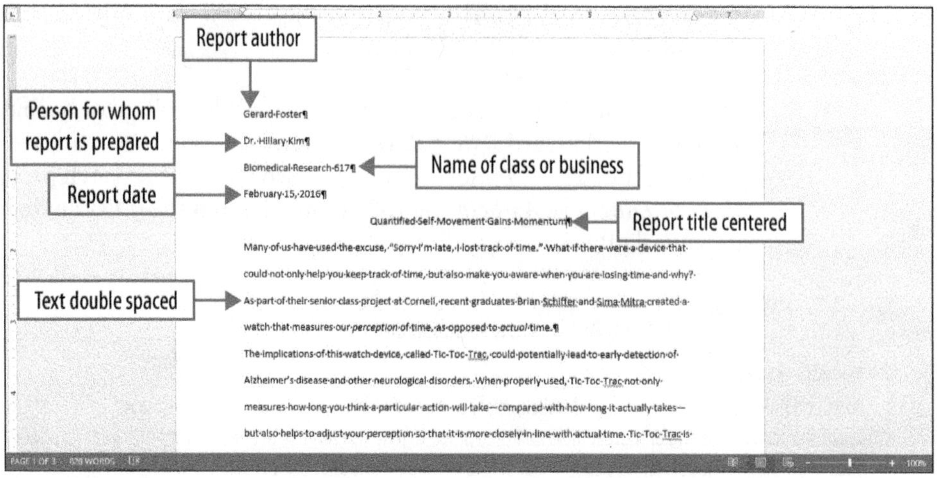

More Knowledge **Creating a Bookmark**

In a document, you can mark a place you want to find again easily. Select the content to which you want to assign the bookmark. On the INSERT tab, in the Links group, click Bookmark, and assign a name. To go to the bookmark, press CTRL + G, select Bookmark, and then click the bookmark name.

Activity 3.02 | Formatting the Page Numbering and Paragraph Indents for a Research Paper

1. On the **INSERT tab**, in the **Header & Footer group**, click **Header**, and then at the bottom of the list, click **Edit Header**.

2. Type **Foster** and then press Spacebar.

   Recall that the text you insert into a header or footer displays on every page of a document. Within a header or footer, you can insert many different types of information; for example, automatic page numbers, the date, the time, the file name, or pictures.

3. Under **HEADER & FOOTER TOOLS**, on the **DESIGN tab**, in the **Header & Footer group**, click **Page Number**, and then point to **Current Position**. In the gallery, under **Simple**, click **Plain Number**. Compare your screen with Figure 3.3.

   Word will automatically number the pages using this number format.

FIGURE 3.3

4. On the **HOME tab**, in the **Paragraph group**, click **Align Right**. Double-click anywhere in the document to close the Header area.

5. Near the top of **Page 1**, locate the paragraph beginning *Many of us*, and then click to position the insertion point at the beginning of the paragraph. By moving the vertical scroll bar, scroll to the end of the document, hold down Shift, and then click to the right of the last paragraph mark to select all of the text from the insertion point to the end of the document. Release Shift.

6 With the text selected, in the **Paragraph group**, click the **Dialog Box Launcher** button to display the **Paragraph** dialog box.

7 On the **INDENTS and SPACING tab**, under **Indentation**, click the **Special arrow**, and then click **First line**. In the **By** box, be sure **0.5"** displays. Click **OK**. Compare your screen with Figure 3.4.

The MLA style uses 0.5-inch indents at the beginning of the first line of every paragraph. *Indenting*—moving the beginning of the first line of a paragraph to the right or left of the rest of the paragraph—provides visual cues to the reader to help divide the document text and make it easier to read.

FIGURE 3.4

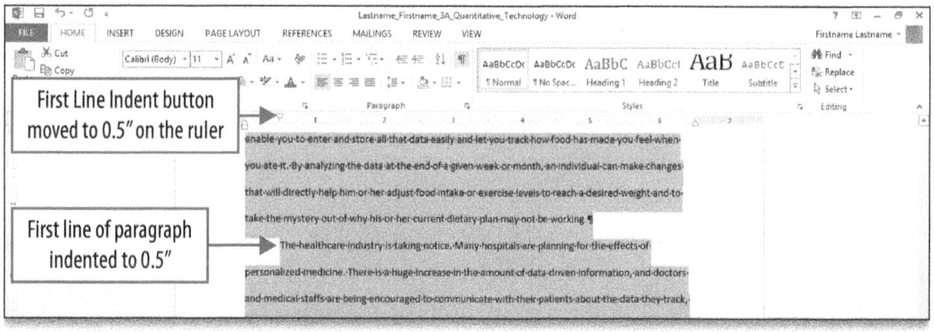

ANOTHER WAY

On the ruler, point to the First Line Indent button, and then drag the button to 0.5" on the horizontal ruler.

8 Press Ctrl + Home to deselect and move to the top of the document. On the **INSERT tab**, in **the Header & Footer group**, click **Footer**, and then at the bottom of the list click **Edit Footer**.

9 In the **Insert group**, click **Document Info**, and then click **File Name**. On the ribbon, click **Close Header and Footer**.

The file name in the footer is *not* part of the research report format, but it is included in projects in this textbook so that you and your instructor can identify your work.

10 **Save** your document.

More Knowledge **Suppressing the Page Number on the First Page of a Document**

Some style guidelines require that the page number and other header and footer information on the first page be hidden from view—***suppressed***. To hide the information contained in the header and footer areas on Page 1 of a document, double-click in the header or footer area. Then, under HEADER & FOOTER TOOLS, on the DESIGN tab, in the Options group, select the Different First Page check box.

Objective 2 Insert Footnotes in a Research Paper

Video W3-2

Reports and research papers typically include information that you find in other sources, and these must be credited. Within report text, numbers mark the location of ***notes***—information that expands on the topic being discussed but that does not fit well in the document text. The numbers refer to ***footnotes***—notes placed at the bottom of the page containing the note, or to ***endnotes***—notes placed at the end of a document or chapter.

Activity 3.03 | Inserting Footnotes

You can add footnotes as you type your document or after your document is complete. Word renumbers the footnotes automatically, so footnotes need not be entered in order, and if one footnote is removed, the remaining footnotes automatically renumber.

1 Scroll to view the upper portion of **Page 2**, and then locate the paragraph that begins *Accurate records.* In the third line of the paragraph, click to position the insertion point to the right of the period after *infancy.*

2 On the **REFERENCES tab**, in the **Footnotes group**, click **Insert Footnote.**

Word creates space for a footnote in the footnote area at the bottom of the page and adds a footnote number to the text at the insertion point location. Footnote *1* displays in the footnote area, and the insertion point moves to the right of the number. A short black line is added just above the footnote area. You do not need to type the footnote number.

3 Type **The U.S. Department of Health & Human Services indicates that the widespread use of Health Information Technology will improve the quality of health care and prevent medical errors.**

This is an explanatory footnote; the footnote provides additional information that does not fit well in the body of the report.

4 Click the **HOME tab**, and then examine the font size and line spacing settings. Notice that the new footnote displays in 10 pt font size and is single-spaced, even though the font size of the document text is 11 pt and the text is double-spaced, as shown in Figure 3.5.

FIGURE 3.5

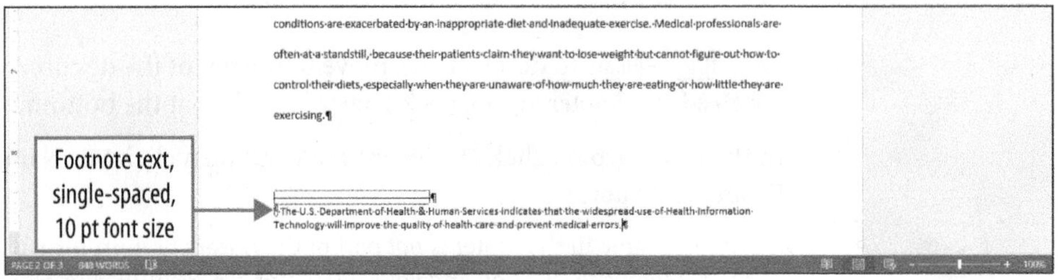

5 Scroll to view the top of **Page 1**, and then locate the paragraph that begins *Many of us.* At the end of the paragraph, click to position the insertion point to the right of the period following *time.*

6 On the **REFERENCES tab**, in the **Footnotes group**, click **Insert Footnote**. Type **Organizations such as airlines and the military could benefit because many employees are involved in time-sensitive operations, where errors can have catastrophic consequences.** Notice that the footnote you just added becomes the new footnote *1*. Click **Save**, and then compare your screen with Figure 3.6.

The first footnote that you typed, which is on Page 2 and begins *The U.S. Department of Health*, is renumbered as footnote *2*.

FIGURE 3.6

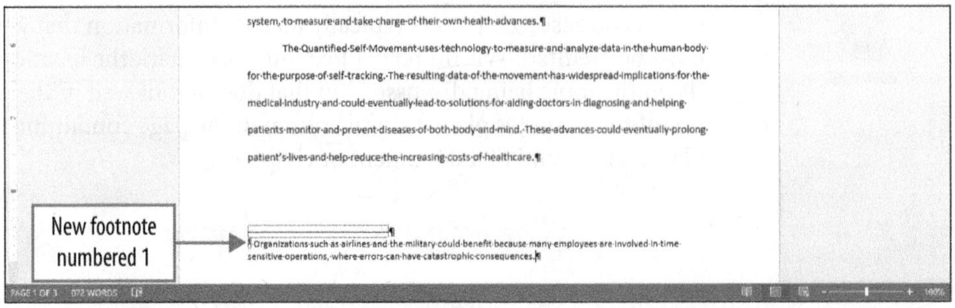

More Knowledge **Using Symbols Rather Than Numbers for Notes**

Instead of using numbers to designate footnotes, you can use standard footnote symbols. The seven traditional symbols, available from the Footnote and Endnote dialog box, in order, are * (asterisk), † (dagger), ‡ (double dagger), § (section mark), || (parallels), ¶ (paragraph mark), and # (number or pound sign). This sequence can be continuous (this is the default setting), or it can begin anew with each page.

Activity 3.04 | Modifying a Footnote Style

Microsoft Word contains built-in paragraph formats called ***styles***—groups of formatting commands, such as font, font size, font color, paragraph alignment, and line spacing—that can be applied to a paragraph with one command.

The default style for footnote text is a single-spaced paragraph that uses a 10-point Calibri font and no paragraph indents. MLA style specifies double-spaced text in all areas of a research paper—including footnotes. According to the MLA style, first lines of footnotes must also be indented 0.5 inch and use the same font size as the report text.

1 At the bottom of **Page 1**, point anywhere in the footnote text you just typed, right-click, and then on the shortcut menu, click **Style**. Compare your screen with Figure 3.7.

The Style dialog box displays, listing the styles currently in use in the document, in addition to some of the word processing elements that come with special built-in styles. Because you right-clicked on the footnote text, the selected style is the Footnote Text style.

FIGURE 3.7

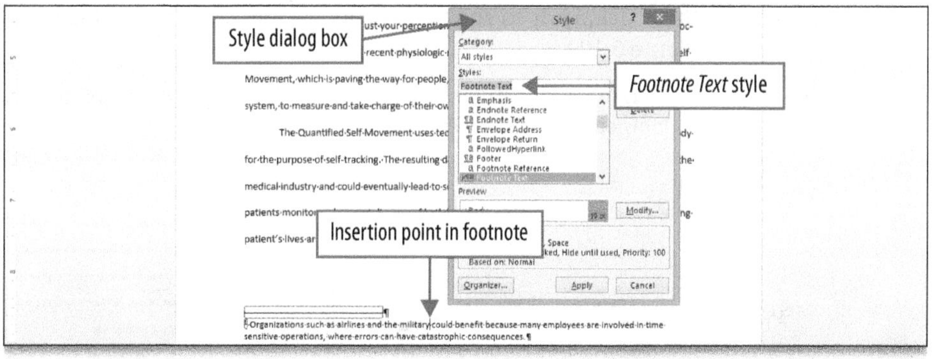

2 In the **Style** dialog box, click **Modify**, and then in the **Modify Style** dialog box, locate the small **Formatting** toolbar in the center of the dialog box. Click the **Font Size button arrow**, click **11**, and then compare your screen with Figure 3.8.

FIGURE 3.8

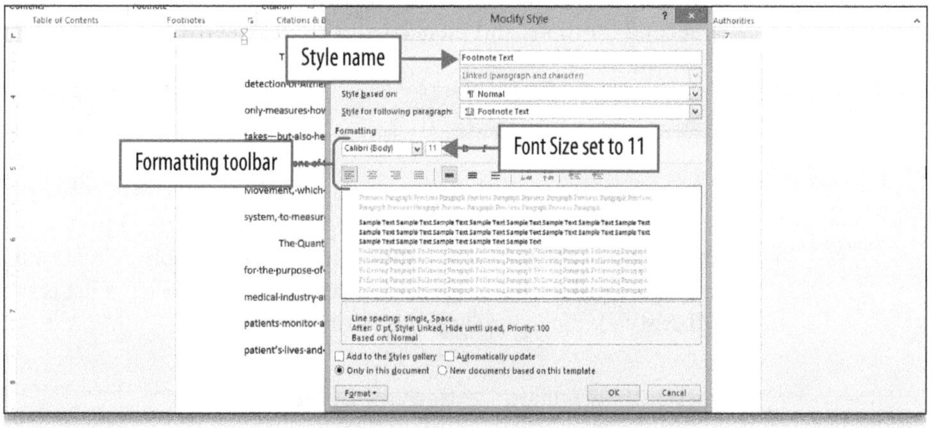

3 In the lower left corner of the dialog box, click **Format**, and then click **Paragraph**. In the **Paragraph** dialog box, on the **Indents and Spacing tab**, under **Indentation**, click the **Special arrow**, and then click **First line**.

4 Under **Spacing**, click the **Line spacing arrow**, and then click **Double**. Compare your dialog box with Figure 3.9.

FIGURE 3.9

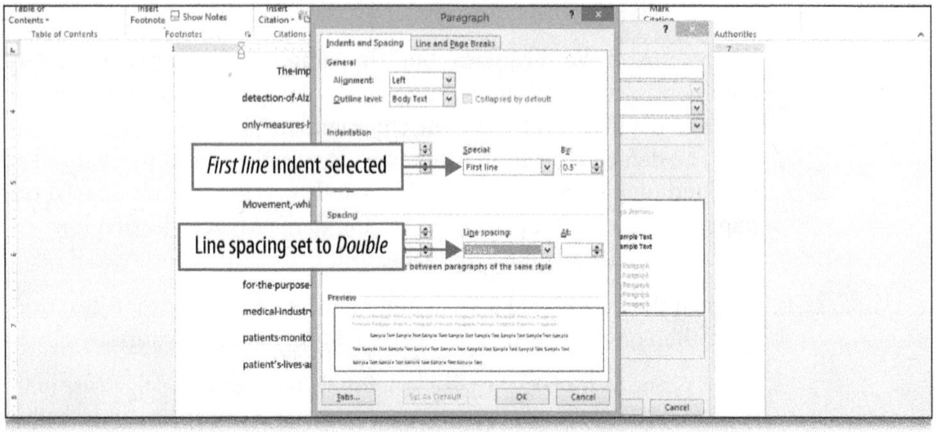

5 Click **OK** to close the **Paragraph** dialog box, click **OK** to close the **Modify Style** dialog box, and then click **Apply** to apply the new style and **close** the dialog box. Compare your screen with Figure 3.10.

Your inserted footnotes are formatted with the modified Footnote Text paragraph style; any new footnotes that you insert will also use this format.

FIGURE 3.10

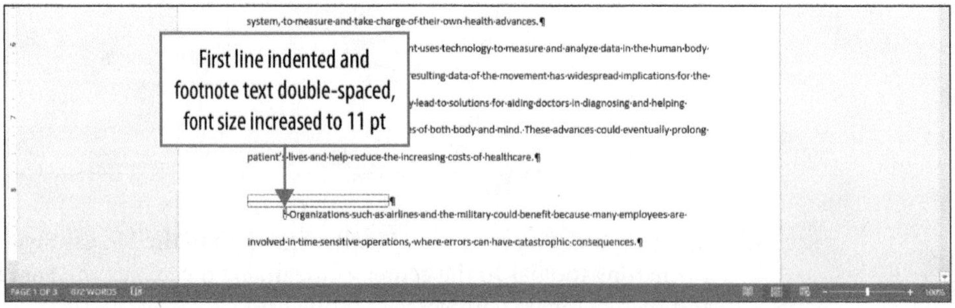

6 Scroll to view the bottom of **Page 2** to confirm that the new format was also applied to the second footnote, and then **Save** your document.

Objective 3 Create Citations and a Bibliography in a Research Paper

Video W3-3

When you use quotations from or detailed summaries of other people's work, you must specify the source of the information. A ***citation*** is a note inserted into the text of a report or research paper that refers the reader to a source in the bibliography. Create a ***bibliography*** at the end of a research paper to list the sources you have referenced. Such a list is typically titled ***Works Cited*** (in MLA style), *Bibliography*, *Sources*, or *References*.

Activity 3.05 Adding Citations for a Book

When writing a long research paper, you will likely reference numerous books, articles, and websites. Some of your research sources may be referenced many times, others only one time.

References to sources within the text of your research paper are indicated in an *abbreviated* manner. However, as you enter a citation for the first time, you can also enter the *complete* information about the source. Then, when you have finished your paper, you will be able to automatically generate the list of sources that must be included at the end of your research paper.

1 Scroll to view the middle of **Page 2**. In the paragraph that begins *Accurate records*, at the end of the paragraph, click to position the insertion point to the right of the quotation mark.

The citation in the document points to the full source information in the bibliography, which typically includes the name of the author, the full title of the work, the year of publication, and other publication information.

2 On the **REFERENCES tab**, in the **Citations & Bibliography group**, click the **Style button arrow**, and then click **MLA** to insert a reference using MLA bibliography style.

3 Click **Insert Citation**, and then click **Add New Source**. Click the **Type of Source arrow**, and then click **Book**. Add the following information, and then compare your screen with Figure 3.11:

Author:	**Sopol, Eric J.**
Title:	**The Creative Destruction of Medicine**
Year:	**2012**
City:	**New York**
Publisher:	**Basic Books**
Medium	**Print**

FIGURE 3.11

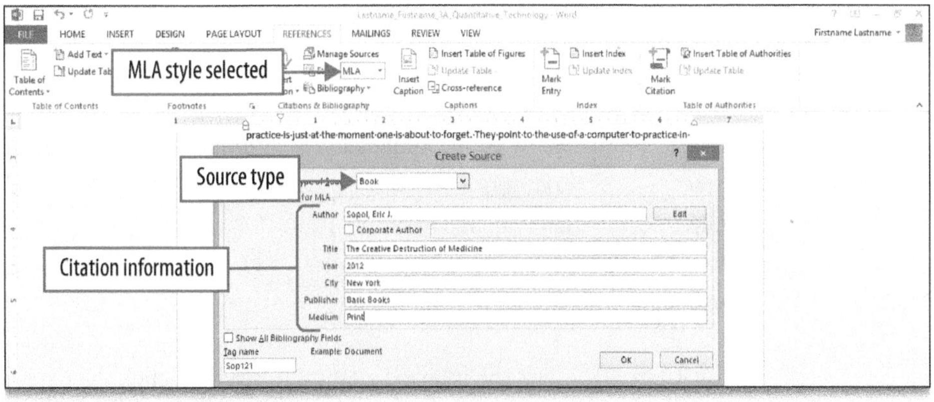

NOTE **Citing Corporate Authors and Indicating the Medium**

If the author of a document is only identified as the name of an organization, select the Corporate Author check box and type the name of the organization in the Corporate Author box.

In the Seventh edition of the *MLA Handbook for Writers of Research Papers*, the category Medium was added and must be included for any item on the Works Cited page. Entries for this category can include Print, Web, Performance, and Photograph, among many others.

4 Click **OK** to insert the citation. Point to *(Sopol)* and click one time to select the citation.

In the MLA style, citations that refer to items on the *Works Cited* page are placed in parentheses and are referred to as ***parenthetical references***—references that include the last name of the author or authors and the page number in the referenced source, which you add to the reference. No year is indicated, and there is no comma between the name and the page number.

5 Save the document.

Activity 3.06 | Editing Citations

1 In the lower right corner of the box that surrounds the reference, point to the small arrow to display the ScreenTip *Citation Options*. Click this **Citation Options arrow**, and then on the list of options, click **Edit Citation.**

2 In the **Edit Citation** dialog box, under **Add**, in the **Pages** box, type **5** to indicate that you are citing from Page 5 of this source. Compare your screen with Figure 3.12.

FIGURE 3.12

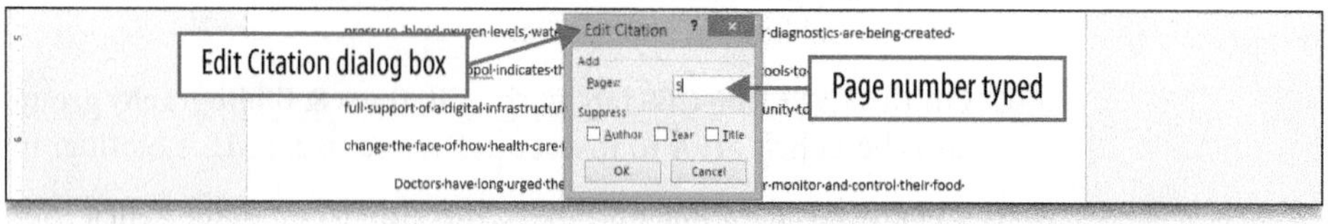

3 Click **OK** to display the page number of the citation. Click outside of the citation box to deselect it. Then type a period to the right of the citation, and delete the period to the left of the quotation mark.

In the MLA style, if the reference occurs at the end of a sentence, the parenthetical reference always displays to the left of the punctuation mark that ends the sentence.

4 Press Ctrl + End to move to the end of the document, and then click to position the insertion point after the letter *e* in *disease* and to the left of the period.

5 In the **Citations & Bibliography group**, click **Insert Citation**, and then click **Add New Source.** Click the **Type of Source arrow**, if necessary scroll to the top of the list, click **Book**, and then add the following information:

Author:	**Glaser, John P. and Claudia Salzberg**
Title:	**The Strategic Application of Information Technology in Health Care Organizations**
Year:	**2011**
City:	**San Francisco**
Publisher:	**Jossey-Bass**
Medium:	**Print**

6 Click **OK**. Click the inserted citation to select it, click the **Citation Options arrow**, and then click **Edit Citation.**

7 In the **Edit Citation** dialog box, under **Add**, in the **Pages** box, type **28** to indicate that you are citing from page 28 of this source. Click **OK.**

8 On the **REFERENCES tab**, in the **Citations & Bibliography group**, click **Manage Sources**, and then compare your screen with Figure 3.13.

The Source Manager dialog box displays. Other citations on your computer display in the Master List box. The citations for the current document display in the Current List box. Word maintains the Master List so that if you use the same sources regularly, you can copy sources from your Master List to the current document. A preview of the bibliography entry also displays at the bottom of the dialog box.

FIGURE 3.13

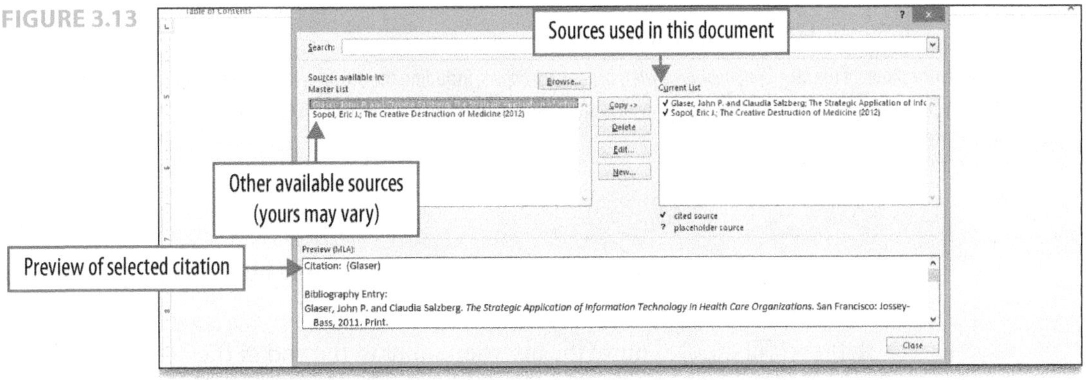

9 At the bottom of the **Source Manager** dialog box, click **Close**. Click anywhere in the document to deselect the parenthetical reference, and then **Save** your document.

Activity 3.07 | Adding Citations for a Website

1 In the lower portion of **Page 2**, in the paragraph that begins *Doctors have long*, in the third line, click to position the insertion point after the s in *States* and to the left of the period.

2 In the **Citations & Bibliography group**, click **Insert Citation**, and then click **Add New Source**. Click the **Type of Source arrow**, scroll down as necessary, and then click **Web site**. Type the following information:

Author:	**Ogden, Cynthia L., Margaret D. Carroll, Brian K. Kit, and Katherine M. Flegal.**
Name of Web Page:	**NCHS Data Brief Number 82**
Year:	**2012**
Month:	**January**
Day:	**15**
Year Accessed:	**2016**
Month Accessed:	**January**
Day Accessed:	**17**
Medium	**Web**

3 Click **OK**. **Save** , and then compare your screen with Figure 3.14.

A parenthetical reference is added. Because the cited web page has no page numbers, only the author name is used in the parenthetical reference.

FIGURE 3.14

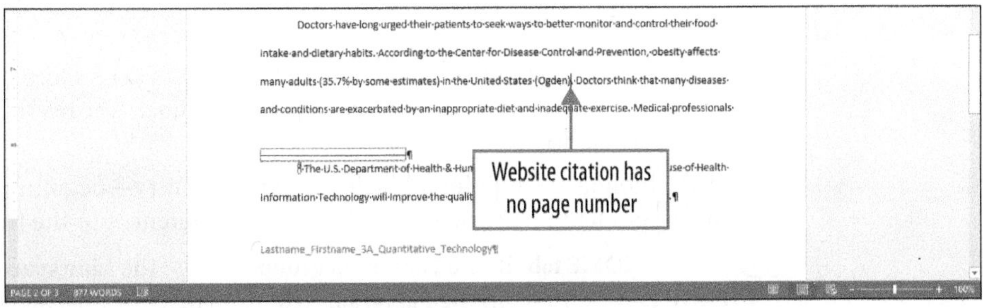

More Knowledge **Including URLs of Web Sources**

With the Seventh edition of the *MLA Handbook for Writers of Research Papers*, including the URL of web sources is recommended only when the reader would have difficulty finding the source without it or if your instructor requires it. Otherwise, readers will likely find the resource by using search tools. If you include the URL, enclose it in angle brackets and end with a period.

Activity 3.08 | Inserting Page Breaks

Your bibliography must begin on a new page, so at the bottom of the last page of your report, you must insert a manual page break.

1 Press Ctrl + End to move the insertion point to the end of the document.

If there is a footnote on the last page, the insertion point will display at the end of the final paragraph, but above the footnote—a footnote is always associated with the page that contains the citation.

2 Press Ctrl + Enter to insert a manual page break.

A ***manual page break*** forces a page to end at the insertion point location, and then places any subsequent text at the top of the next page. Recall that the new paragraph retains the formatting of the previous paragraph, so in this instance the first line is indented.

A ***page break indicator***, which shows where a manual page break was inserted, displays at the bottom of Page 3.

3 On the **HOME tab**, in the **Paragraph group**, click the **Dialog Box Launcher** button to display the **Paragraph** dialog box.

4 On the **Indents and Spacing tab**, under **Indentation**, click the **Special arrow**, and then click **(none)**. Click **OK**, and then **Save** your document.

ANOTHER WAY On the ruler, point to the First Line Indent button, and then drag the button to 0" on the horizontal ruler.

Activity 3.09 | Creating a Reference Page

At the end of a report or research paper, include a list of each source referenced. *Works Cited* is the reference page heading used in the MLA style guidelines. Other styles may refer to this page as a *Bibliography* (Business Style) or *References* (APA Style). Always display this information on a separate page.

1 With the insertion point blinking in the first line of **Page 4**, type **Works Cited** and then press Enter. On the **REFERENCES tab**, in the **Citations & Bibliography group**, in the **Style** box, be sure *MLA* displays.

2 In the **Citations & Bibliography group**, click **Bibliography**, and then near the bottom of the list, click **Insert Bibliography**.

3 Scroll as necessary to view the entire list of three references, and then click anywhere in the inserted text.

The bibliography entries that you created display as a field, which is indicated by the gray shading. This field links to the Source Manager for the citations. The references display alphabetically by the author's last name.

4 In the bibliography, point to the left of the first entry—beginning *Glaser, John P.*—to display the pointer. Drag down to select all three references in the field.

5 On the **HOME tab**, in the **Paragraph group**, change the **Line spacing** to **2.0**, and then on the **PAGE LAYOUT tab**, in the **Paragraph group**, change the **Spacing After** to **0 pt**.

The entries display according to MLA guidelines; the text is double-spaced, the extra space between paragraphs has been removed, and each entry uses a ***hanging indent***—the first line of each entry extends 0.5 inch to the left of the remaining lines of the entry.

ANOTHER WAY Display the Paragraph dialog box. Under Spacing, click the Line spacing arrow, and then click Double. Under Spacing, in the After box, type 0.

6 At the top of **Page 4**, click anywhere in the title text *Works Cited*, and then press Ctrl + E to center the title. Compare your screen with Figure 3.15, and then **Save** your document.

In MLA style, the *Works Cited* title is centered.

FIGURE 3.15

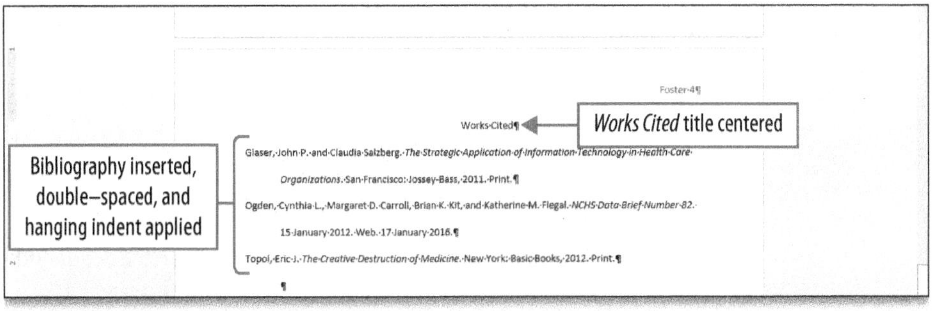

Activity 3.10 Managing and Modifying Sources for a Document

Use the Source Manager to organize the sources cited in your document. For example, in the Source Manager dialog box, you can copy sources from the master list to the current list, delete a source, edit a source, or search for a source. You can also display a preview of how your citations will appear in your document.

1 On the **REFERENCES tab**, in the **Citations & Bibliography group**, click **Manage Sources**.

2 On the left, in the **Master List**, click the entry for *Sopol, Eric J.* and then between the **Master List** and the **Current List**, click **Edit**.

The name of this source should be *Topol* instead of *Sopol*.

3 In the **Edit Source** dialog box, in the **Author** box, delete *S* and type **T**

4 Click **OK**. When the message box indicates *This source exists in your master list and current document. Do you want to update both lists with these changes?* click **Yes**. Compare your screen with Figure 3.16.

In the lower portion of the Source Manager dialog box, a preview of the corrected entry displays.

FIGURE 3.16

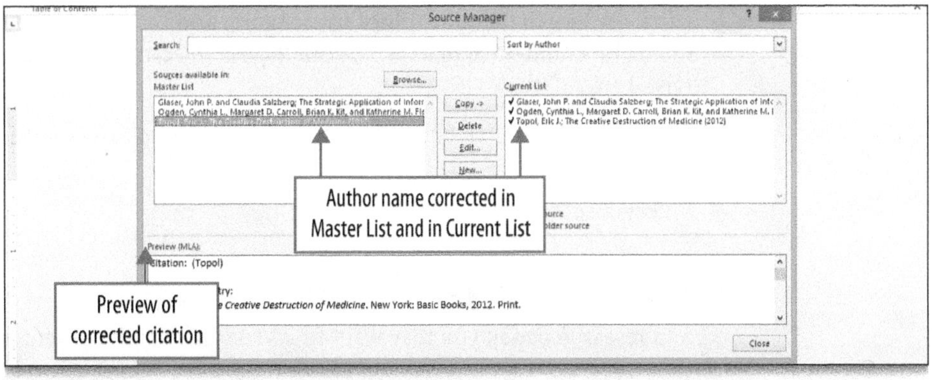

5 In the lower right corner, click **Close**. On your **Works Cited page**, notice that the author name is *not* corrected. Scroll to view the lower portion of **Page 2**, and notice that the author name *is* corrected and the citation is selected.

6 On the selected citation *(Topol 5)*, click the **Citation Options arrow**, and then click **Update Citations and Bibliography**. Press Ctrl + End, and notice that this action updates the **Works Cited page** with the corrected name.

Editing a source in Source Manager updates only the sources in the document; to update the Works Cited page, use the Update Citations and Bibliography command on the citation.

7 Drag to select all the lines for the three references. On the **HOME tab**, in the **Paragraph group**, click **Line and Paragraph Spacing**, and then click **2.0**. Click **Save**.

Activity 3.11 | Using the Navigation Pane to Go to a Specific Page

In a multipage document, use the navigation pane to move to a specific page or to find specific objects in the document.

1 Press Ctrl + Home to move to the top of the document. Click the **VIEW tab**, and then in the **Show group**, select the **navigation pane** check box.

2 In the **navigation pane**, on the right end of the **Search document** box, click the **Search for more things arrow**, and then compare your screen with Figure 3.17.

FIGURE 3.17

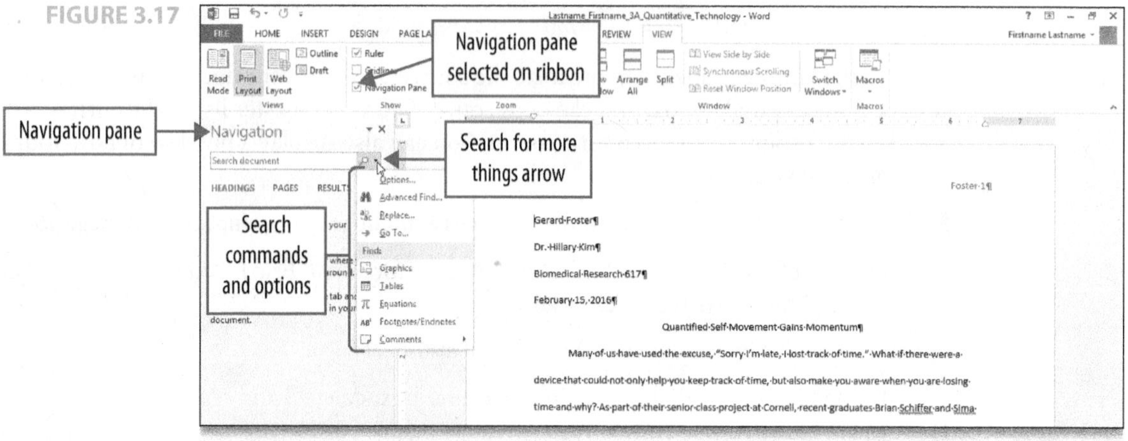

3 Under **Find**, click **Footnotes/Endnotes**. Notice that the first numbered footnote is selected.

4 In the **navigation pane,** to the right of *Result 1 of 2*, click the down arrow to move to the next numbered footnote.

5 Click the **Search for more things arrow** again, and then click **Go To**. In the **Find and Replace** dialog box, under **Go to what**, be sure **Page** is selected, and then in the **Enter page number** box, type **4**

6 Click **Go To**, and then click **Close**. Notice that **Page 4** displays. **Close** the **navigation pane.**

The navigation pane is useful when you need to navigate to find various elements, especially in a lengthy document.

Activity 3.12 | Managing Document Properties

For a research paper, you may want to add additional document properties.

1 Press Ctrl + Home to return to the top of your document. Click the **FILE tab** to display **Backstage** view, and then in the lower right corner of the screen, click **Show All Properties.**

2 As the document **Title**, type **Quantified Self Movement Gains Momentum** and then as the **Tags**, type **quantified self, physiologic monitoring, research paper**

3. Click in the **Comments** box and type **Draft copy of a research report that will be distributed to class members** and then in the **Categories** box, type **Biomedical Research**

4. In the **Subject** box, type your course name and section number. In the **Company** box, select and delete any existing text, and then type **University Medical Center**

5. Click in the **Manager** box and type **Dr. Hillary Kim** Be sure your name displays as the **Author** and edit if necessary.

6. At the top of the **Properties** list, click the text *Properties*, and then click **Advanced Properties**. In the dialog box, click the **Summary tab**, and then compare your screen with Figure 3.18.

   In the Advanced Properties dialog box, you can view and modify additional document properties.

FIGURE 3.18

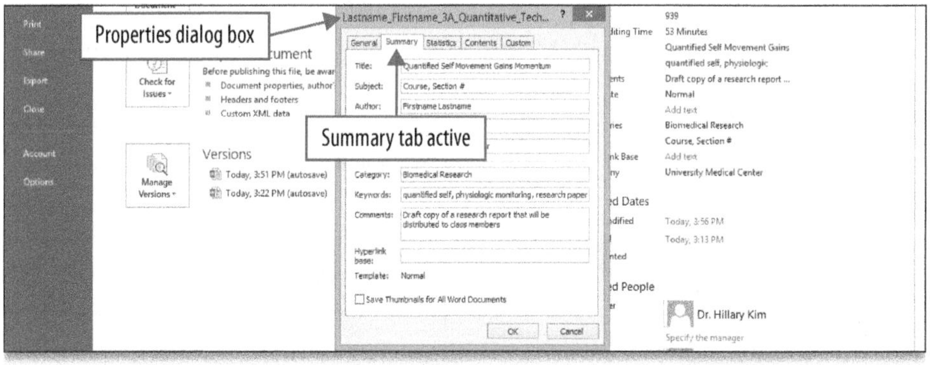

7. Click the **Statistics tab**.

   The document statistics show the number of revisions made to the document, the last time the document was edited, and the number of paragraphs, lines, words, and characters in the document. Additional information categories are available by clicking the Custom tab.

8. **Close** [X] the dialog box, and then on the left, click **Save** to save and return to your document.

Objective 4 Use Read Mode and PDF Reflow

Video W3-4

Read Mode optimizes the view of the Word screen for the times when you are *reading* Word documents on the screen and not creating or editing them. Microsoft's research indicates that two-thirds of user sessions in Word contain no editing—meaning that people are simply reading the Word document on the screen. The Column Layout feature of Read Mode reflows the document to fit the size of the device you are reading so that the text is as easy to read on a tablet device as on a 24-inch screen. The Object Zoom feature of Read Mode resizes graphics to fit the screen you are using, but you can click or tap to zoom in on the graphic.

PDF Reflow provides the ability to import PDF files into Word so that you can transform a PDF back into a fully editable Word document. This is useful if you have lost the original Word file or if someone sends you a PDF that you would like to modify. PDF Reflow is not intended to act as a viewer for PDF files—for that you will still want to use the desktop app known as Adobe Reader or the ***Windows Reader app***, with which you can open a PDF or XPS file, zoom, find words or phrases, take notes, save changes, and then print or share the file.

Activity 3.13 Using Read Mode

1. If necessary, press Ctrl + Home to move to the top of your document. On the **VIEW tab**, in the **Views group**, click **Read Mode**, and notice that **Read Mode** keeps footnotes displayed on the page associated with the footnote.

ANOTHER WAY On the right side of the status bar, click the Read Mode button.

2 In the upper left corner, click **TOOLS**.

You can use these tools to find something within the document or jump out to Bing to conduct an Internet search.

3 Click **Find**, and then in the **Search** box, type **Topol** Notice that Word displays the first page where the search term displays and highlights the term in yellow. Compare your screen with Figure 3.19.

FIGURE 3.19

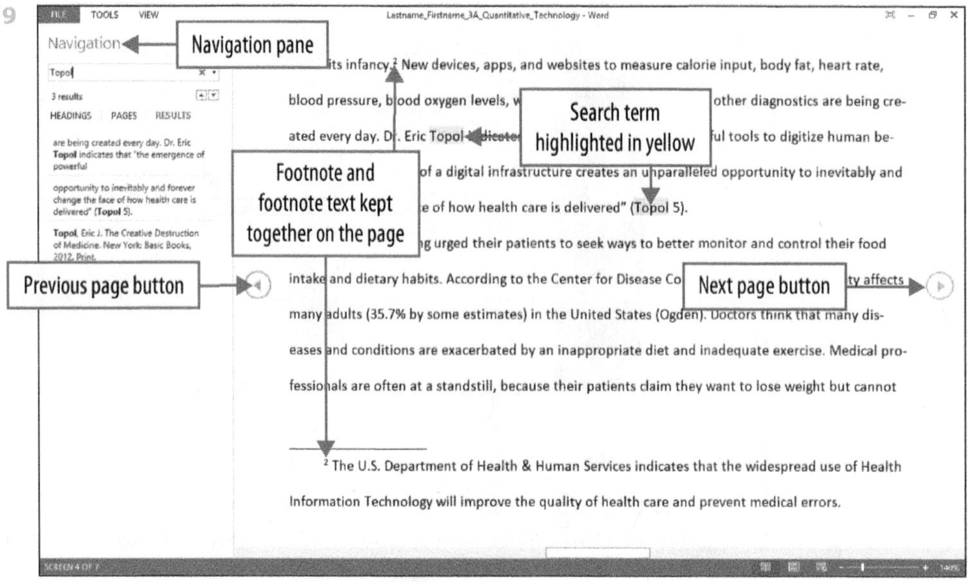

4 In the upper left corner, click **VIEW**, and then take a moment to study the table in Figure 3.20.

FIGURE 3.20

VIEW COMMANDS IN READ MODE

VIEW COMMAND	ACTION
Edit Document	Return to Print Layout view to continue editing the document.
Navigation Pane	Search for specific text or click a heading or page to move to that location.
Show Comments	See comments, if any, within the document.
Column Width	Change the display of the document to fit more or less text on each line.
Page Color	Change the colors used to show the document to make it easier to read. Some readers prefer a sepia (brownish-gray) shading as the background or a black background with white text.
Layout	Read in different layouts. Select Column Layout, which is the default, or Paper Layout, which mimics the 8.5 × 11 format but without the ribbon.

5 On the **VIEW** menu, click **Edit Document** to return to **Print Layout** view. **Close** the **navigation pane.**

ANOTHER WAY On the status bar on the right, click the Print Layout button.

Activity 3.14 | Using PDF Reflow

1. **Save** your document. Click the **FILE tab**, and then on the left, click **Close** to close your document but leave Word open.

2. Press Ctrl + F12 to display the **Open** dialog box, navigate to your student data files, and then click **w03A_PDF**. In the lower right corner, click **Open**. If a message indicates that *Word will now convert the PDF to an editable Word document…*, click **OK**.

3. If necessary, on the right side of the status bar, click **Print Layout**.

4. In the newsletter heading, change the **Volume** number to **3** Insert a footer, and then, using your own name, type **Lastname_Firstname_3A_PDF_Reflow** as shown in Figure 3.21.

FIGURE 3.21

5. Close the footer area. Press F12 to display the **Save As** dialog box, and then navigate to your **Word Chapter 3** folder. In the lower portion of the dialog box, click the **Save as type arrow**, and then click **PDF**.

6. In the **File name** box, type **Lastname_Firstname_3A_PDF_Reflow** and then in the lower right corner, click **Save** or press Enter.

   This action re-saves the document as a PDF file.

ANOTHER WAY

Click the FILE tab, on the left click Export, click Create PDF/XPS, navigate to the desired folder, and then click Publish.

7. **Close** the **w03A_PDF** document without saving. **Close** Word. Print or submit electronically the two files that are the result of this project.

More Knowledge | **Inserting Watermarks**

You can add ghost text such as *Draft* or *Confidential* behind the content of a page. To do so, on the DESIGN tab, in the Page Background group, click Watermark, and select or create the watermark you want to use.

END | You have completed Project 3A

GO! with Office Online (formerly Web Apps)

Objective Insert a Link and Highlight Text in a Word Online Document

You can use Word Online to insert a link to a website.

> **ALERT! Working with Web-Based Applications and Services**
>
> Computer programs and services on the web receive continuous updates and improvements, so the steps to complete this web-based activity may differ from the ones shown. You can often look at the screens and the information presented to determine how to complete the activity.

Activity | Inserting a Link and Highlighting a Text Selection

Word Web Online does not include the commands on the REFERENCES tab, so if you open a report that contains footnotes or citations created in the Word desktop app, you cannot edit them in Word Online. However, you can still make common text edits as you have practiced in other Office Online projects. You can also insert a link to a website. In this activity, you will use Word Online to insert a link in a report, which you might want to do before sharing the report electronically for review by others.

1 From the desktop, start Internet Explorer. Navigate to **http://onedrive.com**, and then sign in to your Microsoft account. Open your **GO! Web Projects** folder; or create this folder if you have not done so.

2 In the OneDrive menu bar, click **Upload**. Navigate to your student data files, click **w03_3A_Web**, and then click **Open**.

3 Point to the uploaded file **w03_3A_Web**, and then right-click. On the shortcut menu, scroll as necessary, and then click **Rename**. Using your own last name and first name, type **Lastname_Firstname_WD_3A_Web** and then press Enter to rename the file.

4 Click the file that you just renamed, and then click **EDIT DOCUMENT**. On the list, click **Edit in Word Online**.

5 In the paragraph that begins *The implications*, drag to select *Tic-Toc-Trac*, and then on the **HOME tab**, in the **Font group**, click **Text Highlight Color**. Click the **Yellow** block to highlight this text in yellow.

6 Press Ctrl + End to move to the end of the document, and then press Enter.

7 On the **INSERT tab**, in the **Links group**, click **Link**. In the **Display text** box, type **See how Tic-Toc-Trac works!**

8 In the **Address** box, type **www.tictoctrac.com** and then click **Insert**. Compare your screen with Figure A.

9 To test the link, point to it, hold down Ctrl and then click one time. The site opens on a new tab.

10 In your browser, close the **TicTocTrac** tab.

11 Submit as directed by your instructor. Sign out of your OneDrive.

FIGURE A

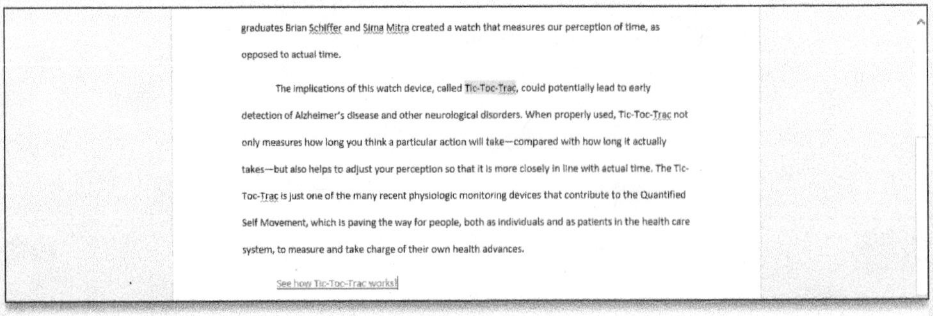

Newsletter with Mailing Labels

MyITLab®
Project 3B Training

PROJECT ACTIVITIES

In Activities 3.15 through 3.29, you will edit a newsletter that University Medical Center is sending to the board of directors and create the necessary mailing labels. Your completed documents will look similar to Figure 3.22.

PROJECT FILES

For Project 3B, you will need the following files:

New blank Word document
w03B_Environment_Newsletter
w03B_Addresses
w03B_Recycling

You will save your documents as:

Lastname_Firstname_3B_Mailing_Labels
Lastname_Firstname_3B_Addresses
Lastname_Firstname_3B_Environment_Newsletter

PROJECT RESULTS

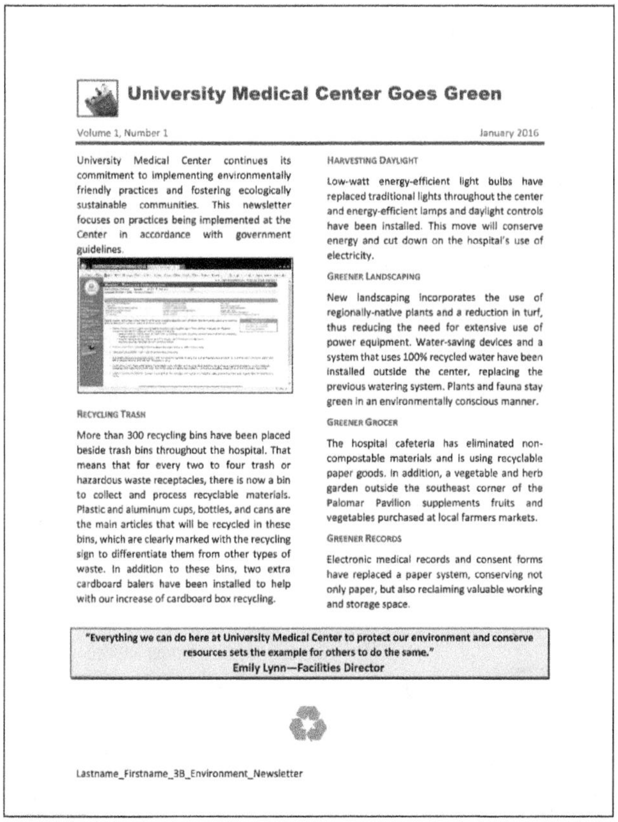

University Medical Center Goes Green

Volume 1, Number 1 January 2016

University Medical Center continues its commitment to implementing environmentally friendly practices and fostering ecologically sustainable communities. This newsletter focuses on practices being implemented at the Center in accordance with government guidelines.

RECYCLING TRASH

More than 300 recycling bins have been placed beside trash bins throughout the hospital. That means that for every two to four trash or hazardous waste receptacles, there is now a bin to collect and process recyclable materials. Plastic and aluminum cups, bottles, and cans are the main articles that will be recycled in these bins, which are clearly marked with the recycling sign to differentiate them from other types of waste. In addition to these bins, two extra cardboard balers have been installed to help with our increase of cardboard box recycling.

HARVESTING DAYLIGHT

Low-watt energy-efficient light bulbs have replaced traditional lights throughout the center and energy-efficient lamps and daylight controls have been installed. This move will conserve energy and cut down on the hospital's use of electricity.

GREENER LANDSCAPING

New landscaping incorporates the use of regionally-native plants and a reduction in turf, thus reducing the need for extensive use of power equipment. Water-saving devices and a system that uses 100% recycled water have been installed outside the center, replacing the previous watering system. Plants and fauna stay green in an environmentally conscious manner.

GREENER GROCER

The hospital cafeteria has eliminated non-compostable materials and is using recyclable paper goods. In addition, a vegetable and herb garden outside the southeast corner of the Palomar Pavilion supplements fruits and vegetables purchased at local farmers markets.

GREENER RECORDS

Electronic medical records and consent forms have replaced a paper system, conserving not only paper, but also reclaiming valuable working and storage space.

"Everything we can do here at University Medical Center to protect our environment and conserve resources sets the example for others to do the same."
Emily Lynn—Facilities Director

Lastname_Firstname_3B_Environment_Newsletter

Sherry Andersen 9000 S. Susan Creek Dr. Germantown, TN 38139	Kelley Ballen 179 Auburn Court Collierville, TN 38017	Janice Barnett 2361 Bluebird Lane #8 Memphis, TN 38107
Nancy Chang 2221 S. Flowers Road Memphis, TN 38103	Samuel Connor 124 Whitworth Drive #352 Memphis, TN 38134	Mauricio Diaz 82 E. Ramona Blvd. Arlington, TN 38002
Jackie Epps 653 Constitution Ave. #D Lakeland, TN 38002	Michael Feingold 1821 Alturas St. #1442 Germantown, TN 38138	Anthony Johnson 2820 Clairewood Dr. Collierville, TN 38017
Jason Lau 975 Treetop Place #G Germantown, TN 38138	Ronald Longoria 36 S. Delowe St. #D Bartlett, TN 38135	Ruth Marigold 4220 Thornewood Dr. #320 Memphis, TN 38112
Ami Mehta 3418 Longview Drive #320 Memphis, TN 38112	Taylor Mines 189 Ventura Street Millington, TN 38053	Karlie Nichols 2000 St. Luke Place Millington, TN 38053
Julian Omdahl 34 Gloucester Pl. Bartlett, TN 38133	Jacob Orr 1550 Glenrosa Drive #1550 Memphis, TN 38104	Walter Parsons 2495 Sunset Drive Arlington, TN 38002
Jessica Pyun 1255 Miravista Street Memphis, TN 38122	Mia Rodriguez 8720 Natchez Trail Millington, TN 38053	Steven Scroggins 1518 Orchard Place Arlington, TN 38002
Michelle Trevino 648 Pine Cliff St. Bartlett, TN 38133	Leonard Wang 600 County Line NE Memphis, TN 38117	Monica Warren 5626 Summer Road #234 Lakeland, TN 38002
Alex Washington 15 Harwell Rd. Memphis, TN 38111	Sharon Williams 1251 Parker Road #843 Memphis, TN 38123	Bin Wu 676 North St. Clair St. Memphis, TN 38120

Lastname_Firstname_3B_Mailing_Labels

FIGURE 3.22 Project 3B Newsletter with Mailing Labels

Objective 5 Format a Multiple-Column Newsletter

Video W3-5

A ***newsletter*** is a periodical that communicates news and information to a specific group. Newsletters, as well as all newspapers and most magazines, use multiple columns for articles because text in narrower columns is easier to read than text that stretches across a page. You can create a newsletter in Word by changing a single column of text into two or more columns. If a column does not end where you want it to, you can end the column at a location of your choice by inserting a ***manual column break***—an artificial end to a column to balance columns or to provide space for the insertion of other objects.

Activity 3.15 | Changing One Column of Text to Two Columns

Newsletters are usually two or three columns wide. When using 8.5 × 11-inch paper in portrait orientation, avoid creating four or more columns because they are so narrow that word spacing looks awkward, often resulting in one long word on a line by itself.

1. Start Word. On Word's opening screen, in the lower left, click **Open Other Documents**. Navigate to your student files, and then locate and open the document **w03B_Environment_Newsletter**. If necessary, display the formatting marks and rulers. **Save** the file in your **Word Chapter 3** folder as **Lastname_Firstname_3B_Environment_Newsletter** and then add the file name to the footer.

2. Select the first paragraph of text—*University Medical Center Goes Green*. On the mini toolbar, change the **Font** to **Arial Black** and the **Font Size** to **18**.

3. Select the first two paragraphs—the title and the Volume information and date. On the mini toolbar, click the **Font Color button arrow**, and then under **Theme Colors**, in the fifth column, click the last color—**Blue, Accent 1, Darker 50%**.

4. With the text still selected, on the **HOME tab**, in the **Paragraph group**, click the **Borders button arrow**, and then at the bottom, click **Borders and Shading**.

5. In the **Borders and Shading** dialog box, on the **Borders tab**, click the **Color arrow**, and then under **Theme Colors**, in the fifth column, click the last color—**Blue, Accent 1, Darker 50%**.

6. Click the **Width arrow**, and then click **3 pt**. In the **Preview** box at the right, point to the *bottom* border of the preview and click one time. Compare your screen with Figure 3.23.

FIGURE 3.23

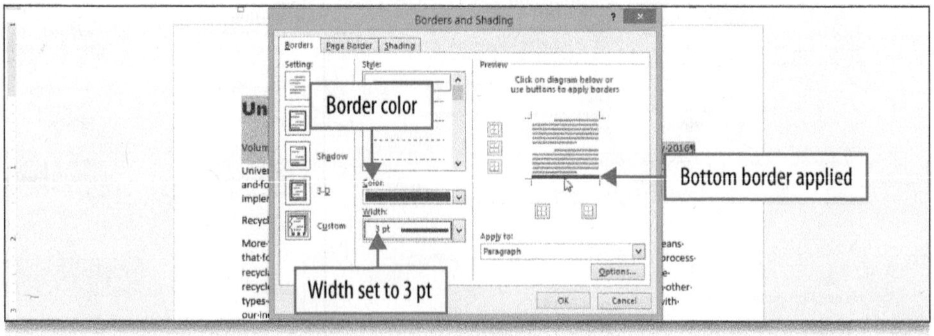

ANOTHER WAY In the Preview area, click the Bottom Border button.

7. In the **Borders and Shading** dialog box, click **OK**.

The line visually defines the newsletter's ***nameplate***—the banner on the front page of a newsletter that identifies the publication.

8 Below the Volume information, click at the beginning of the paragraph that begins *University Medical Center continues.* By using the vertical scroll box, scroll to view the lower portion of the document, hold down Shift, and then click after the paragraph mark at the end of the paragraph that begins *Electronic medical records* to select all of the text between the insertion point and the sentence ending with the word *space.* Be sure that the paragraph mark is included in the selection. Compare your screen with Figure 3.24.

Use Shift to define a selection that may be difficult to select by dragging.

FIGURE 3.24

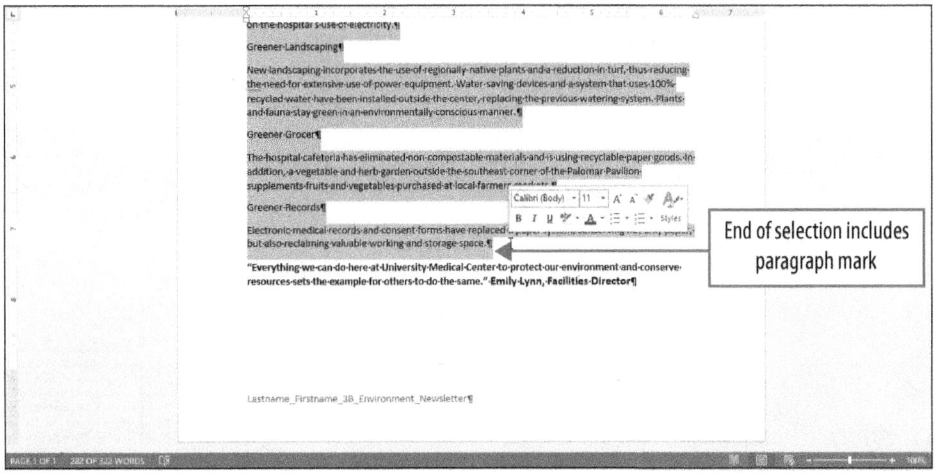

9 On the **PAGE LAYOUT tab**, in the **Page Setup group**, click **Columns**, and then click **Two.** Compare your screen with Figure 3.25, and then **Save** your newsletter.

Word divides the text into two columns and inserts a ***section break*** at the end of the selection, dividing the one-column section of the document from the two-column section of the document. A ***section*** is a portion of a document that can be formatted differently from the rest of the document. A section break marks the end of one section and the beginning of another section.

FIGURE 3.25

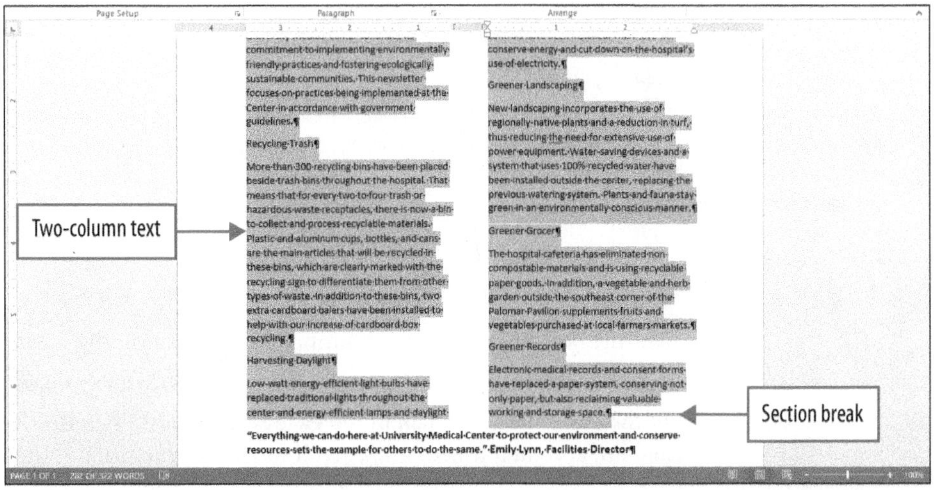

Activity 3.16 | Formatting Multiple Columns

The uneven right margin of a single page-width column is easy to read. When you create narrow columns, justified text is sometimes preferable. Depending on the design and layout of your newsletter, you might decide to reduce extra space between paragraphs and between columns to improve the readability of the document.

1 With the two columns of text still selected, on the **PAGE LAYOUT tab**, in the **Paragraph group**, click the **Spacing After down spin arrow** one time to change the spacing after to **6 pt**.

2 On the **HOME tab**, in the **Paragraph group**, click **Justify** .

3 Click anywhere in the document to deselect the text, compare your screen with Figure 3.26, and then **Save** .

FIGURE 3.26

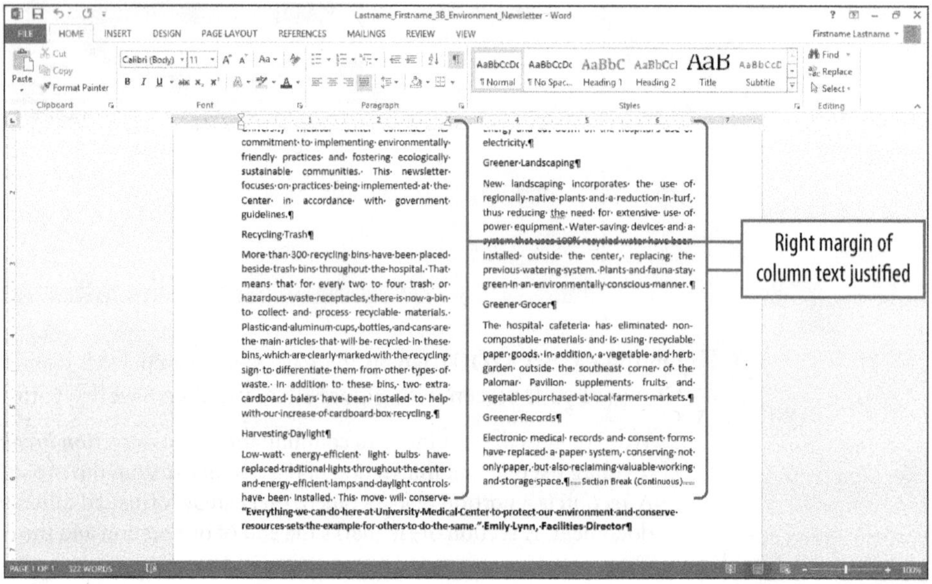

More Knowledge **Justifying Column Text**

Although many magazines and newspapers still justify text in columns, there are a variety of opinions about whether to justify the columns, or to use left alignment and leave the right edge uneven. Justified text tends to look more formal and cleaner, but in a word processing document, it also results in uneven spacing between words. It is the opinion of some authorities that justified text is more difficult to read, especially in a page-width document. Let the overall look and feel of your newsletter be your guide.

Activity 3.17 | Inserting a Column Break

1 Near the bottom of the first column, click to position the insertion point at the beginning of the line *Harvesting Daylight*.

2 On the **PAGE LAYOUT tab**, in the **Page Setup group**, click **Breaks**. Under **Page Breaks**, click **Column**, and then if necessary, scroll to view the bottom of the first column.

A column break displays at the bottom of the first column; text to the right of the column break moves to the top of the next column.

3 Compare your screen with Figure 3.27, and then **Save** .

A ***column break indicator***—a dotted line containing the words ***Column Break***—displays at the bottom of the column.

FIGURE 3.27

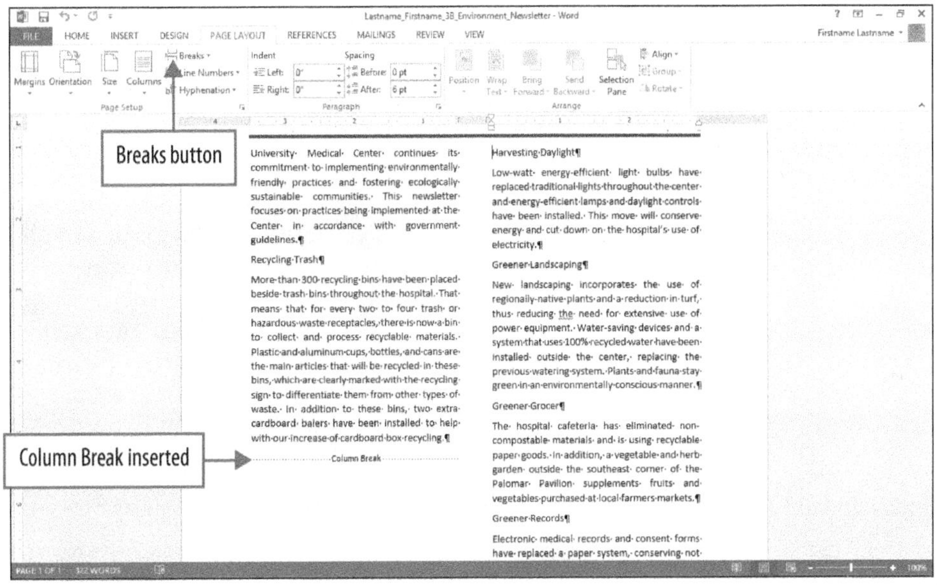

Activity 3.18 | Inserting an Online Picture

You can search for and insert online pictures in your document without saving the images to your computer. Pictures can make your document visually appealing and more interesting.

1. Press Ctrl + Home. On the **INSERT tab**, in the **Illustrations group**, click **Online Pictures.**

2. In the **Office.com Clip Art** search box, type **recycling bottles** so that Word can search for images that contain the keywords *recycling* and *bottles*. Press Enter.

3. Click the image of the recycle bin on a black background. Compare your screen with Figure 3.28. If the image does not display, close the Insert Pictures dialog box. Then, on the **INSERT tab**, in the **Illustrations group**, click **Pictures,** navigate to your student data files, and then double-click **w03B_Recycling.**

FIGURE 3.28

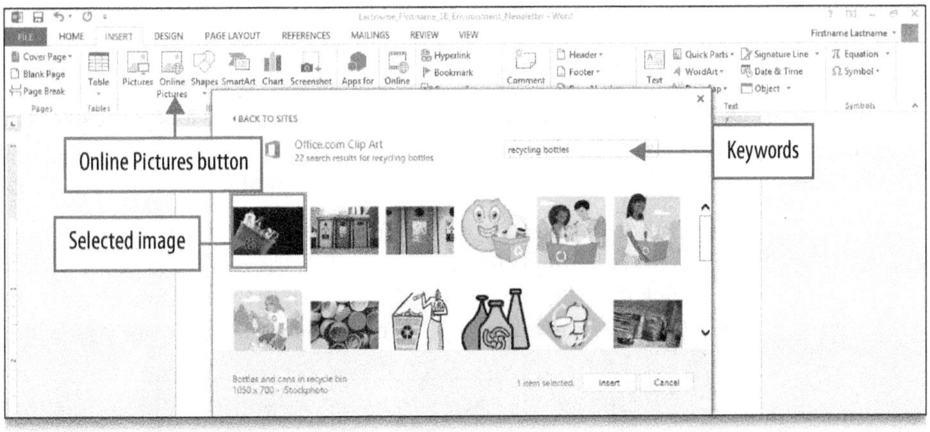

4 Click **Insert**, and then compare your screen with Figure 3.29.

FIGURE 3.29

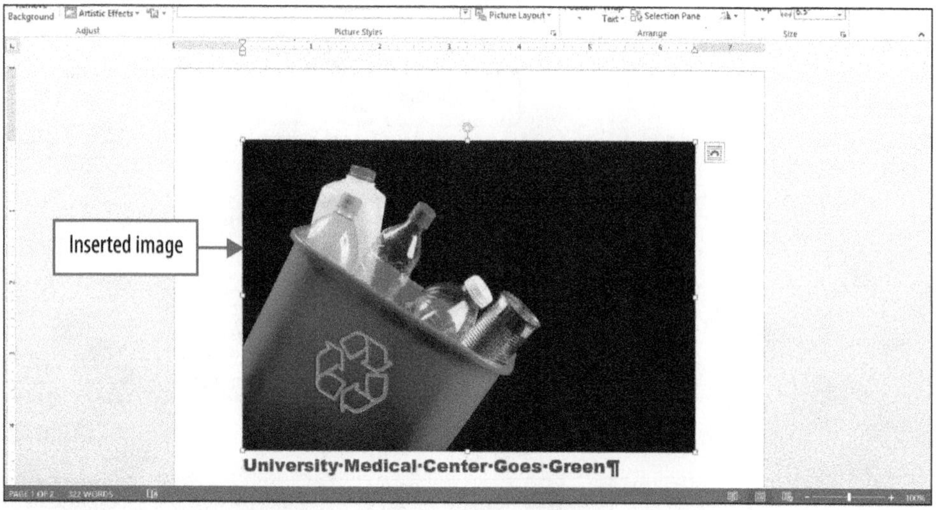

5 Press Ctrl + End to move to the end of the document. On the **INSERT tab**, in the **Illustrations group**, click **Online Pictures**. In the **Office.com Clip Art** search box, type **green recycling symbol** and then press Enter.

6 Click the first recycling symbol and then compare your screen with Figure 3.30. If the picture is not available, choose a similar picture.

FIGURE 3.30

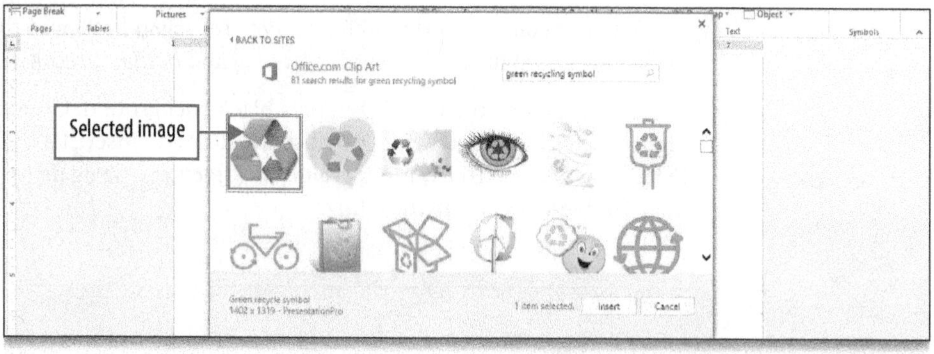

7 Click **Insert**. With the picture selected, on the **FORMAT tab**, in the **Size group**, click in the **Height** box. Type **0.5** and then press Enter. To the right of the picture, click **Layout Options**, and then click **Square**. At the bottom of the **Layout Options gallery**, click **See more**.

8 On the **Position tab**, under **Horizontal**, click the **Alignment** option button. Click the **Alignment arrow**, and then click **Centered**. Click the **relative to arrow** and then click **Page**. Under **Vertical**, click the **Alignment** option button. Click the **Alignment arrow**, and then click **Bottom**. Click the **relative to arrow**, and then click **Margin**. Compare your screen with Figure 3.31.

FIGURE 3.31

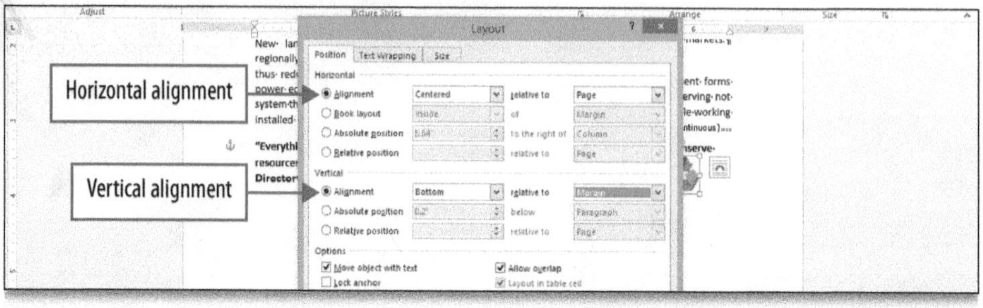

9 Click **OK**, scroll to the bottom of the page, and then notice that the recycle image displays at the bottom of the second page. **Save** the document.

ANOTHER WAY Drag the image to visually position the image.

Activity 3.19 | Cropping a Picture and Resizing a Picture by Scaling

In this activity, you will edit the recycle bin image by cropping and scaling the picture. When you ***crop*** a picture, you remove unwanted or unnecessary areas of the picture. When you ***scale*** a picture, you resize it to a percentage of its size.

1 Press Ctrl + Home to move to the top of the document, and then click the recycle bin picture to select it. On the **FORMAT tab**, in the **Size group**, click the upper portion of the **Crop** button to display crop handles around the picture. Compare your screen with Figure 3.32.

Crop handles are used like sizing handles to define unwanted areas of the picture.

FIGURE 3.32

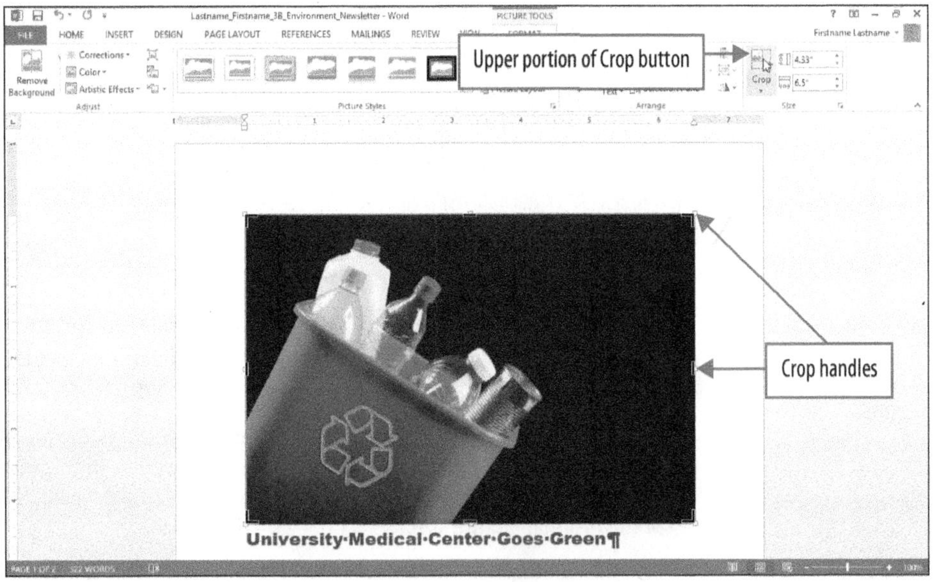

2 Point to the center right crop handle to display the pointer. Compare your screen with Figure 3.33.

Use the ***crop pointer*** to crop areas of a picture.

FIGURE 3.33

3 With the crop pointer displayed, hold down the left mouse button and drag to the left to approximately **5 inches on the horizontal ruler**, and then release the mouse button. Compare your screen with Figure 3.34.

The portion of the image to be removed displays in gray.

FIGURE 3.34

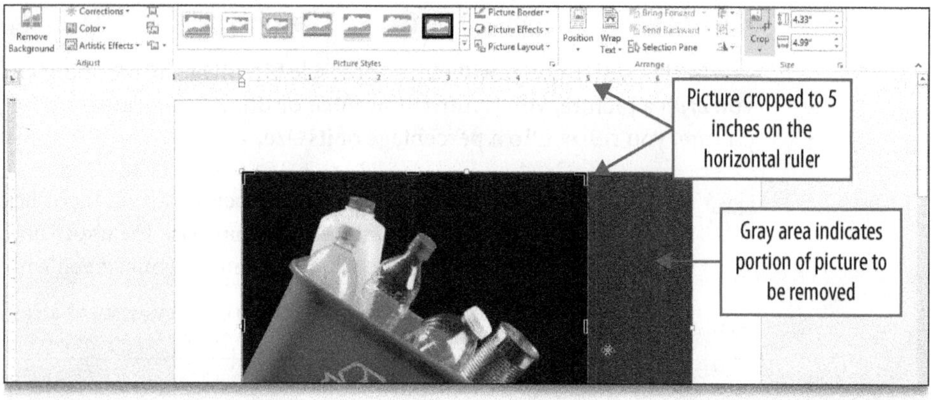

4 Click anywhere in the document outside of the image to apply the crop.

ANOTHER WAY Click the upper portion of the Crop button to apply the crop.

5 Click to select the picture again. On the **FORMAT tab**, in the **Size group**, click the **Dialog Box Launcher** button.

6 In the **Layout dialog box**, on the **Size tab**, under **Scale**, be sure that the **Lock aspect ratio** and **Relative to original picture size** check boxes are selected. Select the number in the **Height box**, type **10** and then press Tab. Compare your screen with Figure 3.35.

When *Lock aspect ratio* is selected, the height and width of the picture are sized proportionately and only one scale value is necessary. The second value—in this instance Width—adjusts proportionately. When *Relative to original picture size* is selected, the scale is applied as a percentage of the original picture size.

FIGURE 3.35

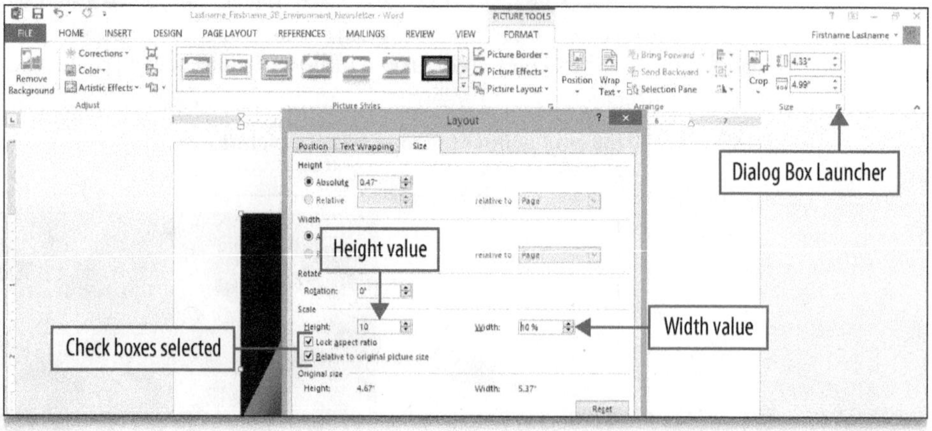

7 In the **Layout** dialog box, click the **Text Wrapping tab**. Under **Wrapping style**, click **Square**.

8 Click the **Position tab**, and then under **Horizontal**, click the **Alignment** option button. Be sure that the **Alignment** indicates **Left** and **relative to Column**. Under **Vertical**, click the **Alignment** option button, and then change the alignment to **Top relative to Margin**. Click **OK**, and then compare your screen with Figure 3.36.

FIGURE 3.36

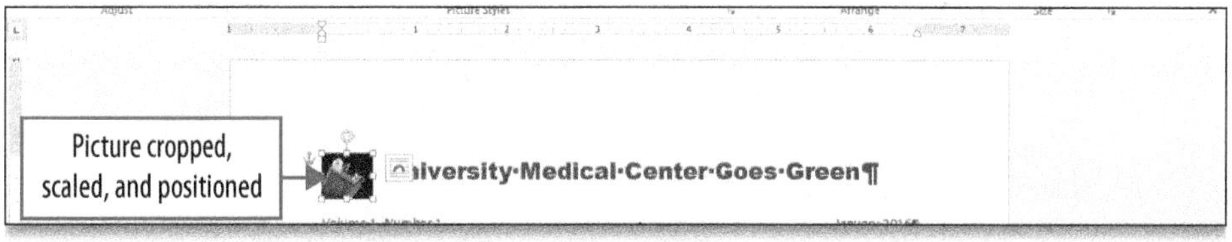

Activity 3.20 | Setting Transparent Color and Recoloring a Picture

You can make one color in a picture transparent using the Set Transparent Color command. When you ***recolor*** a picture, you change all the colors in the picture to shades of a single color.

1. On the **VIEW tab**, in the **Zoom group**, click **Zoom**, and then click **200%**. Click **OK**. Drag the scroll bars as necessary so that you can view the recycle bin picture at the top of the document.
2. If necessary, select the recycle bin picture. On the **FORMAT tab**, in the **Adjust group**, click **Color**, and then below the gallery, click **Set Transparent Color**. Move the pointer into the document to display the [pointer icon] pointer.
3. Point anywhere in the black background of the recycle bin picture, and then click to apply the transparent color to the background. Compare your screen with Figure 3.37.

FIGURE 3.37

4. Press Ctrl + End to move to the end of your document, and then select the picture of the recycle symbol. On the **FORMAT tab**, in the **Adjust group**, click **Color** to display a gallery of recoloring options. Under **Recolor**, in the last row, click the fourth option— **Olive Green, Accent color 3 Light**. Compare your screen with Figure 3.38, and then **Save** [Save icon] the document.

FIGURE 3.38

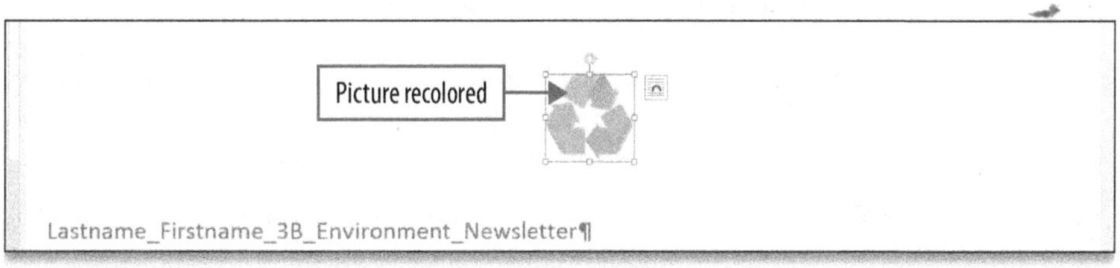

Activity 3.21 | Adjusting the Brightness and Contrast of a Picture

Brightness is the relative lightness of a picture. ***Contrast*** is the difference between the darkest and lightest area of a picture.

1. If necessary, select the recycle symbol. On the **FORMAT tab**, in the **Adjust group**, click **Corrections**. Under **Brightness/Contrast**, point to several of the options to view the effect that the settings have on the picture.

2 Under **Brightness/Contrast**, in the last row, click the first setting—**Brightness: -40% Contrast: +40%**. Compare your screen with Figure 3.39.

FIGURE 3.39

3 On the **VIEW tab**, in the **Zoom group**, click **100%**, and then **Save** the document.

Activity 3.22 | Applying a Border to a Picture and Flipping a Picture

The ***flip*** commands create a reverse image of a picture or object.

1 Press Ctrl + Home to move to the top of the document, and then select the picture of the recycle bin. On the **FORMAT tab**, in the **Picture Styles group**, click the **Picture Border button arrow**. Under **Theme Colors**, in the fourth column, click the first color—**Dark Blue, Text 2**.

2 Click the **Picture Border arrow** again, and then point to **Weight**. Click **1 1/2 pt** to change the thickness of the border.

3 On the **FORMAT tab**, in the **Arrange group**, click **Rotate Objects**, and then click **Flip Horizontal**. Click anywhere in the document to deselect the picture. **Save**, and then compare your screen with Figure 3.40.

FIGURE 3.40

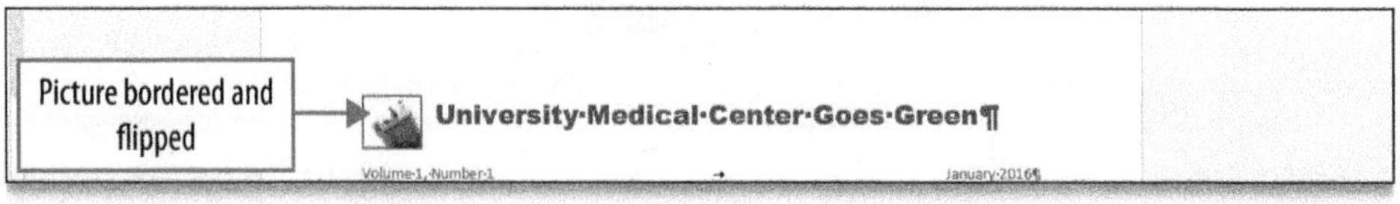

Activity 3.23 | Inserting a Screenshot

A ***screenshot*** is an image of an active window on your computer that you can paste into a document. Screenshots are especially useful when you want to insert an image of a website into your Word document. You can insert a screenshot of any open window on your computer.

1 In the paragraph that begins *University Medical Center continues*, click after the period at the end of the paragraph. Start Internet Explorer, and then navigate to **www.epa.gov/osw/conserve** and press Enter.

2 From the taskbar, redisplay your **3B_Environment_Newletter** document.

3 With the insertion point positioned at the end of the paragraph, on the **INSERT tab**, in the **Illustrations group**, click **Screenshot**.

All of your open windows display in the Available Windows gallery and are available to paste into the document.

4 In the **Screenshot** gallery, click the browser window that contains the EPA site to insert the screenshot at the insertion point. If a message box displays asking if you want to hyperlink the screenshot, click No, and then notice that the image is inserted and is sized to fit between the margins of the first column. Compare your screen with Figure 3.41.

By selecting No in the message box, you are inserting a screenshot without links to the actual website. Choose Yes, if you want to link the image to the website.

FIGURE 3.41

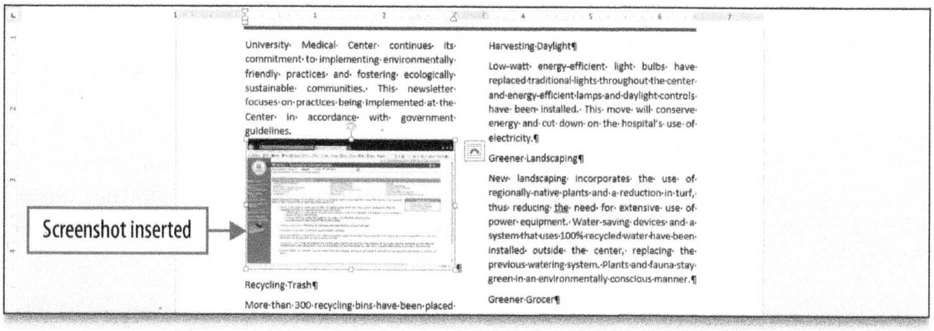

5 With the inserted screenshot selected, on the **FORMAT tab**, in the **Picture Styles group**, click the **Picture Border button arrow**, and then under **Theme Colors**, in the second column, click the first color—**Black, Text 1**.

6 **Save** the document.

Objective 6 Use Special Character and Paragraph Formatting

Video W3-6

Special text and paragraph formatting is useful to emphasize text, and it makes your newsletter look more professional. For example, you can place a border around one or more paragraphs or add shading to a paragraph. When adding shading, use light colors; dark shading can make the text difficult to read.

Activity 3.24 | Applying the Small Caps Font Effect

For headlines and titles, ***small caps*** is an attractive font effect. The effect changes lowercase letters to uppercase letters, but with the height of lowercase letters.

1 Under the screenshot, select the paragraph *Recycling Trash* including the paragraph mark.

2 Right-click the selected text, and then on the shortcut menu, click **Font** to display the **Font** dialog box. Click the **Font color arrow**, and then change the color to **Blue, Accent 1, Darker 50%**—in the fifth column, the last color.

3 Under **Font style**, click **Bold**. Under **Effects**, select the **Small caps** check box. Compare your screen with Figure 3.42.

The Font dialog box provides more options than are available on the ribbon and enables you to make several changes at the same time. In the Preview box, the text displays with the selected formatting options applied.

FIGURE 3.42

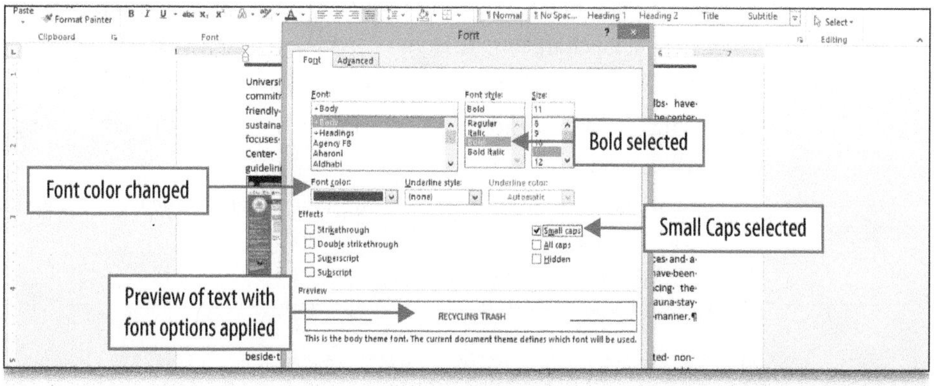

4 Click **OK**. With the text still selected, right-click, and then on the mini toolbar, double-click **Format Painter** . Then, in the second column, with the pointer, select each of the heading paragraphs—*Harvesting Daylight*, *Greener Landscaping*, *Greener Grocer*, and *Greener Records*—to apply the same formats. Press Esc to turn off **Format Painter**.

5 In the first column below the screenshot, notice that the space between the *Recycling Trash* subheading and the screenshot is fairly small. Click anywhere in the *Recycling Trash* subheading, and then on the **PAGE LAYOUT tab**, in the **Paragraph group**, click the **Before up spin arrow** two times to set the spacing to **12 pt**.

6 Compare your screen with Figure 3.43, and then **Save** your document.

FIGURE 3.43

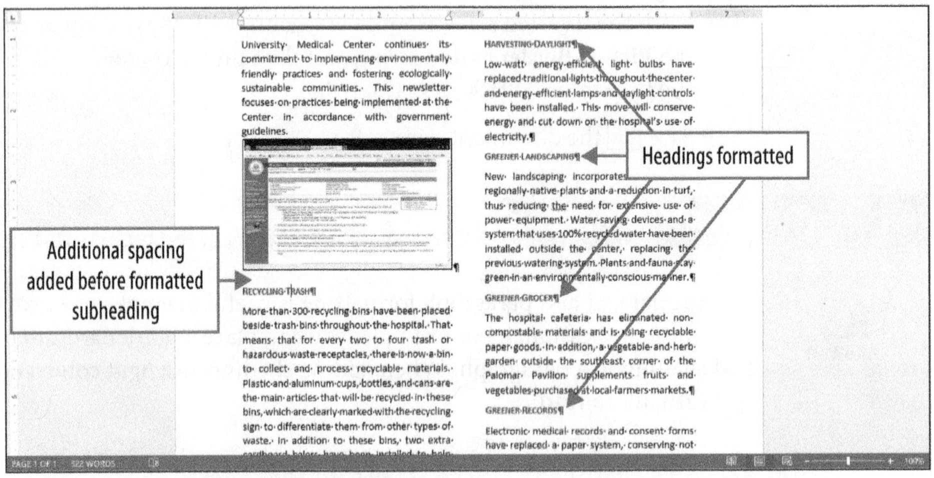

Activity 3.25 | Inserting Symbols and Special Characters

You can insert symbols and special characters in a Word document, including copyright symbols, trademark symbols, and em dashes. An ***em dash*** is a punctuation symbol used to indicate an explanation or emphasis.

1 Press Ctrl + End to move to the end of the document, and then after the name *Emily Lynn* delete the comma and the space that separates her name from her job title—*Facilities Director*.

2 With the insertion point positioned before the *F* in *Facilities*, on the **INSERT tab**, in the **Symbols group**, click **Symbol**. Below the gallery, click **More Symbols** to display the **Symbol** dialog box.

Here you can choose the symbol that you want to insert in your document.

3 In the **Symbol** dialog box, click the **Special Characters tab**. Scroll the list to view the types of special characters that you can insert; notice that some of the characters can be inserted using a Shortcut key.

4 Click **Em Dash**, and then in the lower right portion of the dialog box, click **Insert**. Compare your screen with Figure 3.44.

An em dash displays between the name *Lynn* and the word *Facilities*.

FIGURE 3.44

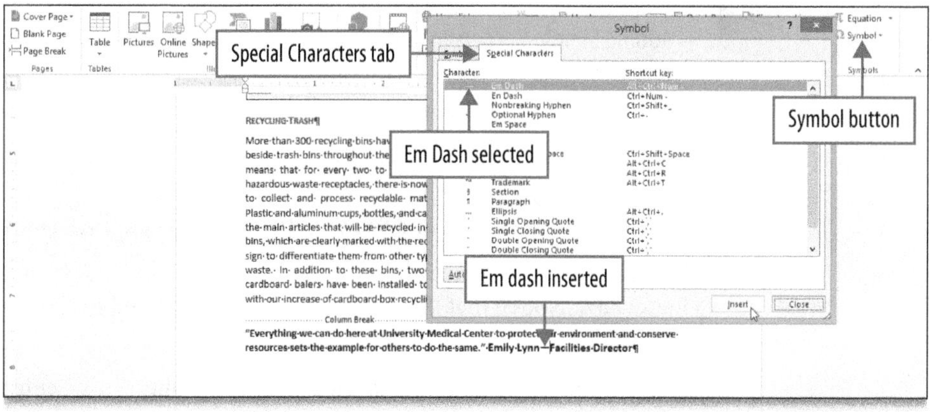

5 In the **Symbol** dialog box, click **Close**, and then **Save** your document.

Activity 3.26 | Adding Borders and Shading to a Paragraph and Inserting a Manual Line Break

Paragraph borders provide strong visual cues to the reader. You can use paragraph shading with or without borders; however, combined with a border, light shading can be very effective in drawing the reader's eye to the text.

1 At the end of the document, select the two lines of bold text that begin *"Everything we can do.*

The recycle picture may also be selected because it is anchored to the paragraph.

2 On the **HOME tab**, in the **Paragraph group**, click the **Borders button arrow**, and then click **Borders and Shading**.

3 In the **Borders and Shading** dialog box, be sure the **Borders tab** is selected. Under **Setting**, click **Shadow**. Click the **Color arrow**, and then in the fifth column, click the last color—**Blue, Accent 1, Darker 50%**. Click the **Width arrow**, and then click **1 pt**. Compare your screen with Figure 3.45.

In the lower right portion of the Borders and Shading dialog box, the *Apply to* box indicates *Paragraph*. The *Apply to* box directs where the border will be applied—in this instance, the border will be applied only to the selected paragraph.

FIGURE 3.45

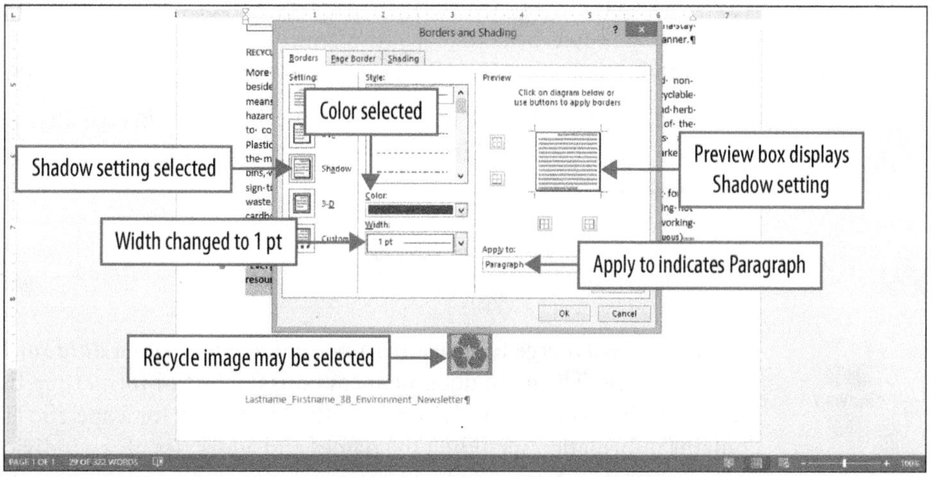

NOTE **Adding Simple Borders to Text**

You can add simple borders from the Borders button gallery, located in the Paragraph group. This button offers less control over the border appearance, however, because the line thickness and color applied will match the most recently used on this computer. The Borders and Shading dialog box enables you to make your own custom selections.

4 At the top of the **Borders and Shading** dialog box, click the **Shading tab**.

5 Click the **Fill arrow**, and then in the fifth column, click the second color—**Blue, Accent 1, Lighter 80%**. Notice that the shading change is reflected in the **Preview area** on the right side of the dialog box.

6 Click **OK**. On the **HOME tab**, in the **Paragraph group**, click **Center**.

7 Click anywhere in the document to deselect, and then compare your screen with Figure 3.46.

FIGURE 3.46

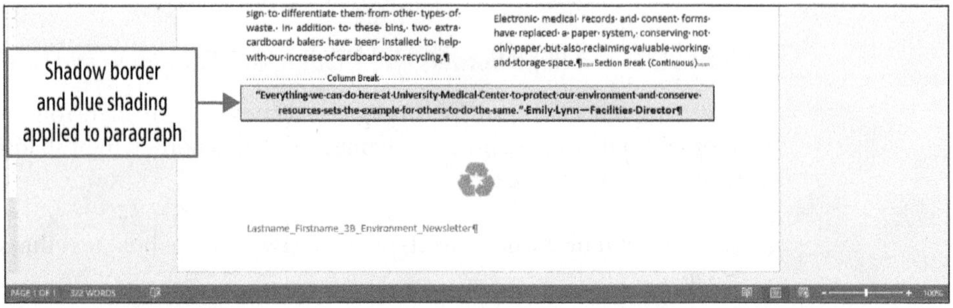

8 In the shaded paragraph, in the second line, click in front of the *E* in the name *Emily*. Hold down Shift and then press Enter.

Holding down Shift while pressing Enter inserts a ***manual line break***, which moves the text to the right of the insertion point to a new line while keeping the text in the same paragraph. A ***line break indicator***, in the shape of a bent arrow, indicates a manual line break.

9 Press Ctrl + Home to move the insertion point to the top of the document. Click the **FILE tab** to display **Backstage** view. On the right, at the bottom of the **Properties** list, click **Show All Properties**.

10 On the list of **Properties**, click to the right of **Tags**, and then type **newsletter, January**

11 Click to the right of **Subject**, and then type your course name and section number. Under **Related People**, be sure that your name displays as the author. If necessary, right-click the author name, click **Edit Property**, type your name, and click **OK**.

12 On the left, click **Print** to display the **Print Preview**, make any necessary corrections, and then **Save** the document. **Close** Word; hold this file until you complete this project. If necessary, close Internet Explorer.

Objective 7 Create Mailing Labels Using Mail Merge

Video W3-7

Word's ***mail merge*** feature joins a ***main document*** and a ***data source*** to create customized letters or labels. The main document contains the text or formatting that remains constant. For labels, the main document contains the formatting for a specific label size. The data source contains information including the names and addresses of the individuals for whom the labels are being created. Names and addresses in a data source might come from a Word table, an Excel worksheet, or an Access database.

The easiest way to perform a mail merge is to use the Mail Merge Wizard, which asks you questions and, based on your answers, walks you step by step through the mail merge process.

Activity 3.27 | Starting the Mail Merge Wizard Template

In this activity, you will open the data source for the mail merge, which is a Word table containing names and addresses.

1 Start Word and display a new blank document. Display formatting marks and rulers. **Save** the document in your **Word Chapter 3** folder as **Lastname_Firstname_3B_Mailing_Labels**

2 With your new document open on the screen, from your student files, **Open** the file **w03B_Addresses. Save** the address file in your **Word Chapter 3** folder as **Lastname_Firstname_3B_Addresses** and then add the file name to the footer.

This document contains a table of addresses. The first row contains the column names. The remaining rows contain the names and addresses.

3 Click to position the insertion point in the last cell in the table, and then press Tab to create a new row. Enter the following information, and then compare your table with Figure 3.47.

FIRST NAME	LAST NAME	ADDRESS 1	UNIT	CITY	STATE	ZIP CODE
Monica	Warren	5626 Summer Road	#234	Lakeland	TN	38002

FIGURE 3.47

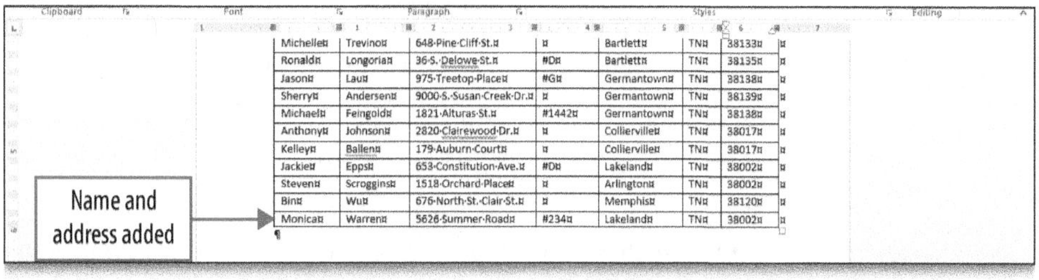

4 **Save** , and then **Close** the table of addresses. Be sure that your blank **Lastname_Firstname_3B_Mailing_Labels** document displays.

5 Click the **MAILINGS tab**. In the **Start Mail Merge group**, click **Start Mail Merge**, and then click **Step-by-Step Mail Merge Wizard** to display the **Mail Merge** pane on the right.

6 In the **Mail Merge** pane, under **Select document type**, click **Labels**. At the bottom of the **Mail Merge** pane, click **Next: Starting document** to display Step 2 of 6.

7 Under **Select starting document**, be sure **Change document layout** is selected, and then under **Change document layout**, click **Label options**.

8 In the **Label Options** dialog box, under **Printer information**, click the **Tray arrow**, and then if necessary, click **Default tray** (Automatically Select)—the exact wording may vary depending on your printer, but select the *Default* or *Automatic* option so that you can print the labels on regular paper rather than manually inserting labels in the printer.

9 Under **Label information**, click the **Label vendors arrow**, and then click **Avery US Letter**. Under **Product number**, scroll about halfway down the list, and then click **5160 Easy Peel Address Labels**. Compare your screen with Figure 3.48.

The Avery 5160 address label is a commonly used label. The precut sheets contain three columns of 10 labels each—for a total of 30 labels per sheet.

FIGURE 3.48

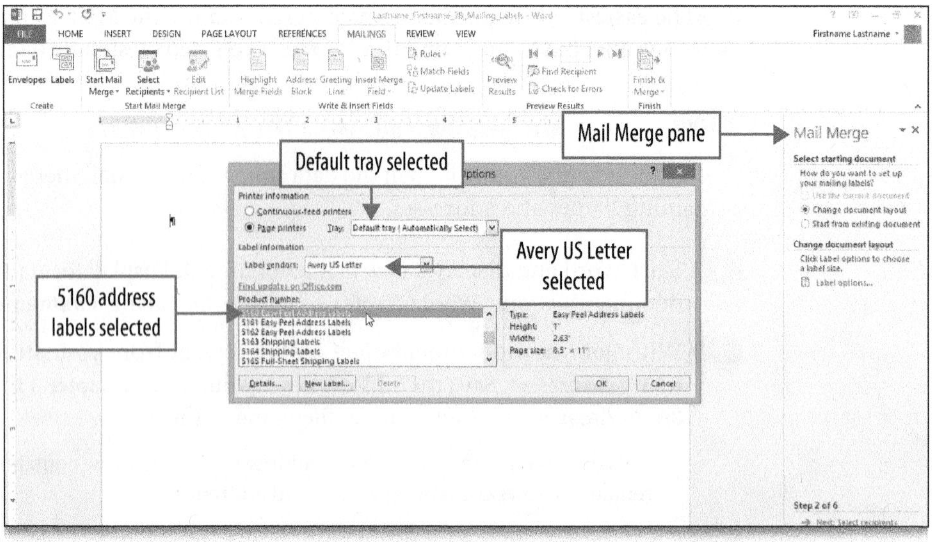

10 At the bottom of the **Label Options** dialog box, click **OK**. If a message box displays, click **OK** to set up the labels. If the gridlines do not display, on the **Layout tab**, in the **Table** group, click **View Gridlines**. At the bottom of the **Mail Merge** pane, click **Next: Select recipients**.

The label page is set up with three columns and ten rows. Here, in Step 3 of the Mail Merge Wizard, you must identify the recipients—the data source. For your recipient data source, you can choose to use an existing list—for example, a list of names and addresses that you have in an Access database, an Excel worksheet, a Word table, or your Outlook contacts list. If you do not have an existing data source, you can type a new list at this point in the wizard.

11 In the **Mail Merge** pane, under **Select recipients**, be sure the **Use an existing list** option button is selected. Under **Use an existing list**, click **Browse**.

12 Navigate to your **Word Chapter 3** folder, select your **Lastname_Firstname_3B_Addresses** file, and then click **Open** to display the **Mail Merge Recipients** dialog box. Compare your screen with Figure 3.49.

In the Mail Merge Recipients dialog box, the column headings are formed from the text in the first row of your Word table of addresses. Each row of information that contains data for one person is referred to as a ***record***. The column headings—for example, *Last_Name* and *First_Name*—are referred to as ***fields***. An underscore replaces the spaces between words in the field name headings.

FIGURE 3.49

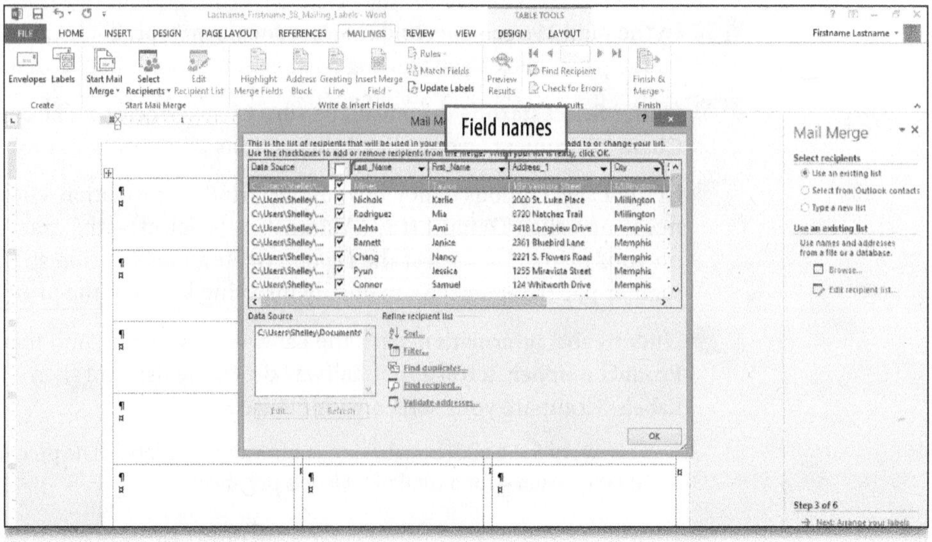

13 In the lower left portion of the **Mail Merge Recipients** dialog box, in the **Data Source** box, click the path that contains your file name. Then, at the bottom of the **Mail Merge Recipients** dialog box, click **Edit**.

14 In the upper right corner of the **Data Form** dialog box, click **Add New**. In the blank record, type the following, pressing Tab to move from field to field, and then compare your **Data Form** dialog box with Figure 3.50.

FIRST_NAME	LAST_NAME	ADDRESS_1	UNIT	CITY	STATE	ZIP CODE
Sharon	Williams	1251 Parker Road	#843	Memphis	TN	38123

FIGURE 3.50

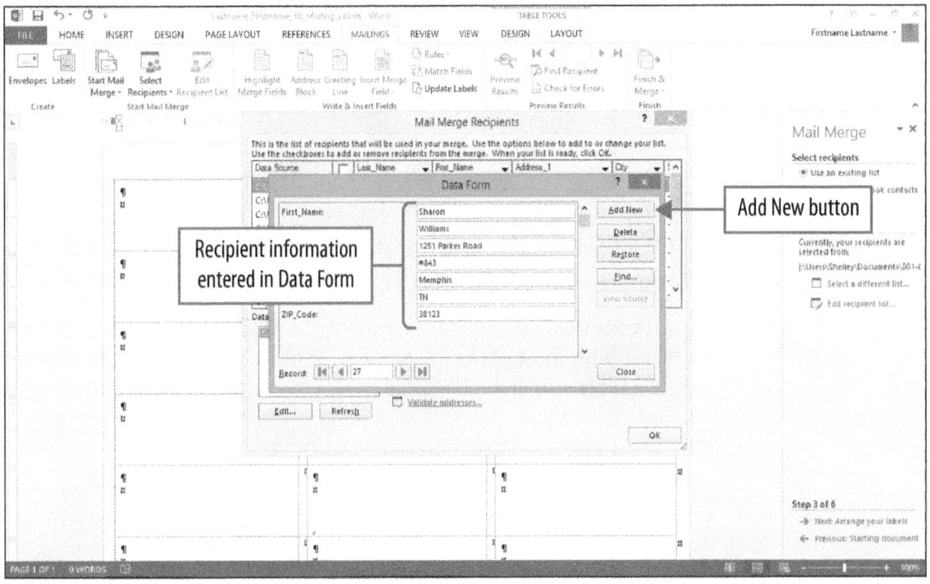

15 In the lower right corner of the **Data Form** dialog box, click **Close**. Scroll to the end of the recipient list to confirm that the record for *Sharon Williams* that you just added is in the list. At the bottom of the **Mail Merge Recipients** dialog box, click **OK**.

Activity 3.28 | Completing the Mail Merge Wizard

You can add or edit names and addresses while completing the Mail Merge. You can also match your column names with preset names used in Mail Merge.

1 At the bottom of the **Mail Merge** pane, click **Next: Arrange your labels.**

2 Under **Arrange your labels**, click **Address block**. In the **Insert Address Block** dialog box, under **Specify address elements**, examine the various formats for names. If necessary, under *Insert recipient's name in this format*, select the *Joshua Randall Jr.* format. Compare your dialog box with Figure 3.51.

FIGURE 3.51

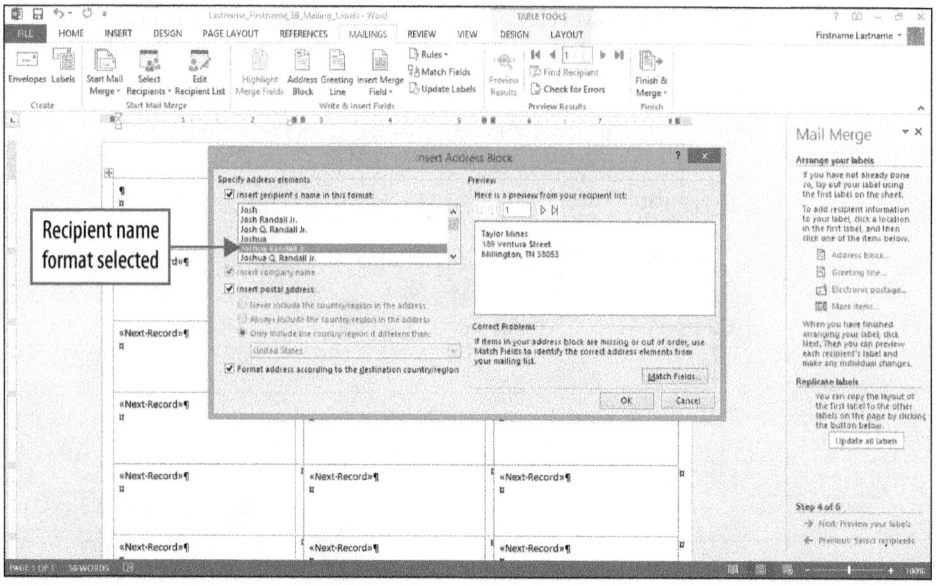

3 In the lower right corner of the **Insert Address Block** dialog box, click **Match Fields**, and then compare your screen with Figure 3.52.

If your field names are descriptive, the Mail Merge program will identify them correctly, as is the case with most of the information in the *Required for Address Block* section. However, the Address 2 field is unmatched—in the source file, this column is named *Unit*.

FIGURE 3.52

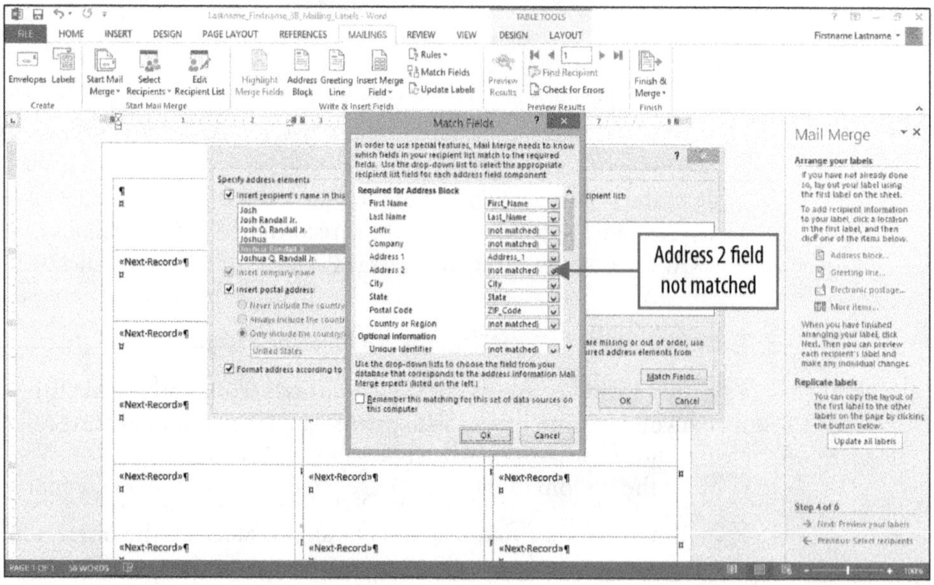

4 Click the **Address 2 arrow**, and then from the list of available fields, click **Unit** to match the Mail Merge field with the field in your data source.

5 At the bottom of the **Match Fields** dialog box, click **OK**. At the bottom of the **Insert Address Block** dialog box, click **OK**.

Word inserts the Address block in the first label space surrounded by double angle brackets. The *AddressBlock* field name displays, which represents the address block you saw in the Preview area of the Insert Address Block dialog box.

6 In the **Mail Merge** pane, under **Replicate labels**, click **Update all labels** to insert an address block in each label space for each subsequent record.

7 At the bottom of the **Mail Merge** pane, click **Next: Preview your labels**. Notice that for addresses with four lines, the last line of the address is cut off.

8 Press Ctrl + A to select all of the label text, click the **PAGE LAYOUT tab**, and then in the **Paragraph group**, click in the **Spacing Before** box. Type **3** and press Enter.

9 Click in any label to deselect, and notice that 4-line addresses are no longer cut off. Compare your screen with Figure 3.53.

FIGURE 3.53

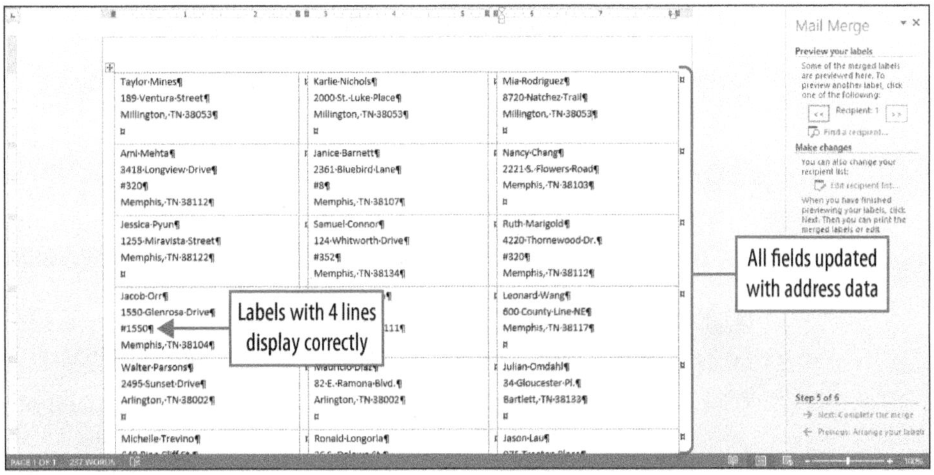

10 At the bottom of the **Mail Merge** pane, click **Next: Complete the merge.**

Step 6 of the Mail Merge displays. At this point you can print or edit your labels, although this is done more easily in the document window.

11 **Save** your labels, and then on the right, **Close** the **Mail Merge** pane.

Activity 3.29 | Sorting Mail Merge Results

If you discover that you need to make further changes to your labels, you can still make them even though the Mail Merge task pane is closed.

1 Add the file name to the footer, close the footer area, and then move to the top of Page 2. Click anywhere in the empty table row, and then click the **LAYOUT tab**. In the **Rows & Columns group**, click **Delete**, and then click **Delete Rows**.

Adding footer text to a label sheet replaces the last row of labels on a page with the footer text, and moves the last row of labels to the top of the next page. In this instance, a blank second page is created, which you can delete by deleting the blank row.

2 Notice that the labels do not display in alphabetical order. Click the **MAILINGS tab**, and then in the **Start Mail Merge group**, click **Edit Recipient List** to display the list of names and addresses.

3 In the **Mail Merge Recipients** dialog box, click the **Last_Name** field heading, and notice that the names are sorted alphabetically by the recipient's last name.

Mailing labels are often sorted by either last name or by ZIP Code.

4 Click the **Last_Name** field heading again, and notice that the last names are sorted in descending order. Click the **Last_Name** field one more time to return to ascending order, and then click **OK**. Press Ctrl + Home, and then compare your screen with Figure 3.54.

FIGURE 3.54

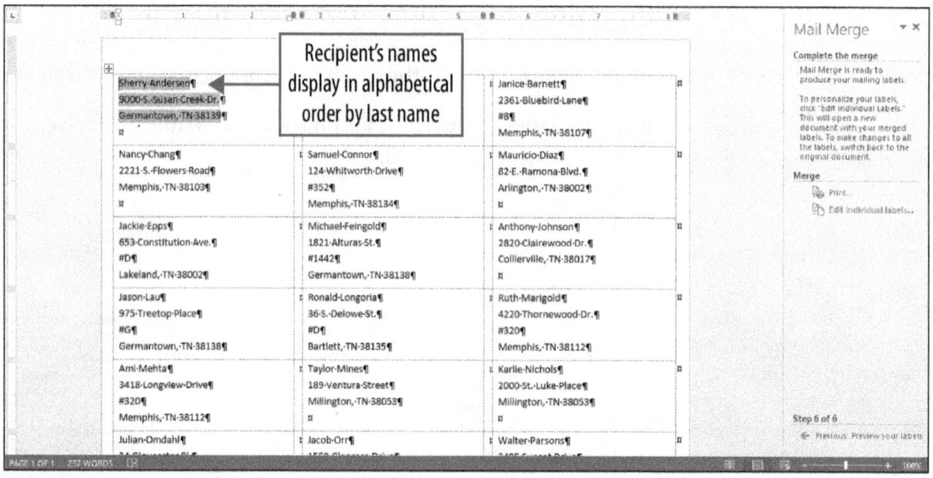

5 Click the **FILE tab**. On the right, at the bottom of the **Properties** list, click **Show All Properties**. On the list of **Properties**, click to the right of **Tags**, and then type **labels**

6 Click to the right of **Subject**, and then type your course name and section number. Be sure that your name displays as the author. If necessary, right-click the author name, click **Edit Property**, type your name, and click **OK**. **Save** the file. **Close** the document, and click **Yes** to save the data source.

7 As directed by your instructor, print or submit electronically.

If you print, the labels will print on whatever paper is in the printer; unless you have preformatted labels available, the labels will print on a sheet of paper. Printing the labels on plain paper enables you to proofread the labels before you print them on more expensive label sheets.

8 In addition to your labels and address document, print or submit your **Lastname_Firstname_3B_Environment_Newsletter** document as directed. **Close** Word.

END | You have completed Project 3B

GO! with Office Online (formerly Web Apps)

Objective Format a Single-Column Newsletter in Word Online

You can use Word Online to insert clip art and to format text. You can change fonts and font color, and modify paragraph spacing.

ALERT! Working with Web-Based Applications and Services

Computer programs and services on the web receive continuous updates and improvements, so the steps to complete this web-based activity may differ from the ones shown. You can often look at the screens and the information presented to determine how to complete the activity.

Activity | Formatting a Single-Column Newsletter

In this activity, you will use Word Online to edit a single-column newsletter similar to the one you edited in Project 3B.

1 From the desktop, start Internet Explorer. Navigate to **http://onedrive.com**, and then sign in to your Microsoft account. Open your **GO! Web Projects** folder; or create this folder if necessary.

2 In the OneDrive menu bar, click **Upload**. Navigate to your student data files, click **w03_3B_Web**, and then click **Open**.

3 Point to the uploaded file **w03_3B_Web**, and then right-click. On the shortcut menu, scroll as necessary, and then click **Rename**. Using your own last name and first name, type **Lastname_Firstname_WD_3B_Web** and then press Enter to rename the file.

4 Click the file that you just renamed, and then click **EDIT DOCUMENT**. On the list, click **Edit in Word Online**.

5 Drag to select the newsletter title—*University Medical Center Goes Green*. On the **HOME tab**, in the **Font group**, locate and click the **Grow Font button** two times to change the font size to **18**. With the newsletter title still selected, on the **HOME tab**, in the **Font group**, click **Font Color**, and then in the fifth column, click the last color—**Blue Gray, Accent 1, Darker 50%**. Apply the same **Font Color** to the five subheadings—*Recycling Trash*, *Harvesting Daylight*, *Greener Landscaping*, *Greener Grocer*, and *Greener Records*.

6 Drag to select the first subheading—*Recycling Trash*. On the **PAGE LAYOUT tab**, in the **Paragraph group**, click in the **After box**. Type **12** and then press Enter—or click the arrow as necessary. Apply the same **Spacing After** to the remaining four subheadings—*Harvesting Daylight*, *Greener Landscaping*, *Greener Grocer*, and *Greener Records*. Click anywhere in the document, and then press Ctrl + Home to move to the top of the document. Compare your screen with Figure A.

FIGURE A

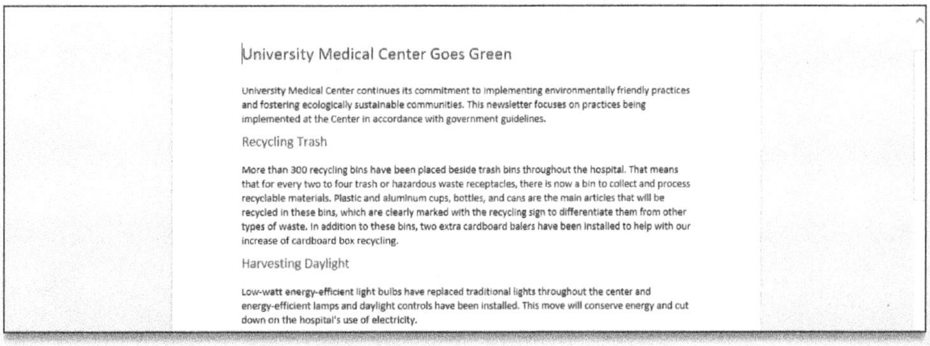

(GO! with Office Online (formerly Web Apps) continues on the next page)

7 Be sure the insertion point is positioned at the top of the document. On the **PAGE LAYOUT tab**, in the **Page Setup group**, click **Margins**, and then click **Custom Margins**. Click in the **Top** box and type **0.5** and then click in the **Bottom** box. Type **0.5** and then click **OK**.

8 On the **INSERT tab**, in the **Pictures group**, click **Picture**. Navigate to your student data files, and then click **w03B_Recycling**. Click **Insert**.

9 On the **FORMAT tab**, in the **Image Size group**, click in the **Scale** box. Type **5** to replace the existing number, and then press Enter. On the **FORMAT tab**, in the **Picture Styles group**, use the ScreenTips to locate and then click **Reflected Rounded Rectangle**.

10 Deselect the picture. Press Ctrl + End to move to the end of the document, and then press Enter. On the **INSERT tab**, in the **Pictures group**, click **Clip Art**. In the **Search** box, type **green recycle symbol** and then press Enter. Click the image of the green recycle symbol that you used in Project 3B. If the image is not available, choose a similar picture. Click **Insert**.

11 On the **FORMAT tab**, in the **Image Size group**, click in the **Scale** box. Type **5** to replace the existing number, and then press Enter. On the **HOME tab**, in the **Paragraph group**, click **Center**.

12 In the last paragraph of the newsletter, click to position the insertion point between the second quotation mark and the letter *E* in *Emily*. Hold down Shift and then press Enter to insert a manual line break. On the **HOME tab**, in the **Paragraph group**, click **Center** to center the three lines of text in the last paragraph. Deselect the picture and then compare your screen with Figure B.

13 Submit your file as directed by your instructor. Sign out of your OneDrive and close Internet Explorer.

FIGURE B

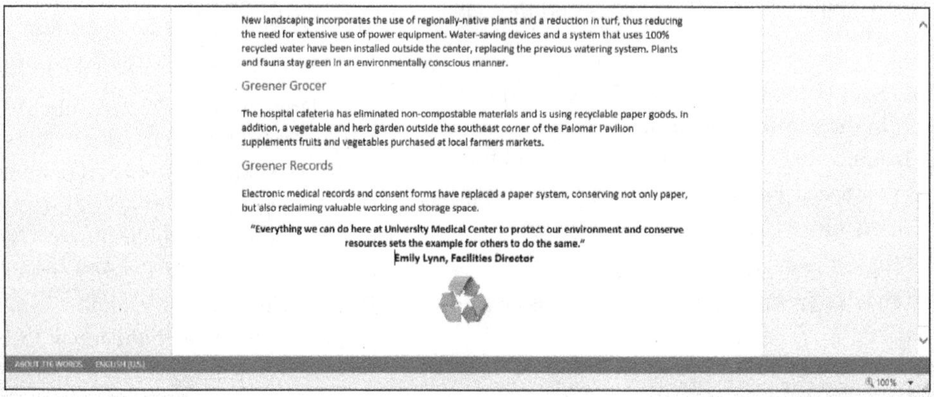

GO! with Microsoft Office 365

Andrew Rodriguez / Fotolia; FotolEdhar/ Fotolia; apops/ Fotolia; Yuri Arcurs/ Fotolia

The advantage of using Office 365 is that your organization does not have to purchase and install server hardware and software for sophisticated business applications and does not need a full-time IT person or staff just to manage the technology your teams need.

By using Office 365, you are able to have business-class services for your employees without investing in expensive hardware, software, and personnel. However, at least one person in an organization must be designated as the ***Office 365 Administrator***—the person who creates and manages the account, adds new users, sets up the services your organization wants to use, sets permission levels, and manages the SharePoint team sites. You can have more than one Administrator if you want to share these tasks with others.

Microsoft provides easy-to-use instructions and videos to get you started, and you might also have contact with a Microsoft representative. You will probably find, however, that subscribing to and setting up the account, adding users, and activating services is a straightforward process that requires little or no assistance.

After purchasing the required number of licenses, you will add each team member as a user that includes his or her email address.

The Admin Overview page, as shown in the Figure below, assists the Office 365 Administrator. On the left, there are links to manage the users and domains in your Office 365 account. This is where you can add new users, delete users, set permission levels, enter and change passwords, and update the user properties and the licenses.

In the center, you can see the various services available to you in Office 365. In the site shown in Figure A, Outlook, Lync, SharePoint (team sites), and a public-facing website are all part of the services.

Activity | Using a Team Site to Collaborate

This group project relates to the **Bell Orchid Hotels.** If your instructor assigns this project to your class, you can expect to use a SharePoint team site in **Office 365** to collaborate on the following tasks for this chapter:

- If you are in the **Accounting Group**, you and your teammates will finalize the report to shareholders, merge the letter with the labels, and post the final report on the SharePoint team site.
- If you are in the **Engineering Group**, you and your teammates will finalize the report to the three insurance companies, merge the letter with the labels, and post the final report on the SharePoint team site.
- If you are in the **Food and Beverage Group**, you and your teammates will finalize the letter to customers planning a banquet, merge the letter with the labels, and post the final letter on the SharePoint team site.
- If you are in the **Human Resources Group**, you and your teammates will finalize the memo to employees, merge the memo with the labels, and post the final memo on the SharePoint team site.
- If you are in the **Operations Group**, you and your teammates will finalize the letter to job applicants, merge the letter with the labels, and post the final letter on the SharePoint team site.
- If you are in the **Sales and Marketing Group**, you and your teammates will finalize the letter to the 20 professional associations, merge the letter with the labels, and post the final letter on the SharePoint team site.

FIGURE A

END OF CHAPTER

SUMMARY

Word assists you in formatting a research paper for college or business by providing built-in styles and applies the most commonly used footnote and citation styles for research papers—MLA and APA.

Word helps you create the bibliography for your research paper by recording all of your citations in the Source Manager, and then generating the bibliography—in MLA, called Works Cited—for you.

Newsletters are often used by organizations to communicate information to a specific group. A newsletter can be formatted in two columns with a nameplate at the top that identifies the publication.

The Mail Merge Wizard enables you to easily merge a main document and a data source to create customized letters or labels. The data source can be a Word table, Excel spreadsheet, or Access database.

GO! LEARN IT ONLINE

Review the concepts and key terms in this chapter by completing these online challenges, which you can find at **www.pearsonhighered.com/go**.

Matching and Multiple Choice: Answer matching and multiple choice questions to test what you learned in this chapter. MyITLab®

Crossword Puzzle: Spell out the words that match the numbered clues, and put them in the puzzle squares.

Flipboard: Flip through the definitions of the key terms in this chapter and match them with the correct term.

GO! FOR JOB SUCCESS

Video: Email Etiquette

Your instructor may assign this video to your class, and then ask you to think about, or discuss with your classmates, these questions:

FotolEdhar / Fotolia

Why do you think it is important to follow specific etiquette when composing email?

Why is it important to include a greeting and sign every email that you send?

What are the differences between sending a business email and a personal email, and what are three specific things you should never do in a business email?

END OF CHAPTER

REVIEW AND ASSESSMENT GUIDE FOR WORD CHAPTER 3

Your instructor may assign one or more of these projects to help you review the chapter and assess your mastery and understanding of the chapter.

Review and Assessment Guide for Word Chapter 3			
Project	**Apply Skills from These Chapter Objectives**	**Project Type**	**Project Location**
3C	Objectives 1-4 from Project 3A	**3C Skills Review** A guided review of the skills from Project 3A.	On the following pages
3D	Objectives 5-7 from Project 3B	**3D Skills Review** A guided review of the skills from Project 3B.	On the following pages
3E	Objectives 1-4 from Project 3A	**3E Mastery (Grader Project)** A demonstration of your mastery of the skills in Project 3A with extensive decision making.	In MyITLab and on the following pages
3F	Objectives 5-7 from Project 3B	**3F Mastery (Grader Project)** A demonstration of your mastery of the skills in Project 3B with extensive decision making.	In MyITLab and on the following pages
3G	Objectives 1-7 from Projects 3A and 3B	**3G Mastery (Grader Project)** A demonstration of your mastery of the skills in Projects 3A and 3B with extensive decision making.	In MyITLab and on the following pages
3H	Combination of Objectives from Projects 3A and 3B	**3H GO! Fix It** A demonstration of your mastery of the skills in Projects 3A and 3B by creating a correct result from a document that contains errors you must find.	Online
3I	Combination of Objectives from Projects 3A and 3B	**3I GO! Make It** A demonstration of your mastery of the skills in Projects 3A and 3B by creating a result from a supplied picture.	Online
3J	Combination of Objectives from Projects 3A and 3B	**3J GO! Solve It** A demonstration of your mastery of the skills in Projects 3A and 3B, your decision-making skills, and your critical thinking skills. A task-specific rubric helps you self-assess your result.	Online
3K	Combination of Objectives from Projects 3A and 3B	**3K GO! Solve It** A demonstration of your mastery of the skills in Projects 3A and 3B, your decision-making skills, and your critical thinking skills. A task-specific rubric helps you self-assess your result.	On the following pages
3L	Combination of Objectives from Projects 3A and 3B	**3L GO! Think** A demonstration of your understanding of the chapter concepts applied in a manner that you would outside of college. An analytic rubric helps you and your instructor grade the quality of your work by comparing it to the work an expert in the discipline would create.	On the following pages
3M	Combination of Objectives from Projects 3A and 3B	**3M GO! Think** A demonstration of your understanding of the chapter concepts applied in a manner that you would outside of college. An analytic rubric helps you and your instructor grade the quality of your work by comparing it to the work an expert in the discipline would create.	Online
3N	Combination of Objectives from Projects 3A and 3B	**3N You and GO!** A demonstration of your understanding of the chapter concepts applied in a manner that you would in a personal situation. An analytic rubric helps you and your instructor grade the quality of your work.	Online
3O	Combination of Objectives from Projects 3A and 3B	**3O Cumulative Group Project for Word Chapter 3** A demonstration of your understanding of concepts and your ability to work collaboratively in a group role-playing assessment, requiring both collaboration and self-management.	Online
Capstone Project for Word Chapters 1-3	Combination of Objectives from Projects 1A, 1B, 2A, 2B, 3A, and 3B	A demonstration of your mastery of the skills in Chapters 1-3 with extensive decision making. **(Grader Project)**	In MyITLab and online

GLOSSARY

GLOSSARY OF CHAPTER KEY TERMS

American Psychological Association (APA) One of two commonly used style guides for formatting research papers.

Bibliography A list of cited works in a report or research paper; also referred to as Works Cited, Sources, or References, depending upon the report style.

Brightness The relative lightness of a picture.

Citation A note inserted into the text of a research paper that refers the reader to a source in the bibliography.

Column break indicator A dotted line containing the words *Column Break* that displays at the bottom of the column.

Contrast The difference between the darkest and lightest area of a picture.

Crop A command that removes unwanted or unnecessary areas of a picture.

Crop handles Handles used to define unwanted areas of a picture.

Crop pointer The pointer used to crop areas of a picture.

Data source A document that contains a list of variable information, such as names and addresses, that is merged with a main document to create customized form letters or labels.

Em dash A punctuation symbol used to indicate an explanation or emphasis.

Endnote In a research paper, a note placed at the end of a document or chapter.

Fields In a mail merge, the column headings in the data source.

Flip A command that creates a reverse image of a picture or object.

Footnote In a research paper, a note placed at the bottom of the page.

Hanging indent An indent style in which the first line of a paragraph extends to the left of the remaining lines and that is commonly used for bibliographic entries.

Line break indicator A non-printing character in the shape of a bent arrow that indicates a manual line break.

Mail merge A feature that joins a main document and a data source to create customized letters or labels.

Main document In a mail merge, the document that contains the text or formatting that remains constant.

Manual column break An artificial end to a column to balance columns or to provide space for the insertion of other objects.

Manual line break A break that moves text to the right of the insertion point to a new line while keeping the text in the same paragraph.

Manual page break The action of forcing a page to end and placing subsequent text at the top of the next page.

Modern Language Association (MLA) One of two commonly used style guides for formatting research papers.

Nameplate The banner on the front page of a newsletter that identifies the publication.

Newsletter A periodical that communicates news and information to a specific group.

Note In a research paper, information that expands on the topic, but that does not fit well in the document text.

Office 365 Administrator—the person who creates and manages the account, adds new users, sets up the services your organization wants to use, sets permission levels, and manages the SharePoint team sites.

Page break indicator A dotted line with the text *Page Break* that indicates where a manual page break was inserted.

Parenthetical references References that include the last name of the author or authors, and the page number in the referenced source.

PDF Reflow The ability to import PDF files into Word so that you can transform a PDF back into a fully editable Word document.

Read Mode A view in Word that optimizes the Word screen for the times when you are reading Word documents on the screen and not creating or editing them.

Recolor A feature that enables you to change all colors in the picture to shades of a single color.

Record Each row of information that contains data for one person.

Scale A command that resizes a picture to a percentage of its size.

Screenshot An image of an active window on your computer that you can paste into a document.

Section A portion of a document that can be formatted differently from the rest of the document.

Section break A double dotted line that indicates the end of one section and the beginning of another section.

Small caps A font effect that changes lowercase letters to uppercase letters, but with the height of lowercase letters.

Style A group of formatting commands, such as font, font size, font color, paragraph alignment, and line spacing that can be applied to a paragraph with one command.

Style guide A manual that contains standards for the design and writing of documents.

Suppress A Word feature that hides header and footer information, including the page number, on the first page of a document.

Windows Reader app A Windows Store app with which you can open a PDF or XPS file, zoom, find words or phrases, take notes, save changes, and then print or share the file.

Works Cited In the MLA style, a list of cited works placed at the end of a research paper or report.

CHAPTER REVIEW

Apply 3A skills from these Objectives:

1. Create a Research Paper
2. Insert Footnotes in a Research Paper
3. Create Citations and a Bibliography in a Research Paper
4. Use Read Mode and PDF Reflow

Skills Review Project 3C Diet and Exercise Report

In the following Skills Review, you will edit and format a research paper that contains information about the effects of diet and exercise. This paper was created by Rachel Holder, a medical intern at University Medical Center, for distribution to her classmates studying physiology. Your completed document will look similar to the one shown in Figure 3.55.

PROJECT FILES

For Project 3C, you will need the following file:

w03C_Diet_Exercise

You will save your document as:

Lastname_Firstname_3C_Diet_Exercise

PROJECT RESULTS

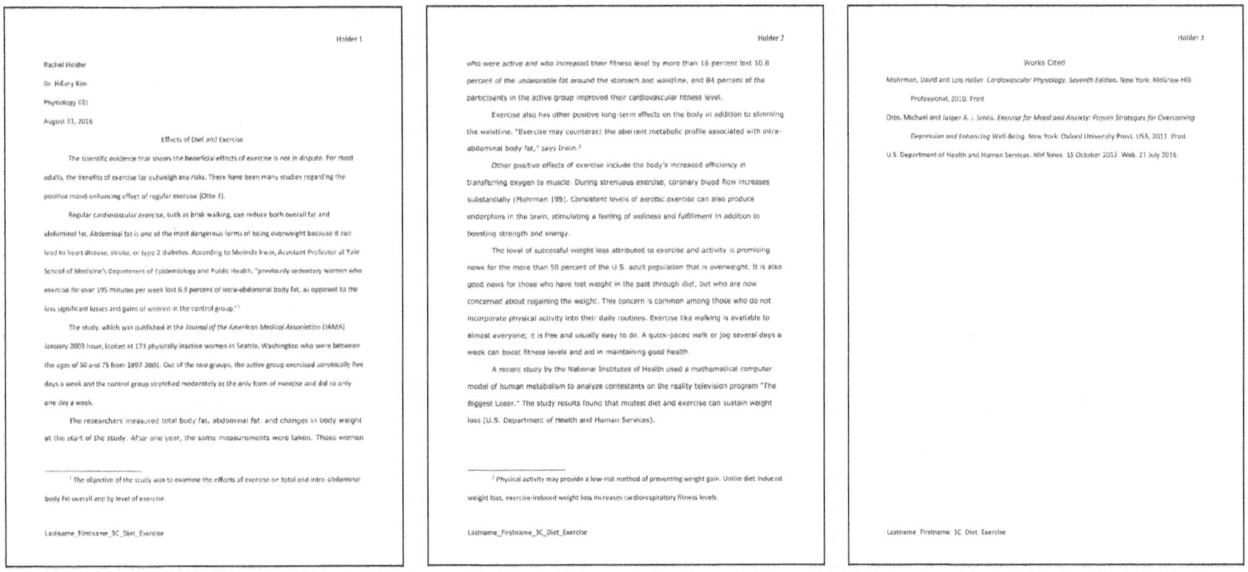

Holder 1

Rachel Holder

Dr. Hillary Kim

Physiology 621

August 31, 2016

Effects of Diet and Exercise

The scientific evidence that shows the beneficial effects of exercise is not in dispute. For most adults, the benefits of exercise far outweigh any risks. There have been many studies regarding the positive mood-enhancing effect of regular exercise (Otto 3).

Regular cardiovascular exercise, such as brisk walking, can reduce both overall fat and abdominal fat. Abdominal fat is one of the most dangerous forms of being overweight because it can lead to heart disease, stroke, or type 2 diabetes. According to Melinda Irwin, Assistant Professor at Yale School of Medicine's Department of Epidemiology and Public Health, "previously sedentary women who exercise for over 195 minutes per week lost 6.9 percent of intra-abdominal body fat, as opposed to the less significant losses and gains of women in the control group."[1]

The study, which was published in the *Journal of the American Medical Association* (JAMA) January 2003 issue, looked at 173 physically inactive women in Seattle, Washington who were between the ages of 50 and 75 from 1997-2001. Out of the two groups, the active group exercised aerobically five days a week and the control group stretched moderately as the only form of exercise and did so only one day a week.

The researchers measured total body fat, abdominal fat, and changes in body weight at the start of the study. After one year, the same measurements were taken. Those women

[1] The objective of the study was to examine the effects of exercise on total and intra-abdominal body fat overall and by level of exercise.

Lastname_Firstname_3C_Diet_Exercise

Holder 2

who were active and who increased their fitness level by more than 16 percent lost 10.8 percent of the undesirable fat around the stomach and waistline, and 84 percent of the participants in the active group improved their cardiovascular fitness level.

Exercise also has other positive long-term effects on the body in addition to slimming the waistline. "Exercise may counteract the aberrant metabolic profile associated with intra-abdominal body fat," says Irwin.[2]

Other positive effects of exercise include the body's increased efficiency in transferring oxygen to muscle. During strenuous exercise, coronary blood flow increases substantially (Mohrman 195). Consistent levels of aerobic exercise can also produce endorphins in the brain, stimulating a feeling of wellness and fulfillment in addition to boosting strength and energy.

The level of successful weight loss attributed to exercise and activity is promising news for the more than 50 percent of the U.S. adult population that is overweight. It is also good news for those who have lost weight in the past through diet, but who are now concerned about regaining the weight. This concern is common among those who do not incorporate physical activity into their daily routines. Exercise like walking is available to almost everyone; it is free and usually easy to do. A quick-paced walk or jog several days a week can boost fitness levels and aid in maintaining good health.

A recent study by the National Institutes of Health used a mathematical computer model of human metabolism to analyze contestants on the reality television program "The Biggest Loser." The study results found that modest diet and exercise can sustain weight loss (U.S. Department of Health and Human Services).

[2] Physical activity may provide a low-risk method of preventing weight gain. Unlike diet-induced weight loss, exercise-induced weight loss increases cardiorespiratory fitness levels.

Lastname_Firstname_3C_Diet_Exercise

Holder 3

Works Cited

Mohrman, David and Lois Heller. *Cardiovascular Physiology, Seventh Edition.* New York: McGraw-Hill Professional, 2010. Print.

Otto, Michael and Jasper A. J. Smits. *Exercise for Mood and Anxiety: Proven Strategies for Overcoming Depression and Enhancing Well-Being.* New York: Oxford University Press, USA, 2011. Print.

U.S. Department of Health and Human Services. *NIH News.* 15 October 2012. Web. 21 July 2016.

Lastname_Firstname_3C_Diet_Exercise

FIGURE 3.55

(Project 3C Diet and Exercise Report continues on the next page)

CHAPTER REVIEW

Skills Review Project 3C Diet and Exercise Report (continued)

1 Start Word. From your student files, locate and open the document **w03C_Diet_Exercise**. Display the formatting marks and rulers. **Save** the file in your **Word Chapter 3** folder as **Lastname_Firstname_3C_Diet_Exercise**

a. Press Ctrl + A to select all the text. On the **HOME tab**, in the **Paragraph group**, click **Line and Paragraph Spacing**, and then change the line spacing to **2.0**. On the **PAGE LAYOUT tab**, change the **Spacing After** to **0 pt**.

b. Press Ctrl + Home, press Enter to create a blank line at the top of the document, and then click to position the insertion point in the new blank line. Type **Rachel Holder** and press Enter. Type **Dr. Hillary Kim** and press Enter. Type **Physiology 621** and press Enter. Type **August 31, 2016** and press Enter.

c. Type **Effects of Diet and Exercise** and then press Ctrl + E to center the title you just typed.

2 On the **INSERT tab**, in the **Header & Footer group**, click **Header**, and then at the bottom of the list, click **Edit Header**. Type **Holder** and then press Spacebar.

a. Under **HEADER & FOOTER TOOLS**, on the **DESIGN tab**, in the **Header & Footer group**, click **Page Number**, and then point to **Current Position**. Under **Simple**, click **Plain Number**.

b. On the **HOME tab**, in the **Paragraph group**, click **Align Right**. Double-click anywhere in the document to close the Header area.

c. Near the top of **Page 1**, locate the paragraph beginning *The scientific evidence*, and then click to position the insertion point at the beginning of that paragraph. Scroll to the end of the document, hold down Shift, and then click to the right of the last paragraph mark to select all of the text from the insertion point to the end of the document.

d. On the **HOME tab**, in the **Paragraph group**, click the **Dialog Box Launcher** button. In the **Paragraph** dialog box, on the **Indents and Spacing tab**, under **Indentation**, click the **Special arrow**, and then click **First line**. Click **OK**.

e. On the **INSERT tab**, in the **Header & Footer group**, click **Footer**, and then click **Edit Footer**. In the **Insert group**, click **Document Info**, and then click **File Name**. Click **Close Header and Footer**.

3 Scroll to view the top of **Page 2**, locate the paragraph that begins *Exercise also has*, and then at the end of that paragraph, click to position the insertion point to the right of the period following *Irwin*. On the **REFERENCES tab**, in the **Footnotes group**, click **Insert Footnote**.

a. As the footnote text, type **Physical activity may provide a low-risk method of preventing weight gain. Unlike diet-induced weight loss, exercise-induced weight loss increases cardiorespiratory fitness levels.**

b. In the upper portion of **Page 1**, locate the paragraph that begins *Regular cardiovascular exercise*. Click to position the insertion point at the end of the paragraph and insert a footnote.

c. As the footnote text, type **The objective of the study was to examine the effects of exercise on total and intra-abdominal body fat overall and by level of exercise. Save** your document.

4 At the bottom of **Page 1**, right-click in the footnote you just typed. On the shortcut menu, click **Style**. In the **Style** dialog box, click **Modify**. In the **Modify Style** dialog box, locate the small Formatting toolbar in the center of the dialog box, click the **Font Size button arrow**, and then click **11**.

a. In the lower left corner of the dialog box, click **Format**, and then click **Paragraph**. In the **Paragraph** dialog box, under **Indentation**, click the **Special arrow**, and then click **First line**. Under **Spacing**, click the **Line spacing button arrow**, and then click **Double**.

b. Click **OK** to close the **Paragraph** dialog box, click **OK** to close the **Modify Style** dialog box, and then click **Apply** to apply the new style. **Save** your document.

5 Scroll to view the top of **Page 1**, and then in the paragraph that begins *The scientific evidence*, click to position the insertion point to the left of the period at the end of the paragraph.

a. On the **REFERENCES tab**, in the **Citations & Bibliography group**, click the **Style button arrow**, and then click **MLA** to insert a reference using MLA style. Click **Insert Citation**, and then click **Add New Source**. Click the **Type of Source arrow**, scroll as

(Project 3C Diet and Exercise Report continues on the next page)

Skills Review Project 3C Diet and Exercise Report (continued)

necessary to locate and click **Book**, and then add the following information:

Author	**Otto, Michael and Jasper A. J. Smits**
Title	**Exercise for Mood and Anxiety: Proven Strategies for Overcoming Depression and Enhancing Well-Being**
Year	**2011**
City	**New York**
Publisher	**Oxford University Press, USA**
Medium	**Print**

b. Click **OK** to insert the citation. In the paragraph, click to select the citation, click the **Citation Options arrow**, and then click **Edit Citation**. In the **Edit Citation** dialog box, under **Add**, in the **Pages** box, type **3** and then click **OK**.

c. On the upper portion of **Page 2**, in the paragraph that begins *Other positive effects*, in the third line, click to position the insertion point to the left of the period following *substantially*. In the **Citations & Bibliography group**, click **Insert Citation**, and then click **Add New Source**. Click the **Type of Source arrow**, click **Book**, and then add the following information:

Author	**Lohrman, David and Lois Heller**
Title	**Cardiovascular Physiology, Seventh Edition**
Year	**2010**
City	**New York**
Publisher	**McGraw-Hill Professional**
Medium	**Print**

d. Click **OK**. Click to select the citation in the paragraph, click the **Citation Options arrow**, and then click **Edit Citation**. In the **Edit Citation** dialog box, under **Add**, in the **Pages** box, type **195** and then click **OK**.

6 Press Ctrl + End to move to the end of the last paragraph in the document. Click to the left of the period following *loss*. In the **Citations & Bibliography group**, click **Insert Citation**, and then click **Add New Source**. Click the **Type of Source arrow**, click **Web site**, and then select the **Corporate Author** check box. Add the following information:

Corporate Author	**U.S. Department of Health and Human Services**
Name of Web Page	**NIH News**
Year	**2012**
Month	**October**
Day	**15**
Year Accessed	**2016**
Month Accessed	**July**
Day Accessed	**21**
Medium	**Web**

a. Click **OK**. Press Ctrl + End to move the insertion point to the end of the document. Press Ctrl + Enter to insert a manual page break. On the **HOME tab**, in the **Paragraph group**, click the **Dialog Box Launcher** button. In the **Paragraph** dialog box, on the **Indents and Spacing tab**, under **Indentation**, click the **Special arrow**, and then click **(none)**. Click **OK**.

b. Type **Works Cited** and then press Enter. On the **REFERENCES tab**, in the **Citations & Bibliography group**, be sure **MLA** displays in the **Style** box. In the **Citations & Bibliography group**, click **Bibliography**, and then at the bottom, click **Insert Bibliography**.

c. Click anywhere in the *Works Cited* title, and then press Ctrl + E to center the title. **Save** your document.

7 On the **REFERENCES tab**, in the **Citations & Bibliography group**, click **Manage Sources**. On the left, on the **Master List**, click the entry for *Lohrman, David*, and then click **Edit**. In the **Edit Source** dialog box, in the **Author** box, change the *L* in *Lohrman* to **M** Click **OK**, click **Yes**, and then click **Close**.

a. On **Page 2**, in the paragraph that begins *Other positive effects*, in the third line, on the selected citation, click the **Citation Options arrow**, and then click **Update Citations and Bibliography**.

(Project 3C Diet and Exercise Report continues on the next page)

Skills Review Project 3C Diet and Exercise Report (continued)

b. In the bibliography, move the pointer to the left of the first entry—beginning *Mohrman*—to display the [pointer icon] pointer. Drag down to select all three references in the field. On the **HOME tab**, in the **Paragraph group**, set the **Line spacing** to **2.0**. On the **PAGE LAYOUT tab**, set the **Spacing After** to **0 pt**.

c. Click the **FILE tab**, and then in the lower right corner, click **Show All Properties**. Add the following information:

Title	**Diet and Exercise**
Tags	**weight loss, exercise, diet**
Comments	**Draft copy of report for class**
Categories	**biomedical research**
Company	**University Medical Center**
Manager	**Dr. Hillary Kim**

d. In the **Subject** box, type your course name and section number. Be sure that your name displays as the Author and edit if necessary. On the left, click **Save** to redisplay your document. On the **VIEW tab**, in the **Views group**, click **Read Mode**. In the upper left, click **TOOLS**, click **Find**, and then in the search box, type **Yale** and notice that the text you searched for is highlighted in the document.

e. In the upper left, click **VIEW**, and then click **Edit Document** to return to **Print Layout** view. **Close** the **navigation pane**. **Save** your document, view the **Print Preview**, and then print or submit electronically as directed by your instructor. **Close** Word.

END | You have completed Project 3C

CHAPTER REVIEW

Apply 3B skills from these Objectives:

5 Format a Multiple-Column Newsletter

6 Use Special Character and Paragraph Formatting

7 Create Mailing Labels Using Mail Merge

Skills Review Project 3D Career Newsletter

In the following Skills Review, you will format a newsletter regarding professional development opportunities offered by University Medical Center, and you will create mailing labels for staff interested in these opportunities. Your completed document will look similar to Figure 3.56.

PROJECT FILES

For Project 3D, you will need the following files:

New blank Word document
w03D_Career_Newsletter
w03D_Addresses

You will save your documents as:

Lastname_Firstname_3D_Career_Newsletter
Lastname_Firstname_3D_Addresses
Lastname_Firstname_3D_Mailing_Labels

PROJECT RESULTS

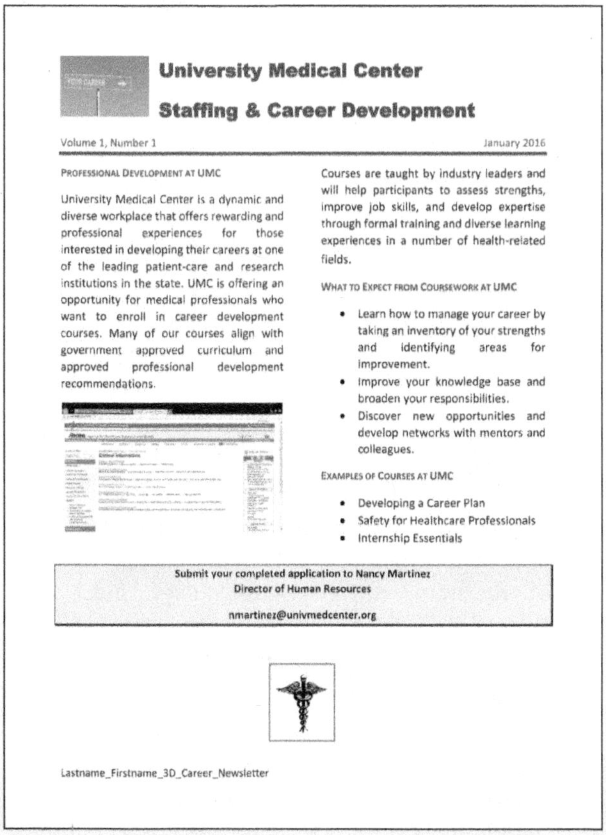

University Medical Center

Staffing & Career Development

Volume 1, Number 1 January 2016

PROFESSIONAL DEVELOPMENT AT UMC

University Medical Center is a dynamic and diverse workplace that offers rewarding and professional experiences for those interested in developing their careers at one of the leading patient-care and research institutions in the state. UMC is offering an opportunity for medical professionals who want to enroll in career development courses. Many of our courses align with government approved curriculum and approved professional development recommendations.

Courses are taught by industry leaders and will help participants to assess strengths, improve job skills, and develop expertise through formal training and diverse learning experiences in a number of health-related fields.

WHAT TO EXPECT FROM COURSEWORK AT UMC

- Learn how to manage your career by taking an inventory of your strengths and identifying areas for improvement.
- Improve your knowledge base and broaden your responsibilities.
- Discover new opportunities and develop networks with mentors and colleagues.

EXAMPLES OF COURSES AT UMC

- Developing a Career Plan
- Safety for Healthcare Professionals
- Internship Essentials

Submit your completed application to Nancy Martinez
Director of Human Resources
nmartinez@univmedcenter.org

Lastname_Firstname_3D_Career_Newsletter

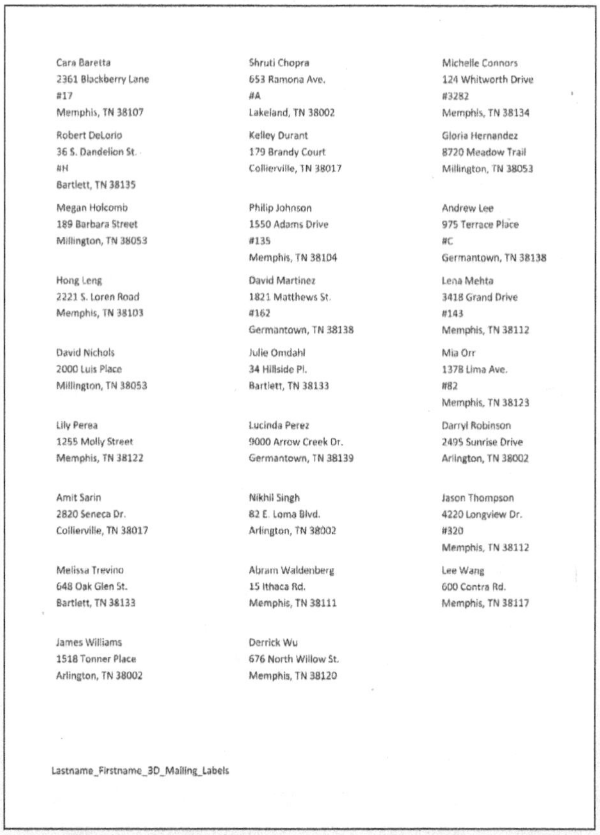

Cara Baretta 2361 Blackberry Lane #17 Memphis, TN 38107	Shruti Chopra 653 Ramona Ave. #A Lakeland, TN 38002	Michelle Connors 124 Whitworth Drive #3282 Memphis, TN 38134
Robert DeLorio 36 S. Dandelion St. #H Bartlett, TN 38135	Kelley Durant 179 Brandy Court Collierville, TN 38017	Gloria Hernandez 8720 Meadow Trail Millington, TN 38053
Megan Holcomb 189 Barbara Street Millington, TN 38053	Philip Johnson 1550 Adams Drive #135 Memphis, TN 38104	Andrew Lee 975 Terrace Place #C Germantown, TN 38138
Hong Leng 2221 S. Loren Road Memphis, TN 38103	David Martinez 1821 Matthews St. #162 Germantown, TN 38138	Lena Mehta 3418 Grand Drive #143 Memphis, TN 38112
David Nichols 2000 Luis Place Millington, TN 38053	Julie Omdahl 34 Hillside Pl. Bartlett, TN 38133	Mia Orr 1378 Lima Ave. #82 Memphis, TN 38123
Lily Perea 1255 Molly Street Memphis, TN 38122	Lucinda Perez 9000 Arrow Creek Dr. Germantown, TN 38139	Darryl Robinson 2495 Sunrise Drive Arlington, TN 38002
Amit Sarin 2820 Seneca Dr. Collierville, TN 38017	Nikhil Singh 82 E. Loma Blvd. Arlington, TN 38002	Jason Thompson 4220 Longview Dr. #320 Memphis, TN 38112
Melissa Trevino 648 Oak Glen St. Bartlett, TN 38133	Abram Waldenberg 15 Ithaca Rd. Memphis, TN 38111	Lee Wang 600 Contra Rd. Memphis, TN 38117
James Williams 1518 Tonner Place Arlington, TN 38002	Derrick Wu 676 North Willow St. Memphis, TN 38120	

Lastname_Firstname_3D_Mailing_Labels

FIGURE 3.56

(Project 3D Career Newsletter continues on the next page)

CHAPTER REVIEW

Skills Review Project 3D Career Newsletter (continued)

1 Start Word. On Word's opening screen, in the lower left, click **Open Other Documents**. Navigate to your student files, and then locate and open **w03D_Career_ Newsletter**. **Save** the file in your **Word Chapter 3** folder as **Lastname_Firstname_3D_Career_Newsletter** and then add the file name to the footer.

a. Select the first two lines of the document. On the mini toolbar, change the **Font** to **Arial Black** and the **Font Size** to **18**. Select the first three lines of the document. Click the **Font Color button arrow**, and then under **Theme Colors**, in the fifth column, click the last color—**Blue, Accent 1, Darker 50%**.

b. With the text still selected, on the **HOME tab**, in the **Paragraph group**, click the **Borders button arrow**, and then at the bottom, click **Borders and Shading**. In the **Borders and Shading** dialog box, on the **Borders tab**, click the **Color arrow**, and then under **Theme Colors**, in the fifth column, click the last color—**Blue, Accent 1, Darker 50%**.

c. Click the **Width arrow**, and then click **3 pt**. In the **Preview** box, click the bottom border. Click **OK**.

d. Click at the beginning of the paragraph that begins *Professional Development*. Scroll the document, hold down Shift, and then click after the paragraph mark at the end of the *Internship Essentials* line. On the **PAGE LAYOUT tab**, in the **Page Setup group**, click **Columns**, and then click **Two**. With the two columns of text selected, on the **HOME tab**, in the **Paragraph group**, click **Justify**.

e. In the first column, click at the beginning of the paragraph that begins *Courses are taught*. On the **PAGE LAYOUT tab**, in the **Page Setup group**, click **Breaks**. Under **Page Breaks**, click **Column**.

2 Press Ctrl + Home. On the **INSERT tab**, in the **Illustrations group**, click **Online Pictures**. In the **Office.com Clip Art** search box, type **career** and then press Enter. Click the image of the sign with the text *Your Career*. If the image does not display, select a similar picture. Click **Insert**.

a. On the **FORMAT tab**, in the **Size group**, click the **Dialog Box Launcher** button. In the **Layout** dialog box, on the **Size tab**, under **Scale**, be sure the **Lock aspect ratio** and **Relative to original picture size** check boxes are selected. Select the number in the **Height** box, type **10** and then press Tab.

b. In the **Layout** dialog box, click the **Text Wrapping tab**. Under **Wrapping style**, click **Square**.

c. Click the **Position tab**, and then under **Horizontal**, click the **Alignment** option button. Be sure that the **Alignment** indicates **Left** and **relative to Column**. Under **Vertical**, click the **Alignment** option button, and then change the alignment to **Top relative to Margin**. Click **OK**. **Save** your newsletter.

3 Press Ctrl + End to move to the end of the document. On the **INSERT tab**, in the **Illustrations group**, click **Online Pictures**. In the **Office.com Clip Art** search box, search for **caducei healthcare symbol** and then insert the picture of the gray caducei with a gray shadow. If the image does not display, select a similar picture.

a. On the **FORMAT tab**, in the **Size group**, click the upper portion of the **Crop** button. Point to the center right crop handle, and then drag to the left to approximately **5.5 inches on the horizontal ruler**. Point to the center left crop handle, and then drag to the right to approximately **1.5 inches on the horizontal ruler**. Click the upper portion of the **Crop** button to apply the crop.

b. On the **FORMAT tab**, in the **Adjust group**, click **Color**, and then click **Set Transparent Color**. In the lower left area of the picture, click in the gray shadow to apply the transparent color.

c. With the picture selected, on the **FORMAT tab**, in the **Size group**, click in the **Height** box. Type **1** and then press Enter. On the **FORMAT tab**, in the **Arrange group**, click **Position**, and then click **More Layout Options** to display the **Layout** dialog box. Click the **Text Wrapping tab**, and then under **Wrapping Style**, click **Square**.

d. On the **Position tab**, under **Horizontal**, click the **Alignment** option button, and then change the **Alignment** to **Centered relative to Page**. Under **Vertical**, click the **Alignment** option button, and then change the **Alignment** to **Bottom relative to Margin**. Click **OK**.

e. On the **FORMAT tab**, in the **Picture Styles group**, click the **Picture Border button arrow**. Under **Theme Colors**, in the fourth column, click the first color—**Dark Blue, Text 2**. Click the **Picture Border button arrow** again, and then point to **Weight**. Click **1 pt**.

(Project 3D Career Newsletter continues on the next page)

f. On the **FORMAT tab**, in the **Adjust group**, click **Color**. Under **Recolor**, in the first row, click the last option—**Black and White, 75%**. On the **FORMAT tab**, in the **Adjust group**, click **Corrections**. Under **Brightness/Contrast**, in the second row, click the fourth setting—**Brightness: +20% Contrast: -20%**.

4 In the paragraph that begins *University Medical Center is a dynamic*, click after the period at the end of the paragraph, and then press Enter. Start Internet Explorer, maximize the window, and then navigate to **www.ahrq.gov/clinic/**

a. Redisplay your **3D_Career_Newletter** document. With the insertion point positioned in the blank line above the column break, on the **INSERT tab**, in the **Illustrations group**, click **Screenshot**. In the **Screenshot** gallery, click the browser window that contains the website; click **No** in the message that displays.

b. Select the subheading *Professional Development at UMC* including the paragraph mark. Right-click the selected text, and then on the shortcut menu, click **Font**. In the **Font** dialog box, click the **Font color arrow**, and then in the fifth column, click the last color—**Blue, Accent 1, Darker 50%**. Under **Font style**, click **Bold**, and then under **Effects**, select **Small caps**. Click **OK**.

c. With the text still selected, right-click, and then on the mini toolbar, double-click **Format Painter**. In the second column, with the [Format Painter] pointer, select each of the subheadings—*What to Expect from Coursework at UMC* and *Example of Courses at UMC*. Press Esc to turn off **Format Painter**.

5 Press Ctrl + End to move to the end of the document, and then select the two lines of bold text—the graphic will also be selected. On the **HOME tab**, in the **Paragraph group**, click the **Borders button arrow**, and then click **Borders and Shading**.

a. In the **Borders and Shading** dialog box, on the **Borders tab**, under **Setting**, click **Shadow**. Click the **Color arrow**, and then in the fifth column, click the last color—**Blue, Accent 1, Darker 50%**. Click the **Width arrow**, and then click **1 pt**.

b. In the **Borders and Shading** dialog box, click the **Shading tab**. Click the **Fill arrow**, and then in the fifth column, click the second color—**Blue, Accent 1, Lighter 80%**. Click **OK**. On the **HOME tab**, in the **Paragraph group**, click **Center**. In the shaded paragraph, click in front of the *D* in the word *Director*. Hold down Shift and then press Enter.

c. Press Ctrl + Home, and then click the **FILE tab**. At the bottom of the **Properties** list, click **Show All Properties**. Click to the right of **Tags**, and then type **newsletter, careers** Click to the right of **Subject**, and then type your course name and section number. Under **Related People**, if necessary, type your name in the Author box. Display the **Print Preview** and make any necessary corrections. **Save** the document; close Word and close Internet Explorer.

6 Start Word and display a new blank document. **Save** the document in your **Word Chapter 3** folder as **Lastname_Firstname_3D_Mailing_Labels** With your new document open on the screen, from your student files, **Open** the file **w03D_Addresses**. **Save** the address file in your **Word Chapter 3** folder as **Lastname_Firstname_3D_Addresses** and then add the file name to the footer. **Save** and then **Close** the file. Be sure that your **Lastname_Firstname_3D_Mailing_Labels** document displays.

a. Click the **MAILINGS tab**. In the **Start Mail Merge group**, click **Start Mail Merge**, and then click **Step-by-Step Mail Merge Wizard**. In the **Mail Merge** pane, under **Select document type**, click **Labels**. At the bottom of the **Mail Merge** pane, click **Next: Starting document**.

b. Under **Select starting document**, under **Change document layout**, click **Label options**. In the **Label Options** dialog box, under **Printer information**, be sure that the **Default tray** is selected.

c. Under **Label information**, click the **Label vendors arrow**, and then click **Avery US Letter**. Under **Product number**, scroll about halfway down the list, and then click **5160 Easy Peel Address Labels**. At the bottom of the **Label Options** dialog box, click **OK**. At the bottom of the **Mail Merge** pane, click **Next: Select recipients**.

d. In the **Mail Merge** pane, under **Select recipients**, under **Use an existing list**, click **Browse**. Navigate to your **Word Chapter 3** folder, select your **Lastname_Firstname_3D_Addresses** file, and then click **Open**.

(Project 3D Career Newsletter continues on the next page)

CHAPTER REVIEW

Skills Review Project 3D Career Newsletter (continued)

7 In the lower left portion of the **Mail Merge Recipients** dialog box, in the **Data Source** box, click the path that contains your file name. Then, at the bottom of the **Mail Merge Recipients** dialog box, click **Edit**. In the upper right corner of the **Data Form** dialog box, click **Add New**. In the blank record, type the following, pressing Tab to move from field to field:

First_Name:	**Mia**
Last_Name:	**Orr**
Address_1:	**1378 Lima Ave.**
Unit:	**#82**
City:	**Memphis**
State:	**TN**
ZIP_Code:	**38123**

a. In the lower right corner of the **Data Form** dialog box, click **Close**. At the bottom of the **Mail Merge Recipients** dialog box, click **OK**.

b. At the bottom of the **Mail Merge** pane, click **Next: Arrange your labels**. Under **Arrange your labels**, click **Address block**. In the lower right corner of the **Insert Address Block** dialog box, click **Match Fields**.

c. Click the **Address 2 arrow**, and then from the list of available fields, click **Unit**. Click **OK** two times.

d. In the **Mail Merge** pane, under **Replicate labels**, click **Update all labels**. At the bottom of the **Mail Merge** pane, click **Next: Preview your labels**. Press Ctrl + A to select all of the label text, click the **PAGE LAYOUT tab**, and then in the **Paragraph group**, click in the **Spacing Before** box. Type **3** and press Enter. At the bottom of the **Mail Merge** pane, click **Next: Complete the merge**.

e. Click the **MAILINGS tab**, and then in the **Start Mail Merge group**, click **Edit Recipient List** to display the list of names and addresses. In the **Mail Merge Recipients** dialog box, click the **Last_Name** field heading to sort the names. Click **OK**. **Close** the **Mail Merge** pane.

f. Scroll the document and then click anywhere in the empty table row at the bottom. Click the **LAYOUT tab**. In the **Rows & Columns group**, click **Delete**, and then click **Delete Rows**. Add the file name to the footer, close the footer area, and then click the **FILE tab**. Click **Show All Properties**. As the **Tags**, type **labels** and as the **Subject**, type your course name and section number. Be sure your name displays as the **Author**, and then **Save** your file.

g. As directed by your instructor, print or submit electronically. **Close** the document, click **Yes** to save the data source, and then if necessary, click **Save** to save the labels. In addition to your labels and address document, submit your **3D_Career_Newsletter** document as directed. **Close** Word.

END | You have completed Project 3D

CONTENT-BASED ASSESSMENTS

Mastering Word Project 3E Skin Protection Report

MyITLab® grader

Apply 3A skills from these Objectives:

1. Create a Research Paper
2. Insert Footnotes in a Research Paper
3. Create Citations and a Bibliography in a Research Paper
4. Use Read Mode and PDF Reflow

In the following Mastering Word project, you will edit and format a research paper that contains information about skin protection and the use of sunblocks and sunscreens. This paper was created by Rachel Holder, a medical intern at University Medical Center, for distribution to her classmates studying dermatology. Your completed document will look similar to the one shown in Figure 3.57.

PROJECT FILES

For Project 3E, you will need the following file:

w03E_Skin_Protection

You will save your document as:

Lastname_Firstname_3E_Skin_Protection

PROJECT RESULTS

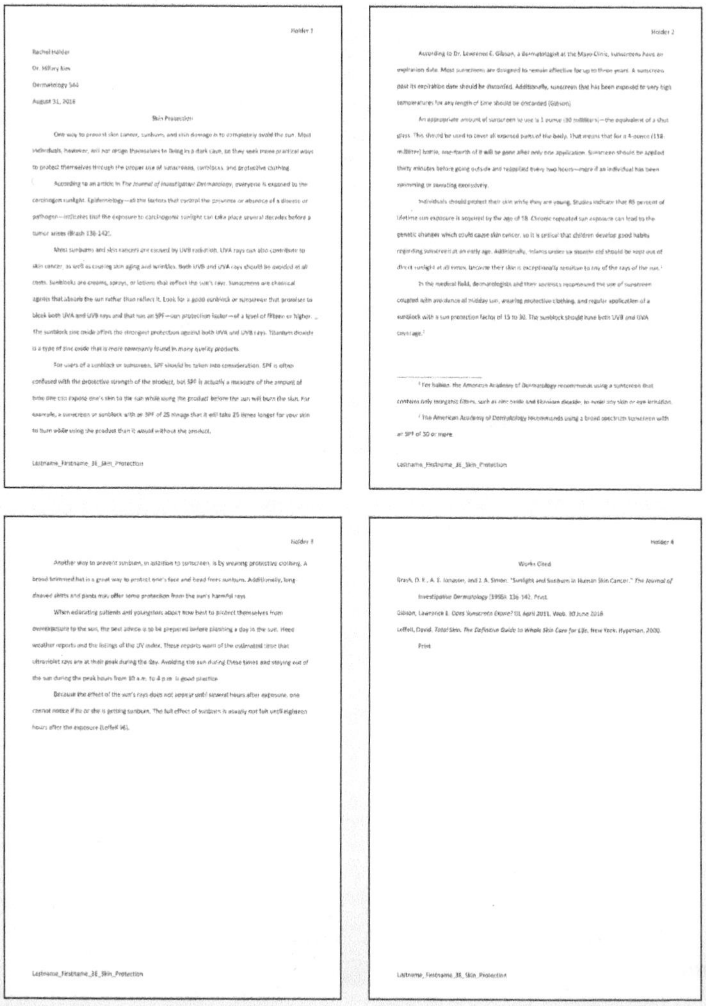

FIGURE 3.57

(Project 3E Skin Protection Report continues on the next page)

CONTENT-BASED ASSESSMENTS

Mastering Word | Project 3E Skin Protection Report (continued)

1 Start Word. From your student files, locate and open the document **w03E_Skin_Protection**. Display formatting marks and rulers. Save the file in your **Word Chapter 3** folder as **Lastname_Firstname_3E_Skin_Protection**

2 Select all the text, change the **Line Spacing** to **2.0**, and then change the **Spacing After** to **0 pt**. At the top of the document, insert a new blank paragraph, and then in the new paragraph, type **Rachel Holder** Press Enter. Type **Dr. Hillary Kim** and press Enter. Type **Dermatology 544** and press Enter. Type **August 31, 2016** and press Enter. Type **Skin Protection** and then press Ctrl + E to center the title you just typed.

3 Insert a header, type **Holder** and then press Spacebar. Display the **Page Number gallery**, and then in the **Current Position**, add the **Plain Number** style. Apply **Align Right** formatting to the header. Insert a footer with the file name. Starting with the paragraph that begins *One way to prevent*, select all the text in the document, and then set a **First line** indent of **0.5"**.

4 On **Page 2**, at the end of the paragraph that begins *In the medical field*, insert a footnote with the following text: **The American Academy of Dermatology recommends using a broad spectrum sunscreen with an SPF of 30 or more.**

5 On **Page 2**, at the end of the paragraph that begins *Individuals should protect*, insert a footnote with the following text: **For babies, the American Academy of Dermatology recommends using a sunscreen that contains only inorganic filters, such as zinc oxide and titanium dioxide, to avoid any skin or eye irritation.**

6 Modify the **Footnote Text** style so that the **Font Size** is **11**, there is a **First line indent** of **0.5"**, and the spacing is **Double**, and then apply the style.

7 On **Page 1**, at the end of the paragraph that begins *According to an article*, click to the left of the period, and then using **MLA** format, insert a citation for a **Journal Article** with the following information:

Author	**Frash, D. E., A. S. Jonason, and J. A. Simon**
Title	**Sunlight and Sunburn in Human Skin Cancer**
Journal Name	**The Journal of Investigative Dermatology**
Year	**1996**
Pages	**136-142**
Medium	**Print**

8 In the report, select the citation you just created, display the **Citation Options**, and then edit the citation to include **Pages 136-142** At the end of the last paragraph of the report, click to the left of the period, and then insert a citation for a **Book** with the following information:

Author	**Leffell, David**
Title	**Total Skin: The Definitive Guide to Whole Skin Care for Life**
Year	**2000**
City	**New York**
Publisher	**Hyperion**
Medium	**Print**

9 In the report, select the citation you just created, display the **Citation Options**, and then edit the citation to include **Page 96** At the top of **Page 2**, at the end of the paragraph that begins *According to Dr.*, click to the left of the period, and then insert a citation for a **Web site** with the following information:

Author	**Gibson, Lawrence E.**
Name of Web Page	**Does Sunscreen Expire?**
Year	**2011**
Month	**April**
Day	**01**
Year Accessed	**2016**
Month Accessed	**June**
Day Accessed	**30**
Medium	**Web**

10 Move to the end of the document, and then insert a manual page break to create a new page. Display the **Paragraph** dialog box, and then change the **Indentation** under **Special** to **(none)**. Add a **Works Cited** title, press Enter, and then click **Insert Bibliography**. **Center** the *Works Cited* title.

(Project 3E Skin Protection Report continues on the next page)

Mastering Word Project 3E Skin Protection Report (continued)

11 By using the **Manage Sources** command, display the **Source Manager**. On the **Master List**, select the entry for **Frash, D. E.**, and then **Edit** this source—the last name should be **Brash** instead of *Frash*. In the message that displays, update both lists. Locate the citation in the text of the report, display the **Citation Options**, and then **Update Citations and Bibliography**. On the Works Cited page, select the references, apply **Double** line spacing, and then set the **Spacing After** paragraphs to **0 pt**.

12 Update the **Document Properties** with the following information:

Title	**Skin Protection**
Tags	**sunscreen, sun exposure**
Comments	**Draft copy of report for class**
Categories	**Dermatology**
Company	**University Medical Center**
Manager	**Dr. Hillary Kim**

13 In the **Subject** box, type your course name and section number. Be sure that your name displays as the **Author** and edit if necessary. On the left, click **Print** to view the **Print Preview**, and then click **Save** to redisplay your document. Print or submit electronically as directed by your instructor. **Close** Word.

END | You have completed Project 3E

CONTENT-BASED ASSESSMENTS

MyITLab® grader

Mastering Word | Project 3F Dogs Newsletter and Mailing Labels

Apply 3B skills from these Objectives:

5 Format a Multiple-Column Newsletter
6 Use Special Character and Paragraph Formatting
7 Create Mailing Labels Using Mail Merge

In the following Mastering Word project, you will format a newsletter with information about the therapy dogs handled by volunteers at the University Medical Center. You will also create mailing labels so that the newsletter can be sent to the volunteer staff. Your completed documents will look similar to Figure 3.58.

PROJECT FILES

For Project 3F, you will need the following files:

New blank Word document
w03F_Dogs_Newsletter
w03F_Addresses

You will save your documents as:

Lastname_Firstname_3F_Dogs_Newsletter
Lastname_Firstname_3F_Addresses
Lastname_Firstname_3F_Mailing_Labels

PROJECT RESULTS

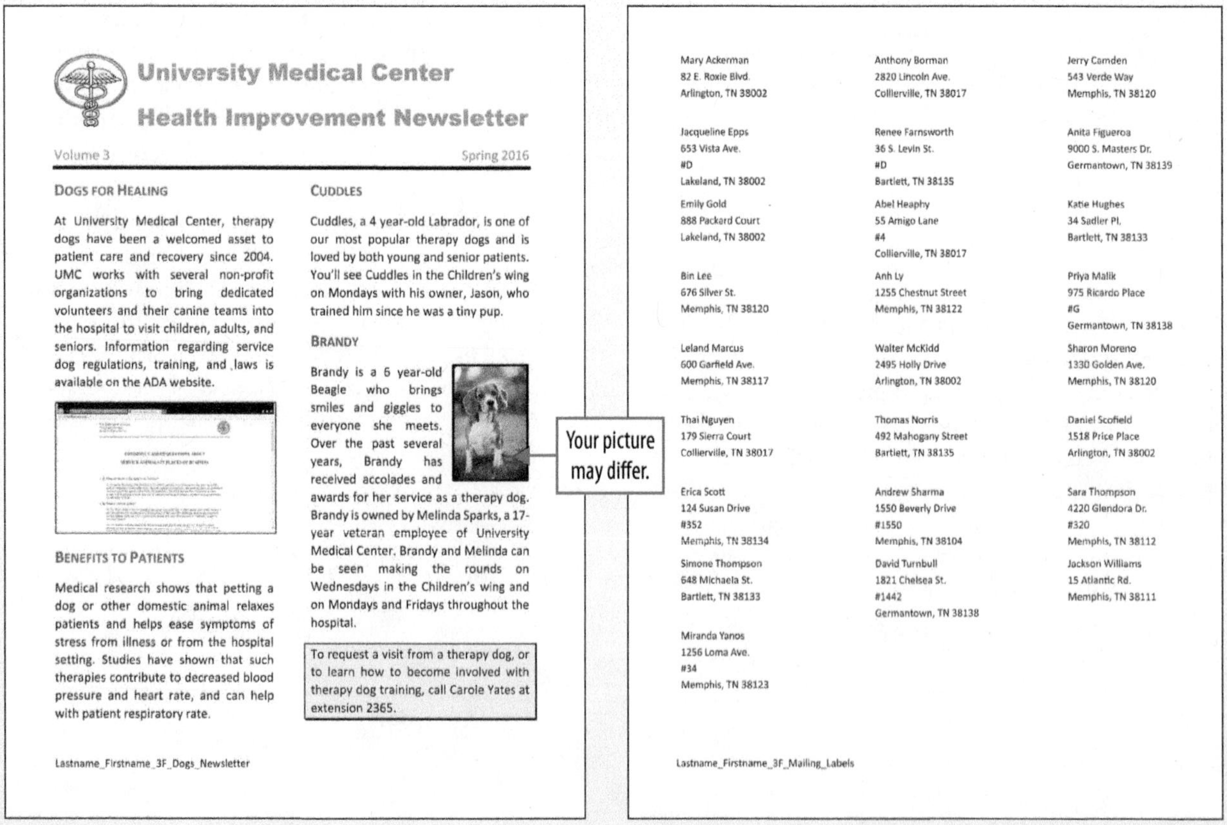
University Medical Center
Health Improvement Newsletter
Volume 3 Spring 2016

DOGS FOR HEALING

At University Medical Center, therapy dogs have been a welcomed asset to patient care and recovery since 2004. UMC works with several non-profit organizations to bring dedicated volunteers and their canine teams into the hospital to visit children, adults, and seniors. Information regarding service dog regulations, training, and laws is available on the ADA website.

BENEFITS TO PATIENTS

Medical research shows that petting a dog or other domestic animal relaxes patients and helps ease symptoms of stress from illness or from the hospital setting. Studies have shown that such therapies contribute to decreased blood pressure and heart rate, and can help with patient respiratory rate.

CUDDLES

Cuddles, a 4 year-old Labrador, is one of our most popular therapy dogs and is loved by both young and senior patients. You'll see Cuddles in the Children's wing on Mondays with his owner, Jason, who trained him since he was a tiny pup.

BRANDY

Brandy is a 6 year-old Beagle who brings smiles and giggles to everyone she meets. Over the past several years, Brandy has received accolades and awards for her service as a therapy dog. Brandy is owned by Melinda Sparks, a 17-year veteran employee of University Medical Center. Brandy and Melinda can be seen making the rounds on Wednesdays in the Children's wing and on Mondays and Fridays throughout the hospital.

To request a visit from a therapy dog, or to learn how to become involved with therapy dog training, call Carole Yates at extension 2365.

Lastname_Firstname_3F_Dogs_Newsletter

Your picture may differ.

Mary Ackerman 82 E. Roxie Blvd. Arlington, TN 38002	Anthony Borman 2820 Lincoln Ave. Collierville, TN 38017	Jerry Camden 543 Verde Way Memphis, TN 38120
Jacqueline Epps 653 Vista Ave. #D Lakeland, TN 38002	Renee Farnsworth 36 S. Levin St. #D Bartlett, TN 38135	Anita Figueroa 9000 S. Masters Dr. Germantown, TN 38139
Emily Gold 888 Packard Court Lakeland, TN 38002	Abel Heaphy 55 Amigo Lane #4 Collierville, TN 38017	Katie Hughes 34 Sadler Pl. Bartlett, TN 38133
Bin Lee 676 Silver St. Memphis, TN 38120	Anh Ly 1255 Chestnut Street Memphis, TN 38122	Priya Malik 975 Ricardo Place #G Germantown, TN 38138
Leland Marcus 600 Garfield Ave. Memphis, TN 38117	Walter McKidd 2495 Holly Drive Arlington, TN 38002	Sharon Moreno 1330 Golden Ave. Memphis, TN 38120
Thai Nguyen 179 Sierra Court Collierville, TN 38017	Thomas Norris 492 Mahogany Street Bartlett, TN 38135	Daniel Scofield 1518 Price Place Arlington, TN 38002
Erica Scott 124 Susan Drive #352 Memphis, TN 38134	Andrew Sharma 1550 Beverly Drive #1550 Memphis, TN 38104	Sara Thompson 4220 Glendora Dr. #320 Memphis, TN 38112
Simone Thompson 648 Michaela St. Bartlett, TN 38133	David Turnbull 1821 Chelsea St. #1442 Germantown, TN 38138	Jackson Williams 15 Atlantic Rd. Memphis, TN 38111
Miranda Yanos 1256 Loma Ave. #34 Memphis, TN 38123		

Lastname_Firstname_3F_Mailing_Labels

FIGURE 3.58

(Project 3F Dogs Newsletter and Mailing Labels continues on the next page)

CONTENT-BASED ASSESSMENTS

Mastering Word Project 3F Dogs Newsletter and Mailing Labels (continued)

1 Start Word. From your student files, open **w03F_Dogs_Newsletter**. **Save** the file in your **Word Chapter 3** folder as **Lastname_Firstname_3F_Dogs_Newsletter** and then add the file name to the footer. Select the first three lines of the document, and then change the **Font Color** to **Olive Green, Accent 3, Darker 25%**—in the seventh column, the fifth color. With the text selected, display the **Borders and Shading** dialog box. Apply a **3 pt** bottom border in **Black, Text 1**.

2 Click at the beginning of the newsletter title *University Medical Center*. Insert an online picture from **Office.com Clip Art** by searching for **caducei** Insert the picture of the physician symbol on top of the green oval with a blue outline. Use the **Set Transparent Color** command to make the green background transparent. Change the **Brightness/Contrast** to **Brightness: 0% (Normal) Contrast: +40%.**

3 **Scale** the picture to **50%** of its **Height**, and then change the **Text Wrapping** to **Square**. Change the **Horizontal Alignment** to **Left relative** to **Margin** and the **Vertical Alignment** to **Top relative** to **Margin**.

4 Starting with the paragraph that begins *Dogs for Healing*, select all of the text from that point to the end of the document. Change the **Spacing After** to **10 pt**, format the text in two columns, and apply **Justify** alignment. Insert a **Column break** before the subheading *Cuddles*.

5 Click at the beginning of the sentence that begins with *Brandy is a 6 year-old Beagle*. Insert an online picture from **Office.com Clip Art** by searching for **dog sitting up begging** and then insert the picture that displays. Insert the picture of the beagle sitting on the grass. If the picture is not available, from your student data files insert w03F_Dog. Rotate the picture using **Flip Horizontal**. Change the picture **Height** to **1.5** and then apply the **Square** layout option. Change the **Horizontal Alignment** to **Right relative** to **Margin** and the **Vertical Alignment** to **Top relative** to **Line**. Apply a **Black, Text 1 Picture Border** and change the **Weight** to **2 1/4 pt**.

6 Start Internet Explorer, navigate to **www.ada.gov/qasrvc.htm** and then maximize your browser window. In your **3F_Dogs_Newsletter** file, click at the end of the paragraph below the *Dogs for Healing* subheading, and then press Enter. In the blank line, insert a **Screenshot** of the website; do not link to the URL. Apply a **Black, Text 1 Picture Border** and change the **Weight** to **1 pt**.

7 Select the subheading *Dogs for Healing* including the paragraph mark. By using the **Font** dialog box, change the **Size** to **16**, apply **Bold**, apply the **Small caps** effect, and change the **Font color** to **Olive Green, Accent 3, Darker 50%**—in the seventh column, the last color. Apply the same formatting to the subheadings *Benefits to Patients*, *Cuddles*, and *Brandy*.

8 Select the last paragraph in the newsletter, and then apply a **1 pt Shadow** border, in **Black, Text 1**. Shade the paragraph with a **Fill** color of **Olive Green, Accent 3, Lighter 80%**—in the seventh column, the second color. Click the **FILE tab**, and then click **Show All Properties**. As the **Tags**, type **dogs, newsletter** As the **Subject**, type your course name and section number. Under **Related People**, if necessary, type your name in the **Author box**. **Print Preview** the document and make any necessary corrections. **Save** the document and **close** Word.

9 Start Word and display a new blank document. **Save** the document in your **Word Chapter 3** folder as **Lastname_Firstname_3F_Mailing_Labels** From your student files, **Open** the file **w03F_Addresses**. **Save** the address file in your **Word Chapter 3** folder as **Lastname_Firstname_3F_Addresses** and then add the file name to the footer. **Save** and **Close** the file. Be sure that your **Lastname_Firstname_3F_Mailing_Labels** document displays.

10 Start the **Step-by-Step Mail Merge Wizard** to create **Labels**. Be sure that the **Default tray** is selected and that the label vendor is **Avery US Letter**. The **Product number** is **5160 Easy Peel Address Labels**. Select the **Use an existing list** option, and then from your **Word Chapter 3** folder, open your **Lastname_Firstname_3F_Addresses** file. Add the following record to your file:

First Name	**Miranda**
Last Name	**Yanos**
Address 1	**1256 Loma Ave.**
Unit	**#34**
City	**Memphis**
State	**TN**
ZIP Code	**38123**

(Project 3F Dogs Newsletter and Mailing Labels continues on the next page)

CONTENT-BASED ASSESSMENTS

Mastering Word Project 3F Dogs Newsletter and Mailing Labels (continued)

11 Insert an **Address block** and match the fields. Match the **Address 2** field to the **Unit** field, and then update the labels. Preview the labels, and then select the entire document. Change the **Spacing Before** to **3** and then **Complete the merge**. Delete the last row from the bottom of the table, and then add the file name to the footer.

12 Display the document properties. As the **Tags** type **labels** and as the **Subject** type your course name and section number. Be sure your name displays in the **Author box**, and then **Save** your file. As directed by your instructor, print or submit electronically. In addition to your labels and address document, submit your **3F_Dogs_Newsletter** document as directed. **Close** Word and Internet Explorer.

END | You have completed Project 3F

CONTENT-BASED ASSESSMENTS

MyITLab® grader

Mastering Word | Project 3G Research Paper, Newsletter, and Mailing Labels

Apply 3A and 3B skills from these Objectives:

1. Create a Research Paper
2. Insert Footnotes in a Research Paper
3. Create Citations and a Bibliography in a Research Paper
4. Use Read Mode and PDF Reflow
5. Format a Multiple-Column Newsletter
6. Use Special Character and Paragraph Formatting
7. Create Mailing Labels Using Mail Merge

In the following Mastering Word project, you will edit and format a research paper and a newsletter, and you will create mailing labels. Your completed documents will look similar to Figure 3.59.

PROJECT FILES

For Project 3G, you will need the following files:

New blank Word document
w03G_Electronic_Records
w03G_Newsletter
w03G_Addresses

You will save your documents as:

Lastname_Firstname_3G_Electronic_Records
Lastname_Firstname_3G_Newsletter
Lastname_Firstname_3G_Mailing_Labels
Lastname_Firstname_3G_Addresses

PROJECT RESULTS

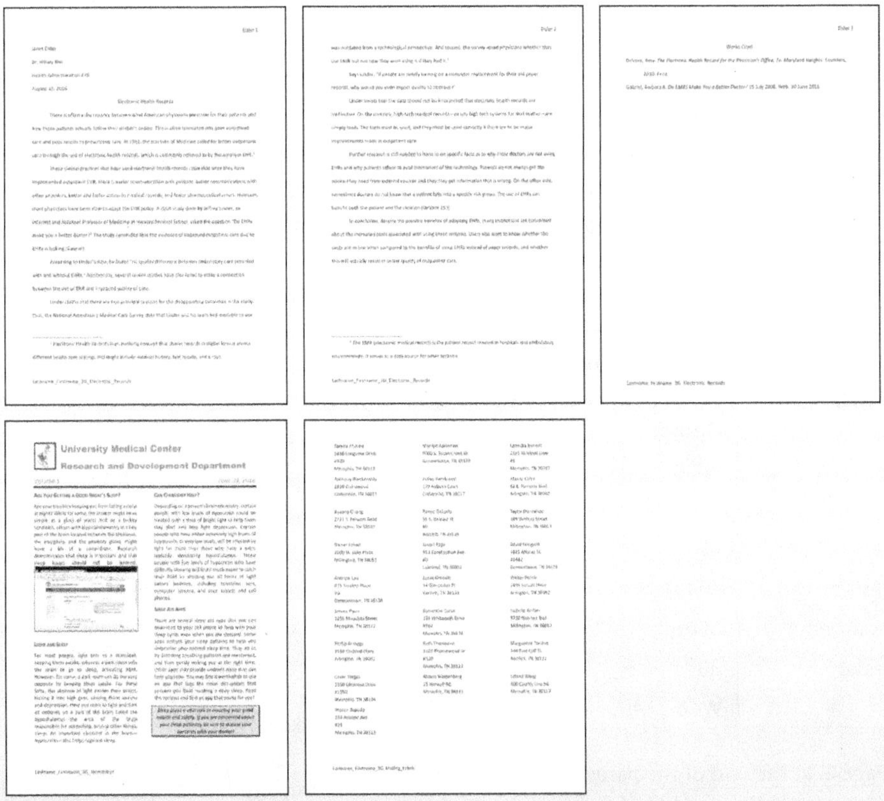

FIGURE 3.59

(Project 3G Research Paper, Newsletter, and Mailing Labels continues on the next page)

Mastering Word Project 3G Research Paper, Newsletter, and Mailing Labels (continued)

1 Start Word. From your student files, locate and open the document **w03G_Electronic_Records**, and then **Save** it in your **Word Chapter 3** folder as **Lastname_Firstname_3G_Electronic_Records** Display the header area, type **Eisler** and then press Spacebar. From the **Header & Footer group**, add a **Plain Number** page number from the **Current Position** gallery. Apply **Align Right** formatting to the header. Move to the footer area and add the file name to the footer.

Select all the text in the document, change the **Line Spacing** to **2.0**, and then change the **Spacing After** to **0 pt**. **Center** the title *Electronic Health Records*. Beginning with text below the centered title, select the text from that point to the end of the document, and then set a **First line** indent of **0.5"**.

2 At the top of **Page 1**, at the end of the paragraph that begins *There is often*, insert a footnote with the following text: **Electronic Health Records is an evolving concept that shares records in digital format across different health care settings and might include medical history, test results, and x-rays.**

At the top of **Page 2**, in the second line, at the end of the sentence that ends *if they had it*, insert a footnote with the following text: **The EMR (electronic medical record) is the patient record created in hospitals and ambulatory environments; it serves as a data source for other systems.**

3 On **Page 1**, at the end of the paragraph that begins *Those clinical practices*, click to the left of the period, and then using **MLA** format, insert a citation for a **Web site** with the following information:

Author	**Sabriel, Barbara A.**
Name of Web Page	**Do EMRS Make You a Better Doctor?**
Year	**2008**
Month	**July**
Day	**15**
Year Accessed	**2016**
Month Accessed	**June**
Day Accessed	**30**
Medium	**Web**

On **Page 2**, at the end of the paragraph that begins *Further research*, click to the left of the period, and then using **MLA** format, insert a citation for a **Book** with the following information:

Author	**DeVore, Amy**
Title	**The Electronic Health Record for the Physician's Office, 1e**
Year	**2010**
City	**Maryland Heights**
Publisher	**Saunders**
Medium	**Print**

In the report, select the citation you just created, display the **Citation Options**, and then edit the citation to include **Pages 253**

4 Insert a manual page break at the end of the document. On the new **Page 3**, display the **Paragraph** dialog box, and then change the **Special** indentation to **(none)**. Type **Works Cited** and then press Enter. On the **REFERENCES tab**, click **Bibliography**, and then click **Insert Bibliography**. **Center** the *Works Cited* title.

Use the **Source Manager** to change the name of the reference *Sabriel* to **Gabriel** and update both lists. Then in the selected citation in the report, display the **Citation Options** and click **Update Citations and Bibliography**. On the Works Cited page, select the references, apply **Double** line spacing, and then set the **Spacing After** paragraphs to **0 pt**.

Update the **Document Properties** with the following information:

Title	**Electronic Records**
Tags	**EMR, health records**
Comments	**Draft copy of report for class**
Categories	**Health Administration**
Subject	(insert your course name and section number)
Company	**University Medical Center**
Manager	**Dr. Hillary Kim**

On the left, click **Print** to display the **Print Preview**, make any necessary corrections, **save** and **close** the document; leave Word open. Hold this file until you complete this project.

(Project 3G Research Paper, Newsletter, and Mailing Labels continues on the next page)

Mastering Word | Project 3G Research Paper, Newsletter, and Mailing Labels (continued)

5 From your student files, open **w03G_ Newsletter. Save** the file in your **Word Chapter 3** folder as **Lastname_ Firstname_3G_Newsletter** and then add the file name to the footer. Select the first three lines of the document and apply a **3 pt** bottom border in **Black, Text 1**.

Click at the beginning of the newsletter title *University Medical Center*. Insert an online picture from **Office.com Clip Art** by searching for **microscope** Insert a picture of a black and white microscope. **Recolor** the picture by applying **Blue, Accent color 1 Light**. Apply a **Black, Text 1 Picture Border** and change the **Weight** to **2 1/4 pt**.

Scale the picture to **10%** of its **Height**, and then change the **Text Wrapping** to **Square**. Change the **Horizontal Alignment** to **Left relative to Margin** and the **Vertical Alignment** to **Top relative to Margin**.

6 Starting with the paragraph that begins *Are You Getting a Good Night's Sleep?*, select all of the text from that point to the end of the document. Format the text in two columns, and apply **Justify** alignment. Insert a **Column break** before the subheading *Can Chemistry Help?*

Start and maximize Internet Explorer, and then navigate to **www.nhlbi.nih.gov/health** and then in the middle of the page, click **Sleep Disorders**. In your **3G_Newsletter** file, click at the end of the paragraph below the *Are You Getting a Good Night's Sleep* subheading, and then press Enter. In the blank line, insert a **Screenshot** of the website; do not link to the URL. Apply a **Black, Text 1 Picture Border** and change the **Weight** to **1 pt**.

Select the subheading *Are You Getting a Good Night's Sleep?* including the paragraph mark. From the **Font** dialog box, apply **Bold** and **Small Caps** and change the **Font color** to **Dark Blue, Text 2**—in the fourth column, the first color. Apply the same formatting to the subheadings *Light and Sleep*, *Can Chemistry Help?* and *Sleep Aid Apps*.

7 Select the last paragraph in the newsletter, and then apply a **1 pt Shadow** border using **Black, Text 1**. Shade the paragraph with the **Fill** color **Dark Blue, Text 2, Lighter 80%**—in the fourth column, the second color. **Center** the text.

Click the **FILE tab**, and then click **Show All Properties**. As the Tags, type **sleep, newsletter** As the **Subject**, type your course name and section number. Under **Related People**, if necessary, type your name in the **Author box**. On the left, click **Print** to display the **Print Preview**. Make any necessary corrections. **Save** the document and **Exit** Word.

8 Start Word and display a new blank document. **Save** the document in your **Word Chapter 3** folder as **Lastname_Firstname_3G_Mailing_Labels** From your student files, **Open** the file **w03G_Addresses. Save** the address file in your **Word Chapter 3** folder as **Lastname_ Firstname_3G_Addresses** and then add the file name to the footer. **Save** and **Close** the file. Be sure that your **Lastname_Firstname_3G_Mailing_Labels** document displays.

9 Start the **Step-by-Step Mail Merge Wizard** to create **Labels**. Be sure that the **Default tray** is selected and that the label vendor is **Avery US Letter**. The **Product number** is **5160 Easy Peel Address Labels**. Select the **Use an existing list option**, and then from your **Word Chapter 3** folder, **Open** your **Lastname_Firstname_3G_Addresses** file. Add the following record to your file:

First Name	**Mason**
Last Name	**Zepeda**
Address 1	**134 Atlantic Ave.**
Unit	**#21**
City	**Memphis**
State	**TN**
ZIP Code	**38123**

10 Insert an **Address block** and match the fields. Match the **Address 2** field to the **Unit** field, and then update the labels. Preview the labels, and then select the entire document. Change the **Spacing Before** to **3** and then **Complete the merge**. Delete the last row from the bottom of the table, and then add the file name to the footer.

Display the document properties. As the **Tags** type **labels** and as the **Subject** type your course name and section number. Be sure your name displays in the **Author box**, and then **Save** your file. As directed by your instructor, print or submit your work electronically. In addition to your labels and address document, submit your **3G_Newsletter** and **3G_Electronic_Records** documents as directed. **Close** Word and Internet Explorer.

END | You have completed Project 3G

CONTENT-BASED ASSESSMENTS

Apply a combination of the 3A and 3B skills.

GO! Fix It | Project 3H Hospital Materials | Online

GO! Make It | Project 3I Health Newsletter | Online

GO! Solve It | Project 3J Colds and Flu | Online

Build from Scratch

GO! Solve It | Project 3K Cycling Newsletter

PROJECT FILES

For Project 3K, you will need the following file:

w03K_Cycling_Newsletter

You will save your document as:

Lastname_Firstname_3K_Cycling_Newsletter

The UMC Emergency Department publishes a newsletter focusing on safety and injury prevention. The topic for the current newsletter is bicycle safety. From your student data files, open w03K_Cycling_Newsletter, add the file name to the footer, and then save the file in your Word Chapter 3 folder as **Lastname_Firstname_3K_Cycling_Newsletter**.

Using the techniques that you practiced in this chapter, format the document in two-column, newsletter format. Format the nameplate so that it is clearly separate from the body of the newsletter. Insert column breaks as necessary and apply appropriate formatting to subheadings. Insert and format at least one appropriate online picture and insert a screenshot of a relevant website. Apply a border and shading to the last paragraph.

Add your name, your course name and section number, and the keywords **safety, newsletter** to the Properties area. Submit as directed.

CONTENT-BASED ASSESSMENTS

GO! Solve It Project 3K Cycling Newsletter (continued)

Performance Level

Performance Criteria	Exemplary: You consistently applied the relevant skills	Proficient: You sometimes, but not always, applied the relevant skills	Developing: You rarely or never applied the relevant skills
Format nameplate	The nameplate is formatted attractively and in a manner that clearly indicates that it is the nameplate.	The nameplate includes some formatting but is not clearly separated from the body of the newsletter.	The newsletter does not include a nameplate.
Insert and format at least one online picture	An sized and positioned online picture image is included.	An online picture is inserted but is either inappropriate, or is formatted or positioned poorly.	No online picture is included.
Border and shading added to a paragraph	The last paragraph displays an attractive border with shading.	An appropriate border or shading is displayed but not both.	No border or shading is applied.
Insert a screenshot	A relevant screenshot is inserted in one of the columns.	A screenshot is inserted in the document but does not relate to the content of the article.	No screenshot is inserted.

END | You have completed Project 3K

OUTCOMES-BASED ASSESSMENTS

RUBRIC

The following outcomes-based assessments are *open-ended assessments*. That is, there is no specific correct result; your result will depend on your approach to the information provided. Make *Professional Quality* your goal. Use the following scoring rubric to guide you in *how* to approach the problem and then to evaluate *how well* your approach solves the problem.

The *criteria*—Software Mastery, Content, Format and Layout, and Process—represent the knowledge and skills you have gained that you can apply to solving the problem. The *levels of performance*—Professional Quality, Approaching Professional Quality, or Needs Quality Improvements—help you and your instructor evaluate your result.

	Your completed project is of Professional Quality if you:	Your completed project is Approaching Professional Quality if you:	Your completed project Needs Quality Improvements if you:
1-Software Mastery	Choose and apply the most appropriate skills, tools, and features and identify efficient methods to solve the problem.	Choose and apply some appropriate skills, tools, and features, but not in the most efficient manner.	Choose inappropriate skills, tools, or features, or are inefficient in solving the problem.
2-Content	Construct a solution that is clear and well organized, contains content that is accurate, appropriate to the audience and purpose, and is complete. Provide a solution that contains no errors in spelling, grammar, or style.	Construct a solution in which some components are unclear, poorly organized, inconsistent, or incomplete. Misjudge the needs of the audience. Have some errors in spelling, grammar, or style, but the errors do not detract from comprehension.	Construct a solution that is unclear, incomplete, or poorly organized; contains some inaccurate or inappropriate content; and contains many errors in spelling, grammar, or style. Do not solve the problem.
3-Format & Layout	Format and arrange all elements to communicate information and ideas, clarify function, illustrate relationships, and indicate relative importance.	Apply appropriate format and layout features to some elements, but not others. Overuse features, causing minor distraction.	Apply format and layout that does not communicate information or ideas clearly. Do not use format and layout features to clarify function, illustrate relationships, or indicate relative importance. Use available features excessively, causing distraction.
4-Process	Use an organized approach that integrates planning, development, self-assessment, revision, and reflection.	Demonstrate an organized approach in some areas, but not others; or, use an insufficient process of organization throughout.	Do not use an organized approach to solve the problem.

Apply a combination of the 3A and 3B skills.

OUTCOMES-BASED ASSESSMENTS

GO! Think Project 3L Influenza Report

Build from Scratch

PROJECT FILES

For Project 3L, you will need the following file:

New blank Word document

You will save your document as:

Lastname_Firstname_3L_Influenza

As part of the ongoing research conducted by University Medical Center in the area of community health and contagious diseases, Dr. Hillary Kim has asked Sarah Stanger to create a report on influenza—how it spreads, and how it can be prevented in the community.

Create a new file and save it as **Lastname_Firstname_3L_Influenza** Create the report in MLA format. The report should include at least two footnotes, at least two citations, and should include a *Works Cited* page.

The report should contain an introduction, and then information about what influenza is, how it spreads, and how it can be prevented. A good place to start is at http://health.nih.gov/topic/influenza.

Add the file name to the footer. Add appropriate information to the Document Properties and submit it as directed.

END | You have completed Project 3L

OUTCOMES-BASED ASSESSMENTS

Build from Scratch

GO! Think Project 3M Volunteer Newsletter **Online**

Build from Scratch

You and GO! Project 3N College Newsletter **Online**

GO! Cumulative Group Project Project 3O Bell Orchid Hotels **Online**

Introduction to Microsoft Excel 2013

E
Excel 2013

modern financial analysis / Fotolia

Excel 2013: Introduction

Video EA

Quantitative information! Defined as a type of information that can be counted or that communicates the quantity of something, quantitative information can be either easy or hard to understand—depending on how it is presented. According to Stephen Few in his book *Show Me the Numbers*: "Quantitative information forms the core of what businesses must know to operate effectively."

Excel 2013 is a tool to communicate quantitative business information effectively. Sometimes you need to communicate quantitative relationships. For example, the number of units sold per geographic region shows a relationship of sales to geography. Sometimes you need to summarize numbers. A list of every student enrolled at your college with his or her major is not as informative as a summary of the total number of students in each major. In business, the most common quantitative information is some measure of money—costs, sales, payroll, expenses—and so on.

Rather than just a tool for making calculations, Excel is now a tool for you to communicate and collaborate with others. When you want to communicate visually with tables and graphs, Excel 2013 has many new features to help you do so. Microsoft Excel 2013 works best on a Windows 8 PC—desktop, laptop, or tablet—because if your PC is touch-enabled, you will be able to use your fingers to work with Excel.

Creating a Worksheet and Charting Data

1

EXCEL 2013

GO! to Work Video E1

PROJECT 1A

OUTCOMES
Create a sales report with an embedded column chart and sparklines.

PROJECT 1B

OUTCOMES
Calculate the value of an inventory.

OBJECTIVES

1. Create, Save, and Navigate an Excel Workbook
2. Enter Data in a Worksheet
3. Construct and Copy Formulas and Use the SUM Function
4. Format Cells with Merge & Center, Cell Styles, and Themes
5. Chart Data to Create a Column Chart and Insert Sparklines
6. Print a Worksheet, Display Formulas, and Close Excel

OBJECTIVES

7. Check Spelling in a Worksheet
8. Enter Data by Range
9. Construct Formulas for Mathematical Operations
10. Edit Values in a Worksheet
11. Format a Worksheet

Warren Goldswain / Fotolia

In This Chapter

In this chapter, you will use Microsoft Excel 2013 to create and analyze data organized into columns and rows. After entering data in a worksheet, you can perform complex calculations, analyze the data to make logical decisions, and create informative charts that help readers visualize your data in a way they can understand and that is meaningful. In this chapter, you will create and modify Excel workbooks. You will practice the basics of worksheet design; create a footer; enter and edit data in a worksheet; chart data; and then save, preview, and print workbooks. You will also construct formulas for mathematical operations.

The projects in this chapter relate to **Pro Fit Marietta**, a distributor of fitness equipment and apparel to private gyms, personal trainers, health clubs, corporate wellness centers, hotels, college athletic facilities, physical therapy practices, and multi-unit residential properties. The company's mission is to find, test, and distribute the highest quality fitness products in the world to its customers for the benefit of consumers. Their popular blog provides useful tips on how to use the latest workout and fitness equipment. The company is located in Marietta, Georgia, which is metropolitan Atlanta's largest suburb.

Sales Report with Embedded Column Chart and Sparklines

PROJECT 1A

MyITLab®
Project 1A Training

PROJECT ACTIVITIES

In Activities 1.01 through 1.17, you will create an Excel worksheet for Michelle Barry, the President of Pro Fit Marietta. The worksheet displays the second quarter sales of cardio equipment for the current year and includes a chart to visually represent the data. Your completed worksheet will look similar to Figure 1.1.

PROJECT FILES

For Project 1A, you will need the following file:
New blank Excel workbook

You will save your workbook as:
Lastname_Firstname_1A_Quarterly_Sales

PROJECT RESULTS

Build from Scratch

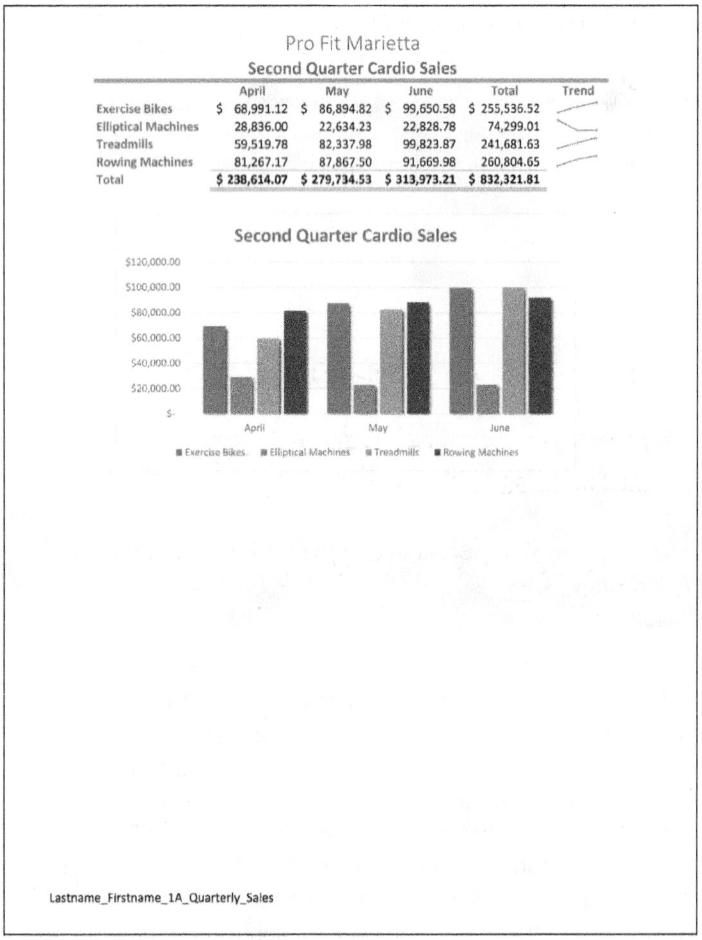
Pro Fit Marietta

Second Quarter Cardio Sales

	April	May	June	Total	Trend
Exercise Bikes	$ 68,991.12	$ 86,894.82	$ 99,650.58	$ 255,536.52	
Elliptical Machines	28,836.00	22,634.23	22,828.78	74,299.01	
Treadmills	59,519.78	82,337.98	99,823.87	241,681.63	
Rowing Machines	81,267.17	87,867.50	91,669.98	260,804.65	
Total	**$ 238,614.07**	**$ 279,734.53**	**$ 313,973.21**	**$ 832,321.81**	

Lastname_Firstname_1A_Quarterly_Sales

FIGURE 1.1 Project 1A Sales Report with Embedded Column Chart and Sparklines

NOTE **If You Are Using a Touchscreen**

- Tap an item to click it.
- Press and hold for a few seconds to right-click; release when the information or commands displays.
- Touch the screen with two or more fingers and then pinch together to zoom in or stretch your fingers apart to zoom out.
- Slide your finger on the screen to scroll—slide left to scroll right and slide right to scroll left.
- Slide to rearrange—similar to dragging with a mouse.
- Swipe from edge: from right to display charms; from left to expose open apps, snap apps, or close apps; from top or bottom to show commands or close an app.
- Swipe to select—slide an item a short distance with a quick movement—to select an item and bring up commands, if any.

Objective 1 Create, Save, and Navigate an Excel Workbook

Video E1-1

On startup, Excel displays a new blank ***workbook***—the Excel document that stores your data—which contains one or more pages called a ***worksheet***. A worksheet—or ***spreadsheet***—is stored in a workbook and is formatted as a pattern of uniformly spaced horizontal rows and vertical columns. The intersection of a column and a row forms a box referred to as a ***cell***.

Activity 1.01 Starting Excel, Navigating Excel, and Naming and Saving a Workbook

1. Start Excel, and then on the opening screen, click **Blank workbook**. In the lower right corner of the window, on the status bar, if necessary, click the Normal button, and then to the right, locate the zoom—magnification—level.

   Your zoom level should be 100%, although some figures in this textbook may be shown at a higher zoom level. The ***Normal view*** maximizes the number of cells visible on your screen and keeps the column letters and row numbers closer.

BY TOUCH

On Excel's opening screen, tap Blank workbook.

2. Press F12 to display the **Save As** dialog box, and then navigate to the location where you will store your workbooks for this chapter.
3. In your storage location, create a new folder named **Excel Chapter 1** Open the new folder to display its folder window, and then in the **File name** box, notice that *Book1* displays as the default file name.
4. In the **File name** box, if necessary click *Book1* to select it, and then using your own name, type **Lastname_Firstname_1A_Quarterly_Sales** being sure to include the underscore (_) instead of spaces between words.
5. In the **Save As** dialog box, click **Save**. Compare your screen with Figure 1.2, and then take a moment to study the Excel window parts in the table in Figure 1.3.

More Knowledge **Creating a New Workbook by Using a Template**

On Excel's opening screen, you can select a professional-look template instead of a blank workbook. Templates have some formatting completed; you just add and modify what you want. You can select or search for a template to match your needs from Excel's opening screen; or, from the Excel window, click FILE, and then click New to search for online templates.

FIGURE 1.2

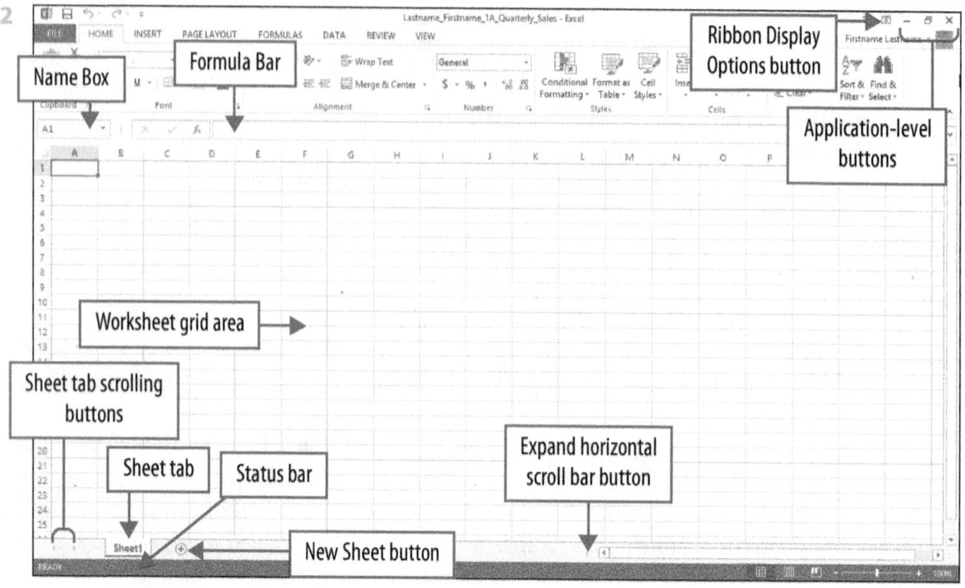

FIGURE 1.3

PARTS OF THE EXCEL WINDOW	
WINDOW PART	**DESCRIPTION**
Expand horizontal scroll bar button	Increases the width of the horizontal scroll bar.
Formula Bar	Displays the value or formula contained in the active cell; also permits entry or editing.
Sheet tab	Identifies the worksheet in the workbook.
New sheet button	Inserts an additional worksheet.
Name Box	Displays the name of the selected cell, table, chart, or object.
Sheet tab scrolling buttons	Display sheet tabs that are not in view when there are numerous sheet tabs.
Status bar	Displays the current cell mode, page number, worksheet information, view and zoom buttons, and for numerical data, common calculations such as Sum and Average.
Application-level buttons	Minimize, close, or restore the previous size of the displayed workbook.
Ribbon Display Options button	Displays various ways you can display the ribbon—the default is Show Tabs and Commands.
Worksheet grid area	Displays the columns and rows that intersect to form the worksheet's cells.

6 Take a moment to study Figure 1.4 and the table in Figure 1.5 to become familiar with the Excel workbook window.

FIGURE 1.4

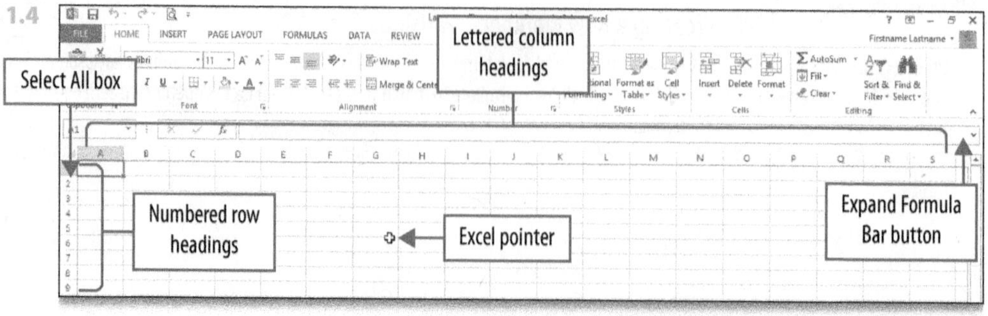

FIGURE 1.5

EXCEL WORKBOOK WINDOW ELEMENTS	
WORKBOOK WINDOW ELEMENT	**DESCRIPTION**
Excel pointer	Displays the location of the pointer.
Expand Formula Bar button	Increases the height of the Formula Bar to display lengthy cell content.
Lettered column headings	Indicate the column letter.
Numbered row headings	Indicate the row number.
Select All box	Selects all the cells in a worksheet.

7 In the lower right corner of the screen, in the horizontal scroll bar, click the **right scroll arrow** one time to shift **column A** out of view.

A ***column*** is a vertical group of cells in a worksheet. Beginning with the first letter of the alphabet, *A*, a unique letter identifies each column—this is called the ***column heading***. Clicking one of the horizontal scroll bar arrows shifts the window either left or right one column at a time.

8 Point to the **right scroll arrow**, and then hold down the left mouse button until the columns begin to scroll rapidly to the right; release the mouse button when you begin to see pairs of letters as the column headings.

BY TOUCH

Anywhere on the worksheet, slide your finger to the left to scroll to the right.

9 Slowly drag the horizontal scroll box to the left, and notice that just above the scroll box, ScreenTips with the column letters display as you drag. Drag the horizontal scroll box left or right—or click the **left or right scroll arrow**—as necessary to position **column Z** near the center of your screen.

Column headings after column Z use two letters starting with AA, AB, and so on through ZZ. After that, columns begin with three letters beginning with AAA. This pattern provides 16,384 columns. The last column is XFD.

10 In the vertical scroll bar, click the **down scroll arrow** one time to move **Row 1** out of view.

A ***row*** is a horizontal group of cells. Beginning with number 1, a unique number identifies each row—this is the ***row heading***, located at the left side of the worksheet. A single worksheet can handle 1 million rows of data.

11 Use the skills you just practiced to scroll horizontally to display **column A**, and if necessary, **row 1**.

12 Click **Save**.

Objective 2 Enter Data in a Worksheet

Video E1-2

Cell content, which is anything you type in a cell, can be one of two things: either a ***constant value***—referred to simply as a ***value***—or a ***formula***. A formula is an equation that performs mathematical calculations on values in your worksheet. The most commonly used values are ***text values*** and ***number values***, but a value can also include a date or a time of day. A text value is also referred to as a ***label***.

Activity 1.02 | Entering Text, Using AutoComplete, and Using the Name Box to Select a Cell

A text value usually provides information about number values in other worksheet cells. For example, a title such as Second Quarter Cardio Sales gives the reader an indication that the data in the worksheet relates to information about sales of cardio equipment during the three-month period April through June.

1 Point to and then click the cell at the intersection of **column A** and **row 1** to make it the ***active cell***—the cell is outlined in black and ready to accept data.

The intersecting column letter and row number form the ***cell reference***—also called the ***cell address***. When a cell is active, its column letter and row number are highlighted. The cell reference of the selected cell, *A1*, displays in the Name Box.

2 With cell **A1** as the active cell, type the worksheet title **Pro Fit Marietta** and then press Enter. Compare your screen with Figure 1.6.

Text or numbers in a cell are referred to as ***data***. You must confirm the data you type in a cell by pressing Enter or by some other keyboard movement, such as pressing Tab or an arrow key. Pressing Enter moves the active cell to the cell below.

FIGURE 1.6

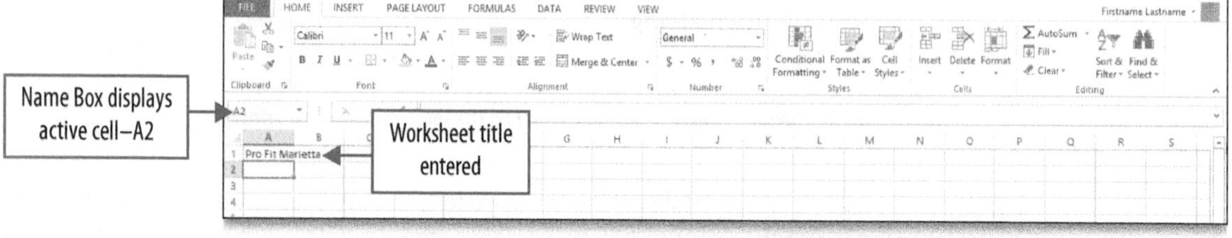

3 In cell **A1**, notice that the text does not fit; the text extends into cell **B1** to the right.

If text is too long for a cell and cells to the right are empty, the text will display. If the cells to the right contain other data, only the text that will fit in the cell displays.

4 In cell **A2**, type the worksheet subtitle **Second Quarter Cardio Sales** and then press Enter. Compare your screen with Figure 1.7.

FIGURE 1.7

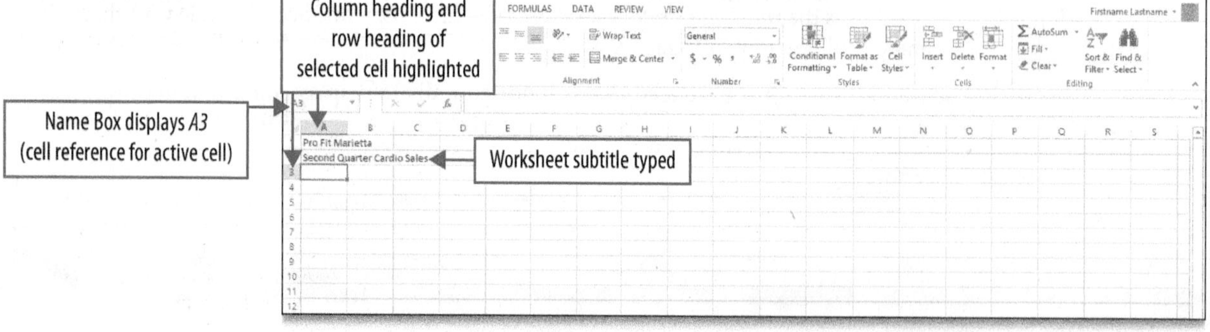

5 Above **column A**, click in the **Name Box** to select the cell reference *A3*, and then type **a4** Press Enter to make cell **A4** the active cell. In cell **A4**, type **Exercise Bikes** to form the first row title, and then press Enter.

The text characters that you typed align at the left edge of the cell—referred to as ***left alignment***—and cell A5 becomes the active cell. Left alignment is the default for text values. You can type a cell address in the Name Box and press Enter to move to a specific cell quickly.

6 In cell **A5**, type **E** and notice the text from the previous cell displays.

If the first characters you type in a cell match an existing entry in the column, Excel fills in the remaining characters for you. This feature, called ***AutoComplete***, assists only with alphabetic values.

7 Continue typing the remainder of the row title **lliptical Machines** and press Enter.

The AutoComplete suggestion is removed when the entry you are typing differs from the previous value.

8 In cell **A6**, type **Treadmills** and press Enter. In cell **A7**, type **Rowing Machines** and press Enter. In cell **A8**, type **Total** and press Enter. On the **Quick Access Toolbar**, click **Save**.

ANOTHER WAY Use the keyboard shortcut Ctrl + S to save changes to your workbook.

Activity 1.03 | Using Auto Fill and Keyboard Shortcuts

1 Click cell **B3**. Type **A** and notice that when you begin to type in a cell, on the **Formula Bar**, the **Cancel** and **Enter** buttons become active, as shown in Figure 1.8.

FIGURE 1.8

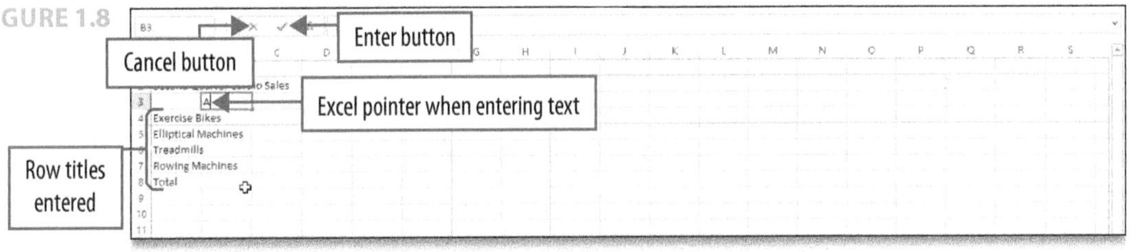

2 Continue to type **pril** On the **Formula Bar**, notice that values you type in a cell also display there. Then, on the **Formula Bar**, click **Enter** to confirm the entry and keep cell **B3** active.

3 With cell **B3** active, locate the small square in the lower right corner of the selected cell.

You can drag this ***fill handle***—the small square in the lower right corner of a selected cell—to adjacent cells to fill the cells with values based on the first cell.

4 Point to the **fill handle** until the + pointer displays, hold down the left mouse button, drag to the right to cell **D3**, and as you drag, notice the ScreenTips *May* and *June*. Release the mouse button.

5 Under the text that you just filled, click the **Auto Fill Options** button that displays, and then compare your screen with Figure 1.9.

Auto Fill generates and extends a ***series*** of values into adjacent cells based on the value of other cells. A series is a group of things that come one after another in succession; for example, *April, May, June.*

The Auto Fill Options button displays options to fill the data; options vary depending on the content and program from which you are filling, and the format of the data you are filling.

Fill Series is selected, indicating the action that was taken. Because the options are related to the current task, the button is referred to as being ***context sensitive***.

FIGURE 1.9

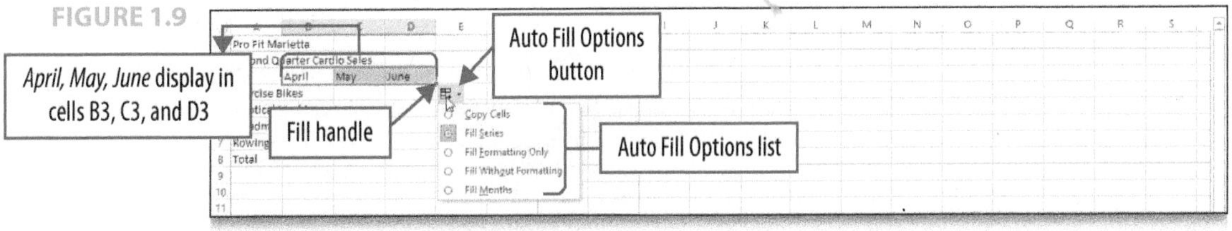

6 Click in any cell to cancel the display of the list.

The list no longer displays; the button will display until you perform some other screen action.

7 Press Ctrl + Home, which is the keyboard shortcut to make cell **A1** active.

8 On the **Quick Access Toolbar**, click **Save** to save the changes you have made to your workbook.

9 Take a moment to study the table in Figure 1.10 to become familiar with keyboard shortcuts with which you can navigate the Excel worksheet.

FIGURE 1.10

KEYBOARD SHORTCUTS TO NAVIGATE THE EXCEL WINDOW	
TO MOVE THE LOCATION OF THE ACTIVE CELL:	**PRESS:**
Up, down, right, or left one cell	↑, ↓, →, ←
Down one cell	Enter
Up one cell	Shift + Enter
Up one full screen	PageUp
Down one full screen	PageDown
To column A of the current row	Home
To the last cell in the last column of the active area (the rectangle formed by all the rows and columns in a worksheet that contain entries)	Ctrl + End
To cell A1	Ctrl + Home
Right one cell	Tab
Left one cell	Shift + Tab
To the cell one worksheet window to the right	Alt + PageDown
To the cell one worksheet window to the left	Alt + PageUp
To the cell containing specific content that you enter in the Find and Replace dialog box	Shift + F5
To the cell that corresponds with the cell reference you enter in the Go To dialog box	F5

Activity 1.04 | Aligning Text and Adjusting the Size of Columns

1 In the **column heading area**, point to the vertical line between **column A** and **column B** to display the ✛ pointer, press and hold down the left mouse button, and then compare your screen with Figure 1.11.

A ScreenTip displays information about the width of the column. The default width of a column is 64 ***pixels***. A pixel, short for ***picture element***, is a point of light measured in dots per square inch. Sixty-four pixels equal 8.43 characters, which is the average number of characters that will fit in a cell using the default font. The default font in Excel is Calibri and the default font size is 11.

FIGURE 1.11

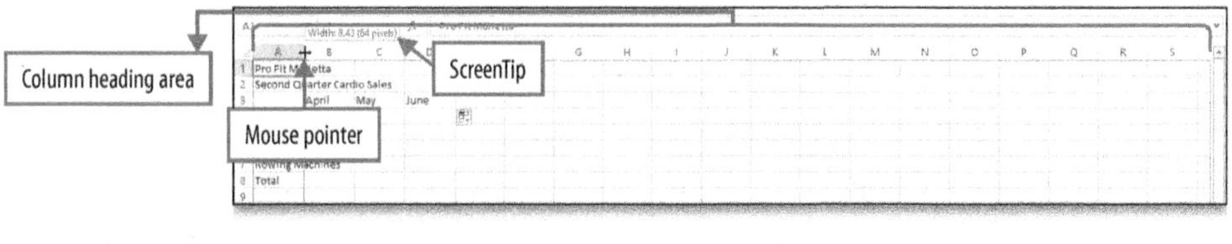

2 Drag to the right, and when the number of pixels indicated in the ScreenTip reaches **120 pixels**, release the mouse button. If you are not satisfied with your result, click Undo on the Quick Access Toolbar and begin again.

This width accommodates the longest row title in cells A4 through A8—*Elliptical Machines*. The worksheet subtitle in cell A2 spans more than one column and still does not fit in column A.

3 Point to cell **B3** and then drag across to select cells **B3, C3,** and **D3**. Compare your screen with Figure 1.12; if you are not satisfied with your result, click anywhere and begin again.

The three cells, B3 through D3, are selected and form a ***range***—two or more cells on a worksheet that are adjacent (next to each other) or nonadjacent (not next to each other). This range of cells is referred to as *B3:D3*. When you see a colon (:) between two cell references, the range includes all the cells between the two cell references.

A range of cells you select this way is indicated by a dark border, and Excel treats the range as a single unit so you can make the same changes to more than one cell at a time. The selected cells in the range are highlighted except for the first cell in the range, which displays in the Name Box.

When you select a range of data, the ***Quick Analysis tool*** displays in the lower right corner of the selected range with which you can analyze your data by using Excel tools such as charts, color-coding, and formulas.

FIGURE 1.12

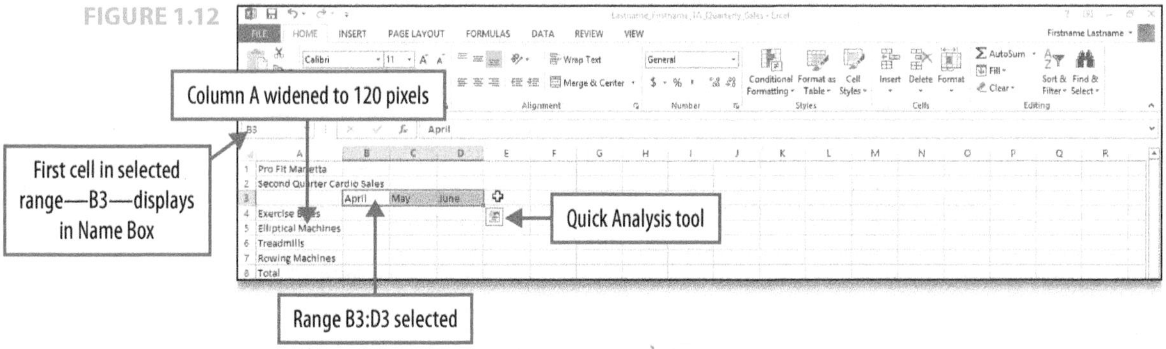

BY TOUCH

To select a range, tap and hold the first cell, and then when the circular gripper displays, drag it to the right, or to the right and down, to define the beginning and end of a range.

4 With the range **B3:D3** selected, point anywhere over the selected range, right-click, and then on the mini toolbar, click **Center**. On the **Quick Access Toolbar**, click **Save**.

The column titles *April*, *May*, *June* align in the center of each cell.

Activity 1.05 | Entering Numbers

To type number values, use either the number keys across the top of your keyboard or the numeric keypad if you have one—laptop computers may not have a numeric keypad.

1 Under *April*, click cell **B4**, type **68991.12** and then on the **Formula Bar**, click **Enter** to maintain cell **B4** as the active cell. Compare your screen with Figure 1.13.

By default, *number* values align at the right edge of the cell. The default ***number format***—a specific way in which Excel displays numbers—is the ***general format***. In the default general format, whatever you type in the cell will display, with the exception of trailing zeros to the right of a decimal point. For example, in the number 237.50 the *0* following the *5* is a trailing zero and will not display.

Data that displays in a cell is the ***displayed value***. Data that displays in the Formula Bar is the ***underlying value***. The number of digits or characters that display in a cell—the displayed value—depends on the width of the column. Calculations on numbers will always be based on the underlying value, not the displayed value.

FIGURE 1.13

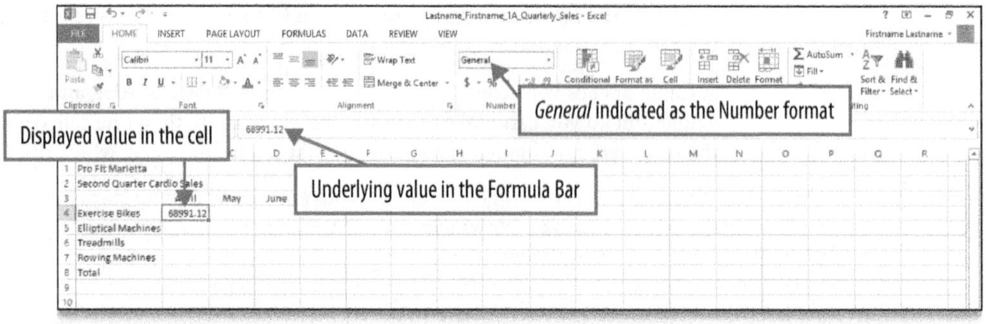

2 Press Tab to make cell **C4** active. Type **86894.82** and then press Tab to move to cell **D4**. Type **99650.58** and then press Enter to move to cell **B5** in the next row. Then, by using the same technique, enter the remaining sales numbers as shown:

	APRIL	MAY	JUNE
Elliptical Machines	**28836**	**22634.23**	**22828.78**
Treadmills	**59519.78**	**82337.98**	**99823.87**
Rowing Machines	**81267.17**	**87867.50**	**91669.98**

3 Compare the numbers you entered with Figure 1.14, and then **Save** your workbook.

In the default General format, trailing zeros to the right of a decimal point will not display. For example, when you type *87867.50*, the cell displays 87867.5 instead.

FIGURE 1.14

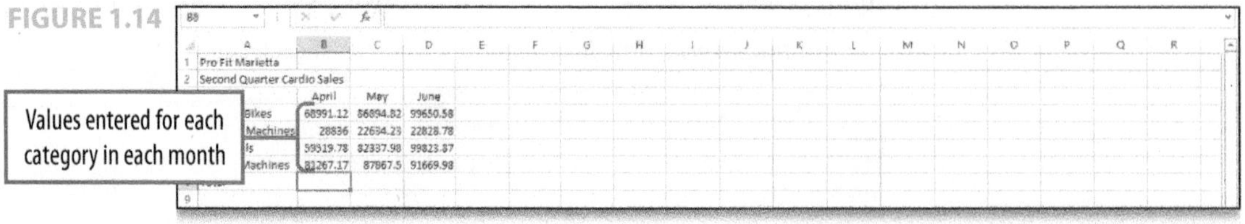

Objective 3 Construct and Copy Formulas and Use the SUM Function

Video E1-3

A cell contains either a constant value (text or numbers) or a formula. A formula is an equation that performs mathematical calculations on values in other cells, and then places the result in the cell containing the formula. You can create formulas or use a ***function***—a prewritten formula that looks at one or more values, performs an operation, and then returns a value.

Activity 1.06 Constructing a Formula and Using the SUM Function

In this activity, you will practice three different ways to sum a group of numbers in Excel.

1 Click cell **B8** to make it the active cell and type **=**

The equal sign (=) displays in the cell with the insertion point blinking, ready to accept more data.

All formulas begin with the = sign, which signals Excel to begin a calculation. The Formula Bar displays the = sign, and the Formula Bar Cancel and Enter buttons display.

2 At the insertion point, type **b4** and then compare your screen with Figure 1.15.

A list of Excel functions that begin with the letter *B* may briefly display—as you progress in your study of Excel, you will use functions of this type. A blue border with small corner boxes surrounds cell B4, which indicates that the cell is part of an active formula. The color used in the box matches the color of the cell reference in the formula.

FIGURE 1.15

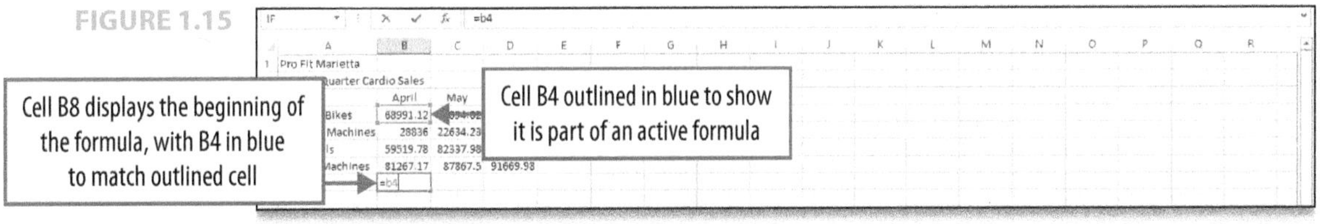

3 At the insertion point, type **+** and then type **b5**

A border of another color surrounds cell B5, and the color matches the color of the cell reference in the active formula. When typing cell references, it is not necessary to use uppercase letters.

4 At the insertion point, type **+b6+b7** and then press Enter.

The result of the formula calculation—*238614.1*—displays in the cell. Recall that in the default General format, trailing zeros do not display.

5 Click cell **B8** again, look at the **Formula Bar**, and then compare your screen with Figure 1.16.

The formula adds the values in cells B4 through B7, and the result displays in cell B8. In this manner, you can construct a formula by typing. Although cell B8 displays the *result* of the formula, the formula itself displays in the Formula Bar. This is referred to as the ***underlying formula***.

Always view the Formula Bar to be sure of the exact content of a cell—*a displayed number may actually be a formula.*

FIGURE 1.16

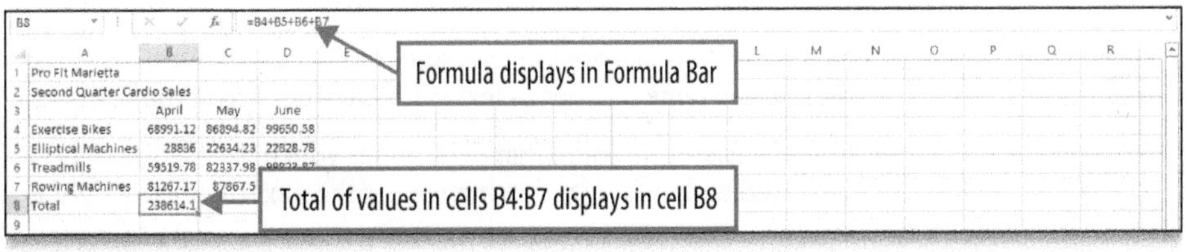

6 Click cell **C8** and type **=** to signal the beginning of a formula. Then, point to cell **C4** and click one time.

The reference to the cell C4 is added to the active formula. A moving border surrounds the referenced cell, and the border color and the color of the cell reference in the formula are color coded to match.

7 At the insertion point, type **+** and then click cell **C5**. Repeat this process to complete the formula to add cells **C6** and **C7**, and then press Enter.

The result of the formula calculation—*279734.5*—displays in the cell. This method of constructing a formula is the ***point and click method***.

8 Click cell **D8**. On the **HOME tab**, in the **Editing group**, click **AutoSum** [Σ AutoSum ▾], and then compare your screen with Figure 1.17.

SUM is an Excel function—a prewritten formula. A moving border surrounds the range D4:D7 and *=SUM(D4:D7)* displays in cell D8.

The = sign signals the beginning of a formula, *SUM* indicates the type of calculation that will take place (addition), and *(D4:D7)* indicates the range of cells on which the sum calculation will be performed. A ScreenTip provides additional information about the action.

FIGURE 1.17

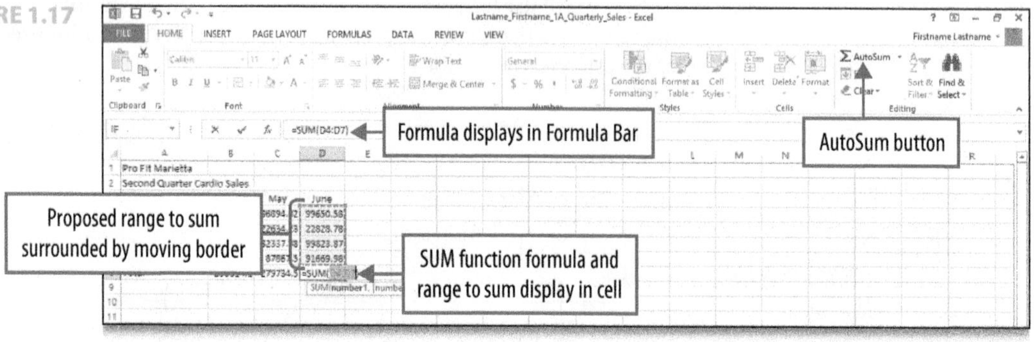

ANOTHER WAY Use the keyboard shortcut Alt + =; or, on the Formulas tab, in the Function Library group, click the AutoSum button.

9 Look at the **Formula Bar**, and notice that the formula also displays there. Then, look again at the cells surrounded by the moving border.

When you activate the ***Sum function***, Excel first looks *above* the active cell for a range of cells to sum. If no range is above the active cell, Excel will look to the *left* for a range of cells to sum. If the proposed range is not what you want to calculate, you can select a different group of cells.

10 Press Enter to construct a formula by using the prewritten SUM function.

Your total is *313973.2*. Because the Sum function is frequently used, it has its own button in the Editing group on the Home tab of the ribbon. A larger version of the button also displays on the FORMULAS tab in the Function Library group. This button is also referred to as ***AutoSum***.

11 Notice that the totals in the range **B8:D8** display only one decimal place. Click **Save**.

Number values that are too long to fit in the cell do *not* spill over into the unoccupied cell to the right in the same manner as text values. Rather, Excel rounds the number to fit the space.

Rounding is a procedure that determines which digit at the right of the number will be the last digit displayed and then increases it by one if the next digit to its right is 5, 6, 7, 8, or 9.

Activity 1.07 | Copying a Formula by Using the Fill Handle

You have practiced three ways to create a formula—by typing, by using the point-and-click technique, and by using a Function button from the ribbon. You can also copy formulas. When you copy a formula from one cell to another, Excel adjusts the cell references to fit the new location of the formula.

1 Click cell **E3**, type **Total** and then press Enter.

The text in cell E3 is centered because the centered format continues from the adjacent cell.

2 With cell **E4** as the active cell, hold down Alt, and then press =. Compare your screen with Figure 1.18.

Alt + = is the keyboard shortcut for the Sum function. Recall that Excel first looks above the selected cell for a proposed range of cells to sum, and if no data is detected, Excel looks to the left and proposes a range of cells to sum.

FIGURE 1.18

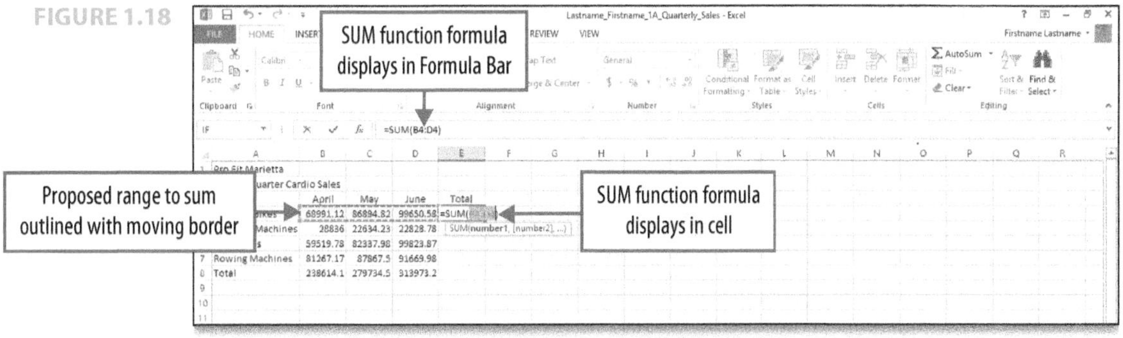

3 On the **Formula Bar**, click **Enter** ✓ to display the result and keep cell **E4** active.

The total dollar amount of *Exercise Bikes* sold in the quarter is *255536.5*. In cells E5:E8, you can see that you need a formula similar to the one in E4, but formulas that refer to the cells in row 5, row 6, and so on.

4 With cell **E4** active, point to the **fill handle** in the lower right corner of the cell until the + pointer displays. Then, drag down through cell **E8**; if you are not satisfied with your result, on the Quick Access Toolbar, click Undo and begin again. Compare your screen with Figure 1.19.

FIGURE 1.19

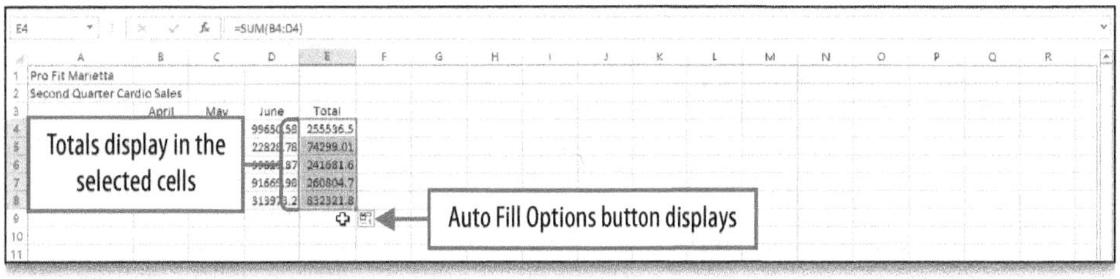

5 Click cell **E5**, look at the **Formula Bar**, and notice the formula *=SUM(B5:D5)*. Click cell **E6**, look at the **Formula Bar**, and then notice the formula *=SUM(B6:D6)*.

In each row, Excel copied the formula but adjusted the cell references *relative to* the row number. This is called a ***relative cell reference***—a cell reference based on the relative position of the cell that contains the formula and the cells referred to in the formula.

The calculation is the same, but it is performed on the cells in that particular row. Use this method to insert numerous formulas into spreadsheets quickly.

6 Click cell **F3**, type **Trend** and then press Enter. **Save** your workbook.

Objective 4 Format Cells with Merge & Center, Cell Styles, and Themes

Video E1-4

Format—change the appearance of—cells to make your worksheet attractive and easy to read.

Activity 1.08 | Using Merge & Center and Applying Cell Styles

1. Select the range **A1:F1**, and then in the **Alignment group**, click **Merge & Center**. Then, select the range **A2:F2** and click **Merge & Center**.

   The ***Merge & Center*** command joins selected cells into one larger cell and centers the contents in the merged cell; individual cells in the range B1:F1 and B2:F2 can no longer be selected—they are merged into cell A1 and A2 respectively.

ANOTHER WAY Select the range, right-click over the selection, and then on the mini toolbar, click the Merge & Center button.

2. Click cell **A1**. In the **Styles group**, click **Cell Styles**, and then compare your screen with Figure 1.20.

   A ***cell style*** is a defined set of formatting characteristics, such as font, font size, font color, cell borders, and cell shading.

FIGURE 1.20

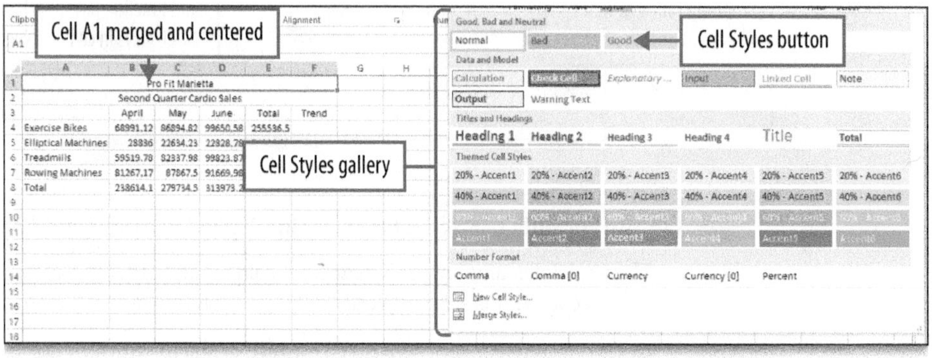

3. In the displayed gallery, under **Titles and Headings**, click **Title** and notice that the row height adjusts to accommodate the larger font size.

4. Click cell **A2**, display the **Cell Styles** gallery, and then under **Titles and Headings**, click **Heading 1**.

   Use cell styles to maintain a consistent look in a worksheet and across worksheets in a workbook.

5. Select the horizontal range **B3:F3**, hold down Ctrl, and then select the vertical range **A4:A8** to select the column titles and the row titles.

   Use this technique to select two or more ranges that are nonadjacent—not next to each other.

6. Display the **Cell Styles** gallery, click **Heading 4** to apply this cell style to the column titles and row titles, and then **Save** your workbook.

Activity 1.09 | Formatting Financial Numbers

1 Select the range **B4:E4**, hold down Ctrl, and then select the range **B8:E8**.

This range is referred to as *b4:e4,b8:e8* with a comma separating the references to the two nonadjacent ranges.

ANOTHER WAY In the Name Box type b4:e4,b8:e8 and then press Enter.

2 On the **HOME tab**, in the **Number group**, click **Accounting Number Format** [$]. Compare your screen with Figure 1.21.

The ***Accounting Number Format*** applies a thousand comma separator where appropriate, inserts a fixed U.S. dollar sign aligned at the left edge of the cell, applies two decimal places, and leaves a small amount of space at the right edge of the cell to accommodate a parenthesis when negative numbers are present. Excel widens the columns to accommodate the formatted numbers.

At the bottom of your screen, in the status bar, Excel displays the results for some common calculations that might be made on the range; for example, the Average of the numbers selected and the Count—the number of items selected.

FIGURE 1.21

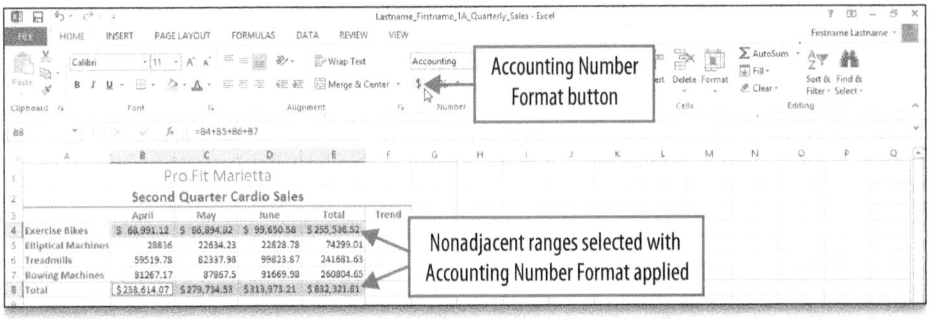

ANOTHER WAY Display the Cell Styles gallery, and under Number Format, click Currency.

3 Select the range **B5:E7**, and then in the **Number group**, click **Comma Style** [,].

The ***Comma Style*** inserts a thousand comma separator where appropriate and applies two decimal places. Comma Style also leaves space at the right to accommodate a parenthesis when negative numbers are present.

When preparing worksheets with financial information, the first row of dollar amounts and the total row of dollar amounts are formatted in the Accounting Number Format; that is, with thousand comma separators, dollar signs, two decimal places, and space at the right to accommodate a parenthesis for negative numbers, if any. Rows that are *not* the first row or the total row should be formatted with the Comma Style.

4 Select the range **B8:E8**. In the **Styles group**, display the **Cell Styles** gallery, and then under **Titles and Headings**, click **Total**. Click any blank cell to cancel the selection, and then compare your screen with Figure 1.22.

This is a common way to apply borders to financial information. The single border indicates that calculations were performed on the numbers above, and the double border indicates that the information is complete. Sometimes financial documents do not display values with cents; rather, the values are rounded up. You can do this by selecting the cells, and then clicking the Decrease Decimal button two times.

FIGURE 1.22

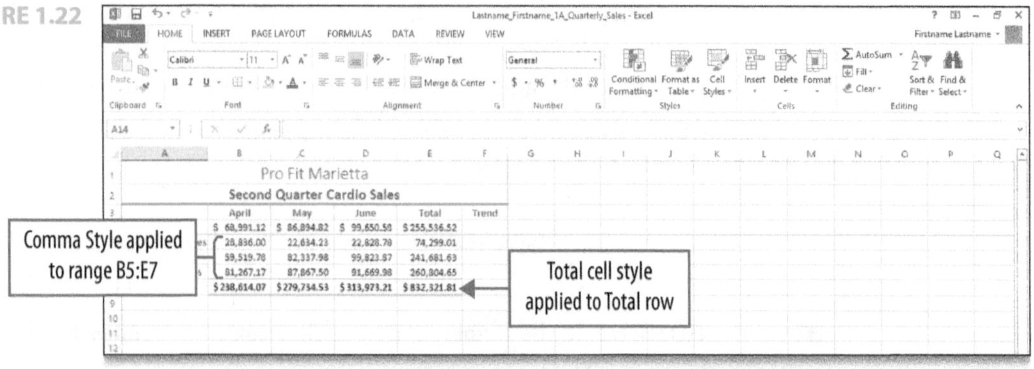

Activity 1.10 | Changing the Workbook Theme

A ***theme*** is a predefined set of colors, fonts, lines, and fill effects that coordinate for an attractive look.

1. Click the **PAGE LAYOUT tab**, and then in the **Themes group**, click **Themes**.

2. Click the **Retrospect** theme, and notice that the cell styles change to match the new theme. Click **Save** [Save icon].

More Knowledge | **Formatting a Cell's Font, Style, Size, or Color with Individual Commands**

Instead of using Cell Styles, you could use a combination of individual commands to format a cell. For example, on the HOME tab, in the Font group, you can change a cell's font by clicking the Font arrow and selecting a different font. You can change the font size by clicking the Font Size arrow and selecting a size. From the same group, you can apply various styles to the cell—such as Bold or Italic or Underline. To change a cell's font color, in the Font Group, click the Font Color arrow and select a different color.

Objective 5 Chart Data to Create a Column Chart and Insert Sparklines

Video E1-5

A ***chart*** is a graphic representation of data in a worksheet. Data in a chart is easier to understand than a table of numbers. ***Sparklines*** are tiny charts embedded in a cell that give a visual trend summary alongside your data. A sparkline makes a pattern more obvious to the eye.

Activity 1.11 | Charting Data and Using Recommended Charts to Select and Insert a Column Chart

Recommended Charts is an Excel feature that displays a customized set of charts that, according to Excel's calculations, will best fit your data based on the range of data that you select. In this activity, you will create a ***column chart*** showing the monthly sales of cardio equipment by category during the second quarter. A column chart is useful for illustrating comparisons among related numbers. The chart will enable the company president, Michelle Barry, to see a pattern of overall monthly sales.

1. Select the range **A3:D7**.

   When charting data, typically you should *not* include totals—include only the data you want to compare.

2 With the data that you want to compare selected, click the **INSERT tab**, and then in the **Charts group**, click **Recommended Charts**. Compare your screen with Figure 1.23.

The Insert Chart dialog box displays a list of recommended charts on the left and a preview of the first chart, which is selected, on the right. The second tab of the Insert Chart dialog box includes all chart types—even those that are not recommended by Excel for this type of data.

By using different ***chart types***, you can display data in a way that is meaningful to the reader—common examples are column charts, pie charts, and line charts.

FIGURE 1.23

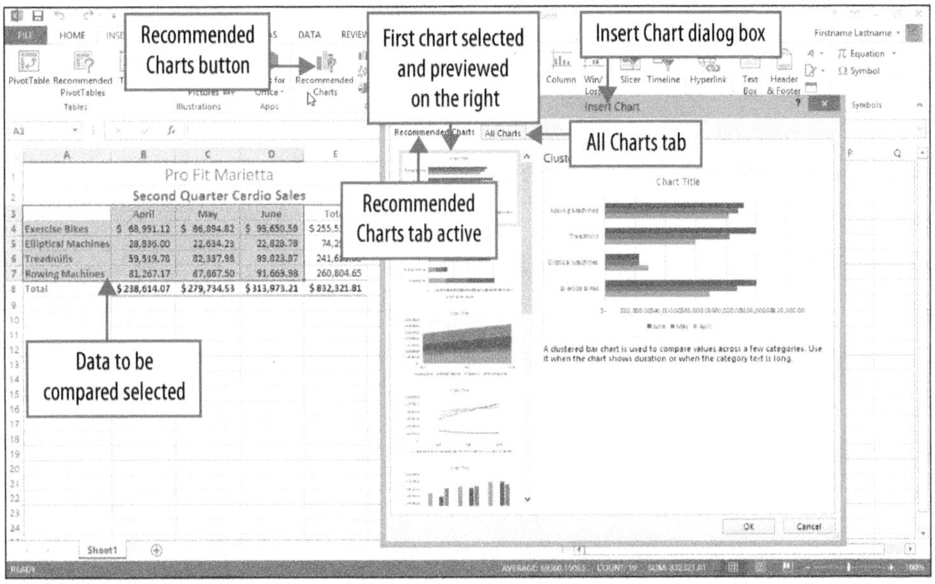

3 In the **Insert Chart** dialog box, use the scroll bar to scroll down about one-third of the way, and then click the second Clustered Column chart. Compare your screen with Figure 1.24.

Here, *each type of cardio equipment* displays its *sales for each month*. A clustered column chart is useful to compare values across a few categories, especially if the order of categories is not important.

FIGURE 1.24

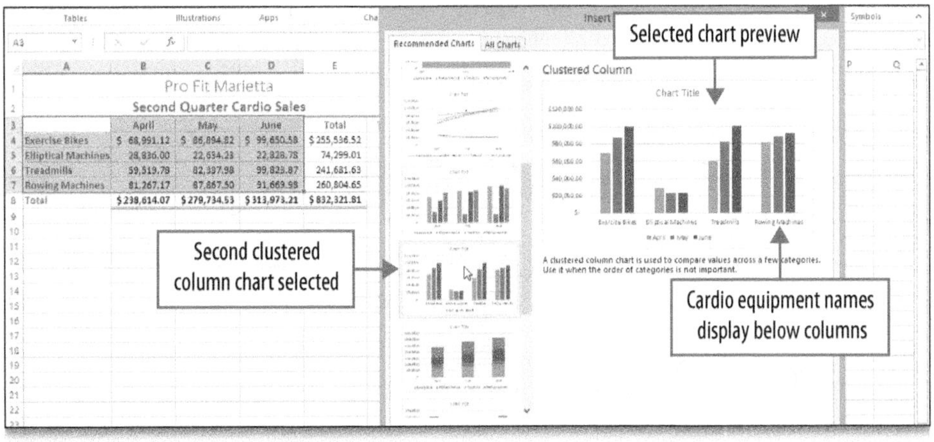

4 In the **Insert Chart** dialog box, click the chart directly above the selected chart—the first clustered column chart. Compare your screen with Figure 1.25.

In this clustered column chart, *each month* displays its *sales for each type of cardio equipment*. When constructing a chart, you can switch the row and column data in this manner to display the data in a way that is most useful to the reader. Here, the president of Pro Fit Marietta wants to compare sales of each type of equipment by month to detect patterns.

The comparison of data—either by month or by type of equipment—depends on the type of analysis you want to perform. You can select either chart, or, after your chart is complete, you can use the ***Switch/Row Column*** command on the ribbon to swap the data over the axis; that is, data being charted on the vertical axis will move to the horizontal axis and vice versa.

FIGURE 1.25

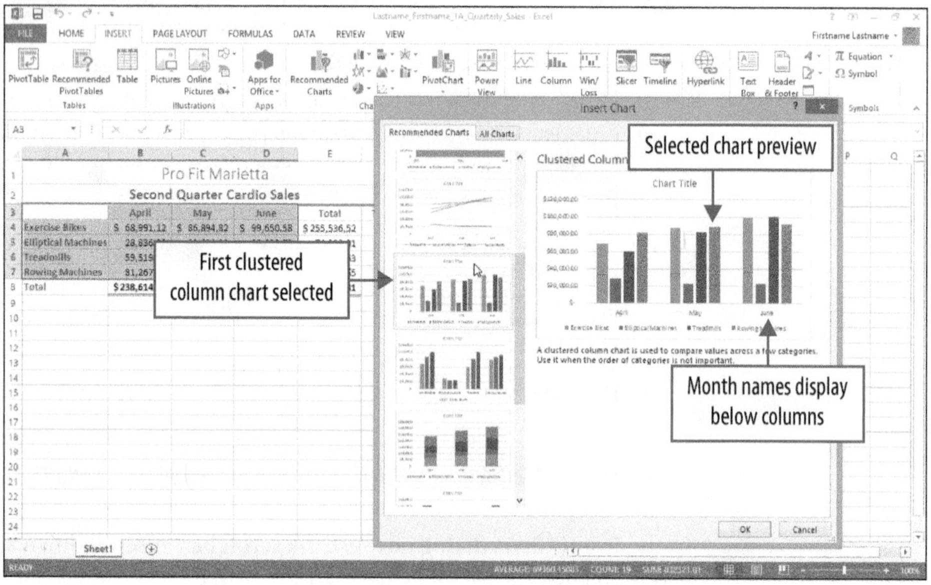

5 In the lower right corner of the **Insert Chart** dialog box, click **OK** to insert the selected chart into the worksheet. Compare your screen with Figure 1.26.

Your selected column chart displays in the worksheet, and the charted data is bordered by colored lines. Because the chart object is selected—surrounded by a border and displaying sizing handles—contextual tools named *CHART TOOLS* display and add contextual tabs next to the standard tabs on the ribbon.

FIGURE 1.26

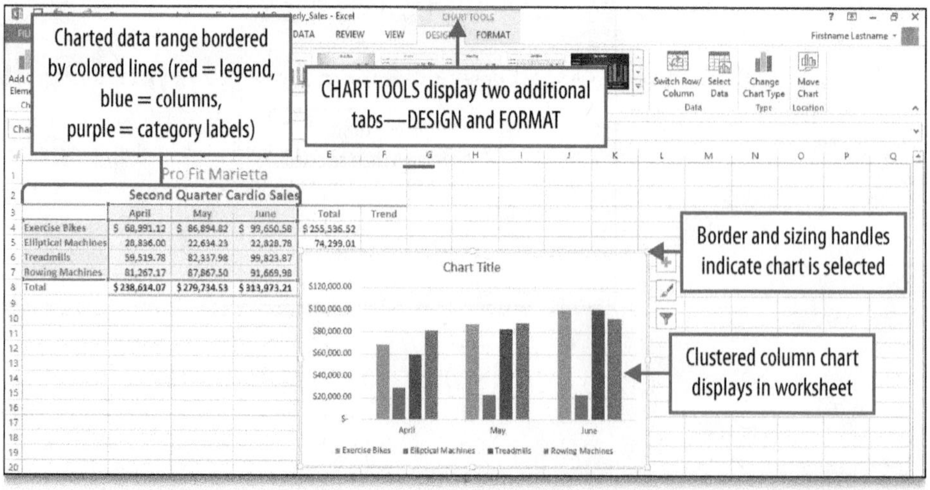

Activity 1.12 | Using the Chart Tools to Apply Chart Styles

1 On the ribbon, locate the contextual tabs under **CHART TOOLS—DESIGN** and **FORMAT**.

When a chart is selected, CHART TOOLS become available and these two tabs provide commands for working with the chart.

Based on the data you selected in your worksheet and the chart you selected in the Insert Chart dialog box, Excel constructs a column chart and adds ***category labels***—the labels that display along the bottom of the chart to identify the category of data. This area is referred to as the ***category axis*** or the ***x-axis***.

Depending on which arrangement of row and column data you select in the Insert Chart dialog box, Excel arranges either the row titles or the column titles as the category names. Here, based on your selection, the column titles that form the category labels are bordered in purple, indicating the cells that contain the category names.

On the left side of the chart, Excel includes a numerical scale on which the charted data is based; this is the ***value axis*** or the ***y-axis***. Along the lower edge of the chart, a ***legend***, which is a chart element that identifies the patterns or colors that are assigned to the categories in the chart, displays. Here, the row titles are bordered in red, indicating the cells containing the legend text.

2 To the right of the chart, notice the three buttons, and then point to each button to display its ScreenTip, as shown in Figure 1.27.

The ***Chart Elements button*** enables you to add, remove, or change chart elements such as the title, legend, gridlines, and data labels.

The ***Chart Styles button*** enables you to set a style and color scheme for your chart.

The ***Chart Filters button*** enables you to change which data displays in the chart—for example, to see only the data for *May* and *June* or only the data for *Treadmills* and *Rowing Machines*.

FIGURE 1.27

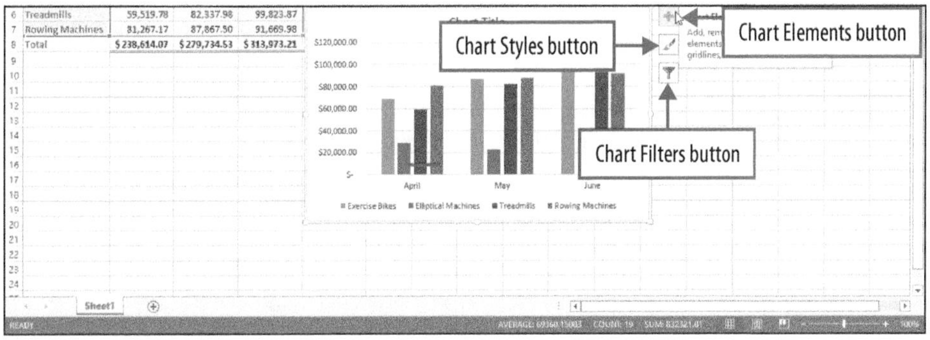

3 In the worksheet data, locate the group of cells bordered in blue.

Each of the twelve cells bordered in blue is referred to as a ***data point***—a value that originates in a worksheet cell. Each data point is represented in the chart by a ***data marker***—a column, bar, area, dot, pie slice, or other symbol in a chart that represents a single data point.

Related data points form a ***data series***; for example, there is a data series for *April*, for *May*, and for *June*. Each data series has a unique color or pattern represented in the chart legend.

4 On the **DESIGN tab**, in the **Chart Layouts group**, click **Quick Layout**, and then compare your screen with Figure 1.28.

In the Quick Layout gallery, you can change the overall layout of the chart by selecting a predesigned ***chart layout***—a combination of chart elements, which can include a title, legend, labels for the columns, and the table of charted cells.

FIGURE 1.28

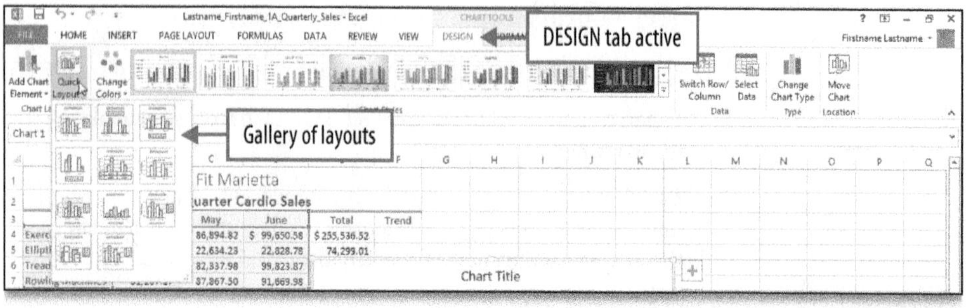

5 *Point* to several different layouts to see how Live Preview displays the effect on your chart, and then click the **Quick Layout** button again *without* changing the layout.

6 In the chart, click anywhere in the text *Chart Title* to select the title box, watch the **Formula Bar** as you begin to type **Second** and notice that AutoComplete fills in the subtitle for you. Press Enter at any point to insert the subtitle as the chart title.

7 Click in a white area just slightly *inside* the chart border to deselect the chart title but keep the chart selected. To the right of the chart, click **Chart Styles**, and then at the top of the **Chart Styles** gallery, be sure that **Style** is selected. Compare your screen with Figure 1.29.

The ***Chart Styles gallery*** displays an array of pre-defined ***chart styles***—the overall visual look of the chart in terms of its colors, backgrounds, and graphic effects such as flat or shaded columns. You can also select Chart Styles from the Chart Styles group on the ribbon, but having the gallery closer to the chart makes it easier to use a touch gesture on a touch device to format a chart.

FIGURE 1.29

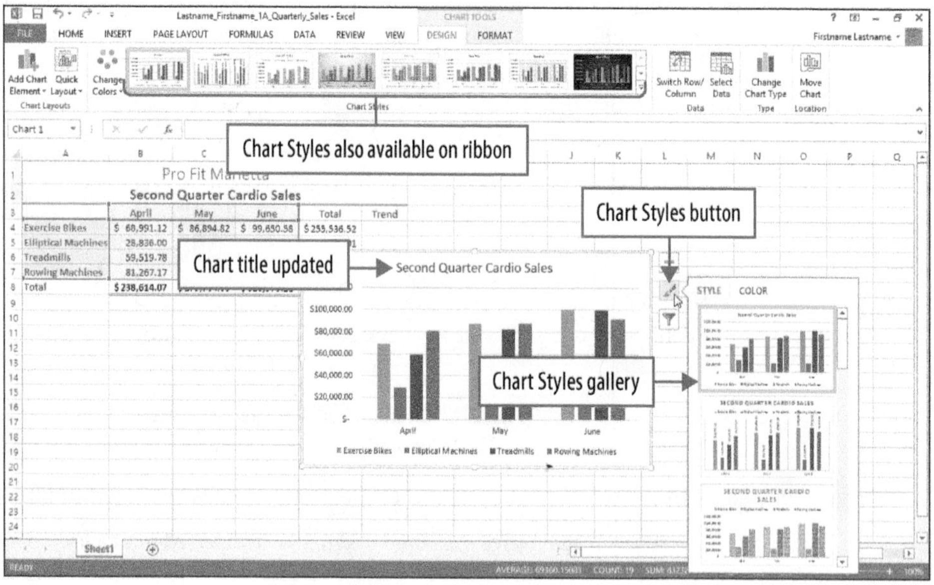

8 On the right side of the **Style** gallery, scroll down about halfway, and then by using the ScreenTips as your guide, locate and click **Style 6**.

This style uses a white background, formats the columns with theme colors, and applies a slight shadowed effect to the columns. With this clear visual representation of the data, the president can see the sales of all product categories in each month, and can see that the sale of exercise bikes and treadmills has risen markedly during the quarter.

9 At the top of the gallery, click **COLOR**. Under **Colorful**, point to the third row of colors to display the ScreenTip *Color 3*, and then click to apply the **Color 3** variation of the theme colors.

10 Point to the top border of the chart to display the [pointer icon] pointer, and then drag the upper left corner of the chart just inside the upper left corner of cell **A10**, approximately as shown in Figure 1.30.

FIGURE 1.30

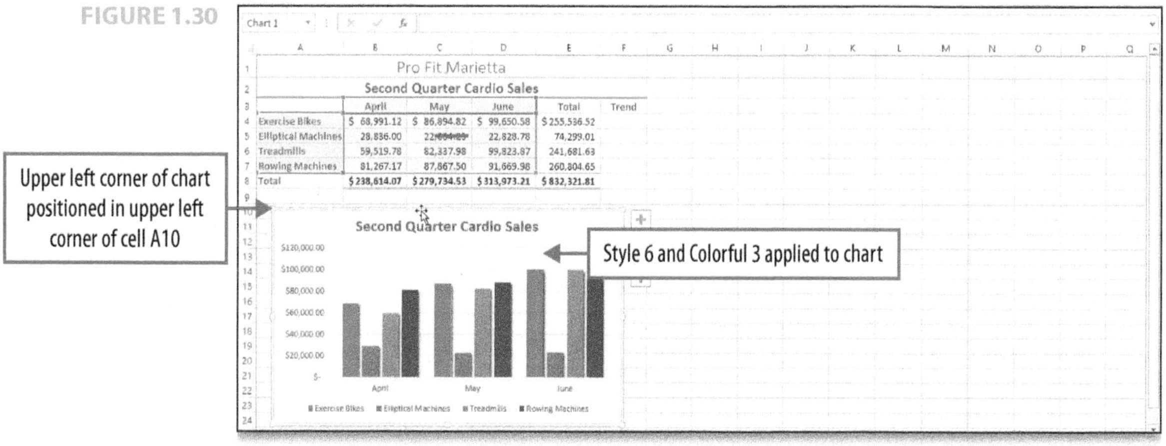

11 Click any cell to deselect the chart, and notice that the chart buttons no longer display to the right of the chart and the CHART TOOLS no longer display on the ribbon. Click **Save** [Save icon].

Contextual tabs display when an object is selected and then are removed from view when the object is deselected.

Activity 1.13 Creating and Formatting Sparklines

By creating sparklines, you provide a context for your numbers. Your readers will be able to see the relationship between a sparkline and its underlying data quickly.

1 Select the range **B4:D7**, which represents the monthly sales figures for each product and for each month. Click the **INSERT tab**, and then in the **Sparklines group**, click **Line**. In the displayed **Create Sparklines** dialog box, notice that the selected range *B4:D7* displays as the Data Range.

2 With the insertion point blinking in the **Location Range** box, type **f4:f7** which is the range of cells where you want the sparklines to display. Compare your screen with Figure 1.31.

FIGURE 1.31

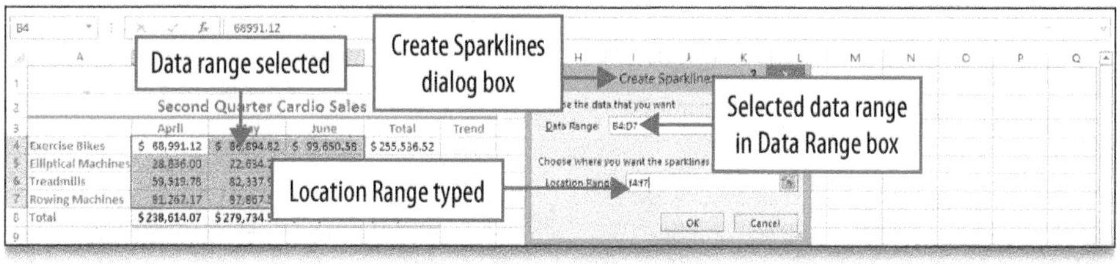

ANOTHER WAY In the worksheet, select the range F4:F7 to insert it into the Location Range box.

3 Click **OK** to insert the sparklines in the range **F4:F7**, and then on the **DESIGN tab**, in the **Show group**, click the **Markers** check box to select it.

Alongside each row of data, the sparkline provides a quick visual trend summary for sales of each cardio item over the three-month period. For example, you can see instantly that of the four items, only Elliptical Machines had declining sales for the period.

4 On the **DESIGN tab**, in the **Style group**, click **More** . In the second row, click the fourth style—**Sparkline Style Accent 4, Darker 25%.** Press Ctrl + Home to deselect the range and make cell **A1** the active cell. Click **Save** , and then compare your screen with Figure 1.32.

Use markers, colors, and styles in this manner to further enhance your sparklines.

FIGURE 1.32

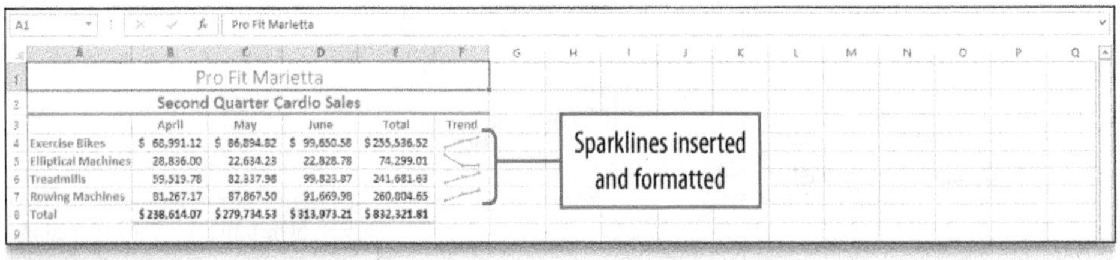

Objective 6 Print a Worksheet, Display Formulas, and Close Excel

Video E1-6

Use the Show Formulas command to display the formula in each cell instead of the resulting value. Use the commands on the PAGE LAYOUT tab to prepare for printing.

Activity 1.14 | Creating a Footer and Centering a Worksheet

For each Excel project in this textbook, you will create a footer containing the file name, which includes your name and the project name. You will also center the data horizontally on the page to create an attractive result if your worksheet is printed.

1 If necessary, click cell **A1** to deselect the chart. Click the **PAGE LAYOUT tab**, and then in the **Page Setup group**, click **Margins**. At the bottom of the **Margins** gallery, click **Custom Margins**, to display the **Page Setup** dialog box. Compare your screen with Figure 1.33.

FIGURE 1.33

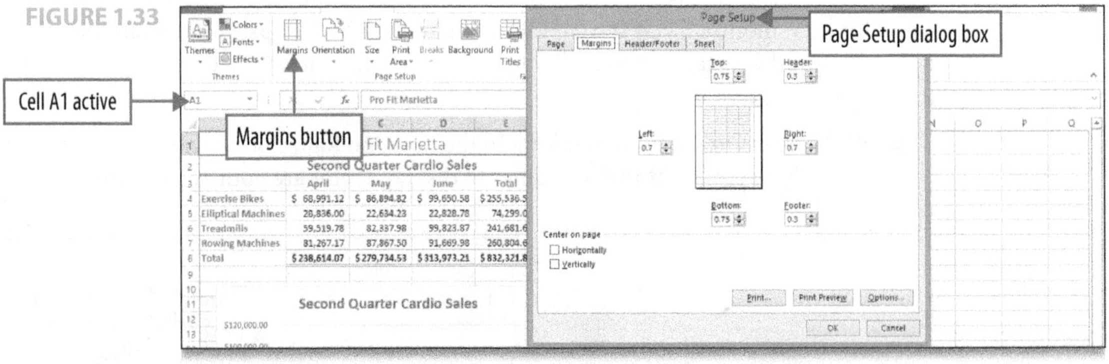

2 On the **Margins tab**, under **Center on page**, select the **Horizontally** check box.

This action will center the data and chart horizontally on the page, as shown in the Preview area.

3 Click the **Header/Footer tab**, and then in the center of the dialog box, click **Custom Footer**. In the **Footer** dialog box, with your insertion point blinking in the **Left section**, on the row of buttons, click **Insert File Name** . Compare your screen with Figure 1.34.

&[File] displays in the Left section. Here you can type or insert information from the row of buttons into the left, middle, or right section of the footer. The Custom Header button displays a similar screen to enter information in the header of the worksheet.

FIGURE 1.34

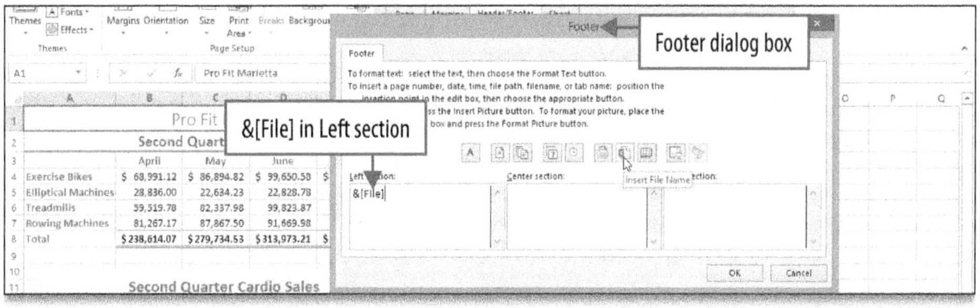

4 Click **OK** two times.

The vertical dotted line between columns indicates that as currently arranged, only the columns to the left of the dotted line will print on the first page. The exact position of the vertical line may depend on your default printer setting.

ANOTHER WAY

Deselect the chart. On the INSERT tab, in the Text group, click Header & Footer to display Page Layout view. Click in the Left section of the displayed footer, and then in the Header & Footer Elements group, click File Name. Click any cell in the workbook to deselect the footer area, and then on the status bar, click the Normal button to return to Normal view.

Activity 1.15 | Adding Document Properties and Printing a Workbook

1 In the upper left corner of your screen, click the **FILE tab** to display **Backstage** view. In the lower right corner, click **Show All Properties**.

2 As the **Tags**, type **cardio sales** In the **Subject** box, type your course name and section number. Be sure your name displays as the author and edit if necessary.

3 On the left, click **Print** to view the **Print Preview**. Compare your screen with Figure 1.35.

FIGURE 1.35

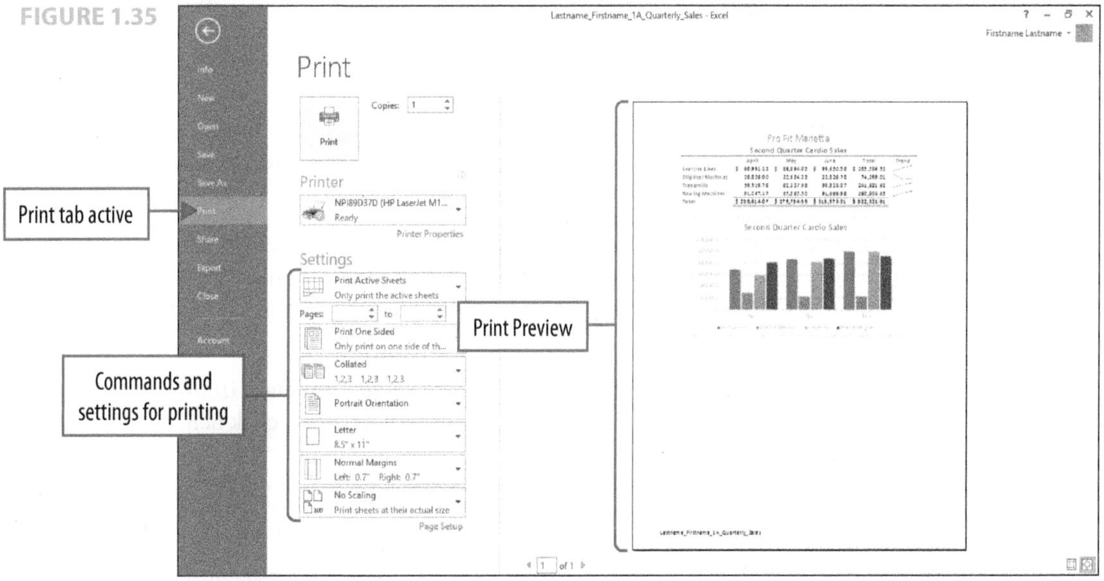

4 Note any adjustments that need to be made, and then on the left, click **Save** to save and return to the workbook.

5 If you are directed to print on paper, be sure that a printer is available to your system. Press Ctrl + F2, which is the keyboard shortcut to display the **Print Preview**, and then under **Print**, click the **Print** button.

6 If you are directed to create an electronic printout, click the **FILE tab**, on the left click **Export**, and then on the right, click **Create PDF/XPS**. In the **Publish as PDF or XPS** dialog box, navigate to your storage location, in the **Save as type** box, be sure **PDF** is indicated, and then click **Publish** to create the PDF file.

Activity 1.16 | Printing a Section of the Worksheet

From Backstage view, you can print only the portion of the worksheet that you select, and there are times you might want to do this.

1 Select the range **A2:F5** to select only the subtitle and the data for *Exercise Bikes* and *Elliptical Machines* and the column titles

2 Press Ctrl + F2 to display **Print Preview**, and then under **Settings**, click the first arrow, which currently displays *Print Active Sheets*. On the list that displays, click **Print Selection**, and then compare your screen with Figure 1.36.

FIGURE 1.36

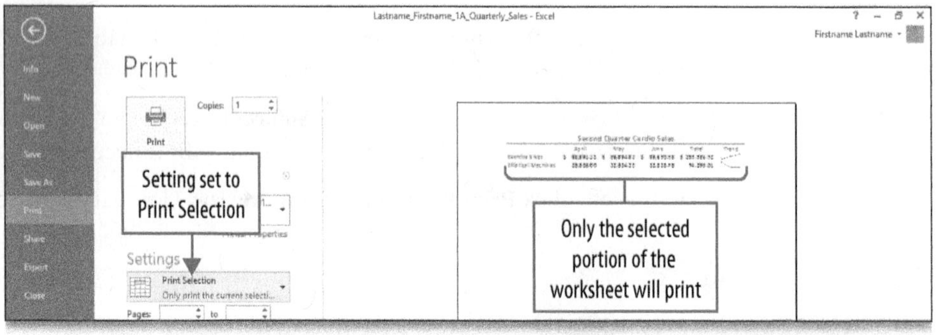

3 To print on paper or create an electronic printout, follow Steps 3-5; otherwise read through the steps and move to Step 6. To print on paper, if directed to do so by your instructor, click **Print**.

4 To create an electronic printout, if directed to do so by your instructor, complete this step and Step 5. On the left click **Export**, and then on the right, click **Create PDF/XPS**. In the **Publish as PDF or XPS** dialog box, navigate to your storage location, in the **Save as type** box, be sure **PDF** is indicated.

5 In the **File name**, to the end of the file name, add **_selection** In the lower right corner of the dialog box, click **Options**, and then under **Publish what**, click **Selection**. Click **OK**, and then click **Publish**.

6 Redisplay the workbook, press Ctrl + Home, and then click **Save**.

Activity 1.17 | Changing Page Orientation and Displaying, Printing, and Hiding Formulas

When you type a formula in a cell, the cell displays the *results* of the formula calculation. Recall that this value is called the displayed value. You can view and print the underlying formulas in the cells. When you do so, a formula often takes more horizontal space to display than the result of the calculation.

1 If necessary, redisplay your worksheet. Because you will make some temporary changes to your workbook, on the **Quick Access Toolbar**, click **Save** to be sure your work is saved up to this point.

2 On the **FORMULAS tab**, in the **Formula Auditing group**, click **Show Formulas**.

ANOTHER WAY Hold down Ctrl, and then press ` (usually located below Esc).

3 In the **column heading area**, point to the **column A** heading to display the ↓ pointer, hold down the left mouse button, and then drag to the right to select columns **A:F**. Compare your screen with Figure 1.37.

FIGURE 1.37

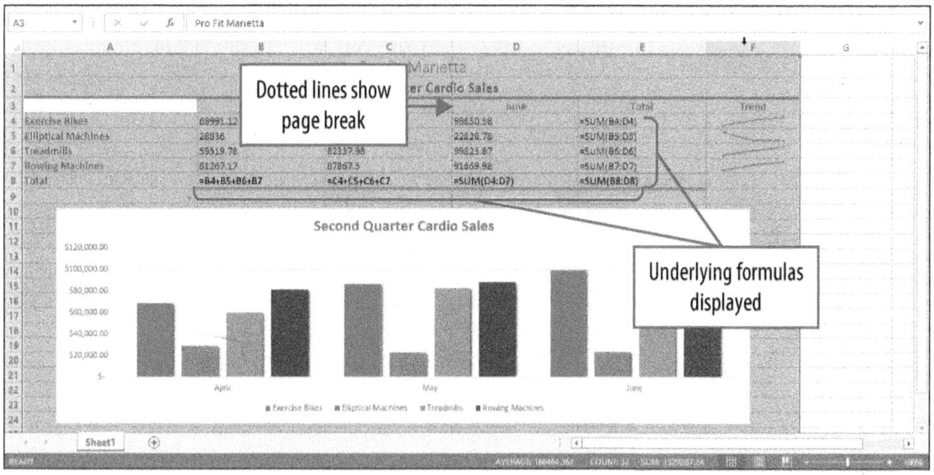

NOTE	Turning the Display of Formulas On and Off

The Show Formulas button is a toggle button. Clicking it once turns the display of formulas on—the button will be shaded. Clicking the button again turns the display of formulas off.

4 Point to the column heading boundary between any two of the selected columns to display the ✛ pointer, and then double-click to AutoFit the selected columns.

AutoFit adjusts the width of a column to fit the cell content of the *widest* cell in the column.

ANOTHER WAY With the columns selected, on the HOME tab, in the Cells group, click Format, and then click AutoFit Column Width.

5 On the **PAGE LAYOUT tab**, in the **Page Setup group**, click **Orientation**, and then click **Landscape**. In the **Scale to Fit** group, click the **Width arrow**, and then click **1 page** to scale the data to fit onto one page.

Scaling shrinks the width or height of the printed worksheet to fit a maximum number of pages, and is convenient for printing formulas. Although it is not always the case, formulas frequently take up more space than the actual data.

ANOTHER WAY In the Scale to Fit group, click the Dialog Box Launcher button to display the Page tab of the Page Setup dialog box. Then, under Scaling, click the Fit to option button.

6 In the **Page Setup group**, click **Margins**, click **Custom Margins**, and then on the **Margins tab**, under **Center on page**, be sure the **Horizontally** check box is selected—select it if necessary.

7 Click **OK** to close the dialog box. Check to be sure your chart is centered below the data and the left and right edges are slightly inside column A and column F—use the pointer to drag a chart edge and then deselect the chart if necessary.

8 Click any cell so that the chart is not selected, and then press Ctrl + F2 to display the **Print Preview**. Under **Settings**, if necessary switch back to the option to **Print Active Sheets**. If directed to do so by your instructor, print on paper or click Save As and name the worksheet **Lastname_Firstname_1A_Quarterly_Sales_fomulas**

9 On the left, click **Close**, and when prompted, click **Don't Save** so that you do *not* save the changes you made—displaying formulas, changing column widths and orientation, and scaling—to print your formulas.

10 In the upper right corner of your screen, click **Close** × to close Excel.

***More* Knowledge** **Inserting a Watermark**

Excel does not have a watermark feature like the watermark in Word, but there are two ways you can achieve the same effect. To use WordArt to mimic a watermark, on the INSERT tab, in the Text group, click Insert WordArt, and then click the style you want to use. Type the text and resize as necessary. Then, right-click the WordArt, click Format Text Effects, click Text Fill & Outline, and then drag one or both transparency sliders to the percentage you want. Or, simply create an image of a watermark and insert the image in the worksheet header or footer.

END | You have completed Project 1A

GO! with Office Online (formerly Web Apps)

Objective Create a Sales Report with an Embedded Column Chart Using Excel Online

If you are working on a computer that does not have Microsoft Office installed, you can still create new workbooks in your web browser by using Excel Office Online.

ALERT! **Working with Web-Based Applications and Services**

Computer programs and services on the web receive continuous updates and improvements, so the steps to complete this web-based activity may differ from the ones shown. You can often look at the screens and the information presented to determine how to complete the activity.

Activity Creating a Sales Report with Embedded Column Chart Using Excel Online

In this activity, you will use Excel Online to create a sales report and chart similar to the one you created in Project 1A.

1. Start Excel, open a new blank workbook, and then if necessary, in the upper right corner, log into Office with your Microsoft account. In cell **A1**, type **Pro Fit Marietta** press Enter, and then click the **FILE tab**. On the left, click **Save As**, and then on the right, click the name of your OneDrive—the path to your GO! Web Projects folder on the OneDrive may display under Recent Folders and if so, you can click there.

2. In the **Save As** dialog box for your OneDrive, if necessary open your **GO! Web Projects** folder, and then save the file as **Lastname_Firstname_EX_1A_Web** Close Excel, launch Internet Explorer, go to http://onedrive.com, sign in, and then from your **GO! Web Projects** folder, open the file you just saved there.

3. To help you create this project quickly and to eliminate extra typing, you will import the data from a Word table. From the taskbar, open **File Explorer**, navigate to the student data files that accompany this textbook, and then open the Word document **e01_1A_Web**. Press Ctrl + A to select all of the text, right-click anywhere over the selection, and then click **Copy**. **Close** Word and **Close** File Explorer.

4. Click cell **A2**, on the Excel Online ribbon, in the **Clipboard group**, click the upper portion of the **Paste** button; if necessary click **Allow access**. Notice that number symbols display when numeric data is too wide for the cell.

5. Select column headings **A:E**, point to the border between any two selected column headings to display the pointer, and then double-click to resize all the columns to display all data.

6. Drag to select the range **A1:E1**, and then in the **Alignment group**, click **Merge & Center**. Merge and center the worksheet's subtitle in the same manner. Select the range **A1:A2**, and then in the **Font group**, apply **Bold** and change the **Font Color** to **Dark Blue**.

7. Select the range **B4:E4**. In the **Number group**, click the **Number Format arrow**, and then click **Currency**. Apply the same format to the range **B8:E8**.

FIGURE A

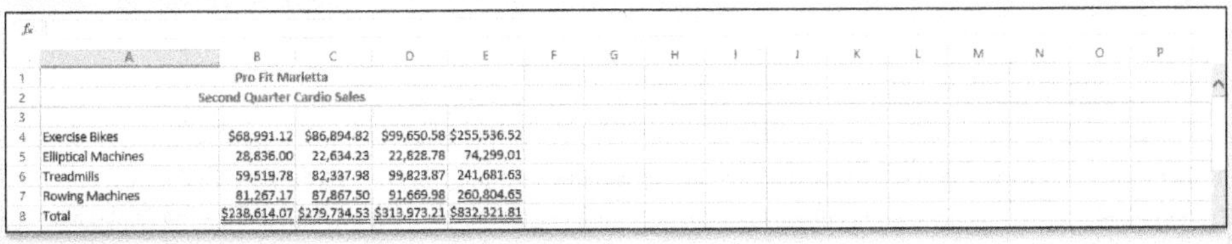

	A	B	C	D	E
1	Pro Fit Marietta				
2	Second Quarter Cardio Sales				
3					
4	Exercise Bikes	$68,991.12	$86,894.82	$99,650.58	$255,536.52
5	Elliptical Machines	28,836.00	22,634.23	22,828.78	74,299.01
6	Treadmills	59,519.78	82,337.98	99,823.87	241,681.63
7	Rowing Machines	81,267.17	87,867.50	91,669.98	260,804.65
8	Total	$238,614.07	$279,734.53	$313,973.21	$832,321.81

(GO! with Office Online (formerly Web Apps) continues on the next page)

8 Select the range **B7:E7**, and then in the **Font group**, click **Underline** [U]. Select the range **B8:E8**, and then in the **Font group** click **Double Underline** [D]. Click any empty cell, and then compare your screen with Figure A.

9 Click cell **B3**, type **April** and press Enter, and then click the cell **B3** again. Drag the fill handle to select cells **C3:D3** to complete the series. In cell **E3** type **Total** Select these four column titles and apply **Center** and **Bold** [B].

10 Select the range **A3:D7**—the data without the totals. On the **INSERT tab**, in the **Charts group**, click **Column**, and then click the first chart type—**Clustered Column**. In the **Data group**, click **Switch Row/Column**.

11 Drag the chart so that the upper left corner of the chart is inside the upper left portion of cell **A9**. From the **Labels group**, add a **Chart Title** in the **Above Chart** position with the text **2nd Quarter Cardio Sales**

12 Click cell **A1**, and then compare your screen with Figure B.

In Excel Online, you do not have the same set of features available that you have in the full version of Office; for example, you do not have Cell Styles, sparklines, and chart styles. But you can still create the data and chart in a meaningful way.

13 If you are instructed to submit your file, use one of the methods outlined in the Note box below. In Excel Online, there is no Save button because your workbook is being saved automatically. Sign out of your OneDrive and close Internet Explorer.

FIGURE B

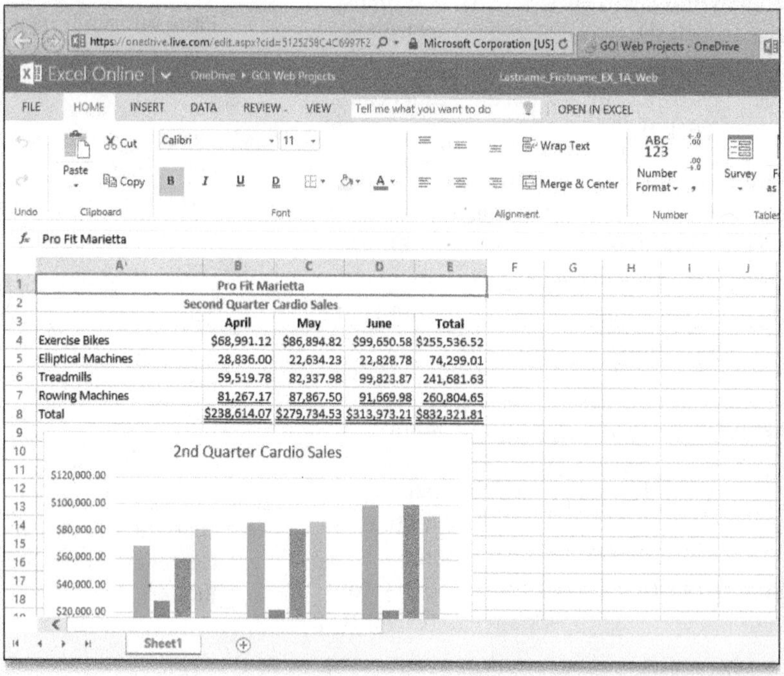

NOTE Printing or Creating an Electronic File from Excel Online

To print on paper, click the FILE tab, click Print, click the Print button, and then click Print. In the Print Preview display, click Print. In the displayed Print dialog box, click Print to print on the printer connected to your system. To create an electronic file of your printout, from the Print dialog box, click the printer labeled *Send to OneNote 2013*, and then click Print. You may have to open and then close OneNote first if you have never opened it before. When OneNote opens, click the Quick Notes section of the displayed notebook, and then click OK. On the ribbon, click the FILE tab, click Export, and then create a PDF of the page. Navigate to an appropriate location and give the file an appropriate name. Close OneNote.

PROJECT
1B Inventory Valuation

MyITLab® Project 1B Training

1 EXCEL

PROJECT ACTIVITIES

In Activities 1.18 through 1.27 you will create a workbook for Josh Feingold, Operations Manager, which calculates the retail value of an inventory of plyometric training products. Your completed worksheet will look similar to Figure 1.38.

PROJECT FILES

For Project 1B, you will need the following file:
New blank Excel workbook

You will save your workbook as:
Lastname_Firstname_1B_Plyo_Products

PROJECT RESULTS

Build from Scratch

Pro Fit Marietta

Plyometric Products Inventory Valuation

As of September 30

	Warehouse Location	Quantity in Stock	Retail Price	Total Retail Value	Percent of Total Retail Value
Power Hurdle	Atlanta	125	$ 32.95	$ 4,118.75	1.41%
Speed Hurdle	Atlanta	995	59.95	59,650.25	20.37%
Stackable Steps	Marietta	450	251.59	113,215.50	38.65%
Pro Jump Rope	Marietta	1,105	49.95	55,194.75	18.84%
Plyometric Box Set	Marietta	255	158.05	40,302.75	13.76%
Plyometric Mat	Atlanta	215	94.99	20,422.85	6.97%
Total Retail Value for All Products				**$ 292,904.85**	

Lastname_Firstname_1B_Plyo_Products

FIGURE 1.38 Project 1B Inventory Valuation

Objective 7 Check Spelling in a Worksheet

Video E1-7

In Excel, the spelling checker performs similarly to the other Microsoft Office programs.

Activity 1.18 | Checking Spelling in a Worksheet

1. **Start** Excel and display a new blank workbook. In cell **A1**, type **Pro Fit Marietta** and press Enter. In cell **A2**, type **Plyometric Products Inventory** and press Enter.

2. Press F12 to display the **Save As** dialog box, and then navigate to your **Excel Chapter 1** folder. As the **File name**, using your own name, type **Lastname_Firstname_1B_Plyo_Products** and then click **Save**.

3. Press Tab to move to cell **B3**, type **Quantity** and press Tab. In cell **C3**, type **Average Cost** and press Tab. In cell **D3**, type **Retail Price** and press Tab.

4. Click cell **C3**, and then look at the **Formula Bar**. Notice that in the cell, the displayed value is cut off; however, in the **Formula Bar**, the entire text value—the underlying value—displays. Compare your screen with Figure 1.39.

   Text that is too long to fit in a cell extends into cells on the right only if they are empty. If the cell to the right contains data, the text in the cell to the left is truncated—cut off. The entire value continues to exist, but is not completely visible.

FIGURE 1.39

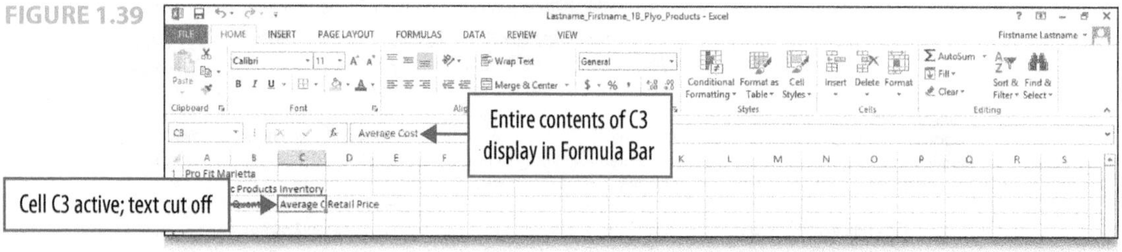

5. Click cell **E3**, type **Total Retail Value** and press Tab. In cell **F3**, type **Percent of Total Retail Value** and press Enter.

6. Click cell **A4**. *Without* correcting the spelling error, type **Powr Hurdle** and then press Enter. In the range **A5:A10**, type the remaining row titles shown below. Then compare your screen with Figure 1.40.

   Speed Hurdle
   Stackable Steps
   Pro Jump Rope
   Plyometric Box Set
   Plyometric Mat
   Total Retail Value for All Products

FIGURE 1.40

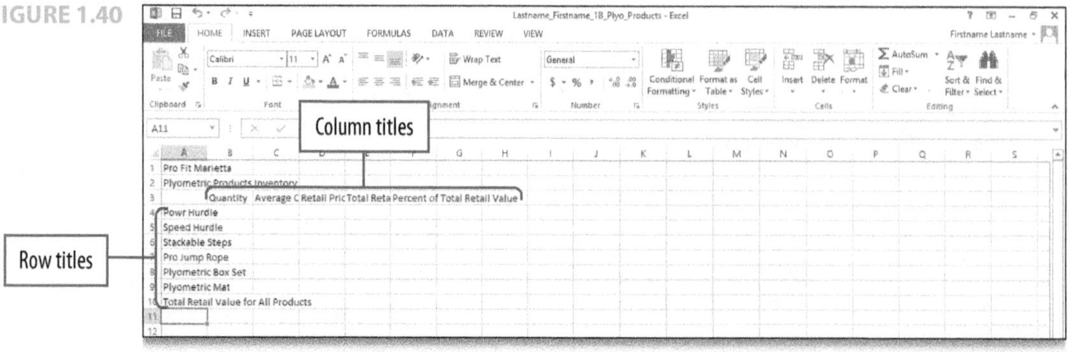

1

EXCEL

7 In the **column heading area**, point to the right boundary of **column A** to display the [+] pointer, and then drag to the right to widen **column A** to **215** pixels.

8 Select the range **A1:F1**, **Merge & Center** the text, and then from the **Cell Styles** gallery, apply the **Title** style.

9 Select the range **A2:F2**, **Merge & Center** the text, and then from the **Cell Styles** gallery, apply the **Heading 1** style. Press Ctrl + Home to move to the top of your worksheet.

10 With cell **A1** as the active cell, click the **REVIEW tab**, and then in the **Proofing group**, click **Spelling**. Compare your screen with Figure 1.41.

FIGURE 1.41

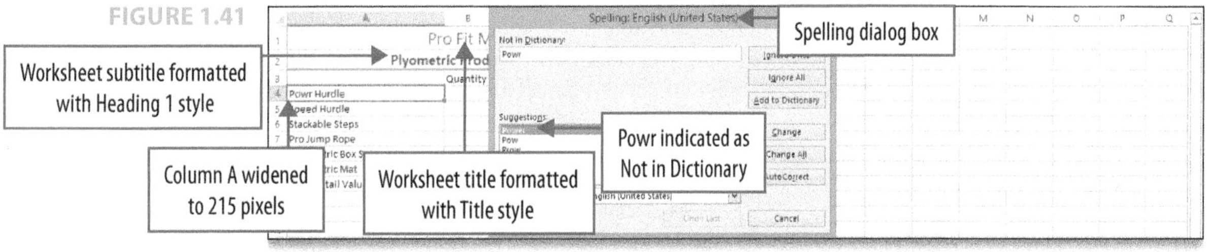

ALERT! **Does a Message Display Asking if You Want to Continue Checking at the Beginning of the Sheet?**

If a message displays asking if you want to continue checking at the beginning of the sheet, click Yes. The Spelling command begins its checking process with the currently selected cell and moves to the right and down. If your active cell was a cell after A1, this message may display.

ANOTHER WAY Press F7, which is the keyboard shortcut for the Spelling command.

11 In the **Spelling** dialog box, under **Not in Dictionary**, notice the word *Powr*.

The spelling tool does not have this word in its dictionary. Under *Suggestions*, Excel provides a list of suggested spellings.

12 Under **Suggestions**, click **Power**, and then click **Change**.

Powr, a typing error, is changed to *Power*. A message box displays *Spell check complete. You're good to go!*—unless you have additional unrecognized words. Because the spelling check begins its checking process starting with the currently selected cell, it is good practice to return to cell A1 before starting the Spelling command.

13 Correct any other errors you may have made. When the message displays, *Spell check complete. You're good to go!*, click **OK**. **Save** your workbook.

Objective 8 Enter Data by Range

Video E1-8

You can enter data by first selecting a range of cells. This is a time-saving technique, especially if you use the numeric keypad to enter the numbers.

Activity 1.19 | Entering Data by Range

1 Select the range **B4:D9**, type **125** and then press Enter.

The value displays in cell B4, and cell B5 becomes the active cell.

2 With cell **B5** active in the range, and pressing Enter after each entry, type the following, and then compare your screen with Figure 1.42:

1125
450
1105
255
215

After you enter the last value and press Enter, the active cell moves to the top of the next column within the selected range. Although it is not required to enter data in this manner, you can see that selecting the range before you enter data saves time because it confines the movement of the active cell to the selected range. When you select a range of data, the Quick Analysis button displays.

FIGURE 1.42

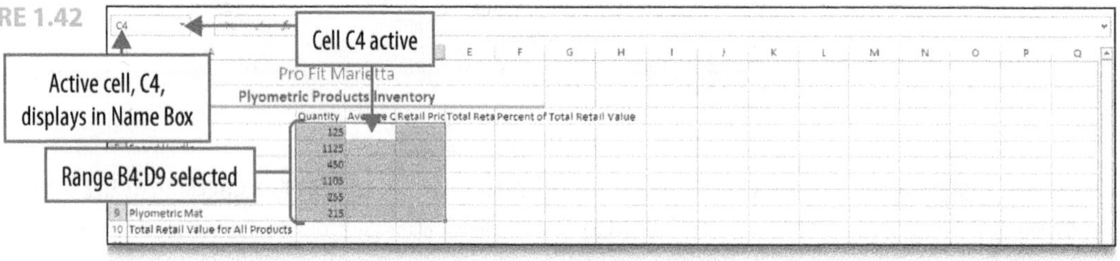

3 With the selected range still active, from the following table, beginning in cell **C4** and pressing Enter after each entry, enter the data for the **Average Cost** column and then the **Retail Price** column. If you prefer, deselect the range to enter the values—typing in a selected range is optional.

AVERAGE COST	RETAIL PRICE
15.50	32.95
29.55	59.95
125.95	251.59
18.75	49.95
85.25	159.05
49.95	94.99

Recall that the default number format for cells is the *General* number format, in which numbers display exactly as you type them and trailing zeros do not display, even if you type them.

4 Click any blank cell, and then compare your screen with Figure 1.43. Correct any errors you may have made while entering data, and then click **Save**.

FIGURE 1.43

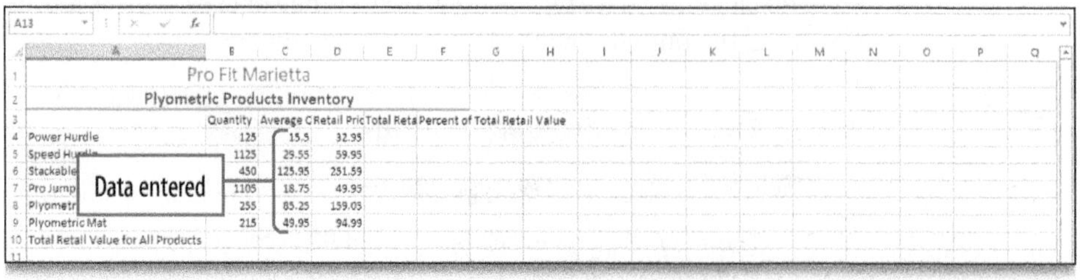

Objective 9 Construct Formulas for Mathematical Operations

Video E1-9

Operators are symbols with which you can specify the type of calculation you want to perform in a formula.

Activity 1.20 | Using Arithmetic Operators

1 Click cell **E4**, type **=b4*d4** and notice that the two cells are outlined as part of an active formula. Then press Enter.

The *Total Retail Value* of all *Power Hurdle* items in inventory—*4118.75*—equals the *Quantity* (125) times the *Retail Price* (selling price) of 32.95. In Excel, the asterisk (*) indicates multiplication.

2 Take a moment to study the symbols you will use to perform basic mathematical operations in Excel as shown in the table in Figure 1.44, which are referred to as ***arithmetic operators***.

FIGURE 1.44

SYMBOLS USED IN EXCEL FOR ARITHMETIC OPERATORS	
OPERATOR SYMBOL	**OPERATION**
+	Addition
–	Subtraction (also negation)
*	Multiplication
/	Division
%	Percent
^	Exponentiation

3 Click cell **E4**.

You can see that in cells E5:E9, you need a formula similar to the one in E4, but one that refers to the cells in row 5, row 6, and so forth. Recall that you can copy formulas and the cell references will change *relative to* the row number.

4 With cell **E4** selected, position your pointer over the fill handle in the lower right corner of the cell until the + pointer displays. Then, drag down through cell **E9** to copy the formula.

5 Select the range **B4:B9**, and then on the **HOME tab**, in the **Number group**, click **Comma Style**. In the **Number group**, click **Decrease Decimal** two times to remove the decimal places from these values.

Comma Style formats a number with two decimal places; because these are whole numbers referring to quantities, no decimal places are necessary.

ANOTHER WAY Select the range, display the Cell Styles gallery, and then under Number Format, click Comma [0].

6 Select the range **E4:E9**, and then at the bottom of your screen, in the status bar, notice the displayed values for **Average**, **Count**, and **Sum**—*50158.89167*, *6* and *300953.35*.

When you select a range of numerical data, Excel's ***AutoCalculate*** feature displays three calculations in the status bar by default—Average, Count, and Sum. Here, Excel indicates that if you averaged the selected values, the result would be *50158.89167*, there are *6* cells in the selection that contain values, and that if you added the values the result would be *300953.35*.

You can display three additional calculations to this area by right-clicking the status bar and selecting them—Numerical Count, Minimum, and Maximum.

Activity 1.21 | Using the Quick Analysis Tool

Recall that the Quick Analysis button displays when you select a range of data. Quick Analysis is convenient because it keeps common commands close to your mouse pointer and also displays commands in a format that is easy to touch with your finger if you are using a touchscreen device.

1 In the lower right corner of the selected range, click **Quick Analysis**, and then in the displayed gallery, click **TOTALS**. *Point to*, but do not click, the first **Sum** button, which shows blue cells at the bottom. Compare your screen with Figure 1.45.

Here, the shaded cells on the button indicate what will be summed and where the result will display, and a preview of the result displays in the cell bordered with a gray shadow.

FIGURE 1.45

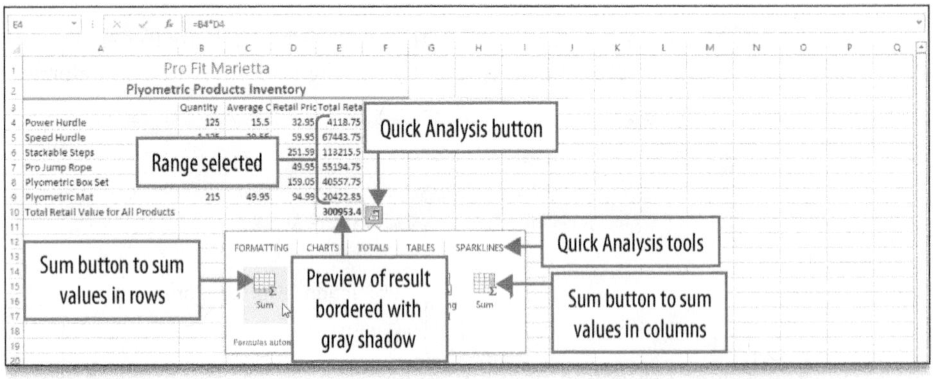

2 Click the first **Sum** button to display the column total *300953.4* formatted in Bold.

Sums calculated using the Quick Analysis tool are formatted in Bold.

3 Select the range **C5:E9** and apply the **Comma Style**; notice that Excel widens the columns to accommodate the data.

4 Select the range **C4:E4**, hold down Ctrl, and then click cell **E10**. Release Ctrl, and then apply the **Accounting Number Format** $. Notice that Excel widens the columns as necessary.

5 Click cell **E10**, and then in the **Cell Styles** gallery, apply the **Total** style. Click any blank cell, **Save** your workbook, and then compare your screen with Figure 1.46.

FIGURE 1.46

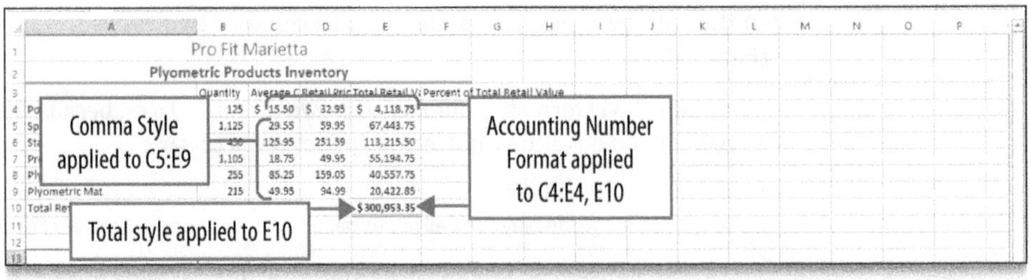

Activity 1.22 | Copying Formulas Containing Absolute Cell References

In a formula, a relative cell reference refers to a cell by its position *relative to* the cell that contains the formula. An ***absolute cell reference***, on the other hand, refers to a cell by its *fixed* position in the worksheet, for example, the total in cell E10.

A relative cell reference automatically adjusts when a formula is copied. In some calculations, you do *not* want the cell reference to adjust; rather, you want the cell reference to remain the same when the formula is copied.

1 Click cell **F4**, type **=** and then click cell **E4**. Type **/** and then click cell **E10**.

The formula =*E4/E10* indicates that the value in cell E4 will be *divided* by the value in cell E10. Why? Because Mr. Feingold wants to know the percentage by which each product's Total Retail Value makes up the Total Retail Value for All Products.

Arithmetically, the percentage is computed by dividing the *Total Retail Value* for each product by the *Total Retail Value for All Products*. The result will be a percentage expressed as a decimal.

2 Press Enter. Click cell **F4** and notice that the formula displays in the **Formula Bar**. Then, point to cell **F4** and double-click.

The formula, with the two referenced cells displayed in color and bordered with the same color, displays in the cell. This feature, called the ***range finder***, is useful for verifying formulas because it visually indicates which workbook cells are included in a formula calculation.

3 Press Enter to redisplay the result of the calculation in the cell, and notice that .013686, which is approximately 1% of the total retail value of the inventory, is made up of Power Hurdles.

4 Click cell **F4** again, and then drag the fill handle down through cell **F9**. Compare your screen with Figure 1.47.

Each cell displays an error message—*#DIV/0!* and a green triangle in the upper left corner of each cell indicates that Excel detects an error.

Like a grammar checker, Excel uses rules to check for formula errors and flags errors in this manner. Additionally, the Auto Fill Options button displays, from which you can select formatting options for the copied cells.

FIGURE 1.47

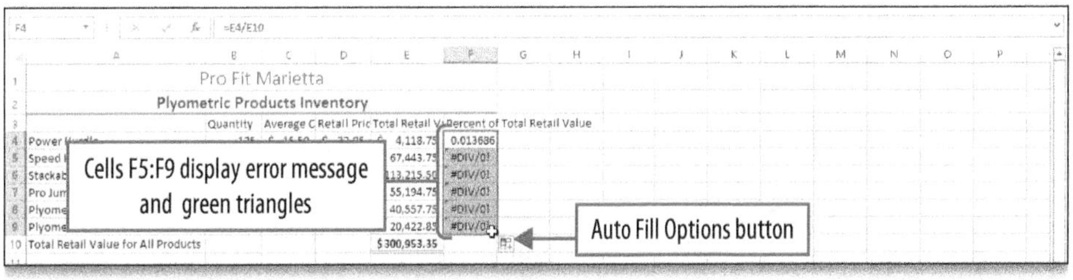

5 Click cell **F5**, and to the left of the cell, point to the **Error Checking** button to display its ScreenTip—*The formula or function used is dividing by zero or empty cells.*

In this manner, Excel suggests the cause of an error.

6 Look at the **Formula Bar** and examine the formula.

The formula is =E5/E11. The cell reference to E5 is correct, but the cell reference following the division operator (/) is *E11*, and E11 is an *empty* cell.

7 Click cell **F6**, point to the **Error Checking** button, and in the **Formula Bar** examine the formula.

Because the cell references are relative, Excel builds the formulas by increasing the row number for each equation. But in this calculation, the divisor must always be the value in cell E10—the *Total Retail Value for All Products.*

8 Point to cell **F4**, and then double-click to place the insertion point within the cell.

9 Within the cell, use the arrow keys as necessary to position the insertion point to the left of *E10*, and then press F4. Compare your screen with Figure 1.48.

Dollar signs ($) display, which changes the reference to cell E10 to an absolute cell reference. The use of the dollar sign to denote an absolute reference is not related in any way to whether or not the values you are working with are currency values. It is simply the symbol that Excel uses to denote an absolute cell reference.

FIGURE 1.48

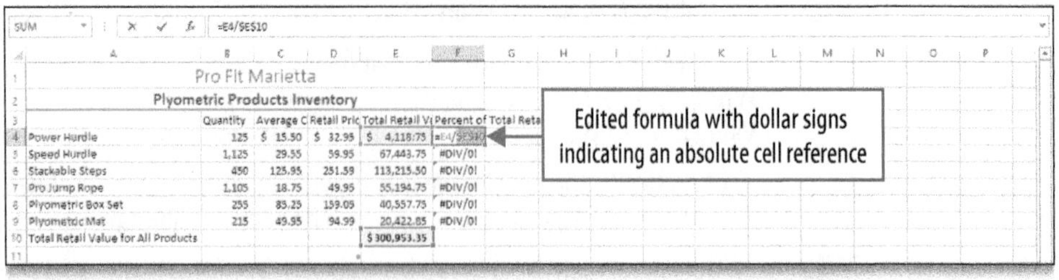

ANOTHER WAY Edit the formula so that it indicates *=E4/E10.*

10 On the **Formula Bar**, click **Enter** so that **F4** remains the active cell. Then, drag the fill handle to copy the new formula down through cell **F9**. Compare your screen with Figure 1.49.

FIGURE 1.49

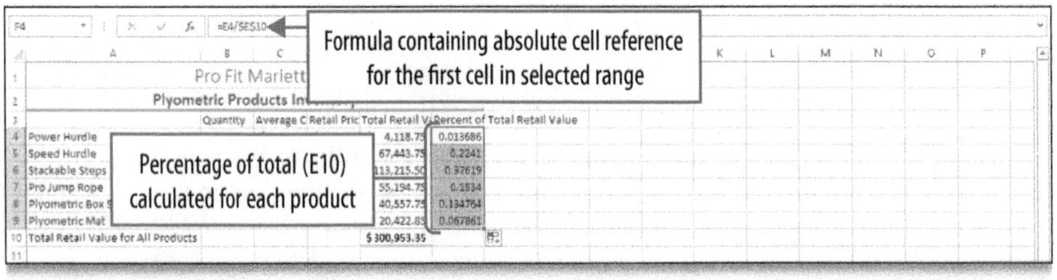

11 Click cell **F5**, examine the formula in the **Formula Bar**, and then examine the formulas for cells **F6**, **F7**, **F8**, and **F9**.

For each formula, the cell reference for the *Total Retail Value* of each product changed relative to its row; however, the value used as the divisor—*Total Retail Value for All Products* in cell E10—remained absolute. You can see that by using either relative or absolute cell references, it is easy to duplicate formulas without typing them.

12 **Save** your workbook.

More Knowledge **Calculate a Percentage if You Know the Total and the Amount**

Using the equation *amount/total = percentage*, you can calculate the percentage by which a part makes up a total—with the percentage formatted as a decimal. For example, if on a test you score 42 points correctly out of 50, your percentage of correct answers is 42/50 = 0.84 or 84%.

Objective 10 Edit Values in a Worksheet

Video E1-10

Excel performs calculations on numbers; that is why you use Excel. If you make changes to the numbers, Excel automatically *re*-calculates the results. This is one of the most powerful and valuable features of Excel.

Activity 1.23 | Editing Values in a Worksheet

You can edit text and number values directly within a cell or in the Formula Bar.

1 In cell **E10**, notice the column total *$300,953.35*. Then, click cell **B5**, and to change its value type **995** Watch cell **E5** and press Enter.

Excel formulas *re-calculate* if you change the value in a cell that is referenced in a formula. It is not necessary to delete the old value in a cell; selecting the cell and typing a new value replaces the old value with your new typing.

The *Total Retail Value* of all *Speed Hurdle* items recalculates to *59,650.25* and the total in cell E10 recalculates to *$293,159.85*. Additionally, all of the percentages in column F recalculate.

2 Point to cell **D8**, and then double-click to place the insertion point within the cell. Use the arrow keys to move the insertion point to left or right of *9*, and use either Del or Backspace to delete *9* and then type **8** so that the new Retail Price is *158.05*.

3 Watch cell **E8** and **E10** as you press Enter, and then notice the recalculation of the formulas in those two cells.

Excel recalculates the value in cell E8 to *40,302.75* and the value in cell E10 to *$292,904.85*. Additionally, all of the percentages in column F recalculate because the *Total Retail Value for All Products* recalculated.

4 Point to cell **A2** so that the pointer is positioned slightly to the right of the word *Inventory*, and then double-click to place the insertion point in the cell. Edit the text to add the word **Valuation** pressing Spacebar as necessary, and then press Enter.

5 Click cell **B3**, and then in the **Formula Bar**, click to place the insertion point after the letter *y*. Press Spacebar one time, type **in Stock** and then on the **Formula Bar**, click **Enter** . Click **Save** , and then compare your screen with Figure 1.50.

Recall that if text is too long to fit in the cell and the cell to the right contains data, the text is truncated—cut off—but the entire value still exists as the underlying value.

FIGURE 1.50

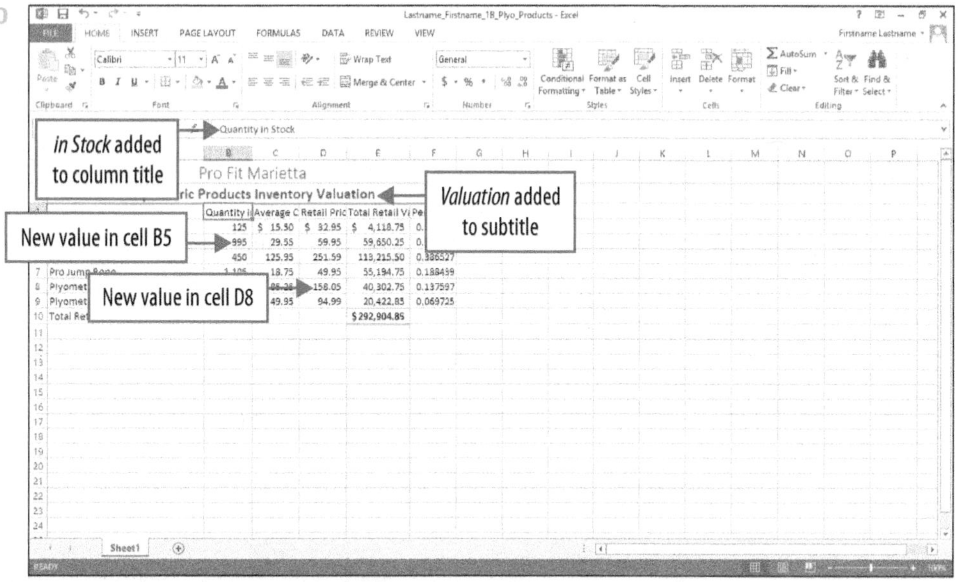

Activity 1.24 | Formatting Cells with the Percent Style

A percentage is part of a whole expressed in hundredths. For example, 75 cents is the same as 75 percent of one dollar. The Percent Style button formats the selected cell as a percentage rounded to the nearest hundredth.

1 Click cell **F4**, and then in the **Number group**, click **Percent Style** [%].

Your result is 1%, which is *0.014062* rounded to the nearest hundredth and expressed as a percentage. Percent Style displays the value of a cell as a percentage.

2 Select the range **F4:F9**, right-click over the selection, and then on the mini toolbar, click **Percent Style** [%], click **Increase Decimal** two times, and then click **Center**.

Percent Style may not offer a percentage precise enough to analyze important financial information—adding additional decimal places to a percentage makes data more precise.

3 Click any cell to cancel the selection, **Save** your workbook, and then compare your screen with Figure 1.51.

FIGURE 1.51

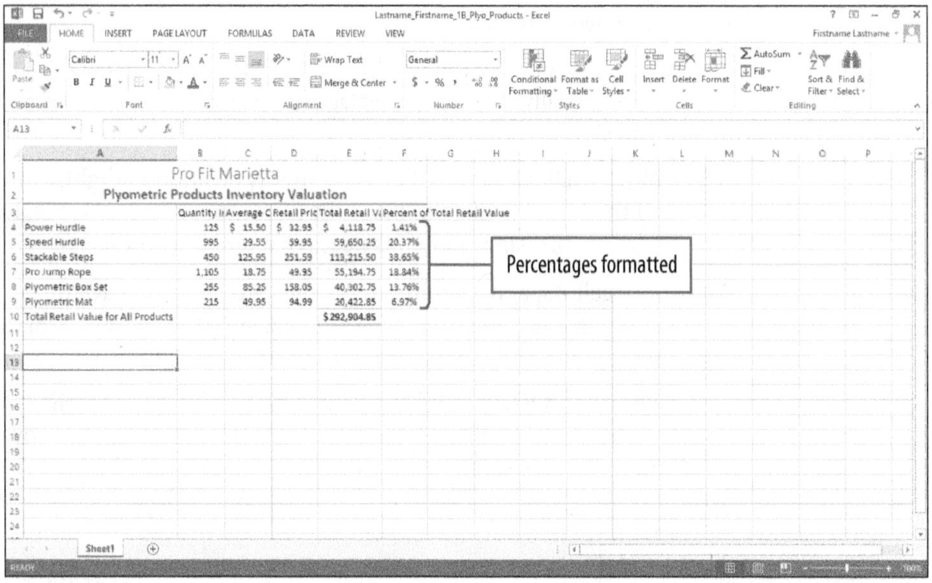

Objective 11 Format a Worksheet

Video E1-11

Formatting refers to the process of specifying the appearance of cells and the overall layout of your worksheet. Formatting is accomplished through various commands on the ribbon, for example, applying Cell Styles, and also from commands on shortcut menus, using keyboard shortcuts, and in the Format Cells dialog box.

Activity 1.25 | Inserting and Deleting Rows and Columns

1 In the **row heading area** on the left side of your screen, point to the row heading for **row 3** to display the [→] pointer, and then right-click to simultaneously select the row and display a shortcut menu.

2 On the shortcut menu, click **Insert** to insert a new **row 3** above the selected row.

The rows below the new row 3 move down one row, and the Insert Options button displays. By default, the new row uses the formatting of the row *above*.

ANOTHER WAY Select the row, on the Home tab, in the Cells group, click the Insert button arrow, and then click Insert Sheet Rows. Or, select the row and click the Insert button—the default setting of the button inserts a new sheet row above the selected row.

3 Click cell **E11**. On the **Formula Bar**, notice that the range changed to sum the new range **E5:E10**. Compare your screen with Figure 1.52.

If you move formulas by inserting additional rows or columns in your worksheet, Excel automatically adjusts the formulas. Excel adjusted all of the formulas in the worksheet that were affected by inserting this new row.

FIGURE 1.52

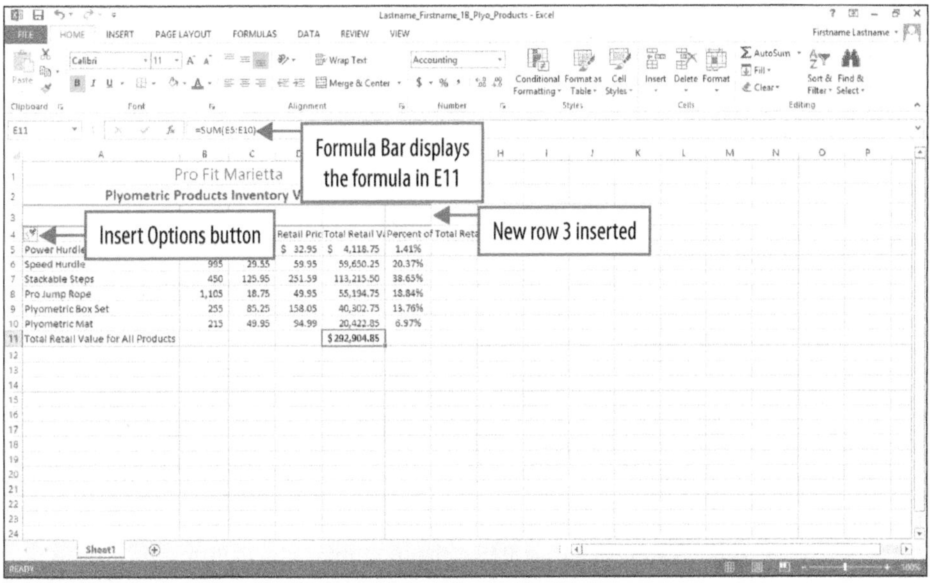

4 Click cell **A3**, type **As of September 30** and then on the **Formula Bar**, click **Enter** to maintain **A3** as the active cell. **Merge & Center** the text across the range **A3:F3**, and then apply the **Heading 2** cell style.

5 In the **column heading area**, point to **column B** to display the pointer, right-click, and then click **Insert**.

A column is inserted to the left of column B. By default, the new column uses the formatting of the column to the *left*.

ANOTHER WAY

Select the column, on the Home tab, in the Cells group, click the Insert button arrow, and then click Insert Sheet Columns. Or, select the column and click the Insert button—the default setting of the button inserts a new sheet column to the right of the selected column.

6 Click cell **B4**, type **Warehouse Location** and then press Enter.

7 In cell **B5**, type **Atlanta** and then type **Atlanta** again in cells **B6** and **B10**. Use AutoComplete to speed your typing by pressing Enter as soon as the AutoComplete suggestion displays. In cells **B7**, **B8**, and **B9**, type **Marietta**

8 In the **column heading area**, point to **column D**, right-click, and then click **Delete**.

The remaining columns shift to the left, and Excel adjusts all the formulas in the worksheet accordingly. You can use a similar technique to delete a row in a worksheet.

9 Compare your screen with Figure 1.53, and then **Save** your workbook.

FIGURE 1.53

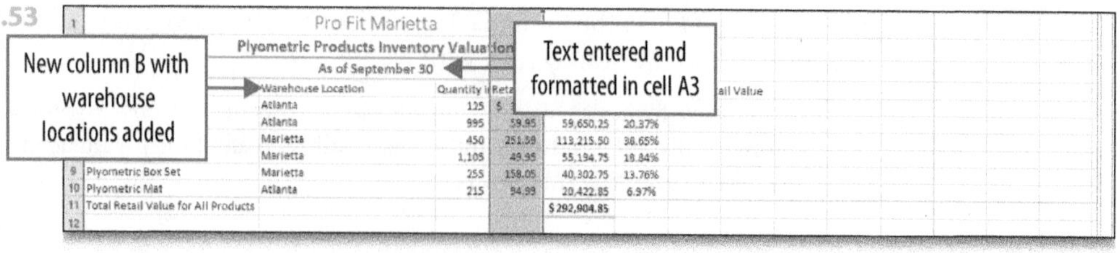

More Knowledge **Hiding Rows and Columns**

To hide a row or column from view, select the row or column, right-click, and then click Hide. A border displays to indicate that data is hidden from view. To unhide, select the rows above and below—or the adjacent columns—right-click, and then click Unhide.

Activity 1.26 | Adjusting Column Widths and Wrapping Text

Use the Wrap Text command to display the contents of a cell on multiple lines.

1 In the **column heading area**, point to the **column B** heading to display the [↓] pointer, and then drag to the right to select **columns B:F**.

2 With the columns selected, in the **column heading area**, point to the right boundary of any of the selected columns to display the [+] pointer, and then drag to set the width to **95 pixels**.

Use this technique to format multiple columns or rows simultaneously.

3 Select the range **B4:F4** that comprises the column titles, and then on the **HOME tab**, in the **Alignment group**, click **Wrap Text**. Notice that the row height adjusts to display the titles on multiple lines.

4 With the range **B4:F4** still selected, in the **Alignment group**, click **Center** and **Middle Align**. With the range **B4:F4** still selected, apply the **Heading 4** cell style.

The Middle Align command aligns text so that it is centered between the top and bottom of the cell.

5 Select the range **B5:B10**, right-click, and then on the mini toolbar, click **Center**. Click cell **A11**, and then from the **Cell Styles** gallery, under **Themed Cell Styles**, click **40% - Accent1**. **Save** your workbook.

Activity 1.27 | Changing Theme Colors

You can change only the Theme colors of a workbook—without changing the theme fonts or effects.

1 On the **PAGE LAYOUT tab**, in the **Themes group**, click the **Colors arrow**, and then click **Green** to change the theme color. Click any blank cell, and then compare your screen with Figure 1.54.

FIGURE 1.54

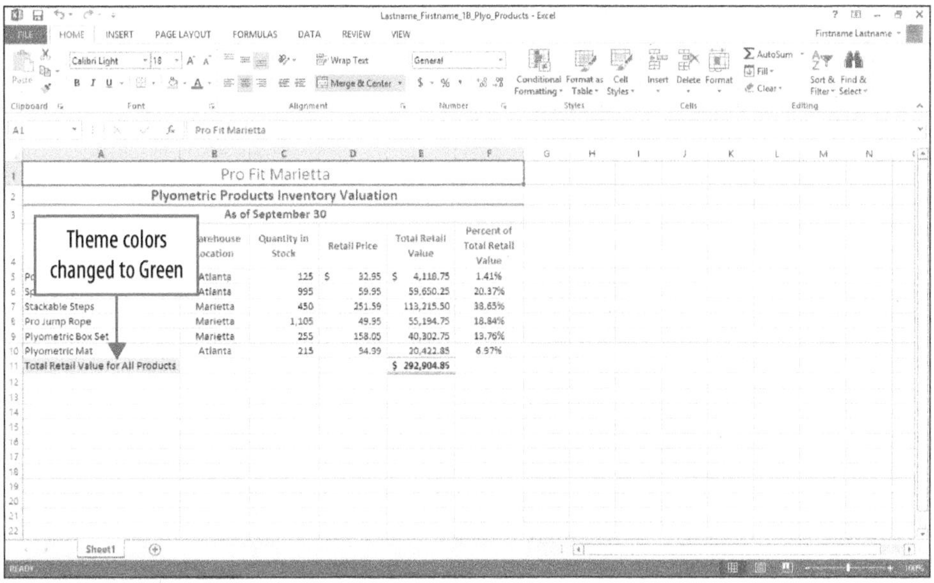

2. On the **PAGE LAYOUT tab**, in the **Page Setup group**, click **Margins**, and then click **Custom Margins**.

3. In the **Page Setup** dialog box, on the **Margins tab**, under **Center on page**, select the **Horizontally** check box.

   This action will center the data and chart horizontally on the page, as shown in the Preview area.

4. In the displayed **Page Setup** dialog box, click the **Header/Footer tab**, and then in the center of the dialog box, click **Custom Footer**. In the **Footer** dialog box, with your insertion point blinking in the **Left section**, on the row of buttons, click **Insert File Name**.

   &[File] displays in the Left section. Here you can type or insert information from the row of buttons into the left, middle, or right section of the footer. The Custom Header button displays a similar screen to enter information in the header of the worksheet.

5. Click **OK** two times.

6. Click the **FILE tab** to display **Backstage** view, and then in the lower right corner, click **Show All Properties**.

7. As the **Tags**, type **plyo products, inventory** and as the **Subject**, type your course name and section number. Be sure your name displays as the author.

8. On the left, click **Print** to view the **Print Preview**. At the bottom of the **Print Preview**, click **Next Page**, and notice that as currently formatted, the worksheet occupies two pages.

9. Under **Settings**, click **Portrait Orientation**, and then click **Landscape Orientation**. Compare your screen with Figure 1.55.

   You can change the orientation on the Page Layout tab, or here, in Print Preview. Because it is in the Print Preview that you will often see adjustments that need to be made, commonly used settings display on the Print tab in Backstage view.

FIGURE 1.55

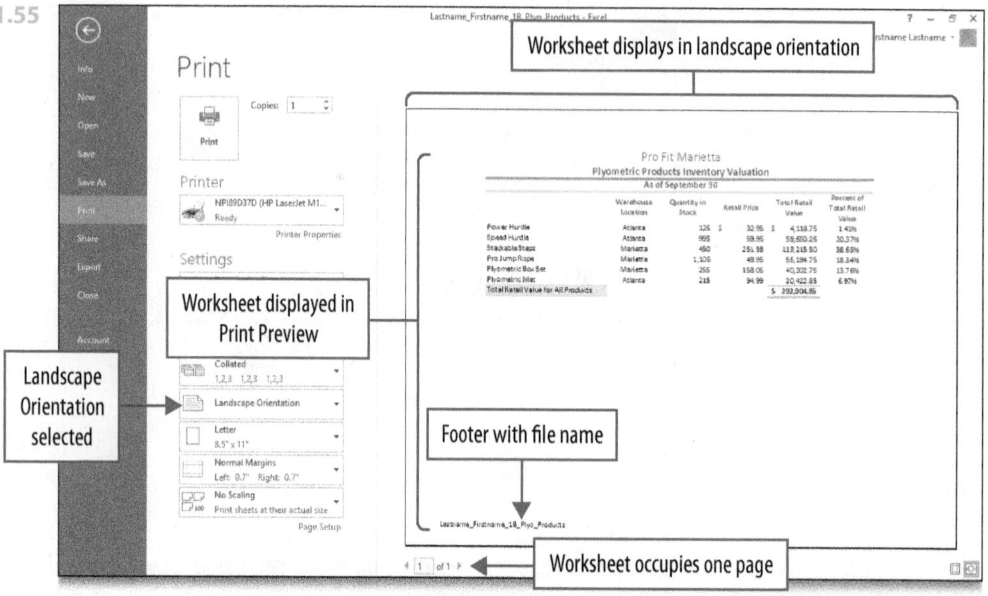

10 By using the techniques you practiced in Project 1A, print or submit electronically as directed by your instructor. If required by your instructor, print or create an electronic version of your worksheet with formulas displayed.

11 Close your workbook and Close Excel.

END | You have completed Project 1B

GO! with Office Online (formerly Web Apps)

Objective Calculate the Value of an Inventory in Excel Online

If you are working on a computer that does not have Microsoft Office installed, you can still create new workbooks in your web browser by using Excel Online.

ALERT! **Working with Web-Based Applications and Services**

Computer programs and services on the web receive continuous updates and improvements, so the steps to complete this web-based activity may differ from the ones shown. You can often look at the screens and the information presented to determine how to complete the activity.

Activity | Creating an Inventory Valuation Report in Excel Online

In this activity, you will use Excel Online to create an inventory valuation similar to the one you created in Project 1B.

1. From the desktop, start Internet Explorer. Navigate to **http://onedrive.com**, and then sign in to your Microsoft account. Open your **GO! Web Projects** folder—or create and then open this folder if necessary.
2. Near the top of the screen, click **Create**, and then click **Excel workbook**. Above the ribbon, click Book1 to select the text. Using your own name, as the file name type **Lastname_Firstname_EX_1B_Web** Click cell **1A**.
3. To help you create this project quickly and to eliminate extra typing, you will import the data from a Word table. From the taskbar, open **File Explorer**, navigate to the student data files that accompany this textbook, and then open the Word document **e01_1B_Web**. Press Ctrl + A to select all of the text, right-click anywhere over the selection, and then click **Copy**. **Close** Word and File Explorer.
4. With cell **A1** selected, on the Excel Online ribbon, in the **Clipboard group**, click the upper portion of the **Paste** button; if necessary click **Allow access**.
5. Select column headings **A:D**, point to the border between any two selected column headings to display the pointer, and then double-click to resize the selected columns to display all the data.
6. In cell **E3** type **Total Retail Value** and press Enter. Select the range **B3:E3**, and then in the **Alignment group**, click **Center**, **Middle Align**, and **Wrap Text**. Widen **column E** so that *Total Retail* is on one line and *Value* is on the second line.
7. Click cell **E4** and type **=c4*d4** to create the formula and press Enter; your result is *4118.75*. Click cell **E4** again, and then drag the fill handle down through cell **E9** to calculate each row. Compare your screen with Figure A.

FIGURE A

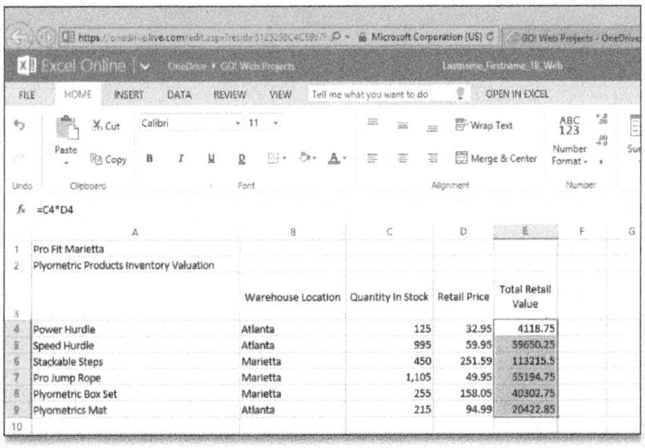

(GO! with Office Online (formerly Web Apps) continues on the next page)

8 Click cell **E10**, and then in the **Editing group**, click **AutoSum** and press Enter to total the column.

9 In cell **F3** type **Percent of Total Retail Value** and then apply **Center**, **Middle Align**, and **Wrap Text**. Widen the column to display the column title on three lines. In cell **F4** type the formula to calculate the percent of total value **=e4/e10** and press Enter, and then copy the formula down through cell **F9**. With the range **F4:F9** still selected, from the **Number Format arrow**, click **Percentage**.

10 Select the range **E4:E10** and then from the **Number Format arrow**, apply **Currency** format. Click cell **E9**, and then in the **Font group**, click **Underline**. Click cell **E10**, and then in the **Font group**, click **Double Underline**.

11 Select the range **A1:F1**, and then in the **Alignment group**, click **Merge & Center**. Merge and center the worksheet's subtitle in the same manner. Select the range **A1:A2**, and then in the **Font group**, apply **Bold** and change the **Font Color** to **Orange, Darker 50%**.

12 Click cell **B3**, and then adjust the width of **column B** so that the column title displays on two lines. Click cell **C3** and adjust in the same manner.

13 In cell **A10** type **Total Retail Value for All Products** and then AutoFit **column A**.

14 Click cell **A1**, and then compare your screen with Figure B.

15 If you are instructed to submit your file, use one of the methods outlined in the Note box below. Recall that in Excel Online, there is no Save button because your workbook is being saved automatically. Sign out and close Internet Explorer.

FIGURE B

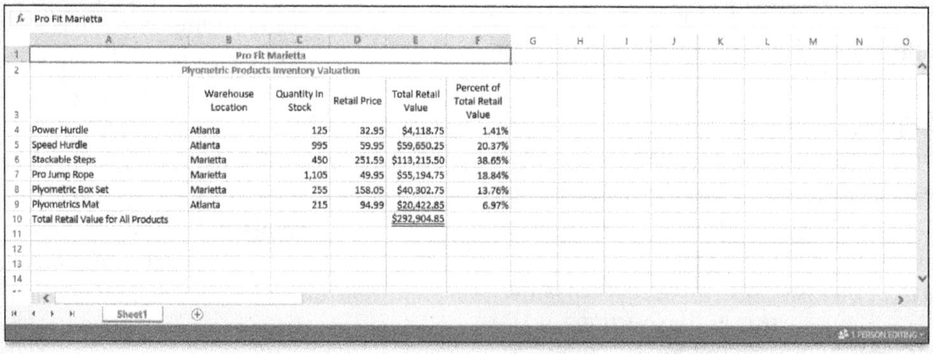

Pro Fit Marietta

	A	B	C	D	E	F
1	Pro Fit Marietta					
2	Plyometric Products Inventory Valuation					
3		Warehouse Location	Quantity In Stock	Retail Price	Total Retail Value	Percent of Total Retail Value
4	Power Hurdle	Atlanta	125	32.95	$4,118.75	1.41%
5	Speed Hurdle	Atlanta	995	59.95	$59,650.25	20.37%
6	Stackable Steps	Marietta	450	251.59	$113,215.50	38.65%
7	Pro Jump Rope	Marietta	1,105	49.95	$55,194.75	18.84%
8	Plyometric Box Set	Marietta	255	158.05	$40,302.75	13.76%
9	Plyometrics Mat	Atlanta	215	94.99	$20,422.85	6.97%
10	Total Retail Value for All Products				$292,904.85	

Sheet1

NOTE

Printing or Creating an Electronic File from Excel Online

To print on paper, click the FILE tab, click Print, click the Print button, and then click Print. In the Print Preview display, click Print. In the displayed Print dialog box, click Print to print on the printer connected to your system. To create an electronic file of your printout, from the Print dialog box, click the printer labeled *Send to OneNote 2013*, and then click Print. You may have to open and then close OneNote first if you have never opened it before. When OneNote opens, click the Quick Notes section of the displayed notebook, and then click OK. On the ribbon, click the FILE tab, click Export, and then create a PDF of the page. Navigate to an appropriate location and give the file an appropriate name. Close OneNote.

GO! with Microsoft Office 365

Andrew Rodriguez / Fotolia; FotolEdhar/ Fotolia; apops/ Fotolia; Yuri Arcurs/ Fotolia

In every job, you must work and communicate with other people. A group of workers tasked with working together to solve a problem, make a decision, or create a work product is referred to as a ***team***. For a team to succeed, the team members must be able to communicate with one another easily.

If all the team members work at the same location and work the same hours, communication is easy. You schedule face-to-face meetings and exchange documents and information among yourselves. But that is a rare arrangement in today's organizations. Rather, it is more likely that the members of your team work in different locations—even different countries—and work different hours or travel extensively away from the headquarters location. Also, for specific projects, teams are frequently organized across different departments of an organization or even across different organizations entirely. Then when the project is complete, the team disbands.

Collaboration is when you work together with others as a team in an intellectual endeavor to complete a shared task or achieve a shared goal; for example, when you and one or more of your classmates work together on a class project. Collaboration involves giving feedback to and receiving feedback from others on the team, and then revising the strategies to achieve the goal or produce the work product based on the feedback.

Microsoft Office 365 is a set of secure online services that enable people in an organization to communicate and collaborate by using any Internet-connected device—a computer, a tablet, or a mobile phone. Because Office 365 offers access from anywhere to email, Web conferencing, documents, and calendars, everyone on a team can work together easily. Office 365 is intended for use by multiple users in an organization and is offered on a monthly subscription basis to organizations starting as low as $6 per month per user.

Activity | Using the Exchange Online Outlook Meeting Tool to Collaborate

This team project relates to the **Bell Orchid Hotels**. If your instructor assigns this project to your class, in this chapter you can expect to use the **Outlook Meeting tool** in **Office 365 Exchange Online** to collaborate on the following tasks for this chapter:

- If you are in the **Accounting Group**, you and your teammates will meet virtually to plan a workbook to summarize hotel rooms sold over a four-week period in April.
- If you are in the **Engineering Group**, you and your teammates will meet virtually to plan a workbook summarizing Maintenance Expenses for the first quarter.
- If you are in the **Food and Beverage Group**, you and your teammates will meet virtually to plan a Menu Analysis workbook to analyze the profitability of the ten most popular entrees in the hotel's restaurant.
- If you are in the **Human Resources Group**, you and your teammates will meet virtually to plan a Salary Analysis workbook summarizing the pay of salaried employees over the first six months of operation.
- If you are in the **Operations Group**, you and your teammates will meet virtually to plan a workbook for Rooms and Housekeeping Service Analysis that will be used to determine ongoing needs for housekeeping service.
- If you are in the **Sales and Marking Group**, you and your teammates will meet virtually to plan a Rooms Sold Analysis workbook summarizing rooms sold by four salespersons during January-June that will be used to develop a marketing plan for the rest of the year.

FIGURE A

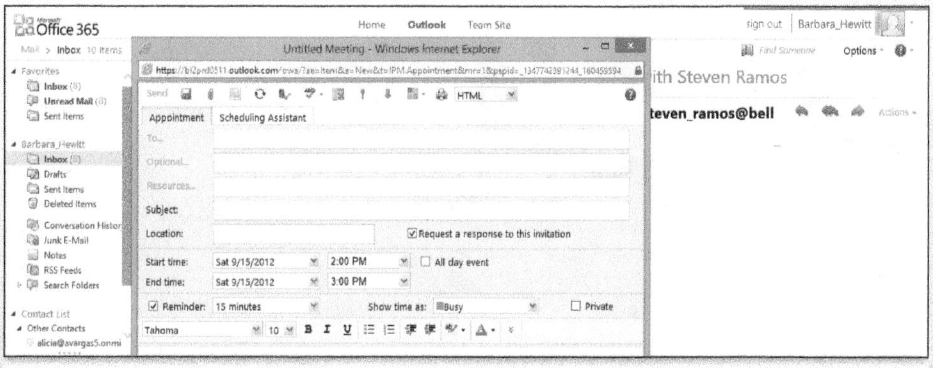

END OF CHAPTER

SUMMARY

In Excel, you work with worksheets that are contained in a workbook. A worksheet is formatted as a pattern of uniformly spaced horizontal rows and vertical columns, the intersection of which forms a cell.

A cell can contain a constant value—referred to as a value—or a formula, which is an equation that performs mathematical calculations on the values in your worksheet. Common values are text and numbers.

You can insert sparklines in an Excel worksheet, which are tiny charts embedded in a cell that give a visual trend summary alongside your data. A sparkline makes a pattern more obvious to the eye.

Charts provide a graphic representation of data in a worksheet. Use the Recommended Charts feature to display customized charts that, according to Excel's calculations, will best represent your data.

GO! LEARN IT ONLINE

Review the concepts and key terms in this chapter by completing these online challenges, which you can find at **www.pearsonhighered.com/go**.

Matching and Multiple Choice: Answer matching and multiple choice questions to test what you learned in this chapter. MyITLab®

Crossword Puzzle: Spell out the words that match the numbered clues, and put them in the puzzle squares.

Flipboard: Flip through the definitions of the key terms in this chapter and match them with the correct term.

GO! FOR JOB SUCCESS

Video: Dress to Impress

Your instructor may assign this video to your class, and then ask you to think about, or discuss with your classmates, these questions:

FotolEdhar / Fotolia

If you were interviewing people for your company, what would you look for in terms of their dress and personal presentation?

What might you want to change about your personal dress for work or for an interview?

Do you feel that it's right to "judge a book by its cover"? Why or why not?

END OF CHAPTER

REVIEW AND ASSESSMENT GUIDE FOR EXCEL CHAPTER 1

Your instructor may assign one or more of these projects to help you review the chapter and assess your mastery and understanding of the chapter.

Review and Assessment Guide for Excel Chapter 1

Project	Apply Skills from These Chapter Objectives	Project Type	Project Location
1C	Objectives 1–6 from Project 1A	**1C Skills Review** A guided review of the skills from Project 1A.	On the following pages
1D	Objectives 7–11 from Project 1B	**1D Skills Review** A guided review of the skills from Project 1B.	On the following pages
1E	Objectives 1–6 from Project 1A	**1E Mastery (Grader Project)** A demonstration of your mastery of the skills in Project 2A with extensive decision making.	In MyITLab and on the following pages
1F	Objectives 7–11 from Project 1B	**1F Mastery (Grader Project)** A demonstration of your mastery of the skills in Project 1B with extensive decision making.	In MyITLab and on the following pages
1G	Objectives 1–11 from Projects 1A and 1B	**1G Mastery (Grader Project)** A demonstration of your mastery of the skills in Projects 1A and 1B with extensive decision making.	In MyITLab and on the following pages
1H	Combination of Objectives from Projects 1A and 1B	**1H GO! Fix It** A demonstration of your mastery of the skills in Projects 1A and 1B by creating a correct result from a document that contains errors you must find.	Online
1I	Combination of Objectives from Projects 1A and 1B	**1I GO! Make It** A demonstration of your mastery of the skills in Projects 1A and 1B by creating a result from a supplied picture.	Online
1J	Combination of Objectives from Projects 1A and 1B	**1J GO! Solve It** A demonstration of your mastery of the skills in Projects 1A and 1B, your decision-making skills, and your critical thinking skills. A task-specific rubric helps you self-assess your result.	Online
1K	Combination of Objectives from Projects 1A and 1B	**1K GO! Solve It** A demonstration of your mastery of the skills in Projects 1A and 1B, your decision-making skills, and your critical thinking skills. A task-specific rubric helps you self-assess your result.	On the following pages
1L	Combination of Objectives from Projects 1A and 1B	**1L GO! Think** A demonstration of your understanding of the chapter concepts applied in a manner that you would outside of college. An analytic rubric helps you and your instructor grade the quality of your work by comparing it to the work an expert in the discipline would create.	On the following pages
1M	Combination of Objectives from Projects 1A and 1B	**1M GO! Think** A demonstration of your understanding of the chapter concepts applied in a manner that you would outside of college. An analytic rubric helps you and your instructor grade the quality of your work by comparing it to the work an expert in the discipline would create.	Online
1N	Combination of Objectives from Projects 1A and 1B	**1N You and GO!** A demonstration of your understanding of the chapter concepts applied in a manner that you would in a personal situation. An analytic rubric helps you and your instructor grade the quality of your work.	Online
1O	Combination of Objectives from Projects 1A and 1B	**1O Cumulative Group Project for Excel Chapter 1** A demonstration of your understanding of concepts and your ability to work collaboratively in a group role-playing assessment, requiring both collaboration and self-management.	Online

GLOSSARY

GLOSSARY OF CHAPTER KEY TERMS

Absolute cell reference A cell reference that refers to cells by their fixed position in a worksheet; an absolute cell reference remains the same when the formula is copied.

Accounting Number Format The Excel number format that applies a thousand comma separator where appropriate, inserts a fixed U.S. dollar sign aligned at the left edge of the cell, applies two decimal places, and leaves a small amount of space at the right edge of the cell to accommodate a parenthesis for negative numbers.

Active cell The cell, surrounded by a black border, ready to receive data or be affected by the next Excel command.

Arithmetic operators The symbols +, −, *, /, %, and ^ used to denote addition, subtraction (or negation), multiplication, division, percentage, and exponentiation in an Excel formula.

Auto Fill An Excel feature that generates and extends values into adjacent cells based on the values of selected cells.

AutoCalculate A feature that displays three calculations in the status bar by default—Average, Count, and Sum—when you select a range of numerical data.

AutoComplete A feature that speeds your typing and lessens the likelihood of errors; if the first few characters you type in a cell match an existing entry in the column, Excel fills in the remaining characters for you.

AutoFit An Excel feature that adjusts the width of a column to fit the cell content of the widest cell in the column.

AutoSum A button that provides quick access to the SUM function.

Category axis The area along the bottom of a chart that identifies the categories of data; also referred to as the x-axis.

Category labels The labels that display along the bottom of a chart to identify the categories of data; Excel uses the row titles as the category names.

Cell The intersection of a column and a row.

Cell address Another name for a cell reference.

Cell content Anything typed into a cell.

Cell reference The identification of a specific cell by its intersecting column letter and row number.

Cell style A defined set of formatting characteristics, such as font, font size, font color, cell borders, and cell shading.

Chart The graphic representation of data in a worksheet; data presented as a chart is usually easier to understand than a table of numbers.

Chart Elements button A button that enables you to add, remove, or change chart elements such as the title, legend, gridlines, and data labels.

Chart Filters button A button that enables you to change which data displays in the chart.

Chart layout The combination of chart elements that can be displayed in a chart such as a title, legend, labels for the columns, and the table of charted cells.

Chart style The overall visual look of a chart in terms of its graphic effects, colors, and backgrounds; for example, you can have flat or beveled columns, colors that are solid or transparent, and backgrounds that are dark or light.

Chart Styles button A button that enables you to set a style and color scheme for your chart.

Chart Styles gallery A group of predesigned chart styles that you can apply to an Excel chart.

Chart types Various chart formats used in a way that is meaningful to the reader; common examples are column charts, pie charts, and line charts.

Column A vertical group of cells in a worksheet.

Column chart A chart in which the data is arranged in columns and that is useful for showing how data changes over a period of time or for illustrating comparisons among items.

Column heading The letter that displays at the top of a vertical group of cells in a worksheet; beginning with the first letter of the alphabet, a unique letter or combination of letters identifies each column.

Comma Style The Excel number format that inserts thousand comma separators where appropriate and applies two decimal places; Comma Style also leaves space at the right to accommodate a parenthesis when negative numbers are present.

Constant value Numbers, text, dates, or times of day that you type into a cell.

Context sensitive A command associated with the currently selected or active object; often activated by right-clicking a screen item.

Data Text or numbers in a cell.

Data marker A column, bar, area, dot, pie slice, or other symbol in a chart that represents a single data point; related data points form a data series.

Data point A value that originates in a worksheet cell and that is represented in a chart by a data marker.

Data series Related data points represented by data markers; each data series has a unique color or pattern represented in the chart legend.

Displayed value The data that displays in a cell.

Excel pointer An Excel window element with which you can display the location of the pointer.

Expand Formula Bar button An Excel window element with which you can increase the height of the Formula Bar to display lengthy cell content.

Expand horizontal scroll bar button An Excel window element with which you can increase the width of the horizontal scroll bar.

Fill handle The small black square in the lower right corner of a selected cell.

Format Changing the appearance of cells and worksheet elements to make a worksheet attractive and easy to read.

Formula An equation that performs mathematical calculations on values in a worksheet.

Formula Bar An element in the Excel window that displays the value or formula contained in the active cell; here you can also enter or edit values or formulas.

Function A predefined formula—a formula that Excel has already built for you—that performs calculations by using specific values in a particular order.

General format The default format that Excel applies to numbers; this format has no specific characteristics—whatever you type in the cell will display, with the exception that trailing zeros to the right of a decimal point will not display.

Label Another name for a text value, and which usually provides information about number values.

Left alignment The cell format in which characters align at the left edge of the cell; this is the default for text entries and is an example of formatting information stored in a cell.

Legend A chart element that identifies the patterns or colors that are assigned to the categories in the chart.

Lettered column headings The area along the top edge of a worksheet that identifies each column with a unique letter or combination of letters.

Merge & Center A command that joins selected cells in an Excel worksheet into one larger cell and centers the contents in the merged cell.

Name Box An element of the Excel window that displays the name of the selected cell, table, chart, or object.

Normal view A screen view that maximizes the number of cells visible on your screen and keeps the column letters and row numbers close to the columns and rows.

Number format A specific way in which Excel displays numbers in a cell.

Number values Constant values consisting of only numbers.

Numbered row headings The area along the left edge of a worksheet that identifies each row with a unique number.

Operators The symbols with which you can specify the type of calculation you want to perform in an Excel formula.

Page Layout view A screen view in which you can use the rulers to measure the width and height of data, set margins for printing, hide or display the numbered row headings and the lettered column headings, and change the page orientation; this view is useful for preparing your worksheet for printing.

Picture element A point of light measured in dots per square inch on a screen; 64 pixels equals 8.43 characters, which is the average number of characters that will fit in a cell in an Excel worksheet using the default font.

Pixel The abbreviated name for a picture element.

Point and click method The technique of constructing a formula by pointing to and then clicking cells; this method is convenient when the referenced cells are not adjacent to one another.

Quick Analysis tool A tool that displays in the lower right corner of a selected range with which you can analyze your data by using Excel tools such as charts, color-coding, and formulas.

Range Two or more selected cells on a worksheet that are adjacent or nonadjacent; because the range is treated as a single unit, you can make the same changes or combination of changes to more than one cell at a time.

Range finder An Excel feature that outlines cells in color to indicate which cells are used in a formula; useful for verifying which cells are referenced in a formula.

Recommended Charts An Excel feature that displays a customized set of charts that, according to Excel's calculations, will best fit your data based on the range of data that you select.

Relative cell reference In a formula, the address of a cell based on the relative positions of the cell that contains the formula and the cell referred to in the formula.

Rounding A procedure in which you determine which digit at the right of the number will be the last digit displayed and then increase it by one if the next digit to its right is 5, 6, 7, 8, or 9.

Row A horizontal group of cells in a worksheet.

Row heading The numbers along the left side of an Excel worksheet that designate the row numbers.

Scaling The process of shrinking the width and/or height of printed output to fit a maximum number of pages.

Select All box A box in the upper left corner of the worksheet grid that, when clicked, selects all the cells in a worksheet.

Series A group of things that come one after another in succession; for example, January, February, March, and so on.

Sheet tab scrolling buttons Buttons to the left of the sheet tabs used to display Excel sheet tabs that are not in view; used when there are more sheet tabs than will display in the space provided.

Sheet tabs The labels along the lower border of the Excel window that identify each worksheet.

Show Formulas A command that displays the formula in each cell instead of the resulting value.

Sparkline A tiny chart in the background of a cell that gives a visual trend summary alongside your data; makes a pattern more obvious.

Spreadsheet Another name for a worksheet.

Status bar The area along the lower edge of the Excel window that displays, on the left side, the current cell mode, page number, and worksheet information; on the right side, when numerical data is selected, common calculations such as Sum and Average display.

SUM function A predefined formula that adds all the numbers in a selected range of cells.

Switch Row/Column A charting command to swap the data over the axis—data being charted on the vertical axis will move to the horizontal axis and vice versa.

Text values Constant values consisting of only text, and which usually provide information about number values; also referred to as labels.

Theme A predefined set of colors, fonts, lines, and fill effects that coordinate with each other.

Underlying formula The formula entered in a cell and visible only on the Formula Bar.

Underlying value The data that displays in the Formula Bar.

Value Another name for a constant value.

Value axis A numerical scale on the left side of a chart that shows the range of numbers for the data points; also referred to as the Y-axis.

Workbook An Excel file that contains one or more worksheets.

Workbook-level buttons Buttons at the far right of the ribbon tabs that minimize or restore a displayed workbook.

Worksheet The primary document that you use in Excel to work with and store data, and which is formatted as a pattern of uniformly spaced horizontal and vertical lines.

Worksheet grid area A part of the Excel window that displays the columns and rows that intersect to form the worksheet's cells.

X-axis Another name for the horizontal (category) axis.

Y-axis Another name for the vertical (value) axis.

CHAPTER REVIEW

Apply 1A skills from these Objectives:

1. Create, Save, and Navigate an Excel Workbook
2. Enter Data in a Worksheet
3. Construct and Copy Formulas and Use the SUM Function
4. Format Cells with Merge & Center, Cell Styles, and Themes
5. Chart Data to Create a Column Chart and Insert Sparklines
6. Print a Worksheet, Display Formulas, and Close Excel

Build from Scratch

Skills Review Project 1C Step Sales

In the following Skills Review, you will create a new Excel worksheet with a chart that summarizes the first quarter sales of fitness equipment for step training. Your completed worksheet will look similar to Figure 1.56.

PROJECT FILES

For Project 1C, you will need the following file:

New blank Excel workbook

You will save your workbook as:

Lastname_Firstname_1C_Step_Sales

PROJECT RESULTS

Pro Fit Marietta

First Quarter Step Sales

	January	February	March	Total	Trend
Basic Step Box	$ 75,826.99	$ 81,657.32	$ 72,431.22	$ 229,915.53	
Step Storage Box	85,245.90	92,618.95	88,337.68	266,202.53	
Stackable Steps	68,751.64	71,997.48	78,951.23	219,700.35	
Step Mats	63,255.10	58,742.67	67,995.20	189,992.97	
Total	**$ 293,079.63**	**$ 305,016.42**	**$ 307,715.33**	**$ 905,811.38**	

Lastname_Firstname_1C_Step_Sales

FIGURE 1.56

(Project 1C Step Sales continues on the next page)

CHAPTER REVIEW

Skills Review Project 1C Step Sales (continued)

1 **Start** Excel and open a new blank workbook. Click the **FILE tab** to display **Backstage** view, click **Save As**, and then navigate to your **Excel Chapter 1** folder. In the **File name** box, using your own name, type **Lastname_Firstname_1C_Step_Sales** and then press Enter.

a. With cell **A1** as the active cell, type the worksheet title **Pro Fit Marietta** and then press Enter. In cell **A2**, type the worksheet subtitle **First Quarter Step Sales** and then press Enter.

b. Leave row 3 blank, click in cell **A4**, type **Basic Step Box** and then press Enter. In cell **A5**, type **Step Storage Box** and then press Enter. In cell **A6**, type **Stackable Steps** and then press Enter. In cell **A7**, type **Step Mats** and then press Enter. In cell **A8**, type **Total** and then press Enter.

c. Click cell **B3**. Type **January** and then in the **Formula Bar**, click **Enter** to keep cell **B3** the active cell. With **B3** as the active cell, point to the **fill handle** in the lower right corner of the selected cell, drag to the right to cell **D3**, and then release the mouse button to enter the text *February* and *March*.

d. Press Ctrl + Home to make cell **A1** the active cell. In the **column heading area**, point to the vertical line between **column A** and **column B** to display the ⟷ pointer, hold down the left mouse button, and drag to the right to increase the column width to **130 pixels**.

e. Point to cell **B3**, and then drag across to select cells **B3** and **C3** and **D3**.With the range **B3:D3** selected, point anywhere over the selected range, right-click, and then on the mini toolbar, click **Center**.

f. Click cell **B4**, type **75826.99** and press Tab to make cell **C4** active. Enter the remaining values, as shown below in **Table 1**, pressing Tab to move across the rows and Enter to move down the columns.

TABLE 1

	January	February	March
Basic Step Box	75826.99	**81657.32**	**72431.22**
Step Storage Rack	**85245.90**	**92618.95**	**88337.68**
Stackable Steps	**68751.64**	**71997.48**	**78951.23**
Step Mats	**63255.10**	**58742.67**	**67995.20**

2 Click cell **B8** to make it the active cell and type **=**

a. At the insertion point, type **b4** and then type **+** Type **b5** and then type **+b6+b7** Press Enter. Your result is *293079.6*.

b. Click in cell **C8**. Type **=** and then click cell **C4**. Type **+** and then click cell **C5**. Repeat this process to complete the formula to add cells **C6** and **C7** to the formula, and then press Enter. Your result is *305016.4*.

c. Click cell **D8**. On the **HOME tab**, in the **Editing group**, click **AutoSum**, and then press Enter to construct a formula by using the SUM function. Your result is *307715.3*.

d. In cell **E3** type **Total** and press Enter. With cell **E4** as the active cell, hold down Alt, and then press =. On the **Formula Bar**, click **Enter** to display the result and keep cell **E4** active.

e. With cell **E4** active, point to the **fill handle** in the lower right corner of the cell. Drag down through cell **E8**, and then release the mouse button to copy the formula with relative cell references down to sum each row.

3 Click cell **F3**. Type **Trend** and then press Enter.

a. Select the range **A1:F1**, and then on the **HOME tab**, in the **Alignment group**, click **Merge & Center**. Select the range **A2:F2** and **Merge & Center** the selection.

b. Click cell **A1**. In the **Styles group**, click **Cell Styles**. Under **Titles and Headings**, click **Title**. Click cell **A2**, display the **Cell Styles** gallery, and then click **Heading 1**.

c. Select the range **B3:F3**, hold down Ctrl, and then select the range **A4:A8**. From the **Cell Styles** gallery, click **Heading 4** to apply this cell style to the column and row titles.

d. Select the range **B4:E4**, hold down Ctrl, and then select the range **B8:E8**. On the **HOME tab**, in the **Number group**, click **Accounting Number Format**. Select the range **B5:E7**, and then in the **Number group**, click **Comma Style**. Select the range **B8:E8**. From the **Styles group**, display the **Cell Styles** gallery, and then under **Titles and Headings**, click **Total**.

e. On the ribbon, click the **PAGE LAYOUT tab**, and then in the **Themes group**, click **Themes** to display the **Themes** gallery. Click the **Basis** theme. (This theme widens the columns slightly). On the **Quick Access Toolbar**, click **Save**.

(Project 1C Step Sales continues on the next page)

CHAPTER REVIEW

Skills Review Project 1C Step Sales (continued)

4 Select the range **A3:D7**, which includes the row titles, the column titles and the data without the totals. Click the **INSERT tab**, and then in the **Charts group**, click **Recommended Charts**. In the **Insert Chart** dialog box, scroll down and click the fifth recommended chart—a **Clustered Column** chart in which *each month* displays its *sales for each type of step training equipment*. Click **OK**.

a. In the chart, click anywhere in the text *Chart Title* to select the text box. Watch the **Formula Bar** as you type **First** and then let AutoComplete complete the title by pressing Enter.

b. Click in a white area just slightly *inside* the chart border to deselect the chart title but keep the chart selected. To the right of the chart, click the second button—the **Chart Styles** button. Be sure the **STYLE** tab is selected. Use the scroll bar to scroll down, and then by using the ScreenTips, locate and click **Style 6**.

c. At the top of the gallery, click **COLOR**. Under **Colorful**, point to the fourth row of colors to display the ScreenTip *Color 4*, and then click to apply the **Color 4** variation of the theme colors.

d. Point to the top border of the chart to display the pointer, and then drag the upper left corner of the chart just to the center of cell **A10** to visually center it below the data.

5 Select the range **B4:D7**. Click the **INSERT tab**, and then in the **Sparklines group**, click **Line**. In the **Create Sparklines** dialog box, in the **Location Range** box, type **f4:f7** and then click **OK** to insert the sparklines.

a. On the **DESIGN tab**, in the **Show group**, select the **Markers** check box to display markers in the sparklines.

b. On the **DESIGN tab**, in the **Style group**, click **More** and then in the second row, click the fourth style—**Sparkline Style Accent 4, Darker 25%**.

6 Click cell **A1** to deselect the chart. Click the **PAGE LAYOUT tab**, and then in the **Page Setup group**, click **Margins**. At the bottom, click **Custom Margins** to display the **Page Setup** dialog box, and then on the **Margins tab**, under **Center on page**, select the **Horizontally** check box.

a. In the dialog box, click the **Header/Footer tab**, and then click **Custom Footer**. With your insertion point in the **Left section**, click **Insert File Name**. Click **OK** two times.

b. Click the **FILE tab** to display **Backstage** view. In the lower right corner, click **Show All Properties**. As the **Tags**, type **step sales, 1st quarter** In the **Subject** box, type your course name and section number. Be sure your name displays as the Author—edit if necessary.

c. On the left, click **Save**.

d. Print or submit your workbook electronically as directed by your instructor. If required by your instructor, print or create an electronic version of your worksheet with formulas displayed by using the instructions in Project 1A. **Close** Excel without saving so that you do not save the changes you made to print formulas.

END | You have completed Project 1C

CHAPTER REVIEW

Skills Review Project 1D Band and Tubing Inventory

Apply 1B skills from these Objectives:

7 Check Spelling in a Worksheet
8 Enter Data by Range
9 Construct Formulas for Mathematical Operations
10 Edit Values in a Worksheet
11 Format a Worksheet

Build from Scratch

In the following Skills Review, you will create a worksheet that summarizes the inventory of band and tubing exercise equipment. Your completed worksheet will look similar to Figure 1.57.

PROJECT FILES

For Project 1D, you will need the following file:

New blank Excel workbook

You will save your workbook as:

Lastname_Firstname_1D_Band_Inventory

PROJECT RESULTS

Pro Fit Marietta

Band and Tubing Inventory

As of June 30

	Material	Quantity in Stock	Retail Price	Total Retail Value	Percent of Total Retail Value
Super Strength Bands	Latex	225	$ 48.98	$ 11,020.50	25.16%
Medium Tubing	Rubber	198	27.95	5,534.10	12.64%
Resistance Band, Average	Latex	165	42.95	7,086.75	16.18%
Mini Bands, Medium	Latex	245	25.95	6,357.75	14.52%
Mini Bands, Heavy	Rubber	175	32.95	5,766.25	13.17%
Heavy Tubing	Latex	187	42.95	8,031.65	18.34%
Total Retail Value for All Products				$ 43,797.00	

Lastname_Firstname_1D_Band_Inventory

FIGURE 1.57

(Project 1D Band and Tubing Inventory continues on the next page)

Skills Review Project 1D Band and Tubing Inventory (continued)

1 **Start** Excel and display a new blank workbook. **Save** the workbook in your **Excel Chapter 1** folder as **Lastname_Firstname_1D_Band_Inventory** In cell **A1** type **Pro Fit Marietta** and in cell **A2** type **Band and Tubing Inventory**

a. Click cell **B3**, type **Quantity in Stock** and press Tab. In cell **C3** type **Average Cost** and press Tab. In cell **D3**, type **Retail Price** and press Tab. In cell **E3**, type **Total Retail Value** and press Tab. In cell **F3** type **Percent of Total Retail Value** and press Enter.

b. Click cell **A4**, type **Super Strength Bands** and press Enter. In the range **A5:A10**, type the remaining row titles as shown below, including any misspelled words.

Medium Tubing

Resistnce Band, Average

Mini Bands, Medium

Mini Bands, Heavy

Heavy Tubing

Total Retail Value for All Products

c. Press Ctrl + Home to move to the top of your worksheet. On the **REVIEW tab**, in the **Proofing group**, click **Spelling.** Correct *Resistnce* to **Resistance** and any other spelling errors you may have made, and then when the message displays, *Spell check complete. You're good to go!* click **OK.**

d. In the **column heading area**, point to the right boundary of **column A** to display the ✛ pointer, and then drag to the right to widen **column A** to **225 pixels.**

e. In the **column heading area**, point to the **column B** heading to display the ↓ pointer, and then drag to the right to select **columns B:F**. With the columns selected, in the **column heading area**, point to the right boundary of any of the selected columns, and then drag to the right to set the width to **100 pixels.**

f. Select the range **A1:F1**. On the **HOME tab**, in the **Alignment group**, click **Merge & Center**, and then in the **Cell Styles** gallery, apply the **Title** style. Select the range **A2:F2**. **Merge & Center** the text across the selection, and then in the **Cell Styles** gallery, apply the **Heading 1** style.

2 On the **PAGE LAYOUT tab**, in the **Themes group**, change the **Colors** to **Blue Green**. Select the empty range **B4:D9**. With cell **B4** active in the range, type **225** and then press Enter.

a. With cell **B5** active in the range, and pressing Enter after each entry, type the following data in the *Quantity in Stock* column:

198

265

245

175

187

b. With the selected range still active, from the following table, beginning in cell **C4** and pressing Enter after each entry, enter the following data for the **Average Cost** column and then the **Retail Price** column. If you prefer, type without selecting the range first; recall that this is optional.

Average Cost	Retail Price
22.75	48.98
15.95	27.95
26.90	42.95
12.95	25.95
18.75	32.95
26.90	42.95

3 In cell **E4**, type **=b4*d4** and then press Enter to construct a formula that calculates the *Total Retail Value* of the *Super Strength Bands* (Quantity in Stock × Retail Price).

a. Click cell **E4**, position your pointer over the fill handle, and then drag down through cell **E9** to copy the formula with relative cell references.

b. Select the range **B4:B9**, and then on the **HOME tab**, in the **Number group**, click **Comma Style**. Then, in the **Number group**, click **Decrease Decimal** two times to remove the decimal places from these non-currency values.

c. To calculate the *Total Retail Value for All Products*, select the range **E4:E9**, and then in the lower right corner of the selected range, click the **Quick Analysis** button.

(Project 1D Band and Tubing Inventory continues on the next page)

CHAPTER REVIEW

Skills Review Project 1D Band and Tubing Inventory (continued)

d. In the gallery, click **TOTALS**, and then click the *first* **Sum** button, which visually indicates that the column will be summed with a result at the bottom of the column.

e. Select the range **C5:E9** and apply the **Comma Style**. Select the range **C4:E4**, hold down Ctrl, and then click cell **E10**. With the nonadjacent cells selected, apply the **Accounting Number Format**. Click cell **E10**, and then from the **Cell Styles** gallery, apply the **Total** style.

f. Click cell **F4**, type **=** and then click cell **E4**. Type **/** and then click cell **E10**. Press F4 to make the reference to cell *E10* absolute, and then on the **Formula Bar**, click ✓ so that cell **F4** remains the active cell. Drag the **fill handle** to copy the formula down through cell **F9**.

g. Point to cell **B6**, and then double-click to place the insertion point within the cell. Use the arrow keys to move the insertion point to the left or right of *2*, and use either Delete or Backspace to delete *2*, and then type **1** and press Enter so that the new *Quantity in Stock* is *165*. Notice the recalculations in the worksheet.

4 Select the range **F4:F9**, right-click over the selection, and then on the mini toolbar, click **Percent Style**. Click **Increase Decimal** two times, and then **Center** the selection.

a. In the **row heading area** on the left side of your screen, point to **row 3** to display the ➡ pointer, and then right-click to simultaneously select the row and display a shortcut menu. On the shortcut menu, click **Insert** to insert a new **row 3**.

b. Click cell **A3**, type **As of June 30** and then on the **Formula Bar**, click ✓ to keep cell **A3** as the active cell. **Merge & Center** the text across the range **A3:F3**, and then apply the **Heading 2** cell style.

5 In the **column heading area**, point to **column B**. When the ⬇ pointer displays, right-click, and then click **Insert** to insert a new column.

a. Click cell **B4**, type **Material** and then press Enter. In cell **B5**, type **Latex** and then press Enter. In cell **B6**, type **Rubber** and then press Enter.

b. Using AutoComplete to speed your typing by pressing Enter as soon as the AutoComplete suggestion displays, in cells **B7**, **B8**, and **B10** type **Latex** and in cell **B9** type **Rubber**

c. In the **column heading area**, point to the right boundary of **column B**, and then drag to the left and set the width to **90 pixels**. In the **column heading area**, point to **column D**, right-click, and then click **Delete**.

d. Select the column titles in the range **B4:F4**, and then on the **HOME tab**, in the **Alignment group**, click **Wrap Text**, **Center**, and **Middle Align**. With the range still selected, apply the **Heading 4** cell style.

e. Click cell **A11**, and then in the **Cell Styles** gallery, under **Themed Cell Styles**, click **40% - Accent1**.

6 Click the **PAGE LAYOUT tab**, in the **Page Setup group**, click **Margins**, and then click **Custom Margins**. In the **Page Setup** dialog box, on the **Margins tab**, under **Center on page**, select the **Horizontally** check box.

a. Click the **Header/Footer tab**, and then click **Custom Footer**. With your insertion point in the **Left section**, click **Insert File Name**. Click **OK** two times.

b. In the **Page Setup group**, click **Orientation**, and then click **Landscape**.

c. Click the **FILE tab** to display **Backstage** view. In the lower right corner, click **Show All Properties**. As the **Tags**, type **bands, tubing, inventory** In the **Subject** box, type your course name and section number. Be sure your name displays as the author—edit if necessary.

d. On the left, click **Save** to be sure that you have saved your work up to this point.

e. Print or submit your workbook electronically as directed by your instructor. If required by your instructor, print or create an electronic version of your worksheet with formulas displayed by using the instructions in Project 1A. **Close** Excel without saving so that you do not save the changes you made to print formulas.

END | You have completed Project 1D

CONTENT-BASED ASSESSMENTS

MyITLab® grader

Mastering Excel | Project 1E Gym Sales

Apply 1A skills from these Objectives:

1. Create, Save, and Navigate an Excel Workbook
2. Enter Data in a Worksheet
3. Construct and Copy Formulas and Use the SUM Function
4. Format Cells with Merge & Center, Cell Styles, and Themes
5. Chart Data to Create a Column Chart and Insert Sparklines
6. Print a Worksheet, Display Formulas, and Close Excel

Build from Scratch

In the following Mastering Excel project, you will create a worksheet comparing the sales of different types of home gym equipment sold in the second quarter. Your completed worksheet will look similar to Figure 1.58.

PROJECT FILES

For Project 1E, you will need the following files:

New blank Excel workbook

You will save your workbook as:

Lastname_Firstname_1E_Gym_Sales

PROJECT RESULTS

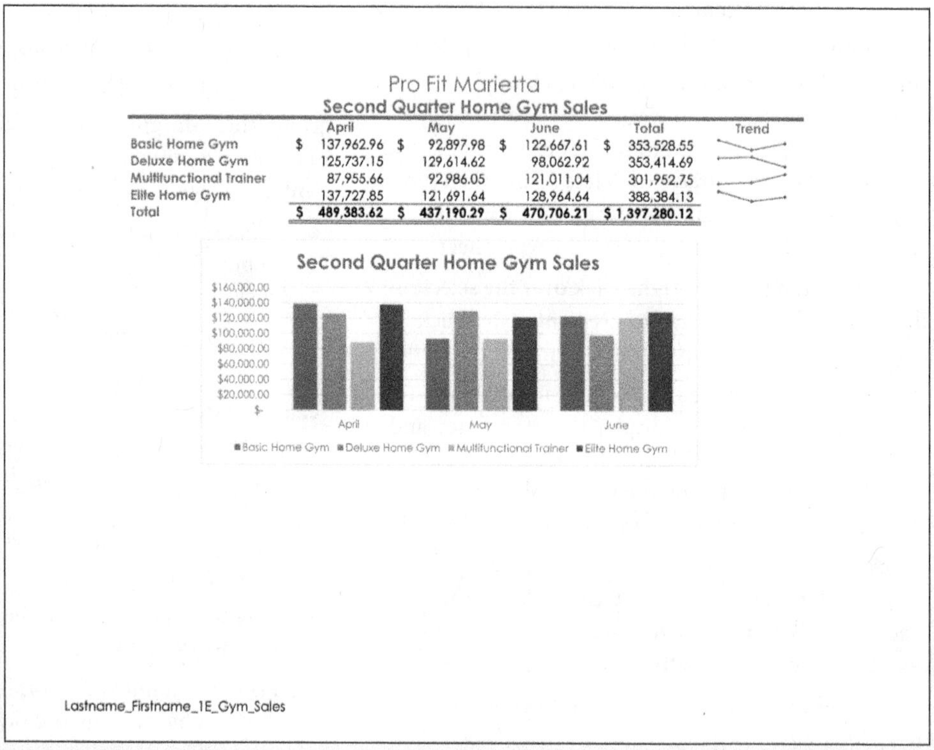

Pro Fit Marietta

Second Quarter Home Gym Sales

	April	May	June	Total	Trend
Basic Home Gym	$ 137,962.96	$ 92,897.98	$ 122,667.61	$ 353,528.55	
Deluxe Home Gym	125,737.15	129,614.62	98,062.92	353,414.69	
Multifunctional Trainer	87,955.66	92,986.05	121,011.04	301,952.75	
Elite Home Gym	137,727.85	121,691.64	128,964.64	388,384.13	
Total	**$ 489,383.62**	**$ 437,190.29**	**$ 470,706.21**	**$ 1,397,280.12**	

FIGURE 1.58

(Project 1E Gym Sales continues on the next page)

CONTENT-BASED ASSESSMENTS

Mastering Excel Project 1E Gym Sales (continued)

1 Start Excel and display a new blank workbook. In cell **A1**, type **Pro Fit Marietta** and in cell **A2**, type **Second Quarter Home Gym Sales** Change the **Theme** to **Wisp**, and then **Save** the workbook in your **Excel Chapter 1** folder as **Lastname_Firstname_1E_Gym_Sales**

2 In cell **B3**, type **April** and then fill the months *May* and *June* in the range **C3:D3**. In cell **E3**, type **Total** and in cell **F3**, type **Trend**

3 **Center** the column titles in the range **B3:F3**. **Merge & Center** the title across the range **A1:F1**, and apply the **Title** cell style. **Merge & Center** the subtitle across the range **A2:F2**, and then apply the **Heading 1** cell style.

4 Widen **column A** to **180 pixels**, and then in the range **A4:A8**, type the following row titles:

Basic Home Gym

Deluxe Home Gym

Multifunctional Trainer

Elite Home Gym

Total

5 Widen columns **B:F** to **115 pixels**, and then in the range **B4:D7**, enter the monthly sales figures for each type of gym, as shown in the table below:

	April	May	June
Basic Home Gym	137962.96	92897.98	122667.61
Deluxe Home Gym	125737.15	129614.62	98062.92
Multifunctional Trainer	87955.66	92986.05	121011.04
Elite Home Gym	137727.85	121691.64	128964.64

6 Select the range that represents April sales, and then on the **HOME tab**, in the **Editing group**, click **AutoSum**. Copy the formula across to cells **C8:D8**. Select the range that represents the sales of the *Basic Home Gym*, and then on the **HOME tab**, in the **Editing group**, click **AutoSum**. Copy the formula down to cells **E5:E8**.

7 Apply the **Heading 4** cell style to the row titles and the column titles. Apply the **Total** cell style to the totals in the range **B8:E8**. Apply the **Accounting Number Format** to the first row of sales figures and to the total row. Apply the **Comma Style** to the remaining sales figures.

8 To compare the monthly sales of each product visually, select the range that represents the sales figures for the three months, including the month names and the product names—do not include any totals in the range. With this data selected, use **Recommended Charts** to insert a **Clustered Column** chart with the month names displayed on the category axis and the product names displayed in the legend.

9 Drag the center right sizing handle to widen the chart slightly so that all the legend items display on one line, and then position the chart so that it is visually centered below the data with its top edge aligned with the top edge of row 10 approximately as shown in Figure 1.58. Apply **Chart Style 6** and **Color 2** under **Colorful**. Change the **Chart Title** to **Second Quarter Home Gym Sales**

10 In the range **F4:F7**, insert **Line** sparklines that compare the monthly data. Do not include the totals. Show the sparkline **Markers** and apply **Sparkline Style Accent 2, Darker 50%**.

11 Center the worksheet **Horizontally** on the page, and then insert a **Footer** with the **File Name** in the **Left section**. Change the **Orientation** to **Landscape**. Display the document properties, and then as the **Tags** type **home gym, sales** As the **Subject**, type your course name and section number. Be sure your name displays as the author. Check your worksheet by previewing it in **Print Preview**, and then make any necessary corrections.

12 **Save** your workbook, and then print or submit electronically as directed. If required by your instructor, print or create an electronic version of your worksheet with formulas displayed by using the instructions in Project 1A. **Close** Excel without saving so that you do not save the changes you made to print formulas.

END | You have completed Project 1E

CONTENT-BASED ASSESSMENTS

MyITLab® grader

Mastering Excel | Project 1F Balance Sales

Apply 1B skills from these Objectives:

7 Check Spelling in a Worksheet
8 Enter Data by Range
9 Construct Formulas for Mathematical Operations
10 Edit Values in a Worksheet
11 Format a Worksheet

In the following Mastering Excel project, you will create a worksheet that summarizes the sales of balance and stabilization equipment that Pro Fit Marietta is marketing. Your completed worksheet will look similar to Figure 1.59.

PROJECT FILES

For Project 1F, you will need the following file:

New blank Excel workbook

You will save your workbook as:

Lastname_Firstname_1F_Balance_Sales

PROJECT RESULTS

Build from Scratch

Pro Fit Marietta

Balance and Stabilization Sales

Month Ending March 31

	Quantity Sold	Retail Price	Total Sales	Percent of Total Sales
Balance Pillow	275	$ 22.95	$ 6,311.25	5.43%
Slide Board	382	75.50	28,841.00	24.82%
Foam Roller	251	39.50	9,914.50	8.53%
Rebounder	162	139.95	22,671.90	19.51%
Stability Ball	380	51.50	19,570.00	16.84%
Balance Board	206	84.95	17,499.70	15.06%
Balance Pad	150	75.99	11,398.50	9.81%
Total Sales for All Products			**$ 116,206.85**	

Lastname_Firstname_1F_Balance_Sales

FIGURE 1.59

(Project 1F Balance Sales continues on the next page)

Mastering Excel Project 1F Balance Sales (continued)

1 Start Excel and display a new blank workbook. **Save** the workbook in your **Excel Chapter 1** folder as **Lastname_Firstname_1F_Balance_Sales** In cell **A1**, type **Pro Fit Marietta** In cell **A2**, type **Balance and Stabilization Sales** and then **Merge & Center** the title and the subtitle across **columns A:F**. Apply the **Title** and **Heading 1** cell styles respectively.

2 Beginning in cell **B3**, type the following column titles: **Product Number** and **Quantity Sold** and **Retail Price** and **Total Sales** and **Percent of Total Sales**

3 Beginning in cell **A4**, type the following row titles, including misspelled words:

Balance Pillow
Silde Board
Foam Roller
Rebounder
Stability Ball
Balance Board
Balance Pad
Total Sales for All Products

4 Make cell **A1** the active cell, and then check spelling in your worksheet. Correct *Silde* to **Slide**, and make any other necessary corrections. Widen **column A** to **180 pixels** and **columns B:F** to **95 pixels**.

5 In the range **B4:D10**, type the following data:

	Product Number	Quantity Sold	Retail Price
Balance Pillow	BP-3	275	22.95
Slide Board	SB-8	382	99.95
Foam Roller	FR-2	251	39.50
Rebounder	RB-4	162	139.95
Stability Ball	SB-5	380	51.50
Balance Board	BB-6	206	84.95
Balance Pad	BP-8	220	75.99

6 In cell **E4**, construct a formula to calculate the *Total Sales* of the *Balance Pillow* by multiplying the *Quantity Sold* times the *Retail Price*. Copy the formula down for the remaining products. Select the range **E4:E10**, and then use the **Quick Analysis tool** to **Sum** the *Total Sales for All Products*, which will be formatted in **Bold**. To the total in cell **E11**, apply the **Total** cell style.

7 Using absolute cell references as necessary so that you can copy the formula, in cell **F4**, construct a formula to calculate the *Percent of Total Sales* for the first product. Copy the formula down for the remaining products. To the computed percentages, apply **Percent Style** with two decimal places, and then **Center** the percentages.

8 Apply the **Comma Style** with no decimal places to the *Quantity Sold* figures. To cells **D4**, **E4**, and **E11** apply the **Accounting Number Format**. To the range **D5:E10**, apply the **Comma Style**.

9 Change the *Retail Price* of the *Slide Board* to **75.50** and the *Quantity Sold* of the *Balance Pad* to **150** Delete **column B**, and then **Insert** a new **row 3**. In cell **A3**, type **Month Ending March 31** and then **Merge & Center** the text across the range **A3:E3**. Apply the **Heading 2** cell style. To cell **A12**, apply the **20%-Accent1** cell style. Select the four column titles, apply **Wrap Text**, **Middle Align**, and **Center** formatting, and then apply the **Heading 3** cell style.

10 Center the worksheet **Horizontally** on the page, and then insert a **Footer** with the **File Name** in the **Left section**. Display the document properties, and then as the **Tags**, type **balance, stability, sales** In the **Subject** box, add your course name and section number. Be sure your name displays as the author.

11 **Save** your workbook, and then print or submit electronically as directed. If required by your instructor, print or create an electronic version of your worksheet with formulas displayed by using the instructions in Project 1A. **Close** Excel without saving so that you do not save the changes you made to print formulas.

END | You have completed Project 1F

CONTENT-BASED ASSESSMENTS

MyITLab® grader

Mastering Excel | Project 1G Regional Sales

Apply a combination of 1A and 1B skills:

1. Create, Save, and Navigate an Excel Workbook
2. Enter Data in a Worksheet
3. Construct and Copy Formulas and Use the SUM Function
4. Format Cells with Merge & Center, Cell Styles, and Themes
5. Chart Data to Create a Column Chart and Insert Sparklines
6. Print a Worksheet, Display Formulas, and Close Excel
7. Check Spelling in a Worksheet
8. Enter Data by Range
9. Construct Formulas for Mathematical Operations
10. Edit Values in a Worksheet
11. Format a Worksheet

Build from Scratch

In the following Mastering Excel project, you will create a new worksheet that compares annual sales by region. Your completed worksheet will look similar to Figure 1.60.

PROJECT FILES

For Project 1G, you will need the following file:

New blank Excel workbook

You will save your workbook as:

Lastname_Firstname_1G_Regional_Sales

PROJECT RESULTS

Pro Fit Marietta

2016 Regional Sales to Fitness Clubs

	Quarter 1	Quarter 2	Quarter 3	Quarter 4	Total	% of Total Sales	Trend
Northeast	$ 225,684.50	$ 210,760.45	$ 181,555.32	$ 228,634.85	$ **846,635.12**	28.67%	
Southeast	128,698.12	144,465.29	132,106.81	155,874.75	**561,144.97**	19.00%	
Midwest	110,985.45	118,674.91	100,548.50	120,621.17	**450,830.03**	15.26%	
West	292,416.67	247,941.48	262,774.12	291,698.99	**1,094,831.26**	37.07%	
Total Sales	**$ 757,784.74**	**$ 721,842.13**	**$ 676,984.75**	**$ 796,829.76**	**$ 2,953,441.38**		

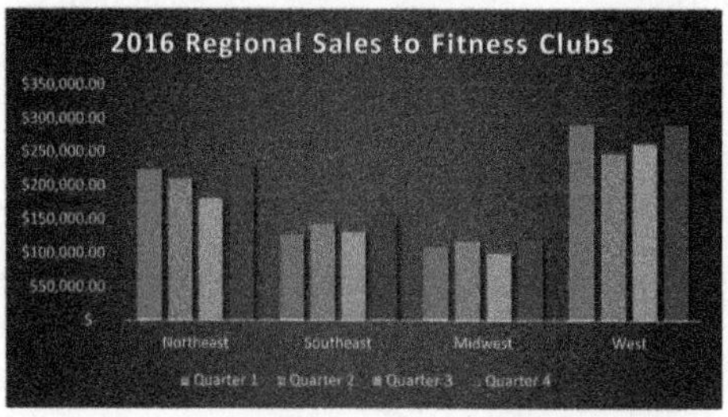

Lastname_Firstname_1G_Regional_Sales

FIGURE 1.60

(Project 1G Regional Sales continues on the next page)

CONTENT-BASED ASSESSMENTS

Mastering Excel Project 1G Regional Sales (continued)

1 Start Excel and display a new blank workbook. Change the **Theme** to **Retrospect**. In cell **A1**, type **Pro Fit Marietta** In cell **A2**, type **2016 Regional Sales to Fitness Clubs** and then **Save** the workbook in your **Excel Chapter 1** folder as **Lastname_Firstname_1G_Regional_Sales**

2 In cell **B3**, type **Quarter 1** and fill *Quarter 2*, *Quarter 3*, and *Quarter 4* in the range **C3:E3**. In cell **F3**, type **Total** In cell **G3**, type **% of Total Sales** and in cell **H3**, type **Trend**

3 In the range **A4:A7**, type the following row titles: **Northeast** and **Southeast** and **West** and **Total Sales**

4 Set the width of **column A** to **80 pixels** and the width of columns **B:H** to **110 pixels**. **Merge & Center** the title across the range **A1:H1**, and then apply the **Title** cell style. **Merge & Center** the subtitle across the range **A2:H2**, and then apply the **Heading 1** cell style. Select the seven column titles, apply **Center** formatting, and then apply the **Heading 4** cell style.

5 In the range **B4:E6**, enter the sales values for each Quarter as shown below.

	Quarter 1	Quarter 2	Quarter 3	Quarter 4
Northeast	225684.50	210760.45	181555.32	228634.85
Southeast	128698.12	144465.29	132106.81	155874.75
West	292416.67	247941.48	262774.12	291698.99

6 By using the **Quick Analysis tool**, **Sum** the *Quarter 1* sales, and then copy the formula across for the remaining Quarters. By using the **Quick Analysis tool**, **Sum** the sales for the *Northeast* region, and then copy the formula down through cell **F7**. Recall that the **Quick Analysis tool** formats sums in **Bold**. Apply the **Accounting Number Format** to the first row of sales figures and to the total row, and apply the **Comma Style** to the remaining sales figures. Format the totals in **row 7** with the **Total** cell style.

7 **Insert** a new **row 6** with the row title **Midwest** and the following sales figures for each quarter: **110985.45** and **118674.91** and **100548.50** and **120621.17** Copy the formula in cell **F5** down to cell **F6** to sum the new row.

8 Using absolute cell references as necessary so that you can copy the formula, in cell **G4** construct a formula to calculate the *Percent of Total Sales* for the first region. Copy the formula down for the remaining regions. To the computed percentages, apply **Percent Style** with two decimal places, and then **Center** the percentages.

9 Insert **Line** sparklines in the range **H4:H7** that compare the quarterly data. Do not include the totals. Show the sparkline **Markers** and apply the second style in the second row—**Sparkline Style Accent 2, Darker 25%**.

10 **Save** your workbook. To compare the quarterly sales of each region visually, select the range that represents the sales figures for the four quarters, including the quarter names and each region—do not include any totals in the range. With this data selected, by using **Recommended Charts**, insert a **Clustered Column** with the regions as the category axis and the Quarters as the legend.

11 Apply **Chart Style 8** and **Color 3** under **Colorful**. Position the top edge of the chart in **row 10** and visually center it below the worksheet data. Change the **Chart Title** to **2016 Regional Sales to Fitness Clubs**

12 Deselect the chart. Change the page **Orientation** to **Landscape**, center the worksheet **Horizontally** on the page, and then insert a footer with the file name in the Left section.

13 Show the document properties. As the **Tags**, type **fitness clubs, sales** In the **Subject** box, type your course name and section number. Be sure your name displays as the author.

14 **Save** your workbook, and then print or submit electronically as directed. If required by your instructor, print or create an electronic version of your worksheet with formulas displayed by using the instructions in Project 1A. **Close** Excel without saving so that you do not save the changes you made to print formulas.

END | You have completed Project 1G

CONTENT-BASED ASSESSMENTS

Apply a combination of the 1A and 1B skills.

GO! Fix It | Project 1H Team Sales | Online

Build from Scratch

GO! Make It | Project 1I Agility Sales | Online

GO! Solve It | Project 1J Kettlebell Sales | Online

GO! Solve It | Project 1K Commission

PROJECT FILES

For Project 1K, you will need the following file:

e01K_Commission

You will save your workbook as:

Lastname_Firstname_1K_Commission

Open the file **e01K_Commission** and save it as **Lastname_Firstname_1K_Commission** Complete the worksheet by using Auto Fill to complete the month headings, and then calculating the Total Commission for each month and for each region. Insert and format appropriate sparklines in the Trend column. Format the worksheet attractively with a title and subtitle, check spelling, adjust column width, and apply appropriate financial formatting. Insert a chart that compares the total sales commission for each region with the months displaying as the categories, and format the chart attractively. Include the file name in the footer, add appropriate properties, and submit as directed.

Performance Level

Performance Criteria	Exemplary: You consistently applied the relevant skills	Proficient: You sometimes, but not always, applied the relevant skills	Developing: You rarely or never applied the relevant skills
Create formulas	All formulas are correct and are efficiently constructed.	Formulas are correct but not always constructed in the most efficient manner.	One or more formulas are missing or incorrect, or only numbers were entered.
Create a chart	Chart created properly.	Chart was created but incorrect data was selected.	No chart was created.
Insert and format sparklines	Sparklines inserted and formatted properly.	Sparklines were inserted but incorrect data was selected or sparklines were not formatted.	No sparklines were inserted.
Format attractively and appropriately	Formatting is attractive and appropriate.	Adequately formatted but difficult to read or unattractive.	Inadequate or no formatting.

END | You have completed Project 1K

OUTCOMES-BASED ASSESSMENTS

RUBRIC

The following outcomes-based assessments are *open-ended assessments*. That is, there is no specific correct result; your result will depend on your approach to the information provided. Make *Professional Quality* your goal. Use the following scoring rubric to guide you in *how* to approach the problem and then to evaluate *how well* your approach solves the problem.

The *criteria*—Software Mastery, Content, Format and Layout, and Process—represent the knowledge and skills you have gained that you can apply to solving the problem. The *levels of performance*—Professional Quality, Approaching Professional Quality, or Needs Quality Improvements—help you and your instructor evaluate your result.

	Your completed project is of Professional Quality if you:	Your completed project is Approaching Professional Quality if you:	Your completed project Needs Quality Improvements if you:
1-Software Mastery	Choose and apply the most appropriate skills, tools, and features and identify efficient methods to solve the problem.	Choose and apply some appropriate skills, tools, and features, but not in the most efficient manner.	Choose inappropriate skills, tools, or features, or are inefficient in solving the problem.
2-Content	Construct a solution that is clear and well organized, contains content that is accurate, appropriate to the audience and purpose, and is complete. Provide a solution that contains no errors in spelling, grammar, or style.	Construct a solution in which some components are unclear, poorly organized, inconsistent, or incomplete. Misjudge the needs of the audience. Have some errors in spelling, grammar, or style, but the errors do not detract from comprehension.	Construct a solution that is unclear, incomplete, or poorly organized; contains some inaccurate or inappropriate content; and contains many errors in spelling, grammar, or style. Do not solve the problem.
3-Format & Layout	Format and arrange all elements to communicate information and ideas, clarify function, illustrate relationships, and indicate relative importance.	Apply appropriate format and layout features to some elements, but not others. Overuse features, causing minor distraction.	Apply format and layout that does not communicate information or ideas clearly. Do not use format and layout features to clarify function, illustrate relationships, or indicate relative importance. Use available features excessively, causing distraction.
4-Process	Use an organized approach that integrates planning, development, self-assessment, revision, and reflection.	Demonstrate an organized approach in some areas, but not others; or, use an insufficient process of organization throughout.	Do not use an organized approach to solve the problem.

OUTCOMES-BASED ASSESSMENTS

Apply a combination of the 1A and 1B skills.

GO! Think Project 1L Video Sales

PROJECT FILES

Build from Scratch

For Project 1L, you will need the following file:

New blank Excel workbook

You will save your workbook as:

Lastname_Firstname_1L_Video_Sales

Michelle Barry, President of Pro Fit Marietta, needs a worksheet that summarizes the following data regarding the first quarter sales of training videos. Michelle would like the worksheet to include a calculation of the total sales for each type of video and a total of the sales of all of the videos. She would also like to know each type of video's percentage of total sales.

	Number Sold	Price
Pilates	**156**	**29.99**
Step	**392**	**14.99**
Weight Training	**147**	**54.99**
Kickboxing	**282**	**29.99**
Yoga	**165**	**34.99**

Create a worksheet that provides Michelle with the information needed. Include appropriate worksheet, column, and row titles. Using the formatting skills that you practiced in this chapter, format the worksheet in a manner that is professional and easy to read and understand. Insert a footer with the file name and add appropriate document properties. Save the file as **Lastname_Firstname_1L_Video_Sales** and print or submit as directed by your instructor.

END | You have completed Project 1L

Build from Scratch

GO! Think Project 1M Planner **Online**

Build from Scratch

You and GO! Project 1N Personal Expenses **Online**

GO! Cumulative Group Project Project 1O Bell Orchid Hotels **Online**

Using Functions, Creating Tables, and Managing Large Workbooks

GO! to Work Video E2

2

EXCEL 2013

PROJECT 2A

OUTCOMES
Analyze inventory by applying statistical and logical calculations to data and by sorting and filtering data.

OBJECTIVES

1. Use Flash Fill and the SUM, AVERAGE, MEDIAN, MIN, and MAX Functions
2. Move Data, Resolve Error Messages, and Rotate Text
3. Use COUNTIF and IF Functions and Apply Conditional Formatting
4. Use Date & Time Functions and Freeze Panes
5. Create, Sort, and Filter an Excel Table
6. View, Format, and Print a Large Worksheet

PROJECT 2B

OUTCOMES
Summarize the data on multiple worksheets.

OBJECTIVES

7. Navigate a Workbook and Rename Worksheets
8. Enter Dates, Clear Contents, and Clear Formats
9. Copy and Paste by Using the Paste Options Gallery
10. Edit and Format Multiple Worksheets at the Same Time
11. Create a Summary Sheet with Column Sparklines
12. Format and Print Multiple Worksheets in a Workbook

In This Chapter

In this chapter, you will use the Statistical functions to calculate the average of a group of numbers and use other Logical and Date & Time functions. Excel's statistical functions are useful for common calculations that you probably encounter frequently. You will also use Excel's new Flash Fill to automatically fill in values, use the counting functions, and apply different types of conditional formatting to make data easy to visualize. You will create a table to organize related information and analyze the table's information by sorting and filtering. You will summarize a workbook that contains multiple worksheets.

The projects in this chapter relate to **Rosedale Landscape and Garden**, which grows and sells trees and plants suitable for all areas of North America. Throughout its 75 year history, the company has introduced many new plants for the enjoyment of home gardeners. The company has nurseries and stores in the major metropolitan areas in the United States and Canada. In addition to high-quality plants and trees, Rosedale sells garden tools and outdoor furniture. Rosedale also offers professional landscape design and installation for both commercial and residential clients. The company headquarters is in Pasadena, California.

PROJECT 2A Inventory Status Report

MyITLab® Project 2A Training

PROJECT ACTIVITIES

In Activities 2.01 through 2.20 you will edit a worksheet for Holman Hill, President, detailing the current inventory of trees at the Pasadena nursery. Your completed worksheet will look similar to Figure 2.1.

PROJECT FILES

For Project 2A, you will need the following file:
e02A_Tree_Inventory

You will save your workbook as:
Lastname_Firstname_2A_Tree_Inventory

PROJECT RESULTS

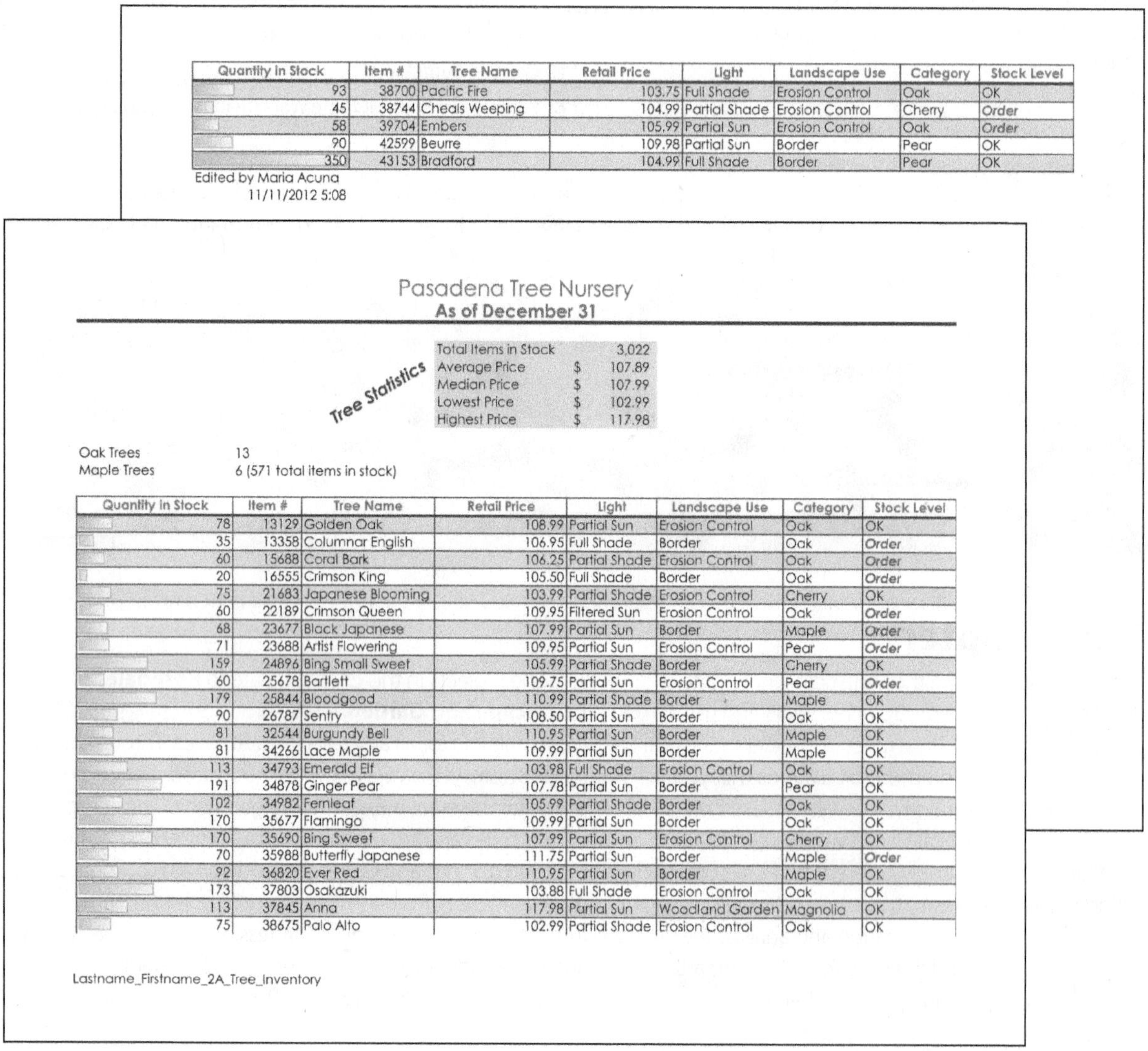

Quantity in Stock	Item #	Tree Name	Retail Price	Light	Landscape Use	Category	Stock Level
93	38700	Pacific Fire	103.75	Full Shade	Erosion Control	Oak	OK
45	38744	Cheals Weeping	104.99	Partial Shade	Erosion Control	Cherry	Order
58	39704	Embers	105.99	Partial Sun	Erosion Control	Oak	Order
90	42599	Beurre	109.98	Partial Sun	Border	Pear	OK
350	43153	Bradford	104.99	Full Shade	Border	Pear	OK

Edited by Maria Acuna
11/11/2012 5:08

Pasadena Tree Nursery
As of December 31

Tree Statistics

Total Items in Stock		3,022
Average Price	$	107.89
Median Price	$	107.99
Lowest Price	$	102.99
Highest Price	$	117.98

Oak Trees 13
Maple Trees 6 (571 total items in stock)

Quantity in Stock	Item #	Tree Name	Retail Price	Light	Landscape Use	Category	Stock Level
78	13129	Golden Oak	108.99	Partial Sun	Erosion Control	Oak	OK
35	13358	Columnar English	106.95	Full Shade	Border	Oak	Order
60	15688	Coral Bark	106.25	Partial Shade	Erosion Control	Oak	Order
20	16555	Crimson King	105.50	Full Shade	Border	Oak	Order
75	21683	Japanese Blooming	103.99	Partial Shade	Erosion Control	Cherry	OK
60	22189	Crimson Queen	109.95	Filtered Sun	Erosion Control	Oak	Order
68	23677	Black Japanese	107.99	Partial Sun	Border	Maple	Order
71	23688	Artist Flowering	109.95	Partial Sun	Erosion Control	Pear	Order
159	24896	Bing Small Sweet	105.99	Partial Shade	Border	Cherry	OK
60	25678	Bartlett	109.75	Partial Sun	Erosion Control	Pear	Order
179	25844	Bloodgood	110.99	Partial Shade	Border	Maple	OK
90	26787	Sentry	108.50	Partial Sun	Border	Oak	OK
81	32544	Burgundy Bell	110.95	Partial Sun	Border	Maple	OK
81	34266	Lace Maple	109.99	Partial Sun	Border	Maple	OK
113	34793	Emerald Elf	103.98	Full Shade	Erosion Control	Oak	OK
191	34878	Ginger Pear	107.78	Partial Sun	Border	Pear	OK
102	34982	Fernleaf	105.99	Partial Shade	Border	Oak	OK
170	35677	Flamingo	109.99	Partial Sun	Border	Oak	OK
170	35690	Bing Sweet	107.99	Partial Sun	Erosion Control	Cherry	OK
70	35988	Butterfly Japanese	111.75	Partial Sun	Border	Maple	Order
92	36820	Ever Red	110.95	Partial Sun	Border	Maple	OK
173	37803	Osakazuki	103.88	Full Shade	Erosion Control	Oak	OK
113	37845	Anna	117.98	Partial Sun	Woodland Garden	Magnolia	OK
75	38675	Palo Alto	102.99	Partial Shade	Erosion Control	Oak	OK

Lastname_Firstname_2A_Tree_Inventory

FIGURE 2.1 Project 2A Inventory Status Report

Objective 1 Use Flash Fill and the SUM, AVERAGE, MEDIAN, MIN, and MAX Functions

Video E2-1

Flash Fill recognizes a pattern in your data, and then automatically fills in values when you enter examples of the output that you want. Use Flash Fill to split data from two or more cells or to combine data from two cells.

A ***function*** is the name given to a predefined formula—a formula that Excel has already built for you—that performs calculations by using specific values that you insert in a particular order or structure. ***Statistical functions***, which include the AVERAGE, MEDIAN, MIN, and MAX functions, are useful to analyze a group of measurements.

Activity 2.01 | Using Flash Fill

1. Start Excel, and then in the lower left corner of Excel's opening screen, click **Open Other Workbooks**.

ANOTHER WAY Press Ctrl + F12 to display the Open dialog box.

2. Navigate to the student files that accompany this textbook, and then locate and open **e02A_Tree_Inventory**. Press F12 to display the **Save As** dialog box, and then navigate to the location where you are storing your projects for this chapter.

3. Create a new folder named **Excel Chapter 2** and open the new folder. In the **File name** box, using your own name, type **Lastname_Firstname_2A_Tree_Inventory** and click **Save** or press Enter.

4. Scroll down. Notice that the worksheet contains data related to types of trees in inventory, including information about the *Quantity in Stock, Item #/Category, Tree Name, Retail Price, Light*, and *Landscape Use*.

5. In the **column heading area**, point to **column C** to display the ↓ pointer, and then drag to the right to select **columns C:D**. On the **HOME tab**, in the **Cells group**, click the **Insert button arrow**, and then click **Insert Sheet Columns**.

   New columns for C and D display and the remaining columns move to the right.

ANOTHER WAY Select the columns, right-click anywhere over the selected columns, and then on the shortcut menu, click Insert.

6. Click cell **C11**, type **13129** and then on the **Formula Bar**, click ✓ to confirm the entry and keep **C11** as the active cell.

7. On the **HOME tab**, in the **Editing group**, click **Fill**, and then click **Flash Fill**. Compare your screen with Figure 2.2.

   Use this technique to split a column of data based on what you type. Flash Fill looks to the left and sees the pattern you have established, and then fills the remaining cells in the column with only the Item #. The Flash Fill Options button displays.

FIGURE 2.2

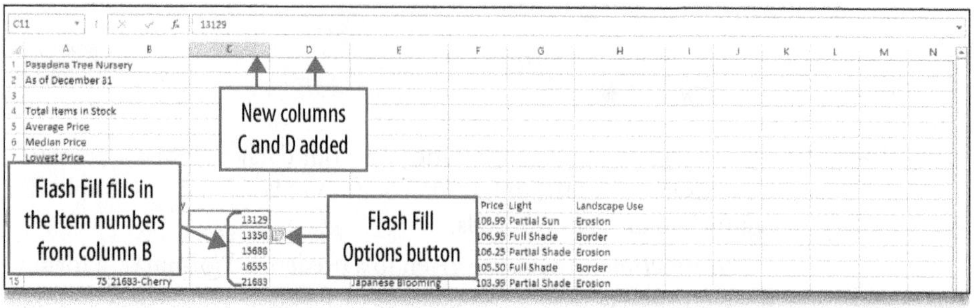

8 Near the lower right corner of cell **C11**, click the **Flash Fill Options** button, and notice that here you can *Undo Flash Fill, Accept suggestions*, or *Select all 28 changed cells*, for example, to apply specific formatting. Click the button again to close it.

If Excel is not sure what pattern to use, it suggests a pattern by filling with pale gray characters, and then you can use the Accept suggestions command to accept or start again.

9 Click cell **D11**, type **Oak** On the **Formula Bar**, click [✓] to confirm the entry and keep **D11** as the active cell, and then press Ctrl + E, which is the keyboard shortcut for Flash Fill.

Flash Fill extracts the text from the *Item#/Category* column and also inserts *Category* as the column name. Now that *Item #* and *Category* are in two separate columns, Mr. Hill can sort and filter by both Item # and Category.

10 Select **column B**, and then in the **Cells group**, click the **Delete button arrow**. Click **Delete Sheet Columns**. On the Quick Access Toolbar, click **Save** [Save].

ANOTHER WAY Select the column, right-click anywhere over the selected column, and then on the shortcut menu, click Delete.

Activity 2.02 | Moving a Column

1 In cell **B10** type **Item #** and press Enter. Select **column C**, and then on the **HOME tab**, in the **Clipboard group**, click **Cut** [Cut]. Notice that the column is surrounded by a moving border. Click cell **H1**, and then in the **Clipboard group**, click the upper portion of the **Paste** button.

ANOTHER WAY Press Ctrl + X to cut and Ctrl + V to paste.

2 Select and then delete **column C**. Select **columns A:G**. In the **Cells group**, click **Format**, and then click **AutoFit Column Width**.

ANOTHER WAY Select the columns, in the column heading area point to any of the column borders to display the [+] pointer, and then double-click to AutoFit the columns.

3 Press Ctrl + Home to deselect and make cell **A1** the active cell.

4 **Merge & Center** cell **A1** across the range **A1:H1**, and then apply the **Title** cell style. **Merge & Center** cell **A2** across the range **A2:H2**, and apply the **Heading 1** cell style. Compare your screen with Figure 2.3. **Save** [Save] your workbook.

FIGURE 2.3

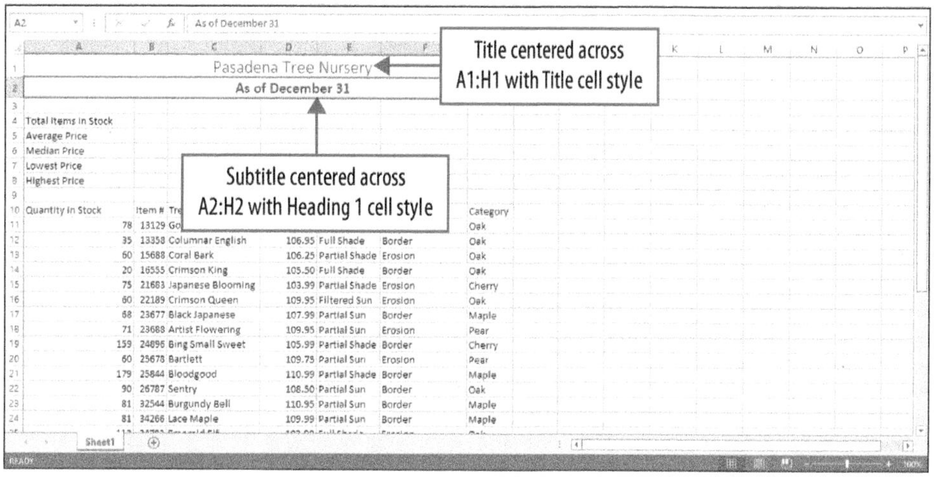

Activity 2.03 | Using the SUM and AVERAGE Functions

Mr. Hill has a worksheet with information about the inventory of trees currently in stock at the Pasadena nursery. In this activity, you will use the SUM and AVERAGE functions to gather information about the product inventory.

1. Click cell **B4**. Click the **FORMULAS tab**, and then in the **Function Library group**, click the upper portion of the **AutoSum** button. Compare your screen with Figure 2.4.

   The ***SUM function*** that you have used is a predefined formula that adds all the numbers in a selected range of cells. Because it is frequently used, there are several ways to insert the function. For example, you can insert the function from the HOME tab's Editing group, or by using the keyboard shortcut Alt + =, or from the Function Library group on the Formulas tab, or from the Math & Trig button in that group.

FIGURE 2.4

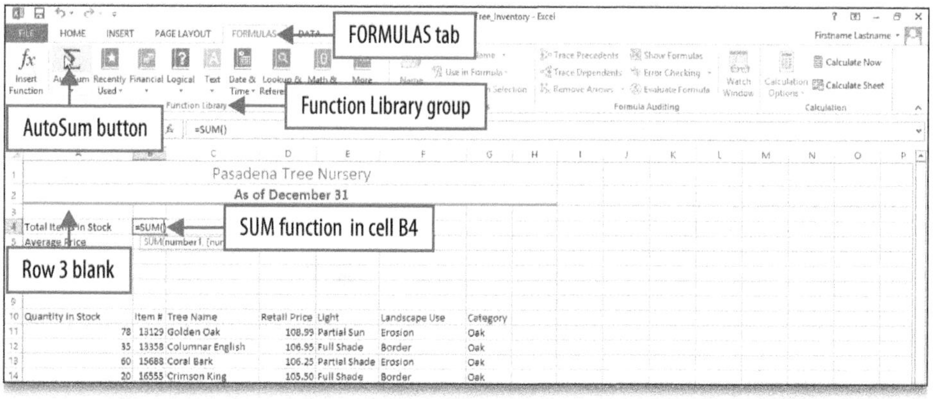

2. With the insertion point blinking in the function, type the cell range **a11:a39** to sum all the values in the **Quantity in Stock** column, and then press Enter; your result is *3022*.

3. Click cell **B4**, look at the **Formula Bar**, and then compare your screen with Figure 2.5.

   SUM is the name of the function. The values in parentheses are the ***arguments***—the values that an Excel function uses to perform calculations or operations. In this instance, the argument consists of the values in the range A11:A39.

FIGURE 2.5

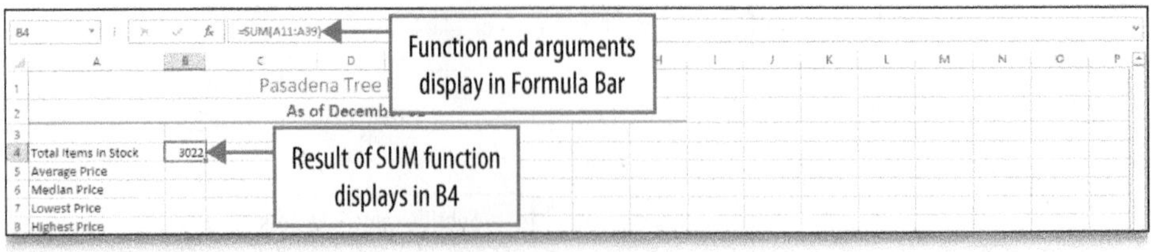

4 Click cell **B5**. In the **Function Library group**, click **More Functions**, point to **Statistical**, point to **AVERAGE**, and notice the ScreenTip. Compare your screen with Figure 2.6.

The ScreenTip describes how the AVERAGE function will compute the calculation.

FIGURE 2.6

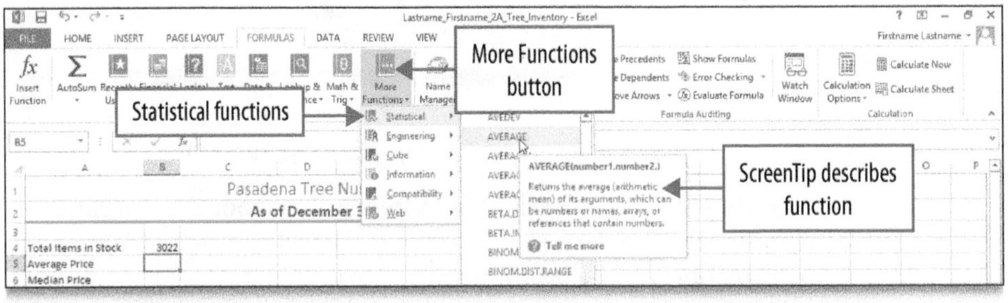

5 Click **AVERAGE**, and then if necessary, drag the title bar of the **Function Arguments** dialog box down and to the right so you can view the **Formula Bar** and cell **B5**.

The ***AVERAGE function*** adds a group of values, and then divides the result by the number of values in the group. In the cell, the Formula Bar, and the dialog box, Excel proposes to average the value in cell B4. Recall that Excel functions will propose a range if there is data above or to the left of a selected cell.

6 In the **Function Arguments** dialog box, notice that *B4* is highlighted. Press Del to delete the existing text, type **d11:d39** and then compare your screen with Figure 2.7.

Because you want to average the values in the range D11:D39—and not cell B4—you must edit the proposed range.

FIGURE 2.7

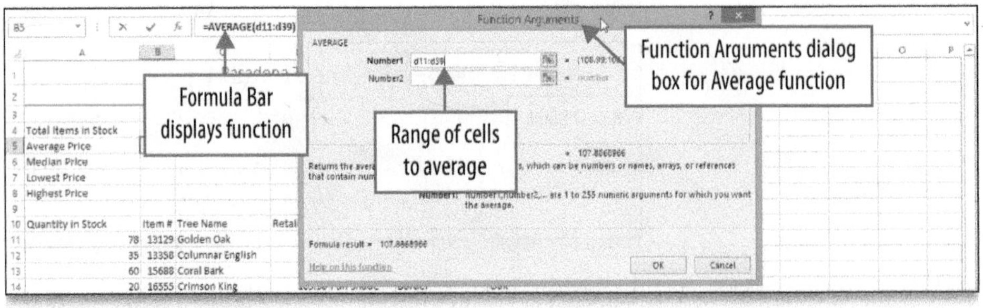

7 In the **Function Arguments** dialog box, click **OK**, and then click **Save**.

The result indicates that the average Retail Price of all products is *107.89*.

Activity 2.04 | Using the MEDIAN Function

The ***MEDIAN function*** is a statistical function that describes a group of data—it is commonly used to describe the price of houses in a particular geographical area. The MEDIAN function finds the middle value that has as many values above it in the group as are below it. It differs from

AVERAGE in that the result is not affected as much by a single value that is greatly different from the others.

1 Click cell **B6**. In the **Function Library group**, click **More Functions**, display the list of **Statistical** functions, scroll down as necessary, and then click **MEDIAN**.

2 Press Del to delete the text in the **Number1** box, and then type **d11:d39** Compare your screen with Figure 2.8.

When indicating which cells you want to use in the function's calculation—known as *defining the arguments*—you can either select the values with your mouse or type the range of values, whichever you prefer.

FIGURE 2.8

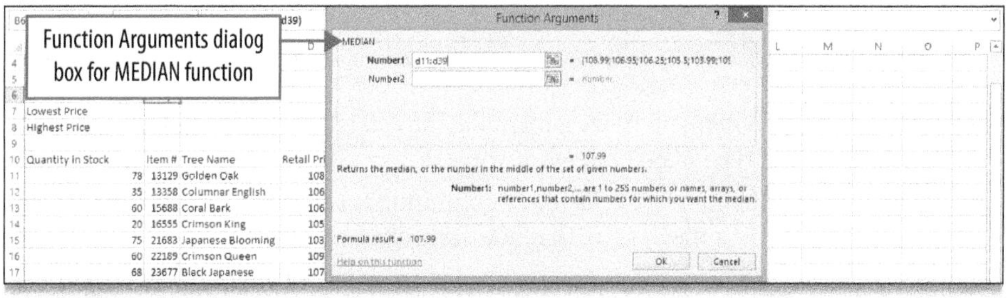

3 Click **OK** to display *107.99* in cell **B6**. Click **Save**, and then compare your screen with Figure 2.9.

In the range of prices, 107.99 is the middle value. Half of all trees in inventory are priced *above* 107.99 and half are priced *below* 107.99.

FIGURE 2.9

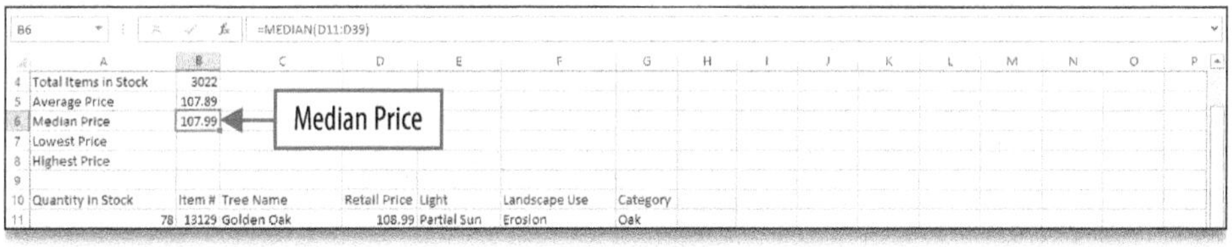

Activity 2.05 Using the MIN and MAX Functions

The statistical ***MIN function*** determines the smallest value in a selected range of values. The statistical ***MAX function*** determines the largest value in a selected range of values.

1 Click cell **B7**. On the **FORMULAS tab**, in the **Function Library group**, click **More Functions**, display the list of **Statistical** functions, scroll as necessary, and then click **MIN**.

2 Press Del, and then in the **Number1** box, type **d11:d39** Click **OK**.

The lowest Retail Price is *102.99*.

3 Click cell **B8**, and then by using a similar technique, insert the **MAX** function to determine the highest **Retail Price**, then check to see that your result is *117.98*.

4 Press Ctrl + Home. Point to cell **B4**, right-click, and then on the mini toolbar, click **Comma Style** one time and **Decrease Decimal** two times.

5 Select the range **B5:B8**, apply the **Accounting Number Format**, click **Save**, and then compare your screen with Figure 2.10.

FIGURE 2.10

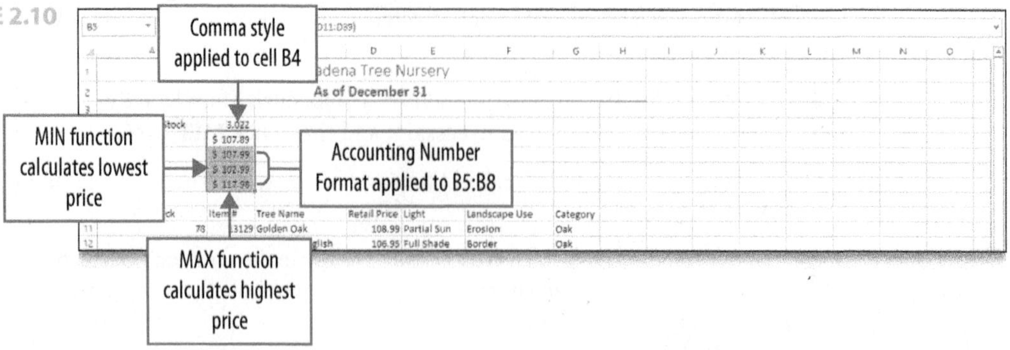

Objective 2 Move Data, Resolve Error Messages, and Rotate Text

Video E2-2

When you move a formula, the cell references within the formula do not change, no matter what type of cell reference you use.

If you move cells into a column that is not wide enough to display number values, Excel will display a message so that you can adjust as necessary.

You can reposition data within a cell at an angle by rotating the text.

Activity 2.06 Moving Data and Resolving a # # # # # Error Message

1 Select **column E** and set the width to **50 pixels**. Select the range **A4:B8**. Point to the right edge of the selected range to display the pointer, and then compare your screen with Figure 2.11.

FIGURE 2.11

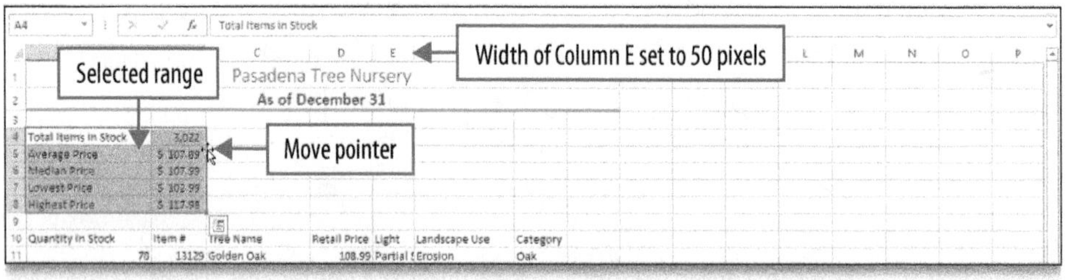

2 Drag the selected range to the right until the ScreenTip displays *D4:E8*, release the mouse button, and then notice that a series of # symbols displays in **column E**. Point to any of the cells that display # symbols, and then compare your screen with Figure 2.12.

Using this technique, cell contents can be moved from one location to another; this is referred to as ***drag and drop***.

If a cell width is too narrow to display the entire number, Excel displays the ##### message, because displaying only a portion of a number would be misleading. The underlying values remain unchanged and are displayed in the Formula Bar for the selected cell. An underlying value also displays in the ScreenTip if you point to a cell containing # symbols.

FIGURE 2.12

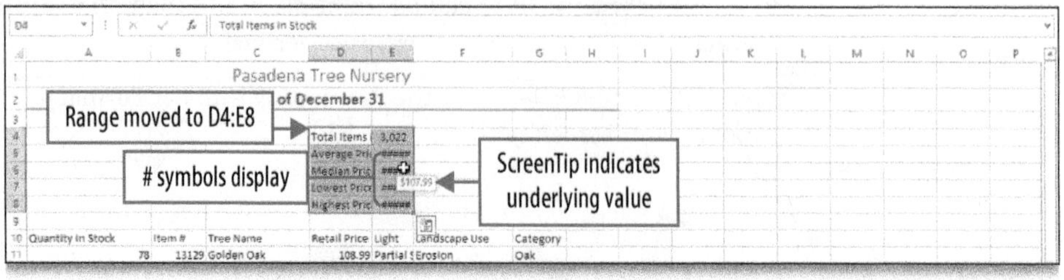

3. Select **column E** and widen it to **60** pixels, and notice that four cells are still not wide enough to display the cell contents.

4. Select **columns D:E**, and then in the **column heading area**, point to the right boundary of **column E** to display the [+] pointer. Double-click to AutoFit the column to accommodate the widest entry.

5. Select the range **D4:E8**. On the **HOME tab**, in the **Styles group**, display the **Cell Styles** gallery. Under **Themed Cell Styles**, click **20%-Accent1**. Click **Save** [icon].

Activity 2.07 | Rotating Text

1. In cell **C6**, type **Tree Statistics** Select the range **C4:C8**, right-click over the selection, and then on the shortcut menu, click **Format Cells.**

2. In the **Format Cells** dialog box, click the **Alignment tab**. Under **Text control**, select the **Merge cells** check box.

3. Under **Orientation**, click in the **Degrees** box, select the existing text, type **30** and then compare your screen with Figure 2.13.

ANOTHER WAY In the upper right portion of the dialog box, under Orientation, point to the red diamond, and then drag the diamond upward until the Degrees box indicates 30.

FIGURE 2.13

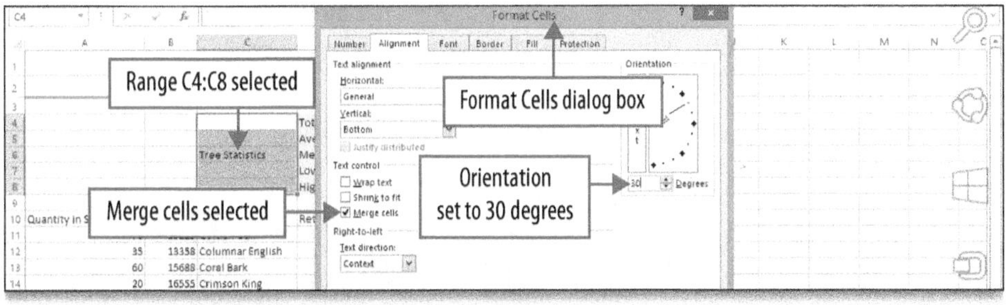

4. In the lower right corner of the **Format Cells** dialog box, click **OK.**

5. With the merged cell still selected, on the **HOME tab**, in the **Font group**, change the **Font Size** [11] to **14**, and then apply **Bold** [B] and **Italic** [I]. Click the **Font Color arrow** [A], and then in the fifth column, click the first color—**Blue, Accent 1.**

6. In the **Alignment group**, apply **Align Right** [icon]. Press Ctrl + Home, **Save** [icon] your workbook, and then compare your screen with Figure 2.14.

FIGURE 2.14

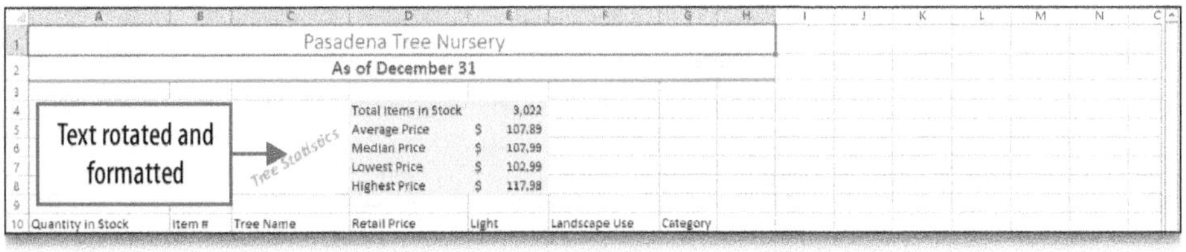

7. In the **row heading area**, point to **row 9** and right-click to select the row and display the shortcut menu. Click **Insert**, and then press F4 two times to repeat the last action and insert three blank rows.

   F4 is useful to repeat commands in Microsoft Office programs. Most commands can be repeated in this manner.

8 From the **row heading area**, select **rows 9:11**. On the **HOME tab**, in the **Editing group**, click **Clear** and then click **Clear Formats** to remove the blue accent color in columns D and E from the new rows. Click **Save**.

When you insert rows or columns, formatting from adjacent rows or columns repeats in the new cells.

Objective 3 Use COUNTIF and IF Functions and Apply Conditional Formatting

Video E2-3

Recall that statistical functions analyze a group of measurements. Another group of Excel functions, referred to as ***logical functions***, test for specific conditions. Logical functions typically use conditional tests to determine whether specified conditions—called ***criteria***—are true or false.

Activity 2.08 Using the COUNT and COUNTIF Functions

The ***Count function*** counts the number of cells in a range that contain numbers. The ***COUNTIF function*** is a statistical function that counts the number of cells within a range that meet the given condition—the criteria that you provide. The COUNTIF function has two arguments—the range of cells to check and the criteria.

The trees of Rosedale Landscape and Garden will be featured on an upcoming segment of a TV gardening show. In this activity, you will use the COUNTIF function to determine the number of *Oak* trees currently available in inventory that can be featured in the TV show.

1 Click cell **E4**, look at the **Formula Bar**, and then notice that the arguments of the **SUM** function adjusted and refer to the appropriate cells in rows 14:42.

The referenced range updates to *A14:A42* after you insert the three new rows. In this manner, Excel adjusts the cell references in a formula relative to their new locations.

2 Click cell **A10**, type **Oak Trees** and then press Tab.

3 With cell **B10** as the active cell, on the **FORMULAS tab**, in the **Function Library group**, click **More Functions**, and then display the list of **Statistical** functions. Click **COUNTIF**.

The COUNTIF function counts the number of cells within a range that meet the given condition.

4 In the **Range** box, type **g14:g42** Click in the **Criteria** box, type **Oak** and then compare your screen with Figure 2.15.

FIGURE 2.15

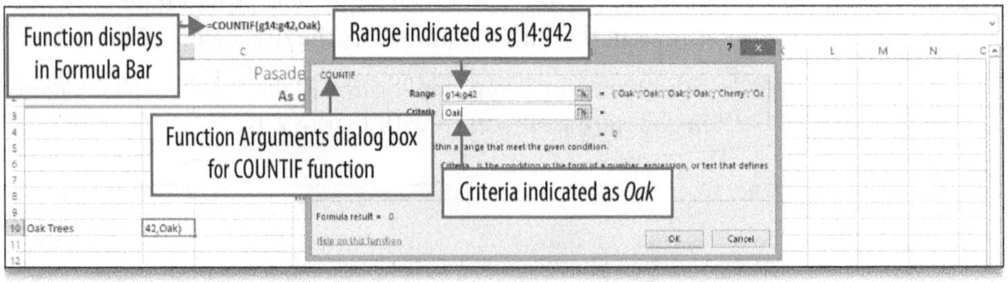

5 In the lower right corner of the **Function Arguments** dialog box, click **OK**.

There are *13* different *Oak* trees available to feature on the TV show.

6 On the **HOME tab**, in the **Alignment group**, click **Align Left** to place the result closer to the row title. **Save** your workbook.

Activity 2.09 | Using the IF Function

A ***logical test*** is any value or expression that you can evaluate as being true or false. The ***IF function*** uses a logical test to check whether a condition is met, and then returns one value if true, and another value if false.

For example, *C14=228* is an expression that can be evaluated as true or false. If the value in cell C14 is equal to 228, the expression is true. If the value in cell C14 is not 228, the expression is false.

In this activity, you will use the IF function to determine the inventory levels and determine if more products should be ordered.

1. Click cell **H13**, type **Stock Level** and then press Enter.

2. In cell **H14**, on the **FORMULAS tab**, in the **Function Library group**, click **Logical**, and then in the list, click **IF**. Drag the title bar of the **Function Arguments** dialog box up or down to view **row 14** on your screen.

3. With the insertion point in the **Logical_test** box, type **a14 < 75**

   This logical test will look at the value in cell A14, which is *78*, and then determine if the number is less than 75. The expression *<75* includes the < ***comparison operator***, which means *less than*. Comparison operators compare values.

4. Examine the table in Figure 2.16 for a list of comparison operator symbols and their definitions.

FIGURE 2.16

COMPARISON OPERATORS	
COMPARISON OPERATORS	**SYMBOL DEFINITION**
=	Equal to
>	Greater than
<	Less than
>=	Greater than or equal to
<=	Less than or equal to
<>	Not equal to

5. Press Tab to move the insertion point to the **Value_if_true** box, and then type **Order**

   If the result of the logical test is true—the Quantity in Stock is less than 75—cell H14 will display the text *Order* indicating that additional trees must be ordered.

6. Press Tab to move to the **Value_if_false** box, type **OK** and then compare your screen with Figure 2.17.

   If the result of the logical test is false—the Quantity in Stock is *not* less than 75—then Excel will display *OK* in the cell.

FIGURE 2.17

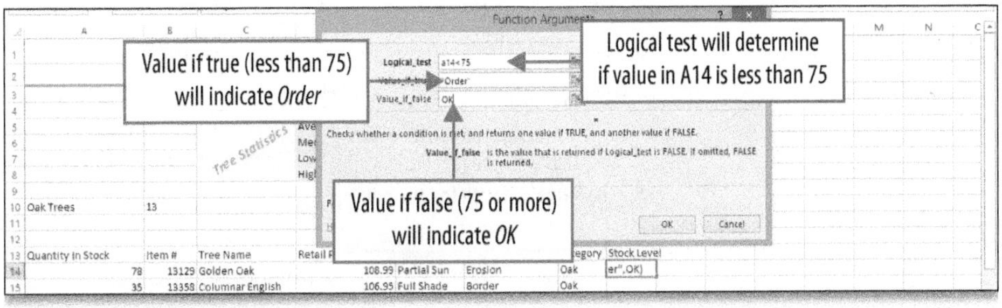

7 Click **OK** to display the result *OK* in cell **H14**.

8 Using the fill handle, copy the function in cell **H14** down through cell **H42**. Then scroll as necessary to view cell **A18**, which contains the value *75*. Look at cell **H18** and notice that the **Stock Level** is indicated as *OK*. **Save** your workbook. Compare your screen with Figure 2.18.

The comparison operator indicated <75 (less than 75) and therefore a value of *exactly* 75 is indicated as OK.

FIGURE 2.18

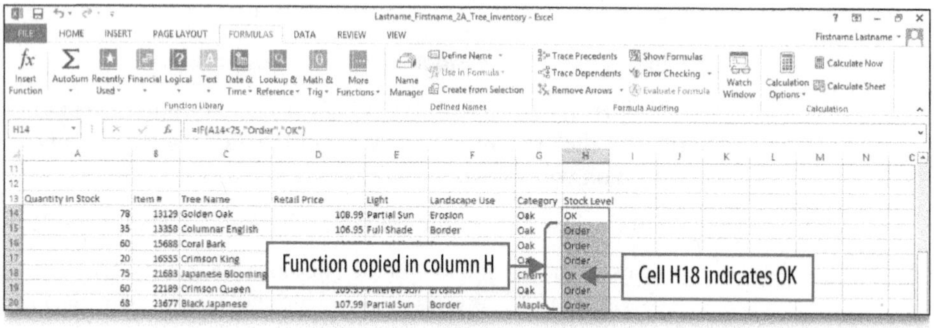

Activity 2.10 | Applying Conditional Formatting by Using Highlight Cells Rules and Data Bars

A ***conditional format*** changes the appearance of a cell based on a condition—a criteria. If the condition is true, the cell is formatted based on that condition; if the condition is false, the cell is *not* formatted. In this activity, you will use conditional formatting as another way to draw attention to the Stock Level of trees.

1 Be sure the range **H14:H42** is selected. On the **HOME tab**, in the **Styles group**, click **Conditional Formatting**. In the list, point to **Highlight Cells Rules**, and then click **Text that Contains.**

2 In the **Text That Contains** dialog box, with the insertion point blinking in the first box, type **Order** and notice that in the selected range, the text *Order* displays with the default format—Light Red Fill with Dark Red Text.

3 In the second box, click the **arrow**, and then in the list, click **Custom Format.**

Here, in the Format Cells dialog box, you can select any combination of formats to apply to the cell if the condition is true. The custom format you specify will be applied to any cell in the selected range if it contains the text *Order*.

4 On the **Font tab**, under **Font style**, click **Bold Italic**. Click the **Color arrow**, and then under **Theme Colors**, in the last column, click the first color—**Green, Accent 6**. Click **OK**. Compare your screen with Figure 2.19.

In the range, if the cell meets the condition of containing *Order*, the font color will change to Bold Italic, Green, Accent 6.

FIGURE 2.19

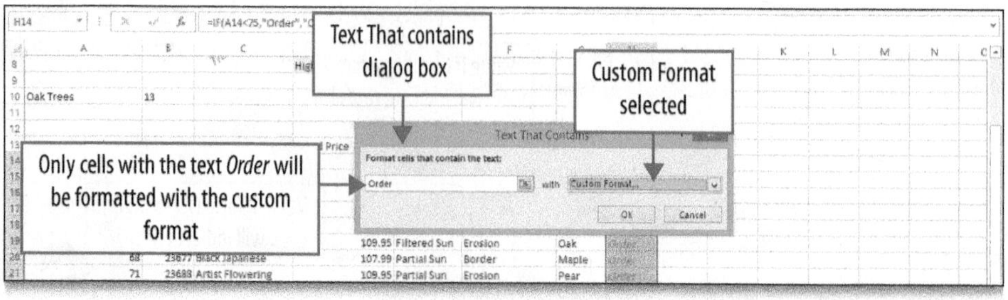

5 In the **Text That Contains** dialog box, click **OK**.

6 Select the range **A14:A42**. In the **Styles group**, click **Conditional Formatting**. Point to **Data Bars**, and then under **Gradient Fill**, click **Orange Data Bar**. Click anywhere to cancel the selection, click **Save**, and then compare your screen with Figure 2.20.

A ***data bar*** provides a visual cue to the reader about the value of a cell relative to other cells. The length of the data bar represents the value in the cell. A longer bar represents a higher value and a shorter bar represents a lower value. Data bars are useful for identifying higher and lower numbers quickly within a large group of data, such as very high or very low levels of inventory.

FIGURE 2.20

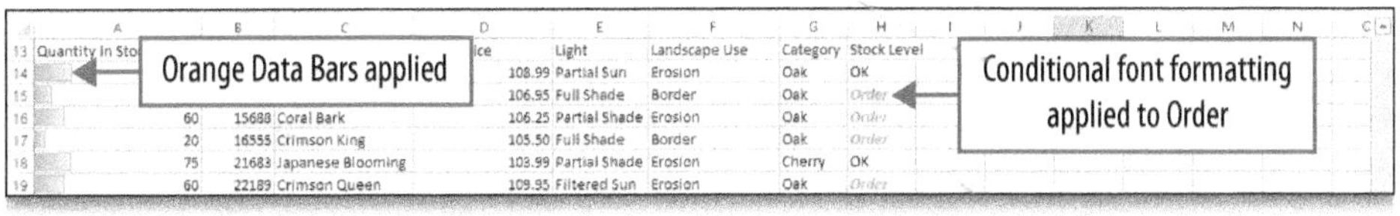

Activity 2.11 Using Find and Replace

The ***Find and Replace*** feature searches the cells in a worksheet—or in a selected range—for matches, and then replaces each match with a replacement value of your choice.

Comments from customers on the company's blog indicate that using the term *Erosion Control* would be clearer than *Erosion* when describing the best landscape use for specific trees. Therefore, all products of this type will be re-labeled accordingly. In this activity, you will replace all occurrences of *Erosion* with *Erosion Control.*

1 Select the range **F14:F42**.

Restrict the find and replace operation to a specific range in this manner, especially if there is a possibility that the name occurs elsewhere.

2 On the **HOME tab**, in the **Editing group**, click **Find & Select**, and then click **Replace**.

3 Type **Erosion** to fill in the **Find what** box. In the **Replace with** box, type **Erosion Control** and then compare your screen with Figure 2.21.

FIGURE 2.21

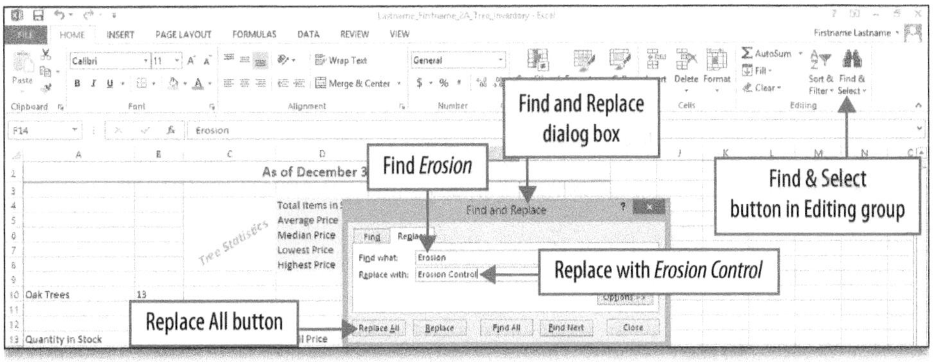

4 Click **Replace All**. In the message box, notice that 13 replacements were made, and then click **OK**. In the lower right corner of the **Find and Replace** dialog box, click **Close**. Click **Save**.

Objective 4 Use Date & Time Functions and Freeze Panes

Video E2-4

Excel can obtain the date and time from your computer's calendar and clock and display this information on your worksheet.

By freezing or splitting panes, you can view two areas of a worksheet and lock rows and columns in one area. When you freeze panes, you select the specific rows or columns that you want to remain visible when scrolling in your worksheet.

Activity 2.12 | Using the NOW Function to Display a System Date

The ***NOW function*** retrieves the date and time from your computer's calendar and clock and inserts the information into the selected cell. The result is formatted as a date and time.

1. To the left of the **Formula Bar**, click in the **Name Box**, type **a44** and then press Enter. Notice that cell **A44** is the active cell. In cell **A44**, type **Edited by Maria Acuna** and then press Enter.

2. With cell **A45** as the active cell, on the **FORMULAS tab**, in the **Function Library group**, click **Date & Time**. In the list of functions, click **NOW**. Compare your screen with Figure 2.22.

FIGURE 2.22

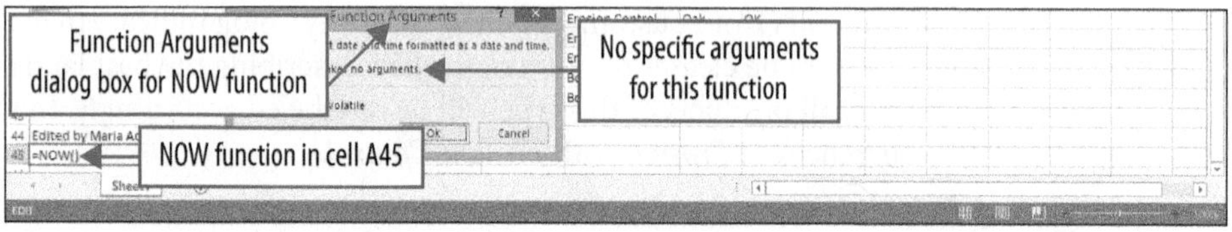

3. Read the description in the **Function Arguments** dialog box, and notice that this result is *Volatile.*

   The Function Arguments dialog box displays a message indicating that this function does not require an argument. It also states that this function is ***volatile***, meaning the date and time will not remain as entered, but rather the date and time will automatically update each time you open this workbook.

4. In the **Function Arguments** dialog box, click **OK** to close the dialog box and display the current date and time in cell **A45**. **Save** your workbook.

More Knowledge | **NOW Function Recalculates Each Time a Workbook Opens**

The NOW function updates each time the workbook is opened. With the workbook open, you can force the NOW function to update by pressing F9, for example, to update the time.

Activity 2.13 | Freezing and Unfreezing Panes

In a large worksheet, if you scroll down more than 25 rows or scroll beyond column O (the exact row number and column letter varies, depending on your screen resolution), you will no longer see the top rows or first column of your worksheet where identifying information about the data is usually placed. You will find it easier to work with your data if you can always view the identifying row or column titles.

The ***Freeze Panes*** command enables you to select one or more rows or columns and then freeze (lock) them into place. The locked rows and columns become separate panes. A ***pane*** is a portion of a worksheet window bounded by and separated from other portions by vertical or horizontal bars.

1 Press Ctrl + Home to make cell **A1** the active cell. Scroll down until **row 21** displays at the top of your Excel window, and notice that all of the identifying information in the column titles is out of view.

2 Press Ctrl + Home again, and then from the **row heading area**, select **row 14**. Click the **VIEW tab**, and then in the **Window group**, click **Freeze Panes**. In the list, click **Freeze Panes**. Click any cell to deselect the row, and then notice that a line displays along the upper border of **row 14**.

By selecting row 14, the rows above—rows 1–13—are frozen in place and will not move as you scroll down.

3 Watch the row numbers below **row 13**, and then begin to scroll down to bring **row 21** into view again. Notice that rows 1:13 are frozen in place. Compare your screen with Figure 2.23.

The remaining rows of data continue to scroll. Use this feature when you have long or wide worksheets.

FIGURE 2.23

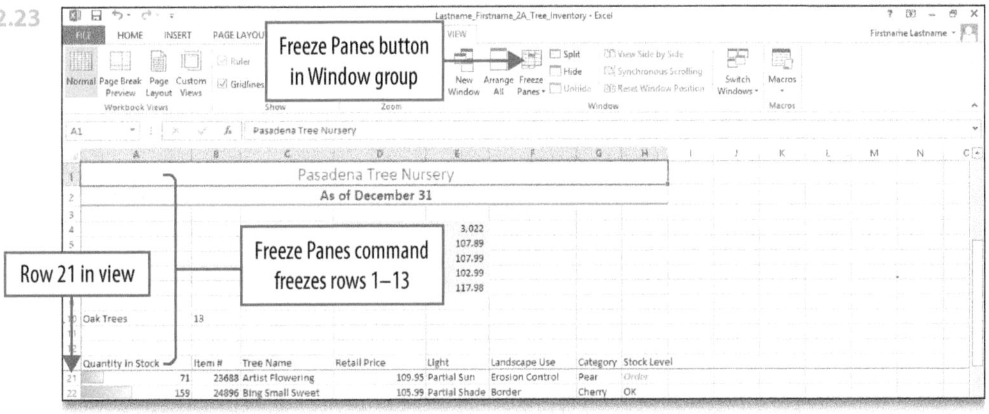

4 In the **Window group**, click **Freeze Panes**, and then click **Unfreeze Panes** to unlock all rows and columns. **Save** your workbook.

More Knowledge **Freeze Columns or Freeze Both Rows and Columns**

You can freeze columns that you want to remain in view on the left. Select the column to the right of the column(s) that you want to remain in view while scrolling to the right, and then click the Freeze Panes command. You can also use the command to freeze both rows and columns; click a *cell* to freeze the rows *above* the cell and the columns to the *left* of the cell.

Objective 5 Create, Sort, and Filter an Excel Table

Video E2-5

To analyze a group of related data, you can convert a range of cells to an ***Excel table***. An Excel table is a series of rows and columns that contains related data that is managed independently from the data in other rows and columns in the worksheet.

Activity 2.14 Creating an Excel Table and Applying a Table Style

1 Be sure that you have applied the Unfreeze Panes command—no rows on your worksheet are locked.

2 Click any cell in the data below row 13. Click the **INSERT tab**. In the **Tables group**, click **Table**. In the **Create Table** dialog box, if necessary, click to select the My table has headers check box, and then compare your screen with Figure 2.24.

The column titles in row 13 will form the table headers. By clicking in a range of contiguous data, Excel will suggest the range as the data for the table. You can adjust the range if necessary.

FIGURE 2.24

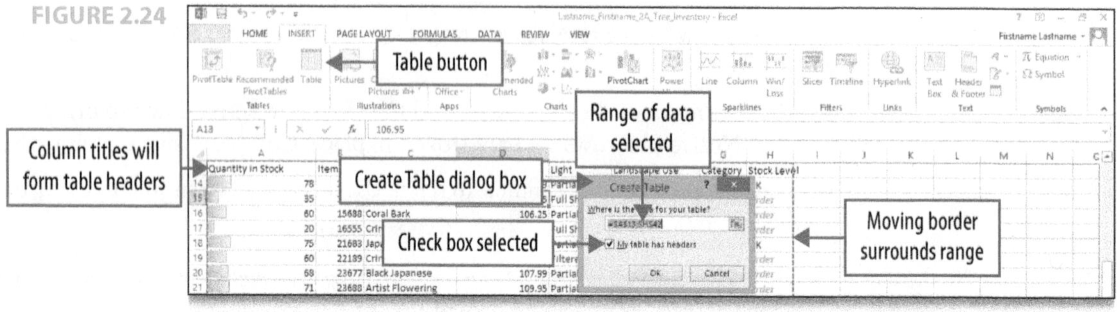

ANOTHER WAY Select the range of cells that make up the table, including the header row, and then click the Table button.

3 Click **OK**. With the range still selected, on the ribbon notice that the **TABLE TOOLS** are active.

4 On the **DESIGN tab**, in the **Table Styles group**, click **More**, and then under **Light**, locate and click **Table Style Light 16**.

5 Press Ctrl + Home. Click **Save**, and then compare your screen with Figure 2.25.

Sorting and filtering arrows display in the table's header row.

FIGURE 2.25

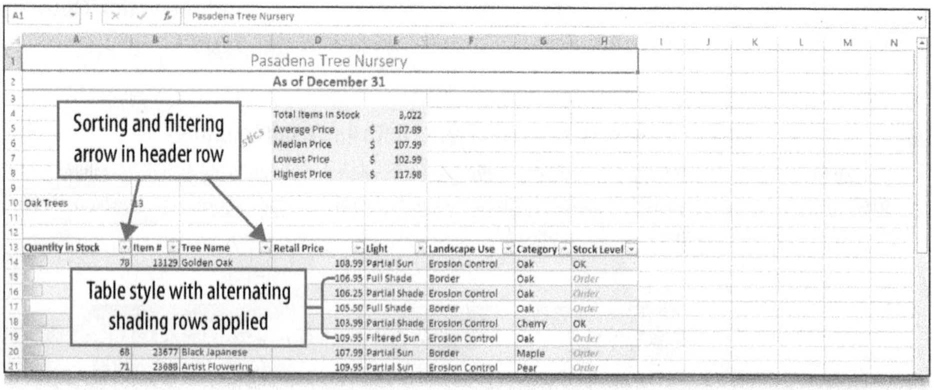

Activity 2.15 | Sorting an Excel Table

You can ***sort*** tables—arrange all the data in a specific order—in ascending or descending order.

1 In the header row of the table, click the **Retail Price arrow**, and then on the menu, click **Sort Smallest to Largest.** Next to the arrow, notice the small **up arrow** indicating an ascending (smallest to largest) sort.

This action sorts the rows in the table from the lowest retail price to highest retail price.

2 In the table's header row, click the **Category arrow**. On the menu, click **Sort A to Z**. Next to the arrow, notice the small **up arrow** indicating an ascending (A to Z) sort.

This action sorts the rows in the table alphabetically by Category, and within a Category, sorts the rows from smallest to largest by Retail Price.

3 Click the **Category arrow** again, and then sort from **Z to A**.

This action sorts the rows in the table in reverse alphabetic order by Category name, and the small arrow points downward, indicating a descending (Z to A) sort. The Retail Price continues to be sorted from smallest to largest within each category.

Activity 2.16 | Filtering an Excel Table and Displaying a Total Row

You can ***filter*** tables—display only a portion of the data based on matching a specific value—to show only the data that meets the criteria that you specify.

1 Click the **Category arrow** again. On the menu, click the **(Select All)** check box to clear all the check boxes. Click to select only the **Maple** check box, and then click **OK**. Compare your screen with Figure 2.26.

Only the rows containing *Maple* in the Category column display—the remaining rows are hidden from view. A small funnel—the filter icon—indicates that a filter is applied to the data in the table. Additionally, the row numbers display in blue to indicate that some rows are hidden from view. A filter hides entire rows in the worksheet.

FIGURE 2.26

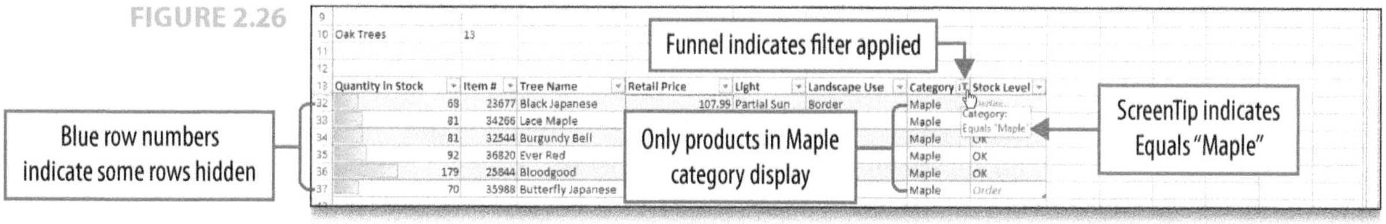

2 Point to the funnel icon to the right of *Category*, and notice that *Equals "Maple"* displays to indicate the filter criteria.

3 Click any cell in the table so that the table is selected. On the ribbon, click the **DESIGN tab**, and then in the **Table Style Options group**, select the **Total Row** check box.

Total displays in cell A43. In cell H43, the number *6* indicates that six rows currently display.

4 Click cell **A43**, click the **arrow** that displays to the right of cell **A43**, and then in the list, click **Sum**.

Excel sums only the visible rows in Column A, and indicates that 571 products in the Maple category are in stock. In this manner, you can use an Excel table to quickly find information about a group of data.

5 Click cell **A11**, type **Maple Trees** and press Tab. In cell **B11**, type **6 (571 total items in stock)** and then press Enter.

6 In the table header row, click the **Category arrow**, and then on the menu, click **Clear Filter From "Category"**.

All the rows in the table redisplay. The Z to A sort on Category remains in effect.

***More* Knowledge** **Band Rows and Columns in a Table**

You can band rows to format even rows differently from odd rows making them easier to read. To band rows or columns, on the DESIGN tab, in the Table Style Options group, select the Banded Rows or Banded Columns check box.

7 Click the **Landscape Use arrow**, click the **(Select All)** check box to clear all the check boxes, and then click to select the **Erosion Control** check box. Click **OK**.

8 Click the **Category arrow**, click the **(Select All)** check box to clear all the check boxes, and then click the **Oak** check box. Click **OK**, **Save** your workbook, and then compare your screen with Figure 2.27.

By applying multiple filters, Mr. Hill can determine quickly that eight tree names identified with a *Landscape Use* of *Erosion Control* are in the *Oak* tree category with a total of 710 such trees in stock.

FIGURE 2.27

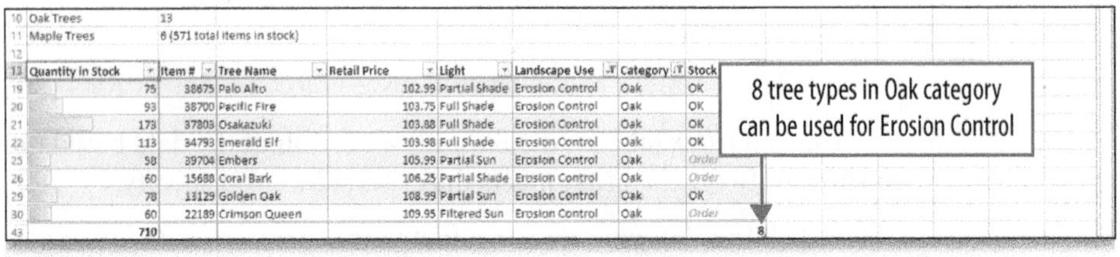

Activity 2.17 | Clearing Filters and Converting a Table to a Range of Data

When you are finished answering questions about the data in a table by sorting, filtering, and totaling, you can convert the table into a normal range. Doing so is useful if you want to use the Table feature only to apply a Table Style to a range. For example, you can insert a table, apply a Table Style, and then convert the table to a normal range of data but keep the formatting.

1 Click the **Category arrow**, and then click **Clear Filter From "Category"**. Use the same technique to remove the filter from the **Landscape Use** column.

2 In the table header row, click the **Item # arrow**, and then click **Sort Smallest to Largest**, which will apply an ascending sort to the data using the *Item #* column.

3 Click anywhere in the table to activate the table and display the **TABLE TOOLS** on the ribbon. Click the **DESIGN tab**, and then in the **Table Style Options group**, click the **Total Row** check box to clear the check mark and remove the Total row from the table.

4 On the **DESIGN tab**, in the **Tools group**, click **Convert to Range**. In the message box, click **Yes**. Click **Save**, and then compare your screen with Figure 2.28.

FIGURE 2.28

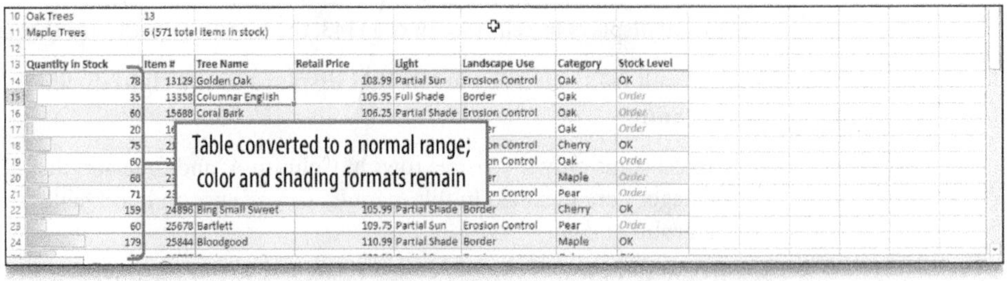

ANOTHER WAY With any table cell selected, right-click, point to Table, and then click Convert to Range.

Objective 6 View, Format, and Print a Large Worksheet

Video E2-6

You can magnify or shrink the view of a worksheet on your screen to either zoom in to view specific data or zoom out to see the entire worksheet. You can also split a worksheet window into panes to view different parts of a worksheet at the same time.

A worksheet might be too wide, too long—or both—to print on a single page. Use Excel's ***Print Titles*** and ***Scale to Fit*** commands to create pages that are attractive and easy to read.

The Print Titles command enables you to specify rows and columns to repeat on each printed page. Scale to Fit commands enable you to stretch or shrink the width, height, or both, of printed output to fit a maximum number of pages.

Activity 2.18 | Modifying and Shrinking the Worksheet View

1. Press Ctrl + Home to display the top of your worksheet. On the **VIEW tab**, in the **Zoom group**, click **Zoom**.

2. In the **Zoom** dialog box, click the **75%** option button, and then click **OK.** Notice that by zooming out in this manner, you can see additional rows of your worksheet on the screen.

3. In the lower right corner of your worksheet, in the status bar, click the **Zoom In** button until the worksheet redisplays at 100%.

Activity 2.19 | Splitting a Worksheet Window into Panes

The ***Split*** command splits the window into multiple resizable panes that contain views of your worksheet. This is useful to view multiple distant parts of your worksheet at one time.

1. Click cell **F9**. On the **VIEW tab**, in the **Window group**, click **Split**.

   Horizontal and vertical split bars display. You can drag the split bars to view any four portions of the worksheet.

2. Notice on the right that separate vertical scroll bars display for the upper and lower panes and at the bottom, separate horizontal scroll bars display for the left and right panes.

3. Drag the lower vertical scroll box down to the bottom of the scroll bar to view **line 44**. Compare your screen with Figure 2.29.

   Here it could be useful to isolate the Tree Statistics at the top and then scroll to the bottom to browse the inventory items or to make a note about who edited the original worksheet.

FIGURE 2.29

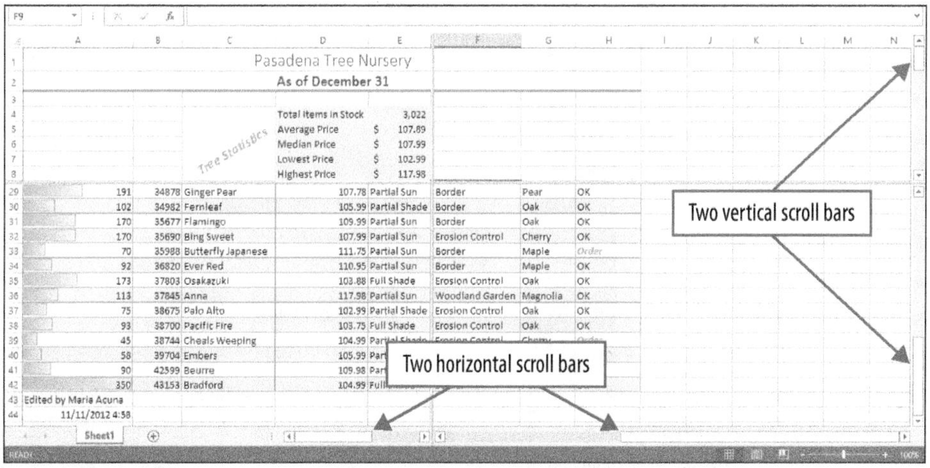

4. On the **VIEW tab**, click **Split** again to remove the split bars.

5. Press Ctrl + Home to display the top of your worksheet. On the **PAGE LAYOUT tab**, in the **Themes group**, click **Themes**, and then click **Slice**.

6. Select the range **A13:H13**. On the **HOME tab**, from the **Styles group**, apply the **Heading 4** cell style, and then apply **Center**. Click cell **A1**.

Activity 2.20 | Printing Titles and Scaling to Fit

1. Click the **PAGE LAYOUT tab**, and then in the **Page Setup group**, click **Margins**. At the bottom of the gallery, click **Custom Margins** to display the **Page Setup** dialog box. Under **Center on page**, select the **Horizontally** check box.

2. Click the **Header/Footer tab**, and then in the center of the dialog box, click **Custom Footer**. In the **Footer** dialog box, with your insertion point blinking in the **Left section**, on the row of buttons, click **Insert File Name**. Click **OK** two times.

3. In the **Page Setup group**, click **Orientation**, and then click **Landscape**.

   The dotted line indicates that as currently formatted, column H will not fit on one page.

4. Press Ctrl + F2 to display the **Print Preview**. At the bottom of the **Print Preview**, click **Next Page**.

   As currently formatted, the worksheet will print on four pages, and the columns will span multiple pages. Additionally, after Page 1, no column titles are visible to identify the data in the columns.

5. Click **Next Page** two times to display **Page 4**, and notice that one column moves to an additional page.

6. In the upper left corner of **Backstage** view, click **Back** to return to the worksheet. In the **Page Setup group**, click **Print Titles**. Under **Print titles**, click in the **Rows to repeat at top** box, and then at the right, click **Collapse Dialog**.

7. From the **row heading area**, select **row 13**, and then in the **Page Setup - Rows to repeat at top** dialog box, click **Expand Dialog**. Click **OK** to print the column titles in row 13 at the top of every page.

   You can collapse and then expand dialog boxes on your screen to enable a better view of your data.

8. Press Ctrl + F2 to display the **Print Preview** again. At the bottom of the **Settings group**, click the **No Scaling arrow**, and then on the displayed list, point to **Fit All Columns on One Page**. Compare your screen with Figure 2.30.

   This action will shrink the width of the printed output to fit all the columns on one page. You can make adjustments like this on the Page Layout tab, or here, in the Print Preview.

FIGURE 2.30

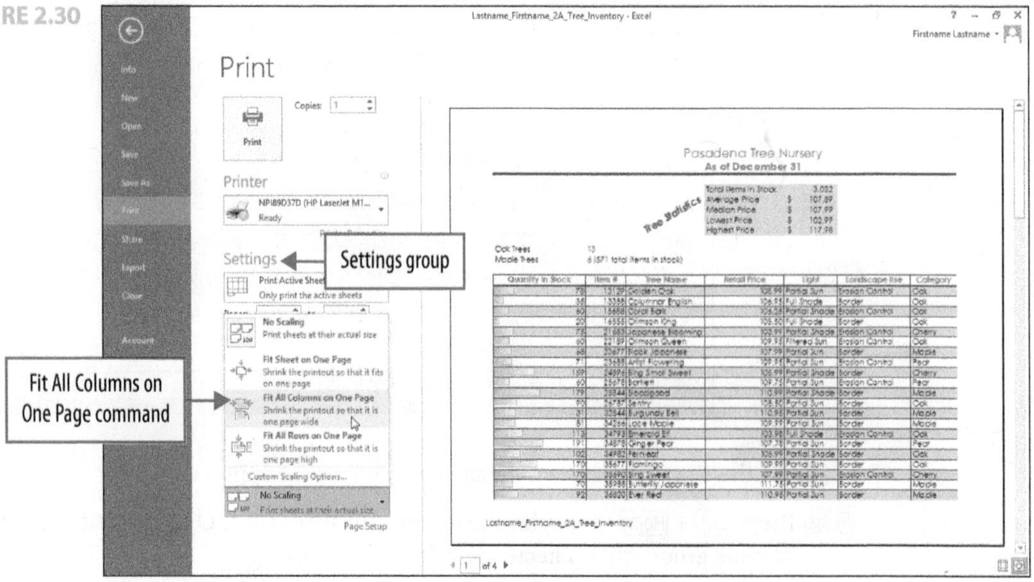

9 Click **Fit All Columns on One Page**. Notice in the **Print Preview** that all the columns display on one page.

ANOTHER WAY With the worksheet displayed, on the Page Layout tab, in the Scale to Fit group, click the Width button arrow, and then click 1 page.

10 At the bottom of the **Print Preview**, click **Next Page** ▶ one time. Notice that the output will now print on two pages and that the column titles display at the top of **Page 2**. Compare your screen with Figure 2.31.

FIGURE 2.31

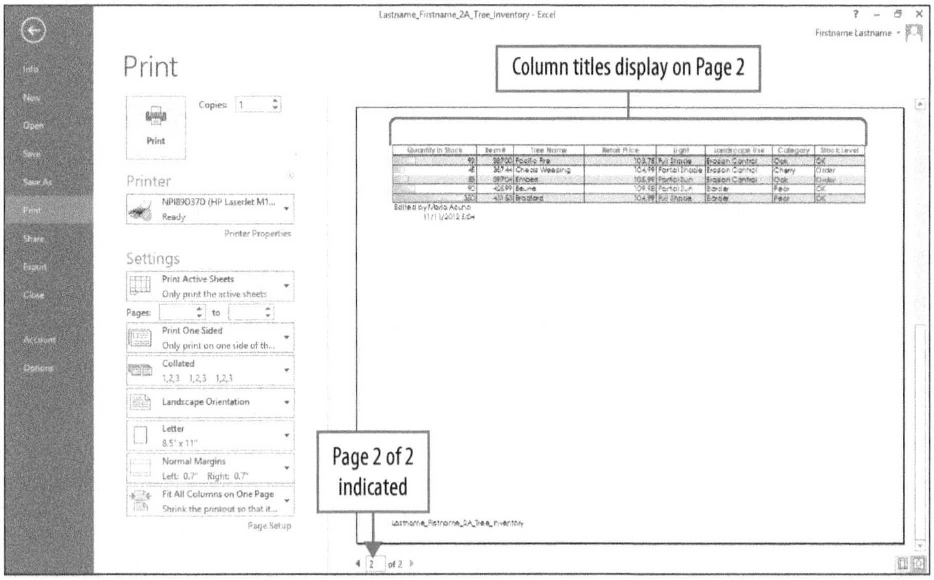

11 On the left, click **Info**, and then click **Show All Properties**. As the **Tags**, type **tree inventory, Pasadena** As the **Subject**, type your course name and section number. Be sure your name displays as the author; edit if necessary.

12 On the left, click **Save**. By using the techniques you practiced in Project 1A, print or submit electronically as directed by your instructor. If required by your instructor, print or create an electronic version of your worksheet with formulas displayed.

13 Close your workbook and close Excel.

More Knowledge **Scaling for Data That Is Slightly Larger Than the Printed Page**

For data just a little too large to fit on a page, you can scale the worksheet to make it fit. Scaling reduces the width and height of the printed data to a percentage of its original size or by the number of pages that you specify. On the Page Layout tab, in the Scale to Fit group, click the Scale arrows to select a percentage.

END | You have completed Project 2A

GO! with Office Online (formerly Web Apps)

Objective | Sort, Filter, and Use Functions in a Table in Excel Online

If you are working on a computer that does not have Microsoft Office installed, you can still create new workbooks with tables in your web browser by using Excel Office Online.

ALERT! **Working with Web-Based Applications and Services**

Computer programs and services on the web receive continuous updates and improvements, so the steps to complete this web-based activity may differ from the ones shown. You can often look at the screens and the information presented to determine how to complete the activity.

Activity | Sort, Filter, and Use Functions in a Table

In this activity, you will use Excel Online to create a table similar to the one you created in Project 2A.

1 Launch your web browser, navigate to **http://onedrive.com**, and then sign in to your Microsoft account. Open your **GO! Web Projects** folder—or create and then open this folder if necessary.

2 Near the top of the screen, click **Create**, and then click **Excel workbook**. Above the ribbon, click Book1 (the number may differ) to select the text. Using your own name, as the file name type **Lastname_Firstname_EX_2A_Web** Click cell **1A**.

3 To help you create this project quickly and to eliminate extra typing, you will import the data from a Word document. From the taskbar, open **File Explorer**, navigate to the student data files that accompany this textbook, and then open the Word document **e02_2A_Web**. Press Ctrl + A to select all of the text, right-click anywhere over the selection, and then click **Copy**. **Close** [x] Word and if necessary **Close** [x] the folder window.

4 With cell **A1** selected, on the Excel Online ribbon, in the **Clipboard group**, click **Paste**; if necessary click Allow access.

5 Select column headings **A:H**, point to the border between any two selected column headings to display the [+] pointer, and then double-click to resize all the columns to display all data.

6 Click cell **A1**, type **Pasadena Nursery: Tree Inventory** Press Enter and then **Merge & Center** the text across the range **A1:H1**. In cell **A2**, type **As of December 31** and **Merge & Center** across the range **A2:H2**. Select the range **A1:A2** and apply **Bold** [B].

7 Click cell **B4**. On the **HOME tab**, in the **Editing group**, click the **AutoSum arrow** and then click **Sum**. Within the formula's parentheses, type **a13:a67** and press Enter for a result of *7085*. In cell **B5**, click the **AutoSum arrow** again, and then click **Average**. With *B4* selected, press Backspace one time, and then within the parentheses type **d13:d67** and press Enter. Your result is *108.09*.

8 With cell **B6** selected, click the **INSERT tab**, and then click **Function**. Click the **Pick a category arrow**, click **Statistical**, and then scroll down and click **MEDIAN**. Click **OK**. Type **d13:d67)** and press Enter for a result of *106.98*.

9 In cell **B7**, click **Function**, from the **Commonly Used** group click **MIN**, click **OK**, type **d13:d67)** and press Enter for a result of *79.99*. In cell **B8**, use the same technique to compute the Highest Price for a result of *131.78*.

10 In cell **B9**, display the list of **Commonly Used** functions, scroll down, click **COUNTIF**, and then click **OK**. Type **g13:g67,"Oak")** and press Enter. Compare your screen with Figure A.

FIGURE A

1	Pasadena Nursery: Tree Inventory	
2	As of December 31	
3		
4	Total Items in Stock	7085
5	Average Price	108.09
6	Median Price	106.98
7	Lowest Price	79.99
8	Highest Price	131.78
9	Oak Trees:	20
10	Magnolia Trees:	
11		

(GO! with Office Online (formerly Web Apps) continues on the next page)

11 Click cell **H13**. From the **Commonly Used** list of functions, insert **IF**, and then type **a13<75,"Order","OK")** and press Enter. Copy this formula down through cell **H67**, which you will have to do in sections due to the way Excel Online scrolls on your screen.

12 Scroll up and click cell **A12**, hold down Shift, drag the vertical scroll box down to view **row 67**, and then click cell **H67** to select the entire range of the table data. On the **INSERT tab**, click **Table**, and then click **OK**. Drag the scroll box back to the top of the vertical scroll bar.

13 Sort the **Retail Price** column in **Ascending** order. Click the **Category arrow**, click **Filter**, and then filter on **Magnolia**.

14 Scroll as necessary to view all the rows in the filtered table, click the **HOME tab**, and then in the **Tables group**, click the **Format as Table arrow**. On the list, click **Toggle Total Row**. Notice that a total row displays and indicates *8* different types of Magnolia trees. In cell **B10** type **8 types** and press Enter.

15 Click any cell in the table. Click the **Format as Table arrow** again, and then click **Toggle Total Row** to turn it off. In the table, click the **Category arrow**, and then clear the filter. Press Ctrl + Home, and then compare your screen with Figure B.

16 If you are instructed to submit your file, use one of the methods outlined in the Note box below. Sign out of your OneDrive and close Internet Explorer.

NOTE **Printing or Creating an Electronic File from Excel Online**

To print on paper, click the FILE tab, click Print, click the Print button, and then click Print. In the Print preview display, click Print. In the displayed Print dialog box, click Print to print on the printer connected to your system. To create an electronic file of your printout, from the Print dialog box, click the printer labeled *Send to OneNote 2013*, and then click Print. You may have to open and then close OneNote first if you have never opened it before. When OneNote opens, click the Quick Notes section of the displayed notebook, and then click OK. On the ribbon, click the FILE tab, click Export, and then create a PDF of the page. Navigate to an appropriate location and give the file an appropriate name. Close OneNote.

FIGURE B

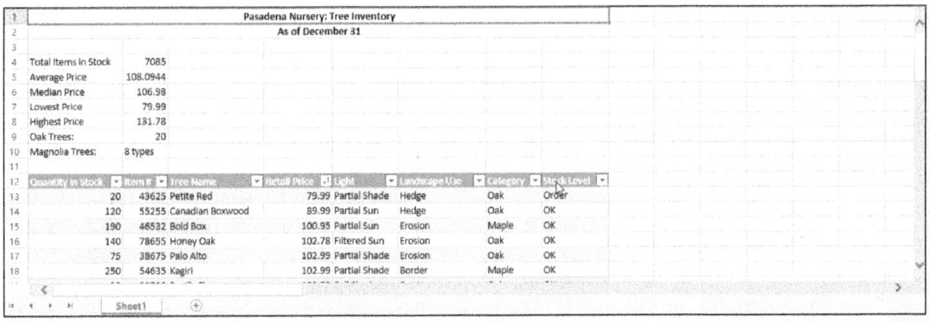

PROJECT

2B Weekly Sales Summary

MyITLab®
Project 2B Training

PROJECT ACTIVITIES

In Activities 2.21 through 2.35, you will edit an existing workbook for the Sales Director, Mariam Daly. The workbook summarizes the online and in-store sales of products during a one-week period in April. The worksheets of your completed workbook will look similar to Figure 2.32.

PROJECT FILES

For Project 2B, you will need the following file:
e02B_Weekly_Sales

You will save your workbook as:
Lastname_Firstname_2B_Weekly_Sales

PROJECT RESULTS

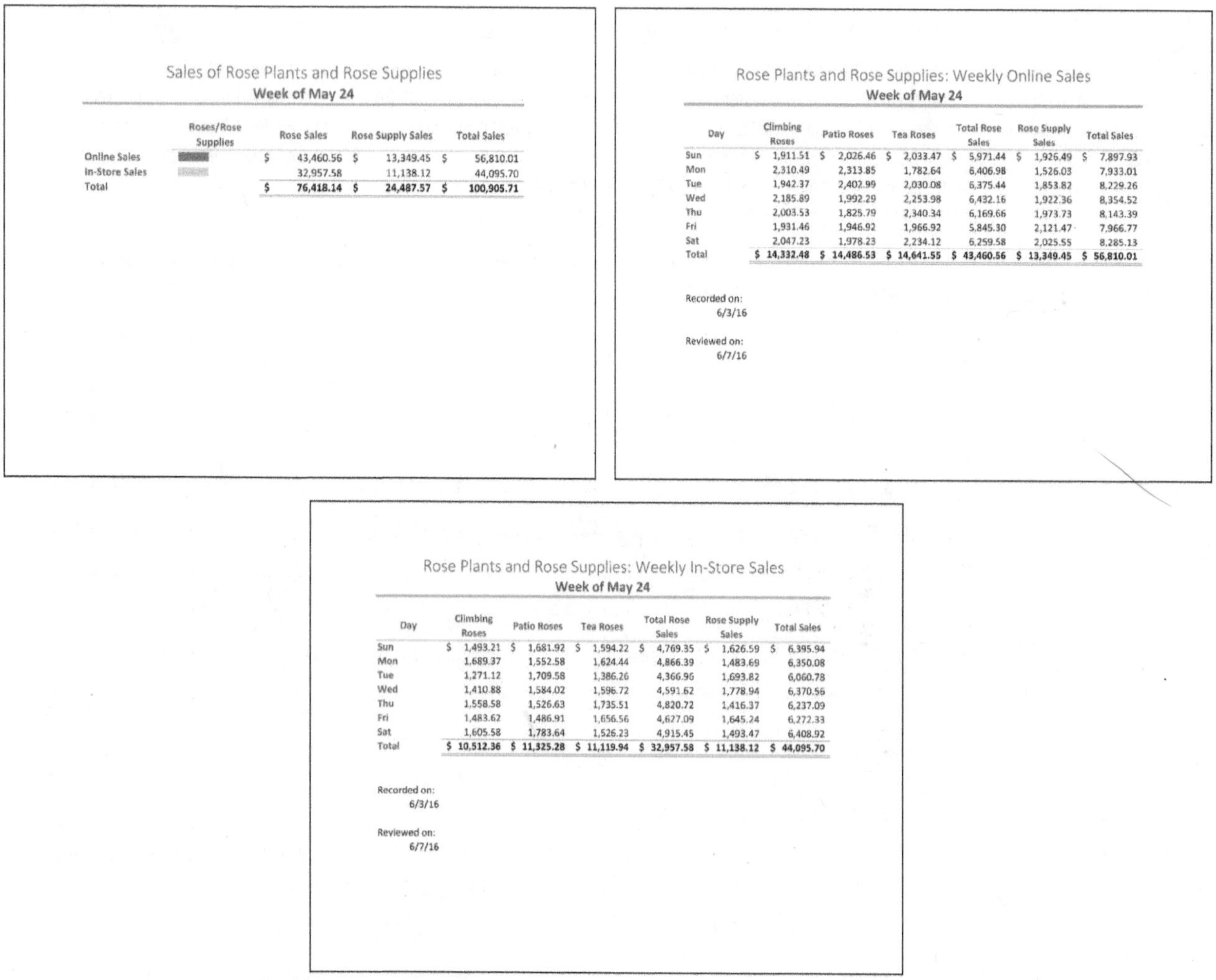

Sales of Rose Plants and Rose Supplies
Week of May 24

	Roses/Rose Supplies	Rose Sales	Rose Supply Sales	Total Sales
Online Sales		$ 43,460.56	$ 13,349.45	$ 56,810.01
In-Store Sales		32,957.58	11,138.12	44,095.70
Total		**$ 76,418.14**	**$ 24,487.57**	**$ 100,905.71**

Rose Plants and Rose Supplies: Weekly Online Sales
Week of May 24

Day	Climbing Roses	Patio Roses	Tea Roses	Total Rose Sales	Rose Supply Sales	Total Sales
Sun	$ 1,911.51	$ 2,026.46	$ 2,033.47	$ 5,971.44	$ 1,926.49	$ 7,897.93
Mon	2,310.49	2,313.85	1,782.64	6,406.98	1,526.03	7,933.01
Tue	1,942.37	2,402.99	2,030.08	6,375.44	1,853.82	8,229.26
Wed	2,185.89	1,992.29	2,253.98	6,432.16	1,922.36	8,354.52
Thu	2,003.53	1,825.79	2,340.34	6,169.66	1,973.73	8,143.39
Fri	1,931.46	1,946.92	1,966.92	5,845.30	2,121.47	7,966.77
Sat	2,047.23	1,978.23	2,234.12	6,259.58	2,025.55	8,285.13
Total	**$ 14,332.48**	**$ 14,486.53**	**$ 14,641.55**	**$ 43,460.56**	**$ 13,349.45**	**$ 56,810.01**

Recorded on:
6/3/16

Reviewed on:
6/7/16

Rose Plants and Rose Supplies: Weekly In-Store Sales
Week of May 24

Day	Climbing Roses	Patio Roses	Tea Roses	Total Rose Sales	Rose Supply Sales	Total Sales
Sun	$ 1,493.21	$ 1,681.92	$ 1,594.22	$ 4,769.35	$ 1,626.59	$ 6,395.94
Mon	1,689.37	1,552.58	1,624.44	4,866.39	1,483.69	6,350.08
Tue	1,271.12	1,709.58	1,386.26	4,366.96	1,693.82	6,060.78
Wed	1,410.88	1,584.02	1,596.72	4,591.62	1,778.94	6,370.56
Thu	1,558.58	1,526.63	1,735.51	4,820.72	1,416.37	6,237.09
Fri	1,483.62	1,486.91	1,656.56	4,627.09	1,645.24	6,272.33
Sat	1,605.58	1,783.64	1,526.23	4,915.45	1,493.47	6,408.92
Total	**$ 10,512.36**	**$ 11,325.28**	**$ 11,119.94**	**$ 32,957.58**	**$ 11,138.12**	**$ 44,095.70**

Recorded on:
6/3/16

Reviewed on:
6/7/16

FIGURE 2.32 Project 2B Weekly Sales Summary

Objective 7 Navigate a Workbook and Rename Worksheets

Video E2-7

Use multiple worksheets in a workbook to organize data in a logical arrangement. When you have more than one worksheet in a workbook, you can ***navigate*** (move) among worksheets by clicking the ***sheet tabs***. Sheet tabs identify each worksheet in a workbook and display along the lower left edge of the window. When you have more worksheets than can display in the sheet tab area, use the sheet tab scrolling buttons to move sheet tabs into and out of view.

Activity 2.21 Navigating Among Worksheets, Renaming Worksheets, and Changing the Tab Color of Worksheets

Excel names the first worksheet in a workbook *Sheet1* and each additional worksheet that you add in order—*Sheet2*, *Sheet3*, and so on. Most Excel users rename their worksheets with meaningful names. In this activity, you will navigate among worksheets, rename worksheets, and change the tab color of sheet tabs.

1 Start Excel, and then in the lower left corner of Excel's opening screen, click **Open Other Workbooks.**

ANOTHER WAY Press Ctrl + F12 to display the Open dialog box.

2 Navigate to the student files that accompany this textbook, and then locate and open **e02B_Weekly_Sales.** Press F12 to display the **Save As** dialog box, and then navigate to your **Excel Chapter 2** folder. In the **File name** box, using your own name, type **Lastname_Firstname_2B_Weekly_Sales** and click **Save** or press Enter

In this workbook, two worksheets display into which some data has already been entered. For example, on the first worksheet, the days of the week and sales data for the one-week period displays.

3 Along the bottom of the Excel window, point to and then click the **Sheet2 tab.**

The second worksheet in the workbook displays and becomes the active worksheet. *Sheet2* displays in bold.

4 In cell **A1**, notice the text *In-Store*—this worksheet will contain data for in-store sales.

5 Click the **Sheet1 tab.** Then, point to the **Sheet1 tab**, and double-click to select the sheet tab name. Type **Online Sales** and press Enter.

The first worksheet becomes the active worksheet, and the sheet tab displays *Online Sales.*

6 Point to the **Sheet2 tab**, right-click, and then from the shortcut menu, click **Rename.** Type **In-Store Sales** and press Enter. Compare your screen with Figure 2.33.

You can use either of these methods to rename a sheet tab.

More Knowledge **Copying a Worksheet**

To copy a worksheet to the same workbook, right-click the sheet tab, on the shortcut menu click Move or Copy, click the sheet before which you want to insert the copied sheet, select the Create a copy check box, and then click OK. To copy to a different workbook, in the Move or Copy dialog box, click the To book arrow, and then select the workbook into which you want to insert the copy.

FIGURE 2.33

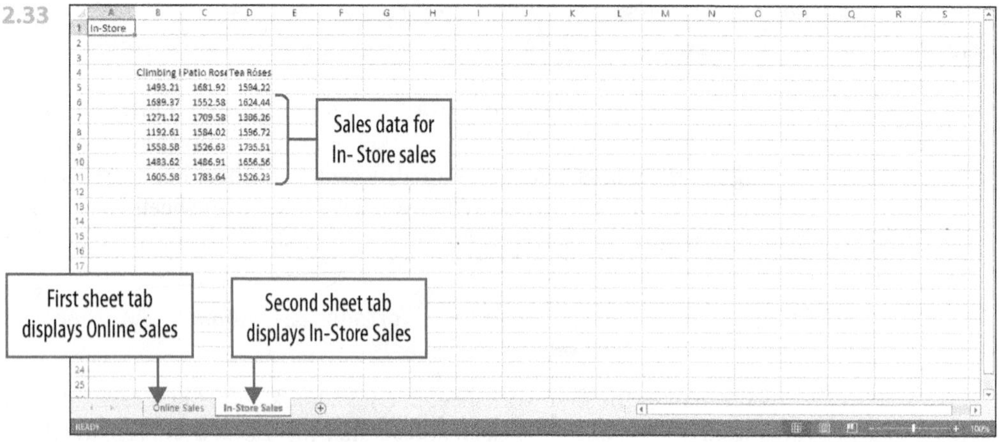

7 Point to the **In-Store Sales sheet tab** and right-click. Point to **Tab Color**, and then in the last column, click the first color—**Green, Accent 6.**

ANOTHER WAY On the Home tab, in the Cells group, click the Format button, and then on the displayed list, point to Tab Color.

8 Using the technique you just practiced, change the tab color of the **Online Sales sheet tab** to **Blue, Accent 5**—in the next to last column, the first color. **Save** your workbook.

Objective 8 Enter Dates, Clear Contents, and Clear Formats

Video E2-8

Dates represent a type of value that you can enter in a cell. When you enter a date, Excel assigns a serial value—a number—to the date. This makes it possible to treat dates like other numbers. For example, if two cells contain dates, you can find the number of days between the two dates by subtracting the older date from the more recent date.

Activity 2.22 Entering and Formatting Dates

In this activity, you will examine the various ways that Excel can format dates in a cell. Date values entered in any of the following formats will be recognized by Excel as a date:

Format	Example
m/d/yy	7/4/2016
d-mmm	4-Jul
d-mmm-yy	4-Jul-16
mmm-yy	Jul-12

On your keyboard, - (the hyphen key) and / (the forward slash key) function identically in any of these formats and can be used interchangeably. You can abbreviate the month name to three characters or spell it out. You can enter the year as two digits, four digits, or even leave it off. When left off, the current year is assumed but does not display in the cell.

A two-digit year value of 30 through 99 is interpreted by the Windows operating system as the four-digit years of 1930 through 1999. All other two-digit year values are assumed to be in the 21st century. If you always type year values as four digits, even though only two digits may display in the cell, you can be sure that Excel interprets the year value as you intended. Examples are shown in Figure 2.34.

FIGURE 2.34

HOW EXCEL INTERPRETS DATES	
DATE TYPED AS:	**COMPLETED BY EXCEL AS:**
7/4/15	7/4/2015
7/4/98	7/4/1998
7/4	4-Jul (current year assumed)
7-4	4-Jul (current year assumed)
July 4	4-Jul (current year assumed)
Jul 4	4-Jul (current year assumed)
Jul/4	4-Jul (current year assumed)
Jul-4	4-Jul (current year assumed)
July 4, 1998	4-Jul-98
July 2012	Jul-12 (first day of month assumed)
July 1998	Jul-98 (first day of month assumed)

1 On the **Online Sales** sheet, click cell **A16** and notice that the cell displays *6/3*. In the **Formula Bar**, notice that the full date of June 3, 2016 displays in the format *6/3/2016*.

2 With cell **A16** selected, on the **HOME tab**, in the **Number group**, click the **Number Format arrow**. At the bottom, click **More Number Formats** to display the **Number tab** of the **Format Cells** dialog box.

Under Category, *Date* is selected, and under Type, *3/14* is selected. Cell A16 uses this format type; that is, only the month and day display in the cell.

3 In the displayed dialog box, under **Type**, click several other date types and watch the **Sample** area to see how applying the selected date format will format your cell. When you are finished, click the **3/14/12** type, and then compare your screen with Figure 2.35.

FIGURE 2.35

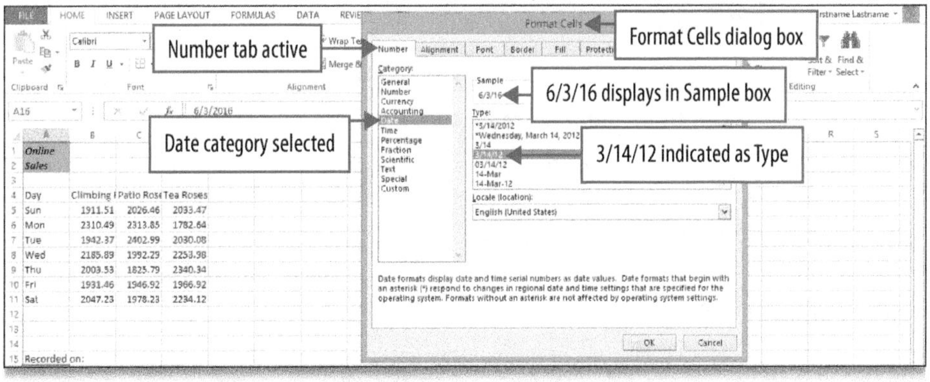

4 At the bottom of the dialog box, click **OK**. Click cell **A19**, type **6-7-16** and then press Enter.

Cell A19 has no special date formatting applied, and displays in the default date format *6/7/2016*.

ALERT! **The Date Does Not Display as 6/7/2016?**

Settings in your Windows operating system determine the default format for dates. If your result is different, it is likely that the formatting of the default date was adjusted on the computer at which you are working.

5 Click cell **A19** again. Hold down Ctrl and press ; (semicolon) on your keyboard. Press Enter to confirm the entry.

Excel enters the current date, obtained from your computer's internal calendar, in the selected cell using the default date format. Ctrl + ; is a quick method to enter the current date.

6 Click cell **A19** again, type **6/7/16** and then press Enter.

Because the year *16* is less than 30, Excel assumes a 21st century date and changes *16* to *2016* to complete the four-digit year. Typing *98* would result in *1998*. For two-digit years that you type that are between 30 and 99, Excel assumes a 20th century date.

7 Click cell **A16**, and then on the **HOME tab**, in the **Clipboard group**, click **Format Painter**. Click cell **A19**, and notice that the date format from cell **A16** is copied to cell **A19**. **Save** your workbook.

Activity 2.23 | Clearing Cell Contents and Formats

A cell has *contents*—a value or a formula—and a cell may also have one or more *formats* applied, for example bold and italic font styles, fill color, font color, and so on. You can choose to clear—delete—the *contents* of a cell, the *formatting* of a cell, or both.

Clearing the contents of a cell deletes the value or formula typed there, but it does *not* clear formatting applied to a cell. In this activity, you will clear the contents of a cell and then clear the formatting of a cell that contains a date to see its underlying content.

1 In the **Online Sales** worksheet, click cell **A1**. In the **Editing group**, click **Clear**, and then click **Clear Contents**. Notice that the text is cleared, but the green formatting remains.

2 Click cell **A2**, and then press Delete.

You can use either of these two methods to delete the *contents* of a cell. Deleting the contents does not, however, delete the formatting of the cell; you can see that the green fill color format applied to the two cells still displays.

3 In cell **A1**, type **Online Sales** and then on the **Formula Bar**, click **Enter** so that cell **A1** remains the active cell.

In addition to the green fill color, the bold italic text formatting remains with the cell.

4 In the **Editing group**, click **Clear**, and then click **Clear Formats**.

Clearing the formats deletes formatting from the cell—the green fill color and the bold and italic font styles—but does not delete the cell's contents.

5 Use the same technique to clear the green fill color from cell **A2**. Click cell **A16**, click **Clear**, and then click **Clear Formats**. In the **Number group**, notice that *General* displays as the number format of the cell.

The box in the Number group indicates the current Number format of the selected cell. Clearing the date formatting from the cell displays the date's serial number. The date, June 3, 2016, is stored as a serial number that indicates the number of days since January 1, 1900. This date is the 42,524th day since the reference date of January 1, 1900.

6 On the Quick Access Toolbar, click **Undo** to restore the date format. **Save** your workbook, and then compare your screen with Figure 2.36.

FIGURE 2.36

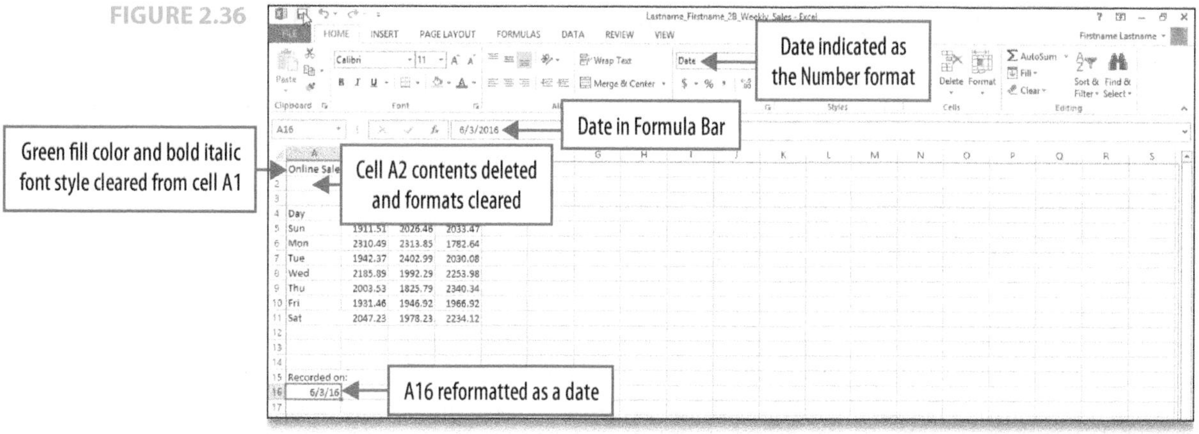

More Knowledge **Clearing an Entire Worksheet**

To clear an entire worksheet, in the upper left corner of the worksheet, click the Select All button, and then on the Home tab, in the Editing group, click Clear, and then click Clear All.

Objective 9 Copy and Paste by Using the Paste Options Gallery

Video E2-9

Data in cells can be copied to other cells in the same worksheet, to other sheets in the same workbook, or to sheets in another workbook. The action of placing cell contents that have been copied or moved to the Clipboard into another location is called ***paste***.

Activity 2.24 | Copying and Pasting by Using the Paste Options Gallery

Recall that the Clipboard is a temporary storage area maintained by your Windows operating system. When you select one or more cells, and then perform the Copy command or the Cut command, the selected data is placed on the Clipboard. From the Clipboard storage area, the data is available for pasting into other cells, other worksheets, other workbooks, and even into other Office programs. When you paste, the ***Paste Options gallery*** displays, which includes Live Preview to preview the Paste formatting that you want.

1 With the **Online Sales** worksheet active, select the range **A4:A19**.

A range of cells identical to this one is required for the *In-Store Sales* worksheet.

2 Right-click over the selection, and then click **Copy** to place a copy of the cells on the Clipboard. Notice that the copied cells display a moving border.

3 At the bottom of the workbook window, click the **In-Store Sales sheet tab** to make it the active worksheet. Point to cell **A4**, right-click, and then on the shortcut menu, under **Paste Options**, *point* to the first button—**Paste**. Compare your screen with Figure 2.37.

Live Preview displays how the copied cells will be placed in the worksheet if you click the Paste button. In this manner, you can experiment with different paste options, and then be sure you are selecting the paste operation that you want. When pasting a range of cells, you need only point to or select the cell in the upper left corner of the ***paste area***—the target destination for data that has been cut or copied using the Clipboard.

FIGURE 2.37

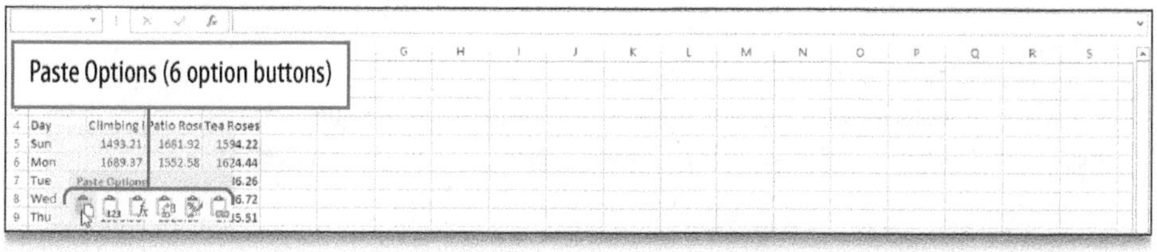

4 Click the first button, **Paste**. In the status bar, notice the message that displays, indicating that your selected range remains available on the Office Clipboard.

5 Display the **Online Sales** worksheet. Press Esc to cancel the moving border. **Save** your workbook.

The status bar no longer displays the message.

Objective 10 Edit and Format Multiple Worksheets at the Same Time

Video E2-10

You can enter or edit data on several worksheets at the same time by selecting and grouping multiple worksheets. Data that you enter or edit on the active sheet is reflected in all selected sheets. If you apply color to the sheet tabs, the name of the sheet tab will be underlined in the color you selected. If the sheet tab displays with a background color, you know the sheet is not selected.

Activity 2.25 | Grouping Worksheets for Editing

1 With the **Online Sales** sheet active, press Ctrl + Home to make cell **A1** the active cell. Point to the **Online Sales sheet tab**, right-click, and then click **Select All Sheets**.

2 At the top of your screen, notice that *[Group]* displays in the title bar. Compare your screen with Figure 2.38.

Both worksheets are selected, as indicated by *[Group]* in the title bar and the sheet tab names underlined. Data that you enter or edit on the active sheet will also be entered or edited in the same manner on all the selected sheets in the same cells.

FIGURE 2.38

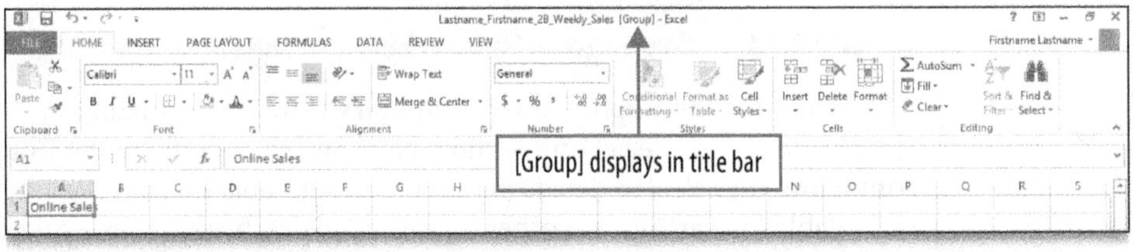

3 Select **columns A:G**, and then set their width to **85 pixels**.

4 Click cell **A2**, type **Week of May 24** and then on the **Formula Bar**, click **Enter** to keep cell **A2** as the active cell. **Merge & Center** the text across the range **A2:G2**, and then apply the **Heading 1** cell style.

5 Click cell **E4**, type **Total Rose Sales** and then press Tab. In cell **F4**, type **Rose Supply Sales** and then press Tab. In cell **G4**, type **Total Sales** and then press Enter.

6 Select the range **A4:G4**, and then apply the **Heading 3** cell style. In the **Alignment group**, click **Center**, **Middle Align**, and **Wrap Text. Save** your workbook.

7 Display the **In-Store Sales** worksheet to cancel the grouping, and then compare your screen with Figure 2.39.

As soon as you select a single sheet, the grouping of the sheets is canceled and *[Group]* no longer displays in the title bar. Because the sheets were grouped, the same new text and formatting were applied to both sheets. In this manner, you can make the same changes to all the sheets in a workbook at one time.

More Knowledge **Hide Worksheets**

You can hide any worksheet in a workbook to remove it from view using this technique:
Select the sheet tabs of the worksheets you want to hide, right-click any of the selected sheet tabs, and then click Hide.

FIGURE 2.39

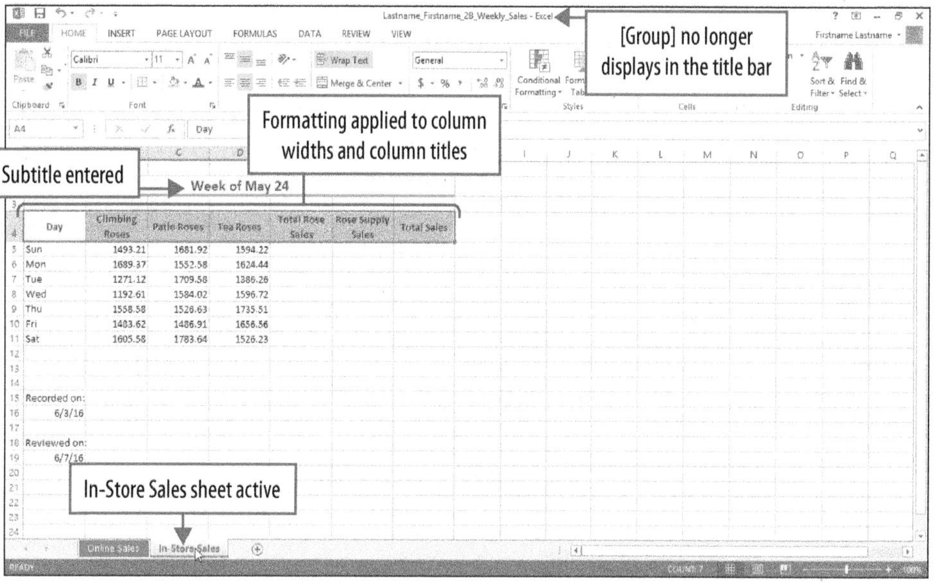

ANOTHER WAY Right-click any sheet tab, and then click Ungroup Sheets.

Activity 2.26 | Formatting and Constructing Formulas on Grouped Worksheets

Recall that formulas are equations that perform calculations on values in your worksheet and that a formula starts with an equal sign (=). Operators are the symbols with which you specify the type of calculation that you want to perform on the elements of a formula. In this activity, you will enter and calculate sales for Rose Supply items from both Online and In-Store sales.

1 Display the **Online Sales** worksheet. Verify that the sheets are not grouped—*[Group]* does *not* display in the title bar.

2 Click cell **A1**, replace *Online Sales* by typing **Rose Plants and Rose Supplies: Weekly Online Sales** and then on the **Formula Bar**, click **Enter** ✓ to keep cell **A1** as the active cell. **Merge & Center** the text across the range **A1:G1**, and then apply the **Title** cell style.

3 In the column titled *Rose Supply Sales*, click cell **F5**, in the range **F5:F11**, type the following data for Rose Supply Sales, and then compare your screen with Figure 2.40.

	ROSE SUPPLY SALES
Sun	**1926.49**
Mon	**1526.03**
Tue	**1853.82**
Wed	**1922.36**
Thu	**1973.73**
Fri	**2121.47**
Sat	**2025.55**

FIGURE 2.40

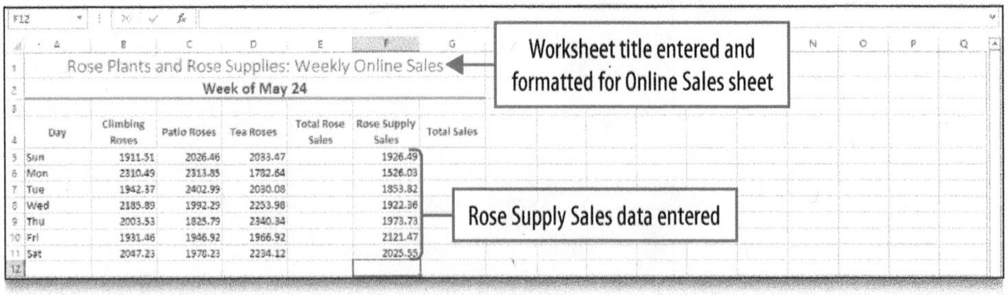

4 Display the **In-Store Sales** sheet. In cell **A1**, replace *In-Store* by typing **Rose Plants and Rose Supplies: Weekly In-Store Sales** and then on the **Formula Bar**, click **Enter** to keep cell **A1** as the active cell. **Merge & Center** the text across the range **A1:G1**, and then apply the **Title** cell style.

5 In the column titled *Rose Supply Sales*, click cell **F5**, in the range **F5:F11**, type the following data for Rose Supply Sales, and then compare your screen with Figure 2.41.

	ROSE SUPPLY SALES
Sun	**1626.59**
Mon	**1483.69**
Tue	**1693.82**
Wed	**1778.94**
Thu	**1416.37**
Fri	**1645.24**
Sat	**1493.47**

FIGURE 2.41

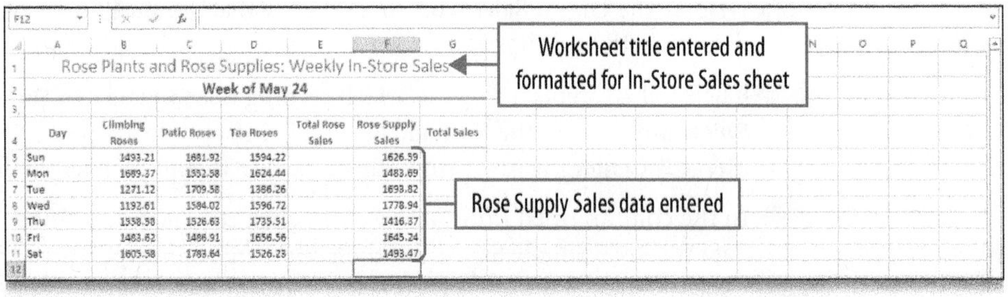

6 **Save** your workbook. Right-click the **Online Sales sheet tab**, and then click **Select All Sheets.**

The first worksheet becomes the active sheet, and the worksheets are grouped. *[Group]* displays in the title bar, and the sheet tabs are underlined in the tab color to indicate they are selected as part of the group. Recall that when grouped, any action that you perform on the active worksheet is *also* performed on any other selected worksheets.

7 With the sheets *grouped* and the **Online Sales** sheet active, click cell **E5**. On the **HOME tab**, in the **Editing group**, click **AutoSum**. Compare your screen with Figure 2.42.

Recall that when you enter the SUM function, Excel looks first above and then left for a proposed range of cells to sum.

FIGURE 2.42

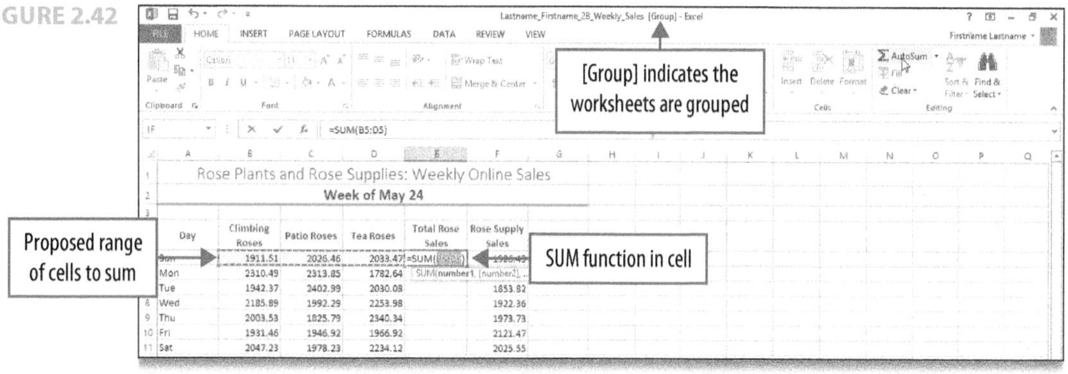

8 Press Enter to display Total Rose Sales for Sunday, which is *5971.44*.

9 Click cell **E5**, and then drag the fill handle down to copy the formula through cell **E11**.

10 Click cell **G5**, type **=** click cell **E5**, type **+** click cell **F5**, and then compare your screen with Figure 2.43.

Using the point-and-click technique to construct this formula is only one of several techniques you can use. Alternatively, you could use any other method to enter the SUM function to add the values in these two cells.

FIGURE 2.43

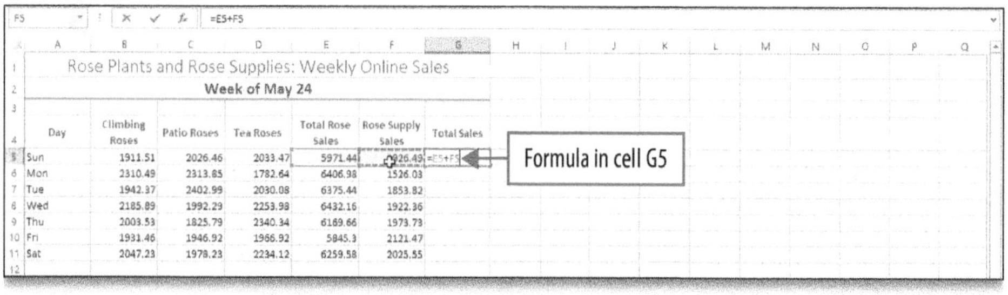

11 Press Enter to display the result *7897.93*, and then copy the formula down through cell **G11**.

Activity 2.27 | Determining Multiple Totals at the Same Time

You can select a contiguous range of cells adjacent to rows or columns of numbers and then click the Sum button—or use Alt + =—to enter the a SUM function for each row or column.

1 **Save** your workbook. With the two worksheets still grouped, in cell **A12**, type **Total** and then select the range **B5:G12**, which is all of the sales data and the empty cells at the bottom of each column of sales data.

2 With the range **B5:G12** selected, hold down Alt and press = to enter the **SUM** function in each empty cell. Click **Save**.

Selecting a range in this manner and then clicking the SUM button, or entering the SUM function with the keyboard shortcut Alt = =, places the Sum function in the empty cells at the bottom of each column.

Activity 2.28 | Formatting Grouped Worksheets

1 With the two worksheets still grouped, select the range **A5:A12**, and then apply the **Heading 4** cell style.

2 To apply financial formatting to the worksheets, select the range **B5:G5**, hold down Ctrl, and then select the range **B12:G12**. With the nonadjacent ranges selected, apply the **Accounting Number Format** $.

3 Select the range **B6:G11** and apply **Comma Style** [,]. Select the range **B12:G12** and apply the **Total** cell style.

4 Press Ctrl + Home to move to the top of the worksheet; compare your screen with Figure 2.44.

FIGURE 2.44

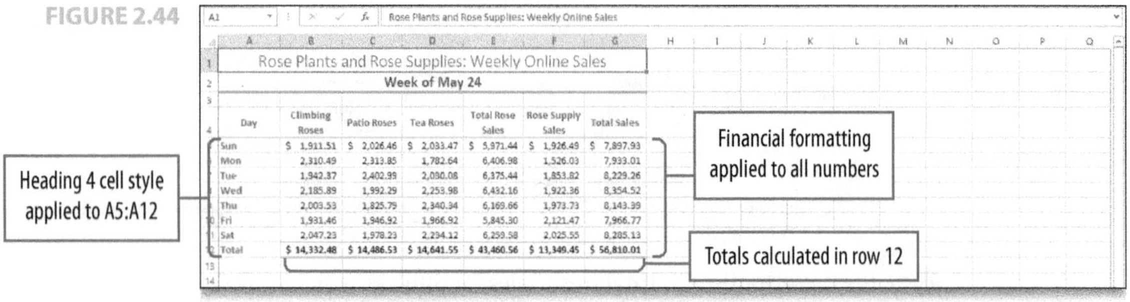

Rose Plants and Rose Supplies: Weekly Online Sales

Week of May 24

Day	Climbing Roses	Patio Roses	Tea Roses	Total Rose Sales	Rose Supply Sales	Total Sales
Sun	$ 1,911.51	$ 2,026.46	$ 2,033.47	$ 5,971.44	$ 1,926.49	$ 7,897.93
Mon	2,310.49	2,313.85	1,782.64	6,406.98	1,526.03	7,933.01
Tue	1,942.37	2,402.99	2,030.08	6,375.44	1,853.82	8,229.26
Wed	2,185.89	1,992.29	2,253.98	6,432.16	1,922.36	8,354.52
Thu	2,003.53	1,825.79	2,340.34	6,169.66	1,973.73	8,143.39
Fri	1,931.46	1,946.92	1,966.92	5,845.30	2,121.47	7,966.77
Sat	2,047.23	1,978.23	2,234.12	6,259.58	2,025.55	8,285.13
Total	$ 14,332.48	$ 14,486.53	$ 14,641.55	$ 43,460.56	$ 13,349.45	$ 56,810.01

Activity 2.29 | Ungrouping Worksheets

1 Click the **In-Store Sales sheet tab** to cancel the grouping and display the second worksheet. Click Save, and then compare your screen with Figure 2.45.

With your worksheets grouped, the calculations and formatting on the first worksheet were also added on the second worksheet. As soon as you click a single sheet tab, the grouping is canceled.

FIGURE 2.45

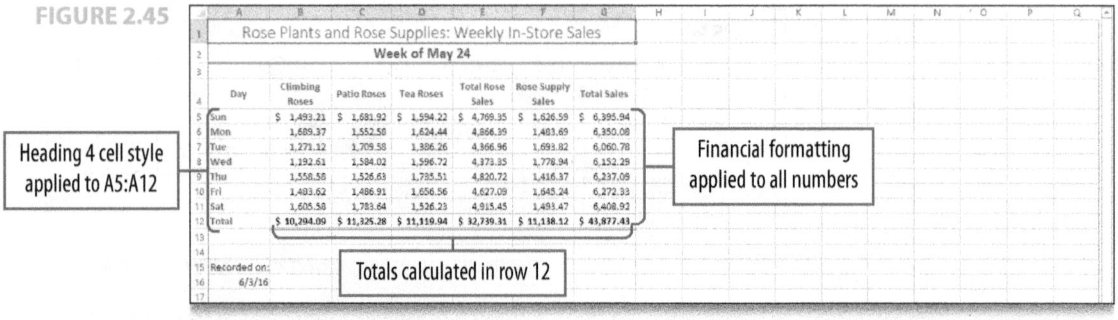

Rose Plants and Rose Supplies: Weekly In-Store Sales

Week of May 24

Day	Climbing Roses	Patio Roses	Tea Roses	Total Rose Sales	Rose Supply Sales	Total Sales
Sun	$ 1,493.21	$ 1,681.92	$ 1,594.22	$ 4,769.35	$ 1,626.59	$ 6,395.94
Mon	1,689.37	1,552.58	1,624.44	4,866.39	1,483.69	6,350.08
Tue	1,271.12	1,709.58	1,386.26	4,366.96	1,693.82	6,060.78
Wed	1,192.61	1,584.02	1,596.72	4,373.35	1,778.94	6,152.29
Thu	1,558.58	1,526.63	1,735.51	4,820.72	1,416.37	6,237.09
Fri	1,483.62	1,486.91	1,656.56	4,627.09	1,645.24	6,272.33
Sat	1,605.58	1,783.64	1,526.23	4,915.45	1,493.47	6,408.92
Total	$ 10,294.09	$ 11,325.28	$ 11,119.94	$ 32,739.31	$ 11,138.12	$ 43,877.43

Recorded on:
6/3/16

Objective 11 Create a Summary Sheet with Column Sparklines

Video E2-11

A ***summary sheet*** is a worksheet where totals from other worksheets are displayed and summarized. Recall that sparklines are tiny charts within a single cell that show a data trend.

Activity 2.30 | Inserting a Worksheet

1 To the right of the **In-Store Sales** sheet tab, click **New sheet** [+].

2 Rename the new worksheet tab **Summary** and change its **Tab Color** to **Gold, Accent 4**.

3 Widen **columns A:E** to **110** pixels. In cell **A1**, type **Sales of Rose Plants and Rose Supplies** **Merge & Center** the title across the range **A1:E1**, and then apply the **Title** cell style.

4 In cell **A2**, type **Week of May 24** and then **Merge & Center** across **A2:E2**; apply the **Heading 1** cell style.

5 Leave **row 3** blank. To form column titles, in cell **B4**, type **Roses/Rose Supplies** and press Tab. In cell **C4**, type **Rose Sales** and press Tab. In cell **D4**, type **Rose Supply Sales** and press Tab. In cell **E4**, type **Total Sales** Press Enter.

6 Select the range **B4:E4**. Apply the **Heading 3** cell style. In the **Alignment group**, click **Center**, **Middle Align**, and **Wrap Text**.

7 To form row titles, in cell **A5**, type **Online Sales** In cell **A6**, type **In-Store Sales** **Save**, and then compare your screen with Figure 2.46.

FIGURE 2.46

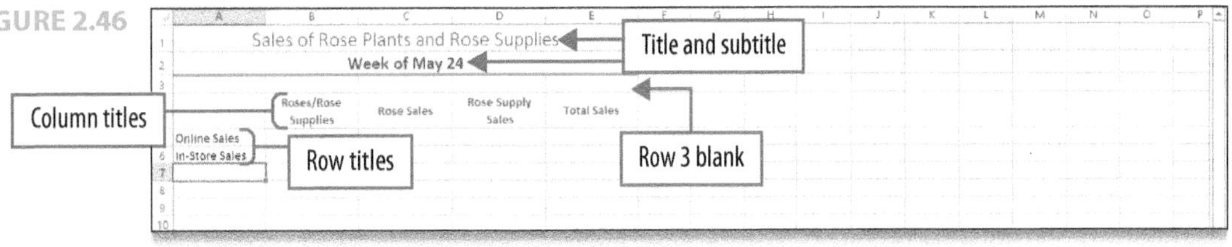

Activity 2.31 Constructing Formulas That Refer to Cells in Another Worksheet

In this activity, you will construct formulas in the Summary worksheet to display the total sales for both online sales and in-store sales that will update the Summary worksheet whenever changes are made to the other worksheet totals.

1 Click cell **C5**. Type = Click the **Online Sales sheet tab**. On the **Online Sales** worksheet, click cell **E12**, and then press Enter to redisplay the **Summary** worksheet and insert the total **Rose Sales** amount of *$43,460.56*.

2 Click cell **C5** to select it again. Look at the **Formula Bar**, and notice that instead of a value, the cell contains a formula that is equal to the value in another cell in another worksheet. Compare your screen with Figure 2.47.

The value in this cell is equal to the value in cell E12 of the *Online Sales* worksheet. The Accounting Number Format applied to the referenced cell is carried over. By using a formula of this type, changes in cell E12 on the *Online Sales* worksheet will be automatically updated in this *Summary* worksheet.

FIGURE 2.47

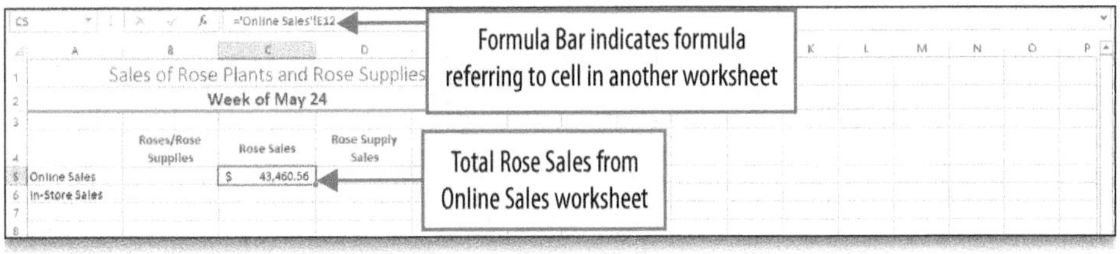

3 Click cell **D5**. Type = and then click the **Online Sales sheet tab**. Click cell **F12**, and then press Enter to redisplay the **Summary** worksheet and insert the total **Rose Supply Sales** amount of *$13,349.45*.

4 By using the techniques you just practiced, in cells **C6** and **D6** insert the total **Rose Sales** and **Rose Supply Sales** data from the **In-Store Sales** worksheet. Click **Save**, and then compare your screen with Figure 2.48.

FIGURE 2.48

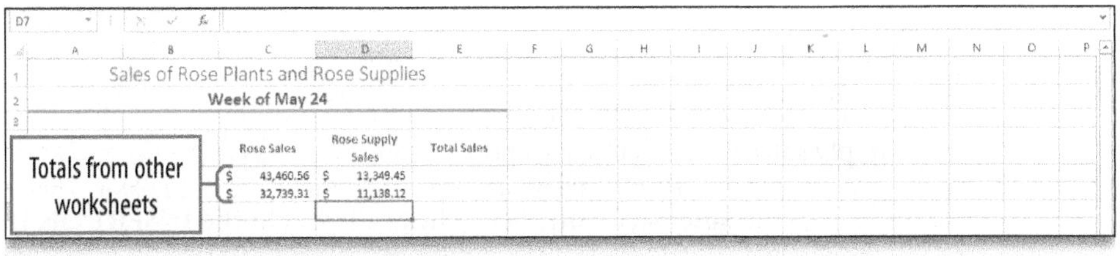

Activity 2.32 | Changing Values in a Detail Worksheet to Update a Summary Worksheet

The formulas in cells C5:D6 display the totals from the other two worksheets. Changes made to any of the other two worksheets—sometimes referred to as ***detail sheets*** because the details of the information are contained there—that affect their totals will display on this Summary worksheet. In this manner, the Summary worksheet accurately displays the current totals from the other worksheets.

1 In cell **A7**, type **Total** Select the range **C5:E6**, and then on the **HOME tab**, in the **Editing group**, click **AutoSum** to total the two rows.

This technique is similar to selecting the empty cells at the bottom of columns and then inserting the SUM function for each column. Alternatively, you could use any other method to sum the rows. Recall that cell formatting carries over to adjacent cells unless two cells are left blank.

2 Select the range **C5:E7**, and then click **AutoSum** to total the three columns. Compare your screen with Figure 2.49.

FIGURE 2.49

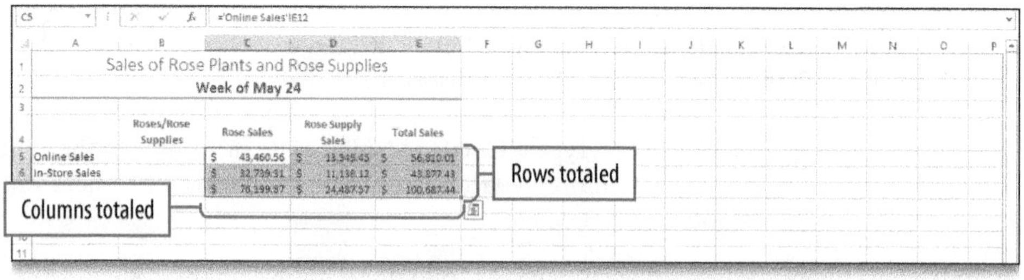

3 In cell **C6**, notice that total **Rose Sales** for **In-Store Sales** is *$32,739.31*, and in cell **C7**, notice the total of *$76,199.87*.

4 Display the **In-Store Sales** worksheet, click cell **B8**, type **1410.88** and then press Enter. Notice that the formulas in the worksheet recalculate.

5 Display the **Summary** worksheet, and notice that in the **Rose Sales** column, both the total for the *In-Store Sales* and the *Total* were recalculated.

In this manner, a Summary sheet recalculates any changes made in the other worksheets.

6 On the **Summary** worksheet, select the range **C6:E6** and change the format to **Comma Style**. Select the range **C7:E7**, and then apply the **Total** cell style. Select the range **A5:A7** and apply the **Heading 4** cell style. **Save** your workbook. Click cell **A1**, and then compare your screen with Figure 2.50.

FIGURE 2.50

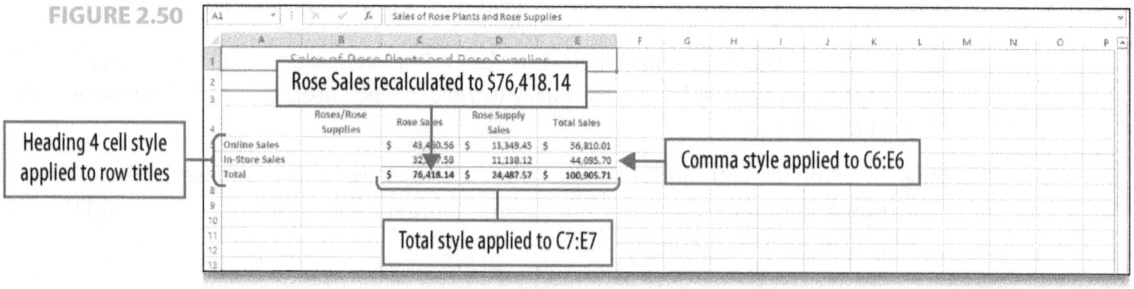

Activity 2.33 | Inserting Column Sparklines

In this activity, you will insert column sparklines to visualize the ratio of Rose sales to Rose Supply sales for both Online and In-Store.

1 On the **Summary** worksheet, click cell **B5**. On the **INSERT tab**, in the **Sparklines group**, click **Column**. In the **Create Sparklines** dialog box, with the insertion point blinking in the **Data Range** box, type **c5:d5** and then compare your screen with Figure 2.51.

FIGURE 2.51

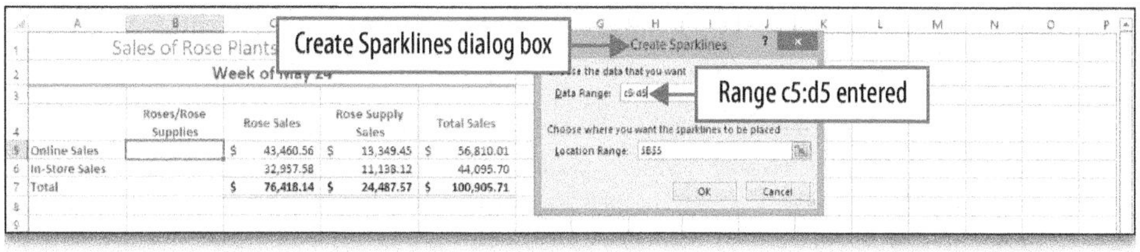

2 Click **OK**. Click cell **B6**, and then **INSERT** a **Column Sparkline** for the range **c6:d6** In the **Style group**, apply **Sparkline Style Accent 4, (no dark or light)**—in the third row, the fourth style. Press Ctrl + Home, click **Save**, and then compare your screen with Figure 2.52.

You can see, at a glance, that for both Online and In-Store sales, Rose sales are much greater than Rose Supply sales.

FIGURE 2.52

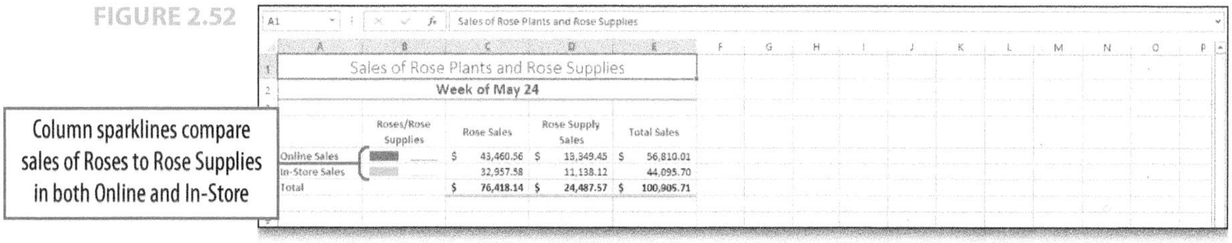

Objective 12 Format and Print Multiple Worksheets in a Workbook

Video E2-12

Each worksheet within a workbook can have different formatting, for example different headers or footers. If all the worksheets in the workbook will have the same header or footer, you can select all the worksheets and apply formatting common to all of the worksheets; for example, you can set the same footer in all of the worksheets.

Activity 2.34 Moving a Worksheet, Repeating Footers, and Formatting Multiple Worksheets in a Workbook

In this activity, you will move the Summary sheet to become the first worksheet in the workbook. Then you will format and prepare your workbook for printing. The three worksheets containing data can be formatted simultaneously.

1 Point to the **Summary sheet tab**, hold down the left mouse button to display a small black triangle—a caret—and then notice that a small paper icon attaches to the mouse pointer.

2 Drag to the left until the caret and mouse pointer are to the left of the **Online Sales sheet tab**, as shown in Figure 2.53, and then release the left mouse button.

Use this technique to rearrange the order of worksheets within a workbook.

FIGURE 2.53

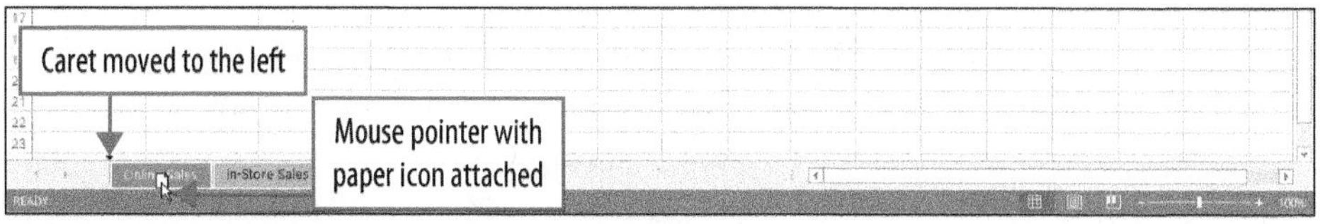

3 Be sure the **Summary** worksheet is the active sheet, point to its sheet tab, right-click, and then click **Select All Sheets** to display *[Group]* in the title bar.

4 Click the **PAGE LAYOUT tab**. In the **Page Setup group**, click **Margins**, and then at the bottom of the gallery, click **Custom Margins** to display the **Page Setup** dialog box.

5 In the **Page Setup** dialog box, on the **Margins tab**, under **Center on page**, select the **Horizontally** check box.

6 Click the **Header/Footer tab**, and then in the center of the dialog box, click **Custom Footer**. In the **Footer** dialog box, with your insertion point blinking in the **Left section**, on the row of buttons, click **Insert File Name** .

7 Click **OK** two times.

The dotted line indicates the page break as currently formatted.

8 Press Ctrl + Home; verify that *[Group]* still displays in the title bar.

By selecting all sheets, you can apply the same formatting to all the worksheets at the same time, for example to repeat headers or footers.

9 Click the **FILE tab** to display **Backstage** view, and then click **Show All Properties**. As the **Tags**, type **weekly sales, online, in-store, rose plants, rose supplies** In the **Subject** box, type your course name and section number. Be sure your name displays as the author.

10 On the left, click **Print** to display the **Print Preview**, and then compare your screen with Figure 2.54.

By grouping, you can view all sheets in Print Preview. If you do not see *1 of 3* at the bottom of the Preview, redisplay the workbook, select all the sheets again, and then redisplay Print Preview.

FIGURE 2.54

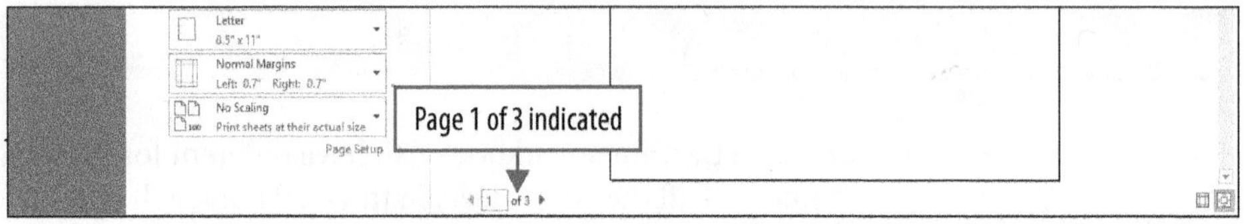

11 At the bottom of the **Print Preview**, click **Next Page** as necessary and take a moment to view each page of your workbook.

Activity 2.35 | Printing All or Individual Worksheets in a Workbook

1 In **Backstage** view, click **Save** to save your workbook before printing. In the displayed workbook, right-click the **Summary sheet tab**, and then click **Ungroup Sheets**.

2 Press Ctrl + F2 to display **Print Preview**, and then at the bottom of the window, notice that *1 of 1* is indicated.

Because the worksheets are no longer grouped, only the active sheet is available for printing.

3 On the left, under **Settings**, click **Print Active Sheets**, and then click **Print Entire Workbook**.

At the bottom of the window, *1 of 3* is indicated. By default, Excel prints only the active worksheet; however, you can use this command to print an entire workbook.

4 By using the techniques you practiced in Project 1A, print or submit electronically as directed by your instructor. If required by your instructor, print or create an electronic version of your worksheet with formulas displayed.

5 Close your workbook and close Excel.

END | You have completed Project 2B

GO! with Office Online (formerly Web Apps)

Objective Summarize the Data on Multiple Worksheets in Excel Online

2 EXCEL

If you are working on a computer that does not have Microsoft Office installed, you can still create new workbooks in your web browser by using Excel Online.

> **ALERT!** **Working with Web-Based Applications and Services**
>
> Computer programs and services on the web receive continuous updates and improvements, so the steps to complete this web-based activity may differ from the ones shown. You can often look at the screens and the information presented to determine how to complete the activity.

Activity | Creating an Inventory Valuation Report in Excel Online

In this activity, you will use Excel Online to add a worksheet to a workbook created in Excel.

1 Launch your web browser, navigate to **http://onedrive.com**, and then sign in to your Microsoft account. Open your **GO! Web Projects** folder—or create and then open this folder if necessary.

2 In the OneDrive menu bar, click **Upload**. In the **Choose File to Upload** dialog box, navigate to your student data files, click the Excel file **e02_2B_Web**, and then click **Open**.

3 Point to the uploaded file **e02_2B_Web**, and then right-click. On the shortcut menu, scroll as necessary, and then click **Rename**. Using your own name, type **Lastname_Firstname_EX_2B_Web** and then press Enter to rename the file.

4 Click the file you just renamed to open it in Excel Online.

5 At the bottom of the workbook, at the right end of the sheet tabs, click **New sheet** ⊕. Double-click the **Sheet4 tab**, and then name the worksheet tab **TV Sales**

6 To help you create this project quickly and to eliminate extra typing, you will import the data from a Word table. From the taskbar, open **File Explorer**, navigate to the student data files that accompany this textbook, and then open the Word document **e02_2B_TV_Sales**. Press Ctrl + A to select all of the text, right-click anywhere over the selection, and then click **Copy**. **Close** Word and the File Explorer window.

7 With cell **A1** selected, on the ribbon, in the **Clipboard group**, click **Paste**; if necessary click Allow access. Notice that # symbols display when numeric data is too wide for the cell.

8 Select the range **A1:G1**, and then in the **Alignment group**, click **Merge & Center**. Merge and center the worksheet's subtitle in the same manner. Select the range **A1:A2**, and then in the **Font group**, apply **Bold**.

9 Select column headings **A:G**, point to the border between any two selected column headings to display the ⟺ pointer, and then double-click to resize all the columns to display all data.

10 Select the range **B5:G12**, and then in the **Editing group**, click **AutoSum** to total all the columns. Compare your screen with Figure A.

FIGURE A

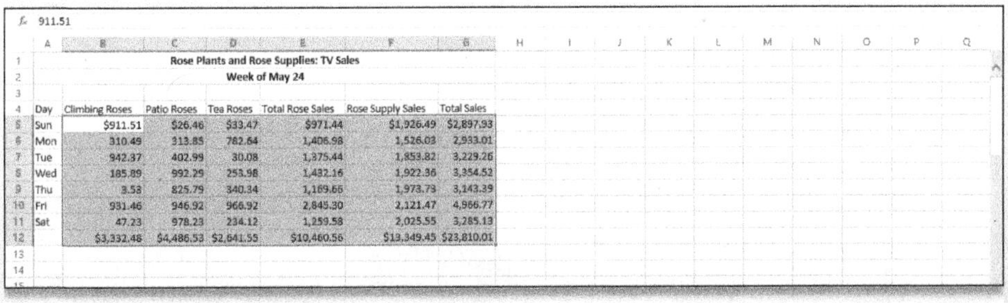

Day	Climbing Roses	Patio Roses	Tea Roses	Total Rose Sales	Rose Supply Sales	Total Sales
Sun	$911.51	$26.46	$33.47	$971.44	$1,926.49	$2,897.93
Mon	310.49	313.85	782.64	1,406.98	1,526.03	2,933.01
Tue	942.37	402.99	30.08	1,375.44	1,853.82	3,229.26
Wed	185.89	992.29	253.98	1,432.16	1,922.36	3,354.52
Thu	3.53	825.79	340.34	1,169.66	1,973.73	3,143.39
Fri	931.46	946.92	966.92	2,845.30	2,121.47	4,966.77
Sat	47.23	978.23	234.12	1,259.58	2,025.55	3,285.13
	$3,332.48	$4,486.53	$2,641.55	$10,460.56	$13,349.45	$23,810.01

(GO! with Office Online (formerly Web Apps) continues on the next page)

11 Display the **Summary** worksheet, and then click cell **A7**. In the **Cells group**, click the **Insert button arrow**, and then click **Insert Rows**. In the new cell A7, type **TV Sales** and then press Tab two times to make cell C7 active.

12 Type **='TV Sales'!E12** and press Enter for a result of *$10,460.56*. Notice that you cannot use the = plus Enter method in Excel Online, but you can simply type the command.

13 Click cell **C7** and drag the fill handle to the right to cell **E7**. Compare your screen with Figure B. Notice that Excel copies the formula and adjusts the cell references to record the Rose Supply Sales and the Total Sales from the TV Sales worksheet. Also, the sparkline is filled in. The TV Sales had higher sales of Rose Supplies than Rose plants.

14 If you are instructed to submit your file, use one of the methods outlined in the Note box below. Sign out of your OneDrive and close Internet Explorer.

NOTE **Printing or Creating an Electronic File from Excel Online**

To print on paper, click the FILE tab, click Print, click the Print button, and then click Print. In the Print preview display, click Print. In the displayed Print dialog box, click Print to print on the printer connected to your system. To create an electronic file of your printout, from the Print dialog box, click the printer labeled *Send to OneNote 2013*, and then click Print. You may have to open and then close OneNote first if you have never opened it before. When OneNote opens, click the Quick Notes section of the displayed notebook, and then click OK. On the ribbon, click the FILE tab, click Export, and then create a PDF of the page. Navigate to an appropriate location and give the file an appropriate name. Close OneNote.

FIGURE B

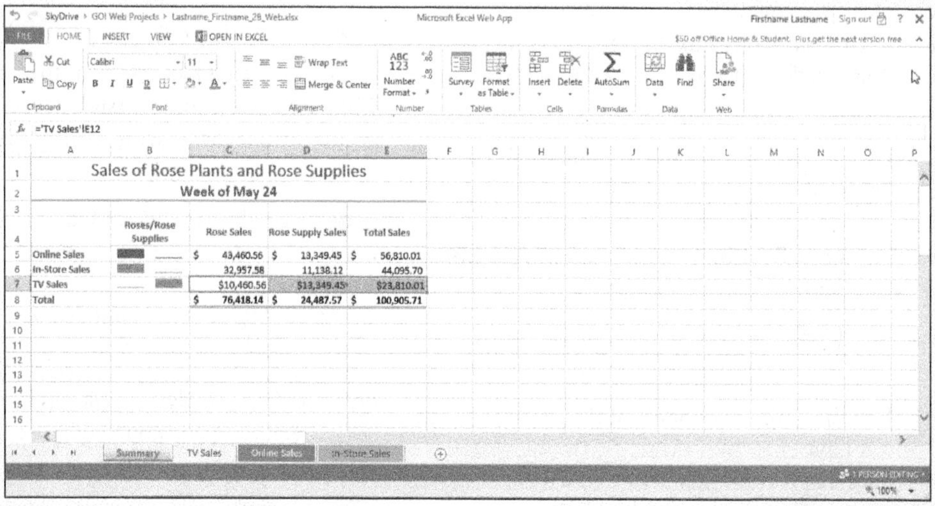

GO! with Microsoft Office 365

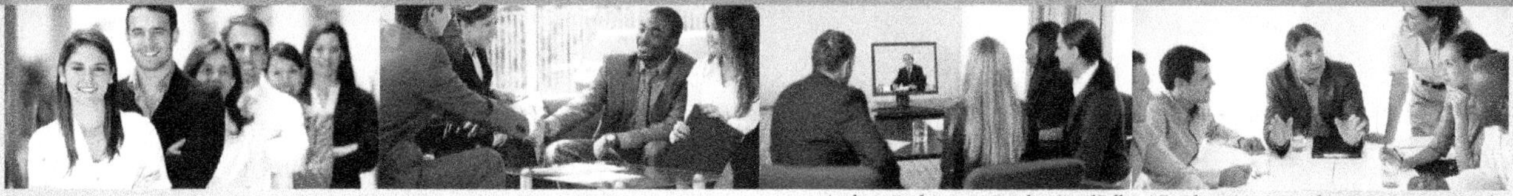

Andrew Rodriguez / Fotolia; FotolEdhar/ Fotolia; apops/ Fotolia; Yuri Arcurs/ Fotolia

Office 365 includes business-class security and is backed by Microsoft. For an organization, what does that mean?

When you and a few classmates work together on a class project, you are not concerned about the security of your data. You probably use free personal email services such as Hotmail, Gmail, or Yahoo Mail to exchange documents, or perhaps you post your documents to free services such as Google Docs.

Organizations, on the other hand—even small ones with only two or three employees—must be concerned with the privacy and security of their data. Organizations cannot entrust their data and confidential communications to free services that may change frequently or that have no legal responsibility for the security of the data.

Organizations must provide each employee with a company email address rather than having each employee use his or her own personal free email address for business communications. Organizations must provide a central storage location for its data rather than having employees store data on flash drives or local hard drives with no control or oversight.

An organization must have a ***secure environment***, which is a system that uses controlled ***servers***—computers that provide services on a network such as an email server or a file server—to ensure the security and privacy of email, to control the storage and use of information, and to protect against the loss of confidential data.

Most small organizations cannot afford to hire the people with the skills necessary to install and maintain servers. So to establish and maintain a secure environment, many small organizations contract with and rely on small IT—the acronym for *Information Technology*—hosting companies to host their email communications and to provide secure storage.

Activity | Using Lync to Collaborate by Using a Video Call

This group project relates to the **Bell Orchid Hotels.** If your instructor assigns this project to your class, you can expect to use **Lync** in **Office 365** to collaborate on the following tasks for this chapter:

- If you are in the **Accounting Group**, you and your teammates will conduct a video call to discuss and agree on a workbook to summarize hotel rooms sold over a four-week period in April.
- If you are in the **Engineering Group**, you and your teammates will conduct a video call to discuss and agree on a workbook summarizing Maintenance Expenses for the first quarter.
- If you are in the **Food and Beverage Group**, you and your teammates will conduct a video call to discuss and agree on a Menu Analysis workbook to analyze the profitability of the ten most popular entrees in the hotel's restaurant.
- If you are in the **Human Resources Group**, you and your teammates will conduct a video call to discuss and agree on a Salary Analysis workbook summarizing the pay of salaried employees over the first six months of operation.
- If you are in the **Operations Group**, you and your teammates will conduct a video call to discuss and agree on a workbook for Rooms and Housekeeping Service Analysis that will be used to determine ongoing needs for housekeeping service.
- If you are in the **Sales and Marking Group**, you and your teammates will conduct a video call to discuss and agree on a Rooms Sold Analysis workbook summarizing rooms sold by four salespersons during January-June that will be used to develop a marketing plan for the rest of the year.

FIGURE A

END OF CHAPTER

SUMMARY

Use Flash Fill to recognize a pattern in data and automatically fill in values when you enter examples of desired output. Flash Fill can split data from two or more cells or combine data from two cells.

Functions are formulas that Excel provides and that perform calculations by using specific values in a particular order or structure. Statistical functions are useful to analyze a group of measurements.

You can navigate among worksheets in a workbook by clicking the sheet tabs, which identify each worksheet in a workbook. Use multiple worksheets in a workbook to organize data in a logical arrangement.

Dates are a value you can enter in a cell to which Excel assigns a serial value—a number—so that you can treat dates like other numbers. For example, you can find the number of days between two dates.

GO! LEARN IT ONLINE

Review the concepts and key terms in this chapter by completing these online challenges, which you can find at **www.pearsonhighered.com/go**.

Matching and Multiple Choice: Answer matching and multiple choice questions to test what you learned in this chapter. MyITLab®

Crossword Puzzle: Spell out the words that match the numbered clues, and put them in the puzzle squares.

Flipboard: Flip through the definitions of the key terms in this chapter and match them with the correct term.

GO! FOR JOB SUCCESS

Video: Customer Service

Your instructor may assign this video to your class, and then ask you to think about, or discuss with your classmates, these questions:

FotolEdhar / Fotolia

How could Lee have been more helpful to the customer?

What did the supervisor, Christine, do to calm the customer?

What might SunTel do on a company-wide basis to create a better customer service experience?

END OF CHAPTER

REVIEW AND ASSESSMENT GUIDE FOR EXCEL CHAPTER 2

Your instructor may assign one or more of these projects to help you review the chapter and assess your mastery and understanding of the chapter.

Review and Assessment Guide for Excel Chapter 2			
Project	**Apply Skills from These Chapter Objectives**	**Project Type**	**Project Location**
2C	Objectives 1-6 from Project 2A	**2C Skills Review** A guided review of the skills from Project 2A.	On the following pages
2D	Objectives 7-12 from Project 2B	**2D Skills Review** A guided review of the skills from Project 2B.	On the following pages
2E	Objectives 1-6 from Project 2A	**2E Mastery (Grader Project)** A demonstration of your mastery of the skills in Project 2A with extensive decision making.	In MyITLab and on the following pages
2F	Objectives 7-12 from Project 2B	**2F Mastery (Grader Project)** A demonstration of your mastery of the skills in Project 2B with extensive decision making.	In MyITLab and on the following pages
2G	Objectives 1-12 from Projects 2A and 2B	**2G Mastery (Grader Project)** A demonstration of your mastery of the skills in Projects 2A and 2B with extensive decision making.	In MyITLab and on the following pages
2H	Combination of Objectives from Projects 2A and 2B	**2H GO! Fix It** A demonstration of your mastery of the skills in Projects 2A and 2B by creating a correct result from a document that contains errors you must find.	Online
2I	Combination of Objectives from Projects 2A and 2B	**2I GO! Make It** A demonstration of your mastery of the skills in Projects 2A and 2B by creating a result from a supplied picture.	Online
2J	Combination of Objectives from Projects 2A and 2B	**2J GO! Solve It** A demonstration of your mastery of the skills in Projects 2A and 2B, your decision-making skills, and your critical thinking skills. A task-specific rubric helps you self-assess your result.	Online
2K	Combination of Objectives from Projects 2A and 2B	**2K GO! Solve It** A demonstration of your mastery of the skills in Projects 2A and 2B, your decision-making skills, and your critical thinking skills. A task-specific rubric helps you self-assess your result.	On the following pages
2L	Combination of Objectives from Projects 2A and 2B	**2L GO! Think** A demonstration of your understanding of the Chapter concepts applied in a manner that you would outside of college. An analytic rubric helps you and your instructor grade the quality of your work by comparing it to the work an expert in the discipline would create.	On the following pages
2M	Combination of Objectives from Projects 2A and 2B	**2M GO! Think** A demonstration of your understanding of the Chapter concepts applied in a manner that you would outside of college. An analytic rubric helps you and your instructor grade the quality of your work by comparing it to the work an expert in the discipline would create.	Online
2N	Combination of Objectives from Projects 2A and 2B	**2N You and GO!** A demonstration of your understanding of the Chapter concepts applied in a manner that you would in a personal situation. An analytic rubric helps you and your instructor grade the quality of your work.	Online
2O	Combination of Objectives from Projects 2A and 2B	**2O Cumulative Group Project for Excel Chapter 2** A demonstration of your understanding of concepts and your ability to work collaboratively in a group role-playing assessment, requiring both collaboration and self-management.	Online

GLOSSARY

GLOSSARY OF CHAPTER KEY TERMS

Arguments The values that an Excel function uses to perform calculations or operations.

AVERAGE function An Excel function that adds a group of values, and then divides the result by the number of values in the group.

Comparison operators Symbols that evaluate each value to determine if it is the same (=), greater than (>), less than (<), or in between a range of values as specified by the criteria.

Conditional format A format that changes the appearance of a cell—for example, by adding cell shading or font color—based on a condition; if the condition is true, the cell is formatted based on that condition, and if the condition is false, the cell is *not* formatted.

COUNT A statistical function that counts the number of cells in a range that contain numbers.

COUNTIF function A statistical function that counts the number of cells within a range that meet the given condition and that has two arguments—the range of cells to check and the criteria.

Criteria Conditions that you specify in a logical function.

Data bar A cell format consisting of a shaded bar that provides a visual cue to the reader about the value of a cell relative to other cells; the length of the bar represents the value in the cell—a longer bar represents a higher value and a shorter bar represents s lower value.

Detail sheets The worksheets that contain the details of the information summarized on a summary sheet.

Drag and drop The action of moving a selection by dragging it to a new location.

Excel table A series of rows and columns that contains related data that is managed independently from the data in other rows and columns in the worksheet.

Filter The process of displaying only a portion of the data based on matching a specific value to show only the data that meets the criteria that you specify.

Find and replace A command that searches the cells in a worksheet—or in a selected range—for matches and then replaces each match with a replacement value of your choice.

Flash Fill Recognizes a pattern in your data, and then automatically fills in values when you enter examples of the output that you want. Use it to split data from two or more cells or to combine data from two cells.

Formula AutoComplete An Excel feature that, after typing an = (equal sign) and the beginning letter or letters of a function name, displays a list of function names that match the typed letter(s), and from which you can insert the function by pointing to its name and pressing the Tab key or double-clicking.

Freeze Panes A command that enables you to select one or more rows or columns and freeze (lock) them into place; the locked rows and columns become separate panes.

Function A predefined formula—a formula that Excel has already built for you—that performs calculations by using specific values in a particular order or structure.

IF function A function that uses a logical test to check whether a condition is met, and then returns one value if true, and another value if false.

Logical functions A group of functions that test for specific conditions and that typically use conditional tests to determine whether specified conditions are true or false.

Logical test Any value or expression that can be evaluated as being true or false.

MAX function An Excel function that determines the largest value in a selected range of values.

MEDIAN function An Excel function that finds the middle value that has as many values above it in the group as are below it; it differs from AVERAGE in that the result is not affected as much by a single value that is greatly different from the others.

MIN function An Excel function that determines the smallest value in a selected range of values.

Navigate The process of moving within a worksheet or workbook.

NOW function An Excel function that retrieves the date and time from your computer's calendar and clock and inserts the information into the selected cell.

Pane A portion of a worksheet window bounded by and separated from other portions by vertical and horizontal bars.

Paste The action of placing cell contents that have been copied or moved to the Clipboard into another location.

Paste area The target destination for data that has been cut or copied using the Office Clipboard.

Paste Options gallery A gallery of buttons that provides a Live Preview of all the Paste options available in the current context.

Print Titles An Excel command that enables you to specify rows and columns to repeat on each printed page.

Scale to Fit Excel commands that enable you to stretch or shrink the width, height, or both, of printed output to fit a maximum number of pages.

Sheet tabs The labels along the lower border of the workbook window that identify each worksheet.

Sort The process of arranging data in a specific order based on the value in each field.

Split Splits the window into multiple resizable panes that contain views of your worksheet. This is useful to view multiple distant parts of your worksheet at one time.

Statistical functions Excel functions, including the AVERAGE, MEDIAN, MIN, and MAX functions, which are useful to analyze a group of measurements.

SUM function A predefined formula that adds all the numbers in a selected range of cells.

Summary sheet A worksheet where totals from other worksheets are displayed and summarized.

Volatile A term used to describe an Excel function that is subject to change each time the workbook is reopened; for example the NOW function updates itself to the current date and time each time the workbook is opened.

Apply 2A skills from these Objectives:

1. Use Flash Fill and the SUM, AVERAGE, MEDIAN, MIN, and MAX Functions
2. Move Data, Resolve Error Messages, and Rotate Text
3. Use COUNTIF and IF Functions and Apply Conditional Formatting
4. Use Date & Time Functions and Freeze Panes
5. Create, Sort, and Filter an Excel Table
6. View, Format, and Print a Large Worksheet

Skills Review Project 2C Roses

In the following Skills Review, you will edit a worksheet detailing the current inventory of Roses at the Pasadena nursery. Your completed workbook will look similar to Figure 2.55.

PROJECT FILES

For Project 2C, you will need the following file:

e02C_Roses

You will save your workbook as:

Lastname_Firstname_2C_Roses

PROJECT RESULTS

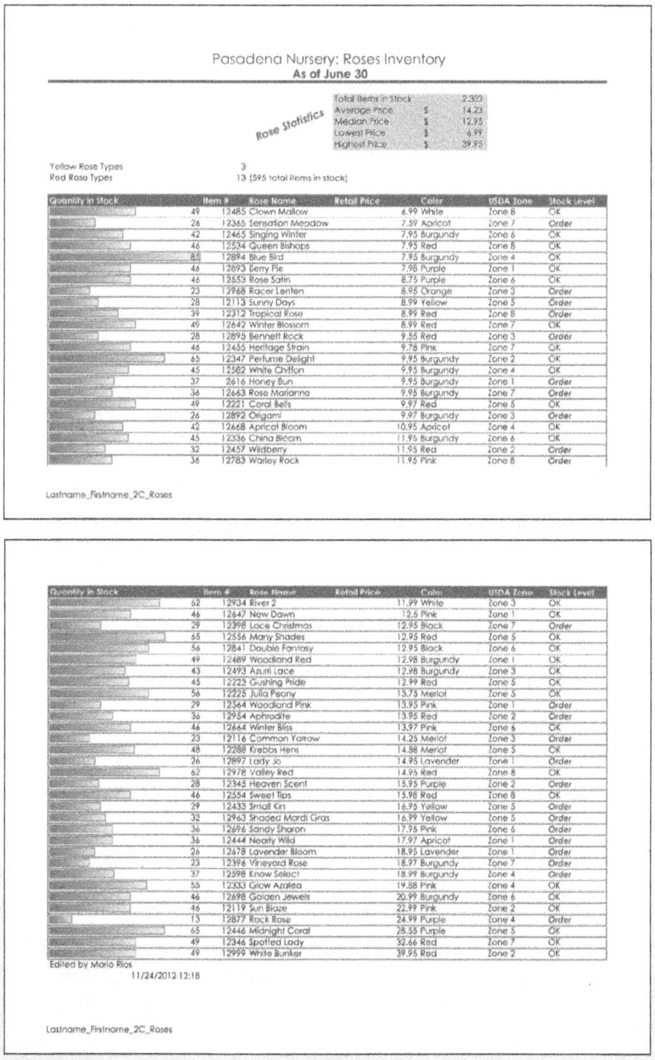

FIGURE 2.55

(Project 2C Roses continues on the next page)

CHAPTER REVIEW

Skills Review Project 2C Roses (continued)

1 Start Excel. From your student files, locate and open **e02C_Roses**. Save the file in your **Excel Chapter 2** folder as **Lastname_Firstname_2C_Roses**

a. In the **column heading area**, point to **column C** to display the [↓] pointer, and then drag to the right to select **columns C:D**. On the **HOME tab**, in the **Cells group**, click the **Insert button arrow**, and then click Insert **Sheet Columns**.

b. Click cell **C14**, type **12113** and then on the **Formula Bar**, click **Enter** to confirm the entry and keep cell **C14** as the active cell. On the **HOME tab**, in the **Editing group**, click **Fill**, and then click **Flash Fill**.

c. Click cell **D14**, type **Zone 5** On the **Formula Bar**, click **Enter** to confirm the entry and keep the cell active. Press Ctrl + E, which is the keyboard shortcut for Flash Fill.

d. Select **column B**, and then in the **Cells group**, click the **Delete button arrow**. Click **Delete Sheet Columns**.

2 In cell **B13** type **Item #** and press Enter.

a. Select **column C**, and then on the **HOME tab**, in the **Clipboard group**, click **Cut**. Click cell **G1**, and then in the **Clipboard group**, click the upper portion of the **Paste** button.

b. Select and then delete **column C**. In cell **F13** type **USDA Zone** and in cell **G13** type **Stock Level**

c. Select columns **A:G**. In the **Cells group**, click **Format**, and then click **AutoFit Column Width**.

d. Press Ctrl + Home. **Merge & Center** cell **A1** across the range **A1:G1**, and then apply the **Title** cell style. **Merge & Center** cell **A2** across the range **A2:G2**, and then apply the **Heading 1** cell style. Click **Save**.

3 Click cell **B4**. On the **FORMULAS tab**, in the **Function Library group**, click **AutoSum**, and then within the parentheses, type **a14:a68** which is the range containing the quantities for each item.

a. Click cell **B5**, in the **Function Library group**, click **More Functions**. Point to **Statistical**, click **AVERAGE**, and then in the **Number1** box, type **d14:d68** which is the range containing the *Retail Price* for each item. Click **OK**.

b. Click cell **B6**. In the **Function Library group**, click **More Functions**, point to **Statistical**, and then click **MEDIAN**. In the **Function Arguments** dialog box, to the right of the **Number1** box, click **Collapse Dialog**, and then select the range **D14:D68**. Click **Expand Dialog**, and then click **OK**. Recall that you can select or type a range and that you can collapse the dialog box to make it easier to view your selection.

c. Click cell **B7**, and then by typing or selecting, insert the **MIN** function to determine the lowest **Retail Price**. Click cell **B8**, and then insert the **MAX** function to determine the highest **Retail Price**.

4 Select cell **B4**. On the **HOME tab**, apply **Comma Style**, and then click **Decrease Decimal** two times. Select the range **B5:B8**, and then apply the **Accounting Number Format**.

a. Select the range **A4:B8**. Point to the right edge of the selected range to display the [move] pointer. Drag the selected range to the right until the ScreenTip displays *D4:E8*, and then release the mouse button. AutoFit **column D**.

b. With the range **D4:E8** selected, on the **HOME tab**, in the **Styles group**, display the **Cell Styles** gallery, and then apply **20%—Accent1**.

c. In cell **C6**, type **Rose Statistics** Select the range **C4:C8**, right-click over the selection, and then click **Format Cells**. In the **Format Cells** dialog box, click the **Alignment tab**. Under **Text control**, select the **Merge cells** check box.

d. In the upper right portion of the dialog box, under **Orientation**, point to the **red diamond**, and then drag the diamond upward until the **Degrees** box indicates *20*. Click **OK**.

e. With the merged cell still selected, change the **Font Size** to **14**, and then apply **Bold** and **Italic**. Click the **Font Color button arrow**, and then in the fifth column, click the first color—**Blue, Accent 1**. Apply **Middle Align** and **Center** to the cell.

5 Click cell **B10**. On the **FORMULAS tab**, in the **Function Library group**, click **More Functions**, and then display the list of **Statistical** functions. Click **COUNTIF**.

a. As the range, type **e14:e68** which is the range with the color of each item. Click in the **Criteria** box, type **Yellow** and then click **OK** to calculate the number of yellow rose types.

(Project 2C Roses continues on the next page)

Skills Review Project 2C Roses (continued)

b. Click cell **G14**. On the **FORMULAS tab**, in the **Function Library group**, click **Logical**, and then on the list, click **IF**. If necessary, drag the title bar of the **Function Arguments** dialog box up or down so that you can view **row 14** on your screen.

c. With the insertion point in the **Logical_test** box, click cell **A14**, and then type **<40** Press Tab to move the insertion point to the **Value_if_true** box, and then type **Order** Press Tab to move the insertion point to the **Value_if_false** box, type **OK** and then click **OK**. Using the fill handle, copy the function in cell **G14** down through cell **G68**.

6 With the range **G14:G68** selected, on the **HOME tab**, in the **Styles group**, click **Conditional Formatting**. In the list, point to **Highlight Cells Rules**, and then click **Text that Contains**.

a. In the **Text That Contains** dialog box, with the insertion point blinking in the first box, type **Order** and then in the second box, click the arrow. On the list, click **Custom Format**.

b. In the **Format Cells** dialog box, on the **Font tab**, under **Font style**, click **Bold Italic**. Click the **Color arrow**, and then under **Theme Colors**, in the fourth column, click the first color—**Blue-Gray, Text 2**. Click **OK** two times to apply the font color, bold, and italic to the cells that contain the word *Order*.

c. Select the range **A14:A68**. In the **Styles group**, click **Conditional Formatting**. In the list, point to **Data Bars**, and then under **Gradient Fill**, click **Red Data Bar**. Click anywhere to cancel the selection.

d. Select the range **E14:E68**. On the **HOME tab**, in the **Editing group**, click **Find & Select**, and then click **Replace**. In the **Find and Replace** dialog box, in the **Find what** box, type **Deep Burgundy** and then in the **Replace with** box type **Burgundy** Click **Replace All** and then click **OK**. In the lower right corner of the **Find and Replace** dialog box, click **Close**.

e. Scroll down as necessary, and then click cell **A70**. Type **Edited by Maria Rios** and then press Enter. With cell **A71** as the active cell, on the **FORMULAS tab**, in the **Function Library group**, click **Date & Time**. In the list of functions, click **NOW**, and then click **OK** to enter the current date and time. **Save** your workbook.

7 Click any cell in the data below row 13. Click the **INSERT tab**, and then in the **Tables group**, click **Table**. In the **Create Table** dialog box, be sure the **My table has headers** check box is selected, and then click **OK**. On the **DESIGN tab**, in the **Table Styles group**, click **More** and then under **Light**, locate and click **Table Style Light 9**.

a. In the header row of the table, click the **Retail Price arrow**, and then from the menu, click **Sort Smallest to Largest**. Click the **Color arrow**. On the menu, click the **(Select All)** check box to clear all the check boxes. Scroll as necessary and then select only the **Red** check box. Click OK.

b. Click anywhere in the table. On the **DESIGN tab**, in the **Table Style Options group**, select the **Total Row** check box. Click cell **A69**, click the arrow that displays to the right of cell **A69**, and then click **Sum**. In cell **B11**, type the result **13** and then press Tab. In cell **C11**, type **(595 total items in stock)** and then press Enter.

c. In the header row of the table, click the **Color arrow** and then click **Clear Filter From "Color"** to redisplay all of the data. Click anywhere in the table. Click the **DESIGN tab**, in the **Table Style Options group**, clear the **Total Row** check box, and then in the **Tools group**, click **Convert to Range**. Click **Yes**.

8 On the **PAGE LAYOUT tab**, in the **Themes group**, click **Themes** and then click the **Ion** theme. Change the **Orientation** to **Landscape**.

a. In the **Page Setup group**, click **Margins**, and then click **Custom Margins** to display the **Page Setup** dialog box.

b. On the **Margins tab**, under **Center on page**, select the **Horizontally** check box. On the **Header/Footer tab**, display the **Custom Footer**, and then in the **Left section**, insert the file name. Click **OK** two times.

c. In the **Page Setup** group, click **Print Titles** to redisplay the **Page Setup** dialog box. Under **Print titles**, click in the **Rows to repeat at top** box, and then at the right, click **Collapse Dialog**. From the **row heading area**, select **row 13**, and then click **Expand Dialog**. Click **OK** to print the column titles in row 13 at the top of every page.

d. Press Ctrl + F2 to display the **Print Preview**. At the bottom of the **Settings group**, click **No Scaling**, and

(Project 2C Roses continues on the next page)

CHAPTER REVIEW

Skills Review | Project 2C Roses (continued)

then on the displayed list, point to **Fit All Columns on One Page**.

e. On the left, click **Info**, and then in the lower right corner, click **Show All Properties**. As the **Tags**, type **inventory, Pasadena, roses** In the **Subject** box, type your course name and section number. Be sure your name displays as the author.

9 **Save** your workbook. Print or submit electronically as directed by your instructor. If required by your instructor, print or create an electronic version of your worksheets with formulas displayed by using the instructions in Excel Project 1A, and then Close Excel without saving so that you do not save the changes you made to print formulas.

END | You have completed Project 2C

CHAPTER REVIEW

Apply 2B skills from these Objectives:

7 Navigate a Workbook and Rename Worksheets
8 Enter Dates, Clear Contents, and Clear Formats
9 Copy and Paste by Using the Paste Options Gallery
10 Edit and Format Multiple Worksheets at the Same Time
11 Create a Summary Sheet with Column Sparklines
12 Format and Print Multiple Worksheets in a Workbook

Skills Review Project 2D Canada

In the following Skills Review, you will edit a workbook that summarizes sales in the Eastern and Western region of Canada. Your completed workbook will look similar to Figure 2.56.

PROJECT FILES

For Project 2D, you will need the following file:

e02D_Canada

You will save your workbook as:

Lastname_Firstname_2D_Canada

PROJECT RESULTS

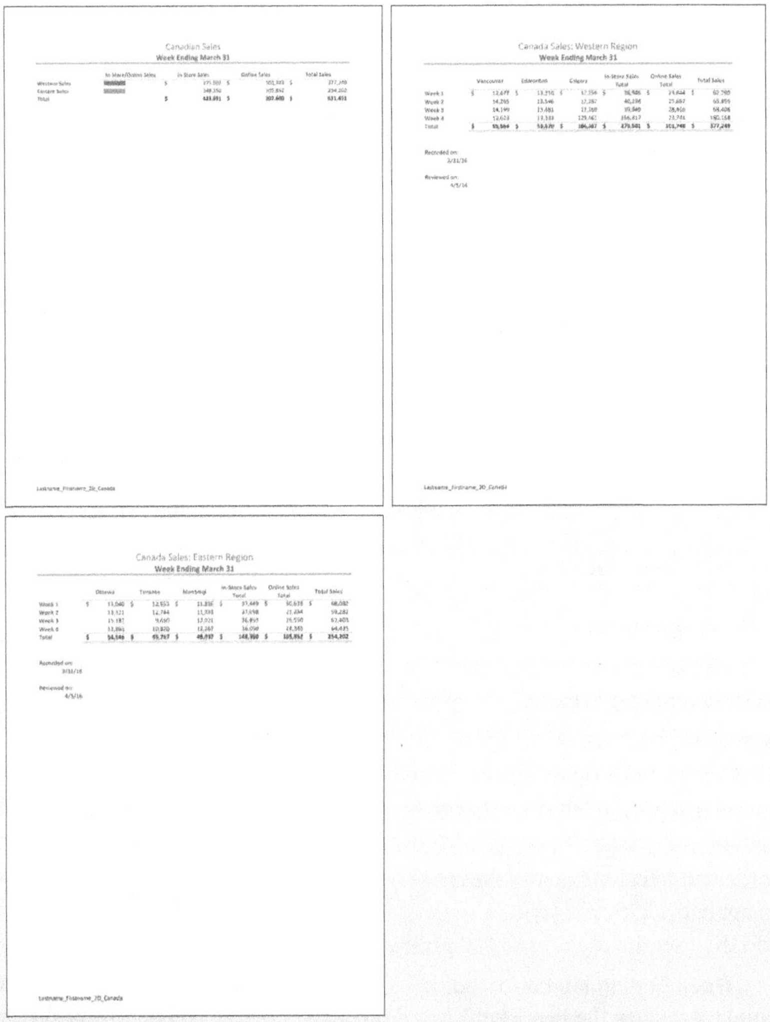

FIGURE 2.56

(Project 2D Canada continues on the next page)

CHAPTER REVIEW

Skills Review Project 2D Canada (continued)

1 Start Excel. From your student files, locate and open **e02D_Canada**. Save the file in your **Excel Chapter 2** folder as **Lastname_Firstname_2D_Canada**

a. Point to the **Sheet1 tab**, and then double-click to select the sheet tab name. Type **Western Sales** and then press Enter.

b. Point to the **Sheet2 tab**, right-click, and then from the shortcut menu, click **Rename**. Type **Eastern Sales** and press Enter.

c. Point to the **Western Sales sheet tab** and right-click. On the shortcut menu, point to **Tab Color**, and then in the last column, click the first color—**Green, Accent 6**. Change the **Tab Color** of the **Eastern Sales sheet tab** to **Blue, Accent 5**.

d. Click the **Western Sales sheet tab**, and then click cell **A13**. On the **HOME tab**, in the **Number group**, click the **Number Format arrow**. At the bottom of the list, click **More Number Formats** to display the **Number tab** of the **Format Cells** dialog box. Click the **3/14/12** type, and then click **OK**.

e. Click cell **A16**, type **4/5/16** and then press Enter. Click cell **A13**, and then on the **HOME tab**, in the **Clipboard group**, click **Format Painter**. Click cell **A16** to copy the date format from cell **A13** to cell **A16**.

f. Click cell **A1**. In the **Editing group**, click **Clear**, and then click **Clear Formats**.

g. Select the range **A5:A16**. On the **HOME tab**, in the **Clipboard group**, click **Copy**. At the bottom of the workbook window, click the **Eastern Sales sheet tab** to make it the active worksheet. Right-click cell **A5**, and then under **Paste Options**, click the first button—**Paste**. Display the **Western Sales** sheet. Press Esc to cancel the moving border.

2 With the **Western Sales** sheet active, make cell **A1** the active cell. Point to the sheet tab, right-click, and then on the shortcut menu, click **Select All Sheets**. Verify that *[Group]* displays in the title bar.

a. **Merge & Center** the text in cell **A1** across the range **A1:G1**, and then apply the **Title** cell style. Select **columns A:G**, and then set their widths to **100 pixels**.

b. Click cell **A2**, type **Week Ending March 31** and then on the **Formula Bar**, click the **Enter** button to keep cell **A2** as the active cell. **Merge & Center** the text across the range **A2:G2**, and then apply the **Heading 1** cell style.

c. Select the range **B4:G4**, and then apply the **Heading 3** cell style. In the **Alignment group**, click **Center**, **Middle Align**, and **Wrap Text**.

d. With the sheets still grouped and the **Western Sales** sheet active, click cell **E5**. On the **HOME tab**, in the **Editing group**, click **AutoSum**, and then press Enter. Click cell **E5**, and then drag the fill handle down to copy the formula through cell **E8**.

e. Click cell **G5**, type = click cell **E5**, type + click cell **F5**, and then press Enter. Copy the formula down through cell **G8**. In cell **A9**, type **Total** Select the range **B5:G9**, and then hold down Alt and press = to enter the SUM function for all the columns. Select the range **A5:A9**, and then apply the **Heading 4** cell style.

f. Select the range **B5:G5**, hold down Ctrl, and then select the range **B9:G9**. Apply the **Accounting Number Format** and decrease the decimal places to zero. Select the range **B6:G8**, and then apply **Comma Style** with zero decimal places. Select the range **B9:G9**, and then apply the **Total** cell style.

3 Click the **Eastern Sales sheet tab** to cancel the grouping and display the second worksheet.

a. To the right of the **Eastern Sales sheet tab**, click the **New sheet** button. **Rename** the new worksheet tab **Summary** and then change the **Tab Color** to **Gold, Accent 4**.

b. Widen **columns A:E** to **150** pixels. In cell **A1**, type **Canadian Sales** and then **Merge & Center** the title across the range **A1:E1**. Apply the **Title** cell style. In cell **A2**, type **Week Ending March 31** and then **Merge & Center** the text across the range **A2:E2**. Apply the **Heading 1** cell style. In cell **A5**, type **Western Sales** and in cell **A6**, type **Eastern Sales**

c. In cell **B4**, type **In-Store/Online Sales** and in cell **C4**, type **In-Store Sales** In cell **D4**, type **Online Sales** and in cell **E4**, type **Total Sales** Select the range **B4:E4**, apply the **Heading 3** cell style, and then **Center** these column titles.

d. Click cell **C5**. Type = and then click the **Western Sales sheet tab**. In the **Western Sales** worksheet, click cell **E9**, and then press Enter. Click cell **D5**. Type = and

(Project 2D Canada continues on the next page)

then click the **Western Sales sheet tab**. Click cell **F9**, and then press Enter.

e. By using the same technique, in cells **C6** and **D6**, insert the total **In-Store Sales** and **Online Sales** data from the **Eastern Sales** worksheet.

f. Select the range **C5:E6**, and then click **AutoSum** to total the two rows. In cell **A7**, type **Total** Select the range **C5:E6** again. In the lower right corner of the selection, click the **Quick Analysis** button, click **Totals**, and then click the first **Sum** button. Recall there are many ways to sum a group of cells.

g. Select the nonadjacent ranges **C5:E5** and **C7:E7**, and then apply **Accounting Number Format** with zero decimal places. Select the range **C6:E6**, and then apply **Comma Style** with zero decimal places. Select the range **C7:E7**, and then apply the **Total** cell style. Select the range **A5:A7** and apply the **Heading 4** cell style.

h. Click cell **B5**. On the **INSERT tab**, in the **Sparklines group**, click **Column**. In the **Create Sparklines** dialog box, with the insertion point blinking in the **Data Range** box, select the range **C5:D5** and then click **OK**.

i. Click cell **B6**, and then insert a **Column Sparkline** for the range **C6:D6**. With the **Eastern Sales** sparkline selected, in the **Style group**, click More [▾]. Apply the second style in the third row—**Sparkline Style Accent 2, (no dark or light)**.

4 Point to the **Summary sheet tab**, hold down the left mouse button to display a small black triangle, and drag to the left until the triangle and mouse pointer are to the left of the **Western Sales sheet tab**, and then release the left mouse button to move the sheet to the first position in the workbook.

a. Be sure the **Summary** worksheet is the active sheet, and then press Ctrl + Home to move to cell **A1**. Point to the **Summary sheet tab**, right-click, and then click **Select All Sheets** to display [*Group*] in the title bar. On the **PAGE LAYOUT tab**, in the **Page Setup group**, click **Margins**, and then click **Custom Margins** to display the **Page Setup** dialog box. On the **Margins tab**, center the worksheets **Horizontally**. On the **Header/Footer tab**, insert the file name in the **left section** of the footer.

b. Display the **Print Preview** of the worksheets. Under **Settings**, click **No Scaling**, and then click **Fit All Columns on One Page**. Use the **Next** button to view all three worksheets.

c. On the left, click **Info**, and then in the lower right corner of the screen, click **Show All Properties**. As the **Tags**, type **Canada, sales** In the **Subject** box, type your course name and section number. Be sure your name displays as the author.

d. On the left, click **Save**. Print or submit electronically as directed by your instructor. If required by your instructor, print or create an electronic version of your worksheets with formulas displayed by using the instructions in Excel Project 1A, and then **Close** Excel without saving so that you do not save the changes you made to print formulas.

END | You have completed Project 2D

CONTENT-BASED ASSESSMENTS

MyITLab® grader

Apply 2A skills from these Objectives:

1. Use Flash Fill and the SUM, AVERAGE, MEDIAN, MIN, and MAX Functions
2. Move Data, Resolve Error Messages, and Rotate Text
3. Use COUNTIF and IF Functions and Apply Conditional Formatting
4. Use Date & Time Functions and Freeze Panes
5. Create, Sort, and Filter an Excel Table
6. View, Format, and Print a Large Worksheet

Mastering Excel Project 2E Plants

In the following project, you will edit a worksheet detailing the current inventory of plants at the Pasadena facility. Your completed worksheet will look similar to Figure 2.57.

PROJECT FILES

For Project 2E, you will need the following file:

e02E_Plants

You will save your workbook as:

Lastname_Firstname_2E_Plants

PROJECT RESULTS

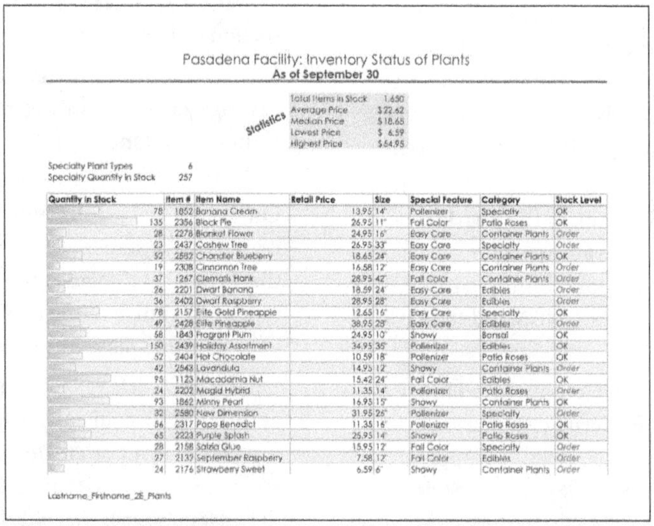

Pasadena Facility: Inventory Status of Plants

As of September 30

Statistics

Total Items in Stock	1,650
Average Price	$22.62
Median Price	$18.65
Lowest Price	$ 6.59
Highest Price	$54.95

Specialty Plant Types	6
Specialty Quantity in Stock	257

Quantity in Stock	Item #	Item Name	Retail Price	Size	Special Feature	Category	Stock Level
78	1852	Banana Cream	13.95	14"	Pollenizer	Specialty	OK
135	2356	Black Pie	26.95	11"	Fall Color	Patio Roses	OK
28	2278	Blanket Flower	24.95	16"	Easy Care	Container Plants	Order
23	2437	Cashew Tree	26.95	33"	Easy Care	Specialty	Order
52	2582	Chandler Blueberry	18.65	24"	Easy Care	Container Plants	OK
19	2308	Cinnamon Tree	16.58	12"	Easy Care	Container Plants	Order
37	1267	Clematis Hank	28.95	42"	Fall Color	Container Plants	Order
26	2201	Dwarf Banana	18.59	24"	Easy Care	Edibles	Order
36	2402	Dwarf Raspberry	28.95	28"	Easy Care	Edibles	Order
78	2157	Elite Gold Pineapple	12.65	16"	Easy Care	Specialty	OK
49	2428	Elite Pineapple	38.95	28"	Easy Care	Edibles	Order
58	1843	Fragrant Plum	24.95	10"	Showy	Bonsai	OK
150	2439	Holiday Assortment	34.95	35"	Pollenizer	Edibles	OK
52	2404	Hot Chocolate	10.59	18"	Pollenizer	Patio Roses	OK
42	2543	Lavandula	14.95	12"	Showy	Container Plants	Order
95	1123	Macadamia Nut	15.42	24"	Fall Color	Edibles	OK
24	2202	Magid Hybrid	11.35	14"	Pollenizer	Patio Roses	Order
93	1862	Minny Pearl	16.95	15"	Showy	Container Plants	OK
32	2580	New Dimension	31.95	26"	Pollenizer	Specialty	Order
56	2317	Pops Benedict	11.35	16"	Pollenizer	Patio Roses	OK
65	2223	Purple Splash	25.95	14"	Showy	Patio Roses	OK
28	2158	Salzia Glue	15.95	12"	Fall Color	Specialty	Order
27	2139	September Raspberry	7.58	12"	Fall Color	Edibles	Order
24	2176	Strawberry Sweet	6.59	6"	Showy	Container Plants	Order

Lastname_Firstname_2E_Plants

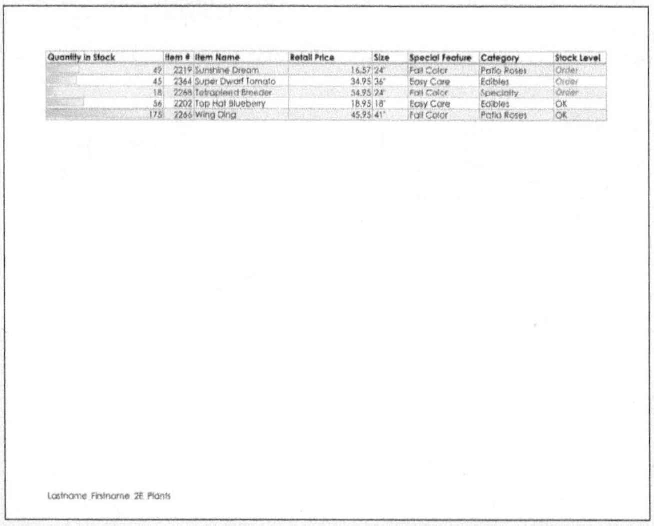

Quantity in Stock	Item #	Item Name	Retail Price	Size	Special Feature	Category	Stock Level
49	2219	Sunshine Dream	16.57	24"	Fall Color	Patio Roses	Order
45	2364	Super Dwarf Tomato	34.95	36"	Easy Care	Edibles	Order
18	2268	Tetraploid Breeder	54.95	24"	Fall Color	Specialty	Order
56	2202	Top Hat Blueberry	18.95	18"	Easy Care	Edibles	OK
175	2266	Wing Ding	45.95	41"	Fall Color	Patio Roses	OK

Lastname_Firstname_2E_Plants

FIGURE 2.57

(Project 2E Plants continues on the next page)

CONTENT-BASED ASSESSMENTS

Mastering Excel Project 2E Plants (continued)

1 Start Excel. From your student files, locate and open **e02E_Plants**, and then **Save** the file in your **Excel Chapter 2** folder as **Lastname_Firstname_2E_Plants**

2 To the right of **column B**, insert two new columns to create **new blank columns C and D**. By using **Flash Fill** in the two new columns, split the data in **column B** into a column for *Item #* in **column C** and *Category* in **column D**. As necessary, type **Item #** as the column title in **column C** and **Category** as the column title in **column D**.

3 Delete **column B**. By using the **Cut** and **Paste** commands, cut **column C**—*Category*—and paste it to **column H**, and then delete the empty **column C**. Apply **AutoFit** to **columns A:G**.

4 In cell **B4**, insert a function to calculate the **Total Items in Stock** by summing the **Quantity in Stock** data, and then apply **Comma Style** with zero decimal places to the result. In each cell in the range **B5:B8**, insert functions to calculate the Average, Median, Lowest, and Highest retail prices, and then apply the **Accounting Number Format** to each result.

5 Move the range **A4:B8** to the range **D4:E8**, apply the **40%—Accent4** cell style to the range, and then select **columns D:E** and **AutoFit**. In cell **C6**, type **Statistics** and then select the range **C4:C8**. In the **Format Cells** dialog box, merge the selected cells, and change the text **Orientation** to **25 Degrees**. Format the cell with **Bold**, a **Font Size** of **14 pt**, and then change the **Font Color** to **Blue-Gray, Text 2**. Apply **Middle Align** and **Align Right**.

6 In the **Category** column, **Replace All** occurrences of **Vine Roses** with **Patio Roses** In cell **B10**, use the **COUNTIF** function to count the number of **Specialty** plant types in the **Category** column.

7 In cell **H13**, type **Stock Level** In cell **H14**, enter an **IF** function to determine the items that must be ordered. If the **Quantity in Stock** is less than **50** the **Value_if_true** is **Order** Otherwise the **Value_if_false** is **OK** Fill the formula down through cell **H42**. Apply **Conditional Formatting** to the **Stock Level** column so that cells that contain the text *Order* are formatted with **Bold Italic** and with a **Color** of **Green, Accent 6**. Apply conditional formatting to the **Quantity in Stock** column by applying a **Gradient Fill Green Data Bar**.

8 Format the range **A13:H42** as a **Table** with headers, and apply the style **Table Style Light 20**. Sort the table from A to Z by **Item Name**, and then filter on the **Category** column to display the **Specialty** types. Display a **Total Row** in the table, and then in cell **A43**, **Sum** the **Quantity in Stock** for the **Specialty** items. Type the result in cell **B11**. Click in the table, and then on the **DESIGN tab**, remove the total row from the table. Clear the **Category** filter, and convert the table to a range.

9 **Merge & Center** the title and subtitle across **columns A:H**, and apply **Title** and **Heading 1** styles respectively. Change the theme to **Mesh**, and then select and **AutoFit** all the columns. Set the orientation to **Landscape**. In the **Page Setup** dialog box, center the worksheet **Horizontally**, insert a custom footer in the **left section** with the file name, and set **row 13** to repeat at the top of each page. Display the **Print Preview**. Apply the **Fit All Columns on One Page** setting.

10 As the **Tags**, type **plants inventory, Pasadena** As the **Subject**, type your course name and section number. Be sure your name displays as the **Author**. In **Backstage** view, on the left click **Save**, and then print or submit electronically as directed. If required by your instructor, print or create an electronic version of your worksheet with formulas displayed by using the instructions in Project 1A, and then close Excel without saving so that you do not save the changes you made to print formulas.

END | You have completed Project 2E

CONTENT-BASED ASSESSMENTS

Mastering Excel | Project 2F Bonus

MyITLab® grader

Apply 2B skills from these Objectives:

7 Navigate a Workbook and Rename Worksheets
8 Enter Dates, Clear Contents, and Clear Formats
9 Copy and Paste by Using the Paste Options Gallery
10 Edit and Format Multiple Worksheets at the Same Time
11 Create a Summary Sheet with Column Sparklines
12 Format and Print Multiple Worksheets in a Workbook

In the following project, you will edit a workbook that summarizes the compensation for the commercial salespersons who qualified for bonuses in the Western and Eastern Canadian regions. Your completed worksheets will look similar to Figure 2.58.

PROJECT FILES

For Project 2F, you will need the following file:

e02F_Bonus

You will save your workbook as:

Lastname_Firstname_2F_Bonus

PROJECT RESULTS

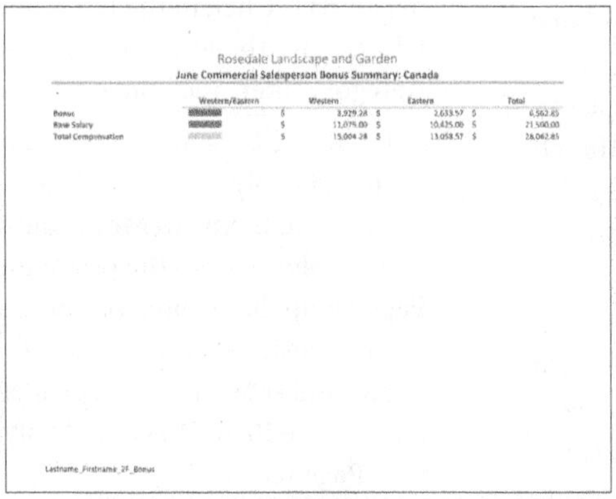

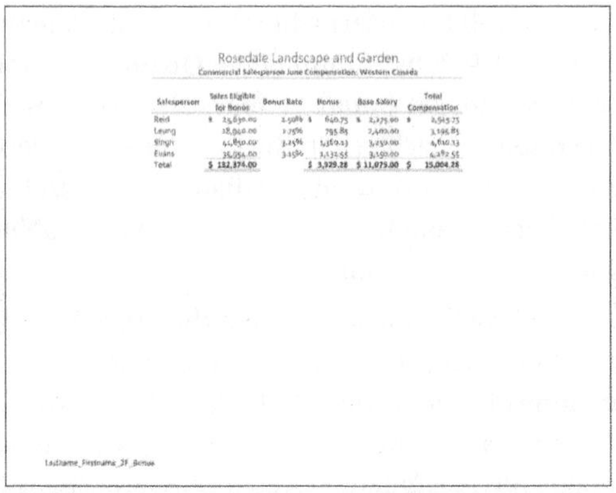

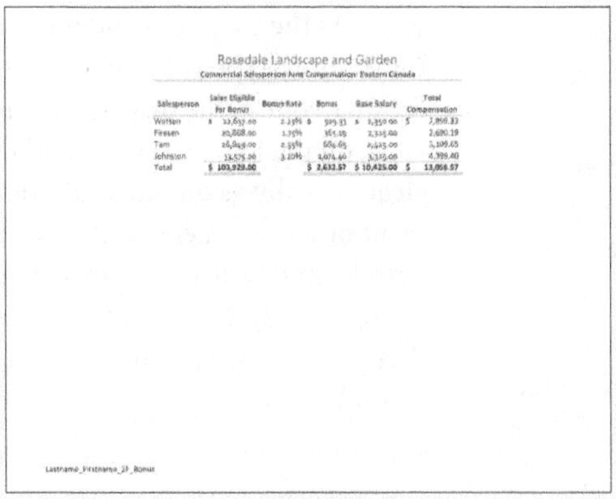

FIGURE 2.58

(Project 2F Bonus continues on the next page)

Mastering Excel Project 2F Bonus (continued)

1 **Start** Excel. From your student files, open **e02F_Bonus**, and then save the file in your **Excel Chapter 2** folder as **Lastname_Firstname_2F_Bonus**

2 Rename **Sheet1** as **Western** and change the **Tab Color** to **Brown, Accent 2**. Rename **Sheet2** as **Eastern** and change the **Tab Color** to **Orange, Accent 1**.

3 Click the **Western sheet tab** to make it the active sheet, and then group the worksheets. In cell **A1**, type **Rosedale Landscape and Garden** and then **Merge & Center** the text across the range **A1:F1**. Apply the **Title** cell style. **Merge & Center** the text in cell **A2** across the range **A2:F2**, and then apply the **Heading 3** cell style.

4 With the sheets still grouped, in cell **D5** calculate the **Bonus** for *Reid* by multiplying the **Sales Eligible for Bonus** times the **Bonus Rate**. Copy the formula down through cell **D8**. In cell **F5**, calculate **Total Compensation** by summing the **Bonus** and **Base Salary** for *Reid*. Copy the formula down through the cell **F8**.

5 In **row 9**, sum the columns for **Sales Eligible for Bonus, Bonus, Base Salary**, and **Total Compensation**. Apply the **Accounting Number Format** with two decimal places to the appropriate cells in **row 5** and **row 9** (do not include the percentages). Apply the **Comma Style** with two decimal places to the appropriate cells in **rows 6:8** (do not include the percentages). Apply the **Total** cell style to the appropriate cells in the Total row.

6 Click the **Eastern** sheet tab to ungroup the sheets, and then insert a new worksheet. Change the sheet name to **Summary** and then change the **Tab Color** to **Brown, Text 2**. Widen **column A** to **210** pixels, widen **columns B:E** to **155** pixels, and then move the **Summary** sheet so that it is the first sheet in the workbook. In cell **A1** of the **Summary** sheet, type **Rosedale Landscape and Garden** and then **Merge & Center** the title across the range **A1:E1**. Apply the **Title** cell style. In cell **A2**, type **June Commercial Salesperson Bonus Summary: Canada** and then **Merge & Center** the text across the range **A2:E2**. Apply the **Heading 1** cell style.

7 In the range **A5:A7**, type the following row titles and then apply the **Heading 4** cell style:

Bonus

Base Salary

Total Compensation

8 In the range **B4:E4**, type the following column titles, and then **Center** and apply the **Heading 3** cell style.

Western/Eastern

Western

Eastern

Total

9 In cell **C5**, enter a formula that references cell **D9** in the **Western** worksheet so that the total bonus amount for the Western region displays in **C5**. Create similar formulas to enter the total **Base Salary** for the Western region in cell **C6**. Using the same technique, enter formulas in the range **D5:D6** so that the **Eastern** totals display.

10 Sum the **Bonus** and **Base Salary** rows, and then calculate **Total Compensation** for the **Western, Eastern**, and **Total** columns.

11 In cell **B5**, insert a **Column Sparkline** for the range **C5:D5**. In cells **B6** and **B7**, insert **Column** sparklines for the appropriate ranges to compare Western totals with Eastern totals. To the sparkline in cell **B5**, apply the second style in the third row—**Sparkline Style Accent 2, (no dark or light)**. To the sparkline in cell **B6**, apply the first style in the fifth row—**Sparkline Style Dark #1**. To the sparkline in cell **B7**, apply the first style in the fourth row—**Sparkline Style Accent 1, Lighter 40%**.

12 **Group** the three worksheets, and then in the **Page Setup** dialog box, center the worksheets **Horizontally** on the page, and insert a **Custom Footer** in the **left section** with the file name. Change the **Orientation** to **Landscape**.

13 As the **Tags**, type **June, bonus, compensation** As the **Subject**, type your course name and section number. Be sure your name displays as the **Author**. Click **Save**, and then print or submit your workbook electronically as directed. If required by your instructor, print or create an electronic version of your worksheets with formulas displayed by using the instructions in Project 1A, and then close Excel without saving so that you do not save the changes you made to print formulas.

END | You have completed Project 2F

CONTENT-BASED ASSESSMENTS

MyITLab® grader

Mastering Excel | Project 2G Inventory

Apply a combination of 2A and 2B skills:

1 Use Flash Fill and the SUM, AVERAGE, MEDIAN, MIN, and MAX Functions
2 Move Data, Resolve Error Messages, and Rotate Text
3 Use COUNTIF and IF Functions and Apply Conditional Formatting
4 Use Date & Time Functions and Freeze Panes
5 Create, Sort, and Filter an Excel Table
6 View, Format and Print a Large Worksheet
7 Navigate a Workbook and Rename Worksheets
8 Enter Dates, Clear Contents, and Clear Formats
9 Copy and Paste by Using the Paste Options Gallery
10 Edit and Format Multiple Worksheets at the Same Time
11 Create a Summary Sheet with Column Sparklines
12 Format and Print Multiple Worksheets in a Workbook

In the following project, you will edit a worksheet that summarizes the inventory of bulbs and trees at the Pasadena facility. Your completed workbook will look similar to Figure 2.59.

PROJECT FILES

For Project 2G, you will need the following file:

e02G_Inventory

You will save your workbook as

Lastname_Firstname_2G_Inventory

PROJECT RESULTS

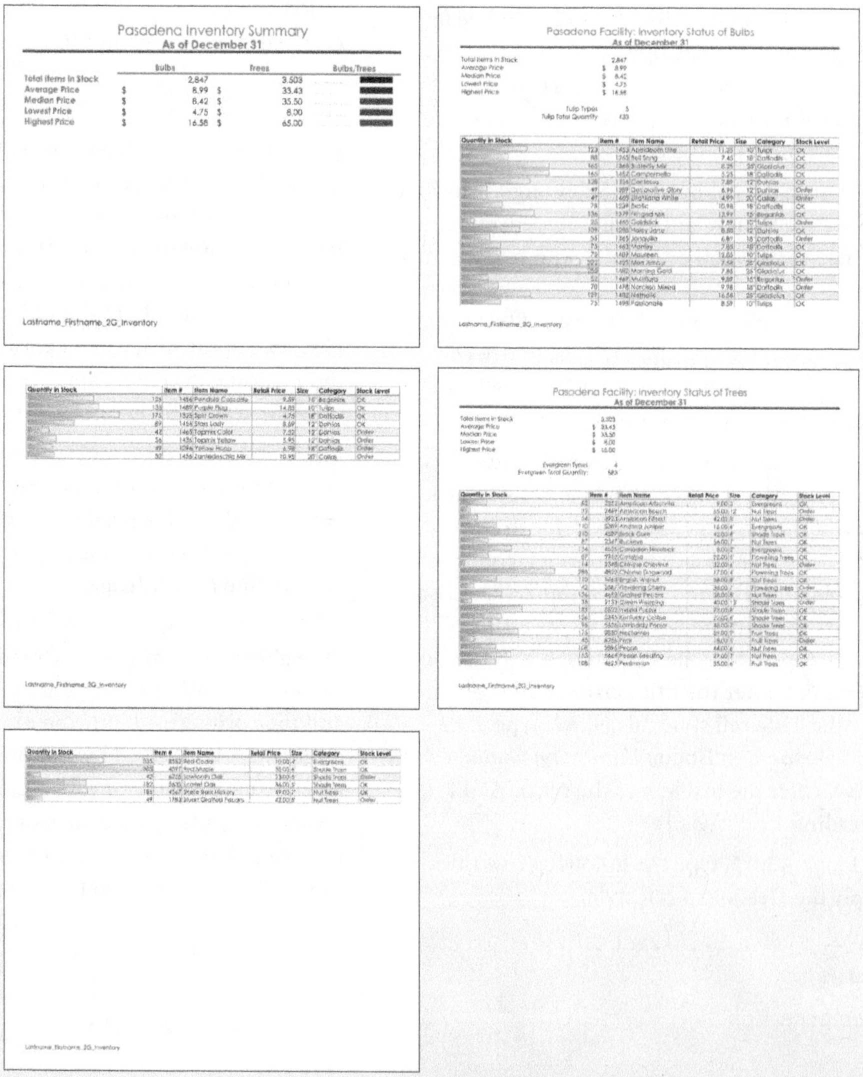

FIGURE 2.59

(Project 2G Inventory continues on the next page)

Mastering Excel Project 2G Inventory (continued)

1 Start Excel. From your student files, open **e02G_ Inventory**. Save the file in your **Excel Chapter 2** folder as **Lastname_Firstname_2G_Inventory.**

2 Change the **Theme** to **Slice**. Rename **Sheet1** as **Bulbs** and **Sheet2** as **Trees** Click the **Bulbs sheet tab** to make it the active sheet.

3 To the right of **column B**, insert two new columns to create **new blank columns C and D**. By using **Flash Fill** in the two new columns, split the data in **column B** into a column for *Item #* in **column C** and *Category* in **column D**. As necessary, type **Item #** as the column title in **column C** and **Category** as the column title in **column D**.

4 Delete **column B**. By using the **Cut** and **Paste** commands, cut **column C**—*Category*—and paste it to **column G**, and then delete the empty **column C**. Apply **AutoFit** to **columns A:F**.

5 Display the **Trees** worksheet, and then repeat Steps 3 and 4 on this worksheet.

6 Make the following calculations in each of the two worksheets *without* grouping the sheets:

- In cell **B4**, enter a function to sum the **Quantity in Stock** data, and then apply **Comma Style** with zero decimal places to the result.
- In cells **B5:B8**, enter formulas to calculate the Average, Median, Lowest, and Highest retail prices, and then apply the **Accounting Number Format.**

7 In each of the two worksheets, make the following calculations *without* grouping the sheets:

- In cell **B10**, enter a COUNTIF function to determine how many different types of **Tulips** are in stock on the **Bulbs** sheet and how many different types of **Evergreens** are in stock on the **Trees** worksheet.
- In cell **G14** type **Stock Level** In cell **G15**, enter an **IF** function to determine the items that must be ordered. If the **Quantity in Stock** is less than **75** the **Value_if_true** is **Order** Otherwise the **Value_ if_false** is **OK** Fill the formula down through all the rows.
- Apply **Conditional Formatting** to the **Stock Level** column so that cells that contain the text *Order* are formatted with **Bold Italic** with a **Font Color** of **Dark Blue, Text 2**. Apply **Gradient Fill Blue Data Bars** to the **Quantity in Stock** column.

8 In the **Bulbs** sheet, format the range **A14:G42** as a table with headers and apply **Table Style Light 20**. Insert a **Total Row**, filter by **Category** for **Tulips**, and then **Sum** the **Quantity in Stock** column. Record the result in cell **B11**.

9 Select the table, clear the filter, **Sort** the table on the **Item Name** column from **A to Z**, remove the **Total Row**, and then convert the table to a range. On the **Page Layout tab**, set **Print Titles** so that **row 14** repeats at the top of each page.

10 In the **Trees** sheet, format the range **A14:G42** as a table with headers and apply **Table Style Light 19**. Insert a **Total Row**, filter by **Category** for **Evergreens**, and then **Sum** the **Quantity in Stock** column. Record the result in cell **B11**.

11 Select the table, clear the filter, **Sort** the table on the **Item Name** column from **A to Z**, remove the **Total Row**, and then convert the table to a range.

12 On the **Page Layout tab**, set **Print Titles** so that **row 14** repeats at the top of each page, and then **Save** your workbook. **Group** the two worksheets. Center the title in cell **A1** across the range **A1:G1** and apply the **Title** cell style. Center the subtitle in cell **A2** across the range **A2:G2** and apply the **Heading 1** cell style. **Center** the worksheets **Horizontally**, change the **Orientation** to **Landscape**, display the **Print Preview**, and then change the **Settings** to **Fit All Columns on One Page**.

13 In **Backstage** view, on the left click **Save**, and then click the **Trees sheet tab** to cancel the grouping. Insert a new worksheet. Change the sheet name to **Summary** and then widen **columns A:D** to **170** pixels. Move the **Summary** sheet so that it is the first sheet in the workbook. In cell **A1**, type **Pasadena Inventory Summary** and then **Merge & Center** the title across **A1:D1**. Apply the **Title** cell style. In cell **A2**, type **As of December 31** and then **Merge & Center** the text across the range **A2:D2**. Apply the **Heading 1** cell style.

14 On the **Bulbs sheet**, **Copy** the range **A4:A8**. Display the **Summary sheet** and **Paste** the selection to cell **A5**. Apply the **Heading 4** cell style to the selection. In the **Summary sheet**, in cell **B4**, type **Bulbs** In cell **C4** type **Trees** In cell **D4** type **Bulbs/Trees** and then **Center** the column titles. Apply the **Heading 3** cell style.

(Project 2G Inventory continues on the next page)

CONTENT-BASED ASSESSMENTS

Mastering Excel | Project 2G Inventory (continued)

15 In cell **B5**, enter a formula that references cell **B4** in the **Bulbs sheet** so that the **Bulbs Total Items in Stock** displays in **B5**. Create similar formulas to enter the **Average Price**, **Median Price**, **Lowest Price**, and **Highest Price** from the **Bulbs sheet** into the **Summary** sheet in the range **B6:B9**. Enter formulas in the range **C5:C9** that reference the appropriate cells in the **Trees** worksheet.

16 To the range **B5:C5**, apply **Comma Style** with zero decimal places, and to the range **B6:C9**, apply **Accounting Number Format**. In cells **D5**, **D6**, **D7**, **D8**, and **D9**, insert **Column** sparklines using the values in the *Bulbs* and *Trees* columns. Format each sparkline using the first five Sparkline styles in the first row.

17 Center the **Summary** worksheet **Horizontally** and change the **Orientation** to **Landscape. Group** the worksheets and insert a footer in the left section with the **File Name**. As the **Tags**, type **Pasadena inventory** As the **Subject**, type your course name and section number. Be sure your name displays as the **Author**.

18 In **Backstage** view, on the left click **Save**, and then print or submit electronically as directed. If required by your instructor, print or create an electronic version of your worksheet with formulas displayed by using the instructions in Project 1A, and then close Excel without saving so that you do not save the changes you made to print formulas.

END | You have completed Project 2G

CONTENT-BASED ASSESSMENTS

Apply a combination of the 2A and 2B skills.

GO! Fix It | Project 2H Planters | Online

GO! Make It | Project 2I Salary | Online

GO! Solve It | Project 2J Sod | Online

GO! Solve It | Project 2K Products

PROJECT FILES

For Project 2K, you will need the following file:

e02K_Products

You will save your workbook as:

Lastname_Firstname_2K_Products

From your student data files, open the file e02K_Products and save it as **Lastname_Firstname_2K_Products** This workbook contains two worksheets: one for U.S. sales data by product and one for Canadian sales data by product. Complete the two worksheets by calculating totals by product and by month. Then calculate the Percent of Total for all products by dividing the Product Total by the Monthly Total, using absolute cell references as necessary. Format the percentages with two decimal places and center in the cells. Format the worksheets attractively and apply financial formatting. Insert a new worksheet that summarizes the monthly totals for the U.S. and Canada. Enter the months as the column titles and the countries as the row titles. Include a Product Total column and a column for sparklines titled **April/May/June** Format the Summary worksheet attractively with a title and subtitle, insert column sparklines that compare the months, and apply financial formatting. Include the file name in the footer, add appropriate document properties, and submit as directed.

(Project 2K Products continues on the next page)

GO! Solve It Project 2K Products (continued)

Performance Level

Performance Criteria	Exemplary: You consistently applied the relevant skills	Proficient: You sometimes, but not always, applied the relevant skills	Developing: You rarely or never applied the relevant skills
Create formulas	All formulas are correct and are efficiently constructed.	Formulas are correct but not always constructed in the most efficient manner.	One or more formulas are missing or incorrect; or only numbers were entered.
Create Summary worksheet	Summary worksheet created properly.	Summary worksheet was created but the data, sparklines, or formulas were incorrect.	No Summary worksheet was created.
Format attractively and appropriately	Formatting is attractive and appropriate.	Adequately formatted but difficult to read or unattractive.	Inadequate or no formatting.

END | You have completed Project 2K

OUTCOMES-BASED ASSESSMENTS

RUBRIC

The following outcomes-based assessments are open-ended assessments. That is, there is no specific correct result; your result will depend on your approach to the information provided. Make Professional Quality your goal. Use the following scoring rubric to guide you in how to approach the problem and then to evaluate how well your approach solves the problem.

The *criteria*—Software Mastery, Content, Format and Layout, and Process—represent the knowledge and skills you have gained that you can apply to solving the problem. The *levels of performance*—Professional Quality, Approaching Professional Quality, or Needs Quality Improvements—help you and your instructor evaluate your result.

	Your completed project is of Professional Quality if you:	Your completed project is Approaching Professional Quality if you:	Your completed project Needs Quality Improvements if you:
1-Software Mastery	Choose and apply the most appropriate skills, tools, and features and identify efficient methods to solve the problem.	Choose and apply some appropriate skills, tools, and features, but not in the most efficient manner.	Choose inappropriate skills, tools, or features, or are inefficient in solving the problem.
2-Content	Construct a solution that is clear and well organized, contains content that is accurate, appropriate to the audience and purpose, and is complete. Provide a solution that contains no errors in spelling, grammar, or style.	Construct a solution in which some components are unclear, poorly organized, inconsistent, or incomplete. Misjudge the needs of the audience. Have some errors in spelling, grammar, or style, but the errors do not detract from comprehension.	Construct a solution that is unclear, incomplete, or poorly organized; contains some inaccurate or inappropriate content; and contains many errors in spelling, grammar, or style. Do not solve the problem.
3-Format & Layout	Format and arrange all elements to communicate information and ideas, clarify function, illustrate relationships, and indicate relative importance.	Apply appropriate format and layout features to some elements, but not others. Overuse features, causing minor distraction.	Apply format and layout that does not communicate information or ideas clearly. Do not use format and layout features to clarify function, illustrate relationships, or indicate relative importance. Use available features excessively, causing distraction.
4-Process	Use an organized approach that integrates planning, development, self-assessment, revision, and reflection.	Demonstrate an organized approach in some areas, but not others; or, use an insufficient process of organization throughout.	Do not use an organized approach to solve the problem.

OUTCOMES-BASED ASSESSMENTS

Apply a combination of the 2A and 2B skills.

GO! Think Project 2L Palms

PROJECT FILES

For Project 2L, you will need the following file:

e02L_Palms

You will save your workbook as:

Lastname_Firstname_2L_Palms

Melanie Castillo, Product Manager for Rosedale Landscape and Garden, has requested a worksheet that summarizes the palm tree inventory data for the month of March. Melanie would like the worksheet to include the total Quantity in Stock and Number of Items for each of the four categories of palm trees, and she would like the items to be sorted from lowest to highest retail price. She would also like a separate column for Item # and for Category.

Edit the workbook to provide Melanie with the information requested, and use the Table feature to find the data requested. Format the worksheet titles and data and include an appropriately formatted table so that the worksheet is professional and easy to read and understand. Insert a footer with the file name and add appropriate document properties. Save the file as **Lastname_Firstname_2L_Palms** and print or submit as directed by your instructor.

END | You have completed Project 2L

GO! Think Project 2M Contracts Online

Build from Scratch

You and GO! Project 2N Annual Expenses Online

GO! Cumulative Group Project Project 2O Bell Orchid Hotels Online

Analyzing Data with Pie Charts, Line Charts, and What-If Analysis Tools

GO! to Work Video E3

3

EXCEL 2013

PROJECT 3A

OUTCOMES
Present fund data in a pie chart.

OBJECTIVES

1. Chart Data with a Pie Chart
2. Format a Pie Chart
3. Edit a Workbook and Update a Chart
4. Use Goal Seek to Perform What-If Analysis

PROJECT 3B

OUTCOMES
Make projections by using what-if analysis and present projections in a line chart.

OBJECTIVES

5. Design a Worksheet for What-If Analysis
6. Answer What-If Questions by Changing Values in a Worksheet
7. Chart Data with a Line Chart

In This Chapter

In this chapter, you will work with two different types of commonly used charts that make it easy to visualize data. You will create a pie chart in a separate chart sheet to show how the parts of a fund contribute to a total fund. Pie charts are one type of chart you can use to show part-to-whole relationships. You will also practice by using parentheses in a formula, calculate the percentage rate of an increase, answer what-if questions, and then chart data in a line chart to show the flow of data over time and the flow of one value to the next. In this chapter, you will also practice formatting the axes in a line chart.

The projects in this chapter relate to the city of **Pacifica Bay**, a coastal city south of San Francisco. The city's access to major transportation provides both residents and businesses an opportunity to compete in the global marketplace. The city's mission is to create a more beautiful and more economically viable community for its residents. Each year the city welcomes a large number of tourists who enjoy exploring the rocky coastline and seeing the famous landmarks in San Francisco. The city encourages best environmental practices and partners with cities in other countries to promote sound government at the local level.

PROJECT

3A Enterprise Fund Pie Chart

MyITLab® Project 3A Training

PROJECT ACTIVITIES

In Activities 3.01 through 3.12, you will edit a worksheet for Michael Larsen, City Manager, that reports the adjusted figures for Enterprise Fund Expenditures for the next fiscal year, and then present the data in a pie chart. Your completed worksheets will look similar to Figure 3.1.

PROJECT FILES

For Project 3A, you will need the following file:
e03A_Enterprise_Fund

You will save your workbook as:
Lastname_Firstname_3A_Enterprise_Fund

PROJECT RESULTS

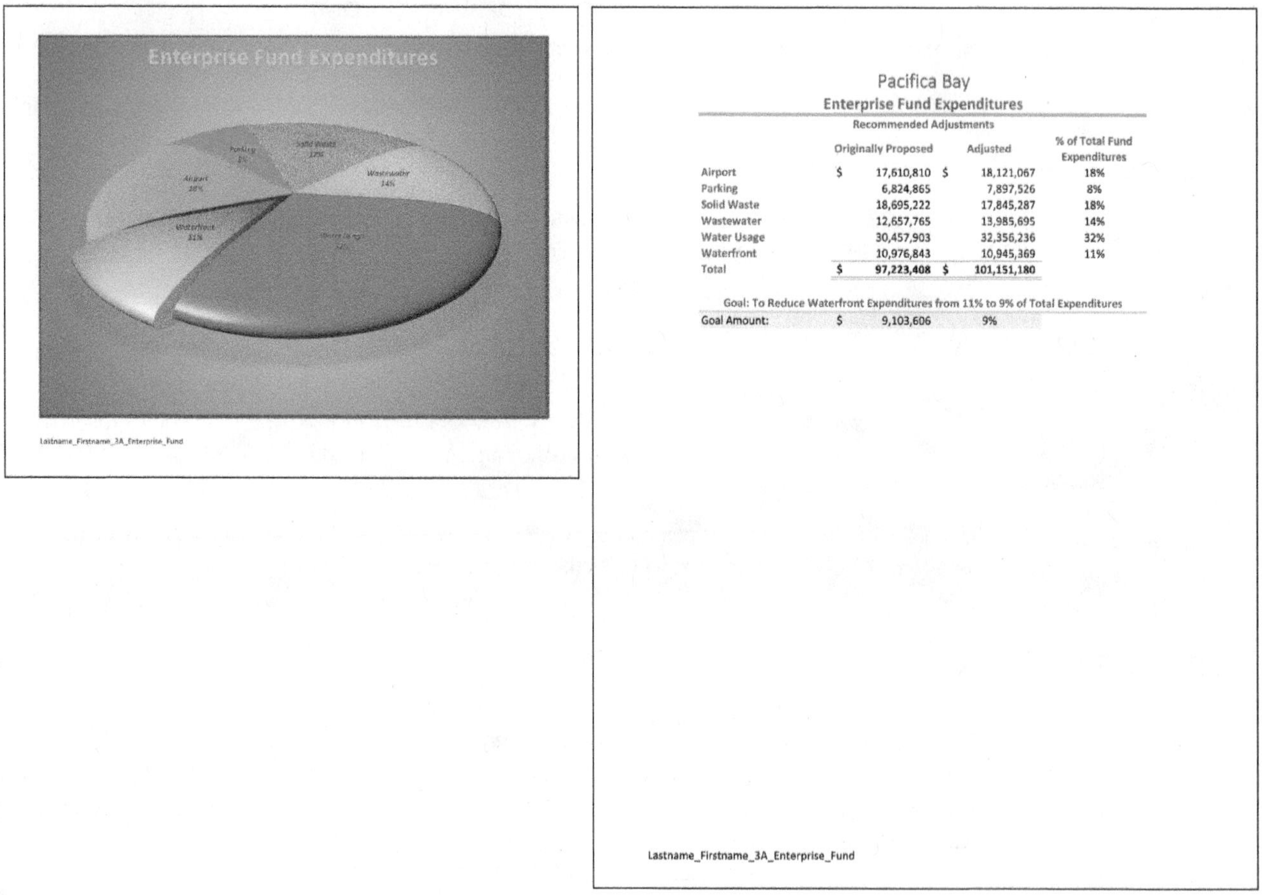

Pacifica Bay
Enterprise Fund Expenditures

	Recommended Adjustments		
	Originally Proposed	Adjusted	% of Total Fund Expenditures
Airport	$ 17,610,810	$ 18,121,067	18%
Parking	6,824,865	7,897,526	8%
Solid Waste	18,695,222	17,845,287	18%
Wastewater	12,657,765	13,985,695	14%
Water Usage	30,457,903	32,356,236	32%
Waterfront	10,976,843	10,945,369	11%
Total	$ 97,223,408	$ 101,151,180	

Goal: To Reduce Waterfront Expenditures from 11% to 9% of Total Expenditures

Goal Amount:	$ 9,103,606	9%

Lastname_Firstname_3A_Enterprise_Fund

FIGURE 3.1 Project 3A Enterprise Fund Pie Chart

Objective 1 Chart Data with a Pie Chart

Video E3-1

A ***pie chart*** shows the relationship of each part to a whole. The size of each pie slice is equal to its value compared to the total value of all the slices. The pie chart style charts data that is arranged in a single column or single row, and shows the size of items in a single data series proportional to the sum of the items. Whereas a column or bar chart can have two or more data series in the chart, a pie chart can have only one data series.

Consider using a pie chart when you have only one data series to plot, you do not have more than seven categories, and the categories represent parts of a total value.

Activity 3.01 | Calculating Values for a Pie Chart

A ***fund*** is a sum of money set aside for a specific purpose. In a municipal government like the city of Pacifica Bay, the ***general fund*** is money set aside for the normal operating activities of the city, such as police, fire, and administering the everyday functions of the city.

Municipal governments also commonly establish an ***enterprise fund*** to report income and expenditures related to municipal services for which a fee is charged in exchange for goods or services. For example, Pacifica Bay receives income from airport landing fees, parking fees, water usage fees, and rental fees along public beaches, but there are costs—expenditures—related to building and maintaining these facilities and services from which income is received.

1 Start Excel. From the student files that accompany this textbook, open **e03A_Enterprise_Fund**. From **Backstage** view, display the **Save As** dialog box. Navigate to the location where you are storing your projects for this chapter.

2 Create a new folder named **Excel Chapter 3** and open the new folder. In the **File name** box, using your name, type **Lastname_Firstname_3A_Enterprise_Fund** Click **Save** or press Enter.

The worksheet indicates the originally proposed and adjusted expenditures from the Enterprise Fund for the next fiscal year.

3 Click cell **D5**, and then type = to begin a formula.

4 Click cell **C5**, which is the first value that is part of the total Fund Expenditures, to insert it into the formula. Type / to indicate division, and then click cell **C11**, which is the total adjusted expenditures.

Recall that to determine the percentage by which a value makes up a total, you must divide the value by the total. The result will be a percentage expressed as a decimal.

5 Press F4 to make the reference to the value in cell **C11** absolute, which will enable you to copy the formula. Compare your screen with Figure 3.2.

Recall that an ***absolute cell reference*** refers to a cell by its fixed position in the worksheet—the cell reference will not change when you copy the formula. The reference to cell C5 is a ***relative cell reference***, because when you copy the formula, you want the reference to change *relative* to its row. Recall also that dollar signs display to indicate that a cell reference is absolute. A ***mixed cell*** reference occurs when only the column or row reference must be absolute, and the other is relative-such as $A10 or A$10. When the cell is copied, only the relative reference changes.

FIGURE 3.2

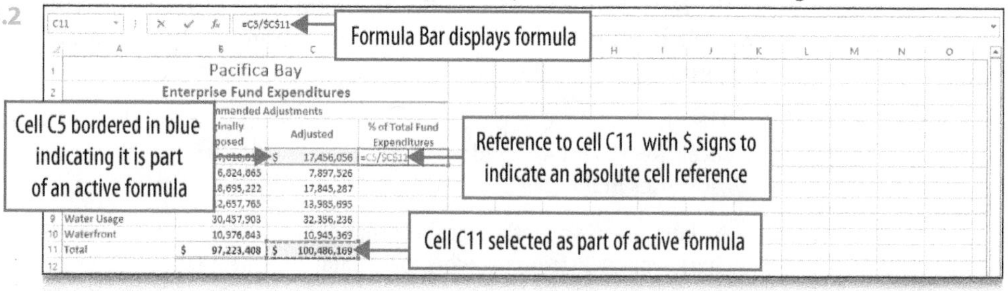

6 On the **Formula Bar**, click **Enter** to confirm the entry and to keep cell **D5** the active cell. Copy the formula down through cell **D10**, and then compare your screen with Figure 3.3.

FIGURE 3.3

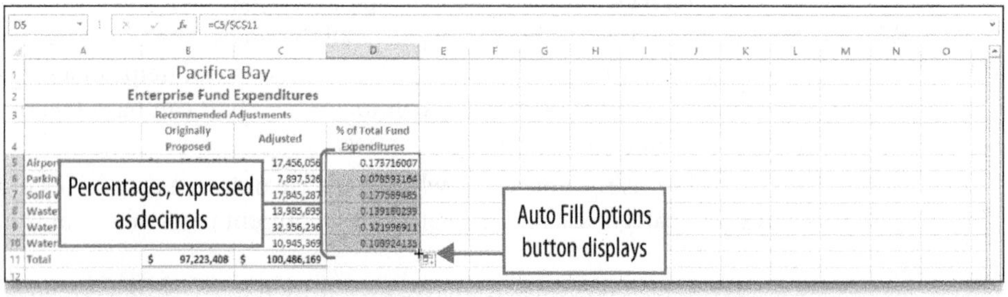

7 With the range **D5:D10** still selected, right-click over the selection, and then on the mini toolbar, click **Percent Style** and **Center**. Click cell **A1** to cancel the selection, and then **Save** your workbook. Compare your screen with Figure 3.4.

FIGURE 3.4

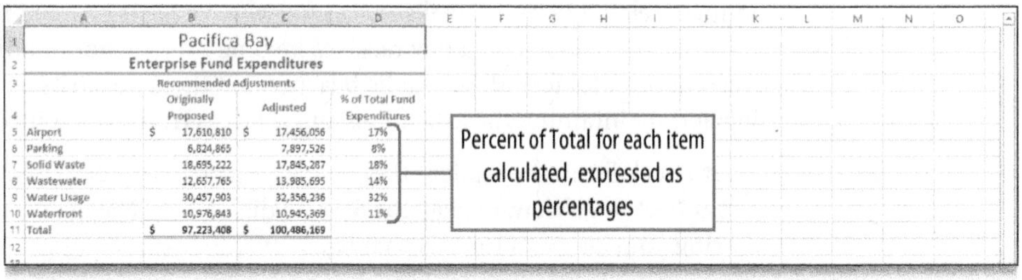

Activity 3.02 | Creating a Pie Chart in a Chart Sheet

1 Select the range **A5:A10**, hold down Ctrl, and then select the range **C5:C10** to select the nonadjacent ranges with the item names and the adjusted expenditure for each item.

To create a pie chart, you must select two ranges. One range contains the labels for each slice of the pie chart, and the other range contains the values that add up to a total. The two ranges must have the same number of cells and the range with the values should *not* include the cell with the total.

The item names (Airport, Parking, and so on) are the category names and will identify the slices of the pie chart. Each projected expenditure is a ***data point***—a value that originates in a worksheet cell and that is represented in a chart by a ***data marker***. In a pie chart, each pie slice is a data marker. Together, the data points form the ***data series***—related data points represented by data markers—and determine the size of each pie slice.

2 With the nonadjacent ranges selected, click the **INSERT tab**, and then in the **Charts group**, click **Insert Pie or Doughnut Chart**. Under **3-D Pie**, click the chart **3-D Pie** to create the chart on your worksheet and to display the **CHART TOOLS** on the ribbon.

3 On the **DESIGN tab**, at the right end of the ribbon in the **Location group**, click **Move Chart**. In the **Move Chart** dialog box, click the **New sheet** option button.

4 In the **New sheet** box, replace the highlighted text *Chart1* by typing **Expenditures Chart** and then click **OK** to display the chart on a separate worksheet in your workbook. Compare your screen with Figure 3.5.

The pie chart displays on a separate new sheet in your workbook, and a ***legend*** identifies the pie slices. Recall that a legend is a chart element that identifies the patterns or colors assigned to the categories in the chart.

A ***chart sheet*** is a workbook sheet that contains only a chart; it is useful when you want to view a chart separately from the worksheet data. The sheet tab indicates *Expenditures Chart.*

FIGURE 3.5

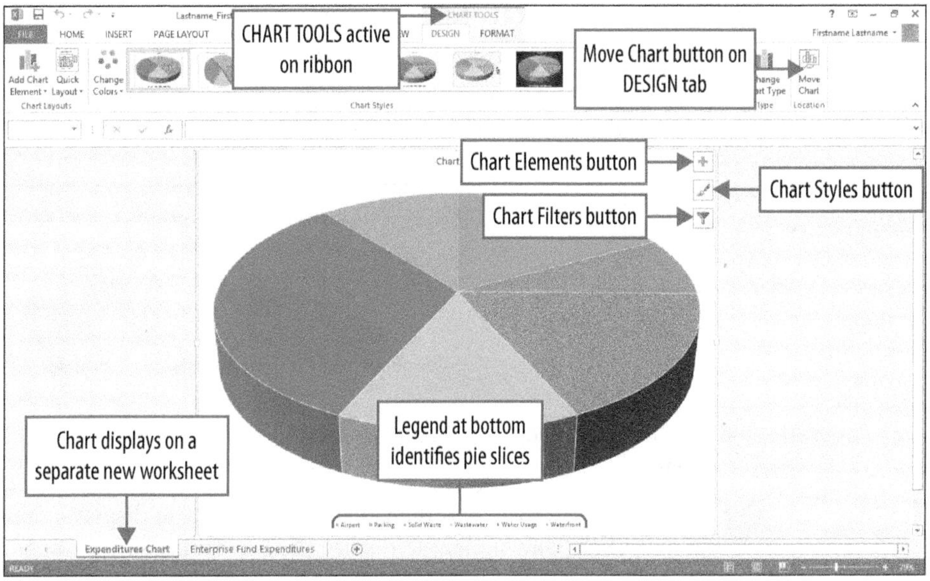

Objective 2 Format a Pie Chart

Activity 3.03 Formatting a Chart Title by Applying a WordArt Style and Changing Font Size

Video E3-2

1. Click the text *Chart Title* to surround it with selection handles, and then watch the **Formula Bar** as you type **Enterprise Fund Expenditures** Press Enter to create the new chart title in the box.

2. Click the **FORMAT tab**, and then in the **WordArt Styles group**, click **More**. In the first row, click the last style—**Fill - Gold, Accent 4, Soft Bevel.**

3. With the I pointer, drag to select the chart title text, and then on the mini toolbar, change the **Font Size** to **32**. Click the edge of the chart to deselect the title, and then compare your screen with Figure 3.6.

FIGURE 3.6

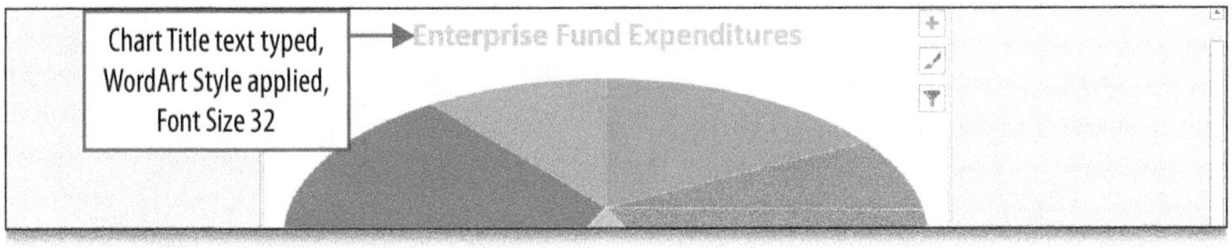

Activity 3.04 Formatting Chart Elements by Removing a Legend and Adding and Formatting Data Labels

In your worksheet, for each budget item, you calculated the percent of the total in column D. These percentages can also be calculated by the Chart feature and added to the pie slices as labels.

1 If necessary, click the edge of the chart to display the three chart buttons on the right, and then click **Chart Elements** [+]. Compare your screen with Figure 3.7.

Use the Chart Elements button to add, remove, or change chart elements such as the chart title, the legend, and the data labels.

FIGURE 3.7

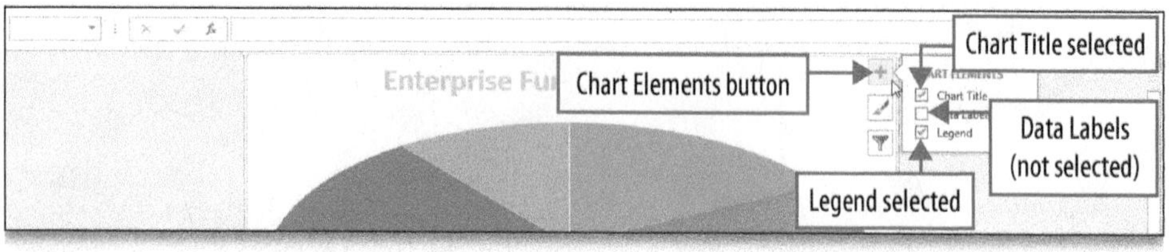

2 Click the **Legend** check box to deselect it and remove the legend from the bottom of the chart.

3 *Point* to **Data Labels**, and then click the [▶] arrow to display a menu. At the bottom of the menu, click **More Options** to display the **Format Data Labels** pane on the right.

The Format Data Labels pane displays and data labels representing the values display on each pie slice.

4 In the **Format Data Labels** pane, under **LABEL OPTIONS**, click as necessary to select the **Category Name** and **Percentage** check boxes. Click to *clear* any other check boxes in this group. Under **Label Position**, click the **Center** option button. Compare your screen with Figure 3.8.

All of the data labels are selected and display both the category name and the percentage. In the worksheet, you calculated the percent of the total in column D. Here, the percentage will be calculated by the Chart feature and added to the chart as a label.

FIGURE 3.8

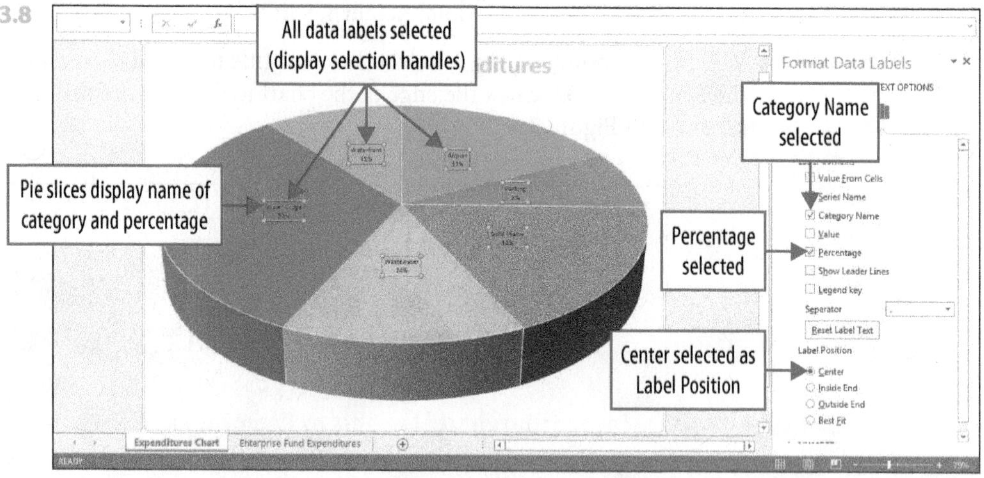

5 Point to any of the selected data labels, right-click to display a shortcut menu, and then click **Font** to display the **Font** dialog box.

6 In the **Font** dialog box, on the **Font tab**, click the **Font style arrow**, and then click **Bold Italic**. In the **Size** box, drag to select *9* and type **11** Compare your screen with Figure 3.9.

FIGURE 3.9

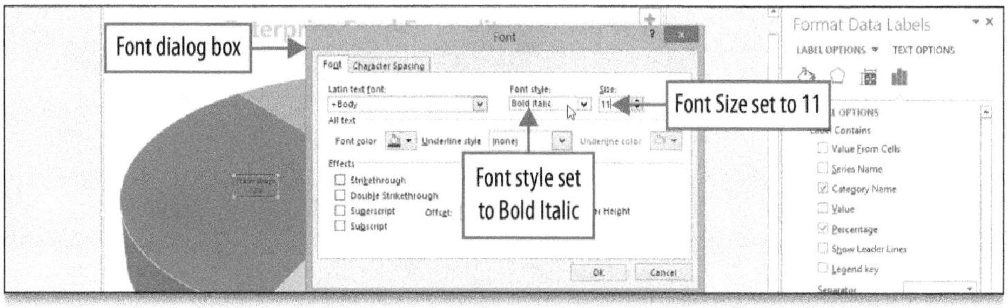

7 Click **OK** to close the dialog box and apply the formatting to the data labels. In the upper right corner of the **Format Data Labels** pane, click **Close** [X].

Activity 3.05 | Formatting a Data Series with 3-D Effects

3-D, which is short for *three-dimensional*, refers to an image that appears to have all three spatial dimensions—length, width, and depth.

1 In any pie slice, point anywhere outside of the selected label, and then double-click to display the **Format Data Series** pane on the right.

ANOTHER WAY

Right-click outside the label of any pie slice, and then click Format Data Series to display the Format Data Series pane. Or, on the FORMAT tab, in the Current Selection group, click the Chart Elements arrow, click Series 1, and then click Format Selection.

2 In the **Format Data Series** pane, under **SERIES OPTIONS**, click **Effects** [icon], and then click **3-D FORMAT**. Compare your screen with Figure 3.10.

FIGURE 3.10

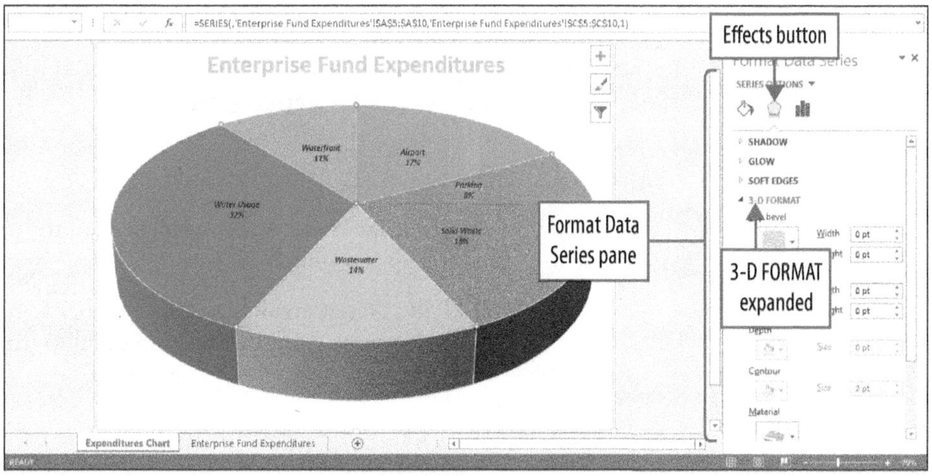

3 Click the **Top bevel arrow**, and then in the gallery, under **Bevel**, click the first bevel—**Circle**—as shown in Figure 3.11.

Bevel is a shape effect that uses shading and shadows to make the edges of a shape appear to be curved or angled.

FIGURE 3.11

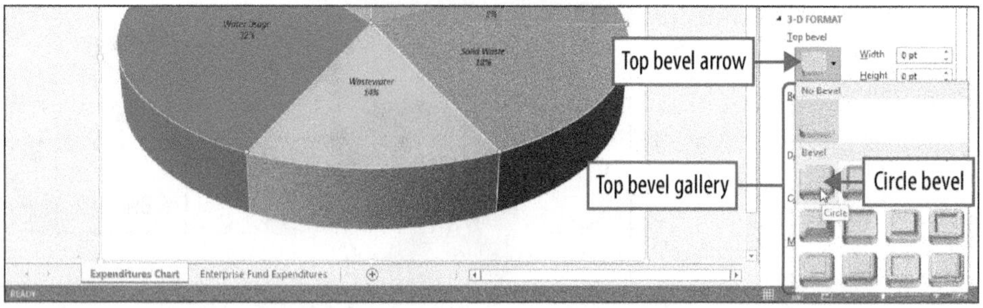

4 Under **Top bevel**, in the **Width** box, select the existing text and type **512 pt** Use the same technique to change the **Height** to **512 pt**

5 Under **Bottom bevel**, use the technique you just practiced to apply a **Circle** bevel with **Width** of **512 pt** and **Height** of **512 pt** Compare your screen with Figure 3.12.

FIGURE 3.12

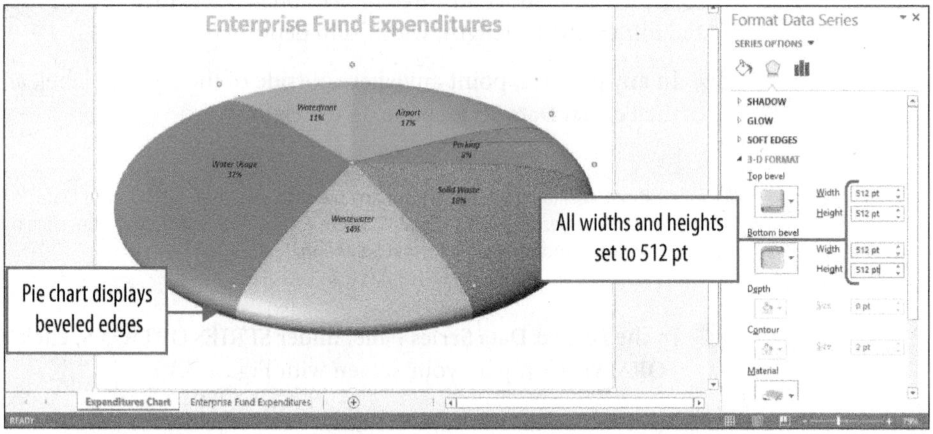

6 In the **Format Data Series** pane, scroll down as necessary, and then click the **Material arrow**. Under **Standard**, click the third material—**Plastic**.

Activity 3.06 | Formatting a Data Series with a Shadow Effect

1 If necessary, in the **Format Data Series** pane, scroll back to the top of the pane, and then click **SHADOW** to expand the options for this effect.

2 Under **SHADOW**, click the **Presets arrow**, use the scroll bar to move to the bottom of the gallery, and then under **Perspective**, in the first row, point to the third effect to display the ScreenTip *Below*. Compare your screen with Figure 3.13.

FIGURE 3.13

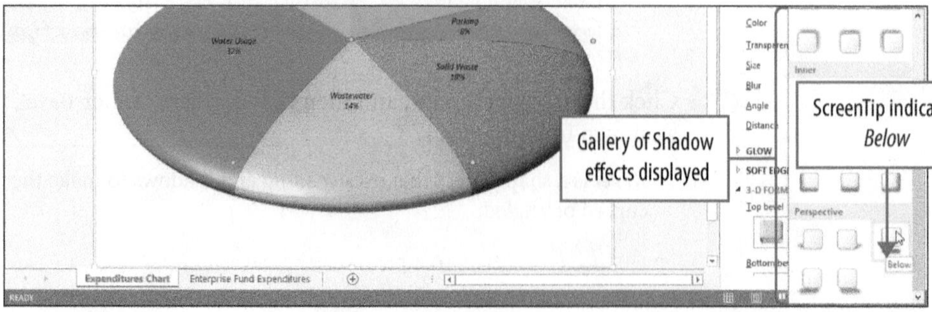

3 Click **Below** to apply the shadow to the chart.

Activity 3.07 | Rotating a Pie Chart by Changing the Angle of the First Slice

The order in which the data series in pie charts are plotted in Excel is determined by the order of the data on the worksheet. To gain a different view of the chart, you can rotate the chart within the 360 degrees of the circle of the pie shape to present a different visual perspective of the chart.

1. Notice the position of the **Water Usage** and **Waterfront** slices in the chart. Then, with the pie chart still selected—sizing handles surround the pie—in the **Format Data Series** pane, under **SERIES OPTIONS**, click **Series Options** [icon].

2. Under **Angle of first slice**, in the box to the right, drag to select **0°**, type **250** and then press Enter to rotate the chart 250 degrees to the right.

ANOTHER WAY Drag the slider to 250°, or click the spin box up arrow as many times as necessary.

3. Click **Save** [icon], and then compare your screen with Figure 3.14.

   Rotating the chart can provide a better perspective to the chart. Here, rotating the chart in this manner emphasizes that Water Usage is the largest enterprise fund expenditure.

FIGURE 3.14

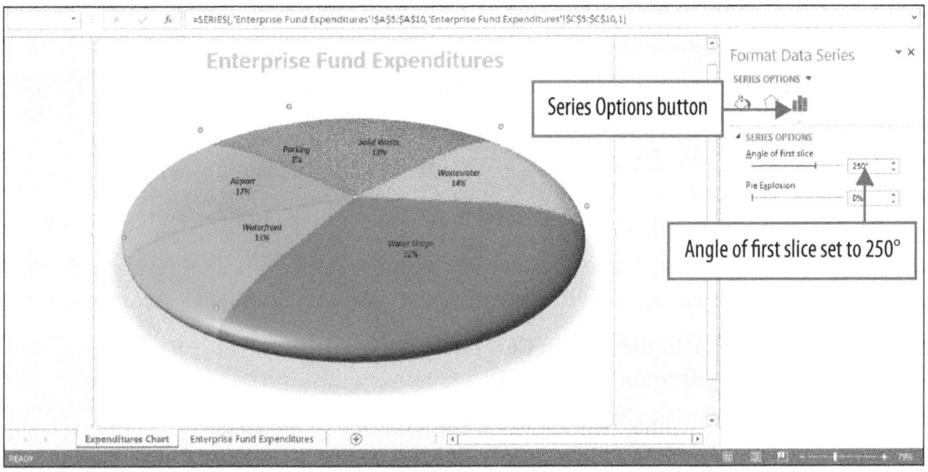

Activity 3.08 | Exploding and Coloring a Pie Slice

You can pull out—***explode***—one or more slices of a pie chart to emphasize a specific slice or slices.

1. In the **Format Data Series** pane, under **SERIES OPTIONS**, notice the slider and box for *Pie Explosion*.

   When all the pie slices are selected, as they currently are, you can use this command to explode *all* of the pie pieces away from the center by varying degrees to emphasize all the individual slices of the pie chart. An exploded pie chart visualizes the contribution of each value to the total, while at the same time emphasizing individual values.

2. On the pie chart, click the green **Waterfront** slice to select only that slice, and then on the right, notice that the **Format Data Point** pane displays.

   Excel adjusts the pane, depending on what you have selected, so that the commands you need are available.

3. In the **Format Data Point** pane, in the **Point Explosion** box, select the existing text, type **10%** and then press Enter.

4. With the **Waterfront** slice still selected, in the **Format Data Point** pane, under **SERIES OPTIONS**, click **Fill & Line** [icon], and then click **FILL** to expand its options.

5 Click the **Gradient fill** option button, click the **Preset gradients arrow**, and then in the fourth row, click the last gradient—**Bottom Spotlight - Accent 6**. Click **Save**, and then compare your screen with Figure 3.15.

FIGURE 3.15

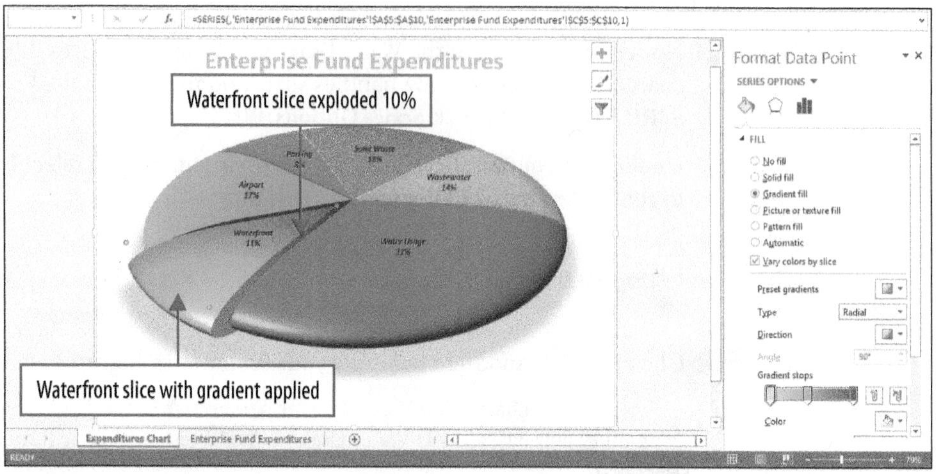

Activity 3.09 | Formatting the Chart Area

The entire chart and all of its elements comprise the ***chart area***.

1 Point to the white area just inside the border of the chart to display the ScreenTip *Chart Area*. Click one time, and notice that on the right, the **Format Chart Area** pane displays.

2 Under **CHART OPTIONS**, click **Fill & Line**, and be sure the **FILL** options are still displayed.

3 Click the **Gradient fill** option button, click the **Preset gradients arrow**, and then in the fourth row, click the first gradient—**Bottom Spotlight - Accent 1**.

4 In the **Format Chart Area** pane, click **FILL** to collapse the options, and then click **BORDER** to expand its options.

5 Under **Border**, click **Solid line**, click the **Color arrow** to display the Outline colors, and then in the fourth column, click the first color—**Blue - Gray, Text 2**. In the **Width** box, drag to select the existing width, and then type **5 pt**

6 **Close** the **Format Chart Area** pane, and then click outside of the Chart Area to deselect the chart. Click **Save**, and then compare your screen with Figure 3.16.

FIGURE 3.16

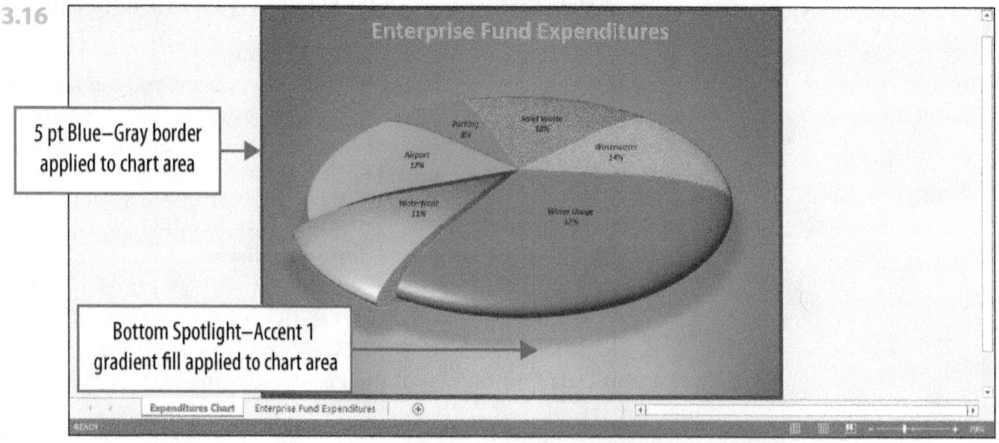

Objective 3 Edit a Workbook and Update a Chart

Activity 3.10 | Editing a Workbook and Updating a Chart

Video E3-3

If you edit the data in your worksheet, the chart data markers—in this instance the pie slices—will adjust automatically to accurately represent the new values.

1. On the pie chart, notice that *Airport* represents 17% of the total projected expenses.
2. In the sheet tab area at the bottom of the workbook, click the **Enterprise Fund Expenditures tab** to redisplay the worksheet.
3. Click cell **C5**, type **18121067** and then press Enter. Notice that the Accounting Number Format is retained in the cell.

ANOTHER WAY Double-click the cell to position the insertion point in the cell and edit.

4. Notice that the total in cell **C11** is recalculated to *$101,151,180* and the percentages in **column D** are also recalculated.
5. Display the **Expenditures Chart** sheet. Notice that the pie slices adjust to show the recalculation—*Airport* is now *18%* of the adjusted expenditures. Click **Save**, and then compare your screen with Figure 3.17.

FIGURE 3.17

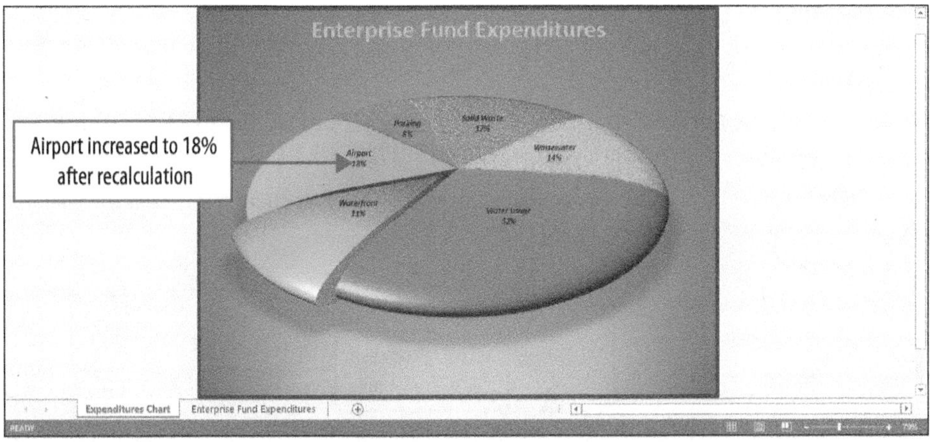

Objective 4 Use Goal Seek to Perform What-If Analysis

Activity 3.11 | Using Goal Seek to Perform What-If Analysis

Video E3-4

The process of changing the values in cells to see how those changes affect the outcome of formulas in your worksheet is referred to as ***what-if analysis***. One what-if analysis tool in Excel is ***Goal Seek***, which finds the input needed in one cell to arrive at the desired result in another cell.

1. Click the **Enterprise Fund Expenditures sheet tab** to redisplay the worksheet. In cell **A13**, type **Goal: To Reduce Waterfront Expenditures from 11% to 9% of Total Expenditures** **Merge & Center** the text across the range **A13:D13**, and then apply the **Heading 3** Cell Style.
2. In cell **A14**, type **Goal Amount:** and press Enter.
3. Select the range **C10:D10**, right-click over the selection, and then click **Copy**. Point to cell **B14**, right-click, and then under **Paste Options**, click **Paste**.

4 Press Esc to cancel the moving border, click cell **C14**, and then compare your screen with Figure 3.18.

FIGURE 3.18

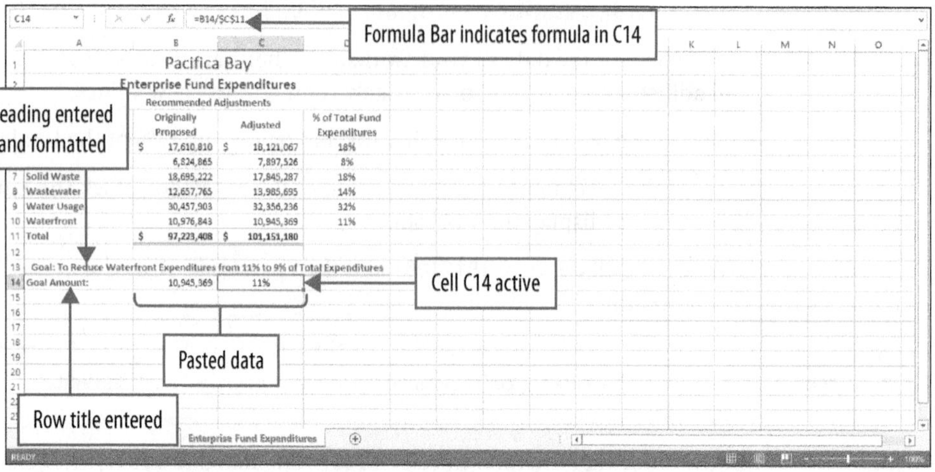

5 Be sure cell **C14** is the active cell. On the **DATA tab**, in the **Data Tools group**, click **What-If Analysis**, and then click **Goal Seek.**

6 In the **Goal Seek** dialog box, notice that the active cell, **C14**, is indicated in the **Set cell** box. Press Tab to move to the **To value** box, and then type **9%**

C14 is the cell in which you want to set a specific value; 9% is the percentage of the total expenditures that is your goal for the Waterfront Expenditure. The Set cell box contains the formula that calculates the information you seek.

7 Press Tab to move the insertion point to the **By changing cell** box, and then click cell **B14**. Compare your screen with Figure 3.19.

Cell B14 contains the value that Excel changes to reach the goal. Excel formats this cell as an absolute cell reference.

FIGURE 3.19

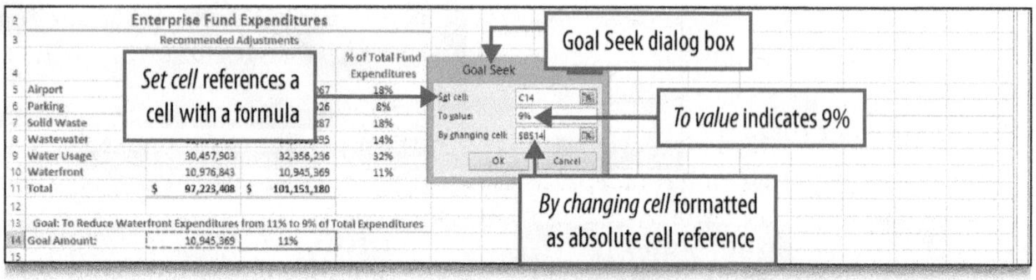

8 Click **OK**. In the displayed **Goal Seek Status** dialog box, click **OK**.

9 Select the range **A14:C14**. On the **HOME tab**, display the **Cell Styles** gallery. Under **Themed Cell Styles**, apply **20% - Accent1**.

10 Click cell **B14**, display the **Cell Styles** gallery again, and then at the bottom, under **Number Format**, click **Currency [0]**.

Use this cell style when you want to apply currency formatting with no decimal places quickly.

11 Press Ctrl + Home, click **Save**, and then compare your screen with Figure 3.20.

Excel calculates that the city must budget for *$9,103,606* in Waterfront expenditures in order for this item to become 9% of the total projected budget.

FIGURE 3.20

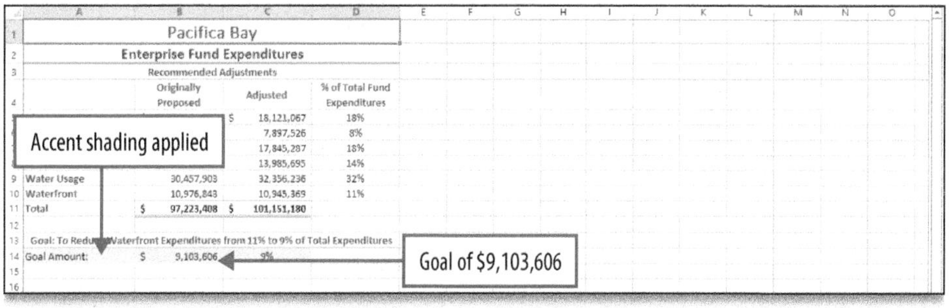

Activity 3.12 Preparing and Printing a Workbook with a Chart Sheet

1 Click the **PAGE LAYOUT tab**. In the **Page Setup group**, click **Margins**, and then click **Custom Margins.**

2 In the **Page Setup** dialog box, on the **Margins tab**, under **Center on page**, select the **Horizontally** check box.

3 Click the **Header/Footer tab**, and then in the center of the dialog box, click **Custom Footer**. In the **Footer** dialog box, with your insertion point blinking in the **Left section**, on the row of buttons, click **Insert File Name**.

4 Click **OK** two times.

The dotted line indicates the page break as currently formatted.

5 Display the **Expenditures Chart**, which must have its footer formatted separately. In the **Page Setup group**, click the **Dialog Box Launcher**.

Chart sheets are automatically centered on the page.

6 Click the **Header/Footer tab**, and then in the center of the dialog box, click **Custom Footer**. In the **Footer** dialog box, with your insertion point blinking in the **Left section**, on the row of buttons, click **Insert File Name**.

7 Click **OK** two times. Click the **FILE tab**, and then click **Show All Properties**. As the **Tags**, type **enterprise fund, expenditures** As the **Subject**, type your course name and section number. Be sure your name displays as the author.

8 On the left, click **Save.** Right-click the **Expenditures Chart sheet tab**, and then click **Select All Sheets**. Verify that *[Group]* displays in the title bar.

Recall that by selecting all sheets, you can view all of the workbook pages in Print Preview.

9 Press Ctrl + F2 to display the **Print Preview**. Examine the first page, and then at the bottom of the **Print Preview**, click **Next Page** to view the second page of your workbook.

NOTE **Printing a Chart Sheet Uses More Toner**

Printing a chart that displays on a chart sheet will use more toner or ink than a small chart that is part of a worksheet. If you are printing your work, check with your instructor to verify whether or not you should print the chart sheet.

10 On the left, click **Save** to redisplay the workbook.

11 By using the techniques you practiced in Project 1A, print or submit electronically as directed by your instructor. If required by your instructor, print or create an electronic version of your worksheet with formulas displayed.

12 **Close** your workbook and close **Excel**.

END | You have completed Project 3A

GO! with Office Online (formerly Web Apps)

Objective Create a JPEG Photo of a Chart and Upload to a OneNote Online Notebook

Recall that ***OneNote*** is a Microsoft application with which you can create a digital notebook that gives you a single location where you can gather and organize information in the form of notes. OneNote Online enables you to share your OneNote notebooks on the web.

ALERT! Working with Web-Based Applications and Services

Computer programs and services on the web receive continuous updates and improvements, so the steps to complete this web-based activity may differ from the ones shown. You can often look at the screens and the information presented to determine how to complete the activity.

Activity | Creating a JPEG Photo of a Chart and Uploading It to a OneNote Online Notebook

In this activity, you will create a JPEG image of a chart, and then upload the image to a OneNote Online notebook.

1. From File Explorer, navigate to your **Excel Chapter 3** folder, and then open your file **Lastname_Firstname_3A_Enterprise_Fund** workbook. Display the **Expenditures Chart** worksheet.

2. Display the **Start** screen and type **snipping** Click the **Snipping Tool** program to start it.

3. In the Snipping Tool dialog box, click the **New arrow**, and then click **Rectangular Snip**. With the pointer, point to the upper left corner of the chart, hold down the left mouse button, and then drag down to the lower right corner of the chart to create a red rectangle around the chart. Release the mouse button. Compare your screen with Figure A.

4. On the **Snipping Tool** mark-up window toolbar, click **Save Snip**. In the **Save As** dialog box, navigate to your **Excel Chapter 3** folder. Be sure the **Save as type** box displays **JPEG file**. In the **File name** box, type **Lastname_Firstname_EX_3A_Web** and then click **Save**. **Close** the **Snipping Tool** window and **Close** Excel.

5. Launch Internet Explorer, navigate to **http://onedrive.com** and then sign in to your **Microsoft** account. Click your **GO! Web Projects** folder to open it; if necessary, create this folder.

FIGURE A

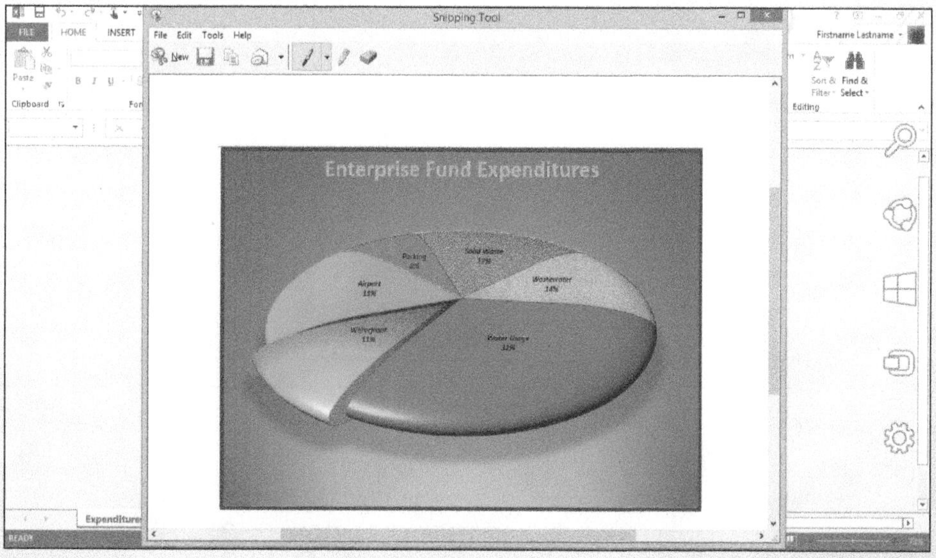

(GO! with Office Online (formerly Web Apps) continues on the next page)

6 In the OneDrive menu bar, click **Create**, and then click **OneNote notebook** to create a new notebook. In the **New Microsoft OneNote notebook** box, using your own name, type **Lastname_Firstname_EX_3A_Web** and then click **Create**.

7 Point to the text *Untitled Section*, right-click, and then click **New Section**. As the **Section Name**, type **Fund Reports** and then click **OK**.

8 With the insertion point blinking at the top of the notebook page, type **Chart of Enterprise Fund Expenditures** and press Enter. With the insertion point in the blank page, on the ribbon, click the **INSERT tab**, and then in the **Pictures group**, click **Picture**.

9 In the **Choose File to Upload** dialog box, navigate to your **Excel Chapter 3** folder, and then click the **EX_3A_Web** JPEG file that you created with the Snipping Tool. Click **Open**.

Use this technique to insert a picture to store in a OneNote notebook.

10 With the insertion point blinking below the inserted picture, click the **HOME tab**, and then in the **Tags group**, click **Tag** to display a list of tags. Click **Important**. Below the picture, click to the right of the tag—a gold star—to position the insertion point there. Type **Attention Council Members: The expenditures from the Enterprise Fund will be discussed at the August City Council meeting.** Compare your screen with Figure B.

A note tag can help you locate specific information quickly. A note tag is both a descriptive term representing a category, such as *Important* or *To Do*, and a related icon that can be associated with a specific note. When this notebook on your OneDrive is shared with all of the City Council members, each will be able to view the chart and see that it is important.

11 If you are instructed to submit your file, use one of the methods outlined in the Note box below. In OneNote Online, there is no Save button because your notebook is being saved automatically.

12 Sign out of your Microsoft account, and then close all windows.

NOTE **Printing or Creating an Electronic File of a Online OneNote Page**

You can use Snipping Tool to create an electronic file or to paste the snip into a document to save and print. In the OneNote Online, in which you can open this page, you can print pages directly to a printer.

FIGURE B

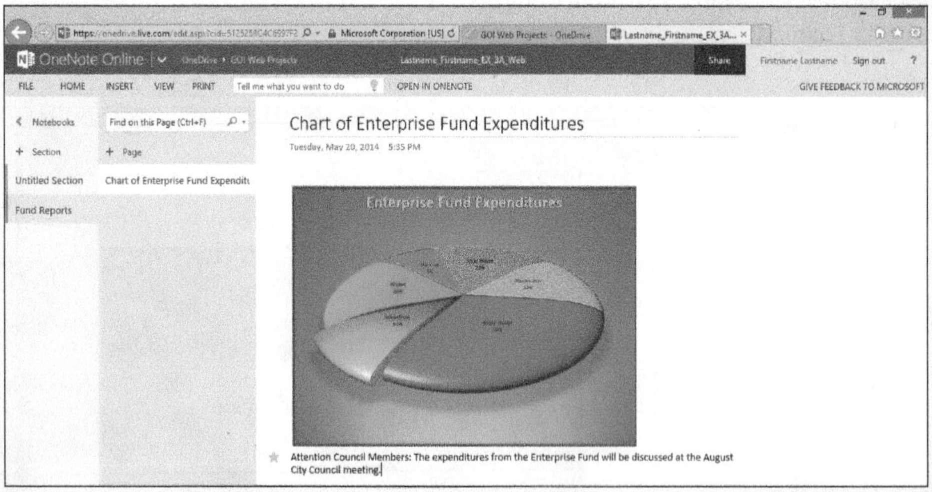

PROJECT 3B Tourism Spending Projection with Line Chart

MyITLab® Project 3B Training

3 EXCEL

PROJECT ACTIVITIES

In Activities 3.13 through 3.20, you will assist Michael Larsen, City Manager, in creating a worksheet to estimate future tourism spending based on two possible growth rates. You will also create a line chart to display past visitor spending. Your resulting worksheet and chart will look similar to Figure 3.21.

PROJECT FILES

Build from Scratch

For Project 3B, you will need the following files:

New blank Excel file
e03B_Surfers

You will save your workbook as:

Lastname_Firstname_3B_Tourism

PROJECT RESULTS

Pacifica Bay

Tourism Spending 2010 to 2014

Year	2010	2011	2012	2013	2014
Tourism Spending	$ 4,644,325	$ 5,605,958	$ 7,235,397	$ 8,824,638	$ 11,086,354
Percent Increase		21%	29%	22%	26%

Projected Tourism Spending

Estimated Growth Rate ***21%***

Year	2014	2015	2016	2017	2018
	$ 11,086,354	$ 13,414,488	$ 16,231,531	$ 19,640,152	$ 23,764,584

Estimated Growth in Tourism Spending 2014 to 2018

Year	2014	2015	2016	2017	2018
25% Growth Rate	$ 11,086,354	$ 13,857,943	$ 17,322,428	$ 21,653,035	$ 27,066,294
21% Growth Rate	$ 11,086,354	$ 13,414,488	$ 16,231,531	$ 19,640,152	$ 23,764,584

Lastname_Firstname_3B_Tourism

FIGURE 3.21 Project 3B Tourism Spending Projection with Line Chart

Objective 5 Design a Worksheet for What-If Analysis

Video E3-5

If you change the value in a cell referenced in a formula, Excel automatically recalculates the result of the formula. This means that you can change cell values to see *what* would happen *if* you tried different values. Recall that this process of changing the values in cells to see how those changes affect the outcome of formulas in your worksheet is referred to as what-if analysis.

Activity 3.13 | Using Parentheses in a Formula to Calculate a Percentage Rate of Increase

Mr. Larsen has the city's tourism spending figures for the recent 5-year period. In each year, tourism spending has increased. In this activity, you will construct a formula to calculate the ***percentage rate of increase***—the percent by which one number increases over another number—for each year since 2010. From this information, future tourism spending growth can be estimated.

Excel follows a set of mathematical rules called the ***order of operations***, which has four basic parts:

- Expressions within parentheses are processed first.
- Exponentiation, if present, is performed before multiplication and division.
- Multiplication and division are performed before addition and subtraction.
- Consecutive operators with the same level of precedence are calculated from left to right.

1 Start Excel and open a new blank workbook. In cell **A1**, type **Pacifica Bay** and in cell **A2**, type **Tourism Spending 2010 to 2014** and then **Merge & Center** cell **A1** across the range **A1:F1** and apply the **Title** cell style. **Merge & Center** cell **A2** across the range **A2:F2** and apply the **Heading 1** cell style.

2 Widen **column A** to **150 pixels** and widen **columns B:F** to **90 pixels**. Press F12 to display the **Save As** dialog box. Navigate to your **Excel Chapter 3** folder, and then in the **File name** box, using your own name, type **Lastname_Firstname_3B_Tourism** Click **Save** or press Enter.

3 Leave **row 3** blank, and then click cell **A4**. Type **Year** and then press Tab. In cell **B4**, type **2010** and then press Tab.

4 In cell **C4**, type **2011** and then press Tab. Select the range **B4:C4**, and then drag the fill handle to the right through cell **F4** to extend the series to *2014*. Apply the **Heading 3** cell style to the selected range. Compare your screen with Figure 3.22.

By establishing a pattern of 1-year intervals with the first two cells, you can use the fill handle to continue the series. The AutoFill feature will do this for any pattern that you establish with two or more cells.

FIGURE 3.22

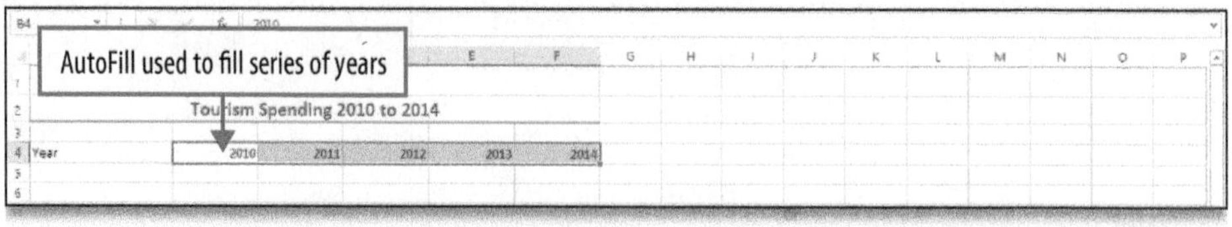

5 In cell **A5**, type **Tourism Spending** and press Enter. In cell **A6**, type **Percent Increase** and press Enter.

6 Click cell **B5**, and then beginning in cell **B5** and pressing Tab to move across the row, enter the following values for tourism spending in the years listed:

2010	2011	2012	2013	2014
4644325	5605958	7235397	8824638	11086354

7 Click cell **C6**. Being sure to include the parentheses, type **=(c5-b5)/b5** and then on the **Formula Bar**, click **Enter** to keep cell **C6** active; your result is *0.207055492*. Compare your screen with Figure 3.23.

Recall that as you type, a list of Excel functions that begin with the letter *C* and *B* may briefly display. This is ***Formula AutoComplete***, an Excel feature which, after typing an = (equal sign) and the beginning letter or letters of a function name, displays a list of function names that match the typed letter(s). In this instance, the letters represent cell references, *not* the beginning of a function name.

FIGURE 3.23

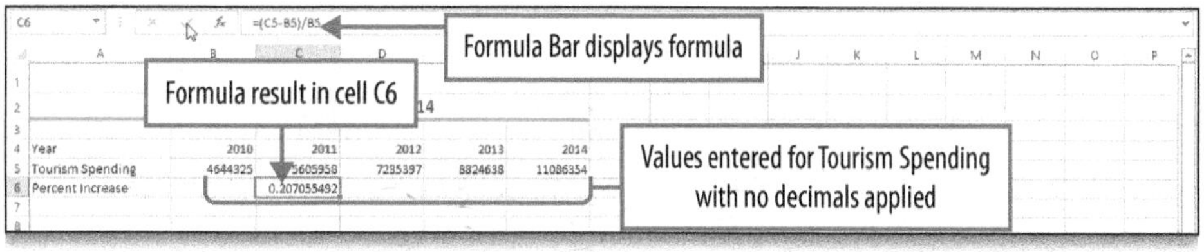

8 With cell **C6** selected, drag the fill handle to the right to copy the formula through cell **F6**.

Because this formula uses relative cell references—that is, for each year, the formula is the same but the values used are relative to the formula's location—you can copy the formula in this manner. For example, the result for 2012 uses the 2011 value as the base, the result for 2013 uses the 2012 value as the base, and the result for 2014 uses the 2013 value as the base.

9 Select the range **B5:F5**, right-click, on the mini toolbar, click **Accounting Number Format**, and then click **Decrease Decimal** two times. Select the range **C6:F6**, right-click, and then apply **Percent Style**. Click cell **C6** and look at the **Formula Bar**.

The mathematical formula ***rate* = *amount of increase/base*** is used to calculated the percentage rate of tourism spending increase from 2010 to 2011. The formula is applied as follows:

First, determine the *amount of increase* by subtracting the ***base***—the starting point represented by the 2010 tourism spending—from the 2011 tourism spending. Therefore, the *amount of increase* = $5,605,958 - $4,644,325 or $961,633. Between 2010 and 2011 tourism spending increased by $961,633. In the formula, this calculation is represented by *C5-B5*.

Second, calculate the *rate*—what the amount of increase ($961,633) represents as a percentage of the base (2010's tourism spending of $4,644,325). Determine this by dividing the amount of increase ($961,633) by the base ($4,644,325). Therefore $961,633 divided by $4,644,325 is equal to *0.207055492* or, when formatted as a percent and rounded up, 21%.

10 In the **Formula Bar**, locate the parentheses enclosing *C5-B5*.

Recall that Excel follows a set of mathematical rules called the order of operations, in which expressions within parentheses are processed first, multiplication and division are performed before addition and subtraction, and consecutive operators with the same level of precedence are calculated from left to right.

11 **Save** your workbook, and then compare your screen with Figure 3.24.

FIGURE 3.24

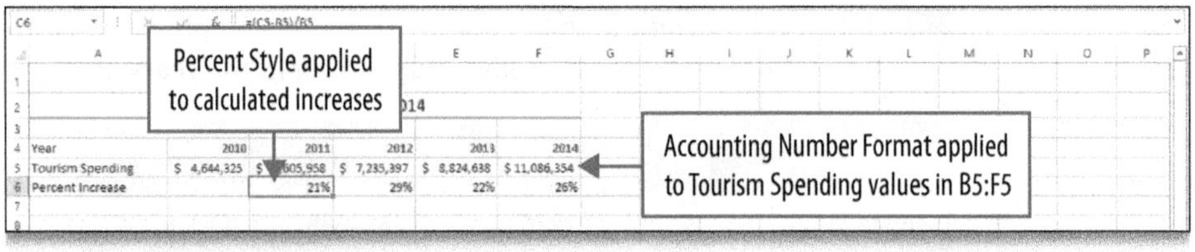

More Knowledge **Use of Parentheses in a Formula**

When writing a formula in Excel, use parentheses to specify the order in which the operations should occur. For example, to average three test scores of 100, 50, and 90 that you scored on three different tests, you would add the test scores and then divide by the number of test scores in the list. If you write this formula as =100+50+90/3, the result would be 180, because Excel would first divide 90 by 3 and then add 100+50+30. Excel would do so because the order of operations states that multiplication and division are calculated *before* addition and subtraction.

The correct way to write this formula is =(100+50+90)/3. Excel will add the three values, and then divide the result by 3, or 240/3 resulting in a correct average of 80. Parentheses play an important role in ensuring that you get the correct result in your formulas.

Activity 3.14 | Using Format Painter

In this activity, you will use Format Painter to copy text (non-numeric) formats.

1. Leave **row 7** blank, and then click cell **A8**. Type **Projected Tourism Spending** and then press Enter.

2. Point to cell **A2**, right-click, on the mini toolbar, click **Format Painter**, and then click cell **A8** to copy the format.

   The format of cell **A2** is *painted*—applied to—cell **A8**, including the merging and centering of the text across the range **A8:F8**.

BY TOUCH On the Home tab, in the Clipboard group, tap the Format Painter button.

3. Leave **row 9** blank, and then click cell **A10**. Type **Estimated Growth Rate** and then press Tab.

4. In cell **B10**, type **25%** and press Enter. Select the range **A10:B10**, right-click over the selection, and then from the mini toolbar, apply **Bold** B and **Italic** I.

5. Leave **row 11** blank. Click cell **A12**, type **Year** and then press Tab. In cell **B12**, type **2014** and press Tab. In cell **C12**, type **2015** and press Tab.

6. Select the range **B12:C12**, and then drag the fill handle through cell **F12** to extend the pattern of years to *2018*. Apply the **Heading 3** cell style to the selected range.

7. Point to cell **F5**, right-click, and then click **Copy**. Point to cell **B13**, right-click, and then click **Paste**. Compare your screen with Figure 3.25, and then **Save** your workbook.

FIGURE 3.25

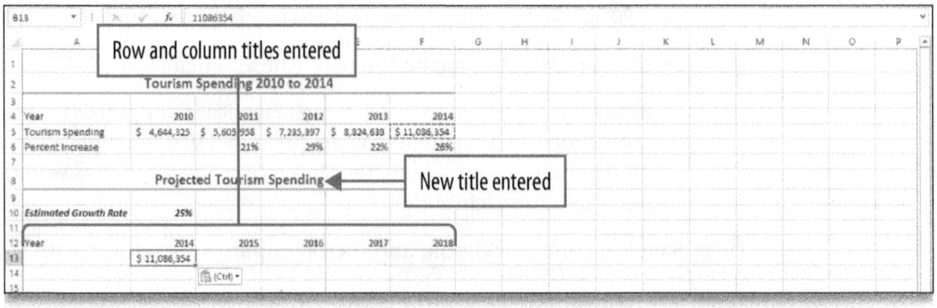

> **More Knowledge** **Percentage Calculations**
>
> When you type a percentage into a cell—for example *25%*—the percentage format, without decimal points, displays in both the cell and the Formula Bar. Excel will, however, use the decimal value of *0.25* for actual calculations.

Activity 3.15 | Calculating a Value After an Increase

A growth in tourism spending means that the city can plan for additional revenues and also plan more hotel and conference space to accommodate the increasing number of visitors. Therefore, city planners in Pacifica Bay want to estimate how much tourism spending will increase in the future. The calculations you made in the previous activity show that tourism spending has increased at varying rates during each year from 2010 to 2014, ranging from a low of 21% to a high of 29% per year.

Economic data suggests that future growth will trend close to that of the recent past. To plan for the future, Mr. Larsen wants to prepare a forecast of tourism spending based on the percentage increase halfway between the high of 29% and the low of 21%; that is, for 25%. In this activity, you will calculate the tourism spending that would result from a 25% increase.

1 Click cell **C13**. Type **=b13*(100%+b10)** and then on the **Formula Bar**, click **Enter** ✓ to display a result of *13857942.5*. Point to cell **B13**, right-click, click **Format Painter**, and then click cell **C13** to copy the format. Compare your screen with Figure 3.26.

This formula calculates what tourism spending will be in the year 2015 assuming an increase of 25% over 2014's tourism spending. Use the mathematical formula ***value after increase* = *base*** × ***percent for new value*** to calculate a value after an increase as follows:

First, establish the *percent for new value*. The ***percent for new value* = *base percent* + *percent of increase***. The *base percent* of 100% represents the base tourism spending and the *percent of increase*—in this instance is 25%. Therefore, the tourism spending will equal 100% of the base year plus 25% of the base year. This can be expressed as 125% or 1.25. In this formula, you will use 100% + the rate in cell **B10**, which is 25%, to equal 125%.

Second, enter a reference to the cell that contains the *base*—the tourism spending in 2014. The base value resides in cell **B13**—*$11,086,354*.

Third, calculate the *value after increase*. Because in each future year the increase will be based on 25%—an absolute value located in cell **B10**—this cell reference can be formatted as absolute by typing dollar signs.

FIGURE 3.26

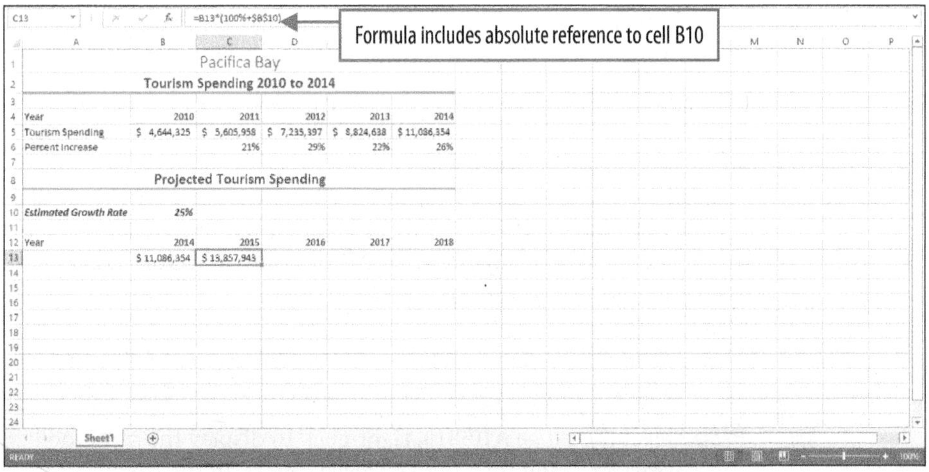

2 With cell **C13** as the active cell, drag the fill handle to copy the formula to the range **D13:F13**. Click an empty cell to cancel the selection, click **Save** and then compare your screen with Figure 3.27.

This formula uses a relative cell address—B13—for the *base*; the tourism spending in the year is used in each of the formulas in cells D13:F13 as the *base* value. Because the reference to the *percent of increase* in cell B10 is an absolute reference, each *value after increase* is calculated with the value from cell B10.

The tourism spending projected for 2015—*$13,857,943*—is an increase of 25% over the spending in 2014. The projected spending in 2016—*$17,322,428*—is an increase of 25% over the spending in 2015, and so on.

FIGURE 3.27

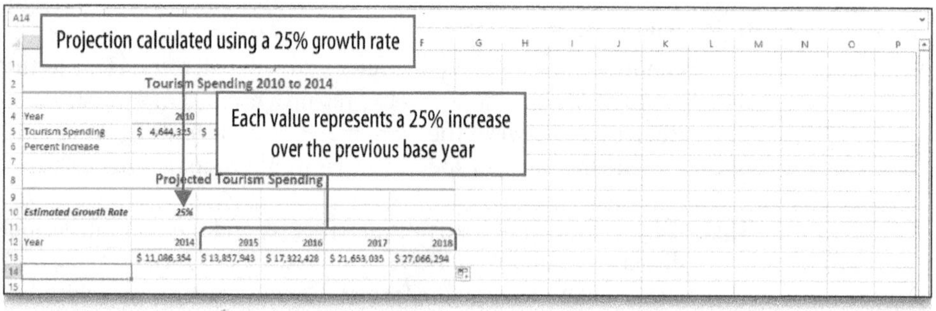

More Knowledge **Percent Increase or Decrease**

The basic formula for calculating an increase or decrease can be done in two parts. First determine the percent by which the base value will be increased or decreased, and then add or subtract the results to the base. The formula can be simplified by using (1+amount of increase) or (1–amount of decrease), where 1, rather than 100%, represents the whole. Therefore, the formula used in Step 1 of Activity 3.15 could also be written =b13*(1+b10), or =(b13*b10)+b13.

Objective 6 Answer What-If Questions by Changing Values in a Worksheet

Video E3-6

If a formula depends on the value in a cell, you can see what effect it will have if you change the value in that cell. Then, you can copy the value computed by the formula and paste it into another part of the worksheet where you can compare it to other values.

Activity 3.16 | Answering What-If Questions and Using Paste Special

A growth rate of 25% in tourism spending in each year will result in tourism spending of approximately $27 million by 2018. The city planners will likely ask: *What if* tourism spending grows at the lowest rate of 21%?

Because the formulas are constructed to use the growth rate displayed in cell **B10**, Mr. Larsen can answer that question quickly by entering a different percentage into that cell. To keep the results of the new calculation so it can be compared, you will paste the results of the what-if question into another area of the worksheet.

1 Leave **row 14** blank, and then click cell **A15**. Type **Estimated Growth in Tourism Spending 2014 to 2018** and then press Enter. Use **Format Painter** to copy the format from cell **A8** to cell **A15**.

2 Select the range **A10:B10**, right-click to display the mini toolbar, click the **Fill Color button arrow**, and then under **Theme Colors**, in the first column, click the third color—**White, Background 1, Darker 15%**.

3 Leave **row 16** blank, and then in the range **A17:A19**, type the following row titles:

Year

25% Growth Rate

21% Growth Rate

4 Select the range **B12:F12**, right-click over the selection, and then on the shortcut menu, click **Copy**.

ANOTHER WAY Press Ctrl + C; or, on the Home tab, in the Clipboard group, click the Copy button.

5 Point to cell **B17**, right-click, and then on the shortcut menu, under **Paste Options**, click **Paste**.

Recall that when pasting a group of copied cells to a target range, you need only point to or select the first cell of the range.

6 Select and **Copy** the range **B13:F13**, and then **Paste** it beginning in cell **B18**.

7 Click cell **C18**. On the **Formula Bar**, notice that the *formula* was pasted into the cell, as shown in Figure 3.28.

This is *not* the desired result. The actual *calculated values*—not the formulas—are needed in the range.

FIGURE 3.28

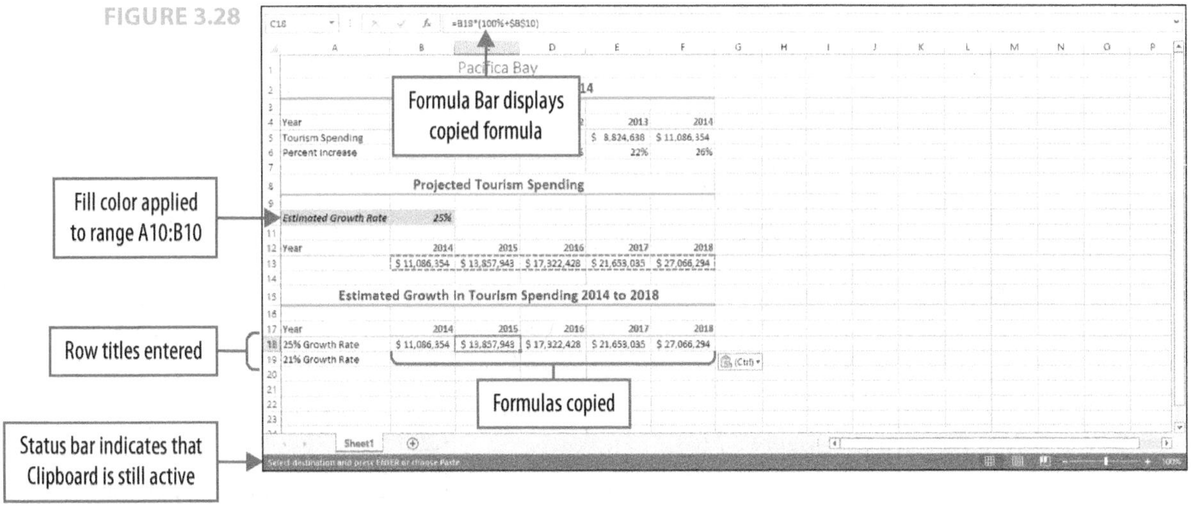

8 On the **Quick Access Toolbar**, click **Undo**. With the range **B13:F13** still copied to the Clipboard—as indicated by the message in the status bar and the moving border—point to cell **B18**, and then right-click to display the shortcut menu.

9 Under **Paste Options**, point to **Paste Special** to display another gallery, and then under **Paste Values**, point to **Values & Number Formatting** to display the ScreenTip as shown in Figure 3.29.

The ScreenTip *Values & Number Formatting (A)* indicates that you can paste the calculated values that result from the calculation of formulas along with the formatting applied to the copied cells. *(A)* is the keyboard shortcut for this command.

FIGURE 3.29

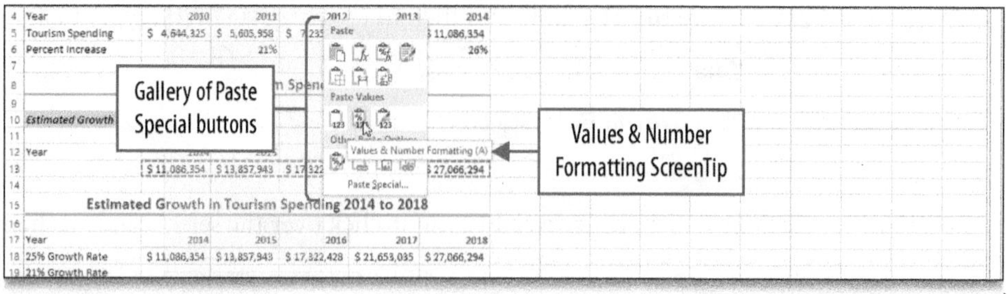

10 Click **Values & Number Formatting** [icon], click cell **C18** and notice on the **Formula Bar** that the cell contains a *value*, not a formula. Press Esc to cancel the moving border. Compare your screen with Figure 3.30.

The calculated estimates based on a 25% growth rate are pasted along with their formatting.

FIGURE 3.30

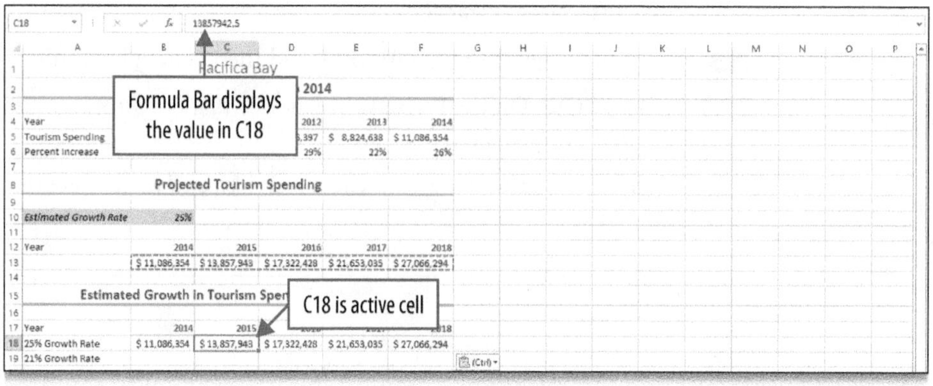

11 Click cell **B10**. Type **21** and then watch the values in **C13:F13** *recalculate* as, on the **Formula Bar**, you click **Enter** [icon].

The value *21%* is the lowest percent increase for the past 5-year period.

12 Select and **Copy** the new values in the range **B13:F13**. Point to cell **B19**, right-click, and then on the shortcut menu, point to **Paste Special**. Under **Paste Values**, click **Values & Number Formatting** [icon].

13 Press Esc to cancel the moving border, click cell **A1**, click **Save** [icon], and then compare your screen with Figure 3.31.

With this information, Mr. Larsen can answer what-if questions about the projected increase in tourism spending based on the rates of increase over the past 5 years.

FIGURE 3.31

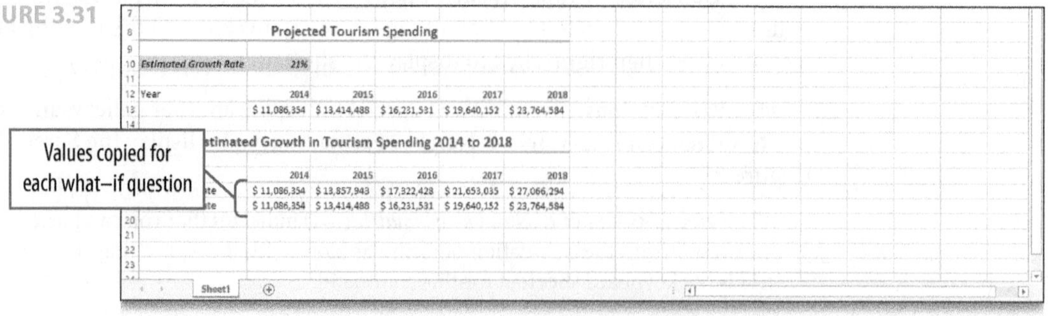

Objective 7 Chart Data with a Line Chart

Video E3-7

A ***line chart*** displays trends over time. Time is displayed along the bottom axis and the data point values connect with a line. The curve and direction of the line make trends obvious to the reader.

The columns in a column chart and the pie slices in a pie chart emphasize the distinct values of each data point. A line chart, on the other hand, emphasizes the flow from one data point value to the next.

Activity 3.17 | Inserting Multiple Rows and Creating a Line Chart

So that City Council members can see how tourism spending has increased over the past five years, in this activity, you will chart the actual tourism spending from 2010 to 2014 in a line chart.

1 Click the **PAGE LAYOUT tab**. In the **Themes group**, click the **Colors arrow**, and then change the **Theme Colors** to **Orange**.

2 In the **row header area**, point to **row 8** to display the [→] pointer, and then drag down to select **rows 8:24**. Right-click over the selection, and then click **Insert** to insert the same number of blank rows as you selected. Compare your screen with Figure 3.32.

Use this technique to insert multiple rows quickly.

FIGURE 3.32

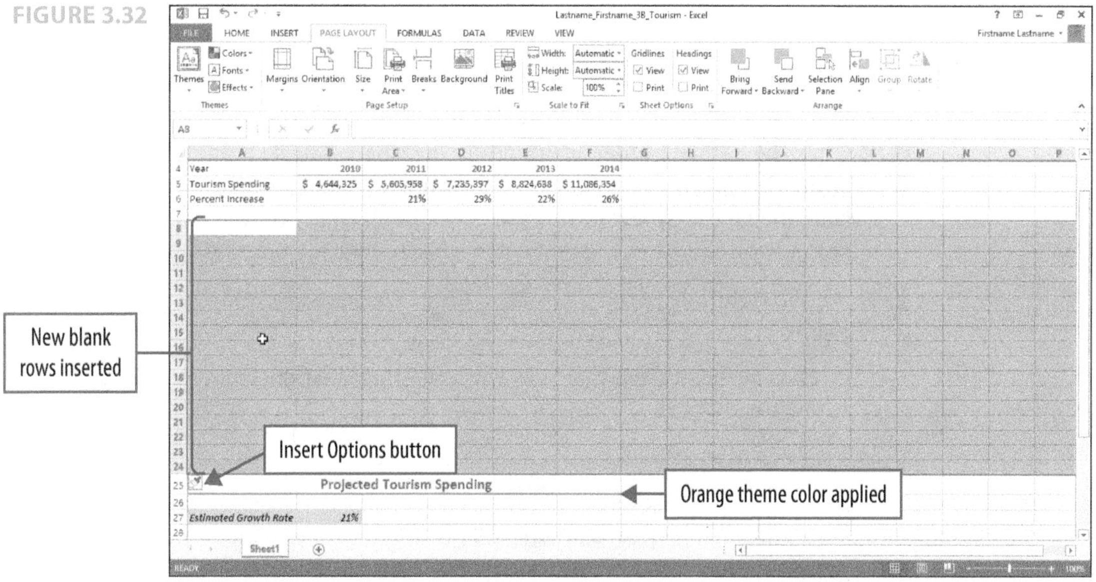

3 Near **row 25**, click **Insert Options** [icon], and then click the **Clear Formatting** option button to clear any formatting from these rows.

You will use this blank area to position your line chart.

4 Press Ctrl + Home to deselect the rows and move to the top of your worksheet. Select the range **A5:F5**. On the **INSERT tab**, in the **Charts group**, click **Insert Line Chart** [icon].

5 In the gallery of line charts, in the second row, point to the first chart type to display the ScreenTip *Line with Markers*. Compare your screen with Figure 3.33.

FIGURE 3.33

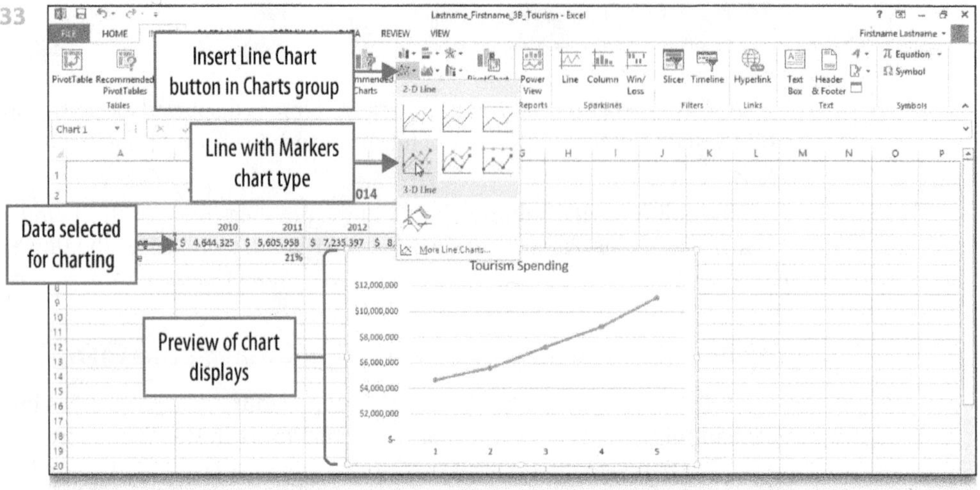

6 Click the **Line with Markers** chart type to create the chart as an embedded chart in the worksheet.

7 Point to the border of the chart to display the [pointer icon] pointer, and then drag the chart so that its upper left corner is positioned in cell **A8**, aligned approximately under the *t* in the word *Percent* above.

Excel uses the label in cell A5—*Tourism Spending*—as the suggested chart title.

8 Point to the **Chart Title** *Tourism Spending* and right-click. On the shortcut menu, click **Edit Text** to place the insertion point in the title. Type **Pacifica Bay** and press Enter. Press End to move to the end of *Spending*, press Spacebar, and then type **2010 to 2014**

9 Click the dashed border surrounding the **Chart Title** so that it is a solid line, indicating the entire title is selected. Right-click over the title, and then click **Font**. In the **Font** dialog box, click the **Font style arrow**, and then click **Bold**. Click the **Font color arrow**, and then in the second column, click the first color—**Black, Text 1**. Click **OK**.

10 On the right side of the chart, click **Chart Elements** [+], and then compare your screen with Figure 3.34.

Three of the available chart elements are included for this chart by default—the axes, the chart title, and the gridlines.

FIGURE 3.34

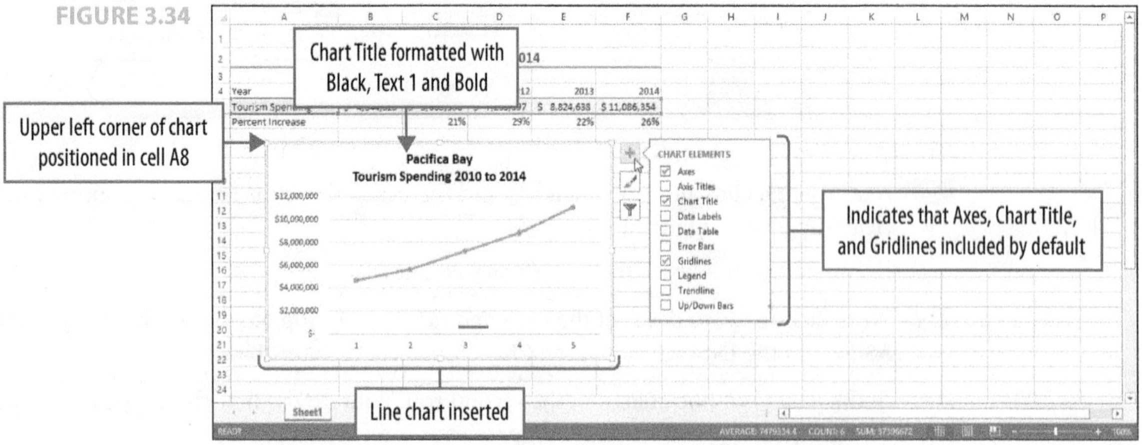

Activity 3.18 | Formatting Axes in a Line Chart

An ***axis*** is a line that serves as a frame of reference for measurement; it borders the chart ***plot area***. The plot area is the area bounded by the axes, including all the data series. Recall that the area along the bottom of a chart that identifies the categories of data is referred to as the ***category axis*** or the ***x-axis***. Recall also that the area along the left side of a chart that shows the range of numbers for the data points is referred to as the ***value axis*** or the ***y-axis***.

In this activity, you will change the category axis to include the years 2010 to 2014 and adjust the numeric scale of the value axis.

1 Be sure the chart is still selected. At the bottom of the chart, point to any of the numbers *1* through *5* to display the ScreenTip *Horizontal (Category) Axis*, and then right-click. On the shortcut menu, click **Select Data**.

BY TOUCH On the ribbon, tap the DESIGN tab, and then in the Data group, tap Select Data.

2 On the right side of the **Select Data Source** dialog box, under **Horizontal (Category) Axis Labels**, locate **Edit**, as shown in Figure 3.35.

Here you can change the labels on the category axis to the years that are represented in the chart.

FIGURE 3.35

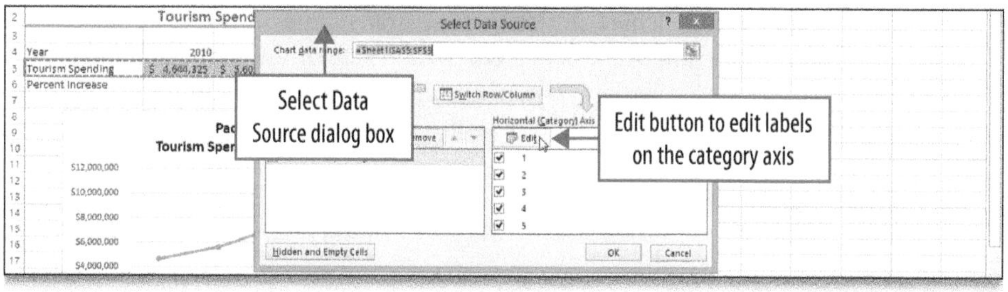

3 In the right column, click **Edit**. If necessary, drag the title bar of the **Axis Labels** dialog box to the right of the chart so that it is not blocking your view of the data, and then select the years in the range **B4:F4**. Compare your screen with Figure 3.36.

FIGURE 3.36

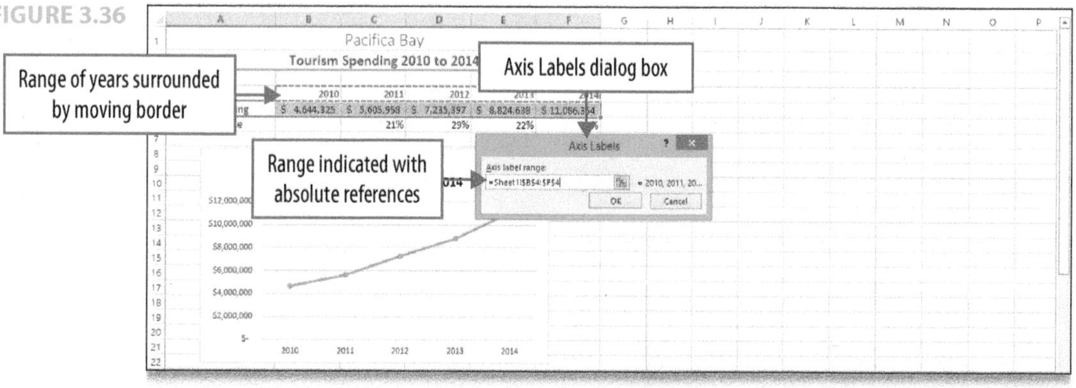

4 In the **Axis Labels** dialog box, click **OK**, and notice that in the right column of the **Select Data Source** dialog box, the years display as the category labels. Click **OK** to close the **Select Data Source** dialog box. Compare your screen with Figure 3.37.

FIGURE 3.37

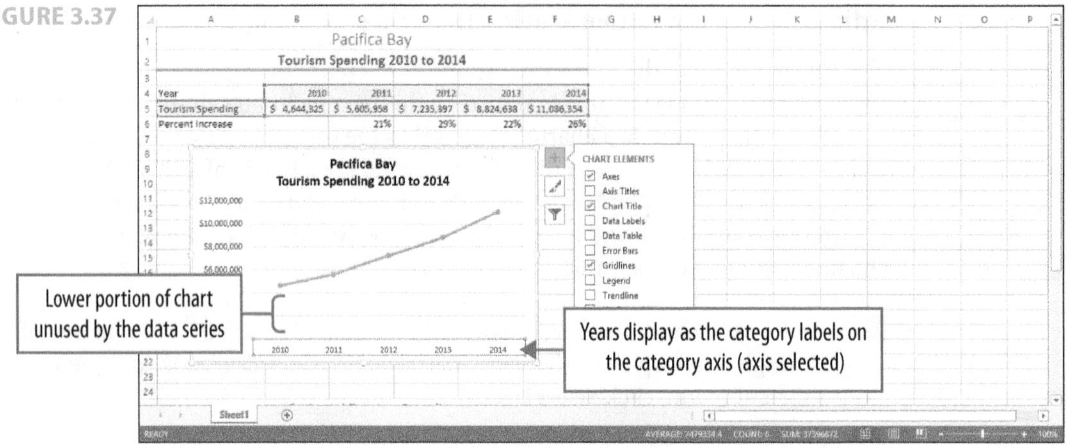

5 With the **Horizontal (Category) Axis** still selected, click the **Chart Elements** button [+], point to **Axes**, click the [▶] **arrow**, and then click **More Options** to display the **Format Axis** pane.

6 Under **AXIS OPTIONS**, click **Fill & Line** [icon], if necessary click **LINE** to expand the options, and then click the **No line** option button so that the line can become a gridline at the bottom of the chart when you format the plot area. **Close** [x] the **Format Axis** pane.

7 On the chart, notice that the orange line—the data series—does not display in the lower portion of the chart. On the left side of the chart, point to any of the dollar values to display the ScreenTip *Vertical (Value) Axis*, and then right-click. On the shortcut menu, click **Format Axis** to display the **Format Axis** pane again on the right. Compare your screen to Figure 3.38.

FIGURE 3.38

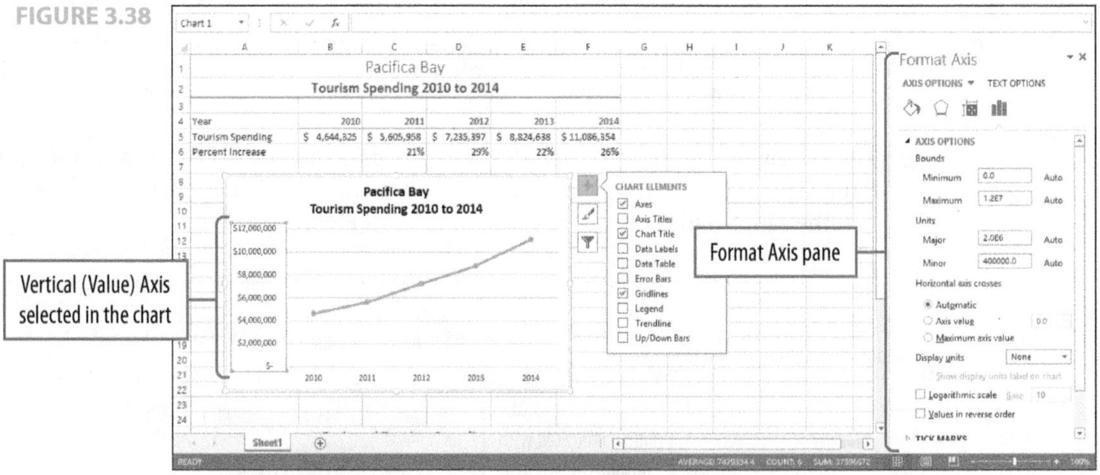

ANOTHER WAY

On the FORMAT tab, in the Current Selection group, click the Chart Elements arrow, click Vertical (Value) Axis, and then click Format Selection. Or, click the Chart Elements button, point to Axes, click the arrow, click More Options, and then in the Format Axis pane, click the AXIS OPTIONS arrow. On the displayed list, click Vertical (Value) Axis.

8 In the **Format Axis** pane, under **Bounds**, click in the **Minimum** box, select the existing text *0.0*, and then type **4000000**

Because none of the spending figures are under $4,000,000, changing the Minimum number to $4,000,000 will enable the data series to occupy more of the plot area.

9 Under **Units**, in the **Major** box, select the text *2.0E6*, type **2000000** and press Enter. Click **Save**, and then compare your screen with Figure 3.39.

The ***Major unit*** value determines the spacing between the gridlines in the plot area. By default, Excel started the values at zero and increased in increments of $2,000,000. By setting the Minimum value on the value axis to $4,000,000 and changing the Major unit to $2,000,000, the line chart shows a clearer and more pronounced trend in tourism spending.

Numbers that display E + a number are expressed by Excel in the Scientific format, which displays a number in exponential notation.

FIGURE 3.39

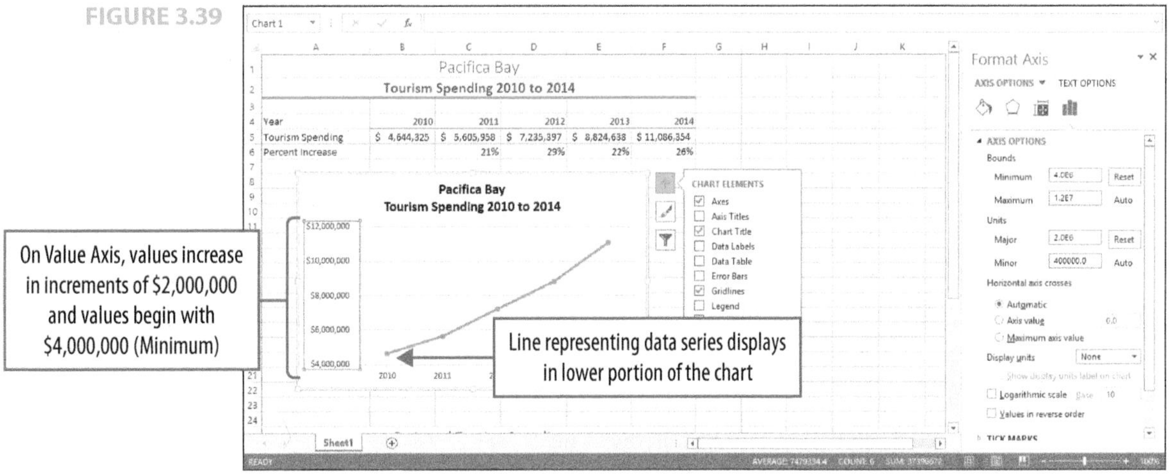

Activity 3.19 | Formatting the Chart Area in a Line Chart

An Excel chart has two background elements—the plot area and the chart area—which, by default display a single fill color. To add visual appeal to a chart, you can insert a graphic image as the background.

1 Near the top of the **Format Axis** pane, click the **AXIS OPTIONS arrow**, and then click **Chart Area** to display the **Format Chart Area** pane. Then click **Fill & Line**.

When formatting chart elements, Excel provides multiple ways to display the panes that you need. You can right-click the area you want to format and choose a command on the shortcut menu. You can use an existing pane to move to a different pane. And you can use the FORMAT tab on the ribbon to navigate among various chart elements in the Current Selection group. Use whatever method is easiest for you.

ANOTHER WAY

On the FORMAT tab, in the Current Selection group, click the Chart Elements arrow, click Chart Area, and then click Format Selection. Or, right-click slightly inside the chart to display the shortcut menu, and then click Format Chart Area.

2 In the **Format Chart Area** pane, click **FILL** to expand the options, and then click the **Picture or texture fill** option button.

A default texture displays in the chart area.

3 In the **Format Chart Area** pane, under **Insert picture from**, click **File**. In the **Insert Picture** dialog box, navigate to the student data files that accompany this textbook, and then click **e03B_Surfers**. Click **Insert**. Compare your screen with Figure 3.40.

FIGURE 3.40

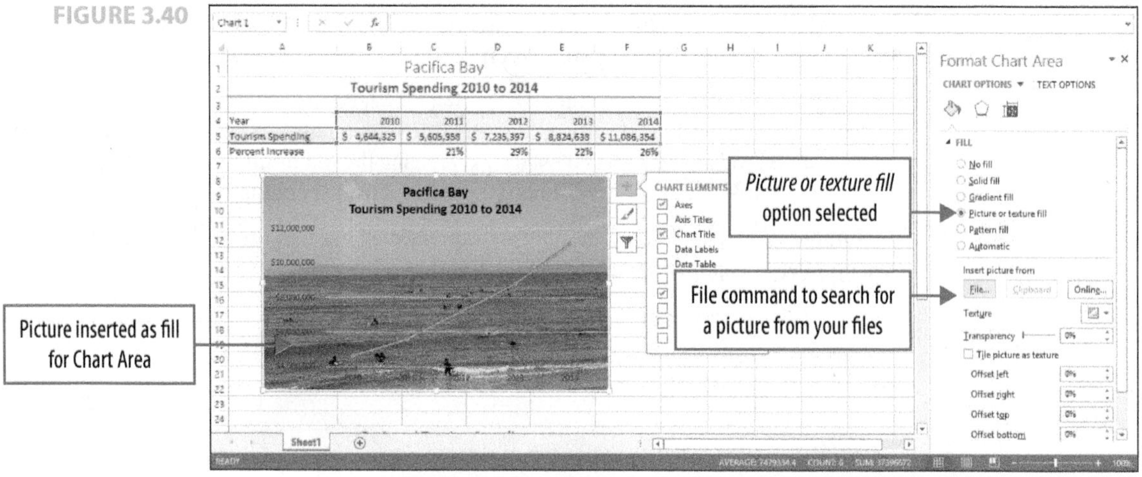

4 In the **Format Chart Area** pane, click **FILL** to collapse the options, and then click **BORDER** to expand the options. Click the **Solid line** option button, click the **Color arrow**, and then under **Theme Colors**, in the fifth column, notice that the first color—**Orange, Accent 1**—is already selected by default.

5 Click the **Color arrow** again to accept the default color and close the color palette.

6 Set the **Width** to **4 pt** either by selecting the existing text in the Width box and typing or by clicking the up spin box arrow as necessary.

7 Use the scroll bar on the right side of the **Format Chart Area** pane if necessary to scroll to the bottom of the pane, and then select the **Rounded corners** check box. On the **Quick Access Toolbar**, click **Save**, and then compare your screen with Figure 3.41.

FIGURE 3.41

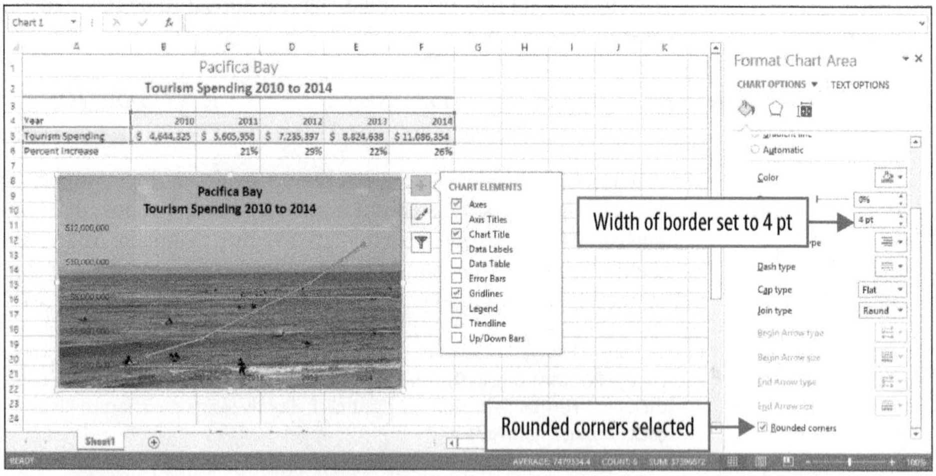

Activity 3.20 | Formatting the Plot Area Gridlines and Axis Fonts in a Line Chart

1 To the right of the chart, if necessary click **Chart Elements** to display the list of elements, point to **Gridlines**, click the **arrow**, and then click **More Options** to display the **Format Major Gridlines** pane. Compare your screen with Figure 3.42.

FIGURE 3.42

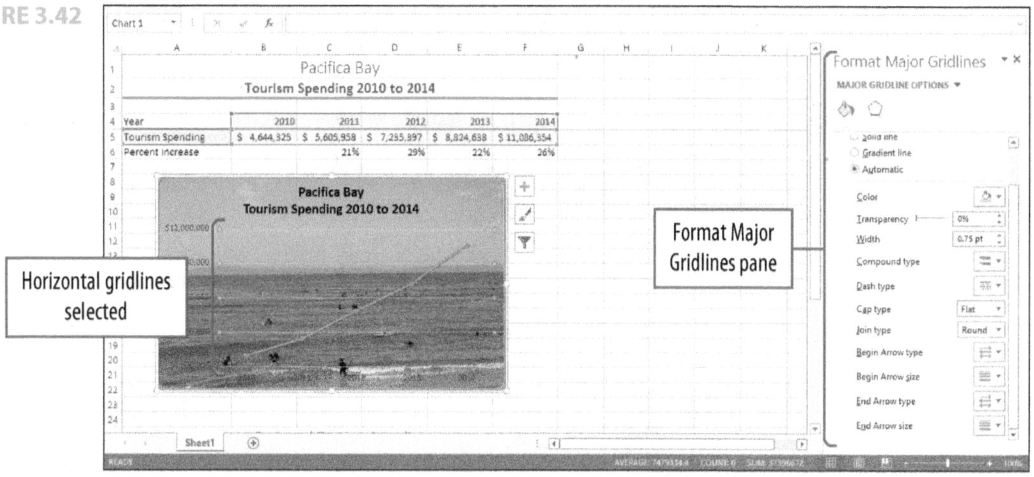

2 If necessary, in the pane, scroll to the top and click to expand **LINE**. Click the **Solid line** option button. Click the **Color arrow**, and be sure that **Orange, Accent 1**—in the fifth column, the first color—is selected.

3 Set the **Width** to **1 pt**.

4 In the chart, point to any of the dollar values on the **Vertical (Value) Axis**, right-click, and then click **Font**.

5 In the **Font** dialog box, change the **Font style** to **Bold**, and then change the **Font color** to **Black, Text 1**—in the second column, the first color. Click **OK**.

6 Use the same technique to format the font of the **Horizontal (Category) Axis** to **Bold** with **Black, Text 1**.

7 **Close** [X] the **Format Axis** pane. Click cell **A1** to deselect the chart. Click **Save** [Save icon], and then compare your screen with Figure 3.43.

FIGURE 3.43

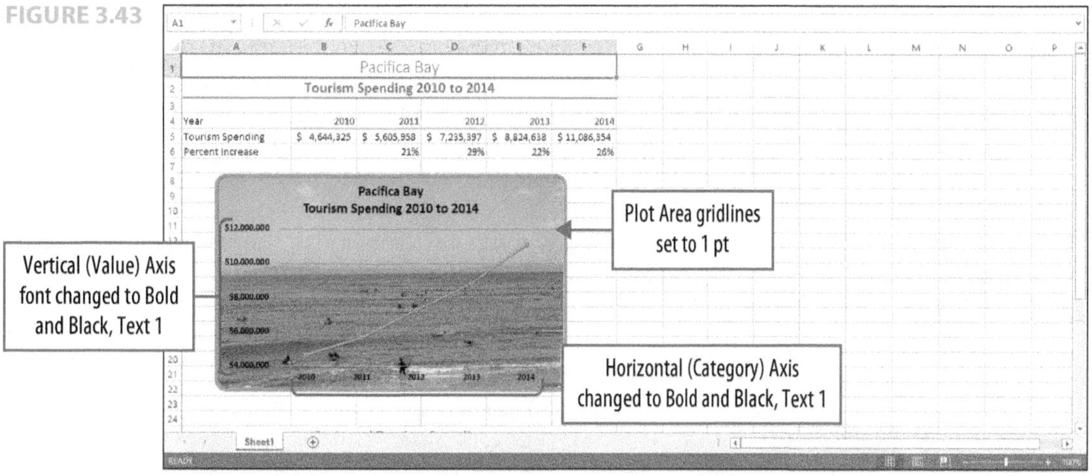

8 Click the **PAGE LAYOUT tab**. In the **Page Setup group**, click **Margins**, and then click **Custom Margins**.

9 In the **Page Setup** dialog box, on the **Margins tab**, under **Center on page**, select the **Horizontally** check box.

10 Click the **Header/Footer tab**, and then in the center of the dialog box, click **Custom Footer**. In the **Footer** dialog box, with your insertion point blinking in the **Left section**, on the row of buttons, click **Insert File Name**.

11 Click **OK** two times. Click the **FILE tab**, and then click **Show All Properties**. As the **Tags**, type **tourism spending** As the **Subject**, type your course name and section number. Be sure your name displays as the author.

12 On the left, click **Print** to display the **Print Preview**, and then compare your screen with Figure 3.44. If necessary return to the worksheet and make any corrections.

FIGURE 3.44

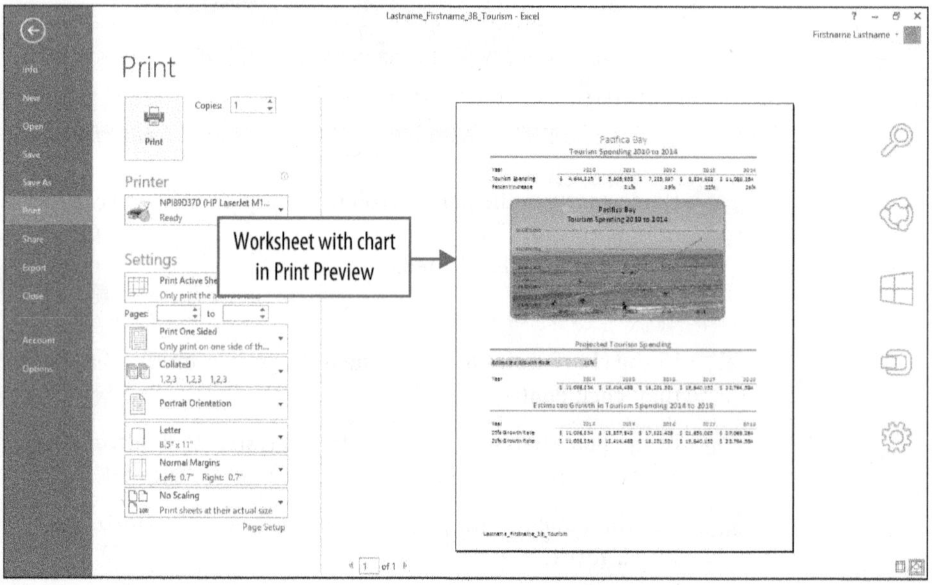

13 On the left, click **Save** to redisplay the workbook.

14 Using the techniques you practiced in Project 1A, print or submit electronically as directed by your instructor. If required by your instructor, print or create an electronic version of your worksheet with formulas displayed.

15 Close your workbook and close Excel.

***More* Knowledge** **Resizing a Chart**

To resize a chart, on the CHART TOOLS FORMAT tab, in the Size group, type the dimensions in the Shape Height or Shape Width box. Or:

- To change the width of a chart, drag a left or right sizing handle.
- To change the height of a chart, drag a top or bottom sizing handle.
- To size a chart proportionately, drag a corner sizing handle.

END | You have completed Project 3B

GO! with Office Online (formerly Web Apps)

3 EXCEL

Objective Convert an Excel Worksheet to a Google Docs Spreadsheet with a Chart

Google Docs is Google's free, web-based word processor, spreadsheet, slide show, and form service that, along with free data storage, is known as ***Google Drive***. You can convert an Excel worksheet to a Google Docs spreadsheet. Google Drive and Google Docs are similar to OneDrive and Office Online—both are free, cloud-based productivity tools.

ALERT! Working with Web-Based Applications and Services

Computer programs and services on the web receive continuous updates and improvements, so the steps to complete this web-based activity may differ from the ones shown. You can often look at the screens and the information presented to determine how to complete the activity.

Activity | Converting an Excel Worksheet to a Google Docs Spreadsheet with a Chart

In this activity, you will convert an Excel worksheet to a Google Docs spreadsheet and create a column chart.

1 If you do *not* have a Google account, skip to Step 2. If you already have a Google account, start Internet Explorer, in the address bar, type **http://docs.google.com** and then press Enter. Sign in to your Google account your Google Drive. Now skip to Step 3.

2 From the desktop, start Internet Explorer. In the address bar, type **http://docs.google.com** and then press Enter. Locate and click the button to sign up for a new account, and then complete the information. As your email address, you can use your Microsoft account or other email address. Sign in to your new Google account.

3 Locate and click **CREATE**, and then click **Spreadsheet**. Under **Untitled spreadsheet**, click **File**, and then click **Import**. Click **Upload**, and then click **Select a file from your computer**. In the **Choose File to Upload** dialog box, navigate to your student data files and click **e03_3B_Web**. In the lower right corner of the dialog box, click **Open**, and then click **Import**.

4 When the screen indicates that the file was imported successfully, click **Open now**. Compare your screen with Figure A.

5 Drag to select the years and values in the range **A4:F5**, and then on the menu bar, click **Insert**. On the menu, click **Chart**.

6 On the **Chart Editor** screen, under **Recommended charts**, click the second chart—the **Column chart**. On the left above **Recommended charts**, click to select the first check box—**Switch rows/columns**, and then the second check box **Use column A as headers**, and then the third check box, **Use row 4 as labels**.

FIGURE A

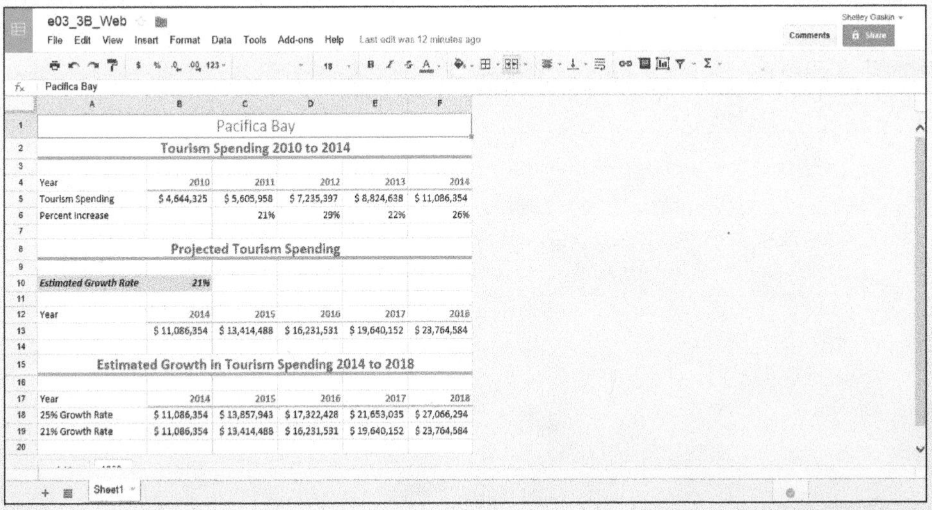

	A	B	C	D	E	F
1	Pacifica Bay					
2	Tourism Spending 2010 to 2014					
3						
4	Year	2010	2011	2012	2013	2014
5	Tourism Spending	$ 4,644,325	$ 5,605,958	$ 7,235,397	$ 8,824,638	$ 11,086,354
6	Percent Increase		21%	29%	22%	26%
7						
8	Projected Tourism Spending					
9						
10	*Estimated Growth Rate*	21%				
11						
12	Year	2014	2015	2016	2017	2018
13		$ 11,086,354	$ 13,414,488	$ 16,231,531	$ 19,640,152	$ 23,764,584
14						
15	Estimated Growth in Tourism Spending 2014 to 2018					
16						
17	Year	2014	2015	2016	2017	2018
18	25% Growth Rate	$ 11,086,354	$ 13,857,943	$ 17,322,428	$ 21,653,035	$ 27,066,294
19	21% Growth Rate	$ 11,086,354	$ 13,414,488	$ 16,231,531	$ 19,640,152	$ 23,764,584
20						

(GO! with Office Online (formerly Web Apps) continues on the next page)

7 In the lower left corner, click **Insert**. In the upper right corner, click the down arrow and then click **Move to own sheet.**

8 On the displayed chart, click the text *Chart title*. In the box that displays, with the text selected, and then using your own name, type **2010 – 2014 Tourism Spending Prepared by Firstname Lastname** Press Enter.

9 In the upper right corner of the chart, click the small square labeled *Tourism Spending*, and then click one time to edit the legend. In the toolbar that displays above, click **Right**, and then on the displayed list, click **None**. Compare your screen with Figure B.

10 In the upper right, click **Save image**, and then in the **Notification bar** at the bottom, click the **Save arrow**. Click **Save as**, and then in the **Save As** dialog box, navigate to your **Excel Chapter 3** folder. In the **File name** box, using your own name, type **Lastname_Firstname_EX_3B_Web** and then press Enter.

11 In the upper right corner, click your Google name, and then click **Sign out**. Close Internet Explorer.

It is not necessary to save your spreadsheet, because Google Drive saves your work automatically. Your image is saved as a ***.png*** file, which is the file extension for an image in the *Portable Network Graphics* format. This format, like JPEG, is commonly used for graphics on the web.

12 Submit your .png image file to your instructor as directed.

FIGURE B

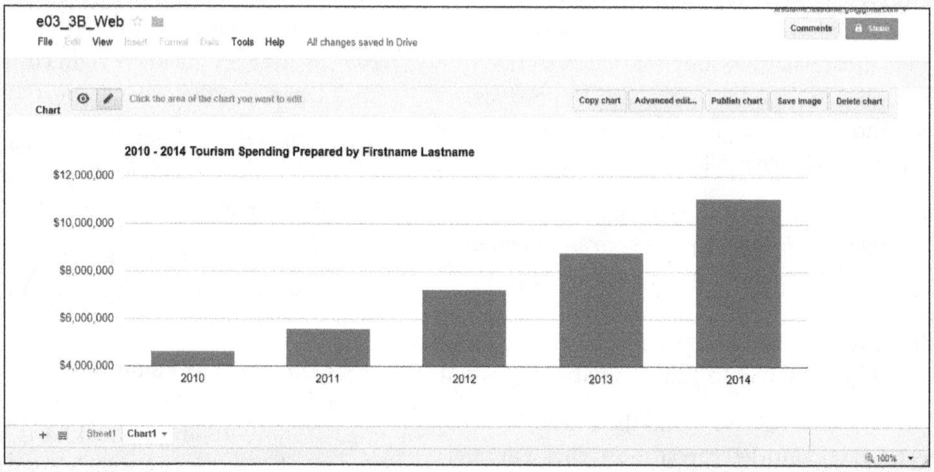

GO! with Microsoft Office 365

Andrew Rodriguez / Fotolia; FotolEdhar/ Fotolia; apops/ Fotolia; Yuri Arcurs/ Fotolia

The advantage of using Office 365 is that your organization does not have to purchase and install server hardware and software for sophisticated business applications and does not need a full-time IT person or staff just to manage the technology your teams need.

By using Office 365, you are able to have business-class services for your employees without investing in expensive hardware, software, and personnel. However, at least one person in an organization must be designated as the ***Office 365 Administrator***—the person who creates and manages the account, adds new users, sets up the services your organization wants to use, sets permission levels, and manages the SharePoint team sites. You can have more than one Administrator if you want to share these tasks with others.

Microsoft provides easy-to-use instructions and videos to get you started, and you might also have contact with a Microsoft representative. You will probably find, however, that subscribing to and setting up the account, adding users, and activating services is a straightforward process that requires little or no assistance.

After purchasing the required number of licenses, you will add each team member as a user that includes his or her email address.

The Office 365 Administrator can manage the team sites, as shown in Figure A. On the left there are links to manage the site pages in the Office 365 account. Here the administrator can manage permissions, specifying which users can access and edit which team sites. The administrator can also manage and modify the look and feel of the team site.

Activity | Using a Team Site to Collaborate

This group project relates to the **Bell Orchid Hotels.** If your instructor assigns this project to your class, you can expect to use **Lync** in **Office 365** to collaborate on the following tasks for this chapter:

- If you are in the **Accounting Group**, you and your teammates will finalize the workbook to summarize hotel rooms sold over a four-week period in April and post it to your team site.
- If you are in the **Engineering Group**, you and your teammates will finalize your workbook summarizing Maintenance Expenses for the first quarter and post it to your team site.
- If you are in the **Food and Beverage Group**, you and your teammates will finalize your workbook to analyze the profitability of the ten most popular entrees in the hotel's restaurant and post it to your team site.
- If you are in the **Human Resources Group**, you and your teammates will finalize your workbook summarizing the pay of salaried employees over the first six months of operation and post it to your team site.
- If you are in the **Operations Group**, you and your teammates will finalize your workbook for Rooms and Housekeeping Service Analysis that will be used to determine ongoing needs for housekeeping service and post it to your team site.
- If you are in the **Sales and Marketing Group**, you and your teammates will finalize your Rooms Sold Analysis workbook summarizing rooms sold by four salespersons during January-June that will be used to develop a marketing plan for the rest of the year and post it to your team site.

FIGURE A

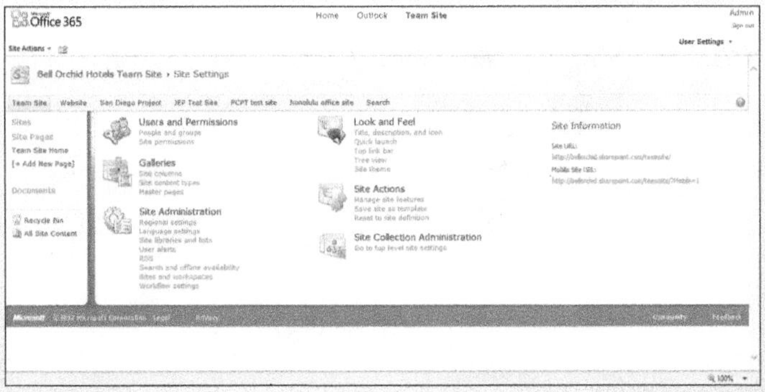

END OF CHAPTER

SUMMARY

Use pie charts when you want to show the relationship of each part to a whole. Consider using a pie chart when you have only one data series to plot and you do not have more than seven categories.

To create a pie chart, you must select two ranges. One range contains the labels for each pie slice; the other contains the values that add up to a total. Both ranges must have the same number of cells.

In formulas, Excel follows rules called the order of operations; expressions within parentheses are processed first, and multiplication and division are performed before addition and subtraction.

Use a line chart when you want to show trends over time. Time displays along the bottom axis and the data point values connect with a line. The curve and direction of the line make trends obvious.

GO! LEARN IT ONLINE

Review the concepts and key terms in this chapter by completing these online challenges, which you can find at **www.pearsonhighered.com/go**.

Matching and Multiple Choice: Answer matching and multiple choice questions to test what you learned in this chapter. MyITLab®

Crossword Puzzle: Spell out the words that match the numbered clues, and put them in the puzzle squares.

Flipboard: Flip through the definitions of the key terms in this chapter and match them with the correct term.

GO! FOR JOB SUCCESS

Video: Planning and Managing Your Career

Your instructor may assign this video to your class, and then ask you to think about, or discuss with your classmates, these questions:

FotolEdhar / Fotolia

When did you start career planning and what were the main steps you took to plan your career?

What have been your best sources for networking?

What advice would you give to others about how to stay employable throughout your career?

END OF CHAPTER

REVIEW AND ASSESSMENT GUIDE FOR EXCEL CHAPTER 3

Your instructor may assign one or more of these projects to help you review the chapter and assess your mastery and understanding of the chapter.

Review and Assessment Guide for Excel Chapter 3			
Project	**Apply Skills from These Chapter Objectives**	**Project Type**	**Project Location**
3C	Objectives 1-4 from Project 3A	**3C Skills Review** A guided review of the skills from Project 3A.	On the following pages
3D	Objectives 5-7 from Project 3B	**3D Skills Review** A guided review of the skills from Project 3B.	On the following pages
3E	Objectives 1-4 from Project 3A	**3E Mastery (Grader Project)** A demonstration of your mastery of the skills in Project 3A with extensive decision making.	In MyITLab and on the following pages
3F	Objectives 5-7 from Project 3B	**3F Mastery (Grader Project)** A demonstration of your mastery of the skills in Project 3B with extensive decision making.	In MyITLab and on the following pages
3G	Objectives 1-7 from Projects 3A and 3B	**3G Mastery (Grader Project)** A demonstration of your mastery of the skills in Projects 3A and 3B with extensive decision making.	In MyITLab and on the following pages
3H	Combination of Objectives from Projects 3A and 3B	**3H GO! Fix It** A demonstration of your mastery of the skills in Projects 3A and 3B by creating a correct result from a document that contains errors you must find.	Online
3I	Combination of Objectives from Projects 3A and 3B	**3I GO! Make It** A demonstration of your mastery of the skills in Projects 3A and 3B by creating a result from a supplied picture.	Online
3J	Combination of Objectives from Projects 3A and 3B	**3J GO! Solve It** A demonstration of your mastery of the skills in Projects 3A and 3B, your decision-making skills, and your critical thinking skills. A task-specific rubric helps you self-assess your result.	Online
3K	Combination of Objectives from Projects 3A and 3B	**3K GO! Solve It** A demonstration of your mastery of the skills in Projects 3A and 3B, your decision-making skills, and your critical thinking skills. A task-specific rubric helps you self-assess your result.	On the following pages
3L	Combination of Objectives from Projects 3A and 3B	**3L GO! Think** A demonstration of your understanding of the Chapter concepts applied in a manner that you would outside of college. An analytic rubric helps you and your instructor grade the quality of your work by comparing it to the work an expert in the discipline would create.	On the following pages
3M	Combination of Objectives from Projects 3A and 3B	**3M GO! Think** A demonstration of your understanding of the Chapter concepts applied in a manner that you would outside of college. An analytic rubric helps you and your instructor grade the quality of your work by comparing it to the work an expert in the discipline would create.	Online
3N	Combination of Objectives from Projects 3A and 3B	**3N You and GO!** A demonstration of your understanding of the Chapter concepts applied in a manner that you would in a personal situation. An analytic rubric helps you and your instructor grade the quality of your work.	Online
3O	Combination of Objectives from Projects 3A and 3B	**3O Cumulative Group Project for Excel Chapter 3** A demonstration of your understanding of concepts and your ability to work collaboratively in a group role-playing assessment, requiring both collaboration and self-management.	Online
Capstone Project for Excel Chapters 1-3	Combination of Objectives from Projects 1A, 1B, 2A, 2B, 3A, and 3B	A demonstration of your mastery of the skills in Chapters 1-3 with extensive decision making. **(Grader Project)**	In MyITLab and online

GLOSSARY

GLOSSARY OF CHAPTER KEY TERMS

3-D The shortened term for *three-dimensional*, which refers to an image that appears to have all three spatial dimensions—length, width, and depth.

Absolute cell reference A cell reference that refers to cells by their fixed position in a worksheet; an absolute cell reference remains the same when the formula is copied.

Axis A line that serves as a frame of reference for measurement and which borders the chart plot area.

Base The starting point when you divide the amount of increase by it to calculate the rate of increase.

Bevel A shape effect that uses shading and shadows to make the edges of a shape appear to be curved or angled.

Category axis The area along the bottom of a chart that identifies the categories of data; also referred to as the x-axis.

Chart area The entire chart and all of its elements.

Chart sheet A workbook sheet that contains only a chart.

Data marker A column, bar, area, dot, pie slice, or other symbol in a chart that represents a single data point; related data points form a data series.

Data point A value that originates in a worksheet cell and that is represented in a chart by a data marker.

Data series Related data points represented by data markers; each data series has a unique color or pattern represented in the chart legend.

Enterprise fund A municipal government fund that reports income and expenditures related to municipal services for which a fee is charged in exchange for goods or services.

Explode The action of pulling out one or more pie slices from a pie chart for emphasis.

Formula AutoComplete An Excel feature which, after typing an = (equal sign) and the beginning letter or letters of a function name, displays a list of function names that match the typed letter(s).

Fund A sum of money set aside for a specific purpose.

General fund The term used to describe money set aside for the normal operating activities of a government entity such as a city.

Goal Seek A what-if analysis tool that finds the input needed in one cell to arrive at the desired result in another cell.

Google Docs Google's free, web-based word processor, spreadsheet, slide show, and form service, that along with free data storage, is known as Google Drive.

Google Drive Google's free web-based word processor, spreadsheet, slide show, and form service, that includes free data storage.

Legend A chart element that identifies the patterns or colors that are assigned to the categories in the chart.

Line chart A chart type that displays trends over time; time displays along the bottom axis and the data point values are connected with a line.

Major unit The value in a chart's value axis that determines the spacing between tick marks and between the gridlines in the plot area.

Order of operations The mathematical rules for performing multiple calculations within a formula.

Percent for new value = base percent + percent of increase The formula for calculating a percentage by which a value increases by adding the base percentage—usually 100%—to the percent increase.

Percentage rate of increase The percent by which one number increases over another number.

Pie chart A chart that shows the relationship of each part to a whole.

Plot area The area bounded by the axes of a chart, including all the data series.

Rate = amount of increase/base The mathematical formula to calculate a rate of increase.

Relative cell reference In a formula, the address of a cell based on the relative position of the cell that contains the formula and the cell referred to.

Value after increase = base x percent for new value The formula for calculating the value after an increase by multiplying the original value—the base—by the percent for new value (see the *Percent for new value* formula).

Value axis A numerical scale on the left side of a chart that shows the range of numbers for the data points; also referred to as the Y-axis.

What-if analysis The process of changing the values in cells to see how those changes affect the outcome of formulas in a worksheet.

x-axis Another name for the category axis.

y-axis Another name for the value axis.

CHAPTER REVIEW

Apply 3A skills from these Objectives:

1. Chart Data with a Pie Chart
2. Format a Pie Chart
3. Edit a Workbook and Update a Chart
4. Use Goal Seek to Perform What-If Analysis

Skills Review Project 3C Parks

In the following Skills Review, you will edit a worksheet for Jerry Silva, City Parks Manager, which details the revenue generated from city parks and structures. Your completed worksheets will look similar to Figure 3.45.

PROJECT FILES

For Project 3C, you will need the following file:

e03C_Parks

You will save your workbook as:

Lastname_Firstname_3C_Parks

PROJECT RESULTS

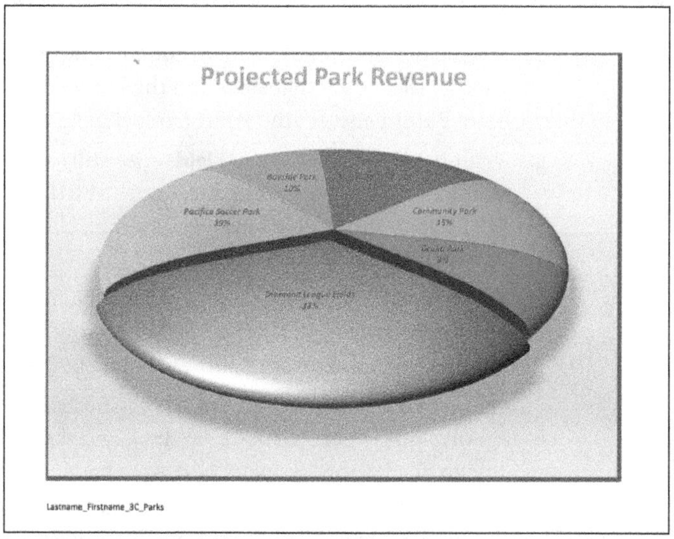

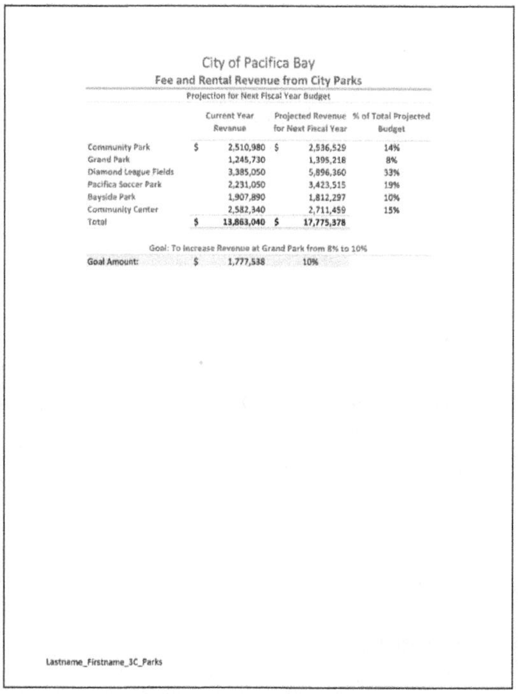

City of Pacifica Bay

Fee and Rental Revenue from City Parks

Projection for Next Fiscal Year Budget

	Current Year Revenue	Projected Revenue for Next Fiscal Year	% of Total Projected Budget
Community Park	$ 2,510,980	$ 2,536,529	14%
Grand Park	1,245,730	1,395,218	8%
Diamond League Fields	3,385,050	5,896,360	33%
Pacifica Soccer Park	2,231,050	3,423,515	19%
Bayside Park	1,907,890	1,812,297	10%
Community Center	2,582,340	2,711,459	15%
Total	$ 13,863,040	$ 17,775,378	

Goal: To Increase Revenue at Grand Park from 8% to 10%

Goal Amount:	$ 1,777,538	10%

Lastname_Firstname_3C_Parks

FIGURE 3.45

(Project 3C Parks continues on the next page)

CHAPTER REVIEW

Skills Review Project 3C Parks (continued)

1 Start Excel. From your student data files, open the file **e03C_Parks**. Save the file in your **Excel Chapter 3** folder as **Lastname_Firstname_3C_Parks**

a. Click cell **D5**, and then type = to begin a formula. Click cell **C5**, type / and then click cell **C11**. Press F4 to make the reference to the value in cell **C11** absolute. On the **Formula Bar**, click **Enter**, and then fill the formula down through cell **D10**.

b. With the range **D5:D10** selected, right-click over the selection, and then on the mini toolbar, click **Percent Style** and **Center**.

2 Select the nonadjacent ranges **A5:A10** and **C5:C10** to select the park names and the projected revenue. Click the **INSERT tab**, and then in the **Charts group**, click **Insert Pie or Doughnut Chart**. Under **3-D Pie**, click the chart type **3-D Pie**.

a. On the **DESIGN tab**, in the **Location group**, click **Move Chart**. In the **Move Chart** dialog box, click the **New sheet** option button. In the **New sheet** box, replace the highlighted text *Chart1* by typing **Projected Park Revenue Chart** and then click **OK**.

b. Click the text *Chart Title*, and then type **Projected Park Revenue** Press Enter to create the new chart title.

c. With the title selected, on the **FORMAT tab**, in the **WordArt Styles group**, click **More** to display the gallery. In the second row, select the fifth style—**Fill - Olive Green, Accent 3, Sharp Bevel**. Drag to select the chart title text, and then on the mini toolbar, change the **Font Size** to **32**.

d. Click in a white area of the chart to deselect the chart title. Click **Chart Elements** [+], and then click the **Legend** check box to remove the legend.

e. In the list of **CHART ELEMENTS**, point to **Data Labels**, click the **arrow** that displays, and then click **More Options**. In the **Format Data Labels** pane on the right, under **LABEL OPTIONS**, select the **Category Name** and **Percentage** check boxes, and *clear* all other check boxes. Under **Label Position**, click **Center**.

f. Point to any of the selected labels, right-click to display a shortcut menu, and then click **Font**. In the **Font** dialog box, on the **Font tab**, change the **Font style** to **Bold Italic** and change the **Size** to **11** Click **OK**.

3 In any pie slice, point anywhere outside the selected label, and then double-click to display the **Format Data Series** pane. Under **SERIES OPTIONS**, click **Effects**, and then click **3-D FORMAT**.

a. Click the **Top bevel arrow**, and then under **Bevel**, click the first button—**Circle**. Apply the **Circle** bevel to the **Bottom bevel**.

b. Set the **Width** and **Height** of both the **Top bevel** and the **Bottom bevel** to **512 pt**

c. Scroll down, click the **Material arrow**, and then under **Standard**, click the third material—**Plastic**.

d. Scroll to the top of the **Format Data Series** pane, click **SHADOW**, and then click the **Presets arrow**. Scroll down, and then under **Perspective**, in the first row, click the third effect—**Below**.

e. In the **Format Data Series** pane, under **SERIES OPTIONS**, click the third button—**Series Options**. Set the **Angle of first slice** to **50**

f. On the pie chart, click the **Diamond League Fields** slice to select only that slice, and then in the **Format Data Point** pane, set the Point Explosion to **10%**

g. With the **Diamond League Fields** slice still selected, in the **Format Data Point** pane, under **SERIES OPTIONS**, click **Fill & Line**, and then click **FILL** to expand the options.

h. Click the **Gradient fill** option button, click the **Preset gradients arrow**, and then in the fourth row, click the third gradient—**Bottom Spotlight - Accent 3**.

4 Point to the white area just inside the border of the chart to display the ScreenTip *Chart Area*, and then click one time to display the **Format Chart Area** pane.

a. Under **CHART OPTIONS**, click **Fill & Line**, and be sure the **FILL** options are still displayed.

b. Click the **Gradient fill** option button, click the **Preset gradients arrow**, and then in the first row, click the fifth gradient—**Light Gradient - Accent 5**.

c. In the **Format Chart Area** pane, click **FILL** to collapse the options, and then click **BORDER** to expand the options.

d. Click the **Solid line** option button, click the **Color arrow**, and then in the fifth column, click the last color—**Ice Blue, Accent 1, Darker 50%**. Set the **Width** of the border to **5 pt** Close the pane, and then **Save** your workbook.

(Project 3C Parks continues on the next page)

Skills Review Project 3C Parks (continued)

5 In the sheet tab area at the bottom of the workbook, click the **Sheet1 tab**. In cell **A13**, type **Goal: To Increase Revenue at Grand Park from 8% to 10%** and then **Merge & Center** the text across the range **A13:D13**. Apply the **Heading 3** cell style.

a. In cell **A14**, type **Goal Amount:** and press Enter. Select the range **C6:D6**, right-click over the selection, and then click **Copy**. Point to cell **B14**, right-click, and then under **Paste Options**, click **Paste**. Press Esc to cancel the moving border.

b. Click cell **C14**. On the **DATA tab**, in the **Data Tools group**, click **What-If Analysis**, and then click **Goal Seek**. In the **Goal Seek** dialog box, press Tab to move to the **To value** box, and then type **10%**

c. Press Tab to move the insertion point to the **By changing cell** box, and then click cell **B14**. Click **OK**. In the displayed **Goal Seek Status** dialog box, click **OK**.

d. Select the range **A14:C14**. From the **HOME tab**, display the **Cell Styles** gallery. Under **Themed Cell Styles**, apply **20% - Accent6**. Click cell **B14**, and then from the **Cell Styles** gallery, under **Number Format**, apply the **Currency** [**0**] cell style.

6 With your worksheet displayed, in the sheet tab area, double-click *Sheet1* to select the text, and then type **Projected Park Revenue Data** and press Enter.

a. Click the **PAGE LAYOUT tab**. In the **Page Setup Group**, click **Margins**, click **Custom Margins**, and then in the **Page Setup** dialog box, on the **Margins tab**, under **Center on page**, select the **Horizontally** check box.

b. Click the **Header/Footer tab**, click **Custom Footer**, and then with your insertion point in the **Left section**, on the row of buttons, click **Insert File Name**. Click **OK** two times.

c. Display the **Projected Park Revenue Chart**—recall a chart sheet must have its footer formatted separately. Display the **Page Setup** dialog box.

d. Click the **Header/Footer tab**, click **Custom Footer**, and then in the **Left section**, click the **Insert File Name** button. Click **OK** two times.

e. Click the **FILE tab**, and then click **Show All Properties**. As the **Tags**, type **park revenue** As the **Subject**, type your course name and section number. Be sure your name displays as the **Author**.

f. On the left, click **Save**. Right-click the **Projected Park Revenue Chart sheet tab**, and then click **Select All Sheets**. Print or submit electronically as directed by your instructor. If required by your instructor, print or create an electronic version with formulas displayed by using the instructions in Project 1A. Close Excel without saving so that you do not save the changes you made to print formulas.

END | You have completed Project 3C

CHAPTER REVIEW

Apply 3B skills from these Objectives:

5 Design a Worksheet for What-If Analysis
6 Answer What-If Questions by Changing Values in a Worksheet
7 Chart Data with a Line Chart

Skills Review Project 3D Housing Permits

In the following Skills Review, you will edit a worksheet that forecasts the revenue from new housing permits that the City of Pacifica Bay expects to collect in the five-year period 2014–2018. Your completed worksheet will look similar to Figure 3.46.

PROJECT FILES

For Project 3D, you will need the following files:

New blank workbook
e03D_Housing

Build from Scratch

You will save your workbook as:

Lastname_Firstname_3D_Housing

PROJECT RESULTS

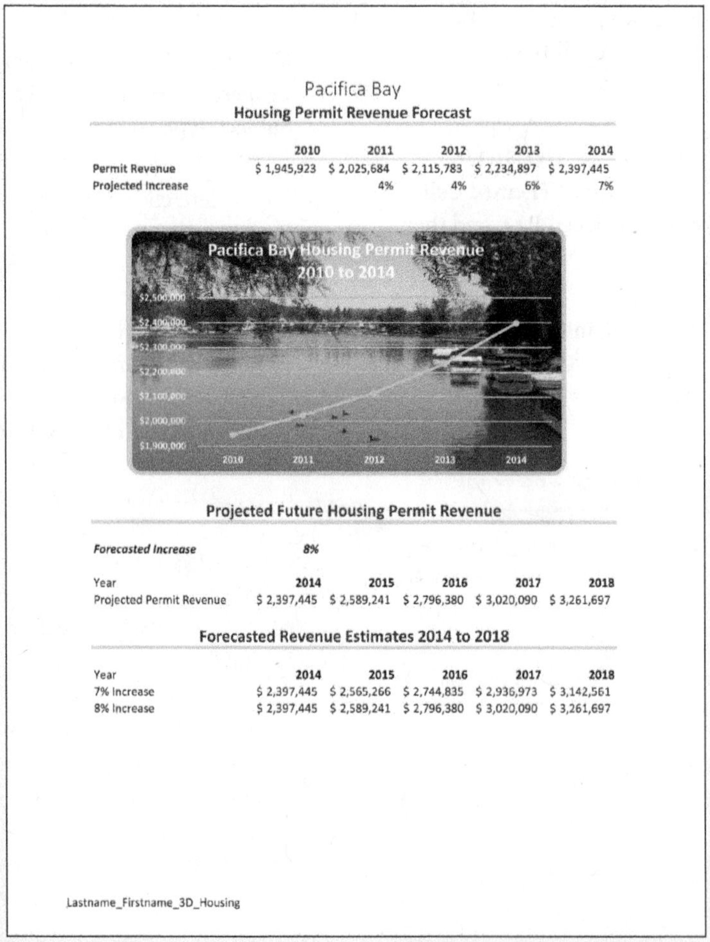
Pacifica Bay
Housing Permit Revenue Forecast

	2010	2011	2012	2013	2014
Permit Revenue	$ 1,945,923	$ 2,025,684	$ 2,115,783	$ 2,234,897	$ 2,397,445
Projected Increase		4%	4%	6%	7%

Projected Future Housing Permit Revenue

Forecasted Increase 8%

Year	2014	2015	2016	2017	2018
Projected Permit Revenue	$ 2,397,445	$ 2,589,241	$ 2,796,380	$ 3,020,090	$ 3,261,697

Forecasted Revenue Estimates 2014 to 2018

Year	2014	2015	2016	2017	2018
7% Increase	$ 2,397,445	$ 2,565,266	$ 2,744,835	$ 2,936,973	$ 3,142,561
8% Increase	$ 2,397,445	$ 2,589,241	$ 2,796,380	$ 3,020,090	$ 3,261,697

Lastname_Firstname_3D_Housing

FIGURE 3.46

(Project 3D Housing Permits continues on the next page)

CHAPTER REVIEW

Skills Review Project 3D Housing Permits (continued)

1 Start Excel and display a new blank workbook. By using your own name, save the file in your **Excel Chapter 3** folder as **Lastname_Firstname_3D_Housing**

a. In cell **A1**, type **Pacifica Bay** and in cell **A2** type **Housing Permit Revenue Forecast**

b. **Merge & Center** the title and subtitle across **columns A:F**. To **A1** apply the **Title** cell style and to **A2** apply the **Heading 1** cell style.

c. Widen **column A** to **175 pixels**, and widen **columns B:F** to **80 pixels**.

d. In cell **A5**, type **Permit Revenue** and in cell **A6** type **Projected Increase** Apply the **Heading 4** cell style to both cells. In cell **B4**, type **2010** Press Tab, and then in **C4**, type **2011** Use the fill handle to fill the remaining years through **column F** so that the last year that displays is 2014. Apply the **Heading 3** cell style to the years.

e. In the range **B5:F5**, type the values **1945923** and **2025684** and **2115783** and **2234897** and **2397445** Select the values you just typed, display the **Cell Styles** gallery, and then at the bottom, apply the **Currency [0]** cell style.

2 Click cell **C6**. Being sure to include the parentheses, type **=(c5-b5)/b5** and then press Enter. Select cell **C6**, and then apply **Percent Style**.

a. With cell **C6** selected, drag the fill handle to the right through cell **F6**.

b. In cell **A8**, type **Projected Future Housing Permit Revenue** and then press Enter. Point to cell **A2**, right-click, on the mini toolbar, click **Format Painter**, and then click cell **A8**. In cell **A10**, type **Forecasted Increase** leave row 11 blank, and then in cell **A12**, type **Year**

c. In cell **A13**, type **Projected Permit Revenue** and then in cell **B12**, type **2014** and press Tab. In cell **C12**, type **2015** and then press Tab. Select the range **B12:C12**, and then drag the fill handle through cell **F12** to extend the pattern of years to *2018*. Apply **Bold** to the selection.

d. Right-click cell **F5**, and then click **Copy**. Right-click over cell **B13**, and then click **Paste**.

e. In cell **B10**, type **7%** which is the percent of increase from 2013 to 2014. Select the range **A10:B10**, and then from the mini toolbar, apply **Bold** and **Italic**.

3 Click cell **C13**. Type **=b13*(100%+b10)** and then on the **Formula Bar**, click **Enter** to keep the cell active. With cell C13 as the active cell, drag the fill handle to copy the formula to the range **D13:F13**.

a. Point to cell **B13**, right-click, click **Format Painter**, and then select the range **C13:F13**.

b. Click cell **A15**. Type **Forecasted Revenue Estimates 2014 to 2018** and then press Enter. Use **Format Painter** to copy the format from cell **A8** to cell **A15**.

c. In the range **A17:A19**, type the following row titles:

Year

7% Increase

8% Increase

4 Select the range **B12:F12**, right-click over the selection, and then on the shortcut menu, click **Copy**. **Paste** the selection to the range **B17:F17**.

a. Select the range **B13:F13**, right-click over the selection, and then on the shortcut menu, click **Copy**. Point to cell **B18**, right-click, and then from the shortcut menu, point to **Paste Special**. Under **Paste Values**, click the second button—**Values & Number Formatting**. Press Esc to cancel the moving border.

b. Click cell **B10**. Type **8** and then press Enter. Copy the new values in the range **B13:F13**. Point to cell **B19**, right-click, and then point to **Paste Special**. Under **Paste Values**, click **Values & Number Formatting**. **Save** your workbook.

5 In the **row header area**, point to **row 8** to display the pointer, and then drag down to select **rows 8:24**. Right-click over the selection, and then click **Insert** to insert the same number of blank rows as you selected. Under the selection area near cell **A25**, click **Insert Options**, and then click the **Clear Formatting** option button to clear any formatting from these rows.

a. On the **PAGE LAYOUT tab**, in the **Themes group**, click the **Colors arrow**, and then click **Yellow**. Select the range **A5:F5**. On the **INSERT tab**, in the **Charts group**, click **Insert Line Chart**. In the displayed gallery of line charts, in the second row, click the **Line with Markers** chart type to create the chart as an embedded chart in the worksheet.

b. Point to the border of the chart to display the pointer, and then drag the chart so that its upper left corner is positioned in cell **A9**, aligned approximately under the *c* in the word *Projected* above.

(Project 3D Housing Permits continues on the next page)

Skills Review Project 3D Housing Permits (continued)

c. Point to the Chart Title *Permit Revenue* and right-click. On the shortcut menu, click **Edit Text** so that the insertion point is positioned before the word *Permit*. Type **Pacifica Bay Housing** and then press Spacebar. Press End and then press Enter to create a second line. Type **2010 to 2014**

6 At the bottom of the chart, point to any of the numbers *1* through *5*, and then right-click. On the shortcut menu, click **Select Data**. On the right side of the **Select Data Source** dialog box, click **Edit**. In the worksheet, select the years in the range **B4:F4**, and then click **OK** two times to enter the years as the category labels.

a. With the **Horizontal (Category) Axis** still selected, click **Chart Elements** [+], point to **Axes**, click the [▸] **arrow**, and then click **More Options**. In the **Format Axis** pane, under **AXIS OPTIONS**, click **Fill & Line** [icon], if necessary click **LINE** to expand the options, and then click the **No line** option button. **Close** the **Format Axis** pane.

b. On the left side of the chart, point to any of the dollar values, right-click, and then click **Format Axis**. In the **Format Axis** pane, under **Bounds**, select the text in the **Minimum** box, and then type **1900000**

c. Under **Units**, in the **Major** box, select the existing text, and then type **100000**

d. Near the top of the **Format Axis** pane, click the **AXIS OPTIONS arrow**, and then click **Chart Area** to display the **Format Chart Area** pane. Then, click **Fill & Line** [icon].

e. In the **Format Chart Area** pane, click **FILL** to expand the options, and then click the **Picture or texture fill** option button. Under **Insert picture from**, click **File**. In the **Insert Picture** dialog box, navigate to your student data files, and then click **e03D_Housing**. Click **Insert**.

f. In the **Format Chart Area** pane, click **FILL** to collapse the options, and then click **Border** to expand the options. Click the **Solid line** option button, click the **Color arrow**, and then under **Theme Colors**, in the fifth column, click the first color—**Gold Accent 1**. Set the **Width** to **4 pt** Scroll to the bottom of the pane, and then select the **Rounded corners** check box

g. Right-click the chart title, and then on the shortcut menu, click **Font**. In the **Font** dialog box, change the **Font style** to **Bold**, change the **Size** to **16**, and change the **Font color** to **White, Background 1**—in the first column, the first color. Click **OK**.

7 To the right of the chart, click **Chart Elements** [+], point to **Gridlines**, click the **arrow**, and then click **More Options** to display the **Format Major Gridlines** pane.

a. Under **LINE**, click the **Solid line** option button. Click the **Color arrow**, and be sure that **Gold, Accent 1** is the selected color. Set the **Width** to **1 pt**

b. In the chart, point to any of the dollar values on the **Vertical (Value) Axis**, right-click, and then click **Font**. In the **Font** dialog box, change the **Font style** to **Bold**, and then change the **Font color** to **White, Background 1**—in the first column, the first color. Click **OK**.

c. By using the same technique, format the **Font** of the **Horizontal (Category) Axis** to **Bold** with **White, Background 1** as the font color.

d. **Close** the **Format Axis** pane, and then click cell **A1** to deselect the chart. Click the **PAGE LAYOUT tab**. In the **Page Setup group**, click **Margins**, and then click **Custom Margins**. In the **Page Setup** dialog box, on the **Margins tab**, select the **Horizontally** check box. Click the **Header/Footer tab**, click **Custom Footer**, and then in the **Left section**, insert the file name. Click **OK** two times.

e. Click the **FILE tab**, and then click **Show All Properties**. As the **Tags**, type **housing permit revenue, forecast** In the **Subject** box, type your course name and section number. Be sure your name displays as the **Author**.

f. View the **Print Preview**, and then **Save** your workbook. Print or submit electronically as directed by your instructor. If required by your instructor, print or create an electronic version of your worksheet with formulas displayed by using the instructions in Project 1A, and then **Close** Excel without saving so that you do not save the changes you made to print formulas.

END | You have completed Project 3D

CONTENT-BASED ASSESSMENTS

MyITLab® grader

Mastering Excel Project 3E Revenue

Apply 3A skills from these Objectives:

1. Chart Data with a Pie Chart
2. Format a Pie Chart
3. Edit a Workbook and Update a Chart
4. Use Goal Seek to Perform What-If Analysis

In the following project, you will edit a worksheet that summarizes the revenue budget for the City of Pacifica Bay. Your completed worksheets will look similar to Figure 3.47.

PROJECT FILES

For Project 3E, you will need the following file:

e03E_Revenue

You will save your workbook as:

Lastname_Firstname_3E_Revenue

PROJECT RESULTS

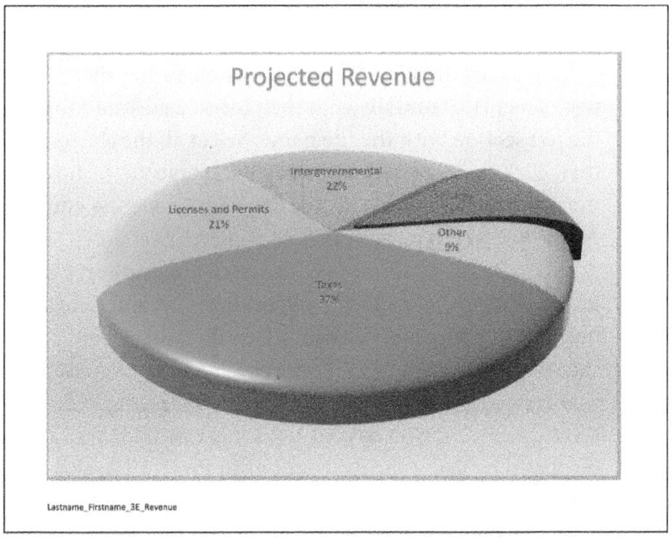

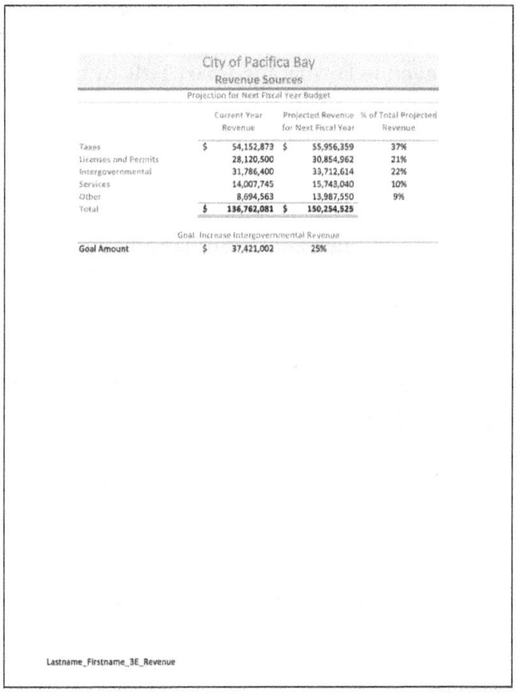

City of Pacifica Bay
Revenue Sources
Projection for Next Fiscal Year Budget

	Current Year Revenue	Projected Revenue for Next Fiscal Year	% of Total Projected Revenue
Taxes	$ 54,152,873	$ 55,956,359	37%
Licenses and Permits	28,120,500	30,854,962	21%
Intergovernmental	31,786,400	33,712,614	22%
Services	14,007,745	15,743,040	10%
Other	8,694,563	13,987,550	9%
Total	$ 136,762,081	$ 150,254,525	

Goal: Increase Intergovernmental Revenue

Goal Amount	$ 37,421,002	25%

Lastname_Firstname_3E_Revenue

FIGURE 3.47

(Project 3E Revenue continues on the next page)

Mastering Excel | Project 3E Revenue (continued)

1 Start Excel. From your student data files, locate and open **e03E_Revenue**. **Save** the file in your **Excel Chapter 3** folder as **Lastname_Firstname_3E_Revenue**

2 In cells **B10** and **C10**, enter formulas to calculate totals for each column. In cell **D5**, construct a formula to calculate the **% of Total Projected Revenue** from **Taxes** by dividing the **Projected Revenue for Next Fiscal Year** for **Taxes** by the **Total Projected Revenue for Next Fiscal Year**. Use absolute cell references as necessary, format the result in **Percent Style**, and **Center** the percentage. Fill the formula down through cell **D9**.

3 Select the nonadjacent ranges **A5:A9** and **C5:C9** as the data for a pie chart, and then insert a **3-D Pie** chart. Move the chart to a **New sheet** named **Projected Revenue Chart** As the text for the **Chart Title** element, type **Projected Revenue** Format the **Chart Title** by using the **WordArt Style Fill - Aqua, Accent 1, Shadow**—in the first row, the second style and a **Font Size** of **32**.

4 Remove the **Legend** chart element, and then add the **Data Labels** chart element formatted so that only the **Category Name** and **Percentage** display positioned in the **Center**. Format the data labels with a **Font style** of **Bold** and a **Font Size** of **14**.

5 Format the **Data Series** by using a **3-D Format** effect. Change the **Top bevel** and **Bottom bevel** to **Art Deco**. Set the **Top bevel Width** and **Height** to **350 pt** and then set the **Bottom bevel Width** and **Height** to **0 pt** Change the **Material** to the second **Special Effect—Soft Edge**.

6 Display the **Series Options**, and then set the **Angle of first slice** to **115** so that the **Taxes** slice is in the front of the pie. Select the **Services** slice, and then explode the slice **10%**. Change the **Fill Color** of the **Services** slice to a **Solid fill** by using **Gray-50%, Accent 4**—in the eighth column, the first color.

7 Format the **Chart Area** by applying a **Gradient fill** by using the **Preset gradients Light Gradient - Accent 4**. Format the **Border** of the **Chart Area** by applying a **Solid line** border by using **Gray-50%, Accent 4** and a **5 pt Width**. Close any panes that are open on the right.

8 Display the **Page Setup** dialog box, and then for this chart sheet, insert a **Custom Footer** in the **left section** with the file name.

9 Display **Sheet1** and rename the sheet as **Revenue Sources** Click in any blank cell to cancel any selections. In cell **A12**, type **Goal: Increase Intergovernmental Revenue** and then **Merge & Center** the text across the range **A12:D12**. Apply the **Heading 3** cell style. In cell **A13**, type **Goal Amount**

10 **Copy** the range **C7:D7** to the range **B13:C13**. Click cell **C13**, and then use **Goal Seek** to determine the projected amount of Intergovernmental Revenue in cell **B13** if the value in **C13** is **25%**

11 Select the range **A13:C13**, and then apply the **20% - Accent4** cell style. In **B13**, from the **Cell Styles** gallery, apply the **Currency [0]** cell style.

12 Display the **Page Setup** dialog box, center the worksheet **Horizontally**, and then insert a custom footer in the **left section** with the file name. Select all the sheets, and then click the **FILE tab** to display **Backstage** view. Show all the properties, and then as the **Tags**, type **revenue sources** As the **Subject**, type your course name and section number. Be sure your name displays as the **Author**. On the left, click **Print** to display the **Print Preview**, and note any necessary changes or corrections. In **Backstage** view, on the left click **Save**, and then print or submit electronically as directed. If required by your instructor, print or create an electronic version of your worksheet with formulas displayed by using the instructions in Project 1A, and then close Excel without saving so that you do not save the changes you made to print formulas.

END | You have completed Project 3E

CONTENT-BASED ASSESSMENTS

MyITLab® grader

Mastering Excel | Project 3F Streets

Apply 3B skills from these Objectives:

5 Design a Worksheet for What-If Analysis

6 Answer What-If Questions by Changing Values in a Worksheet

7 Chart Data with a Line Chart

Build from Scratch

In the following project, you will create a worksheet that the City of Pacifica Bay Facilities Director will use to prepare a five-year forecast of the costs associated with street maintenance. Your completed worksheet will look similar to Figure 3.48.

PROJECT FILES

For Project 3F, you will need the following file:

New blank Excel workbook

You will save your workbook as:

Lastname_Firstname_3F_Streets

PROJECT RESULTS

City of Pacifica Bay

Street Maintenance Costs 2012 to 2016

	2012	2013	2014	2015	2016
Annual Street Costs	$ 2,194,374	$ 2,438,156	$ 2,497,489	$ 2,614,252	$ 2,716,008
Percent Increase		11%	2%	5%	4%

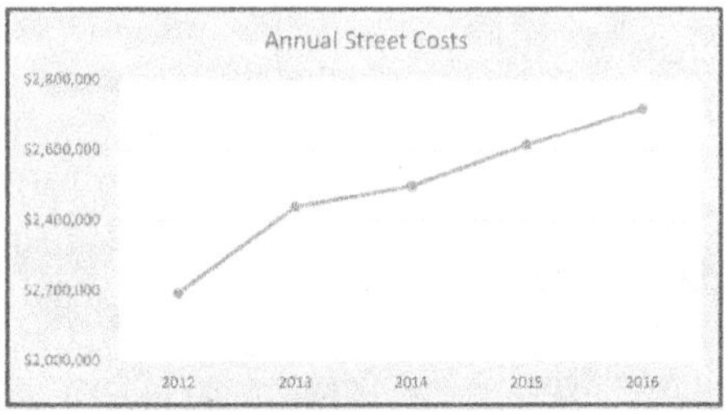

Projected Street Maintenance Costs

Projected Increase ***4%***

Year	2016	2017	2018	2019	2020
Projected Costs	$ 2,716,008	$ 2,824,648	$ 2,937,634	$ 3,055,140	$ 3,177,345

Projected Estimates 2016 to 2020

Year	2016	2017	2018	2019	2020
6% Increase	$ 2,716,008	$ 2,878,968	$ 3,051,707	$ 3,234,809	$ 3,428,898
4% Increase	$ 2,716,008	$ 2,824,648	$ 2,937,634	$ 3,055,140	$ 3,177,345

Lastname_Firstname_3F_Streets

FIGURE 3.48

(Project 3F Streets continues on the next page)

CONTENT-BASED ASSESSMENTS

Mastering Excel Project 3F Streets (continued)

1 Start Excel and display a new Blank workbook. Change the **Theme Colors** to **Paper**, and then **Save** the file in your **Excel Chapter 3** folder as **Lastname_Firstname_3F_Streets**

2 In cell **A1**, type the title **City of Pacifica Bay** and then in cell **A2** type the subtitle **Street Maintenance Costs 2012 to 2016 Merge & Center** both the title and the subtitle across **columns A:F**, and then apply the **Title** and **Heading 1** cell styles respectively.

3 In the range **B4:F4**, fill the year range with the values 2012 through 2016. In cell **A5** type **Annual Street Costs** and in cell **A6** type **Percent Increase** Change the width of **column A** to **150 pixels**, and then change the width of **columns B:F** to **85 pixels**. In the range **B5:F5** type **2194374** and **2438156** and **2497489** and **2614252** and **2716008**

4 Apply the **Currency [0]** cell style to the values in **B5:F5**. Apply the **Heading 1** cell style to the years, and apply the **Heading 4** cell style to the range **A5:A6**.

5 In cell **C6**, construct a formula to calculate the percent of increase in annual street maintenance costs from 2012 to 2013. Format the result with the **Percent Style** and then fill the formula through cell **F6** to calculate the percent of increase in each year.

6 In cell **A8**, type **Projected Street Maintenance Costs** and then use **Format Painter** to copy the formatting from cell **A2** to cell **A8**. In cell **A10**, type **Projected Increase** and then in cell **A12**, type **Year** In cell **A13**, type **Projected Costs** and then in the range **B12:F12**, use the fill handle to enter the years 2016 through 2020. Apply **Bold** to the years. **Copy** the value in cell **F5** to cell **B13**. In cell **B10**, type **6%** which is the projected increase estimated by the City financial analysts. To the range **A10:B10**, apply **Bold** and **Italic**.

7 In cell **C13**, construct a formula to calculate the annual projected street maintenance costs for the year 2017 after the projected increase of 6% is applied. Fill the formula through cell **F13**, and then use **Format Painter** to copy the formatting from cell **B13** to the range **C13:F13**.

8 In cell **A15**, type **Projected Estimates 2016 to 2020** and then use **Format Painter** to copy the format from cell **A8** to cell **A15**. In cells **A17:A19**, type the following row titles:

Year

6% Increase

4% Increase

9 **Copy** the range **B12:F12**, and then **Paste** the selection to **B17:F17**. Copy the range **B13:F13** and then paste the **Values & Number Formatting** to the range **B18:F18**. Complete the Projected Estimates section of the worksheet by changing the *Projected Increase* in **B10** to **4%** and then copying and pasting the **Values & Number Formatting** to the appropriate range in the worksheet. **Save** your workbook.

10 Select **rows 8:24**, and then **Insert** the same number of blank rows as you selected. **Clear Formatting** from the inserted rows. By using the data in **A4:F5**, insert a **Line with Markers** chart in the worksheet. Move the chart so that its upper left corner is positioned in cell **A9** and visually centered under the data above.

11 Format the **Bounds** of the **Vertical (Value) Axis** so that the **Minimum** is **2000000** and the **Major unit** is at **200000** Format the **Fill** of the **Chart Area** with a **Texture fill** by applying the **Parchment** texture—in the third row, the fifth texture. Format the **Plot Area** with a **Solid fill** by using **White, Background 1**—in the first column, the first color. Format the **Chart Area** with a **Border** by applying a **Solid line** by using **Olive Green, Accent 1, Darker 50%**—in the fifth column, the last color. Change the **Width** of the border to **2**

12 Click cell **A1** to deselect the chart. From the **Page Setup** dialog box, center the worksheet **Horizontally**, and then insert a **Custom Footer** in the **left section** with the file name.

13 Show all the properties, and then as the **Tags**, type **street maintenance costs** As the **Subject**, type your course name and section number. Be sure your name displays as the **Author**. In **Backstage** view, on the left, click **Print** to view the Print Preview. Print or submit electronically as directed. **Save** your workbook. If required by your instructor, print or create an electronic version of your worksheet with formulas displayed by using the instructions in Project 1A, and then close Excel without saving so that you do not save the changes you made to print formulas.

END | You have completed Project 3F

MyITLab® grader

Apply a combination of 3A and 3B skills:

1. Chart Data with a Pie Chart
2. Format a Pie Chart
3. Edit a Workbook and Update a Chart
4. Use Goal Seek to Perform What-If Analysis
5. Design a Worksheet for What-If Analysis
6. Answer What-If Questions by Changing Values in a Worksheet
7. Chart Data with a Line Chart

Mastering Excel Project 3G Operations

In the following project, you will edit a workbook for Jennifer Carson, City Finance Manager, that summarizes the operations costs for the Public Works Department. Your completed worksheets will look similar to Figure 3.49.

PROJECT FILES

For Project 3G, you will need the following file:

e03G_Expenses

You will save your workbook as

Lastname_Firstname_3G_Expenses

PROJECT RESULTS

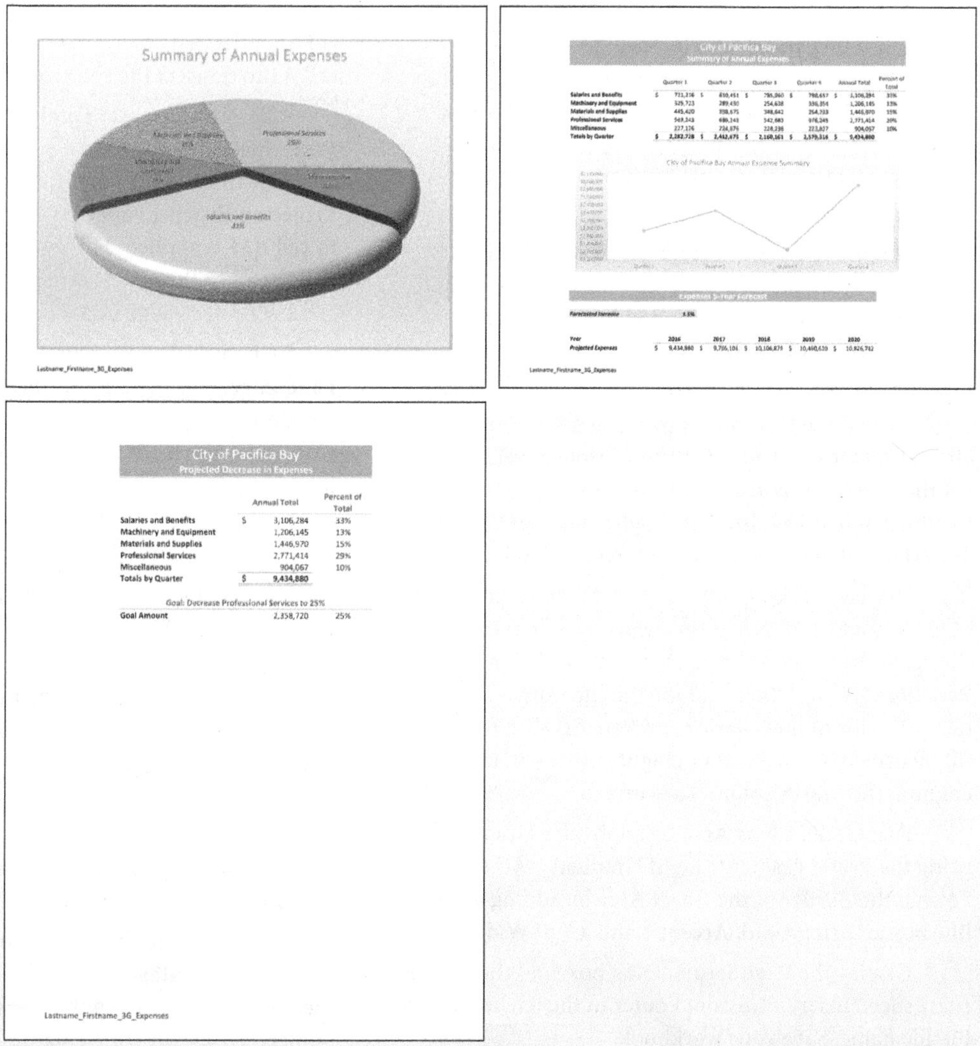

FIGURE 3.49

(Project 3G Operations continues on the next page)

Mastering Excel Project 3G Operations (continued)

1 Start Excel. From your student data files, open **e03G_Expenses**. **Save** the file in your **Excel Chapter 3** folder as **Lastname_Firstname_3G_Expenses**

2 In the **Expenses** worksheet, calculate row totals for each expense item in the range **F5:F9**. Format the range **F6:F9** by applying the cell style **Comma [0]**. Calculate column totals for each quarter and for the Annual Total in the range **B10:F10**. In cell **G5**, construct a formula to calculate the **Percent of Total** by dividing the **Annual Total** for **Salaries and Benefits** by the **Annual Total** for all quarters. Use absolute cell references as necessary, format the result in **Percent Style**, and then **Center**. Fill the formula down through cell **G9**.

3 Use a **3-D Pie** chart to chart the **Annual Total** for each item. Move the chart to a **New sheet**; name the sheet **Annual Expenses Chart** As the text for the **Chart Title** element, type **Summary of Annual Expenses** Format the **Chart Title** by using **WordArt Style Fill - Blue, Accent 1, Shadow**—in the first row, the second style and a **Font Size** of **28**.

4 Remove the **Legend** from the chart, and then add **Data Labels** formatted so that only the **Category Name** and **Percentage** display positioned in the **Center**. Format the data labels with **Bold** and **Italic** and a **Font Size** of **12**.

5 Format the **Data Series** by using a **3-D Format** effect. Change the **Top bevel** and **Bottom bevel** to **Circle**. Set the **Top bevel Width** and **Height** to **50 pt** and then set the **Bottom bevel Width** and **Height** to **256 pt** Change the **Material** to the fourth **Standard Effect—Metal**.

6 Display the **Series Options**, and then set the **Angle of first slice** to **125** so that the **Salaries and Benefits** slice is in the front of the pie. Select the **Salaries and Benefits** slice, and then explode the slice **10%**. Change the **Fill Color** of the **Salaries and Benefits** slice to a **Solid fill** by using **Green, Accent 6, Lighter 40%**—in the last column, the fourth color.

7 Format the **Chart Area** by applying a **Gradient fill** using the **Preset gradients Light Gradient – Accent 4**. Format the **Border** of the **Chart Area** by adding a **Solid line** border using **Gold, Accent 4** and a **5 pt Width**.

8 Display the **Page Setup** dialog box, and then for this chart sheet, insert a **Custom Footer** in the **left section** with the file name. **Save** your workbook.

9 Display the **Expenses** worksheet, and then by using the Quarter names and the Totals by Quarter, insert a **Line with Markers** chart in the worksheet. Move the chart so that its upper left corner is positioned slightly inside the upper left corner of cell **A12**, and then drag the right sizing handle so that the chart extends slightly inside the right border of **column G**. As the **Chart Title** type **City of Pacifica Bay Annual Expense Summary**

10 Format the **Bounds** of the **Vertical (Value) Axis** so that the **Minimum** is **2100000** and the **Major unit** is at **50000** Format the **Fill** of the **Chart Area** with a **Gradient fill** by applying the preset **Light Gradient - Accent 3**—in the first row, the third gradient. Format the **Plot Area** with a **Solid fill** by using **White, Background 1**—in the first column, the first color. Close any panes on the right, click cell **A1** to deselect the chart, and then **Save** your workbook.

11 **Copy** the **Annual Total** in cell **F10** and then use **Paste Special** to paste **Values & Number Formatting** in cell **B35**. In cell **C35**, construct a formula to calculate the **Projected Expenses** after the forecasted increase of **3.5%** in cell **B31** is applied. Fill the formula through cell **F35**, and then use **Format Painter** to copy the formatting from cell **B35** to the range **C35:F35**.

12 Change the **Orientation** of this worksheet to **Landscape**, and then use the **Scale to Fit** options to fit the **Height** to **1 page**. In the **Page Setup** dialog box, center this worksheet **Horizontally**, and insert a **Custom Footer** in the **left section** with the file name. **Save** your workbook.

13 Display the **Projected Decrease** worksheet. In cell **C5**, calculate the **Percent of Total** for the first expense, apply **Percent Style**, and then copy the formula down for the remaining expenses.

14 **Copy** cell **B8**, and then use **Paste Special** to paste the **Values & Number Formatting** to cell **B13**. **Copy** and **Paste** cell **C8** to cell **C13**. With cell **C13** selected, use **Goal Seek** to determine the goal amount of Professional Services expenses in cell **B13** if the value in **C13** is set to **25%**

15 In the **Page Setup** dialog box, center this worksheet **Horizontally**, and insert a **Custom Footer** in the **left section** with the file name.

16 Select all the sheets, and then click the **FILE tab** to display **Backstage** view. Show all the properties, and then as the **Tags**, type **annual expense summary** As the **Subject**, type your course name and section number. Be sure your name displays as the **Author**. On the left, click

(Project 3G Operations continues on the next page)

Mastering Excel Project 3G Operations (continued)

Print to display the **Print Preview**, and view all three worksheets. Note any necessary changes or corrections. In **Backstage** view, on the left click **Save**, and then print or submit electronically as directed. If required by your instructor, print or create an electronic version of your worksheet with formulas displayed by using the instructions in Project 1A, and then close Excel without saving so that you do not save the changes you made to print formulas.

END | You have completed Project 3G

CONTENT-BASED ASSESSMENTS

Apply a combination of the 3A and 3B skills.

GO! Fix It | Project 3H Schools | Online

Build from Scratch

GO! Make It | Project 3I Tax | Online

GO! Solve It | Project 3J Staffing | Online

GO! Solve It | Project 3K Water Usage

Build from Scratch

PROJECT FILES

For Project 3K, you will need the following files:

New blank Excel workbook
e03K_Beach

You will save your workbook as:

Lastname_Firstname_3K_Water_Usage

Pacifica Bay is a growing community and the City Council has requested an analysis of future resource needs. In this project, you will create a worksheet for the Department of Water and Power that illustrates residential water usage over a five-year period. Create a worksheet with the following data:

	2014	2015	2016	2017	2018
Water Use in Acre Feet	62518	65922	71864	76055	82542

Calculate the percent increase for the years 2015 to 2018. Below the Percent Increase, insert a line chart that illustrates the city's water usage from 2014 to 2018. Format the chart and worksheet attractively with a title and subtitle, and apply appropriate formatting. If you choose to format the chart area with a picture, you can use e03K_Beach located with your student files. Include the file name in the footer and enter appropriate document properties. Save the workbook as **Lastname_Firstname_3K_Water_Usage** and submit as directed.

Performance Level

Performance Criteria	Exemplary: You consistently applied the relevant skills	Proficient: You sometimes, but not always, applied the relevant skills	Developing: You rarely or never applied the relevant skills
Create formulas	All formulas are correct and are efficiently constructed.	Formulas are correct but not always constructed in the most efficient manner.	One or more formulas are missing or incorrect or only numbers were entered.
Insert and format a line chart	Line chart created correctly and is attractively formatted.	Line chart was created but the data was incorrect or the chart was not appropriately formatted.	No line chart was created.
Format attractively and appropriately	Formatting is attractive and appropriate.	Adequately formatted but difficult to read or unattractive.	Inadequate or no formatting.

END | You have completed Project 3K

OUTCOMES-BASED ASSESSMENTS

RUBRIC

The following outcomes-based assessments are open-ended assessments. That is, there is no specific correct result; your result will depend on your approach to the information provided. Make Professional Quality your goal. Use the following scoring rubric to guide you in how to approach the problem and then to evaluate how well your approach solves the problem.

The *criteria*—Software Mastery, Content, Format and Layout, and Process—represent the knowledge and skills you have gained that you can apply to solving the problem. The *levels of performance*—Professional Quality, Approaching Professional Quality, or Needs Quality Improvements—help you and your instructor evaluate your result.

	Your completed project is of Professional Quality if you:	Your completed project is Approaching Professional Quality if you:	Your completed project Needs Quality Improvements if you:
1-Software Mastery	Choose and apply the most appropriate skills, tools, and features and identify efficient methods to solve the problem.	Choose and apply some appropriate skills, tools, and features, but not in the most efficient manner.	Choose inappropriate skills, tools, or features, or are inefficient in solving the problem.
2-Content	Construct a solution that is clear and well organized, contains content that is accurate, appropriate to the audience and purpose, and is complete. Provide a solution that contains no errors in spelling, grammar, or style.	Construct a solution in which some components are unclear, poorly organized, inconsistent, or incomplete. Misjudge the needs of the audience. Have some errors in spelling, grammar, or style, but the errors do not detract from comprehension.	Construct a solution that is unclear, incomplete, or poorly organized; contains some inaccurate or inappropriate content; and contains many errors in spelling, grammar, or style. Do not solve the problem.
3-Format & Layout	Format and arrange all elements to communicate information and ideas, clarify function, illustrate relationships, and indicate relative importance.	Apply appropriate format and layout features to some elements, but not others. Overuse features, causing minor distraction.	Apply format and layout that does not communicate information or ideas clearly. Do not use format and layout features to clarify function, illustrate relationships, or indicate relative importance. Use available features excessively, causing distraction.
4-Process	Use an organized approach that integrates planning, development, self-assessment, revision, and reflection.	Demonstrate an organized approach in some areas, but not others; or, use an insufficient process of organization throughout.	Do not use an organized approach to solve the problem.

OUTCOMES-BASED ASSESSMENTS

Apply a combination of the 3A and 3B skills.

GO! Think Project 3L Employment

PROJECT FILES

Build from Scratch

For Project 3L, you will need the following file:

New blank Excel workbook

You will save your workbook as:

Lastname_Firstname_3L_Employment

Sandy Ingram, the Director of the Employment Development Department for the city of Pacifica Bay, has requested an analysis of employment sectors in the city. Employment data for the previous two years is listed below:

Job Sector	2015 Employment	2016 Employment
Government	1,795	1,524
Healthcare	2,832	2,952
Retail	2,524	2,480
Food Service	3,961	3,753
Industrial	1,477	1,595
Professional	2,515	2,802

Create a workbook to provide Sandy with the employment information for each sector and the total employment for each year. Insert a column to calculate the percent change from 2015 to 2016. Note that some of the results will be negative numbers. Format the percentages with two decimal places. Insert a pie chart in its own sheet that illustrates the 2016 employment figures, and format the chart attractively. Format the worksheet so that it is professional and easy to read and understand. Insert a footer with the file name and add appropriate document properties. Save the file as **Lastname_Firstname_3L_Employment** and print or submit as directed by your instructor.

END | You have completed Project 3L

Build from Scratch

GO! Think Project 3M Population Online

Build from Scratch

You and GO! Project 3N Expense Analysis Online

Build from Scratch

GO! Cumulative Group Project Project 3O Bell Orchid Hotels Online

Introduction to Microsoft Access 2013

A
Access 2013

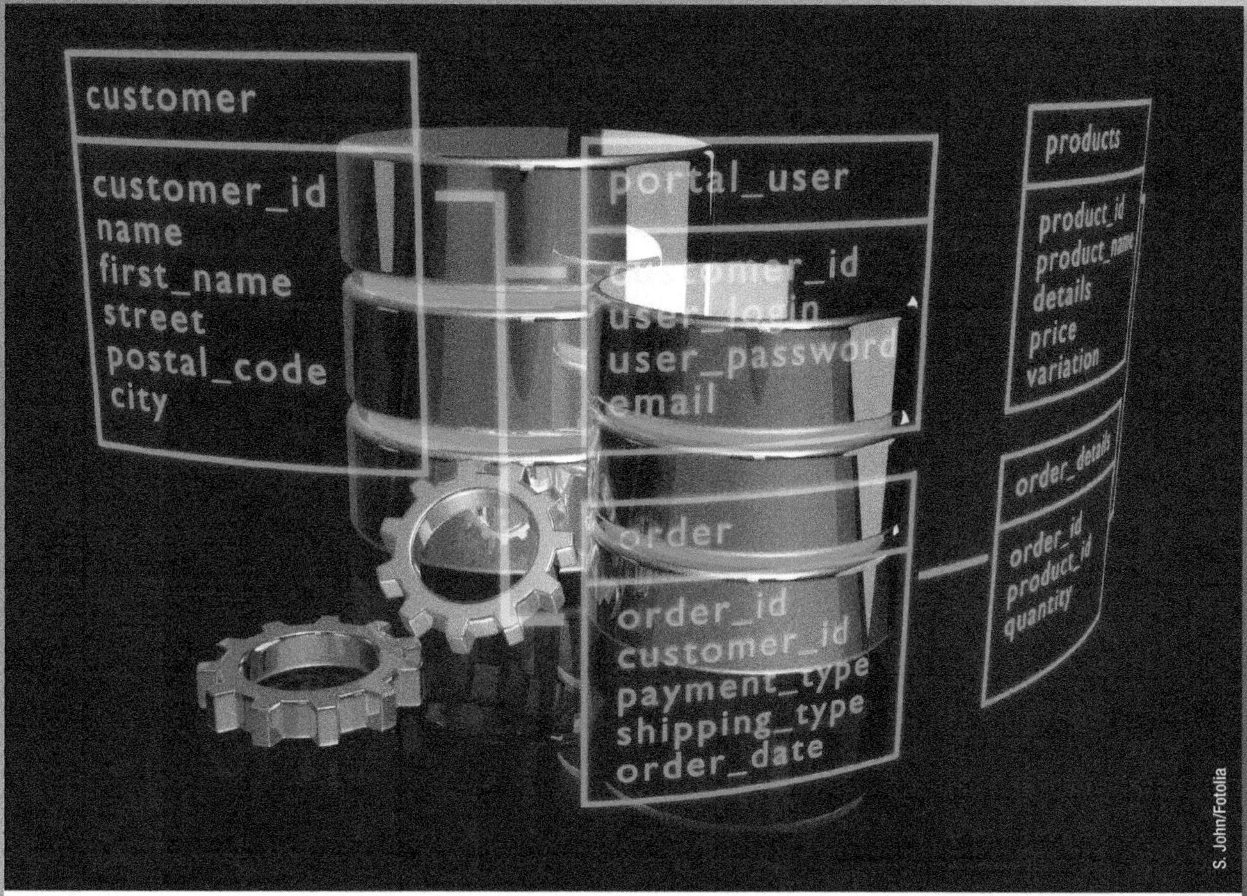

S. John/Fotolia

Access 2013: Introduction

Video AA

Microsoft Access 2013 provides a convenient way to organize data that makes it easy for you to retrieve information. Access uses tables to store data. Like Excel spreadsheets, data is stored in rows and columns in a table. So why use a database rather than an Excel spreadsheet? By using a database, you can manipulate and work with data in a more robust manner. For example, if you have thousands of records about patients in a hospital, you can easily find all of the records that pertain to the patients who received a specific type of medicine on a particular day. Information from one table can be used to retrieve information from another table. For example, by knowing a patient's ID number, you can view immunization records or view insurance information or view hospitalization records. Having information stored in an Access database enables you to make bulk changes to data at one time even when it is stored in different tables.

It's easy to get started with Access by using one of the many prebuilt database templates. For example, a nonprofit organization can track events, donors, members, and donations. A small business can use a prebuilt database to track inventory, create invoices, keep track of projects, manage pricing, track competitors, and manage quotes.

Getting Started with Microsoft Access 2013

GO! to Work Video A1

1

ACCESS 2013

PROJECT 1A

OUTCOMES
Create a new database.

PROJECT 1B

OUTCOMES
Create a database from a template.

OBJECTIVES

1. Identify Good Database Design
2. Create a Table and Define Fields in a Blank Desktop Database
3. Change the Structure of Tables and Add a Second Table
4. Create a Query, Form, and Report
5. Close a Database and Exit Access

OBJECTIVES

6. Use a Template to Create a Database
7. Organize Objects in the Navigation Pane
8. Create a New Table in a Database Created with a Template
9. Print a Report and a Table

Riccardo Piccinini/Fotolia

In This Chapter

In this chapter, you use Microsoft Access 2013 to organize a collection of related information. You will create new databases, create tables, and enter data into the tables. You will create a query, a form, and a report—all of which are Access objects that make a database useful for finding and analyzing information. You will also create a complete database from a template that you can use as provided, or that you can modify to suit your needs. In this chapter, you will also learn how to apply good database design principles to your Access database and to define the structure of a database.

The projects in this chapter relate to **Texas Lakes Community College**, which is located in the Austin, Texas, area. Its four campuses serve over 30,000 students and offer more than 140 certificate programs and degrees. The college has a highly acclaimed Distance Education program and an extensive Workforce Development program. The college makes positive contributions to the community through cultural and athletic programs and has significant partnerships with businesses and nonprofit organizations. Popular fields of study include nursing and health care, solar technology, computer technology, and graphic design.

PROJECT

1A Student Advising Database with Two Tables

MyITLab®
Project 1A Training

PROJECT ACTIVITIES

In Activities 1.01 through 1.17, you will assist Dr. Daniel Martinez, vice president of Student Services at Texas Lakes Community College, in creating a new database for tracking students and their faculty advisors. Your completed database objects will look similar to Figure 1.1.

PROJECT FILES

For Project 1A, you will need the following files:

Blank desktop database
a01A_Students (Excel workbook)
a01A_Faculty_Advisors (Excel workbook)

You will save your database as:

Lastname_Firstname_1A_Advising

Build from Scratch

PROJECT RESULTS

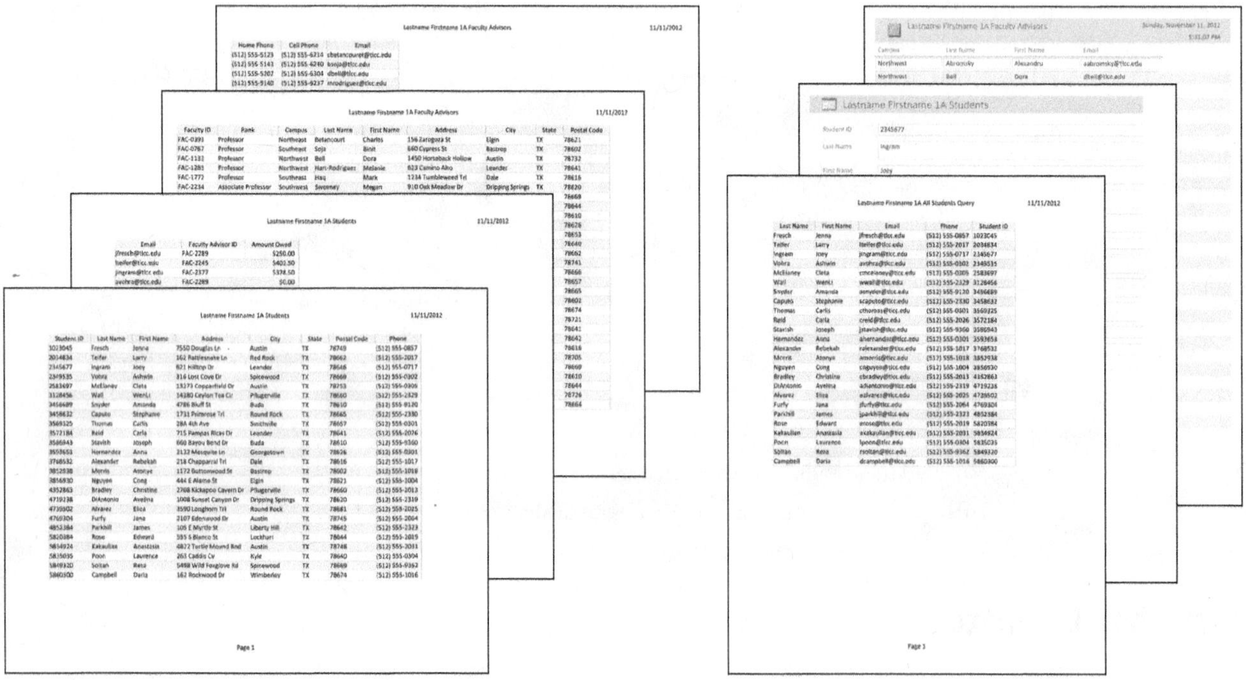

FIGURE 1.1 Project 1A Advising

NOTE **If You Are Using a Touchscreen**

- Tap an item to click it.
- Press and hold for a few seconds to right-click; release when the information or commands display.
- Touch the screen with two or more fingers and then pinch together to zoom in or stretch your fingers apart to zoom out.
- Slide your finger on the screen to scroll—slide left to scroll right and slide right to scroll left.
- Slide to rearrange—similar to dragging with a mouse.
- Swipe from edge: from right to display charms; from left to expose open apps, snap apps, or close apps; from top or bottom to show commands or close an app.
- Swipe to select—slide an item a short distance with a quick movement—to select an item and bring up commands, if any.

Objective 1 Identify Good Database Design

Video A1-1

A ***database*** is an organized collection of ***data***—facts about people, events, things, or ideas—related to a specific topic or purpose. ***Information*** is data that is organized in a useful manner. Your contact list is a type of database because it is a collection of data about one topic—the people with whom you communicate. A simple database of this type is called a ***flat database*** because it is not related or linked to any other collection of data. Another example of a simple database is a list of your music collection. You do not keep information about your music collection in your contact list because the data is not related to the people in your contact list.

A more sophisticated type of database is a ***relational database***, so-called because multiple collections of data in the database are related to one another; for example, data about the students, the courses, and the faculty members at a college. Microsoft Access 2013 is a relational ***database management system***—also referred to as a ***DBMS***—which is software that controls how related collections of data are stored, organized, retrieved, and secured.

Activity 1.01 Using Good Design Techniques to Plan a Database

Before creating a new database, the first step is to determine the information you want to keep track of by asking yourself, *What questions should this database be able to answer?* The purpose of a database is to store the data in a manner that makes it easy to get the information you need by asking questions. For example, in a student database for Texas Lakes Community College, the questions to be answered might include:

- How many students are enrolled at the college?
- How many students have not yet been assigned a faculty advisor?
- Which students live in Austin, Texas?
- Which students owe money for tuition?
- Which students are majoring in Information Systems Technology?

Tables are the foundation of an Access database because all of the data is stored in one or more tables. A table is similar in structure to an Excel worksheet because data is organized into rows and columns. Each table row is a ***record***—all of the categories of data pertaining to one person, place, event, thing, or idea. Each table column is a ***field***—a single piece of information for every record. For example, in a table storing student contact information, each row forms a record for only one student. Each column forms a field for every record; for example, the student ID number or the student last name.

When organizing the fields of information in your table, break each piece of information into its smallest, most useful part. For example, create three fields for the name of a student—one field for the last name, one field for the first name, and one field for the middle name or initial.

The ***first principle of good database design*** is to organize data in the tables so that ***redundant***—duplicate—data does not occur. For example, record the student contact information in only *one* table, so that if a student's address changes, you can change the information in just one place. This conserves space, reduces the likelihood of errors when recording new data, and does not require remembering all of the different places where the student's address is stored.

The ***second principle of good database design*** is to use techniques that ensure the accuracy and consistency of data as it is entered into the table. Typically, many different people enter data into a database—think of all the people who enter data about students at your college. When entering a state in a student contacts table, one person might enter the state as *Texas*, while another might enter the state as *TX*. Use design techniques to help those who enter data into a database to enter the data more accurately and consistently.

Normalization is the process of applying design rules and principles to ensure that your database performs as expected. Taking the time to plan and create a database that is well designed will ensure that you can retrieve meaningful information from the database.

The tables of information in a relational database are linked or joined to one another by a ***common field***—a field in two or more tables that stores the same data. For example, a Students table includes the Student ID, name, and address of every student. The Student Activities table includes the club name and the Student ID of members, but not the name or address, of each student in the club. Because the two tables share a common field—Student ID—you can create a list of names and addresses of all of the students in the Photography Club. The names and addresses are stored in the Students table, and the Student IDs of the Photography Club members are stored in the Student Activities table.

Objective 2 Create a Table and Define Fields in a Blank Desktop Database

Video A1-2

There are three methods to create a new Access database. One method is to create a new database using a ***database template***—a preformatted database designed for a specific purpose. A second method is to create a new database from a ***blank desktop database***. A blank desktop database is stored on your computer or other storage device. It has no data and has no database tools; you create the data and the tools as you need them. A third method is to create a ***custom web app*** database from scratch or by using a template that you can publish and share with others over the Internet.

Regardless of the method you use, you must name and save the database before you can create any ***objects*** in it. Objects are the basic parts of a database; you create objects to store your data, to work with your data, and to display your data. The most common database objects are tables, queries, forms, and reports. Think of an Access database as a container for the objects that you create.

Activity 1.02 | Starting with a Blank Desktop Database

1. Start Access using the same technique you used to locate and open other Office desktop apps. Take a moment to compare your screen with Figure 1.2 and study the parts of the Microsoft Access opening screen described in the table in Figure 1.3.

   From this Access opening screen, you can open an existing database, create a custom web app, create a blank desktop database, or create a new web app or desktop database from a template.

FIGURE 1.2

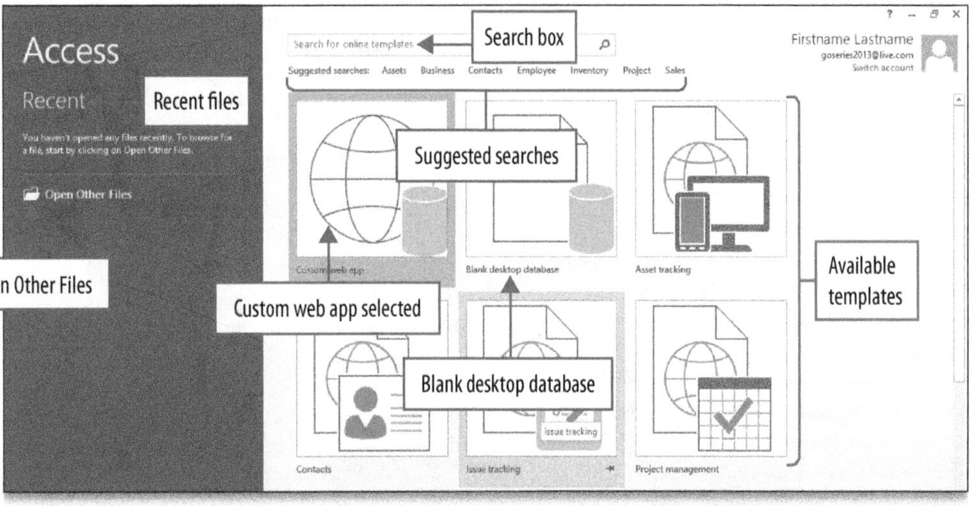

FIGURE 1.3

MICROSOFT ACCESS OPENING SCREEN ELEMENTS	
SCREEN ELEMENT	**DESCRIPTION**
Available templates	Starts a database for a specific purpose that includes built-in objects and tools ready for use.
Blank desktop database	Starts a blank database that is stored on your computer or on a storage device.
Custom web app	Starts a web app database that can be published and shared on the Internet.
Open Other Files	Enables you to open a database file from your computer, a shared location, or other location that you have designated.
Recent files	Displays a list of database files that have been recently opened.
Search box	Enables you to search the Microsoft Office website for templates.
Suggested searches	Enables you to click on a category to start an online search for a template.

2 In the Access opening screen, click **Blank desktop database**. In the **Blank desktop database** dialog box, to the right of the **File Name** box, click **Browse**. In the **File New Database** dialog box, navigate to the location where you are saving your databases for this chapter, create a **New folder** named **Access Chapter 1** and then press Enter. With the folder name selected, in the **File New Database** dialog box, click **Open**.

In the File name box, *Database1* displays as the default file name—the number at the end of your file name might differ if you have saved a database previously with the default name. In the Save as type box, the default database type is *Microsoft Access 2007 – 2013 Databases*, which means that you can open a database created in Access 2013 by using Access 2007, Access 2010, or Access 2013.

3 Click in the **File name** box. Using your own name, replace the existing text with **Lastname_Firstname_1A_Advising** and then click **OK** or press Enter. Compare your screen with Figure 1.4.

In the Blank desktop database dialog box, in the File Name box, the name of your database displays. Under the File Name box, the drive and folder where the database will be stored displays. An Access database has a file extension of *.accdb*.

FIGURE 1.4

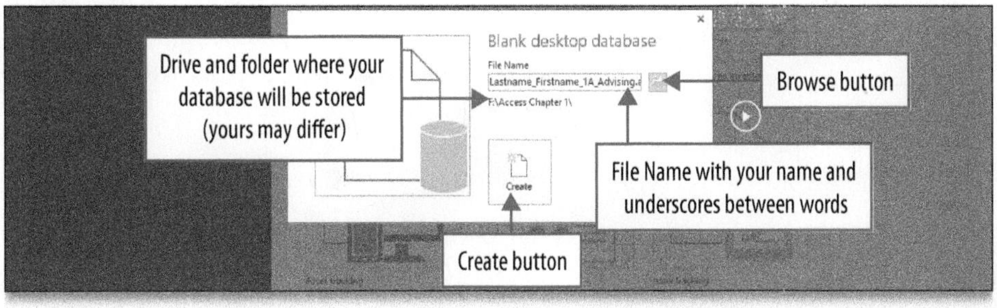

4 In the **Blank desktop database** dialog box, click **Create**. Compare your screen with Figure 1.5, and then take a moment to study the screen elements described in the table in Figure 1.6.

Access creates the new database and opens *Table1*. Recall that a table is an Access object that stores data in columns and rows, similar to the format of an Excel worksheet. Table objects are the foundation of a database because tables store the data that is used by other database objects.

FIGURE 1.5

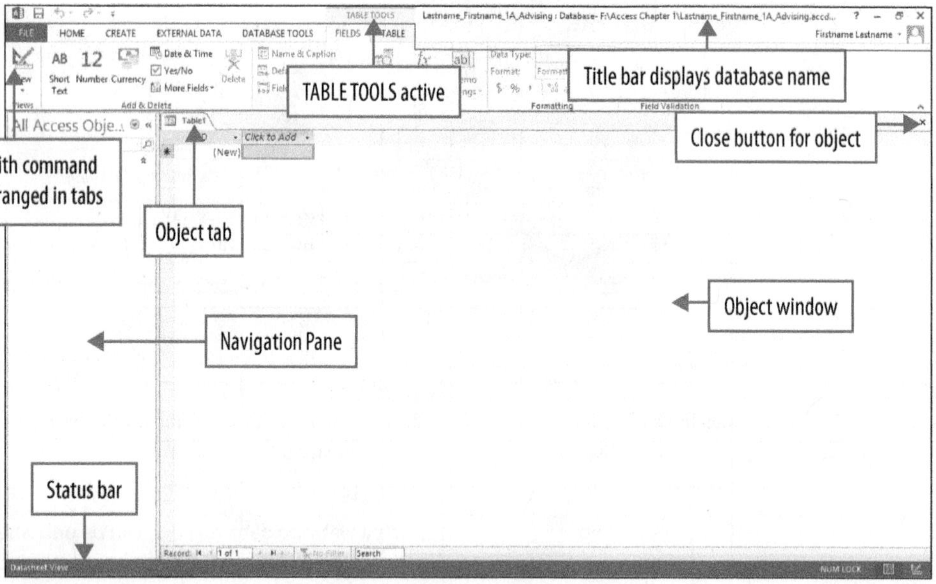

FIGURE 1.6

MICROSOFT ACCESS DATABASE WINDOW ELEMENTS	
ACCESS WINDOW ELEMENT	**DESCRIPTION**
Navigation Pane	Displays the database objects that you can open in the object window.
Object tab	Identifies and enables you to work with the open object.
Object window	Displays the active or open object (table, query, or other object).
Close button for object	Closes the active object (table, query, or other object).
Ribbon with command groups arranged in tabs	Groups the commands for performing related database tasks on tabs.
Status bar	Indicates the active view and the status of action occurring within the database on the left; provides buttons on the right to switch between Datasheet view and Design view.
Table Tools	Provides tools for working with a table object—only available when a table object is active.
Title bar	Displays the database name.

Activity 1.03 | Assigning the Data Type and Name to Fields

After you have named and saved your database, the next step is to consult your database design plan and then create the tables for your data. Limit the data in each table to *one* subject. For example, in this project, your database will have two tables—one for student information and one for faculty advisor information.

Recall that each column in a table is a field; field names display at the top of each column of the table. Recall also that each row in a table is a record—all of the data pertaining to one person, place, thing, event, or idea. Each record is broken up into its smallest usable parts—the fields. Use meaningful names for fields; for example, *Last Name*.

1. Notice the new blank table that displays in **Datasheet** view, and then take a moment to study the elements of the table's object window. Compare your screen with Figure 1.7.

   The table displays in ***Datasheet view***, which displays the data in columns and rows similar to the format of an Excel worksheet. Another way to view a table is in ***Design view***, which displays the underlying design—the ***structure***—of the table's fields. The ***object window*** displays the open object—in this instance, the table object.

   In a new blank database, there is only one object—a new blank table. Because you have not yet named this table, the object tab displays a default name of *Table1*. Access creates the first field and names it *ID*. In the ID field, Access assigns a unique sequential number—each number incremented by one—to each record as it is entered into the table.

FIGURE 1.7

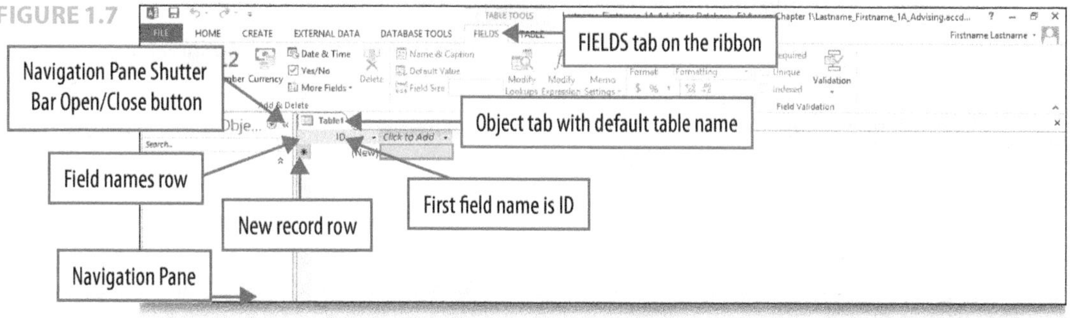

2. In the **Navigation Pane**, click **Shutter Bar Open/Close Button** « to collapse the **Navigation Pane** to a narrow bar on the left.

   The ***Navigation Pane*** displays and organizes the names of the objects in a database. From the Navigation Pane, you can open objects. Collapse or close the Navigation Pane to display more of the object—in this case, the table.

ANOTHER WAY Press F11 to close or open the Navigation Pane.

3. In the field names row, click anywhere in the text *Click to Add* to display a list of data types. Compare your screen with Figure 1.8.

   A ***data type*** defines the kind of data that you can store in a field, such as numbers, text, or dates. A field in a table can have only one data type. The data type of each field should be included in your database design. After selecting the data type, you can name the field.

ANOTHER WAY To the right of *Click to Add*, click the arrow.

FIGURE 1.8

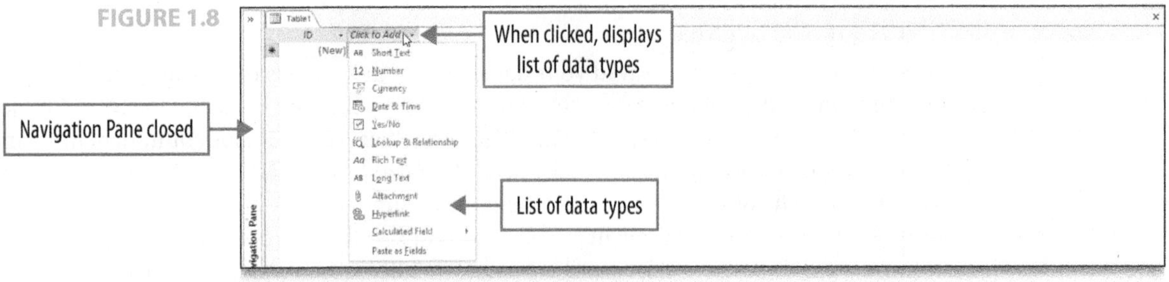

4 On the list of data types, click **Short Text**, and notice that in the second column, *Click to Add* changes to *Field1*, which is selected. Type **Last Name** and then press Enter.

The second column displays *Last Name* as the field name, and, in the third column, the data type list displays. The ***Short Text data type*** describes text, a combination of text and numbers, or numbers that are not used in calculations, such as the Postal Code. This data type enables you to enter up to 255 characters in the field.

ANOTHER WAY With the list of data types displayed, type the character that is underscored to select the data type. For example, type *t* to select Short Text or type *u* to select Currency.

5 In the third field name box, type **t** to select *Short Text*, type **First Name** and then press Enter.

6 In the fourth field name box, click **Short Text**, type **Middle Initial** and then press Enter.

7 Create the remaining fields from the table given by first selecting the data type, typing the field name, and then pressing Enter. The field names in the table will display on one line—do not be concerned if the field names do not completely display in the column; you will adjust the column widths later.

Data Type		Short Text	Short Text	Short Text	Short Text	Short Text	Short Text	Short Text	Short Text	Short Text	Short Text	Currency
Field Name	ID	Last Name	First Name	Middle Initial	**Address**	**City**	**State**	**Postal Code**	**Phone**	**Email**	**Faculty Advisor ID**	**Amount Owed**

The Postal Code and Phone fields are assigned a data type of Short Text because the numbers are never used in calculations. The Amount Owed field is assigned the ***Currency data type***, which describes monetary values and numeric data that can be used in calculations and that have one to four decimal places. A U.S. dollar sign ($) and two decimal places are automatically included for all of the numbers in a field with the Currency data type.

8 If necessary, scroll to bring the first column—**ID**—into view, and then compare your screen with Figure 1.9.

Access automatically created the ID field, and you created 11 additional fields in the table.

FIGURE 1.9

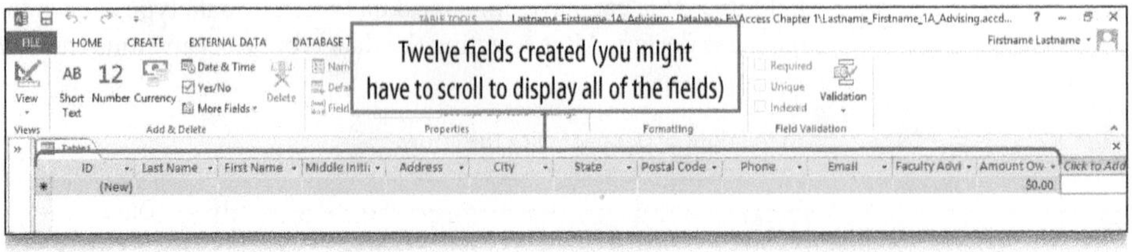

More Knowledge **Create Fields by Entering Data**

You can create a new field in Datasheet view by typing the data in a new column. Access automatically assigns a data type based on the data you enter. For example, if you enter a date, Access assigns the Date/Time data type. If you enter a monetary amount, Access assigns the Currency data type. If Access cannot determine the data type based on the data entered, the Short Text data type is assigned. You can always change the data type if an incorrect data type is assigned. If you use this method to create fields, you must check the assigned data types to be sure they are correct. You must also rename the fields because Access assigns the names as *Field1*, *Field2*, and so on.

Activity 1.04 | Renaming Fields and Changing Data Types in a Table

1 In the first column, click anywhere in the text *ID*. On the ribbon, under **TABLE TOOLS**, on the **FIELDS tab**, in the **Properties group**, click **Name & Caption**. In the **Enter Field Properties** dialog box, in the **Name** box, change *ID* to **Student ID**

The field name *Student ID* is a clearer and more precise description of this field's data. In the Enter Field Properties dialog box, you have the option to change the ***Caption*** to display a name for a field other than the name that displays in the Name box. Many database designers do not use spaces in field names; instead, they might name a field *LastName* or *LName* and then create a caption for the field so it displays as *Last Name* in tables, forms, or reports. In the Enter Field Properties dialog box, you can also provide a description for the field.

ANOTHER WAY Right-click the field name to display the shortcut menu, and then click Rename Field; or, double-click the field name to select the existing text, and then type the new field name.

2 Click **OK** to close the **Enter Field Properties** dialog box. On the ribbon, in the **Formatting group**, notice that the **Data Type** for the **Student ID** field is *AutoNumber*. Click the **Data Type arrow**, click **Short Text**, and then compare your screen with Figure 1.10.

In the new record row, the Student ID field is selected. By default, Access creates an ID field for all new tables and sets the data type for the field to AutoNumber. The ***AutoNumber data type*** describes a unique sequential or random number assigned by Access as each record is entered. Changing the data type of this field to Short Text enables you to enter a custom student ID number.

When records in a database have *no* unique value, such as a book ISBN or a license plate number, the AutoNumber data type is a useful way to automatically create a unique number. In this manner, you are sure that every record is different from the others.

FIGURE 1.10

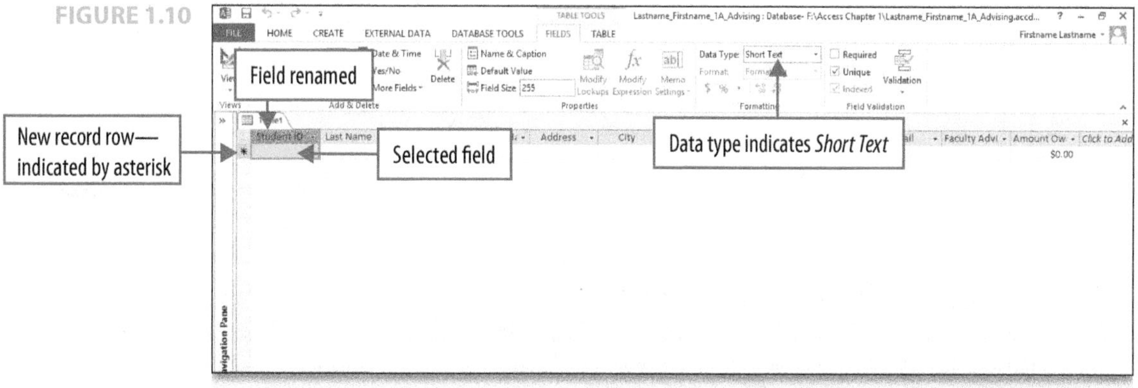

Activity 1.05 | Adding a Record to a Table

A new contact list is not useful until you fill it with names and phone numbers. Likewise, a new database is not useful until you ***populate*** it by filling one or more tables with data. You can populate a table with records by typing data directly into the table.

1 In the new record row, click in the **Student ID** field to display the insertion point, type **1023045** and then press Enter. Compare your screen with Figure 1.11.

The pencil icon in the ***record selector box*** indicates that a record is being entered or edited. The record selector box is the small box at the left of a record in Datasheet view. When clicked, the entire record is selected.

ANOTHER WAY Press Tab to move the insertion point to the next field.

FIGURE 1.11

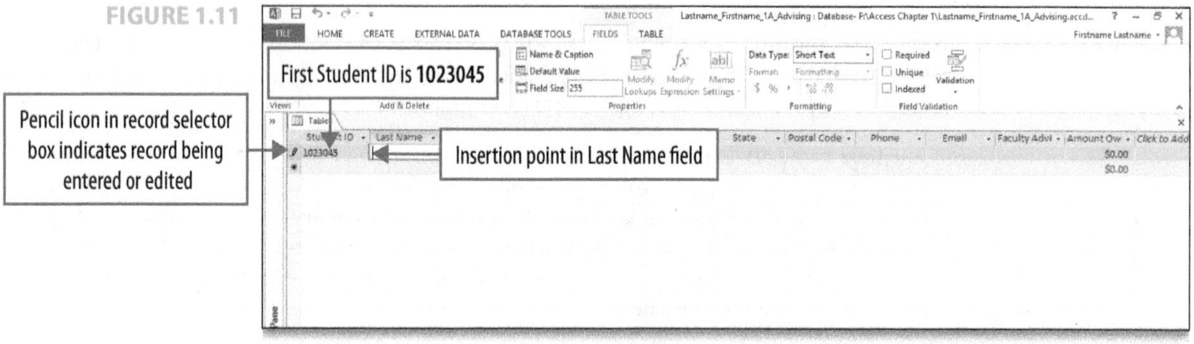

2 With the insertion point positioned in the **Last Name** field, type **Fresch** and then press Enter.

NOTE **Correcting Typing Errors**

Correct any typing errors you make by using the techniques you have practiced in other Office applications. For example, use Backspace to remove characters to the left of the insertion point. Use Del to remove characters to the right of the insertion point. Or select the text you want to replace and type the correct information. Press Esc to exit out of a record that has not been completely entered.

3 In the **First Name** field, type **Jenna** and then press Enter.

4 In the **Middle Initial** field, type **A** and then press Enter.

5 In the **Address** field, type **7550 Douglas Ln** and then press Enter.

Do not be concerned if the data does not completely display in the column. As you progress in your study of Access, you will adjust column widths so that you can view all of the data.

6 Continue entering data in the fields as indicated in the table given, pressing Enter to move to the next field.

City	State	Postal Code	Phone	Email	Faculty Advisor ID
Austin	**TX**	**78749**	**(512) 555-0857**	**jfresch@tlcc.edu**	**FAC-2289**

NOTE **Format for Typing Telephone Numbers in Access**

Access does not require a specific format for typing telephone numbers in a record. The examples in this textbook use the format of Microsoft Outlook. Using such a format facilitates easy transfer of Outlook information to and from Access.

7 In the **Amount Owed** field, type **250** and then press Enter. Compare your screen with Figure 1.12.

Pressing Enter or Tab in the last field moves the insertion point to the next row to begin a new record. Access automatically saves the record as soon as you move to the next row; you do not have to take any specific action to save a record.

FIGURE 1.12

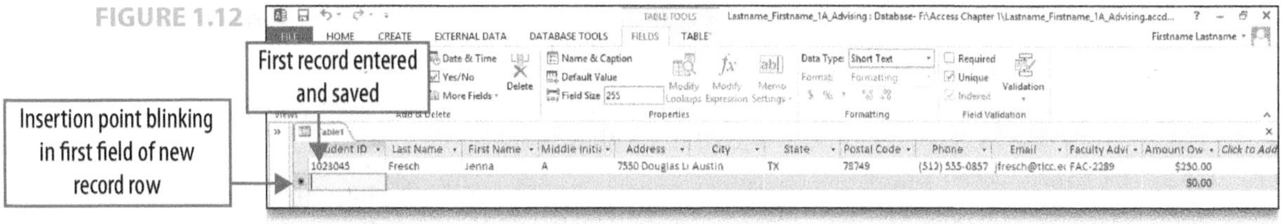

8 To give your table a meaningful name, on the **Quick Access Toolbar**, click **Save**. In the **Save As** dialog box, in the **Table Name** box, using your own name, replace the selected text by typing **Lastname Firstname 1A Students**

Save each database object with a name that identifies the data that it contains. When you save objects within a database, it is not necessary to use underscores in place of the spaces between words. Your name is included as part of the object name so that you and your instructor can identify your printouts or electronic files easily.

9 In the **Save As** dialog box, click **OK**. Notice that the object tab—located directly above the **Student ID** field name—displays the new table name that you just entered.

> ***More* Knowledge** **Renaming or Deleting a Table**
>
> To change the name of a table, close the table, display the Navigation Pane, right-click the table name, and then click Rename. Type the new name or edit as you would any selected text. To delete a table, close the table, display the Navigation Pane, right-click the table name, and then click Delete.

Activity 1.06 Adding Additional Records to a Table

1 In the new record row, click in the **Student ID** field, and then enter the data for two additional students as shown in the table given. Press Enter or Tab to move from field to field. The data in each field will display on one line in the table.

Student ID	Last Name	First Name	Middle Initial	Address	City	State	Postal Code	Phone	Email	Faculty Advisor ID	Amount Owed
2345677	**Ingram**	**Joey**	**S**	**621 Hilltop Dr**	**Leander**	**TX**	**78646**	**(512) 555-0717**	**jingram@tlcc.edu**	**FAC-2377**	**378.5**
3456689	**Snyder**	**Amanda**	**J**	**4786 Bluff St**	**Buda**	**TX**	**78610**	**(512) 555-9120**	**asnyder@tlcc.edu**	**FAC-9005**	**0**

2 Compare your screen with Figure 1.13.

FIGURE 1.13

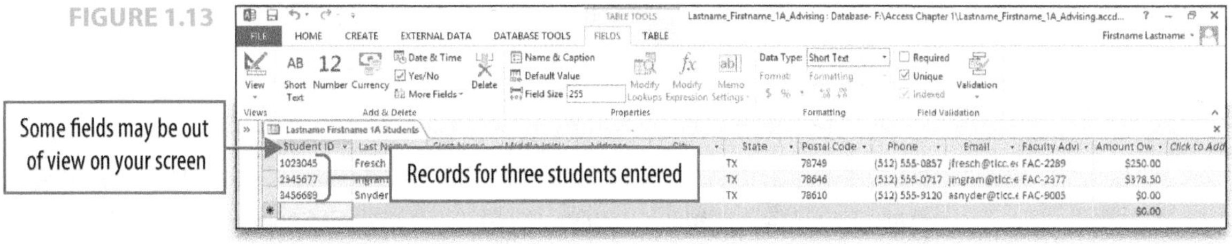

Activity 1.07 Importing Data from an Excel Workbook into an Existing Access Table

You can type records directly into a table. You can also ***import*** data from a variety of sources. Importing is the process of copying data from one source or application to another application. For example, you can import data from a Word table or an Excel spreadsheet into an Access database because the data is arranged in columns and rows, similar to a table in Datasheet view.

In this activity, you will ***append***—add on—data from an Excel spreadsheet to your *1A Students* table. To append data, the table must already be created, and it must be closed.

1. In the upper right corner of the table, below the ribbon, click **Object Close** [×] to close your **1A Students** table. Notice that no objects are open.

2. On the ribbon, click the **EXTERNAL DATA tab**. In the **Import & Link group**, click **Excel**. In the **Get External Data - Excel Spreadsheet** dialog box, click **Browse**.

3. In the **File Open** dialog box, navigate to your student files, double-click the Excel file **a01A_Students**, and then compare your screen with Figure 1.14.

   The path to the ***source file***—the file being imported—displays in the File name box. There are three options for importing data from an Excel spreadsheet: import the data into a *new* table in the current database, append a copy of the records to an existing table, or link the data from the spreadsheet to a linked table in the database. A ***link*** is a connection to data in another file. When linking, Access creates a table that maintains a link to the source data, so that changes to the data in one file are automatically made in the other—linked—file.

ANOTHER WAY Click the file name, and then in the File Open dialog box, click Open.

FIGURE 1.14

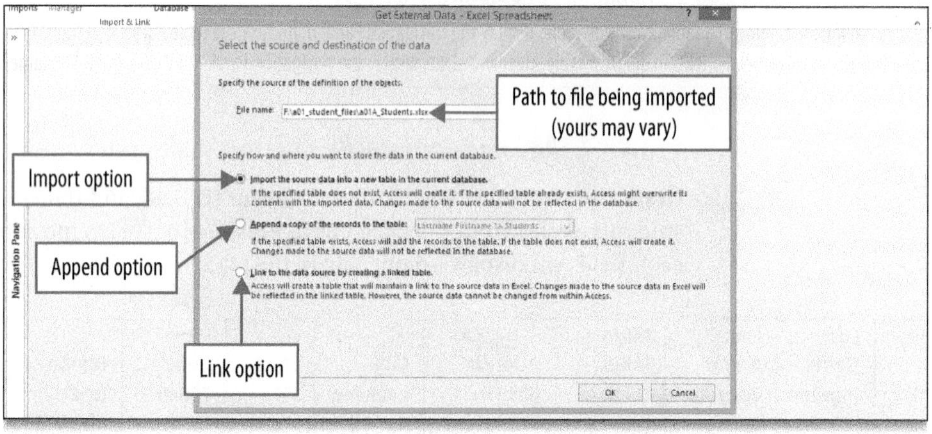

4. Click the **Append a copy of the records to the table** option button, and then, in the box to the right, click the **arrow**.

   Currently, your database has only one table, so no other tables display on the list. However, when a database has multiple tables, click the arrow to select the table to which you want to append records. The table into which you import or append data is referred to as the ***destination table***.

5. Press [Esc] to cancel the list, and in the dialog box, click **OK**. Compare your screen with Figure 1.15.

   The first screen of the Import Spreadsheet Wizard displays, and the presence of scroll bars indicates that records and fields are out of view in this window. To append records from an Excel workbook to an existing database table, the column headings in the Excel worksheet or spreadsheet must be identical to the field names in the table. The ***wizard*** identifies the first row of the spreadsheet as column headings, which are equivalent to field names. A wizard is a feature in a Microsoft Office program that walks you step by step through a process.

FIGURE 1.15

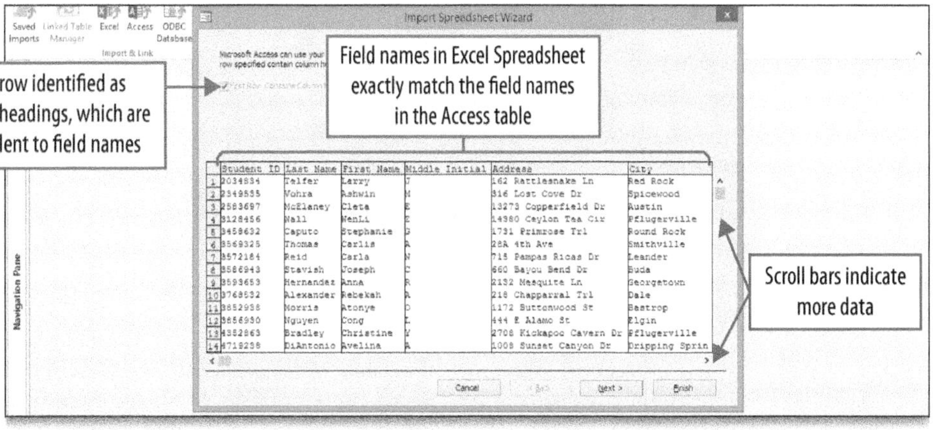

6 In the lower right corner of the wizard, click **Next**. Notice that the name of your table displays under **Import to Table**. In the lower right corner of the wizard, click **Finish**.

7 In the **Get External Data – Excel Spreadsheet** dialog box, click **Close. Open** [»] the **Navigation Pane.**

8 Point to the right edge of the **Navigation Pane** to display the [⇔] pointer. Drag to the right to increase the width of the **Navigation Pane** so that the entire table name displays, and then compare your screen with Figure 1.16.

FIGURE 1.16

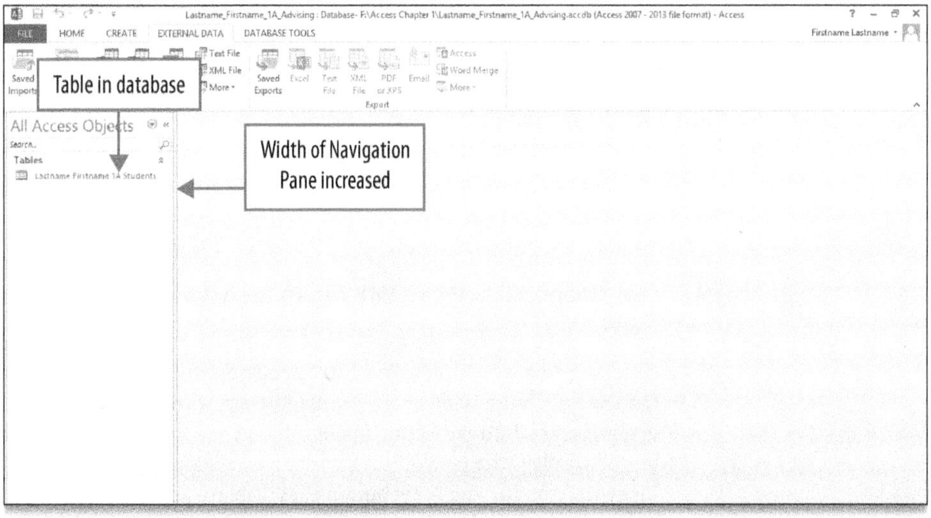

9 In the **Navigation Pane**, double-click your **1A Students** table to open the table in **Datasheet** view, and then **Close** [«] the **Navigation Pane.**

ANOTHER WAY To open an object from the Navigation Pane, right-click the object name, and then click Open.

10 In the lower left corner of your screen, locate the navigation area, and notice that there are a total of **25** records in the table—you entered three records and imported 22 additional records. Compare your screen with Figure 1.17.

The records that you entered and the records you imported from the Excel spreadsheet display in your table; the first record in the table is selected. The ***navigation area*** indicates the number of records in the table and has controls in the form of arrows that you click in order to navigate among the records.

FIGURE 1.17

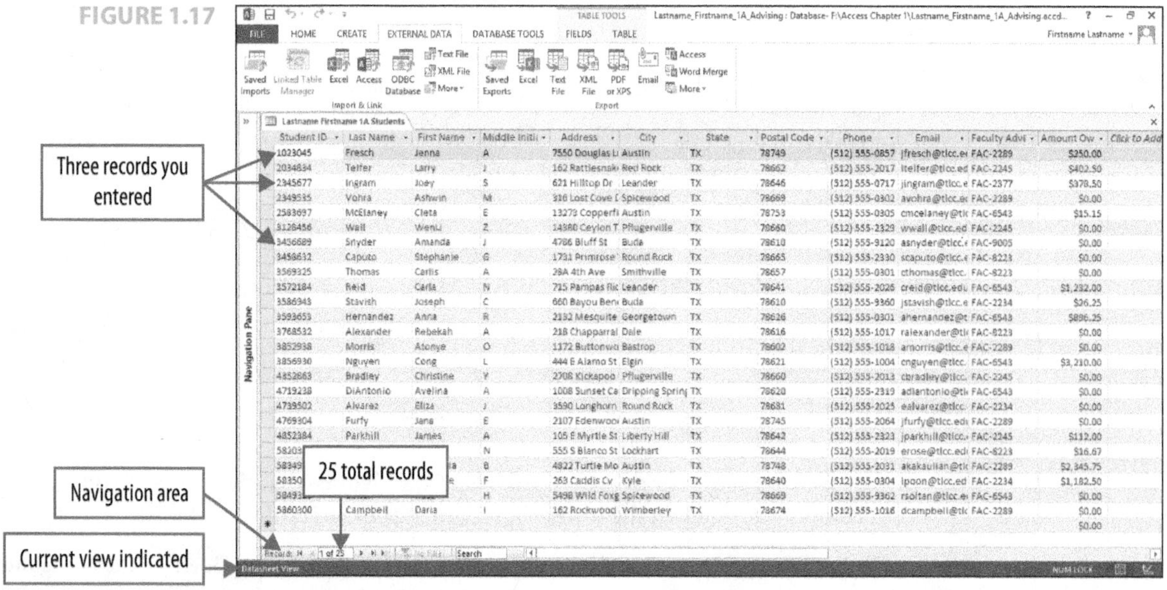

Objective 3 Change the Structure of Tables and Add a Second Table

Video A1-3

Recall that the structure of a table is the underlying design of the table and includes field names and data types. You can create or modify a table in Datasheet view. To define and modify fields, many database experts prefer to work in Design view, where you have more options for defining fields in a table.

Activity 1.08 | Deleting a Table Field in Design View

In this activity, you will delete the *Middle Initial* field from the table.

1. On the ribbon, click the **HOME tab**. In the **Views group**, click the **View arrow** to display a list of views.

   There are two views for tables: Datasheet view and Design view. Other objects have different views. On the list, Design view is represented by a picture of a pencil, a ruler, and an angle. Datasheet view is represented by a picture of a table arranged in columns and rows. In the Views group, if the View button displays the pencil, ruler, and angle, clicking View will switch your view to Design view. Likewise, clicking the View button that displays as a datasheet will switch your view to Datasheet view.

2. On the list, click **Design View**, and then compare your screen with Figure 1.18.

   Design view displays the underlying design—the structure—of the table and its fields. In Design view, the records with the data in the table do not display. You can only view the information about each field's characteristics. Each field name is listed, along with its data type. You can add more descriptive information about a field in the Description column.

   You can decide how each field should look and behave in the Field Properties area. For example, you can set a specific field size in the Field Properties area. In the lower right corner, information displays about the active selection—in this case, the Field Name.

FIGURE 1.18

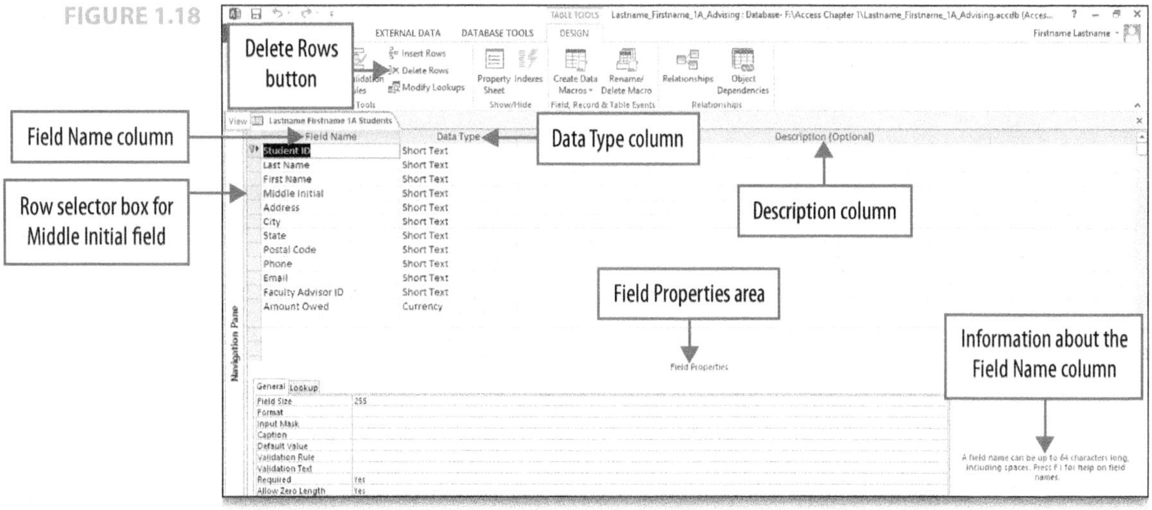

3 In the **Field Name** column, to the left of **Middle Initial**, point to the row selector box to display the [→] pointer, and then click one time to select the entire row.

4 Under **TABLE TOOLS**, on the **DESIGN tab**, in the **Tools group**, click **Delete Rows**. Read the message in the message box, and then click **Yes**.

Deleting a field deletes both the field and its data. After you save the changes, you cannot undo this action, so Access prompts you to be sure you want to proceed. If you change your mind after deleting a field and saving the changes, you must add the field back into the table and then reenter the data for that field for every record.

ANOTHER WAY In Design view, right-click the selected row, and then click Delete Rows; or, in Datasheet view, select the field—column—and on the HOME tab, in the Records group, click Delete.

Activity 1.09 | Changing a Field Size and Adding a Description

Typically, many different individuals in an organization have the ability to enter data into a table. For example, at your college, many registration assistants enter and modify student and course information daily. Two ways to help reduce errors are to restrict what can be typed in a field and to add descriptive information to help the individuals when entering the data.

1 With your table still displayed in **Design** view, in the **Field Name** column, click anywhere in the **Student ID** field name.

2 In the lower area of the screen, under **Field Properties**, click **Field Size** to select *255*, type **7** and then press Enter.

This action limits the size of the Student ID field to no more than seven characters. ***Field properties*** control how the field displays and how data can be entered into the field. You can define properties for each field in the Field Properties area by first clicking on the field name.

The default field size for a Short Text field is 255. Limiting the Field Size property to seven ensures that no more than seven characters can be entered for each Student ID. However, this does not prevent someone from entering seven characters that are incorrect or entering fewer than seven characters. Setting the proper data type for the field and limiting the field size are two ways to *help* reduce errors during data entry.

ANOTHER WAY In Datasheet view, click in the field. On the FIELDS tab, in the Properties group, click in the Field Size box, and then type the number that represents the maximum number of characters for that field.

3 In the **Student ID** row, click in the **Description** box, type **Seven-digit Student ID number** and then press Enter. Compare your screen with Figure 1.19.

Descriptions for fields in a table are optional. Include a description if the field name does not provide an obvious explanation of the type of data to be entered. If a description is provided for a field, when data is entered in that field in Datasheet view, the text in the Description displays on the left side of the status bar to provide additional information for the individuals who are entering the data.

When you enter a description for a field, a Property Update Options button displays below the text you typed, which enables you to copy the description for the field to all other database objects that use this table as an underlying source.

FIGURE 1.19

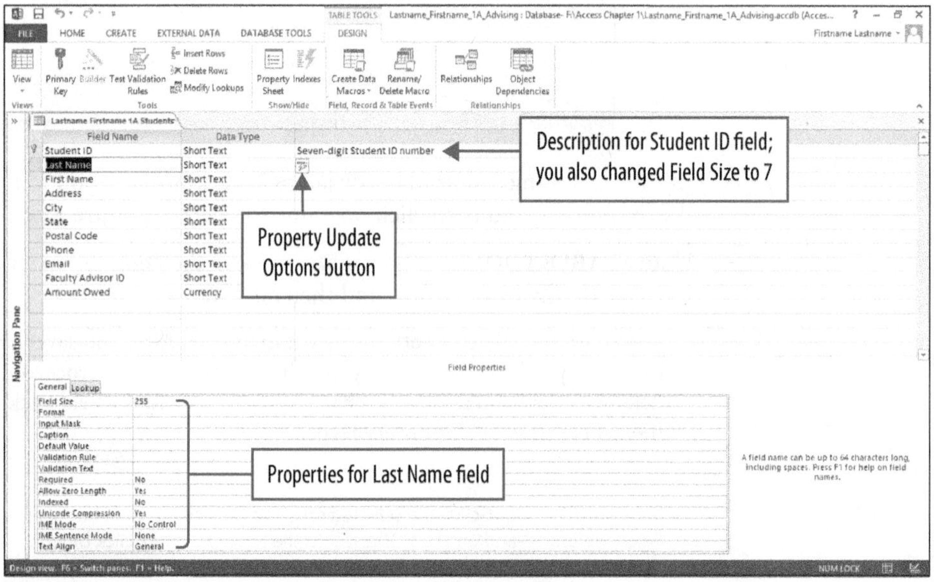

4 Click in the **State** field name box. In the **Field Properties** area, change the **Field Size** to **2** and in the **Description** box for this field, type **Two-character state abbreviation** and then press Enter.

5 Click in the **Faculty Advisor ID** field name box. In the **Field Properties** area, change the **Field Size** to **8** and in the **Description** box for this field, type **Eight-character ID of instructor assigned as advisor** and then press Enter.

6 On the **Quick Access Toolbar**, click **Save** to save the design changes to your table, and then notice the message.

The message indicates that the field size property of one or more fields has changed to a shorter size. If more characters are currently present in the Student ID, State, or Faculty Advisor ID fields than you have set as the field size, the data will be ***truncated***—cut off or shortened—because the fields were not previously restricted to these specific number of characters.

7 In the message box, click **Yes**.

Activity 1.10 | Viewing the Primary Key in Design View

Primary key refers to the field in the table that uniquely identifies a record. For example, in a college registration database, your Student ID number uniquely identifies you—no other student at the college has your exact student number. In the 1A Students table, the Student ID uniquely identifies each student.

When you create a table using the blank desktop database template, Access designates the first field as the primary key field and names the field ID. It is good database design practice to establish a primary key for every table, because doing so ensures that you do not enter the same record more than once. You can imagine the confusion if another student at your college had the same Student ID number as your own.

1. With your table still displayed in **Design** view, in the **Field Name** column, click in the **Student ID** field name box. To the left of the box, notice the small icon of a key, as shown in Figure 1.20.

   Access automatically designates the first field as the primary key field, but you can set any field as the primary key by clicking the field name, and then in the Tools group, clicking Primary Key.

FIGURE 1.20

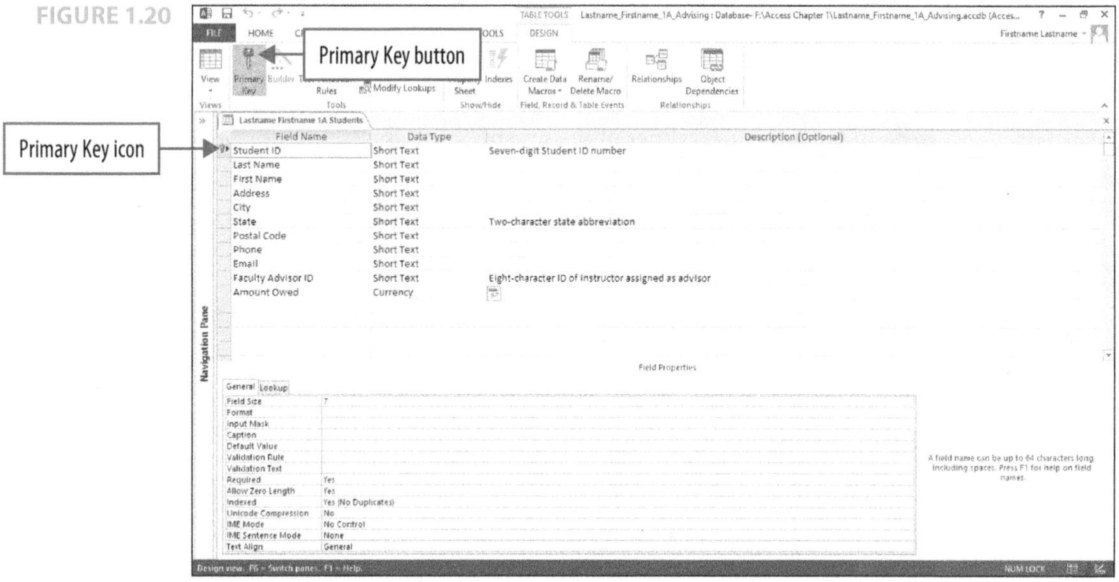

2. On the **DESIGN tab**, in the **Views group**, notice that the **View** button displays a picture of a datasheet, indicating that clicking **View** will switch the view to **Datasheet** view. Click the top of the **View** button.

   If you make design changes to a table and switch views without first saving the table, Access prompts you to save the table before changing views.

Activity 1.11 | Adding a Second Table to a Database by Importing an Excel Spreadsheet

Many Microsoft Office users track data in an Excel spreadsheet. The sorting and filtering capabilities of Excel are useful for a simple database where all of the information resides in one large Excel spreadsheet. However, Excel is limited as a database management tool because it cannot *relate* the information in multiple spreadsheets in a way that you can ask a question and get a meaningful result. Because data in an Excel spreadsheet is arranged in columns and rows, the spreadsheet can easily become an Access table by importing the spreadsheet.

1. On the ribbon, click the **EXTERNAL DATA tab**, and then in the **Import & Link group**, click **Excel**. In the **Get External Data – Excel Spreadsheet** dialog box, click **Browse**.

2. In the **File Open** dialog box, navigate to the location where your student data files are stored, and then double-click **a01A_Faculty_Advisors**. Compare your screen with Figure 1.21.

FIGURE 1.21

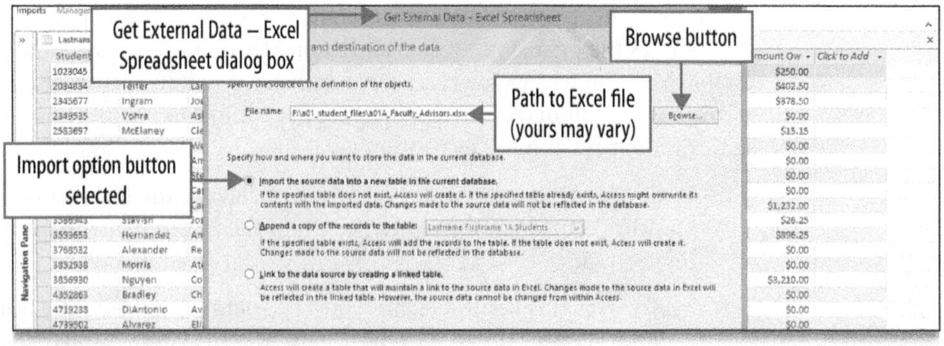

3 Be sure that the **Import the source data into a new table in the current database** option button is selected, click **OK**, and then click **Next**.

The Import Spreadsheet Wizard displays the spreadsheet data.

4 In the upper left corner of the wizard, select the **First Row Contains Column Headings** check box.

The Excel data is framed, indicating that the first row of Excel column titles will become the Access table field names, and the remaining rows will become the individual records in the new Access table.

5 Click **Next.** Notice that the first column—**Faculty ID**—is selected, and in the upper area of the wizard, the **Field Name** and the **Data Type** display. Compare your screen with Figure 1.22.

Here, under Field Options, you can review and change the name or the data type of each selected field. You can also identify fields in the spreadsheet that you do not want to import into the Access table by selecting the Do not import field (Skip) check box.

FIGURE 1.22

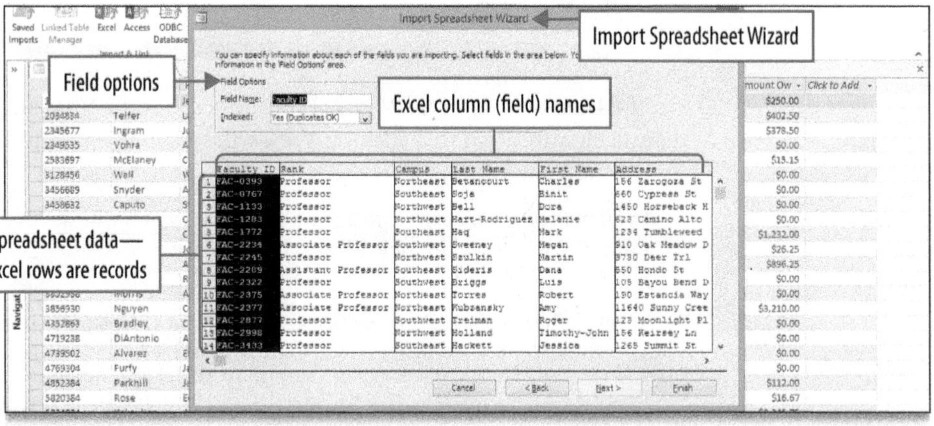

6 Click **Next.** In the upper area of the wizard, click the **Choose my own primary key** option button, and then be sure that **Faculty ID** displays in the box to the right.

In the new table, Faculty ID will be the primary key. No two faculty members have the same Faculty ID. By default, Access selects the first field as the primary key, but you can click the arrow to select a different field.

7 Click **Next.** In the **Import to Table** box, using your own name, type **Lastname Firstname 1A Faculty Advisors** and then click **Finish.**

8 In the **Get External Data - Excel Spreadsheet** dialog box, click **Close. Open** » the **Navigation Pane.**

9 In the **Navigation Pane,** double-click your **1A Faculty Advisors** table to open it in **Datasheet** view, and then **Close** « the **Navigation Pane.**

Two tables that are identified by their object tabs are open in the object window. Your 1A Faculty Advisors table is the active table and displays the 29 records that you imported from the Excel spreadsheet.

10 In your **1A Faculty Advisors** table, click in the **Postal Code** field in the first record. On the ribbon, under **TABLE TOOLS,** click the **FIELDS tab.** In the **Formatting group,** click the **Data Type arrow,** and then click **Short Text.** Compare your screen with Figure 1.23.

When you import data from an Excel spreadsheet, check the data types of all fields to ensure they are correct. Recall that if a field, such as the Postal Code, contains numbers that are not used in calculations, the data type should be set to Short Text. To change the data type of a field, click in the field in any record.

FIGURE 1.23

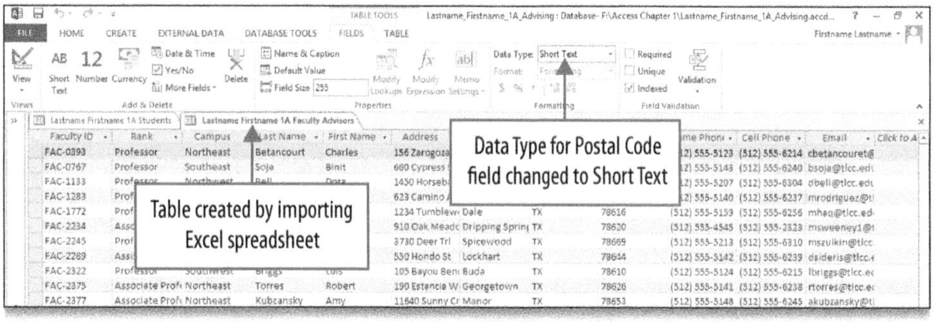

Activity 1.12 Adjusting Column Widths

You can adjust the column widths in a table displayed in Datasheet view by using techniques similar to those you use for Excel spreadsheets.

1 In the object window, click the **object tab** for your **1A Students** table to make it the active object and to display it in the object window.

Clicking the object tabs along the top of the object window enables you to display open objects and make them active so that you can work with them. All of the columns in the datasheet are the same width, regardless of the length of the data in the field, the length of the field name, or the field size that was set. If you print the table as currently displayed, some of the data or field names will not print fully, so you will want to adjust the column widths.

2 In the field names row, point to the right edge of the **Address** field to display the ✛ pointer, and then compare your screen with Figure 1.24.

FIGURE 1.24

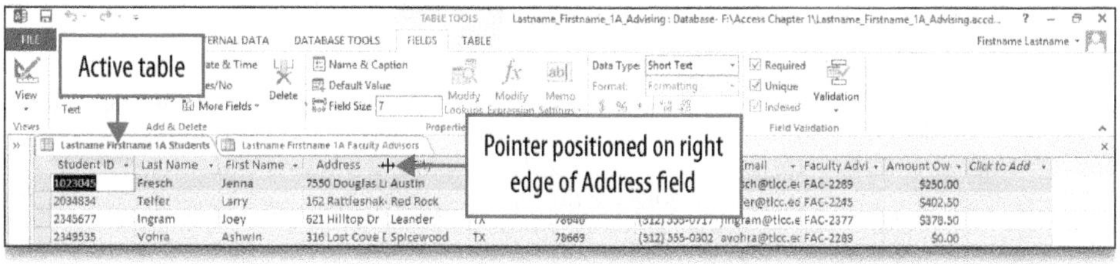

3 With the ✛ pointer positioned as shown in Figure 1.24, double-click the right edge of the **Address** field.

The column width of the Address field widens to display fully the longest entry in the field. In this manner, the width of a column can be increased or decreased to fit its contents in the same manner as a column in an Excel spreadsheet. In Access, adjusting the column width to fit the contents is referred to as ***Best Fit.***

4. Point to the **City** field name to display the pointer, right-click to select the entire column, and then click **Field Width**. In the **Column Width** dialog box, click **Best Fit**.

   This is a second way to adjust column widths.

5. If necessary, scroll to the right to view the last three fields. Point to the **Email** field name to display the pointer, hold down the left mouse button, and then drag to the right to select this column, the **Faculty Advisor ID** column, and the **Amount Owed** column. Point to the right edge of any of the selected columns to display the pointer, and then double-click to apply **Best Fit** to all three columns.

   You can select multiple columns and adjust the widths of all of them at one time by using this technique or by right-clicking any of the selected columns, clicking Field Width, and clicking Best Fit in the Column Width dialog box.

6. If necessary, scroll to the left to view the **Student ID** field. To the left of the **Student ID** field name, click **Select All**. Notice that all of the fields are selected.

7. On the ribbon, click the **HOME tab**. In the **Records group**, click **More**, and then click **Field Width**. In the **Column Width** dialog box, click **Best Fit**. Click anywhere in the **Student ID** field, and then compare your screen with Figure 1.25.

   Using the More command is a third way to adjust column widths. By using Select All, you can adjust the widths of all of the columns at one time. Adjusting the width of columns does not change the data in the table's records; it only changes the *display* of the data.

FIGURE 1.25

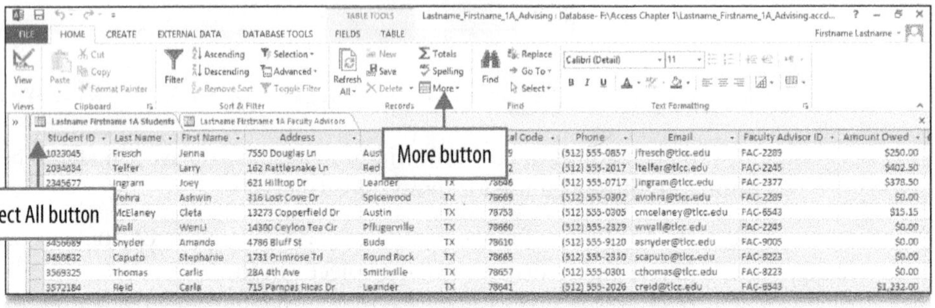

NOTE **Adjusting Column Widths**

After adjusting column widths, scroll horizontally and vertically to be sure that all of the data displays in all of the fields. Access adjusts column widths to fit the screen size based on the displayed data. If data is not displayed on the screen when you adjust column widths—even if you use Select All—the column width might not be adjusted adequately to display all of the data in the field. After adjusting column widths, save the table before performing other tasks. The column width adjustments might not save with the table. When you reopen a table, be sure to readjust the column widths if you plan to print the table or work with the data in the table.

8. On the **Quick Access Toolbar**, click **Save** to save the table design changes—changing the column widths.

   If you do not save the table after making design changes, Access prompts you to save when you close the table.

Activity 1.13 | Printing a Table

There are times when you will want to print a table, even though a report may look more professional. For example, you may need a quick reference, or you may want to proofread the data that has been entered. Before printing a table, be sure to apply Best Fit to all of the columns in the table.

1 On the ribbon, click the **FILE tab**, click **Print**, and then click **Print Preview**. Compare your screen with Figure 1.26.

The table displays in Print Preview with the default zoom setting of Fit to Window, a view that enables you to see how your table will print on the page. It is a good idea to view any object in Print Preview before printing so that you can make changes to the object if needed before actually printing it. In the navigation area, the Next Page button is darker (available), an indication that more than one page will print.

FIGURE 1.26

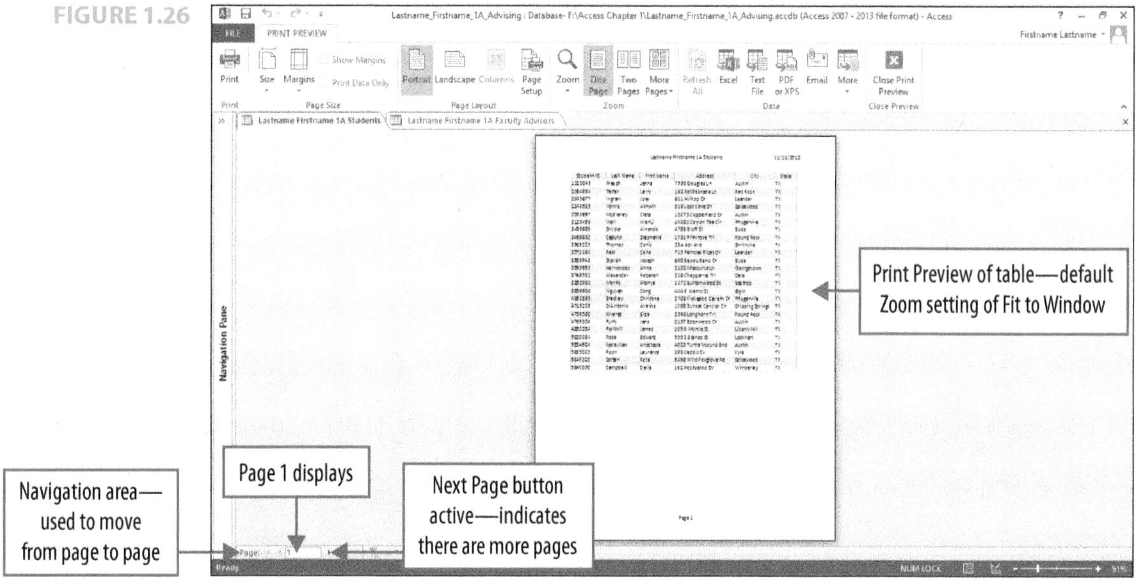

2 In the navigation area, click **Next Page** [▶] to display Page 2. Point to the top of the page to display the [🔍] pointer, click one time to zoom in, and then compare your screen with Figure 1.27.

The Print Preview display enlarges, and the Zoom Out pointer displays. The second page of the table displays the last five fields. The Next Page button is dimmed, indicating that the button is unavailable because there are no more pages after Page 2. The Previous Page button is available, indicating that a page exists before this page.

FIGURE 1.27

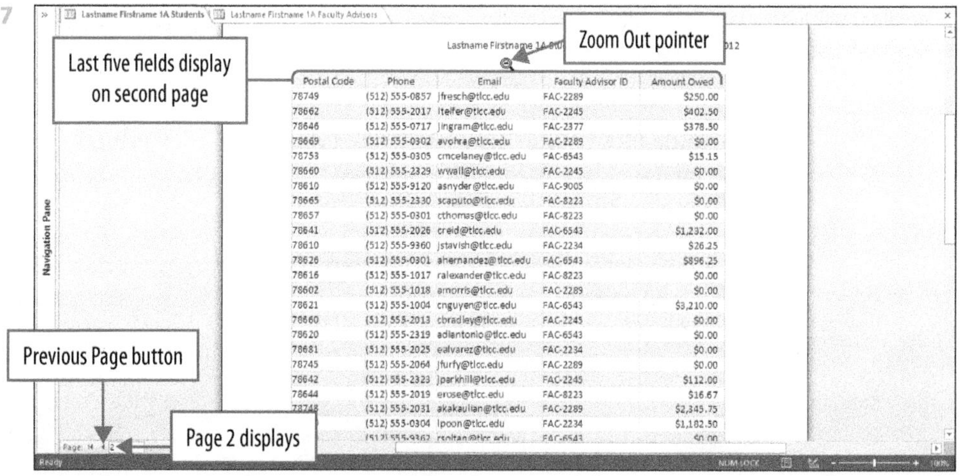

3 On the ribbon, on the **PRINT PREVIEW tab**, in the **Zoom group**, click the top portion of the **Zoom** button to change the zoom setting back to the default setting of Fit to Window.

ANOTHER WAY With the [zoom] pointer displayed on the page, click to zoom back to the Fit to Window setting.

4 In the **Page Layout group**, click **Landscape**, and notice that there are only three fields on Page 2. In the navigation area, click **Previous Page** [◄] to display Page 1, and then compare your screen with Figure 1.28.

The orientation of the page to be printed changes. Included on the page are the table name and current date at the top of the page and the page number at the bottom of the page. The change in orientation from portrait to landscape is not saved with the table. Each time you print, you must check the page orientation, the margins, and any other print parameters so that the object prints as you intend. You should also be sure that Best Fit is applied to each column or to the entire table.

FIGURE 1.28

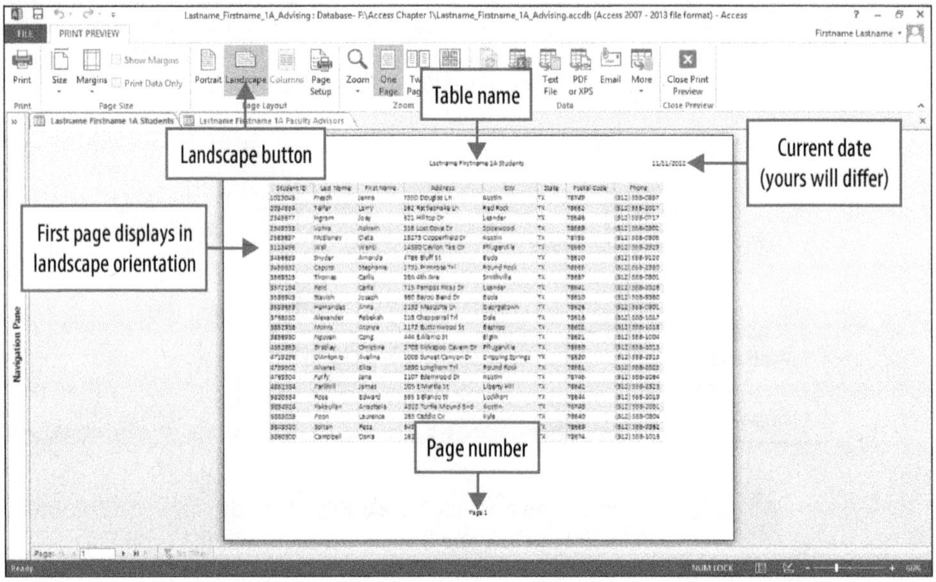

NOTE **Headers and Footers in Access Objects**

The headers and footers in Access tables and queries are controlled by default settings; you cannot enter additional information or edit the information. The object name displays in the center of the header area, and the current date displays on the right. Adding your name to the object name is helpful in identifying your paper or electronic results. The page number displays in the center of the footer area. The headers and footers in Access forms and reports are more flexible; you can add to and edit the information.

5 On the **PRINT PREVIEW tab**, in the **Print group**, click **Print**. In the **Print** dialog box, under **Print Range**, verify that **All** is selected. Under **Copies**, verify that the **Number of Copies** is **1**. Compare your screen with Figure 1.29.

FIGURE 1.29

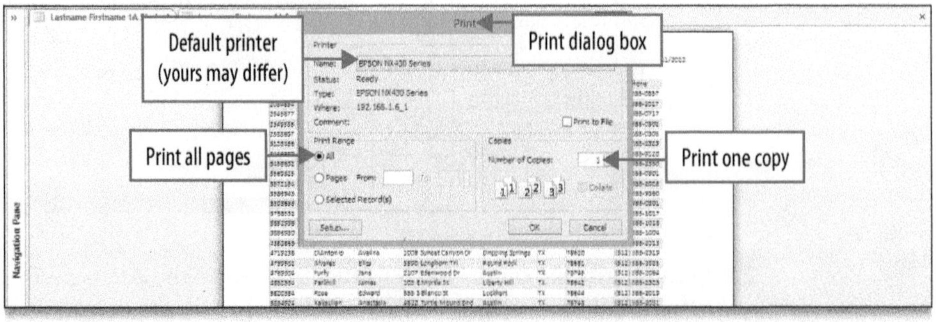

6 Determine whether your instructor wants you to submit your work for this project on paper or electronically. If submitting electronically, determine whether, in addition to submitting your Access database, your instructor wants you to create and submit electronic printouts of individual database objects.

7 To print on paper, in the **Print** dialog box, click **OK**; and then on the ribbon, in the **Close Preview group**, click **Close Print Preview**. If you are required to create and submit electronic printouts, in the **Print** dialog box, click **Cancel**, and then follow the steps in the following Note—or follow the specific directions provided by your instructor.

NOTE **Creating a PDF Electronic Printout of an Access Object**

Display the object (table, query, form, report, and so on) in Print Preview and adjust margins and orientation as needed. On the PRINT PREVIEW tab, in the Data group, click PDF or XPS. In the Publish as PDF or XPS dialog box, navigate to your chapter folder. Use the default file name, or follow your instructor's directions to name the object. If wish to view the PDF file, in the dialog box, select the Open file after publishing check box. In the Publish as PDF or XPS dialog box, click Publish. If necessary, close the Windows 8 Reader, Adobe Reader, or Adobe Acrobat window and the Export – PDF dialog box. On the ribbon, click Close Print Preview; your electronic printout is saved.

8 In the upper right corner of the object window, click **Close Object** [×] to close your **1A Students** table. Notice that the **1A Faculty Advisors** table is the active object in the object window.

ANOTHER WAY In the object window, right-click your 1A Students object tab, and then click Close.

9 In your **1A Faculty Advisors** table, to the left of the **Faculty ID** field name, click **Select All** [ ] to select all of the columns. On the **HOME tab**, in the **Records group**, click **More**, and then click **Field Width**. In the **Column Width** dialog box, click **Best Fit** to adjust the widths of all of the columns so that all of the data display. Scroll horizontally and vertically to be sure that all of the data display in each field; if necessary, use the techniques you practiced to apply **Best Fit** to individual columns. **Save** the changes you made to the table's column widths, and then click in any record to cancel the selection.

10 On the ribbon, click the **FILE tab**, click **Print**, and then click **Print Preview**. On the **PRINT PREVIEW tab**, in the **Page Layout group**, click **Landscape**. Notice that the table will print on more than one page. In the **Page Size group**, click **Margins**, click **Normal**, and then notice that one more column moved to the first page—your results may differ depending upon your printer's capabilities.

In addition to changing the page orientation to Landscape, you can change the margins to Normal to see if all of the fields will print on one page. In this instance, there are still too many fields to print on one page, although the Postal Code field moved from Page 2 to Page 1.

11 If directed to do so by your instructor, create a paper or electronic printout of your **1A Faculty Advisors** table, and then click **Close Print Preview**.

12 In the object window, **Close** [×] your **1A Faculty Advisors** table.

All of your database objects—your *1A Students* table and your *1A Faculty Advisors* table—are closed; the object window is empty.

Objective 4 Create a Query, Form, and Report

Video A1-4

Recall that tables are the foundation of an Access database because all of the data is stored in one or more tables. You can display the data stored in tables in other database objects such as queries, forms, and reports.

Activity 1.14 | Creating a Query by Using the Simple Query Wizard

A ***query*** is a database object that retrieves specific data from one or more database objects—either tables or other queries—and then, in a single datasheet, displays only the data that you specify when you design the query. Because the word *query* means *to ask a question*, think of a query as a question formed in a manner that Access can answer.

A ***select query*** is one type of Access query. A select query, also called a ***simple select query***, retrieves (selects) data from one or more tables or queries and then displays the selected data in a datasheet. A select query creates a subset of the data to answer specific questions; for example, *Which students live in Austin, TX?*

The objects from which a query selects the data are referred to as the query's ***data source***. In this activity, you will create a simple select query using a wizard that walks you step by step through the process. The process involves selecting the data source and indicating the fields that you want to include in the query results. The query—the question you want to ask—is *What is the last name, first name, email address, phone number, and Student ID of every student?*

1. On the ribbon, click the **CREATE tab**, and then in the **Queries group**, click **Query Wizard**. In the **New Query** dialog box, be sure **Simple Query Wizard** is selected, and then click **OK**. Compare your screen with Figure 1.30.

FIGURE 1.30

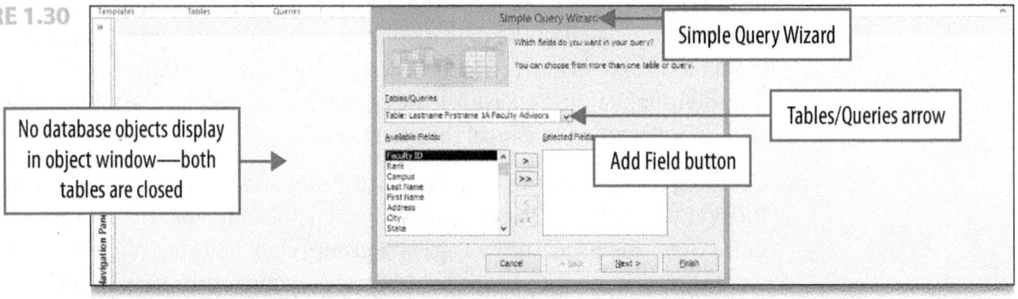

2. In the wizard, click the **Tables/Queries arrow**, and then click **Table: Lastname Firstname 1A Students.**

   In the wizard, the displayed table or query name is the object that was last selected on the Navigation Pane. The last object you worked with was your 1A Faculty Advisors table, so that object name displayed in the wizard.

   To create a query, first select the data source—the object from which the query is to select the data. The information you need to answer the question is stored in your 1A Students table, so this table is your data source.

3. Under **Available Fields**, click **Last Name**, and then click **Add Field** [>] to move the field to the **Selected Fields** list on the right. Double-click the **First Name** field to add the field to the **Selected Fields** list.

   Use either method to add fields to the Selected Fields list—you can add fields in any order.

4 By using **Add Field** [>] or by double-clicking the field name, add the following fields to the **Selected Fields** list in the order specified: **Email, Phone,** and **Student ID**. Compare your screen with Figure 1.31.

Selecting these five fields will answer the question, *What is the last name, first name, email address, phone number, and Student ID of every student?*

FIGURE 1.31

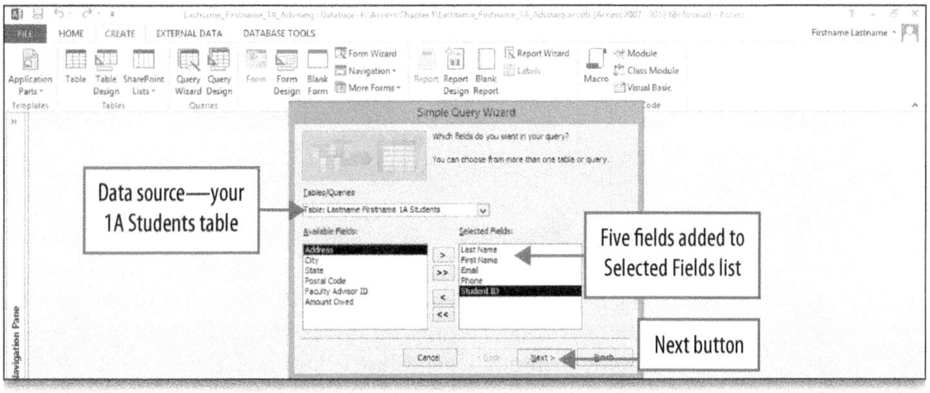

5 In the wizard, click **Next**. Click in the **What title do you want for your query?** box. Using your own name, edit as necessary so that the query name is **Lastname Firstname 1A All Students Query** and then compare your screen with Figure 1.32.

FIGURE 1.32

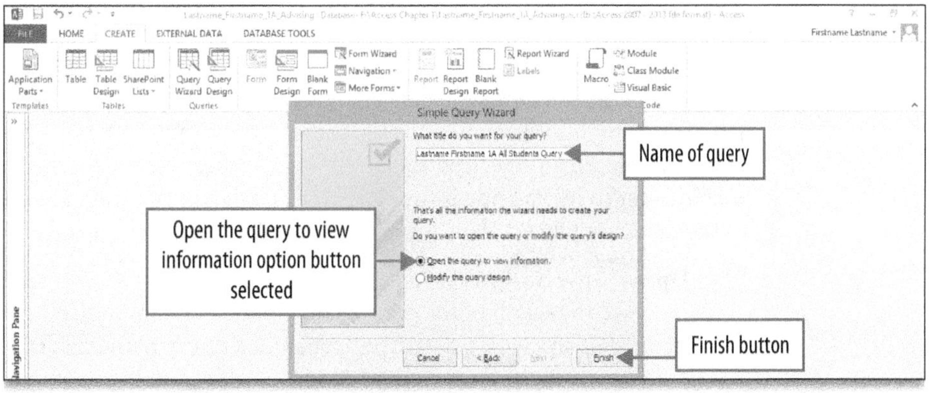

6 In the wizard, click **Finish**. Select all of the columns, apply **Best Fit**, and then **Save** [Save icon] the query. In the first record, click in the **Last Name** field to cancel the selection. Compare your screen with Figure 1.33.

Access ***runs*** the query—performs the actions indicated in your query design—by searching the records in the specified data source, and then finds the records that match specified criteria. The records that match the criteria display in a datasheet. A select query *selects*—finds and displays—*only* the information from the data source that you request, including the specified fields.

In the object window, Access displays every student from your 1A Students table—the data source—but displays *only* the five fields that you moved to the Selected Fields list in the Simple Query Wizard.

FIGURE 1.33

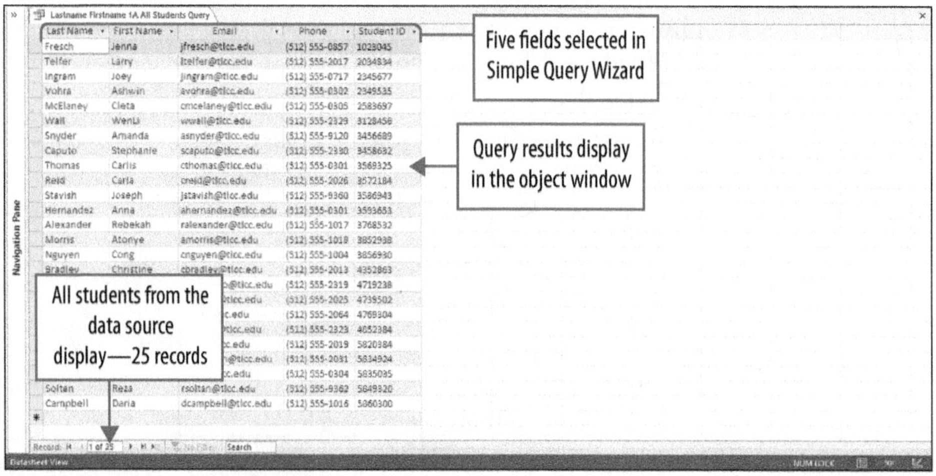

7 On the ribbon, click the **FILE tab**, click **Print**, and then click **Print Preview**. Notice that the query results will print on one page. As directed by your instructor, create a paper or electronic printout. Click **Close Print Preview**.

8 In the object window, **Close** [×] the query.

Activity 1.15 | Creating and Printing a Form

A ***form*** is an Access object with which you can enter data, edit data, or display data from a table or query. In a form, the fields are laid out in an attractive format on the screen, which makes working with the database easier for those who must enter and look up data.

One type of form displays only one record at a time. Such a form is useful not only to the individual who performs the data entry—typing in the records—but also to anyone who has the job of viewing information in the database. For example, when you visit the Records office at your college to obtain a transcript, someone displays your record on the screen. For the viewer, it is much easier to look at one record at a time, using a form, than to look at all of the student records in the database table.

1 **Open** [»] the **Navigation Pane**. Drag the right edge of the **Navigation Pane** to the right to increase the width of the pane so that all object names display fully. Notice that a table name displays with a datasheet icon, and a query name displays an icon of two overlapping datasheets. Right-click your **1A Students** table, and then compare your screen with Figure 1.34.

FIGURE 1.34

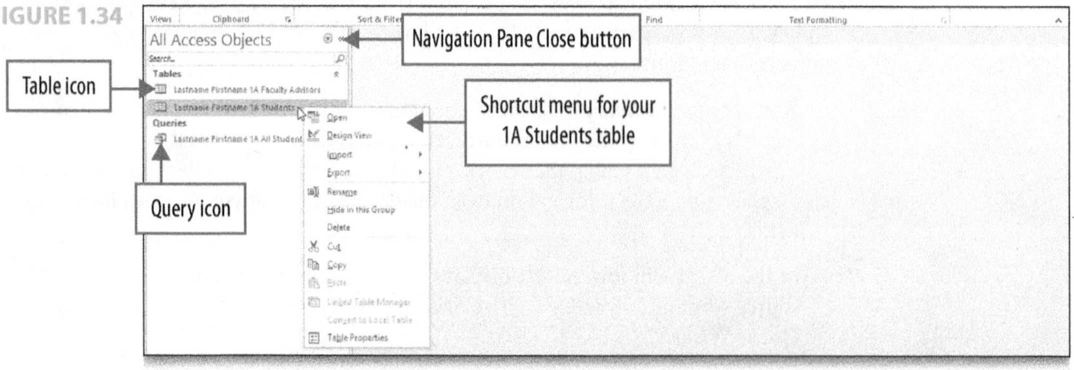

2 On the shortcut menu, click **Open** to display the table in the object window, and then **Close** [«] the **Navigation Pane** to maximize your object window space.

ANOTHER WAY On the Navigation Pane, double-click the object name to open it.

3 Notice that there are 11 fields in the table. On the **CREATE tab**, in the **Forms group**, click **Form**, and then compare your screen with Figure 1.35.

The Form tool creates a form based on the active object—your 1A Students table. The form displays all of the fields from the underlying data source—one record at a time—in a simple top-to-bottom format with all 11 fields lined up in a single column. You can use this new form immediately, or you can modify it. Records that you create or edit in a form are automatically added to or updated in the underlying table or data source.

The new form displays in ***Layout view***—the Access view in which you can make changes to an object while the object is open and displaying the data from the data source. Each field in the form displayed in Figure 1.35 displays the data for the first student record—*Jenna Fresch*—from your 1A Students table.

FIGURE 1.35

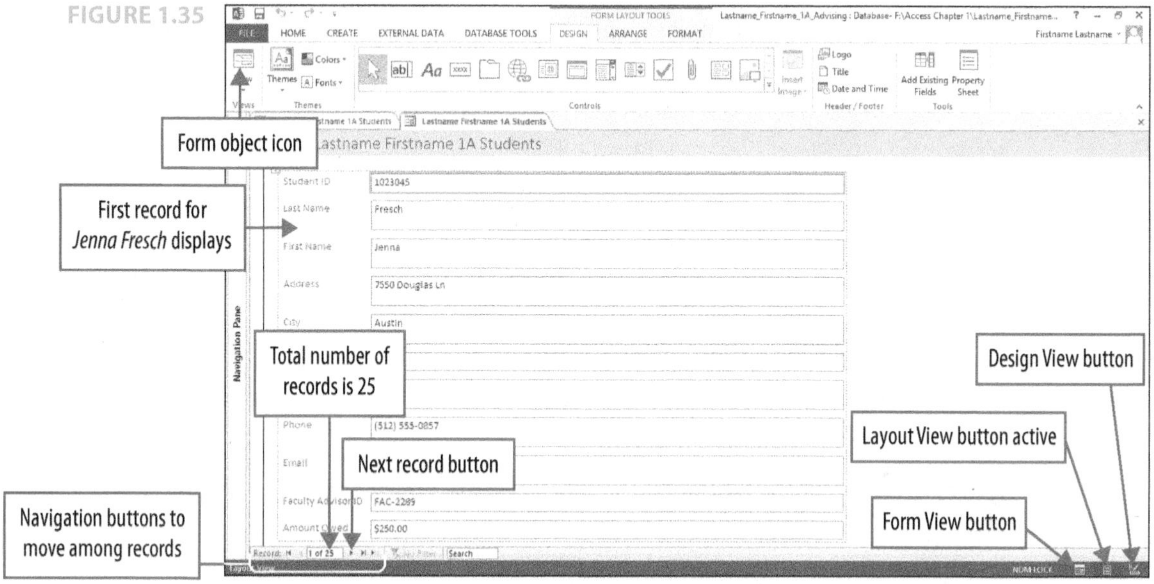

4 At the right side of the status bar, notice the three buttons. Point to each button to display its ScreenTip, and notice that **Layout View** is active, indicating that the form is displayed in Layout view.

5 In the status bar, click **Form View**.

In ***Form view***, you can view the records, create a new record, edit a record, and delete a record. You cannot change the layout or design of the form. Form view is useful for individuals who *access records* in your database. Layout view is useful for individuals who *design* the form.

ANOTHER WAY On the DESIGN tab, or on the HOME tab, in the Views group, click the top portion of the View button when it displays an icon of a form.

6 In the navigation area, click **Next record** two times to display the third record—the record for *Joey Ingram*.

Use the navigation buttons to scroll among the records and to display any single record.

7 Using your own name, **Save** the form as **Lastname Firstname 1A Student Form**

8. Be sure that Record 3 displays. On the ribbon, click the **FILE tab**, click **Print**, and then on the right, click **Print**—do *not* click **Print Preview** because you are going to print a *single* record—not all of the records.

9. In the **Print** dialog box, under **Print Range**, click the **Selected Record(s)** option button, and then click **Setup**.

10. In the **Page Setup** dialog box, click the **Columns tab**. Under **Column Size**, double-click in the **Width** box to select the existing value, type **7.5** and then click **OK**.

    Forms are usually not printed, so the default width for a form created with the Form command is larger than most printers can handle to print on one page. If you do not change the width, the form will print on two pages because the last column flows over the margins allowed by the printer. If, after changing the Width to 7.5, your form still prints on two pages, try entering a different Width; for example, 7 or 6.5.

11. If instructed to print your objects, in the **Print** dialog box, click **OK** to print the record for *Joey Ingram* on one page; otherwise, click **Cancel**. If instructed to print an electronic copy, follow the steps in the following Note or the directions provided by your instructor.

    After printing, along the left edge of the record, the narrow bar—the ***record selector bar***—displays in black, indicating that the record is selected.

NOTE

Printing a Single Form in PDF

On the FILE tab, click Print, and then on the right, click Print. In the Print dialog box, click Setup. In the Page Setup dialog box, click the Columns tab. Under Column Size, double-click in the Width box, type 7.5 and then click OK. In the Print dialog box, click Cancel. On the left edge of the form, click the record selector bar so that it is black—selected.

On the ribbon, click the EXTERNAL DATA tab. In the Export group, click PDF or XPS. In the Publish as PDF or XPS dialog box, navigate to your chapter folder, and at the lower right corner of the dialog box, click Options. In the Options dialog box, under Range, click the Selected records option button, and then click OK. In the Publish as PDF or XPS dialog box, click Publish. If necessary, close the Window 8 Reader, Adobe Reader, or Adobe Acrobat window.

12. **Close** [×] your **1A Student Form** object; leave your **1A Students** table open.

Activity 1.16 | Creating, Modifying, and Printing a Report

A ***report*** is a database object that displays the fields and records from a table or query in an easy-to-read format suitable for printing. Create professional-looking reports to summarize database information.

1. **Open** [»] the **Navigation Pane**, and then open your **1A Faculty Advisors** table by double-clicking the table name or by right-clicking the table name and clicking **Open**. **Close** [«] the **Navigation Pane**.

2. On the ribbon, click the **CREATE tab**. In the **Reports group**, click **Report**.

    The Report tool creates a report in Layout view and includes all of the fields and all of the records in the data source—your 1A Faculty Advisors table. Dotted lines indicate how the report will break across pages if you print it now. In Layout view, you can make quick changes to the report layout while viewing the data from the table.

3. In the report, click the **Faculty ID** field name, and then on the ribbon, under **REPORT LAYOUT TOOLS**, click the **ARRANGE tab**. In the **Rows & Columns group**, click **Select Column**, and then press [Del]. Using the same technique, delete the **Rank** field.

    The Faculty ID and Rank fields, along with the data, are deleted from the report. The fields readjust by moving to the left. Deleting the fields from the report does *not* delete the fields and data from the data source—your 1A Faculty Advisors table.

ANOTHER WAY Right-click the field name, click Select Entire Column, and then press Del.

4 Click the **Address** field name, and then by using the scroll bar at the bottom of the screen, scroll to the right to display the **Cell Phone** field; be careful not to click in the report.

5 Hold down Shift, and then click the **Cell Phone** field name to select all of the fields from *Address* through *Cell Phone*. With the six field names selected—surrounded by a colored border—in the **Rows & Columns group**, click **Select Column**, and then press Del.

Use this method to select and delete multiple columns in Layout view.

6 Scroll to the left, and notice that the four remaining fields display within the dotted lines—they are within the margins of the report. Click the **Campus** field name. Hold down Shift, and then click the **First Name** field name to select the first three fields.

7 On the ribbon, under **REPORT LAYOUT TOOLS**, click the **DESIGN tab**. In the **Tools group**, click **Property Sheet**.

The ***Property Sheet*** for the selected columns displays on the right side of the screen. Every object and every item in an object has an associated Property Sheet where you can make precise changes to the properties—characteristics—of selected items.

8 In the **Property Sheet**, if necessary, click the **Format tab**. Click **Width**, type **1.5** and then press Enter. Compare your screen with Figure 1.36.

The width of the three selected field names and the columns changes to 1.5", and the fields readjust by moving to the left. When you change the Width property, you do not need to select the entire column. Change the Width property if you need to move columns within the margins of a report. In this report, the fields already displayed within the margins, but some reports may need this minor adjustment to print on one page.

ANOTHER WAY Select the column, and then drag the right edge of the column to the left to decrease the width of the field, or drag to the right to increase the width of the field.

FIGURE 1.36

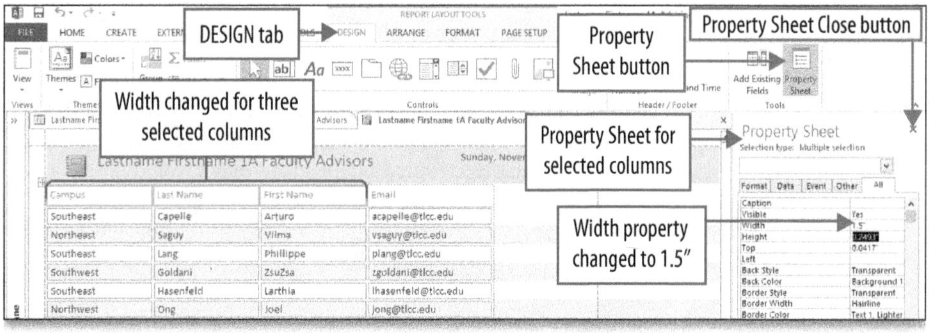

9 Close the **Property Sheet**. Click the **Last Name** field name. On the ribbon, click the **HOME tab**, and then in the **Sort & Filter group**, click **Ascending**.

Access sorts the report in ascending alphabetical order by the Last Name field. By default, tables are sorted in ascending order by the primary key field—in this instance, the Faculty ID field. Changing the sort order in the report does *not* change the sort order in the underlying table.

10 At the top of the report, to the right of the green report icon, click anywhere in the title of the report to select the title. On the **HOME tab**, in the **Text Formatting group**, click the **Font Size arrow**, and then click **14**. **Save** the report. In the **Save As** dialog box, in the **Report Name** box, add **Report** to the end of *Lastname Firstname 1A Faculty Advisors*, and then click **OK**.

11 On the **FILE tab**, click **Print**, and then click **Print Preview**. On the **PRINT PREVIEW tab**, in the **Zoom group**, click **Two Pages**, and then compare your screen with Figure 1.37.

As currently formatted, the report will print on two pages because the page number at the bottom of the report is positioned beyond the right margin of the report.

FIGURE 1.37

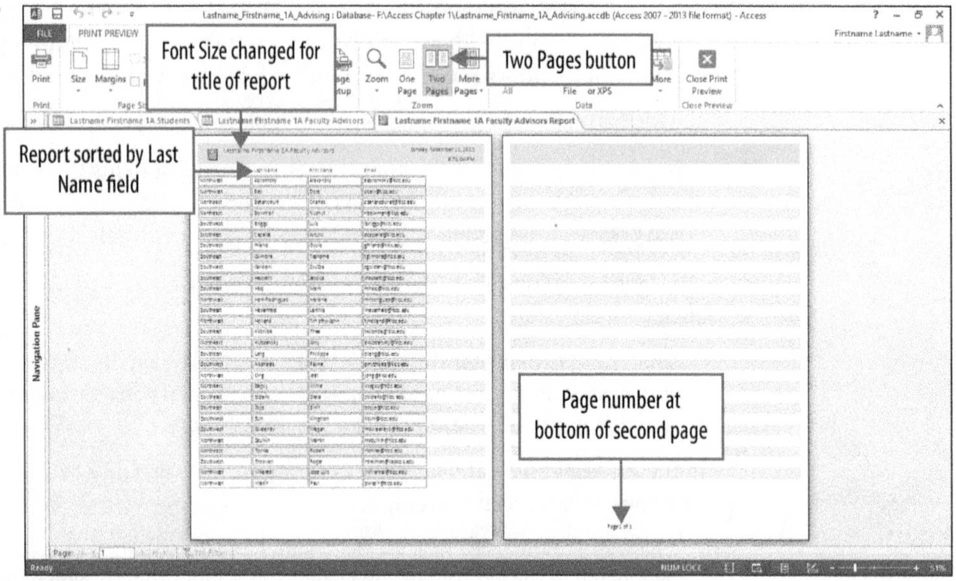

12 In the **Close Preview group**, click **Close Print Preview**. Scroll down to display the bottom of the report, and then, if necessary, scroll to the right to display the page number. Click the page number—**Page 1 of 1**—and then press Del.

Because all of the data will print on one page, the page number is not necessary for this report. If you want the page number to display, you can drag it within the margins of the report.

13 Display the report in **Print Preview**, and notice that the report will now print on one page. In the **Zoom group**, click **One Page**. Click **Save** to save the changes to the design of the report, and then create a paper or electronic printout as directed. Click **Close Print Preview**.

When you create a report by using the Report tool, the default margins are 0.25 inch. Some printers require a greater margin, so your printed report may result in two pages. As you progress in your study of Access, you will practice making these adjustments. Also, if a printer is not installed on your system, the electronic PDF printout may result in a two-page report.

14 In the object window, right-click any **object tab**, and then click **Close All** to close all of the open objects. Notice that the object window is empty.

Objective 5 Close a Database and Exit Access

Video A1-5

When you close a table, any changes made to the records are saved automatically. If you make changes to the structure or adjust column widths, you are prompted to save the table when you close the table or when you switch views. Likewise, you are prompted to save queries, forms, and reports if you make changes to the layout or design. If the Navigation Pane is open when you exit Access, it will display when you reopen the database. When you are finished using your database, close the database, and then exit Access.

Activity 1.17 | Closing a Database and Exiting Access

1 **Open** [»] the **Navigation Pane**. If necessary, increase the width of the **Navigation Pane** so that all object names display fully. Notice that your report object displays with a green report icon. Compare your screen with Figure 1.38.

FIGURE 1.38

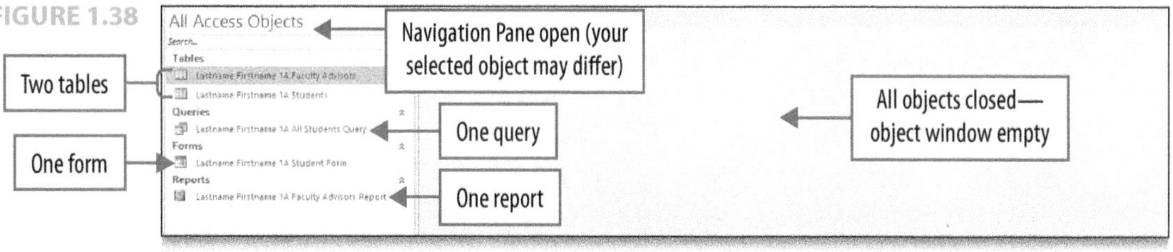

2 On the ribbon, click the **FILE tab**. Click **Close** to close the database but leave Access open. This action enables you to continue working in Access with another database if you want to do so. In the Access opening screen, in the upper right corner, click **Close** [×] to exit Access. As directed by your instructor, submit your database and the paper or electronic printouts of the five objects—two tables, one query, one form, and one report—that are the results of this project. Specifically, in this project, using your own name, you created the following database and printouts or electronic printouts:

1. Lastname_Firstname_1A_Advising	Database file
2. Lastname Firstname 1A Students	Table (printout or electronic printout – two pages)
3. Lastname Firstname 1A Faculty Advisors	Table (printout or electronic printout – two pages)
4. Lastname Firstname 1A All Students Query	Query (printout or electronic printout)
5. Lastname Firstname 1A Student Form	Form (printout or electronic printout – Record 3)
6. Lastname Firstname 1A Faculty Advisors Report	Report (printout or electronic printout)

ANOTHER WAY

On the left side of the title bar, click [A] and then click Close, or on the right side of the title bar, click [×] to close the database and to exit Access.

END | You have completed Project 1A

GO! with Office Online (formerly Web Apps)

Objective: Export an Access Table to an Excel Spreadsheet, Save to OneDrive, Edit a Record, and Save to Your Computer

Access web apps are designed to work with Microsoft's ***SharePoint***, an application for setting up websites to share and manage documents. Your college may not have SharePoint installed, so you will use other tools to share objects from your database so that you can work collaboratively with others. Recall that Window's OneDrive is a free file storage and file sharing service. For Access, you can export a database object to an Excel worksheet, a PDF file, or a text file, and then save the file to OneDrive.

ALERT! **Working with Web-Based Applications and Services**

Computer programs and services on the web receive continuous updates and improvements. Therefore, the steps to complete this web-based activity may differ from the ones shown. You can often look at the screens and the information presented to determine how to complete the activity.

Activity: Exporting an Access Table to an Excel Spreadsheet, Saving the Spreadsheet to OneDrive, Editing a Record in OneDrive, and Saving to Your Computer

In this activity, you will ***export***—copy data from one file into another file—your 1A Students table to an Excel spreadsheet, upload your Excel file to OneDrive, edit a record in OneDrive, and then download a copy of the edited spreadsheet to your computer.

1 Start Access, navigate to your **Access Chapter 1** folder, and then open your **1A_Advising** database file. If necessary, on the Message Bar, click Enable Content. In the **Navigation Pane**, click your **1A Students** table to select it—do not open it.

2 On the ribbon, click the **EXTERNAL DATA tab**, and then in the **Export group**, click **Excel**. In the **Export – Excel Spreadsheet** dialog box, click **Browse**, and then navigate to your **Access Chapter 1** folder. In the **File Save** dialog box, click in the **File name** box, type **Lastname_Firstname_AC_1A_Web** and then click **Save**.

3 In the **Export – Excel Spreadsheet** dialog box, under **Specify export options**, select the first two check boxes—**Export data with formatting and layout** and **Open the destination file after the export operation is complete**—and then click **OK**. In the **Microsoft Excel** window, in the column headings row, to the left of column **A**, click **Select All**. On the **HOME tab**, in the **Cells group**, click **Format**, and then click **AutoFit Column Width**. Click in cell **A1** to cancel the selection, and then compare your screen with Figure A.

4 **Save** the spreadsheet, and then **Close** Excel. In the **Export – Excel Spreadsheet** dialog box, click **Close**, and then **Close** Access.

5 From the desktop, start Internet Explorer. Navigate to **http://onedrive.com**, and then sign in to your Microsoft account. Open your **GO! Web Projects** folder—or create and then open this folder if necessary.

6 On the menu bar, click **Upload**. In the **Choose File to Upload** dialog box, navigate to your **Access Chapter 1** folder, and then double-click your **AC_1A_Web** Excel file to upload it to OneDrive.

FIGURE A

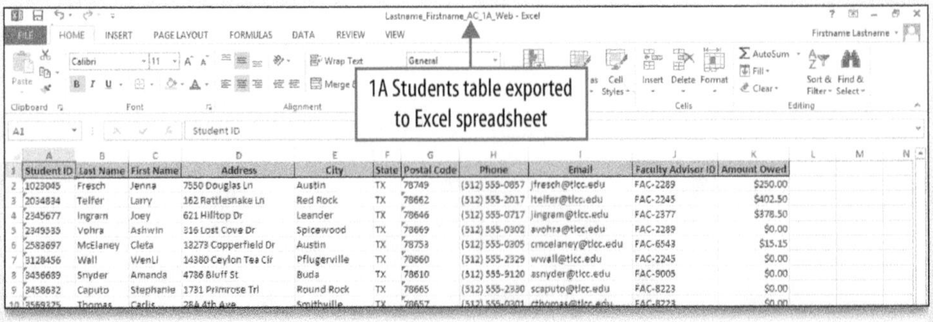

(GO! with Office Online (formerly Web Apps) continues on the next page)

7 When the upload is completed, in your **GO! Web Projects** folder, click your **AC_1A_Web** file to open it in Excel Online.

On the ribbon, notice that you can open this worksheet in Excel instead of using Excel Online. If you are working on a computer that does not have Microsoft Excel installed, you can still create and modify workbooks in your web browser by using Excel Online.

8 In the first record, click in the **Last Name** field. Using your own last name, type **Lastname** and then press Tab to replace *Fresch* with your last name. In the **First Name** field, using your own first name, type **Firstname** to replace *Jenna* with your own first name, and then press ↓ to save the record. Compare your screen with Figure B.

9 On the ribbon, click the **FILE tab**, click **Save As**, and then click **Download a Copy**. In the message box—usually displays at the bottom of your screen—click the **Save arrow**, and then click **Save as**. In the **Save As** dialog box, navigate to your **Access Chapter 1** folder, and then click in the **File name** box. Type **Lastname_Firstname_AC_1A_Web_Download** and then click **Save**. **Close** the message box.

10 In OneDrive, on the title bar, click **OneDrive** to return to your home page. At the top right corner of your screen, click your OneDrive name, and then click **Sign out**. **Close** your browser window.

11 Start Excel. In the Excel opening screen, click **Open Other Workbooks**. Under **Open**, click **Computer**. Under **Computer**, click **Browse**. Navigate to your **Access Chapter 1** folder, and then double-click your **AC_1A_Web** Excel file. Notice that this file is the original file—the first record is not changed. If you are required to print your documents, use one of the methods in the Note box given. **Close** your Excel file, saving the changes to your worksheet, and then **Open** and print your **AC_1A_Web_Download** file by using one of the methods in the following Note. **Close** Excel, saving the changes to your worksheet. As directed by your instructor, submit your two workbooks and the two paper or electronic printouts that are the results of this project.

NOTE

Adding the File Name to the Footer and Printing or Creating an Electronic Printout of an Excel Spreadsheet on One Page

Click the FILE tab, click Print, and then click Page Setup. In the Page Setup dialog box, on the Page tab, under Orientation, click Landscape. Under Scaling, click the Fit to option button. In the Page Setup dialog box, click the Header/Footer tab, and then click Custom Footer. With the insertion point blinking in the Left section box, click the Insert File Name button, and then click OK. In the Page Setup dialog box, click OK.

To print on paper, click Print. To create an electronic file of your printout, on the left side of your screen, click Export. Under Export, be sure Create PDF/XPS Document is selected, and then, on the right, click Create PDF/XPS. Navigate to your Access Chapter 1 folder, and then click Publish to save the file with the default name and an extension of pdf.

FIGURE B

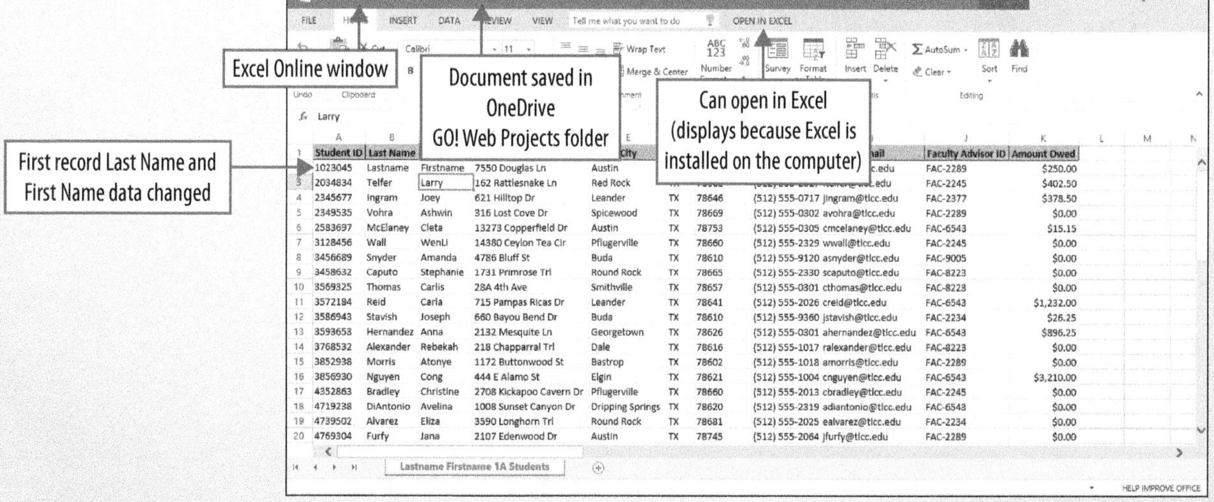

PROJECT

1B Student Workshops Database

MyITLab®
Project 1B Training

PROJECT ACTIVITIES

In Activities 1.18 through 1.25, you will assist Dr. Miriam Yong, director of student activities, in creating a database to store information about student workshops held at Texas Lakes Community College campuses. You will use a database template that tracks event information, add workshop information to the database, and then print the results. Your completed report and table will look similar to Figure 1.39.

PROJECT FILES

For Project 1B, you will need the following files:

Desktop Event Management template
a01B_Workshops (Excel workbook)

You will save your database as:

Lastname_Firstname_1B_Student_Workshops

PROJECT RESULTS

Build from Scratch

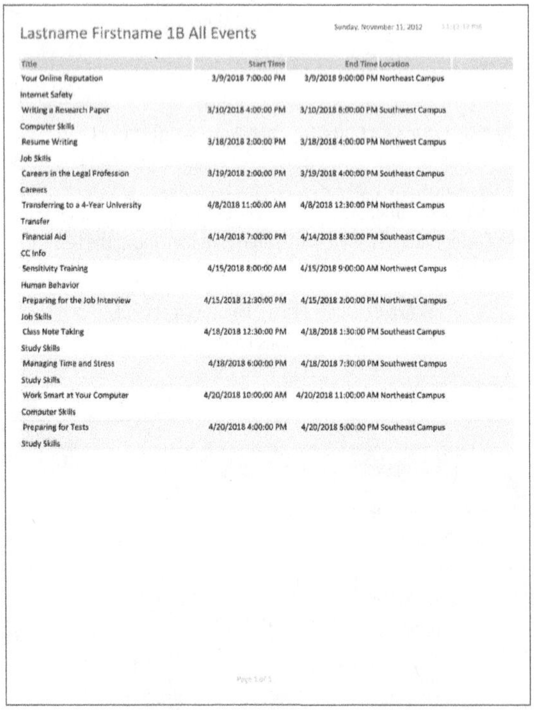

Lastname Firstname 1B All Events

Sunday, November 11, 2012

Title	Start Time	End Time	Location
Your Online Reputation	3/9/2018 7:00:00 PM	3/9/2018 9:00:00 PM	Northeast Campus
Internet Safety			
Writing a Research Paper	3/10/2018 4:00:00 PM	3/10/2018 6:00:00 PM	Southwest Campus
Computer Skills			
Resume Writing	3/18/2018 2:00:00 PM	3/18/2018 4:00:00 PM	Northwest Campus
Job Skills			
Careers in the Legal Profession	3/19/2018 2:00:00 PM	3/19/2018 4:00:00 PM	Southeast Campus
Careers			
Transferring to a 4-Year University	4/8/2018 11:00:00 AM	4/8/2018 12:30:00 PM	Northeast Campus
Transfer			
Financial Aid	4/14/2018 7:00:00 PM	4/14/2018 8:30:00 PM	Southeast Campus
CC Info			
Sensitivity Training	4/15/2018 8:00:00 AM	4/15/2018 9:00:00 AM	Northwest Campus
Human Behavior			
Preparing for the Job Interview	4/15/2018 12:30:00 PM	4/15/2018 2:00:00 PM	Northwest Campus
Job Skills			
Class Note Taking	4/18/2018 12:30:00 PM	4/18/2018 1:30:00 PM	Southeast Campus
Study Skills			
Managing Time and Stress	4/18/2018 6:00:00 PM	4/18/2018 7:30:00 PM	Southwest Campus
Study Skills			
Work Smart at Your Computer	4/20/2018 10:00:00 AM	4/20/2018 11:00:00 AM	Northeast Campus
Computer Skills			
Preparing for Tests	4/20/2018 4:00:00 PM	4/20/2018 5:00:00 PM	Southeast Campus
Study Skills			

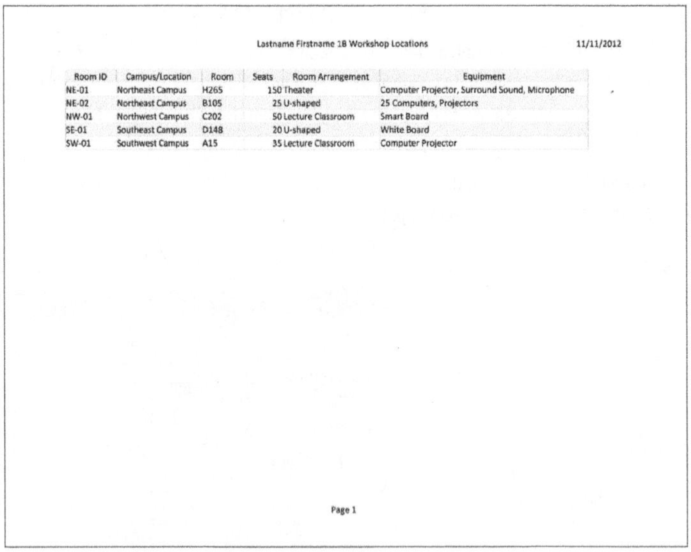

Lastname Firstname 1B Workshop Locations 11/11/2012

Room ID	Campus/Location	Room	Seats	Room Arrangement	Equipment
NE-01	Northeast Campus	H265	150	Theater	Computer Projector, Surround Sound, Microphone
NE-02	Northeast Campus	B105	25	U-shaped	25 Computers, Projectors
NW-01	Northwest Campus	C202	50	Lecture Classroom	Smart Board
SE-01	Southeast Campus	D148	20	U-shaped	White Board
SW-01	Southwest Campus	A15	35	Lecture Classroom	Computer Projector

Page 1

FIGURE 1.39 Project 1B Student Workshops

Objective 6 Use a Template to Create a Database

Video A1-6

A ***database template*** contains prebuilt tables, queries, forms, and reports that perform a specific task, such as tracking a large number of events. For example, your college may hold events such as athletic contests, plays, lectures, concerts, and club meetings. Using a predefined template, your college's activities director can quickly create a database to manage these events. The advantage of using a template to start a new database is that you do not have to create the objects—all you need to do is enter the data and modify the prebuilt objects to suit your needs.

The purpose of the database in this project is to track the student workshops that are held by Texas Lakes Community College. The questions to be answered might include:

- What workshops will be offered, and when will they be offered?
- In what rooms and on what campuses will the workshops be held?
- Which workshop locations have a computer projector for PowerPoint presentations?

Activity 1.18 | Using a Template to Create a Database

There are two types of database templates—those that will be stored on your desktop and those that are designed to share with others over the Internet. In this activity, you will use a desktop template to create your database.

1 Start Access. In the Access opening screen, scroll down until the last templates display. Notice that there is a **Task management** template and a **Desktop task management** template. Compare your screen with Figure 1.40.

These templates are included with the Access program. To store a database to manage tasks on your desktop, select the *Desktop task management* template. To publish a database to manage tasks and share it with others, select the *Task management* template—the one that displays a globe image. The names of templates designed to create databases stored on your computer start with the word *Desktop*.

You can search the Microsoft Office website for more templates. You can also click on a category under the search box, where templates will be suggested.

FIGURE 1.40

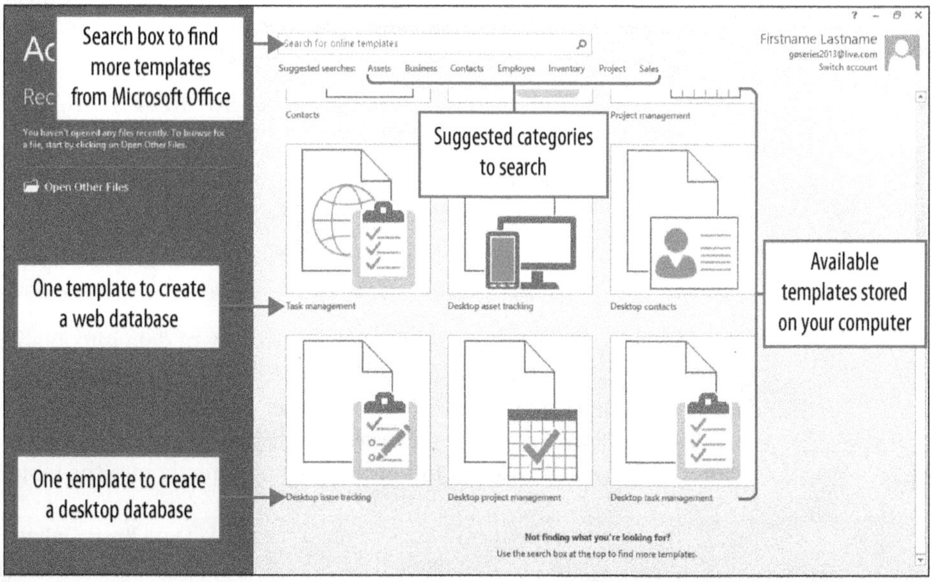

2 At the top of the window, click in the **Search for online templates** box, type **event** and then press Enter. Compare your screen with Figure 1.41.

You must have an Internet connection to search for online templates. Access displays several templates, including the Desktop Event Management template.

FIGURE 1.41

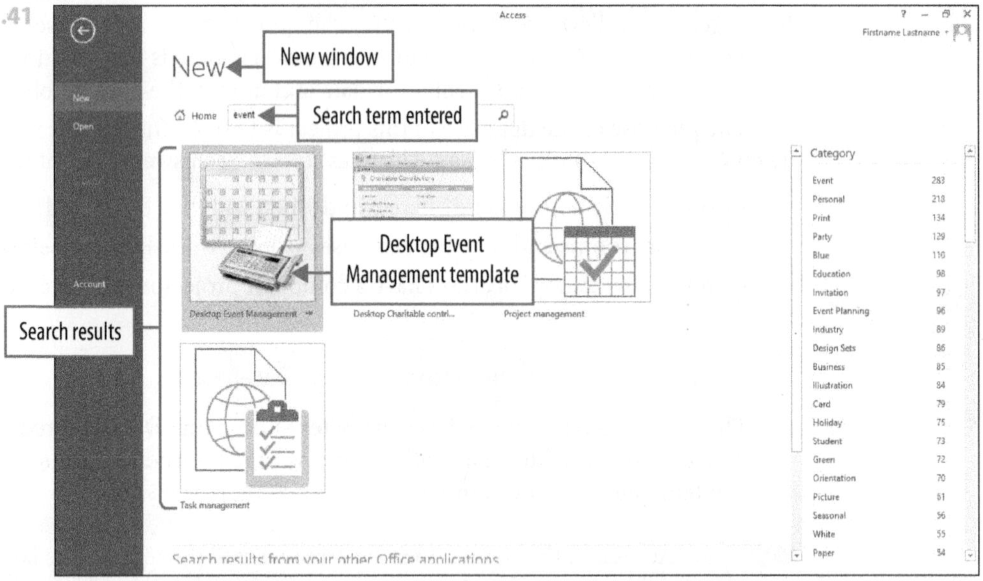

3 Click the **Desktop Event Management** template. In the dialog box, to the right of the **File Name** box, click **Browse**, and then navigate to your **Access Chapter 1** folder.

4 In the **File New Database** dialog box, click in the **File name** box to select the existing text. Using your own name, type **Lastname_Firstname_1B_Student_Workshops** and then press Enter.

5 In the **Desktop Event Management** dialog box, click **Create** to download the template and to save the database.

Access creates the *1B_Student_Workshops* database, and the database name displays in the title bar. A predesigned *form*—Event List—automatically displays in the object window. Although you can enter events for any date, when you open the database in the future, the Event List form will display only those events for the current date and future dates.

6 Under the ribbon, on the **Message Bar**, a *SECURITY WARNING* displays. On the **Message Bar**, click **Enable Content.**

Databases provided by Microsoft are safe to use on your computer.

Activity 1.19 | Building a Table by Entering Records in a Multiple-Items Form and a Single-Record Form

One purpose of a form is to simplify the entry of data into a table—either for you or for others who enter data. In Project 1A, you created a simple form that enabled you to display or enter records in a table, one record at a time. The Desktop Event Management template contains a ***multiple-items form*** that enables you to display or enter *multiple* records in a table, but with an easier and simplified layout rather than typing directly into the table itself.

1 In the new record row, click in the **Title** field. Type **Your Online Reputation** and then press Tab. In the **Start Time** field, type **3/9/18 7p** and then press Tab.

Access formats the date and time. As you enter dates and times, a small calendar displays to the right of the field. You can use the calendar to select a date instead of typing it.

2 In the **End Time** field, type **3/9/18 9p** and then press Tab. In the **Description** field, type **Internet Safety** and then press Tab. In the **Location** field, type **Northeast Campus** and then press Tab three times to move to the **Title** field in the new record row. Compare your screen with Figure 1.42.

Because the workshops have no unique value, Access uses the AutoNumber data type in the ID field to assign a unique, sequential number to each record.

FIGURE 1.42

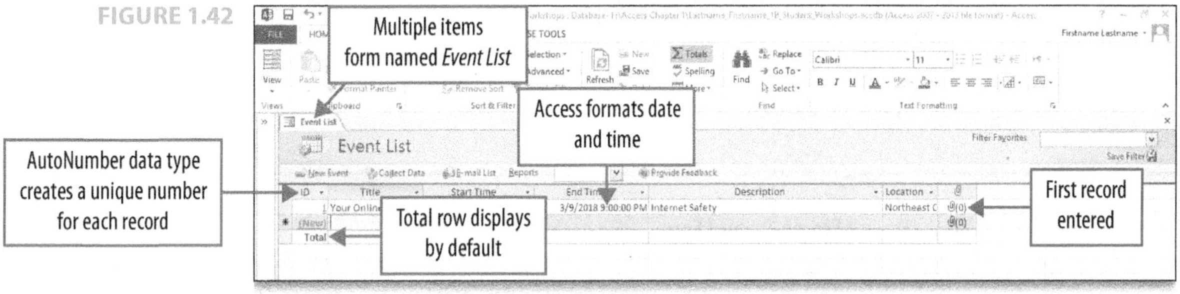

3 In the form, directly above the field names row, click **New Event**.

A ***single-record form*** with the name *Event Details* displays, similar to the simple form you created in Project 1A. A single-record form enables you to display or enter one record at a time into a table.

4 Using Tab to move from field to field, enter the following record in the **Event Details** form—press Tab three times to move from the **End Time** field to the **Description** field. Then compare your screen with Figure 1.43.

Title	Location	Start Time	End Time	Description
Writing a Research Paper	**Southwest Campus**	**3/10/18 4p**	**3/10/18 6p**	**Computer Skills**

FIGURE 1.43

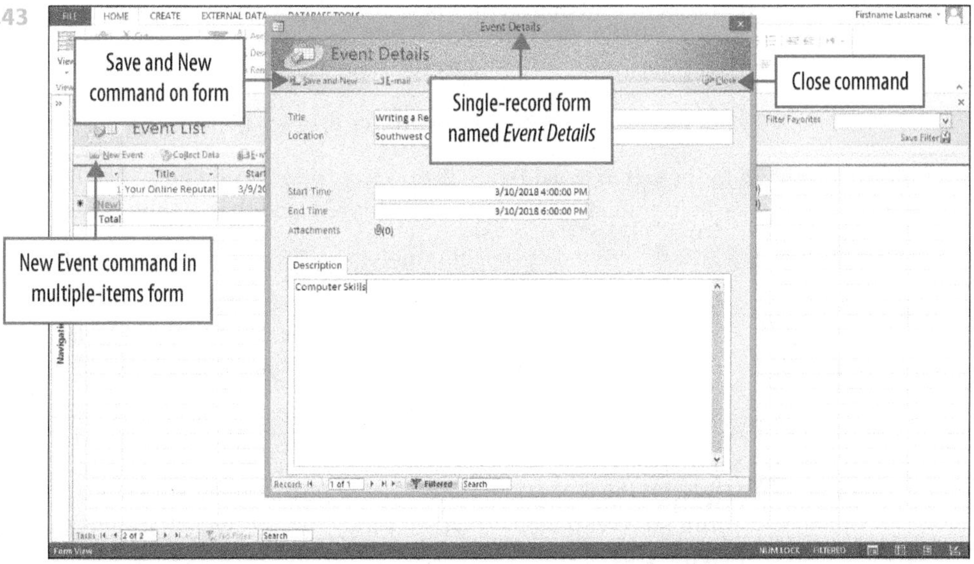

5 In the **Event Details** single-record form, in the upper right corner, click **Close**, and notice that the new record displays in the multiple-items form—*Event List*.

6 Enter the following records by using either the **Event List** form—the multiple-items form—or the **Event Details** form—the single-record form that is accessed by clicking the *New Event* command on the **Event List** form. The data in the table given is arranged in the same order as the **Event List** form. Be sure the multiple-items form displays, and then compare your screen with Figure 1.44.

ID	Title	Start Time	End Time	Description	Location
3	**Resume Writing**	**3/18/18 2p**	**3/18/18 4p**	**Job Skills**	**Northwest Campus**
4	**Careers in the Legal Profession**	**3/19/18 2p**	**3/19/18 4p**	**Careers**	**Southeast Campus**

ALERT! **Does a Single-Record Form—*Event Details*–Open?**

In the multiple-items form, pressing Enter three times at the end of the row to begin a new record will display the single-record form—*Event Details*. If you prefer to use the multiple-items form—Event List—close the single-record form and continue entering records, using the Tab key to move from field to field.

FIGURE 1.44

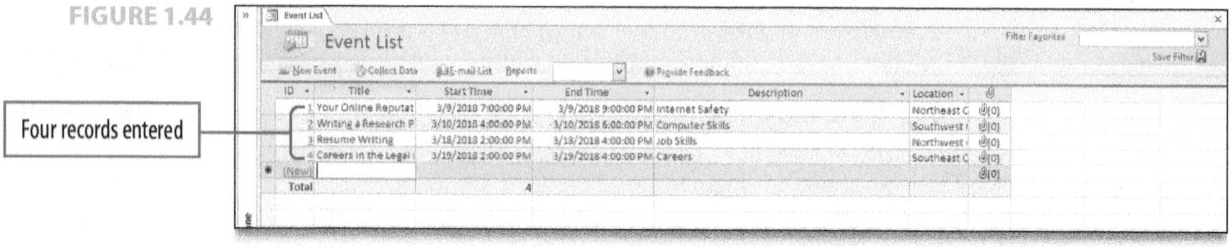

7 In the object window, click **Close** ☒ to close the **Event List** form.

Activity 1.20 | Appending Records by Importing from an Excel Spreadsheet

In this activity, you will append records to the table that stores the data that displays in the Events List form. You will import the records from an Excel spreadsheet.

1 On the ribbon, click the **EXTERNAL DATA tab**. In the **Import & Link group**, click **Excel**.

2 In the **Get External Data - Excel Spreadsheet** dialog box, click **Browse**. Navigate to the location where your student data files are stored, and then double-click **a01B_Workshops**.

3 Click the second option button—**Append a copy of the records to the table**—and then click **OK**.

The table that stores the data is named *Events*. Recall that other objects, such as forms, queries, and reports, display data from tables; so the Event Details form displays data that is stored in the Events table.

4 In the **Import Spreadsheet Wizard**, click **Next**, and then click **Finish**. In the **Get External Data - Excel Spreadsheet** dialog box, click **Close**.

5 **Open** » the **Navigation Pane**. Double-click **Event List** to open the form that displays data from the **Events** table, and then **Close** « the **Navigation Pane**. Compare your screen with Figure 1.45.

A total of 12 records display; you entered four records, and you appended eight records from the a01B_Workshops Excel workbook. The data is truncated in several fields because the columns are not wide enough to display all of the data.

FIGURE 1.45

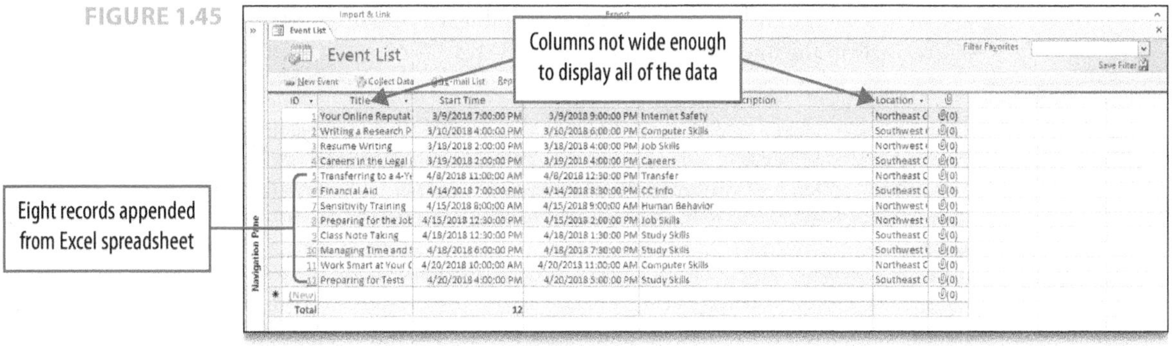

6 To the left of the **ID** field name, click **Select All** ☐ to select all of the columns and rows.

7 In the field names row, point to the right edge of any of the selected columns to display the ✛ pointer, and then double-click to apply **Best Fit** to all of the columns. **Save** 🖫 the form, and then click in any field to cancel the selection.

Objective 7 Organize Objects in the Navigation Pane

Video A1-7

Use the Navigation Pane to open objects, organize database objects, and perform common tasks, such as renaming an object or deleting an object.

Activity 1.21 | Grouping Database Objects in the Navigation Pane

The Navigation Pane groups and displays your database objects and can do so in predefined arrangements. In this activity, you will group your database objects using the ***Tables and Related Views*** category, which groups objects by the table to which the objects are related. This grouping is useful because you can determine easily the table that is the data source of queries, forms, and reports.

1 **Open** » the **Navigation Pane**. At the top right side of the **Navigation Pane**, click ⊙. On the list, under **Navigate To Category**, click **Tables and Related Views**. Compare your screen with Figure 1.46.

In the Navigation Pane, you can see the number of objects that are included in the Desktop Event Management template, including the table named *Events*. Other objects in the database that display data from the Events table include one query, two forms, and five reports. In the Navigation Pane, the Event List form is selected because it is open in the object window and is the active object. Other objects might display on the Navigation Pane; for example, Filters and Unrelated Objects. These filters are objects created for use by the Desktop Event Management template.

FIGURE 1.46

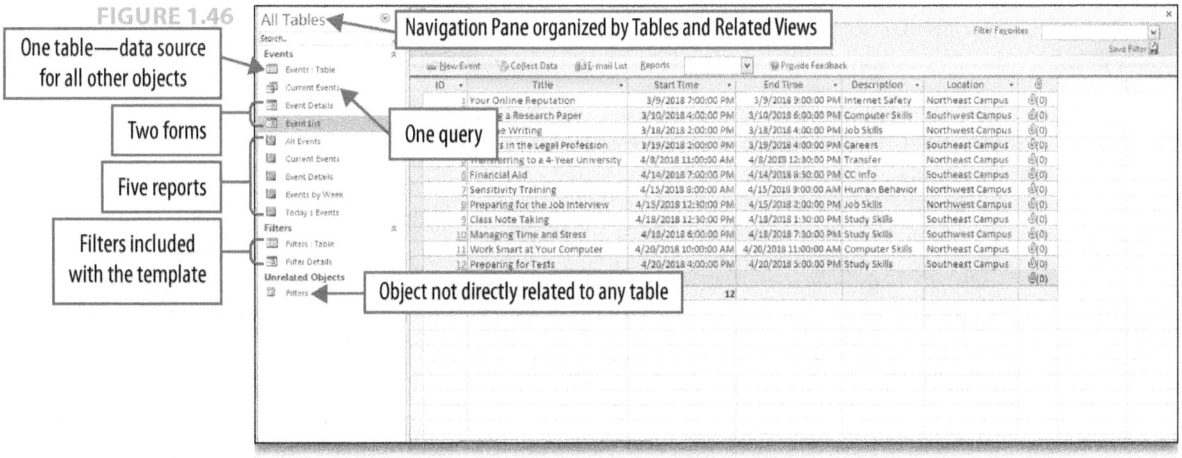

2 In the **Navigation Pane**, point to **Events: Table**, right-click, and then click **Open** to display the records in the underlying table.

The Events table is the active object in the object window. Use the Navigation Pane to open objects for use. The 12 records that display in the Event List multiple-items form are stored in this table. Recall that tables are the foundation of your database because your data must be stored in a table. You can enter records directly into a table or you can use a form to enter records.

ANOTHER WAY Double-click the table name to open it in the object window.

3 In the object window, click the **Event List tab** to display the form as the active object in the object window.

Recall that a form presents a more user-friendly screen for entering records into a table.

4 In the **Navigation Pane**, double-click the **Current Events** *report* (green icon) to open the report. Compare your screen with Figure 1.47.

An advantage of using a template to create a database is that many objects, such as reports, are already designed for you.

FIGURE 1.47

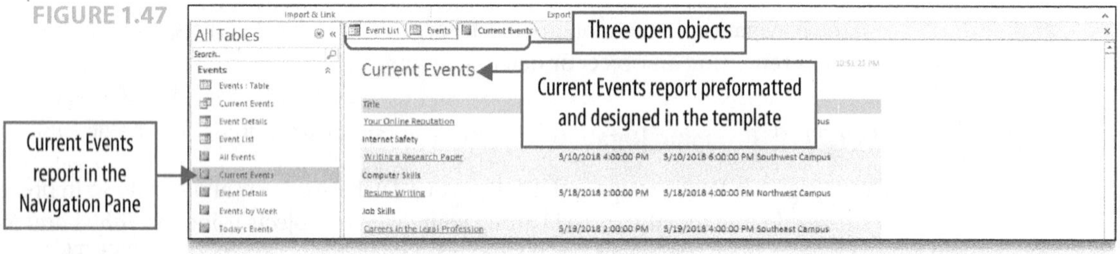

5 In the object window, **Close** [×] the **Current Events** report.

6 By double-clicking or right-clicking, from the **Navigation Pane**, open the **Events by Week** report.

In this predesigned report, the events are displayed by week. After entering records in the form or table, the preformatted reports are updated with the records from the table.

7 In the object window, right-click any one of the **object tabs**, and then click **Close All** to close all of the objects. **Close** [«] the **Navigation Pane**.

Objective 8 Create a New Table in a Database Created with a Template

Video A1-8

The Desktop Event Management template included only one table—the *Events* table. It is easy to start a database with a template, and then you can add additional objects as needed.

Activity 1.22 | Using the Table Tool to Create a New Table

Dr. Yong has information about the various locations where workshops are held. For example, on the Northeast Campus, she has information about the room, seating arrangements, number of seats, and multimedia equipment. In the Events table, workshops are scheduled in rooms at each of the four campuses. It would not make sense to store information about the campus rooms multiple times in the same table. It is *not* considered good database design to have duplicate information in a table.

When data becomes redundant, it is usually an indication that you need a new table to store that information. In this activity, you will create a table to track the workshop locations, the equipment, and the seating arrangements in each location.

1. On the ribbon, click the **CREATE tab**, and then in the **Tables group**, click **Table**.

2. In the field names row, click **Click to Add**, click **Short Text**, type **Campus/Location** and then press Enter.

3. In the third column, click **Short Text**, type **Room** and then press Enter. In the fourth column, click **Number**, type **Seats** and then press Enter.

   The ***Number data type*** describes numbers that may be used in calculations. For the Seats field, you may need to determine the number of seats remaining after reservations are booked for a room. In the new record row, a *0* displays in the field.

4. In the fifth column, type **t** to select *Short Text*, type **Room Arrangement** and then press Enter. In the sixth column, type **t** and then type **Equipment** On your keyboard, press ↓.

   With the data type list displayed, you can select the data type by either clicking it or typing the letter that is underscored for the data type.

   This table has six fields. Access automatically creates the first field in the table—the ID field—to ensure that every record has a unique value. Before naming each field, you must define the data type for the field.

5. Right-click the **ID** field name, and then click **Rename Field**. Type **Room ID** and then press Enter. On the ribbon, under **TABLE TOOLS**, on the **FIELDS tab**, in the **Formatting group**, click the **Data Type arrow**, and then click **Short Text**. On the ribbon, in the **Field Validation group**, notice that **Unique** is selected.

   Recall that, by default, Access creates the ID field with the AutoNumber data type so that the field can be used as the primary key. Here, this field will store a unique room ID that is a combination of letters, symbols, and numbers; therefore, it is appropriate to change the data type to Short Text. In Datasheet view, the primary key field is identified by the selection of the Unique check box.

Activity 1.23 | Entering Records into a New Table

1. If necessary, in the new record row, click in the **Room ID** field. Enter the following record, pressing Enter or Tab to move from one field to the next. Do not be concerned that all of your text does not display; you will adjust the column widths later. After entering the record, compare your screen with Figure 1.48.

   Recall that Access saves a record when you move to another row within the table. You can press either Enter or Tab to move between fields in a table.

Room ID	Campus/ Location	Room	Seats	Room Arrangement	Equipment
NE-01	**Northeast Campus**	**H265**	**150**	**Theater**	**Computer Projector, Surround Sound, Microphone**

FIGURE 1.48

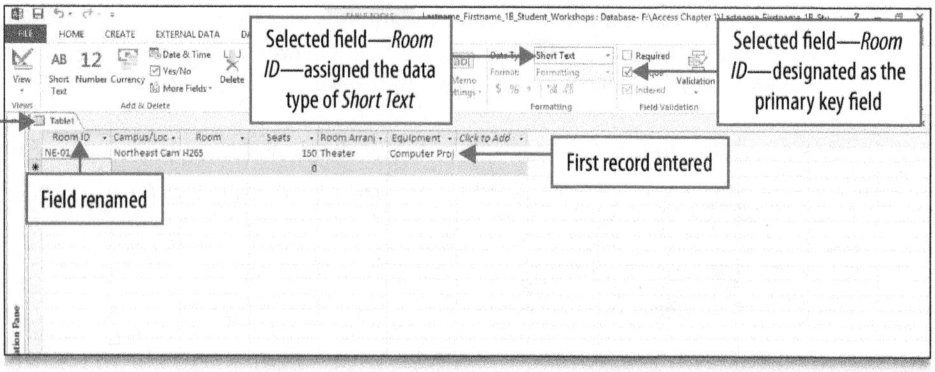

2 In the **Views group**, click the top of the **View** button to switch to **Design** view. In the **Save As** dialog box, in the **Table Name** box, using your own name, type **Lastname Firstname 1B Workshop Locations** and then click **OK**.

Recall that when you switch views or when you close a table, Access prompts you to save the table if you have not previously saved it.

ANOTHER WAY On the right side of the status bar, click Design View to switch to Design view.

3 In the **Field Name** column, to the left of **Room ID**, notice the key icon.

In Design view, the key icon indicates that the field—Room ID—is the primary key field.

4 In the **Views group**, click the top of the **View** button to switch back to **Datasheet** view.

ANOTHER WAY On the right side of the status bar, click Datasheet View to switch to Datasheet view.

5 In the new record row, click in the **Room ID** field. Enter the following records, pressing Enter or Tab to move from one field to the next.

Room ID	Campus/Location	Room	Seats	Room Arrangement	Equipment
SW-01	**Southwest Campus**	**A15**	**35**	**Lecture Classroom**	**Computer Projector**
NW-01	**Northwest Campus**	**C202**	**50**	**Lecture Classroom**	**Smart Board**
SE-01	**Southeast Campus**	**D148**	**20**	**U-shaped**	**White Board**
NE-02	**Northeast Campus**	**B105**	**25**	**U-shaped**	**25 Computers, Projector**

6 To the left of the **Room ID** field name, click **Select All** to select all of the columns and rows in the table. On the **HOME tab**, in the **Records group**, click **More**, and then click **Field Width**. In the **Column Width** dialog box, click **Best Fit** to display all of the data in each column. **Save** the changes to the table, and then click in any field to cancel the selection. In the object window, **Close** your **1B Workshop Locations** table.

7 **Open** the **Navigation Pane**, and notice that your new table name displays in its own group. Point to the right edge of the **Navigation Pane** to display the pointer. Drag to the right to increase the width of the **Navigation Pane** so that your entire table name displays. Compare your screen with Figure 1.49.

Recall that by organizing the Navigation Pane by Tables and Related Views, the Navigation Pane groups the objects by each table and displays the related objects under each table name.

FIGURE 1.49

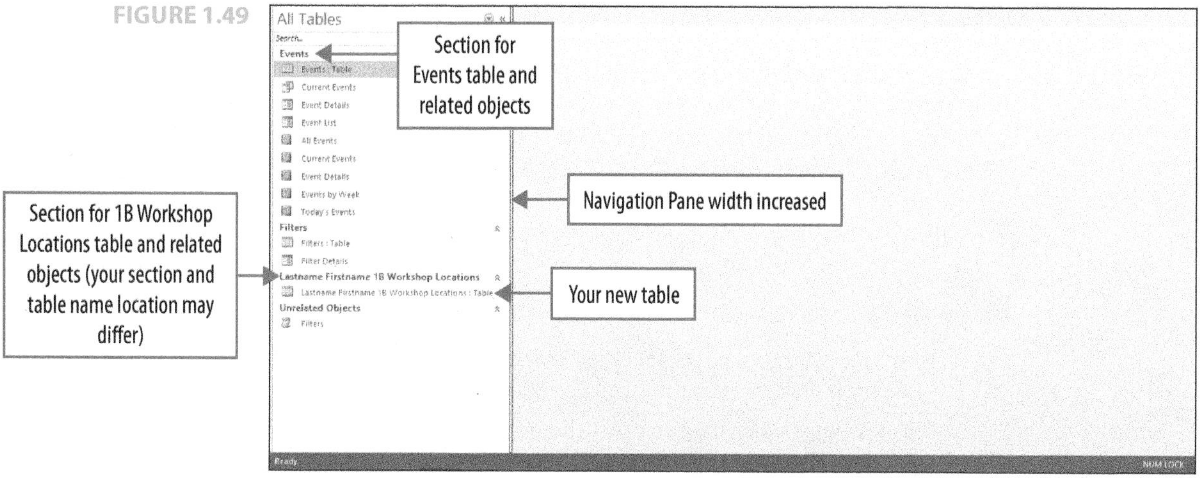

Objective 9 Print a Report and a Table

Video A1-9

Recall that one advantage to starting a new database with a template, instead of from a blank database, is that many report objects are already created for you.

Activity 1.24 | Viewing Reports and Printing a Report

1 In the **Navigation Pane**, double-click the report (not the form) named **Event Details** to open it in the object window.

This prebuilt Event Details report displays in an attractively arranged format.

2 **Close** the **Event Details** report. Open the **All Events** report, and then **Close** the **Navigation Pane**. On the **HOME** tab, in the **Views group**, click the top of the **View** button to switch to **Layout** view.

Recall that Layout view enables you to make changes to an object while viewing the data in the fields. Each prebuilt report displays the records in the table in different useful formats.

ANOTHER WAY On the right side of the status bar, click Layout View to switch to Layout view.

3 At the top of the report, click the title—*All Events*—to display a colored border around the title. Click to the left of the letter *A* to place the insertion point there. Using your own name, type **Lastname Firstname 1B** and then press Spacebar. Press Enter, and then **Save** the report.

Including your name in the title will help you and your instructor identify any submitted work.

4 On the right side of the status bar, click **Print Preview**. In the navigation area, notice that the navigation arrows are unavailable, an indication that this report will print on one page.

ANOTHER WAY On the HOME tab, in the Views group, click the View arrow, and then click Print Preview. Or, on the FILE tab, click Print, and then click Print Preview. Or, right-click the object tab, and then click Print Preview.

5 Create a paper or electronic printout as instructed. Click **Close Print Preview**, and then **Close** the report.

Activity 1.25 | Printing a Table

When printing a table, use the Print Preview command to determine whether the table will print on one page or if you need to adjust column widths, margins, or page orientation. Recall that there will be occasions when you print a table for a quick reference or for proofreading. For a more professional-looking format, create and print a report.

1 **Open** [»] the **Navigation Pane**, double-click your **1B Workshop Locations** table to open it in the object window, and then **Close** [«] the **Navigation Pane.**

2 On the ribbon, click the **FILE tab**, click **Print**, and then click **Print Preview**.

The table displays showing how it will look when printed. Generally, tables are not printed, so there is no Print Preview option on the View button or on the status bar.

The navigation area displays *1* in the Pages box, and the navigation arrows to the right of the box are active, an indication that the table will print on more than one page.

3 In the navigation area, click **Next Page** [▶].

The second page of the table displays the last field. Whenever possible, try to print all of the fields horizontally on one page. Of course, if there are many records, more than one page may be needed to print all of the records and all of the fields.

4 On the **PRINT PREVIEW tab**, in the **Page Layout group**, click **Landscape**, and then compare your screen with Figure 1.50. In landscape orientation, notice that the entire table will print on one page—all of the navigation buttons are unavailable.

FIGURE 1.50

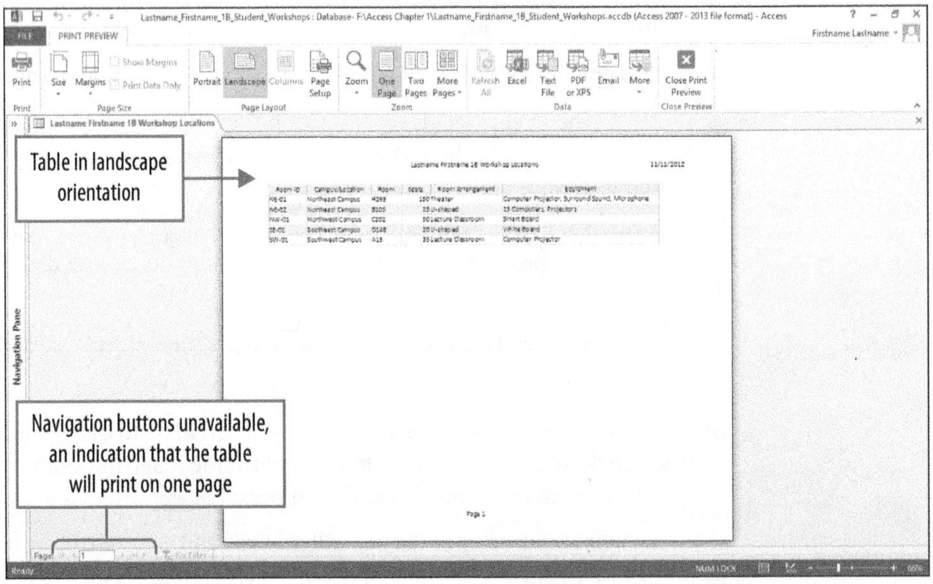

5 Create a paper or electronic printout as instructed, and then click **Close Print Preview**.

6 **Close** [×] your **1B Workshop Locations** table. For the convenience of the next individual opening the database, **Open** [»] the **Navigation Pane**.

7 On the right side of the title bar, click **Close** [×] to close the database and to exit Access. As directed by your instructor, submit your database and the paper or electronic printouts of the two objects—one report and one table—that are the results of this project. Specifically, in this project, using your own name, you created the following database and printouts or electronic printouts:

1. Lastname_Firstname_1B_Student_Workshops	Database file
2. All Events	Report (printout or electronic printout)
3. Lastname Firstname 1B Workshop Locations	Table (printout or electronic printout)

END | You have completed Project 1B

GO! with Office Online (formerly Web Apps)

Objective Export an Access Table to an Excel Spreadsheet, Save to Google Drive, Add a Record, and Save to Your Computer

Access web apps are designed to work with Microsoft's SharePoint, a service for setting up websites to share and manage documents. Your college may not have SharePoint installed, so you will use other tools to share objects from your database so that you can work collaboratively with others. Recall that Google Docs is Google's free, web-based word processor, spreadsheet, slide show, form, and data storage service. Google Drive is Google's free file storage and sharing service. For Access, you can export a database object to an Excel worksheet, a PDF file, or a text file, and then save the file to Google Drive.

ALERT! Working with Web-Based Applications and Services

Computer programs and services on the web receive continuous updates and improvements. Therefore, the steps to complete this web-based activity may differ from the ones shown. You can often look at the screens and the information presented to determine how to complete the activity.

Activity | Exporting an Access Table to an Excel Spreadsheet, Saving the Spreadsheet to Google Drive, Editing a Record in Google Drive, and Saving to Your Computer

In this activity, you will export your 1B Workshop Locations table to an Excel spreadsheet, upload your Excel file to Google Drive as a Google Doc, add a record in Google Drive, and then download a copy of the edited spreadsheet to your computer.

1 Start Access, navigate to your **Access Chapter 1** folder, and then **Open** your **1B_Student_Workshops** database file. If necessary, on the Message Bar, click Enable Content, and then **Close** the **Event List** form. In the **Navigation Pane**, click your **1B Workshop Locations** table to select it—do not open it.

2 On the ribbon, click the **EXTERNAL DATA tab**, and then in the **Export group**, click **Excel**. In the **Export – Excel Spreadsheet** dialog box, click **Browse**, and then navigate to your **Access Chapter 1** folder. In the **File Save** dialog box, click in the **File name** box, type **Lastname_Firstname_AC_1B_Web** and then click **Save**.

3 In the **Export – Excel Spreadsheet** dialog box, under **Specify export options**, select the first two check boxes—**Export data with formatting and layout** and **Open the destination file after the export operation is complete**—and then click **OK**. Take a moment to examine the data in the file, and then **Close** Excel. In the **Export – Excel Spreadsheet** dialog box, click **Close**, and then **Close** Access.

4 From the desktop, start Internet Explorer, navigate to **http://drive.google.com**, and sign in to your Google account; if necessary, create a new Google account and then sign in. On the right side of the screen, click the **Settings arrow**, and then point to **Upload settings**. Be sure that **Convert uploaded files to Google Docs format** is selected.

If this setting is not selected, your document will upload as a pdf file and cannot be edited without further action.

5 Open your **GO! Web Projects** folder—or create and then open this folder by clicking **New folder**. Under **Drive**, to the right of **Create**, click **Upload**, and then click **Files**. In the **Choose File to Upload** dialog box, navigate to your **Access Chapter 1** folder, and then double-click your **AC_1B_Web** Excel file to upload it to Google Drive. When the title bar of the message box indicates *Upload complete*, **Close** the message box. Compare your screen with Figure A.

FIGURE A

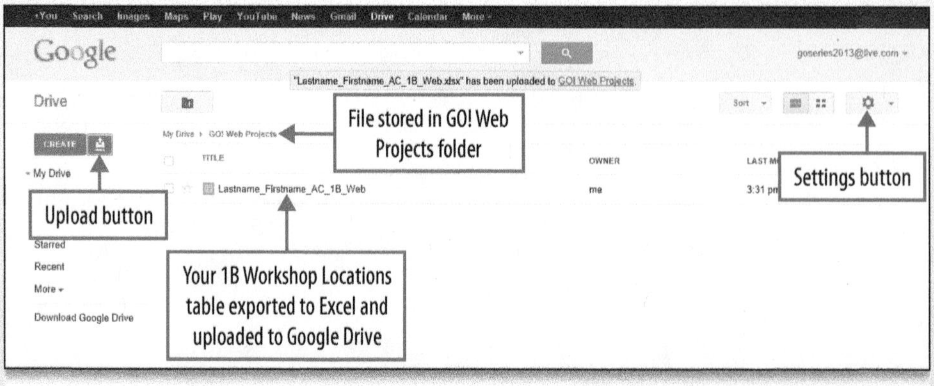

(GO! with Office Online (formerly Web Apps) continues on the next page)

6 Click your **AC_1B_Web** file to open the file in Google Drive. If necessary, maximize the window.

The worksheet displays column letters, row numbers, and data.

7 Click in cell **A7**, type **SW-02** and then press Tab. In cell **B7**, type **Southwest Campus** and then press Tab. In cell **C7**, type **B101** and then press Tab. In cell **D7**, type **25** and then press ↓ to save the record.

The new record might display with a different font than the other records.

8 Above row **1** and to the left of column **A**, click **Select All** ☐. On the menu bar, click **Format**, and then click **Clear formatting** so that the font is the same for all data. Click in cell **A8**, and then compare your screen with Figure B.

9 On the menu, click **File**, point to **Download as**, and then click **Microsoft Excel (.xlsx)**. In the message box—usually displays at the bottom of your screen—click the **Save arrow**, and then click **Save as**. In the **Save As** dialog box, navigate to your **Access Chapter 1** folder, click in the **File name** box, type **Lastname_Firstname_AC_1B_Web_Download** and then click **Save**. **Close** the message box.

10 In Google Drive, at the top right corner of your screen, click your user name, and then click **Sign out**. **Close** your browser window.

11 Start Excel. In the Excel opening screen, click **Open Other Workbooks**. Under **Open**, click **Computer**. On the right, under **Computer**, click **Browse**. Navigate to your **Access Chapter 1** folder, and then double-click your **AC_1B_Web** Excel file. Notice that this file is the original file—the new record is not entered. If you are required to print your documents, use one of the methods in following Note. **Close** your Excel file; and, if prompted, save the changes to your worksheet. Then **Open** and print your **AC_1B_Web_Download** Excel file using one of the methods in the following Note. **Close** Excel; and, if prompted, save the changes to your worksheet. As directed by your instructor, submit your two workbooks and the two paper or electronic printouts that are the results of this project.

NOTE

Adding the File Name to the Footer and Printing or Creating an Electronic Printout of an Excel Spreadsheet on One Page

Click the FILE tab, click Print, and then click Page Setup. In the Page Setup dialog box, on the Page tab, under Orientation, click Landscape. Under Scaling, click the Fit to option button. In the Page Setup dialog box, click the Header/Footer tab, and then click Custom Footer. With the insertion point blinking in the Left section box, click the Insert File Name button, and then click OK. In the Page Setup dialog box, click OK.

To print on paper, click Print. To create an electronic file of your printout, on the left side of your screen, click Export. Under Export, be sure Create PDF/XPS Document is selected, and then, on the right, click Create PDF/XPS. Navigate to your Access Chapter 1 folder, and then click Publish to save the file with the default name and an extension of pdf.

FIGURE B

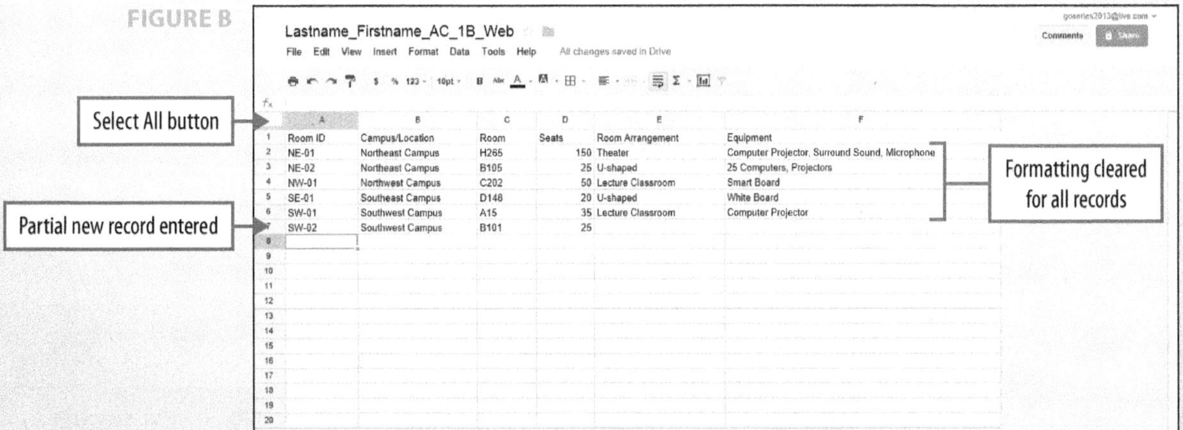

GO! with Microsoft Office 365

Andrew Rodriguez/Fotolia; FotolEdhar/Fotolia; apops/Fotolia; Yuri Arcurs/Fotolia

Office 365 includes business-class security and is backed by Microsoft. For an organization, what does that mean?

When you and a few classmates work together on a class project, you are not concerned about the security of your data. You probably use free personal email services such as Hotmail, Gmail, or Yahoo Mail to exchange documents, or perhaps you post your documents to free services such as Google Docs.

Organizations, on the other hand—even small ones with only two or three employees—must be concerned with the privacy and security of their data. Organizations cannot entrust their data and confidential communications to free services that may change frequently or that have no legal responsibility for the security of the data.

Organizations must provide each employee with a company email address rather than having each employee use his or her own personal free email address for business communications. Organizations must provide a central storage location for its data rather than having employees store data on flash drives or local hard drives with no control or oversight.

An organization must have a ***secure environment***, which is a system that uses controlled ***servers***—computers that provide services on a network such as an email server or a file server—to ensure the security and privacy of email, to control the storage and use of information, and to protect against the loss of confidential data.

Most small organizations cannot afford to hire the people with the skills necessary to install and maintain servers. So to establish and maintain a secure environment, many small organizations contract with and rely on small IT—the acronym for *Information Technology*—hosting companies to host their email communications and to provide secure storage.

Activity | Using the Exchange Online Outlook Meeting Tool to Collaborate

This group project relates to the **Bell Orchid Hotels**. If your instructor assigns this project to your class, you can expect to use the **Outlook Meeting tool** in **Office 365 Exchange Online** to collaborate on the following tasks for this chapter:

- If you are in the **Accounting Group**, you and your teammates will meet virtually to create a Stockholders Database to track individuals who have purchased stock in the hotel.
- If you are in the **Engineering Group**, you and your teammates will meet virtually to create a Subcontractors Database to track companies used by the Hotel for maintenance and renovation projects.
- If you are in the **Food and Beverage Group**, you and your teammates will meet virtually to create a Banquet Clients Database to track the types of functions taking place in the Hotel's banquet rooms.
- If you are in the **Human Resources Group**, you and your teammates will meet virtually to create an Employee Database for salaried employees.
- If you are in the **Operations Group**, you and your teammates will meet virtually to create a Guests Database to track guest information, as well as room rates and availability.
- If you are in the **Sales and Marketing Group**, you and your teammates will meet virtually to create an Associations Database to track industry and trade associations that book conventions for large groups.

FIGURE A

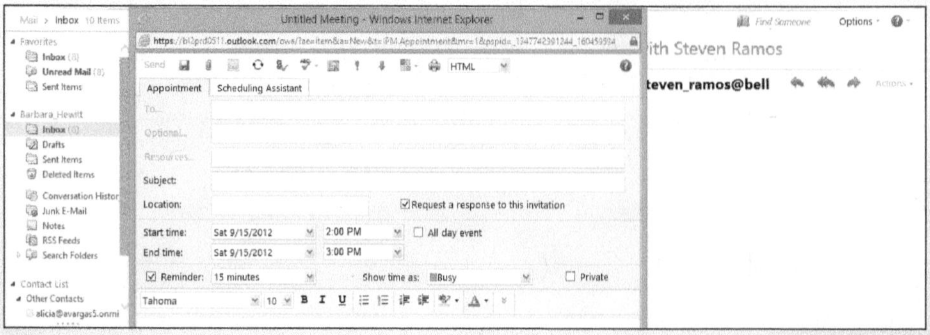

END OF CHAPTER

SUMMARY

Principles of good database design, also known as normalization, help ensure that the data in your database is accurate and organized in a way that you can retrieve information that is useful.

Databases can be created from scratch by using the blank desktop database template or a custom web app or by using a template that contains prebuilt tables, queries, forms, reports, and other objects.

Before entering records in a table, which is the foundation of a database, you must define data types and name the fields. Common data types are Short Text, Number, Currency, and Date/Time.

Forms are used to enter data into a table or view the data in a table. Queries are used to retrieve information from tables, and reports display information from tables in a professional-looking format.

GO! LEARN IT ONLINE

Review the concepts and key terms in this chapter by completing these online challenges, which you can find at **www.pearsonhighered.com/go.**

Matching and Multiple Choice: Answer matching and multiple choice questions to test what you learned in this chapter. MyITLab®

Crossword Puzzle: Spell out the words that match the numbered clues, and put them in the puzzle squares.

Flipboard: Flip through the definitions of the key terms in this chapter and match them with the correct term.

GO! FOR JOB SUCCESS

Video: Goal Setting

Your instructor may assign this video to your class, and then ask you to think about, or discuss with your classmates, these questions:

FotolEdhar/Fotolia

Is there anything you would change about Theo's behavior at his performance evaluation? Why or why not?

SMART goals are goals that are specific, measurable, achievable, realistic, and time-frame specific. Is Theo's first goal of beating his sales numbers by 10 percent next year a SMART goal?

How important do you think it is to set career development goals for yourself? Why?

END OF CHAPTER

REVIEW AND ASSESSMENT GUIDE FOR ACCESS CHAPTER 1

Your instructor may assign one or more of these projects to help you review the chapter and assess your mastery and understanding of the chapter.

Review and Assessment Guide for Access Chapter 1

Project	Apply Skills from These Chapter Objectives	Project Type	Project Location
1C	Objectives 1-5 from Project 1A	**1C Skills Review** A guided review of the skills from Project 1A.	On the following pages
1D	Objectives 6-9 from Project 1B	**1D Skills Review** A guided review of the skills from Project 1B.	On the following pages
1E	Objectives 1-5 from Project 1A	**1E Mastery (Grader Project)** A demonstration of your mastery of the skills in Project 1A with extensive decision making.	In MyITLab and on the following pages
1F	Objectives 6-9 from Project 1B	**1F Mastery (Grader Project)** A demonstration of your mastery of the skills in Project 1B with extensive decision making.	In MyITLab and on the following pages
1G	Objectives 1-9 from Projects 1A and 1B	**1G Mastery (Grader Project)** A demonstration of your mastery of the skills in Projects 1A and 1B with extensive decision making.	In MyITLab and on the following pages
1H	Combination of Objectives from Projects 1A and 1B	**1H GO! Fix It** A demonstration of your mastery of the skills in Projects 1A and 1B by creating a correct result from a document that contains errors you must find.	Online
1I	Combination of Objectives from Projects 1A and 1B	**1I GO! Make It** A demonstration of your mastery of the skills in Projects 1A and 1B by creating a result from a supplied picture.	Online
1J	Combination of Objectives from Projects 1A and 1B	**1J GO! Solve It** A demonstration of your mastery of the skills in Projects 1A and 1B, your decision-making skills, and your critical thinking skills. A task-specific rubric helps you self-assess your result.	Online
1K	Combination of Objectives from Projects 1A and 1B	**1K GO! Solve It** A demonstration of your mastery of the skills in Projects 1A and 1B, your decision-making skills, and your critical thinking skills. A task-specific rubric helps you self-assess your result.	On the following pages
1L	Combination of Objectives from Projects 1A and 1B	**1L GO! Think** A demonstration of your understanding of the chapter concepts applied in a manner that you would outside of college. An analytic rubric helps you and your instructor grade the quality of your work by comparing it to the work an expert in the discipline would create.	On the following pages
1M	Combination of Objectives from Projects 1A and 1B	**1M GO! Think** A demonstration of your understanding of the chapter concepts applied in a manner that you would outside of college. An analytic rubric helps you and your instructor grade the quality of your work by comparing it to the work an expert in the discipline would create.	Online
1N	Combination of Objectives from Projects 1A and 1B	**1N You and GO!** A demonstration of your understanding of the chapter concepts applied in a manner that you would in a personal situation. An analytic rubric helps you and your instructor grade the quality of your work.	Online
1O	Combination of Objectives from Projects 1A and 1B	**1O Cumulative Group Project for Access Chapter 1** A demonstration of your understanding of concepts and your ability to work collaboratively in a group role-playing assessment, requiring both collaboration and self-management.	Online

GLOSSARY

GLOSSARY OF CHAPTER KEY TERMS

Append To add on to the end of an object; for example, to add records to the end of an existing table.

AutoNumber data type A data type that describes a unique sequential or random number assigned by Access as each record is entered and that is useful for data that has no distinct field that can be considered unique.

Best Fit An Access command that adjusts the width of a column to accommodate the column's longest entry.

Blank desktop database A database that has no data and has no database tools—you must create the data and tools as you need them; the database is stored on your computer or other storage device.

Caption A property setting that displays a name for a field in a table, query, form, or report other than that listed as the field name.

Common field A field in two or more tables that stores the same data.

Currency data type An Access data type that describes monetary values and numeric data that can be used in mathematical calculations involving values with one to four decimal places.

Custom web app A database that you can publish and share with others over the Internet.

Data Facts about people, events, things, or ideas.

Data source The table or tables from which a query, form, or report retrieves its data.

Data type The characteristic that defines the kind of data that can be stored in a field, such as numbers, text, or dates.

Database An organized collection of facts about people, events, things, or ideas related to a specific topic or purpose.

Database management system (DBMS) Database software that controls how related collections of data are stored, organized, retrieved, and secured; also known as a DBMS.

Database template A preformatted database that contains prebuilt tables, queries, forms, and reports that perform a specific task, such as tracking events.

Datasheet view The Access view that displays data organized in columns and rows similar to an Excel worksheet.

DBMS An acronym for database management system.

Design view An Access view that displays the detailed structure of a table, query, form, or report. For forms and reports, may be the view in which some tasks must be performed, and only the controls, and not the data, display in this view.

Destination table The table to which you import or append data.

Export The process of copying data from one file into another file, such as an Access table into an Excel spreadsheet.

Field A single piece of information that is stored in every record; represented by a column in a database table.

Field properties Characteristics of a field that control how the field displays and how data can be entered in the field.

First principle of good database design A principle of good database design stating that data is organized in tables so that there is no redundant data.

Flat database A simple database file that is not related or linked to any other collection of data.

Form An Access object you can use to enter new records into a table, edit or delete existing records in a table, or display existing records.

Form view The Access view in which you can view records, but you cannot change the layout or design of the form.

Import The process of copying data from another file, such as a Word table or an Excel workbook, into a separate file, such as an Access database.

Information Data that is organized in a useful manner.

Layout view The Access view in which you can make changes to a form or report while the object is open—the data from the underlying data source displays.

Link A connection to data in another file.

Multiple-items form A form that enables you to display or enter multiple records in a table.

Navigation area An area at the bottom of the Access window that indicates the number of records in the table and contains controls in the form of arrows that you click to navigate among the records.

Navigation Pane An area of the Access window that displays and organizes the names of the objects in a database; from here, you open objects for use.

Normalization The process of applying design rules and principles to ensure that your database performs as expected.

Number data type An Access data type that describes numbers that might be used in calculations.

Object tab In the object window, a tab that identifies the object and which enables you to make the open object active.

Object window An area of the Access window that displays open objects, such as tables, queries, forms, or reports; by default, each object displays on its own tab.

Objects The basic parts of a database that you create to store your data and to work with your data; for example, tables, queries, forms, and reports.

Populate The action of filling a database table with records.

Primary key The field in a table that uniquely identifies a record; for example, a Student ID number at a college.

Property Sheet A list of characteristics—properties—for fields or controls on a form or report in which you can make precise changes to each property associated with the field or control.

Query A database object that retrieves specific data from one or more database objects—either tables or other queries—and then, in a single datasheet, displays only the data you specify.

Record All of the categories of data pertaining to one person, place, event, thing, or idea; represented by a row in a database table.

Record selector bar The bar at the left edge of a record when it is displayed in a form, and which is used to select an entire record.

Record selector box The small box at the left of a record in Datasheet view that, when clicked, selects the entire record.

Redundant In a database, information that is duplicated in a manner that indicates poor database design.

Relational database A sophisticated type of database that has multiple collections of data within the file that are related to one another.

Report A database object that summarizes the fields and records from a table or query in an easy-to-read format suitable for printing.

Run The process in which Access searches the records in the table(s) included in the query design, finds the records that match the specified criteria, and then displays the records in a datasheet; only the fields that have been included in the query design display.

Second principle of good database design A principle stating that appropriate database techniques are used to ensure the accuracy and consistency of data as it is entered into the table.

Secure environment A system that uses controlled servers to ensure the security and privacy of email, to control the storage and use of information and to protect against the loss of confidential data.

Select query A type of Access query that retrieves (selects) data from one or more tables or queries, displaying the selected data in a datasheet; also known as a simple select query.

Server A computer that provides services on a network such as an email server or a file server.

SharePoint A Microsoft application used for setting up websites to share and manage documents.

Short Text data type An Access data type that describes text, a combination of text and numbers, or numbers that are not used in calculations, such as a Postal Code.

Simple select query Another name for a select query.

Single-record form A form that enables you to display or enter one record at a time in a table.

Source file When importing a file, refers to the file being imported.

Structure In Access, the underlying design of a table, including field names, data types, descriptions, and field properties.

Table A format for information that organizes and presents text and data in columns and rows; the foundation of a database.

Tables and Related Views An arrangement in the Navigation Pane that groups objects by the table to which they are related.

Truncated Refers to data that is cut off or shortened because the field or column is not wide enough to display all of the data or the field size is too small to contain all of the data.

Wizard A feature in Microsoft Office that walks you step by step through a process.

CHAPTER REVIEW

Apply 1A skills from these Objectives:

1. Identify Good Database Design
2. Create a Table and Define Fields in a Blank Desktop Database
3. Change the Structure of Tables and Add a Second Table
4. Create a Query, Form, and Report
5. Close a Database and Exit Access

Skills Review Project 1C College Administrators

In the following Skills Review, you will create a database to store information about the administrators of Texas Lakes Community College and their departments. Your completed database objects will look similar to Figure 1.51.

PROJECT FILES

For Project 1C, you will need the following files:

Blank desktop database
a01C_Administrators (Excel workbook)
a01C_Departments (Excel workbook)

You will save your database as:

Lastname_Firstname_1C_College_Administrators

Build from Scratch

PROJECT RESULTS

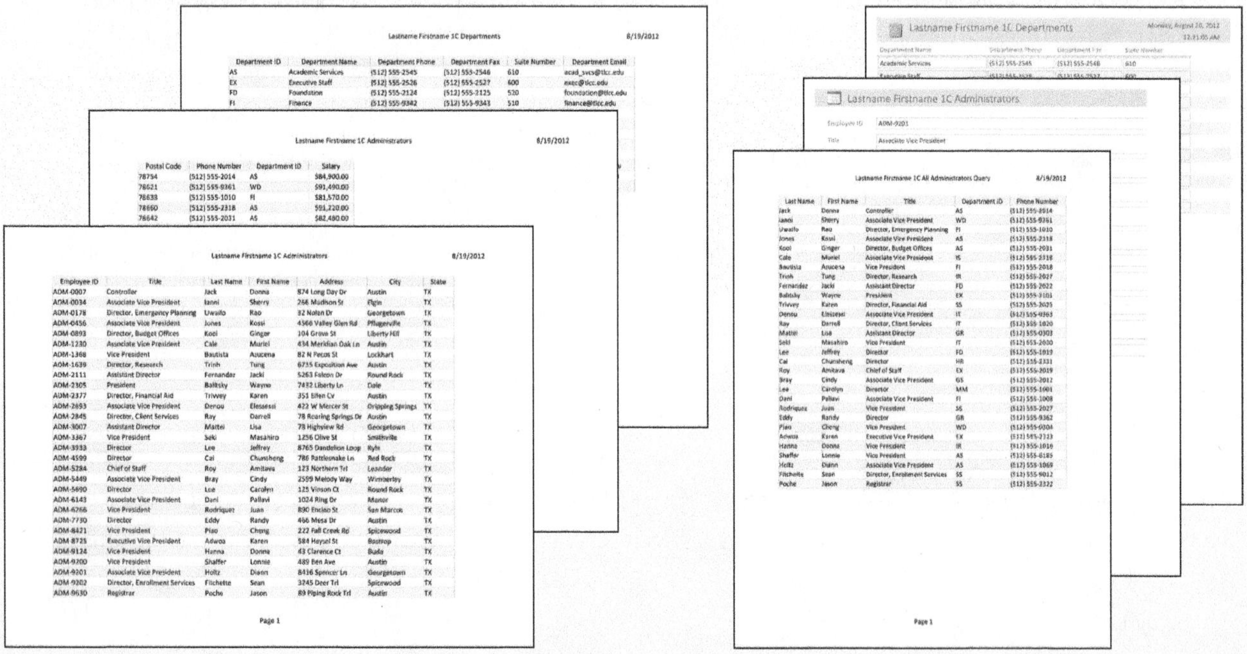

FIGURE 1.51

(Project 1C College Administrators continues on the next page)

CHAPTER REVIEW

Skills Review Project 1C College Administrators (continued)

1 Start Access. In the Access opening screen, click **Blank desktop database**. In the **Blank desktop database** dialog box, to the right of the **File Name** box, click **Browse**. In the **File New Database** dialog box, navigate to your **Access Chapter 1** folder. In the **File New Database** dialog box, click in the **File name** box, type **Lastname_Firstname_1C_College_Administrators** and then press Enter. In the **Blank desktop database** dialog box, click **Create**.

a. **Close** the **Navigation Pane**. In the field names row, click in the text *Click to Add*, and then click **Short Text**. Type **Title** and then press Enter.

b. In the third field name box, click **Short Text**, type **Last Name** and then press Enter. In the fourth field name box, click **Short Text**, type **First Name** and then press Enter. Create the remaining fields shown in **Table 1**, pressing Enter after the last field name. All of the data is typed on one line.

c. If necessary, scroll to bring the first column into view, and then click the **ID** field name. Under **TABLE TOOLS**, on the **FIELDS tab**, in the **Properties group**, click **Name & Caption**. In the **Name** box, change *ID* to **Employee ID** and then click **OK**. On the ribbon, in the **Formatting group**, click the **Data Type arrow**, and then click **Short Text**.

d. In the new record row, click in the **Employee ID** field, type, **ADM-9200** and press Enter. In the **Title** field, type **Vice President** and press Enter. Continue entering data in the fields shown in **Table 2**, pressing Enter or Tab to move to the next field and to the next row.

e. On the **Quick Access Toolbar**, click **Save**. In the **Save As** dialog box, in the **Table Name** box, using your own name, replace the selected text by typing **Lastname Firstname 1C Administrators** and then click **OK**.

f. In the new record row, enter the data for two college administrators shown in **Table 3**, pressing Enter or Tab to move from field to field and to the next row.

TABLE 1

Data Type		Short Text	Short Text	Short Text	Short Text	Short Text	Short Text	Short Text	Short Text	Short Text	Short Text	Currency
Field Name	ID	Title	Last Name	First Name	**Middle Initial**	**Address**	**City**	**State**	**Postal Code**	**Phone Number**	**Department ID**	**Salary**

(Return to Step 1c)

TABLE 2

Last Name	First Name	Middle Initial	Address	City	State	Postal Code	Phone Number	Department ID	Salary
Shaffer	**Lonnie**	**J**	**489 Ben Ave**	**Austin**	**TX**	**78734**	**(512) 555-6185**	**AS**	**123500**

(Return to Step 1e)

TABLE 3

Employee ID	Title	Last Name	First Name	Middle Initial	Address	City	State	Postal Code	Phone Number	Department ID	Salary
ADM-9201	**Associate Vice President**	**Holtz**	**Diann**	**S**	**8416 Spencer Ln**	**Georgetown**	**TX**	**78627**	**(512) 555-1069**	**AS**	**101524**
ADM-9202	**Director, Enrollment Services**	**Fitchette**	**Sean**	**H**	**3245 Deer Trl**	**Spicewood**	**TX**	**78669**	**(512) 555-9012**	**SS**	**45070**

(Return to Step 1g)

(Project 1C College Administrators continues on the next page)

Skills Review Project 1C College Administrators (continued)

g. **Close** your **1C Administrators** table. On the ribbon, click the **EXTERNAL DATA tab**, in the **Import & Link group**, click **Excel**. In the **Get External Data – Excel Spreadsheet** dialog box, click **Browse**. In the **File Open** dialog box, navigate to your student data files, and then double-click the **a01C_Administrators** Excel file.

h. Click the **Append a copy of the records to the table** option button, and then click **OK**. In the **Import Spreadsheet Wizard**, click **Next**, and then click **Finish**. In the **Get External Data – Excel Spreadsheet** dialog box, click **Close**.

i. **Open** the **Navigation Pane**. Point to the right edge of the **Navigation Pane** to display the [⟺] pointer, and then drag to the right so that the entire table name displays. In the **Navigation Pane**, double-click your **1C Administrators** table to open it, and then **Close** the **Navigation Pane**—there are 30 records in this table.

2 Click the **HOME tab**, and then in the **Views group**, click the top of the **View** button to switch to **Design** view. In the **Field Name** column, to the left of **Middle Initial**, click the row selector box to select the entire row. Under **TABLE TOOLS**, on the **DESIGN tab**, in the **Tools group**, click **Delete Rows**. In the message box, click **Yes**.

a. Click in the **Employee ID** field name box. Under **Field Properties**, click **Field Size** to select the existing text. Type **8** and then in the **Employee ID** field row, click in the **Description** box. Type **Eight-character Employee ID** and then press Enter.

b. Click in the **State** field name box. In the **Field Properties** area, click **Field Size**, and then type **2** In the **State Description** box, type **Two-character state abbreviation** and then press Enter.

c. **Save** the design changes to your table, and in the message box, click **Yes**. On the **DESIGN tab**, in the **Views group**, click the top of the **View** button to switch to **Datasheet** view.

d. On the ribbon, click the **EXTERNAL DATA tab**, and then in the **Import & Link group**, click **Excel**. In the **Get External Data – Excel Spreadsheet** dialog box, to the right of the **File name** box, click **Browse**. In the **File Open** dialog box, navigate to your student data files, and then double-click **a01C_Departments**. Be sure that the **Import the source data into a new table in the current database** option button is selected, and then click **OK**.

e. In the upper left corner of the wizard, select the **First Row Contains Column Headings** check box, and then click **Next**. Click **Next** again. Click the **Choose my own primary key** option button, be sure that **Department ID** displays, and then click **Next**. In the **Import to Table** box, type **Lastname Firstname 1C Departments** and then click **Finish**. In the **Get External Data – Excel Spreadsheet** dialog box, click **Close**.

f. **Open** the **Navigation Pane**, double-click your **1C Departments** table, and then **Close** the **Navigation Pane**. There are 12 records in your **1C Departments** table.

g. To the left of the **Department** field name, click **Select All**. On the ribbon, click the **HOME tab**. In the **Records group**, click **More**, and then click **Field Width**. In the **Column Width** dialog box, click **Best Fit**. **Save** the table, and then click in any field to cancel the selection. In the object window, click the **object tab** for your **1C Administrators** table. Using the techniques you just practiced, apply **Best Fit** to the columns, **Save** the table, and then cancel the selection.

h. With your **1C Administrators** table displayed, on the ribbon, click the **FILE tab**, click **Print**, and then click **Print Preview**. On the **PRINT PREVIEW tab**, in the **Page Layout group**, click **Landscape**. Create a paper or electronic printout as directed by your instructor—two pages result. On the ribbon, click **Close Print Preview**, and then **Close** your **1C Administrators** table.

i. With your **1C Departments** table displayed, view the table in **Print Preview**. Change the orientation to **Landscape**, and then create a paper or electronic printout as directed by your instructor—one page results. Click **Close Print Preview**, and then **Close** your **1C Departments** table.

(Project 1C College Administrators continues on the next page)

CHAPTER REVIEW

Skills Review Project 1C College Administrators (continued)

3 On the ribbon, click the **CREATE tab**, and then in the **Queries group**, click **Query Wizard**. In the **New Query** dialog box, be sure **Simple Query Wizard** is selected, and then click **OK**. In the wizard, click the **Tables/Queries arrow**, and then, if necessary, click **Table: Lastname Firstname 1C Administrators.**

a. Under **Available Fields**, click **Last Name**, and then click **Add Field** to move the field to the **Selected Fields** list on the right. Double-click the **First Name** field to move it to the **Selected Fields** list. By using **Add Field** or by double-clicking the field name, add the following fields to the **Selected Fields** list in the order specified: **Title**, **Department ID**, and **Phone Number**. This query will answer the question, *What is the last name, first name, title, Department ID, and phone number of every administrator?*

b. In the wizard, click **Next**. Click in the **What title do you want for your query?** box. Using your own name, edit as necessary so that the query name is **Lastname Firstname 1C All Administrators Query** and then click **Finish**. If necessary, apply **Best Fit** to the columns, and then **Save** the query. Display the query in **Print Preview**, and then create a paper or electronic printout as directed—one page results. Click **Close Print Preview**, and then **Close** the query.

c. **Open** the **Navigation Pane**, right-click your **1C Administrators** table, and then click **Open** to display the table in the object window. **Close** the **Navigation Pane**. Notice that the table has 11 fields. On the ribbon, click the **CREATE tab**, and in the **Forms group**, click **Form**. On the **Quick Access Toolbar**, click **Save**. In the **Save As** dialog box, click in the **Form Name** box, edit to name the form **Lastname Firstname 1C Administrator Form** and then click **OK**.

d. In the navigation area, click **Last record**, and then click **Previous record** two times to display the record for *Diann Holtz*. Using the instructions in Activity 1.15, print or create an electronic printout of only this record on one page. **Close** the form object, saving it if prompted. Your **1C Administrators** table object remains open.

e. **Open** the **Navigation Pane**, open your **1C Departments** table by double-clicking the table name or by right-clicking the table name and clicking **Open**. **Close** the **Navigation Pane**. On the **CREATE tab**, in the **Reports group**, click **Report**.

f. Click the **Department ID** field name, and then on the ribbon, click the **ARRANGE tab**. In the **Rows & Columns group**, click **Select Column**, and then press Del. Using the same technique, delete the **Department Email** field.

g. Click the **Department Phone** field name. Hold down Shift, and then click the **Suite Number** field name to select the last three field names. On the ribbon, click the **DESIGN tab**, and then in the **Tools group**, click **Property Sheet**. In the **Property Sheet**, on the **Format tab**, click **Width**, type **1.5** and then press Enter. **Close** the **Property Sheet**.

h. Click the **Department Name** field name. On the ribbon, click the **HOME tab**. In the **Sort & Filter group**, click **Ascending** to sort the report in alphabetic order by *Department Name*. At the bottom of the report, on the right side, click **Page 1 of 1**, and then press Del.

i. **Save** the report as **Lastname Firstname 1C Departments Report** and then click **OK**. Display the report in **Print Preview**, and then create a paper or electronic printout of the report as directed. Click **Close Print Preview**. In the object window, right-click any **object tab**, and then click **Close All** to close all open objects, leaving the object window empty.

(Project 1C College Administrators continues on the next page)

CHAPTER REVIEW

Skills Review Project 1C College Administrators (continued)

4 **Open** the **Navigation Pane**. If necessary, increase the width of the **Navigation Pane** so that all object names display fully. On the right side of the title bar, click **Close** to close the database and to exit Access. As directed by your instructor, submit your database and the paper or electronic printouts of the five objects—two tables, one query, one form, and one report—that are the results of this project. Specifically, in this project, using your own name, you created the following database and printouts or electronic printouts:

1. Lastname_Firstname_1C_College_Administrators	Database file
2. Lastname Firstname 1C Administrators	Table (printout or electronic printout – two pages)
3. Lastname Firstname 1C Departments	Table (printout or electronic printout)
4. Lastname Firstname 1C All Administrators Query	Query (printout or electronic printout)
5. Lastname Firstname 1C Administrator Form	Form (printout or electronic printout – Record 28)
6. Lastname Firstname 1C Departments Report	Report (printout or electronic printout)

END | You have completed Project 1C

CHAPTER REVIEW

Apply 1B skills from these Objectives:

6 Use a Template to Create a Database
7 Organize Objects in the Navigation Pane
8 Create a New Table in a Database Created with a Template
9 Print a Report and a Table

Skills Review Project 1D Certification Events

In the following Skills Review, you will create a database to store information about certification test preparation events at Texas Lakes Community College. Your completed report and table will look similar to Figure 1.52.

PROJECT FILES

For Project 1D, you will need the following files:

Desktop Event Management template
a01D_Certification_Events (Excel workbook)

You will save your database as:

Lastname_Firstname_1D_Certification_Events

Build from Scratch

PROJECT RESULTS

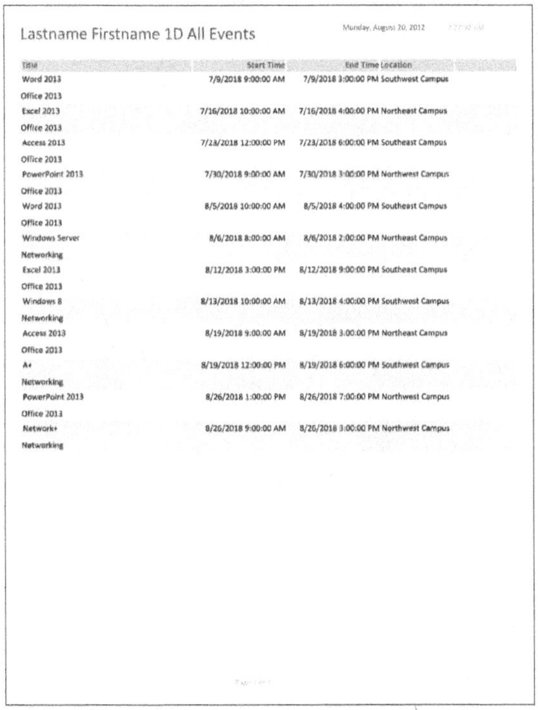

Lastname Firstname 1D All Events

Monday, August 20, 2012

Title	Start Time	End Time	Location
Word 2013	7/9/2018 9:00:00 AM	7/9/2018 3:00:00 PM	Southwest Campus
Office 2013			
Excel 2013	7/16/2018 10:00:00 AM	7/16/2018 4:00:00 PM	Northeast Campus
Office 2013			
Access 2013	7/23/2018 12:00:00 PM	7/23/2018 6:00:00 PM	Southeast Campus
Office 2013			
PowerPoint 2013	7/30/2018 9:00:00 AM	7/30/2018 3:00:00 PM	Northwest Campus
Office 2013			
Word 2013	8/5/2018 10:00:00 AM	8/5/2018 4:00:00 PM	Southeast Campus
Office 2013			
Windows Server	8/6/2018 8:00:00 AM	8/6/2018 2:00:00 PM	Northeast Campus
Networking			
Excel 2013	8/12/2018 3:00:00 PM	8/12/2018 9:00:00 PM	Southeast Campus
Office 2013			
Windows 8	8/13/2018 10:00:00 AM	8/13/2018 4:00:00 PM	Southwest Campus
Networking			
Access 2013	8/19/2018 9:00:00 AM	8/19/2018 3:00:00 PM	Northeast Campus
Office 2013			
A+	8/19/2018 12:00:00 PM	8/19/2018 6:00:00 PM	Southwest Campus
Networking			
PowerPoint 2013	8/26/2018 1:00:00 PM	8/26/2018 7:00:00 PM	Northwest Campus
Office 2013			
Network+	8/26/2018 9:00:00 AM	8/26/2018 3:00:00 PM	Northwest Campus
Networking			

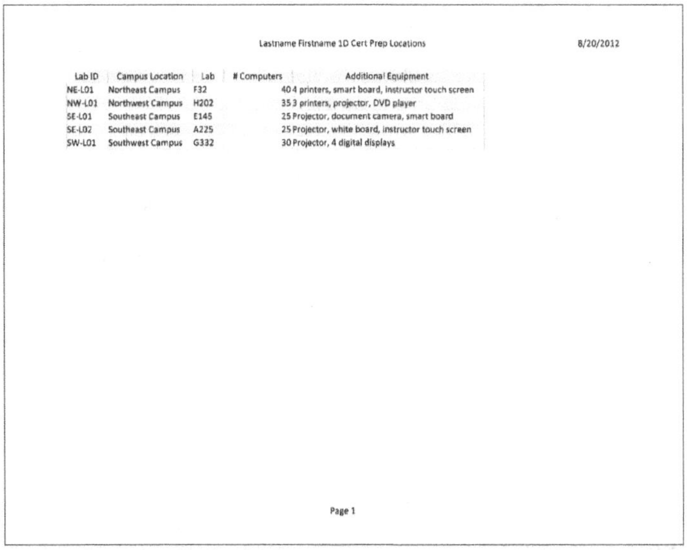

Lastname Firstname 1D Cert Prep Locations 8/20/2012

Lab ID	Campus Location	Lab	# Computers	Additional Equipment
NE-L01	Northeast Campus	F32	40	4 printers, smart board, instructor touch screen
NW-L01	Northwest Campus	H202	35	3 printers, projector, DVD player
SE-L01	Southeast Campus	E145	25	Projector, document camera, smart board
SE-L02	Southeast Campus	A225	25	Projector, white board, instructor touch screen
SW-L01	Southwest Campus	G332	30	Projector, 4 digital displays

Page 1

FIGURE 1.52

(Project 1D Certification Events continues on the next page)

CHAPTER REVIEW

Skills Review Project 1D Certification Events (continued)

1 Start Access. In the Access opening screen, click in the **Search** box, type **event** and then press Enter to search for a template to manage events. Click the **Desktop Event Management** template. In the **Desktop Event Management** dialog box, to the right of the **File Name** box, click **Browse**, and then navigate to your **Access Chapter 1** folder. In the **File New Database** dialog box, click in the **File name** box to select the existing text. Using your own name, type **Lastname_Firstname_1D_Certification_Events** and then press Enter. In the **Desktop Event Management** dialog box, click **Create** to download the template and to save the database. Under the ribbon, on the **Message Bar**, click **Enable Content**.

a. In the first row, click in the **Title** field, type **Word 2013** and then press Tab. In the **Start Time** field, type **7/9/18 9a** and then press Tab. In the **End Time** field, type **7/9/18 3p** and then press Tab. In the **Description** field, type **Office 2013** and then press Tab. In the **Location** field, type **Southwest Campus** and then press Tab three times to move to the **Title** field in the new record row.

b. In the form, directly above the field names row, click **New Event** to open the **Event Details** single-record form. Using Tab to move from field to field, enter the record shown in **Table 1**. Press Tab three times to move from the **End Time** field to the **Description** field.

c. In the **Events Detail** form, click **Close**. Using either the **Event List** multiple-items form or the **Event Details** single-record form, enter the records shown in **Table 2**. If you use the **Events Detail** form, be sure to close it after entering records to display the records in the **Event List** form.

d. **Close** the **Event List** form. On the ribbon, click the **EXTERNAL DATA tab**, and in the **Import & Link group**, click **Excel**. In the **Get External Data – Excel Spreadsheet** dialog box, click **Browse**. Navigate to your student data files, and then double-click **a01D_Certification_Events**. Click the second option button—**Append a copy of the records to the table**—and then click **OK**.

e. In the **Import Spreadsheet Wizard**, click **Next**, and then click **Finish**. In the **Get External Data – Excel Spreadsheet** dialog box, click **Close**. **Open** the **Navigation Pane**, and then double-click **Event List** to open the form that displays data stored in the **Events** table—12 total records display. **Close** the **Navigation Pane**.

f. To the left of the **ID** field name, click **Select All**. In the field names row, point to the right edge of any of the selected columns to display the ✢ pointer, and then double-click to apply **Best Fit** to all of the columns. **Save** the form, and then click in any field to cancel the selection.

2 **Open** the **Navigation Pane**. At the top of the **Navigation Pane**, click the arrow. On the list, under **Navigate To Category**, click **Tables and Related Views**.

a. In the **Navigation Pane**, point to **Events: Table**, right-click, and then click **Open** to display the records in the underlying table. In the **Navigation Pane**, double-click the **Current Events** *report* (green icon) to view this predesigned report. From the **Navigation Pane**, open the **Events by Week** report to view this predesigned report.

TABLE 1

Title	Location	Start Time	End Time	Description
Excel 2013	**Northeast Campus**	**7/16/18 10a**	**7/16/18 4p**	**Office 2013**

(Return to Step 1c)

TABLE 2

ID	Title	Start Time	End Time	Description	Location
3	**Access 2013**	**7/23/18 12p**	**7/23/18 6p**	**Office 2013**	**Southeast Campus**
4	**PowerPoint 2013**	**7/30/18 9a**	**7/30/18 3p**	**Office 2013**	**Northwest Campus**

(Return to Step 1d)

(Project 1D Certification Events continues on the next page)

b. In the object window, right-click any of the **object tabs**, and then click **Close All**. **Close** the **Navigation Pane**.

3 On the ribbon, click the **CREATE tab**, and in the **Tables group**, click **Table**.

a. In the field names row, click **Click to Add**, click **Short Text**, type **Campus Location** and then press Enter. In the third column, click **Short Text**, type **Lab** and then press Enter. In the fourth column, click **Number**, type **# Computers** and then press Enter. In the fifth column, click **Short Text**, type **Additional Equipment** and then press ↓.

b. Right-click the **ID** field name, and then click **Rename Field**. Type **Lab ID** and then press Enter. On the **FIELDS tab**, in the **Formatting group**, click the **Data Type arrow**, and then click **Short Text**.

c. In the new record row, click in the **Lab ID** field, and then enter the records shown in **Table 3**, pressing Enter or Tab to move from one field to the next.

d. In the **Views group**, click the top of the **View** button to switch to **Design** view. In the **Save As** dialog box, in the **Table Name** box, using your own name, type **Lastname Firstname 1D Cert Prep Locations** and then click **OK**. Notice that the **Lab ID** field is the **Primary Key**. On the **DESIGN tab**, in the **Views group**, click the top of the **View** button to switch to **Datasheet** view.

e. To the left of the **Lab ID** field name, click **Select All** to select all of the columns and rows in the table. On the **HOME tab**, in the **Records group**, click **More**, and then click **Field Width**. In the **Column Width** dialog box, click **Best Fit**. **Save** the changes to the table, and then click in any field to cancel the selection. **Close** the table, and then **Open** the **Navigation Pane**. Increase the width of the **Navigation Pane** so that your entire table name displays.

4 In the **Navigation Pane**, double-click the **All Events** report to open it in the object window. **Close** the **Navigation Pane**. On the **HOME tab**, in the **Views group**, click the top of the **View** button to switch to **Layout** view. At the top of the report, click the title—*All Events*—to display a colored border around the title. Click to the left of the letter *A* to place the insertion point there. Using your own name, type **Lastname Firstname 1D** and then press Spacebar. Press Enter, and then **Save** the report.

a. On the right side of the status bar, click **Print Preview**, and notice that the report will print on one page. Create a paper or electronic printout as instructed. Click **Close Print Preview**, and then **Close** the report.

b. **Open** the **Navigation Pane**, double-click your **1D Cert Prep Locations** table, and then **Close** the **Navigation Pane**. On the ribbon, click the **FILE tab**, click **Print**, and then click **Print Preview**. On the **PRINT PREVIEW tab**, in the **Page Layout group**, click **Landscape**. Create a paper or electronic printout as directed, and then click **Close Print Preview**. Close your **1D Cert Prep Locations** table.

TABLE 3

Lab ID	Campus Location	Lab	# Computers	Additional Equipment
NW-L01	**Northwest Campus**	**H202**	**35**	**3 printers, projector, DVD player**
SE-L01	**Southeast Campus**	**E145**	**25**	**Projector, document camera, smart board**
NE-L01	**Northeast Campus**	**F32**	**40**	**4 printers, smart board, instructor touch screen**
SW-L01	**Southwest Campus**	**G332**	**30**	**Projector, 4 digital displays**
SE-L02	**Southeast Campus**	**A225**	**25**	**Projector, white board, instructor touch screen**

(Return to Step 3d)

(Project 1D Certification Events continues on the next page)

Skills Review Project 1D Certification Events (continued)

c. **Open** the **Navigation Pane**. On the right side of the title bar, click **Close** to close the database and to exit Access. As directed by your instructor, submit your database and the paper or electronic printouts of the two objects—one report and one table—that are the results of this project. Specifically, in this project, using your own name, you created the following database and printouts or electronic printouts:

1. Lastname_Firstname_1D_Certification_Events	Database file
2. Lastname Firstname 1D Cert Prep Locations	Table (printout or electronic printout)
3. All Events	Report (printout or electronic printout)

END | You have completed Project 1D

CONTENT-BASED ASSESSMENTS

Mastering Access Project 1E Kiosk Inventory

MyITLab® grader

Apply 1A skills from these Objectives:

1. Identify Good Database Design
2. Create a Table and Define Fields in a Blank Desktop Database
3. Change the Structure of Tables and Add a Second Table
4. Create a Query, Form, and Report
5. Close a Database and Exit Access

In the following Mastering Access project, you will create a database to track information about the inventory of items for sale in the kiosk located in the snack bar at the Southeast Campus of Texas Lakes Community College. Your completed database objects will look similar to Figure 1.53.

PROJECT FILES

For Project 1E, you will need the following files:

Blank desktop database
a01E_Inventory (Excel workbook)
a01E_Inventory_Storage (Excel workbook)

You will save your database as:

Lastname_Firstname_1E_Kiosk_Inventory

PROJECT RESULTS

Build from Scratch

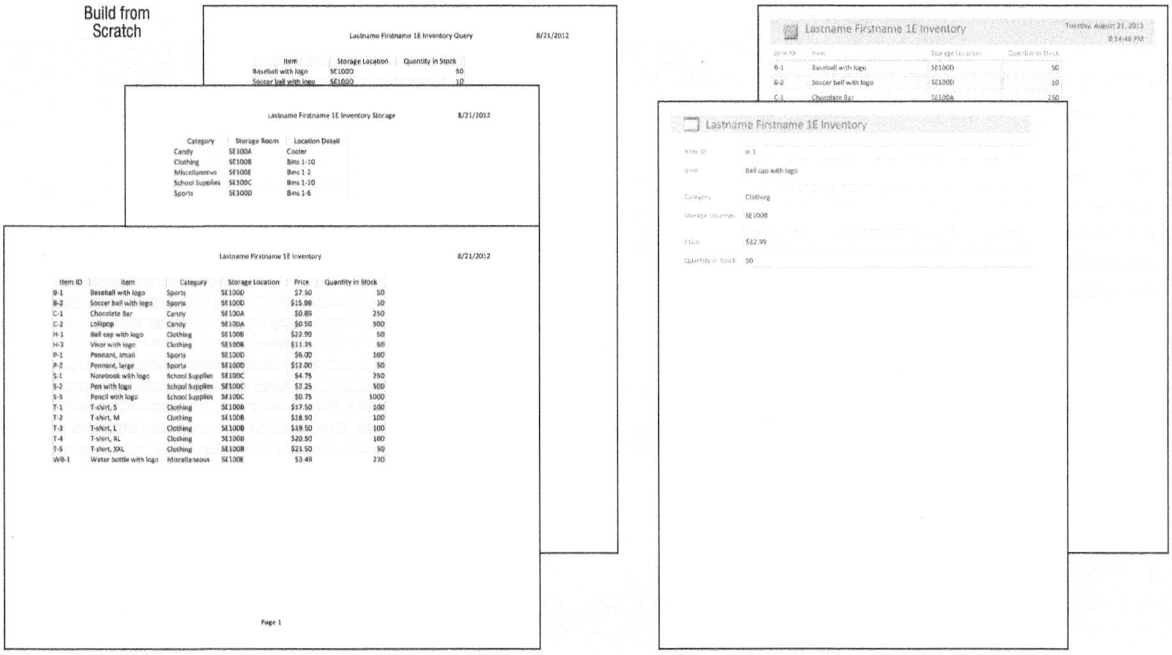

FIGURE 1.53

(Project 1E Kiosk Inventory continues on the next page)

CONTENT-BASED ASSESSMENTS

Mastering Access | Project 1E Kiosk Inventory (continued)

1 Start Access. Create a **Blank desktop database** in your **Access Chapter 1** folder. Name the database **Lastname_Firstname_1E_Kiosk_Inventory** and then **Close** the **Navigation Pane**. Create the fields shown in **Table 1**.

2 For the **ID** field, change the **Data Type** to **Short Text**, rename the field to **Item ID** and then enter the records shown in **Table 2**.

3 **Save** the table as **Lastname Firstname 1E Inventory** and then **Close** the table. From your student data files, import and then **Append** the data in the Excel file **a01E_Inventory** to your **1E Inventory** table. After importing, open your **1E Inventory** table—17 records display.

4 In **Design** view, delete the **Campus** field, which is redundant data. For the **Category** field, change the **Field Size** to **25** and enter a **Description** of **Enter the category of the item** For the **Item ID** field, change the **Field Size** to **10** and then **Save** the changes to your table. Switch to **Datasheet** view, apply **Best Fit** to all of the fields in the table, and then **Save** your changes. Display the table in **Print Preview**, change the orientation to **Landscape**, and then create a paper or electronic printout as directed by your instructor. **Close Print Preview**, and then **Close** the table.

5 From your student data files, import the **Excel** file **a01E_Inventory_Storage** into the database as a new table; designate the first row as column headings and the **Category** field as the primary key. In the wizard, name the table **Lastname Firstname 1E Inventory Storage** and then open your **1E Inventory Storage** table—five records display. In **Design** view, for the **Location Detail** field, change the **Field Size** to **30** and enter a **Description** of **Room and bin number or alternate location of inventory item** **Save** the design changes, switch to **Datasheet** view, apply **Best Fit** to all of the fields, and then **Save** your changes. Display the table in **Print Preview**, create a paper or electronic printout as directed, **Close Print Preview**, and then **Close** the table.

6 Use the **Query Wizard** to create a simple query based on your **1E Inventory** table. Include only the three fields that will answer the question, *For all item names, what is the storage location and quantity in stock?* In the wizard, accept the default name for the query. Display the query in **Print Preview**, create a paper or electronic printout as directed, **Close Print Preview**, and then **Close** the query.

TABLE 1

Data Type		Short Text	Short Text	Short Text	Short Text	Currency	Number
Field Name	ID	Item	Category	Campus	Storage Location	Price	Quantity in Stock

(Return to Step 2)

TABLE 2

Item ID	Item	Category	Campus	Storage Location	Price	Quantity in Stock
C-1	Chocolate Bar	Candy	Southeast	SE100A	.89	250
C-2	Lollipop	Candy	Southeast	SE100A	.5	500
T-1	T-shirt, S	Clothing	Southeast	SE100B	17.5	100

(Return to Step 3)

(Project 1E Kiosk Inventory continues on the next page)

Mastering Access Project 1E Kiosk Inventory (continued)

7 Open your **1E Inventory** table, and then create a **Form** for this table. **Save** the form as **Lastname Firstname 1E Inventory Form** and then display and select the fifth record. By using the instructions in Activity 1.15, create a paper or electronic printout of only this record on one page, as directed by your instructor. **Close** the form object, saving changes if prompted.

8 With your **1E Inventory** table open, create a **Report**. Delete the **Category** and **Price** fields, and then sort the **Item ID** field in **Ascending** order. Using the **Property Sheet**, for the **Item ID** field, change the **Width** to **0.75** and then for the **Storage Location** field, change the **Width** to **1.5** Scroll to display the bottom of the report, and then delete the page number—**Page 1 of 1**. **Save** the report as **Lastname Firstname 1E Inventory Report** and then display the report in **Print Preview**. Create a paper or electronic printout as directed. Click **Close Print Preview**.

9 **Close All** open objects. **Open** the **Navigation Pane** and be sure that all object names display fully. **Close** the database, and then **Close** Access. As directed by your instructor, submit your database and the paper or electronic printouts of the five objects—two tables, one query, one form, and one report—that are the results of this project. Specifically, in this project, using your own name, you created the following database and printouts or electronic printouts:

1. Lastname_Firstname_1E_Kiosk_Inventory	Database file
2. Lastname Firstname 1E Inventory	Table (printout or electronic printout)
3. Lastname Firstname 1E Inventory Storage	Table (printout or electronic printout)
4. Lastname Firstname 1E Inventory Query	Query (printout or electronic printout)
5. Lastname Firstname 1E Inventory Form	Form (printout or electronic printout - Record 5)
6. Lastname Firstname 1E Inventory Report	Report (printout or electronic printout)

END | You have completed Project 1E

CONTENT-BASED ASSESSMENTS

Mastering Access Project 1F Recruiting Events

MyITLab® grader

Apply 1B skills from these Objectives:

6 Use a Template to Create a Database
7 Organize Objects in the Navigation Pane
8 Create a New Table in a Database Created with a Template
9 Print a Report and a Table

Build from Scratch

In the following Mastering Access project, you will create a database to store information about the recruiting events that are scheduled to attract new students to Texas Lakes Community College. Your completed report and tables will look similar to Figure 1.54.

PROJECT FILES

For Project 1F, you will need the following files:

Desktop Event Management template
a01F_Recruiting_Events (Excel workbook)

You will save your database as:

Lastname_Firstname_1F_Recruiting_Events

PROJECT RESULTS

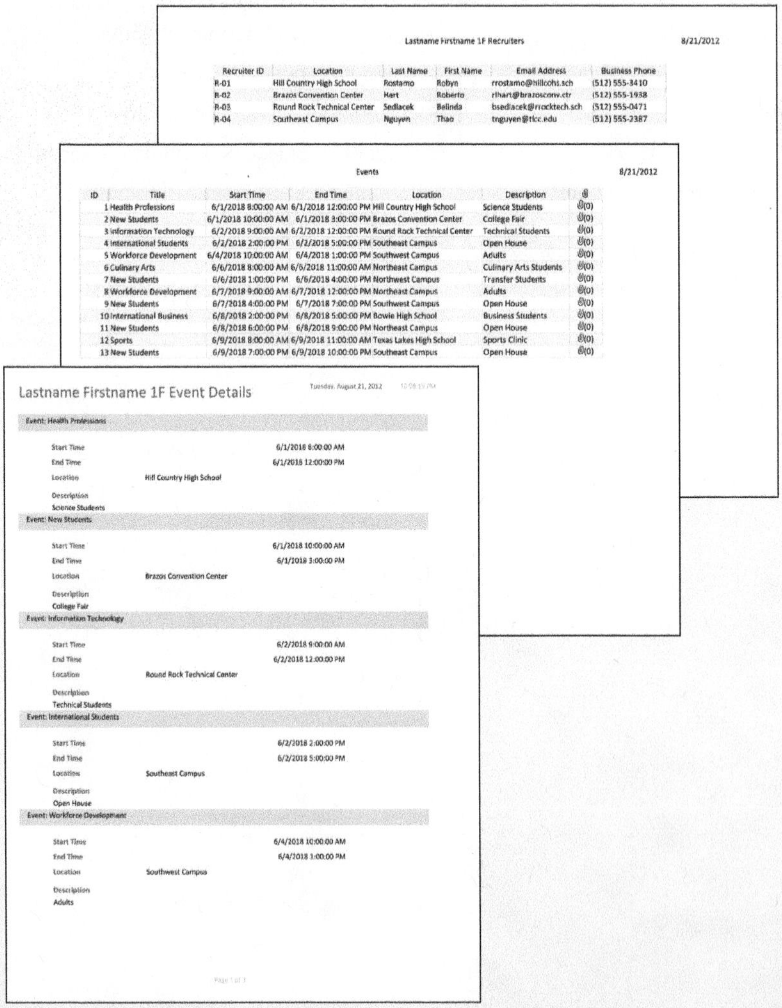
Lastname Firstname 1F Recruiters 8/21/2012

Recruiter ID	Location	Last Name	First Name	Email Address	Business Phone
R-01	Hill Country High School	Rostamo	Robyn	rrostamo@hillcohs.sch	(512) 555-3410
R-02	Brazos Convention Center	Hart	Roberto	rlhart@brazosconv.ctr	(512) 555-1938
R-03	Round Rock Technical Center	Sedlacek	Belinda	bsedlacek@rrocktech.sch	(512) 555-0471
R-04	Southeast Campus	Nguyen	Thao	tnguyen@tlcc.edu	(512) 555-2387

Events 8/21/2012

ID	Title	Start Time	End Time	Location	Description	
1	Health Professions	6/1/2018 8:00:00 AM	6/1/2018 12:00:00 PM	Hill Country High School	Science Students	(0)
2	New Students	6/1/2018 10:00:00 AM	6/1/2018 3:00:00 PM	Brazos Convention Center	College Fair	(0)
3	Information Technology	6/2/2018 9:00:00 AM	6/2/2018 12:00:00 PM	Round Rock Technical Center	Technical Students	(0)
4	International Students	6/2/2018 2:00:00 PM	6/2/2018 5:00:00 PM	Southeast Campus	Open House	(0)
5	Workforce Development	6/4/2018 10:00:00 AM	6/4/2018 1:00:00 PM	Southwest Campus	Adults	(0)
6	Culinary Arts	6/6/2018 8:00:00 AM	6/6/2018 11:00:00 AM	Northeast Campus	Culinary Arts Students	(0)
7	New Students	6/6/2018 1:00:00 PM	6/6/2018 4:00:00 PM	Northwest Campus	Transfer Students	(0)
8	Workforce Development	6/7/2018 9:00:00 AM	6/7/2018 12:00:00 PM	Northeast Campus	Adults	(0)
9	New Students	6/7/2018 4:00:00 PM	6/7/2018 7:00:00 PM	Southwest Campus	Open House	(0)
10	International Business	6/8/2018 2:00:00 PM	6/8/2018 5:00:00 PM	Bowie High School	Business Students	(0)
11	New Students	6/8/2018 6:00:00 PM	6/8/2018 9:00:00 PM	Northeast Campus	Open House	(0)
12	Sports	6/9/2018 8:00:00 AM	6/9/2018 11:00:00 AM	Texas Lakes High School	Sports Clinic	(0)
13	New Students	6/9/2018 7:00:00 PM	6/9/2018 10:00:00 PM	Southeast Campus	Open House	(0)

Lastname Firstname 1F Event Details Tuesday, August 21, 2012

Event: Health Professions
Start Time 6/1/2018 8:00:00 AM
End Time 6/1/2018 12:00:00 PM
Location Hill Country High School
Description
Science Students

Event: New Students
Start Time 6/1/2018 10:00:00 AM
End Time 6/1/2018 3:00:00 PM
Location Brazos Convention Center
Description
College Fair

Event: Information Technology
Start Time 6/2/2018 9:00:00 AM
End Time 6/2/2018 12:00:00 PM
Location Round Rock Technical Center
Description
Technical Students

Event: International Students
Start Time 6/2/2018 2:00:00 PM
End Time 6/2/2018 5:00:00 PM
Location Southeast Campus
Description
Open House

Event: Workforce Development
Start Time 6/4/2018 10:00:00 AM
End Time 6/4/2018 1:00:00 PM
Location Southwest Campus
Description
Adults

FIGURE 1.54

(Project 1F Recruiting Events continues on the next page)

Mastering Access Project 1F Recruiting Events (continued)

1 Start Access. In the Access opening screen, search for **event** and then click the **Desktop Event Management** template. Save the database in your **Access Chapter 1** folder as **Lastname_Firstname_1F_Recruiting_Events** and on the **Message Bar**, click **Enable Content**.

2 In the **Event List** multiple-items form or the **Event Details** single-record form—open by clicking **New Event** on the **Event List** form—enter the records shown in **Table 1**.

3 **Close** the **Event List** form. From your student data files, import and append the data from the **Excel** file **a01F_Recruiting_Events** to the **Events** table. **Open** the **Navigation Pane**, organize the objects by **Tables and Related Views**, and then open the **Events** table to display 13 records. **Close** the table, and then **Close** the **Navigation Pane**.

4 Create a new **Table** defining the new fields shown in **Table 2**.

5 For the **ID** field, change the **Data Type** to **Short Text**, rename the field to **Recruiter ID** and then enter the records shown in **Table 3**.

TABLE 1

ID	Title	Start Time	End Time	Description	Location
1	**Health Professions**	**6/1/18 8a**	**6/1/18 12p**	**Science Students**	**Hill Country High School**
2	**New Students**	**6/1/18 10a**	**6/1/18 3p**	**College Fair**	**Brazos Convention Center**
3	**Information Technology**	**6/2/18 9a**	**6/2/18 12p**	**Technical Students**	**Round Rock Technical Center**
4	**International Students**	**6/2/18 2p**	**6/2/18 5p**	**Open House**	**Southeast Campus**

(Return to Step 3)

TABLE 2

Data Type		Short Text	Short Text	Short Text	Short Text	Short Text
Field Name	ID	**Location**	**Last Name**	**First Name**	**Email Address**	**Business Phone**

(Return to Step 5)

TABLE 3

Recruiter ID	Location	Last Name	First Name	Email Address	Business Phone
R-01	**Hill Country High School**	**Rostamo**	**Robyn**	**rrostamo@hillcohs.sch**	**(512) 555-3410**
R-02	**Brazos Convention Center**	**Hart**	**Roberto**	**rlhart@brazosconv.ctr**	**(512) 555-1938**
R-03	**Round Rock Technical Center**	**Sedlacek**	**Belinda**	**bsedlacek@rrocktech.sch**	**(512) 555-0471**
R-04	**Southeast Campus**	**Nguyen**	**Thao**	**tnguyen@tlcc.edu**	**(512) 555-2387**

(Return to Step 6)

(Project 1F Recruiting Events continues on the next page)

CONTENT-BASED ASSESSMENTS

Mastering Access | Project 1F Recruiting Events (continued)

6 Apply **Best Fit** to all of the columns. **Save** the table as **Lastname Firstname 1F Recruiters** and then **Close** the table.

7 From the **Navigation Pane**, open the **Event Details** *report* (green icon). Switch to **Layout** view. In the report, click in the title—*Event Details*—and then click to position the insertion point to the left of the word *Event*. Using your own name, type **Lastname Firstname 1F** and then press Spacebar and Enter. If necessary, decrease the font size of the title so that the title does not overlap the date on the right side or does not extend to two lines.

Save the report, and then display it in **Print Preview**. If directed to create a paper printout, in the **Print group**, click **Print**. In the **Print** dialog box, under **Print Range**, to the right of **Pages**, click in the **From** box, type **1** and then click in the **To** box and type **1** and then click **OK** to print only the first page. If directed to create an electronic printout, in the **Publish as PDF or XPS** dialog box, click **Options**, and then under **Range**, click the **Pages** option button, and then click **OK**. **Close Print Preview**, and then **Close** the report.

8 From the **Navigation Pane**, open the **Events** table, select all of the columns, and then apply **Best Fit** to all of the columns by double-clicking the right edge of any one of the selected columns. **Save** the table, and then cancel the selection. Display the table in **Print Preview**, change the orientation to **Landscape**, change the **Margins** to **Normal**, and then create a paper or electronic printout as directed. **Close Print Preview**, and then **Close** the table.

9 From the **Navigation Pane**, open your **1F Recruiters** table. Display the table in **Print Preview**, change the orientation to **Landscape**, and then create a paper or electronic printout as directed. **Close Print Preview**, and then **Close** the table.

10 Open the **Navigation Pane**, and be sure that all object names display fully. **Close** Access. As directed by your instructor, submit your database and the paper or electronic printouts of the three objects—one report and two tables—that are the results of this project. Specifically, in this project, using your own name, you created the following database and printouts or electronic printouts:

1. Lastname_Firstname_1F_Recruiting_Events	Database file
2. Event Details	Report (printout or electronic printout – Page 1)
3. Events	Table (printout or electronic printout)
4. Lastname Firstname 1F Recruiters	Table (printout or electronic printout)

END | You have completed Project 1F

MyITLab® grader

CONTENT-BASED ASSESSMENTS

Mastering Access Project 1G College Construction

Apply 1A and 1B skills from these Objectives:

1. Identify Good Database Design
2. Create a Table and Define Fields in a Blank Desktop Database
3. Change the Structure of Tables and Add a Second Table
4. Create a Query, Form, and Report
5. Close a Database and Exit Access
6. Use a Template to Create a Database
7. Organize Objects in the Navigation Pane
8. Create a New Table in a Database Created with a Template
9. Print a Report and a Table

Build from Scratch

In the following Mastering Access project, you will create one database to store information about construction projects for Texas Lakes Community College and a second database to store information about the public events related to the construction projects. Your completed database objects will look similar to Figure 1.55.

PROJECT FILES

For Project 1G, you will need the following files:

Blank desktop database
a01G_Projects (Excel workbook)
a01G_Contractors (Excel workbook)
Desktop Event Management template

You will save your databases as:

Lastname_Firstname_1G_College_Construction
Lastname_Firstname_1G_Public_Events

PROJECT RESULTS

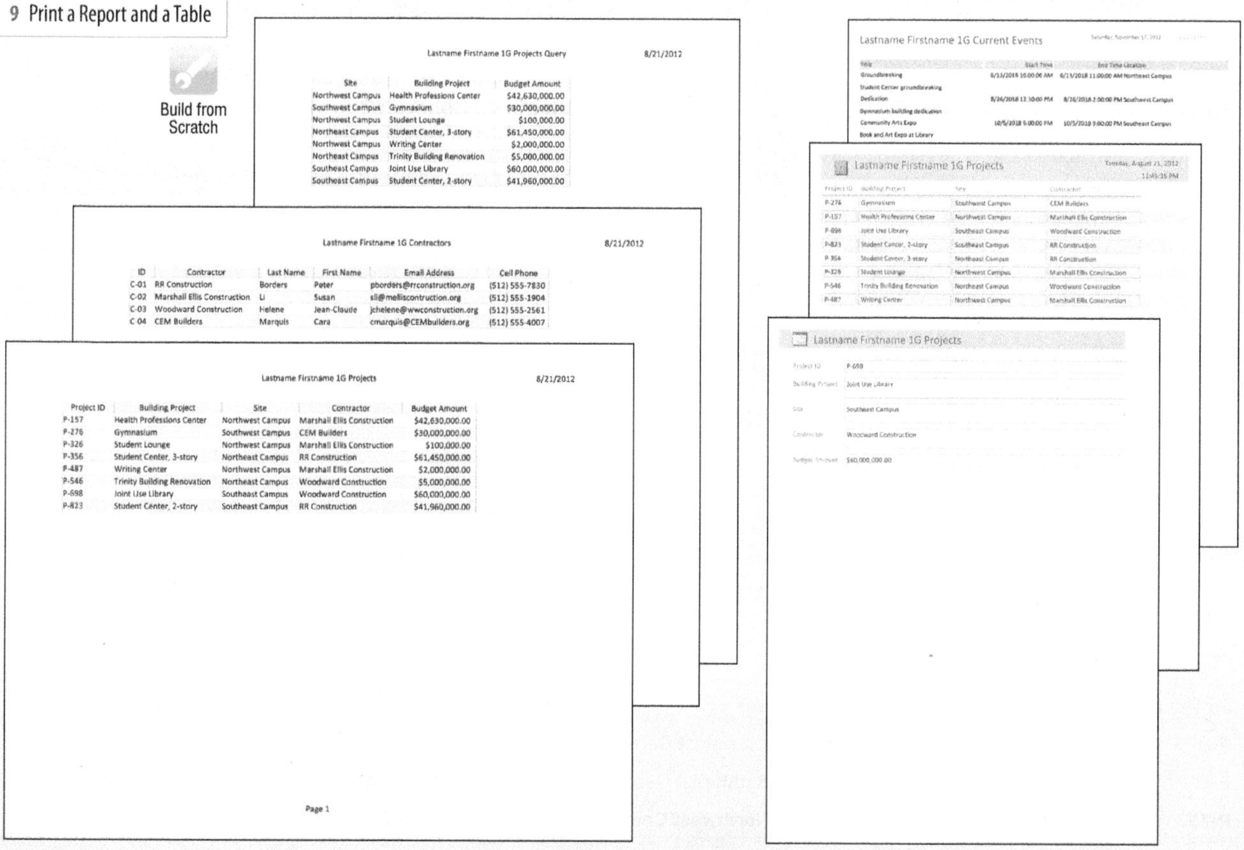

Lastname Firstname 1G Projects Query 8/21/2012

Site	Building Project	Budget Amount
Northwest Campus	Health Professions Center	$42,630,000.00
Southwest Campus	Gymnasium	$30,000,000.00
Northwest Campus	Student Lounge	$100,000.00
Northeast Campus	Student Center, 3-story	$61,450,000.00
Northwest Campus	Writing Center	$2,000,000.00
Northeast Campus	Trinity Building Renovation	$5,000,000.00
Southeast Campus	Joint Use Library	$60,000,000.00
Southeast Campus	Student Center, 2-story	$41,960,000.00

Lastname Firstname 1G Contractors 8/21/2012

ID	Contractor	Last Name	First Name	Email Address	Cell Phone
C-01	RR Construction	Borders	Peter	pborders@rrconstruction.org	(512) 555-7830
C-02	Marshall Ellis Construction	Li	Susan	sli@melliscontruction.org	(512) 555-1904
C-03	Woodward Construction	Helene	Jean-Claude	jchelene@wwconstruction.org	(512) 555-2561
C-04	CEM Builders	Marquis	Cara	cmarquis@CEMbuilders.org	(512) 555-4007

Lastname Firstname 1G Projects 8/21/2012

Project ID	Building Project	Site	Contractor	Budget Amount
P-157	Health Professions Center	Northwest Campus	Marshall Ellis Construction	$42,630,000.00
P-276	Gymnasium	Southwest Campus	CEM Builders	$30,000,000.00
P-326	Student Lounge	Northwest Campus	Marshall Ellis Construction	$100,000.00
P-356	Student Center, 3-story	Northeast Campus	RR Construction	$61,450,000.00
P-487	Writing Center	Northwest Campus	Marshall Ellis Construction	$2,000,000.00
P-546	Trinity Building Renovation	Northeast Campus	Woodward Construction	$5,000,000.00
P-698	Joint Use Library	Southeast Campus	Woodward Construction	$60,000,000.00
P-823	Student Center, 2-story	Southeast Campus	RR Construction	$41,960,000.00

Page 1

FIGURE 1.55

(Project 1G College Construction continues on the next page)

CONTENT-BASED ASSESSMENTS

Mastering Access | Project 1G College Construction (continued)

1 Start Access. Create a **Blank desktop database** in your **Access Chapter 1** folder. Name the database **Lastname_Firstname_1G_College_Construction** and then **Close** the **Navigation Pane**. Create the fields shown in **Table 1**.

2 For the **ID** field, change the **Data Type** to **Short Text**, rename the field to **Project ID** and then enter the three records shown in **Table 2**.

3 **Save** the table as **Lastname Firstname 1G Projects** and then **Close** the table. From your student data files, import and then append the data in the **Excel** file **a01G_Projects** to your **1G Projects** table. After importing, open your **1G Projects** table—eight records display.

4 In **Design** view, for the **Project ID** field, change the **Field Size** to **5** and then enter a **Description** of **Enter the Project ID using the format P-###** **Save** the changes to your table. Switch to **Datasheet** view, apply **Best Fit** to all of the fields in the table, and then **Save** your changes. Display the table in **Print Preview**, change the orientation to **Landscape**, and then create a paper or electronic printout as directed by your instructor. **Close Print Preview**, and then **Close** the table.

5 From your student data files, import the **Excel** file **a01G_Contractors** into the database as a new table; designate the first row as column headings and the **ID** field as the primary key. In the wizard, name the table **Lastname Firstname 1G Contractors** and then open your **1G Contractors** table—four records display. Apply **Best Fit** to all of the fields, and then **Save** your changes. Display the table in **Print Preview**, change the orientation to **Landscape**, and then create a paper or electronic printout as directed. **Close Print Preview**, and then **Close** the table.

6 Use the **Query Wizard** to create a simple query based on your **1G Projects** table. Include only the three fields that will answer the question, *For every site, what is the building project and the budget amount?* In the wizard, accept the default name for the query. Display the query in **Print Preview**, create a paper or electronic printout as directed, **Close Print Preview**, and then **Close** the query.

7 Open your **1G Projects** table, and then create a **Form** for this table. **Save** the form as **Lastname Firstname 1G Project Form** and then display and select the seventh record. By using the instructions in Activity 1.15, create a paper or electronic printout of only this record on one page as directed by your instructor. **Close** the form object, saving changes if prompted.

8 With your **1G Projects** table open, create a **Report**. Delete the **Budget Amount** field, and then sort the **Building Project** field in **Ascending** order. For the **Building Project**, **Site**, and **Contractor** fields, using the **Property Sheet**, change the **Width** of all three fields to **2** At the bottom of the report, delete the page number—**Page 1 of 1**. **Save** the report as **Lastname Firstname 1G Projects Report** and then display the report in **Print Preview**. Create a paper or electronic printout as directed. **Close Print Preview**.

9 **Close All** open objects. **Open** the **Navigation Pane**, arrange the objects by **Tables and Related Views**, and be sure that all object names display fully. **Close** the database, but do *not* close Access.

TABLE 1

Data Type		Short Text	Short Text	Short Text	Currency
Field Name	ID	**Building Project**	**Site**	**Contractor**	**Budget Amount**

(Return to Step 2)

TABLE 2

Project ID	Building Project	Site	Contractor	Budget Amount
P-356	**Student Center, 3-story**	**Northeast Campus**	**RR Construction**	**61450000**
P-823	**Student Center, 2-story**	**Southeast Campus**	**RR Construction**	**41960000**
P-157	**Health Professions Center**	**Northwest Campus**	**Marshall Ellis Construction**	**42630000**

(Return to Step 3)

(Project 1G College Construction continues on the next page)

CONTENT-BASED ASSESSMENTS

Mastering Access | Project 1G College Construction (continued)

10 In the Access opening screen, search for **event** and then click the **Desktop Event Management** template. Save the database in your **Access Chapter 1** folder as **Lastname_Firstname_1G_Public_Events** and on the **Message Bar**, click **Enable Content.**

11 In the **Event List** multiple-items form or the **Event Details** single-record form—open by clicking **New Event** on the **Event List** form—enter the three records shown in **Table 3**.

12 **Close** the **Event List** form. **Open** the **Navigation Pane**, organize the objects by **Tables and Related Views**, and then open the **Current Events** *report* (green icon). Switch to **Layout** view. In the report, click in the title—*Current Events*—and then click to position the insertion point to the left of the letter *C*. Using your own name, type **Lastname Firstname 1G** and then press Spacebar and Enter. If necessary, decrease the font size of the title so that the title does not overlap the date on the right side or does not extend to two lines. **Save** the report, display it in **Print Preview**, and then create a paper or electronic printout as directed. **Close Print Preview**, and then **Close** the report.

13 Open the **Navigation Pane**, and be sure that all object names display fully. **Close** Access. As directed by your instructor, submit your database and the paper or electronic printouts of the six objects—two tables, one query, one form, and two reports—that are the results of this project. Specifically, in this project, using your own name, you created the following database and printouts or electronic printouts:

1. Lastname_Firstname_1G_College_Construction	Database file
2. Lastname_Firstname_1G_Public_Events	Database file
3. Lastname Firstname 1G Projects	Table (printout or electronic printout)
4. Lastname Firstname 1G Contractors	Table (printout or electronic printout)
5. Lastname Firstname 1G Projects Query	Query (printout or electronic printout)
6. Lastname Firstname 1G Project Form	Form (printout or electronic printout - Record 7)
7. Lastname Firstname 1G Projects Report	Report (printout or electronic printout)
8. Current Events	Report (printout or electronic printout)

TABLE 3

ID	Title	Start Time	End Time	Description	Location
1	**Groundbreaking**	**6/13/18 10a**	**6/13/18 11a**	**Student Center groundbreaking**	**Northeast Campus**
2	**Dedication**	**8/26/18 12:30 p**	**8/26/18 2p**	**Gymnasium building dedication**	**Southwest Campus**
3	**Community Arts Expo**	**10/5/18 6p**	**10/5/18 9p**	**Book and Art Expo at Library**	**Southeast Campus**

(Return to Step 12)

END | You have completed Project 1G

CONTENT-BASED ASSESSMENTS

Apply a combination of the 1A and 1B skills.

GO! Fix It | Project 1H Scholarships | Online

Build from Scratch

GO! Make It | Project 1I Theater Events | Online

Build from Scratch

GO! Solve It | Project 1J Athletic Scholarships | Online

GO! Solve It | Project 1K Student Activities

Build from Scratch

PROJECT FILES

For Project 1K, you will need the following files:

Desktop Event Management template
a01K_Student_Activities (Word document)

You will save your database as:

Lastname_Firstname_1K_Student_Activities

Use the Desktop Event Management template to create a database, and save it in your Access Chapter 1 folder as **Lastname_Firstname_1K_Student_Activities** From your student data files, use the information in the Word document a01K_Student_Activities to enter data into the Event List multiple-items form. Each event begins at 6 p.m. and ends at 10 p.m.

After entering the records, close the form, and arrange the Navigation Pane by Tables and Related Views. Open the Event Details *report*, and then add **Lastname Firstname 1K** to the beginning of the report title. If necessary, decrease the font size of the title so that it does not overlap the date and so that it displays on one line. Create a paper or electronic printout as directed—two pages result. As directed, submit your database and the paper or electronic printout of the report that are the results of this project. Specifically, in this project, using your own name, you created the following database and printout or electronic printout:

1. Lastname_Firstname_1K_Student_Activities	Database file
2. Lastname Firstname 1K Event Details	Report (printout or electronic printout)

Performance Level

Performance Criteria	Exemplary	Proficient	Developing
Create database using Desktop Event Management template and enter data	Database created using the correct template, named correctly, and all data entered correctly.	Database created using the correct template, named correctly, but not all data entered correctly.	Database created using the correct template, but numerous errors in database name and data.
Modify report	Event Details report title includes name and project on one line.	Event Details report title includes name and project, but not on one line.	Event Details report title does not include name and project.
Create report printout	Event Details report printout is correct.	Event Details printout is incorrect.	Event Details report printout not created.

END | You have completed Project 1K

OUTCOMES-BASED ASSESSMENTS

RUBRIC

The following outcomes-based assessments are *open-ended assessments*. That is, there is no specific correct result; your result will depend on your approach to the information provided. Make *Professional Quality* your goal. Use the following scoring rubric to guide you in *how* to approach the problem and then to evaluate *how well* your approach solves the problem.

The *criteria*—Software Mastery, Content, Format & Layout, and Process—represent the knowledge and skills you have gained that you can apply to solving the problem. The *levels of performance*—Professional Quality, Approaching Professional Quality, or Needs Quality Improvements—help you and your instructor evaluate your result.

	Your completed project is of Professional Quality if you:	Your completed project is Approaching Professional Quality if you:	Your completed project Needs Quality Improvements if you:
1-Software Mastery	Choose and apply the most appropriate skills, tools, and features and identify efficient methods to solve the problem.	Choose and apply some appropriate skills, tools, and features, but not in the most efficient manner.	Choose inappropriate skills, tools, or features, or are inefficient in solving the problem.
2-Content	Construct a solution that is clear and well organized, contains content that is accurate, appropriate to the audience and purpose, and is complete. Provide a solution that contains no errors in spelling, grammar, or style.	Construct a solution in which some components are unclear, poorly organized, inconsistent, or incomplete. Misjudge the needs of the audience. Have some errors in spelling, grammar, or style, but the errors do not detract from comprehension.	Construct a solution that is unclear, incomplete, or poorly organized; contains some inaccurate or inappropriate content; and contains many errors in spelling, grammar, or style. Do not solve the problem.
3-Format & Layout	Format and arrange all elements to communicate information and ideas, clarify function, illustrate relationships, and indicate relative importance.	Apply appropriate format and layout features to some elements, but not others. Overuse features, causing minor distraction.	Apply format and layout that does not communicate information or ideas clearly. Do not use format and layout features to clarify function, illustrate relationships, or indicate relative importance. Use available features excessively, causing distraction.
4-Process	Use an organized approach that integrates planning, development, self-assessment, revision, and reflection.	Demonstrate an organized approach in some areas, but not others; or, use an insufficient process of organization throughout.	Do not use an organized approach to solve the problem.

Apply a combination of the 1A and 1B skills.

OUTCOMES-BASED ASSESSMENTS

GO! Think Project 1L Student Clubs

Build from Scratch

PROJECT FILES

For Project 1L, you will need the following files:

Blank desktop database
a01L_Clubs (Word document)
a01L_Student_Clubs (Excel workbook)
a01L_Club_Presidents (Excel workbook)

You will save your database as

Lastname_Firstname_1L_Student_Clubs

Dr. Daniel Martinez, vice president of Student Services, needs a database that tracks information about student clubs. The database should contain two tables—one for club information and one for contact information for the club presidents.

Create a desktop database, and save the database in your Access Chapter 1 folder as **Lastname_Firstname_1L_Student_Clubs** From your student data files, use the information in the Word document a01L_Clubs to create the first table and to enter two records. Name the table appropriately to include your name and 1L, and then append the 23 records from the Excel workbook a01L_Student_Clubs to your table. For the Club ID and President ID fields, add a description and change the field size.

Create a second table in the database by importing 25 records from the Excel workbook a01L_Club_Presidents, and name the table appropriately to include your name and 1L. For the State and Postal Code fields, add a description and change the field size. Be sure that the field data types are correct—recall that numbers that are not used in calculations should have a data type of Short Text. Be sure all of the data and field names display in each table.

Create a simple query based on the Clubs table that answers the question, *What is the club name, meeting day, meeting time, campus, and Room ID for all of the clubs?* Create a form based on the Clubs table, saving it with an appropriate name that includes your name and 1L. Create a report based on the Presidents table, saving it with an appropriate name that includes your name and 1L, that displays the president's last name (in ascending order), the president's first name, and the phone number of every president. Change the width of the three fields so that there is less space between them, but being sure that each record prints on a single line. Delete the page number from the report.

Create paper or electronic printouts of the two tables, the query, only Record 21 of the form, and the report as directed and being sure that each object prints on one page. Organize the objects on the Navigation Pane by Tables and Related Views, and be sure that all object names display fully. As directed, submit your database and the paper or electronic printouts of the five objects—two tables, one query, one form, and one report—that are the results of this project.

END | You have completed Project 1L

Build from Scratch

GO! Think Project 1M Faculty Training — Online

Build from Scratch

You and GO! Project 1N Personal Contacts — Online

Build from Scratch

GO! Cumulative Group Project Project 1O Bell Orchid Hotels — Online

Sort and Query a Database

GO! to Work Video A2

2

ACCESS 2013

PROJECT 2A

OUTCOMES
Sort and query a database.

OBJECTIVES

1. Open and Save an Existing Database
2. Create Table Relationships
3. Sort Records in a Table
4. Create a Query in Design View
5. Create a New Query from an Existing Query
6. Sort Query Results
7. Specify Criteria in a Query

PROJECT 2B

OUTCOMES
Create complex queries.

OBJECTIVES

8. Specify Numeric Criteria in a Query
9. Use Compound Criteria in a Query
10. Create a Query Based on More Than One Table
11. Use Wildcards in a Query
12. Create Calculated Fields in a Query
13. Calculate Statistics and Group Data in a Query
14. Create a Crosstab Query
15. Create a Parameter Query

In This Chapter

In this chapter, you will sort Access database tables and create and modify queries. To convert data into meaningful information, you must manipulate your data in a way that you can answer questions. One question might be: *Which students have a grade point average of 3.0 or higher?* By having this list of students, you could send information about scholarships or internships to those who meet the grade point average criteria. Queries are one of the most powerful tools in an Access database—a query not only answers questions, but it also provides data for meaningful reports.

The projects in this chapter relate to **Texas Lakes Community College**, which is located in the Austin, Texas, area. Its four campuses serve more than 30,000 students and offer more than 140 certificate programs and degrees. The college has a highly acclaimed Distance Education program and an extensive Workforce Development program. The college makes positive contributions to the community through cultural and athletic programs and has significant partnerships with businesses and nonprofit organizations. Popular fields of study include nursing and health care, solar technology, computer technology, and graphic design.

PROJECT

2A Instructors and Courses Database

MyITLab®
Project 2A Training

PROJECT ACTIVITIES

In Activities 2.01 through 2.17, you will assist Dr. Carolyn Judkins, dean of the Business Division at the Northeast Campus of Texas Lakes Community College, in locating information about instructors and courses in the division. Your completed database objects will look similar to Figure 2.1.

PROJECT FILES

For Project 2A, you will need the following file:
a02A_Instructors_Courses

You will save your database as:
Lastname_Firstname_2A_Instructors_Courses

PROJECT RESULTS

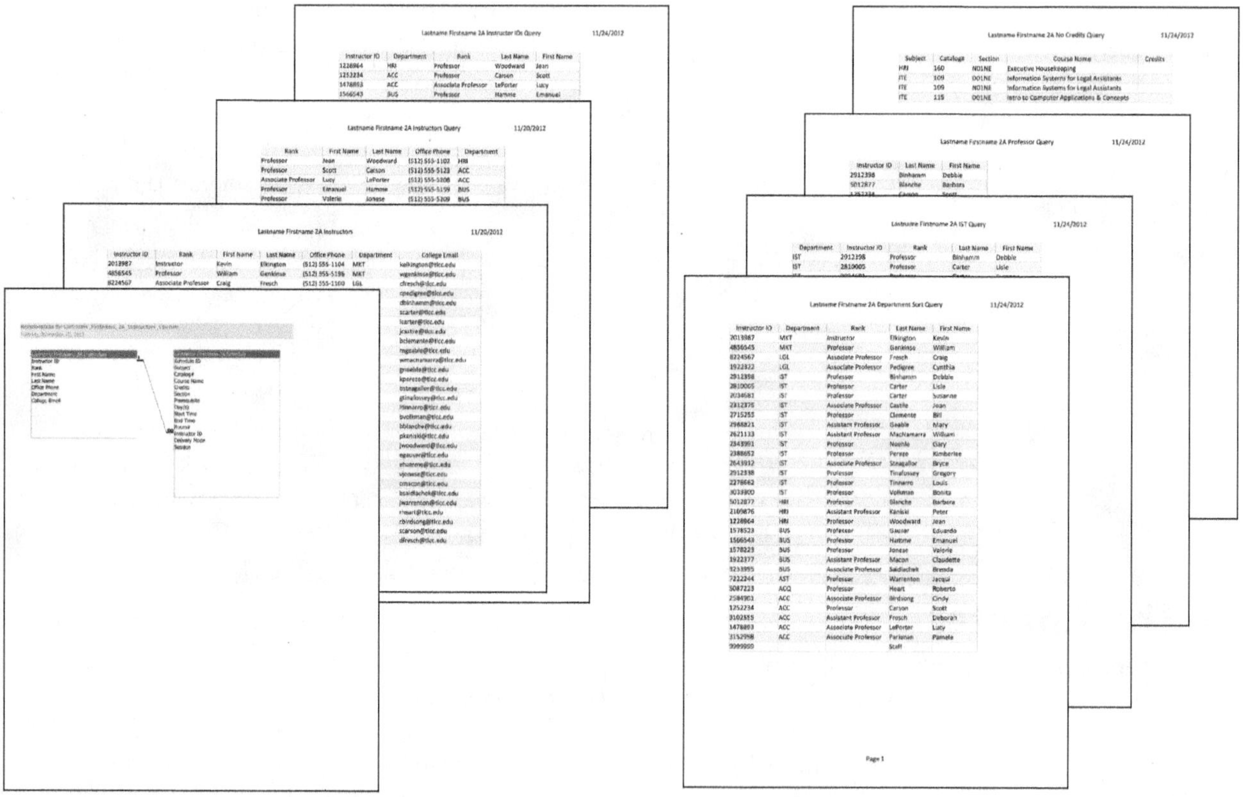

FIGURE 2.1 Project 2A Instructors and Courses

NOTE | **If You Are Using a Touchscreen**

- Tap an item to click it.
- Press and hold for a few seconds to right-click; release when the information or command displays.
- Touch the screen with two or more fingers and then pinch together to zoom in or stretch your fingers apart to zoom out.
- Slide your finger on the screen to scroll—slide left to scroll right and slide right to scroll left.
- Slide to rearrange—similar to dragging with a mouse.
- Swipe from edge: from right to display charms; from left to expose open apps, snap apps, or close apps; from top or bottom to show commands or close an app.
- Swipe to select—slide an item a short distance with a quick movement—to select an item and bring up commands, if any.

Objective 1 Open and Save an Existing Database

Video A2-1

There will be instances when you need to work with a database and still keep the original, unaltered version of the database. Like the other Microsoft Office 2013 applications, you can open a database file and save it with another name.

Activity 2.01 | Opening and Saving an Existing Database

1. **Start** Access. In the Access opening screen, click **Open Other Files**. Under **Open**, click **Computer**, and then on the right, click **Browse**. In the **Open** dialog box, navigate to the location where your student data files for this chapter are stored, and then double-click **a02A_Instructors_Courses** to open the database.

2. On the ribbon, click the **FILE tab**, and then click **Save As**. Under **File Types**, be sure **Save Database As** is selected. On the right, under **Database File Types**, be sure **Access Database** is selected, and then at the bottom of the screen, click **Save As**.

   The Access Database file type saves your database in a format that enables the database to be opened with Access 2007, Access 2010, or Access 2013. If you are sharing your database with individuals who have an earlier version of Access, you can save the database in a version that is compatible with that application, although some functionality might be lost if an earlier version of Access does not have the same feature as the later version of Access.

3. In the **Save As** dialog box, navigate to the location where you are saving your databases. Create a **New folder** named **Access Chapter 2**, and then **Open** the folder. Click in the **File name** box, drag to select the existing text, and using your own name, type **Lastname_Firstname_2A_Instructors_Courses** and then click **Save** or press Enter.

   Use this technique when you need to keep a copy of the original database file.

4. On the **Message Bar**, notice the **SECURITY WARNING**. In the **Navigation Pane**, notice that this database contains two table objects. Compare your screen with Figure 2.2.

FIGURE 2.2

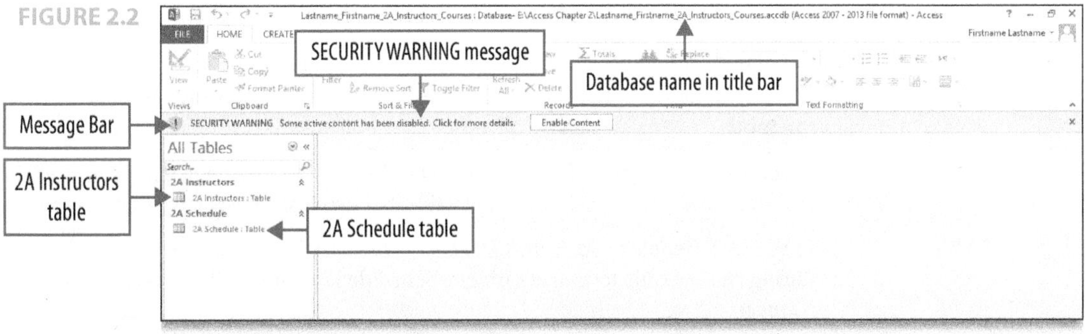

Activity 2.02 | Resolving Security Alerts and Renaming Tables

The ***Message Bar*** is the area directly below the ribbon that displays information such as security alerts when there is potentially unsafe, active content in an Office document that you open. Settings that determine the alerts that display on your Message Bar are set in the Access ***Trust Center***, an area in Access where you can view the security and privacy settings for your Access installation.

You may not be able to change the settings in the Trust Center, depending upon decisions made by your organization. To display the Trust Center, click the FILE tab, click Options, and then click Trust Center.

1. On the **Message Bar**, click **Enable Content**.

   When working with the student data files that accompany this textbook, repeat this action each time you see the security warning. Databases for this textbook are safe to use on your computer.

2. In the **Navigation Pane**, right-click the **2A Instructors** table, and then click **Rename**. With the table name selected and using your own name, type **Lastname Firstname 2A Instructors** and then press Enter to rename the table. Use the same technique to **Rename** the **2A Schedule** table to **Lastname Firstname 2A Schedule**

   Including your name in the table enables you and your instructor to easily identify your work, because Access includes the table name in the header of your paper or electronic printouts.

3. Point to the right edge of the **Navigation Pane** to display the ⟺ pointer. Drag to the right to increase the width of the pane until both table names display fully.

Objective 2 Create Table Relationships

Video A2-2

Access databases are relational databases because the tables in the database can relate—actually connect—to other tables through common fields. Recall that common fields are fields in two or more tables that store the same data; for example, a Student ID number may be stored in two tables in the same database.

After you have a table for each subject in your database, you must provide a way to connect the data in the tables when you need to obtain meaningful information from the stored data. To do this, create common fields in the related tables, and then define table ***relationships***. A relationship is an association that you establish between two tables based on common fields. After the relationship is established, you can create a query, form, or report that displays information from more than one table.

Activity 2.03 | Selecting the Tables and Common Field to Establish the Table Relationship

In this activity, you will select the two tables in the database that you will use to establish the table relationship and identify the common field that will connect the tables.

1. In the **Navigation Pane**, double-click your **2A Instructors** table to open it in the object window. Examine the fields in the table. Double-click your **2A Schedule** table, and examine the fields in the table.

   In the 2A Instructors table, *Instructor ID* is the primary key field, which ensures that each instructor has only one record in the table. No two instructors have the same Instructor ID.

   In the 2A Schedule table, *Schedule ID* is the primary key field. Every scheduled course section during an academic term has a unique Schedule ID. Some colleges refer to this as the *Section Number*.

2 In the **2A Schedule** table, scroll to display the **Instructor ID** field—third from last column—and then compare your screen with Figure 2.3.

Both the 2A Instructors table and the 2A Schedule table include the *Instructor ID* field, which is the common field of the two tables. Because *one* instructor can teach *many* different courses, *one* Instructor ID can be present *many* times in the 2A Schedule table. When the relationship is established, it will be a ***one-to-many relationship***, which is the most common type of relationship in a relational database.

FIGURE 2.3

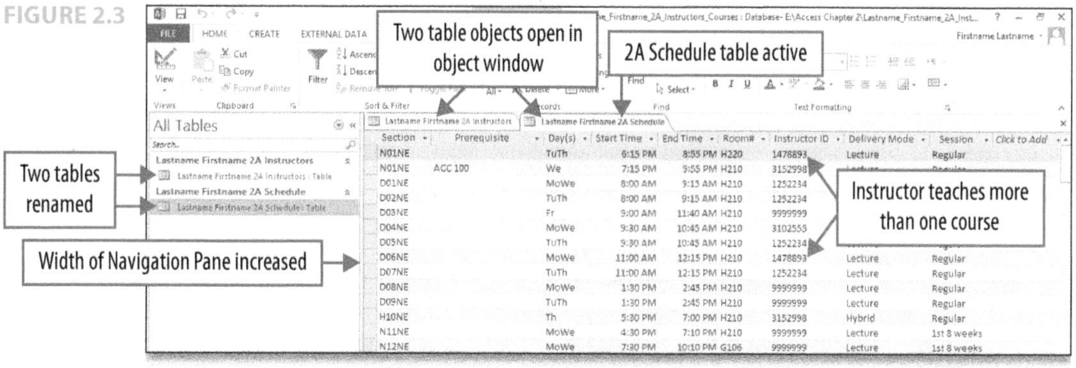

3 In the object window, right-click the **2A Schedule object tab**, and then click **Close All** to close both tables. On the ribbon, click the **DATABASE TOOLS tab**, and then in the **Relationships group**, click **Relationships**. Compare your screen with Figure 2.4.

You can close all of the open objects by right-clicking any object tab. The Show Table dialog box displays in the Relationships window. In the Show Table dialog box, the Tables tab displays the two tables that are in this database.

FIGURE 2.4

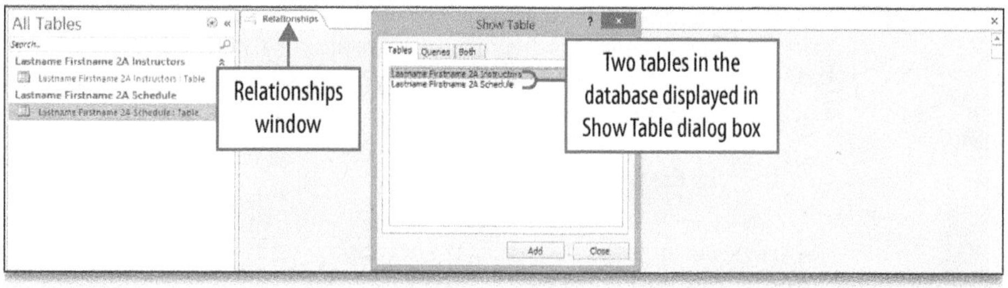

4 Point to the title bar of the **Show Table** dialog box, and then drag downward and to the right to move the dialog box away from the top of the **Relationships** window.

Moving the Show Table dialog box enables you to see the tables as they are added to the Relationships window.

5 In the **Show Table** dialog box, if necessary, click your **2A Instructors** table, and then click **Add**. In the **Show Table** dialog box, double-click your **2A Schedule** table to add it to the **Relationships** window. In the **Show Table** dialog box, click **Close**, and then compare your screen with Figure 2.5.

You can use either technique to add a table to the Relationships window. A ***field list***—a list of the field names in a table—for each of the two table objects displays, and each table's primary key is identified by the key icon. Although this database has only two tables, larger databases have many tables. Scroll bars in a field list indicate that there are fields that are not currently in view.

FIGURE 2.5

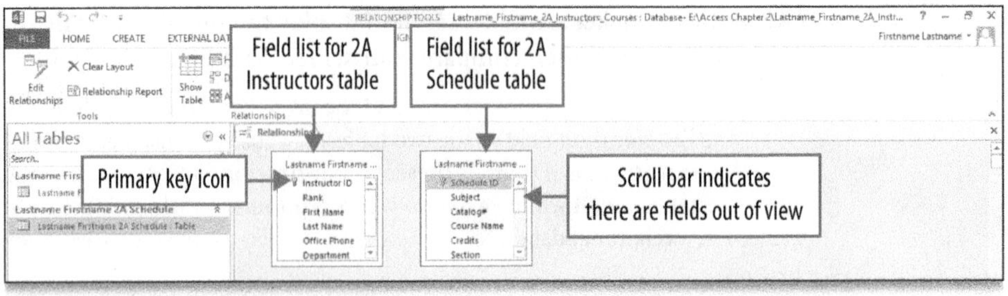

ALERT! **Are There More Than Two Field Lists in the Relationships Window?**

In the Show Table dialog box, if you double-click a table name more than one time, a duplicate field list displays in the Relationships window. To remove a field list from the Relationships window, right-click the title bar of the field list, and then click Hide Table. Alternatively, click anywhere in the field list, and then on the DESIGN tab, in the Relationships group, click Hide Table.

6 In the **2A Schedule** field list—the field list on the right—point to the title bar to display the [pointer icon] pointer. Drag the field list to the right until there are about two inches of space between the field lists.

7 In the **2A Instructors** field list—the field list on the left—point to the lower right corner of the field list to display the [resize icon] pointer, and then drag downward and to the right to increase the height and width of the field list until the entire name of the table in the title bar displays and all of the field names display.

This action enables you to see all of the available fields and removes the vertical scroll bar.

8 Use the same technique to resize the **2A Schedule** field list so that the table name and all of the field names display as shown in Figure 2.6.

Recall that *one* instructor can teach *many* scheduled courses. The arrangement of field lists in the Relationships window displays the *one table* on the left side and the *many table* on the right side. Recall also that the primary key in each table is the field that contains the data that uniquely identifies each record in the table. In the 2A Instructors table, each instructor is uniquely identified by the Instructor ID. In the 2A Schedule table, each scheduled course section is uniquely identified by the Schedule ID.

FIGURE 2.6

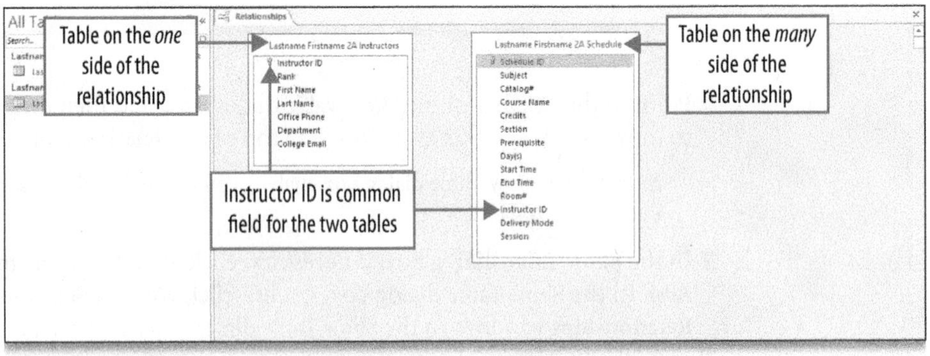

NOTE **The Field That Is Highlighted Does Not Matter**

After you rearrange the field lists in the Relationships window, the highlighted field name indicates the active field list, which is the list that you moved or resized last. This is of no consequence for this activity.

9 In the **2A Instructors** field list, point to **Instructor ID**, and then drag the field name downward and to the right into the **2A Schedule** field list until the pointer's arrow is on top of **Instructor ID**. Release the mouse button to display the **Edit Relationships** dialog box.

As you drag, a small graphic displays to indicate that you are dragging a field name from one field list to another. A table relationship works by matching data in two fields—the common field. In these two tables, the common field has the same name—*Instructor ID*. Common fields are not required to have the same name; however, they must have the same data type and field size.

ANOTHER WAY On the DESIGN tab, in the Tools group, click Edit Relationships. In the Edit Relationships dialog box, click Create New. In the Create New dialog box, designate the tables and fields that will create the relationship and click OK.

10 Point to the title bar of the **Edit Relationships** dialog box, and then drag the dialog box downward and to the right below the two field lists as shown in Figure 2.7.

By dragging the common field, you create the *one-to-many* relationship. In the 2A Instructors table, Instructor ID is the primary key. In the 2A Schedule table, Instructor ID is the ***foreign key*** field. The foreign key is the field in the related table used to connect to the primary key in another table. The field on the *one* side of the relationship is typically the primary key.

FIGURE 2.7

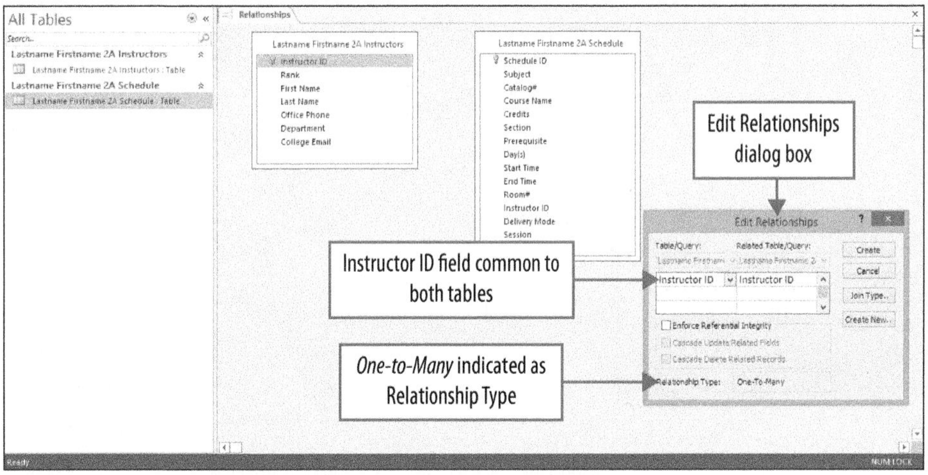

Activity 2.04 | Setting Relationship Options

In this activity, you will set relationship options that enable you to work with records in the two related tables.

1 In the **Edit Relationships** dialog box, click to select the **Enforce Referential Integrity** check box. Notice that the two options under **Enforce Referential Integrity** are now available.

Referential integrity is a set of rules that Access uses to ensure that the data between related tables is valid. Enforcing referential integrity ensures that an Instructor ID cannot be added to a course in the 2A Schedule table if the Instructor ID is *not* included in the 2A Instructors table. Similarly, enforcing referential integrity without selecting a cascade option below ensures that you cannot delete an instructor from the 2A Instructors table if there is a course that has been assigned to that instructor in the 2A Schedule table.

After selecting Enforce Referential Integrity, ***cascade options***—relationship options that enable you to update records in related tables when referential integrity is enforced—become available for use.

2 In the **Edit Relationships** dialog box, click to select the **Cascade Update Related Fields** check box.

The ***Cascade Update Related Fields*** option enables you to change the data in the primary key field for the table on the *one* side of the relationship, and updates that change to any fields in the related table that store the same data. For example, in the 2A Instructors table, if you change the data in the Instructor ID field for one instructor, Access automatically finds every scheduled course assigned to that instructor in the 2A Schedule table and changes the data in the common field, in this case, the Instructor ID field. Without this option, if you try to change the Instructor ID number for an instructor, an error message displays if there is a related record in the related table on the *many* side of the relationship.

3 In the **Edit Relationships** dialog box, click to select the **Cascade Delete Related Records** check box, and then compare your screen with Figure 2.8.

The ***Cascade Delete Related Records*** option enables you to delete a record in the table on the *one* side of the relationship and also delete all of the related records in related tables. For example, if an instructor retires or leaves the college and the courses that the instructor teaches must be canceled because no other instructor can be found, you can delete the instructor's record from the 2A Instructors table, and then all of the courses that are assigned to that instructor in the 2A Schedule table are also deleted. Without this option, an error message displays if you try to delete the instructor's record from the 2A Instructors table.

FIGURE 2.8

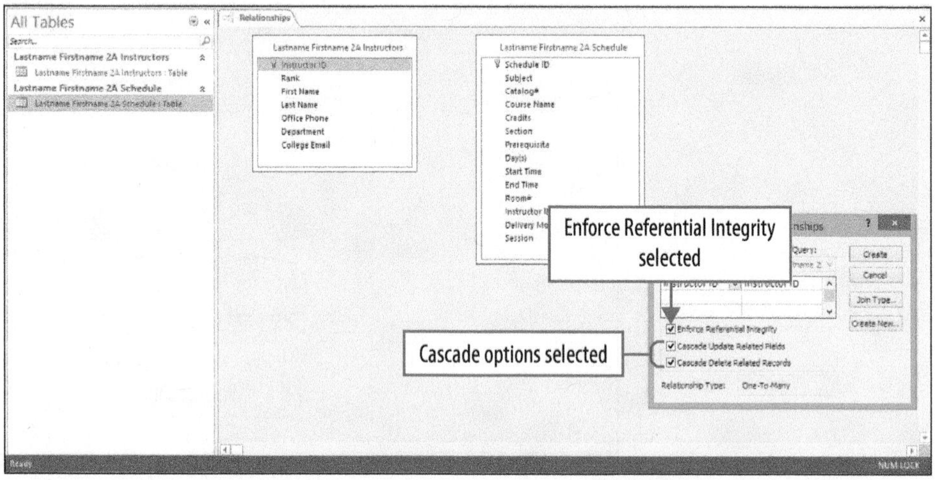

4 In the **Edit Relationships** dialog box, click **Create**, and then compare your screen with Figure 2.9.

The Edit Relationships dialog box closes and a ***join line***—the line connecting or joining the two tables—displays between the two field lists. The join line connects the primary key field—Instructor ID—in the 2A Instructors field list to the common field—Instructor ID—in the 2A Schedule field list. On the join line, *1* indicates the *one* side of the relationship, and the infinity symbol (∞) indicates the *many* side of the relationship. These symbols display when referential integrity is enforced.

FIGURE 2.9

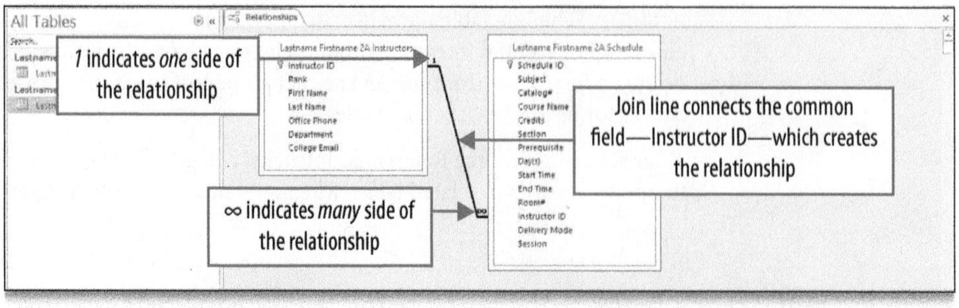

Activity 2.05 | Printing and Saving a Relationship Report

The Relationships window provides a map of how your database tables are related, and you can print and save this information as a report.

1. Under **RELATIONSHIP TOOLS**, on the **DESIGN tab**, in the **Tools group**, click **Relationship Report**.

   The report is created and displays in the object window in Print Preview.

2. On the **PRINT PREVIEW tab**, in the **Page Size group**, click **Margins**, and then click **Normal** to increase the margins slightly—some printers cannot print with narrow margins. Compare your screen with Figure 2.10. Create a paper or electronic printout of the relationship report as directed.

FIGURE 2.10

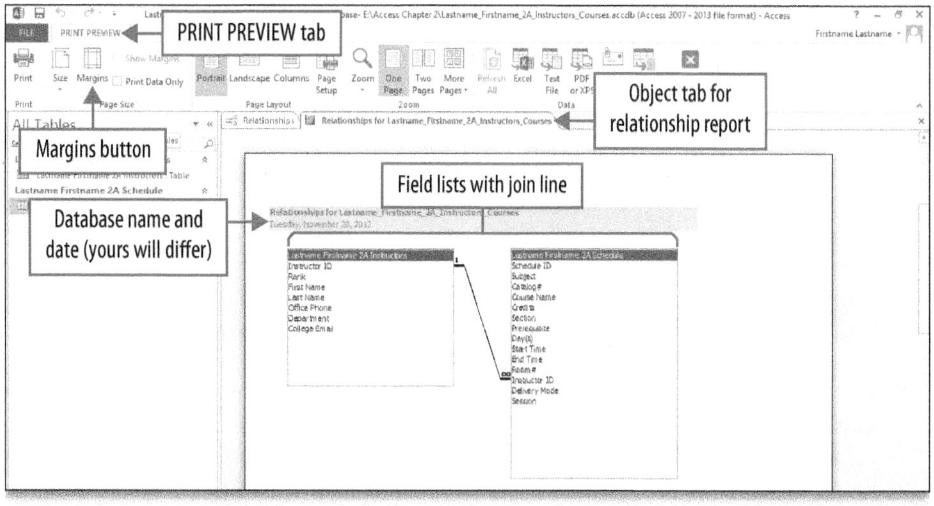

3. On the **Quick Access Toolbar**, click **Save** [Save icon]. In the **Save As** dialog box, click **OK** to accept the default report name.

   The report name displays in the Navigation Pane under *Unrelated Objects*. Because the report is just a map of the relationship between the tables, and not a report containing records from a table, it is not associated with or related to any tables.

4. In the object window, click **Close** [×] to close the report, and then **Close** [×] the **Relationships** window.

> **NOTE** **Close Print Preview and the Relationship Report**
>
> If you click Close Print Preview when the report is displayed in Print Preview, the Relationship Report displays in Design view in the object window. If this happens, you can Close the object while it is displayed in this view.

Activity 2.06 | Displaying Subdatasheet Records

When you open the table on the *one* side of the relationship, the related records from the table on the *many* side are available for you to view and to modify.

1. In the **Navigation Pane**, double-click your **2A Instructors** table to open it in the object window, and then **Close** [«] the **Navigation Pane**.

2 On the left side of the first record—*Instructor ID* of *1224567*—click [+], and then compare your screen with Figure 2.11.

The [+] symbol to the left of a record in a table indicates that *related* records may exist in another table. Click [+] to display the related records in a ***subdatasheet***. In the first record for *Craig Fresch*, you can see that related records exist in the 2A Schedule table—he is scheduled to teach five LGL (Legal) courses. The [+] symbol to the left of each record displays because you created a relationship between the two tables using the Instructor ID field—the common field.

When you click [+] to display the subdatasheet, the symbol changes to [−], an indication that the subdatasheet is expanded. Click [−] to collapse the subdatasheet.

FIGURE 2.11

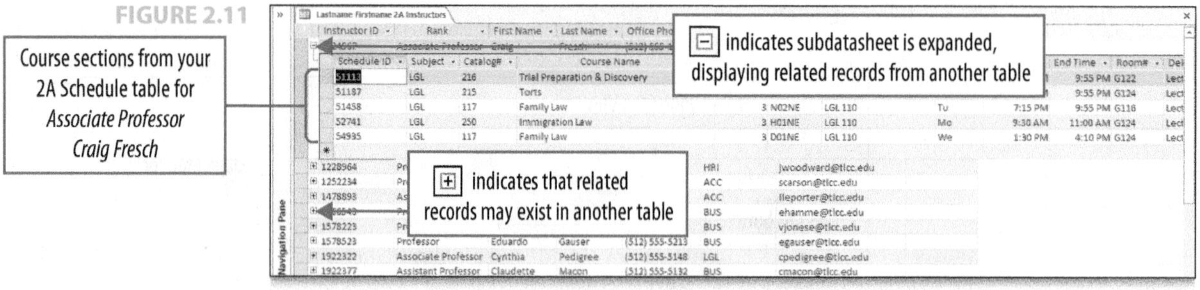

More Knowledge **Other Types of Relationships: One-to-One and Many-to-Many**

The type of relationship is determined by the placement of the primary key field. A one-to-one relationship exists between two tables when a record in one table is related to only one record in a second table. In this case, both tables use the same field as the primary key. This is most often used when data is placed in a separate table because access to that information is restricted; for example, using an Employee ID field as the primary key field, there is one table for contact information and a second table with payroll information.

A many-to-many relationship between tables exists when many records in one table are related to many records in another table. For example, many students can enroll in many courses. To create a many-to-many relationship, you must create a third table that contains the primary key fields from both tables. In the Relationships window, you create a join line from this table to the other two tables. In effect, you create multiple one-to-many relationships.

Activity 2.07 | Testing Cascade Options

Recall that cascade options enable you to make changes to records on the *one* side table of the relationship and update or delete records in the table on the *many* side of the relationship. In this activity, you will change the data in the Instructor ID field—the primary key field—for one instructor, and then delete all of the records associated with another instructor from both tables.

1 In the subdatasheet for the first record—*Instructor ID* of *1224567*—notice that the first course that this instructor is scheduled to teach has a *Schedule ID* of *51113—LGL 216*. In the **2A Instructors** table, to the left of the first record, click [−] to collapse the subdatasheet.

2 If necessary, in the first record, in the **Instructor ID** field, select the data—**1224567**. Type **8224567** and then press [↓] to save the record.

Because you enabled Cascade Update Related Fields in the Edit Relationships dialog box, you can change the data in the Instructor ID field—the primary key field—and all records in the 2A Schedule table that store that Instructor ID number are automatically updated. If this option is not enabled, an error message displays.

3 **Open** [»] the **Navigation Pane**. In the **Navigation Pane**, double-click your **2A Schedule** table to open it, and then **Close** [«] the **Navigation Pane**.

ANOTHER WAY Press [F11] to open or close the Navigation Pane.

4 Scroll to locate the record with a **Schedule ID** of **51113**—*LGL 216*. If necessary, scroll to the right to display the **Instructor ID** field, and notice that for this record, the **Instructor ID** is **8224567**. Compare your screen with Figure 2.12.

The Cascade Update Related Fields option enables you to change the data in the primary key field in your 2A Instructors table, and the five related records for *Craig Fresch* in the 2A Schedule table were updated to store his new Instructor ID of *8224567*.

FIGURE 2.12

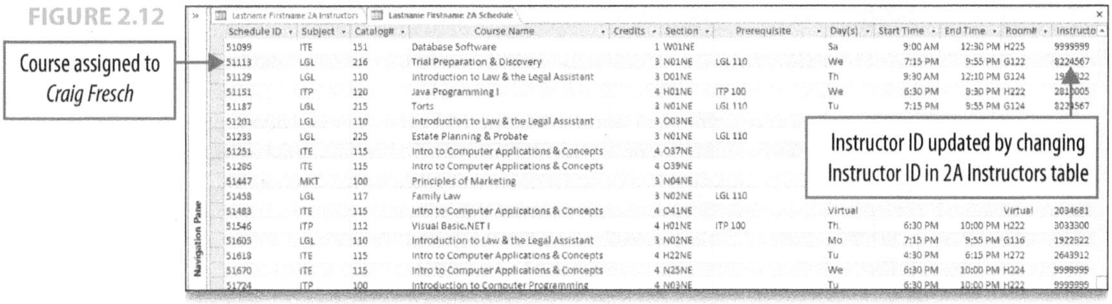

5 **Close** [×] your **2A Schedule** table. In your **2A Instructors** table, scroll to display the last few records. On the left side of the record for **Instructor ID** of **6145288**—*Professor Ivey Clarke*—click [+] to display the subdatasheet. Notice that this instructor is scheduled to teach two courses—*Schedule IDs* of *42837* and *42930*.

6 Click [−] to collapse the subdatasheet. For the same record—*Instructor ID* of *6145288*—point to the record selector box to display the [→] pointer, and then click to select the record. On the **HOME tab**, in the **Records group**, click **Delete**.

A message displays warning you that this record and related records in related tables will be deleted. The record you selected does not display in the table, and the next record is selected. Because you enabled Cascade Delete Related Records, you are able to delete the record for Professor Ivey Clarke and delete the two courses she is scheduled to teach from the 2A Schedule table—with no error message.

ANOTHER WAY With the record selected, press [Del]; or with the record selected, right-click within the record, and then click Delete Record.

7 In the message box, click **Yes**.

The record for *Instructor ID* of *6145288* is deleted, and the two courses she was scheduled to teach are deleted from the 2A Schedule table. On the Quick Access Toolbar, Undo is unavailable—if you mistakenly delete a record and its related records, you must enter them again in both tables.

8 **Open** [»] the **Navigation Pane**, open your **2A Schedule** table, and then **Close** [«] the **Navigation Pane**. Scroll through the records and notice that the records for a **Schedule ID** of **42837** and **42930** have been deleted from the table.

The Cascade Delete Related Records option in the Edit Relationships dialog box enables you to delete a record in the table on the *one* side of the relationship—2A Instructors—and simultaneously delete the records in the table on the *many* side of the relationship—2A Schedule—that are related to the deleted record.

9 In the object window, right-click either **object tab**, and then click **Close All** to close both tables.

Objective 3 Sort Records in a Table

Video A2-3

Sorting is the process of arranging data in a specific order based on the value in a field. For example, you can sort the names in your contact list alphabetically by each person's last name, or you can sort your music collection by the artist. Initially, records in an Access table display in the order they are entered into the table. After you close the table and reopen it, the records display in order by the primary key field.

Activity 2.08 | Sorting Records in a Table in Ascending or Descending Order

In this activity, you will determine the departments of the faculty in the Business Division by sorting the data. Data can be sorted in either ***ascending order*** or ***descending order***. Ascending order sorts text alphabetically (A to Z) and sorts numbers from the lowest number to the highest number. Descending order sorts text in reverse alphabetical order (Z to A) and sorts numbers from the highest number to the lowest number.

1. **Open** [»] the **Navigation Pane**, open your **2A Instructors** table, and then **Close** [«] the **Navigation Pane**. Notice that the records in the table are sorted in ascending order by the **Instructor ID** field, which is the primary key field.

2. In the field names row, click the **Department arrow**, click **Sort A to Z**, and then compare your screen with Figure 2.13.

   To sort records in a table, click the arrow to the right of the field name in the column on which you want to sort, and then click the sort order. After a field is sorted, a small arrow in the field name box indicates the sort order. For the Department field, the small arrow points upward, indicating an ascending sort; on the ribbon, Ascending is selected.

   The records display in alphabetical order by the Department field. Because the department names are now grouped together, you can quickly scroll through the table to see the instructors for each department. The first record in the table has no data in the Department field because the *Instructor ID* of *9999999* is reserved for *Staff*, a designation that is used until a scheduled course has been assigned to a specific instructor.

ANOTHER WAY

Click in the field in any record, and then on the HOME tab, in the Sort & Filter group, click Ascending; or right-click in the field in any record, and then click Sort A to Z.

FIGURE 2.13

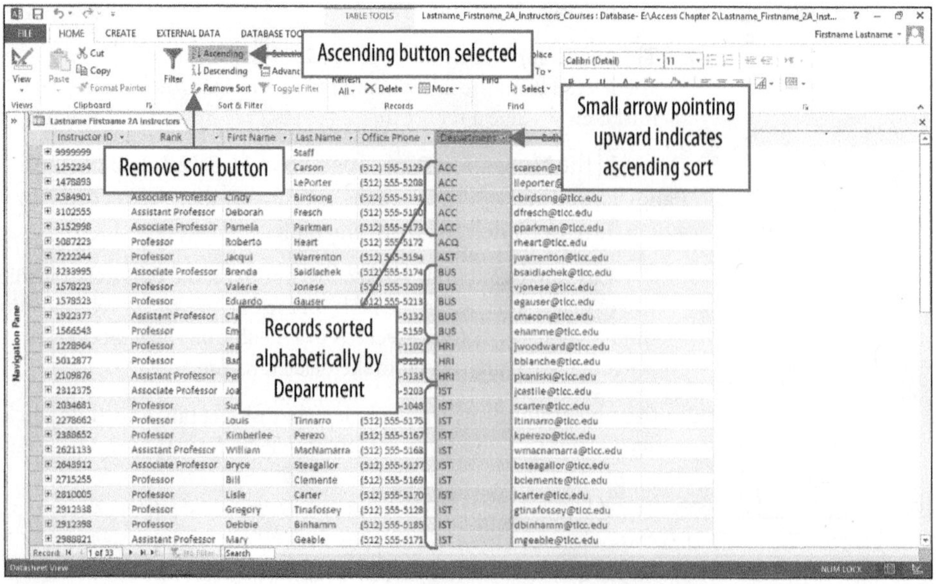

3 On the **HOME tab**, in the **Sort & Filter group**, click **Remove Sort** to clear the sort and to return the records to the default sort order, which is by the primary key field—**Instructor ID**.

4 Click the **Last Name arrow**, and then click **Sort Z to A**.

The records in the table are sorted by the Last Name field in reverse alphabetical order. The small arrow in the field name box points downward, indicating a descending sort. On the ribbon, Descending is selected.

5 In the **Sort & Filter group**, click **Remove Sort** to clear the sort.

Activity 2.09 | Sorting Records in a Table on Multiple Fields

To sort a table on two or more fields, first identify the fields that will act as the ***outermost sort field*** and the ***innermost sort field***. The outermost sort field is the first level of sorting, and the innermost sort field is the second level of sorting. To alphabetize a table by Last Name and then First Name—also called First Name within Last Name—the Last Name field is identified as the outermost sort field. If there are duplicate last names, the records should be further sorted by the First Name field—the innermost sort field. For tables, you sort the *innermost* field *first* and then sort the outermost field.

In this activity, you will sort the records by Last Name—innermost sort field—within the Department—outermost sort field.

1 In the **Last Name** field, click in any record. On the ribbon, on the **HOME tab**, in the **Sort & Filter group**, click **Ascending**.

The records are sorted in ascending order by Last Name—the innermost sort field.

2 In any record, point in the **Department** field, right-click, and then click **Sort Z to A**. Compare your screen with Figure 2.14.

The records are sorted in descending order first by Department—the outermost sort field. Within each Department grouping, the records are sorted in ascending order by Last Name—the innermost sort field. Records can be sorted on multiple fields using both ascending and descending order.

FIGURE 2.14

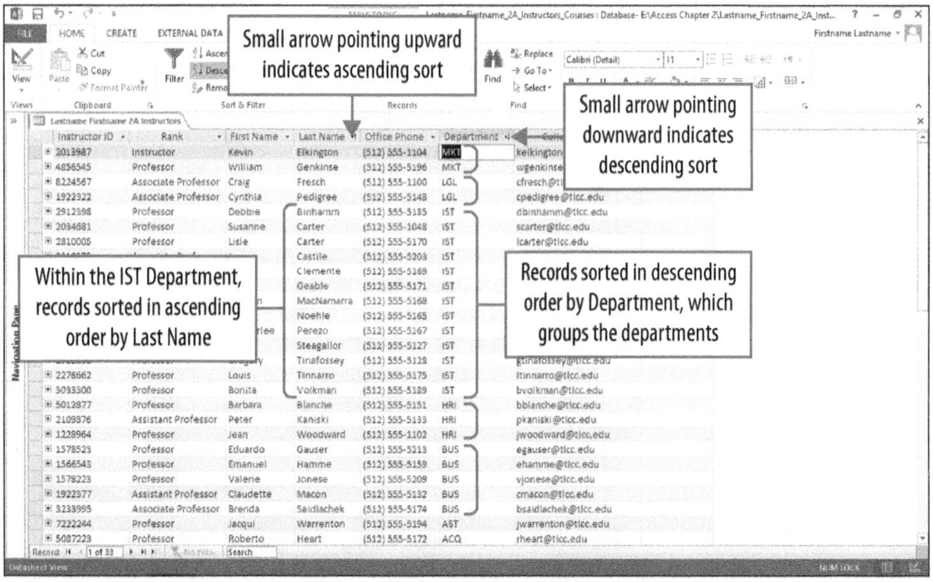

3 On the ribbon, click the **FILE tab**, click **Print**, and then click **Print Preview**. On the **PRINT PREVIEW tab**, in the **Page Layout group**, click **Landscape**. In the **Zoom group**, click **Two Pages**, and notice that the table will print on two pages.

4 In the **Print group**, click **Print**. In the **Print** dialog box, under **Print Range**, click in the **From** box, type **1** and then click in the **To** box. Type **1** to print only the first page. If directed to submit a paper printout, click **OK**. If directed to create an electronic printout, in the **Print** dialog box, click **Cancel**. On the **PRINT PREVIEW tab**, in the **Data group**, click **PDF or XPS**, click **Options**, and then under **Range**, click the **Pages** option button, click **OK**, and then click **Publish**.

5 In the object window, **Close** [×] the table. In the message box, click **Yes** to save the changes to the sort order.

6 **Open** [»] the **Navigation Pane**, double-click your **2A Instructors** table to open it, and then **Close** [«] the **Navigation Pane**. Notice that the table displays the sort order you specified.

7 On the **HOME tab**, in the **Sort & Filter group**, click **Remove Sort**. **Close** [×] the table, and in the message box, click **Yes** to save the table with the sort removed.

Generally, tables are not stored with the data sorted. Instead, queries are created that sort the data, and then reports are created to display the sorted data.

Objective 4 Create a Query in Design View

Video A2-4

Recall that a select query is a database object that retrieves (selects) specific data from one or more tables and then displays the specified data in a table in Datasheet view. A query answers a question, such as *Which instructors teach courses in the IST department?* Unless a query has already been designed to ask this question, you must create a new query.

Database users rarely need to see all of the records in all of the tables. That is why a query is so useful; it creates a ***subset*** of records—a portion of the total records—according to your specifications and then displays only those records.

Activity 2.10 Creating a New Select Query in Design View

Previously, you created a query using the Query Wizard. To create more complex queries, use Query Design view. The table (or tables) from which a query selects its data is referred to as the ***data source***.

1 On the ribbon, click the **CREATE tab**, and then in the **Queries group**, click **Query Design**. Compare your screen with Figure 2.15.

A new query opens in Design view, and the Show Table dialog box displays, which lists both tables in the database.

FIGURE 2.15

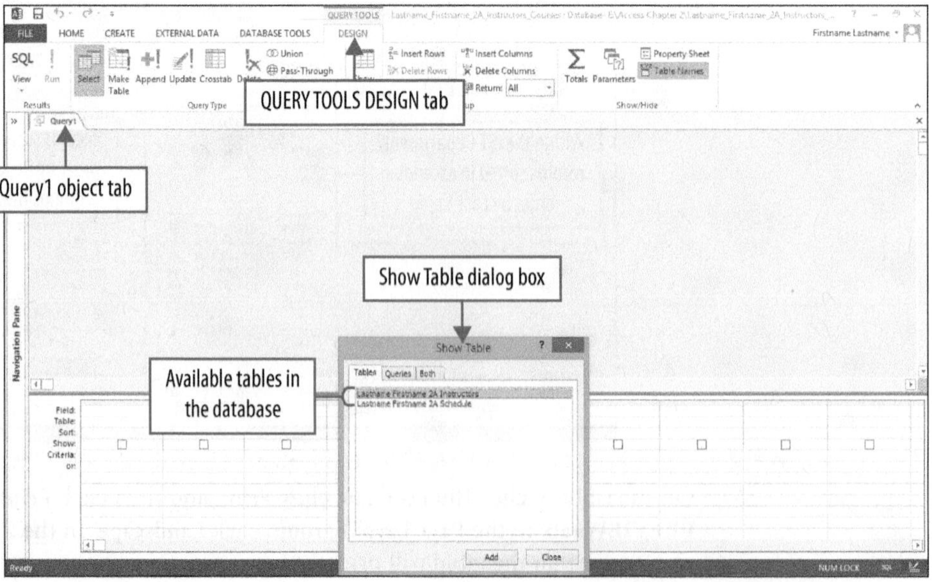

2 In the **Show Table** dialog box, double-click **2A Instructors**, and then, in the dialog box, click **Close.**

A field list for your 2A Instructors table displays in the upper area of the query window. Instructor ID is the primary key field in this table.

The query window has two parts: the upper area called the ***table area*** that displays the field lists for tables that are used in the query, and the lower area called the ***design grid*** that displays the design of the query.

ALERT! **Is There More Than One Field List in the Table Area?**

If you double-click a table more than one time, a duplicate field list displays in the table area of the query window. To remove a field list from the query window, right-click the title bar of the field list, and then click Remove Table.

3 Point to the lower right corner of the field list to display the [pointer] pointer, and then drag downward and to the right to resize the field list, displaying all of the field names and the entire table name. In the **2A Instructors** field list, double-click **Rank**, and then look at the design grid.

The Rank field name displays in the design grid in the Field row. You limit the fields that display in the query results by placing only the desired field names in the design grid.

4 In the **2A Instructors** field list, point to **First Name**, drag the field name down into the design grid until the [pointer] pointer displays in the **Field** row in the second column, and then release the mouse button. Compare your screen with Figure 2.16.

This is a second way to add field names to the design grid. As you drag the field, a small rectangular shape attaches to the mouse pointer. When you release the mouse button, the field name displays in the Field row.

FIGURE 2.16

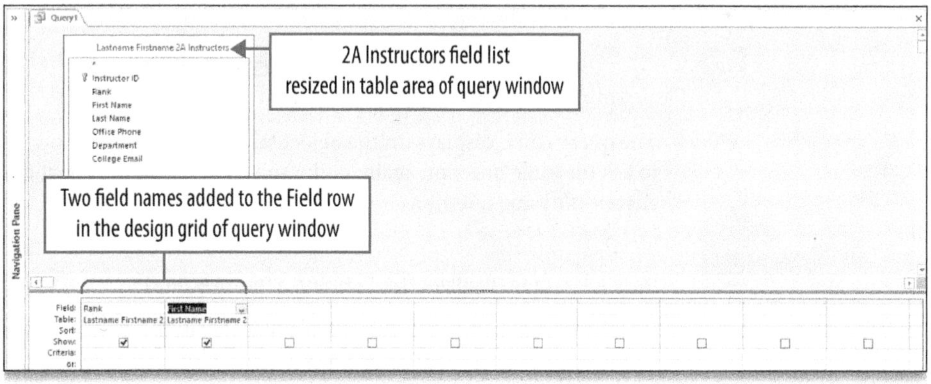

5 In the design grid, in the **Field** row, click in the third column, and then click the **arrow** that displays. From the list, click **Last Name** to add the field to the design grid.

This is a third way to add field names to the design grid.

6 Using one of the three techniques you just practiced, add the **Office Phone** field to the fourth column and the **Department** field to the fifth column in the design grid.

ALERT! **Is There a Duplicate Field Name or an Incorrect Field Name in the Design Grid?**

If you double-click a field name more than one time, a duplicate field name displays in the design grid. To remove a duplicate field name, in the design grid, in the Field row, right-click the duplicate field name, and then click Cut. Use this same method to delete a field name that you placed in the design grid by mistake. As you progress in your study of query design, you will learn alternate ways to delete field names from the design grid.

Activity 2.11 | Running, Saving, Printing, and Closing a Query

After you design a query, you ***run*** the query to display the results. When you run a query, Access looks at the records in the table (or tables) you have included in the query, finds the records that match the specified conditions (if any), and displays only those records in a datasheet. Only the fields that you have added to the design grid display in the query results. The query always runs using the current table or tables, presenting the most up-to-date information.

1. Under **QUERY TOOLS**, on the **DESIGN tab**, in the **Results group**, click **Run**, and then compare your screen with Figure 2.17.

   This query answers the question, *What is the rank, first name, last name, office phone number, and department of all of the instructors in the 2A Instructors table?* A query is a subset of the records in the table, arranged in Datasheet view, using the fields and conditions that you specify in the design grid. The five fields you specified in the design grid display in columns, and the records from the 2A Instructors table display in rows.

ANOTHER WAY On the DESIGN tab, in the Results group, click the top portion of the View button, which runs the query by switching to Datasheet view.

FIGURE 2.17

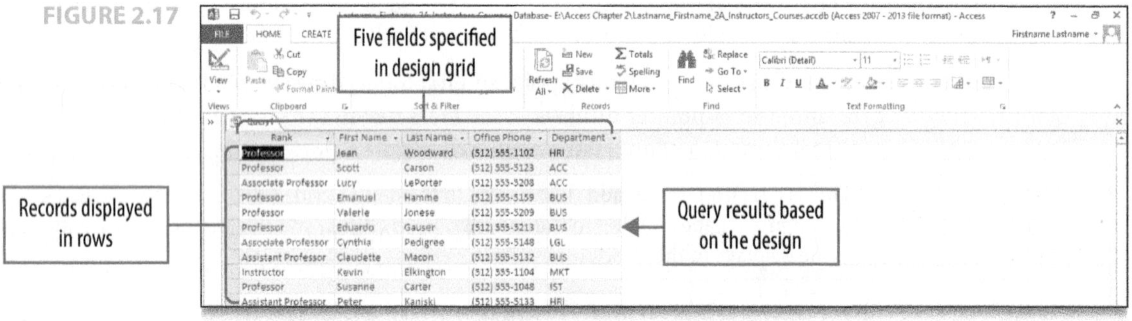

2. On the **Quick Access Toolbar**, click **Save**. In the **Save As** dialog box, type **Lastname Firstname 2A Instructors Query** and then click **OK**.

   The query name displays on the object tab in the object window. Save your queries if you are likely to ask the same question again; doing so will save you the effort of creating the query again to answer the same question.

ALERT! **Does a Message Display After Entering a Query Name?**

Query names are limited to 64 characters. For all projects, if you have a long last name or first name that results in your query name exceeding the 64-character limit, use your first initial instead of your first name.

3. On the ribbon, click the **FILE tab**, click **Print**, and then click **Print Preview**. Create a paper or electronic printout as directed, and then click **Close Print Preview**.

   Queries answer questions and gather information from the data in tables. Typically, queries are created as a basis for a report, but query results can be printed just like any table of data.

4. **Close** the query. **Open** the **Navigation Pane**, and then notice that your **2A Instructors Query** object displays under your **2A Instructors** table object.

   The new query name displays in the Navigation Pane under the table with which it is related—the 2A Instructors table, which is the data source. Only the design of the query is saved; the records reside in the table object. Each time you open a query, Access runs it again and displays the results based on the data stored in the data source. Thus, the results of the query always reflect the most up-to-date information.

Objective 5 Create a New Query from an Existing Query

Video A2-5

You can create a new query from scratch, or you can copy an existing query and modify the design to answer another question. Using an existing query saves you time if your new query uses all or some of the same fields and conditions in an existing query.

Activity 2.12 Copying an Existing Query

1 In the **Navigation Pane**, right-click your **2A Instructors Query**, and then click **Copy**.

ANOTHER WAY To create a copy of the query, in the Navigation Pane, click the query name to select it. On the HOME tab, in the Clipboard group, click Copy.

2 In the **Navigation Pane**, point to a blank area, right-click, and then click **Paste**.

The Paste As dialog box displays, which enables you to name the copied query.

ANOTHER WAY On the HOME tab, in the Clipboard group, click Paste.

3 In the **Paste As** dialog box, type **Lastname Firstname 2A Instructor IDs Query** and then click **OK**.

A new query, based on a copy of your 2A Instructors Query is created and displays in the Navigation Pane under its data source—your 2A Instructors table object.

4 In the **Navigation Pane**, double-click your **2A Instructor IDs Query** to run the query and open the query results in **Datasheet** view. **Close** « the **Navigation Pane**.

Activity 2.13 Modifying the Design of a Query

1 On the **HOME tab**, in the **Views group**, click the top portion of the **View** button to switch to **Design** view.

ANOTHER WAY On the HOME tab, in the Views group, click the View arrow, and then click Design View; or on the right side of the status bar, click Design View. If the query is not open, in the Navigation Pane, right-click the query name, and then click Design View.

2 In the design grid, point to the thin gray selection bar above the **Office Phone** field name to display the ↓ pointer, and then compare your screen with Figure 2.18.

FIGURE 2.18

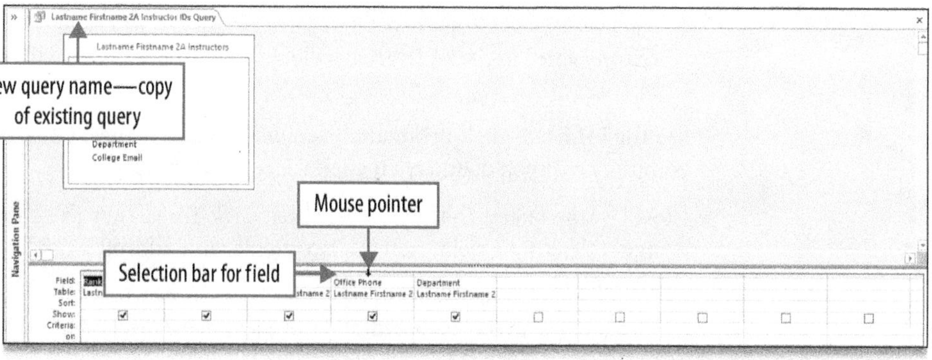

3 With the [↓] pointer displayed in the selection bar above the **Office Phone** field name, click to select the column, and then press [Del].

This action deletes the field from the query design only—it has no effect on the field in the data source—2A Instructors table. The Department field moves to the left. Similarly, by using the selection bar, you can drag to select multiple fields and delete them at one time.

ANOTHER WAY In the design grid, click in the field name. On the DESIGN tab, in the Query Setup group, click Delete Columns; or right-click the field name, and then click Cut; or select the column, and on the HOME tab, in the Records group, click Delete.

4 Point to the selection bar above the **First Name** column, and then click to select the column. In the selected column, point to the selection bar, hold down the left mouse button to display the [pointer] pointer, and then drag to the right until a dark vertical line displays on the right side of the **Last Name** column. Release the mouse button to position the **First Name** field in the third column.

To rearrange fields in a query, first select the field to move, and then drag it to a new position in the design grid.

5 Using the technique you just practiced, move the **Department** field to the left of the **Rank** field.

6 From the field list, drag the **Instructor ID** field down to the first column in the design grid until the [pointer] pointer displays, and then release the mouse button. Compare your screen with Figure 2.19.

The Instructor ID field displays in the first column, and the remaining four fields move to the right. Use this method to insert a field to the left of a field already displayed in the design grid.

FIGURE 2.19

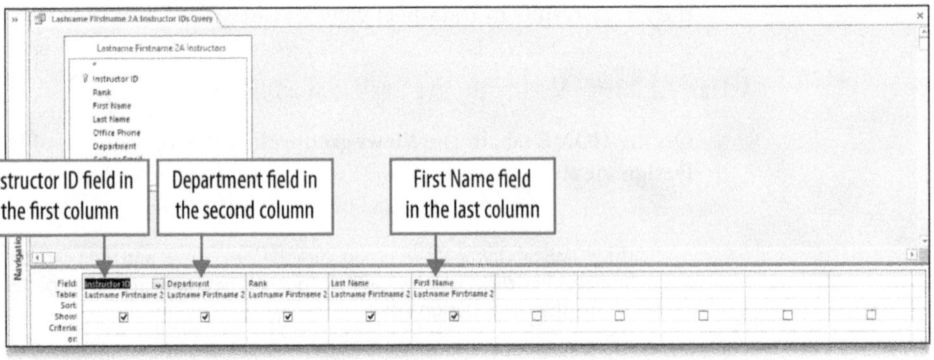

7 On the **DESIGN tab**, in the **Results group**, click **Run**.

This query answers the question, *What is the instructor ID, department, rank, last name, and first name of every instructor in the 2A Instructors table?* The results of the query are a subset of the records stored in the 2A Instructors table. The records are sorted by the table's primary key field—Instructor ID.

8 On the **FILE tab**, click **Print**, and then click **Print Preview**. Create a paper or electronic printout as directed, and then click **Close Print Preview**.

9 **Close** [×] the query. In the message box, click **Yes** to save the changes to the query design—deleting a field, moving two fields, and adding a field. **Open** [»] the **Navigation Pane**.

The query is saved and closed, and the query name displays in the Navigation Pane under the related table. Recall that only the *design* of the query is saved; the records reside in the related table.

Objective 6 Sort Query Results

Video A2-6

You can sort the results of a query in ascending or descending order in either Datasheet view or Design view. Use Design view if your query results should always display in a specified sort order or if you intend to use the sorted results in a report.

Activity 2.14 | Sorting Query Results

In this activity, you will copy an existing query and then sort the query results by using the Sort row in Design view.

1. In the **Navigation Pane**, right-click your **2A Instructor IDs Query**, and then click **Copy**. In the **Navigation Pane**, point to a blank area, right-click, and then click **Paste**.

2. In the **Paste As** dialog box, type **Lastname Firstname 2A Department Sort Query** and then click **OK**. Increase the width of the **Navigation Pane** so that the names of all of the objects display fully.

   A new query is created based on a copy of your 2A Instructor IDs Query; that is, the new query includes the same fields in the same order as the query that you copied.

3. In the **Navigation Pane**, right-click your **2A Department Sort Query**, and then click **Design View**. **Close** « the **Navigation Pane**.

   Use this technique to display the query in Design view if you are redesigning the query. Recall that if you double-click a query name in the Navigation Pane, Access runs the query and displays the query results.

4. In the design grid, in the **Sort** row, under **Last Name**, click to display the insertion point and an arrow. Click the **arrow**, click **Ascending**, and then compare your screen with Figure 2.20.

FIGURE 2.20

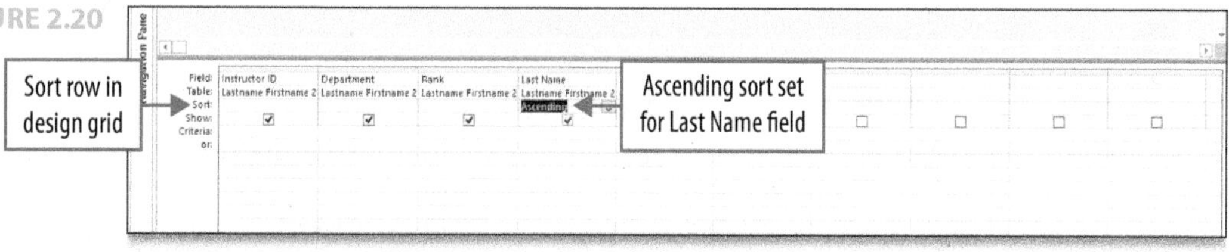

5. On the **DESIGN tab**, in the **Results group**, click **Run**.

   In the query results, the records are sorted in ascending order by the Last Name field, and two instructors have the same last name of *Carter—Susanne* and *Lisle*.

6. On the **HOME tab**, in the **Views group**, click the top of the **View** button to switch to **Design** view.

7. In the design grid, click in the **Sort** row under **First Name**, click the **arrow**, and then click **Ascending**. **Run** the query.

   In the query results, the records are sorted first by the Last Name field. If two instructors have the same last name, then those records are sorted by the First Name field. The two instructors with the same last name of *Carter* are sorted by their first names, and the two records with the same last name of *Fresch* are sorted by their first names.

8 Switch to **Design** view. In the design grid, click in the **Sort** row under **Department**, click the **arrow**, and then click **Descending**. **Run** the query, and then compare your screen with Figure 2.21.

In Design view, fields with a Sort setting are sorted from left to right. That is, the sorted field on the left becomes the outermost sort field, and the sorted field on the right becomes the innermost sort field. Thus, the records in this query are sorted first in descending order by the Department field—the leftmost sort field. Then, within each department, the records are sorted in ascending order by the Last Name field. And, finally, within each duplicate last name, the records are sorted in ascending order by the First Name field.

If you run a query and the sorted results are not what you intended, be sure the fields are displayed from left to right according to the groupings that you desire.

FIGURE 2.21

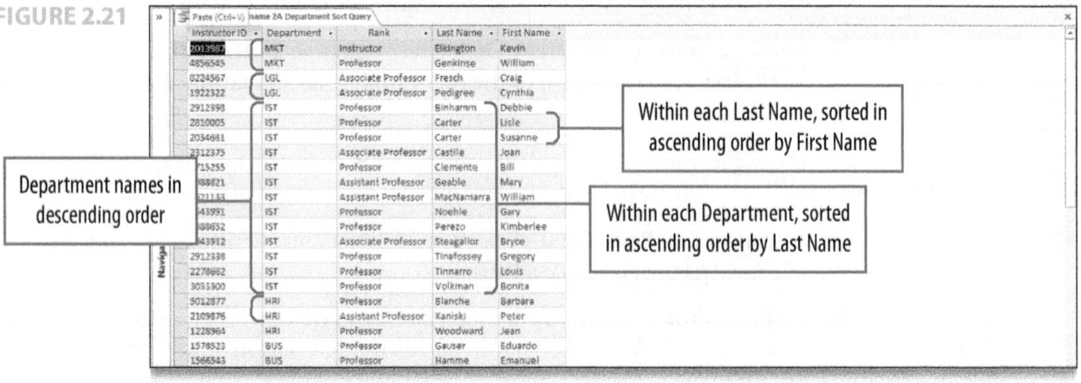

9 Display the query results in **Print Preview**. Create a paper or electronic printout as directed, and then click **Close Print Preview**. **Close** [×] the query. In the message box, click **Yes** to save the changes to the query design.

More Knowledge **Sorting in Design View or Datasheet View**

If you add a sort order to the *design* of a query, it remains as a permanent part of the query design. If you use the sort buttons in Datasheet view, the sort order will override the sort order of the query design and can be saved as part of the query. A sort order designated in Datasheet view does not display in the Sort row of the query design grid. As with sorting tables, in Datasheet view, a small arrow displays to the right of the field name to indicate the sort order of the field.

Objective 7 Specify Criteria in a Query

Video A2-7

Queries locate information in a table based on ***criteria*** that you specify as part of the query design. Criteria are conditions that identify the specific records that you are looking for. Criteria enable you to ask a more specific question; therefore, you will get a more specific result. For example, to find out how many instructors are in the IST department, limit the results to display only that specific department by entering criteria in the design grid.

Activity 2.15 | Specifying Text Criteria in a Query

In this activity, you will assist Dean Judkins by creating a query to answer the question, *How many instructors are in the IST Department?*

1 On the ribbon, click the **CREATE tab**, and then in the **Queries group**, click **Query Design**.

2 In the **Show Table** dialog box, double-click your **2A Instructors** table to add it to the table area, and then **Close** the **Show Table** dialog box.

3 By dragging the lower right corner downward and to the right, resize the field list to display all of the field names and the table name. Add the following fields to the design grid in the order given: **Department, Instructor ID, Rank, Last Name,** and **First Name.**

4 In the design grid, click in the **Criteria** row under **Department,** type **IST** and then press Enter. Compare your screen with Figure 2.22.

Access places quotation marks around the criteria to indicate that this is a ***text string***—a sequence of characters. Use the Criteria row to specify the criteria that will limit the results of the query to your exact specifications. The criteria is not case sensitive; you can type *ist* instead of *IST*.

FIGURE 2.22

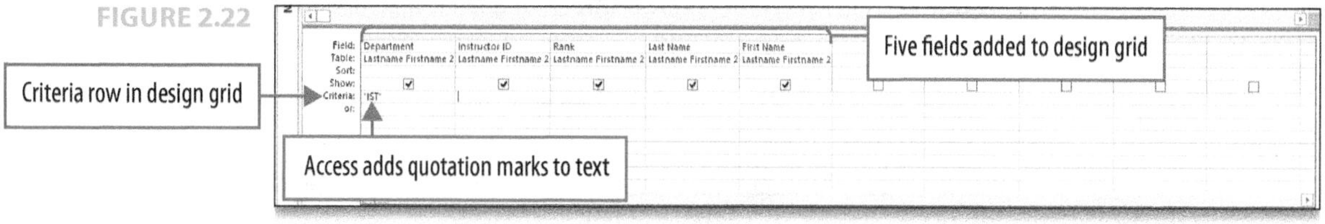

NOTE **Pressing Enter After Adding Criteria**

After adding criteria, when you press Enter or click in another column or row in the query design grid, you can see how Access alters the criteria so it can interpret what you have typed. Sometimes there is no change, such as when you add criteria to a field that stores a numeric or currency value. Other times, Access capitalizes a letter or adds quotation marks, words, or other symbols to clarify the criteria. Pressing Enter after adding criteria has no effect on the query results; it is used here to help you see how the program behaves.

5 In the design grid, click in the **Sort** row under **Last Name,** click the **arrow,** and then click **Ascending.** Click in the **Sort** row under **First Name,** click the **arrow,** and then click **Ascending.**

6 **Run** the query, and then compare your screen with Figure 2.23.

Thirteen records display. There are 13 instructors in the IST Department; or, more specifically, there are 13 records that have *IST* in the Department field. The records are sorted in ascending order, first by the Last Name field and then by the First Name field.

FIGURE 2.23

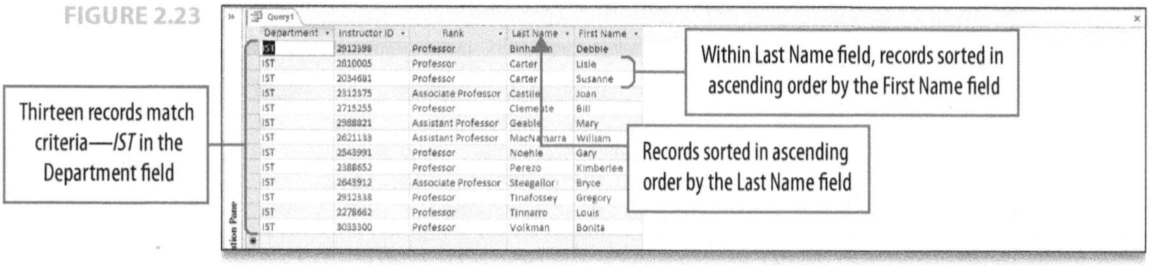

ALERT! **Do Your Query Results Differ?**

If you mistype the criteria, or enter it under the wrong field, or make some other error, the query results will display no records. This indicates that there are no records in the table that match the criteria as you entered it. If this occurs, return to Design view and examine the query design. Verify that the criteria is entered in the Criteria row, under the correct field, and without typing errors. Then, run the query again.

7 **Save** the query as **Lastname Firstname 2A IST Query** and then display the query results in **Print Preview.** Create a paper or electronic printout as directed, and then click **Close Print Preview.**

8 **Close** [×] the query, **Open** [»] the **Navigation Pane**, and then notice that your **2A IST Query** object name displays under your **2A Instructors** table—its data source.

Recall that in the Navigation Pane, queries display an icon of two overlapping datasheets.

Activity 2.16 | Specifying Criteria and Hiding the Field in the Query Results

So far, all of the fields that you included in the query design have also been included in the query results. There are times when you need to use the field in the query design, but you do not need to display that field in the results, usually, when the data in the field is the same for all of the records. In this activity, you will create a query to answer the question, *Which instructors have a rank of professor?*

1 **Close** [«] the **Navigation Pane.** On the ribbon, click the **CREATE tab**, and then in the **Queries group**, click **Query Design**.

2 In the **Show Table** dialog box, double-click your **2A Instructors** table to add it to the table area, and then **Close** the **Show Table** dialog box.

3 Resize the field list, and then add the following fields to the design grid in the order given: **Instructor ID, Last Name, First Name,** and **Rank.**

4 Click in the **Sort** row under **Last Name,** click the **arrow**, and then click **Ascending**. Click in the **Sort** row under **First Name,** click the **arrow,** and then click **Ascending.**

5 Click in the **Criteria** row under **Rank**, type **professor** and then press Enter. Compare your screen with Figure 2.24.

Recall that criteria is not case sensitive. As you start typing *professor*, a list of functions displays, from which you can select if a function is included in your criteria. After pressing Enter, the insertion point moves to the next criteria box, and quotation marks are added around the text string that you entered.

FIGURE 2.24

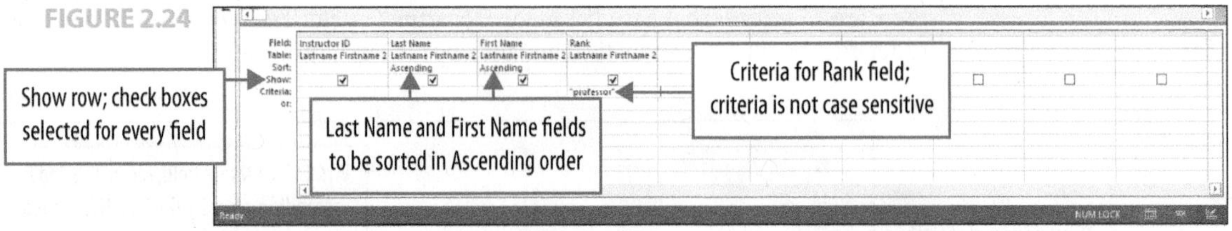

6 In the design grid, in the **Show** row, notice that a check box is selected for every field. **Run** the query.

Eighteen records meet the criteria—*professor* in the *Rank* field. In the Rank column, every record displays *Professor*, and the records are sorted in ascending order by the First Name field within the Last Name field.

7 Switch to **Design** view. In the design grid, in the **Show** row under **Rank**, click to clear the check box.

Because it is repetitive and not particularly useful to display *Professor* for every record in the query results, clear the Show check box so that the field is hidden and does not display. It is good practice, however, to run the query first before clearing the Show check box to be sure that the correct records display.

8 **Run** the query, and then notice that the *Rank* field does not display even though it is used to specify criteria in the query.

The same 18 records display, but the *Rank* field is hidden from the query results. Although the Rank field is included in the query design so that you can specify the criteria of *professor*, it is not necessary to display the field in the results. When appropriate, clear the Show check box to avoid cluttering the query results with data that is not useful.

9 **Save** the query as **Lastname Firstname 2A Professor Query** and then display the query results in **Print Preview**. Create a paper or electronic printout as directed, and then click **Close Print Preview**. **Close** [×] the query.

Activity 2.17 | Using *Is Null* Criteria to Find Empty Fields

Sometimes you must locate records where data is missing. You can locate such records by using ***Is Null*** as the criteria in a field. *Is Null* is used to find empty fields. Additionally, you can display only the records where data has been entered in the field by using the criteria of ***Is Not Null***, which excludes records where the specified field is empty. In this activity, you will design a query to answer the question, *Which scheduled courses have no credits listed?*

1 On the ribbon, click the **CREATE tab**, and then in the **Queries group**, click **Query Design**. In the **Show Table** dialog box, double-click your **2A Schedule** table to add it to the table area, and then **Close** the **Show Table** dialog box.

2 Resize the field list, and then add the following fields to the design grid in the order given: **Subject**, **Catalog#**, **Section**, **Course Name**, and **Credits**.

3 Click in the **Criteria** row under **Credits**, type **is null** and then press Enter.

Access capitalizes *is null*. The criteria *Is Null* examines the Credits field and locates records that do *not* have any data entered in the field.

4 Click in the **Sort** row under **Subject**, click the **arrow**, and then click **Ascending**. **Sort** the **Catalog#** field in **Ascending** order, and then **Sort** the **Section** field in **Ascending** order. Compare your screen with Figure 2.25.

FIGURE 2.25

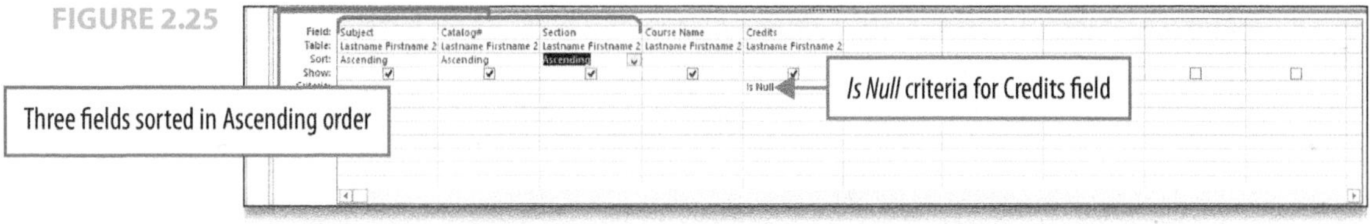

5 **Run** the query, and then compare your screen with Figure 2.26.

Four scheduled courses do not have credits listed—the Credits field is empty. The records are sorted in ascending order first by the Subject field. Within the Subject field, the records are sorted in ascending order by the Catalog# field. Within the Catalog# field, the records are sorted in ascending order by the Section field. Using the information displayed in the query results, a course scheduler can more easily locate the records in the table and enter the credits for these courses.

FIGURE 2.26

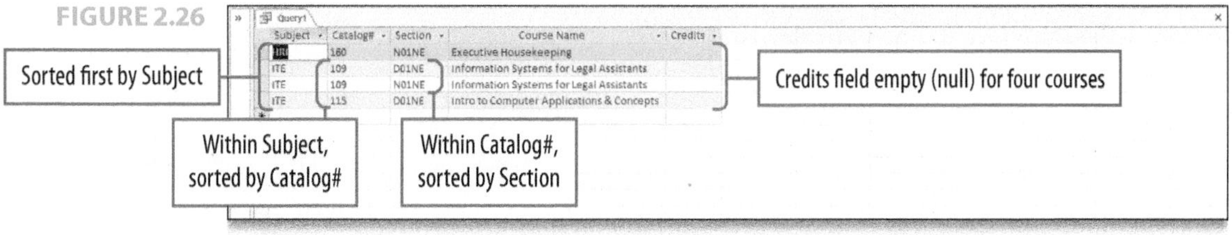

6 **Save** [icon] the query as **Lastname Firstname 2A No Credits Query**, and then display the query results in **Print Preview**. Create a paper or electronic printout as instructed, click **Close Print Preview**, and then **Close** [×] the query.

7 **Open** [»] the **Navigation Pane**, and then notice that your **2A No Credits Query** object displays under your **2A Schedule** table object, its data source.

8 On the right side of the title bar, click **Close** [×] to close the database and to exit Access. As directed by your instructor, submit your database and the paper or electronic printouts of the eight objects—relationship report, sorted table, and six queries—that are the results of this project. Specifically, in this project, using your own name, you created the following database and printouts or electronic printouts:

1. Lastname_Firstname_2A_Instructors_Courses	Database file
2. Relationships for Lastname_Firstname_2A_Instructors_Courses	Relationships Report (printout or electronic printout)
3. Lastname Firstname 2A Instructors table sorted (not saved)	Table sorted (printout or electronic printout - Page 1)
4. Lastname Firstname 2A Instructors Query	Query (printout or electronic printout)
5. Lastname Firstname 2A Instructor IDs Query	Query (printout or electronic printout)
6. Lastname Firstname 2A Department Sort Query	Query (printout or electronic printout)
7. Lastname Firstname 2A IST Query	Query (printout or electronic printout)
8. Lastname Firstname 2A Professor Query	Query (printout or electronic printout)
9. Lastname Firstname 2A No Credits Query	Query (printout or electronic printout)

END | You have completed Project 2A

GO! with Office Online (formerly Web Apps)

2 ACCESS

Objective Export an Access Query to a PDF File, Save to OneDrive, and Add a Description to the PDF File

Access web apps are designed to work with Microsoft's SharePoint, an application for setting up websites to share and manage documents. Your college may not have SharePoint installed, so you will use other tools to share objects from your database so that you can work collaboratively with others. When you have information that you want to share with others, you can upload files to OneDrive. Some files can be opened in OneDrive; some can only be downloaded. Because database files are typically large in size, and free storage space on OneDrive is limited, you can export database objects to different formats and then upload those files to OneDrive.

ALERT! Working with Web-Based Applications and Services

Computer programs and services on the web receive continuous updates and improvements. Thus, the steps to complete this web-based activity may differ from the ones shown. You can often look at the screens and the information presented to determine how to complete the activity.

Activity Exporting an Access Query to a PDF File, Uploading a PDF File to OneDrive, and Adding a Description to a PDF File

In this activity, you will export your 2A No Credits Query object to a PDF file, upload your PDF file to OneDrive, and then add a description to the PDF File. Recall that PDF stands for Portable Document Format—a file format that creates an image that preserves the look of your file, but that cannot be easily changed. The results of the query will be available for individuals with whom you have shared your OneDrive files or folders.

1 **Start** Access, navigate to your **Access Chapter 2** folder, and then **Open** your **2A_Instructors_Courses** database file. If necessary, on the Message Bar, click Enable Content. In the **Navigation Pane**, click your **2A No Credits Query** object to select it—do not open it.

2 On the ribbon, click the **EXTERNAL DATA tab**, and then in the **Export group**, click **PDF or XPS**. In the **Publish as PDF or XPS** dialog box, navigate to your **Access Chapter 2** folder. Click in the **File name** box, type **Lastname_Firstname_AC_2A_Web** and then be sure the **Open file after publishing** check box is selected, and the **Minimum size (publishing online)** option button is selected. Click **Publish**, and then compare your screen with Figure A.

The PDF file is created and opens in the Windows 8 Reader, Adobe Reader, or Adobe Acrobat, depending on the software that is installed on your computer.

3 **Close** your **AC_2A_Web** file. In the **Export - PDF** dialog box, click **Close**, and then **Close** Access.

4 From the desktop, start Internet Explorer, navigate to **http://onedrive.com**, and then sign in to your Microsoft account. Open your **GO! Web Projects** folder—or create and then open this folder if necessary.

FIGURE A

Your 2A No Credits Query exported as a PDF file and opened in Adobe Reader (yours may open in Windows 8 Reader or Adobe Acrobat)

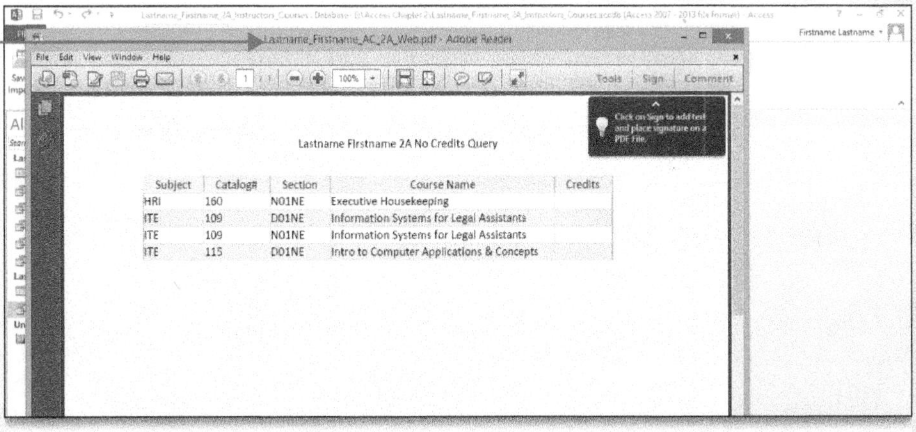

(GO! with Office Online (formerly Web Apps) continues on the next page)

5 On the menu bar, click **Upload**. In the **Choose File to Upload** dialog box, navigate to your **Access Chapter 2** folder, and then double-click your **AC_2A_Web** file to upload it to OneDrive.

6 In your **GO! Web Projects** folder, right-click your **AC_2A_Web** file, and then click **Properties**.

A properties panel displays on the right side of the window.

7 In the properties panel, click **Add a description**. In the box, type **This query displays courses in the schedule that do not have credits assigned to them.** and then press Enter. Compare your screen with Figure B.

8 On your keyboard, press the [Windows] key, type **snip**, and then click **Snipping Tool**. In the **Snipping Tool** dialog box, click the **New arrow**, and then click **Full-screen snip**.

9 On the **Snipping Tool** toolbar, click **Save Snip** [icon]. In the **Save As** dialog box, navigate to your **Access Chapter 2** folder. Click in the **File name** box, type **Lastname_Firstname_AC_2A_Web_Snip** and then click the **Save as type arrow**. Click **JPEG file**, and then click **Save**. **Close** [icon] the **Snipping Tool** window.

10 In OneDrive, on the title bar, click **OneDrive** to return to your home page. At the top right corner of your screen, click your OneDrive name, and then click **Sign out**. **Close** your browser window.

11 If directed to submit a paper printout of your pdf and snip file, follow the directions given in the Note. As directed by your instructor, submit your pdf file and your snip file that are the results of this project.

NOTE **Printing Your PDF and Snip .jpeg File**

Using Windows Explorer, navigate to your Access Chapter 2 folder. Locate and double-click your AC_2A_Web file. On the toolbar, click the Print file button. Then Close the Windows 8 Reader, Adobe Reader, or Adobe Acrobat window. In your Access Chapter 2 folder, locate and double-click your AC_2A_Web_Snip file. If this is the first time you have tried to open a .jpeg file, you will be asked to identify a program. If you are not sure which program to use, select Windows Photo Viewer. From the ribbon, menu bar, or toolbar, click the Print command, and then Close the program window.

FIGURE B

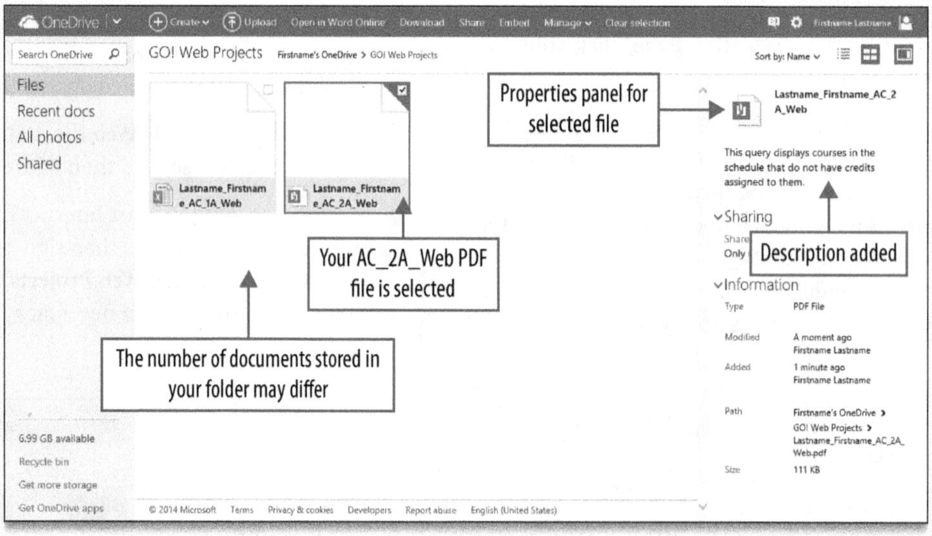

PROJECT 2B

Athletic Scholarships Database

MyITLab® Project 2B Training

PROJECT ACTIVITIES

In Activities 2.18 through 2.33, you will assist Roberto Garza, athletic director for Texas Lakes Community College, in creating queries to locate information about athletic scholarships that are awarded to students. Your completed database objects will look similar to Figure 2.27.

PROJECT FILES

For Project 2B, you will need the following files:

a02B_Athletes_Scholarships
a02B_Athletes (Excel workbook)

You will save your database as:

Lastname_Firstname_2B_Athletes_Scholarships

PROJECT RESULTS

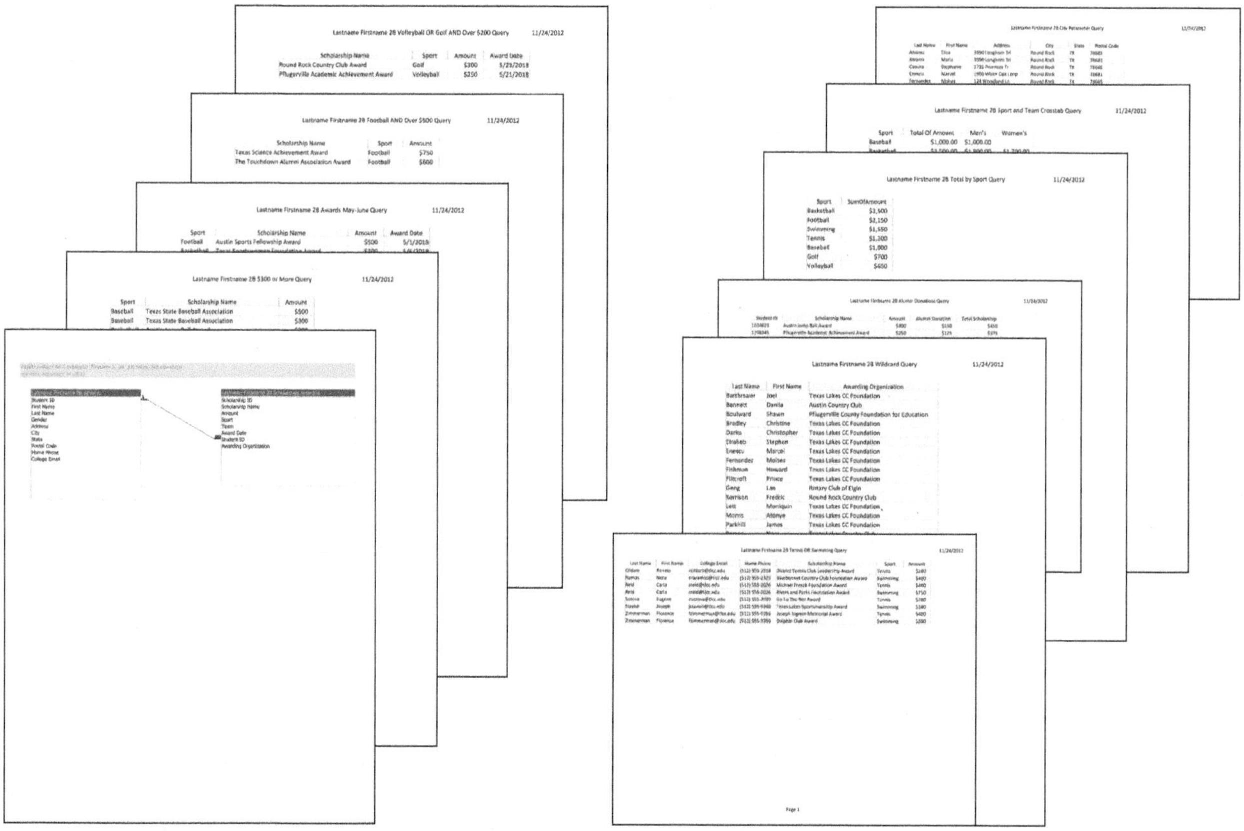

FIGURE 2.27 Project 2B Athletic Scholarships

Objective 8 Specify Numeric Criteria in a Query

Video A2-8

Criteria can be set for fields containing numeric data. When you design your table, set the appropriate data type for fields that will contain numbers, currency, or dates so that mathematical calculations can be performed.

Activity 2.18 | Opening, Renaming, and Saving an Existing Database and Importing a Spreadsheet as a New Table

In this activity, you will open, rename, and save an existing database, and then import an Excel spreadsheet as a new table in the database.

1. **Start** Access. In the Access opening screen, click **Open Other Files**. Under **Open**, click **Computer**. Under **Recent Folders**, if displayed, click the location where your student data files are stored; otherwise, click **Browse** and then navigate to the location where your student data files are stored. Double-click **a02B_Athletes_Scholarships** to open the database.

2. Click the **FILE tab**, click **Save As**, and then under **File Types**, be sure **Save Database As** is selected. On the right, under **Database File Types**, be sure **Access Database** is selected, and then click **Save As**. In the **Save As** dialog box, navigate to your **Access Chapter 2** folder, click in the **File name** box, type **Lastname_Firstname_2B_Athletes_Scholarships** and then press Enter.

3. On the **Message Bar**, click **Enable Content**. In the **Navigation Pane**, right-click **2B Scholarships Awarded**, and then click **Rename**. Using your own name, type **Lastname Firstname 2B Scholarships Awarded** and then press Enter. In the **Navigation Pane**, double-click the table name to open it in **Datasheet** view. **Close** « the **Navigation Pane**, and then examine the data in the table. Compare your screen with Figure 2.28.

   In this table, Mr. Garza tracks the names and amounts of scholarships awarded to student athletes. Students are identified only by their Student ID numbers, and the primary key is the Scholarship ID field.

FIGURE 2.28

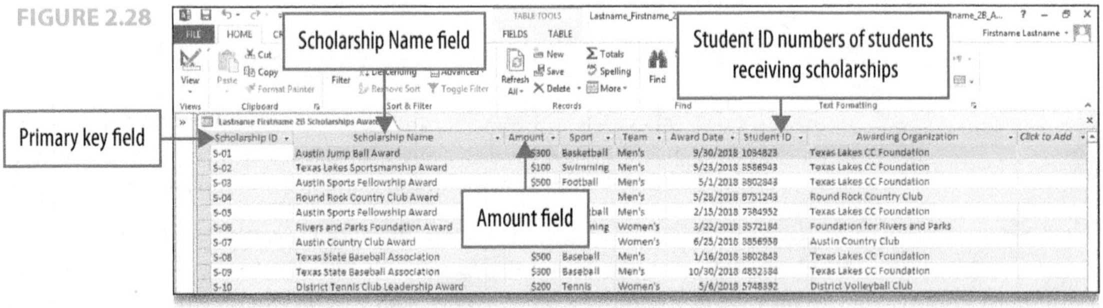

4. **Close** × the table. On the ribbon, click the **EXTERNAL DATA tab**, and then in the **Import & Link group**, click **Excel**. In the **Get External Data – Excel Spreadsheet** dialog box, to the right of the **File name** box, click **Browse**.

5. In the **File Open** dialog box, navigate to your student data files, and then double-click **a02B_Athletes**. Be sure that the **Import the source data into a new table in the current database** option button is selected, and then click **OK**.

   The Import Spreadsheet Wizard opens and displays the spreadsheet data.

6. In the wizard, click **Next**. In the upper left area of the wizard, select the **First Row Contains Column Headings** check box, click **Next**, and then click **Next** again.

7 In the wizard, click the **Choose my own primary key** option button, and then be sure that **Student ID** displays in the box.

In the new table, Student ID will be designated as the primary key. No two students have the same Student ID.

8 Click **Next**. With the text selected in the **Import to Table** box, type **Lastname Firstname 2B Athletes** and then click **Finish**. In the **Get External Data – Excel Spreadsheet** dialog box, click **Close**.

9 **Open** [»] the **Navigation Pane**, and increase the width of the pane so that the two table names display fully. In the **Navigation Pane**, right-click your **2B Athletes** table, and then click **Design View**. **Close** [«] the **Navigation Pane**.

10 To the right of **Student ID**, click in the **Data Type** box, click the **arrow**, and then click **Short Text**. For the **Postal Code** field, change the **Data Type** to **Short Text**, and in the **Field Properties** area, click **Field Size**, type **5** and then press Enter. In the **Field Name** column, click **State**, set the **Field Size** to **2** and then press Enter. Compare your screen with Figure 2.29.

Recall that numeric data that is not used in a calculation, such as the Student ID and Postal Code, should be assigned a data type of Short Text.

FIGURE 2.29

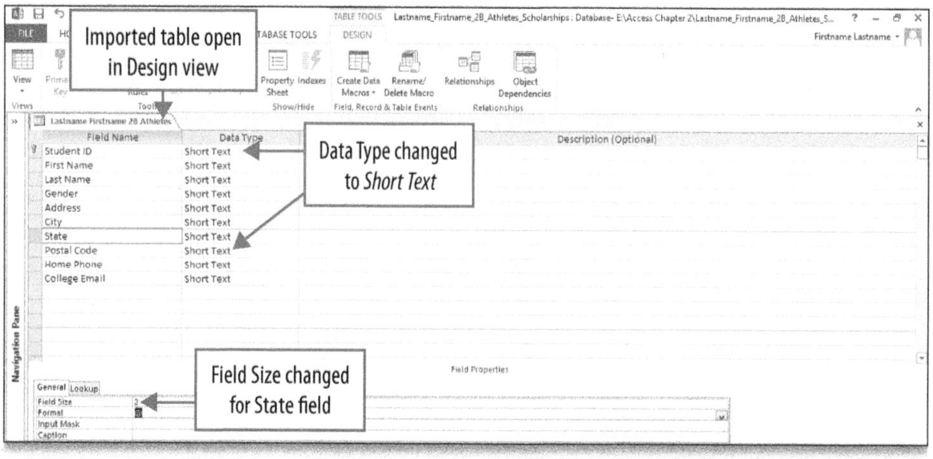

11 On the **DESIGN tab**, in the **Views group**, click the top of the **View** button to switch to **Datasheet** view. In the message box, click **Yes** to save the table. In the second message box, click **Yes**—no data will be lost. Take a moment to examine the data in the imported table.

12 In the datasheet, to the left of the **Student ID** field name, click **Select All** [ ]. On the **HOME tab**, in the **Records group**, click **More**, and then click **Field Width**. In the **Column Width** dialog box, click **Best Fit**. **Save** [💾] the table, click in any record to cancel the selection, and then **Close** [×] the table.

Activity 2.19 | Creating a One-to-Many Table Relationship

In this activity, you will create a one-to-many relationship between your 2B Athletes table and your 2B Scholarships Awarded table by using the common field—*Student ID*.

1 On the ribbon, click the **DATABASE TOOLS tab**, and then in the **Relationships group**, click **Relationships**.

2 In the **Show Table** dialog box, double-click your **2B Athletes** table, and then double-click your **2B Scholarships Awarded** table to add both tables to the **Relationships** window. **Close** the **Show Table** dialog box.

3 Point to the title bar of the field list on the right, and drag the field list to the right until there are approximately three inches of space between the field lists. By dragging the lower right corner of the field list downward and to the right, resize each field list to display all of the field names and the entire table name.

Repositioning and resizing the field lists are not required, but doing so makes it easier for you to view the field names and the join line when creating relationships.

4 In the **2B Athletes** field list, point to **Student ID**, and then drag the field name into the **2B Scholarships Awarded** field list on top of **Student ID**. Release the mouse button to display the **Edit Relationships** dialog box.

5 Point to the title bar of the **Edit Relationships** dialog box, and then drag it downward below the two field lists. In the **Edit Relationships** dialog box, be sure that **Student ID** displays as the common field for both tables.

Repositioning the Edit Relationships dialog is not required, but doing so enables you to see the field lists. The Relationship Type is *One-To-Many*—*one* athlete can have *many* scholarships. The common field in both tables is the *Student ID* field. In the 2B Athletes table, Student ID is the primary key. In the 2B Scholarships Awarded table, Student ID is the foreign key.

6 In the **Edit Relationships** dialog box, click to select the **Enforce Referential Integrity** check box, the **Cascade Update Related Fields** check box, and the **Cascade Delete Related Records** check box. Click **Create,** and then compare your screen with Figure 2.30.

The one-to-many relationship is established. The *1* and ∞ symbols indicate that referential integrity is enforced, which ensures that a scholarship cannot be awarded to a student whose Student ID is not included in the 2B Athletes table. Recall that the Cascade options enable you to update and delete records automatically on the *many* side of the relationship when changes are made in the table on the *one* side of the relationship.

FIGURE 2.30

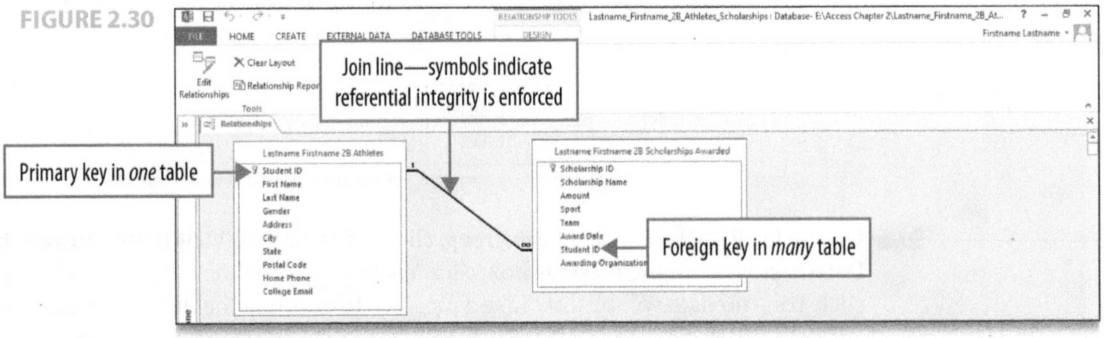

7 Under **RELATIONSHIP TOOLS,** on the **DESIGN tab**, in the **Tools group**, click **Relationship Report.** On the **PRINT PREVIEW tab**, in the **Page Size group**, click **Margins**, and then click **Normal. Save** the report as **Lastname Firstname 2B Relationships** and then create a paper or electronic printout as directed.

8 In the object window, right-click either **object tab**, and then click **Close All** to close the **Relationship Report** and the **Relationships** window.

9 **Open** » the **Navigation Pane**, double-click your **2B Athletes** table to open it, and then **Close** « the **Navigation Pane.** On the left side of the first record, click ⊞ to display the subdatasheet for the record.

In the first record, for *Joel Barthmaier*, one related record exists in the 2B Scholarships Awarded table. Joel has been awarded the *Austin Jump Ball Award* in the amount of *$300.* The subdatasheet displays because you created a relationship between the two tables using Student ID as the common field.

10 **Close** [×] the **2B Athletes** table.

When you close the table, the subdatasheet collapses—you do not need to click [⊟] before closing a table.

Activity 2.20 | Specifying Numeric Criteria in a Query

In this activity, you will create a query to answer the question, *Which scholarships are in the amount of $300, and for which sports?*

1 On the ribbon, click the **CREATE tab**. In the **Queries group**, click **Query Design**.

2 In the **Show Table** dialog box, double-click your **2B Scholarships Awarded** table to add it to the table area, and then **Close** the **Show Table** dialog box. Resize the field list to display all of the fields and the entire table name.

3 Add the following fields to the design grid in the order given: **Sport**, **Scholarship Name**, and **Amount**.

4 Click in the **Sort** row under **Sport**, click the **arrow**, and then click **Ascending**. Click in the **Sort** row under **Scholarship Name**, click the **arrow**, and then click **Ascending**.

The records will be sorted in ascending order by the Scholarship Name field within the Sport field.

5 Click in the **Criteria** row under **Amount**, type **300** and then press [Enter]. Compare your screen with Figure 2.31.

When you enter currency values as criteria, do not type the dollar sign. Include a decimal point only if you are looking for a specific amount that includes cents; for example, 300.49. Access does not insert quotation marks around the criteria because the data type of the field is Currency, which is a numeric format.

FIGURE 2.31

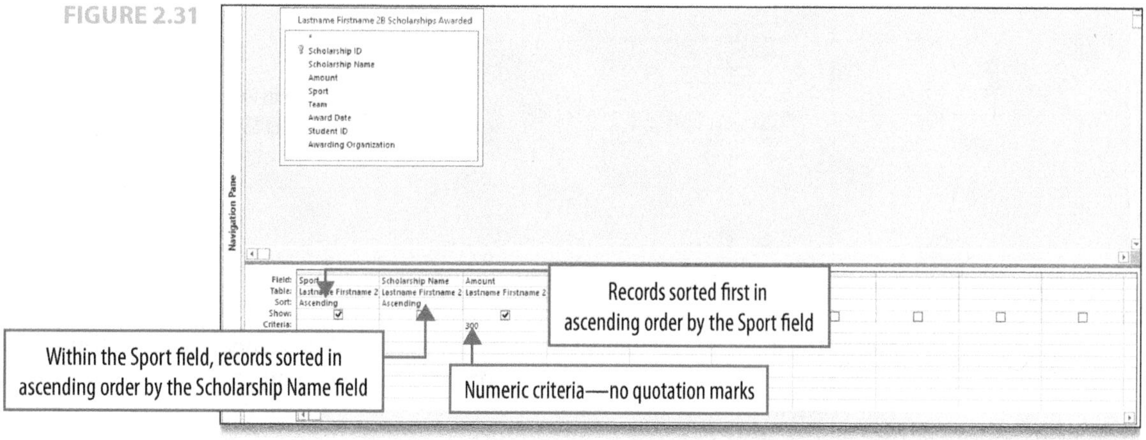

6 Under **QUERY TOOLS**, on the **DESIGN tab**, in the **Results group**, click **Run** to display the query results.

Five scholarships in the exact amount of $300 were awarded to student athletes. In the navigation area, *1 of 5* displays—1 represents the first record that is selected, and 5 represents the total number of records that meet the criteria.

7 On the **HOME tab**, in the **Views group**, click the top of the **View** button to switch to **Design** view.

Activity 2.21 | Using Comparison Operators in Criteria

Comparison operators are symbols you can use to evaluate data in the field to determine if it is the same (=), greater than (>), less than (<), or in between a range of values as specified by the criteria. If no comparison operator is specified, equal (=) is assumed. For example, in the previous activity, you created a query to display only those records where the *Amount* is *300*. The comparison operator of = was assumed, and the query results displayed only those records that had values in the Amount field equal to 300.

1 In the design grid, in the **Criteria** row under **Amount**, select the existing criteria of *300*. Type **>300** and then press Enter. **Run** the query.

Fourteen records display, and each has a value *greater than* $300 in the Amount field; there are no records for which the Amount is *equal to* $300.

2 Switch to **Design** view. In the **Criteria** row under **Amount**, select the existing criteria of *>300*. Type **<300** and then press Enter. **Run** the query.

Eleven records display, and each has a value *less than* $300 in the Amount field; there are no records for which the Amount is *equal to* $300.

3 Switch to **Design** view. In the **Criteria** row under **Amount**, select the existing criteria of *<300*. Type **>=300** and then press Enter. **Run** the query, and then compare your screen with Figure 2.32.

Nineteen records display, including the records for scholarships in the exact amount of $300. The records include scholarships *greater than* or *equal to* $300. In this manner, comparison operators can be combined. This query answers the question, *Which scholarships have been awarded in the amount of $300 or more, and for which sports, arranged alphabetically by sport?*

FIGURE 2.32

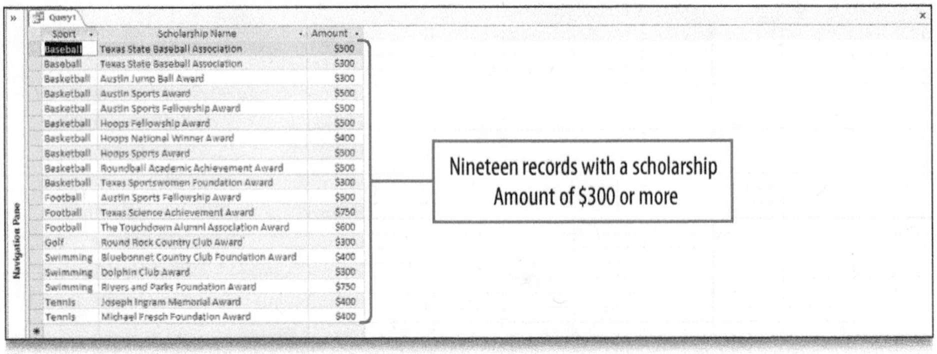

Sport	Scholarship Name	Amount
Baseball	Texas State Baseball Association	$300
Baseball	Texas State Baseball Association	$300
Basketball	Austin Jump Ball Award	$300
Basketball	Austin Sports Award	$500
Basketball	Austin Sports Fellowship Award	$500
Basketball	Hoops Fellowship Award	$500
Basketball	Hoops National Winner Award	$400
Basketball	Hoops Sports Award	$300
Basketball	Roundball Academic Achievement Award	$500
Basketball	Texas Sportswomen Foundation Award	$300
Football	Austin Sports Fellowship Award	$500
Football	Texas Science Achievement Award	$750
Football	The Touchdown Alumni Association Award	$600
Golf	Round Rock Country Club Award	$300
Swimming	Bluebonnet Country Club Foundation Award	$400
Swimming	Dolphin Club Award	$300
Swimming	Rivers and Parks Foundation Award	$750
Tennis	Joseph Ingram Memorial Award	$400
Tennis	Michael Fresch Foundation Award	$400

4 **Save** the query as **Lastname Firstname 2B $300 or More Query** and then display the query results in **Print Preview**. Create a paper or electronic printout as directed, and then click **Close Print Preview**.

5 **Close** the query. **Open** the **Navigation Pane**, and notice that this new query displays under *2B Scholarships Awarded*, its data source.

Activity 2.22 | Using the Between … And Comparison Operator

The ***Between … And operator*** is a comparison operator that looks for values within a range. It is useful when you need to locate records that are within a range of dates; for example, scholarships awarded between May 1 and June 30.

In this activity, you will create a new query from an existing query, and then add criteria to look for values within a range of dates. The query will answer the question, *Which scholarships were awarded between May 1 and June 30?*

1 In the **Navigation Pane**, right-click your **2B $300 or More Query** object, and then click **Copy**. In the **Navigation Pane**, point to a blank area, right-click, and then click **Paste**.

2 In the **Paste As** dialog box, type **Lastname Firstname 2B Awards May-June Query** and then click **OK**.

A new query, based on a copy of your 2B $300 or More Query is created and displays in the Navigation Pane under its data source—your 2B Scholarships Awarded table.

3 In the **Navigation Pane**, right-click your **2B Awards May-June Query** object, click **Design View**, and then **Close** [«] the **Navigation Pane**.

4 In the **2B Scholarships Awarded** field list, double-click **Award Date** to add it as the fourth column in the design grid.

5 In the **Criteria** row under **Amount**, select the existing criteria of *>=300*, and then press [Del] so that the query is not restricted by a monetary value.

6 Click in the **Criteria** row under **Award Date**, type **between 5/1/18 and 6/30/18** and then press [Enter].

7 Click in the **Sort** row under **Sport**, click the **arrow**, and then click **(not sorted)** to remove the sort from this field. Click in the **Sort** row under **Scholarship Name**, click the **arrow**, and then click **(not sorted)** to remove the sort from this field. Click in the **Sort** row under **Award Date**, click the **arrow**, and then click **Ascending**.

8 In the selection bar of the design grid, point to the right edge of the **Award Date** column to display the [+] pointer, and then double-click to apply Best Fit to this column. Compare your screen with Figure 2.33.

The width of the Award Date column is increased to fit the longest entry in the column, which enables you to see all of the criteria. Access places pound signs (#) around the dates and capitalizes *between* and *and*. This criteria instructs Access to look for values in the Award Date field that begin with 5/1/18 and end with 6/30/18. Both the beginning and ending dates will be included in the query results.

FIGURE 2.33

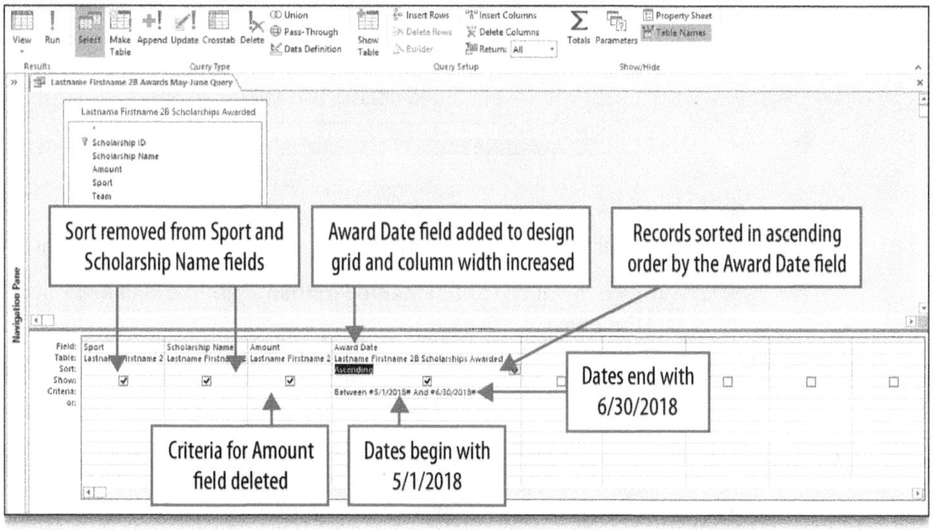

9 **Run** the query, and notice that eight scholarships were awarded between 5/1/2018 and 6/30/2018.

10 Display the query results in **Print Preview**, create a paper or electronic printout as directed, and then click **Close Print Preview**. **Close** [×] the query, and in the message box, click **Yes** to save the changes to the query design.

Objective 9 Use Compound Criteria in a Query

Video A2-9

You can specify more than one condition—criteria—in a query; this is called ***compound criteria***. Compound criteria use ***logical operators*** such as AND and OR. Logical operators evaluate data to determine if a condition is met (true) or not met (false). The AND and OR logical operators enable you to enter multiple criteria for the same field or for different fields.

Activity 2.23 | Using AND Criteria in a Query

The ***AND condition*** is an example of a compound criteria you can use to display records that match all parts of the specified criteria. In this activity, you will design a query to answer the question, *Which scholarships over $500 were awarded for football?*

1 On the ribbon, click the **CREATE tab**, and in the **Queries group**, click **Query Design**. In the **Show Table** dialog box, double-click your **2B Scholarships Awarded** table to add it to the table area, and then **Close** the **Show Table** dialog box. Resize the field list to display all of the fields and the entire table name.

2 Add the following fields to the design grid in the order given: **Scholarship Name**, **Sport**, and **Amount**.

3 Click in the **Criteria** row under **Sport**, type **football** and then press Enter.

4 In the **Criteria** row under **Amount**, type **>500** and then press Enter. Compare your screen with Figure 2.34.

You create the AND condition by placing the criteria for both fields on the same line in the Criteria row. The criteria indicates that records should be located that contain *Football* in the Sport field AND a value greater than *500* in the Amount field. Both conditions must exist or be true for the records to display in the query results.

FIGURE 2.34

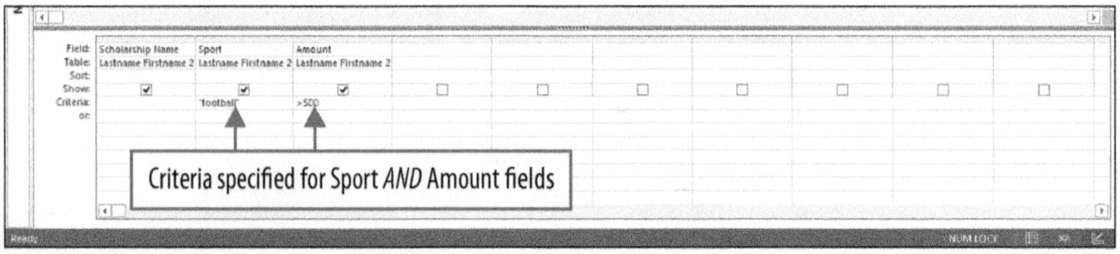

5 **Run** the query, and notice that two records display that match both conditions—*Football* in the **Sport** field AND a value greater than *$500* in the **Amount** field.

6 **Save** the query as **Lastname Firstname 2B Football AND Over $500 Query** and then **Close** the query.

7 **Open** » the **Navigation Pane**, and then click to select your **2B Football AND Over $500 Query** object. On the ribbon, click the **FILE tab**, click **Print**, and then click **Print Preview**.

You can view an object in Print Preview or print any selected object in the Navigation Pane—the object does not need to be open in the object window to print it.

8 Create a paper or electronic printout as directed, and then click **Close Print Preview**. **Close** « the **Navigation Pane**.

Activity 2.24 | Using OR Criteria in a Query

The ***OR condition*** is an example of a compound criteria you can use to display records that meet one or more parts of the specified criteria. The OR condition can specify criteria in a single field or in different fields. In this activity, you will help Mr. Garza answer the question, *Which scholarships over $200 were awarded for volleyball or golf, and what is the award date of each?*

1 On the ribbon, click the **CREATE tab**. In the **Queries group**, click **Query Design**.

2 In the **Show Table** dialog box, double-click your **2B Scholarships Awarded** table to add it to the table area, and then **Close** the **Show Table** dialog box. Resize the field list, and then add the following fields to the design grid in the order given: **Scholarship Name**, **Sport**, **Amount**, and **Award Date**.

3 In the design grid, click in the **Criteria** row under **Sport**, type **volleyball** and then press ↓.

The insertion point is blinking in the *or* row under Sport.

4 In the **or** row under **Sport**, type **golf** and then press Enter. **Run** the query.

Six records were located in the 2B Scholarships Awarded table that have either *volleyball* OR *golf* stored in the Sport field. This is an example of using the OR condition to locate records that meet one or more parts of the specified criteria in a single field—*Sport*.

5 Switch to **Design** view. In the **or** row under **Sport**, select *"golf"* and then press Del. In the **Criteria** row under **Sport**, select and delete *"volleyball"*. Type **volleyball or golf** and then press Enter.

6 In the **Criteria** row under **Amount**, type **>200** and then press Enter. Compare your screen with Figure 2.35.

This is an alternative way to enter the OR condition in the Sport field and is a good method to use when you add an AND condition to the criteria. Access will locate records where the Sport field contains *volleyball* OR *golf* AND where the Amount field contains a value greater than *200*.

If you enter *volleyball* in the Criteria row, and *golf* in the or row for the Sport field, then you must enter *>200* in both the Criteria row and the or row for the Amount field so that the correct records are located when you run the query.

FIGURE 2.35

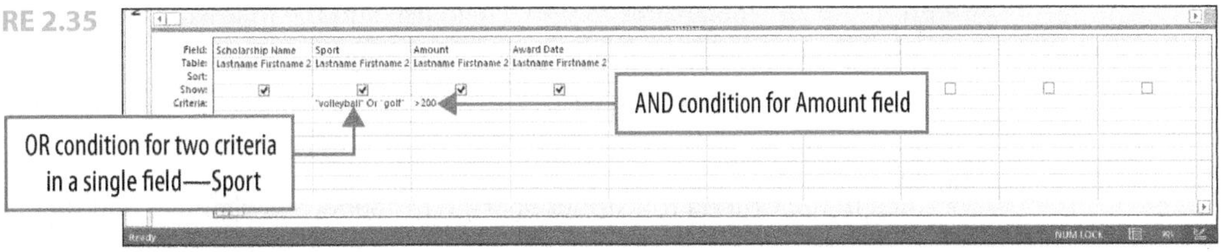

7 **Run** the query.

Two records were located in the 2B Scholarships Awarded table that have either *Volleyball* OR *Golf* stored in the Sport field AND a value greater than $200 stored in the Amount field. This is an example of using the OR condition in combination with an AND condition.

8 **Save** the query as **Lastname Firstname 2B Volleyball OR Golf AND Over $200 Query** and then display the query results in **Print Preview**. Create a paper or electronic printout as directed, click **Close Print Preview**, and then **Close** × the query.

Objective 10 Create a Query Based on More Than One Table

Video A2-10

In a relational database, you can retrieve information from more than one table. Recall that a table in a relational database contains all of the records about a single topic. Tables are joined to one another by relating the primary key in one table to the foreign key in another table. This common field is used to create the relationship and is used to find records from multiple tables when the query is created and run.

For example, the Athletes table stores all of the data about the student athletes—name, address, and so on. The Scholarships Awarded table stores data about the scholarship name, the amount, and so on. When an athlete receives a scholarship, only the Student ID of the athlete is used to identify the athlete in the Scholarships Awarded table. It is not necessary to include any other data about the athlete in the Scholarships Awarded table; doing so would result in redundant data.

Activity 2.25 | Creating a Query Based on More Than One Table

In this activity, you will create a query that selects records from two tables. This is possible because you created a relationship between the two tables in the database. The query will answer the questions, *What is the name, email address, and phone number of athletes who have received a scholarship for tennis or swimming, and what is the name and amount of the scholarship?*

1. On the ribbon, click the **CREATE tab**, and then in the **Queries group**, click **Query Design**. In the **Show Table** dialog box, double-click your **2B Athletes** table, and then double-click your **2B Scholarships Awarded** table to add both tables to the table area. In the **Show Table** dialog box, click **Close**. Drag the **2B Scholarships Awarded** field list—the field list on the right—to the right so that there are approximately three inches of space between the two field lists, and then resize each field list to display all of the field names and the table names.

   The join line displays because you created a one-to-many relationship between the two tables using the common field of Student ID; *one* athlete can receive *many* scholarships.

2. From the **2B Athletes** field list, add the following fields to the design grid in the order given: **Last Name, First Name, College Email,** and **Home Phone.**

3. From the **2B Scholarships Awarded** field list, add the following fields to the design grid in the order given: **Scholarship Name, Sport,** and **Amount.**

4. Click in the **Sort** row under **Last Name**, click the **arrow**, and then click **Ascending**. Click in the **Sort** row under **First Name**, click the **arrow**, and then click **Ascending.**

5. Click in the **Criteria** row under **Sport**, type **tennis or swimming** and then press Enter.

6. In the selection bar of the design grid, point to the right edge of the **Home Phone** column to display the + pointer, and then double-click to increase the width of the column and to display the entire table name on the **Table** row. Using the same technique, increase the width of the **Scholarship Name** column. If necessary, scroll to the right to display both of these columns in the design grid, and then compare your screen with Figure 2.36.

   When locating data from multiple tables, the information in the Table row is helpful, especially when different tables include the same field name, such as Address. Although the field name is the same, the data may be different; for example, you might have an athlete's address or a coach's address from two different related tables.

FIGURE 2.36

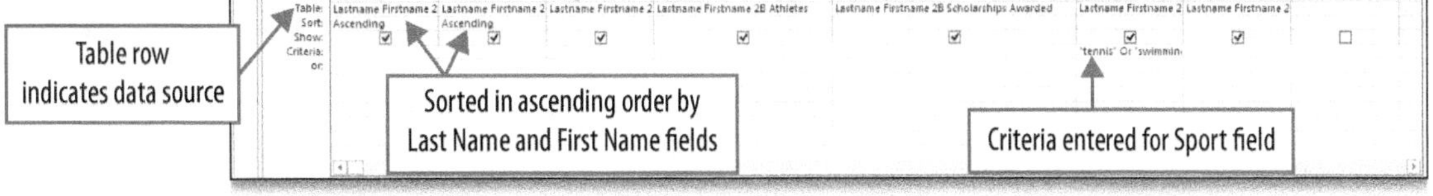

7 **Run** the query, and then compare your screen with Figure 2.37.

Eight records display for athletes who received either a Tennis *or* Swimming scholarship, and the records are sorted in ascending order by the Last Name field, and then the First Name field. Because the common field of Student ID is included in both tables, Access can locate the specified fields in both tables by using one query. Two students—*Carla Reid* and *Florence Zimmerman*—received two scholarships, one for tennis and one for swimming. Recall that *one* student athlete can receive *many* scholarships.

FIGURE 2.37

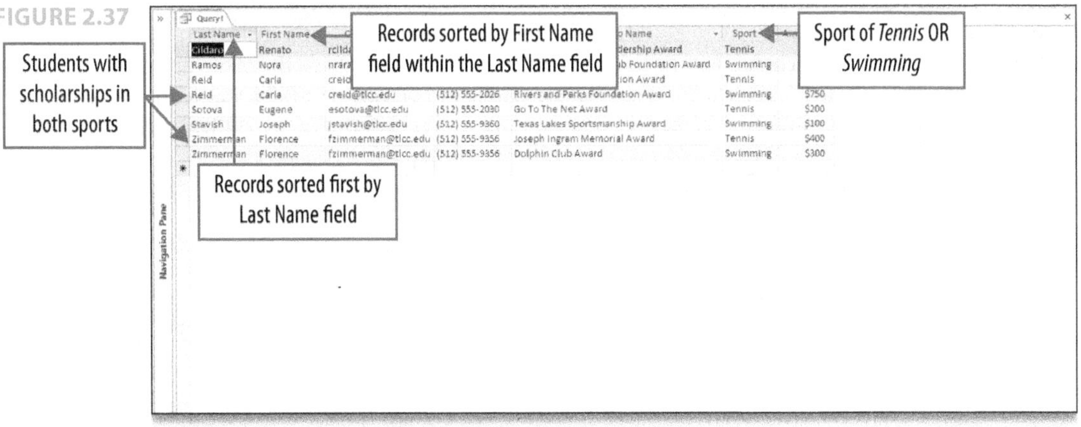

8 **Save** the query as **Lastname Firstname 2B Tennis OR Swimming Query** and then display the query results in **Print Preview**. Change the orientation to **Landscape**, and the **Margins** to **Normal**. Create a paper or electronic printout as directed, and then click **Close Print Preview**.

9 **Close** the query, **Open** the **Navigation Pane**, increase the width of the **Navigation Pane** to display all object names fully, and then compare your screen with Figure 2.38.

Your *2B Tennis OR Swimming Query* object name displays under both tables from which it selected records.

FIGURE 2.38

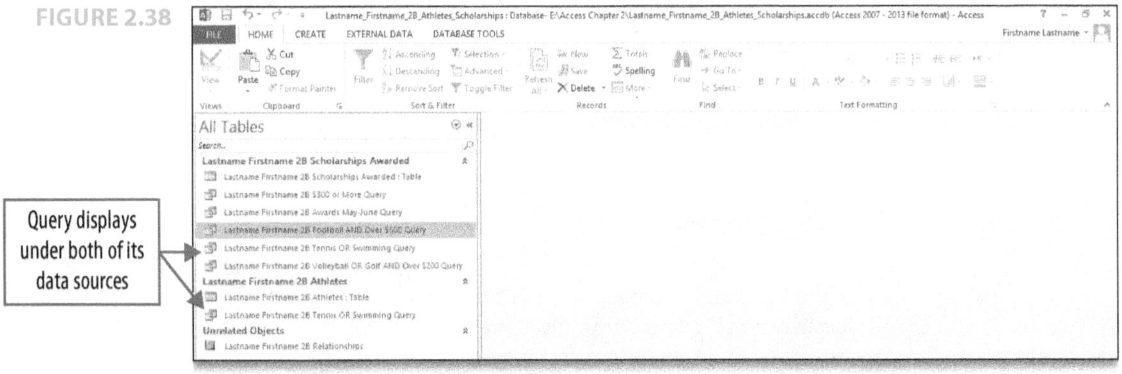

10 **Close** the **Navigation Pane**.

Objective 11 Use Wildcards in a Query

Video A2-11

Wildcard characters serve as a placeholder for one or more unknown characters in criteria. When you are unsure of the specific character or set of characters to include in the criteria, use a wildcard character in place of the character.

Activity 2.26 | Using a Wildcard in a Query

Use the asterisk (*) wildcard character to represent one or more unknown characters. For example, entering Fo* as the criteria in a last name field will result in displaying records containing last names of Foster, Forrester, Fossil, or any other last name that begins with *Fo*. In this activity, you will use the asterisk (*) wildcard character in criteria to answer the question, *Which athletes received scholarships from local rotary clubs, country clubs, or foundations?*

1 On the ribbon, click the **CREATE tab**, and then in the **Queries group**, click **Query Design**. In the **Show Table** dialog box, double-click your **2B Athletes** table, and then double-click your **2B Scholarships Awarded** table to add both tables to the table area. In the **Show Table** dialog box, click **Close**. Drag the **2B Scholarships Awarded** field list to the right so that there are approximately three inches of space between the two field lists, and then resize each field list to display all of the field names and the table names.

2 From the **2B Athletes** field list, add the following fields to the design grid in the order given: **Last Name** and **First Name**. From the **2B Scholarships Awarded** field list, add the **Awarding Organization** field to the design grid.

3 Click in the **Sort** row under **Last Name**, click the **arrow**, and then click **Ascending**. Click in the **Sort** row under **First Name**, click the **arrow**, and then click **Ascending**.

4 Click in the **Criteria** row under **Awarding Organization**, type **rotary*** and then press Enter.

The * wildcard character is a placeholder you can use to match one or more unknown characters. After pressing Enter, Access adds *Like* to the beginning of the criteria and places quotation marks around *rotary**.

5 **Run** the query, and then compare your screen with Figure 2.39.

Three athletes received scholarships from a rotary club from different cities. The results are sorted alphabetically by the Last Name field. If there were two athletes with the same Last Name, the records would be sorted by the First Name field.

FIGURE 2.39

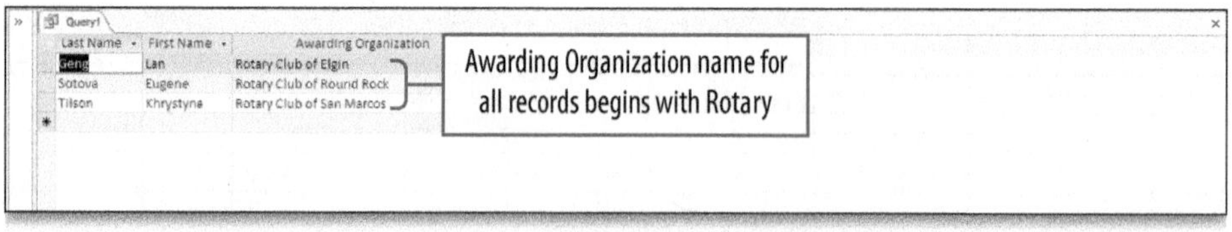

6 Switch to **Design** view. Click in the **or** row under **Awarding Organization**, type ***country club** and then press Enter.

You can use the * wildcard character at the beginning, middle, or end of the criteria. The position of the * determines the location of the unknown characters. By entering **country club*, Access will locate records with an Awarding Organization name that ends in *Country Club*.

7 **Run** the query.

Six records display for students receiving scholarships; three from organizations with a name that begins with *Rotary*, and three from organizations with a name that ends with *Country Club*.

8 Switch to **Design** view. In the design grid under **Awarding Organization** and under **Like "*country club"**, type ***foundation*** and then press Enter. Compare your screen with Figure 2.40.

This query will also display records where the Awarding Organization has *Foundation* anywhere in its name—at the beginning, in the middle, or at the end of the organization name. Three *OR* criteria have been entered for the Awarding Organization field. When run, this query will locate records where the Awarding Organization has a name that begins with *Rotary*, OR ends with *Country Club*, OR has *Foundation* anywhere in its name.

FIGURE 2.40

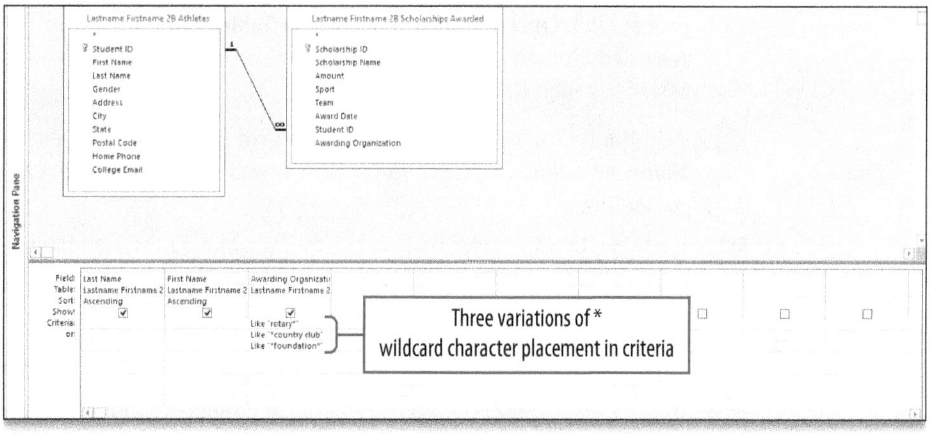

9 **Run** the query.

Twenty-eight scholarships were awarded from organizations where the name of the organization begins with *Rotary*, ends with *Country Club*, or has *Foundation* anywhere in its name. The records are sorted alphabetically by the Last Name field and then by the First Name field.

10 **Save** the query as **Lastname Firstname 2B Wildcard Query** and then display the query results in **Print Preview**. Create a paper or electronic printout as directed, and then click **Close Print Preview**.

11 **Close** the query, and then **Open** the **Navigation Pane**. Notice that your **2B Wildcard Query** displays under both tables because the query selected data from both tables—the data sources.

More Knowledge **Using the ? Wildcard Character to Search for a Single Unknown Character**

You can use the question mark (?) wildcard character to search for a single unknown character. For each question mark included in the criteria, the query results can display any character. For example, entering *b?d* as the criteria will result in the display of words such as *bed*, *bid*, or *bud*, or any three-character word that begins with *b* and ends with *d*. Entering *b??d* as the criteria will result in the display of words such as *bard*, *bend*, or *bind*, or any four-character word that begins with *b* and ends with *d*.

Objective 12 Create Calculated Fields in a Query

Video A2-12

Queries can create calculated values that are stored in a ***calculated field***. A calculated field stores the value of a mathematical operation. For example, you can multiply the value stored in a field named Total Hours Worked by the value stored in a field named Hourly Pay to display the Gross Pay value for each work study student.

There are two steps to create a calculated field in a query. First, name the field that will store the results of the calculation. Second, enter the ***expression***—the formula—that will perform the calculation. When entering the information for the calculated field in the query, the new field name must be followed by a colon (:), and each field name used in the expression must be enclosed within its own pair of brackets.

Activity 2.27 | Creating a Calculated Field in a Query

For each scholarship received by student athletes, the Texas Lakes Community College Alumni Association will donate an amount equal to 50 percent of each scholarship amount. In this activity, you will create a calculated field to determine the amount that the Alumni Association will donate for each scholarship. The query will answer the question, *How much money will the Alumni Association donate for each student athlete who is awarded a scholarship?*

1 **Close** « the **Navigation Pane**. On the ribbon, click the **CREATE tab**, and then in the **Queries group**, click **Query Design**. In the **Show Table** dialog box, double-click your **2B Scholarships Awarded** table to add the table to the table area, **Close** the **Show Table** dialog box, and then resize the field list.

2 Add the following fields to the design grid in the order given: **Student ID**, **Scholarship Name**, and **Amount**. Click in the **Sort** row under **Student ID**, click the **arrow**, and then click **Ascending**.

3 In the **Field** row, right-click in the first empty column to display a shortcut menu, and then click **Zoom**.

Although the calculation can be typed directly in the empty Field box, the Zoom dialog box gives you more working space and enables you to see the entire calculation as you enter it.

4 In the **Zoom** dialog box, type **Alumni Donation:[Amount]*0.5** and then compare your screen with Figure 2.41.

The first element, *Alumni Donation*, is the new field name that will display the result of the calculation when the query is run. The new field name is followed by a colon (:), which separates the new field name from the expression. *Amount* is enclosed in brackets because it is an existing field name in your 2B Scholarships Awarded table; it contains the numeric data on which the calculation is performed. Following the right square bracket is the asterisk (*), the mathematical operator for multiplication. Finally, the percentage expressed as a decimal—*0.5*—displays.

FIGURE 2.41

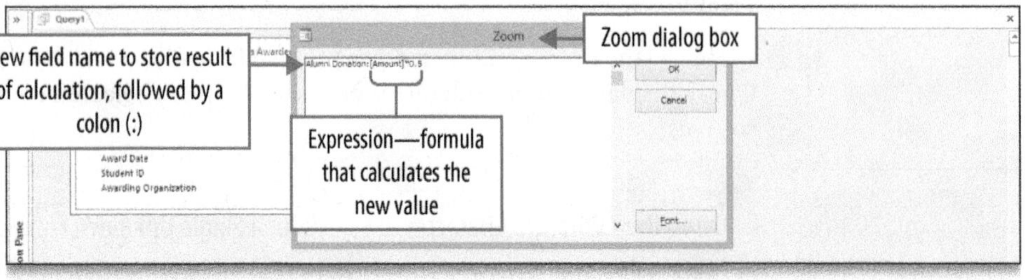

5 In the **Zoom** dialog box, click **OK**, **Run** the query, and then compare your screen with Figure 2.42.

The query results display three fields from your 2B Scholarships Awarded table and a fourth field—*Alumni Donation*—that displays a calculated value. Each calculated value equals the value in the Amount field multiplied by 0.5 or 50%.

FIGURE 2.42

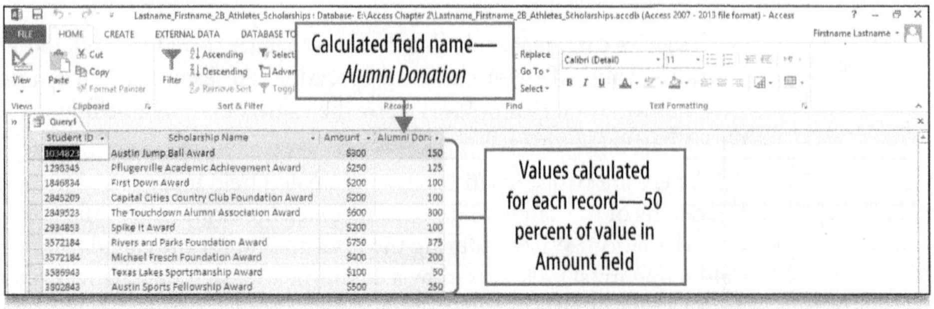

ALERT! **Do Your Query Results Differ from Figure 2.42?**

If your new field name does not display or if the results of the calculation do not display as shown in Figure 2.42, switch to Design view and carefully examine the expression you entered. Spelling or syntax errors prevent calculated fields from working properly.

6 Notice the formatting of the values in the **Alumni Donation** field—there are no dollar signs to match the formatting in the **Amount** field; you will adjust the formatting of this field later.

When using a number, such as 0.5, in an expression, the values that display in the calculated field might not be formatted the same as the existing field that was part of the calculation.

Activity 2.28 | Creating a Second Calculated Field in a Query

In this activity, you will create a calculated field to determine the total value of each scholarship after the Alumni Association donates an additional 50% based on the amount awarded by various organizations. The query will answer the question, *What is the total value of each scholarship after the Alumni Association donates an additional 50%?*

1 Switch to **Design** view. In the **Field** row, right-click in the first empty column to display a shortcut menu, and then click **Zoom.**

2 In the **Zoom** dialog box, type **Total Scholarship:[Amount]+[Alumni Donation]** and then compare your screen with Figure 2.43.

Each existing field name—*Amount* and *Alumni Donation*—must be enclosed in separate pairs of brackets.

FIGURE 2.43

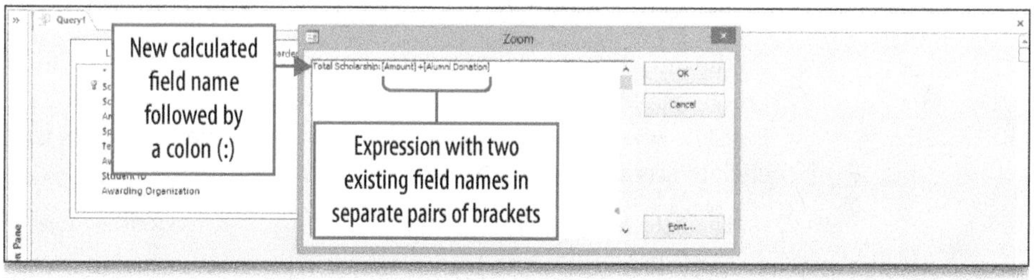

3 In the **Zoom** dialog box, click **OK**, and then **Run** the query.

The value in the *Total Scholarship* field is calculated by adding together the values in the Amount field and the Alumni Donation field. The values in the Total Scholarship field are formatted with dollar signs, commas, and decimal points, which is carried over from the Currency format in the Amount field.

Activity 2.29 | Formatting Calculated Fields

In this activity, you will format the calculated fields so that the values display in a consistent manner.

1 Switch to **Design** view. In the **Field** row, click in the **Alumni Donation** field name box.

2 Under **QUERY TOOLS**, on the **DESIGN tab**, in the **Show/Hide group**, click **Property Sheet.**

The Property Sheet displays on the right. Recall that a Property Sheet enables you to make precise changes to the properties—characteristics—of selected items, in this case, a field.

ANOTHER WAY In the design grid, on the Field row, right-click in the Alumni Donation field name box, and then click Properties.

3 In the **Property Sheet**, on the **General tab**, click **Format**. In the property setting box, click the **arrow**, and then compare your screen with Figure 2.44.

A list of available formats for the Alumni Donation field displays.

FIGURE 2.44

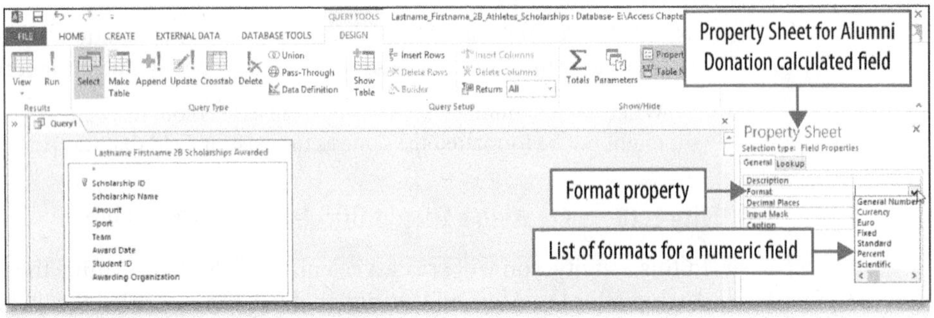

4 On the list, click **Currency**. In the **Property Sheet**, click **Decimal Places**. In the property setting box, click the **arrow**, and then click **0**.

5 In the design grid, in the **Field** row, click in the **Total Scholarship** field name. In the **Property Sheet**, set the **Decimal Places** property setting to **0**.

You do not need to set the Format setting to Currency as the field already displays with the currency symbol.

6 **Close** [×] the **Property Sheet**, and then **Run** the query.

The Alumni Donation and Total Scholarship fields are formatted as Currency with 0 decimal places.

7 To the left of the **Student ID** field name, click **Select All** [ ]. On the **HOME tab**, in the **Records group**, click **More**, and then click **Field Width**. In the **Column Width** dialog box, click **Best Fit**. **Save** [save] the query as **Lastname Firstname 2B Alumni Donations Query** and then click in any field to cancel the selection.

The field widths adjust to display fully the calculated field names.

8 Display the query results in **Print Preview**. On the **PRINT PREVIEW tab**, in the **Page Layout group**, click **Landscape**. Create a paper or electronic printout as directed, and then click **Close Print Preview**. **Close** [×] the query.

Objective 13 Calculate Statistics and Group Data in a Query

Video A2-13

You can use queries to perform statistical calculations known as ***aggregate functions*** on a group of records. For example, you can find the total or average amount for a group of records, or you can find the lowest or highest number in a group of records.

Activity 2.30 | Using the Min, Max, Avg, and Sum Functions in a Query

In this activity, you will use aggregate functions to find the lowest and highest scholarship amounts and the average and total scholarship amounts. The last query in this activity will answer the question, *What is the total dollar amount of all scholarships awarded?*

1 On the ribbon, click the **CREATE tab**, and then in the **Queries group**, click **Query Design**. In the **Show Table** dialog box, double-click your **2B Scholarships Awarded** table to add the table to the table area, **Close** the **Show Table** dialog box, and then resize the field list.

2 Add the **Amount** field to the design grid.

Include only the field to summarize in the design grid, so that the aggregate function is applied only to that field.

3 Under **QUERY TOOLS**, on the **DESIGN tab**, in the **Show/Hide group**, click **Totals** to add a **Total** row as the third row in the design grid. Notice that in the design grid, on the **Total** row under **Amount**, *Group By* displays.

Use the Total row to select an aggregate function for the selected field.

4 In the **Total** row under **Amount**, click in the box that displays *Group By*, and then click the **arrow** to display a list of aggregate functions. Compare your screen with Figure 2.45, and then take a moment to review the available aggregate functions and the purpose of each function as shown in Table 2.46.

FIGURE 2.45

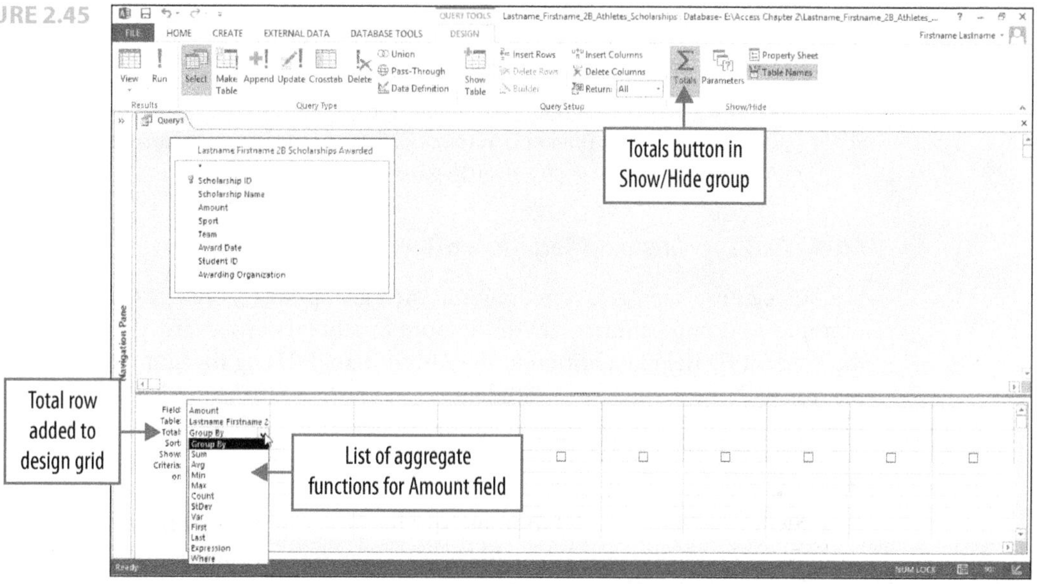

FIGURE 2.46

AGGREGATE FUNCTIONS	
FUNCTION NAME	**PURPOSE**
Group By	Groups the records alphabetically, for example, groups by Sport.
Sum	Totals the values in a field.
Avg	Averages the values in a field.
Min	Locates the smallest value in a field.
Max	Locates the largest value in a field.
Count	Displays the number of records based on a field.
StDev	Calculates the standard deviation for the values in a field.
Var	Calculates the variance for the values in a field.
First	Displays the first value in a field or column.
Last	Displays the last value in a field or column.
Expression	Creates a calculated field that includes an aggregate function.
Where	Limits the records to those that match a condition specified in the Criteria row of a field.

5 In the list of functions, click **Min**, and then **Run** the query. Point to the right edge of the first column to display the ⊞ pointer, and then double-click to apply Best Fit to the field.

Access locates the minimum (smallest) value—*$100*—in the Amount field for all of the records in the 2B Scholarships Awarded table. The field name *MinOfAmount* is automatically created. This query answers the question, *What is the minimum (smallest) scholarship amount awarded to athletes?*

6 Switch to **Design** view. In the **Total** row under **Amount**, click the **arrow**, and then click **Max. Run** the query.

The maximum (largest) value for a scholarship award amount is *$750.00*.

7 Switch to **Design** view. In the **Total** row, under **Amount**, click the **arrow**, and then click **Avg. Run** the query.

The average scholarship award amount is *$358.33*.

8 Switch to **Design** view. In the **Total** row, under **Amount**, click the **arrow**, and then click **Sum. Run** the query.

The values in the Amount field for all records are summed displaying a result of *$10,750.00*. The field name *SumOfAmount* is automatically created. The query answers the question, *What is the total dollar amount of all scholarships awarded?*

Activity 2.31 | Grouping Records in a Query

You can use aggregate functions and then group the records by the data in a field. For example, to group (summarize) the amount of scholarships awarded to each student, you include the Student ID field in addition to the Amount field. Using the Sum aggregate function, the records will be grouped by the Student ID so you can see the total amount of scholarships awarded to each student. Similarly, you can group the records by the Sport field so you can see the total amount of scholarships awarded for each sport.

1 Switch to **Design** view. From the field list, drag the **Student ID** field to the first column of the design grid—the **Amount** field moves to the second column. In the **Total** row, under **Student ID**, notice that *Group By* displays.

This query will group—summarize—the records by Student ID and will calculate a total amount for each student.

2 **Run** the query, and then compare your screen with Figure 2.47.

The query calculates the total amount of all scholarships for each student.

FIGURE 2.47

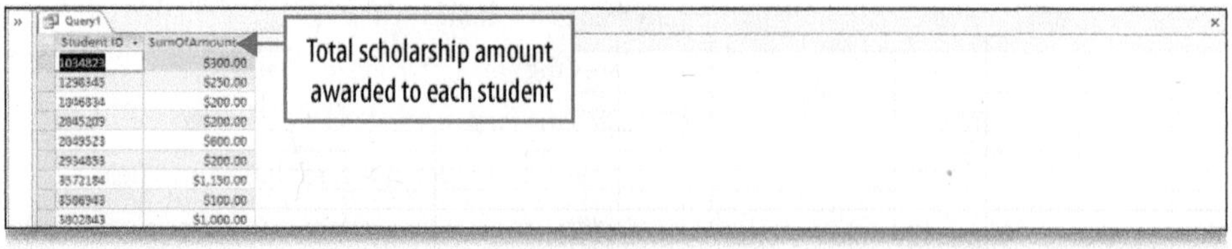

3 Switch to **Design** view. In the design grid, above **Student ID**, point to the selection bar to display the ⬇ pointer. Click to select the column, and then press **Del** to remove the **Student ID** field from the design grid.

4 From the field list, drag the **Sport** field to the first column in the design grid—the **Amount** field moves to the second column. Click in the **Sort** row under **Amount**, click the **arrow**, and then click **Descending**.

5 On the **DESIGN tab**, in the **Show/Hide group**, click **Property Sheet**. In the **Property Sheet**, set the **Decimal Places** property to **0**, and then **Close** [X] the **Property Sheet**.

6 **Run** the query, and then compare your screen with Figure 2.48.

Access groups—summarizes—the records by each sport and displays the groupings in descending order by the total amount of scholarships awarded for each sport. Basketball scholarships were awarded the largest total amount—*$3,500*—and Volleyball scholarships were awarded the smallest total amount—*$650*.

FIGURE 2.48

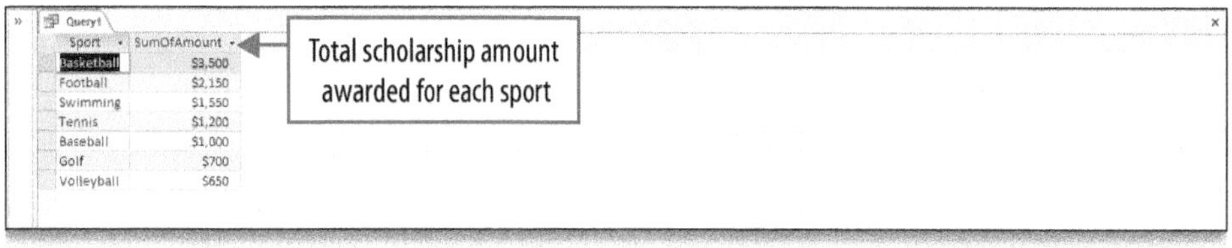

7 **Save** the query as **Lastname Firstname 2B Total by Sport Query** and then display the query results in **Print Preview**. Create a paper or electronic printout as directed, click **Close Print Preview**, and then **Close** [×] the query.

Objective 14 Create a Crosstab Query

Video A2-14

A ***crosstab query*** uses an aggregate function for data that can be grouped by two types of information, and then displays the data in a compact, spreadsheet-like format with column headings and row headings. A crosstab query always has at least one row heading, one column heading, and one summary field. Use a crosstab query to summarize a large amount of data in a compact space that is easy to read.

Activity 2.32 | Creating a Crosstab Query Using the Query Wizard

In this activity, you will create a crosstab query that displays the total amount of scholarships awarded for each sport and for each type of team—men's or women's.

1 On the ribbon, click the **CREATE tab**, and then in the **Queries group**, click **Query Wizard**.

2 In the **New Query** dialog box, click **Crosstab Query Wizard**, and then click **OK**.

3 In the **Crosstab Query Wizard**, click your **Table: 2B Scholarships Awarded**, and then click **Next**.

4 In the wizard under **Available Fields**, double-click **Sport** to move the field to the **Selected Fields** list and to group the scholarship amounts by the sports—the sports will display as row headings. Click **Next**, and then compare your screen with Figure 2.49.

The sport names will be grouped and displayed as row headings, and you are prompted to select column headings.

FIGURE 2.49

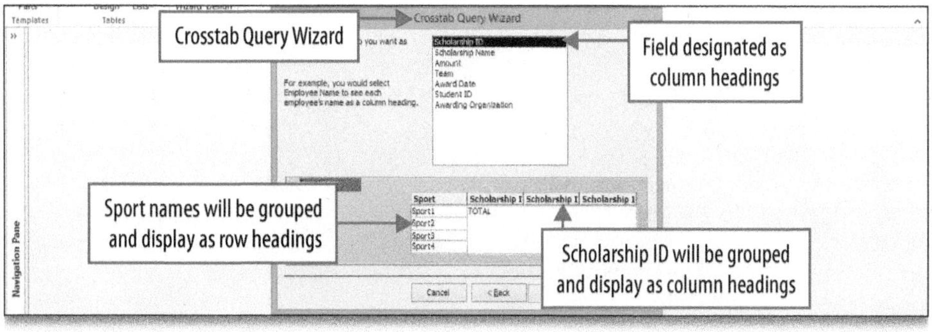

5 In the wizard, in the field list, click **Team** to select the column headings. Click **Next**, and then compare your screen with Figure 2.50.

The Team types—*Men's* and *Women's*—will display as column headings, and you are prompted to select a field to summarize.

FIGURE 2.50

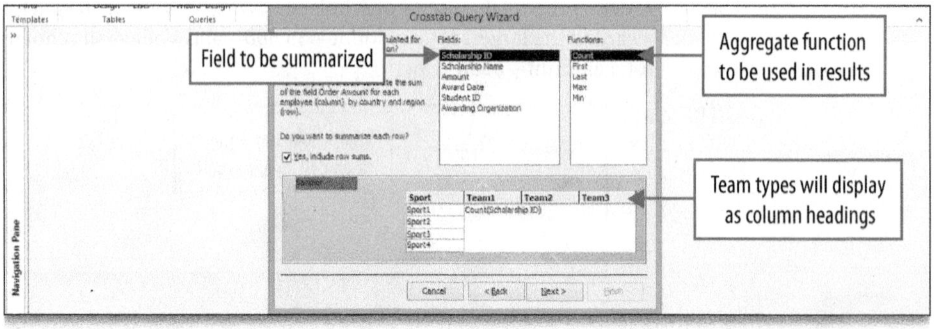

6 In the wizard under **Fields**, click **Amount**. Under **Functions**, click **Sum**.

The crosstab query will calculate the total scholarship amount for each sport and for each type of team.

7 Click **Next**. In the **What do you want to name your query?** box, select the existing text, type **Lastname Firstname 2B Sport and Team Crosstab Query** and then click **Finish**. Apply **Best Fit** to the datasheet, **Save** the query, click in any field to cancel the selection, and then compare your screen with Figure 2.51.

The field widths adjust to display fully the calculated field names.

FIGURE 2.51

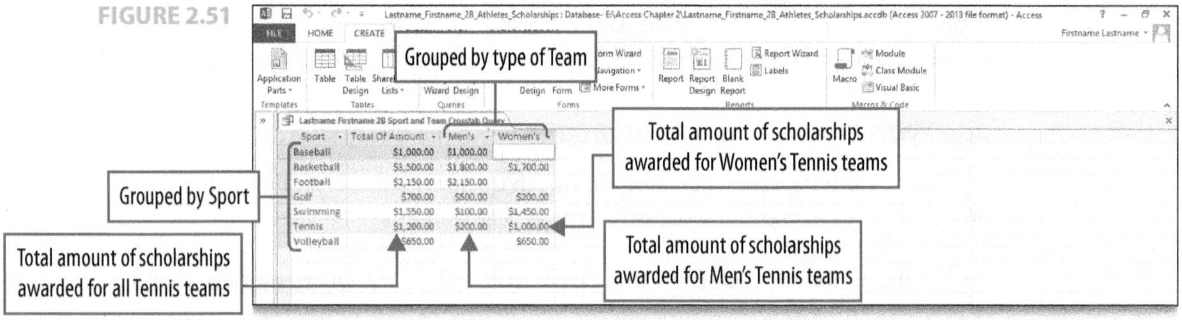

8 Display the query results in **Print Preview**. Create a paper or electronic printout as directed, click **Close Print Preview**, and then **Close** the query.

More Knowledge **Creating a Crosstab Query Using Data from Two Related Tables**

To create a crosstab query using fields from more than one table, you must first create a select query with the fields from both tables, and then use the query as the data source for the crosstab query.

Objective 15 Create a Parameter Query

Video A2-15

A ***parameter query*** prompts you for criteria before running the query. For example, you might need to display the records for students who live in different cities serviced by Texas Lakes Community College. You can create a select query and enter the criteria for a city such as Austin, but when you open the query, only the records for those students who live in Austin will display. To find the students who live in Round Rock, you must open the query in Design view, change the criteria, and then run the query again.

A parameter query eliminates the need to change the design of a select query. You create a single query that prompts you to enter the city; the results are based upon the criteria you enter when prompted.

Activity 2.33 | Creating a Parameter Query with One Criteria

In this activity, you will create a parameter query that displays student athletes from a specified city in the areas serviced by Texas Lakes Community College.

1. On the **CREATE tab**, in the **Queries group**, click **Query Design**.
2. In the **Show Table** dialog box, double-click your **2B Athletes** table to add it to the table area, **Close** the **Show Table** dialog box, and then resize the field list.
3. Add the following fields to the design grid in the order given: **Last Name, First Name, Address, City, State,** and **Postal Code.**
4. Click in the **Sort** row under **Last Name,** click the **arrow,** and then click **Ascending.** Click in the **Sort** row under **First Name,** click the **arrow,** and then click **Ascending.**
5. In the **Criteria** row under **City,** type **[Enter a City]** and then press Enter. Compare your screen with Figure 2.52.

   The bracketed text indicates a ***parameter***—a value that can be changed—rather than specific criteria.

FIGURE 2.52

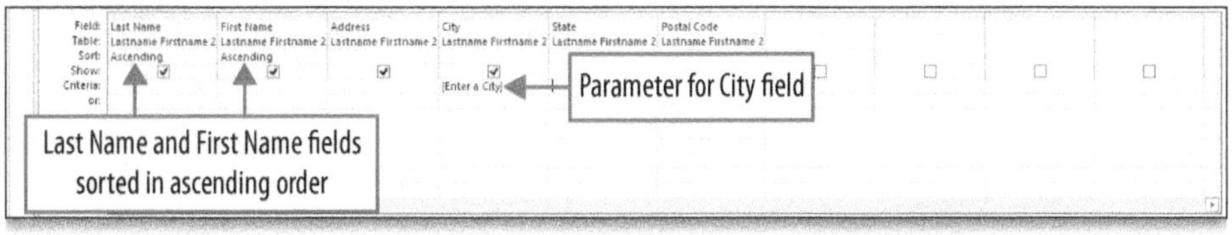

6. **Run** the query. In the **Enter Parameter Value** dialog box, type **austin** and then compare your screen with Figure 2.53.

   The Enter Parameter Value dialog box prompts you to *Enter a City*, which is the text enclosed in brackets that you entered in the Criteria row under City. The city you enter will be set as the criteria for the query. Because you are prompted for the criteria, you can reuse this query without having to edit the Criteria row in Design view. The value you enter is not case sensitive—you can enter *austin, Austin,* or *AUSTIN.*

FIGURE 2.53

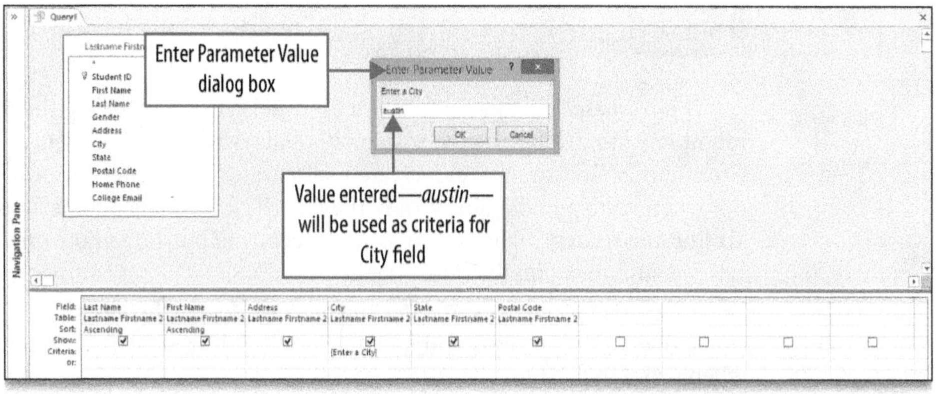

ALERT! Did the Enter Parameter Value Dialog Box Not Display?

If the Enter Parameter Value dialog box does not display, you may have typed the parameter incorrectly in the design grid. Common errors include using parentheses or curly braces instead of brackets around the parameter text, which Access interprets as specific criteria, resulting in no records matching the criteria. If you type curly braces instead of brackets, the query will not run. To correct, display the query in Design view and correct the parameter entered in the Criteria row.

7 In the **Enter Parameter Value** dialog box, click **OK.**

Twenty-three students live in the city of Austin, and the records are sorted in alphabetical order by the Last Name field. If students have the same last name, those records will be sorted by the First Name field.

8 **Save** the query as **Lastname Firstname 2B City Parameter Query** and then **Close** the query.

Recall that only the query design is saved; each time you open a query, it is run using the most up-to-date information from the data source.

9 **Open** » the **Navigation Pane**. In the **Navigation Pane**, under your **2B Athletes** table, double-click your **2B City Parameter Query**. In the **Enter Parameter Value** dialog box, type **round rock** and then click **OK. Close** « the **Navigation Pane.** Compare your screen with Figure 2.54.

Nine students live in the city of Round Rock. Every time you open a parameter query, you are prompted to enter criteria. You may have to apply Best Fit to the columns if all of the data in the fields does not display and you wish to print the query results—the length of the data in the fields changes as new records display depending upon the criteria entered.

FIGURE 2.54

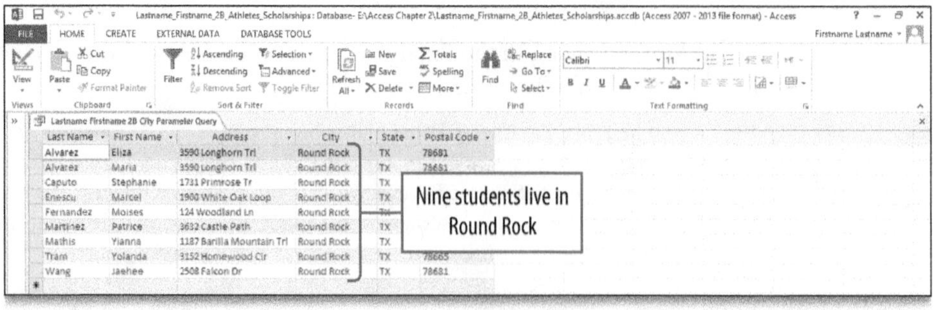

10 Display the query results in **Print Preview**, and change the orientation to **Landscape.** Create a paper or electronic printout as directed, click **Close Print Preview**, and then **Close** the query.

11 **Open** [»] the **Navigation Pane**, and, if necessary increase the width of the pane so that all object names display fully. On the right side of the title bar, click **Close** [X] to close the database and to exit Access. As directed by your instructor, submit your database and the paper or electronic printouts of the 11 objects—relationship report and 10 queries—that are the results of this project. Specifically, in this project, using your own name, you created the following database and printouts or electronic printouts:

1. Lastname_Firstname_2B_Athletes_Scholarships	Database file
2. Lastname Firstname 2B Relationships	Relationships Report (printout or electronic printout)
3. Lastname Firstname 2B $300 or More Query	Query (printout or electronic printout)
4. Lastname Firstname 2B Awards May-June Query	Query (printout or electronic printout)
5. Lastname Firstname 2B Football AND Over $500 Query	Query (printout or electronic printout)
6. Lastname Firstname 2B Volleyball OR Golf AND Over $200 Query	Query (printout or electronic printout)
7. Lastname Firstname 2B Tennis OR Swimming Query	Query (printout or electronic printout)
8. Lastname Firstname 2B Wildcard Query	Query (printout or electronic printout)
9. Lastname Firstname 2B Alumni Donations Query	Query (printout or electronic printout)
10. Lastname Firstname 2B Total by Sport Query	Query (printout or electronic printout)
11. Lastname Firstname 2B Sport and Team Crosstab Query	Query (printout or electronic printout)
12. Lastname Firstname 2B City Parameter Query	Query (printout or electronic printout - Round Rock)

***More* Knowledge** **Parameter Query Prompts**

Be sure that the parameter you enter in the Criteria row as a prompt is not the same as the field name. For example, do not use *[City]* as the parameter. Access interprets this as the field name of *City*. Recall that you entered a field name in brackets when creating a calculated field in a query. If you use a field name as the parameter, the Enter Parameter Value dialog box *will not* display, and all of the records *will* display.

The parameter should inform the individual running the query of the data required to display the correct results. If you want to use the field name by itself as the prompt, type a question mark at the end of the text; for example, *[City?]*. You cannot use a period, exclamation mark (!), curly braces ({ }), another set of brackets ([ ]), or the ampersand (&) as part of the parameter.

END | You have completed Project 2B

GO! with Office Online (formerly Web Apps)

Objective Export an Access Query to a PDF File, Save the PDF File to Google Drive, and Share the File

Access web apps are designed to work with Microsoft's SharePoint, a service for setting up websites to share and manage documents. Your college may not have SharePoint installed, so you will use other tools to share objects from your database so that you can work collaboratively with others. Recall that Google Docs is Google's free, web-based word processor, spreadsheet, slide show, form, and data storage service. Google Drive is Google's free file storage and sharing service. For Access, you can export a database object to an Excel worksheet, a PDF file, or a text file, and then save the file to Google Drive.

ALERT! Working with Web-Based Applications and Services

Computer programs and services on the web receive continuous updates and improvements. Thus, the steps to complete this web-based activity may differ from the ones shown. You can often look at the screens and the information presented to determine how to complete the activity.

Activity | Exporting an Access Query to a PDF File, Saving the PDF file to Google Drive, and Sharing the File

In this activity, you will export your 2B Sport and Team Crosstab Query object to a PDF file, upload your PDF file to Google Drive, and then share the file.

1 **Start** Access, navigate to your **Access Chapter 2** folder, and then **Open** your **2B_Athletes_Scholarships** database file. If necessary, on the Message Bar, click **Enable Content**. In the **Navigation Pane**, click your **2B Sport and Team Crosstab Query** object to select it—do not open it.

2 On the ribbon, click the **EXTERNAL DATA tab**, and then in the **Export group**, click **PDF or XPS**. In the **Publish as PDF or XPS** dialog box, navigate to your **Access Chapter 2** folder. Click in the **File name** box. Using your own name, type **Lastname_Firstname_AC_2B_Web** and then be sure that the **Open file after publishing** check box is selected, and the **Minimum size (publishing online)** option button is selected. Click **Publish**, and then compare your screen with Figure A.

The PDF file is created and opens in Windows 8 Reader, Adobe Reader, or Adobe Acrobat, depending on the software that is installed on your computer.

FIGURE A

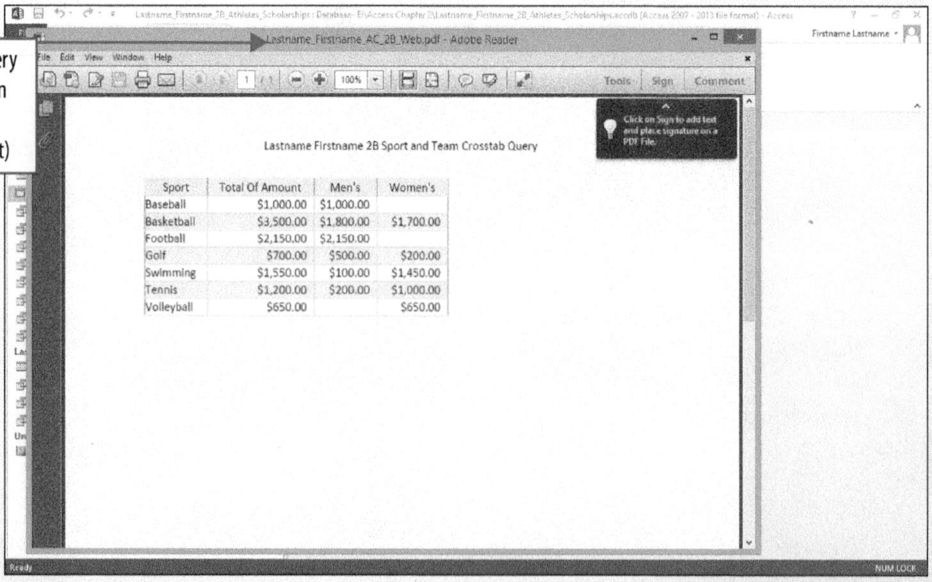

Your 2B Sport and Team Crosstab Query exported as a PDF file and opened in Adobe Reader (yours may open in Windows Reader 8 or Adobe Acrobat)

(GO! with Office Online (formerly Web Apps) continues on the next page)

3 **Close** your AC_2B_Web file. In the **Export - PDF** dialog box, click **Close**, and then **Close** Access.

4 From the desktop, start Internet Explorer, navigate to **http://drive.google.com**, and sign in to your Google account, or create one.

5 Open your **GO! Web Projects** folder—or create and open this folder if necessary. Under **Drive**, to the right of **Create**, click **Upload**, and then click **Files**. In the **Choose File to Upload** dialog box, navigate to your **Access Chapter 2** folder, and then double-click your **AC_2B_Web** file to upload it to Google Drive. When the title bar of the message box indicates *Upload complete*, **Close** the message box.

6 Click your **AC_2B_Web** file to open the file in Google Drive. Notice that it displays as a PDF file on a separate tab in the browser window.

7 In the browser window, locate the tab for the PDF file, and then **Close** the tab to display your folder in Google Drive.

8 Right-click your **AC_2B_Web** file, point to **Share**, and then click **Share**.

9 In the **Sharing settings** dialog box, click in the **Add people** box, and then type your own email address that you use at your college. Click the **Can edit arrow**, and click **Can comment**. Click **Add message**, type **Please share your comments about the results of this crosstab query.** and then compare your screen with Figure B.

10 On your keyboard, press the key, type **snip** and then click **Snipping Tool**. In the **Snipping Tool** dialog box, click the **New arrow**, and then click **Full-screen snip**.

11 On the **Snipping Tool** toolbar, click **Save Snip**. In the **Save As** dialog box, navigate to your **Access Chapter 2** folder. Click in the **File name** box, type **Lastname_Firstname_AC_2B_Web_Snip** and then be sure that the **Save as type** box displays **JPEG file**. Click **Save**, and then **Close** the **Snipping Tool** window.

12 In the **Sharing settings** dialog box, click **Share & save**. In the **Sharing settings** dialog box, click **Done**.

You can change who has access to the file in the Sharing settings dialog box. By default, the file is private and is shared only with specific people you have designated. You can grant access to anyone on the web or to anyone who has the link to this file.

13 In Google Drive, click your Google Drive name, and then click **Sign out**. **Close** your browser window.

14 If directed to submit a paper printout of your pdf and snip file, follow the directions given in the Note. As directed by your instructor, submit your pdf file and your snip file that are the results of this project. Your instructor may also request that you submit a copy of the email that was sent to you notifying you of the shared file.

NOTE **Printing Your PDF and Snip .jpeg File**

Use File Explorer to navigate to your Access Chapter 2 folder. Locate and double-click your AC_2B_Web file. On the toolbar, click the Print file button. Then Close the Windows 8 Reader, Adobe Reader, or Adobe Acrobat window. In your Access Chapter 2 folder, locate and double-click your AC_2B_Web_Snip file. If this is the first time you have tried to open a .jpeg file, you will be asked to identify a program. If you are not sure which program to use, select Windows Photo Viewer. From the ribbon, menu bar, or toolbar, click the Print command, and then Close the program window.

FIGURE B

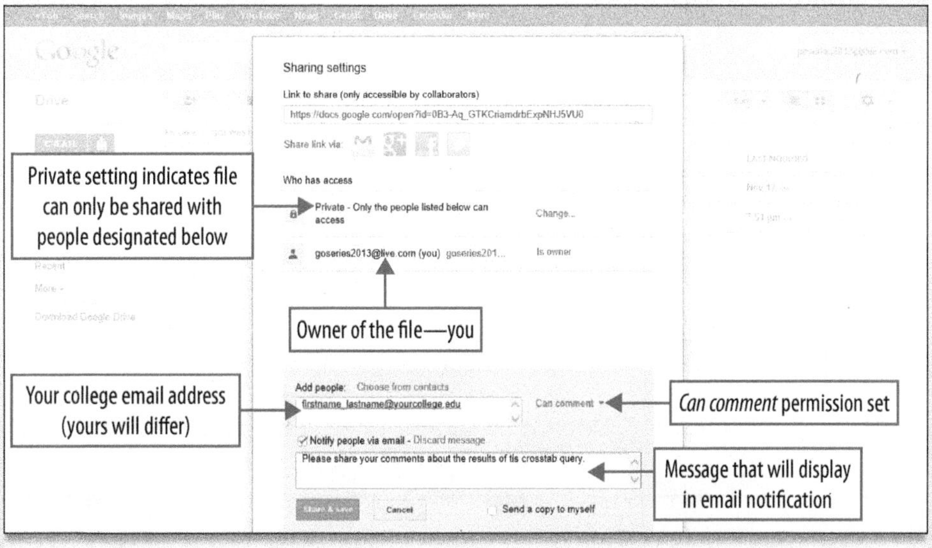

GO! with Microsoft Office 365

Andrew Rodriguez / Fotolia; FotolEdhar/ Fotolia; apops/ Fotolia; Yuri Arcurs/ Fotolia

Sharing Your Calendar in Office 365: With Office 365, you set up your Calendar in Outlook—either in Outlook Web App or on the desktop app—and then you can share your calendar, add appointments and meetings, and see your calendar from anywhere that you have Internet access. Recall that Outlook Web App and the Outlook desktop app work seamlessly together. When you use the desktop app, you have some additional features that are not available in Outlook Web App, but any information you add is available in either app. You will be able to view your calendar—and use email—from your smartphone or from anywhere you have an Internet connection.

In an Office 365 environment, the most important thing to do with your calendar is to share it with others. Recall that Office 365 is specifically designed to help teams work together, and the first step to working together successfully is to share as much information as possible to facilitate good communication.

When you create an appointment in your calendar, Outlook displays one of four indicators associated with your availability for that date and time: Busy, Free, Tentative, or Out of Office. This is referred to as your ***free/busy information***. Outlook's default setting for all appointments is Busy. The free/busy indicators also display when others view your calendar on the Office 365 shared Exchange server. Recall that Exchange Server is Microsoft's system for sharing Outlook information among members on a network. Your free/busy schedule is shared automatically with all other users.

In an Exchange Online environment, you can share your calendar with other Exchange Online users in your organization. Additionally, you can publish your calendar to the Internet and other people so they can access it. You could even share your calendar with a customer or client.

Activity | Sharing Calendars

This group project relates to the **Bell Orchid Hotels.** If your instructor assigns this project to your class, you can expect to use your **Outlook Calendar** in **Office 365 Exchange Online** to set meeting times for the following tasks for this chapter:

- If you are in the **Accounting Group**, you and your teammates will set meeting times to sort, filter, and create queries for the Stockholders database you created in Chapter 1.
- If you are in the **Engineering Group**, you and your teammates will set meeting times to sort, filter, and create queries for the Subcontractors database you created in Chapter 1.
- If you are in the **Food and Beverage Group**, you and your teammates will set meeting times to sort, filter, and create queries for the Banquet Clients database you created in Chapter 1.
- If you are in the **Human Resources Group**, you and your teammates will set meeting times to sort, filter, and create queries for the Employee database you created in Chapter 1.
- If you are in the **Operations Group**, you and your teammates will set meeting times to sort, filter, and create queries for the Guests database you created in Chapter 1.
- If you are in the **Sales and Marketing Group**, you and your teammates will set meeting times to sort, filter, and create queries for the Associations database you created in Chapter 1.

FIGURE A

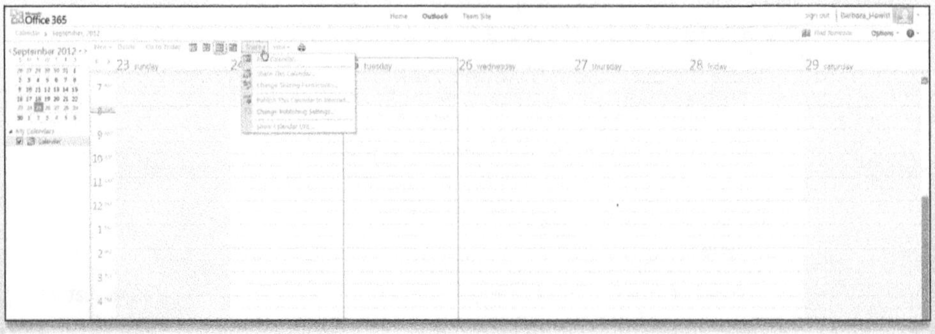

END OF CHAPTER

SUMMARY

Table relationships are created by joining the common fields in tables and provide a means for you to extract information from multiple tables when you create queries, forms, and reports.

Queries are created to answer questions and to extract information from your database tables; saving a query with your database saves you time when you need to answer the question many times.

Queries range from simple queries where you ask a single question to complex queries where you use compound criteria, wildcard characters, logical operators, and create calculated fields.

A crosstab query displays information grouped by two fields that is an easy way to display complex data, and a parameter query prompts you to enter the criteria when you open or run the query.

GO! LEARN IT ONLINE

Review the concepts and key terms in this chapter by completing these online challenges, which you can find at **www.pearsonhighered.com/go**.

Matching and Multiple Choice: Answer matching and multiple choice questions to test what you learned in this chapter. MyITLab®

Crossword Puzzle: Spell out the words that match the numbered clues, and put them in the puzzle squares.

Flipboard: Flip through the definitions of the key terms in this chapter and match them with the correct term.

GO! FOR JOB SUCCESS

Video: Making Ethical Choices

Your instructor may assign this video to your class, and then ask you to think about, or discuss with your classmates, these questions:

FotolEdhar / Fotolia

Which behaviors in this video do you think were unethical?

Is it unethical to "borrow" things from your employer? Why? What would you do if you saw this behavior going on?

What do you think an employer could do to prevent unethical behavior?

END OF CHAPTER

REVIEW AND ASSESSMENT GUIDE FOR ACCESS CHAPTER 2

Your instructor may assign one or more of these projects to help you review the chapter and assess your mastery and understanding of the chapter.

Review and Assessment Guide for Access Chapter 2

Project	Apply Skills from These Chapter Objectives	Project Type	Project Location
2C	Objectives 1-7 from Project 2A	**2C Skills Review** A guided review of the skills from Project 2A.	On the following pages
2D	Objectives 8-15 from Project 2B	**2D Skills Review** A guided review of the skills from Project 2B.	On the following pages
2E	Objectives 1-7 from Project 2A	**2E Mastery (Grader Project)** A demonstration of your mastery of the skills in Project 2A with extensive decision making.	In MyITLab and on the following pages
2F	Objectives 8-15 from Project 2B	**2F Mastery (Grader Project)** A demonstration of your mastery of the skills in Project 2B with extensive decision making.	In MyITLab and on the following pages
2G	Objectives 1-15 from Projects 2A and 2B	**2G Mastery (Grader Project)** A demonstration of your mastery of the skills in Projects 2A and 2B with extensive decision making.	In MyITLab and on the following pages
2H	Combination of Objectives from Projects 2A and 2B	**2H GO! Fix It** A demonstration of your mastery of the skills in Projects 2A and 2B by creating a correct result from a document that contains errors you must find.	Online
2I	Combination of Objectives from Projects 2A and 2B	**2I GO! Make It** A demonstration of your mastery of the skills in Projects 2A and 2B by creating a result from a supplied picture.	Online
2J	Combination of Objectives from Projects 2A and 2B	**2J GO! Solve It** A demonstration of your mastery of the skills in Projects 2A and 2B, your decision-making skills, and your critical thinking skills. A task-specific rubric helps you self-assess your result.	Online
2K	Combination of Objectives from Projects 2A and 2B	**2K GO! Solve It** A demonstration of your mastery of the skills in Projects 2A and 2B, your decision-making skills, and your critical thinking skills. A task-specific rubric helps you self-assess your result.	On the following pages
2L	Combination of Objectives from Projects 2A and 2B	**2L GO! Think** A demonstration of your understanding of the chapter concepts applied in a manner that you would outside of college. An analytic rubric helps you and your instructor grade the quality of your work by comparing it to the work an expert in the discipline would create.	On the following pages
2M	Combination of Objectives from Projects 2A and 2B	**2M GO! Think** A demonstration of your understanding of the chapter concepts applied in a manner that you would outside of college. An analytic rubric helps you and your instructor grade the quality of your work by comparing it to the work an expert in the discipline would create.	Online
2N	Combination of Objectives from Projects 2A and 2B	**2N You and GO!** A demonstration of your understanding of the chapter concepts applied in a manner that you would in a personal situation. An analytic rubric helps you and your instructor grade the quality of your work.	Online
2O	Combination of Objectives from Projects 2A and 2B	**2O Cumulative Group Project for Access Chapter 2** A demonstration of your understanding of concepts and your ability to work collaboratively in a group role-playing assessment, requiring both collaboration and self-management.	Online

GLOSSARY

GLOSSARY OF CHAPTER KEY TERMS

Aggregate functions Calculations such as Min, Max, Avg, and Sum that are performed on a group of records.

AND condition A compound criteria used to display records that match all parts of the specified criteria.

Ascending order A sorting order that arranges text alphabetically (A to Z) and numbers from the lowest number to the highest number.

Between ... And operator A comparison operator that looks for values within a range.

Calculated field A field that stores the value of a mathematical operation.

Cascade Delete Related Records A cascade option that enables you to delete a record in a table on the *one* side of the relationship and also delete all of the related records in related tables.

Cascade options Relationship options that enable you to update records in related tables when referential integrity is enforced.

Cascade Update Related Fields A cascade option that enables you to change the data in the primary key field in the table on the *one* side of the relationship and update that change to any fields storing that same data in related tables.

Comparison operators Symbols that are used to evaluate data in the field to determine if it is the same (=), greater than (>), less than (<), or in between a range of values as specified by the criteria.

Compound criteria Multiple conditions in a query or filter.

Criteria Conditions in a query that identify the specific records you are looking for.

Crosstab query A query that uses an aggregate function for data that can be grouped by two types of information and displays the data in a compact, spreadsheet-like format with column headings and row headings.

Data source The table or tables from which a form, query, or report retrieves its data.

Descending order A sorting order that arranges text in reverse alphabetical order (Z to A) and numbers from the highest number to the lowest number.

Design grid The lower area of the query window that displays the design of the query.

Expression A formula.

Field list A list of field names in a table.

Foreign key The field that is included in the related table so the field can be joined with the primary key in another table for the purpose of creating a relationship.

Free/Busy information In the Outlook calendar, one of four indicators—Busy, Free, Tentative, or Out of Office—associated with your availability for a specific date and time.

Innermost sort field When sorting on multiple fields in Datasheet view, the field that is used for the second level of sorting.

Is Not Null A criteria that searches for fields that are not empty.

Is Null A criteria that searches for fields that are empty.

Join line In the Relationships window, the line joining two tables that visually indicates the common fields and the type of relationship.

Logical operators Operators that are used to evaluate data to determine if a condition is met (true) or not met (false). With two criteria, AND requires that both conditions be met and OR requires that either condition be met for a record to display in the query results.

Message Bar The area directly below the ribbon that displays information such as security alerts when there is potentially unsafe, active content in an Office document that you open.

One-to-many relationship A relationship between two tables where one record in the first table corresponds to many records in the second table—the most common type of relationship in Access.

OR condition A compound criteria used to display records that match at least one of the specified criteria.

Outermost sort field When sorting on multiple fields in Datasheet view, the field that is used for the first level of sorting.

Parameter A value that can be changed.

Parameter query A query that prompts you for criteria before running the query.

Referential integrity A set of rules that Access uses to ensure that the data between related tables is valid.

Relationship An association that you establish between two tables based on common fields.

Run The process in which Access looks at the records in the table(s) included in the query design, finds the records that match the specified criteria, and then displays the records in a datasheet; only the fields included in the query design display.

Sorting The process of arranging data in a specific order based on the value in a field.

Subdatasheet A format for displaying related records when you click ⊞ next to a record in a table on the *one* side of the relationship.

Subset A portion of the total records available.

Table area The upper area of the query window that displays field lists for the tables that are used in a query.

Text string A sequence of characters.

Trust Center An area of Access where you can view the security and privacy settings for your Access installation.

Wildcard character In a query, a character that serves as a placeholder for one or more unknown characters in criteria; an asterisk (*) represents one or more unknown characters, and a question mark (?) represents a single unknown character.

CHAPTER REVIEW

Apply 2A skills from these Objectives:

1. Open and Save an Existing Database
2. Create Table Relationships
3. Sort Records in a Table
4. Create a Query in Design View
5. Create a New Query from an Existing Query
6. Sort Query Results
7. Specify Criteria in a Query

Skills Review Project 2C Freshman Orientation

In the following Skills Review, you will assist Dr. Wendy Bowie, the director of counseling at the Southwest Campus, in using her database to answer several questions about the freshman orientation sessions that will be held prior to class registration. Your completed database objects will look similar to Figure 2.55.

PROJECT FILES

For Project 2C, you will need the following file:

a02C_Freshman_Orientation

You will save your database as:

Lastname_Firstname_2C_Freshman_Orientation

PROJECT RESULTS

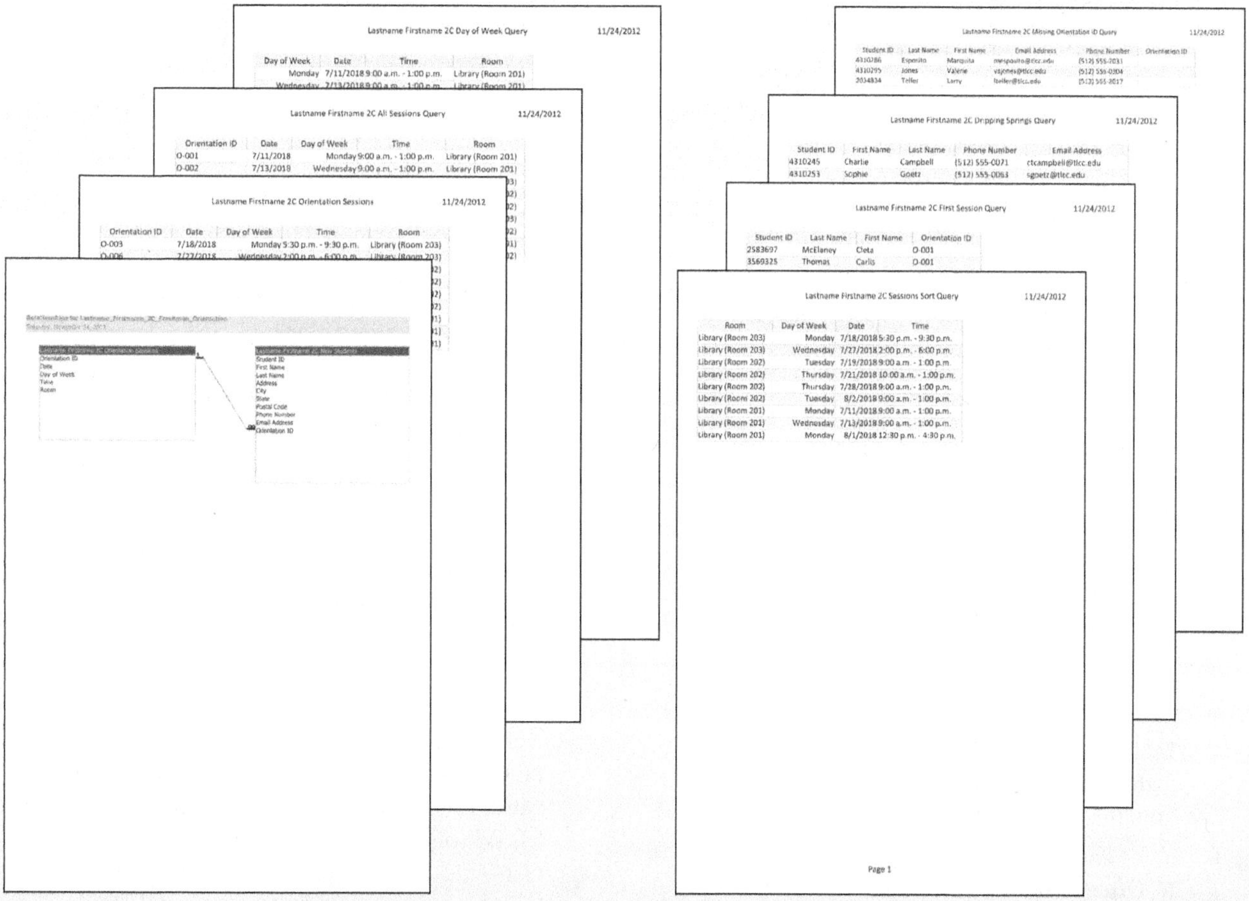

FIGURE 2.55

(Project 2C Freshman Orientation continues on the next page)

CHAPTER REVIEW

Skills Review Project 2C Freshman Orientation (continued)

1 **Start** Access. In the Access opening screen, click **Open Other Files**. Under **Open**, click **Computer**. Under **Recent Folders**, if displayed, click the location where your student data files are stored; otherwise, click **Browse** and then navigate to the location where your student data files are stored. Double-click **a02C_Freshman_Orientation** to open the database.

a. On the ribbon, click the **FILE tab**, and then click **Save As**. Under **File Types**, be sure **Save Database As** is selected. On the right, under **Database File Types**, be sure **Access Database** is selected, and then click **Save As**.

b. In the **Save As** dialog box, navigate to your **Access Chapter 2** folder. Click in the **File name** box, type **Lastname_Firstname_2C_Freshman_Orientation** and then press Enter. On the **Message Bar**, click **Enable Content**.

c. In the **Navigation Pane**, right-click **2C New Students**, and then click **Rename**. With the table name selected and using your own name, type **Lastname Firstname 2C New Students** and then press Enter. **Rename** the 2C Orientation Sessions table to **Lastname Firstname 2C Orientation Sessions** and then point to the right edge of the **Navigation Pane** to display the pointer. Drag to the right to increase the width of the pane until both tables names display fully.

2 In the **Navigation Pane**, double-click your **2C New Students** table to open it in the object window, and examine the fields in the table. Double-click your **2C Orientation Sessions** table, and examine the fields in the table. In the object window, right-click either **object tab**, and then click **Close All** to close both tables. **Close** the **Navigation Pane**.

a. On the ribbon, click the **DATABASE TOOLS tab**, and then in the **Relationships group**, click **Relationships**. Point to the title bar of the **Show Table** dialog box, and then drag downward and slightly to the right to move the dialog box away from the top of the **Relationships** window.

b. In the **Show Table** dialog box, click your **2C Orientation Sessions** table, and then click **Add**. In the **Show Table** dialog box, double-click your **2C New Students** table to add it to the **Relationships** window. In the **Show Table** dialog box, click **Close**.

c. In the **2C New Students** field list—the field list on the right—point to the title bar to display the pointer, and then drag the field list to the right until there are approximately three inches of space between the field lists. In the **2C New Students** field list, point to the lower right corner of the field list to display the pointer, and then drag downward and to the right to resize the field list and display all of the field names and the entire table name. Use the same technique to resize the **2C Orientation Sessions** field list—the field list on the left—so that the table name displays fully.

d. In the **2C Orientation Sessions** field list, point to **Orientation ID**, and then drag the field name downward and to the right into the **2C New Students** field list until the pointer's arrow is on top of **Orientation ID**. Release the mouse button to display the **Edit Relationships** dialog box. Drag the **Edit Relationships** dialog box downward below the two field lists.

e. In the **Edit Relationships** dialog box, click to select the **Enforce Referential Integrity** check box, the **Cascade Update Related Fields** check box, and the **Cascade Delete Related Records** check box. In the **Edit Relationships** dialog box, click **Create** to create a one-to-many relationship—*one* orientation session can be scheduled for *many* new students.

f. Under **RELATIONSHIP TOOLS**, on the **DESIGN tab**, in the **Tools group**, click **Relationship Report**. On the **PRINT PREVIEW tab**, in the **Page Size group**, click **Margins**, and then click **Normal**. Create a paper or electronic printout as directed. On the **Quick Access Toolbar**, click **Save**. In the **Save As** dialog box, click **OK** to accept the default report name. In the object window, **Close** the report, and then **Close** the **Relationships** window.

g. **Open** the **Navigation Pane**, double-click your **2C Orientation Sessions** table to open it in the object window, and then **Close** the **Navigation Pane**. On the left side of the last record—*Orientation ID* of *O-1*—click to display the subdatasheet, and notice that 13 new students are scheduled to attend this orientation session. Click to collapse the subdatasheet.

(Project 2C Freshman Orientation continues on the next page)

Skills Review Project 2C Freshman Orientation (continued)

h. In the last record, in the **Orientation ID** field, select the existing data—*O-1*—and then type **O-001**—the first character is the letter *O* followed by a hyphen, two zeros, and the number *1*— to make the data consistent with the Orientation IDs of the other sessions. The 13 related records in your 2C New Students table are updated with the new Orientation ID because you selected **Cascade Update Related Fields** in the **Edit Relationships** dialog box.

i. Display the subdatasheet for the record with an **Orientation ID** of **O-010**, and notice that one student—*Student ID* of *8273485*—is scheduled for this orientation session. Collapse the subdatasheet. To the left of the record, point to the record selector box to display the [→] pointer, and then click to select the record. On the **HOME tab**, in the **Records group**, click **Delete**. In the message box, click **Yes** to delete this record and the related student record in the **2C New Students** table.

3 In the **Date** field, click in any record. On the **HOME tab**, in the **Sort & Filter group**, click **Ascending** to sort the records by the date. In the field names row, click the **Room arrow**, and then click **Sort Z to A** to sort the rooms from Room 203 to Room 201. The records are sorted first by the **Room** field and then by the **Date** field. On the **FILE tab**, click **Print**, and then click **Print Preview**. Create a paper or electronic printout as directed, and then click **Close Print Preview**. On the **HOME tab**, in the **Sort & Filter group**, click **Remove Sort**. **Close** the table, and in the message box, click **No;** you do not need to save any design changes to the table.

4 On the ribbon, click the **CREATE tab**, and then in the **Queries group**, click **Query Design**. In the **Show Table** dialog box, double-click your **2C Orientation Sessions** table, and then **Close** the **Show Table** dialog box. Point to the lower right corner of the field list to display the [↘] pointer, and then drag downward and to the right to resize the field list, displaying all of the field names and the entire table name.

a. In the field list, double-click **Orientation ID** to add the field to the first column in the design grid. In the field list, point to **Date**, and then drag the field name down into the design grid until the [pointer] pointer displays in the **Field** row in the second column, and then release the mouse button. In the design grid, in the **Field** row, click in the third column, click the **arrow**, and then click **Day of Week** to add the field to the design grid. Using one of the three techniques you just practiced, add the **Time** field to the fourth column and the **Room** field to the fifth column in the design grid.

b. Under **QUERY TOOLS**, on the **DESIGN tab**, in the **Results group**, click **Run**. This query answers the question, *What is the Orientation ID, date, day of week, time, and room for all of the orientation sessions in the 2C Orientation Sessions table?*

c. On the **Quick Access Toolbar**, click **Save**. In the **Save As** dialog box, type **Lastname Firstname 2C All Sessions Query** and then click **OK**. On the ribbon, click the **FILE tab**, click **Print**, and then click **Print Preview**. Create a paper or electronic printout as directed, and then click **Close Print Preview**. **Close** your **2C All Sessions Query**, and then **Open** the **Navigation Pane**.

5 In the **Navigation Pane**, right-click your **2C All Sessions Query** object, and then click **Copy**. In the **Navigation Pane**, point to a blank area, right-click, and then click **Paste**. In the **Paste As** dialog box, type **Lastname Firstname 2C Day of Week Query** and then click **OK** to create a new query based on an existing query.

a. In the **Navigation Pane**, right click your **2C Day of Week Query** object, and then click **Design View**. **Close** the **Navigation Pane**. In the design grid, point to the thin gray selection bar above the **Orientation ID** field name to display the [↓] pointer, click to select the column, and then press [Del].

b. Point to the selection bar above the **Day of Week** field name to display the [pointer] pointer, and then drag to the left until a dark vertical line displays on the left side of the **Date** column. Release the mouse button to position the **Day of Week** field in the first column.

c. **Run** the query. The query results display four fields. This query answers the question, *What is the day of week, date, time, and room for every orientation session in the 2C Orientation Sessions table?*

(Project 2C Freshman Orientation continues on the next page)

Skills Review Project 2C Freshman Orientation (continued)

d. On the **FILE tab**, click **Print**, and then click **Print Preview**. Create a paper or electronic printout as directed, and then click **Close Print Preview**. **Close** the query, and in the message box, click **Yes** to save the changes to the design—you deleted one field and moved another field. **Open** the **Navigation Pane**.

6 In the **Navigation Pane**, right-click your **2C Day of Week Query** object, and then click **Copy**. In the **Navigation Pane**, point to a blank area, right-click, and then click **Paste**. In the **Paste As** dialog box, type **Lastname Firstname 2C Sessions Sort Query** and then click **OK** to create a new query based on an existing query. Increase the width of the **Navigation Pane** so that the names of all of the objects display fully.

a. In the **Navigation Pane**, right-click your **2C Sessions Sort Query** click **Design View**, and then **Close** the **Navigation Pane**. In the design grid, drag the **Room** field to the left of the **Day of Week** field to position it in the first column. In the design grid, click in the **Sort** row under **Room**, click the **arrow**, and then click **Descending**. Click in the **Sort** row under **Date**, click the **arrow**, and then click **Ascending**.

b. **Run** the query. This query answers the question, *For every session, within each room (with the Room field sorted in descending order), what is the day of week, date (with the Date field sorted in ascending order), and time?*

c. Display the query results in **Print Preview**, create a paper or electronic printout as directed, and then click **Close Print Preview**. **Close** the query, and in the message box, click **Yes** to save the changes to the query design.

7 On the ribbon, click the **CREATE tab**, and then in the **Queries group**, click **Query Design**. In the **Show Table** dialog box, double-click your **2C New Students** table to add it to the table area, and then **Close** the **Show Table** dialog box. Resize the field list to display all of the field names and the entire table name. Add the following fields to the design grid in the order given: **Student ID**, **Last Name**, **First Name**, and **Orientation ID**.

a. In the design grid, click in the **Criteria** row under **Orientation ID**, type **O-001**—the first character is the letter *O* followed by a hyphen, two zeros, and the number *1*—and then press Enter.

b. **Run** the query to display 13 records that meet the specified criteria—records that have *O-001* in the *Orientation ID* field. **Save** the query as **Lastname Firstname 2C First Session Query** and then display the query results in **Print Preview**. Create a paper or electronic printout as directed, click **Close Print Preview**, and then **Close** the query.

c. On the ribbon, click the **CREATE tab**, and then in the **Queries group**, click **Query Design**. In the **Show Table** dialog box, double-click your **2C New Students** table to add it to the table area, and then **Close** the **Show Table** dialog box. Resize the field list, and then add the following fields to the design grid in the order given: **Student ID**, **First Name**, **Last Name**, **Phone Number**, **Email Address**, and **City**. Click in the **Criteria** row under **City**, type **dripping springs** and then press Enter.

d. **Run** the query to display the five new students who live in *Dripping Springs*. Switch to **Design** view. In the design grid, in the **Show** row under **City**, click to clear the check box. Recall that if all of the results use the same criteria, such as *dripping springs*, it is not necessary to display that field in the query results. **Run** the query again. **Save** the query as **Lastname Firstname 2C Dripping Springs Query** and then display the query results in **Print Preview**. Create a paper or electronic printout as directed, click **Close Print Preview**, and then **Close** the query.

e. On the ribbon, click the **CREATE tab**, and then in the **Queries group**, click **Query Design**. In the **Show Table** dialog box, double-click your **2C New Students** table to add it to the table area, and then **Close** the **Show Table** dialog box. Resize the field list, and then add the following fields to the design grid in the order given: **Student ID**, **Last Name**, **First Name**, **Email Address**, **Phone Number**, and **Orientation ID**. Click in the **Sort** row under **Last Name**, click the **arrow**, and then click **Ascending**. Click in the **Sort** row under **First Name**, click the **arrow**, and then click **Ascending**. Click in the **Criteria** row under **Orientation ID**, type **is null** and then press Enter.

(Project 2C Freshman Orientation continues on the next page)

CHAPTER REVIEW

Skills Review Project 2C Freshman Orientation (continued)

f. **Run** the query to display the three new students who have not signed up for an orientation session. **Save** the query as **Lastname Firstname 2C Missing Orientation ID Query** and then display the query results in **Print Preview**. On the **PRINT PREVIEW** tab, in the **Page Size group**, click **Margins**, and then click **Normal**. Create a paper or electronic printout as directed, click **Close Print Preview**, and then **Close** the query.

g. **Open** the **Navigation Pane**. If necessary, increase the width of the pane so that all object names display fully. On the right side of the title bar, click **Close** to close the database and to exit Access. As directed by your instructor, submit your database and the paper or electronic printouts of the eight objects—relationship report, sorted table, and six queries—that are the results of this project. Specifically, in this project, using your own name, you created the following database and printouts or electronic printouts:

1. Lastname_Firstname_2C_Freshman_Orientation	Database file
2. Relationships for Lastname_Firstname_2C_Freshman_Orientation	Relationships Report (printout or electronic printout)
3. Lastname Firstname 2C Orientation Sessions table sorted (not saved)	Table sorted (printout or electronic printout)
4. Lastname Firstname 2C All Sessions Query	Query (printout or electronic printout)
5. Lastname Firstname 2C Day of Week Query	Query (printout or electronic printout)
6. Lastname Firstname 2C Sessions Sort Query	Query (printout or electronic printout)
7. Lastname Firstname 2C First Session Query	Query (printout or electronic printout)
8. Lastname Firstname 2C Dripping Springs Query	Query (printout or electronic printout)
9. Lastname Firstname 2C Missing Orientation ID Query	Query (printout or electronic printout)

END | You have completed Project 2C

CHAPTER REVIEW

Apply 2B skills from these Objectives:

8 Specify Numeric Criteria in a Query
9 Use Compound Criteria in a Query
10 Create a Query Based on More Than One Table
11 Use Wildcards in a Query
12 Create Calculated Fields in a Query
13 Calculate Statistics and Group Data in a Query
14 Create a Crosstab Query
15 Create a Parameter Query

Skills Review Project 2D Club Fundraisers

In the following Skills Review, you will assist Dr. Michael Bransford, the student activities director for Texas Lakes Community College, in answering his questions about fundraisers, clubs, donations, dates of fundraiser events, and fundraiser locations. Your completed database objects will look similar to Figure 2.56.

PROJECT FILES

For Project 2D, you will need the following files:

a02D_Club_Fundraisers
a02D_Clubs (Excel workbook)

You will save your database as:

Lastname_Firstname_2D_Club_Fundraisers

PROJECT RESULTS

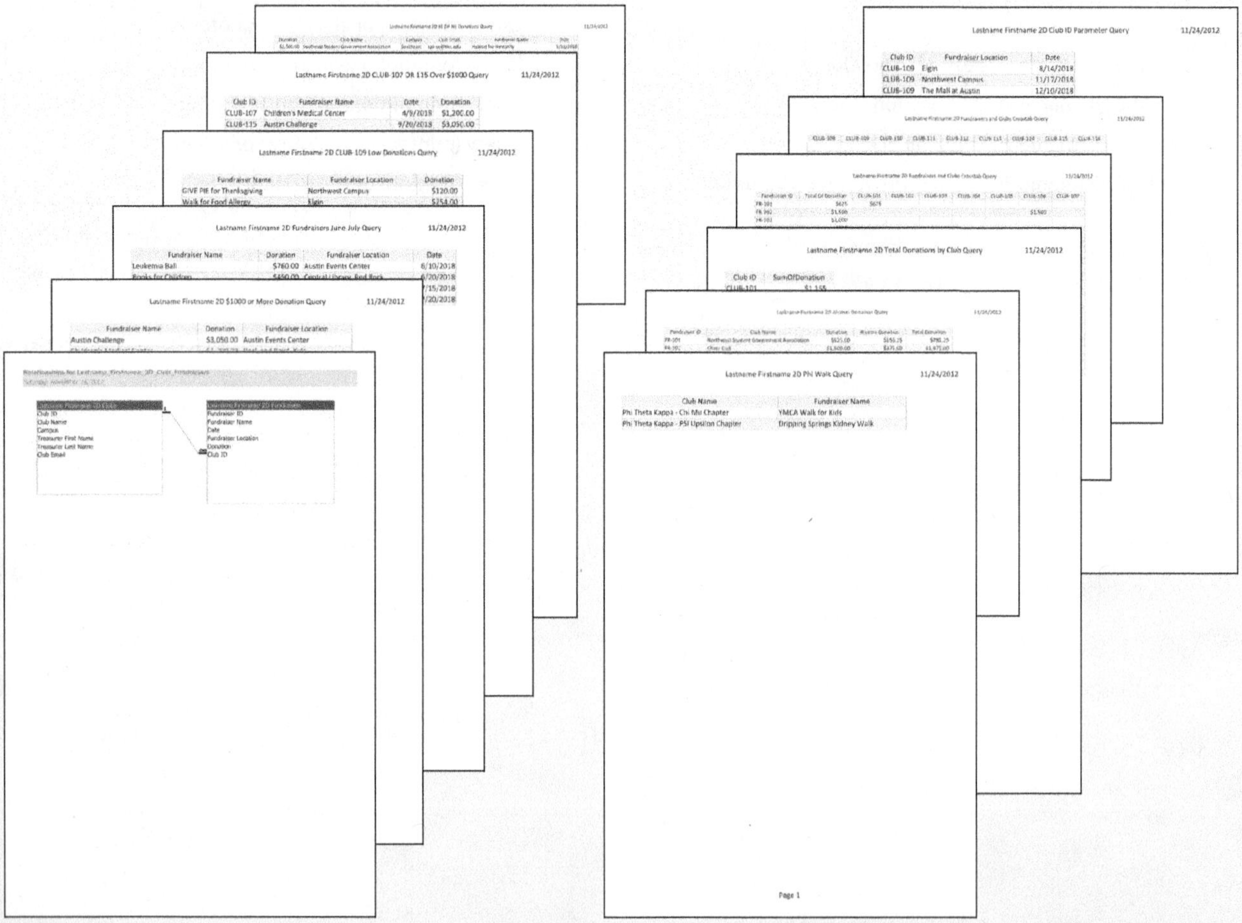

FIGURE 2.56

(Project 2D Club Fundraisers continues on the next page)

CHAPTER REVIEW

Skills Review Project 2D Club Fundraisers (continued)

1 **Start** Access. In the Access opening screen, click **Open Other Files**. Under **Open**, click **Computer**. Under **Recent Folders**, if displayed, click the location where your student data files are stored; otherwise, click **Browse** and then navigate to the location where your student data files are stored. Double-click **a02D_Club_Fundraisers** to open the database.

a. On the ribbon, click the **FILE tab**, and then click **Save As**. Under **File Types**, be sure **Save Database As** is selected. On the right, under **Database File Types**, be sure **Access Database** is selected, and then at the bottom of the screen, click **Save As**. In the **Save As** dialog box, navigate to your **Access Chapter 2** folder. Click in the **File name** box, type **Lastname_Firstname_2D_Club_Fundraisers** and then press Enter. On the **Message Bar**, click **Enable Content**.

b. In the **Navigation Pane**, right-click **2D Fundraisers**, click **Rename**, type **Lastname Firstname 2D Fundraisers** and then press Enter. Increase the width of the **Navigation Pane** to display the entire table name. Double-click the table name to open it, examine the fields in the table, and then **Close** the table.

c. On the ribbon, click the **EXTERNAL DATA tab**, and then in the **Import & Link group**, click **Excel**. In the **Get External Data - Excel Spreadsheet** dialog box, to the right of the **File name** box, click **Browse**. In the **File Open** dialog box, navigate to your student data files, and then double-click **a02D_Clubs**. Be sure that the **Import the source data into a new table in the current database** option button is selected, and then click **OK**.

d. In the upper left area of the wizard, select the **First Row Contains Column Headings** check box, click **Next**, and then click **Next** again. In the wizard, click the **Choose my own primary key** option button, be sure that **Club ID** displays, and then click **Next**. With the text selected in the **Import to Table** box and using your own name, type **Lastname Firstname 2D Clubs**, and then click **Finish**. In the **Get External Data - Excel Spreadsheet** dialog box, click **Close**.

e. In the **Navigation Pane**, right-click your **2D Clubs** table, and then click **Design View**. **Close** the **Navigation Pane**. In the **Field Name** column, click **Club ID**. In the **Field Properties** area, click **Field Size**, type **8** and then press Enter. Under **TABLE TOOLS**, on the **DESIGN tab**, in the **Views group**, click the upper portion of the **View** button to switch to **Datasheet** view. In the message box, click **Yes** to save the design changes. In the second message box, click **Yes**—no data will be lost. Examine the fields and data in the table. To the left of the **Club ID** field name, click **Select All**. On the **HOME tab**, in the **Records group**, click **More**, and then click **Field Width**. In the **Column Width** dialog box, click **Best Fit**. **Save** the table, click in any record to cancel the selection, and then **Close** the table.

f. On the ribbon, click the **DATABASE TOOLS tab**, and then in the **Relationships group**, click **Relationships**. In the **Show Table** dialog box, double-click your **2D Clubs** table, and then double-click your **2D Fundraisers** table to add both tables to the **Relationships** window. **Close** the **Show Table** dialog box. Point to the title bar of the field list on the right, and drag the field list to the right until there are approximately two inches of space between the field lists. By dragging the lower right corner of the field list, resize each field list to display all of the field names and the entire table name.

g. In the **2D Clubs** field list, point to **Club ID**, drag the field name into the **2D Fundraisers** table on top of **Club ID**, and then release the mouse button. Point to the title bar of the **Edit Relationships** dialog box, and then drag it downward below the two field lists. In the **Edit Relationships** dialog box, select the **Enforce Referential Integrity** check box, the **Cascade Update Related Fields** check box, the **Cascade Delete Related Records** check box, and then click **Create**. A *one-to-many* relationship is established; *one* student club can raise money for *many* fundraising events.

h. Under **RELATIONSHIP TOOLS**, on the **DESIGN tab**, in the **Tools group**, click **Relationship Report**. On the **PRINT PREVIEW tab**, in the **Page Size group**, click **Margins**, and then click **Normal**. **Save** the report as **Lastname Firstname 2D Relationships** and then create a paper or electronic printout as directed. In the object window, right-click either **object tab**, and then click **Close All**.

(Project 2D Club Fundraisers continues on the next page)

Skills Review Project 2D Club Fundraisers (continued)

2 On the ribbon, click the **CREATE tab**. In the **Queries group**, click **Query Design**. In the **Show Table** dialog box, double-click your **2D Fundraisers** table to add it to the table area, and then **Close** the **Show Table** dialog box. Resize the field list. Add the following fields to the design grid in the order given: **Fundraiser Name, Donation**, and **Fundraiser Location.**

a. Click in the **Sort** row under **Fundraiser Name**, click the **arrow**, and then click **Ascending**. Click in the **Criteria** row under **Donation**, type **>=1000** and then press Enter. **Run** the query, and notice that seven records match the criteria. This query answers the question, *Where was each fundraiser held (in alphabetical order by the Fundraiser Name field) for fundraisers with a donation greater than or equal to $1,000?*

b. **Save** the query as **Lastname Firstname 2D $1000 or More Donation Query** and then display the query results in **Print Preview**. Create a paper or electronic printout as directed, click **Close Print preview**, and then **Close** your query object. **Open** the **Navigation Pane.**

c. In the **Navigation Pane**, right-click your **2D $1000 or More Donation Query** object, and then click **Copy**. In the **Navigation Pane**, point to a blank area, right-click, and then click **Paste**. In the **Paste As** dialog box, type **Lastname Firstname 2D Fundraisers June-July Query** and then click **OK**. In the **Navigation Pane**, right-click your **2D Fundraisers June-July Query** object, and then click **Design View. Close** the **Navigation Pane.**

d. In the **2D Fundraisers** field list, double-click **Date** to add it to the fourth column in the design grid. Click in the **Sort** row under **Fundraiser Name**, click the **arrow**, and then click **(not sorted)**. Click in the **Sort** row under **Date**, click the **arrow**, and then click **Ascending.**

e. In the **Criteria** row under **Donation**, select the existing criteria of *>=1000*, and then press Del so that the query results are not restricted by a monetary value. Click in the **Criteria** row under **Date**, type **between 6/1/18 and 7/31/18** and then press Enter. **Run** the query, and notice that four records match the criteria. This query answers the question, *What is the fundraiser name, donation, fundraiser location, and date (in chronological order) for events held between June 1, 2018 and July 31, 2018?*

f. Display the query results in **Print Preview**, create a paper or electronic printout as directed, and then click **Close Print Preview. Close** the query, and in the message box, click **Yes** to save the changes to the query design.

3 On the ribbon, click the **CREATE tab**, and in the **Queries group**, click **Query Design**. In the **Show Table** dialog box, double-click your **2D Fundraisers** table to add it to the table area, and then **Close** the **Show Table** dialog box. Resize the field list. Add the following fields to the design grid in the order given: **Fundraiser Name, Fundraiser Location, Donation**, and **Club ID.**

a. Click in the **Sort** row under **Fundraiser Name**, click the **arrow**, and then click **Ascending**. Click in the **Criteria** row under **Club ID**, type **club-109** and then press Enter. Click in the **Criteria** row under **Donation**, type **<=1000** and then press Enter. **Run** the query, and notice that two records match the criteria. Switch back to **Design** view, and in the **Show** row under **Club ID**, clear the check box. **Run** the query again. This query answers the question, *Which fundraiser events with their locations listed had donations raised by CLUB-109 of $1,000 or less?*

b. **Save** the query as **Lastname Firstname 2D CLUB-109 Low Donations Query** and then display the query results in **Print Preview**. Create a paper or electronic printout as directed, click **Close Print Preview**, and then **Close** the query.

c. On the ribbon, click the **CREATE tab**, and then in the **Queries group**, click **Query Design**. In the **Show Table** dialog box, double-click your **2D Fundraisers** table to add it to the table area, and then **Close** the **Show Table** dialog box. Resize the field list. Add the following fields to the design grid in the order given: **Club ID, Fundraiser Name, Date**, and **Donation.**

d. Click in the **Sort** row under **Date**, click the **arrow**, and then click **Ascending**. Click in the **Criteria** row under **Club ID**, type **club-107 or club-115** and then press Enter. Click in the **Criteria** row under **Donation**, type **>1000** and then press Enter. **Run** the query, and notice that two records match the criteria. This query answers the questions, *Which fundraiser events received donations over $1,000 from either CLUB-107 or CLUB-115, and on what dates (in chronological order) were the fundraiser events held?*

(Project 2D Club Fundraisers continues on the next page)

e. **Save** the query as **Lastname Firstname 2D CLUB 107 OR 115 Over $1000 Query** and then display the query results in **Print Preview**. Create a paper or electronic printout as directed, click **Close Print Preview**, and then **Close** the query.

4 On the ribbon, click the **CREATE tab**, and then in the **Queries group**, click **Query Design**. In the **Show Table** dialog box, double-click your **2D Clubs** table, and then double-click your **2D Fundraisers** table to add both tables to the table area. **Close** the **Show Table** dialog box. Drag the field list on the right side to the right until there are approximately two inches of space between the field lists, and then resize each field list.

a. From the **2D Clubs** field list, add the following fields to the design grid in the order given: **Club Name**, **Campus**, and **Club Email**. From the **2D Fundraisers** field list, add the following fields to the design grid in the order given: **Fundraiser Name**, **Date**, and **Donation**. In the design grid, drag the **Donation** field to the left to position it as the first column.

b. Click in the **Sort** row under **Donation**, click the **arrow**, and then click **Descending**. Click in the **Criteria** row under **Campus**, type **southeast** and then press Enter. Click in the **or** row under **Campus**, type **northeast** and then press Enter. **Run** the query, and notice that 10 records match the criteria. This query answers the question, *For the Southeast and Northeast campuses, what is the donation (in descending order), club name, campus name, club email address, fundraiser name, and date of all fundraising events?*

c. **Save** the query as **Lastname Firstname 2D SE OR NE Donations Query** and then display the query results in **Print Preview**. On the **PRINT PREVIEW tab**, in the **Page Layout group**, click **Landscape**. In the **Page Size group**, click **Margins**, and then click **Normal**. Create a paper or electronic printout as directed, click **Close Print Preview**, and then **Close** the query.

5 On the ribbon, click the **CREATE tab**, and then in the **Queries group**, click **Query Design**. In the **Show Table** dialog box, double-click your **2D Clubs** table, and then double-click your **2D Fundraisers** table to add both tables to the table area. **Close** the **Show Table** dialog box. Drag the field list on the right side to the right until there are approximately two inches of space between the field lists, and then resize each field list. From the **2D Clubs** field list, add the **Club Name** field to the design grid. From the **2D Fundraisers** field list, add the **Fundraiser Name** field to the design grid.

a. Click in the **Sort** row under **Club Name**, click the **arrow**, and then click **Ascending**. Click in the **Criteria** row under **Club Name**, type **phi*** and then press Enter. In the **Criteria** row under **Fundraiser Name**, type ***walk*** and then press Enter. **Run** the query, and notice that two records match the criteria—Club Name begins with *Phi* and Fundraiser Name has *Walk* anywhere in its name. This query answers the question, *Which clubs (in alphabetical order) that have names starting with Phi have raised money for fundraisers that involve walking?*

b. **Save** the query as **Lastname Firstname 2D Phi Walk Query** and then display the query results in **Print Preview**. Create a paper or electronic printout as directed, click **Close Print Preview**, and then **Close** the query.

6 On the ribbon, click the **CREATE tab**, and then in the **Queries group**, click **Query Design**. In the **Show Table** dialog box, double-click your **2D Clubs** table, and then double-click your **2D Fundraisers** table to add both tables to the table area. **Close** the **Show Table** dialog box. Drag the field list on the right side to the right until there are approximately two inches of space between the field lists, and then resize each field list. From the field lists, add the following fields to the design grid in the order given: **Fundraiser ID**, **Club Name**, and **Donation**.

a. Click in the **Sort** row under **Fundraiser ID**, click the **arrow**, and then click **Ascending**. Alumni will donate an additional 25 percent based on the value in the **Donation** field. In the **Field** row, right-click in the fourth column, and then click **Zoom**. In the **Zoom** dialog box, type **Alumni Donation:[Donation]*0.25** and then click **OK**. **Run** the query to be sure the new field—*Alumni Donation*—displays. In the first record, the *Alumni Donation* displays as *156.25*.

b. Switch to **Design** view. In the **Field** row, right-click in the first empty column, and then click **Zoom**. In the **Zoom** dialog box, type **Total Donation:[Donation]+[Alumni Donation]** and then click **OK**. **Run** the query to be sure that the new field—*Total Donation*—displays. In the first record, the *Total Donation* displays as *$781.25*.

(Project 2D Club Fundraisers continues on the next page)

Skills Review Project 2D Club Fundraisers (continued)

c. Switch to **Design** view. In the **Field** row, click in the **Alumni Donation** field name box. Under **QUERY TOOLS**, on the **DESIGN tab**, in the **Show/Hide group**, click **Property Sheet**. In the **Property Sheet**, click **Format**. In the property setting box, click the **arrow**, and then click **Currency**. In the **Property Sheet**, click **Decimal Places**. In the property setting box, click the **arrow**, and then click **2**. **Close** the **Property Sheet**, and then **Run** the query. This query answers the question, *In ascending order by Fundraiser ID, what is the club name, donation, alumni donation, and total donation for each fundraising event if the alumni donate an additional 25 percent based on the value in the Donation field?*

d. To the left of the **Fundraiser ID** field name, click **Select All**. On the **HOME tab**, in the **Records group**, click **More**, and then click **Field Width**. In the **Column Width** dialog box, click **Best Fit**. **Save** the query as **Lastname Firstname 2D Alumni Donation Query** and then click in any field to cancel the selection. Display the query results in **Print Preview**. On the **PRINT PREVIEW tab**, in the **Page Layout group**, click **Landscape**. Create a paper or electronic printout as directed, click **Close Print Preview**, and then **Close** the query.

7 On the ribbon, click the **CREATE tab**, and then in the **Queries group**, click **Query Design**. In the **Show Table** dialog box, double-click your **2D Fundraisers** table to add the table to the table area. **Close** the **Show Table** dialog box. Resize the field list, and then add the **Donation** field to the design grid.

a. Under **QUERY TOOLS**, on the **DESIGN tab**, in the **Show/Hide group**, click **Totals** to add a **Total** row as the third row in the design grid. In the **Total** row under **Donation**, click in the box that displays *Group By*, click the **arrow**, and then click **Sum**. In the **Show/Hide group**, click **Property Sheet**. In the **Property Sheet**, set **Decimal Places** to **0**, and then **Close** the **Property Sheet**. **Run** the query. Point to the right edge of the first column to display the [+] pointer, and then double-click to apply Best Fit to the field. The sum of the Donation fields is *$20,259*.

b. Switch to **Design** view. From the field list, drag the **Club ID** field to the first column in the design grid—the **Donation** field moves to the second column. **Run** the query. This query answers the question, *For each club ID, what are the total donations?*

c. **Save** the query as **Lastname Firstname 2D Total Donations by Club Query** and then display the query results in **Print Preview**. Create a paper or electronic printout as directed, click **Close Print Preview**, and then **Close** the query.

8 On the ribbon, click the **CREATE tab**, and then in the **Queries group**, click **Query Wizard**. In the **New Query** dialog box, click **Crosstab Query Wizard**, and then click **OK**. In the **Crosstab Query Wizard**, click your **Table: 2D Fundraisers**, and then click **Next**. In the wizard under **Available Fields**, double-click **Fundraiser ID** to group the records by this field and display the Fundraiser IDs as row headings. Click **Next**.

a. In the wizard, in the field list, click **Club ID** to select the column headings, and then click **Next**. Under **Fields**, click **Donation**. Under **Functions**, click **Sum**, and then click **Next**. In the **What do you want to name your query?** box, select the existing text, type **Lastname Firstname 2D Fundraisers and Clubs Crosstab Query** and then click **Finish**.

b. On the ribbon, click the **HOME** tab, and then switch to **Design** view. In the design grid, click in the **[Donation]** column. Under **QUERY TOOLS**, on the **DESIGN tab**, in the **Show/Hide group**, click **Property Sheet**. In the **Property Sheet**, click **Decimal Places**. In the property settings box, click the **arrow**, and then click **0**. In the design grid, click in the **Total Of Donation** column, set the **Decimal Places** to **0**, and then **Close** the **Property Sheet**. **Run** the query. Select all of the columns, apply **Best Fit**, and then **Save** the query. This query answers the question, *Grouped by Fundraiser ID and Club ID, what are the total donations?*

c. Display the query results in **Print Preview**. On the **PRINT PREVIEW tab**, in the **Page Layout group**, click **Landscape**. Create a paper or electronic printout as directed—two pages result. Click **Close Print Preview**, and then **Close** the query.

9 On the ribbon, click the **CREATE tab**, and then in the **Queries group**, click **Query Design**. In the **Show Table** dialog box, double-click your **2D Fundraisers** table to add the table to the table area. **Close** the **Show Table** dialog box, and then resize the field list. Add the following fields to the design grid in the order given: **Club ID**, **Fundraiser Location**, and **Date**.

(Project 2D Club Fundraisers continues on the next page)

CHAPTER REVIEW

Skills Review Project 2D Club Fundraisers (continued)

a. Click in the **Sort** row under **Date**, click the **arrow**, and then click **Ascending**. In the **Criteria** row under **Club ID**, right-click, and then click **Zoom**. In the **Zoom** dialog box, type **[Enter a Club ID in the format club-###]** and then click **OK**. **Run** the query. In the **Enter Parameter Value** dialog box, type **club-109** and then click **OK**. Three records match the criteria.

b. **Save** the query as **Lastname Firstname 2D Club ID Parameter Query** and then display the query results in **Print Preview**. Create a paper or electronic printout as directed, click **Close Print Preview**, and then **Close** the query.

c. **Open** the **Navigation Pane**, and increase the width of the pane so that all object names display fully. On the right side of the title bar, click **Close** to close the database and to exit Access. As directed by your instructor, submit your database and the paper or electronic printouts of the 11 objects—relationship report and 10 queries, one of which printed on two pages—that are the results of this project. Specifically, in this project, using your own name, you created the following database and printouts or electronic printouts:

1. Lastname_Firstname_2D_Clubs_Fundraisers	Database file
2. Lastname Firstname 2D Relationships	Relationships Report (printout or electronic printout)
3. Lastname Firstname 2D $1000 or More Donation Query	Query (printout or electronic printout)
4. Lastname Firstname 2D Fundraisers June-July Query	Query (printout or electronic printout)
5. Lastname Firstname 2D CLUB-109 Low Donations Query	Query (printout or electronic printout)
6. Lastname Firstname 2D CLUB-107 OR 115 Over $1000 Query	Query (printout or electronic printout)
7. Lastname Firstname 2D SE OR NE Donations Query	Query (printout or electronic printout)
8. Lastname Firstname 2D Phi Walk Query	Query (printout or electronic printout)
9. Lastname Firstname 2D Alumni Donation Query	Query (printout or electronic printout)
10. Lastname Firstname 2D Total Donations by Club Query	Query (printout or electronic printout)
11. Lastname Firstname 2D Fundraisers and Clubs Crosstab Query	Query (printout or electronic printout - two pages)
12. Lastname Firstname 2D Club ID Parameter Query	Query (printout or electronic printout - CLUB-109)

END | You have completed Project 2D

CONTENT-BASED ASSESSMENTS

MyITLab® grader

Mastering Access | Project 2E Biology Supplies

Apply 2A skills from these Objectives:

1. Open and Save an Existing Database
2. Create Table Relationships
3. Sort Records in a Table
4. Create a Query in Design View
5. Create a New Query from an Existing Query
6. Sort Query Results
7. Specify Criteria in a Query

In the following Mastering Access project, you will assist Greg Franklin, chair of the Biology Department at the Southwest Campus, in using his database to answer questions about biology laboratory supplies. Your completed database objects will look similar to Figure 2.57.

PROJECT FILES

For Project 2E, you will need the following file:

a02E_Biology_Supplies

You will save your database as:

Lastname_Firstname_2E_Biology_Supplies

PROJECT RESULTS

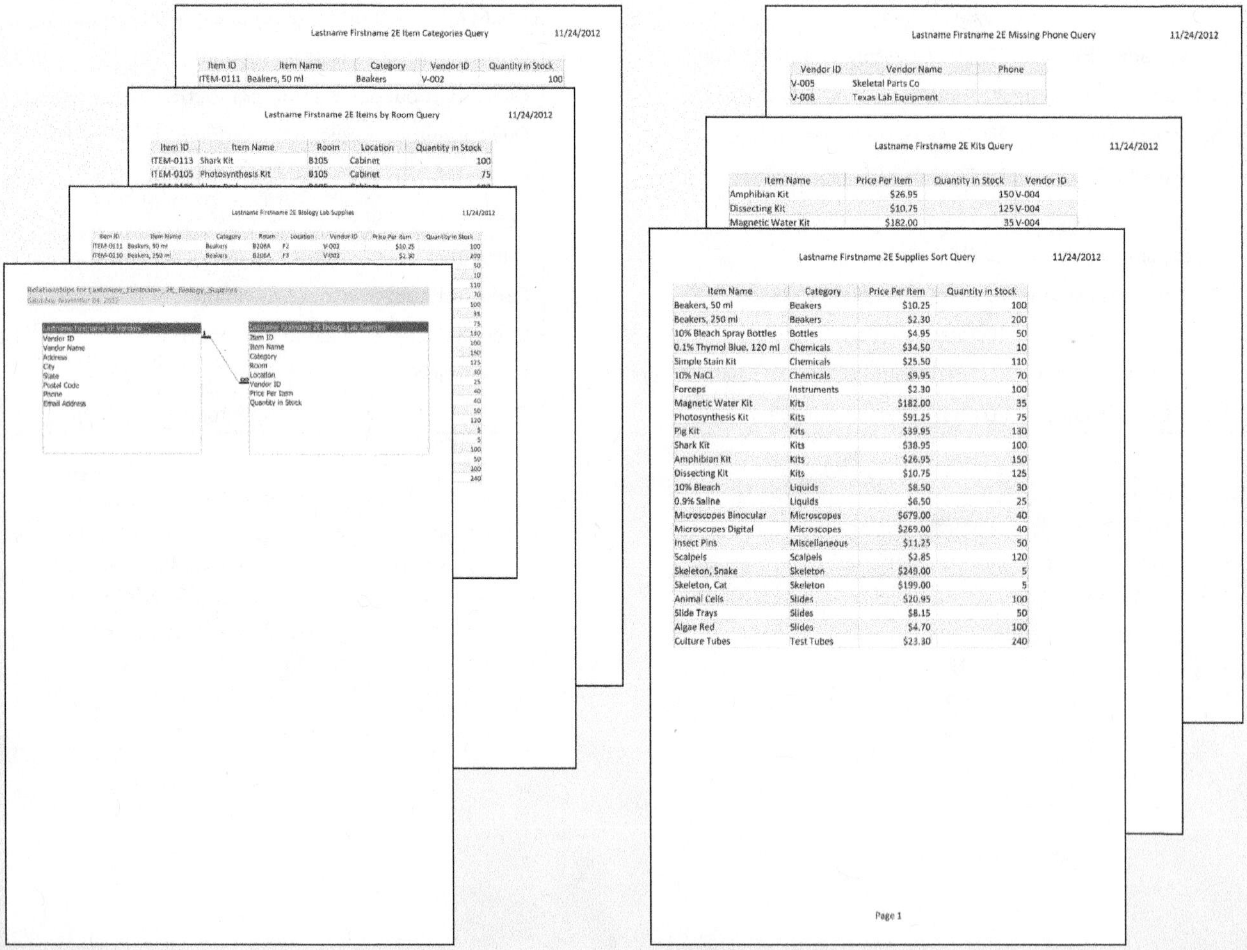

Item Name	Category	Price Per Item	Quantity in Stock
Beakers, 50 ml	Beakers	$10.25	100
Beakers, 250 ml	Beakers	$2.30	200
10% Bleach Spray Bottles	Bottles	$4.95	50
0.1% Thymol Blue, 120 ml	Chemicals	$34.50	10
Simple Stain Kit	Chemicals	$25.50	110
10% NaCL	Chemicals	$9.95	70
Forceps	Instruments	$2.30	100
Magnetic Water Kit	Kits	$182.00	35
Photosynthesis Kit	Kits	$91.25	75
Pig Kit	Kits	$39.95	130
Shark Kit	Kits	$38.95	100
Amphibian Kit	Kits	$26.95	150
Dissecting Kit	Kits	$10.75	125
10% Bleach	Liquids	$8.50	30
0.9% Saline	Liquids	$6.50	25
Microscopes Binocular	Microscopes	$679.00	40
Microscopes Digital	Microscopes	$269.00	40
Insect Pins	Miscellaneous	$11.25	50
Scalpels	Scalpels	$2.85	120
Skeleton, Snake	Skeleton	$249.00	5
Skeleton, Cat	Skeleton	$199.00	5
Animal Cells	Slides	$20.95	100
Slide Trays	Slides	$8.15	50
Algae Red	Slides	$4.70	100
Culture Tubes	Test Tubes	$23.30	240

Page 1

FIGURE 2.57

(Project 2E Biology Supplies continues on the next page)

Mastering Access Project 2E Biology Supplies (continued)

1 **Start** Access. From your student data files, open **a02E_Biology_Supplies.** Save the database in your **Access Chapter 2** folder as **Lastname_Firstname_2E_Biology_Supplies** and then enable the content. In the **Navigation Pane**, **Rename** each table by adding **Lastname Firstname** to the beginning of the table name. Increase the width of the **Navigation Pane** so that all object names display fully.

2 Open both tables to examine the fields and data, and then **Close** both tables. Create a *one-to-many* relationship between your **2E Vendors** table and your **2E Biology Lab Supplies** table using the common field **Vendor ID. Enforce Referential Integrity**, and enable both cascade options. *One* vendor can be the provider of *many* supplies. Create a **Relationship Report** with **Normal Margins**, saving it with the default name. Create a paper or electronic printout as directed, and then **Close All** open objects. Open your **2E Vendors** table. In the last record, in the **Vendor ID** field, select **V-100**, type **V-001** and then press ↓ to save the record. **Close** the table.

3 Open your **2E Biology Lab Supplies** table. Sort the records first in **Descending** order by **Price Per Item** and then in **Ascending** order by **Category**. Using **Landscape** orientation, create a paper or electronic printout as directed. **Close** the table, and do *not* save changes to the table.

4 Create a query in **Query Design** view using your **2E Biology Lab Supplies** table to answer the question, *What is the item ID, item name, room, location, and quantity in stock for all of the items, sorted in ascending order by the Room field and the Location field?* Display the fields in the order listed in the question. **Save** the query as **Lastname Firstname 2E Items by Room Query** and then create a paper or electronic printout as directed. **Close** the query.

5 From the **Navigation Pane**, copy your **2E Items by Room Query** object to create a new query object named **Lastname Firstname 2E Item Categories Query** and then redesign the query to answer the question, *What is the item ID, item name, category, vendor ID, and quantity in stock for all items, sorted in ascending order by the Category field and in ascending order by the Vendor ID field?* Display only the fields necessary to answer the question and in the order listed in the question. Create a paper or electronic printout as directed. **Close** the query, saving the design changes.

6 From the **Navigation Pane**, copy your **2E Items by Room Query** object to create a new query object named **Lastname Firstname 2E Supplies Sort Query** and then redesign the query to answer the question, *What is the item name, category, price per item, and quantity in stock for all supplies, sorted in ascending order by the Category field and then in descending order by the Price Per Item field?* Display only the fields necessary to answer the question and in the order listed in the question. Create a paper or electronic printout as directed. **Close** the query, saving the design changes.

7 From the **Navigation Pane**, copy your **2E Supplies Sort Query** object to create a new query object named **Lastname Firstname 2E Kits Query** and then redesign the query to answer the question, *What is the item name, category, price per item, quantity in stock, and vendor ID for all items that have a category of kits, sorted in ascending order only by the Item Name field?* Do not display the **Category** field in the query results, and display the rest of the fields in the order listed in the question. Six records match the criteria. Create a paper or electronic printout as directed. **Close** the query, saving the design changes.

8 Create a query in **Query Design** view using your **2E Vendors** table to answer the question, *What is the vendor ID and vendor name where the phone number is missing from the table, sorted in ascending order by the Vendor Name field?* Display the fields in the order listed in the question. Two records match the criteria. **Save** the query as **Lastname Firstname 2E Missing Phone Query** and then create a paper or electronic printout as directed. **Close** the query.

(Project 2E Biology Supplies continues on the next page)

CONTENT-BASED ASSESSMENTS

Mastering Access | Project 2E Biology Supplies (continued)

9 Be sure all objects are closed. **Open** the **Navigation Pane**, be sure that all object names display fully, and then **Close** Access. As directed by your instructor, submit your database and the paper or electronic printouts of the seven objects—relationship report, sorted table, and five queries—that are the results of this project. Specifically, in this project, using your own name, you created the following database and printouts or electronic printouts:

1. Lastname_Firstname_2E_Biology_Supplies	Database file
2. Relationships for Lastname_Firstname_2E_Biology_Supplies	Relationships Report (printout or electronic printout)
3. Lastname Firstname 2E Biology Lab Supplies table sorted (not saved)	Table sorted (printout or electronic printout - one page)
4. Lastname Firstname 2E Items by Room Query	Query (printout or electronic printout)
5. Lastname Firstname 2E Item Categories Query	Query (printout or electronic printout)
6. Lastname Firstname 2E Supplies Sort Query	Query (printout or electronic printout)
7. Lastname Firstname 2E Kits Query	Query (printout or electronic printout)
8. Lastname Firstname 2E Missing Phone Query	Query (printout or electronic printout)

END | You have completed Project 2E

CONTENT-BASED ASSESSMENTS

Mastering Access | Project 2F Student Publications

MyITLab® grader

Apply 2B skills from these Objectives:

8 Specify Numeric Criteria in a Query
9 Use Compound Criteria in a Query
10 Create a Query Based on More Than One Table
11 Use Wildcards in a Query
12 Create Calculated Fields in a Query
13 Calculate Statistics and Group Data in a Query
14 Create a Crosstab Query
15 Create a Parameter Query

In the following Mastering Access project, you will assist Siobhan Reiss, the English Writing Lab coordinator, in using her database to answer questions about student publications. Your completed database objects will look similar to Figure 2.58.

PROJECT FILES

For Project 2F, you will need the following files:

a02F_Student_Publications
a02F_Student_Papers (Excel workbook)

You will save your database as:

Lastname_Firstname_2F_Student_Publications

PROJECT RESULTS

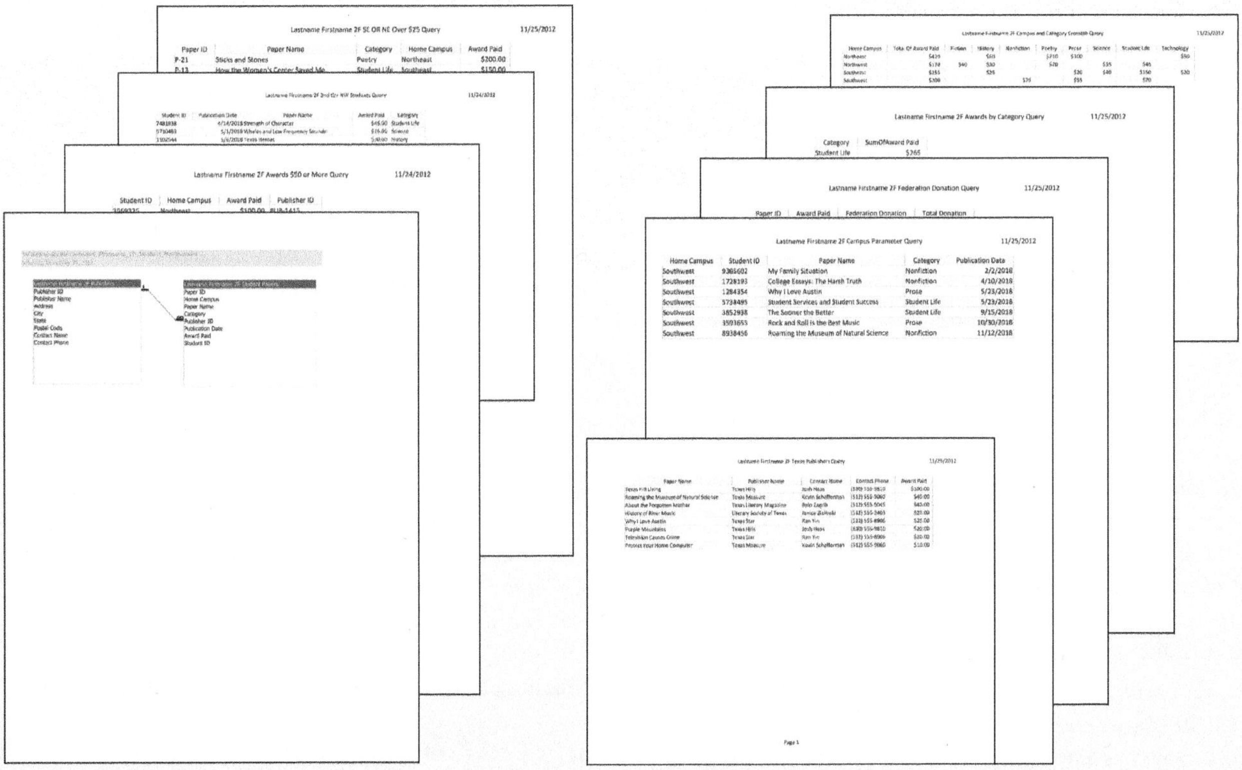

FIGURE 2.58

(Project 2F Student Publications continues on the next page)

Mastering Access Project 2F Student Publications (continued)

1 **Start** Access. From your student data files, open **a02F_Student_Publications**. Save the database in your **Access Chapter 2** folder as **Lastname_Firstname_2F_Student_Publications** and then enable the content. In the **Navigation Pane**, **Rename** the **2F Publishers** table by adding **Lastname Firstname** to the beginning of the table name. From your student data files, import the **a02F_Student_Papers** Excel file as a new table in the database. Designate the first row of the spreadsheet as column headings, and designate **Paper ID** as the primary key. Name the new table **Lastname Firstname 2F Student Papers** and then increase the width of the **Navigation Pane** so that all object names display fully.

Open your **2F Student Papers** table in **Design** view. For the **Student ID** field, change the **Data Type** to **Short Text**. Switch to **Datasheet** view, saving the change, apply **Best Fit** to all of the columns, and then **Save** the table. Examine the fields and data in this table. Open your **2F Publishers** table, examine the fields and data, and then **Close All** open objects.

Create a *one-to-many* relationship between your **2F Publishers** table and your **2F Student Papers** table using the common field **Publisher ID**. **Enforce Referential Integrity**, and enable both cascade options. *One* publisher can publish *many* student papers. Create a **Relationship Report** with **Normal Margins**, saving it as **Lastname Firstname 2F Relationships** and then create a paper or electronic printout as directed. **Close All** open objects.

2 Create a query in **Query Design** view using your **2F Student Papers** table to answer the question, *What is the student ID, home campus, award paid, and publisher ID for awards greater than or equal to $50, sorted in ascending order by the Student ID field?* Display the fields in the order listed in the question. Five records match the criteria. **Save** the query as **Lastname Firstname 2F Awards $50 or More Query** and then create a paper or electronic printout as directed. **Close** the query.

3 From the **Navigation Pane**, copy your **2F Awards $50 or More Query** object to create a new query object named **Lastname Firstname 2F 2nd Qtr NW Students Query** and then redesign the query to answer the questions, *Which students (Student ID) from the Northwest campus had papers published between 4/1/18 and 6/30/18, and what was the paper name, the award paid, and the category, sorted in ascending order only by the Publication Date field?* Do not restrict the results by **Award Paid**. Do not display the **Home Campus** field in the query results, and display the rest of the fields in the order listed in the question. Three records match the criteria. Using **Landscape** orientation, create a paper or electronic printout as directed. **Close** the query, saving the design changes.

4 Create a query in **Query Design** view using your **2F Student Papers** table to answer the question, *Which paper IDs, paper names, and category for students from the Southeast or Northeast campuses were published that had an award paid greater than $25, sorted in descending order by the Award Paid field?* Display the fields in the order listed in the question. Six records match the criteria. **Save** the query as **Lastname Firstname 2F SE OR NE Over $25 Query** and then using **Normal Margins**, create a paper or electronic printout as directed. **Close** the query.

5 Create a query in **Query Design** view using both tables to answer the questions, *Which paper names were published with a publisher name that has Texas as part of its name, what is the contact name and contact phone number, and what was the award paid, sorted in descending order by the Award Paid field?* (Hint: Use a wildcard character in the **Criteria** row.) Display the fields in the order listed in the question. Eight records match the criteria. **Save** the query as **Lastname Firstname 2F Texas Publishers Query** and then using **Landscape** orientation, create a paper or electronic printout as directed. **Close** the query.

6 The college's Federation of English Faculty will donate money to the English Writing Lab based on 50 percent of the awards paid to the students. Create a query in **Query Design** view using your **2F Student Papers** table to answer the question, *In ascending order by the Paper ID field, what will be the total of each donation to the Writing Lab if the Federation donates an additional 50 percent of each award paid to students?* (Hint: First calculate the amount of the donation, naming the new field **Federation Donation**, and then run the query to be sure the correct results display. Then calculate the total donation, naming the new field **Total Donation**.) Change the property settings of the **Federation Donation** field to display with a **Format** of **Currency** and with **Decimal Places** set to **2**. For the **Publisher ID** of **P-20**, the *Federation Donation* is *$22.50*, and the *Total Donation* is *$67.50*. Apply **Best Fit** to all of the columns, **Save** the query as **Lastname Firstname 2F Federation Donation Query** and then create a paper or electronic printout as directed. **Close** the query.

(Project 2F Student Publications continues on the next page)

Mastering Access Project 2F Student Publications (continued)

7 Create a query in **Query Design** view using your **2F Student Papers** table and the **Sum** aggregate function to answer the question, *What are the total awards paid for each category, sorted in descending order by the Award Paid field?* Display the fields in the order listed in the question. Change the property settings of the **Award Paid** field to display with **Decimal Places** set to **0**. For the **Category** of **Student Life**, total awards paid are *$265*. Apply **Best Fit** to the **SumOfAward Paid** column. **Save** the query as **Lastname Firstname 2F Awards by Category Query** and then create a paper or electronic printout as directed. **Close** the query.

8 Use the **Query Wizard** to create a crosstab query based on your **2F Student Papers** table. Select **Home Campus** as the row headings and **Category** as the column headings. **Sum** the **Award Paid** field. Name the query **Lastname Firstname 2F Campus and Category Crosstab Query** In **Design** view, change the property settings of the last two fields to display with **Decimal Places** set to **0**. This query answers the question, *What are the total awards paid for student publications by each home campus and by each category?* Apply **Best Fit** to all of the columns, and then **Save** the query. Using **Landscape** orientation and **Normal Margins**, create a paper or electronic printout as directed. **Close** the query.

9 Create a query in **Query Design** view using your **2F Student Papers** table that prompts you to enter the **Home Campus**, and then answers the question, *What is the home campus, student ID, paper name, category, and publication date for student publications, sorted in ascending order by the Publication Date field?* Display the fields in the order listed in the question. **Run** the query, entering **southwest** when prompted for criteria. Seven records match the criteria. **Save** the query as **Lastname Firstname 2F Campus Parameter Query** and then using **Normal Margins**, create a paper or electronic printout as directed. **Close** the query.

10 Open the **Navigation Pane**, and be sure that all object names display fully. **Close** Access. As directed by your instructor, submit your database and the paper or electronic printouts of the nine objects—relationship report and eight queries—that are the results of this project. Specifically, in this project, using your own name, you created the following database and printouts or electronic printouts:

1. Lastname_Firstname_2F_Student_Publications	Database file
2. Lastname Firstname 2F Relationships	Relationships Report (printout or electronic printout)
3. Lastname Firstname 2F Awards $50 or More Query	Query (printout or electronic printout)
4. Lastname Firstname 2F 2nd Qtr NW Students Query	Query (printout or electronic printout)
5. Lastname Firstname 2F SE OR NE Over $25 Query	Query (printout or electronic printout)
6. Lastname Firstname 2F Texas Publishers Query	Query (printout or electronic printout)
7. Lastname Firstname 2F Federation Donation Query	Query (printout or electronic printout)
8. Lastname Firstname 2F Awards by Category Query	Query (printout or electronic printout)
9. Lastname Firstname 2F Campus and Category Crosstab Query	Query (printout or electronic printout)
10. Lastname Firstname 2F Campus Parameter Query	Query (printout or electronic printout - Southwest)

END | You have completed Project 2F

CONTENT-BASED ASSESSMENTS

MyITLab® grader

Mastering Access | Project 2G Student Scholarships

Apply 2A and 2B skills from these Objectives:

1. Open and Save an Existing Database
2. Create Table Relationships
3. Sort Records in a Table
4. Create a Query in Design View
5. Create a New Query from an Existing Query
6. Sort Query Results
7. Specify Criteria in a Query
8. Specify Numeric Criteria in a Query
9. Use Compound Criteria in a Query
10. Create a Query Based on More Than One Table
11. Use Wildcards in a Query
12. Create Calculated Fields in a Query
13. Calculate Statistics and Group Data in a Query
14. Create a Crosstab Query
15. Create a Parameter Query

In the following Mastering Access project, you will assist Kim Ngo, director of Academic Scholarships, in using her database to answer questions about scholarships awarded to students. Your completed database objects will look similar to Figure 2.59.

PROJECT FILES

For Project 2G, you will need the following file:

a02G_Student_Scholarships

You will save your database as:

Lastname_Firstname_2G_Student_Scholarships

PROJECT RESULTS

FIGURE 2.59

(Project 2G Student Scholarships continues on the next page)

Mastering Access Project 2G Student Scholarships (continued)

1 **Start** Access. From your student data files, open **a02G_Student_Scholarships**. Save the database in your **Access Chapter 2** folder as **Lastname_Firstname_2G_Student_Scholarships** and then enable the content. In the **Navigation Pane**, **Rename** each table by adding **Lastname Firstname** to the beginning of the table name. Increase the width of the **Navigation Pane** so that all object names display fully.

2 Open both tables to examine the fields and data, and then **Close** both tables. Create a *one-to-many* relationship between your **2G Students** table and your **2G Scholarships Awarded** table using the common field **Student ID**. **Enforce Referential Integrity**, and enable both cascade options. *One* student can have *many* scholarships. Create a **Relationship Report** with **Normal Margins**, saving it with the default name. Create a paper or electronic printout as directed, and then **Close All** open objects. Open your **2G Students** table. In the last record, in the **Student ID** field, select **9999999**, type **2839403** and then press ↓ to save the record. **Close** the table.

3 Create a query in **Query Design** view using your **2G Scholarships Awarded** table to answer the question, *What is the scholarship name, amount, and major for scholarships greater than or equal to $500, sorted in ascending order by the Scholarship Name field?* Display the fields in the order listed in the question. Eight records match the criteria. **Save** the query as **Lastname Firstname 2G Amount $500 or More Query** and then create a paper or electronic printout as directed. **Close** the query.

4 From the **Navigation Pane**, copy your **2G Amount $500 or More Query** object to create a new query object named **Lastname Firstname 2G Awards 4th Qtr Query** and then redesign the query to answer the question, *Which scholarships (Scholarship Name) were awarded between 10/1/18 and 12/31/18, for what amount, and for which student (Student ID), sorted in ascending order only by the Award Date field?* Display only the fields necessary to answer the question and in the order listed in the question. Do not restrict the results by amount. Five records match the criteria. Create a paper or electronic printout as directed. **Close** the query, saving the design changes.

5 Create a query in **Query Design** view using your **2G Scholarships Awarded** table to answer the question, *Which scholarships (Scholarship Name) were awarded for either Math or Business majors for amounts of more than $200, sorted in descending order by the Amount field?* Display the fields in the order listed in the question. Four records match the criteria. (Hint: If six records display, switch to **Design** view and combine the majors on one criteria line using OR.) **Save** the query as **Lastname Firstname 2G Math OR Business Over $200 Query** and then create a paper or electronic printout as directed. **Close** the query.

6 Create a query in **Query Design** view using your **2G Students** table and a wildcard character to answer the question, *What is the city, student ID, last name, and first name of students from cities that begin with the letter L, sorted in ascending order by the City field, in ascending order by the Last Name field, and ascending order by the First Name field?* Display the fields in the order listed in the question. Five records match the criteria. **Save** the query as **Lastname Firstname 2G L Cities Query** and then create a paper or electronic printout as directed. **Close** the query.

7 Create a query in **Query Design** view using your **2G Students** table and all of the fields in the same order that they display in the field list to answer the question, *For which students is the Postal Code missing?* Three records match the criteria. **Save** the query as **Lastname Firstname 2G Missing Postal Code Query** and then using **Normal Margins**, create a paper or electronic printout as directed. **Close** the query.

8 The Board of Trustees for the college will donate an amount equal to 50 percent of each scholarship amount. Create a query in **Query Design** view using both tables to answer the question, *In ascending order by the Scholarship Name field, and including the first name and last name of the scholarship recipient, what will be the total value of each scholarship if the Board of Trustees donates an additional 50 percent of each award paid to students?* (Hint: First calculate the amount of the donation, naming the new field **Board Donation**, and then run the query to be sure the correct results display. Then calculate the total donation, naming the new field **Total Donation**.) Change the property settings of the appropriate fields to display with a **Format** of **Currency** and with **Decimal Places** set to **0**. For the **Scholarship Name** of **Amanda Snyder Foundation Scholarship**, the *Board Donation* is *$125*, and the *Total Donation* is *$375*. Apply **Best Fit** to all of the columns, **Save** the query as **Lastname Firstname 2G Board Donation Query** and then using **Landscape** orientation, create a paper or electronic printout as directed. **Close** the query.

(Project 2G Student Scholarships continues on the next page)

Mastering Access Project 2G Student Scholarships (continued)

9 Create a query in **Query Design** view using your **2G Scholarships Awarded** table and the **Sum** aggregate function to answer the question, *For each major, what is the total scholarship amount, sorted in descending order by the Amount field?* Display the fields in the order listed in the question. Change the property settings of the **Amount** field to display with **Decimal Places** set to **0**. For the **Major** of **History**, the total scholarship amount is *$1,850*. Apply **Best Fit** to all of the columns. **Save** the query as **Lastname Firstname 2G Amount by Major Query** and then create a paper or electronic printout as directed. **Close** the query.

10 Use the **Query Wizard** to create a crosstab query based on your **2G Scholarships Awarded** table. Select **Student ID** as the row headings and **Major** as the column headings. **Sum** the **Amount** field. Name the query **Lastname Firstname 2G Student ID and Major Crosstab Query** In **Design** view, change the property settings of the last two fields to display with **Decimal Places** set to **0**. This query answers the question, *What are the total scholarship amounts paid by each student ID and by each major?* Apply **Best Fit** to all of the columns, and then **Save** the query. Using **Landscape** orientation, create a paper or electronic printout as directed—two pages result. **Close** the query.

11 Create a query in **Query Design** view using your **2G Scholarships Awarded** table that prompts you to enter the **Major**, and then answers the question, *What is the scholarship name and amount for a major, sorted in ascending order by the Scholarship Name field?* Display the fields in the order listed in the question. **Run** the query, entering **history** when prompted for criteria. Four records match the criteria. **Save** the query as **Lastname Firstname 2G Major Parameter Query** and then create a paper or electronic printout as directed. **Close** the query.

12 Open the **Navigation Pane**, and be sure that all object names display fully. **Close** Access. As directed by your instructor, submit your database and the paper or electronic printouts of the 10 objects—relationship report and nine queries, one of which prints on two pages—that are the results of this project. Specifically, in this project, using your own name, you created the following database and printouts or electronic printouts:

1. Lastname_Firstname_2G_Student_Scholarships	Database file
2. Relationships for Lastname_Firstname_2G_Student_Scholarships	Relationships Report (printout or electronic printout)
3. Lastname Firstname 2G Amount $500 or More Query	Query (printout or electronic printout)
4. Lastname Firstname 2G Awards 4th Qtr Query	Query (printout or electronic printout)
5. Lastname Firstname 2G Math OR Business Over $200 Query	Query (printout or electronic printout)
6. Lastname Firstname 2G L Cities Query	Query (printout or electronic printout)
7. Lastname Firstname 2G Missing Postal Code Query	Query (printout or electronic printout)
8. Lastname Firstname 2G Board Donation Query	Query (printout or electronic printout)
9. Lastname Firstname 2G Amount by Major Query	Query (printout or electronic printout)
10. Lastname Firstname 2G Student ID and Major Crosstab Query	Query (printout or electronic printout - two pages)
11. Lastname Firstname 2G Major Parameter Query (using History)	Query (printout or electronic printout)

END | You have completed Project 2G

CONTENT-BASED ASSESSMENTS

Apply a combination of the 2A and 2B skills.

GO! Fix It | Project 2H Social Sciences | Online

GO! Make It | Project 2I Faculty Awards | Online

GO! Solve It | Project 2J Student Refunds | Online

GO! Solve It | Project 2K Leave

PROJECT FILES

For Project 2K, you will need the following file:

a02K_Leave

You will save your database as:

Lastname_Firstname_2K_Leave

Start Access, navigate to your student data files, open a02K_Leave, and then save the database in your Access Chapter 2 folder as **Lastname_Firstname_2K_Leave** Add **Lastname Firstname** to the beginning of both table names, create a one-to-many relationship with cascade options between the two tables—*one* employee can have *many* leave transactions—and then create a relationship report saving it as **Lastname Firstname 2K Relationships**

Create and save four queries to answer the following questions:

- What is the last name and first name of employees who have used personal leave, sorted in ascending order by the Last Name and First Name fields? Do not display the Leave field in the query results.
- What is the last name, first name, and email address of employees who have no phone number listed, sorted in ascending order by the Last Name and First Name fields?
- Grouped by the Leave Classification field, what is the total of each type of leave used? (Hint: Use the aggregate function Count.)
- What is the total number of leave transactions grouped in rows by the Employee# field and grouped in columns by the Leave Classification field?

As directed, create paper or electronic printouts of the relationship report and the four queries. Be sure that each object prints on one page, and that the object names display fully in the Navigation Pane. As directed, submit your database and the paper or electronic printouts of the five objects that are the results of this project.

(Project 2K Leave continues on the next page)

CONTENT-BASED ASSESSMENTS

GO! Solve It Project 2K Leave (continued)

Performance Level

Performance Criteria	Exemplary	Proficient	Developing
Create relationship and relationship report	Relationship and relationship report created correctly.	Relationship and relationship report created with one error.	Relationship and relationship report created with two or more errors, or missing entirely.
Create Personal Leave query	Query created with correct name, fields, sorting, and criteria.	Query created with one element incorrect.	Query created with two or more elements incorrect, or missing entirely.
Create Missing Phone query	Query created with correct name, fields, sorting, and criteria.	Query created with one element incorrect.	Query created with two or more elements incorrect, or missing entirely.
Create Type of Leave query	Query created with correct name, fields, and aggregate function.	Query created with one element incorrect.	Query created with two or more elements incorrect, or missing entirely.
Create Crosstab query	Query created with correct name, row headings, column headings, and aggregate function.	Query created with one element incorrect.	Query created with two or more elements incorrect, or missing entirely.

END | You have completed Project 2K

OUTCOMES-BASED ASSESSMENTS

RUBRIC

The following outcomes-based assessments are *open-ended assessments*. That is, there is no specific correct result; your result will depend on your approach to the information provided. Make *Professional Quality* your goal. Use the following scoring rubric to guide you in *how* to approach the problem and then to evaluate *how well* your approach solves the problem.

The *criteria*—Software Mastery, Content, Format & Layout, and Process—represent the knowledge and skills you have gained that you can apply to solving the problem. The *levels of performance*—Professional Quality, Approaching Professional Quality, or Needs Quality Improvements—help you and your instructor evaluate your result.

	Your completed project is of Professional Quality if you:	Your completed project is Approaching Professional Quality if you:	Your completed project Needs Quality Improvements if you:
1-Software Mastery	Choose and apply the most appropriate skills, tools, and features and identify efficient methods to solve the problem.	Choose and apply some appropriate skills, tools, and features, but not in the most efficient manner.	Choose inappropriate skills, tools, or features, or are inefficient in solving the problem.
2-Content	Construct a solution that is clear and well organized, contains content that is accurate, appropriate to the audience and purpose, and is complete. Provide a solution that contains no errors in spelling, grammar, or style.	Construct a solution in which some components are unclear, poorly organized, inconsistent, or incomplete. Misjudge the needs of the audience. Have some errors in spelling, grammar, or style, but the errors do not detract from comprehension.	Construct a solution that is unclear, incomplete, or poorly organized; contains some inaccurate or inappropriate content; and contains many errors in spelling, grammar, or style. Do not solve the problem.
3-Format & Layout	Format and arrange all elements to communicate information and ideas, clarify function, illustrate relationships, and indicate relative importance.	Apply appropriate format and layout features to some elements, but not others. Overuse features, causing minor distraction.	Apply format and layout that does not communicate information or ideas clearly. Do not use format and layout features to clarify function, illustrate relationships, or indicate relative importance. Use available features excessively, causing distraction.
4-Process	Use an organized approach that integrates planning, development, self-assessment, revision, and reflection.	Demonstrate an organized approach in some areas, but not others; or, use an insufficient process of organization throughout.	Do not use an organized approach to solve the problem.

OUTCOMES-BASED ASSESSMENTS

Apply a combination of the 2A and 2B skills.

GO! Think Project 2L Coaches

PROJECT FILES

For Project 2L, you will need the following file:

a02L_Coaches

You will save your database as

Lastname_Firstname_2L_Coaches

Start Access, navigate to your student data files, open a02L_Coaches, and then save the database in your Access Chapter 2 folder as **Lastname_Firstname_2L_Coaches** Add **Lastname Firstname** to the beginning of both table names, create a one-to-many relationship with cascade options between the two tables—*one* coach can participate in *many* activities—and then create a relationship report saving it as **Lastname Firstname 2L Relationships**

Create queries to assist Randy Garza, the athletic director, in answering the following questions about the coaches at Texas Lakes Community College:

- What is the last name and first name of every coach involved in *Dive* activities, sorted in ascending order by the Last Name field and First Name fields?
- What is the last name and first name of every coach involved in basketball or football activities, sorted in ascending order first by the Activity Name field and then by the Last Name and First Name fields?
- Grouped by division, what is the total number of activity names, sorted in descending order by the total number? (Hint: Use the Count aggregate function.)
- What is the skill specialty, last name, first name, and phone number for coaches in a specified position that is entered when prompted for the Position, sorted in ascending order first by the Skill Specialty field and then by the Last Name and First Name fields? (When prompted, enter the position of *director* for your paper or electronic printout.)

As directed, create paper or electronic printouts of the relationship report and the four queries. Be sure that each object prints on one page, and that the object names display fully in the Navigation Pane. As directed, submit your database and the paper or electronic printouts of the five objects that are the results of this project.

END | You have completed Project 2L

GO! Think Project 2M Club Donations Online

Build from Scratch

You and GO! Project 2N Personal Inventory Online

Build from Scratch

GO! Cumulative Group Project Project 2O Bell Orchid Hotels Online

Forms, Filters, and Reports

GO! to Work Video A3

3

ACCESS 2013

PROJECT 3A

OUTCOMES

Create forms to enter and delete records and to display data in a database.

PROJECT 3B

OUTCOMES

Create reports to display database information.

OBJECTIVES

1. Create and Use a Form to Add and Delete Records
2. Filter Records
3. Create a Form by Using the Form Wizard
4. Modify a Form in Layout View and in Design View

OBJECTIVES

5. Create a Report by Using the Report Tool and Modify the Report in Layout View
6. Create a Report by Using the Report Wizard
7. Modify the Design of a Report
8. Keep Grouped Data Together in a Printed Report

Riccardo Piccinini/Fotolia

In This Chapter

In this chapter, you will create forms to enter and delete data and to view data in database tables. Forms can display one record at a time with fields placed in the same order to match a paper source document. Records in a form or table can be filtered to display a subset of the records based on matching specific values. You will modify forms by adding fields, changing field widths, and adding labels to the forms. You will create professional-looking reports that summarize the data stored in a query or table. You will modify the reports by changing the fields in the report, by changing the layout of the report, by grouping data, and by making sure that groupings of data stay together on the printed page.

The projects in this chapter relate to **Texas Lakes Community College**, which is located in the Austin, Texas, area. Its four campuses serve over 30,000 students and offer more than 140 certificate programs and degrees. The college has a highly acclaimed Distance Education program and an extensive Workforce Development program. The college makes positive contributions to the community through cultural and athletic programs and has significant partnerships with businesses and nonprofit organizations. Popular fields of study include nursing and health care, solar technology, computer technology, and graphic design.

PROJECT 3A Students and Majors Database

MyITLab® Project 3A Training

PROJECT ACTIVITIES

In Activities 3.01 through 3.15, you will assist Sean Fitchette, director of Enrollment Services at Texas Lakes Community College, in using his Access database to track new students and their major fields of study. Your completed forms will look similar to Figure 3.1.

PROJECT FILES

For Project 3A, you will need the following file:
a03A_Students_Majors

You will save your database as:
Lastname_Firstname_3A_Students_Majors

PROJECT RESULTS

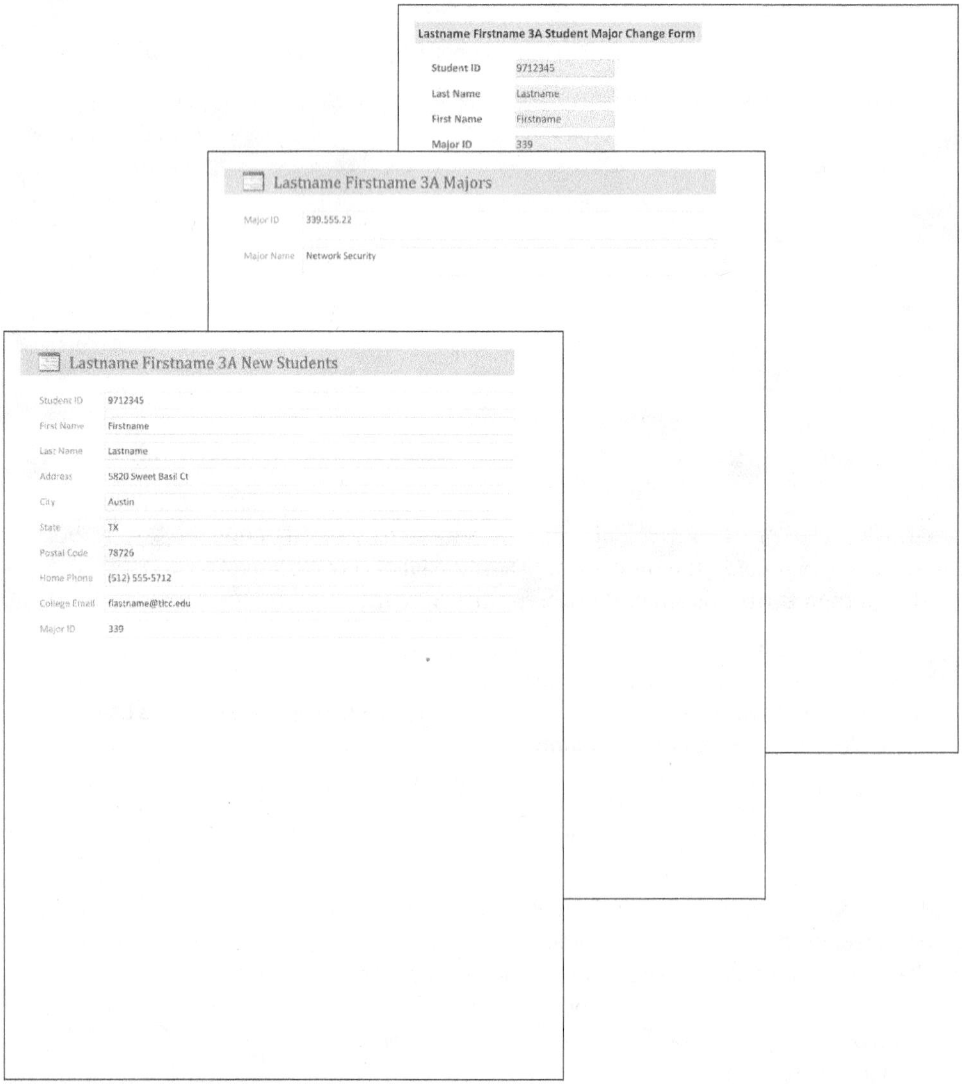

FIGURE 3.1 Project 3A Students and Majors

NOTE **If You Are Using a Touchscreen**

- Tap an item to click it.
- Press and hold for a few seconds to right-click; release when the information or command displays.
- Touch the screen with two or more fingers and then pinch together to zoom in or stretch your fingers apart to zoom out.
- Slide your finger on the screen to scroll—slide left to scroll right and slide right to scroll left.
- Slide to rearrange—similar to dragging with a mouse.
- Swipe from edge: from right to display charms; from left to expose open apps, snap apps, or close apps; from top or bottom to show commands or close an app.
- Swipe to select—slide an item a short distance with a quick movement—to select an item and bring up commands, if any.

Objective 1 Create and Use a Form to Add and Delete Records

Video A3-1

A ***form*** is a database object that you can use to enter new records into a table, or to edit, delete, or display existing records in a table. A form is useful to control access to the data. For example, you can design a form for college registration assistants so that they can see and enter the courses scheduled and fees paid by an individual student. However, they cannot see or enter grades for a student.

Some forms display only one record at a time; other forms display multiple records at the same time. A form that displays only one record at a time is useful not only to the individual who performs the ***data entry***—entering the actual records—but also to anyone who has the job of viewing information in a database. For example, when you request a transcript from your college, someone displays your record on the screen. For the individual viewing your transcript, it is much easier to look at one record at a time, using a form, than to look at all of the student transcripts in the database.

Activity 3.01 Opening and Saving an Existing Database, Renaming Tables, and Viewing a Table Relationship

1. Start Access. In the Access opening screen, click **Open Other Files**. Under **Open**, click **Computer**, and then on the right, click **Browse**. In the **Open** dialog box, navigate to the location where your student data files for this chapter are stored, and then double-click **a03A_Students_Majors** to open the database.

2. On the ribbon, click the **FILE tab**, and then click **Save As**. Under **File Types**, be sure **Save Database As** is selected. On the right, under **Database File Types**, be sure **Access Database** is selected, and then at the bottom of the screen, click **Save As**.

3. In the **Save As** dialog box, navigate to the location where you are saving your databases. Create a **New folder** named **Access Chapter 3**, and then **Open** the folder. In the **File name** box and using your own name, replace the existing text with **Lastname_Firstname_3A_Students_Majors** and then click **Save** or press Enter.

4. On the **Message Bar**, click **Enable Content**. In the **Navigation Pane**, right-click the **3A Majors** table, and then click **Rename**. With the table name selected and using your own name, type **Lastname Firstname 3A Majors** and then press Enter to rename the table. Use the same technique to **Rename** the **3A New Students** table to **Lastname Firstname 3A New Students**

5. Point to the right edge of the **Navigation Pane** to display the ⟺ pointer. Drag to the right to increase the width of the pane until both table names display fully.

6 On the ribbon, click the **DATABASE TOOLS tab**. In the **Relationships group**, click **Relationships**. On the **DESIGN tab**, in the **Relationships group**, click **All Relationships**. If necessary, resize and move the field lists so that the entire table name and fields display for each field list.

Because you renamed the tables, the field lists do not automatically display in the Relationships window.

7 In the **Relationships** window, click the **join line** between the two field lists. In the **Tools group**, click **Edit Relationships**. Point to the title bar of the **Edit Relationships** dialog box, and drag the dialog box downward below the two field lists. Compare your screen with Figure 3.2.

One major is associated with *many* students. A one-to-many relationship is established between your 3A Majors table and your 3A New Students table using the Major ID field as the common field. Recall that Cascade Update Related Fields enables you to change the primary key in the 3A Majors table, and then the data in the foreign key field in the 3A New Students field is automatically updated. Recall that Cascade Delete Related Records enables you to delete a record in the 3A Majors table, and then all related records in the 3A New Students table are automatically deleted.

ANOTHER WAY In the Relationships window, double-click the join line to display the Edit Relationships dialog box.

FIGURE 3.2

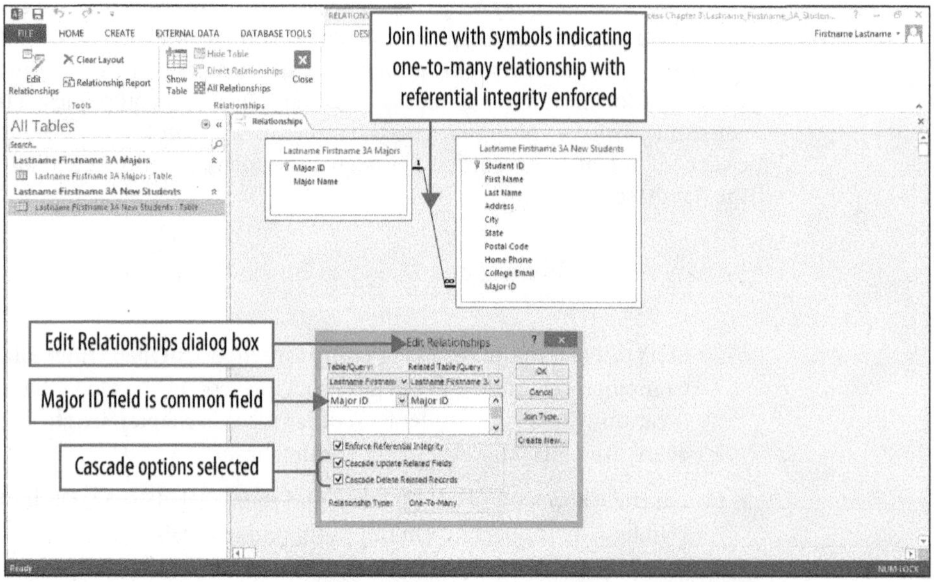

ALERT! **Is Your Edit Relationships Dialog Box Empty?**

The Edit Relationships dialog box does not display any information if you do not first click the join line. If this happens, close the Edit Relationships dialog box, and then be sure that you click the join line—when selected, the join line is darker.

8 **Close** the **Edit Relationships** dialog box, and then **Close** the **Relationships** window. In the message box, click **Yes** to save changes to the layout of the relationships.

Activity 3.02 | Creating a Form and Viewing Records

There are several ways to create a form in Access, but the fastest and easiest way is to use the ***Form tool***. With a single mouse click, all fields from the data source are placed on the form. You can use the new form immediately, or you can modify the form in Layout view or in Design view.

The Form tool uses all of the field names and all of the records from an existing table or query. Records that you create or edit using a form are automatically updated in the underlying table or tables. In this activity, you will create a form and then view records from the underlying table—the data source.

1 In the **Navigation Pane**, double-click your **3A New Students** table to open it. Scroll as needed to view all 10 fields—*Student ID, First Name, Last Name, Address, City, State, Postal Code, Home Phone, College Email,* and *Major ID*. **Close** [×] the table.

2 In the **Navigation Pane**, be sure your **3A New Students** table is selected. On the ribbon, click the **CREATE tab**, and then in the **Forms group**, click **Form**. **Close** [«] the **Navigation Pane**, and then compare your screen with Figure 3.3.

The form is created based on the currently selected object—your 3A New Students table—and displays in ***Layout view***. In Layout view, you can modify the form with the data displayed in the fields. For example, you can adjust the size of the text boxes to fit the data.

The form is created in a simple top-to-bottom layout, with all 10 fields from your 3A New Students table lined up in a single column. The data for the first record in the data source displays.

FIGURE 3.3

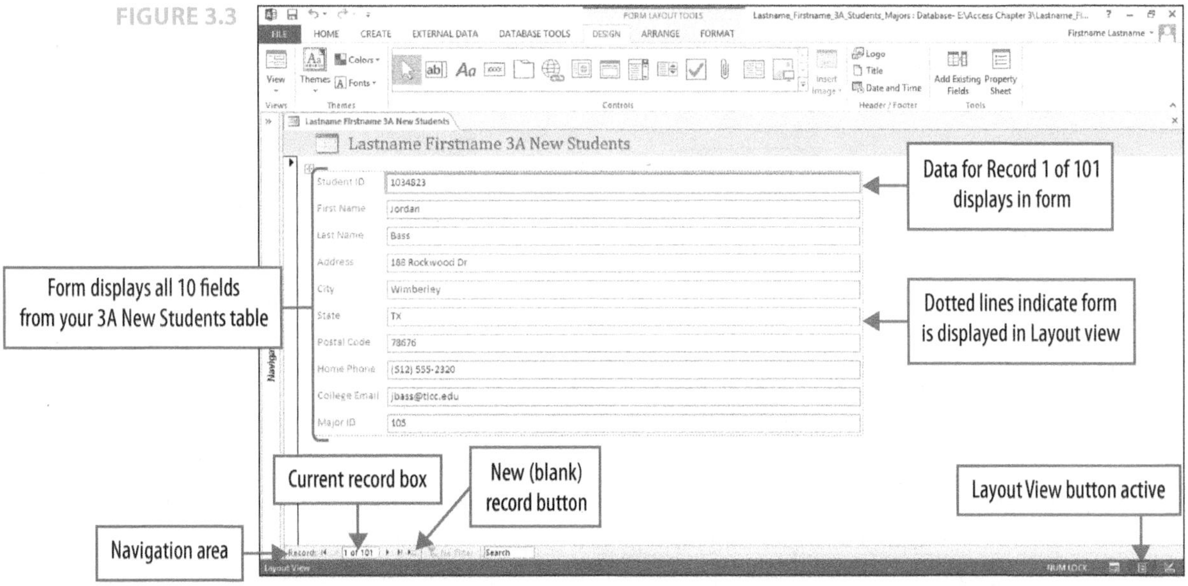

3 In the navigation area, click **Next record** [▶] four times to display the fifth record—*Student ID 1298345*. In the navigation area, select the text in the Current record box, type **62** and then press Enter to display the record for *Student ID 5720358*. In the navigation area, click **Last record** [▶|] to display the record for *Student ID 9583924*, and then click **First record** [|◀] to display the record for *Student ID 1034823*.

Use the navigation buttons to scroll among the records or the Current record box to display any single record.

4 **Save** [💾] the form as **Lastname Firstname 3A New Student Form** and then **Close** [×] the form object.

5 **Open** [»] the **Navigation Pane**. Notice that your new form displays under the table with which it is related—your **3A New Students** table.

Activity 3.03 | Creating a Second Form

In this activity, you will use the Form tool to create a form for your 3A Majors table.

1 In the **Navigation Pane**, click your **3A Majors** table to select it. On the ribbon, click the **CREATE tab**, and then in the **Forms group**, click **Form**. **Close** [«] the **Navigation Pane**, and then compare your screen with Figure 3.4.

Because a one-to-many relationship is established, the form displays related records in the 3A New Students table for each record in the 3A Majors table. Five new students have selected a major of *Diagnostic Medical Sonography—Major ID 105*.

FIGURE 3.4

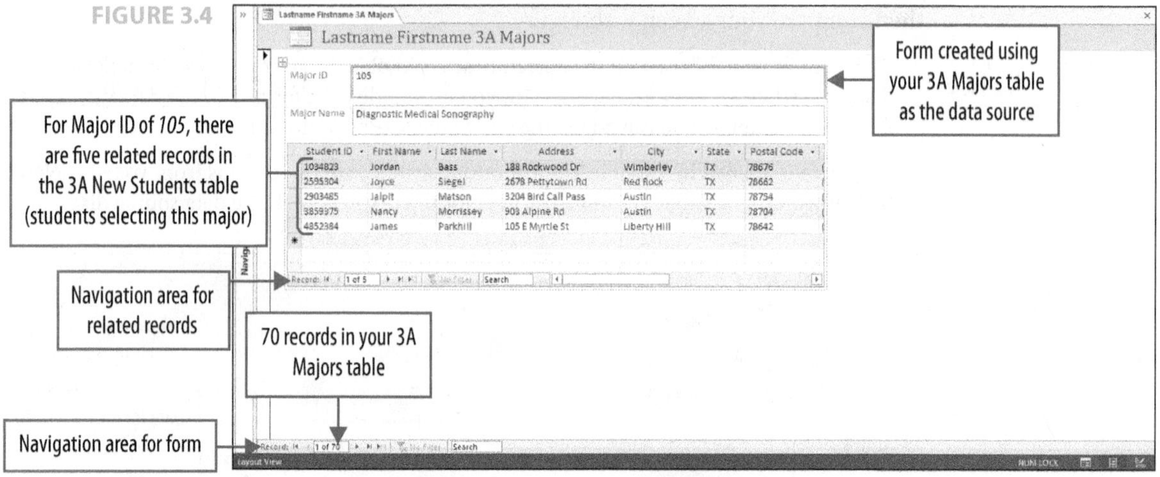

2 **Close** [×] your **3A Majors** form. In the message box, click **Yes**. In the **Save As** dialog box, in the **Form Name** box, type **Lastname Firstname 3A Major Form** and then click **OK**.

Recall that if you do not save an object, you are prompted to do so when you close the object.

3 **Open** [»] the **Navigation Pane**. Notice that your new form displays under the table with which it is related—your **3A Majors** table.

Activity 3.04 | Adding Records to a Table by Using a Form

By using a single-record form to add, modify, and delete records, you can reduce the number of data entry errors, because the individual performing the data entry is looking at only one record at a time. Recall that your database is useful only if the information is accurate—just like your contact list is useful only if it contains accurate phone numbers and email addresses.

Forms are based on—also referred to as ***bound*** to—the table where the records are stored. When a record is entered in a form, the new record is added to the underlying table. The reverse is also true—when a record is added to the table, the new record can be viewed in the related form.

In this activity, you will add a new record to both tables by using the forms that you just created.

1 In the **Navigation Pane**, double-click your **3A New Student Form** object to open it, and then **Close** [«] the **Navigation Pane**. In the navigation area, click **New (blank) record** [▶*] to display a new blank form.

When you open a form, the first record in the underlying table displays in ***Form view***, which is used to view, add, modify, and delete records stored in the table.

2 In the **Student ID** field, type **9712345** and then press [Tab].

Use the [Tab] key to move from field to field in a form. ***Tab order*** is the order in which the insertion point moves from one field to the next when you press the [Tab] key. As you start typing, the pencil icon displays in the ***record selector bar*** at the left—the bar used to select an entire record. The pencil icon displays when a record is being created or edited.

ANOTHER WAY Press the Enter key, provided there are no special links on the form, such as a link to create a new form or a link to print the form.

3 Using your own first name and last name and using the first initial of your first name and your last name for the *College Email* field, continue entering the data shown in the following table, and then compare your screen with Figure 3.5.

Student ID	First Name	Last Name	Address	City	State	Postal Code	Home Phone	College Email	Major ID
9712345	**First Name**	**Last Name**	**5820 Sweet Basil Ct**	**Austin**	**TX**	**78726**	**(512) 555-5712**	**flastname@tlcc.edu**	**339**

FIGURE 3.5

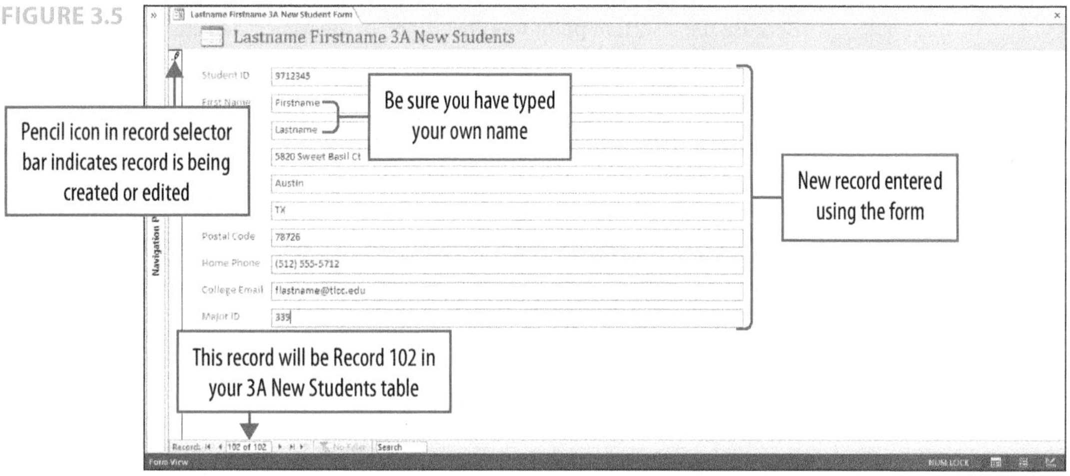

4 With the insertion point positioned in the last field, press Tab to save the record and display a new blank record. **Close** your **3A New Student Form** object.

5 **Open** the **Navigation Pane**, and then double-click your **3A New Students** table to open it. In the navigation area, click **Last record** to verify that the record you entered in the form is stored in the underlying table. **Close** your **3A New Students** table.

6 In the **Navigation Pane**, double-click your **3A Major Form** object to open it. At the bottom of the screen, in the navigation area for the form—*not* the navigation area for the subdatasheet—click **New (blank) record**. In the blank form enter the data shown in the following table:

Major ID	Major Name
339.555.22	**Network Security**

7 **Close** your **3A Major Form** object. In the **Navigation Pane**, double-click your **3A Majors** table, and then scroll to verify that the record for *Major ID 339.555.22 Network Security* displays in the table—records are sorted by the *Major ID* field. **Close** the table.

Activity 3.05 | Deleting Records from a Table by Using a Form

You can delete records from a database table by using a form. In this activity, you will delete the record for *Major ID 800.03* because the program has been discontinued.

1. In the **Navigation Pane**, double-click your **3A Major Form** object to open it, and then **Close** [«] the **Navigation Pane**. On the **HOME tab**, in the **Find group**, click **Find** to open the **Find and Replace** dialog box.

ANOTHER WAY Press [Ctrl] + [F] to open the Find and Replace dialog box.

2. In the **Look In** box, notice that *Current field* displays. In the **Find What** box, type **800.03** and then click **Find Next**. Compare your screen with Figure 3.6, and verify that the record for *Major ID 800.03* displays.

   Because the insertion point was positioned in the *Major ID* field before opening the dialog box, Access will search for data in this field—the *Current field*.

FIGURE 3.6

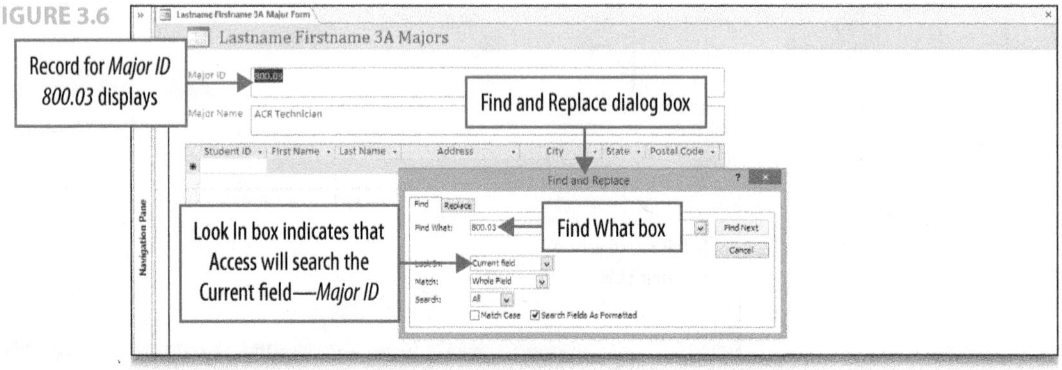

3. **Close** [X] the **Find and Replace** dialog box. On the **HOME tab**, in the **Records group**, click the **Delete arrow**, and then click **Delete Record**.

   The record is removed from the screen, and a message displays alerting you that you are about to delete *1 record(s)*. Once you click *Yes*, you cannot click Undo to reverse this action. If you delete a record by mistake, you must re-create the record by reentering the data. Because no students are associated with this major and the program is being discontinued, you can delete it from the table.

4. In the message box, click **Yes** to delete the record. In the navigation area for the form, notice that the total number of records in the table is *70*. **Close** [×] your **3A Major Form** object.

5. **Open** [»] the **Navigation Pane**, and then double-click your **3A Majors** table to open it. Examine the table to verify that the *Major ID 800.03* record has been deleted from the table, and then **Close** [×] the table.

   Adding and deleting records in a form updates the records stored in the underlying table.

Activity 3.06 | Printing a Form

When a form is displayed, clicking Print causes *all* of the records to print in the form layout. In this activity, you will print only *one* record.

1. In the **Navigation Pane**, double-click your **3A New Student Form** object to open it, and then **Close** [«] the **Navigation Pane**. Press [Ctrl] + [F] to open the **Find and Replace** dialog box. In the **Find What** box, type **9712345** and then click **Find Next** to display the record with your name. **Close** [X] the **Find and Replace** dialog box.

2 On the ribbon, click the **FILE tab**, click **Print**, and then on the right, click **Print**. In the **Print** dialog box, under **Print Range**, click the **Selected Record(s)** option button. In the lower left corner of the dialog box, click **Setup**.

3 In the **Page Setup** dialog box, click the **Columns tab**. Under **Column Size**, double-click in the **Width** box to select the existing value, type **7.5** and then compare your screen with Figure 3.7.

Change the width of the column in this manner so that the form prints on one page. Forms are not typically printed, so the width of the column in a form might be greater than the width of the paper on which you are printing. The maximum column width that you can enter is dependent upon the printer that is installed on your system. This setting is saved when you save or close the form.

FIGURE 3.7

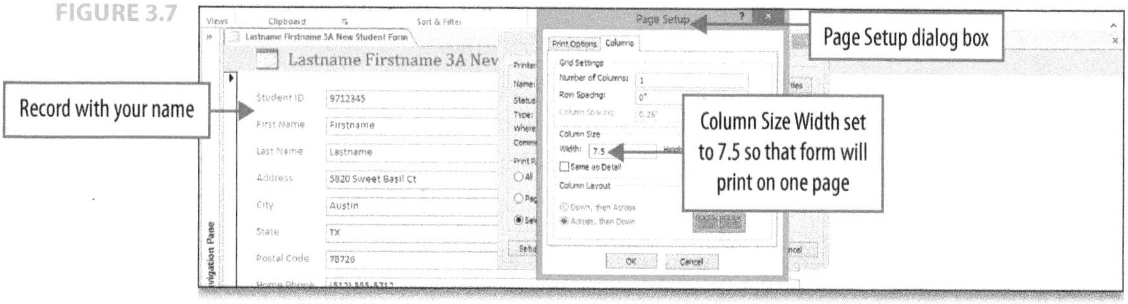

4 In the **Page Setup** dialog box, click **OK**. To create a paper printout, in the **Print** dialog box click **OK**. To create an electronic printout of this single form, click **Cancel** and then follow the instructions in the Note below.

NOTE **Printing a Single Form in PDF**

To create an electronic printout of a single form in PDF, change the column width to 7.5 as described in Step 3 above, and then in the Print dialog box, click Cancel. On the left side of the form, click the Record Selector bar so that it is black—selected. On the ribbon, click the EXTERNAL DATA tab. In the Export group, click PDF or XPS.

In the Publish as PDF or XPS dialog box, navigate to your chapter folder. In the File name box, the form has the same name as the form. Be sure that the Open file after publishing check box is selected, and that the Minimum size (publishing online) option button is selected. In the Publish as PDF or XPS dialog box, Click Options. In the Options dialog box, under Range, click the Selected records option button, click OK, and then click Publish. Close the Windows 8 Reader, Adobe Reader or Adobe Acrobat window, and then submit the file as directed by your instructor.

5 **Close** [×] your **3A New Student Form** object, **Open** [»] the **Navigation Pane**, and then double-click your **3A Major Form** object to open it. **Close** [«] the **Navigation Pane**.

6 Use the techniques you just practiced to **Find** the record for the **Major ID** of **339.555.22**, and then create a paper or electronic printout as directed by your instructor of that record only on one page. After printing, **Close** [×] your **3A Major Form** object.

If there are no related records in the subdatasheet, the empty subdatasheet does not display in the printed form.

Objective 2 Filter Records

Video A3-2

Filtering records in a form displays only a portion of the total records—a ***subset***—based on matching specific values. Filters are commonly used to provide a quick answer, and the result is not generally saved for future use. For example, by filtering records in a form, you can quickly display a subset of records for students majoring in Information Systems Technology, which is identified by the Major ID of 339.

A form provides an interface for the database. For example, because of security reasons, the registration assistants at your college may not have access to the entire student database. Rather, by using a form, they can access and edit only some information—the information necessary for them to do their jobs. Filtering records within a form provides individuals who do not have access to the entire database a way to ask questions of the database without constructing a query. You can save the filter with the form if you are going to use the filter frequently.

Activity 3.07 | Filtering Data by Selection of One Field

In this activity, you will assist a counselor at the college who wants to see records for students majoring in Information Systems Technology. In a form, you can use the ***Filter By Selection*** command to display only the records that contain the value in the selected field and to hide the records that do *not* contain the value in the selected field.

1. **Open** [»] the **Navigation Pane**, double-click your **3A New Student Form** object to open it in **Form** view, and then **Close** [«] the **Navigation Pane.**

2. In the first record, click the **Major ID** field name—or you can click in the field box. Press Ctrl + F to display the **Find and Replace** dialog box. In the **Find What** box, type **339** If necessary, in the Match box, click the arrow, and then click Whole Field. Click **Find Next**, and then compare your screen with Figure 3.8.

   This action finds and displays a record with a *Major ID* of *339*—the major of *Information Systems Technology*. You will use this action to filter the records using the value of *339*.

FIGURE 3.8

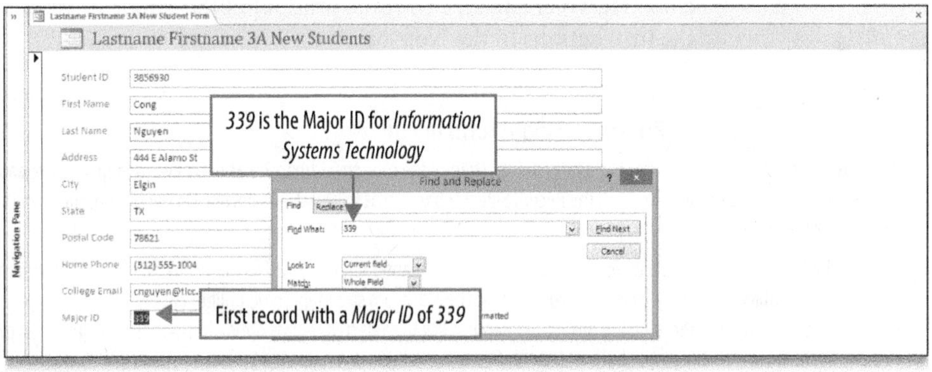

3. **Close** [X] the **Find and Replace** dialog box. On the **HOME tab**, in the **Sort & Filter group**, click **Selection**, and then click **Equals "339"**. Compare your screen with Figure 3.9.

   Seven records match the contents of the selected Major ID field—*339*—the Major ID for the Information Systems Technology major. In the navigation area, *Filtered* with a funnel icon displays next to the number of records. *Filtered* also displays on the right side of the status bar to indicate that a filter is applied. On the HOME tab, in the Sort & Filter group, Toggle Filter is active.

ANOTHER WAY With the data selected in the field, right-click the selection, and then click Equals "339".

FIGURE 3.9

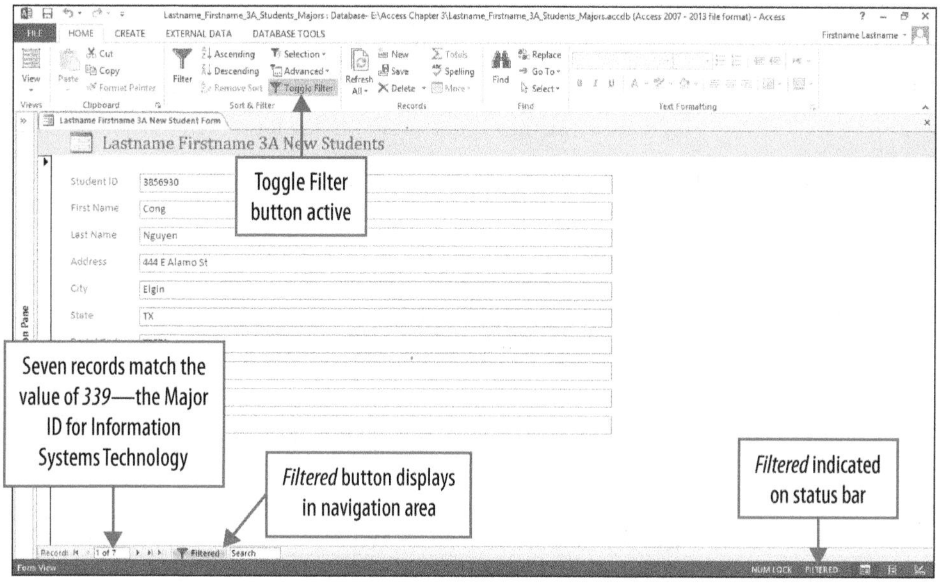

4 On the **HOME tab**, in the **Sort & Filter group**, click **Toggle Filter** to remove the filter and display all 102 records. Notice *Unfiltered* in the navigation area, which indicates a filter is created but is not active.

ANOTHER WAY Click Filtered in the navigation area to remove the filter.

NOTE **The Toggle Filter Button**

On the HOME tab, in the Sort & Filter group, the Toggle Filter button is used to apply or remove a filter. If no filter is created, the button is not available. After a filter is created, the button becomes available. Because it is a toggle button used to apply or remove a filter, the ScreenTip that displays for this button alternates between Apply Filter—when a filter is created but is not currently applied—and Remove Filter—when a filter is applied.

5 Be sure that the first record—for *Jordan Bass*—displays. On the **HOME tab**, in the **Sort & Filter group**, click **Toggle Filter** to reapply the filter. In the navigation area, click **Last record** to display the last of the seven records that match a Major ID of *339*.

The record for *Student ID 9712345* displays—the record with your name. Use Toggle Filter to apply or remove filters as needed.

6 In the navigation area, click **Filtered** to remove the filter and display all of the records.

In the navigation area, *Filtered* changes to *Unfiltered*.

7 In the first record for *Jordan Bass*, in the **Last Name** field, select the first letter—**B**—in *Bass*. In the **Sort & Filter group**, click **Selection**, and then click **Begins with "B"**.

A new filter is applied that displays eight records in which the *Last Name* begins with the letter *B*.

ANOTHER WAY With the letter *B* selected, right-click the selection, and then click Begins with "B".

8 Use either **Toggle Filter** in the **Sort & Filter group** or **Filtered** in the navigation area to remove the filter and display all of the records.

9 In the **Sort & Filter group**, click **Advanced**, and then click **Clear All Filters**. Notice, that in the navigation area, *Unfiltered* changed to *No Filter*.

The filter is removed from the form and must be recreated to apply it. If you toggle the filter off and save the form, the filter is saved with the form even though the filter is not currently applied.

Activity 3.08 | Using Filter By Form

Use the ***Filter By Form*** command to filter the records based on one or more fields, or based on more than one value in the same field. The Filter By Form command offers greater flexibility than the Filter By Selection command and can be used to answer a question that requires matching multiple values. In this activity, you will filter records to help Mr. Fitchette determine how many students live in Dripping Springs or Austin.

1 On the **HOME tab**, in the **Sort & Filter group**, click **Advanced**, and then click **Filter By Form**. Compare your screen with Figure 3.10.

The Filter by Form window displays all of the field names, but without any data. In the empty text box for each field, you can type a value or select a value from a list. The *Look for* and *Or* tabs display at the bottom.

FIGURE 3.10

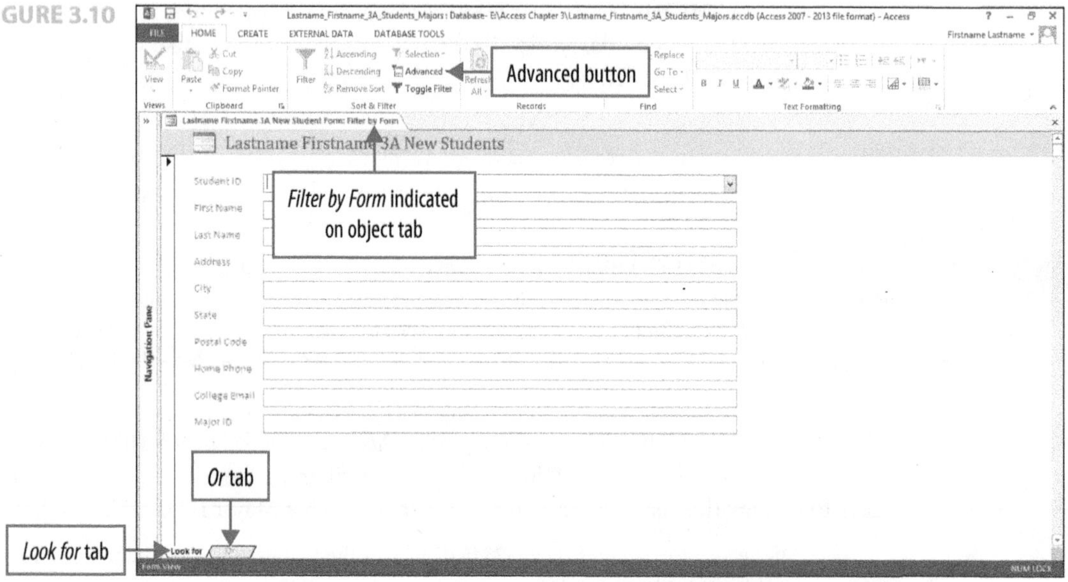

2 In the form, click the **City** field name to position the insertion point in the **City** field box. At the right edge of the **City** field box, click the **arrow**, and then click **Dripping Springs**. In the **Sort & Filter group**, click **Toggle Filter**.

As displayed in the navigation area, four student records have *Dripping Springs* stored in the City field.

3 In the **Sort & Filter group**, click **Advanced**, and then click **Filter By Form**. In the lower left corner of the form, click the **Or tab**. Click the **City** field box **arrow**, and then click **Austin**. In the **Sort & Filter group**, click **Toggle Filter**, and then compare your screen with Figure 3.11.

As displayed in the navigation area, 28 student records have either *Dripping Springs* OR *Austin* stored in the City field. You have created an ***OR condition***; that is, records display where, in this instance, either of two values—Dripping Springs *or* Austin—is present in the selected field.

ANOTHER WAY Click in the field box, and type the criteria separated by the word *or*. For example, in the City field box, type *Dripping Springs or Austin*.

FIGURE 3.11

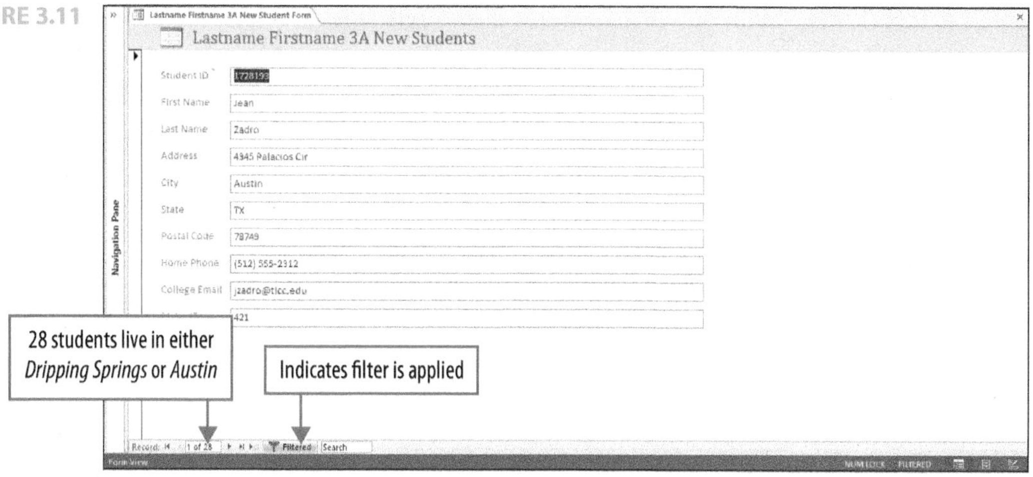

4 In the **Sort & Filter group**, click **Advanced**, and then click **Clear All Filters** to display all 102 records.

Activity 3.09 Using Advanced Filter/Sort

In this activity, you will use the Advanced Filter/Sort command to filter records to locate students who live in Austin with a Major ID of *339*—Information Systems Technology.

1 In the **Sort & Filter group**, click **Advanced**, and then click **Advanced Filter/Sort.**

The Advanced Filter design grid displays, which is similar to the query design grid. A field list for the underlying table of the form displays.

2 In the table area, resize the field list so that the entire table name and all of the field names display.

3 In the **3A New Students** field list, double-click **City**, and then double-click **Major ID** to add both fields to the design grid. In the **Criteria** row under **City**, type **Austin** and then press Enter. In the **Criteria** row under **Major ID**, type **339** and then press Enter. Compare your screen with Figure 3.12.

FIGURE 3.12

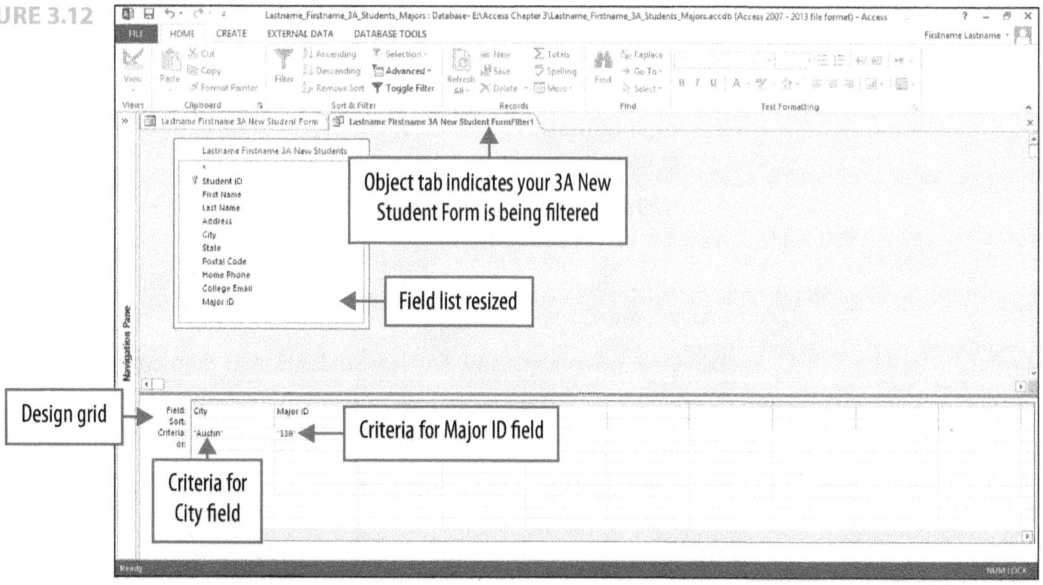

4 In the **Sort & Filter group**, click **Toggle Filter** to display the filtered records.

Three records match the criteria. You have created an ***AND condition***; that is, only records where both values—Austin *and* 339—are present in the selected fields display. There are three students who live in Austin who have declared a major of Information Systems Technology.

5 In the **Sort & Filter group**, click **Toggle Filter** to remove the filter and to display all of the records.

In the navigation area, *Unfiltered* displays, which indicates that a filter has been created for this form. Unless you click Clear All Filters, the filter is saved with the form when the form is closed. When you reopen the form, you can click Toggle Filter or Unfiltered to reapply the filter.

6 **Close** [×] your **3A New Student Form** object, and notice that the Advanced Filter grid also closes.

***More* Knowledge** **Using the Filter Button**

You can filter a form in a manner similar to the way you filter records in a table. Click in the field you wish to use for the filter. On the HOME tab, in the Sort & Filter group, click Filter to display a shortcut menu. Select the (Select All) check box to clear the option, and then select the data by which you want to filter your records by clicking the check boxes preceding the data. To remove the filter, redisplay the menu, and then select the (Select All) check box.

Objective 3 Create a Form by Using the Form Wizard

Video A3-3

The ***Form Wizard*** walks you step by step through the creation of a form and gives you more flexibility in the design, layout, and number of fields in a form than the Form tool. Design a form for the individuals who use the form—either for entering new records or viewing records. For example, when your college counselor displays student information, it may be easier for the counselor to view the information if the fields are arranged in a layout that more closely matches a paper form.

Activity 3.10 | Creating a Form by Using the Form Wizard

In this activity, you will create a form to match the layout of a paper form that a student at Texas Lakes Community College completes when that student changes his or her major. This will make it easier for the individual who changes the data in the database.

1 On the ribbon, click the **CREATE tab**, and then in the **Forms group**, click **Form Wizard.**

The Form Wizard walks you step by step through the process of creating a form by asking questions. In the first wizard screen, you select the fields to include on the form. The fields can come from more than one table or query.

2 In the **Tables/Queries** box, click the **arrow** to display a list of available tables and queries from which you can create the form.

There are two tables in the database from which you can create a new form. The selected table is the one that you last worked with.

3 Click **Table: Lastname Firstname 3A New Students**, and then compare your screen with Figure 3.13.

In the Available Fields list, the field names from your 3A New Students table display.

FIGURE 3.13

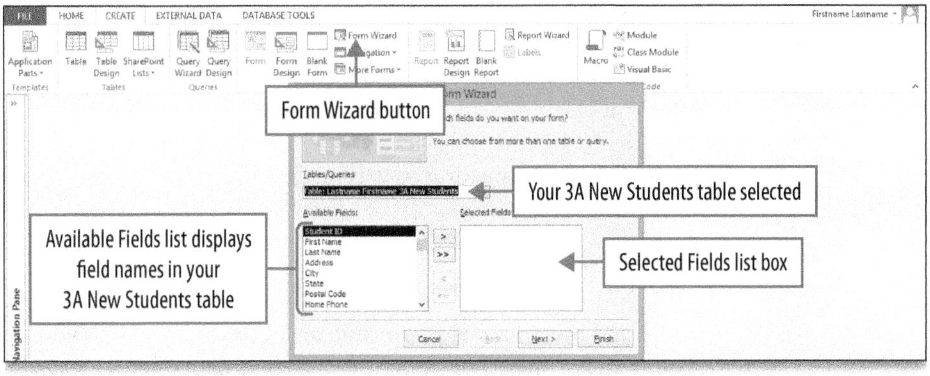

4 In the **Available Fields** list, double-click the following field names in the order given to move them to the **Selected Fields** list: **First Name, Last Name**, and **Major ID**. Compare your screen with Figure 3.14.

Three field names from your 3A New Students table display in the Selected Fields list.

ANOTHER WAY

Click the field name, and then click One Field [>] to move a field from the Available Fields list to the Selected Fields list.

FIGURE 3.14

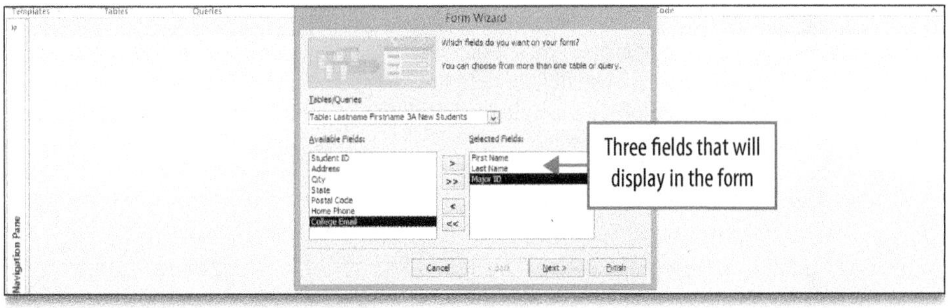

5 Click **Next**. In the wizard, be sure **Columnar** is selected as the layout, and then click **Next**. In the **What title do you want for your form?** box, select the existing text, type **Lastname Firstname 3A Student Major Change Form** and then click **Finish** to close the wizard and create the form.

The three fields and the data from the first record in your 3A New Students table display in Form view.

6 **Open** [»] the **Navigation Pane**. If necessary, increase the width of the Navigation Pane so that all object names display fully. Compare your screen with Figure 3.15.

In the Navigation Pane, the form displays under its data source—your 3A New Students table.

FIGURE 3.15

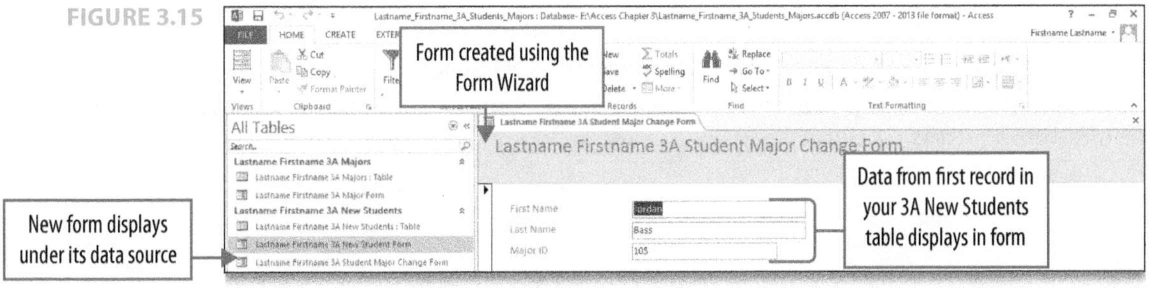

Objective 4 Modify a Form in Layout View and in Design View

Video A3-4

After you create a form, you can make changes to it. For example, you can group the fields, resize the fields, add more fields to the form, and change the style of the form. Layout view enables you to see the data in the form as you modify the form. Most changes to a form can be made in Layout view.

Activity 3.11 | Grouping Controls in Layout View

In this activity, you will group ***controls*** in the form so that you can work with them as one unit. Controls are objects on a form that display data or text, perform actions, and let you view and work with information.

1. **Close** [«] the **Navigation Pane**, and be sure that your **3A Student Major Change Form** object displays in the object window. On the **HOME tab**, in the **Views group**, click the top portion of the **View** button to switch to **Layout** view. If the Field List pane displays on the right side of your screen, click Close [X] to close the pane. Compare your screen with Figure 3.16.

   The field names and data for the first record in your 3A New Students record display in controls. The data for the first record displays in ***text box controls***. The most commonly used control is the text box control, which typically displays data from a field in the underlying table. A text box control is a ***bound control***—its data comes from a field in a table or query.

   The field names—*First Name*, *Last Name*, and *Major ID*—display in ***label controls***. A label control displays to the left of a text box control and contains descriptive information that displays on the form, usually the field name. A control that does not have a data source is an ***unbound control***. Another example of an unbound control is a label control that displays the title of a form.

ANOTHER WAY On the right side of the status bar, click Layout View to switch from Form view to Layout view.

FIGURE 3.16

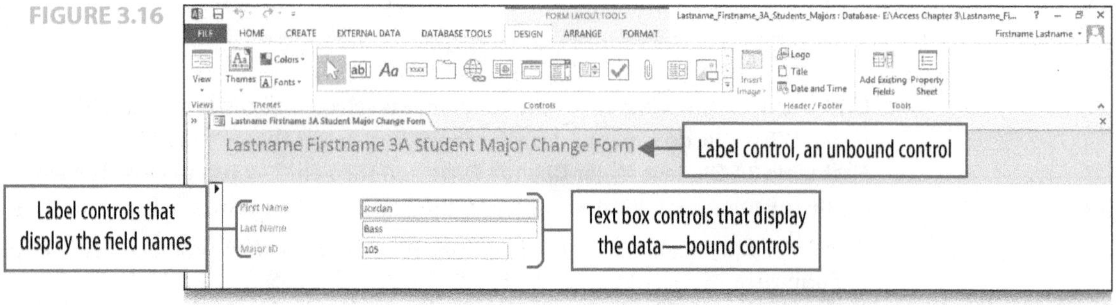

2. Click the **First Name label control**. Hold down [Shift], and then click the **Last Name label control**, the **Major ID label control**, and the three **text box controls** to select all of the label and text box controls on the form.

ALERT! **Do Your Controls Change Order When Selecting?**

If, when selecting multiple controls, the controls change order, click Undo, and then select the controls again. Be careful not to drag the mouse when you are selecting multiple controls.

3. With all six controls selected—surrounded by a colored border—on the ribbon, under **FORM LAYOUT TOOLS**, click the **ARRANGE tab**. In the **Table group**, click **Stacked**. Click the **First Name label control** to cancel the selection of all of the controls and to surround the **First Name label control** with a colored border. Compare your screen with Figure 3.17.

   This action groups the controls together in the ***Stacked layout*** format—a layout similar to a paper form, with labels to the left of each field. Because the controls are grouped, you can move and edit the controls more easily as you redesign your form.

   A dotted line forms a border around the controls, which indicates that the controls are grouped together. Above and to the left of the first label control that displays *First Name*, the ***layout selector*** [⊞] displays. The layout selector is used to select and move or format the entire group of controls.

FIGURE 3.17

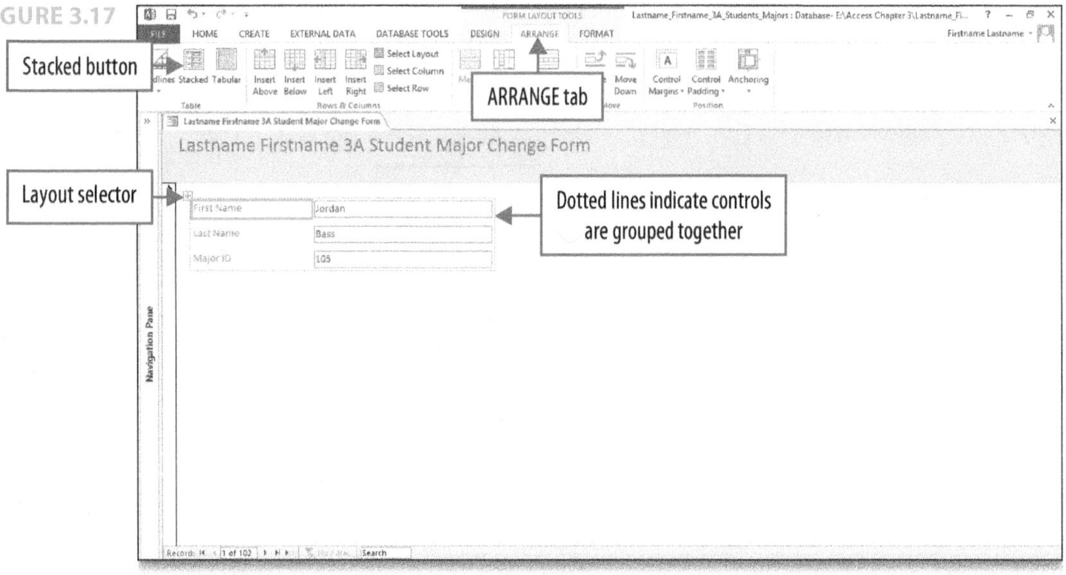

Activity 3.12 | Applying a Theme and Formatting a Form in Layout View

In this activity, you will apply a ***theme*** to the form in Layout view. A theme is a predesigned set of colors, fonts, lines, and fill effects that look good together and that can be applied to all of the objects in the database or to individual objects in the database.

1. On the ribbon, under **FORM LAYOUT TOOLS**, click the **DESIGN tab**. In the **Themes group**, click **Themes**. In the **Themes** gallery, using the ScreenTips, point to the **Retrospect** theme, right-click, and then click **Apply Theme to This Object Only**.

   Right-click a theme so that you can apply the theme to an individual object within the database. Apply a theme before formatting any other controls in your form.

NOTE | **Applying a Theme to an Object and Determining the Applied Theme**

If you click a theme rather than right-clicking it and selecting an option, the theme is applied to all objects in the database. You cannot click Undo to cancel the application of the theme to all objects. To determine the applied theme, in the Themes group, point to Themes. The ScreenTip displays the name of the current theme.

2. Click anywhere in the title of the form—*Lastname Firstname 3A Student Major Change Form*—to select the title. On the ribbon, under **FORM LAYOUT TOOLS**, click the **FORMAT tab**. In the **Font group**, click the **Font Size arrow**, and then click **14**. In the **Font group**, click **Bold** [B]. Click the **Font Color arrow**, and then under **Theme Colors**, in the fourth column, click the last color—**Olive Green, Text 2, Darker 50%**.

Activity 3.13 | Adding, Resizing, and Moving Controls in Layout View

In Layout view, you can change the form's ***control layout***—the grouped arrangement of controls.

1 Be sure that your **3A Student Major Change Form** object displays in **Layout** view. On the ribbon, click the **DESIGN tab**, and in the **Tools group**, click **Add Existing Fields**. Compare your screen with Figure 3.18.

The Field List pane displays, which lists the fields in the underlying table—your 3A New Students table.

FIGURE 3.18

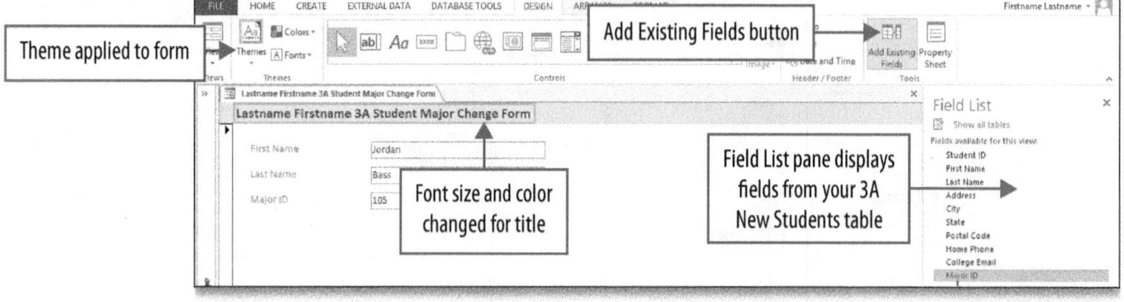

2 In the **Field List** pane, click **Student ID**, and then drag the field name to the left until the pointer displays above the **First Name label control** and a colored line displays above the control. Release the mouse button, and then compare your screen with Figure 3.19. If you are not satisfied with the result, click Undo, and begin again.

This action adds the Student ID label control and text box control to the form above the First Name controls.

FIGURE 3.19

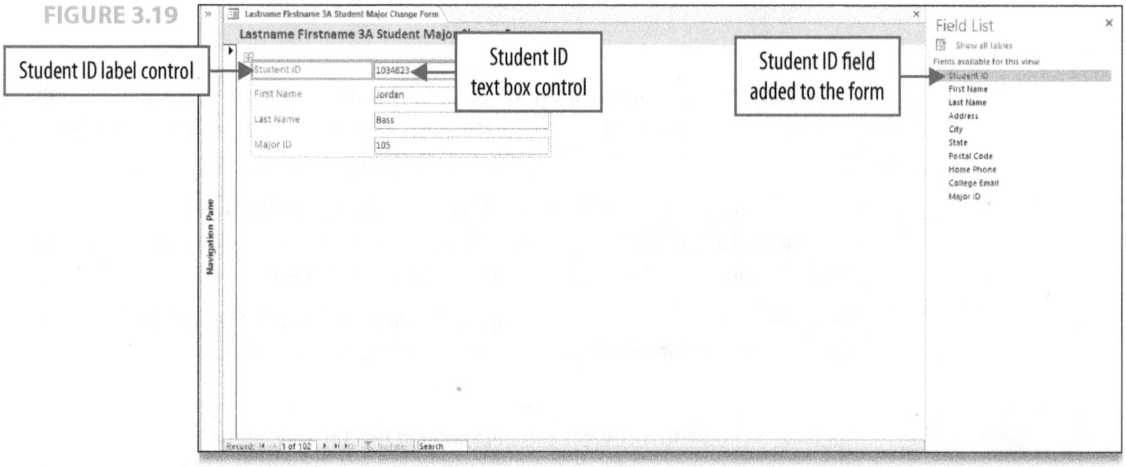

3 **Close** ☒ the **Field List** pane. Click the **Student ID text box control**, which displays *1034823*, to surround it with a border and to remove the border from the label control.

4 On the **DESIGN tab**, in the **Tools group**, click **Property Sheet**.

The Property Sheet for the Student ID text box control displays. Recall that each control has an associated Property Sheet where precise changes to the properties—characteristics—of selected controls can be made. At the top of the Property Sheet, to the right of *Selection type:*, *Text Box* displays because you selected the Student ID text box control.

5 In the **Property Sheet**, click the **Format tab**. Click **Width** to select the property setting, type **1.5** and then press Enter to decrease the width of the text box controls. Compare your screen with Figure 3.20.

All four text box controls are resized simultaneously. Because the controls are grouped together in a stacked layout, you can adjust the width of all of the text box controls at one time without having to select all of the controls. By decreasing the width of the text box controls, you have more space in which to rearrange the form controls. Because you can see the data in Layout view, you can determine visually that the space you have allotted is adequate to display all of the data in every field for every record.

ANOTHER WAY

With the text box control selected, point to the right edge of the text box control until the ↔ pointer displays, and then drag left to the desired location.

FIGURE 3.20

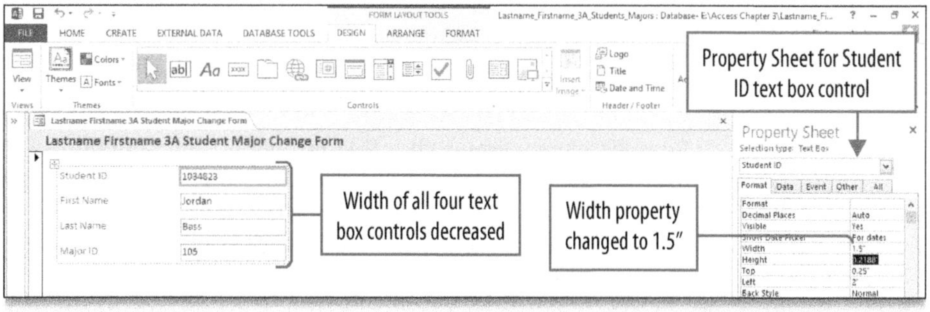

6 **Close** the **Property Sheet**. Click the **Last Name text box control**, which displays *Bass*. On the ribbon, under **FORM LAYOUT TOOLS**, click the **ARRANGE tab**. In the **Rows & Columns group**, click **Select Row** to select the text box control and its associated label control.

7 In the **Move group**, click **Move Up** to move both controls above the **First Name** controls, and then compare your screen with Figure 3.21.

ANOTHER WAY

Drag the selected controls to the desired location and then release the mouse button.

FIGURE 3.21

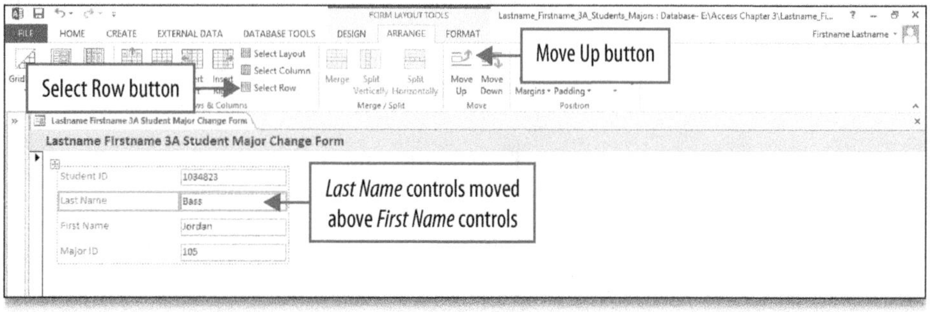

ALERT! **Did the Last Name Label Control Not Move with the Last Name Text Box Control?**

Be sure to select both the text box control and the label control before moving the controls; otherwise, only one of the controls will move. If this happens, click Undo, select both controls, and try again. Controls are stacked from top to bottom, not right to left.

8 **Save** the changes you have made to the design of your form.

Activity 3.14 | Formatting Controls in Layout View

In this activity, you will format and change the property settings for multiple controls.

1 With the form displayed in **Layout** view, click the **Student ID text box control**, which displays *1034823*. On the **ARRANGE tab**, in the **Rows & Columns group**, click **Select Column** to select all four text box controls.

ANOTHER WAY Click the first text box control, hold down Shift, and then click the last text box control to select all four text box controls.

2 With all four text box controls selected, on the ribbon, click the **FORMAT tab**. In the **Font group**, click the **Background Color arrow**. Under **Theme Colors**, in the last column, click the second color—**Green, Accent 6, Lighter 80%.**

All of the text box controls display a background color of light green. This formatting is not applied to the label controls on the left.

3 Click the **Student ID label control**. On the ribbon, click the **ARRANGE tab**, and then in the **Rows & Columns group**, click **Select Column**. On the ribbon, click the **FORMAT tab**, and then click the **Font Color arrow**—*not* the **Background Color arrow**. Under **Theme Colors**, in the fourth column, click the first color—**Olive Green, Text 2**. Click **Bold** B. Click in a blank area of the form to cancel the selection, and then compare your screen with Figure 3.22.

FIGURE 3.22

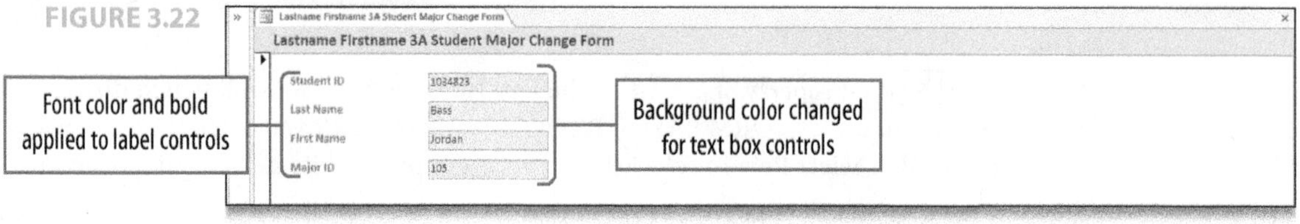

4 Click any **label control** to display the **layout selector**, and then click the **layout selector** to select all of the grouped controls.

Recall that the layout selector, which displays to the left and above the Student ID label control, enables you to select and move the entire group of controls in Layout view.

ANOTHER WAY Click any control, and then on the ARRANGE tab, in the Rows & Columns group, click Select Layout.

5 On the **FORMAT tab**, in the **Font group**, click the **Font Size arrow**, and then click **12** to change the font size of all of the text in all of the controls.

6 With all of the controls still selected, on the ribbon, click the **DESIGN tab**. In the **Tools group**, click **Property Sheet**, and then compare your screen with Figure 3.23.

The Property Sheet for the selected controls displays. At the top of the Property Sheet, to the right of *Selection type:*, *Multiple selection* displays because you have more than one control selected.

FIGURE 3.23

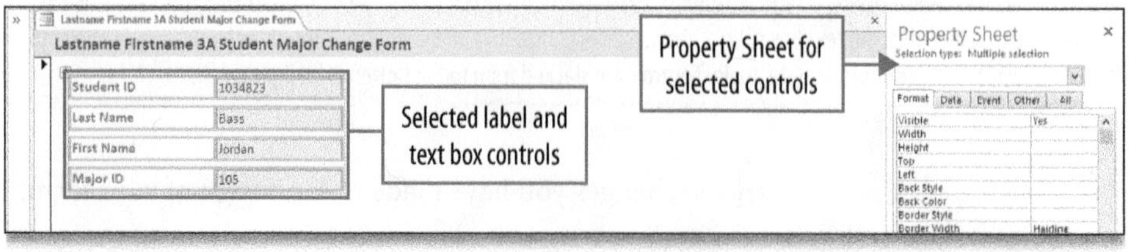

7 In the **Property Sheet**, click **Height**, type **0.25** and then press Enter to change the height of each selected control.

8 Click the **Student ID label control** to cancel the selection of all of the controls and to select only this label control. In the **Property Sheet**, click **Width**, type **1.25** and then press Enter.

The width of every label control changed to 1.25 inches. Recall that because the label controls are arranged in a stacked layout, you can change the width of all controls by selecting only one control. This is one of the few properties that can be changed without first selecting the column.

9 **Close** the **Property Sheet**, and then **Save** the design changes to your form.

Activity 3.15 Modifying a Form in Design View

Design view presents a detailed view of the structure of your form. Because the form is not actually running when displayed in Design view, the data does not display in the text box controls. However, some tasks, such as resizing sections, must be completed in Design view.

1 On the status bar, click **Design View**, and then compare your screen with Figure 3.24.

The form in Design view displays three sections, each designated by a ***section bar*** at the top of each section. The ***Form Header*** contains information, such as the form title, that displays at the top of the screen in Form view or Layout view and is printed at the top of the first page when records are printed as forms. The ***Detail section*** displays the records from the underlying table, and the ***Form Footer*** displays at the bottom of the screen in Form view or Layout view and is printed after the last detail section on the last page of a printout.

ANOTHER WAY On the HOME tab, in the Views group, click the View arrow, and then click Design view; or right-click the object tab, and then click Design View.

FIGURE 3.24

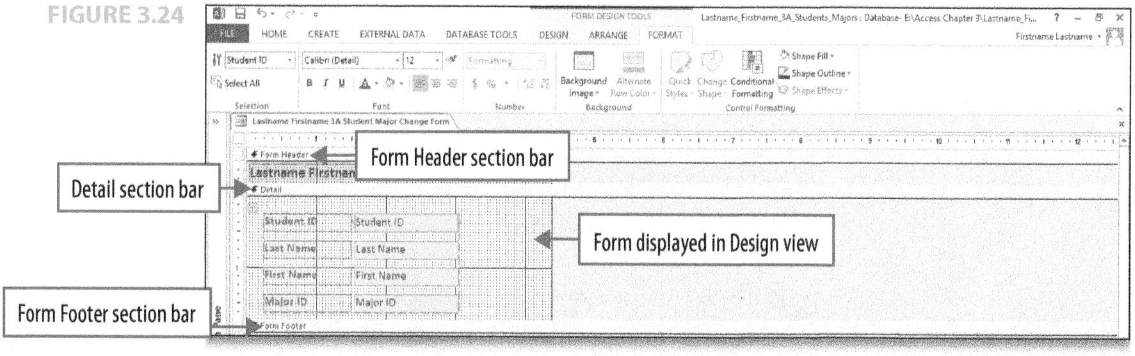

2 At the bottom of the form, click the **Form Footer section bar** to select it. On the ribbon, click the **DESIGN tab**, and in the **Tools group**, click **Property Sheet**. In the **Property Sheet**, on the **Format tab**, click **Height**, type **0.5** and then press Enter. Compare your screen with Figure 3.25.

In addition to properties for controls, you can make precise changes to sections of the form. Because you selected the Form Footer section bar, the Property Sheet displays a *Selection type* of *Section*, and the section is identified as *Form Footer*.

ANOTHER WAY At the bottom of the form, point to the lower edge of the Form Footer section bar to display the pointer, and then drag downward approximately 0.5 inch to increase the height of the section.

FIGURE 3.25

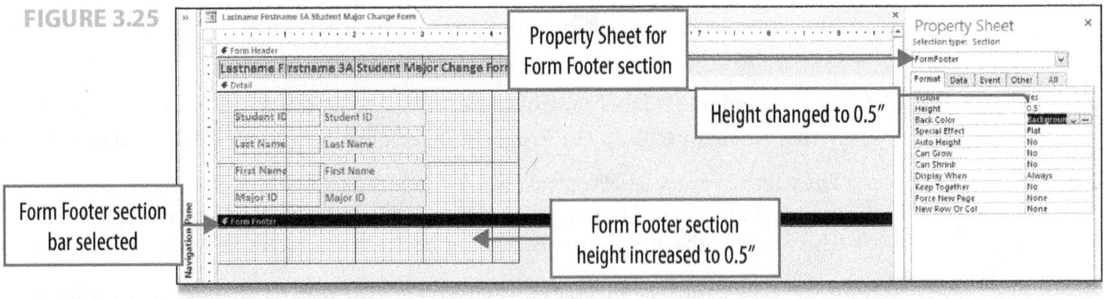

3 On the **DESIGN tab**, in the **Controls group**, click **Label** [Aa]. Move the [+A] pointer into the **Form Footer** section and then position the plus sign of the [+A] pointer at approximately **0.25 inch on the horizontal ruler** and even with the lower edge of the **Form Footer section bar**—the position does not need to be precise. Compare your screen with Figure 3.26.

FIGURE 3.26

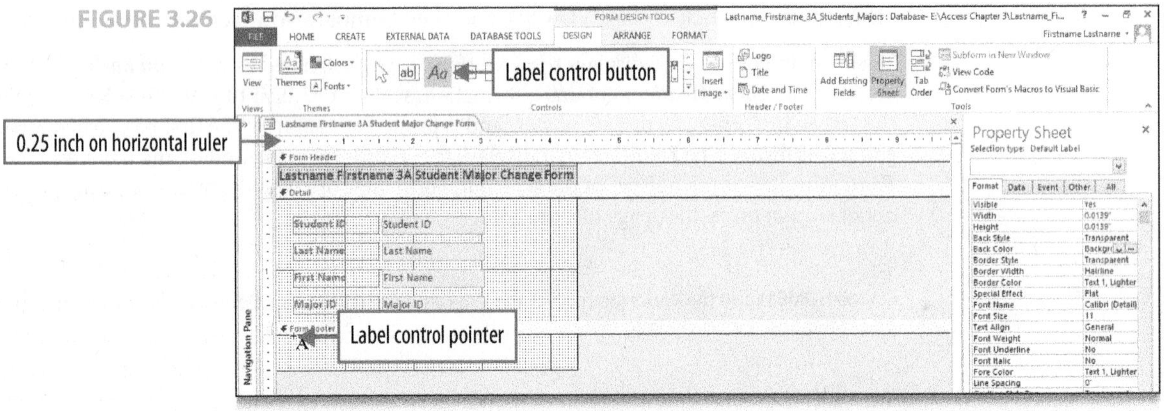

4 Click one time. Type **Texas Lakes Community College** and then press Enter. With the **label control** selected, on the ribbon, click the **FORMAT tab**. In the **Font group**, click **Bold** [B]. Click the **Font Color arrow**, and then under **Theme Colors**, in the fourth column, click the first color—**Olive Green, Text 2.**

5 With the **label control** still selected, in the **Property Sheet**, click **Top**, type **0.1** and then press Enter. In the **Property Sheet**, in the **Left** property setting, type **0.6** and then press Enter. **Close** [X] the **Property Sheet**, and then **Save** [save] the design changes to your form.

The top edge of the label control in the Form Footer section displays 0.1 inch from the lower edge of the Form Footer Section bar. The left edge of the label control aligns at 0.6 inch from the left margin of the form. In this manner, you can place a control in a specific location on the form.

6 On the right side of the status bar, click **Form View** [form view], and then compare your screen with Figure 3.27.

Form Footer text displays on the screen at the bottom of the form and prints only on the last page if all of the forms are printed. Recall, that in Form view, you can add, modify, or delete records stored in the underlying table.

ANOTHER WAY On the HOME tab, in the Views group, click the View arrow, and then click Form View; or right-click the object tab, and then click Form View.

FIGURE 3.27

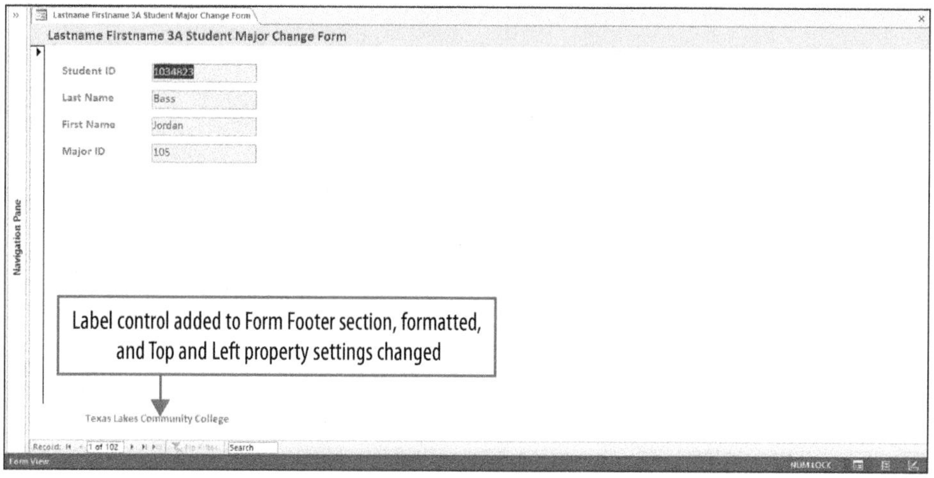

7 In the navigation area, click **Last record** [▶|] to display the record containing your name.

8 On the ribbon, click the **FILE tab**, click **Print**, and then on the right, click **Print**. In the **Print** dialog box, under **Print Range**, click the **Selected Records(s)** option button. Create a paper or electronic printout as directed by your instructor. To create an electronic printout, follow the directions given in the Note in Activity 3.06.

Because you decreased the width of the text box controls, you do *not* have to adjust the Column size Width in the Page Setup dialog box as you did with the form you created by using the Form tool.

9 **Close** [×] all open objects, and then **Open** [»] the **Navigation Pane**. On the right side of the title bar, click **Close** [×] to close the database and to exit Access. As directed by your instructor, submit your database and the paper or electronic printouts of the three forms that are the results of this project. Specifically, in this project, using your own name, you created the following database and printouts or electronic printouts:

1. Lastname_Firstname_3A_Students_Majors	Database file
2. Lastname Firstname 3A New Student Form	Form (printout or electronic printout - Record 102)
3. Lastname Firstname 3A Major Form	Form (printout or electronic printout - Record 33)
4. Lastname Firstname 3A Student Major Change Form	Form (printout or electronic printout - Record 102)

END | You have completed Project 3A

GO! with Office Online (formerly Web Apps)

Objective Export an Access Form to an Excel Spreadsheet, Save to OneDrive, Edit a Record, and Save to Your Computer

Access web apps are designed to work with Microsoft's SharePoint, an application for setting up websites to share and manage documents. Your college may not have SharePoint installed, so you will use other tools to share objects from your database so that you can work collaboratively with others. Recall that Window's OneDrive is a free file storage and file sharing service. For Access, you can export a database object to an Excel worksheet, a PDF file, or a text file, and then save the file to OneDrive.

ALERT! **Working with Web-Based Applications and Services**

Computer programs and services on the web receive continuous updates and improvements. Thus, the steps to complete this web-based activity may differ from the ones shown. You can often look at the screens and the information presented to determine how to complete the activity.

Activity | Exporting an Access Form to an Excel Spreadsheet, Saving the Spreadsheet to OneDrive, Editing a Record in OneDrive, and Saving to Your Computer

In this activity, you will export your 3A Student Major Change Form object to an Excel spreadsheet, upload your Excel file to OneDrive, edit a record in OneDrive, and then download a copy of the edited spreadsheet to your computer.

1 Start Access, navigate to your **Access Chapter 3** folder, and then **Open** your **3A_Students_Majors** database file. If necessary, on the Message Bar, click Enable Content. In the **Navigation Pane**, click your **3A Student Major Change Form** object to select it.

2 On the ribbon, click the **EXTERNAL DATA tab**, and in the **Export group**, click **Excel**. In the **Export – Excel Spreadsheet** dialog box, click **Browse**, and then navigate to your **Access Chapter 3** folder. In the **File Save** dialog box, click in the **File name** box, type **Lastname_Firstname_AC_3A_Web** and then click **Save**.

3 In the **Export – Excel Spreadsheet** dialog box, under **Specify export options**, select the second check box—**Open the destination file after the export operation is complete**—and then click **OK**.

The records from the underlying table of the form display in Excel. When you export a form to Excel, the formatting and layout are automatically saved. For example, notice the olive green background color of the cells, which was the color that was applied to the text box controls in the form.

4 In the **Microsoft Excel** window, in the column headings row, to the left of column **A**, click **Select All** [icon]. On the **HOME tab**, in the **Cells group**, click **Format**, and then click **AutoFit Column Width**. Click in cell **A1** to cancel the selection, and then compare your screen with Figure A.

FIGURE A

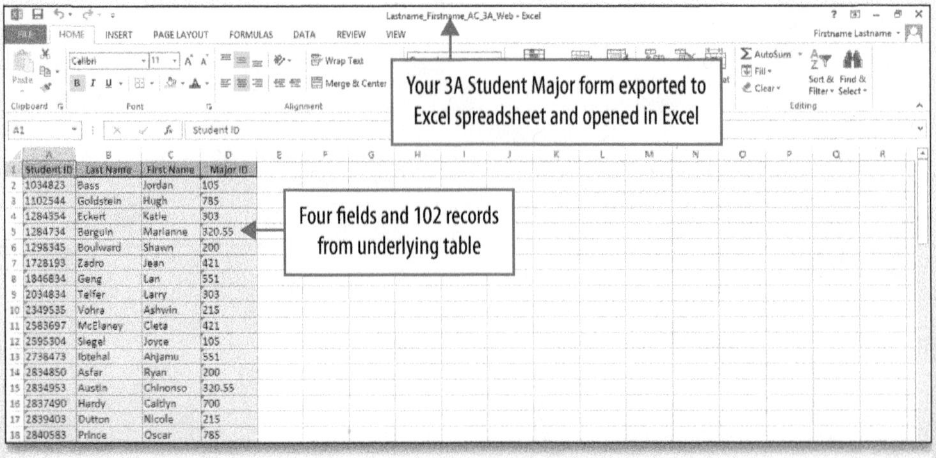

(GO! with Office Online (formerly Web Apps) continues on the next page)

5 **Save** the spreadsheet, and then **Close** Excel. In the **Export - Excel Spreadsheet** dialog box, click **Close**, and then **Close** Access.

6 From the desktop, start Internet Explorer, navigate to **http://onedrive.com**, and then sign in to your Microsoft account. Open your **GO! Web Projects** folder—or create and then open this folder if necessary.

7 On the menu bar, click **Upload**. In the **Choose File to Upload** dialog box, navigate to your **Access Chapter 3** folder, and then double-click your **AC_3A_Web** file to upload it to OneDrive.

8 In your **GO! Web Projects** folder, click your **AC_3A_Web** file to open it in Excel Online.

On the ribbon, notice that you can open this worksheet in Excel instead of using the Excel Online. If you are working on a computer that does not have Microsoft Excel installed, you can still create and modify workbooks in your web browser by using the Excel Online.

9 In the second record, click in the **Last Name** field, using your own last name, type **Lastname** and then press Tab. In the **First Name** field, using your own first name, type **Firstname** and then press ↓ to save the record. Compare your screen with Figure B.

10 On the ribbon, click the **FILE tab**, click **Save As**, and then click **Download a Copy**. In the message box—which usually displays at the bottom of your screen—click the **Save arrow**, and then click **Save as**. In the **Save As** dialog box, navigate to your **Access Chapter 3** folder, click in the **File name** box, and then type **Lastname_Firstname_A3A_Web_Download** and then click **Save**. **Close** the message box.

11 In OneDrive, on the title bar, click **OneDrive** to return to your home page. At the top right corner of your screen, click your OneDrive name, and then click **Sign out**. **Close** your browser window.

12 Start Excel. In the Excel opening screen, click **Open Other Workbooks**. Under **Open**, click **Computer**, and then on the right, click **Browse**. Navigate to your **Access Chapter 3** folder, and then double-click your **A3A_Web** file. Notice that this file is the original file—the second record is not changed. If you are required to print your documents, use one of the methods in the Note box below. **Close** your Excel file, saving the changes to your worksheet, and then **Open** and print your **A3A_Web_Download** file following one of the methods in the Note box below. **Close** Excel, saving the changes to your worksheet. As directed by your instructor, submit your two workbooks and the two paper or electronic printouts that are the results of this project.

NOTE

Adding the File Name to the Footer and Printing or Creating an Electronic Printout of an Excel Spreadsheet of Only One Page

Click the FILE tab, click Print, and then click Page Setup. In the Page Setup dialog box, click the Header/Footer tab, and then click Custom Footer. With the insertion point blinking in the Left section box, click the Insert File Name button, and then click OK. In the Page Setup dialog box, click OK. Under Settings, click the *Pages* spin box up arrow to display *1* in the box. Click the *to* spin box up arrow to display *1* in the box.

To print on paper, click Print. To create an electronic file of your printout, on the left side of your screen, click Export. Under Export, be sure Create PDF/XPS Document is selected, and then click Create PDF/XPS. In the Publish as PDF or XPS dialog box, click Options. In the Options dialog box, under Page range, click Pages, and be sure the From box displays *1* and the To box displays *1*; then click OK. Navigate to your Access Chapter 3 folder, and then click Publish to save the file with the default name and an extension of pdf.

FIGURE B

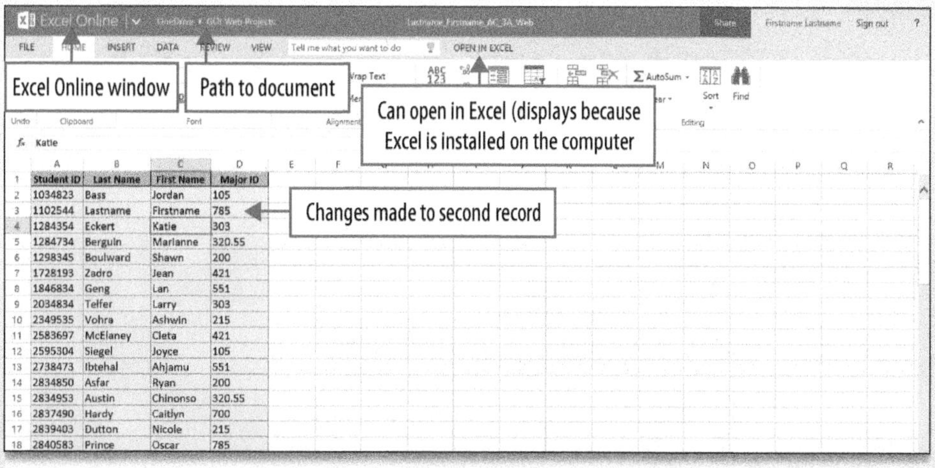

PROJECT

3B Job Openings Database

MyITLab® Project 3B Training

PROJECT ACTIVITIES

In Activities 3.16 through 3.24, you will assist Jack Woods, director of the Career Center for Texas Lakes Community College, in using his Access database to track the employees and job openings advertised for the annual job fair. Your completed reports will look similar to Figure 3.28.

PROJECT FILES

For Project 3B, you will need the following file:
a03B_Job_Openings

You will save your database as:
Lastname_Firstname_3B_Job_Openings

PROJECT RESULTS

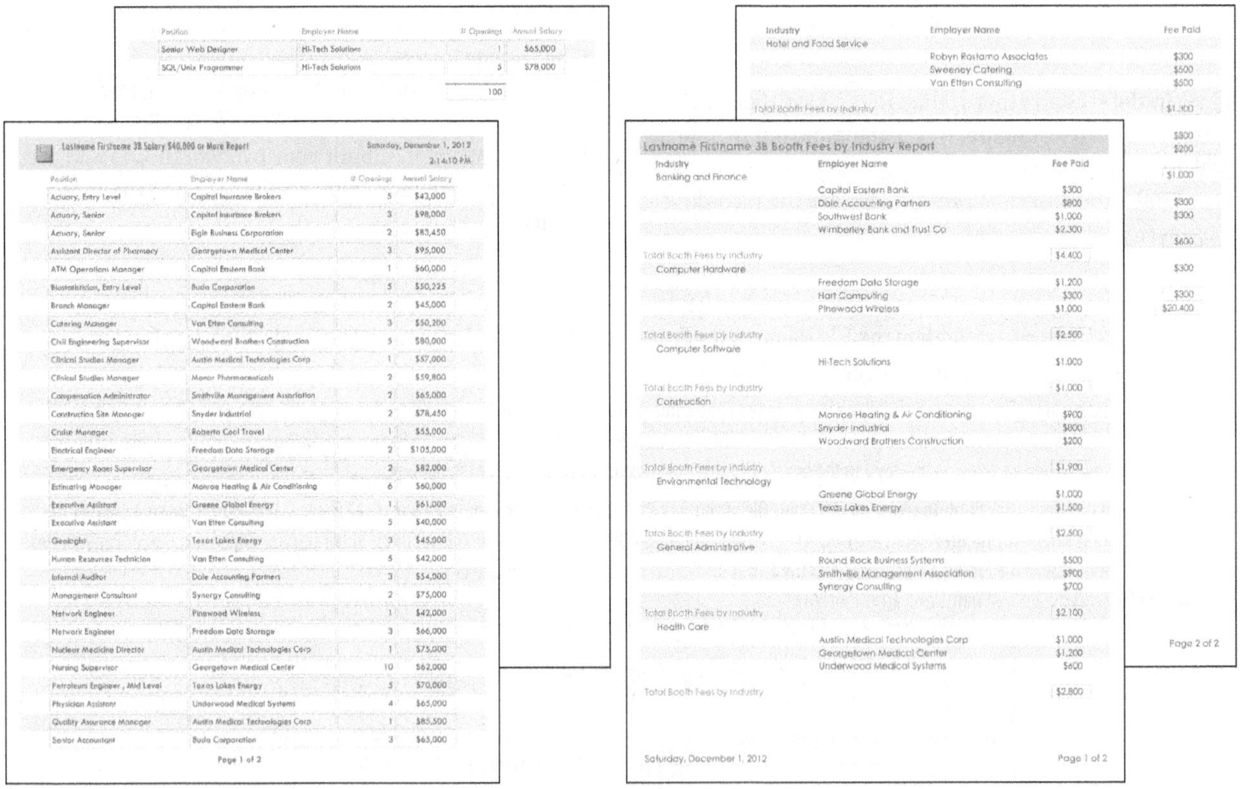

FIGURE 3.28 Project 3B Job Openings

Objective 5 Create a Report by Using the Report Tool and Modify the Report in Layout View

Video A3-5

A ***report*** is a database object that summarizes the fields and records from a query or from a table in an easy-to-read format suitable for printing. A report consists of information extracted from queries or tables and report design controls, such as labels, headings, and graphics. The queries or tables that provide the underlying data for a report are referred to as the report's ***record source***.

Activity 3.16 Opening and Saving an Existing Database, Renaming Objects, and Viewing a Table Relationship

1. Start Access. In the Access opening screen, click **Open Other Files**. Under **Open**, click **Computer**. Under **Recent Folders**, if displayed, click the location where your student data files are stored; otherwise, click **Browse** and then navigate to the location where your student data files are stored. Double-click **a03B_Job_Openings** to open the database.

2. On the **FILE tab**, click **Save As**. Under **File Types**, be sure **Save Database As** is selected. On the right, under **Database File Types**, be sure **Access Database** is selected, and then click **Save As**. In the **Save As** dialog box, navigate to your **Access Chapter 3** folder. In the **File name** box, replace the existing text with **Lastname_Firstname_3B_Job_Openings** and then press Enter.

3. On the **Message Bar**, click **Enable Content**. In the **Navigation Pane**, right-click the **3B Employers** table, and then click **Rename**. With the table name selected and using your own name, type **Lastname Firstname 3B Employers** and then press Enter to rename the table. Use the same technique to **Rename** the **3B Job Openings** table to **Lastname Firstname 3B Job Openings** and then **Rename** the first **3B Salary $40,000 or More Query** object to **Lastname Firstname 3B Salary $40,000 or More Query**

   Recall that a query that selects data from more than one table displays under both table names in the Navigation Pane. When you rename one of the query objects, the name of the second occurrence automatically changes.

4. Point to the right edge of the **Navigation Pane** to display the ⟺ pointer. Drag to the right to increase the width of the pane until all object names display fully.

5. On the ribbon, click the **DATABASE TOOLS tab**. In the **Relationships group**, click **Relationships**. Under **RELATIONSHIP TOOLS**, on the **DESIGN tab**, in the **Relationships group**, click **All Relationships**. Resize and move the field lists so that the entire table name and fields display for each field list.

   Because you renamed the tables, the field lists do not automatically display in the Relationships window.

6. In the **Relationships** window, click the **join line** between the two field lists. In the **Tools group**, click **Edit Relationships**. Point to the title bar of the **Edit Relationships** dialog box, and drag the dialog box downward below the **3B Job Openings** field list. Compare your screen with Figure 3.29.

   One employer is associated with *many* job openings. Thus, a one-to-many relationship is established between the 3B Employers table and the 3B Job Openings table by using Employee ID as the common field. Referential integrity is enforced, and cascade options are selected.

FIGURE 3.29

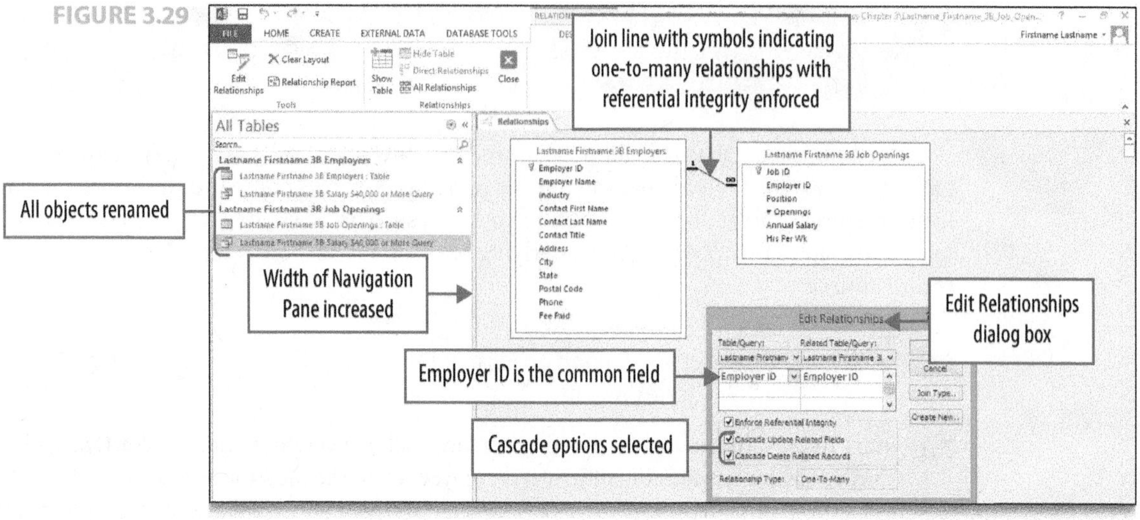

7 **Close** the **Edit Relationships** dialog box, and then **Close** the **Relationships** window. In the message box, click **Yes** to save changes to the layout of the relationships.

8 In the **Navigation Pane**, double-click each table, and then examine the fields and data in each table. Double-click the query object to run the query and examine the query results, apply **Best Fit** to the query results, and then **Save** the query. Switch to **Design** view to examine the design grid.

Because you renamed the tables that are the underlying source of data for the query, you have to reapply Best Fit to the query results. The query answers the question, *What is the Job ID, position, employer name, number of job openings, and annual salary for job openings that have an annual salary of $40,000 or more, in ascending order by the Employer Name field within the Position field?*

9 In the object window, right-click any **object tab**, and then click **Close All**.

Activity 3.17 | Creating a Report by Using the Report Tool and Applying a Theme to the Report

The ***Report tool*** is the fastest way to create a report. This tool displays all of the fields and records from the record source that you select. You can use the Report tool to look at the underlying data quickly in an easy-to-read format, after which you can save the report and modify it in Layout view or in Design view.

In this activity, you will use the Report tool to create a report from a query that lists all of the job openings with an annual salary of at least $40,000 and apply a theme to the report.

1 In the **Navigation Pane**, if necessary, click to select your **3B Salary $40,000 or More Query** object. On the ribbon, click the **CREATE tab**, and in the **Reports group**, click **Report**. **Close** the **Navigation Pane**, and then compare your screen with Figure 3.30.

The report is created using the query as the record source and displays in Layout view. The report includes all of the fields and all of the records from the query and the title of the query. In Layout view, the broken lines indicate the page margins in the report.

FIGURE 3.30

2 Under **REPORT LAYOUT TOOLS**, on the **DESIGN tab**, in the **Themes group**, click **Themes**. In the **Themes** gallery, use the ScreenTips to locate the **Integral** theme, right-click the **Integral** theme, and then click **Apply Theme to This Object Only**.

Recall that right-clicking a theme enables you to apply a predefined format to the active object only, which is a quick way to apply a professional look to a report. Apply a theme before formatting any other controls on the report.

Activity 3.18 | Modifying a Report in Layout View

After you create a report, you can make changes to it. For example, you can add or delete fields, resize the fields, and change the style of the report. Layout view enables you to see the data in the report as you modify the report. Most changes to a report can be made in Layout view.

1 Click the **Job ID** field name. On the ribbon, under **REPORT LAYOUT TOOLS**, click the **ARRANGE tab**. In the **Rows & Columns group**, click **Select Column** to select the field name and all of the data for each record in the field. Press Del to remove the field from the report.

The Job ID field is deleted, and the remaining fields move to the left. No fields extend beyond the right margin of the report.

ANOTHER WAY With the column selected, on the HOME tab, in the Records group, click Delete; or right-click the selected column, and then click Delete or Delete Column.

2 Scroll down, and notice that for the position of *Estimating Manager*, there is an extra blank line in the fields for this record. In the **Employer Name** field, click in the **text box control** that displays *Monroe Heating & Air Conditioning* to select all of the text box controls in this field.

3 On the ribbon, under **REPORT LAYOUT TOOLS**, click the **DESIGN tab**. In the **Tools group**, click **Property Sheet**. In the **Property Sheet**, on the **Format tab**, click **Width**, type **2.5** and then press Enter. Compare your screen with Figure 3.31.

Recall that you can use the Property Sheet to make precise changes to control properties.

ANOTHER WAY Point to the right edge of the text box control to display the ↔ pointer. Drag to the right slightly until the data in the text box control displays on one line.

FIGURE 3.31

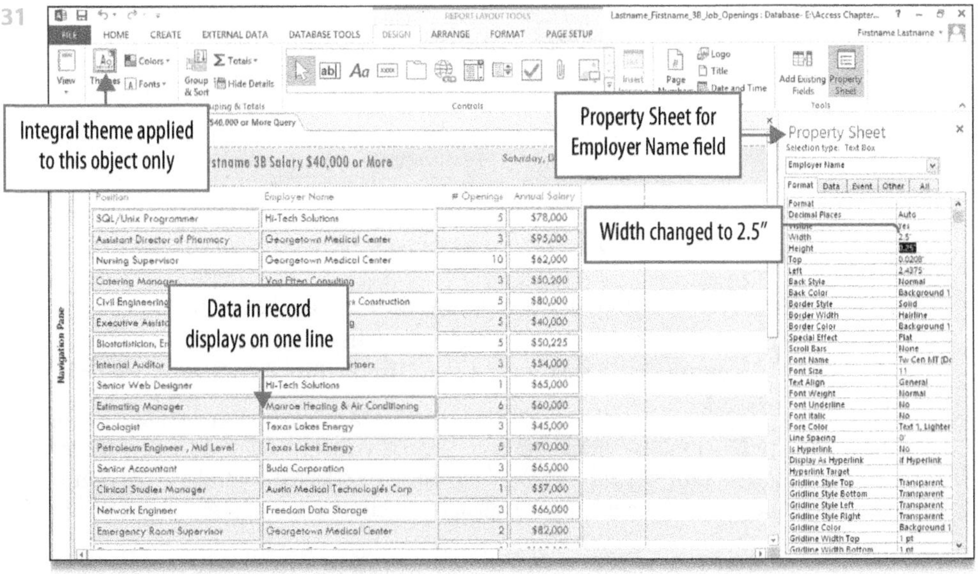

4 **Close** [×] the **Property Sheet**. Click the **Position** field name, and then on the ribbon, click the **HOME tab**. In the **Sort & Filter group**, click **Ascending** to sort the records in ascending order by the Position field.

ANOTHER WAY Right-click the selected field name and then click Sort A to Z.

5 Scroll to the bottom of the report, and then click the **calculated control** that displays *$2,157,625*, which is truncated at the bottom. Press Del to remove this control.

In a report created by using the Report tool, a ***calculated control*** is automatically created to sum any field that is formatted as currency. A calculated control contains an expression, often a formula or a function. Here, the total is not a useful number and thus can be deleted.

6 Scroll to the bottom of the report again, and then under the last column, click the horizontal line that is the border between the last record and the calculated control that you deleted. Press Del to remove this line, and then scroll to the bottom of the report to verify that the line has been deleted.

7 Scroll to the top of the report, and then click the **# Openings** field name. On the ribbon, click the **DESIGN tab**. In the **Grouping & Totals group**, click **Totals**, and then click **Sum**.

8 Scroll to the bottom of the report, and then click the **calculated control** that displays *100*. On the **DESIGN tab**, in the **Tools group**, click **Property Sheet**. In the **Property Sheet**, on the **Format tab**, click **Height**, type **0.25** and then press Enter. Compare your screen with Figure 3.32.

The total number of job openings for positions with a salary of $40,000 or more is 100.

ANOTHER WAY Point to the lower edge of the text box control to display the [↕] pointer, and then double-click to resize the control, or drag downward to increase the height of the control.

FIGURE 3.32

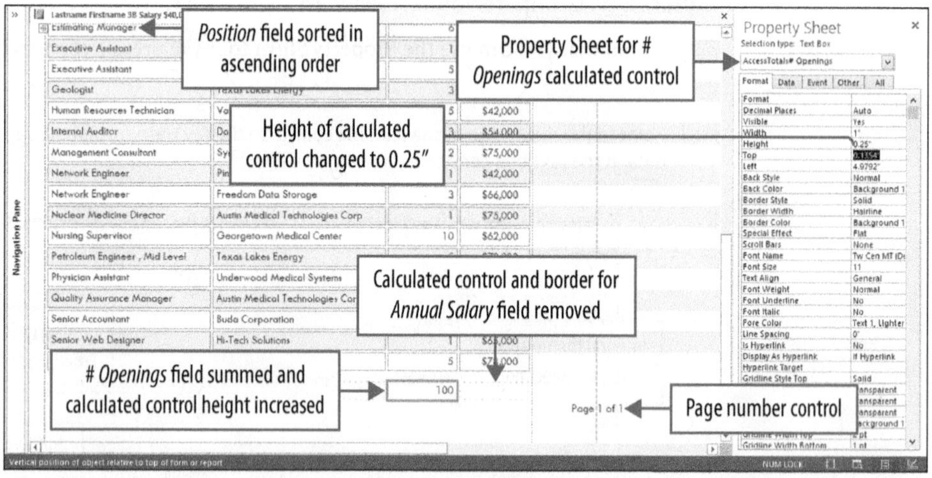

9 At the bottom of the report to the right of the calculated control, notice that the control that displays the page number does not fit entirely within the margins of the report. Click the **control** that displays *Page 1 of 1*. In the **Property Sheet**, click **Left**, type **2.5** and then press Enter.

The control moves within the margins of the report with the left edge of the control 2.5 inches in from the left margin of the report. When you click on different controls in a report or form, the Property Sheet changes to match the selected control. Before printing, always scroll through the report to be sure that all of the controls display on one page and not outside of the margins.

ANOTHER WAY Click the control, point to the selected control to display the pointer, and then drag the control to the left within the margins of the report.

10 Scroll to the top of the report, and then click the **label control** that displays the title of the report—*Lastname Firstname 3B Salary $40,000 or More Query*. On the ribbon, under **REPORT LAYOUT TOOLS**, click the **FORMAT tab**. In the **Font group**, click the **Font Size arrow**, and then click **14**.

11 With the **label control** for the title still selected, double-click **Query** to select the word, type **Report** and then press Enter to change the name of the report to *Lastname Firstname 3B Salary $40,000 or More Report.*

12 Click the **Position** field name. In the **Property Sheet**, click **Left**, type **0.5** and then press Enter to move this field 0.5 inch in from the left margin of the report. Compare your screen with Figure 3.33.

The other fields adjust by moving to the right. The fields are centered approximately within the margins of the report.

ANOTHER WAY Click the layout selector to select all of the controls, and then drag it slightly downward and to the right until the columns are visually centered between the margins of the report. If your columns rearrange, click Undo and begin again.

FIGURE 3.33

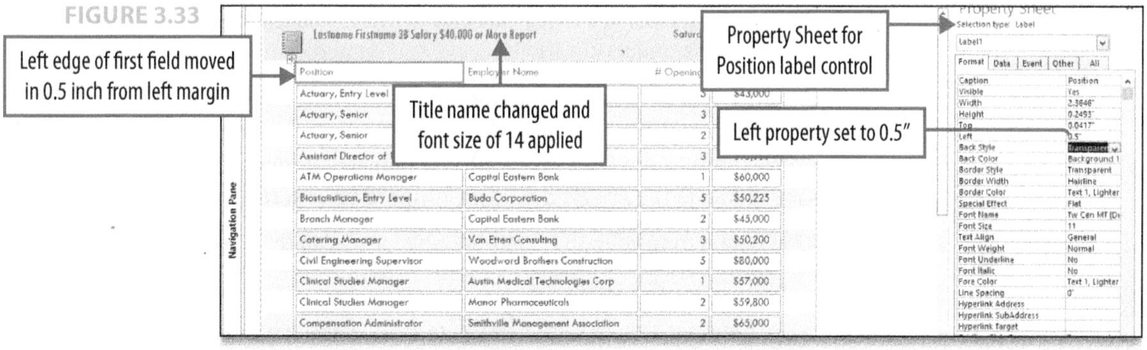

13 Close the **Property Sheet**, and then **Save** the report as **Lastname Firstname 3B Salary $40,000 or More Report**

Activity 3.19 | Printing a Report

In this activity, you will view your report in Print Preview and display the two pages of the report.

1 On the right side of the status bar, click **Print Preview**.

ANOTHER WAY On the DESIGN tab or the HOME tab, in the Views group, click the View arrow, and then click Print Preview; or, in the object window, right-click the object tab, and then click Print Preview.

2 On the **PRINT PREVIEW tab**, in the **Zoom group**, click **Two Pages** to view the two pages of your report. Notice that the page number displays at the bottom of each page.

3 Create a paper or electronic printout as directed—two pages result, and then click **Close Print Preview. Close** [×] the report, and then **Open** [»] the **Navigation Pane.**

The report displays under both tables from which the query was created. The report object name displays with a small green notebook icon.

4 **Close** [«] the **Navigation Pane.**

Objective 6 Create a Report by Using the Report Wizard

Video A3-6

Use the ***Report Wizard*** when you need more flexibility in the design of your report. You can group and sort data by using the wizard and use fields from more than one table or query if you have created the relationships between tables. The Report Wizard is similar to the Form Wizard; the wizard walks you step by step through the process of creating the report by asking you questions and then designs the report based on your answers.

Activity 3.20 | Creating a Report by Using the Report Wizard

In this activity, you will prepare a report for Mr. Woods that displays the employers, grouped by industry, and the total fees paid by employers for renting a booth at the Job Fair.

1 On the ribbon, click the **CREATE tab**, and then in the **Reports group**, click **Report Wizard.**

In the first wizard screen, you select the fields to include on the report. The fields can come from more than one table or query.

2 In the **Tables/Queries** box, click the **arrow**, and then click **Table: Lastname Firstname 3B Employers.** In the **Available Fields** list, double-click the following field names in the order given to move them to the **Selected Fields** list: **Industry, Employer Name,** and **Fee Paid** (scroll as necessary to locate the *Fee Paid* field). Compare your screen with Figure 3.34.

Three field names from your 3B Employers table display in the Selected Fields list.

ANOTHER WAY Click the field name, and then click One Field [>] to move a field from the Available Fields list to the Selected Fields list.

FIGURE 3.34

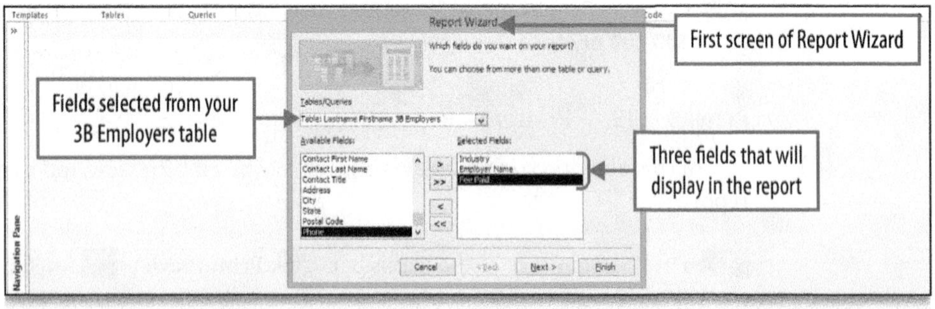

3 Click **Next.** In the wizard, notice that you can add grouping levels and that a preview of the grouping level displays on the right.

Grouping data helps to organize and summarize the data in your report.

4 On the left, double-click **Industry**, and then compare your screen with Figure 3.35.

The preview displays how the data will be grouped in the report. Grouping data in a report places all of the records that have the same data in a field together as a group—in this instance, the records will be grouped by *Industry*. Within each Industry name, the Employer Name and Fee Paid will display.

FIGURE 3.35

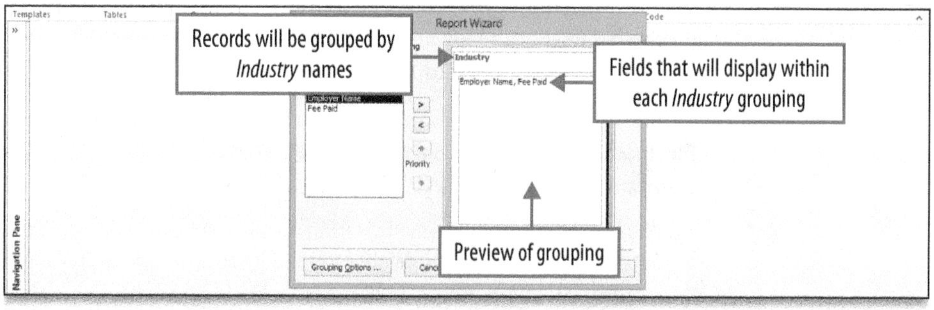

5 Click **Next**. Click the **1** box **arrow**, click **Employer Name**, and then compare your screen with Figure 3.36.

In this step of the wizard, you indicate how you want to sort the records and summarize the information. You can sort up to four fields. The Summary Options button displays because the data is grouped, and at least one of the fields—*Fee Paid*—contains numerical or currency data. Within each Industry grouping, the records will be sorted alphabetically by the Employer Name. Sorting records in a report presents a more organized view of the records.

FIGURE 3.36

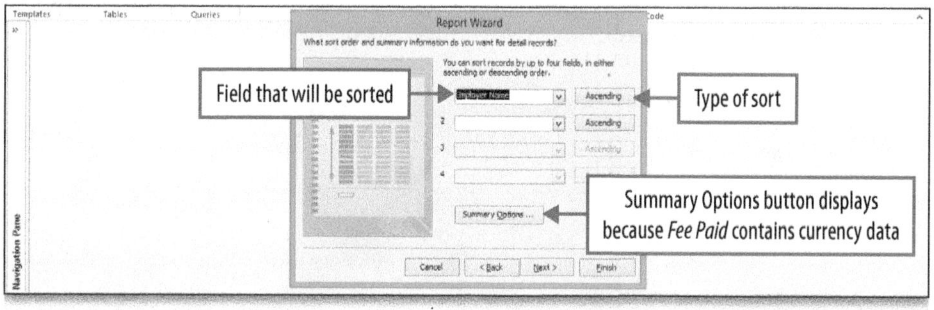

6 In the wizard, click **Summary Options**, and then compare your screen with Figure 3.37.

The Summary Options dialog box displays. The *Fee Paid* field can be summarized by selecting one of the four check boxes for Sum, Avg, Min, or Max. You can also display only summary information or display both the details—each record—and the summary information. The default setting is to display *Detail and Summary*.

FIGURE 3.37

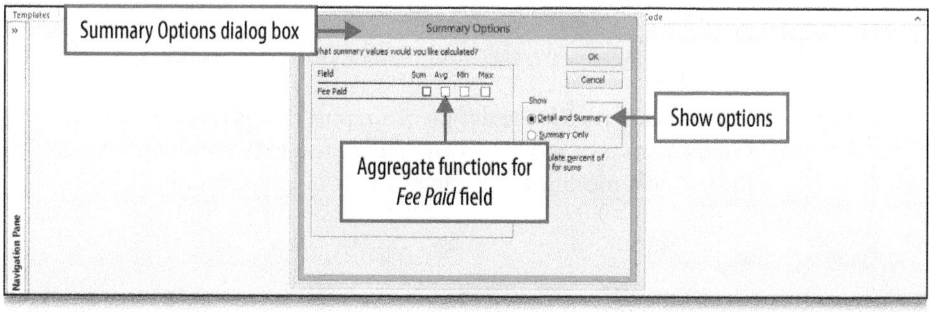

7 In the **Summary Options** dialog box, click to select the **Sum** check box. Under **Show**, be sure that **Detail and Summary** is selected, and then click **OK**. In the wizard, click **Next**.

In this step of the wizard, you select the layout and page orientation. A preview of the layout displays on the left.

8 Click each **Layout** option button, noticing the changes in the preview, and then click **Stepped** to select it as the layout for your report. Under **Orientation**, be sure that **Portrait** is selected. At the bottom of the wizard, be sure that the **Adjust the field width so all fields fit on a page** check box is selected, and then click **Next**.

9 In the **What title do you want for your report?** box, select the existing text, type **Lastname Firstname 3B Booth Fees by Industry Report** and then click **Finish**. Compare your screen with Figure 3.38.

The report is saved and displays in Print Preview using the specifications you defined in the Report Wizard. The records are grouped by Industry. Within each Industry, the records display in ascending order by the Employer Name. Within each Industry grouping, the Fee paid is summed or totaled—the word *Sum* displays at the end of each grouping.

FIGURE 3.38

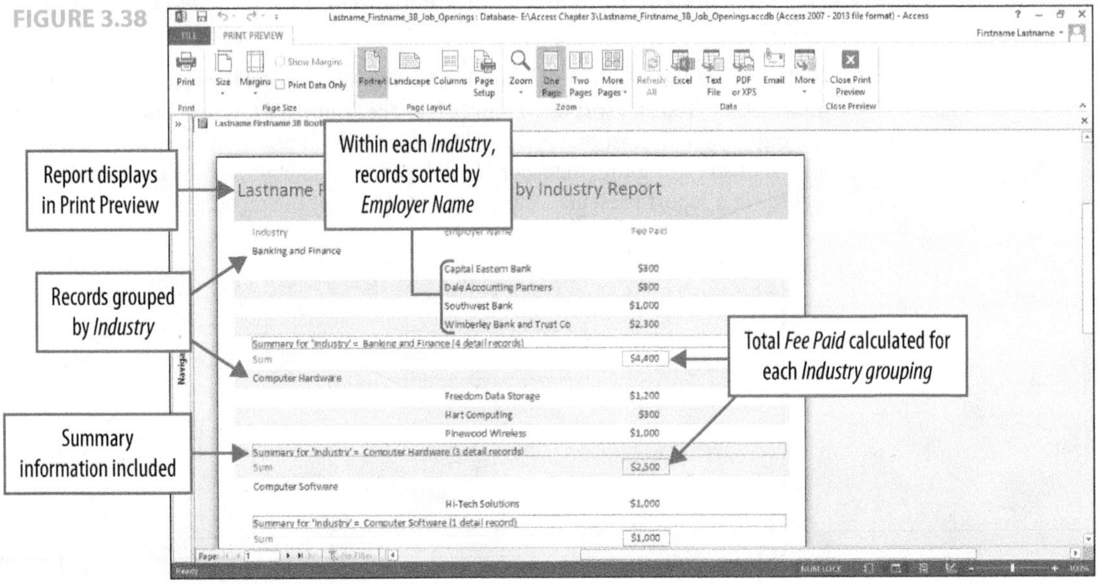

10 In the object window, right-click the **object tab** for the report, and then click **Layout View**.

ANOTHER WAY On the status bar, click Layout View; or click Close Print Preview, and then on the HOME tab or the DESIGN tab, click the View arrow, and then click Layout View.

Objective 7 Modify the Design of a Report

Video A3-7

You can modify the design of a report that is created using the Report Wizard by using the same techniques and tools that you use to modify a report created with the Report tool. Recall that most report modifications can be made in Layout view.

Activity 3.21 | Formatting and Deleting Controls in Layout View

In this activity, you will apply a theme to the report, format the title of the report, and delete the summary information controls.

1 Be sure that your **3B Booth Fees by Industry Report** object is displayed in **Layout** view. Under **REPORT LAYOUT TOOLS**, on the **DESIGN tab**, in the **Themes group**, click **Themes**. In the **Themes** gallery, use the ScreenTips to locate the **Ion Boardroom** theme, right-click the **Ion Boardroom** theme, and then click **Apply Theme to This Object Only**.

Recall that you should apply a theme before applying any other formatting changes. Also, recall that if you click a theme—instead of right-clicking—the theme is applied to all of the objects in the database.

2 At the top of the report, click the title—*Lastname Firstname 3B Booth Fees by Industry*—to display a border around the label control. On the ribbon, under **REPORT LAYOUT TOOLS**, click the **FORMAT tab**. In the **Font group**, click the **Font Size arrow**, and then click **14**. In the **Font group**, click **Bold** [B].

By changing the font size, the report name is no longer truncated and includes the word *Report*.

3 Within each *Industry* grouping, notice the **Summary for 'Industry'** information.

Because you selected Summary Options, a summary line is included at the end of each grouping that details what is being summarized—in this case, summed—and the number of records that are included in the summary total. Now that Mr. Woods has viewed the report, he has decided that this information is not necessary and can be removed.

4 Click any one of the controls that begins with **Summary for 'Industry'**.

The control that you clicked is surrounded by a border, and all of the other summary information controls are surrounded by paler borders to indicate that all controls are selected.

5 Press [Del] to remove the controls from the report, and then compare your screen with Figure 3.39.

ANOTHER WAY Right-click any of the selected controls, and then click Delete to remove the controls from the report.

FIGURE 3.39

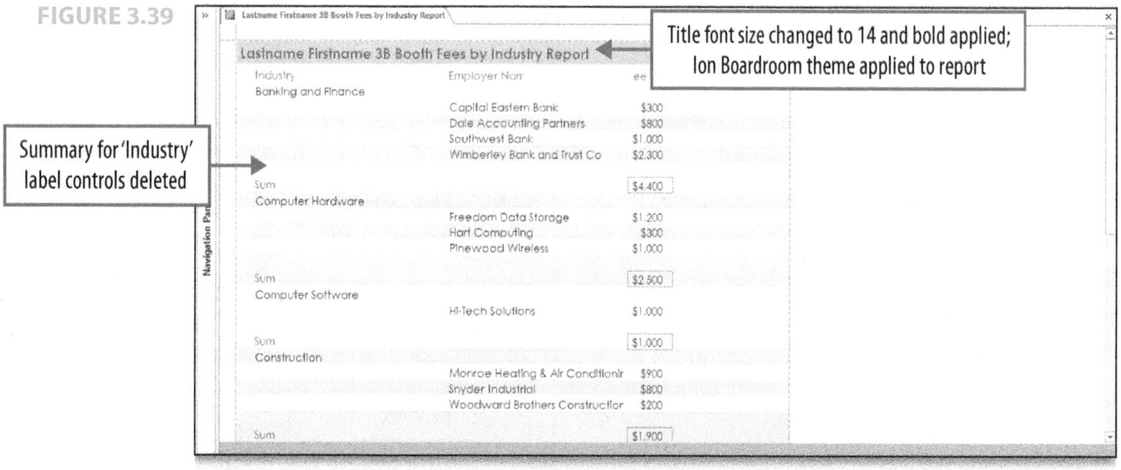

6 **Save** [Save] the changes you have made to the design of the report.

Activity 3.22 | Modifying Controls in Layout View

In this activity, you will modify the text in controls, move controls, resize controls, and add a control to the report in Layout view.

1 On the left side of the report, click a **Sum label control**, which selects all of the related controls. Double-click the control to select the text—*Sum*. Type **Total Booth Fees by Industry** and then press Enter. Compare your screen with Figure 3.40.

This text states more clearly what is being summed.

FIGURE 3.40

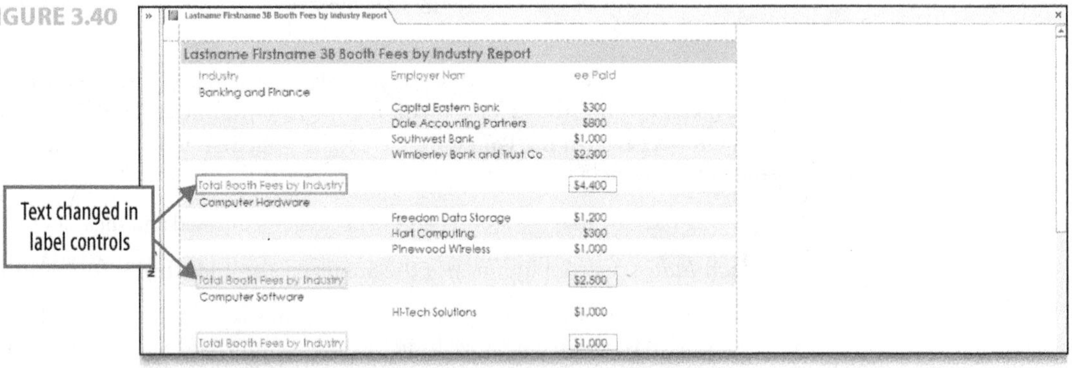

2 At the top of the report, click the **Industry label control** to select it. Hold down Shift, click the **Employer Name label control**, and then click the **Fee Paid label control** to select all three field names. On the **FORMAT tab**, in the **Font group**, click **Bold** B.

Clicking Bold also increases the size of the controls so that the text is no longer truncated.

3 At the top of the report, under the **Fee Paid label control**, click the **text box control** that displays *$300* to select the text box controls for all of the records for this field. On the ribbon, click the **DESIGN tab**. In the **Tools group**, click **Property Sheet**. In the **Property Sheet**, on the **Format tab**, click **Left**, type **7** and then press Enter. Compare your screen with Figure 3.41.

All of the Fee Paid text box controls move to the right—7" in from the left margin. Do not be concerned that the summary total and the field name are not aligned with the data; you will correct this in the next activity. The field is moved to the right so that you can increase the width of the Employer Name text box controls so that all of the data for every record displays.

FIGURE 3.41

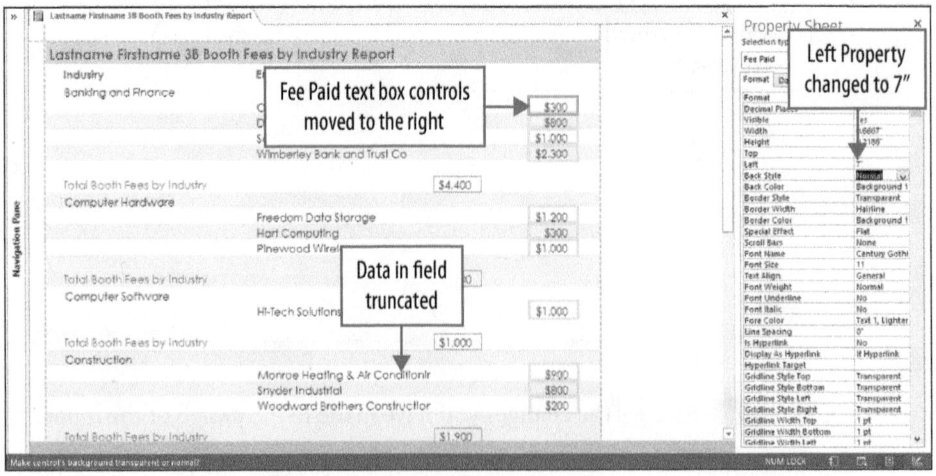

4 Scroll to view the bottom of the report. Click to select the **calculated control** for the **Grand Total,** which displays *20,400* and part of the dollar symbol. In the **Property Sheet**, click **Width**, type **0.8** and then press Enter.

The width of the calculated control increases to display the dollar symbol. Do not be concerned that the right edge of the control no longer aligns with the control above it; you will correct this in the next activity. Recall that a calculated control contains an expression—a formula or function—that displays the result of the expression when the report is displayed in Report view, Print Preview, or Layout view.

ANOTHER WAY Point to the left edge of the control to display the ↔ pointer. Drag to the left slightly to increase the width of the calculated control.

5 At the bottom of the report, on the left side, click the **Grand Total label control.** In the **Property Sheet**, click **Width**, type **1** and then press Enter. Compare your screen with Figure 3.42.

The width of the label control is increased so that all of the text displays.

ANOTHER WAY Point to the right edge of the control to display the ↔ pointer, and then double-click to resize the control.

FIGURE 3.42

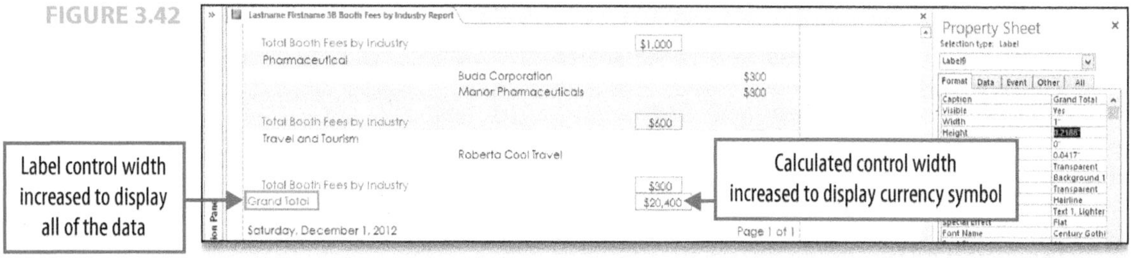

6 Scroll to the top to display the Industry grouping of **Construction**, and notice that the first and third records have truncated data in the **Employer Name** field. In the **Construction** grouping, click, the **Employer Name text box control** that starts with *Monroe Heating* to select all of the text box controls for this field.

7 In the **Property Sheet**, click **Width**, type **3** and then press Enter. **Save** the design changes to your report, and then compare your screen with Figure 3.43.

The width of the Employer Name text box controls is increased so that all of the data in this field for every record displays. Recall that you moved the Fee Paid text box controls to the right to make room for the increased width of these controls.

FIGURE 3.43

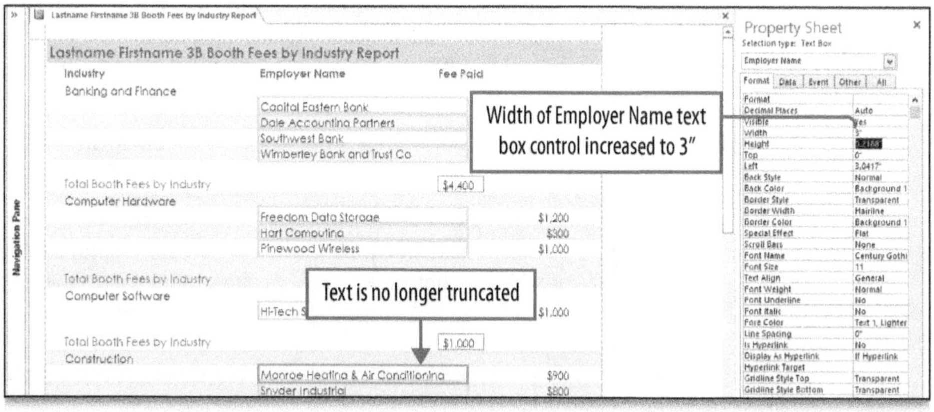

Activity 3.23 | Aligning Controls in Design View

Design view gives you a more detailed view of the structure of your report. You can see the header and footer sections for the report, for the page, and for groups. In Design view, your report is not running, so you cannot see the data from the table in the controls. In the same manner as forms, you can add labels to the Page Footer section or increase the height of sections. Some tasks, such as aligning controls, must be completed in Design view.

1 **Close** the **Property Sheet**. On the status bar, click **Design View**, and then compare your screen with Figure 3.44.

Design view for a report is similar to Design view for a form. You can modify the layout of the report in this view, and use the dotted grid pattern to align controls. This report has several sections. The ***Report Header*** displays information at the top of the *first page* of a report. The ***Page Header*** displays information at the top of *every page* of a report. The ***Group Header*** displays the name of data in the field by which the records are grouped; in this case, the *Industry* name. The ***Detail*** section displays the data for each record. The ***Group Footer*** displays the summary information for each grouping; in this case, the Industry name. The ***Page Footer*** displays information at the bottom of *every page* of the report. The ***Report Footer*** displays information at the bottom of the *last page* of the report.

If you do not group data in a report, the Group Header section and Group Footer section will not display. If you do not summarize the data, the Group Footer section will not display.

FIGURE 3.44

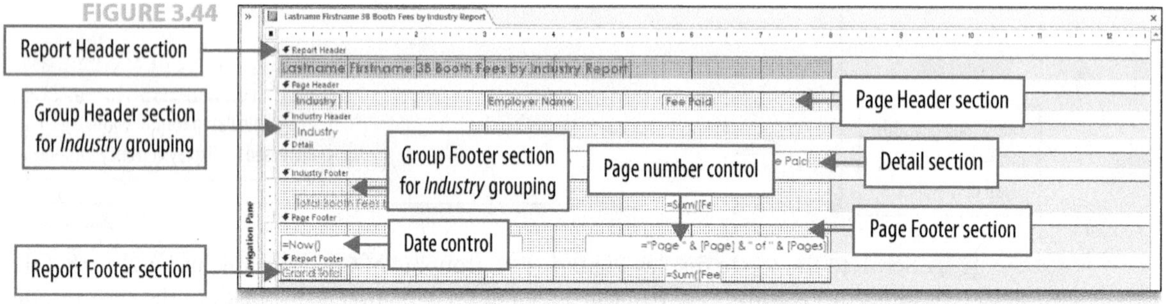

2 In the **Page Footer** section of the report, examine the two controls in this section. Recall that information in the Page Footer section displays at the bottom of every page in the report.

On the left side, the ***date control*** displays *=Now( )*, which inserts the current date each time the report is opened. On the right side, the ***page number control*** displays *="Page " & [Page] & " of " & [Pages]*, which inserts the page number, for example *Page 1 of 2*, when the report is displayed in Print Preview or when printed. Both of these controls contain examples of functions that are used by Access to create controls in a report.

3 In the **Industry Footer** section, click the **Total Booth Fees by Industry label control.** Hold down Shift, and in the **Report Footer** section, click the **Grand Total label control** to select both label controls.

4 On the ribbon, under **REPORT DESIGN TOOLS**, click the **ARRANGE tab.** In the **Sizing & Ordering group**, click **Align**, and then click **Left.**

The left edge of the *Grand Total label control* is aligned with the left edge of the *Total Booth Fees by Industry label control.* When using the Align Left command, the left edges of the selected controls are aligned with the control that is the farthest to the left in the report.

5 In the **Page Header** section, click the **Fee Paid label control**. Hold down Shift while you click the following: in the **Detail** section, click the **Fee Paid text box control**; in the **Industry Footer** section, click the **calculated control** that begins with *=Sum*; and in the **Report Footer** section, click the **calculated control** that begins with *=Sum*.

Four controls are selected.

6 On the **ARRANGE tab**, in the **Sizing & Ordering group**, click **Align**, and then click **Right**. **Save** the design changes to your report, and then compare your screen with Figure 3.45.

The right edges of the four selected controls are aligned with the right edge of the *Fee Paid text box control*. When using the Align Right command, the right edges of the selected controls are aligned with the control that is the farthest to the right in the report.

FIGURE 3.45

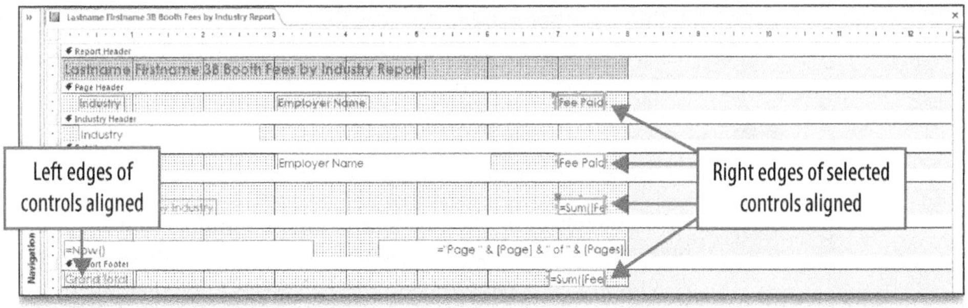

7 On the status bar, click **Layout View** to display the underlying data in the controls. Scroll to view the bottom of the report. On the left side, notice that the **Total Booth Fees by Industry label control** and the **Grand Total label control** are left aligned. Also, notice the right alignment of the controls in the **Fee Paid** column.

Objective 8 Keep Grouped Data Together in a Printed Report

Video A3-8

Before you print a report, examine the report in Print Preview to be sure that all of the labels and data display fully and to be sure that all of the data is properly grouped. Sometimes a page break occurs in the middle of a group of data, leaving the labels on one page and the data or summary information on another page.

Activity 3.24 | Keeping Grouped Data Together in a Printed Report

In this activity, you will preview the document and then will keep the data in each group together so a grouping is not split between two pages of the report. This is possible if the data in a grouping does not exceed the length of a page.

1 On the status bar, click **Print Preview**. On the **PRINT PREVIEW tab**, in the **Zoom group**, click **Two Pages**, and then compare your screen with Figure 3.46.

The report will print on two pages. For the Industry grouping of *Hotel and Food Service*, one record and the summary data display at the top of Page 2 and is separated from the rest of the grouping that displays at the bottom of page 1. Your display may differ depending upon your printer configuration.

In Print Preview, the One Page or Two Pages Zoom view causes the records to be compressed slightly and might display with the bottoms of records truncated. The records, however, will print correctly.

FIGURE 3.46

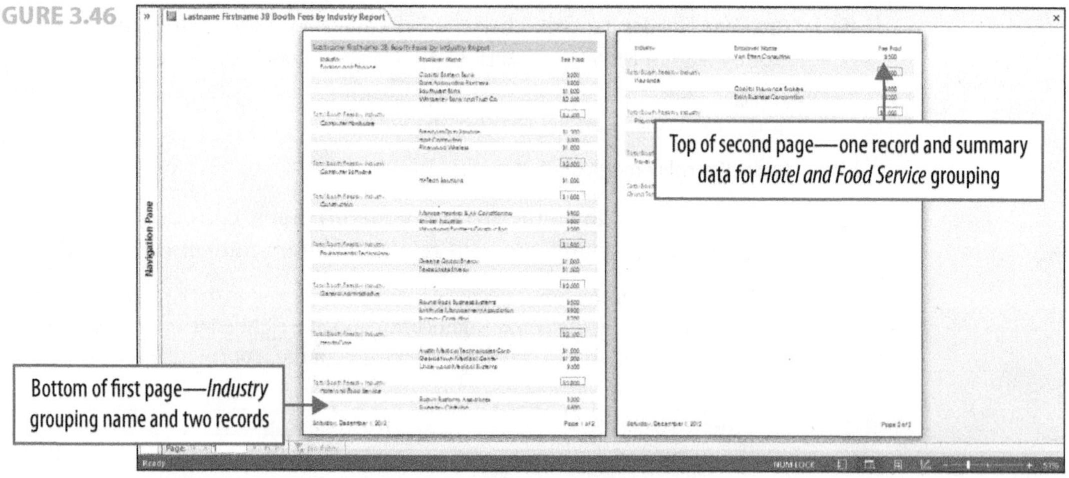

2 On the ribbon, click **Close Print Preview** to return to **Layout** view. On the **DESIGN tab,** in the **Grouping & Totals group,** click **Group & Sort.**

At the bottom of the screen, the ***Group, Sort, and Total pane*** displays. This pane is used to control how information is grouped, sorted, or totaled. Layout view is the preferred view in which to accomplish these tasks because you can see how the changes affect the display of the data in the report.

3 In the **Group, Sort, and Total** pane, on the **Group on Industry** bar, click **More.** To the right of **do not keep group together on one page,** click the **arrow,** and then compare your screen with Figure 3.47.

The *keep whole group together on one page* command keeps each industry group together, from the name in the Group Header section through the summary information in the Group Footer section. The default setting is *do not keep group together on one page.* Next to *Group on Industry, with A on top* indicates that the industry names are sorted in ascending order.

FIGURE 3.47

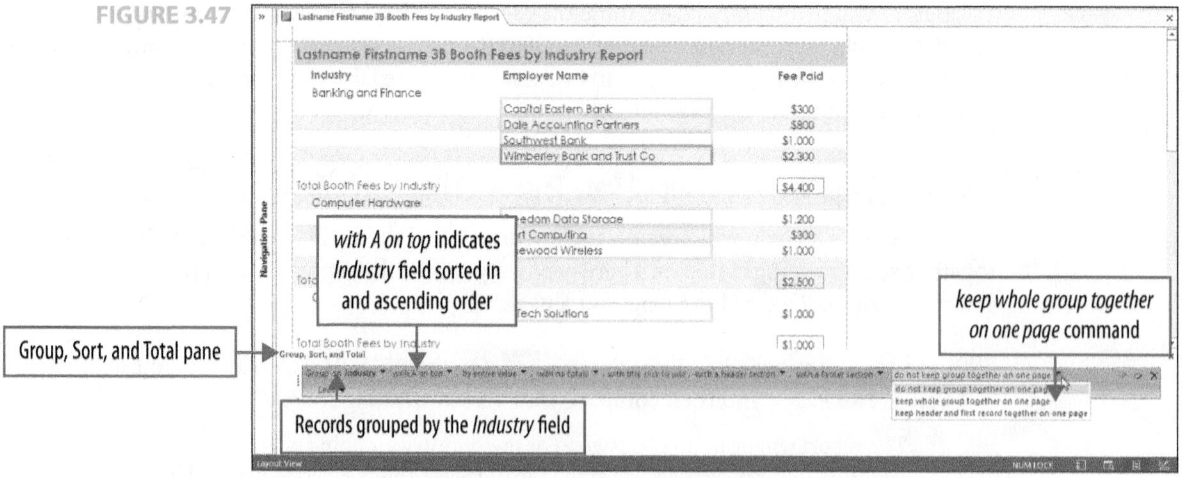

4 Click **keep whole group together on one page.** On the **DESIGN tab,** in the **Grouping & Totals group,** click **Group & Sort** to close the **Group, Sort, and Total** pane.

5 On the status bar, click **Print Preview**. If necessary, in the Zoom group, click Two Pages. Compare your screen with Figure 3.48.

The entire grouping for the Industry of *Hotel and Food Service* displays at the top of page 2. The grouping no longer breaks between page 1 and page 2. Recall that even though the bottoms of records display truncated because of the compressed Print Preview setting of Two Pages, the records will print correctly.

FIGURE 3.48

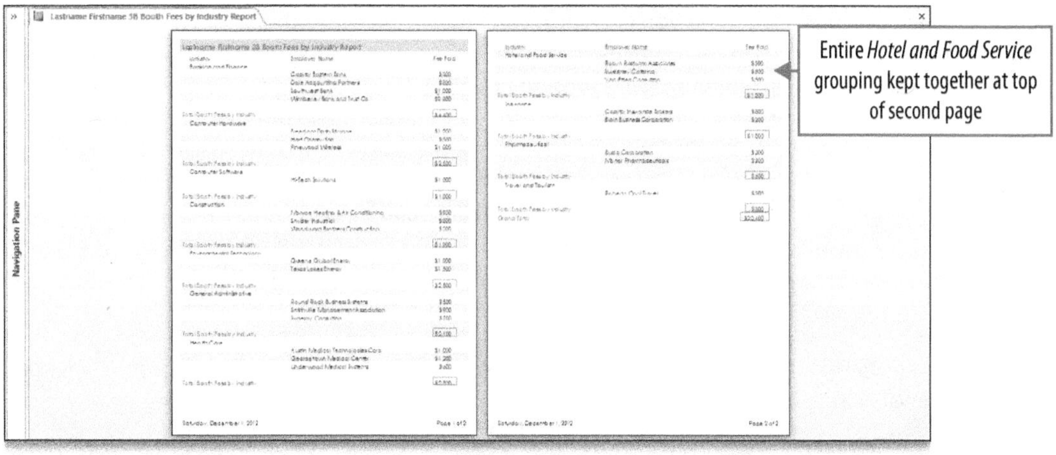

6 **Save** the design changes to your report, and then create a paper or electronic printout of the report as directed—two pages result.

7 **Close** the report, and then **Open** the **Navigation Pane**. If necessary, increase the width of the Navigation Pane so that all object names display fully.

8 On the right side of the title bar, click **Close** to close the database and to exit Access. As directed by your instructor, submit your database and the paper or electronic printouts of the two reports—each report is two pages—that are the results of this project. Specifically, in this project, using your own name you created the following database and printouts or electronic printouts:

1. Lastname_Firstname_3B_Job_Openings	Database file
2. Lastname Firstname 3B Salary $40,000 or More Report	Report (printout or electronic printout - two pages)
3. Lastname Firstname 3B Booth Fees by Industry Report	Report (printout or electronic printout - two pages)

END | You have completed Project 3B

GO! with Office Online (formerly Web Apps)

Objective **Export** an Access Report to a Word File, Save to OneDrive, and Add a Description to the Word File

Access web apps are designed to work with Microsoft's SharePoint, an application for setting up websites to share and manage documents. Your college may not have SharePoint installed, so you will use other tools to share objects from your database so that you can work collaboratively with others. When you have information that you want to share with others, you can upload files to OneDrive. Some files can be opened in OneDrive; some can only be downloaded. Because database files are typically large in size, and free storage space on OneDrive is limited, you can export database objects to different formats and then upload those files to OneDrive.

> **ALERT!** **Working with Web-Based Applications and Services**
>
> Computer programs and services on the web receive continuous updates and improvements. Thus, the steps to complete this web-based activity may differ from the ones shown. You can often look at the screens and the information presented to determine how to complete the activity.

Activity | Exporting an Access Report to a Word File, Uploading the Word File to OneDrive, and Adding a Description to the Word File

In this activity, you will export your 3B Salary $40,000 or More Report object to a Word file, upload your Word file to OneDrive, and then add a description to the Word file. The report will be available for individuals with whom you have shared your OneDrive files or folders.

1 Start Access, navigate to your **Access Chapter 3** folder, and then **Open** your **3B_Job_Openings** database file. If necessary, on the Message Bar, click Enable Content. In the **Navigation Pane**, click your **3B Salary $40,000 or More Report** object to select it.

2 On the ribbon, click the **EXTERNAL DATA tab**, and in the **Export group**, click **More**, and then click **Word**.

The report will be exported as a ***Rich Text Format (RTF)***—a standard file format that contains text and some formatting such as underline, bold, italic, font sizes, and colors. RTF documents can be opened in many word processing programs and text editors.

3 In the **Export – RTF File** dialog box, navigate to your **Access Chapter 3** folder. In the **File Save** dialog box, click in the **File name** box to select the existing text. Type **Lastname_Firstname_AC_3B_Web** and then click **Save**. In the **Export – RTF File** dialog box, select the **Open the destination file after the export operation is complete** check box, and then click **OK**. Compare your screen with Figure A.

The RTF file is created and opens in Word.

4 **Close** [X] Word. In the **Export – RTF File** dialog box, click **Close**, and then **Close** [X] Access.

FIGURE A

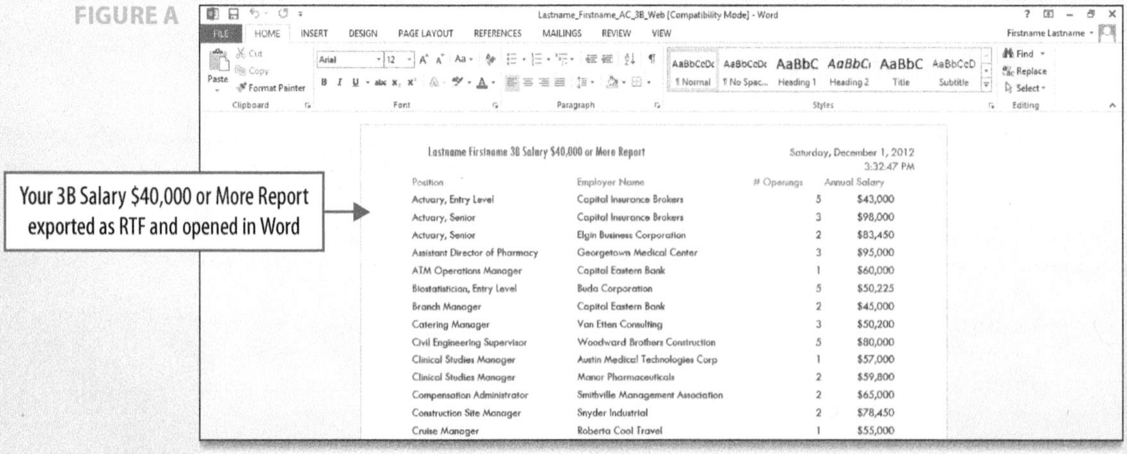

(GO! with Office Online (formerly Web Apps) continues on the next page)

5 From the desktop, start Internet Explorer, navigate to **http://onedrive.com**, and then sign in to your Microsoft account. Open your **GO! Web Projects** folder—or create and then open this folder if necessary.

6 On the menu bar, click **Upload**. In the **Choose File to Upload** dialog box, navigate to your **Access Chapter 3** folder, and then double-click your **AC_3B_Web** file to upload it to OneDrive.

7 After the file is uploaded, in your **GO! Web Projects** folder, right-click your **AC_3B_Web** file, and then click **Properties**.

A Properties panel displays on the right side of your screen.

8 In the **Properties** panel, click **Add a description**. In the box, type **This report displays job openings in our area that have a salary of $40,000 or more for which our students can apply.** Press Enter, and then compare your screen with Figure B.

9 On your keyboard, press the [Windows] key, type **snip**, and then click **Snipping Tool**. In the **Snipping Tool** dialog box, click the **New arrow**, and then click **Full-screen Snip**.

10 On the **Snipping Tool** toolbar, click **Save Snip**. In the **Save As** dialog box, navigate to your **Access Chapter 3** folder. Click in the **File name** box to select the existing text. Type **Lastname_Firstname_AC_3B_Web_Snip** and then, if necessary, click the **Save as type arrow**, and click **JPEG file**. In the **Save As** dialog box, click **Save**, and then **Close** the **Snipping Tool** window.

11 In OneDrive, on the title bar, click **OneDrive** to return to your home page. At the top right corner of your screen, click your OneDrive name, and then click **Sign out**. **Close** your browser window.

12 If directed to submit a paper printout of your RTF document and snip file, follow the directions given in the Note below. As directed by your instructor, submit your RTF document, which is two pages, and your snip file that are the results of this project.

NOTE **Printing your RTF Document and Your Snip .JPEG File**

Using Windows Explorer, navigate to your Access Chapter 3 folder. Locate and double-click your AC_3B_Web file—it will open in Word. On the ribbon, click the FILE tab, and then click Print. To print on paper, on the right, click Print. To create an electronic file of your printout, on the left side of your screen, click Export. Under Export, be sure Create PDF/XPS Document is selected, and then click Create PDF/XPS. Navigate to your Access Chapter 3 folder, and then click Publish to save the file with the default name and an extension of pdf.

In your Access Chapter 3 folder, locate and double-click your AC_3B_Web_Snip file. If this is the first time you have tried to open a .jpeg file, you will be asked to identify a program. If you are not sure which program to use, select Windows Photo Viewer. From the ribbon, menu bar, or toolbar, click the Print command, and then Close the program window.

FIGURE B

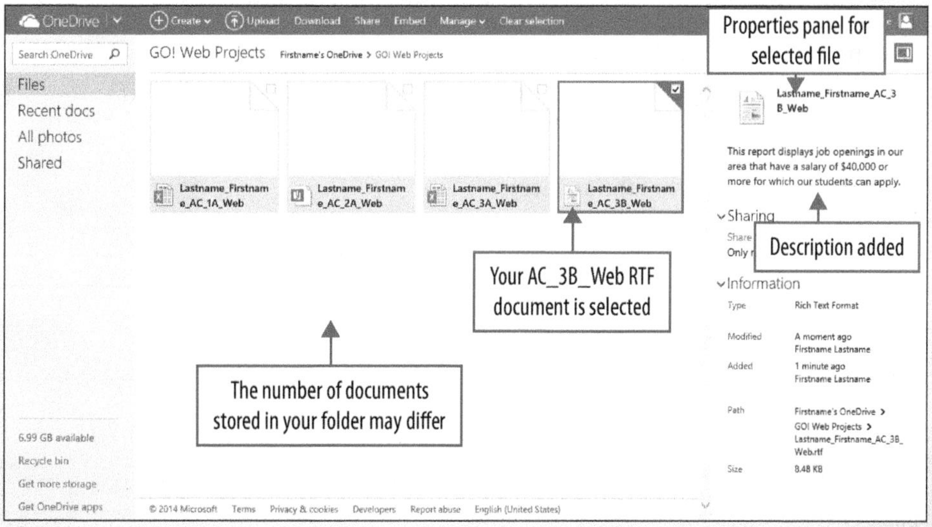

GO! with Microsoft Office 365

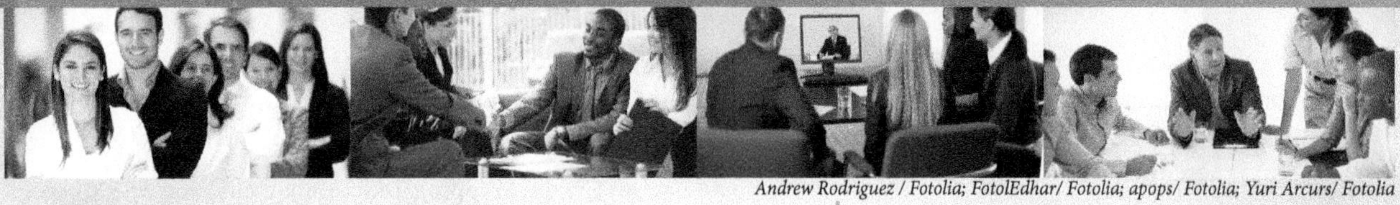

Andrew Rodriguez / Fotolia; FotolEdhar/ Fotolia; apops/ Fotolia; Yuri Arcurs/ Fotolia

The advantage of using Office 365 is that your organization does not have to purchase and install server hardware and software for sophisticated business applications and does not need a full-time IT person or staff just to manage the technology your teams need.

By using Office 365, you are able to have business-class services for your employees without investing in expensive hardware, software, and personnel. However, at least one person in an organization must be designated as the ***Office 365 Administrator***—the person who creates and manages the account, adds new users, sets up the services your organization wants to use, sets permission levels, and manages the SharePoint team sites. You can have more than one administrator if you want to share these tasks with others.

Microsoft provides easy-to-use instructions and videos to get you started, and you might also have contact with a Microsoft representative. You will probably find, however, that subscribing to and setting up the account, adding users, and activating services is a straightforward process that requires little or no assistance.

After purchasing the required number of licenses, you will add each team member as a user that includes his or her email address. The Admin Overview page, as shown in Figure A, assists the Office 365 Administrator. On the left, there are links to manage the users and domains in your Office 365 account. This is where you can add new users, delete users, set permission levels, enter and change passwords, and update the user properties and the licenses.

On this page, you can see the various services available to you in Office 365. In the site shown in Figure A, Outlook, Lync, SharePoint (team sites), and a public-facing website are all part of the services.

Activity | Using a Team Site to Collaborate

This group project relates to the **Bell Orchid Hotels.** If your instructor assigns this project to your class, you will use a SharePoint team site in **Office 365** to collaborate on the following tasks for this chapter:

- If you are in the **Accounting Group**, you and your teammates will finalize the Stockholders database and post it on the SharePoint team site.
- If you are in the **Engineering Group**, you and your teammates will finalize the Subcontractors database and post it on the SharePoint team site.
- If you are in the **Food and Beverage Group**, you and your teammates will finalize Banquet Clients database and post it on the SharePoint team site.
- If you are in the **Human Resources Group**, you and your teammates will finalize the Employees database and post it on the SharePoint team site.
- If you are in the **Operations Group**, you and your teammates will finalize the Guests Database and post it on the SharePoint team site.
- If you are in the **Sales and Marketing Group**, you and your teammates will finalize the Associations database and post it on the SharePoint team site.

FIGURE A

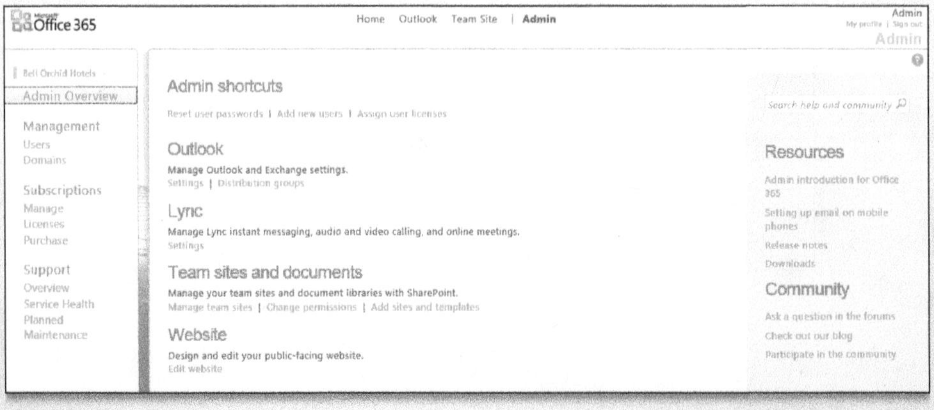

END OF CHAPTER

SUMMARY

A form is a database object that you can use to enter new records into a table, or to edit, delete, or display existing records in a table and can be used to control access to the data in a database.

Filter records in a form to display only a subset of the total records based on matching specific values to provide a quick answer to a question. Filters are generally not saved with a form.

A report is a database object that summarizes the fields and records from a query or from a table, in an easy-to-read format suitable for printing. You can group records and summarize the data in a report.

Most changes to forms and reports can be done in Layout view where the underlying data displays in the controls; however, some modifications, such as aligning controls, must be done in Design view.

GO! LEARN IT ONLINE

Review the concepts and key terms in this chapter by completing these online challenges, which you can find at **www.pearsonhighered.com/go**.

Matching and Multiple Choice: Answer matching and multiple choice questions to test what you learned in this chapter. MyITLab®

Crossword Puzzle: Spell out the words that match the numbered clues, and put them in the puzzle squares.

Flipboard: Flip through the definitions of the key terms in this chapter and match them with the correct term.

GO! FOR JOB SUCCESS

Video: Performance Evaluations

Your instructor may assign this video to your class, and then ask you to think about, or discuss with your classmates, these questions:

FotolEdhar / Fotolia

What kind of message is Sara sending by forgetting to do the self-assessment review she was assigned for her evaluation? Why is it important to do a self-assessment for a review?

How should Sara react to her supervisor's criticisms in her review?

How important is it to follow a company's dress code policy? Do you think Sara's response to not following the dress code is appropriate? Why or why not?

END OF CHAPTER

REVIEW AND ASSESSMENT GUIDE FOR ACCESS CHAPTER 3

Your instructor may assign one or more of these projects to help you review the chapter and assess your mastery and understanding of the chapter.

Review and Assessment Guide for Access Chapter 3

Project	Apply Skills from These Chapter Objectives	Project Type	Project Location
3C	Objectives 1-4 from Project 3A	**3C Skills Review** A guided review of the skills from Project 3A.	On the following pages
3D	Objectives 5-8 from Project 3B	**3D Skills Review** A guided review of the skills from Project 3B.	On the following pages
3E	Objectives 1-4 from Project 3A	**3E Mastery (Grader Project)** A demonstration of your mastery of the skills in Project 3A with extensive decision making.	In MyITLab and on the following pages
3F	Objectives 5-8 from Project 3B	**3F Mastery (Grader Project)** A demonstration of your mastery of the skills in Project 3B with extensive decision making.	In MyITLab and on the following pages
3G	Objectives 1-8 from Projects 3A and 3B	**3G Mastery (Grader Project)** A demonstration of your mastery of the skills in Projects 3A and 3B with extensive decision making.	In MyITLab and on the following pages
3H	Combination of Objectives from Projects 3A and 3B	**3H GO! Fix It** A demonstration of your mastery of the skills in Projects 3A and 3B by creating a correct result from a document that contains errors you must find.	Online
3I	Combination of Objectives from Projects 3A and 3B	**3I GO! Make It** A demonstration of your mastery of the skills in Projects 3A and 3B by creating a result from a supplied picture.	Online
3J	Combination of Objectives from Projects 3A and 3B	**3J GO! Solve It** A demonstration of your mastery of the skills in Projects 3A and 3B, your decision-making skills, and your critical thinking skills. A task-specific rubric helps you self-assess your result.	Online
3K	Combination of Objectives from Projects 3A and 3B	**3K GO! Solve It** A demonstration of your mastery of the skills in Projects 3A and 3B, your decision-making skills, and your critical thinking skills. A task-specific rubric helps you self-assess your result.	On the following pages
3L	Combination of Objectives from Projects 3A and 3B	**3L GO! Think** A demonstration of your understanding of the chapter concepts applied in a manner that you would outside of college. An analytic rubric helps you and your instructor grade the quality of your work by comparing it to the work an expert in the discipline would create.	On the following pages
3M	Combination of Objectives from Projects 3A and 3B	**3M GO! Think** A demonstration of your understanding of the chapter concepts applied in a manner that you would outside of college. An analytic rubric helps you and your instructor grade the quality of your work by comparing it to the work an expert in the discipline would create.	Online
3N	Combination of Objectives from Projects 3A and 3B	**3N You and GO!** A demonstration of your understanding of the chapter concepts applied in a manner that you would in a personal situation. An analytic rubric helps you and your instructor grade the quality of your work.	Online
3O	Combination of Objectives from Projects 3A and 3B	**3O Cumulative Group Project for Access Chapter 3** A demonstration of your understanding of concepts and your ability to work collaboratively in a group role-playing assessment, requiring both collaboration and self-management.	Online
Capstone Project for Access Chapters 1-3	Combination of Objectives from Projects 1A, 1B, 2A, 2B, 3A, and 3B	A demonstration of your mastery of the skills in Chapters 1-3 with extensive decision making. **(Grader Project)**	In MyITLab and online

GLOSSARY

GLOSSARY OF CHAPTER KEY TERMS

AND condition A condition in which records display only when all of the values are present in the selected fields.

Bound A term used to describe objects and controls that are based on data that is stored in tables.

Bound control A control that retrieves its data from an underlying table or query; a text box control is an example of a bound control.

Calculated control A control that contains an expression, often a formula or function, that most often summarizes a field that contains numerical data.

Control An object on a form or report that displays data or text, performs actions, and lets you view and work with information.

Control layout The grouped arrangement of controls on a form or report; for example, the Stacked layout.

Data entry The action of entering the data into a record in a database table or form.

Date control A control on a form or report that inserts the current date each time the form or report is opened.

Design view The Access view that displays the detailed structure of a query, form, or report; for forms and reports, may be the view in which some tasks must be performed, and only the controls, and not the data, display.

Detail section The section of a form or report that displays the records from the underlying table or query.

Filter by Form An Access command that filters the records in a form based on one or more fields, or based on more than one value in the field.

Filter by Selection An Access command that displays only the records that contain the value in the selected field and hides the records that do not contain the value.

Filtering The process of displaying only a portion of the total records (a subset) based on matching specific values to provide a quick answer to a question.

Form A database object that you can use to enter new records into a table, or to edit, delete, and display existing records in a table.

Form Footer Information at the bottom of the screen in Form view or Layout view that is printed after the last detail section on the last page of a printout.

Form Header Information such as a form's title that displays at the top of the screen in Form view or Layout view and is printed at the top of the first page when records are printed as forms.

Form tool An Access tool that creates a form with a single mouse click, which includes all of the fields from the underlying data source (table or query).

Form view The Access view in which you can view, modify, delete, or add records in a table; but you cannot change the layout or design of the form.

Form Wizard An Access tool that walks you step by step through the creation of a form and that gives you more flexibility in the design, layout, and number of fields in a form.

Group Footer Information printed at the end of each group of records; used to display summary information for the group.

Group Header Information printed at the beginning of each new group of records; for example, the group name.

Group, Sort, and Total pane A pane that displays at the bottom of the screen in which you can control how information is sorted and grouped in a report; provides the most flexibility for adding or modifying groups, sort orders, or totals options on a report.

Label control A control on a form or report that contains descriptive information, usually a field name or title.

Layout selector A small symbol that displays in the upper left corner of a selected control layout in a form or report that is displayed in Layout view or Design view; used to move or format an entire group of controls.

Layout view The Access view in which you can make changes to a form or report while the object is running—the data from the underlying data source displays.

Office 365 Administrator In Office 365, the person who creates and manages the account, adds new users, sets up the services your organization wants to use, sets permission levels, and manages the SharePoint team sites.

OR condition A condition in which records display that match at least one of the specified values.

Page Footer Information printed at the bottom of every page in a report; most often includes the page number.

Page Header Information printed at the top of every page in a report.

Page number control A control on a form or report that inserts the page numbers when displayed in Print Preview or when printed.

Record selector bar The vertical bar at the left edge of a record when it is displayed in a form that is used to select an entire record.

Record source The tables or queries that provide the underlying data for a form or report.

Report A database object that summarizes the fields and records from a query or table in an easy-to-read format suitable for printing.

Report Footer Information printed at the bottom of the last page of a report.

Report Header Information printed on the first page of a report; used for logos, titles, and dates.

Report tool An Access tool that creates a report with one mouse click and displays all of the fields and records from the record source that you select.

Report Wizard An Access tool that walks you step by step through the creation of a report and that gives you more flexibility in the design, layout, and number of fields in a report.

Rich Text Format (RTF) A standard file format that contains text and some formatting such as underline, bold, italic, font sizes, and colors; RTF documents can be opened in many word processing programs and text editors.

Section bar In Design view, a gray bar in a form or report that identifies and separates one section from another; used to select the section and to change the size of the section.

Stacked layout A control layout format that is similar to a paper form, with label controls placed to the left of each text box control; the controls are grouped together for easy editing.

Subset A portion of the total records available.

Tab order The order in which the insertion point moves from one field to another in a form when you press the Tab key.

Text box control A bound control on a form or report that displays the data from the underlying table or query.

Theme A predesigned set of colors, fonts, lines, and fill effects that look good together and that can be applied to all of the objects in the database or to individual objects in the database.

Unbound control A control that does not have a source of data, such as the title in a form or report.

CHAPTER REVIEW

Apply 3A skills from these Objectives:

1. Create and Use a Form to Add and Delete Records
2. Filter Records
3. Create a Form by Using the Form Wizard
4. Modify a Form in Layout View and in Design View

Skills Review Project 3C Student Internships

In the following Skills Review, you will assist Erinique Jerlin, the dean of Business at the Northwest Campus, in using her database to track business students and their internship placements for the current semester. Your completed forms will look similar to Figure 3.49.

PROJECT FILES

For Project 3C, you will need the following file:

a03C_Student_Internships

You will save your database as:

Lastname_Firstname_3C_Student_Internships

PROJECT RESULTS

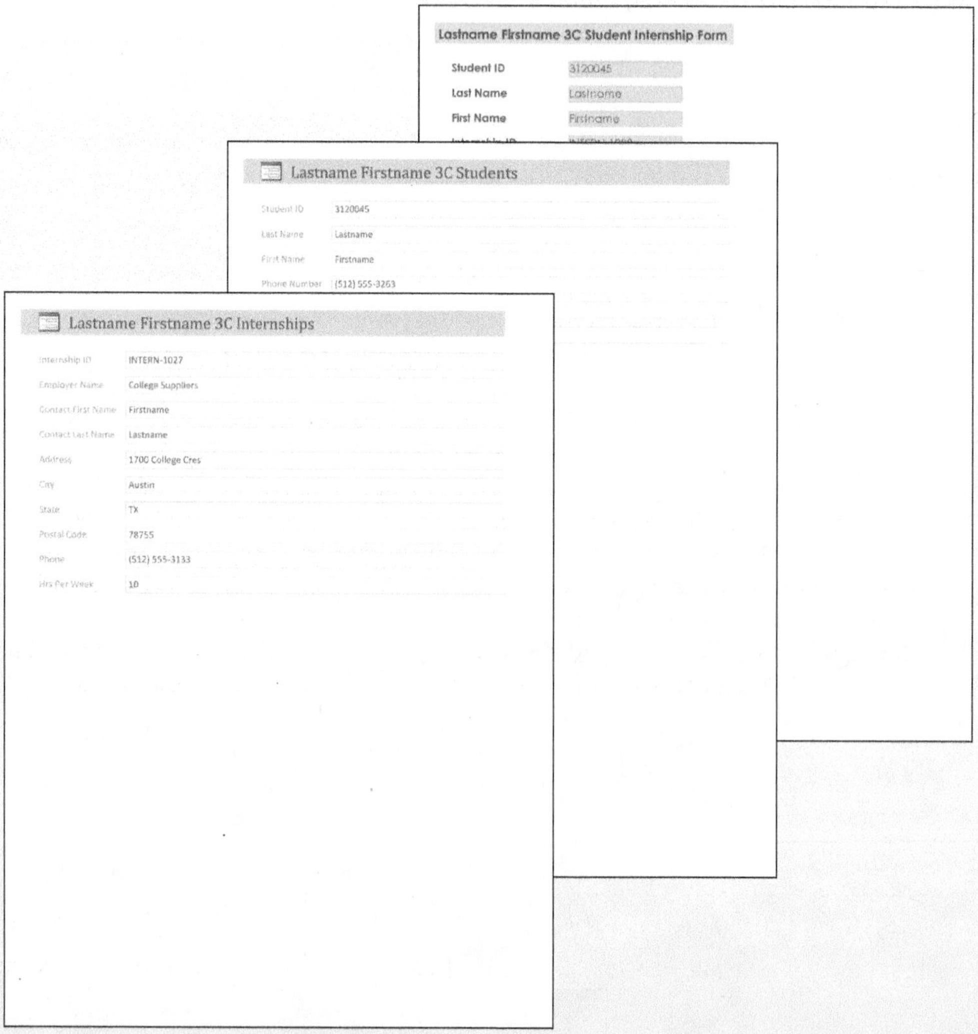

FIGURE 3.49

(Project 3C Student Internships continues on the next page)

CHAPTER REVIEW

3 ACCESS

Skills Review Project 3C Student Internships (continued)

1 Start Access. In the Access opening screen, click **Open Other Files**. Under **Open**, click **Computer**. Under **Recent Folders**, if displayed, click the location where your student data files are stored; otherwise, click **Browse** and then navigate to the location where your student data files are stored. Double-click **a03C_Student_Internships** to open the database.

a. On the ribbon, click the **FILE tab**, and then click **Save As**. Under **File Types**, be sure **Save Database As** is selected. On the right, under **Database File Types**, be sure **Access Database** is selected, and then click **Save As**.

b. In the **Save As** dialog box, navigate to your **Access Chapter 3** folder. In the **File name** box, replace the existing text with **Lastname_Firstname_3C_Student_Internships** and then press Enter. On the **Message Bar**, click **Enable Content**.

c. In the **Navigation Pane**, right-click **3C Students**, and then click **Rename**. With the table name selected and using your own name, type **Lastname Firstname 3C Students** and then press Enter. **Rename** the **3C Internships** table to **Lastname Firstname 3C Internships** and then point to the right edge of the **Navigation Pane** to display the ⇔ pointer. Drag to the right to increase the width of the pane until both tables names display fully.

d. On the ribbon, click the **DATABASE TOOLS tab**, and then in the **Relationships group**, click **Relationships**. Under **RELATIONSHIP TOOLS**, on the **DESIGN tab**, in the **Relationships group**, click **All Relationships**. Resize and move the field lists so that the entire table name and fields display for each field list. In the **Relationships** window, click the **join line** between the two field lists. In the **Tools group**, click **Edit Relationships**. Point to the title bar of the **Edit Relationships** dialog box, and drag the dialog box downward below the two field lists. Notice that a *one-to-many* relationship is established between the two tables by using *Internship ID* as the common field. **Close** the **Edit Relationships** dialog box, and then **Close** the **Relationships** window. In the message box, click **Yes** to save changes to the layout of the relationships.

e. In the **Navigation Pane**, click your **3C Students** table to select it. On the ribbon, click the **CREATE tab**, and then in the **Forms group**, click **Form**. **Save** the form as **Lastname Firstname 3C Student Form** and then **Close** the form object.

f. In the **Navigation Pane**, click your **3C Internships** table to select it. On the ribbon, click the **CREATE tab**, and then in the **Forms group**, click **Form**. Notice that for the first record—*Internship ID INTERN-1000* for *Lakes Realty Inc*—there are two student records in the subdatasheet—two students have been assigned internships for this employer. **Close** the form, and in the message box, click **Yes** to save the form. In the **Save As** dialog box, type **Lastname Firstname 3C Internship Company Form** and then press Enter. If necessary, increase the width of the Navigation Pane so that all object names display fully.

g. In the **Navigation Pane**, double-click your **3C Student Form** object to open it, and then **Close** the **Navigation Pane**. In the navigation area, click **New (blank) record** to display a new blank form. In the **Student ID** field, type **3120045** and then press Tab. Using your own last name and first name, continue entering the data as shown in **Table 1**.

h. With the insertion point positioned in the last field, press Tab to save the record and display a new blank record. **Close** your **3C Student Form** object, and then **Open** the **Navigation Pane**. Double-click your **3C Internship Company Form** object to open it, and then **Close** the **Navigation Pane**. Notice that for the first record, in the subdatasheet, the record you just entered displays. Scroll to view the bottom of

TABLE 1

Student ID	Last Name	First Name	Phone Number	Email	Internship ID
3120045	**Lastname**	**Firstname**	**(512) 555-3263**	**ns3120@tlcc.edu**	**INTERN-1000**

(Return to Step 1-h)

(Project 3C Student Internships continues on the next page)

the form. In the navigation area for the form—*not* the navigation area for the subdatasheet—click **New (blank) record**. In the blank form, using your own first name and last name, enter the data as shown in **Table 2**.

i. In the navigation area for the form, click **First record**. Click in the **Employer Name** field, and then on the **HOME tab**, in the **Find group**, click **Find**. In the **Find and Replace** dialog box, in the **Find What** box, type **Jones Consulting** and then click **Find Next**. **Close** the **Find and Replace** dialog box. On the **HOME tab**, in the **Records group**, click the **Delete arrow**, and then click **Delete Record**. In the message box, click **Yes** to delete the record. In the navigation area for the form, notice that the total number of records is *27*.

j. Use the technique you just practiced to **Find** the form for the **Internship ID** of **INTERN-1027**, and then **Close** the **Find and Replace** dialog box. On the ribbon, click the **FILE tab**, click **Print**, and then on the right, click **Print**. In the **Print** dialog box, under **Print Range**, click the **Selected Record(s)** option button. In the lower left corner of the dialog box, click **Setup**. In the **Page Setup** dialog box, click the **Columns tab**. Under **Column Size**, double-click in the **Width** box to select the existing value, type **7.5** and then click **OK**. If directed to print the form, in the **Print** dialog box, click **OK**. If directed to submit an electronic printout of the form, click **Cancel**, and then follow the directions given in the Note in Activity 3.06.

k. **Close** your **3C Internship Company Form** object, and then **Open** the **Navigation Pane**. In the **Navigation Pane**, double-click your **3C Student Form** object to open it, and then **Close** the **Navigation Pane**. Use the **Find** command to display the record where the **Last Name** field contains your last name, and then create a paper or electronic printout of only that record, being sure to change the **Column Size Width** to **7.5**

2 With your **3C Student Form** object displayed in **Form** view, in the navigation area, click **First record**, and then click the **Internship ID** field name to select the text in the field box. Press Ctrl + F to display the **Find and Replace** dialog box. In the **Find What** box, type **INTERN-1009** and then click **Find Next** to find and display the record for *Michael Fresch*. **Close** the **Find and Replace** dialog box. On the **HOME tab**, in the **Sort & Filter group**, click **Selection**, and then click **Equals "INTERN-1009"**. In the navigation area, notice that two students are assigned internships with the company identified as INTERN-1009.

a. In the **Sort & Filter group**, click **Toggle Filter** to remove the filter and display all 52 records. **Close** the form. If prompted, click **Yes** to save the form.

b. **Open** the **Navigation Pane**, double-click your **3C Internship Company Form** object to open it, and then **Close** the **Navigation Pane**. On the **HOME tab**, in the **Sort & Filter group**, click **Advanced**, and then click **Filter By Form**. In the form, click the **City** field name to position the insertion point in the **City** field box, click the **arrow**, and then click **Georgetown**. In the **Sort & Filter group**, click **Toggle Filter** to display the filtered records. In the navigation area for the form, notice that three internships are located in the *City* of *Georgetown*.

c. In the **Sort & Filter group**, click **Advanced**, and then click **Filter By Form**. In the lower left corner of the form, click the **Or tab**. Click the **City** field box **arrow**, and then click **Elgin**. In the **Sort & Filter group**, click **Toggle Filter**. In the navigation area for the form, notice that five internships are located in either *Georgetown* or *Elgin*. In the **Sort & Filter group**, click **Advanced**, and then click **Clear All Filters** to display all 27 records.

TABLE 2

Internship ID	Employer Name	Contact First Name	Contact Last Name	Address	City	State	Postal Code	Phone	Hrs Per Week
INTERN-1027	**College Suppliers**	**Firstname**	**Lastname**	**1700 College Cres**	**Austin**	**TX**	**78755**	**(512) 555-3133**	**10**

Return to Step 1-i

(Project 3C Student Internships continues on the next page)

Skills Review Project 3C Student Internships (continued)

d. In the **Sort & Filter group**, click **Advanced**, and then click **Advanced Filter/Sort**. Resize the field list. In the **3C Internships** field list, double-click **City**, and then double-click **Hrs Per Week** to add both fields to the design grid. Click in the **Criteria** row under **City**, type **Austin** and then press Enter. In the **Criteria** row under **Hrs Per Week**, type **>10** and then press Enter. In the **Sort & Filter group**, click **Toggle Filter** to display the filtered records, and notice that that there are five internships in the *City* of *Austin* offering *more than 10* hours per week of work. In the **Sort & Filter group**, click **Toggle Filter** to remove the filter and display all 27 records. **Save** and then **Close** your **3C Internship Company Form** object, which also closes the Advanced Filter grid.

3 On the ribbon, click the **CREATE tab**, and then in the **Forms group**, click **Form Wizard**. In the **Tables/Queries** box, click the **arrow**, and then click **Table: Lastname Firstname 3C Students**. In the **Available Fields** list, double-click the following field names in the order given to move them to the **Selected Fields** list: **First Name, Last Name**, and **Internship ID**. Click **Next**. In the wizard, be sure **Columnar** is selected as the layout, and then click **Next**. In the **What title do you want for your form?** box, select the existing text, type **Lastname Firstname 3C Student Internship Form** and then click **Finish** to close the wizard and create the form.

4 On the **HOME tab**, in the **Views group**, click the top portion of the **View** button to switch to **Layout** view. If the **Field List** pane displays on the right side of your screen, close the pane. Click the **First Name label control**. Hold down Shift, and then click the **Last Name label control**, the **Internship ID label control**, and the three **text box controls** to select all of the controls. On the ribbon, under **FORM LAYOUT TOOLS**, click the **ARRANGE tab**. In the **Table group**, click **Stacked** to group all of the controls. Click the **First Name label control** to cancel the selection of all of the controls.

a. On the ribbon, under **FORM LAYOUT TOOLS**, click the **DESIGN tab**. In the **Themes group** click **Themes**. In the **Themes** gallery, using the ScreenTips, point to the **Wisp** theme, right-click, and then click **Apply Theme to This Object Only**. Click anywhere in the title—*Lastname Firstname 3C Student Internship Form*—to select the title. On the ribbon, under **FORM LAYOUT TOOLS**, click the **FORMAT tab**. In the **Font group**, click the **Font Size arrow**, and then click **14**. In the **Font group**, click **Bold**. Click the **Font Color arrow**, and then under **Theme Colors**, in the sixth column, click the last color—**Orange, Accent 2, Darker 50%**.

b. On the ribbon, click the **DESIGN tab**. In the **Tools group**, click **Add Existing Fields**. In the **Field List** pane, click **Student ID**, and then drag the field name to the left until the pointer displays above the **First Name label control** and a colored line displays above the control. Release the mouse button to add the *Student ID* controls to the form, and then **Close** the **Field List** pane.

c. Click the **First Name text box control**, which displays *Jordan*, to select it. On the **DESIGN tab**, in the **Tools group**, click **Property Sheet**. In the **Property Sheet**, on the **Format tab**, click **Width**, type **1.75** and then press Enter to decrease the width of the text box controls. **Close** the **Property Sheet**. Be sure that the **First Name text box control** is still selected. On the ribbon, click the **ARRANGE tab**, and in the **Rows & Columns group**, click **Select Row**. In the **Move group**, click **Move Down** to move both controls below the **Last Name** controls. **Save** the changes you have made to the design of your form.

d. Click the **Student ID text box control**, which displays *1010101*. On the **ARRANGE tab**, in the **Rows & Columns group**, click **Select Column** to select all four text box controls. On the ribbon, click the **FORMAT tab**, and in the **Font group**, click the **Background Color arrow**. Under **Theme Colors**, in the fourth column, click the second color—**Brown, Text 2, Lighter 80%**.

e. Click the **Student ID label control**, and then on the ribbon, click the **ARRANGE tab**. In the **Rows & Columns group**, click **Select Column** to select all four label controls. On the ribbon, click the **FORMAT tab**, and then click the **Font Color arrow**—*not* the **Background Color arrow**. Under **Theme Colors**, in the fourth column, click the first color—**Brown, Text 2**. In the **Font group**, click **Bold**.

(Project 3C Student Internships continues on the next page)

CHAPTER REVIEW

Skills Review Project 3C Student Internships (continued)

f. Click the **layout selector** [icon] to select all of the controls. In the **Font group**, click the **Font Size arrow**, and then click **12**. With all of the controls still selected, on the ribbon, click the **DESIGN tab**, and in the **Tools group**, click **Property Sheet**. In the **Property Sheet**, on the **Format tab**, click **Height**, type **0.25** and then press Enter to change the height of each selected control.

g. Click the **Student ID label control** to select only that control. In the **Property Sheet**, click **Width**, type **1.75** and then press Enter to change the width of all of the label controls. **Save** the design changes to your form.

h. On the status bar, click **Design View**. At the bottom of the form, click the **Form Footer section bar** to select it. In the **Property Sheet**, click **Height**, type **0.5** and then press Enter to increase the height of the **Form Footer** section.

i. On the ribbon, under **FORM DESIGN TOOLS**, click the **DESIGN tab**. In the **Controls group**, click **Label**. Move the pointer into the **Form Footer** section and then position the plus sign of the pointer at approximately **0.25 inch on the horizontal ruler** and even with the lower edge of the **Form Footer section bar**—the placement does not need to be precise. Click one time, type **Texas Lakes Community College** and then press Enter.

j. With the **label control** selected, on the ribbon, click the **FORMAT tab**. In the **Font group**, click **Bold**. Click the **Font Color arrow**, and then under **Theme Colors**, in the fourth column, click the first color—**Brown, Text 2**. If necessary, double-click the right edge of the label control to resize the control so that all of the data displays.

k. With the **label control** still selected, in the **Property Sheet**, click **Top**, type **0.1** and then press Enter. In the **Property Sheet**, in the **Left** property setting box, type **0.9** and then press Enter. **Close** the **Property Sheet**, and then **Save** the design changes to your form.

l. On the right side of the status bar, click **Form View**. In the navigation area, click **Last record** to display the record containing your name. On the ribbon, click the **FILE tab**, and then click **Print**. In the **Print** dialog box, under **Print Range**, click the **Selected Records(s)** option button. Because you changed the field widths, you do not need to change the Column Size Width in the **Print** dialog box. Create a paper or electronic printout as directed by your instructor. To create an electronic printout, follow the directions given in the Note in Activity 3.06.

m. **Close** all open objects, and then **Open** the **Navigation Pane**. If necessary, increase the width of the pane so that all object names display fully. On the right side of the title bar, click **Close** to close the database and to exit Access. As directed by your instructor, submit your database and the paper or electronic printouts of the three forms that are the results of this project. Specifically, in this project, using your own name, you created the following database and printouts or electronic printouts:

1. Lastname_Firstname_3C_Student_Internships	Database file
2. Lastname Firstname 3C Student Form	Form (printout or electronic printout - Record 52)
3. Lastname Firstname 3C Internship Company Form	Form (printout or electronic printout - Record 27)
4. Lastname Firstname 3C Student Internship Form	Form (printout or electronic printout - Record 52)

END | You have completed Project 3C

CHAPTER REVIEW

Skills Review Project 3D Student Parking

Apply 3B skills from these Objectives:

5 Create a Report by Using the Report Tool and Modify the Report in Layout View
6 Create a Report by Using the Report Wizard
7 Modify the Design of a Report
8 Keep Grouped Data Together in a Printed Report

In the following Skills Review, you will assist Carlos Medina, the chief of security, in using his Access database to track the details about students who have paid for parking in designated lots at the Southeast Campus of Texas Lakes Community College. Your completed reports will look similar to Figure 3.50.

PROJECT FILES

For Project 3D, you will need the following file:

a03D_Student_Parking

You will save your database as:

Lastname_Firstname_3D_Student_Parking

PROJECT RESULTS

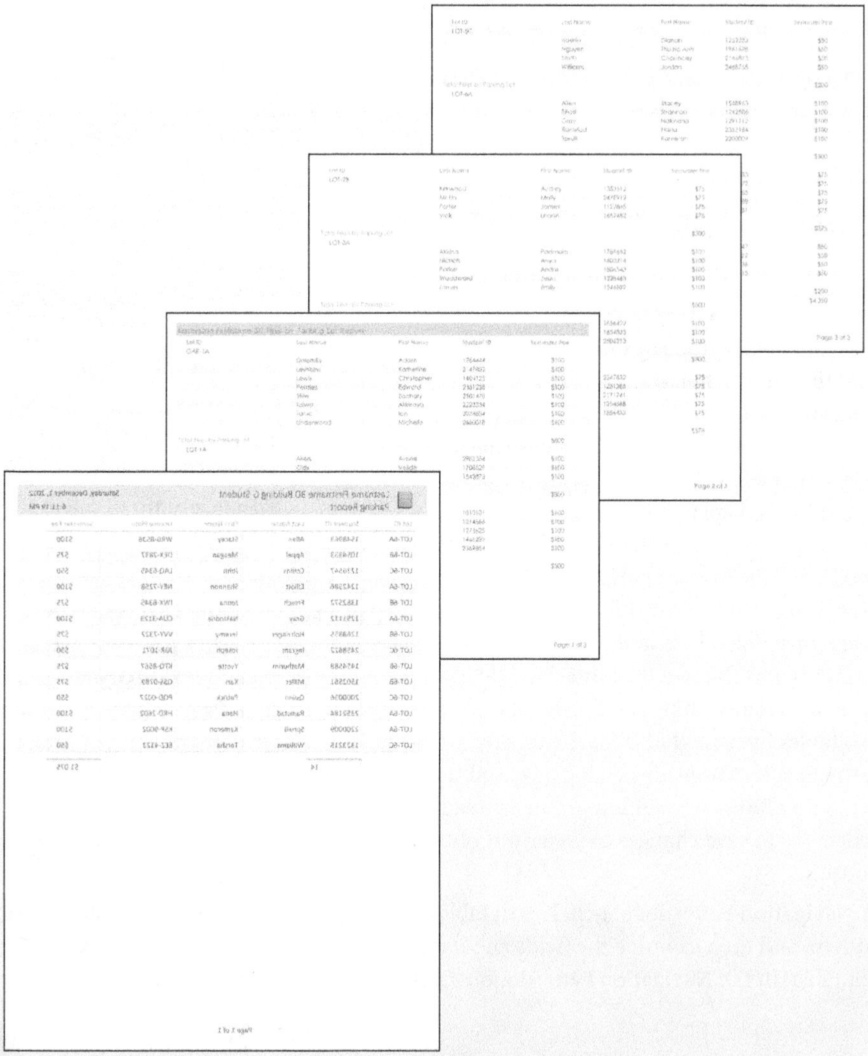

FIGURE 3.50

(Project 3D Student Parking continues on the next page)

CHAPTER REVIEW

Skills Review Project 3D Student Parking (continued)

1 Start Access. In the Access opening screen, click **Open Other Files**. Under **Open**, click **Computer**. Under **Recent Folders**, if displayed, click the location where your student data files are stored; otherwise, click **Browse** and then navigate to the location where your student data files are stored. Double-click **a03D_Student_Parking** to open the database.

a. On the ribbon, click the **FILE tab**, and then click **Save As**. Under **File Types**, be sure **Save Database As** is selected. On the right, under **Database File Types**, be sure **Access Database** is selected, and then at the bottom of the screen, click **Save As**. In the **Save As** dialog box, navigate to your **Access Chapter 3** folder. In the **File name** box, replace the existing text with **Lastname_Firstname_3D_Student_Parking** and then press Enter. On the **Message Bar**, click **Enable Content**.

b. In the **Navigation Pane**, right-click the **3D Parking Lots** table, and then click **Rename**. Using your own name, type **Lastname Firstname 3D Parking Lots** and then press Enter. Use this same technique to add your last name and first name to the beginning of the names of the two queries and the **3D Students** table. Increase the width of the **Navigation Pane** so that all object names display fully.

c. On the ribbon, click the **DATABASE TOOLS tab**, and then in the **Relationships group**, click **Relationships**. On the **DESIGN tab**, in the **Relationships group**, click **All Relationships**. Resize and move the field lists so that the entire table name and fields display for each field list. In the **Relationships** window, click the **join line** between the two field lists. In the **Tools group**, click **Edit Relationships**. Point to the title bar of the **Edit Relationships** dialog box, and drag the dialog box downward below the two field lists. Notice that a *one-to-many* relationship is established between the two tables by using *Lot ID* as the common field. **Close** the **Edit Relationships** dialog box, and then **Close** the **Relationships** window. In the message box, click **Yes** to save changes to the layout of the relationships.

d. In the **Navigation Pane**, double-click each table to open them, and then examine the fields and data in each table. In the **Navigation Pane**, double-click your **3D Building G Student Parking Query** object to run the query and view the results. Apply **Best Fit** to the query results, and then **Save** the query. Switch to **Design** view to examine the design grid. This query answers the question, *What is the lot ID, lot location, student ID, student last name, student first name, license plate, and semester fee for students who have paid for parking in front of Building G, in ascending order by the Last Name field?* In the **Navigation Pane**, double-click your **3D Student Parking by Lots Query** object, apply **Best Fit** to the query results, **Save** the query, and then switch to **Design** view to examine the design grid. This query answers the question, *What is the lot ID, student ID, student last name, student first name, license plate, state, and semester fee for all students?* In the object window, right-click any **object tab**, and then click **Close All**.

e. In the **Navigation Pane**, click to select your **3D Building G Student Parking Query** object. On the ribbon, click the **CREATE tab**, and in the **Reports group**, click **Report**. **Close** the **Navigation Pane**. Under **REPORT LAYOUT TOOLS**, on the **DESIGN tab**, in the **Themes group**, click **Themes**. In the **Themes** gallery, use the ScreenTips to locate the **Retrospect** theme, right-click the **Retrospect** theme, and then click **Apply Theme to This Object Only**.

f. Click the **Lot Location** field name. On the ribbon, under **REPORT LAYOUT TOOLS**, click the **ARRANGE tab**. In the **Rows & Columns group**, click **Select Column** to select the field name and all of the data for each record in the field. Press Del to remove the field from the report.

g. Click the **Last Name** field name, hold down Shift, and then click the **First Name** field name. On the ribbon, click the **DESIGN tab**, and in the **Tools group**, click **Property Sheet**. In the **Property Sheet**, on the **Format tab**, click **Width**, type **1.25** and then press Enter to decrease the width of the two fields. **Close** the **Property Sheet**.

h. Click the **Last Name** field name to cancel the selection of both fields and to select only this field. On the ribbon, click the **HOME tab**, and in the **Sort & Filter group**, click **Ascending** to sort the records in ascending order by the Last Name field.

(Project 3D Student Parking continues on the next page)

CHAPTER REVIEW

Skills Review Project 3D Student Parking (continued)

i. If necessary, scroll to the bottom of the report, and notice that the *Semester Fee* column is automatically totaled. At the top of the report, click the **Student ID** field name. On the ribbon, click the **DESIGN tab.** In the **Grouping & Totals group**, click **Totals**, and then click **Count Records**. If necessary, scroll to the bottom of the report, and notice that *14* students have paid for parking in front of Building G.

j. At the bottom of the report, under **Student ID**, click the **calculated control** that displays *14*. Hold down Ctrl, and then under **Semester Fee**, click the **calculated control** that displays *$1,075*—the two calculated controls are selected. On the **DESIGN tab**, in the **Tools group**, click **Property Sheet**. In the **Property Sheet**, click **Height**, type **0.25** and then press Enter to increase the height of both controls. At the bottom of the report, to the right of the **calculated control** that displays *$1,075*, click the **control** that displays *Page 1 of 1*. In the **Property Sheet**, click **Left**, type **2.5** and then press Enter to move the page number within the margins of the report.

k. At the top of the report, click the **label control** that displays the title of the report—*Lastname Firstname 3D Building G Student Parking Query*. On the ribbon, under **REPORT LAYOUT TOOLS**, click the **FORMAT tab**. In the **Font group**, click the **Font Size arrow**, and then click **14**. With the **label control** still selected, double-click **Query** to select the word, type **Report** and then press Enter to change the title of the report to *Lastname Firstname 3D Building G Student Parking Report*.

l. Click the **Lot ID** field name. In the **Property Sheet**, click **Left**, type **0.25** and then press Enter to move all of the fields slightly to the right from the left margin. **Close** the **Property Sheet**, and then **Save** the report as **Lastname Firstname 3D Building G Student Parking Report**

m. On the right side of the status bar, click **Print Preview**. On the **PRINT PREVIEW tab**, in the **Zoom group**, click **Two Pages**, and notice that the report will print on one page. Create a paper or electronic printout as directed, click **Close Print Preview**, and then **Close** the report.

2 On the ribbon, click the **CREATE tab**, and then in the **Reports group**, click **Report Wizard**. In the **Tables/Queries** box, click the **arrow**, and then click **Query: Lastname Firstname 3D Student Parking by Lots Query**. In the **Available Fields** list, double-click the following field names in the order given to move them to the **Selected Fields** list: **Lot ID**, **Last Name**, **First Name**, **Student ID**, and **Semester Fee**.

a. Click **Next**. In the **How do you want to view your data?** box, click **by Lastname Firstname 3D Students**, and then click **Next**. In the list on the left, double-click **Lot ID** to group the records by this field, and then click **Next**. Click the **1** box **arrow**, and then click **Last Name** to sort the records by the student's last name within each Lot ID.

b. In the wizard, click **Summary Options**. In the **Summary Options** dialog box, to the right of **Semester Fee**, click to select the **Sum** check box. Under **Show**, be sure that **Detail and Summary** is selected, and then click **OK**. In the wizard, click **Next**.

c. In the wizard, under **Layout**, be sure that **Stepped** is selected. Under **Orientation**, click **Landscape**. At the bottom of the wizard, be sure that the **Adjust the field width so all fields fit on a page** check box is selected, and then click **Next**. In the **What title do you want for your report?** box, select the existing text, type **Lastname Firstname 3D Fees by Parking Lot Report** and then click **Finish**. In the object window, right-click the **object tab** for the report, and then click **Layout View**.

3 Under **REPORT LAYOUT TOOLS**, on the **DESIGN tab**, in the **Themes group**, click **Themes**. In the **Themes** gallery, use the ScreenTips to locate the **Ion Boardroom** theme, right-click the **Ion Boardroom** theme, and then click **Apply Theme to This Object Only**. In the report, click the title—*Lastname Firstname 3D Fees by Parking Lot*—to display a border around the label control. On the ribbon, under **REPORT LAYOUT TOOLS**, click the **FORMAT tab**. In the **Font group**, click the **Font Size arrow**, and then click **14**. In the **Font group**, click **Bold**. In the body of the report, click any one of the controls that begins with **Summary for 'Lot ID'**, and then press Del. **Save** the design changes to your report.

a. On the left side of the report, click a **Sum label control**, which will select all of the related controls. Double-click the control to select the text—*Sum*. Type **Total Fees by Parking Lot** and then press Enter.

(Project 3D Student Parking continues on the next page)

Skills Review Project 3D Student Parking (continued)

b. At the top of the report, click the **Lot ID label control** to select it. Hold down Shift, and then click each one of the four other label controls that display the field names to select all five label controls. On the **FORMAT tab**, in the **Font group**, click **Bold.**

c. In the report, under **Last Name**, click the **text box control** that displays *Dolensky*. Hold down Shift, and then under **First Name**, click the **text box control** that displays *Adam*. On the ribbon, click the **DESIGN tab**. In the **Tools group**, click **Property Sheet**. In the **Property Sheet**, click **Width**, type **1.5** and then press Enter.

d. In the report, click the **Student ID label control**. In the **Property Sheet**, click **Left**, type **7.25** and then press Enter. Do not be concerned that the data in the field is not aligned with the field name; you will adjust this later in this project. Scroll to the bottom of the report, and then click the **Grand Total label control**. In the **Property Sheet**, click **Width**, type **1** and then press Enter. **Close** the **Property Sheet**, and then **Save** the design changes to your report.

e. On the status bar, click **Design View**. In the **Lot ID Footer** section, click the **Total Fees by Parking Lot label control**. Hold down Shift, and in the **Report Footer** section, click the **Grand Total label control** to select both controls. On the ribbon, under **REPORT DESIGN TOOLS**, click the **ARRANGE tab**. In the **Sizing & Ordering group**, click **Align**, and then click **Left**.

f. In the report, in the **Page Header** section, click the **Student ID label control**. Hold down Shift, and in the **Detail** section, click the **Student ID text box control**. On the **ARRANGE tab**, in the **Sizing & Ordering group**, click **Align**, and then click **Left**. On the status bar, click **Layout View** and notice the left alignment of the two sets of controls.

4 On the status bar, click **Print Preview**. On the **PRINT PREVIEW tab**, in the **Zoom group**, click **More Pages**, and then click **Four Pages** to view how your report is currently laid out. In the **Zoom group**, click the **Zoom arrow**, and then click **50%**. Notice at the bottom of Page 1 and the top of Page 2, that the grouping for **LOT-2B** breaks across these two pages. Notice at the bottom of Page 2 and the top of Page 3, that the grouping for **LOT-6A** breaks across these two pages. Your pages may display differently depending upon the printer that is installed on your system.

a. On the ribbon, click **Close Print Preview** to return to **Layout** view. On the **DESIGN tab**, in the **Grouping & Totals group**, click **Group & Sort**. In the **Group, Sort, and Total** pane, on the **Group on Lot ID** bar, click **More**. Click the **do not keep group together on one page arrow**, and then click **keep whole group together on one page**. On the **DESIGN tab**, in the **Grouping & Totals group**, click **Group & Sort** to close the **Group, Sort, and Total** pane. **Save** the design changes to your report.

b. On the status bar, click **Print Preview**. Notice that the entire grouping for **LOT-2B** displays at the top of Page 2. Keeping this group together forced the groupings for **LOT-5C** and **LOT-6A** to move to the top of Page 3—your groupings may display differently depending upon the printer that is installed on your system. Create a paper or electronic printout as directed—three pages result.

c. **Close** the report, and then **Open** the **Navigation Pane**. If necessary, increase the width of the pane so that all object names display fully. On the right side of the title bar, click **Close** to close the database and to exit Access. As directed by your instructor, submit your database and the paper or electronic printouts of the two reports—one report is three pages—that are the results of this project. Specifically, in this project, using your own name, you created the following database and printouts or electronic printouts:

1. Lastname_Firstname_3D_Student_Parking	Database file
2. Lastname Firstname 3D Building G Student Parking Report	Report (printout or electronic printout)
3. Lastname Firstname 3D Fees by Parking Lot Report	Report (printout or electronic printout - three pages)

END | You have completed Project 3D

CONTENT-BASED ASSESSMENTS

MyITLab® grader

Apply 3A skills from these Objectives:

1. Create and Use a Form to Add and Delete Records
2. Filter Records
3. Create a Form by Using the Form Wizard
4. Modify a Form in Layout View and in Design View

Mastering Access | Project 3E Textbook Publishers

In the following Mastering Access project, you will assist Donna Rider, manager of the bookstore, in using her database to track textbooks and publishers for courses being offered by the Science Department at the Northeast Campus of Texas Lakes Community College. Your completed forms will look similar to Figure 3.51.

PROJECT FILES

For Project 3E, you will need the following file:

a03E_Textbook_Publishers

You will save your database as:

Lastname_Firstname_3E_Textbook_Publishers

PROJECT RESULTS

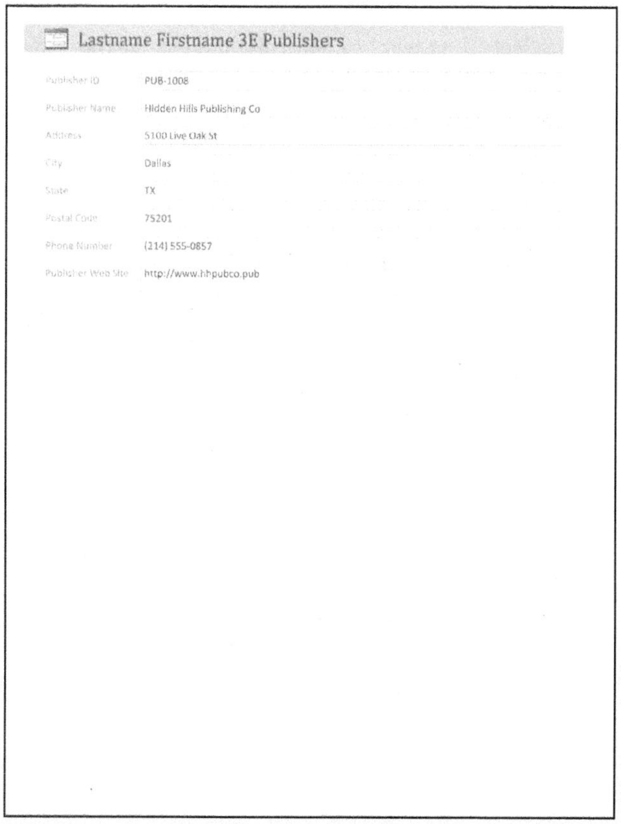

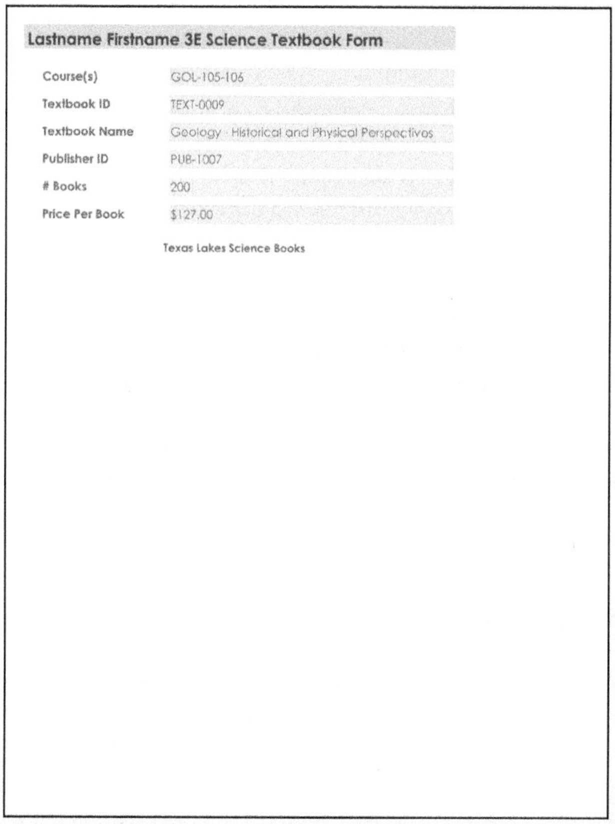

FIGURE 3.51

(Project 3E Textbook Publishers continues on the next page)

CONTENT-BASED ASSESSMENTS

Mastering Access Project 3E Textbook Publishers (continued)

1 Start Access. From your student data files, open **a03E_Textbook_Publishers**. Save the database in your **Access Chapter 3** folder as **Lastname_Firstname_3E_Textbook_Publishers** and then enable the content. In the **Navigation Pane**, **Rename** each table by adding **Lastname Firstname** to the beginning of the table name. Increase the width of the **Navigation Pane** so that all object names display fully. View the relationship between the *3E Publishers* table and the *3E Science Textbooks* table; *one* publisher can provide *many* textbooks for the science courses. Save the changes to the layout of the relationships.

2 Based on your **3E Publishers** table, use the **Form** tool to create a form. **Save** the form as **Lastname Firstname 3E Publisher Form** and then switch to **Form** view. Using the form, add a new record to the underlying table as shown in **Table 1**.

3 Display the first record, and click in the **Publisher ID** field. **Find** the record for the **Publisher ID** of **PUB-1006**, and then **Delete** the record. Display the record you entered for **PUB-1008**, and then, as directed, create a paper or electronic printout of only that record, changing the **Column Size Width** in the **Print** dialog box to **7.5 Save** the design changes to your form.

4 Use the **Filter By Form** tool in your **3E Publisher Form** object to create a filter that displays records with a **State** of **CA** or **TX**. After verifying that three records match this criteria, click **Toggle Filter** to display all seven records. **Save** your form, and then **Close** your form.

5 Use the **Form Wizard** to create a form based on your **3E Science Textbooks** table that includes the following fields in the order given: **Course(s)**, **Textbook Name**, **Publisher ID**, **Price Per Book**, and **# Books**. Apply a **Columnar** layout, and name the form **Lastname Firstname 3E Science Textbook Form.**

6 In **Layout** view, apply the **Stacked** layout to all of the controls, and then apply the **Ion Boardroom** theme to this form only. For the title of the form, change the **Font Size** to **16**, apply **Bold**, and then change the **Font Color** to **Dark Purple, Text 2**—under **Theme Colors**, in the fourth column, the first color. **Save** the design changes to the form.

7 From the **Field List** pane, add the **Textbook ID** field to the form directly above the **Textbook Name** field. Move the **# Books** controls directly above the **Price Per Book** controls. **Close** the **Field List** pane. Display Record 9—this record's textbook name is the longest entry of all records. Click the **Textbook Name text box control**, set the **Width** property to **4** and then **Save** the design changes to your form.

8 Select all six **text box controls**, and change the **Background Color** to **Orange, Accent 4, Lighter 80%**—under **Theme Colors**, in the eighth column, the second color. Select all six **label controls**, and change the **Font Color** to **Orange, Accent 4, Darker 50%**—under **Theme Colors**, in the eighth column, the last color. Apply **Bold** to the **label controls**. With the **label controls** still selected, set the **Width** property to **1.75** and then select all of the **label controls** and all of the **text box controls**. Change the **Font Size** to **12**, set the **Height** property to **0.25** and then **Save** the design changes to your form.

9 In **Design** view, set the **Form Footer** section **Height** property to **0.5** Add a **Label control** to the **Form Footer** section that displays **Texas Lakes Science Books** For this **label control**, change the **Font Color** to **Orange, Accent 4, Darker 50%**—under **Theme Colors**, in the eighth column, the last color—and then apply **Bold**. For this **label control**, set the **Width** property to **2.2** Set the **Top** property to **0.1** and then set the **Left** property to **1.95**

TABLE 1

Publisher ID	Publisher Name	Address	City	State	Postal Code	Phone Number	Publisher Web Site
PUB-1008	**Hidden Hills Publishing Co**	**5100 Live Oak St**	**Dallas**	**TX**	**75201**	**(214) 555-0857**	**http://www.hhpubco.pub**

(Return to Step 3)

(Project 3E Textbook Publishers continues on the next page)

CONTENT-BASED ASSESSMENTS

Mastering Access Project 3E Textbook Publishers (continued)

10 **Close** the **Property Sheet**, **Save** your form, and then switch to **Form** view. **Find** the record for the **Textbook ID** of **TEXT-0009**, and then, as directed, create a paper or electronic printout of only this record. Because you changed the field widths, you do not need to change the Column Size Width in the **Print** dialog box.

11 **Close** all open objects, and then **Open** the **Navigation Pane**. If necessary, increase the width of the pane so that all object names display fully. **Close** Access. As directed by your instructor, submit your database and the paper or electronic printouts of the two forms that are the results of this project. Specifically, in this project, using your own name, you created the following database and printouts or electronic printouts:

1. Lastname_Firstname_3E_Textbook_Publishers	Database file
2. Lastname Firstname 3E Publisher Form	Form (printout or electronic printout - Record 7)
3. Lastname Firstname 3E Science Textbook Form	Form (printout or electronic printout - Record 9)

END | You have completed Project 3E

CONTENT-BASED ASSESSMENTS

MyITLab® grader

Mastering Access | Project 3F Degrees and Students

Apply 3B skills from these Objectives:

5 Create a Report by Using the Report Tool and Modify the Report in Layout View
6 Create a Report by Using the Report Wizard
7 Modify the Design of a Report
8 Keep Grouped Data Together in a Printed Report

In the following Mastering Access project, you will assist Tom Catogrides, the registrar, in using his database to track degrees and grade point averages for honor students in the health professions program in preparation for graduation. Your completed database objects will look similar to Figure 3.52.

PROJECT FILES

For Project 3F, you will need the following file:

a03F_Degrees_Students

You will save your database as:

Lastname_Firstname_3F_Degrees_Students

PROJECT RESULTS

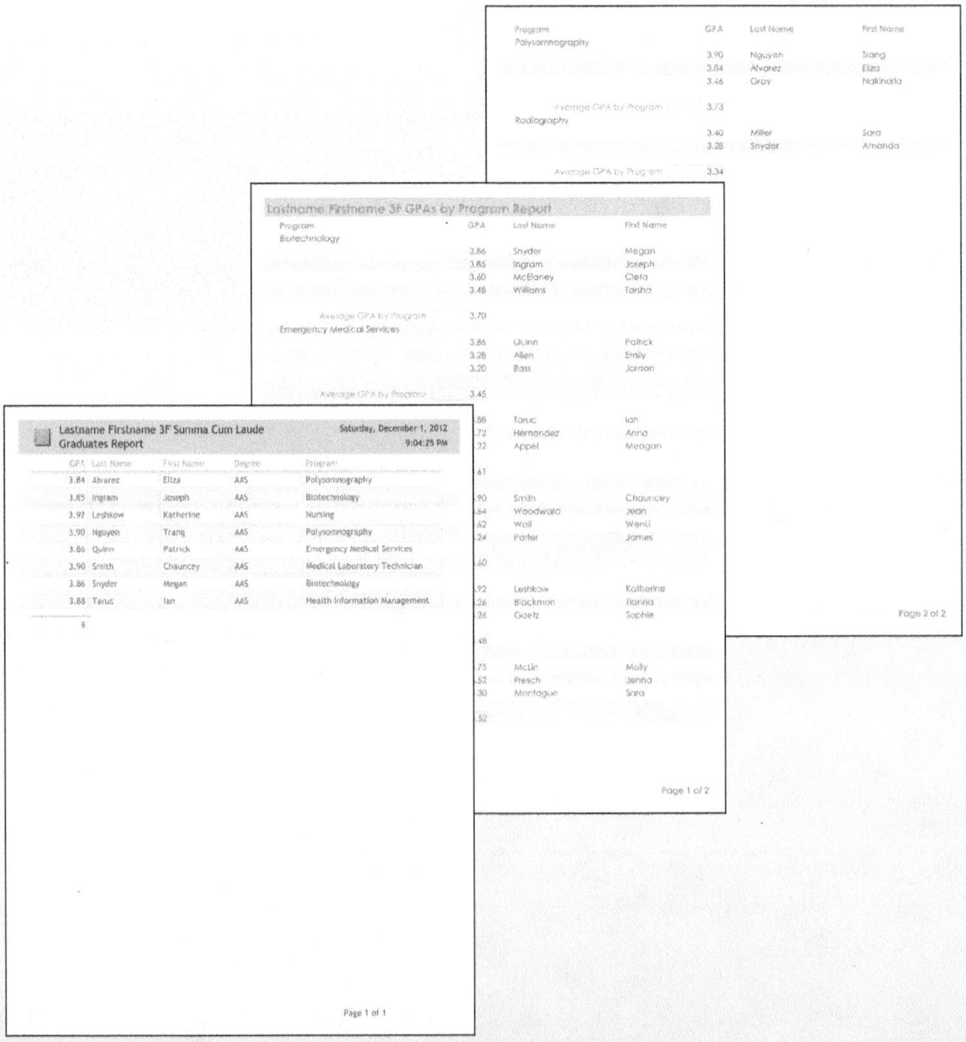

FIGURE 3.52

(Project 3F Degrees and Students continues on the next page)

1 Start Access. From your student data files, open **a03F_Degrees_Students**. **Save** the database in your **Access Chapter 3** folder as **Lastname_Firstname_3F_Degrees_Students** and then enable the content. In the **Navigation Pane**, **Rename** the two tables and two queries by adding **Lastname Firstname** to the beginning of each object name, and then increase the width of the **Navigation Pane** so that all object names display fully. View the relationship that is established between the *3F Degrees* tables and the *3F Students* table—*one* type of degree can be awarded to *many* students. Save the changes to the layout of the relationships. **Run** each query to display the query results, apply **Best Fit**, and then **Save** each query.

Open each query in **Design** view to examine the design grid. The *3F Summa Cum Laude Graduates Query* answers the question, *What is the GPA, student ID, last name, first name, degree, and program for students graduating with a grade point average of 3.8 or higher, in descending order by GPA?* The *3F GPAs by Degree Program Query* answers the question, *What is the program, last name, first name, and GPA for all students, in ascending order by the Last Name field within the Program field?* **Close All** objects.

Based on your **3F Summa Cum Laude Graduates Query** object, use the **Report** tool to create a report. Apply the **Facet** theme to only this report. Delete the **Student ID** field from the report. For the **Last Name**, **First Name**, and **Degree text box controls**, set the **Width** property to **1.25** and then **Sort** the **Last Name** field in **Ascending** order. For the **Program text box controls**, set the **Width** property to **2.5**

At the bottom of the report, for the **calculated control**, which displays *8*, set the **Height** to **0.25** and then for the **page number control**, set the **Left** property to **5** For the title of the report, set the **Font Size** to **14** and change the word *Query* to **Report** For the **GPA** field, set the **Left** property to **0.25** to approximately center the fields within the margins of the report. **Save** the report as **Lastname Firstname 3F Summa Cum Laude Graduates Report** and then create a paper or electronic printout as directed. **Close Print Preview**, **Close** the **Property Sheet**, and then **Close** the report.

2 Use the **Report Wizard** to create a report based on your **3F GPAs by Degree Program Query** object that includes the following fields in the order given: **Program**, **GPA**, **Last Name**, and **First Name**. View your data **by 3F Degrees** and do not add any other grouping to the report. Sort first in **Descending** order by **GPA**, and second in **Ascending** order by **Last Name**. Summarize the report by averaging the **GPA** field. Be sure the layout is **Stepped** and the orientation is **Portrait**. For the report title, type **Lastname Firstname 3F GPAs by Program Report** and then switch to **Layout** view.

3 Apply the **Wisp** theme to only this report. For the report title, change the **Font Size** to **16**, and then apply **Bold**. Delete the controls that begin with **Summary for 'Program'**. Under **Program**, for the **text box controls**, set the **Width** property to **2.75** Change the text in the **Avg label control** to **Average GPA by Program** At the top of the report, select the four **label controls** that display the field names, and then apply **Bold**. Select the **GPA label control**, the **GPA text box controls**, and the **calculated controls** for the average GPA, and then set the **Width** property to **1** and the **Left** property to **3** **Close** the **Property Sheet**. Display the report in **Design** view. Under **Program Header**, click the **Program text box control**, hold down Shift, and under **Program Footer**, click the **Average GPA by Program label control**. **Align** the controls on the **Right**, and then **Save** the design changes to your report.

4 Switch to **Print Preview**, **Zoom** to display **Two Pages** of the report, and examine how the groupings break across the pages. Switch to **Layout** view, display the **Group, Sort, and Total** pane, select **keep whole group together on one page**, and then close the **Group, Sort, and Total** pane. Switch to **Print Preview**, and notice that the groupings are not split between pages. **Save** the report, and then create a paper or electronic printout as directed—two pages result.

(Project 3F Degrees and Students continues on the next page)

CONTENT-BASED ASSESSMENTS

Mastering Access | Project 3F Degrees and Students (continued)

5 **Close Print Preview**, and then **Close** the report. **Open** the **Navigation Pane**, and, if necessary, increase the width of the pane so that all object names display fully. On the right side of the title bar, click **Close** to close the database and to exit Access. As directed by your instructor, submit your database and the paper or electronic printouts of the two reports—one report is two pages—that are the results of this project. Specifically, in this project, using your own name, you created the following database and printouts or electronic printouts:

1. Lastname_Firstname_3F_Degrees_Students	Database file
2. Lastname Firstname 3F Summa Cum Laude Graduates Report	Report (printout or electronic printout)
3. Lastname Firstname 3F GPAs by Program Report	Report (printout or electronic printout - two pages)

END | You have completed Project 3F

CONTENT-BASED ASSESSMENTS

Mastering Access Project 3G Career Books

MyITLab® grader

Apply 3A and 3B skills from these Objectives:

1 Create and Use a Form to Add and Delete Records
2 Filter Records
3 Create a Form by Using the Form Wizard
4 Modify a Form in Layout View and in Design View
5 Create a Report by Using the Report Tool and Modify the Report in Layout View
6 Create a Report by Using the Report Wizard
7 Modify the Design of a Report
8 Keep Grouped Data Together in a Printed Report

In the following Mastering Access project, you will assist Rebecca Hennelly, head librarian at the Southwest Campus of Texas Lakes Community College, in using her database to track publishers and book titles that assist students in finding employment. Your completed forms and report will look similar to Figure 3.53.

PROJECT FILES

For Project 3G, you will need the following file:

a03G_Career_Books

You will save your database as:

Lastname_Firstname_3G_Career_Books

PROJECT RESULTS

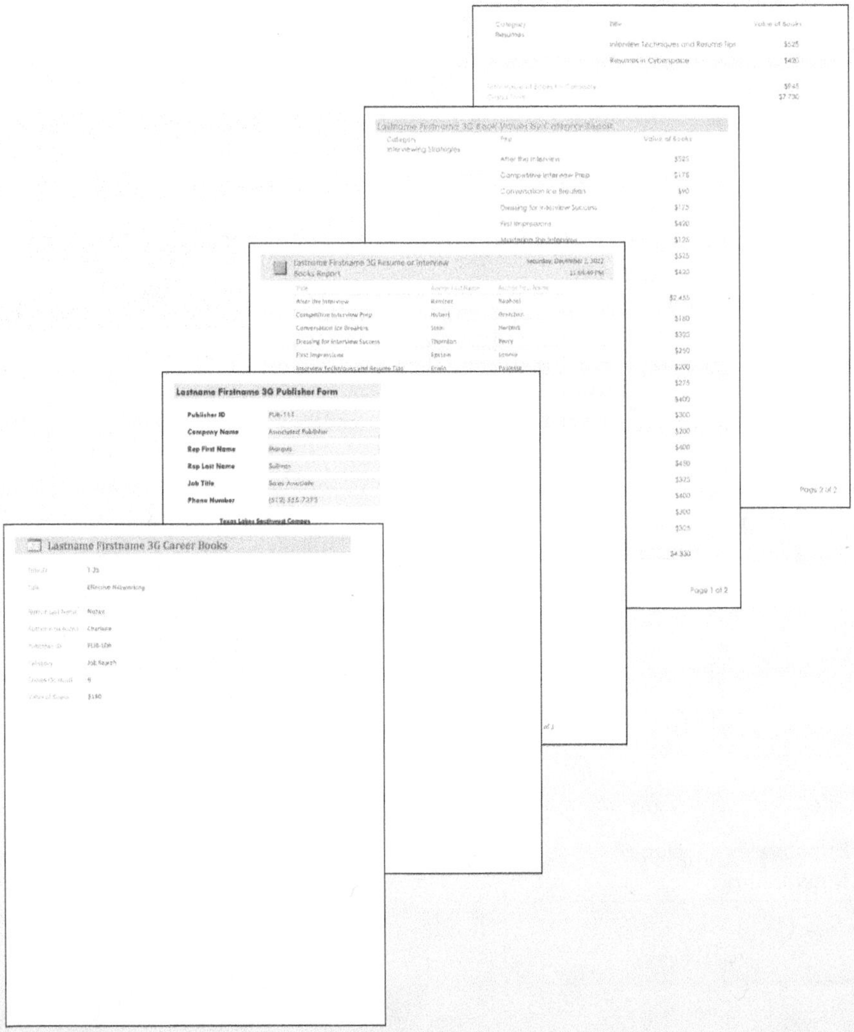

FIGURE 3.53

(Project 3G Career Books continues on the next page)

CONTENT-BASED ASSESSMENTS

Mastering Access Project 3G Career Books (continued)

1 Start Access. From your student data files, open **a03G_Career_Books**. Save the database in your **Access Chapter 3** folder as **Lastname_Firstname_3G_Career_Books** and then enable the content. In the **Navigation Pane, Rename** the two tables and one query by adding **Lastname Firstname** to the beginning of each object name. Increase the width of the **Navigation Pane** so that all object names display fully. View the relationship that is established between the *3G Publishers* tables and the *3G Career Books* table—*one* publisher can publish *many* career books. Save the changes to the layout of the relationships.

Open the **3G Resume or Interview Books Query**, apply **Best Fit**, and then **Save** the query. Switch the query to **Design** view, examine the design of the query, and then **Close** the query object.

2 Based on your **3G Career Books** table, use the **Form** tool to create a form. **Save** the form as **Lastname Firstname 3G Career Book Form** and then switch to **Form** view. Using the form, add a new record to the underlying table as shown in **Table 1**.

3 Display the first record, and click in the **Title ID** field. **Find** the record for the **Title ID** of **T-19**, and then **Delete** the record. Display the record you entered for **T-25**, and then, as directed, create a paper or electronic printout of only that record, changing the **Column Size Width** in the **Print** dialog box to **7.5 Save** the design changes to your form.

4 Use the **Filter By Form** tool in your **3G Career Book Form** object to create a filter that displays records with a **Category** of **Interviewing Strategies** or **Resumes**. After verifying that 10 records match this criteria, click **Toggle Filter** to display all 24 records. **Save** the form, and then **Close** the form.

5 Use the **Form Wizard** to create a form based on your **3G Publishers** table that includes the following fields in the order given: **Company Name, Rep Last Name, Rep First Name, Job Title**, and **Phone Number**. Apply a **Columnar** layout, and name the form **Lastname Firstname 3G Publisher Form**

6 In **Layout** view, apply the **Stacked** layout to all of the controls, and then apply the **Integral** theme to this form only. For the title of the form, change the **Font Size** to **16**, apply **Bold**, and then change the **Font Color** to **Dark Teal, Text 2, Darker 50%**—under **Theme Colors**, in the fourth column, the last color. **Save** the design changes to the form.

7 From the **Field List** pane, add the **Publisher ID** field to the form directly above the **Company Name** field. **Close** the **Field List** pane. Move the **Rep First Name** controls directly above the **Rep Last Name** controls. Click the **Job Title text box control**, set the **Width** property to **2.5** and then **Save** the design changes to your form.

8 Select all six **text box controls**, and change the **Background Color** to **Turquoise, Accent 1, Lighter 80%**—under **Theme Colors**, in the fifth column, the second color. Select all six **label controls**, and change the **Font Color** to **Dark Teal, Text 2, Darker 50%**—under **Theme Colors**, in the fourth column, the last color. Apply **Bold** to the **label controls**. With the **label controls** still selected, set the **Width** property to **1.75** and then select all of the **label controls** and all of the **text box controls**. Change the **Font Size** to **12**, set the **Height** property to **0.25** and then **Save** the design changes to your form.

TABLE 1

Title ID	Title	Author Last Name	Author First Name	Publisher ID	Category	Copies On Hand	Value of Books
T-25	**Effective Networking**	**Nunez**	**Charlene**	**PUB-109**	**Job Search**	**6**	**180**

(Return to Step 3)

(Project 3G Career Books continues on the next page)

CONTENT-BASED ASSESSMENTS

Mastering Access Project 3G Career Books (continued)

9 In **Design** view, set the **Form Footer** section **Height** property to **0.5** Add a **Label** control to the **Form Footer** section that displays **Texas Lakes Southwest Campus** For this **label control**, change the **Font Color** to **Dark Teal, Text 2, Darker 50%**—under **Theme Colors**, in the fourth column, the last color —and then apply **Bold**. For this **label control**, set the **Width** property to **2.2** Set the **Top** property to **0.1** and then set the **Left** property to **1** **Close** the **Property Sheet**, **Save** your form, and then switch to **Form** view. Using the form, add a new record to the underlying table as shown in **Table 2**.

10 Display the record that you just created, and then, as directed, create a paper or electronic printout of only this record. Because you changed the field widths, you do not need to change the Column Size Width in the **Print** dialog box. **Close** the form.

11 Based on your **3G Resume or Interview Books Query** object, use the **Report** tool to create a report. Apply the **Retrospect** theme to only this report. Delete the following fields from the report: **Publisher ID**, **Category**, and **Company Name**. For the **Title text box controls**, set the **Width** property to **3** and then **Sort** the **Title** field in **Ascending** order. For the **Author Last Name text box controls** and the **Author First Name text box controls**, set the **Width** property to **1.5**

12 Click the **Title** field name, and then add a calculated control that counts the number of records. At the bottom of the report, for the **calculated control**, which displays *10*, set the **Height** to **0.25** and then for the **page number control**, set the **Left** property to **5** For the title of the report, set the **Font Size** to **14** and change the word *Query* to **Report** Click the **Title** field name, and then set the **Left** property to **0.75** to move all of the controls to the right. **Save** the report as **Lastname Firstname 3G Resume or Interview Books Report** and then create a paper or electronic printout as directed. **Close Print Preview**, **Close** the **Property Sheet**, and then **Close** the report.

13 Use the **Report Wizard** to create a report based on your **3G Career Books** table that includes the following fields in the order given: **Category**, **Title**, and **Value of Books**. Group your data by **Category**, sort in **Ascending** order by **Title**, and then summarize the report by summing the **Value of Books** field. Be sure the layout is **Stepped** and the orientation is **Portrait**. For the report title, type **Lastname Firstname 3G Book Values by Category Report** and then switch to **Layout** view.

14 Apply the **Ion Boardroom** theme to only this report. For the report title, change the **Font Size** to **14**, and then apply **Bold**. Delete the controls that begin with **Summary for 'Category'**. Select the **Category**, **Title**, and **Value of Books label controls**, and then apply **Bold**. Under **Title**, for the **text box controls**, set the **Width** property to **3.5** For the **Value of Books label control**, set the **Left** property to **6** and then **Save** the design changes to your report.

15 At the bottom of the report in the last column, select the following three controls: **text box control** that displays *$420*, **calculated control** that displays *$945*, and the **calculated control** that displays *7,730*. Set the **Width** property to **1.25** and the **Left** property to **6** For the **Grand Total label control**, set the **Width** property to **1** and then change the text in the **Sum label control** to **Total Value of Books by Category** Click any **Title text box control**, set the **Height** property to **0.35** and then **Save** your report.

16 **Close** the **Property Sheet**, and then display your report in **Design** view. Under **Category Footer**, click the **label control** that displays *Total Value of Books by Category*, hold down Shift, and then under **Report Footer**, click the **Grand Total label control. Align** the controls on the **Left**, and then **Save** the design changes to your report.

TABLE 2

Publisher ID	Company Name	Rep First Name	Rep Last Name	Job Title	Phone Number
PUB-111	**Associated Publishers**	**Marquis**	**Sullivan**	**Sales Associate**	**(512) 555-7373**

(Return to Step 10)

(Project 3G Career Books continues on the next page)

CONTENT-BASED ASSESSMENTS

Mastering Access | Project 3G Career Books (continued)

17 Switch to **Print Preview**, **Zoom** to display **Two Pages** of the report, and examine how the groupings break across the pages. Switch to **Layout** view, display the **Group, Sort, and Total** pane, select **keep whole group together on one page**, and then close the **Group, Sort, and Total** pane. Switch to **Print Preview**, and notice that the groupings are no longer split between pages. **Save** the report, and then create a paper or electronic printout as directed—two pages result.

18 **Close Print Preview**, and then **Close** the report. **Open** the **Navigation Pane**, and, if necessary, increase the width of the pane so that all object names display fully. On the right side of the title bar, click **Close** to close the database and to exit Access. As directed by your instructor, submit your database and the paper or electronic printouts of the two forms and two reports—one report is two pages—that are the results of this project. Specifically, in this project, using your own name, you created the following database and printouts or electronic printouts:

1. Lastname_Firstname_3G_Career_Books	Database file
2. Lastname Firstname 3G Career Book Form	Form (printout or electronic printout - Record 24)
3. Lastname Firstname 3G Publisher Form	Form (printout or electronic printout - Record 12)
4. Lastname Firstname 3G Resume or Interview Books Report	Report (printout or electronic printout)
5. Lastname Firstname 3G Book Values by Category Report	Report (printout or electronic printout - two pages)

END | You have completed Project 3G

Apply a combination of the 3A and 3B skills.

GO! Fix It — Project 3H Resume Workshops — Online

GO! Make It — Project 3I Study Abroad — Online

GO! Solve It — Project 3J Job Offers — Online

GO! Solve It — Project 3K Financial Aid

PROJECT FILES

For Project 3K, you will need the following file:

a03K_Financial_Aid

You will save your database as:

Lastname_Firstname_3K_Financial_Aid

Start Access, navigate to your student data files, open a03K_Financial_Aid, and then save the database in your **Access Chapter 3** folder as **Lastname_Firstname_3K_Financial_Aid** Using your own name, add **Lastname Firstname** to the beginning of both table names and the query name. Sivia Long, the financial aid director, would like you to create an attractive form and a report for this database, using the following guidelines:

- The form will be used to update student records in the 3K FA Students table. Be sure that the Last Name field displays above the First Name field. After the form is created, enter a new record using your own information with a Student ID of **9091246** and Financial Aid ID of **FA-07** and a Home Phone of **(512) 555-9876** and a College Email of **ns246@tlcc.edu** Create a filter that when toggled on displays the records for those students whose last names begin with the letter *S*. Add a footer to the form that displays **Texas Lakes Community College Financial Aid** Save the form as **Lastname Firstname 3K FA Student Update Form** and then create a paper or electronic printout of your record only.
- The report should use the query and list the Award Name, the Student ID, and the Award Amount for financial aid offered to students, grouped by the Award Name field, and sorted in ascending order by the Student ID field. Include a total for the Award Amount field, save the report as **Lastname Firstname 3K FA Amount by Award Report** and be sure the groupings do not break across pages when the report is printed. Create a paper or electronic printout as directed—multiple pages result.

Open the Navigation Pane, be sure that all object names display fully, and then close Access. As directed, submit your database and the paper or electronic printout of the form and report—the report is multiple pages—that are the results of this project. Specifically, in this project, using your own name, you created the following database and printouts or electronic printouts:

1. Lastname_Firstname_3K_Financial_Aid	Database file
2. Lastname Firstname 3K FA Student Update Form	Form (printout or electronic printout - Record 35)
3. Lastname Firstname 3K FA Amount by Award Report	Report (printout or electronic printout - multiple pages)

(Project 3K Financial Aid continues on the next page)

CONTENT-BASED ASSESSMENTS

GO! Solve It Project 3K Financial Aid (continued)

Performance Level

Performance Criteria	Exemplary	Proficient	Developing
Create 3K FA Student Update Form	Form created with correct fields, new record, footer, and filter in an attractive format.	Form created with no more than two missing elements.	Form created with more than two missing elements.
Create 3K FA Amount by Award Report	Report created with correct fields, grouped, sorted, and summarized correctly, with groupings kept together in an attractive format.	Report created with no more than two missing elements.	Report created with more than two missing elements.

END | You have completed Project 3K

OUTCOMES-BASED ASSESSMENTS

RUBRIC

The following outcomes-based assessments are *open-ended assessments*. That is, there is no specific correct result; your result will depend on your approach to the information provided. Make *Professional Quality* your goal. Use the following scoring rubric to guide you in *how* to approach the problem and then to evaluate *how well* your approach solves the problem.

The *criteria*—Software Mastery, Content, Format & Layout, and Process—represent the knowledge and skills you have gained that you can apply to solving the problem. The *levels of performance*—Professional Quality, Approaching Professional Quality, or Needs Quality Improvements—help you and your instructor evaluate your result.

	Your completed project is of Professional Quality if you:	Your completed project is Approaching Professional Quality if you:	Your completed project Needs Quality Improvements if you:
1-Software Mastery	Choose and apply the most appropriate skills, tools, and features and identify efficient methods to solve the problem.	Choose and apply some appropriate skills, tools, and features, but not in the most efficient manner.	Choose inappropriate skills, tools, or features, or are inefficient in solving the problem.
2-Content	Construct a solution that is clear and well organized, contains content that is accurate, appropriate to the audience and purpose, and is complete. Provide a solution that contains no errors in spelling, grammar, or style.	Construct a solution in which some components are unclear, poorly organized, inconsistent, or incomplete. Misjudge the needs of the audience. Have some errors in spelling, grammar, or style, but the errors do not detract from comprehension.	Construct a solution that is unclear, incomplete, or poorly organized; contains some inaccurate or inappropriate content; and contains many errors in spelling, grammar, or style. Do not solve the problem.
3-Format & Layout	Format and arrange all elements to communicate information and ideas, clarify function, illustrate relationships, and indicate relative importance.	Apply appropriate format and layout features to some elements, but not others. Overuse features, causing minor distraction.	Apply format and layout that does not communicate information or ideas clearly. Do not use format and layout features to clarify function, illustrate relationships, or indicate relative importance. Use available features excessively, causing distraction.
4-Process	Use an organized approach that integrates planning, development, self-assessment, revision, and reflection.	Demonstrate an organized approach in some areas, but not others; or, use an insufficient process of organization throughout.	Do not use an organized approach to solve the problem.

OUTCOMES-BASED ASSESSMENTS

Apply a combination of the 3A and 3B skills.

GO! Think Project 3L Food Services

PROJECT FILES

For Project 3L, you will need the following file:

a03L_Food_Services

You will save your database as:

Lastname_Firstname_3L_Food_Services

Start Access, navigate to your student data files, open a03L_Food_Services, save the database in your **Access Chapter 3** folder as **Lastname_Firstname_3L_Food_Services** and then enable the content. Using your own name, add **Lastname Firstname** to the beginning of both table names. Luciano Gonzalez, the hospitality director, would like you to create to create an attractive form and a report to assist him with the staff scheduling of food services for a two-day student orientation workshop using the following guidelines:

- The form will be used to update records in the 3L Staff table. Be sure that the Last Name field displays above the First Name field. After the form is created, enter a new record using your own last name and first name with a Staff ID of **STAFF-1119** and a Phone Number of **(512) 555-0845** and a Title of **Server** Create a filter that when toggled on displays the records for staff with a Title of *Server*. Add a footer to the form that displays **Texas Lakes Community College Hospitality Services** Save the form as **Lastname Firstname 3L Staff Update Form** and then create a paper or electronic printout of your record only.
- The report will be used by Mr. Gonzalez to call staff members when the schedule changes. Add a report footer that displays **Texas Lakes Community College Hospitality Services** and then save the report as **Lastname Firstname 3L Staff Phone List** Create a paper or electronic printout as directed.

Open the Navigation Pane, be sure that all object names display fully, and then close Access. As directed, submit your database and the paper or electronic printout of the form and report that are the results of this project. Specifically, in this project, using your own name, you created the following database and printouts or electronic printouts:

1. Lastname_Firstname_3L_Food_Services	Database file
2. Lastname Firstname 3L Staff Update Form	Form (printout or electronic printout - Record 19)
3. Lastname Firstname 3L Staff Phone List	Report (printout or electronic printout)

END | You have completed Project 3L

GO! Think Project 3M Donor Gifts Online

Build from Scratch

You and GO! Project 3N Personal Inventory Online

Build from Scratch

GO! Cumulative Group Project Project 3O Bell Orchid Hotels Online

Introduction to Microsoft PowerPoint 2013

P
PowerPoint 2013

PowerPoint 2013: Introduction

Video PA

Communication skills are critically important to success in today's business world and when it comes to communicating *your* ideas, presentation is everything! Whether you are planning to deliver your presentation in person or online—to a large audience or to a small group—Microsoft PowerPoint 2013 is a versatile business tool designed to help you create presentations that make a lasting impression. Additionally, collaborating with others to develop a presentation is made easy because you can share the slides you create by using your OneDrive.

New to Microsoft PowerPoint 2013 are a variety of themes that you can apply to a new presentation. Each theme includes several theme variants that coordinate colors, fonts, and effects. The beauty of this approach is that the variations evoke different moods and responses, yet the basic design remains the same. As a result, you can use a similar design within your company to brand your presentations while still changing the colors to make the presentation appropriate to the audience and topic. The best part is that you do not have to determine which colors work well together in the theme you chose. The theme variant does that work for you so that you can concentrate on how best to communicate your message! Focus on creating dynamic, interesting presentations that keep your audience engaged!

Getting Started with Microsoft PowerPoint

GO! to Work Video P1

1

POWERPOINT 2013

PROJECT 1A

OUTCOMES
Creat a company overview presentation.

PROJECT 1B

OUTCOMES
Create a new product announcement presentation.

OBJECTIVES

1. Create a New Presentation
2. Edit a Presentation in Normal View
3. Add Pictures to a Presentation
4. Print and View a Presentation

OBJECTIVES

5. Edit an Existing Presentation
6. Format a Presentation
7. Use Slide Sorter View
8. Apply Slide Transitions

Caleb Foster/Fotolia

In This Chapter

In this chapter you will study presentation skills, which are among the most important skills you will learn. Good presentation skills enhance your communications—written, electronic, and interpersonal. In this technology-enhanced world, communicating ideas clearly and concisely is a critical personal skill. Microsoft PowerPoint 2013 is presentation software with which you create electronic slide presentations. Use PowerPoint to present information to your audience effectively. You can start with a new, blank presentation and add content, pictures, and themes, or you can collaborate with colleagues by inserting slides that have been saved in other presentations.

The projects in this chapter relate to **Kodiak West Travel**, which is a travel agency with offices in Juneau, Anchorage, and Victoria. Kodiak West Travel works closely with local vendors to provide clients with specialized adventure travel itineraries. The company was established in 2001 in Juneau and built a loyal client base that led to the expansion into Anchorage and Victoria. As a full-service travel agency, Kodiak West Travel agents strive to provide their clients with travel opportunities that exceed their expectations. The company works with all major airlines, cruise lines, hotel chains, and vehicle rental companies as well as with small, specialized, boutique hotels.

PROJECT

1A Company Overview

MyITLab®
Project 1A Training

PROJECT ACTIVITIES

In Activities 1.01 through 1.16, you will create the first five slides of a new presentation that Kodiak West Travel tour manager, Ken Dakano, is developing to introduce the tour services that the company offers. Your completed presentation will look similar to Figure 1.1.

PROJECT FILES

For Project 1A, you will need the following files:

New blank PowerPoint presentation
p01A_Glacier
p01A_Bay

You will save your presentation as:

Lastname_Firstname_1A_KWT_Overview

PROJECT RESULTS

Build from Scratch

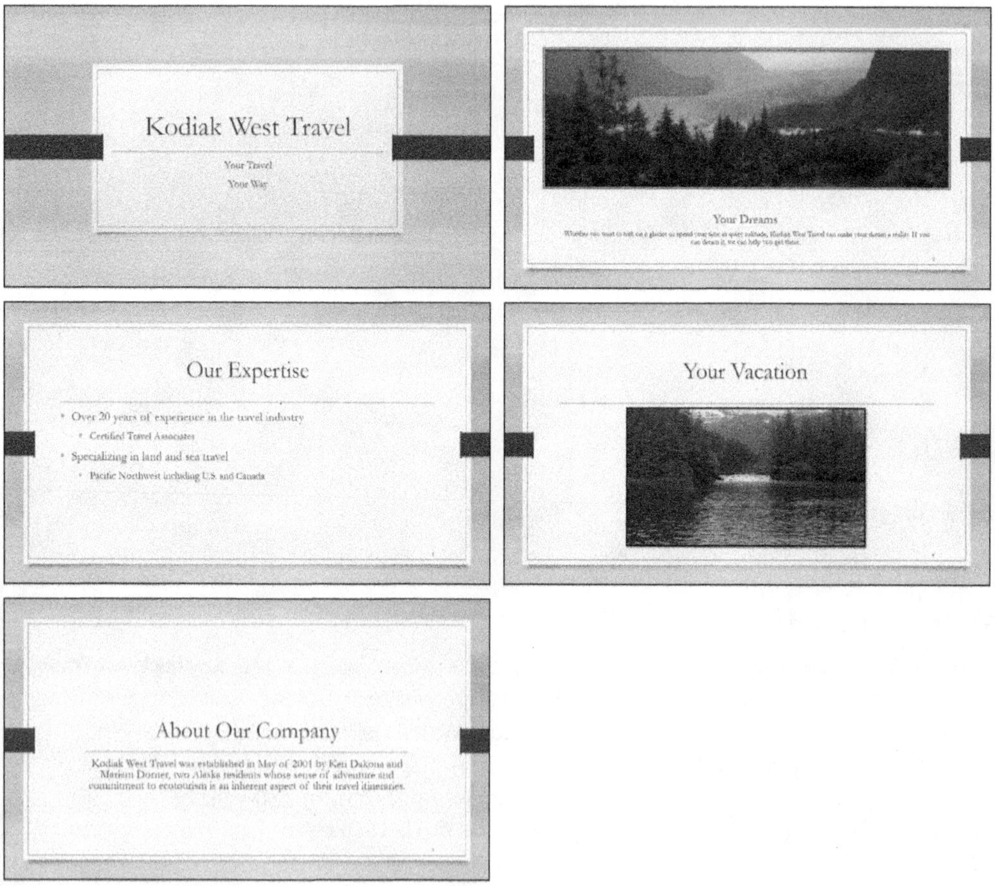

FIGURE 1.1 Project 1A Company Overview

Objective 1 Create a New Presentation

Video P1-1

You can edit and format a blank presentation by adding text, a presentation theme, and pictures. When you start PowerPoint, presentations you have recently opened, if any, display on the left. On the right you can select either a blank presentation or a ***theme***—a set of unified design elements that provides a look for your presentation by applying colors, fonts, and effects.

NOTE **If You Are Using a Touch Screen**

- Tap an item to click it.
- Press and hold for a few seconds to right-click; release when the information or commands displays.
- Touch the screen with two or more fingers and then pinch together to zoom in or stretch your fingers apart to zoom out.
- Slide your finger on the screen to scroll—slide left to scroll right and slide right to scroll left.
- Slide to rearrange—similar to dragging with a mouse.
- Swipe from edge: from right to display charms; from left to expose open apps, snap apps, or close apps; from top or bottom to show commands or close an app.
- Swipe to select—slide an item a short distance with a quick movement—to select an item and bring up commands, if any.

Activity 1.01 Creating a New Presentation and Identifying Parts of the PowerPoint Window

1. Start PowerPoint. On the right, click **Facet** to view a preview of the Facet theme and the color variations associated with this theme. Below the theme preview, click the left and right **More Images** arrows [◄] and [►] to view the manner in which various types of slides in this theme display. To the right of the preview, click each of the color variations. After you have viewed each color, click the original green color.

2. To the right of the preview window, point to the [►] arrow, and then compare your screen with Figure 1.2.

   You can use the left and right arrows to scroll through the available themes.

FIGURE 1.2

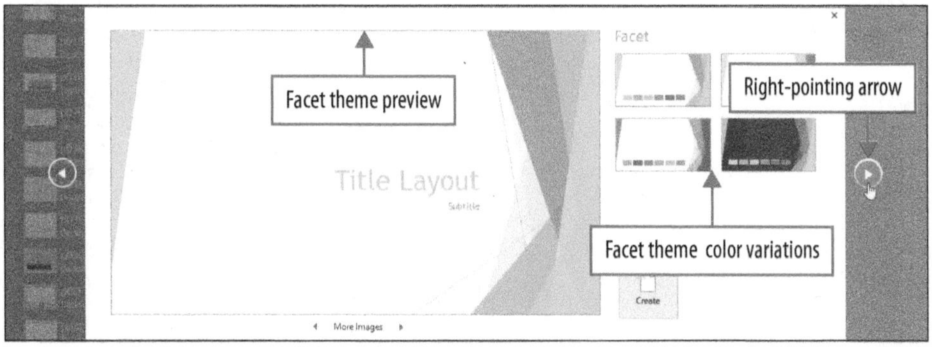

3. Click [►] two times to view the next two available themes. Then, to the left of the preview window, click [◄] two times to return to the **Facet** theme. In the lower right area of the preview window, click **Create** to begin a new presentation using the Facet theme. Compare your screen with Figure 1.3.

   The presentation displays in normal view. ***Normal view*** is the primary editing view in PowerPoint where you write and design your presentations. On the left, a small pane displays miniature images—***thumbnails***—of the slides in your presentation. On the right, the ***Slide pane*** displays a large image of the active slide.

FIGURE 1.3

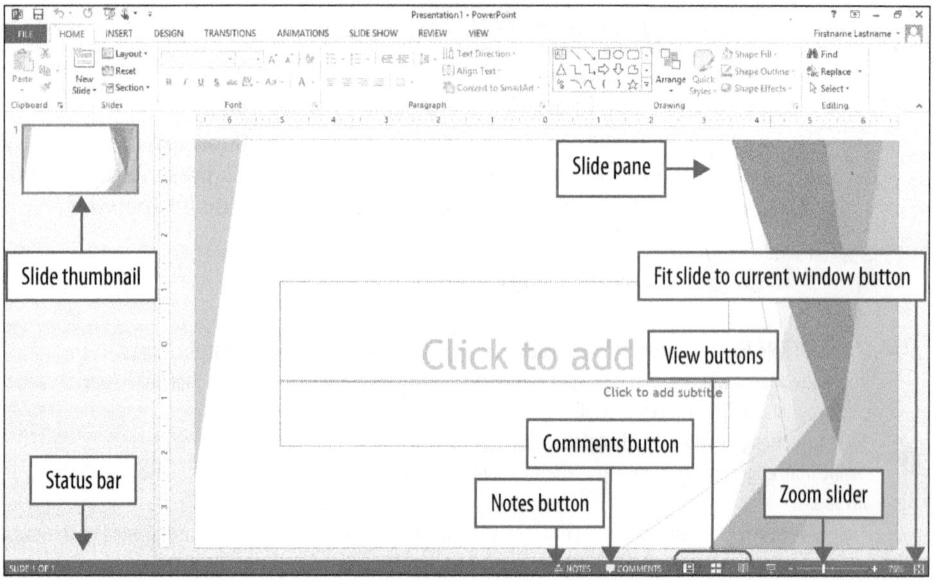

4 Take a moment to study the parts of the PowerPoint window described in the table in Figure 1.4.

FIGURE 1.4

MICROSOFT POWERPOINT SCREEN ELEMENTS	
SCREEN ELEMENT	**DESCRIPTION**
Slide pane	Displays a large image of the active slide.
Slide thumbnails	Miniature images of each slide in the presentation. Clicking a slide thumbnail displays the slide in the Slide pane.
Status bar	Displays, in a horizontal bar at the bottom of the presentation window, the current slide number, number of slides in a presentation, Notes button, Comments button, View buttons, Zoom slider, and Fit slide to current window button; you can customize this area to include additional information.
Notes button	When clicked, displays an area below the Slide pane in which you can type presentation notes.
Comments button	When clicked, displays a Comments pane to the right of the Slide pane, in which reviewers can type comments.
View buttons	Control the look of the presentation window with a set of commands.
Zoom slider	Zooms the slide displayed in the Slide pane, in and out.
Fit slide to current window button	Fits the active slide to the maximum view in the Slide pane.

Activity 1.02 | Entering Presentation Text

When a new presentation is created, PowerPoint displays a new blank presentation with a single slide—a title slide in Normal view. A presentation ***slide***—similar to a page in a document—can contain text, pictures, tables, charts, and other multimedia or graphic objects. The ***title slide*** is most commonly the first slide in a presentation and provides an introduction to the presentation topic.

1 In the **Slide pane**, click in the text *Click to add title*, which is the title placeholder.

A ***placeholder*** is a box on a slide with dotted or dashed borders that holds title and body text or other content such as charts, tables, and pictures. This slide contains two placeholders, one for the title and one for the subtitle.

2 Type **Kodiak West** and then click in the subtitle placeholder. Type **Your Travel** and then press Enter to create a new line in the subtitle placeholder. Type **Your Way** and then compare your screen with Figure 1.5.

FIGURE 1.5

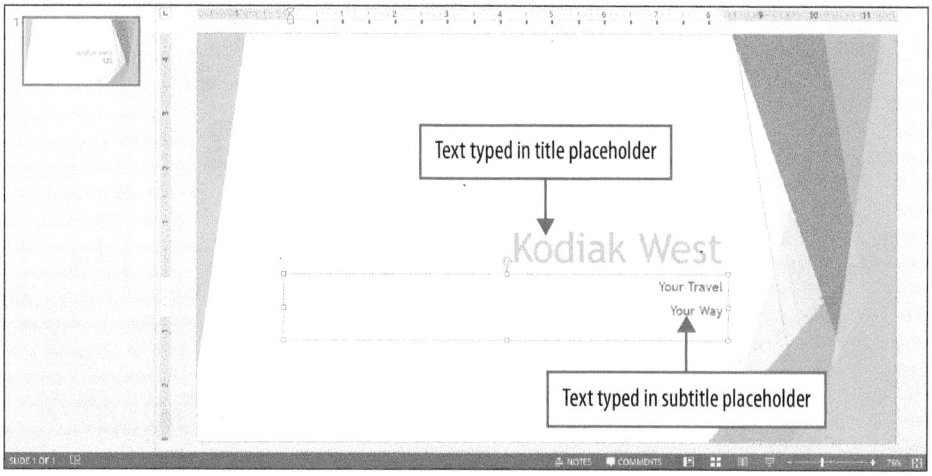

3 On the **Quick Access Toolbar**, click **Save**. Under **Save As**, click **Computer**, and then click **Browse**. Navigate to the location where you are saving your files for this chapter, and then create and open a new folder named **PowerPoint Chapter 1** In the **File name** box, using your own name, replace the existing text with **Lastname_Firstname_1A_KWT_Overview** and then click **Save**.

Activity 1.03 Applying a Presentation Theme

Recall that a theme is a set of unified design elements that provides a look for your presentation by applying colors, fonts, and effects. After you create a presentation, you can change the look of your presentation by applying a different theme.

1 On the ribbon, click the **DESIGN tab**. In the **Themes group**, click **More** to display the **Themes** gallery. Compare your screen with Figure 1.6.

The themes displayed on your system may differ from Figure 1.6.

FIGURE 1.6

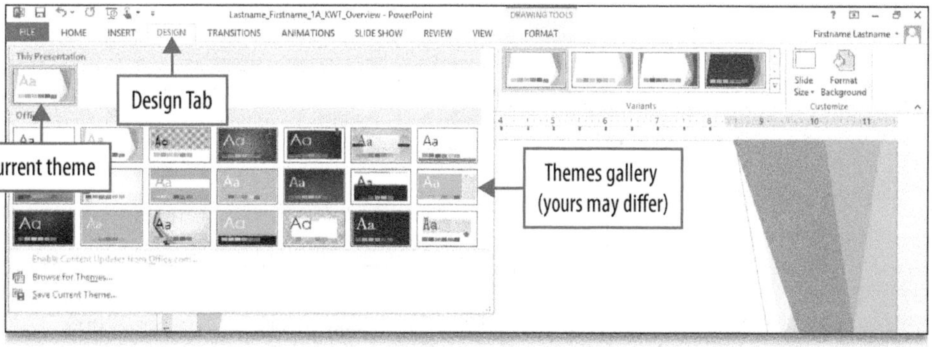

2 Under **Office**, point to several of the themes and notice that a ScreenTip displays the name of each theme and the Live Preview feature displays how each theme would look if applied to your presentation.

The first theme that displays is the Office Theme.

3 Use the ScreenTips to locate the **Organic** theme shown in Figure 1.7.

FIGURE 1.7

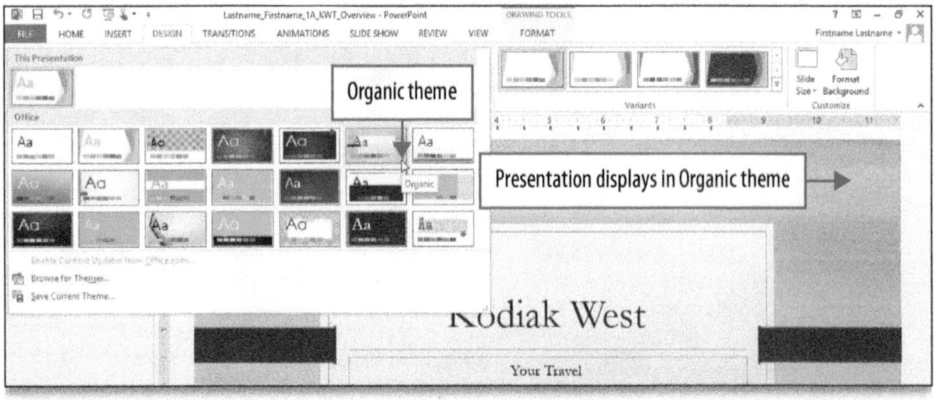

4 Click **Organic** to change the presentation theme, and then **Save** your presentation.

Objective 2 Edit a Presentation in Normal View

Video P1-2

Editing is the process of modifying a presentation by adding and deleting slides or by changing the contents of individual slides.

Activity 1.04 | Inserting a New Slide

To insert a new slide in a presentation, display the slide that will precede the slide that you want to insert.

1 On the **HOME tab**, in the **Slides group**, point to the **New Slide arrow**—the lower part of the New Slide button. Compare your screen with Figure 1.8.

The New Slide button is a ***split button***—a type of button in which clicking the main part of the button performs a command and clicking the arrow opens a menu, list, or gallery. The upper, main part of the New Slide button, when clicked, inserts a slide without displaying any options. The lower part—the New Slide arrow—when clicked, displays a gallery of slide ***layouts***— the arrangement of elements, such as title and subtitle text, lists, pictures, tables, charts, shapes, and movies, on a slide.

FIGURE 1.8

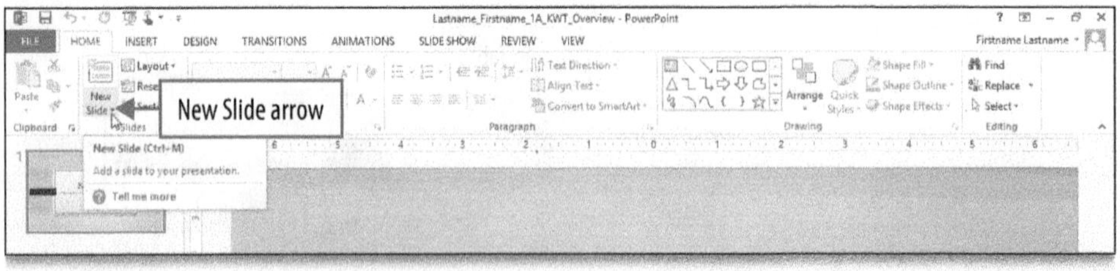

2 In the **Slides group**, click the lower portion of the New Slide button—the **New Slide arrow**—to display the gallery, and then compare your screen with Figure 1.9.

FIGURE 1.9

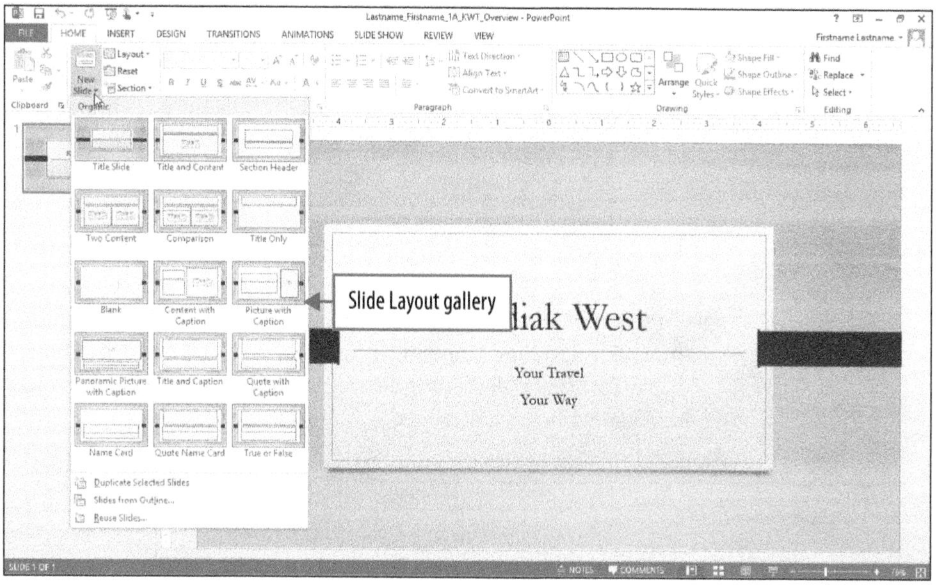

3 In the gallery, in the fourth row, click the first layout—**Panoramic Picture with Caption**—to insert a new slide. Notice that the new blank slide displays in the **Slide pane** and a slide thumbnail displays at the left. Compare your screen with Figure 1.10.

BY TOUCH In the gallery, tap the desired layout to insert a new slide.

FIGURE 1.10

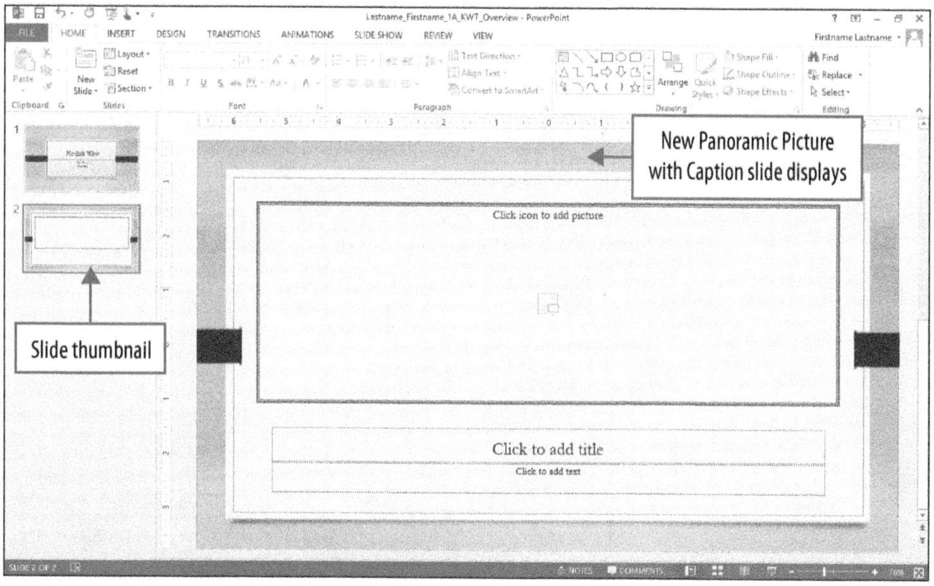

4 On the slide, below the large picture placeholder, click the text *Click to add title*, and then type **Your Dreams**

5 Below the title placeholder, click in the text placeholder. Type **Whether you want to trek on a glacier or spend your time in quiet solitude, Kodiak West Travel can make your dream a reality.** Compare your screen with Figure 1.11.

FIGURE 1.11

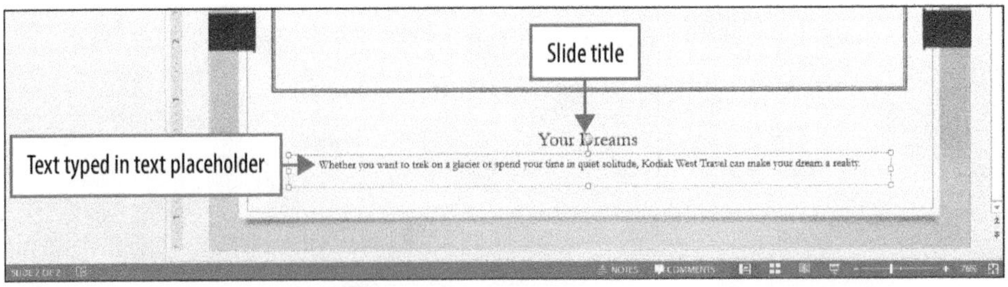

6 On the **HOME tab**, in the **Slides group**, click the **New Slide arrow** to display the gallery, and then click **Title and Content**. In the title placeholder, type **Our Expertise** and then below the title placeholder, click in the content placeholder. Type **Over 20 years of experience in the travel industry**

7 **Save** your presentation.

Activity 1.05 | Increasing and Decreasing List Levels

Text in a PowerPoint presentation can be organized according to ***list levels***. List levels, each represented by a bullet symbol, are similar to outline levels. On a slide, list levels are identified by the bullet style, indentation, and the size of the text. The first level on an individual slide is the title. Increasing the list level of a bullet point increases its indent and results in a smaller text size. Decreasing the list level of a bullet point decreases its indent and results in a larger text size.

1 On **Slide 3**, if necessary, click at the end of the last bullet point after the word *industry*, and then press Enter to insert a new bullet point.

2 Press Tab, and then notice that the bullet is indented. Type **Certified Travel Associates**

By pressing Tab at the beginning of a bullet point, you can increase the list level and indent the bullet point.

3 Press Enter, and then notice that a new bullet point displays at the same level as the previous bullet point.

4 On the **HOME tab**, in the **Paragraph group**, click **Decrease List Level**. Type **Specializing in land and sea travel** and then compare your screen with Figure 1.12.

The indent is removed and the size of the text increases.

FIGURE 1.12

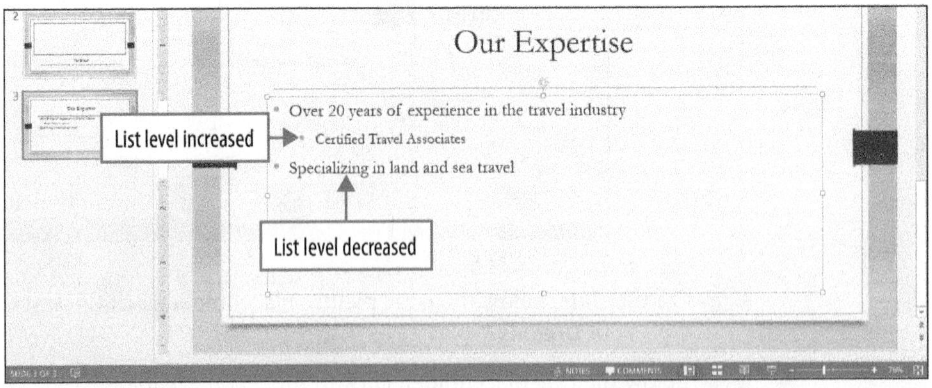

5 Press Enter, and then on the **HOME tab**, click **Increase List Level**. Type **Pacific Northwest including U.S. and Canada**

You can use the Increase List Level button to indent the bullet point.

6 Compare your screen with Figure 1.13, and then **Save** your presentation.

FIGURE 1.13

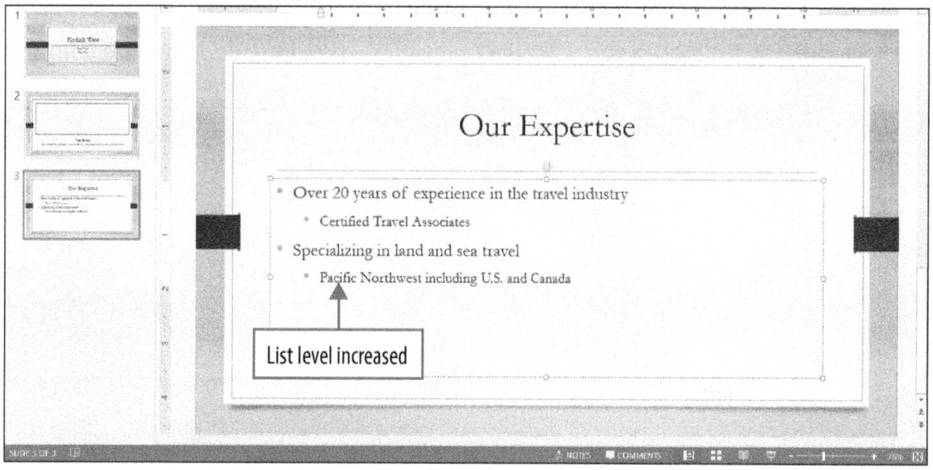

Activity 1.06 Adding Speaker's Notes to a Presentation

The ***Notes pane*** is an area of the Normal view window that displays below the Slide pane with space to type notes regarding the active slide. You can refer to these printouts while making a presentation, thus reminding you of the important points that you want to discuss.

1 With **Slide 3** displayed, in the **Status bar**, click **NOTES**, and then notice that below the Slide pane, the Notes pane displays. Click in the **Notes pane**, and then type **Kodiak West Travel has locations in Juneau, Anchorage, and Victoria.**

2 Compare your screen with Figure 1.14, and then **Save** your presentation.

FIGURE 1.14

Activity 1.07 Displaying and Editing Slides in the Slide Pane

1 At the left side of the PowerPoint window, look at the slide thumbnails, and then notice that the presentation contains three slides. At the right side of the PowerPoint window, in the vertical scroll bar, point to the scroll box, and then hold down the left mouse button to display a ScreenTip indicating the slide number and title.

2 Drag the scroll box up until the ScreenTip displays *Slide: 2 of 3 Your Dreams*. Compare your slide with Figure 1.15, and then release the mouse button to display **Slide 2**.

FIGURE 1.15

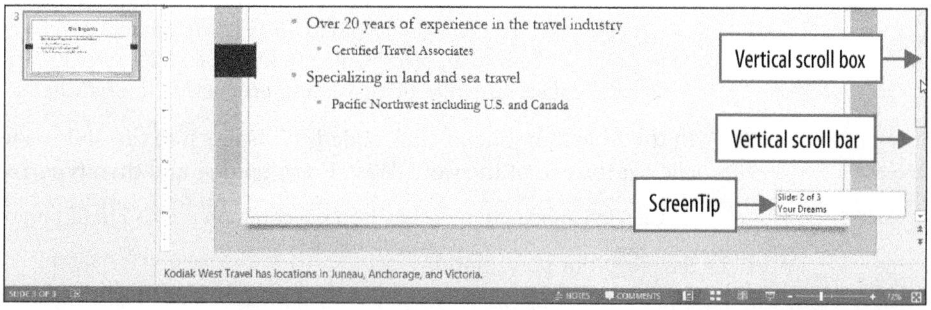

3 At the bottom of the slide, in the content placeholder, click at the end of the sentence, after the period. Press Spacebar, and then type **If you can dream it, we can help you get there.**

4 On the left side of the PowerPoint window, in the slide thumbnails, point to **Slide 3**, and then notice that a ScreenTip displays the slide title. Compare your screen with Figure 1.16.

FIGURE 1.16

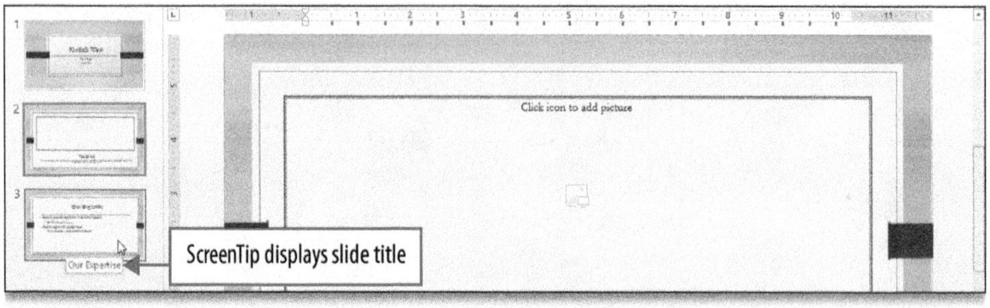

5 Click **Slide 3** to display it in the Slide pane. On the **HOME tab**, in the **Slides group**, click the **New Slide arrow** to display the **Slide Layout** gallery, and then click **Section Header**.

A ***section header*** is a type of slide layout that changes the look and flow of a presentation by providing text placeholders that do not contain bullet points.

6 Click in the title placeholder, and then type **About Our Company**

7 Click in the content placeholder below the title, and then type **Kodiak West Travel was established in May of 2001 by Ken Dakona and Mariam Dorner, two Alaska residents whose sense of adventure and commitment to ecotourism is an inherent aspect of their travel itineraries.** Compare your screen with Figure 1.17.

The placeholder text resizes to fit within the placeholder. The AutoFit Options button displays.

FIGURE 1.17

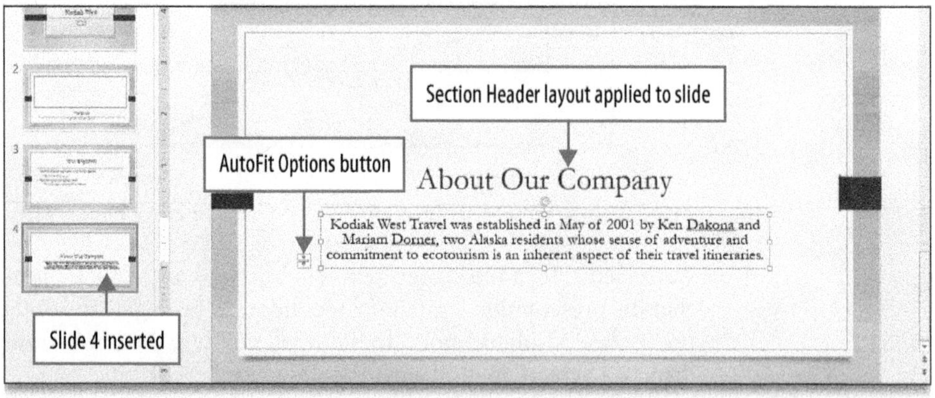

8 Click **AutoFit Options**, and then if necessary, click AutoFit Text to Placeholder.

The *AutoFit Text to Placeholder* option keeps the text contained within the placeholder by reducing the size of the text. The *Stop Fitting Text to This Placeholder* option turns off the AutoFit option so that the text can flow beyond the placeholder border; the text size remains unchanged. You can also choose to split the text between two slides, continue on a new slide, or divide the text into two columns.

9 In the slide thumbnails, click **Slide 1** to display it in the **Slide pane**, and then in the slide title, click at the end of the word *West*. Press Spacebar, and then type **Travel**

Clicking a slide thumbnail is the most common method to display a slide in the Slide pane.

10 **Save** your presentation.

Objective 3 Add Pictures to a Presentation

Video P1-3

Photographic images add impact to a presentation and help the audience visualize your message.

Activity 1.08 Inserting a Picture from a File

Many slide layouts in PowerPoint accommodate digital picture files so that you can easily add pictures you have stored on your system or on a portable storage device.

1. Display **Slide 2**, and then compare your screen with Figure 1.18.

   In the center of the large picture placeholder, the *Pictures* button displays.

FIGURE 1.18

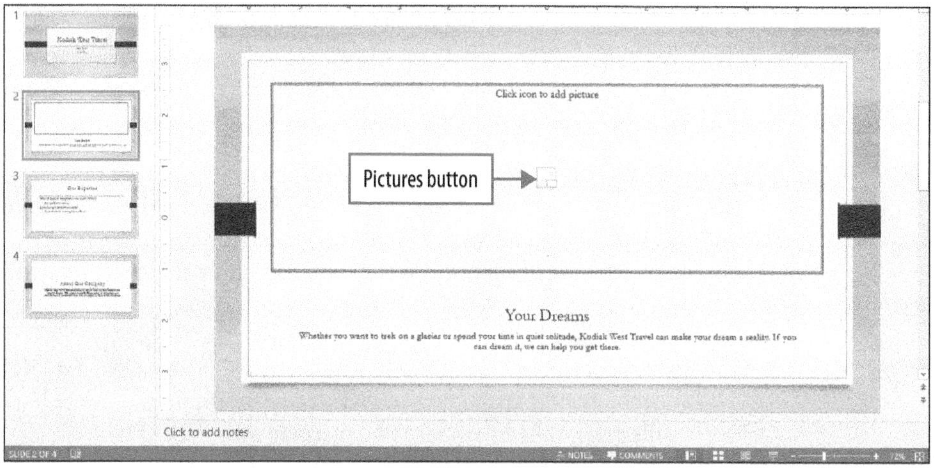

2. In the picture placeholder, click **Pictures** to open the **Insert Picture** dialog box. Navigate to the location in which your student data files are stored, click **p01A_Glacier**, and then click **Insert** to insert the picture in the placeholder. Compare your screen with Figure 1.19.

   Small squares—***sizing handles***—surround the inserted picture and indicate that the picture is selected and can be modified or formatted. The ***rotation handle***—a circular arrow above the picture—provides a way to rotate a selected image. The PICTURE TOOLS are added to the ribbon, providing picture formatting options.

FIGURE 1.19

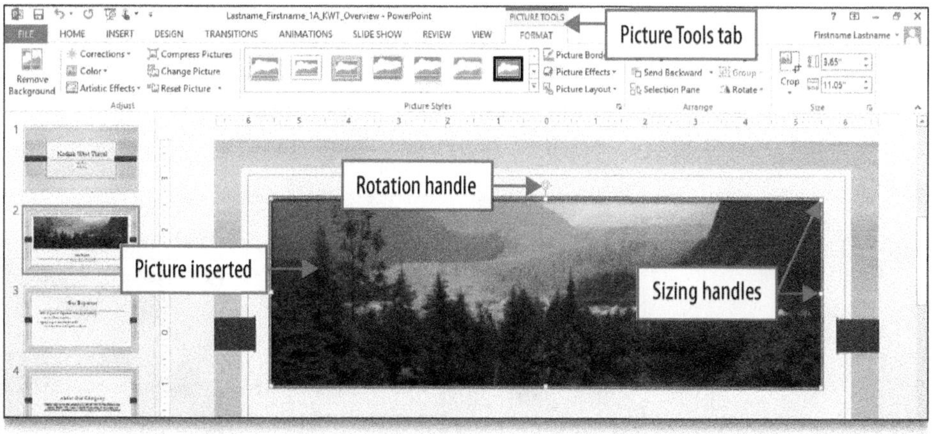

3. Display **Slide 3**. On the **HOME tab**, in the **Slides group**, click the **New Slide arrow**, and then click **Title and Content**. In the title placeholder, type **Your Vacation**

4 In the content placeholder, click **Pictures**. Navigate to your student data files, and then click **p01A_Bay**. Click **Insert**, and then compare your screen with Figure 1.20. **Save** the presentation.

FIGURE 1.20

Activity 1.09 | Applying a Style to a Picture

When a picture is selected, the PICTURE TOOLS display, adding the Format tab to the ribbon. The Format tab provides numerous styles that you can apply to your pictures. A ***style*** is a collection of formatting options that you can apply to a picture, text, or an object.

1 With **Slide 4** displayed, if necessary, click the picture to select it. On the ribbon, notice that the *PICTURE TOOLS* are active and the *FORMAT* tab displays.

2 On the **FORMAT tab**, in the **Picture Styles group**, click **More** to display the **Picture Styles** gallery, and then compare your screen with Figure 1.21.

FIGURE 1.21

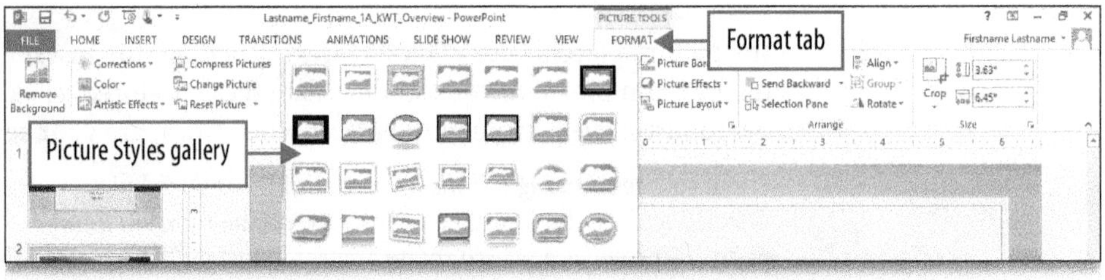

3 In the gallery, point to several of the picture styles to display the ScreenTips and to view the effect on your picture. In the second row, click the second style—**Simple Frame, Black**. Click in a blank area of the slide, compare your screen with Figure 1.22, and then **Save** the presentation.

FIGURE 1.22

Activity 1.10 | Applying and Removing Picture Artistic Effects

Artistic effects are formats applied to images that make pictures resemble sketches or paintings.

1. On **Slide 4**, select the picture. Click the **FORMAT tab**, and then in the **Adjust group**, click **Artistic Effects** to display the **Artistic Effects** gallery. Compare your screen with Figure 1.23.

FIGURE 1.23

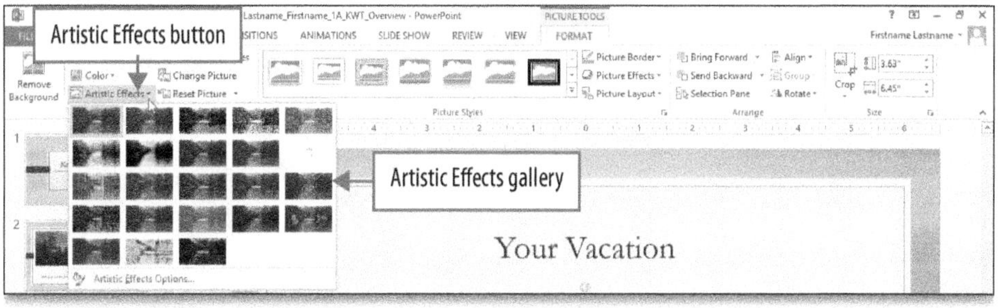

2. In the gallery, point to several of the artistic effects to display the ScreenTips and to have Live Preview display the effect on your picture. Then, in the second row, click the **Glow Diffused** effect.

3. With the picture still selected, on the **FORMAT tab**, in the **Adjust group**, click **Artistic Effects** again to display the gallery. In the first row, click the first effect—**None**—to remove the effect from the picture and restore the previous formatting.

4. **Save** the presentation.

Objective 4 Print and View a Presentation

Video P1-4

There are several print options in PowerPoint. For example, you can print full page images of your slides, presentation handouts to provide your audience with copies of your slides, or Notes pages displaying speaker's notes below an image of the slide.

Activity 1.11 | Viewing a Slide Show

When you view a presentation as an electronic slide show, the entire slide fills the computer screen, and an audience can view your presentation if your computer is connected to a projection system.

1. On the ribbon, click the **SLIDE SHOW tab**. In the **Start Slide Show group**, click **From Beginning**. Compare your screen with Figure 1.24.

   The first slide fills the screen, displaying the presentation as the audience would see it if your computer was connected to a projection system.

ANOTHER WAY Press F5 to start the slide show from the beginning. Or, display the first slide you want to show and click the Slide Show button on the lower right side of the status bar.

FIGURE 1.24

2 Click the left mouse button or press Spacebar to advance to the second slide.

3 Continue to click or press Spacebar until the last slide displays, and then click or press Spacebar one more time to display a ***black slide***—a slide that displays after the last slide in a presentation indicating that the presentation is over.

4 With the black slide displayed, click the left mouse button to exit the slide show and return to the presentation.

Activity 1.12 | Using Presenter View

Presenter View shows the full-screen slide show on one monitor while enabling the presenter to view a preview of the next slide, notes, and a timer on another monitor. Your audience will be able to view only the current slide.

1 On the **SLIDE SHOW tab**, in the **Monitors** group, be sure that the **Use Presenter View** check box is selected. Hold down Alt and press F5. Compare your screen with Figure 1.25.

If you do not have two monitors, you can practice using Presenter View by pressing Alt+F5. Above the upper left corner of the slide, a timer displays. Below the timer, the current slide displays. Below the current slide are slide show option buttons. In the upper right corner, the next slide displays. In the lower right corner, any notes that you typed in the notes pane for the current slide display. Below the notes are buttons that enable you to make the notes smaller or larger. Below the current slide, navigation buttons display.

FIGURE 1.25

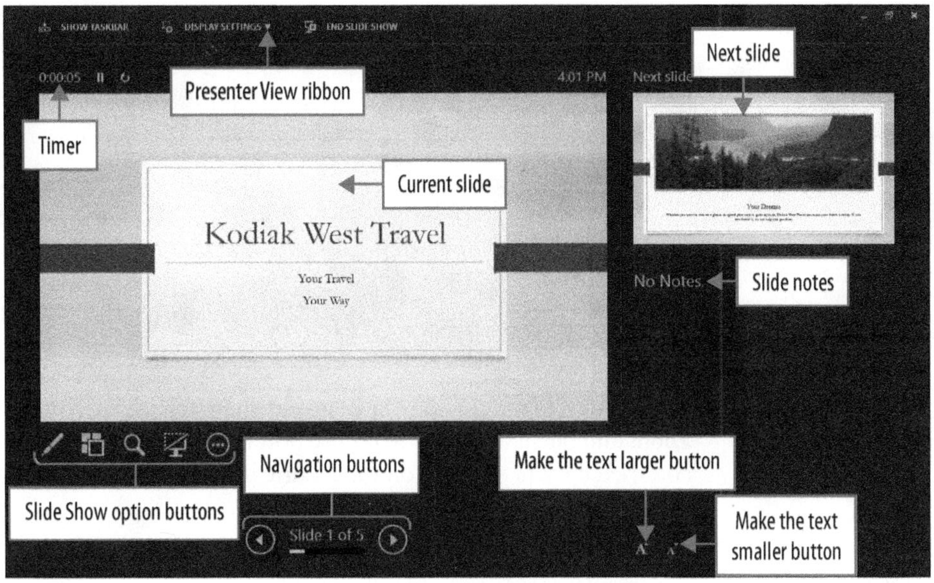

1 POWERPOINT

2 Below the current slide, click **Advance to the next slide** to display **Slide 2**.

BY TOUCH

Advance to the next slide by swiping the current slide to the left.

3 In the upper right corner of the **Presenter View** window, point to the next slide—*Our Expertise*—and then click. Notice that the notes that you typed on **Slide 3** display. Compare your screen with Figure 1.26.

Clicking the image of the next slide advances the presentation.

FIGURE 1.26

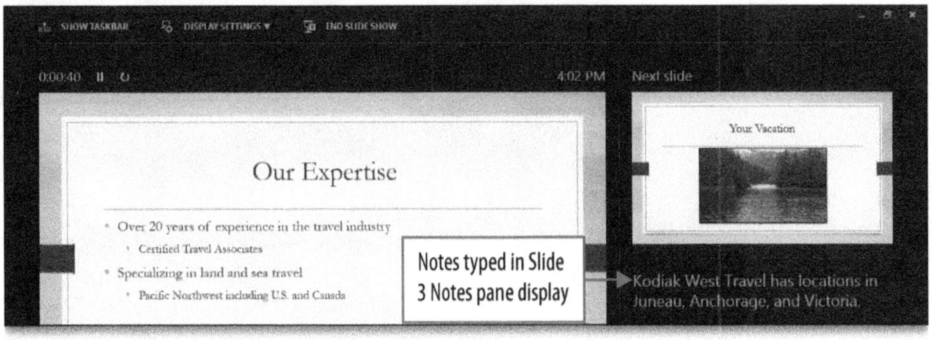

4 Below the notes, click **Make the text larger** one time to increase the font size of the notes in Presenter view, thus increasing readability.

5 Below the current slide, click **See all slides**. Compare your screen with Figure 1.27.

A thumbnail view of all of the slides in your presentation displays. Here you can quickly move to another slide; for example, if you want to review a concept or answer a question related to a slide other than the current slide.

FIGURE 1.27

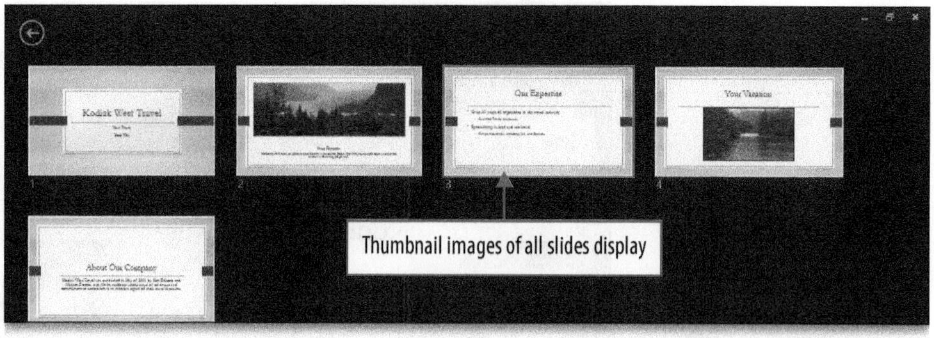

6 Click **Slide 4** to make Slide 4 the current slide in Presenter View. Below the current slide, click **Zoom into the slide** . Move the pointer to the middle of the picture on the current slide, and then click to zoom in on the picture. Notice that the pointer displays. Compare your slide with Figure 1.28.

With the pointer displayed, you can move the zoomed image to draw close-up attention to a particular part of your slide.

BY TOUCH Touch the current slide with two fingers and then pinch together to zoom in or stretch your fingers apart to zoom out.

FIGURE 1.28

7 Below the current slide, click **Advance to the next slide** to display **Slide 5.** At the top of the Presenter View window, click **END SLIDE SHOW** to return to your presentation.

Activity 1.13 | Inserting Headers and Footers on Slide Handouts

A ***header*** is text that prints at the top of each sheet of ***slide handouts*** or ***notes pages***. Slide handouts are printed images of slides on a sheet of paper. Notes pages are printouts that contain the slide image on the top half of the page and notes that you have created on the Notes pane in the lower half of the page.

In addition to headers, you can insert ***footers***—text that displays at the bottom of every slide or that prints at the bottom of a sheet of slide handouts or notes pages.

1 Click the **INSERT tab**, and then in the **Text group**, click **Header & Footer** to display the **Header and Footer** dialog box.

2. In the **Header and Footer** dialog box, click the **Notes and Handouts tab**. Under **Include on page**, select the **Date and time** check box, and as you do so, watch the Preview box in the upper right corner of the Header and Footer dialog box.

   The Preview box indicates the placeholders on the printed Notes and Handouts pages. The two narrow rectangular boxes at the top of the Preview box indicate placeholders for the header text and date. When you select the Date and time check box, the placeholder in the upper right corner is outlined, indicating the location in which the date will display.

3. Be sure that the **Update automatically** option button is selected so that the current date prints on the notes and handouts each time you print the presentation. If it is not selected, click the Update automatically option button.

4. If necessary, *clear* the Header check box to omit this element. Notice that in the **Preview** box, the corresponding placeholder is not selected.

5. Verify that the **Page number** check box is selected and select it if it is not. Select the **Footer** check box, and then click in the **Footer** box. Using your own name, type **Lastname_Firstname_1A_KWT_Overview** so that the file name displays as a footer, and then compare your dialog box with Figure 1.29.

FIGURE 1.29

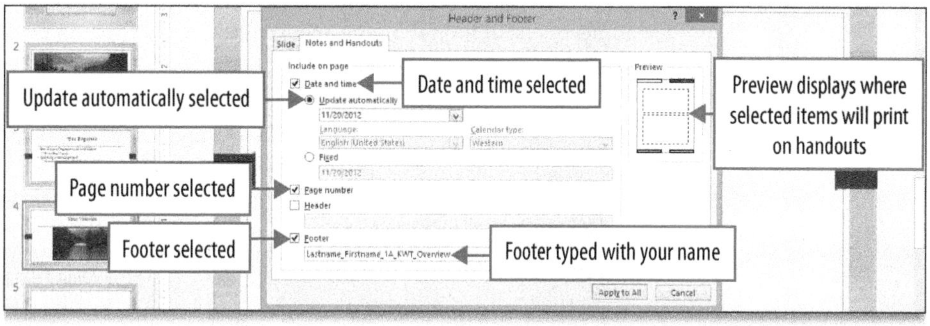

6. In the lower right corner of the dialog box, click **Apply to All**. **Save** your presentation.

Activity 1.14 | Inserting Slide Numbers on Slides

In this activity, you will insert the slide numbers on the presentation slides.

1. Display **Slide 1**. On the **INSERT tab**, in the **Text group**, click **Header & Footer** to display the **Header and Footer** dialog box.

2. In the **Header and Footer** dialog box, if necessary, click the Slide tab. Under **Include on slide**, select the **Slide number** check box, and then select the **Don't show on title slide** check box. Verify that all other check boxes are cleared, and then compare your screen with Figure 1.30.

   Selecting the *Don't show on title slide* check box omits the slide number from the first slide in a presentation.

FIGURE 1.30

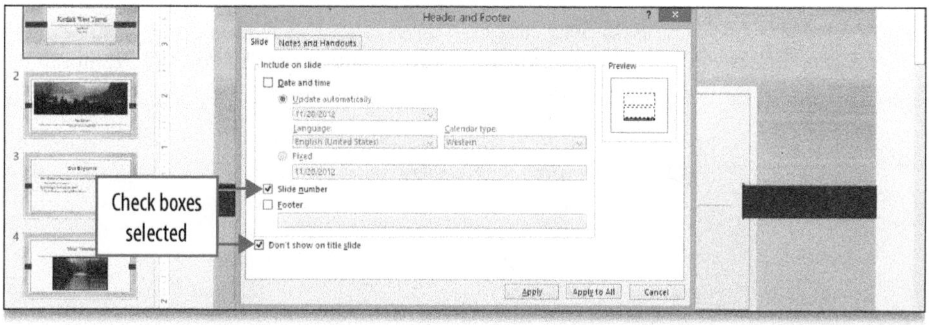

3 Click **Apply to All**, and then notice that on the first slide, the side number does not display.

4 Display **Slide 2**, and then notice that the slide number displays in the lower right area of the slide. Display each slide in the presentation and notice the placement of the slide number.

The position of the slide number and other header and footer information is determined by the theme applied to the presentation.

Activity 1.15 | Printing Presentation Handouts

Use Backstage view to preview the arrangement of slides and to print your presentation.

1 Display **Slide 1**. Click the **FILE tab** to display **Backstage** view, and then click **Print**.

The Print tab in Backstage view displays the tools you need to select your settings and also to view a preview of your presentation. On the right, Print Preview displays your presentation exactly as it will print. If your system is not connected to a color printer, your slide may display in black and white.

2 Under **Settings**, click **Full Page Slides**, and then compare your screen with Figure 1.31.

The gallery displays either the default print setting—Full Page Slides—or the most recently selected print setting. Thus, on your system, this button might indicate the presentation Notes Pages, Outline, or one of several arrangements of slide handouts—depending on the most recently used setting.

FIGURE 1.31

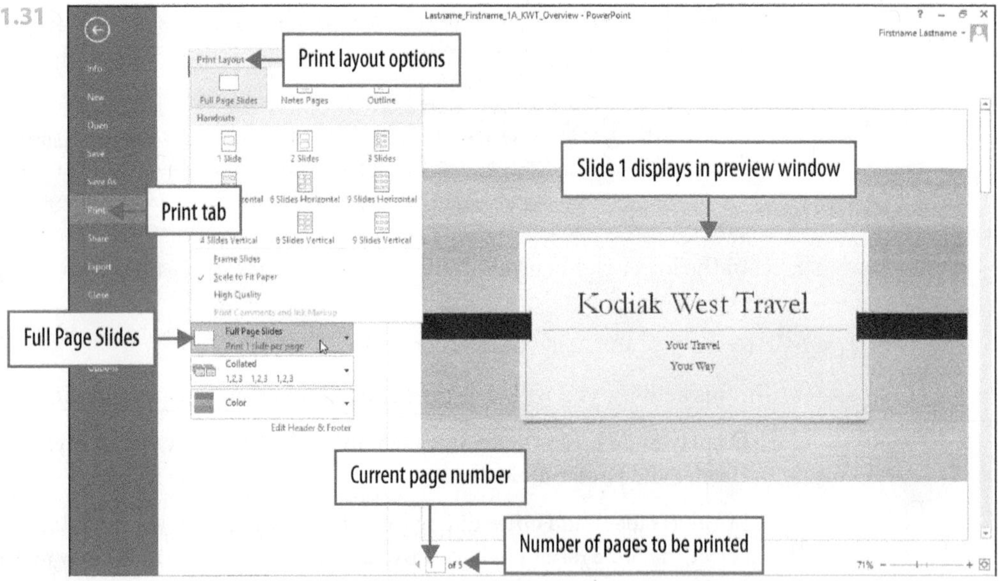

3 In the gallery, under **Handouts**, click **6 Slides Horizontal**. Notice that the **Print Preview** on the right displays the slide handout, and that the current date, file name, and page number display in the header and footer. Compare your screen with Figure 1.32.

In the Settings group, the Portrait Orientation option displays so that you can change the print orientation from Portrait to Landscape. The Portrait Orientation option does not display when Full Page Slides is chosen.

FIGURE 1.32

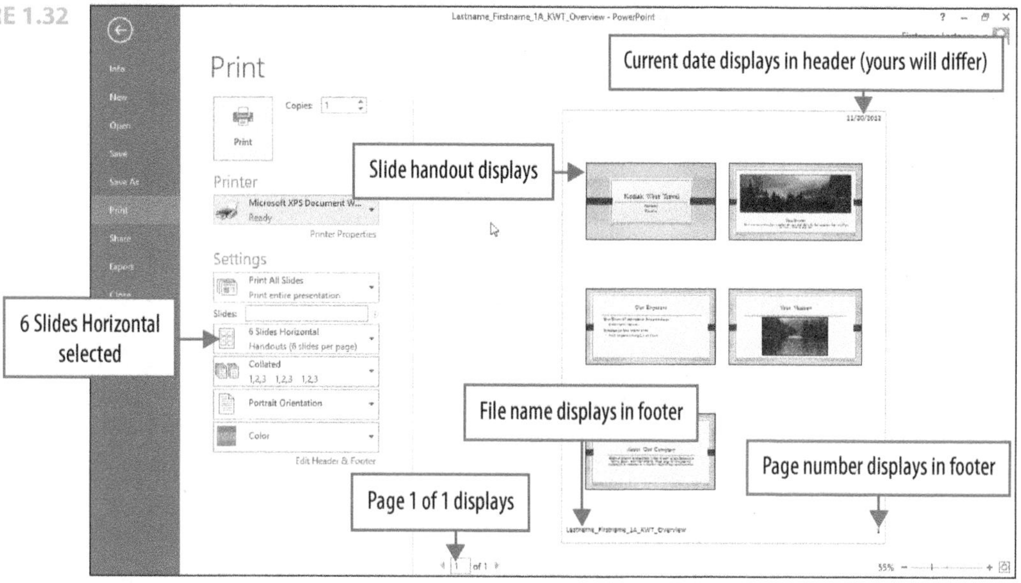

4 To submit your file electronically, skip this step and move to Step 5. To print your document on paper using the default printer on your system, in the upper left portion of the screen, click **Print**.

The handout will print on your default printer—on a black and white printer, the colors will print in shades of gray. Backstage view closes and your file redisplays in the PowerPoint window.

5 To create an electronic file, on the left click **Export**. On the right, click **Create PDF/XPS**. In the **Publish as PDF or XPS** dialog box, navigate to your **PowerPoint Chapter 1** folder, and then click **Publish**. If your Adobe Acrobat or Adobe Reader program displays your PDF, close the program.

More Knowledge **Print a Presentation in Grayscale**

To save toner and ink, you can print a presentation in shades of gray using the grayscale setting. To do so, on the FILE tab, click Print. Under Settings, click the Color arrow, and then click Grayscale.

Activity 1.16 | Printing Speaker Notes

1 Click the **FILE tab**, and then click **Print**. Under **Settings**, click **6 Slides Horizontal**, and then under **Print Layout**, click **Notes Pages** to view the presentation notes for **Slide 1**; recall that you created notes for **Slide 3**.

Indicated below the Notes page are the current slide number and the number of pages that will print when Notes Pages is selected. You can use the Next Page and Previous Page arrows to display each Notes page in the presentation.

2 At the bottom of the **Print Preview**, click **Next Page** ▶ two times so that **Page 3** displays. Notice that the notes you typed for Slide 3 display below the image of the slide. Compare your screen with Figure 1.33.

FIGURE 1.33

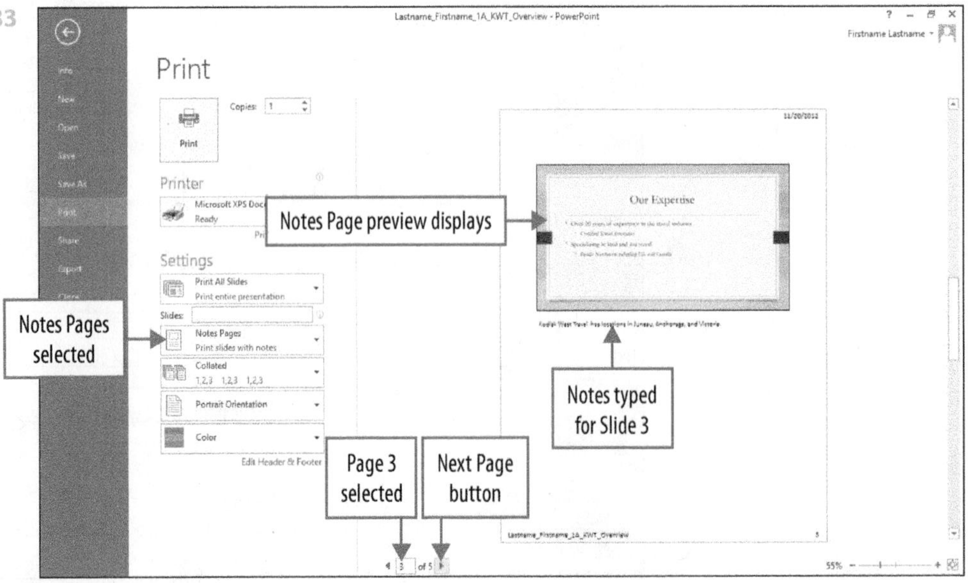

3 Under **Settings**, click in the **Slides box**. Type **3** and then click **Notes Pages**. In the lower section, select **Frame Slides**. To print the notes page, click **Print**.

4 Click the **FILE tab** to display **Backstage** view. On the right, at the bottom of the **Properties** list, click **Show All Properties**. On the list of **Properties**, click to the right of **Tags** to display an empty box, and then type **company overview**

5 Click to the right of **Subject** to display an empty box, and then type your course name and section number. Under **Related People**, be sure that your name displays as the author, and edit if necessary.

6 In the lower right corner, scroll down if necessary, click **Show Fewer Properties**, and then on the left, click **Save**. On the right end of the title bar, click **Close** [x] to close the presentation and close PowerPoint.

END | You have completed Project 1A

GO! with Office Online (formerly Web Apps)

Objective Create a Company Overview Presentation in PowerPoint Online

ALERT! Working with Web-Based Applications and Services

Computer programs and services on the web receive continuous updates and improvements, so the steps to complete this web-based activity may differ from the ones shown. You can often look at the screens and the information presented to determine how to complete the activity.

Activity | Creating a Company Overview Presentation in PowerPoint Online

Build from Scratch

In this activity, you will use PowerPoint Online to create a presentation similar to the one you created in Project 1A.

1 From the desktop, start Internet Explorer. Navigate to **http://onedrive.com**, and then sign in to your Microsoft account. Open your **GO! Web Projects** folder—or create and then open this folder if necessary.

2 On the OneDrive menu bar, click **Create**, and then click **PowerPoint presentation**. On the PowerPoint Online title bar, click Presentation1 so that it is selected. Using your own last name and first name, type **Lastname_Firstname_PPT_1A_Web** and then press Enter to rename the file.

3 On the **DESIGN tab**, in the **Themes group**, click **Organic** to apply a theme.

4 In the title placeholder, type **Kodiak West Travel** and then in the subtitle placeholder type **Your Travel** and press Enter. Type **Your Way** and then click anywhere on the slide outside of the subtitle placeholder to enter the text.

5 On the **HOME Tab**, in the **Slides group**, click **New Slide**. Scroll the **New Slide gallery**, and then click **Panoramic Picture with Caption**. Click **Add Slide**.

6 In the picture placeholder, click **Pictures**, navigate to your student data files, and then click **p01A_Glacier**. Click **Open**.

7 Click in the title placeholder. Type **Your Dreams** and then click in the text placeholder. Type **Let Kodiak West Travel assist you with all of your travel arrangements!** Compare your screen with Figure A.

8 Click outside of the text placeholder. On the **HOME tab**, click **New Slide**, and then click **Title and Content**. Click **Add Slide**. In the title placeholder type **Our Expertise**

9 In the content placeholder, type **Over 20 years of experience in the travel industry** and then press Enter. Press Tab. Type **Certified Travel Associates** and then press Enter. On the **HOME tab**, in the **Paragraph group**, click **Decrease List Level**. Type **Specializing in land and sea travel** and then press Enter. Press Tab and then type **Pacific Northwest including U.S. and Canada**

FIGURE A

(GO! with Office Online (formerly Web Apps) continues on the next page)

10 Click outside the content placeholder, and then insert a **New Slide** with the **Title and Content** layout. In the title placeholder type **Your Vacation** and then in the content placeholder click **Pictures** . From your student data files, insert **p01A_Bay**. On the **PICTURE TOOLS FORMAT** tab, in the **Picture Styles group**, click the **down arrow**, and then in the second row, click the first style **Simple Frame, Black**.

11 Insert a **New Slide** with the **Section Header** layout. In the title placeholder, type **About Our Company** and then click in the text placeholder. Type **Kodiak West Travel was founded in May of 2001 by Ken Dakona and Mariam Dorner.**

12 Click anywhere in a blank area of the slide, and then compare your screen with Figure B.

13 Click **Slide 3**, and then below the slide, click in the Notes pane. Type **Kodiak West Travel has locations in Juneau, Anchorage, and Victoria.**

14 Display **Slide 1**. On the **VIEW tab**, in the **Presentation Views group**, click **Slide Show**. If a Security warning displays at the bottom of your screen, click Allow once. Click the left mouse button to progress through the presentation. When the black slide displays, click the mouse button.

15 If you are instructed to submit your file, create a PDF as indicated in the Note box below. Sign out of OneDrive and close Internet Explorer.

NOTE

Creating a PDF from the PowerPoint Web App

Click the **FILE tab**, click **Print**, and then click **Print to PDF**. In the Microsoft PowerPoint Web App message box, click Click here to view the PDF of your document. In the **Print** dialog box, click **Cancel**. Click **File**, and then click **Save As**. In the Save As dialog box, navigate to your PowerPoint Chapter 1 folder, and then save the file as as **Lastname_Firstname_PPT_1A_Web_PDF.**

FIGURE B

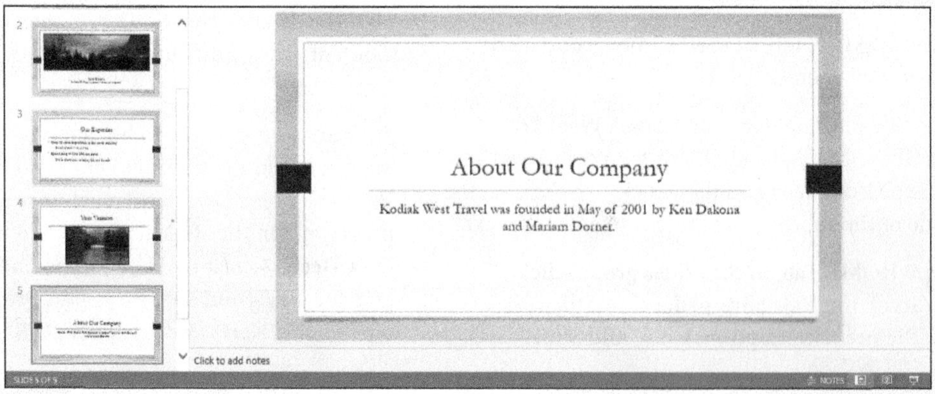

PROJECT

1B Itinerary Presentation

MyITLab® Project 1B Training

PROJECT ACTIVITIES

In Activities 1.17 through 1.33, you will combine two presentations that the marketing team at Kodiak West Travel developed describing itinerary ideas when visiting Seattle before or after a cruise. You will insert slides from one presentation into another, and then you will rearrange and delete slides. You will also apply font formatting and slide transitions to the presentation. Your completed presentation will look similar to Figure 1.34.

PROJECT FILES

For Project 1B, you will need the following files:

p01B_Seattle
p01B_Slides

You will save your presentation as:

Lastname_Firstname_1B_Seattle

PROJECT RESULTS

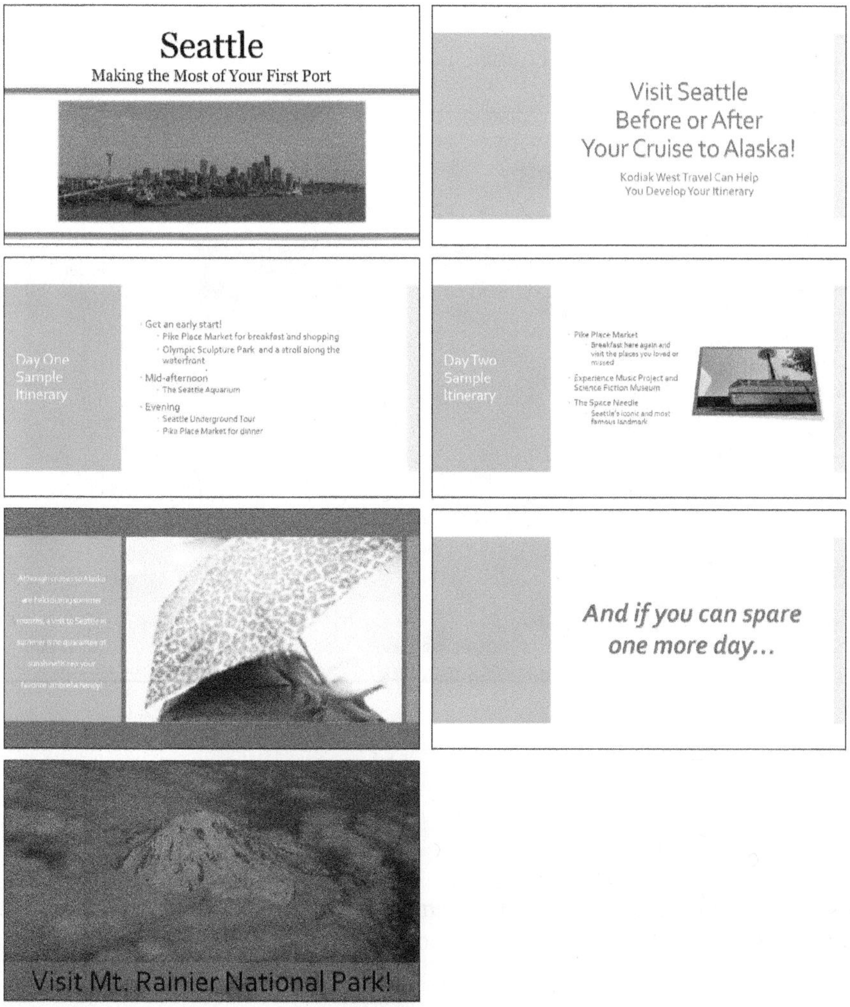

FIGURE 1.34 Project 1B Itinerary Presentation

Objective 5 Edit an Existing Presentation

Video P1-5

Recall that editing refers to the process of adding, deleting, and modifying presentation content. You can edit presentation content in either the Slide pane or in the presentation outline.

Activity 1.17 | Changing Slide Size

Presentations that you create with some of the newer themes in PowerPoint 2013 default to a widescreen format using a 16:9 ***aspect ratio***—the ratio of the width of a display to the height of the display. This slide size is similar to most television and computer monitor screens. Previous versions of PowerPoint used a squarer format with a 4:3 aspect ratio. The widescreen format utilizes screen space more effectively.

1. Start PowerPoint. On the left, under the list of recent presentations, click **Open Other Presentations**. Under **Open**, click **Computer** and then click **Browse**. Navigate to your student data files, and then click **p01B_Seattle**. Click **Open**. On the **FILE tab**, click **Save As**, navigate to your **PowerPoint Chapter 1** folder, and then using your own name, save the file as **Lastname_Firstname_1B_Seattle**

2. Notice that **Slide 1** displays in a square format and that in the **Slide pane**, there is white space on the left and right slides of the slide.

3. On the **DESIGN tab**, in the **Customize group**, click **Slide Size**, and then click **Widescreen (16:9)**. Compare your screen with Figure 1.35 and notice that the slide fills the slide pane.

FIGURE 1.35

4. **Save** the presentation.

Activity 1.18 | Inserting Slides from an Existing Presentation

Presentation content is commonly shared among group members in an organization. Rather than re-creating slides, you can insert slides from an existing presentation into the current presentation. In this activity, you will insert slides from an existing presentation into your 1B_Seattle presentation.

1 With **Slide 1** displayed, on the **HOME tab**, in the **Slides group**, click the **New Slide arrow** to display the **Slide Layout** gallery and additional commands for inserting slides. Compare your screen with Figure 1.36.

FIGURE 1.36

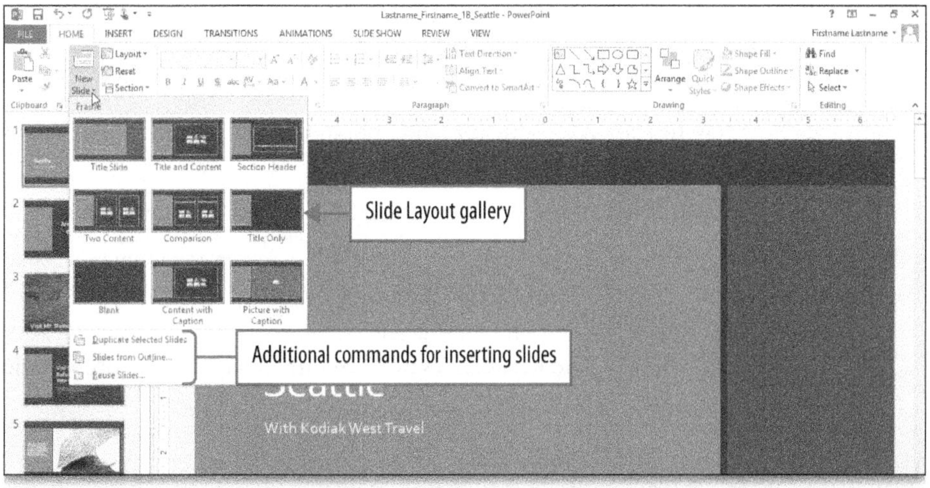

2 Below the gallery, click **Reuse Slides** to open the Reuse Slides pane on the right side of the PowerPoint window.

3 In the **Reuse Slides** pane, click **Browse**, and then click **Browse File**. In the **Browse** dialog box, navigate to the location where your student data files are stored, and then double-click **p01B_Slides** to display the slides from this presentation in the **Reuse Slides** pane.

4 At the bottom of the **Reuse Slides** pane, be sure that the **Keep source formatting** check box is *cleared*, and then compare your screen with Figure 1.37.

When the *Keep source formatting* check box is cleared, the theme formatting of the presentation in which the slides are inserted is applied. When the *Keep source formatting* check box is selected, you retain the formatting applied to the slides when inserted into the existing presentation.

FIGURE 1.37

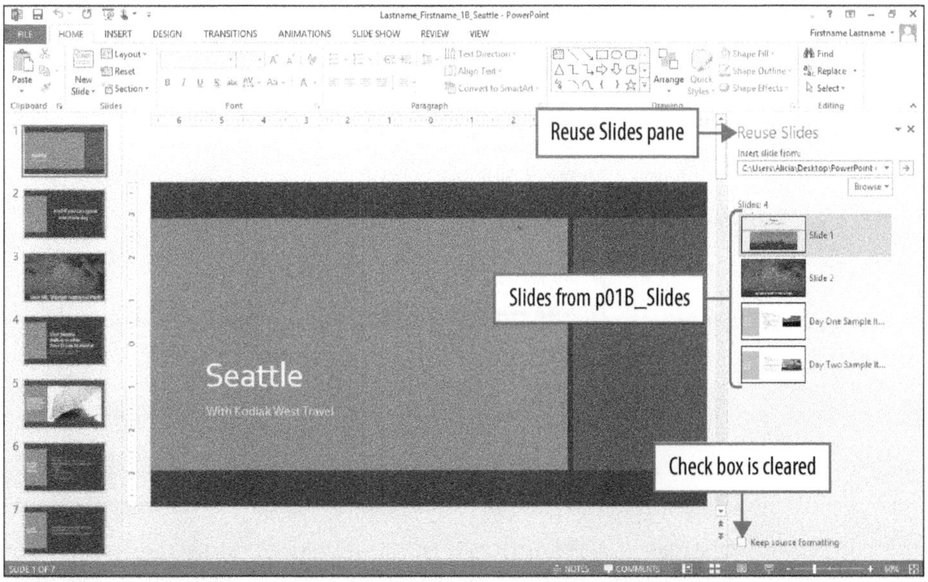

5 In the **Reuse Slides** pane, point to each slide to view a ScreenTip displaying the file name and the slide title.

6 In the **Reuse Slides** pane, click the first slide to insert the slide after Slide 1. Notice that the inserted slide adopts the color of the presentation theme into which the slide was inserted.

> **NOTE** **Inserting Slides**
>
> You can insert slides into your presentation in any order; remember to display the slide that will precede the slide that you want to insert.

7 In your **1B_Seattle** presentation, in the slide thumbnails, click **Slide 7** to display it in the **Slide pane.**

8 In the **Reuse Slides** pane, click the fourth slide to insert it after Slide 7.

Your presentation contains nine slides. When a presentation contains a large number of slides, a scroll box displays to the right of the slide thumbnails so that you can scroll and then select the thumbnails.

9 **Close** [X] the **Reuse Slides** pane, and then **Save** [save icon] the presentation.

> ***More* Knowledge** **Inserting All Slides**
>
> You can insert all of the slides from an existing presentation into the current presentation at one time. In the Reuse Slides pane, right-click one of the slides that you want to insert, and then click Insert All Slides.

Activity 1.19 | Displaying and Editing the Presentation Outline

Outline View displays the presentation outline to the left of the Slide pane. You can use the outline to edit the presentation text. Changes that you make in the outline are immediately displayed in the Slide pane.

1 To the right of the slide thumbnails, drag the scroll box up, and then click **Slide 1** to display it in the Slide pane. On the **VIEW tab**, in the **Presentation Views group**, click **Outline View**. Compare your screen with Figure 1.38.

The outline displays at the left of the PowerPoint window in place of the slide thumbnails. Each slide in the outline displays the slide number, slide icon, and the slide title in bold. Slides that do not display a slide title in the outline use a slide layout that does not include a title, for example, the Blank layout.

FIGURE 1.38

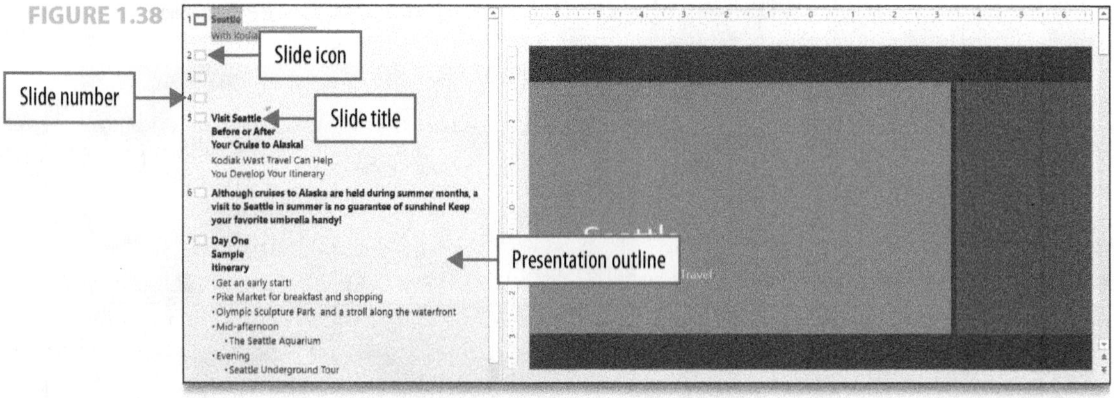

2 In the **Outline**, in **Slide 7**, drag to select the second and third bullet points—*Pike Market for breakfast and shopping*, and *Olympic Sculpture Park and a stroll along the waterfront*. Compare your screen with Figure 1.39.

FIGURE 1.39

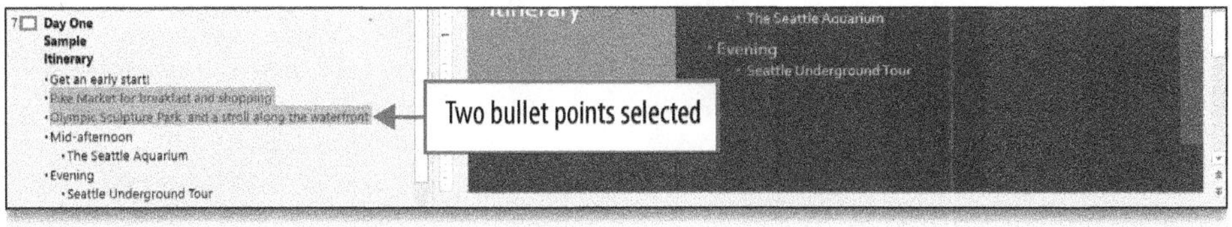

3 On the **HOME tab**, in the **Paragraph group**, click **Increase List Level** one time to increase the list level of the selected bullet points.

When you type in the outline or change the list level, the changes also display in the Slide pane.

4 In the **Outline**, in **Slide 7**, click at the end of the last bullet point after the word *Tour*. Press Enter to create a new bullet point at the same list level as the previous bullet point. Type **Pike Place Market for dinner** and then compare your screen with Figure 1.40.

FIGURE 1.40

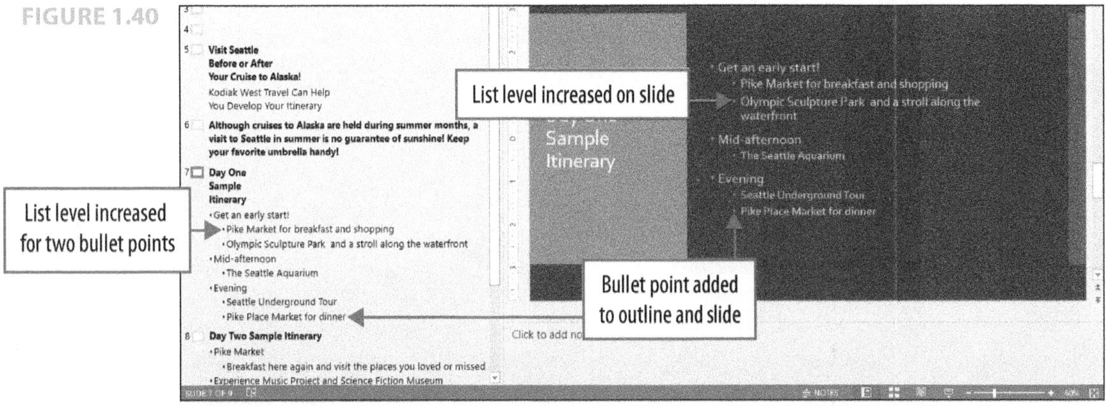

5 In the **Status bar**, click **Normal** to display the slide thumbnails, and then **Save** the presentation.

You can type text in the Slide pane or in the Outline. Displaying the Outline enables you to view the entire flow of the presentation.

Activity 1.20 | Deleting and Moving a Slide

1 To the right of the slide thumbnails, locate the vertical scroll bar and scroll box. If necessary, drag the scroll box down so that **Slide 9** displays in the slide thumbnails. Click **Slide 9** to display it in the Slide pane. Press Del to delete the slide from the presentation.

Your presentation contains eight slides.

2 If necessary, scroll the slide thumbnails so that **Slide 4** displays. Point to **Slide 4**, hold down the left mouse button, and then drag down to position the **Slide 4** thumbnail below the **Slide 8** thumbnail. Release the mouse button and then compare your screen with Figure 1.41.

You can easily rearrange your slides by dragging a slide thumbnail to a new location in the presentation.

BY TOUCH

Use your finger to drag the slide you want to move to a new location in the presentation.

FIGURE 1.41

3 **Save** the presentation.

Activity 1.21 | Finding and Replacing Text

The Replace command enables you to locate all occurrences of specified text and replace it with alternative text.

1 Display **Slide 1**. On the **HOME tab**, in the **Editing group**, click **Replace**. In the **Replace** dialog box, in the **Find what** box, type **Pike Market** and then in the **Replace with** box, type **Pike Place Market** Compare your screen with Figure 1.42.

FIGURE 1.42

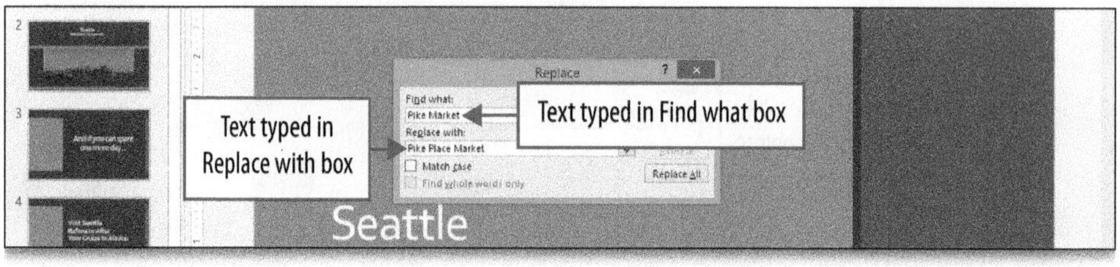

2 In the **Replace** dialog box, click **Replace All** to display a message box indicating that two replacements were made.

3 In the message box, click **OK**. **Close** the **Replace** dialog box, and then click **Save**.

Objective 6 Format a Presentation

Video P1-6

Formatting refers to changing the appearance of the text, layout, and design of a slide.

Activity 1.22 | Applying a Theme Variant

Recall that a theme is a set of unified design elements that provides a look for your presentation by applying colors, fonts, and effects. Each PowerPoint theme includes several ***variants***—variations on the theme style and color.

1 On the **DESIGN tab**, In the **Variants group**, notice that four variants of the current theme—*Frame*—display.

2 Point to each of the variants to view the change to **Slide 1**.

3 With **Slide 1** displayed, in the **Variants group**, point to the **third variant**, and then right-click. Compare your screen with Figure 1.43.

The shortcut menu displays options for applying the variant.

FIGURE 1.43

4 Click **Apply to Selected Slides** to apply the variant to **Slide 1** only.

5 In the **Variants group**, right-click the **blue variant**. On the shortcut menu, click **Apply to All Slides** so that the blue color is applied to all of the slides in the presentation. Compare your screen with Figure 1.44.

FIGURE 1.44

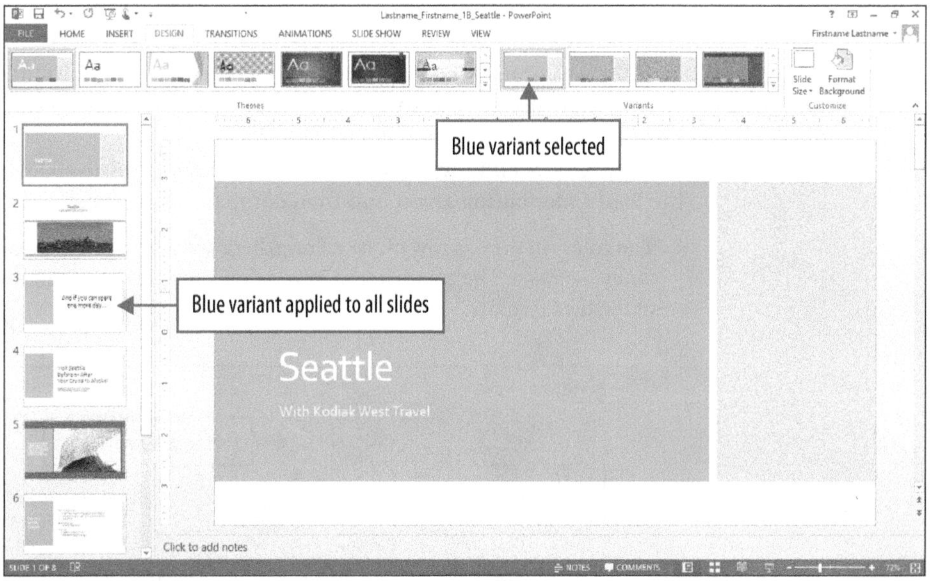

6 **Save** your presentation.

Activity 1.23 | Changing Fonts and Font Sizes

Recall that a font is a set of characters with the same design and shape and that fonts are measured in points. Font styles include bold, italic, and underline, and you can apply any combination of these styles to presentation text. Font styles and font color are useful to provide emphasis and are a visual cue to draw the reader's eye to important text.

1 Display **Slide 2**. Select all of the text in the title placeholder, point to the mini toolbar, and then click the **Font button arrow** to display the available fonts. Scroll the font list, and then click **Georgia**.

2 Select the first line of the title—*Seattle*. On the mini toolbar, click the **Font Size button arrow** and then click **80**.

3 Select the second line of the title—*Making the Most of Your First Port*. On the **HOME tab**, in the **Font group**, click the **Font Size button arrow**, and then click **36**. Click in a blank area of the slide to cancel your selection, and then compare your screen with Figure 1.45. **Save** your presentation.

FIGURE 1.45

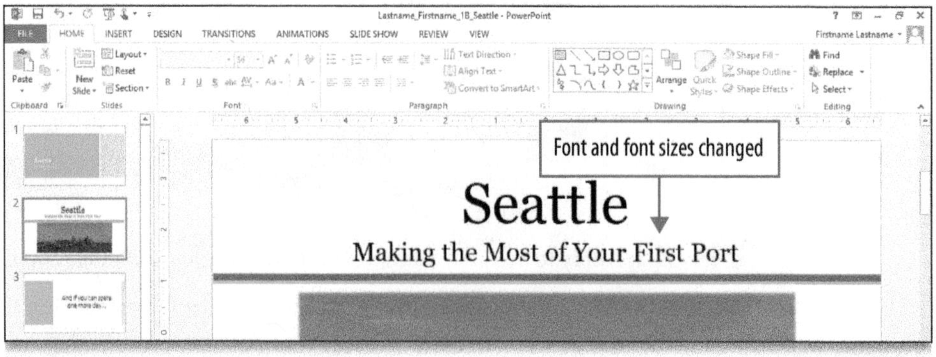

Activity 1.24 | Changing Font Styles and Font Colors

Font styles include bold, italic, and underline, and you can apply any combination of these styles to presentation text. Font styles and font color are useful to provide emphasis and are a visual cue to draw the reader's eye to important text.

1 Display **Slide 3**, and then select both lines of text. On the **HOME tab**, in the **Font group**, click the **Font Color button arrow** and then compare your screen with Figure 1.46.

The colors in the top row of the color gallery are the colors associated with the presentation theme—*Frame*. The colors in the rows below the first row are light and dark variations of the theme colors.

FIGURE 1.46

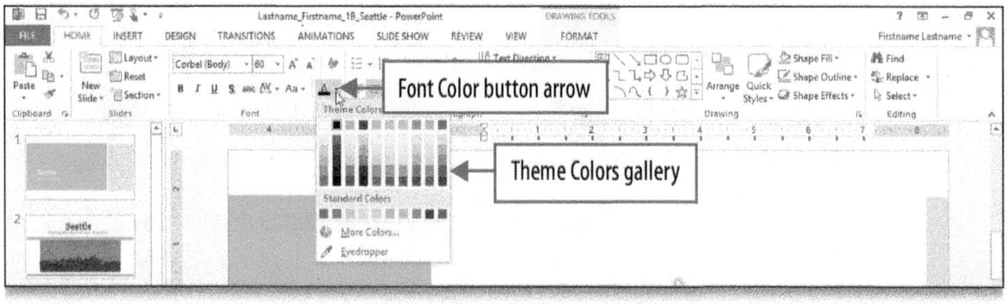

2 Point to several of the colors and notice that a ScreenTip displays the color name and Live Preview displays the selected text in the color to which you are pointing.

3 In the fifth column of colors, click the last color—**Turquoise, Accent 1, Darker 50%**—to change the font color. Notice that on the **HOME tab**, the lower part of the **Font Color** button displays the most recently applied font color—*Turquoise, Accent 1, Darker 50%*.

When you click the Font Color button instead of the Font Color button arrow, the color displayed in the lower part of the Font Color button is applied to selected text without displaying the color gallery.

4 Display **Slide 4**, and then select the title—*Visit Seattle Before or After Your Cruise to Alaska!* On the mini toolbar, click **Font Color** to apply the font color **Turquoise, Accent 1, Darker 50%** to the selection. Select the subtitle—*Kodiak West Travel Can Help You Develop Your Itinerary*—and then change the **Font Color** to **Turquoise, Accent 1, Darker 50%**. Click anywhere on the slide to cancel the selection, and then compare your screen with Figure 1.47.

FIGURE 1.47

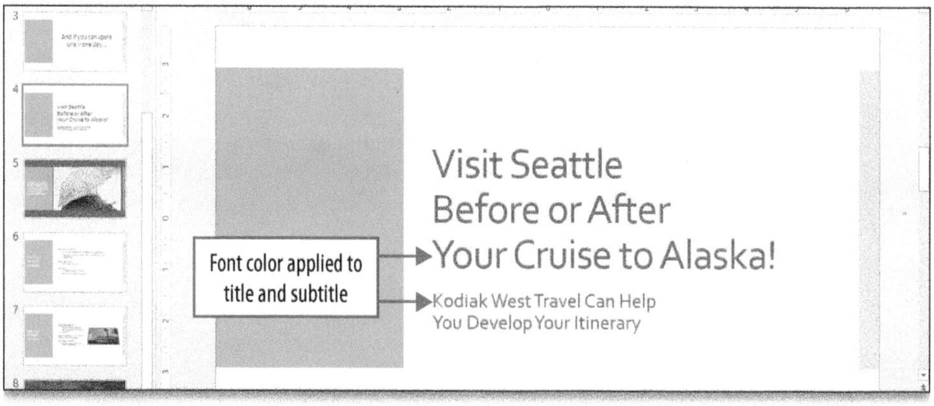

5 Display **Slide 3**, and then select the two lines of text. From the mini toolbar, apply **Bold** [B] and **Italic** [I], and then **Save** your presentation.

Activity 1.25 | Aligning Text

In PowerPoint, ***text alignment*** refers to the horizontal placement of text within a placeholder. You can align left, centered, right, or justified.

1 Display **Slide 5**, and then on the left side of the slide, click anywhere in the paragraph. On the **HOME tab**, in the **Paragraph group**, click **Center** to center the text within the placeholder.

2 Display **Slide 4**, and then click anywhere in the slide title. Press Ctrl + E to use the keyboard shortcut to center the text.

3 On **Slide 4**, using one of the methods that you practiced, **Center** the subtitle. Click in a blank area of the slide. Compare your screen with Figure 1.48, and then **Save** the presentation.

FIGURE 1.48

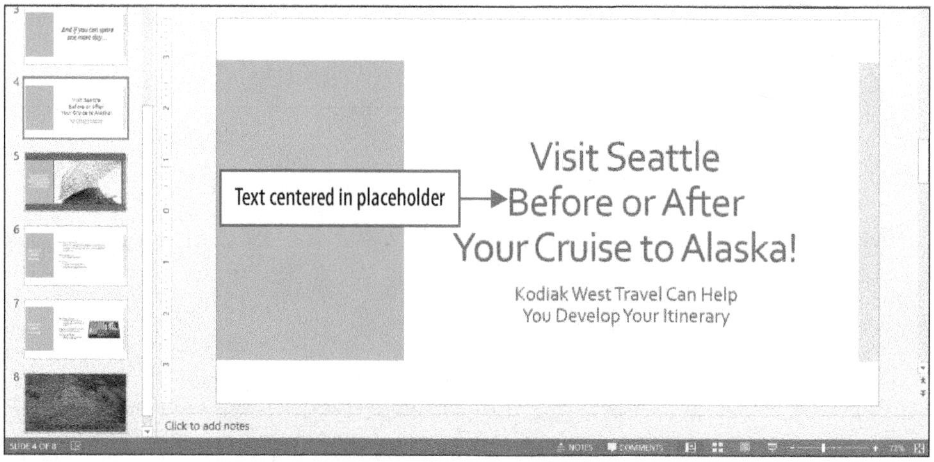

Activity 1.26 | Changing Line Spacing

1 Display **Slide 5**, and then click anywhere in the paragraph. On the **HOME tab**, in the **Paragraph group**, click **Line Spacing**. On the list, click **2.0** to change from single spacing to double spacing between lines of text. Compare your screen with Figure 1.49.

FIGURE 1.49

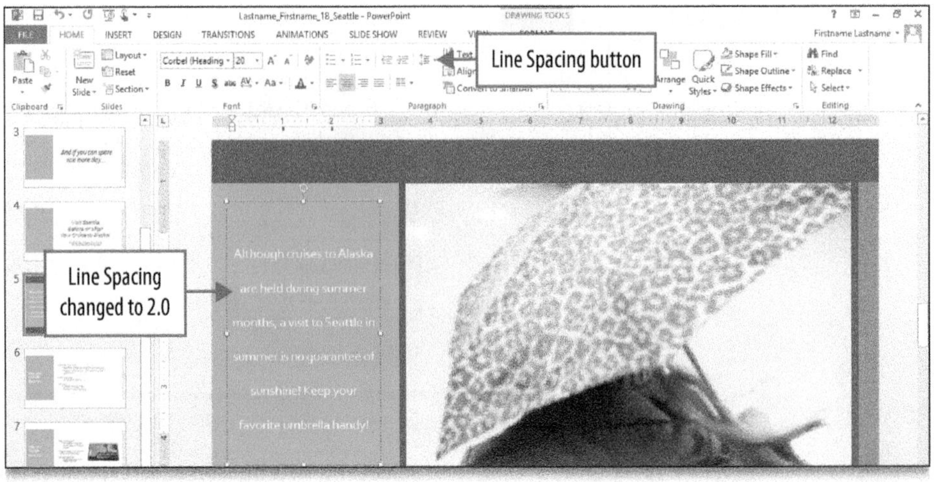

2 **Save** your presentation.

Activity 1.27 | Changing the Slide Layout

Recall that the slide layout defines the placement of the content placeholders on a slide. PowerPoint includes predefined layouts that you can apply to your slide for the purpose of arranging slide elements. For example, a Title Slide contains two placeholder elements—the title and the subtitle. When you design your slides, consider the content that you want to include, and then choose a layout with the elements that will display the message you want to convey in the best way.

1 Display **Slide 1**. On the **HOME tab**, in the **Slides group**, click **Layout** to display the **Slide Layout** gallery. Notice that *Title Slide* is selected, indicating the layout of the current slide.

2 Click **Section Header** to change the slide layout. Compare your screen with Figure 1.50, and then **Save** your presentation.

FIGURE 1.50

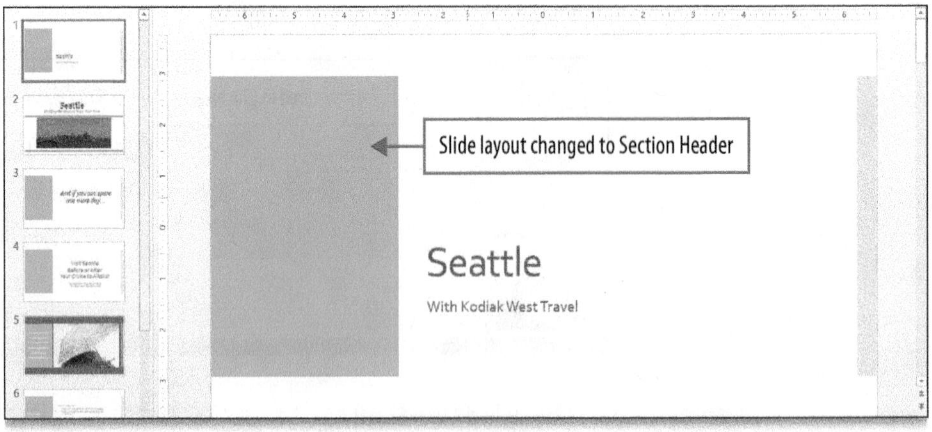

Objective 7 Use Slide Sorter View

Video P1-7

Slide Sorter view displays thumbnails of all of the slides in a presentation. Use Slide Sorter view to rearrange and delete slides and to apply formatting to multiple slides.

Activity 1.28 | Deleting Slides in Slide Sorter View

1 In the lower right corner of the PowerPoint window, click **Slide Sorter** to display all of the slide thumbnails. Compare your screen with Figure 1.51.

Your slides may display larger or smaller than those shown in Figure 1.51.

ANOTHER WAY — On the VIEW tab, in the Presentation Views group, click Slide Sorter.

FIGURE 1.51

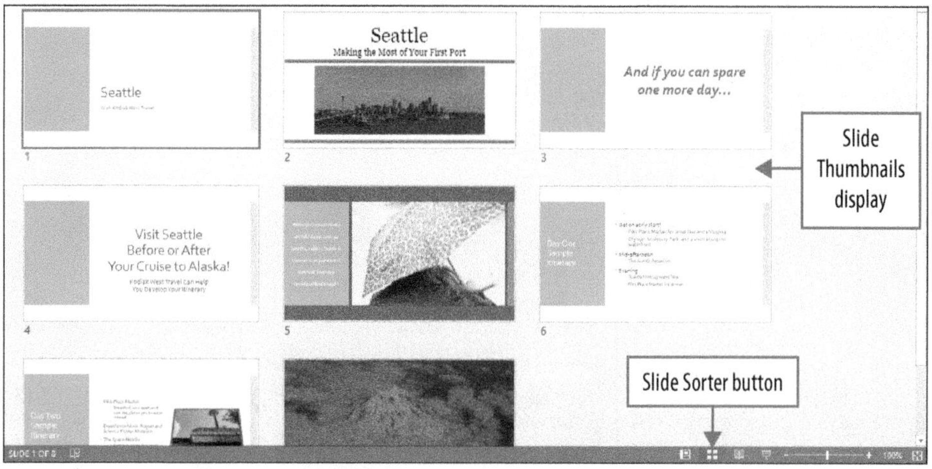

2 Click **Slide 1**, and notice that a thick outline surrounds the slide, indicating that it is selected. On your keyboard, press Delete to delete the slide. Click **Save**.

Activity 1.29 | Moving a Single Slide in Slide Sorter View

1 With the presentation displayed in Slide Sorter view, point to **Slide 2**. Hold down the left mouse button, and then drag to position the slide to the right of **Slide 6**, as shown in Figure 1.52.

FIGURE 1.52

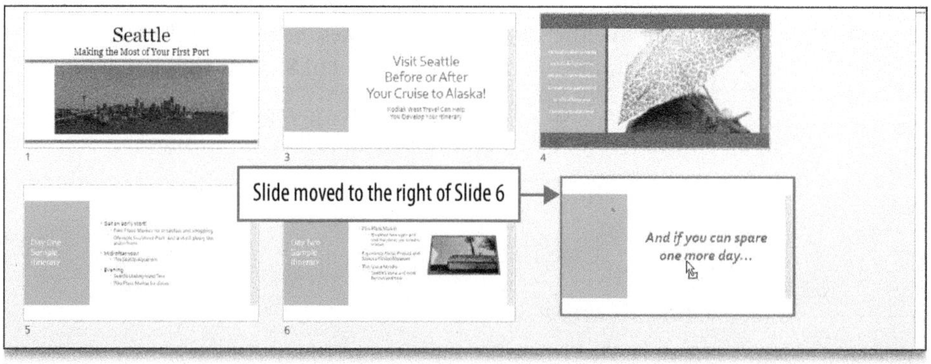

2 Release the mouse button to move the slide to the **Slide 6** position in the presentation. **Save** your presentation.

Activity 1.30 | Selecting Contiguous and Noncontiguous Slides and Moving Multiple Slides

Contiguous slides are slides that are adjacent to each other in a presentation. ***Noncontiguous slides*** are slides that are not adjacent to each other in a presentation.

1 Click **Slide 2**, hold down Ctrl, and then click **Slide 4**. Notice that both slides are selected.

The noncontiguous slides—Slides 2 and 4—are outlined, indicating that both are selected. By holding down Ctrl, you can select noncontiguous slides.

2 Click **Slide 3**, so that only Slide 3 is selected. Hold down Shift, and then click **Slide 5**. Compare your screen with Figure 1.53.

The contiguous slides—Slides 3, 4, and 5—are outlined, indicating that all three slides are selected. By holding down Shift, you can create a group of contiguous selected slides.

FIGURE 1.53

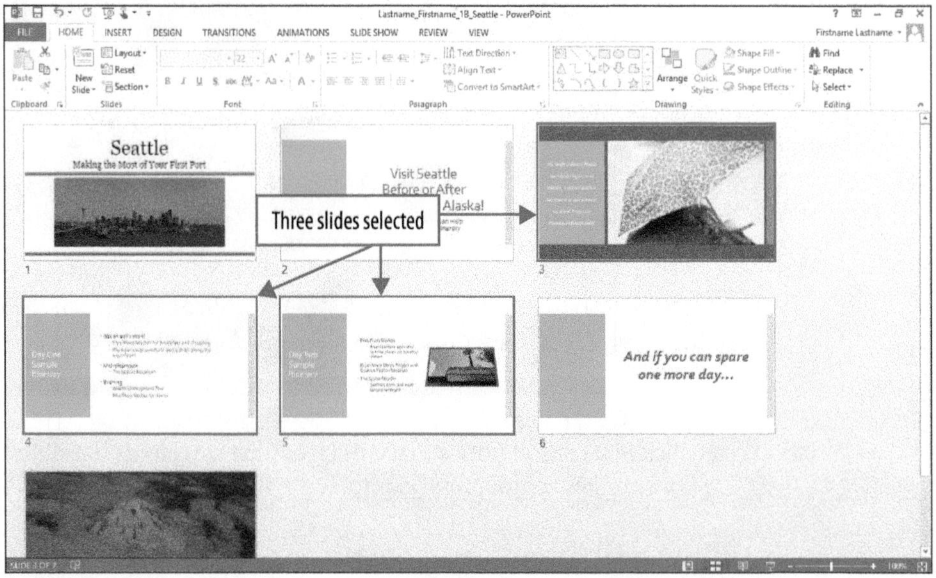

3 With Slides 3, 4, and 5 selected, hold down Ctrl, and then click **Slide 3**. Notice that only slides 4 and 5 are selected.

When a group of slides is selected, you can press Ctrl and then click a selected slide to deselect it.

4 Point to either of the selected slides, hold down the left mouse button, and then drag to position the two slides to the right of **Slide 2**, and then compare your screen with Figure 1.54.

The selected slides are dragged as a group and the number 2 in the upper left area of the selected slides indicates the number of slides that you are moving.

FIGURE 1.54

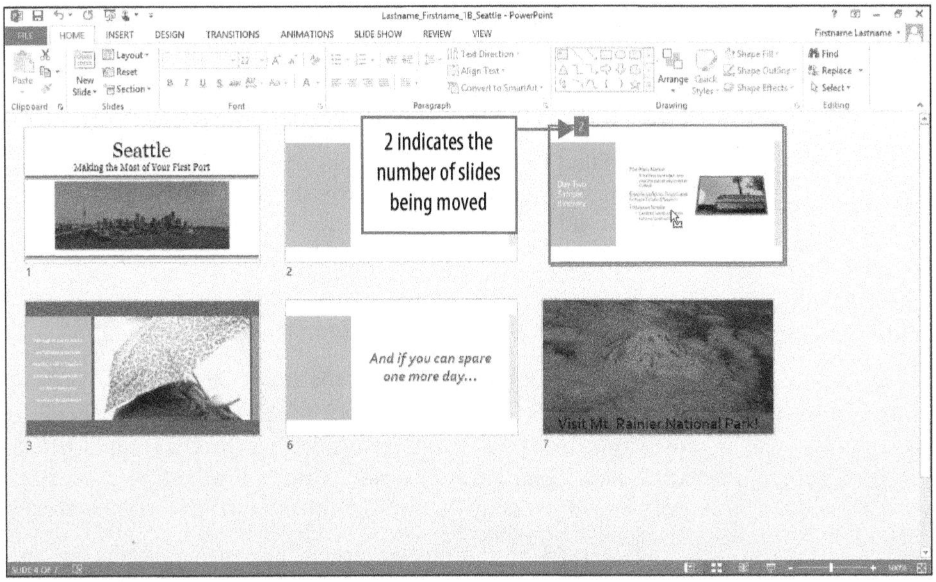

5 Release the mouse button to move the two slides. In the status bar, click **Normal** to return to Normal view. **Save** your presentation.

Objective 8 Apply Slide Transitions

Video P1-8

Slide transitions are the motion effects that occur in Slide Show view when you move from one slide to the next during a presentation. You can choose from a variety of transitions, and you can control the speed and method with which the slides advance.

Activity 1.31 | Applying Slide Transitions to a Presentation

1 Display **Slide 1.** On the **TRANSITIONS tab**, in the **Transition to This Slide group**, click **More** to display the **Transitions** gallery. Compare your screen with Figure 1.55.

FIGURE 1.55

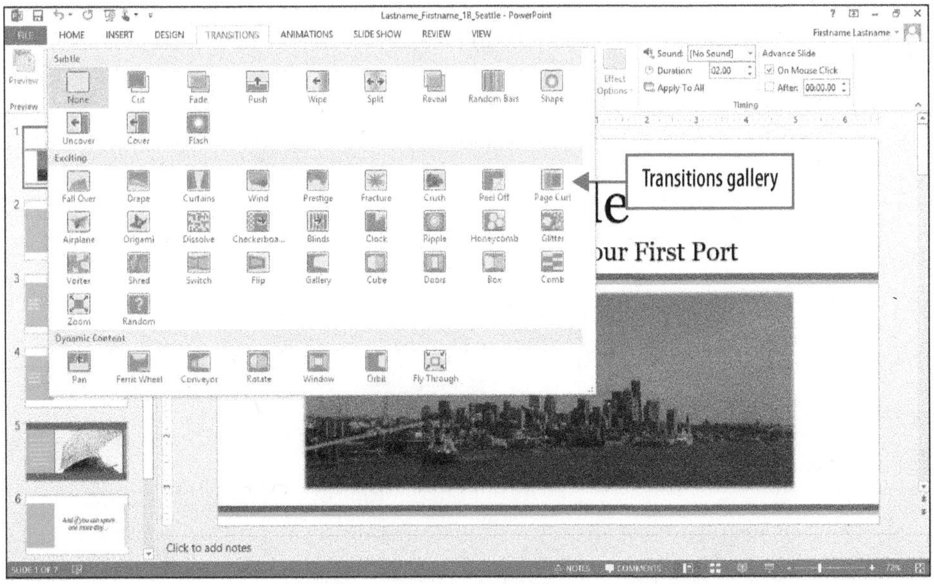

2 Under **Exciting**, click **Doors** to apply and view the transition. In the **Transition to This Slide group**, click **Effect Options** to display the directions from which the slide enters the screen. Click **Horizontal**. In the **Timing group**, click **Apply To All** to apply the *Doors, Horizontal* transition to all of the slides in the presentation. **Save** your presentation.

The Effect Options vary depending upon the selected transition and include the direction from which the slide enters the screen or the shape in which the slide displays during the transition. In the slide thumbnails, a star displays below the slide number providing a visual cue that a transition has been applied to the slide.

Activity 1.32 | Setting Slide Transition Timing Options

1 In the **Timing group**, notice that the **Duration** box displays *01.40*, indicating that the transition lasts 1.40 seconds. Click the **Duration up spin arrow** two times so that *01.75* displays. Under **Advance Slide**, verify that the **On Mouse Click** check box is selected; select it if necessary. Compare your screen with Figure 1.56.

When the On Mouse Click option is selected, the presenter controls when the current slide advances to the next slide by clicking the mouse button or by pressing Spacebar.

FIGURE 1.56

2 In the **Timing group**, click **Apply To All** so that the Duration of *1.75* seconds transition is applied to all of the slides in the presentation.

3 Click the **SLIDE SHOW tab**. In the **Start Slide Show group**, click **From Beginning**, and then view your presentation, clicking the mouse button to advance through the slides. When the black slide displays, click the mouse button one more time to display the presentation in Normal view. **Save** your presentation.

More Knowledge | **Applying Multiple Slide Transitions**

You can apply more than one type of transition in your presentation by displaying the slides one at a time, and then clicking the transition that you want to apply instead of clicking Apply To All.

Activity 1.33 | Displaying a Presentation in Reading View

Organizations frequently conduct online meetings when participants are unable to meet in one location. The ***Reading view*** in PowerPoint displays a presentation in a manner similar to a slide show but the taskbar, title bar, and status bar remain available in the presentation window. This feature enables a presenter to facilitate an online conference easily by switching to another window without closing the slide show.

1. In the lower right corner of the PowerPoint window, click **Reading View**. Compare your screen with Figure 1.57.

   In Reading View, the status bar contains the Next and Previous buttons with which you can navigate in the presentation, and the Menu button from which you can print, copy, and edit slides.

ANOTHER WAY On the VIEW tab, in the Presentation Views group, click Reading View.

FIGURE 1.57

2. Press Spacebar to display **Slide 2**. Click the left mouse button to display **Slide 3**. In the status bar, click **Previous** to display **Slide 2**.

3. In the status bar, click **Menu** to display the Reading view menu, and then click **End Show** to return to Normal view.

ANOTHER WAY Press Esc to exit Reading view and return to Normal view.

4. On the **INSERT tab**, in the **Text group**, click **Header & Footer**, and then click the **Notes and Handouts tab**. Under **Include on page**, select the **Date and time** check box, and if necessary, select **Update automatically**. Clear the **Header** check box if necessary, and then select the **Page number** and **Footer** check boxes. In the **Footer** box, using your own name, type **Lastname_Firstname_1B_Seattle** and then click **Apply to All**.

5. Display **Backstage** view, and then on the right, at the bottom of the **Properties** list, click **Show All Properties**. On the list of properties, click to the right of **Tags**, and type **Seattle** To the right of **Subject**, type your course name and section number. Under **Related People**, be sure that your name displays as the author and edit if necessary.

6 On the left, click **Save**. Submit your presentation electronically or print **Handouts, 4 Slides Horizontal**, as directed by your instructor.

7 **Close** [x] PowerPoint.

***More* Knowledge** **Present a Presentation Online**

You can use the Office Presentation Service to present to people who can watch the presentation in a web browser. You will need a Microsoft account to use this free service. To present online, on the SLIDE SHOW tab, in the Start Slide Show group, click Present Online, and then follow the instructions in the Present Online window.

END | You have completed Project 1B

GO! with Office Online (formerly Web Apps)

Objective Create an Itinerary Presentation in PowerPoint Online

ALERT! **Working with Web-Based Applications and Services**

Computer programs and services on the web receive continuous updates and improvements, so the steps to complete this web-based activity may differ from the ones shown. You can often look at the screens and the information presented to determine how to complete the activity.

Activity | Creating an Itinerary Presentation in PowerPoint Online

In this activity, you will use PowerPoint Online to create a presentation similar to the one you created in Project 1B.

1 From the desktop, start Internet Explorer. Navigate to **http://onedrive.com**, and then sign in to your Microsoft account. Open your **GO! Web Projects** folder—or create and then open this folder if necessary.

2 In the OneDrive menu bar, click **Upload**. Navigate to your student data files, click **p01_1B_Web**, and then click **Open**.

3 Point to the uploaded file **p01_1B_Web**, and then right-click. On the shortcut menu, click **Rename**. Using your own last name and first name, type **Lastname_Firstname_PPT_1B_Web** and then press Enter to rename the file.

4 Click the file that you just renamed, and then click **EDIT PRESENTATION**. On the list, click **Edit in PowerPoint Online**.

5 On the **DESIGN tab**, in the **Variants group**, click the variant that includes a light blue background and notice that the variant is applied to all of the slides in the presentation.

6 On **Slide 1**, double-click in the title, and then drag to select the two lines of text. On the **HOME tab**, in the **Font group**, click the **Font button arrow**, and then click **Georgia**.

7 Select the text *Making the Most of Your First Port*. On the **HOME tab**, in the **Font group**, click the **Font Size button arrow**, and then click **28**. Click in a blank area of the slide, and then compare your screen with Figure A.

8 Click **Slide 2**. On the **HOME tab**, in the **Delete group**, Click **Delete** to remove the slide from the presentation.

9 With **Slide 2**—*Seattle Weather*—displayed, press Delete to remove the slide from your presentation. Notice that the Status bar indicates that the presentation contains 7 slides.

10 Display **Slide 3**, and then double-click in the paragraph on the left side of the slide. Drag to select the text, and then on the **HOME tab**, in the **Font group**, click the **Font Color button arrow**. In the first column, click

FIGURE A

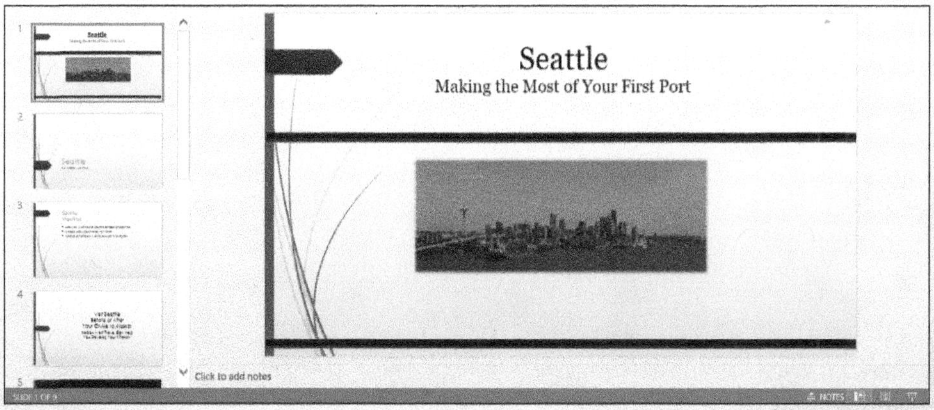

(GO! with Office Online (formerly Web Apps) continues on the next page)

the first color—**White, Background 1**. With the paragraph still selected, in the **Font group**, click **Bold** [B] and **Italic** [I]. In the **Paragraph group**, click **Center** [≡].

11 Click anywhere in a blank area of the slide to cancel the selection and view your formatting changes. Compare your screen with Figure B.

12 In the slide thumbnails, point to **Slide 4**, hold down the left mouse button, and then drag up slightly. Notice that a black bar displays above Slide 4. Continue to drag up until the black bar displays above **Slide 3**. Release the mouse button to move the slide.

13 Using the technique that you just practiced, move **Slide 5** to position it above **Slide 4**.

14 Display **Slide 6**. Click anywhere in the slide text, and then drag to select all three lines of text. On the **HOME tab**, in the **Paragraph group**, click **Center** [≡]. Click anywhere on the slide to cancel the selection.

15 Display **Slide 1**. On the **TRANSITIONS tab**, in the **Transition to This Slide group**, click **Push**. Click **Effect Options**, and then click **From Left**. In the **Transitions group**, click **Apply To All**.

16 Click the **VIEW tab**, and then in the **Presentation Views group**, click **Slide Show**. If a security warning displays at the bottom of your screen, click Allow once. Press [Spacebar] or click the left mouse button to advance through the slides in the presentation. When the black slide displays, click one more time to return to the presentation.

17 Submit your file as instructed by your instructor. Sign out of your OneDrive and close Internet Explorer.

FIGURE B

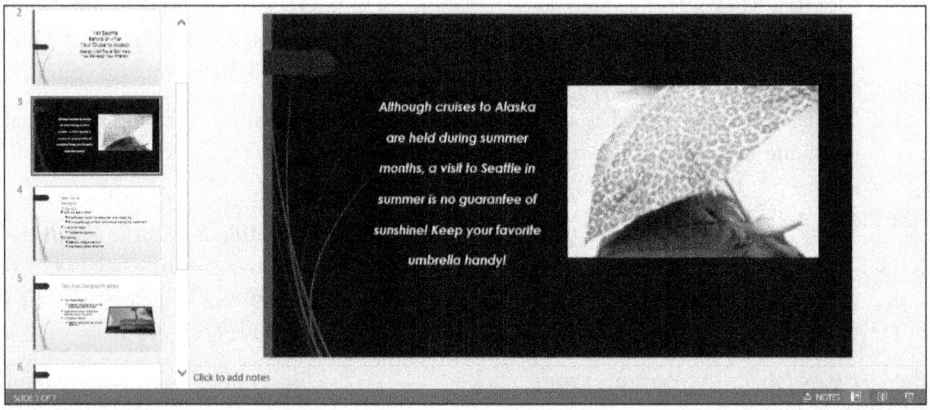

GO! with Microsoft Office 365

Andrew Rodriguez / Fotolia; FotolEdhar/ Fotolia; apops/ Fotolia; Yuri Arcurs/ Fotolia

In every job, you must work and communicate with other people. A group of workers tasked with working together to solve a problem, make a decision, or create a work product is referred to as a ***team***. For a team to succeed, the team members must be able to communicate with one another easily.

If all the team members work at the same location and work the same hours, communication is easy. You schedule face-to-face meetings and exchange documents and information among yourselves. But that is a rare arrangement in today's organizations. Rather, it is more likely that the members of your team work in different locations—even different countries—and work different hours or travel extensively away from the headquarters location. Also, for specific projects, teams are frequently organized across different departments of an organization or even across different organizations entirely. Then when the project is complete, the team disbands.

Collaboration is when you work together with others as a team in an intellectual endeavor to complete a shared task or achieve a shared goal; for example, when you and one or more of your classmates work together on a class project. Collaboration involves giving feedback to and receiving feedback from others on the team, and then revising the strategies to achieve the goal or produce the work product based on the feedback.

Microsoft Office 365 is a set of secure online services that enables people in an organization to communicate and collaborate by using any Internet-connected device—a computer, a tablet, or a mobile phone. Because Office 365 offers access from anywhere to email, web conferencing, documents, and calendars, everyone on a team can work together easily. Office 365 is intended for use by multiple users in an organization.

Activity | Using the Exchange Online Outlook Meeting Tool to Collaborate

This group project relates to the **Bell Orchid Hotels**. If your instructor assigns this project to your class, you can expect to use the **Outlook Meeting tool** in **Office 365 Exchange Online** to collaborate on the following tasks for this chapter:

- If you are in the **Accounting Group**, you and your teammates will meet virtually to create the text and initial formatting for a Loan Presentation to be presented by the Director to the Loan Officers of San Diego's SoCal Bank.
- If you are in the **Engineering Group**, you and your teammates will meet virtually to create the text and initial formatting for a Safety Presentation to be presented to all hotel department heads.
- If you are in the **Food and Beverage Group**, you and your teammates will meet virtually to create the text and initial formatting for a New Menu Item Presentation to be presented by the Director of the F&B Department to restaurant, banquet, and room service managers.
- If you are in the **Human Resources Group**, you and your teammates will meet virtually to create the text and initial formatting for a New Employees Orientation presentation to be presented to new staff hired by the hotel.
- If you are in the **Operations Group**, you and your teammates will meet virtually to create the text and initial formatting for a Front Desk Clerk Training Presentation as part of the hotel's on-the-job training program for Front Desk staff.
- If you are in the **Sales and Marketing Group**, you and your teammates will meet virtually to create the text and initial formatting for a Marketing Plan Presentation to be presented to all department heads and the Executive Office.

FIGURE A

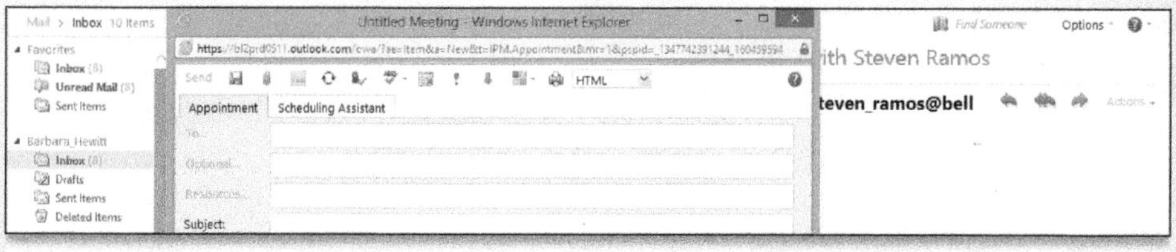

END OF CHAPTER

SUMMARY

When communicating your ideas, PowerPoint is a versatile business tool that will help you create presentations that make a lasting impression. Additionally, you can share slides you create on your OneDrive.

Use a presentation theme to establish a unified presentation design. You can change the color of the presentation theme by applying one of the predefined variants that are supplied with each theme.

Presentations are often organized in a manner similar to how outline levels are organized. List levels represent outline levels and are identified by the bullet style, indentation, and text size.

Slide layout defines the placement of content placeholders on a slide. Each presentation theme includes predefined layouts that you can apply to slides for the purpose of arranging slide elements.

GO! LEARN IT ONLINE

Review the concepts and key terms in this chapter by completing these online challenges, which you can find at **www.pearsonhighered.com/go**.

Matching and Multiple Choice: Answer matching and multiple choice questions to test what you learned in this chapter. MyITLab®

Crossword Puzzle: Spell out the words that match the numbered clues, and put them in the puzzle squares.

Flipboard: Flip through the definitions of the key terms in this chapter and match them with the correct term.

GO! FOR JOB SUCCESS

Video: Managing Priorities and Workspace

Your instructor may assign this video to your class, and then ask you to think about, or discuss with your classmates, these questions:

FotolEdhar / Fotolia

What kind of scheduling tool do you use? Is it on your computer, your cell phone, or other electronic device, or do you write in a notebook or physical calendar? Which kind of scheduling tool will be most effective for you and why?

Name one lifestyle change that you can make today that will help you create more time for your work projects.

What is the *one touch rule* and how do you think it will help you be more efficient?

END OF CHAPTER

REVIEW AND ASSESSMENT GUIDE FOR POWERPOINT CHAPTER 1

Your instructor may assign one or more of these projects to help you review the chapter and assess your mastery and understanding of the chapter.

Review and Assessment Guide for PowerPoint Chapter 1

Project	Apply Skills from These Chapter Objectives	Project Type	Project Location
1C	Objectives 1-4 from Project 1A	**1C Skills Review** A guided review of the skills from Project 1A.	On the following pages
1D	Objectives 5-8 from Project 1B	**1D Skills Review** A guided review of the skills from Project 1B.	On the following pages
1E	Objectives 1-4 from Project 1A	**1E Mastery (Grader Project)** A demonstration of your mastery of the skills in Project 1A with extensive decision making.	In MyITlab and on the following pages
1F	Objectives 5-8 from Project 1B	**1F Mastery (Grader Project)** A demonstration of your mastery of the skills in Project 1B with extensive decision making.	In MyITlab and on the following pages
1G	Objectives 1-8 from Projects 1A and IB	**1G Mastery (Grader Project)** A demonstration of your mastery of the skills in Projects 1A and 1B with extensive decision making.	In MyITlab and on the following pages
1H	Combination of Objectives from Projects 1A and 1B	**1H GO! Fix It** A demonstration of your mastery of the skills in Projects 1A and 1B by creating a correct result from a document that contains errors you must find.	Online
1I	Combination of Objectives from Projects 1A and 1B	**1I GO! Make It** A demonstration of your mastery of the skills in Projects 1A and 1B by creating a result from a supplied picture.	Online
1J	Combination of Objectives from Projects 1A and 1B	**1J GO! Solve It** A demonstration of your mastery of the skills in Projects 1A and 1B, your decision-making skills, and your critical thinking skills. A task-specific rubric helps you self-assess your result.	Online
1K	Combination of Objectives from Projects 1A and 1B	**1K GO! Solve It** A demonstration of your mastery of the skills in Projects 1A and 1B, your decision-making skills, and your critical thinking skills. A task-specific rubric helps you self-assess your result.	On the following pages
1L	Combination of Objectives from Projects 1A and 1B	**1L GO! Think** A demonstration of your understanding of the Chapter concepts applied in a manner that you would outside of college. An analytic rubric helps you and your instructor grade the quality of your work by comparing it to the work an expert in the discipline would create.	On the following pages
1M	Combination of Objectives from Projects 1A and 1B	**1M GO! Think** A demonstration of your understanding of the Chapter concepts applied in a manner that you would outside of college. An analytic rubric helps you and your instructor grade the quality of your work by comparing it to the work an expert in the discipline would create.	Online
1N	Combination of Objectives from Projects 1A and 1B	**1N You and GO!** A demonstration of your understanding of the Chapter concepts applied in a manner that you would in a personal situation. An analytic rubric helps you and your instructor grade the quality of your work.	Online
1O	Combination of Objectives from Projects 1A and 1B	**1O Cumulative Group Project for PowerPoint Chapter 1** A demonstration of your understanding of concepts and your ability to work collaboratively in a group role-playing assessment, requiring both collaboration and self-management.	Online

GLOSSARY

GLOSSARY OF CHAPTER KEY TERMS

Artistic effects Formats applied to images that make pictures resemble sketches or paintings.

Aspect ratio The ratio of the width of a display to the height of the display.

Black slide A slide that displays after the last slide in a presentation indicating that the presentation is over.

Collaboration The action of working with others as a team in an intellectual endeavor to complete a shared task or achieve a shared goal.

Contiguous slides Slides that are adjacent to each other in a presentation.

Editing The process of modifying a presentation by adding and deleting slides or by changing the contents of individual slides.

Footer Text that displays at the bottom of every slide or that prints at the bottom of a sheet of slide handouts or notes pages.

Formatting The process of changing the appearance of the text, layout, and design of a slide.

Header Text that prints at the top of each sheet of slide handouts or notes pages.

Layout The arrangement of elements, such as title and subtitle text, lists, pictures, tables, charts, shapes, and movies, on a slide.

List level An outline level in a presentation represented by a bullet symbol and identified in a slide by the indentation and the size of the text.

Microsoft Office 365 A set of secure online services that enable people in an organization to communicate and collaborate by using any Internet-connected device—a computer, a tablet, or a mobile phone.

Noncontiguous slides Slides that are not adjacent to each other in a presentation.

Normal view The primary editing view in PowerPoint where you write and design your presentations.

Notes page A printout that contains the slide image on the top half of the page and notes that you have created on the Notes pane in the lower half of the page.

Notes pane An area of the Normal view window that displays below the Slide pane with space to type notes regarding the active slide.

Outline View A PowerPoint view that displays the presentation outline to the left of the Slide pane.

Placeholder A box on a slide with dotted or dashed borders that holds title and body text or other content such as charts, tables, and pictures.

Reading view A view in PowerPoint that displays a presentation in a manner similar to a slide show but in which the taskbar, title bar, and status bar remain available in the presentation window.

Rotation handle A circular arrow that provides a way to rotate a selected image.

Section header A type of slide layout that changes the look and flow of a presentation by providing text placeholders that do not contain bullet points.

Sizing handles Small squares surrounding a picture that indicate that the picture is selected.

Slide A presentation page that can contain text, pictures, tables, charts, and other multimedia or graphic objects.

Slide handout Printed images of slides on a sheet of paper.

Slide pane A PowerPoint screen element that displays a large image of the active slide.

Slide Sorter view A presentation view that displays thumbnails of all of the slides in a presentation.

Slide transitions Motion effects that occur in Slide Show view when you move from one slide to the next during a presentation.

Split button A type of button in which clicking the main part of the button performs a command and clicking the arrow opens a menu, list, or gallery.

Style A collection of formatting options that you can apply to a picture, text, or an object.

Team A group of workers tasked with working together to solve a problem, make a decision, or create a work product.

Text alignment The horizontal placement of text within a placeholder.

Theme A set of unified design elements that provides a look for your presentation by applying colors, fonts, and effects.

Thumbnails Miniature images of presentation slides.

Title slide A slide layout—most commonly the first slide in a presentation—that provides an introduction to the presentation topic.

Variant A variation on the presentation theme style and color.

CHAPTER REVIEW

Apply 1A skills from these Objectives:

1 Create a New Presentation
2 Edit a Presentation in Normal View
3 Add Pictures to a Presentation
4 Print and View a Presentation

Build from Scratch

Skills Review Project 1C Glaciers

In the following Skills Review, you will create a new presentation by inserting content and pictures, adding notes and footers, and applying a presentation theme. Your completed presentation will look similar to Figure 1.58.

PROJECT FILES

For Project 1C, you will need the following files:

New blank PowerPoint presentation
p01C_Glacier_Bay
p01C_Ice
p01C_Ship

You will save your presentation as:

Lastname_Firstname_1C_Glaciers

PROJECT RESULTS

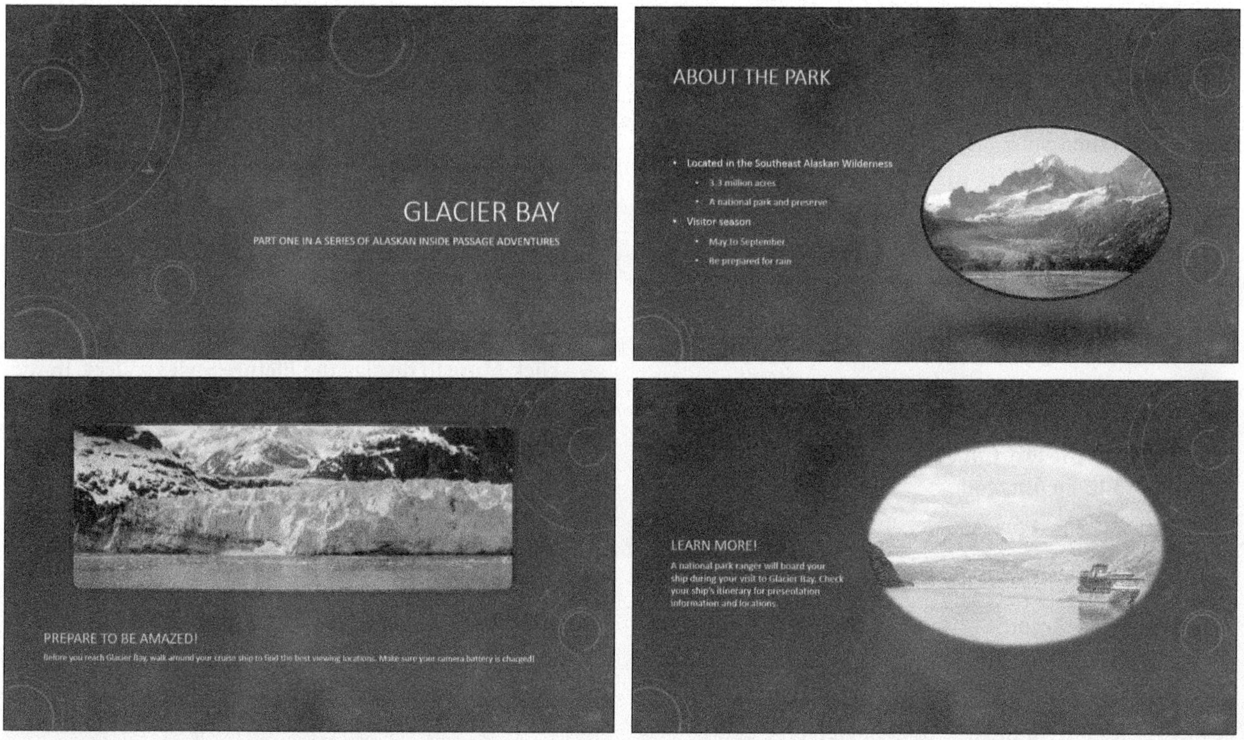

FIGURE 1.58

(Project 1C Glaciers continues on the next page)

CHAPTER REVIEW

Skills Review Project 1C Glaciers (continued)

1 Start PowerPoint. On the right, click **Celestial,** and then click **Create.** In the **Slide pane,** click in the text *Click to add title.* Type **Glacier Bay** and then click in the subtitle placeholder. Type **Part One in a Series of Alaskan Passage Adventures** Notice that the font uses all uppercase letters.

a. On the **Quick Access Toolbar,** click **Save** . Under **Save As,** click **Computer,** and then click **Browse.** Navigate to your **PowerPoint Chapter 1** folder. In the **File name** box, using your own name, replace the existing text with **Lastname_Firstname_1C_Glaciers** and then click **Save.**

b. On the **HOME tab,** in the **Slides group,** click the **New Slide arrow,** and then in the gallery, click **Two Content.** Click the text *Click to add title,* and then type **About the Park**

2 On the left side of the slide, click in the content placeholder. Type **Located in the Southeast Alaskan Wilderness** and then press Enter. Press Tab. Type **3.3 million acres** and then press Enter. Type **A national park and preserve** and then press Enter

a. On the **HOME tab,** in the **Paragraph group,** click **Decrease List Level.** Type **Visitor season** and then press Enter. On the **HOME tab,** in the **Paragraph group,** click **Increase List Level.** Type **May to September**

b. On the **HOME tab,** in the **Slides group,** click the **New Slide arrow,** and then in the gallery, click **Panoramic Picture with Caption.** In the lower portion of the slide, click the text *Click to add title,* and then type **Prepare to be Amazed!**

c. Click in the text placeholder. Type **Before you reach Glacier Bay, walk around your cruise ship to find the best viewing locations. Make sure your camera battery is charged!**

d. On the **HOME tab,** in the **Slides group,** click the **New Slide arrow,** and then in the gallery, click **Content with Caption.** In the title placeholder, type **Learn More!**

e. Click in the text placeholder, and then type **A national park ranger will board your ship during your visit to Glacier Bay. Check your ship's itinerary for presentation information and locations.**

3 With **Slide 4** displayed, in the **Status bar,** click **NOTES.** Click in the **Notes pane,** and then type **Your cruise ship will spend between 6 and 8 hours in Glacier Bay.**

a. On the left side of the PowerPoint window, in the slide thumbnails, click **Slide 1.** Click in the subtitle placeholder after the *n* in *Alaskan.* Press Spacebar, and then type **Inside**

b. In the slide thumbnails, click **Slide 2,** and then click at the end of the last bullet point after the word *September.* Press Enter, and then type **Be prepared for rain**

4 With **Slide** 2 displayed, in the placeholder on the right side of the slide, click **Pictures.** Navigate to your student data files, and then click **p01C_Glacier_Bay.** Click **Insert.**

a. With the picture selected, on the **FORMAT tab,** in the **Picture Styles group,** click **More** to display the **Picture Styles** gallery. In the second row, click the third style—**Beveled Oval, Black.**

b. Display **Slide 3.** In the Picture placeholder, click **Pictures.** Navigate to your student data files, and then click **p01C_Ice.** Click **Insert.**

c. Display **Slide 4.** In the content placeholder on the right side of the slide, click **Pictures.** Navigate to your student data files, and then insert **p01C_Ship.** On the **FORMAT tab,** in the **Picture Styles group,** click **More** to display the **Picture Styles** gallery. In the third row, click the sixth style—**Soft Edge Oval.**

d. With the picture still selected, on the **FORMAT tab,** in the **Adjust group,** click **Artistic Effects** to display the gallery. In the fourth row, click the third effect—**Crisscross Etching.**

5 On the ribbon, click the **SLIDE SHOW tab.** In the **Start Slide Show group,** click **From Beginning.**

a. Click the left mouse button or press Spacebar to advance to the second slide. Continue to click or press Spacebar until the last slide displays, and then click or press Spacebar one more time to display a black slide.

b. With the black slide displayed, click the left mouse button or press Spacebar to exit the slide show and return to the presentation.

(Project 1C Glaciers continues on the next page)

Skills Review Project 1C Glaciers (continued)

6 Click the **INSERT tab**, and then in the **Text group**, click **Header & Footer** to display the **Header and Footer** dialog box.

a. In the **Header and Footer** dialog box, click the **Notes and Handouts tab**. Under **Include on page**, select the **Date and time** check box. If necessary, click the Update automatically option button so that the current date prints on the notes and handouts.

b. If necessary, clear the Header check box to omit this element. Select the **Page number** and **Footer** check boxes. In the **Footer** box, using your own name, type **Lastname_Firstname_1C_Glaciers** and then click **Apply to All**.

c. In the upper left corner of your screen, click the **FILE** tab to display **Backstage** view. On the right, at the bottom of the **Properties list**, click **Show All Properties**.

d. On the list of Properties, click to the right of **Tags** to display an empty box, and then type **Glacier Bay** Click to the right of **Subject** to display an empty box, and then type your course name and section number. Under **Related People**, be sure that your name displays as the author; edit if necessary.

e. **Save** your presentation. Submit your presentation electronically or print **Handouts, 4 Slides Horizontal** as directed by your instructor. **Close** PowerPoint.

END | You have completed Project 1C

CHAPTER REVIEW

Skills Review Project 1D Photography

Apply 1B skills from these Objectives:

5 Edit an Existing Presentation
6 Format a Presentation
7 Use Slide Sorter View
8 Apply Slide Transitions

In the following Skills Review, you will edit an existing presentation by inserting slides from another presentation, applying font and slide formatting, and applying slide transitions. Your completed presentation will look similar to Figure 1.59.

PROJECT FILES

For Project 1D, you will need the following files:

p01D_Photography
p01D_Photography_Slides

You will save your presentation as:

Lastname_Firstname_1D_Photography

PROJECT RESULTS

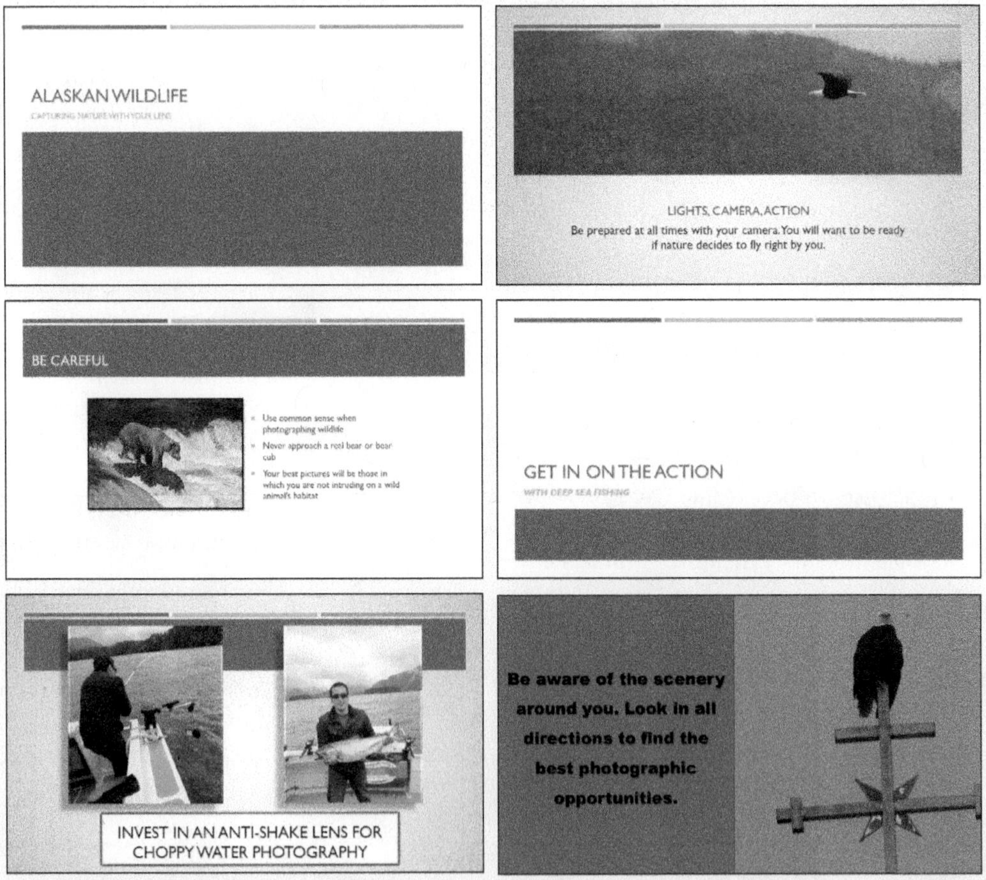

FIGURE 1.59

(Project 1D Photography continues on the next page)

CHAPTER REVIEW

Skills Review Project 1D Photography (continued)

1 Start PowerPoint. On the left, under the list of recent presentations, click **Open Other Presentations**. Under **Open**, click **Computer** and then click **Browse**. Navigate to your student data files, and then click **p01D_Photography**. Click **Open**. On the **FILE tab**, click **Save As**, navigate to your **PowerPoint Chapter 1** folder, and then using your own name, save the file as **Lastname_Firstname_1D_Photography**

a. On the **DESIGN tab**, in the **Customize group**, click **Slide Size**, and then click **Widescreen (16:9)**.

b. With **Slide 1** displayed, on the **HOME tab**, in the **Slides group**, click the **New Slide arrow**, and then click **Reuse Slides**. In the **Reuse Slides** pane, click **Browse**, and then click **Browse File**. In the **Browse** dialog box, navigate to your student data files, and then double-click **p01D_Photography_Slides** to display the slides from this presentation in the Reuse Slides pane.

c. At the bottom of the **Reuse Slides** pane, be sure that the **Keep source formatting** check box is *cleared*. In the **Reuse Slides** pane, click the first slide to insert the slide after Slide 1.

d. At the left of your screen, in the slide thumbnails, click **Slide 6** to display it in the **Slide pane**. In the **Reuse Slides** pane, click the second slide to insert it after Slide 6. **Close** the **Reuse Slides** pane.

2 Display **Slide 1**. On the **VIEW tab**, in the **Presentation Views group**, click **Outline View**.

a. In the **Outline**, in **Slide 7**, drag to select the second and third bullet points—beginning with *Never approach* and ending with *animal's home*.

b. On the **HOME tab**, in the **Paragraph group**, click **Decrease List Level** one time.

c. In the **Outline**, in the same slide, click at the end of the first bullet point after the word *sense*. Press Spacebar, and then type **when photographing wildlife**

d. In the **Status bar**, click **Normal** to display the slide thumbnails.

3 Display **Slide 8**, and then press Delete to delete the slide from the presentation.

a. Display **Slide 1**. On the **HOME tab**, in the **Editing group**, click **Replace**. In the **Replace** dialog box, in the **Find what** box, type **home** and then in the **Replace with** box, type **habitat**

b. In the **Replace** dialog box, click **Replace All** to display a message box indicating that one replacement was made. In the message box, click **OK**. **Close** the **Replace** dialog box.

c. On the **DESIGN tab**, in the **Variants group**, right-click the green variant. On the shortcut menu, click **Apply to All Slides** so that the green color is applied to all of the slides in the presentation.

4 Display **Slide 5**. Select all of the text in the placeholder. On the **HOME tab**, in the **Font group**, click the **Font button arrow**, scroll the font list, and then click **Arial Black**. Click the **Font Size button arrow**, and then click **32**. In the **Paragraph group**, click **Line Spacing**, and then click **1.5**.

a. Display **Slide 2**. On the **HOME tab**, in the **Slides group**, click **Layout** to display the **Slide Layout** gallery. Click **Title Slide** to change the slide layout.

b. On **Slide 2**, select the title—*Alaskan Wildlife*. On the **HOME tab**, in the **Font group**, click the **Font Color button arrow**. In the fifth column, click the first color—**Dark Teal, Accent 1**.

c. Display **Slide 3**, and then select the title—*Lights, Camera, Action*. On the mini toolbar, click **Font Color** to apply the font color **Dark Teal, Accent 1**.

d. Display **Slide 4**, and then, click anywhere in the text. On the **HOME tab**, in the **Paragraph group**, click **Center** to center the text within the placeholder.

e. Display **Slide 6**, and then select the subtitle. From the mini toolbar, apply **Bold** and **Italic**.

f. In the slide thumbnails, point to **Slide 7**, hold down the left mouse button, and then drag up to position the slide between **Slides 3** and **4**.

5 In the lower right corner of the PowerPoint window, click **Slide Sorter** to display all of the slide thumbnails. Click **Slide 1**, so that it is selected. Press Delete to delete the slide.

a. Click **Slide 4**, and then hold down Ctrl and click **Slide 5**. With both slides selected, point to either of the selected slides, hold down the left mouse button, and then drag to position the two slides to the right of **Slide 6**. Release the mouse button to move the two slides. In the status bar, click **Normal** to return to Normal view.

(Project 1D Photography continues on the next page)

Skills Review Project 1D Photography (continued)

b. Display **Slide 1**. On the **TRANSITIONS tab**, in the **Transition to This Slide group**, click **More** to display the **Transitions** gallery.

c. Under **Exciting**, click **Gallery** to apply and view the transition. In the **Transition to This Slide group**, click **Effect Options**, and then click **From Left**. In the **Timing group**, click **Apply To All** to apply the *Gallery, From Left* transition to all of the slides in the presentation.

d. In the **Timing group**, click the **Duration up spin arrow** so that *01.75* displays. Under **Advance Slide**, verify that the **On Mouse Click** check box is selected; select it if necessary. In the **Timing group**, click **Apply To All**.

e. Click the **SLIDE SHOW tab**. In the **Start Slide Show group**, click **From Beginning**, and then view your presentation, clicking the mouse button to advance through the slides. When the black slide displays, click the mouse button one more time to display the presentation in Normal view.

6 Click the **INSERT tab**, and then in the **Text group**, click **Header & Footer** to display the **Header and Footer** dialog box.

a. In the **Header and Footer** dialog box, click the **Notes and Handouts tab**. Under **Include on page**, select the **Date and time** check box. If necessary, click the Update automatically option button so that the current date prints on the notes and handouts.

b. If necessary, clear the Header check box to omit this element. Select the **Page number** and **Footer** check boxes. In the **Footer** box, type **Lastname_Firstname_1D_Photography** and then click **Apply to All**.

c. In the upper left corner of your screen, click the **FILE** tab to display **Backstage** view. On the right, at the bottom of the **Properties list**, click **Show All Properties**.

d. On the list of Properties, click to the right of **Tags** to display an empty box, and then type **photography** Click to the right of **Subject** to display an empty box, and then type your course name and section number. Under **Related People**, be sure that your name displays as the author; edit if necessary.

e. **Save** your presentation. Submit your presentation electronically or print **Handouts, 6 Slides Horizontal** as directed by your instructor. **Close** PowerPoint.

END | You have completed Project 1D

CONTENT-BASED ASSESSMENTS

Mastering PowerPoint | Project 1E Juneau

MyITLab® grader

Apply 1A skills from these Objectives:

1. Create a New Presentation
2. Edit a Presentation in Normal View
3. Add Pictures to a Presentation
4. Print and View a Presentation

Build from Scratch

In the following Mastering PowerPoint project, you will create a new presentation that Kodiak West Travel will use in their promotional materials to describe activities in the city of Juneau. Your completed presentation will look similar to Figure 1.60.

PROJECT FILES

For Project 1E, you will need the following files:

New blank PowerPoint presentation
p01E_Aerial_View
p01E_Whale
p01E_Falls

You will save your presentation as:

Lastname_Firstname_1E_Juneau

PROJECT RESULTS

FIGURE 1.60

(Project 1E Juneau continues on the next page)

CONTENT-BASED ASSESSMENTS

Mastering PowerPoint | Project 1E Juneau (continued)

1 Start PowerPoint and create a presentation using the **Integral** theme. Use the first color variation. As the title of this presentation type **Juneau Highlights** and as the subtitle type **Kodiak West Travel** Save the presentation in your **PowerPoint Chapter 1** folder as **Lastname_Firstname_1E_Juneau**

2 Insert a **New Slide** using the **Content with Caption** layout. In the title placeholder, type **The View from Above** In the content placeholder on the right side of the slide, from your student data files, insert the picture **p01E_Aerial_View**. Format the picture with the **Bevel Rectangle** picture style and the **Paint Brush** artistic effect.

3 In the text placeholder on the left, type **View a glacial ice field from above by plane or helicopter. If you are more adventurous, try glacier trekking in Juneau where you can land on a glacier and climb an ice wall.**

4 Insert a **New Slide** using the **Two Content** layout. In the title placeholder, type **On Land and Sea** In the content placeholder on the left, type the following text, increasing and decreasing the list level as shown below. In this presentation theme, the first level bullet points do not include a bullet symbol.

On the water
- **Whale watching**
- **Kayaking**

Mount Roberts tramway
- **Spectacular views of Juneau**
- **Recreational hiking trails**

5 In the content placeholder on the right, from your student data files, insert the picture **p01D_Whale**. Apply the **Rotated, White** picture style.

6 Insert a new slide with the **Picture with Caption** layout. In the title placeholder, type **Mendenhall Glacier** and then in the picture placeholder, from your student data files, insert the picture **p01E_Falls**.

7 In the text placeholder, type **Walk to Mendenhall Glacier from the Visitor Center to get a close-up view of Nugget Falls.**

8 In the **Notes pane**, type **Mendenhall Glacier is the most famous glacier in Juneau and in some years is visited by over 400,000 people.**

9 Insert a **Header & Footer** on the **Notes and Handouts**. Include the **Date and time** updated automatically, the **Page number**, and a **Footer**—using your own name—with the text **Lastname_Firstname_1E_Juneau** and apply to all the slides.

10 Display the **Document Properties**. As the **Tags** type **Juneau** As the **Subject** type your course and section number. Be sure your name is indicated as the author.

11 **Save** your presentation, and then view the slide show from the beginning. Submit your presentation electronically or print **Handouts, 4 Slides Horizontal** as directed by your instructor. **Close** PowerPoint.

END | You have completed Project 1E

CONTENT-BASED ASSESSMENTS

MyITLab® grader

Apply 1B skills from these Objectives:

5 Edit an Existing Presentation
6 Format a Presentation
7 Use Slide Sorter View
8 Apply Slide Transitions

Mastering PowerPoint Project 1F Refuge

In the following Mastering PowerPoint project, you will edit a presentation regarding a wildlife refuge where Kodiak West Travel conducts tours. Your completed presentation will look similar to Figure 1.61.

PROJECT FILES

For Project 1F, you will need the following files:

p01F_Refuge
p01F_Excursions

You will save your presentation as:

Lastname_Firstname_1F_Refuge

PROJECT RESULTS

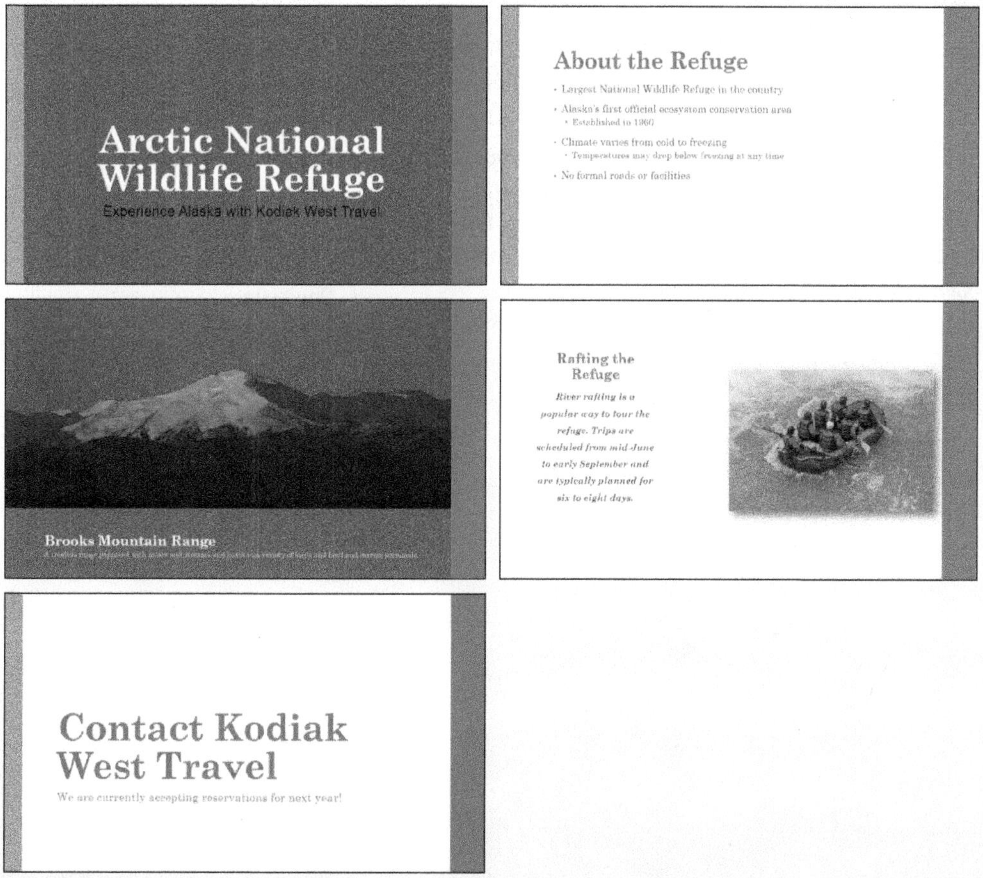

FIGURE 1.61

(Project 1F Refuge continues on the next page)

CONTENT-BASED ASSESSMENTS

Mastering PowerPoint Project 1F Refuge (continued)

1 Start PowerPoint, and then from your student data files, open the file **p01F_Refuge**. In your **PowerPoint Chapter 1** folder, **Save** the file as **Lastname_Firstname_1F_Refuge**

2 Change the **Slide Size** to **Widescreen (16:9)**, and then change the **Variant** for all the slides to the option with the orange bar on the right side.

3 Display the presentation **Outline**. In the **Outline**, on **Slide 2**, increase the list level of the third and the fifth bullet points. Click at the end of the last bullet point after the word *roads*, and then type **or facilities**

4 Return the presentation to **Normal view**, and then display **Slide 4**. Display the **Reuse Slides** pane. Browse to your student data files, and then open **p01F_Excursions**. Make sure the **Keep source formatting** check box is *cleared*. With **Slide 4** in your presentation displayed, insert the last two slides from the **Reuse Slides** pane, and then close the pane.

5 Display **Slide 1**, and then change the layout to **Title Slide**. Select the subtitle—*Experience Alaska with Kodiak West Travel*. Change the **Font** to **Arial**, and the **Font Size** to **28**. Change the **Font Color** to **Black, Background 1**. **Center** the title and the subtitle.

6 Display **Slide 5**, and then select the paragraph in the content placeholder. Apply **Bold** and **Italic**, and then change the **Font Size** to **18**. **Center** the text, and then change the **Line Spacing** to **1.5**. **Center** the slide title.

7 In **Slide Sorter** view, delete **Slide 3**. Move **Slide 5** to position it after **Slide 2**. Move **Slide 4** to the end of the presentation.

8 In **Normal** view, display **Slide 1**. Apply the **Split** transition and change the **Effect Options** to **Horizontal Out**. Change the **Duration** to **1.75**, and the apply the transition to all of the slides in the presentation. View the slide show from the beginning.

9 **Insert** a **Header & Footer** on the **Notes and Handouts**. Include the **Date and time** updated automatically, the **Page number**, and a **Footer** with the text **Lastname_Firstname_1F_Refuge**

10 Display the **Document Properties**. As the **Tags** type **refuge, tours** As the **Subject** type your course and section number. Be sure your name is indicated as the author.

11 **Save** your presentation, and then submit your presentation electronically or print **Handouts, 6 Slides Horizontal** as directed by your instructor. **Close** PowerPoint.

END | You have completed Project 1F

CONTENT-BASED ASSESSMENTS

Mastering PowerPoint | Project 1G Northern Lights

MyITLab® grader

Apply 1A and 1B skills from these Objectives:

1. Create a New Presentation
2. Edit a Presentation in Normal View
3. Add Pictures to a Presentation
4. Print and View a Presentation
5. Edit an Existing Presentation
6. Format a Presentation
7. Use Slide Sorter View
8. Apply Slide Transitions

In the following Mastering PowerPoint project, you will edit an existing presentation that describes the Northern Lights and ideal viewing areas. Your completed presentation will look similar to Figure 1.62.

PROJECT FILES

For Project 1G, you will need the following files:

p01G_Northern_Lights
p01G_Lights
p01G_Slides

You will save your presentation as:

Lastname_Firstname_1G_Northern_Lights

PROJECT RESULTS

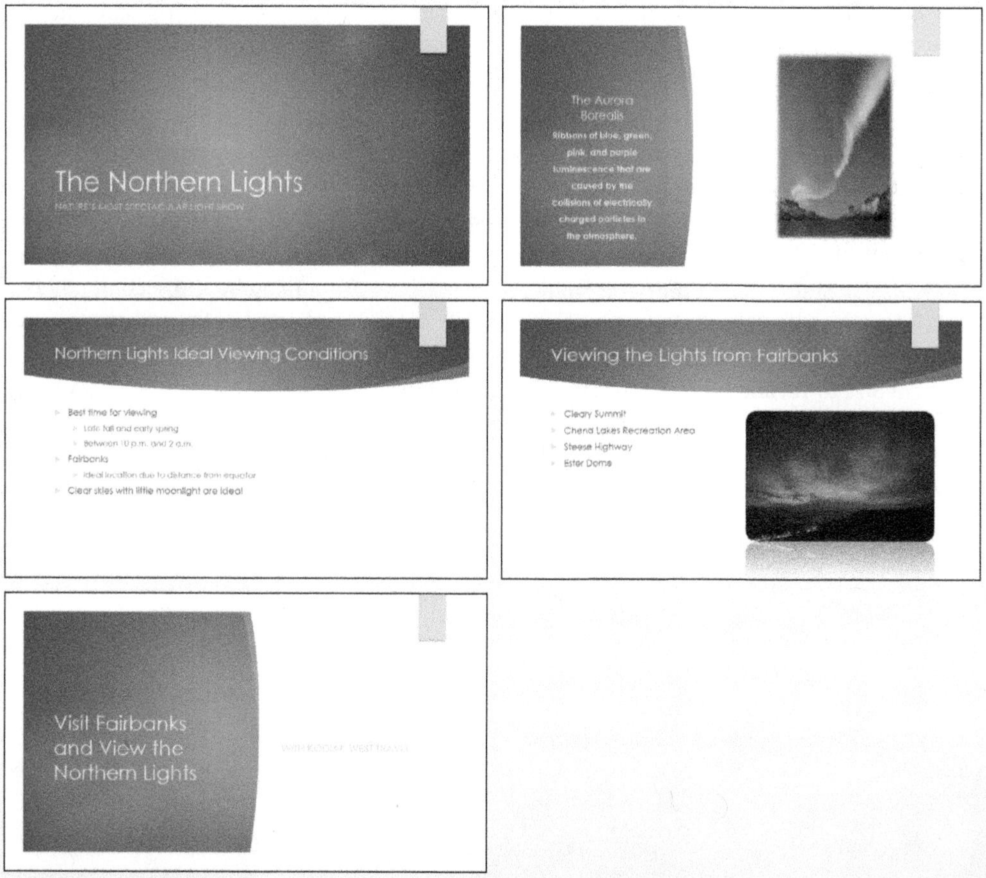

FIGURE 1.62

(Project 1G Northern Lights continues on the next page)

CONTENT-BASED ASSESSMENTS

Mastering PowerPoint | Project 1G Northern Lights (continued)

1 Start PowerPoint, and then from your student data files, open the file **p01G_Northern_Lights**. In your **PowerPoint Chapter 1** folder, **Save** the file as **Lastname_Firstname_1G_Northern_Lights**

2 Replace all occurrences of the text **North** with **Northern** and then change the layout of **Slide 1** to **Title Slide**. Apply the **Ion Boardroom** theme, and then change the **Variant** to the blue variant option. Change the **Slide Size** to **Widescreen (16:9)**.

3 Display **Slide 2**, open the **Reuse Slides** pane, and then from your student data files browse for and open the presentation **p01G_Slides**. If necessary, clear the Keep source formatting check box, and then insert the last two slides from the **p01G_Slides** file.

4 Display **Slide 2**. In either the slide pane or in the slide outline, click at the end of the first bullet point after the word *time*. Add the words **for viewing** and then in the same slide, increase the list level of the second and third bullet points.

5 With **Slide 2** still displayed, select the title and change the **Font Size** to **32**. In the **Notes pane**, type the following notes: **The lights reach their peak in September and March.**

6 Display **Slide 3**. Select the paragraph of text, and then change the **Font Color** to **Green, Accent 6, Lighter 60%**—in the last column, the third color. Change the **Font Size** to **18**, and then apply **Bold**. Change the **Line Spacing** to **1.5**, and then **Center** the paragraph and the slide title.

7 With **Slide 3** still displayed, format the picture with the **Soft Edge Rectangle** picture style and the **Marker** artistic effect.

8 Display **Slide 4**. In the content placeholder on the right, from your student data files, insert the picture **p01G_Lights**. Apply the **Reflected Rounded Rectangle** picture style.

9 Move **Slide 3** between **Slides 1** and **2**, and then display **Slide 4**. Insert a **New Slide** with the **Section Header** layout. In the title placeholder type **Visit Fairbanks and View the Northern Lights!** In the text placeholder type **With Kodiak West Travel**

10 Apply the **Uncover** transition and change the **Effect Options** to **From Top**. Change the **Timing** by increasing the **Duration** to **01.25**. Apply the transition effect to all of the slides. View the slide show from the beginning.

11 **Insert** a **Header & Footer** on the **Notes and Handouts**. Include the **Date and time** updated automatically, the **Page number**, and a **Footer**, using your own name, with the text **Lastname_Firstname_1G_Northern_Lights**

12 Display the **Document Properties**. As the **Tags** type **northern lights, Fairbanks** As the **Subject** type your course and section number. Be sure your name is indicated as the author.

13 **Save** your presentation, and then submit your presentation electronically or print **Handouts, 6 Slides Horizontal** as directed by your instructor. **Close** PowerPoint.

END | You have completed Project 1G

CONTENT-BASED ASSESSMENTS

Apply a combination of the 1A and 1B skills.

Build from Scratch

GO! Fix It Project 1H Rain Forest Online

GO! Make It Project 1I Eagles Online

GO! Solve It Project 1J Packrafting Online

GO! Solve It Project 1K Packing

PROJECT FILES

For Project 1K, you will need the following file:

p01K_Packing

You will save your presentation as:

Lastname_Firstname_1K_Packing

Open the file p01K_Packing and save it as **Lastname_Firstname_1K_Packing** Complete the presentation by applying a theme and changing the variant. Format the presentation attractively by applying appropriate font formatting and by changing text alignment and line spacing. Change the layout of Slide 4 to an appropriate layout. On Slide 2, insert a picture that you have taken yourself, or use one of the pictures in your student data files that you inserted in other projects in this chapter. Apply a style to the picture. Apply slide transitions to all of the slides in the presentation, and then insert a header and footer that includes the date and time updated automatically, the file name in the footer, and the page number. Add your name, your course name and section number, and the tags **packing, weather** to the properties. Save and print or submit as directed by your instructor.

Performance Level

Performance Criteria	Exemplary	Proficient	Developing
Apply a theme and a variant	An appropriate theme and variant were applied to the presentation.	A theme was applied but the variant was not changed.	Neither a theme nor the variant theme were applied.
Apply font and slide formatting	Font and slide formatting is attractive and appropriate.	Adequately formatted but difficult to read or unattractive.	Inadequate or no formatting.
Use appropriate pictures and apply styles attractively	An appropriate picture was inserted and a style is applied attractively.	A picture was inserted but a style was not applied.	Picture was not inserted.
Apply appropriate slide layout to Slide 4	An appropriate layout was applied to the last slide.	The slide layout was changed but is not appropriate for the type of slide.	The slide layout was not changed.

END | You have completed Project 1K

OUTCOMES-BASED ASSESSMENTS

RUBRIC

The following outcomes-based assessments are open-ended assessments. That is, there is no specific correct result; your result will depend on your approach to the information provided. Make Professional Quality your goal. Use the following scoring rubric to guide you in how to approach the problem and then to evaluate how well your approach solves the problem.

The *criteria*—Software Mastery, Content, Format and Layout, and Process—represent the knowledge and skills you have gained that you can apply to solving the problem. The *levels of performance*—Professional Quality, Approaching Professional Quality, or Needs Quality Improvements—help you and your instructor evaluate your result.

	Your completed project is of Professional Quality if you:	Your completed project is Approaching Professional Quality if you:	Your completed project Needs Quality Improvements if you:
1-Software Mastery	Choose and apply the most appropriate skills, tools, and features and identify efficient methods to solve the problem.	Choose and apply some appropriate skills, tools, and features, but not in the most efficient manner.	Choose inappropriate skills, tools, or features, or are inefficient in solving the problem.
2-Content	Construct a solution that is clear and well organized, contains content that is accurate, appropriate to the audience and purpose, and is complete. Provide a solution that contains no errors in spelling, grammar, or style.	Construct a solution in which some components are unclear, poorly organized, inconsistent, or incomplete. Misjudge the needs of the audience. Have some errors in spelling, grammar, or style, but the errors do not detract from comprehension.	Construct a solution that is unclear, incomplete, or poorly organized; contains some inaccurate or inappropriate content; and contains many errors in spelling, grammar, or style. Do not solve the problem.
3-Format & Layout	Format and arrange all elements to communicate information and ideas, clarify function, illustrate relationships, and indicate relative importance.	Apply appropriate format and layout features to some elements, but not others. Overuse features, causing minor distraction.	Apply format and layout that does not communicate information or ideas clearly. Do not use format and layout features to clarify function, illustrate relationships, or indicate relative importance. Use available features excessively, causing distraction.
4-Process	Use an organized approach that integrates planning, development, self-assessment, revision, and reflection.	Demonstrate an organized approach in some areas, but not others; or, use an insufficient process of organization throughout.	Do not use an organized approach to solve the problem.

OUTCOMES-BASED ASSESSMENTS

Apply a combination of the 1A and 1B skills.

GO! Think Project 1L Bears

Build from Scratch

PROJECT FILES

For Project 1L, you will need the following files:

New blank PowerPoint presentation
p01L_Bear

You will save your presentation as:

Lastname_Firstname_1L_Bears

Cindy Barrow, Tour Operations Manager for Kodiak West Travel, is developing a presentation describing brown bear viewing travel experiences that the company is developing. In the presentation, Cindy will be describing the brown bear habitat and viewing opportunities.

Kodiak bears are the largest known size of brown bears on record; they can weigh as much as 2,000 pounds and can get as large as polar bears. Kodiak bears are active during the day and are generally solitary creatures. The Kodiak Bear Travel Experience is a small, personalized travel adventure available to only eight participants at a time. It is an opportunity to peer into the life of these majestic mammals.

The adventure takes place on Kodiak Island near a lake with a high concentration of salmon, making it the perfect natural feeding ground for the Kodiak bears. Travelers can view the bears from boats, kayaks, and recently constructed viewing platforms and guides are available.

This is a true wildlife experience because the area is home to deer, fox, and river otter. Accommodations are available at the Kodiak West Breakfast Inn from mid-June to the end of August. Peak season is early August and reservations can be made up to one year in advance. The cost is $1,800 per person for one week, and includes all meals, use of watercraft, and guided tours.

Using the preceding information, create a presentation that Cindy can show at a travel fair. The presentation should include four to six slides describing the travel experience. Apply an appropriate theme and use slide layouts that will effectively present the content. Insert at least one picture and apply appropriate picture formatting. You may use a picture of your choosing or from your student data files, use the file p01L_Bear. Apply font formatting and slide transitions, and modify text alignment and line spacing as necessary.

Save the file as **Lastname_Firstname_1L_Bears** and then insert a header and footer that include the date and time updated automatically, the file name in the footer, and the page number. Add your name, your course name and section number, and the tags **bears, tours** to the properties. Save and print or submit as directed by your instructor.

END | You have completed Project 1L

OUTCOMES-BASED ASSESSMENTS

Build from Scratch

GO! Think Project 1M Sitka **Online**

Build from Scratch

You and GO! Project 1N Travel **Online**

GO! Cumulative Group Project Project 1O Bell Orchid Hotels **Online**

Formatting PowerPoint Presentations

GO! to Work Video P2

2

POWERPOINT 2013

PROJECT 2A

OUTCOMES
Format a presentation to add visual interest and clarity.

PROJECT 2B

OUTCOMES
Enhance a presentation with WordArt and SmartArt.

OBJECTIVES

1. Format Numbered and Bulleted Lists
2. Insert Online Pictures
3. Insert Text Boxes and Shapes
4. Format Objects

OBJECTIVES

5. Remove Picture Backgrounds and Insert WordArt
6. Create and Format a SmartArt Graphic

In This Chapter

A PowerPoint presentation is a visual aid in which well-designed slides help the audience understand complex information while keeping them focused on the message. Color is an important element that enhances your slides and draws the audience's interest by creating focus. When designing the background and element colors for your presentation, be sure that the colors you use provide contrast so that the text is visible on the background. Graphic elements such as pictures, SmartArt, and shapes can illustrate important information. Choose elements that work well with the presentation design and colors.

The projects in this chapter relate to **Sensation Park Entertainment Group**, an entertainment company that operates 15 regional theme parks across the United States, Mexico, and Canada. Park types include traditional theme parks, water parks, and animal parks. This year the company will launch three of its new "Sensation Parks" where attractions combine fun and the discovery of math and science information, and where teens and adults enjoy the free Friday night concerts. The company focuses on safe and imaginative attractions that appeal to guests with a variety of entertainment interests, including adventure, science, and the arts.

PROJECT 2A Employee Training Presentation

MyITLab®
Project 2A Training

PROJECT ACTIVITIES

In Activities 2.01 through 2.21, you will format a presentation for Marc Johnson, Director of Operations for Sensation Park Entertainment Group, that describes important safety guidelines for employees. Your completed presentation will look similar to Figure 2.1.

PROJECT FILES

For Project 2A, you will need the following file:
p02A_Safety

You will save your presentation as:
Lastname_Firstname_2A_Safety

PROJECT RESULTS

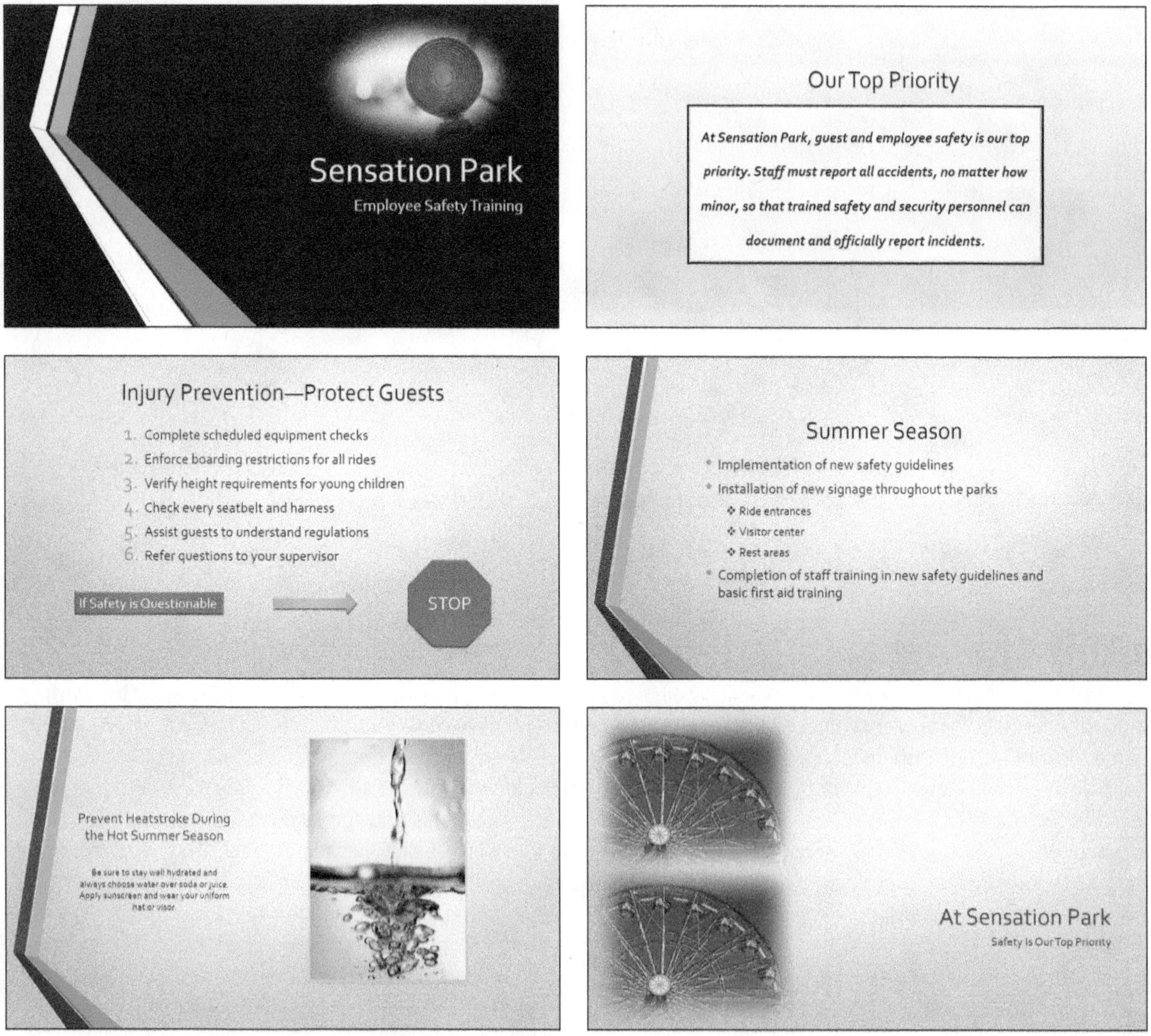

FIGURE 2.1 Project 2A Employee Training Presentation

Objective 1 Format Numbered and Bulleted Lists

Video P2-1

The font, color, and style of a numbered or bulleted list are determined by the presentation theme. You can format slide content by changing the bulleted and numbered list styles and colors.

Activity 2.01 Selecting Placeholder Text

Recall that a placeholder is a box on a slide with dotted or dashed borders that holds title and body text or other content such as charts, tables, and pictures. You can format placeholder contents by selecting text or by selecting the entire placeholder.

1. Start PowerPoint. From the student data files that accompany this textbook, locate and open **p02A_Safety**. Display the **Save As** dialog box, create a **New Folder** with the name **PowerPoint Chapter 2** and then using your own name, save the file in the folder you created as **Lastname_Firstname_2A_Safety**
2. Display **Slide 2**, and then click anywhere in the content placeholder with the single bullet point.
3. Point to the dashed border surrounding the placeholder to display the pointer, and then click one time to display the border as a solid line. Compare your screen with Figure 2.2.

   When a placeholder's border displays as a solid line, all of the text in the placeholder is selected, and any formatting changes that you make will be applied to *all* of the text in the placeholder.

FIGURE 2.2

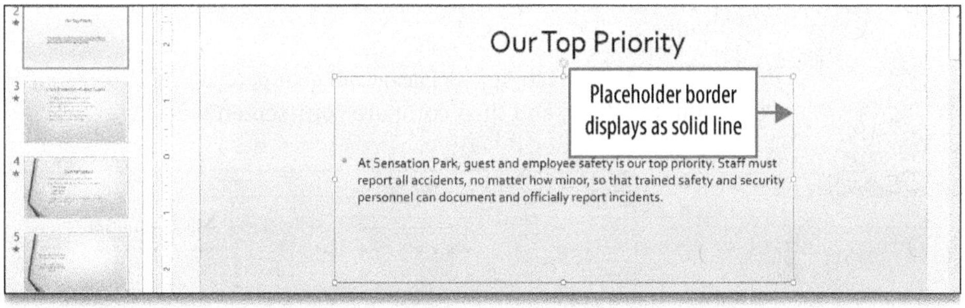

4. With the border of the placeholder displaying as a solid line, change the **Font Size** 20 to **24**. Notice that the font size of *all* of the placeholder text increases.
5. **Save** your presentation.

Activity 2.02 Changing a Bulleted List to a Numbered List

1. Display **Slide 3**, and then click anywhere in the bulleted list. Point to the placeholder dashed border to display the pointer, and then click one time to display the border as a solid line indicating that all of the text is selected.
2. On the **HOME tab**, in the **Paragraph group**, click **Numbering**, and then compare your slide with Figure 2.3.

   All of the bullet symbols are converted to numbers. The color of the numbers is determined by the presentation theme.

FIGURE 2.3

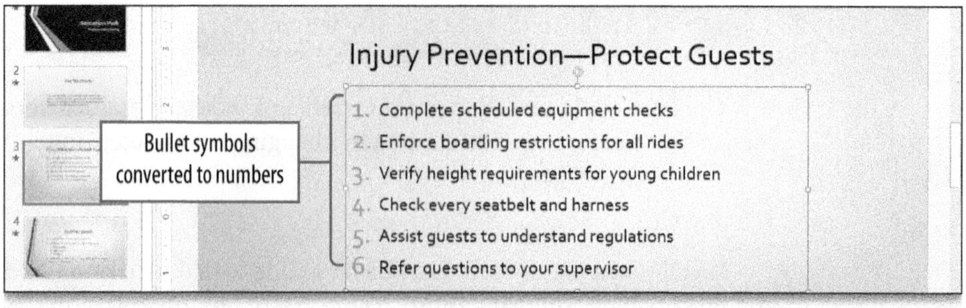

ALERT! Did You Display the Numbering Gallery?

If you clicked the Numbering button arrow instead of the Numbering button, the Numbering gallery displays. Click the Numbering button arrow again to close the gallery, and then click the Numbering button to convert the bullets to numbers.

3 **Save** your presentation.

Activity 2.03 | Changing the Shape and Color of a Bulleted List Symbol

The presentation theme includes default styles for the bullet points in content placeholders. You can customize a bullet by changing its style, color, and size.

1 Display **Slide 4**, and then select the three second-level bullet points—*Ride entrances*, *Visitor center*, and *Rest areas*.

2 On the **HOME tab**, in the **Paragraph group**, click the **Bullets button arrow** to display the **Bullets** gallery, and then compare your screen with Figure 2.4.

FIGURE 2.4

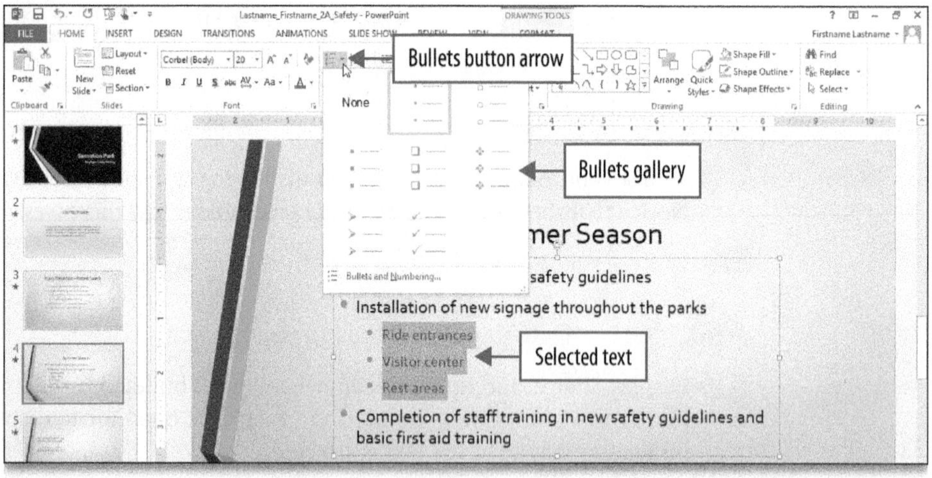

ALERT! Were the Bullets Removed?

If the bullets were removed, then you clicked the Bullets button instead of the Bullets button arrow. Click the Bullets button arrow, and then continue with Step 3.

3 Below the **Bullets** gallery, click **Bullets and Numbering**. In the **Bullets and Numbering** dialog box, point to each bullet style to display its ScreenTip. Then, in the second row, click **Star Bullets**. If the Star Bullets are not available, in the second row of bullets, click the second bullet style, and then click the Reset button.

4 Below the gallery, click the **Color** button. Under **Theme Colors,** in the eighth column, click the last color—**Red, Accent 4, Darker 50%.** In the **Size** box, select the existing number, type **100** and then compare your dialog box with Figure 2.5.

FIGURE 2.5

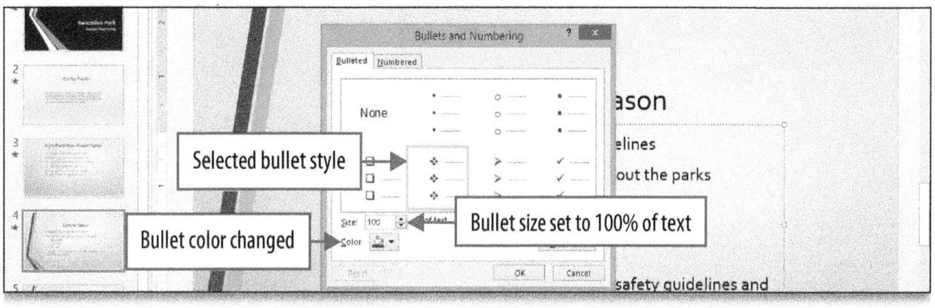

5 Click **OK** to apply the bullet style, and then **Save** your presentation.

More Knowledge **Using Other Symbols as Bullet Characters**

Many bullets styles are available to insert in your presentation. In the Bullets and Numbering dialog box, click Customize to view additional bullet styles.

Activity 2.04 | Removing a Bullet Symbol from a Bullet Point

The Bullets button is a toggle, enabling you to turn the bullet symbol on and off. A slide that contains a single bullet point can be formatted as a single paragraph *without* a bullet symbol.

1 Display **Slide 2,** and then click in the paragraph. On the **HOME tab,** in the **Paragraph group,** click **Bullets**. Compare your screen with Figure 2.6.

The bullet symbol no longer displays, and the Bullets button is no longer selected. Additionally, the indentation associated with the list level is removed.

FIGURE 2.6

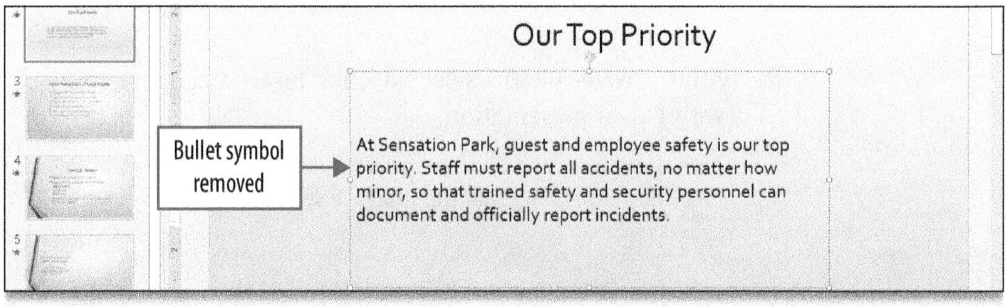

2 **Center** the paragraph. Click the dashed border to display the solid border and to select all of the text in the paragraph, and then apply **Bold** and **Italic**. On the **HOME tab,** in the **Paragraph group,** click **Line Spacing**, and then click **2.0.**

3 **Save** your presentation.

Objective 2 Insert Online Pictures

Video P2-2

There are many sources from which you can insert images into a presentation. One type of image that you can insert is a ***clip***—a single media file such as art, sound, animation, or a movie.

Activity 2.05 | Inserting Online Pictures in a Content Placeholder

1 Display **Slide 5**. In the placeholder on the right side of the slide, click **Online Pictures** to display the **Insert Pictures** dialog box, and then compare your screen with Figure 2.7.

FIGURE 2.7

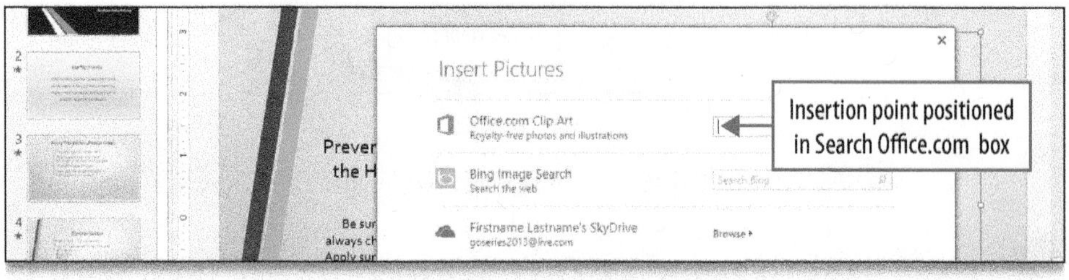

2 With the insertion point in the Search Office.com box, type **pouring water** and then press Enter to search for images that contain the keywords *pouring water*. Click the grayish-blue picture of water being poured. Compare your screen with Figure 2.8. If you are unable to locate the picture, choose another image.

FIGURE 2.8

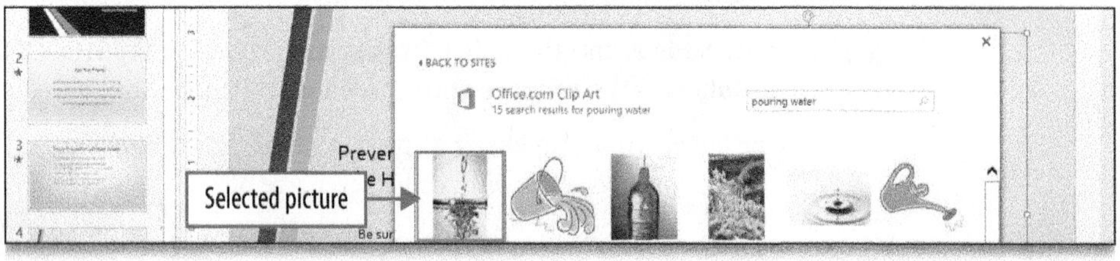

3 With the water picture selected, click **Insert**. Compare your screen with Figure 2.9, and then **Save** your presentation.

On the ribbon, the Picture Tools display, and the water bottle image is surrounded by sizing handles, indicating that the image is selected.

BY TOUCH

Tap the picture that you want to insert, and then tap Insert.

FIGURE 2.9

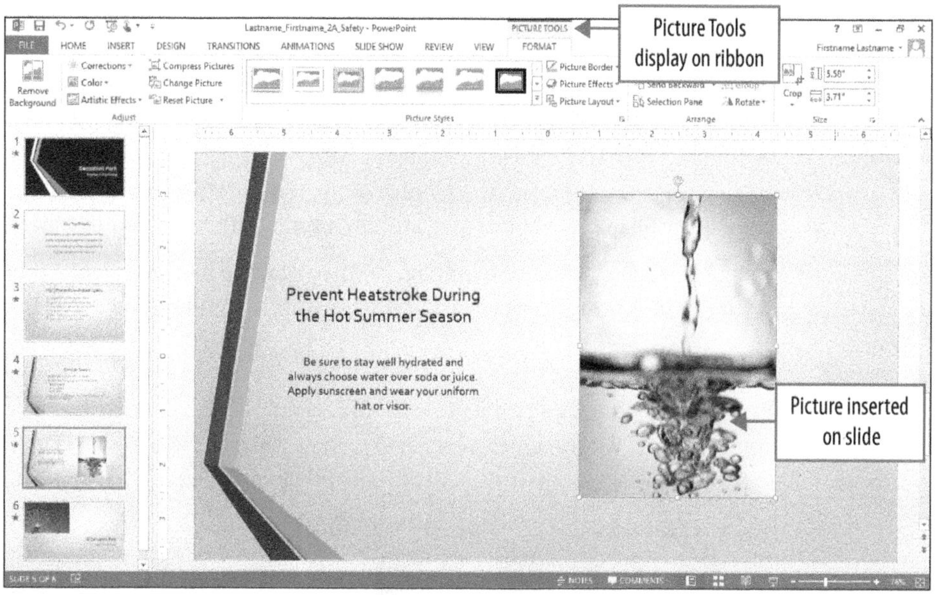

Activity 2.06 | Inserting Online Pictures in Any Location on a Slide

1. Display **Slide 1**. Click the **INSERT tab**, and then in the **Images group**, click **Online Pictures**.

2. In the **Insert Pictures** dialog box, in the **Search Office.com** box, type **red lights** and then press Enter. Click the picture of the single red warning light, and then click **Insert**. Compare your screen with Figure 2.10. If you cannot locate the picture, select another image.

   When you use the Online Pictures button on the ribbon instead of the Online Pictures button in a content placeholder, PowerPoint inserts the image in the center of the slide.

FIGURE 2.10

3. **Save** your presentation.

Activity 2.07 | Sizing a Picture

Recall that a selected image displays sizing handles that you can drag to resize the image. You can also resize an image using the Shape Height and Shape Width boxes on the FORMAT tab.

1. If necessary, select the picture of the red light. On the **FORMAT tab**, in the **Size group**, click in the **Shape Height** box, and then replace the selected number with **3.5**

2. Press Enter to resize the image. Notice that the picture is resized proportionately, and the **Width** box displays *5.26*. Compare your screen with Figure 2.11.

   When a picture is resized in this manner, the width adjusts in proportion to the picture height.

FIGURE 2.11

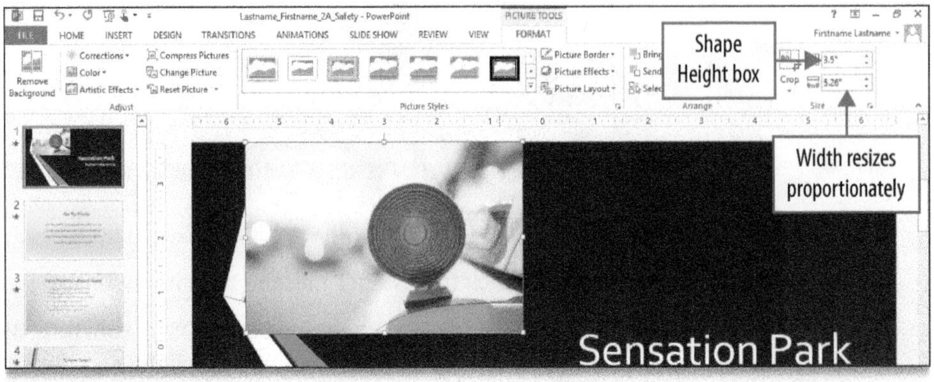

BY TOUCH Drag the corner sizing handle with your finger or mouse to resize the picture proportionately.

3. **Save** your presentation.

Activity 2.08 | Using Smart Guides and the Ruler to Position a Picture

Smart Guides are dashed lines that display on your slide when you are moving an object to assist you with alignment.

1. On **Slide 1**, on the **VIEW tab**, in the **Show group**, verify that the **Ruler** check box is selected and if necessary, select the check box. On the horizontal and vertical rulers, notice that *0* displays in the center.

   Horizontally, the PowerPoint ruler indicates measurements from the center of the slide *out* to the left and to the right. Vertically, the PowerPoint ruler indicates measurements from the center up and down.

2. Point to the picture to display the pointer. Hold down Shift, and then very slowly, drag the picture to the right and notice that dashed red Smart Guides periodically display along the right edge of the picture. When the dashed red Smart Guide displays on the right edge of the picture at approximately **6 inches to the right of zero on the horizontal ruler**, compare your screen with Figure 2.12, and then release the mouse button.

   Smart Guides display when you move an object and the object is aligned with another object on the slide. Here, the Smart Guide displays because the right edge of the picture is aligned with the right edge of the title placeholder. Pressing Shift while dragging an object constrains object movement in a straight line either vertically or horizontally. Here, pressing Shift maintains the vertical placement of the picture at the top edge of the slide.

FIGURE 2.12

3 **Save** the presentation.

> **More Knowledge** **Moving an Object by Using the Arrow Keys**
>
> You can use the directional arrow keys on your keyboard to move a picture, shape, or other object in small increments. Select the object so that its outside border displays as a solid line. Then, on your keyboard, hold down the Ctrl key and press the directional arrow keys to move the selected object in small, precise increments.

Activity 2.09 | Cropping a Picture

When you ***crop*** a picture you remove unwanted or unnecessary areas of the picture.

1 Display **Slide 6**, and then select the ferris wheel picture. On the **FORMAT tab**, in the **Size group**, click the upper portion of the **Crop** button to display the crop handles. Compare your screen with Figure 2.13.

Use the ***crop handles*** like sizing handles to remove unwanted areas of the picture.

FIGURE 2.13

2 Point to the center right crop handle to display the Crop pointer. Compare your screen with Figure 2.14.

The ***crop pointer*** is the mouse pointer that enables you to crop areas of a picture.

FIGURE 2.14

3 With the crop pointer displayed, hold down the left mouse button and drag to the left to approximately **1.5 inches to the left of 0 on the horizontal ruler**, and then release the mouse button. Compare your screen with Figure 2.15.

The portion of the picture to be removed by the crop displays in gray.

FIGURE 2.15

4 Click anywhere on the slide outside of the image to apply the crop, and then **Save** your presentation.

Activity 2.10 | Using Crop to Shape to Change the Shape of a Picture

An inserted picture is rectangular in shape; however, you can modify a picture by changing its shape.

1 Display **Slide 1**, and then select the picture. On the **FORMAT tab**, in the **Size group**, click the lower portion of the Crop button—the **Crop button arrow**—and then compare your screen with Figure 2.16.

FIGURE 2.16

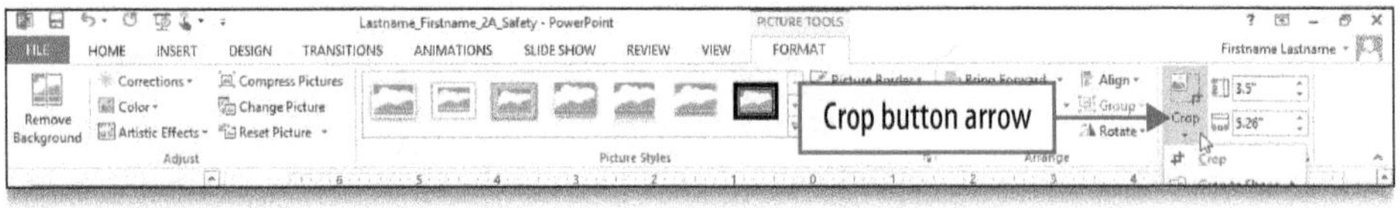

2 Point to **Crop to Shape** to display a gallery of shapes. Compare your screen with Figure 2.17.

FIGURE 2.17

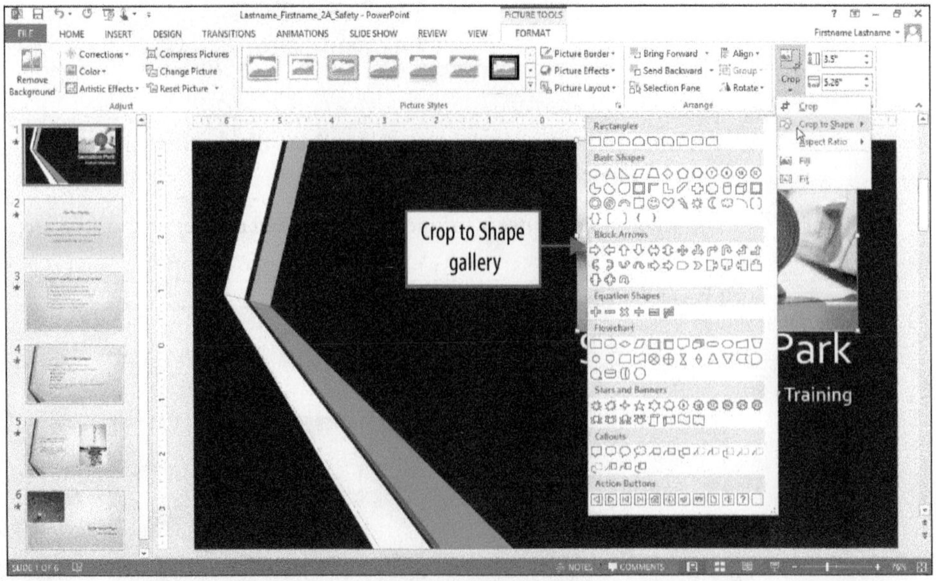

3 Under **Basic Shapes**, in the first row, click the first shape—**Oval**—to change the picture's shape to an oval. **Save** your presentation.

Objective 3 Insert Text Boxes and Shapes

Video P2-3

You can use objects, including text boxes and shapes, to draw attention to important information or to serve as containers for slide text. Many shapes, including lines, arrows, ovals, and rectangles, are available to insert and position anywhere on your slides.

Activity 2.11 Inserting a Text Box

A ***text box*** is an object with which you can position text anywhere on a slide.

1 Display **Slide 3** and verify that the rulers display. Click the **INSERT tab**, and then in the **Text group**, click **Text Box**.

2 Move the pointer to several different places on the slide, and as you do so, in the horizontal and vertical rulers, notice that ***ruler guides***—dotted red vertical and horizontal lines that display in the rulers indicating the pointer's position—move also.

Use the ruler guides to help you position objects on a slide.

3 Position the pointer so that the ruler guides are positioned on the **left half of the horizontal ruler at 4.5 inches** and on the **lower half of the vertical ruler at 2 inches**, and then compare your screen with Figure 2.18.

FIGURE 2.18

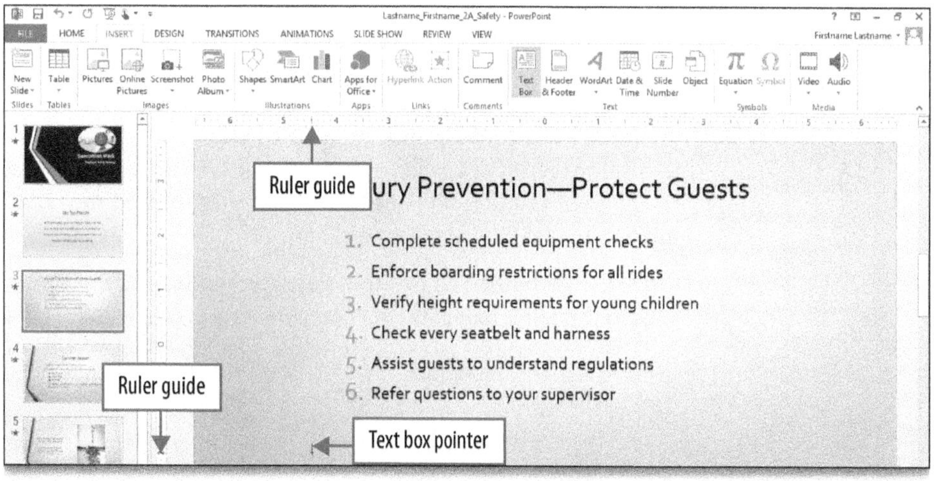

4 Click one time to create a narrow rectangular text box. With the insertion point blinking inside the text box, type **If Safety is Questionable** Notice that as you type, the width of the text box expands to accommodate the text. Compare your screen with Figure 2.19.

Do not be concerned if your text box is not positioned exactly as shown in Figure 2.19.

FIGURE 2.19

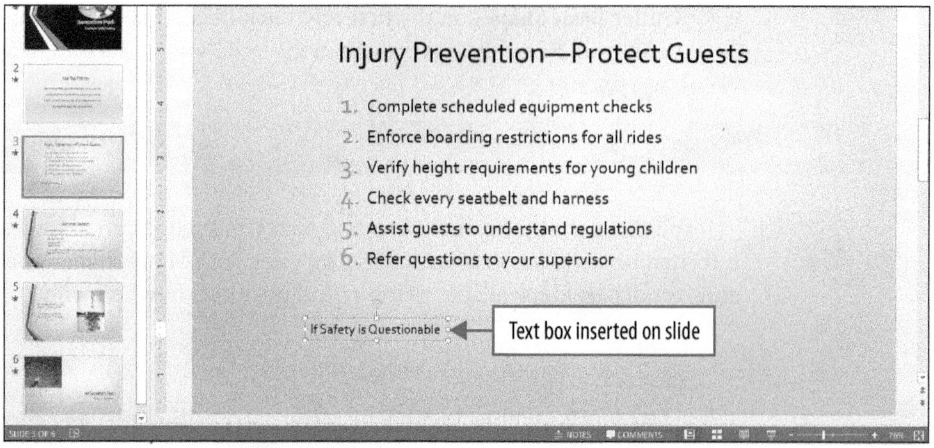

ALERT! **Does the Text in the Text Box Display Vertically, One Character at a Time?**

If you move the pointer when you click to create the text box, PowerPoint sets the width of the text box and does not widen to accommodate the text. If this happens, your text may display vertically instead of horizontally or the text may display on two lines. Click Undo, and then repeat the steps again, being sure that you do not move the mouse when you click to insert the text box.

5. Select the text that you typed, change the **Font Size** to **24** and then **Save** your presentation.

   You can format the text in a text box by using the same techniques that you use to format text in any other placeholder. For example, you can change the font, font style, font size, and font color.

Activity 2.12 | Inserting and Sizing a Shape

Shapes are slide objects such as lines, arrows, boxes, callouts, and banners. You can size and move shapes using the same techniques that you use to size and move pictures.

1. With **Slide 3** displayed, click the **INSERT tab**, and then in the **Illustrations group**, click **Shapes** to display the **Shapes** gallery. Under **Block Arrows**, click the first shape—**Right Arrow**. Move the pointer into the slide until the [+] pointer—called the ***crosshair pointer***—displays, indicating that you can draw a shape.

2. Move the [+] pointer to position the ruler guides at approximately **0 on the horizontal ruler** and on the **lower half of the vertical ruler at 2 inches**. Compare your screen with Figure 2.20.

FIGURE 2.20

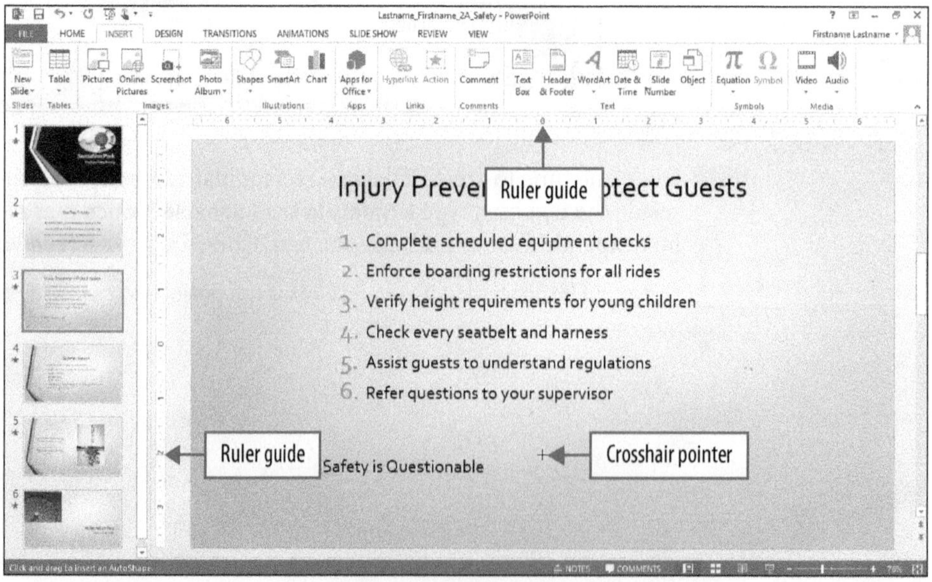

3 Click to insert the arrow. On the **FORMAT tab**, in the **Size group**, click in the **Shape Height** box to select the number. Type **0.5** and then click in the **Shape Width** box. Type **2** and then press Enter to resize the arrow. Compare your screen with Figure 2.21.

FIGURE 2.21

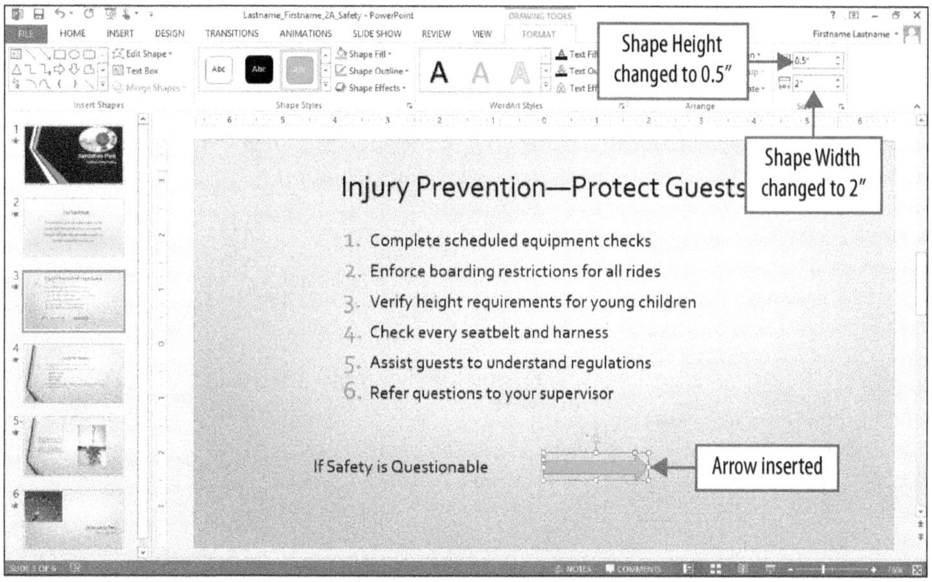

4 On the **FORMAT tab**, in the **Insert Shapes group**, click **More**. In the gallery, under **Basic Shapes**, in the first row, click the second to last shape—**Octagon**.

5 Move the pointer to position the ruler guides on the **right half of the horizontal ruler at 3.5 inches** and on the **lower half of the vertical ruler at 1 inch**, and then click one time to insert an octagon.

6 On the **FORMAT tab**, in the **Size group**, click in the **Shape Height** box to select the number. Type **2** and then click in the **Shape Width** box. Type **2** and then press Enter to resize the octagon. Compare your slide with Figure 2.22. Do not be concerned if your shapes are not positioned exactly as shown in the figure.

FIGURE 2.22

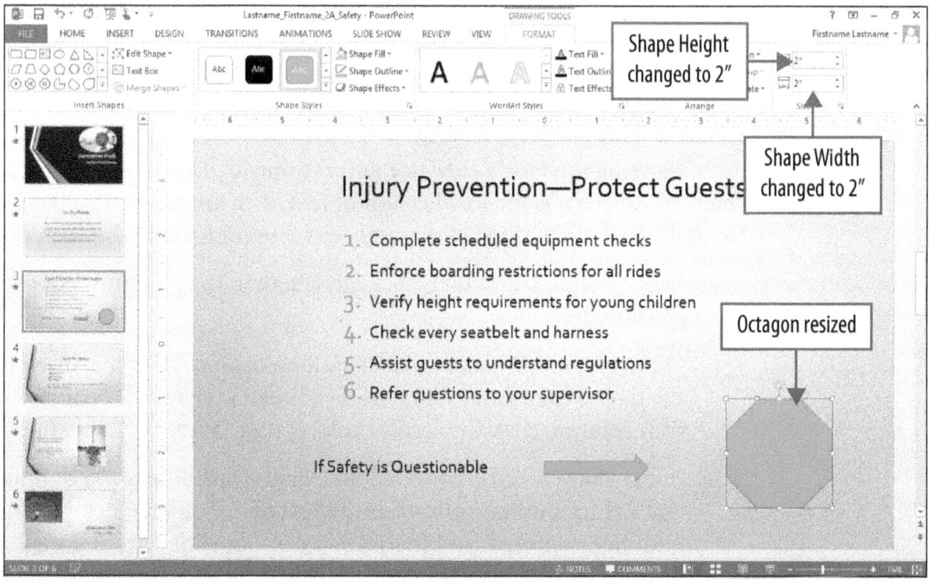

7 **Save** your presentation.

Activity 2.13 | Adding Text to Shapes

Shapes can serve as a container for text. After you add text to a shape, you can change the font and font size, apply font styles, and change text alignment.

1. On **Slide 3**, if necessary, click the octagon so that it is selected. Type **STOP** and notice that the text is centered within the octagon.
2. Select the text *STOP*, and then on the mini toolbar, change the **Font Size** to **32**.
3. Click in a blank area of the slide to cancel the selection, and then compare your screen with Figure 2.23. **Save** your presentation.

FIGURE 2.23

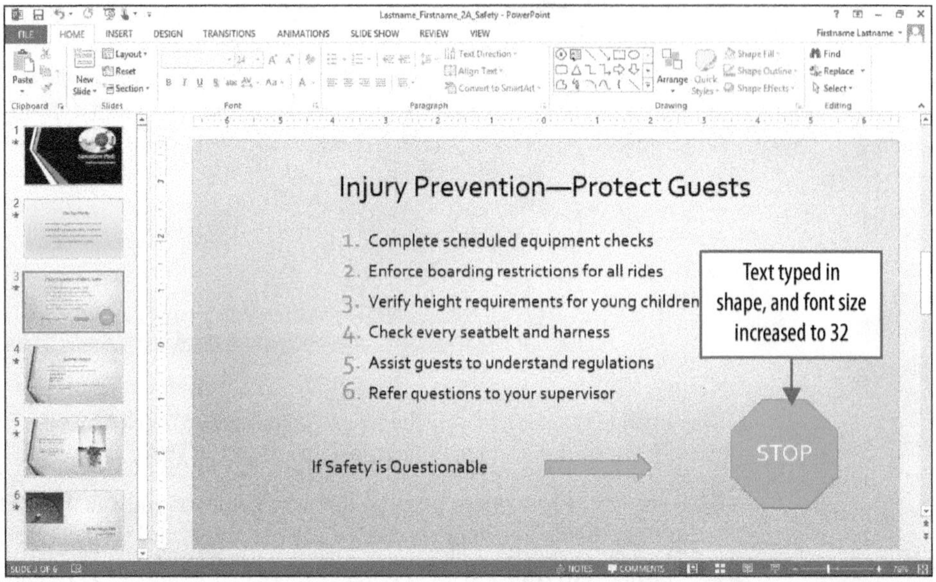

Objective 4 Format Objects

Video P2-4

Apply styles and effects to pictures, shapes, and text boxes to complement slide backgrounds and colors.

Activity 2.14 | Applying Shape Fills and Outlines

Changing the inside ***fill color*** and the outside line color is a distinctive way to format a shape. A fill color is the inside color of text or of an object. Use the Shape Styles gallery to apply predefined combinations of these fill and line colors and also to apply other effects.

1. Display **Slide 2**, and then click anywhere in the paragraph of text to select the content placeholder.
2. On the **FORMAT tab**, in the **Shape Styles group**, click the **Shape Fill arrow**. Point to several of the theme colors and watch as Live Preview changes the inside color of the text box. In the fifth column, click the second color—**Blue, Accent 1, Lighter 80%**.
3. In the **Shape Styles group**, click the **Shape Outline arrow**. Point to **Weight**, click **3 pt**, and notice that a thick outline surrounds the text placeholder. Click in a blank area of the slide so that nothing is selected, and then compare your slide with Figure 2.24.

   You can use combinations of shape fill, outline colors, and weights to format an object.

FIGURE 2.24

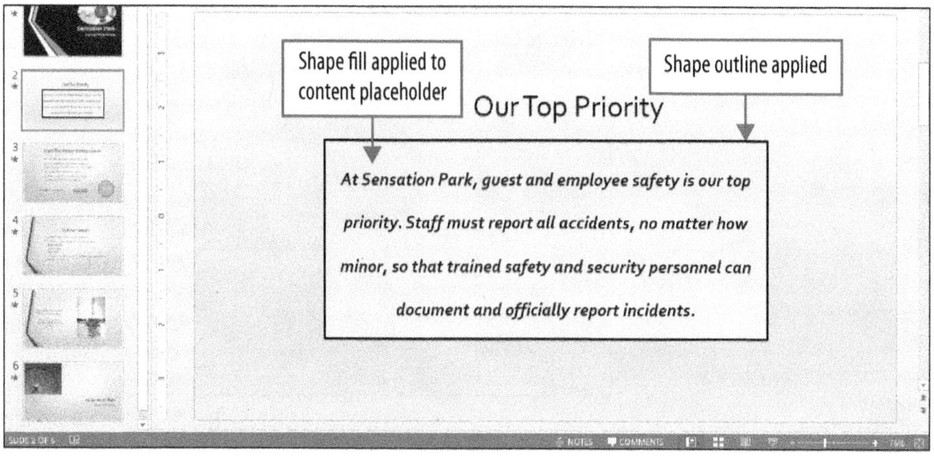

4 **Save** your presentation.

Activity 2.15 | Using the Eyedropper to Change Color

The ***eyedropper*** is a tool that captures the exact color from an object on your screen and then applies the color to any shape, picture, or text. You can use the eyedropper to give your presentation a cohesive look by matching a font color, fill color, border color, or other slide element to any color on any slide.

1 Display **Slide 6**, and then select the title text—*At Sensation Park*.

2 On the **HOME tab**, in the **Font group**, click the **Font Color button arrow**. Below the gallery, click **Eyedropper**, and then move the pointer into the upper right corner of the Ferris wheel picture. Compare your screen with Figure 2.25.

A small square displays next to the pointer indicating the exact color to which you are pointing. When you hover over a color, it's ***RGB*** color coordinates display. RGB is a color model in which the colors red, green, and blue are added together to form another color.

FIGURE 2.25

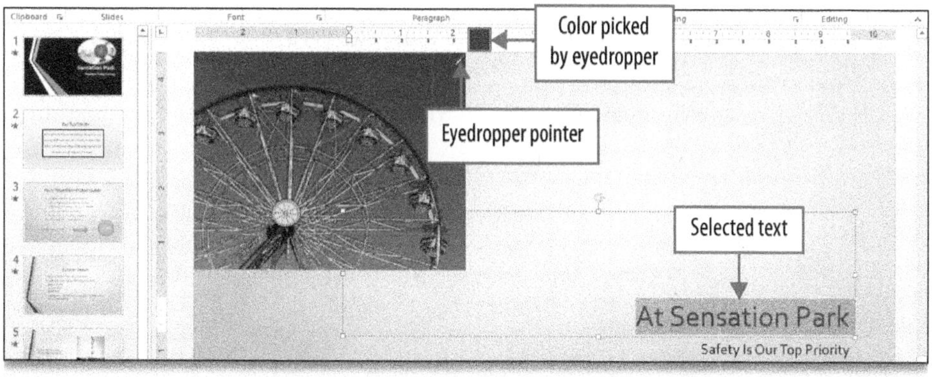

3 With the pointer in the upper right corner of the picture, click one time. Notice that the color is applied to the selected text. Compare your screen with Figure 2.26.

FIGURE 2.26

4 Display **Slide 5**, and then select the title. On the mini toolbar, click the **Font Color button arrow**. Under **Recent Colors**, notice that the color you selected with the eyedropper displays. Point to the color to display the ScreenTip—*Dark Blue*. Click **Dark Blue** to apply the color to the selection.

After a color has been selected with the eyedropper, the color remains available in the presentation each time the color gallery is displayed. When you use the eyedropper in this manner, you can consistently apply the same color throughout your presentation.

5 **Save** your presentation.

Activity 2.16 | Applying Shape Styles

1 Display **Slide 3**, and then select the **arrow shape**. On the **FORMAT tab**, in the **Shape Styles group**, click **More** to display the **Shape Styles** gallery. In the last row, click the second style—**Intense Effect - Blue, Accent 1**.

2 Click anywhere in the text *If Safety is Questionable* to select the text box. On the **FORMAT tab**, in the **Shape Styles group**, click **More**.

3 In the last row, click the fifth style—**Intense Effect - Red, Accent 4**.

4 Select the **octagon** shape, and then apply the same style you applied to the text box—**Intense Effect - Red, Accent 4**.

5 Compare your screen with Figure 2.27, and then **Save** your presentation.

FIGURE 2.27

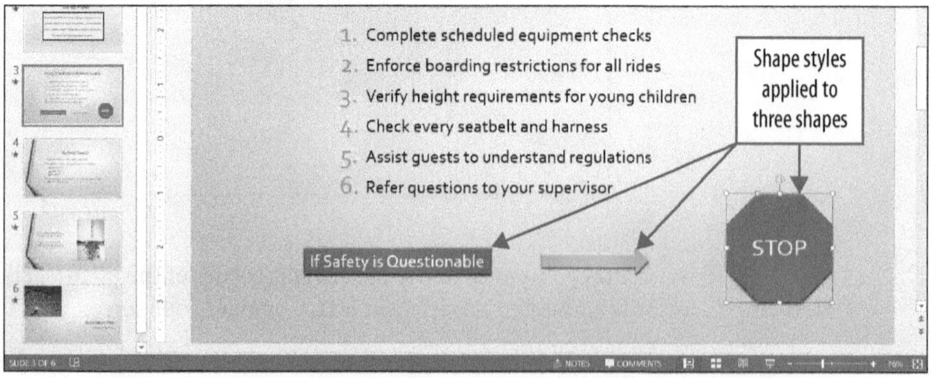

Activity 2.17 | Applying Shape and Picture Effects

1 Display **Slide 1**, and then select the picture. On the **FORMAT tab**, in the **Picture Styles group**, click **Picture Effects**.

A list of effects that you can apply to pictures displays. These effects can also be applied to shapes and text boxes.

2 Point to **Soft Edges**, and then in the **Soft Edges** gallery, point to each style to view its effect on the picture. Click the last **Soft Edges** effect—**50 Point**, and then compare your screen with Figure 2.28.

The soft edges effect softens and blurs the outer edge of the picture so that the picture blends into the slide background.

FIGURE 2.28

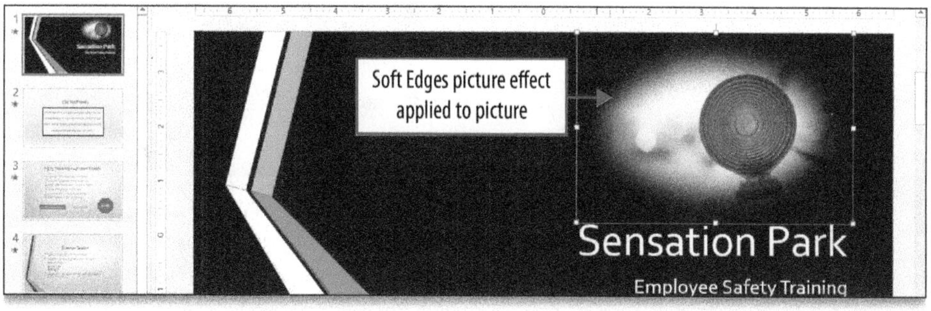

3 Display **Slide 2**, and then select the light blue content placeholder. On the **FORMAT tab**, in the **Shape Styles group**, click **Shape Effects**. Point to **Bevel** to display the **Bevel** gallery. Point to each bevel to view its ScreenTip and to use Live Preview to examine the effect of each bevel on the content placeholder. In the last row, click the last bevel—**Art Deco**.

4 Click in a blank area of the slide and then compare your screen with Figure 2.29.

FIGURE 2.29

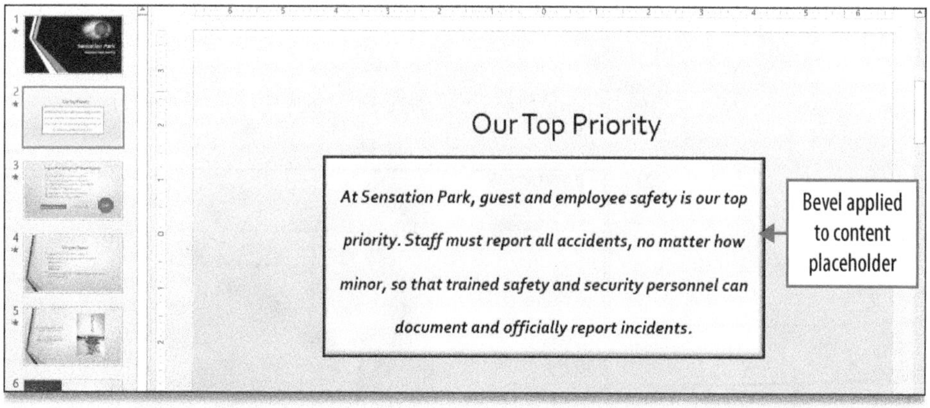

5 Display **Slide 5**, and then select the picture. On the **FORMAT tab**, in the **Picture Styles group**, click **Picture Effects**, and then point to **Glow**.

6 Point to several of the effects to view the effect on the picture, and then under **Glow Variations**, in the second row, click the first glow effect—**Blue, 8 pt glow, Accent color 1**.

The glow effect applies a colored, softly blurred outline to the selected object.

7 **Save** your presentation.

Activity 2.18 | Duplicating Objects

1. Display **Slide 6**, and then select the picture.

2. Press and hold down Ctrl, and then press D one time. Release Ctrl.

   Ctrl + D is the keyboard shortcut to duplicate an object. A duplicate of the picture overlaps the original picture and the duplicated image is selected.

3. Click in a blank area of the slide, and then compare your screen with Figure 2.30. **Save** your presentation.

FIGURE 2.30

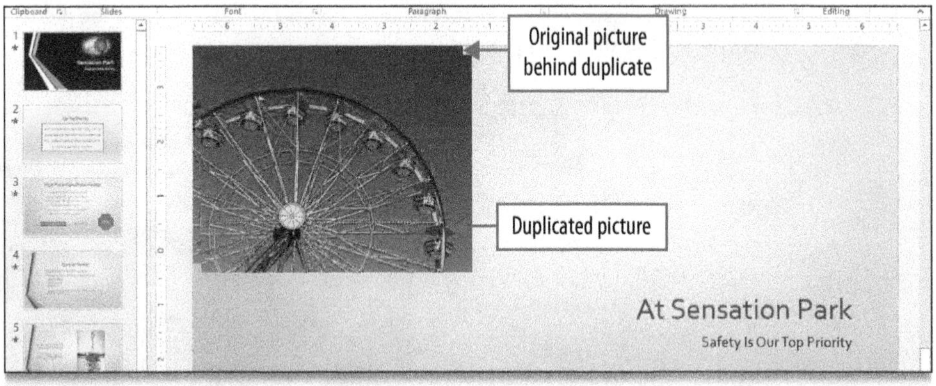

Activity 2.19 | Aligning and Distributing Objects Relative to the Slide

You can select multiple slide objects, and then use ribbon commands to align and distribute the objects precisely.

1. With **Slide 6** displayed, position the pointer in the gray area of the Slide pane just outside the upper left corner of the slide to display the pointer. Drag down and to the right to draw a transparent, gray, selection rectangle that encloses both pictures. Compare your slide with Figure 2.31.

ANOTHER WAY Hold down Shift and then click each object that you want to select.

FIGURE 2.31

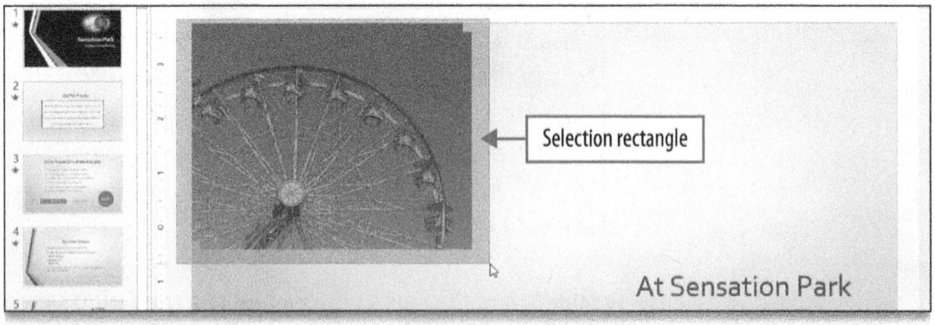

2. Release the mouse button to select the objects, and then compare your screen with Figure 2.32.

   Objects completely enclosed by a selection rectangle are selected when the mouse button is released.

FIGURE 2.32

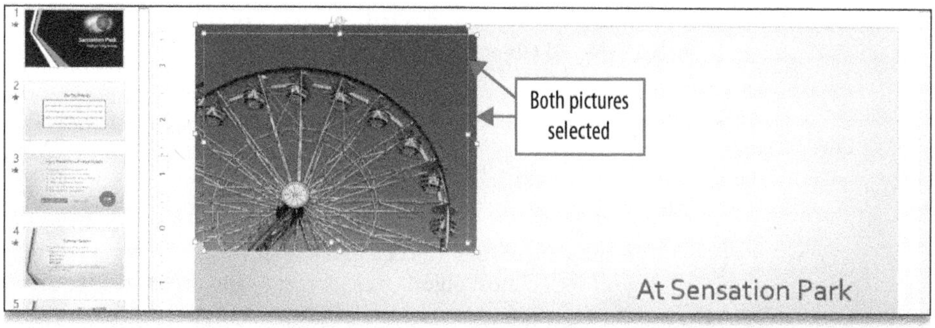

3 Click the **FORMAT tab**, and then in the **Arrange group**, click **Align**. Toward the bottom of the menu, click **Align to Slide** to activate this setting. On the **FORMAT tab**, in the **Arrange group**, click **Align** again, and then click **Align Left**.

The Align to Slide option, in combination with the Align Left option, aligns the left edge of each picture with the left edge of the slide.

4 With both pictures still selected, on the **FORMAT tab**, in the **Arrange group**, click **Align** again, and then click **Distribute Vertically**. Compare your screen with Figure 2.33.

The pictures are distributed evenly down the left edge of the slide between the top and bottom edges of the slide.

FIGURE 2.33

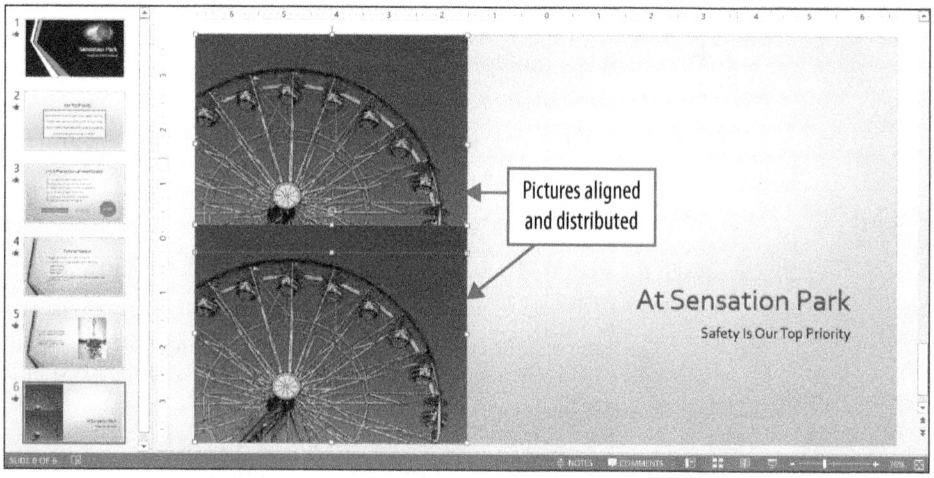

5 With both pictures selected, on the **FORMAT tab**, in the **Picture Styles group**, click the **Picture Effects** button. Point to **Soft Edges**, and then click **50 Point** to apply the picture effect to both images.

6 **Save** the presentation.

Activity 2.20 | Aligning and Distributing Objects Relative to Each Other

1 Display **Slide 3**, hold down Shift, and then at the bottom of the slide, click the **text box**, the **arrow**, and the **octagon** to select all three objects.

BY TOUCH Tap the text box, hold down Shift, and then tap the arrow and the octagon.

2 With the three objects selected, on the **FORMAT tab**, in the **Arrange group**, click **Align**. Click **Align Selected Objects.**

The *Align Selected Objects* option will cause the objects that you select to align relative to each other, rather than relative to the edges of the slide.

3 On the **FORMAT tab**, in the **Arrange group**, click **Align**, and then click **Align Middle**. Click the **Align** button again, and then click **Distribute Horizontally**.

The midpoint of each object aligns and the three objects are distributed evenly between the left edge of the leftmost object—the text box—and the right edge of the rightmost object—the octagon.

4 Click anywhere on the slide so that none of the objects are selected. Compare your screen with Figure 2.34, and then **Save** the presentation.

FIGURE 2.34

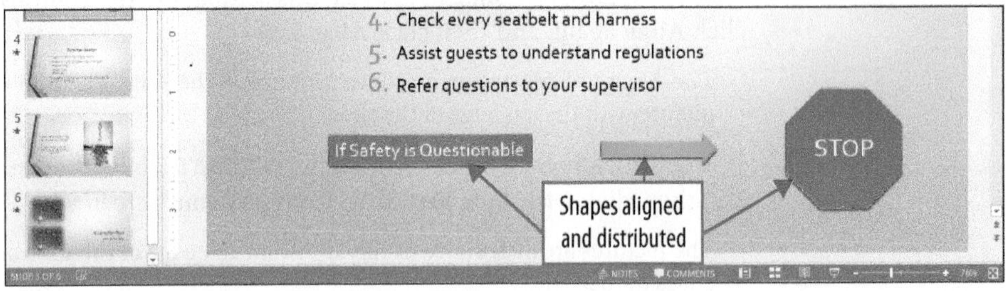

Activity 2.21 | Grouping Objects

You can select multiple objects and group them so that they can be formatted and edited as one object.

1 With **Slide 3** displayed, click the text box, hold down Shift, and then click the arrow and the octagon so that all three objects are selected.

Sizing handles surround each individual object.

2 On the **FORMAT tab**, in the **Arrange group**, click **Group**, and then click **Group**. Compare your screen with Figure 2.35.

The sizing handles surround all three shapes as one, indicating that the three shapes are grouped into one object. The individual objects are not selected. The grouped object can be formatted, aligned, and moved as one object.

FIGURE 2.35

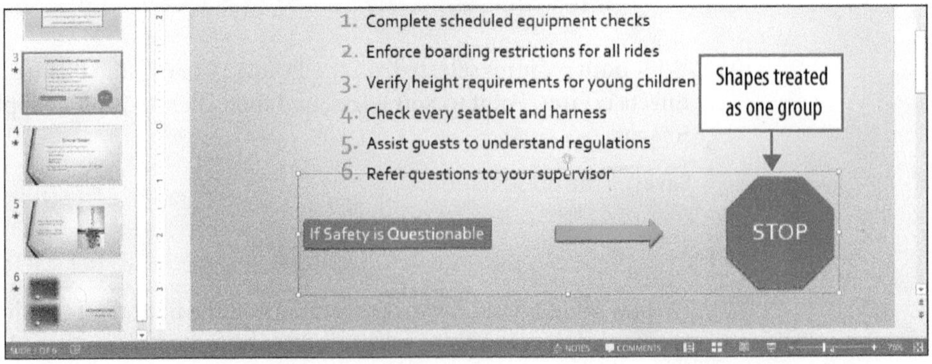

3 On the **FORMAT tab**, in the **Arrange group**, click **Align**, and then click **Align Center**.

The group is centered horizontally on the slide.

4 On the **Slide Show tab**, in the **Start Slide Show group**, click the **From Beginning** button, and then view the slide show. When the black slide displays, press Esc.

5 On the **INSERT tab**, in the **Text group**, click **Header & Footer** to display the **Header and Footer** dialog box. Click the **Notes and Handouts** tab. Under **Include on page**, select the **Date and time** check box, and then select **Update automatically**. If necessary, clear the Header check box. Select the **Page number** and **Footer** check boxes. In the **Footer** box, using your own name, type **Lastname_Firstname_2A_Safety** and then click **Apply to All**.

6 Display the document properties. As the **Tags** type **safety presentation** and as the **Subject** type your course and section number. Be sure your name displays as the author, and then **Save** your file. Print **Handouts 6 Slides Horizontal**, or submit your presentation electronically as directed by your instructor.

7 **Close** PowerPoint.

END | You have completed Project 2A

GO! with Office Online (formerly Web Apps)

Objective Create an Informational Presentation in PowerPoint Online

ALERT! **Working with Web-Based Applications and Services**

Computer programs and services on the web receive continuous updates and improvements, so the steps to complete this web-based activity may differ from the ones shown. You can often look at the screens and the information presented to determine how to complete the activity.

Activity | Creating an Informational Presentation in PowerPoint Online

In this activity, you will use PowerPoint Online to create a presentation similar to the one you created in Project 2A.

1. From the desktop, start Internet Explorer. Navigate to **http://onedrive.com**, and then sign in to your Microsoft account. Open your **GO! Web Projects** folder—or create and then open this folder if necessary.

2. On the OneDrive menu bar, click **Upload**, and then navigate to your student data files and select **p02_2A_Web**. Click **Open**. When the upload is complete, right click **p02_2A_Web**, and then click **Rename**. Using your own name, as the file name type **Lastname_Firstname_PPT_2A_Web** and then press Enter. Click your file, and then click **EDIT PRESENTATION**. Click **Edit in PowerPoint Online**.

3. Display **Slide 5**. In the content placeholder, click the third button—**Online Pictures**. In the **Search** box, type **pouring water** and then press Enter. Insert the picture that you inserted in Project 2A. If the picture is not available, choose another appropriate image.

4. Display **Slide 2**, and then click the paragraph to activate the content placeholder. Click in the paragraph again so that you can edit the paragraph. On the **HOME tab**, in the **Paragraph group**, click **Bullets** to remove the bullet symbol from the paragraph.

5. On the **HOME tab**, in the **Paragraph group**, click **Center** and then select the entire paragraph. Change the **Font Size** to **24** and apply **Bold**.

6. With **Slide 2** displayed and the paragraph selected, click outside of the content placeholder and then click the outer edge so that it displays as a solid line. On the **DRAWING TOOLS FORMAT tab**, in the **Shape Styles group**, click the small down arrow. In the last row, click the second style—**Intense Effect - Blue, Accent 1**. In the **Shape Styles group**, click **Shape Outline**, in the second column, click the first color—**Black, Text 1**. Click **Shape Outline** again, point to **Weight**, and then click **4 1/2 pt**.

7. Click outside the content placeholder to apply your changes, and then compare your screen with Figure A.

8. Display **Slide 3**, and then click in the bulleted list, and then drag to select all of the bullet points. On the **HOME tab**, in the **Paragraph group**, click **Numbering** to apply numbers to all of the bullet points.

FIGURE A

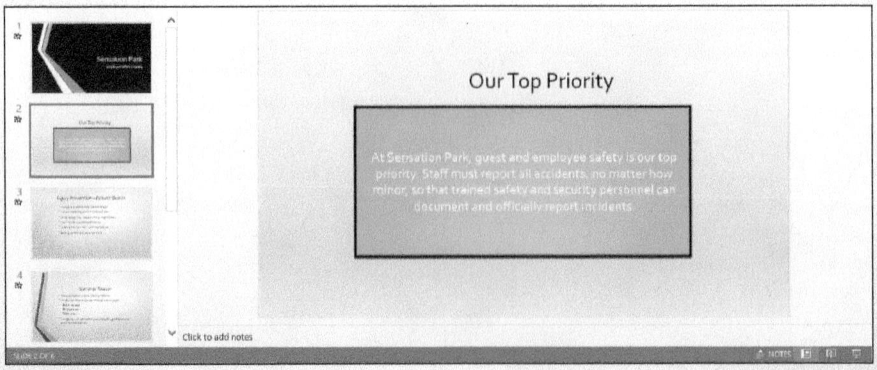

(GO! with Office Online (formerly Web Apps) continues on the next page)

9 Click outside of the content placeholder to deselect it. With **Slide 3** still displayed, on the **INSERT tab**, in the **Text group**, click **Text Box** to insert a text box in the middle of your slide. Point to the text box border, and then drag down and to the left to position the text box so that the circular rotation handle above the center of the text box is positioned below the number 6.

10 Click in the text box and then drag to select *Click to add text*. Type **If Safety is Questionable** and then click outside the text box. Click the text box border, and then on the **FORMAT tab**, in the **Shape Styles group**, click the small down arrow. In the last row, click the fifth style—**Intense Effect - Red, Accent 4**.

11 On the **INSERT tab**, in the **Illustrations group**, click **Right Arrow** to insert an arrow in the middle of your slide. Drag the arrow so that it is aligned horizontally with the text box and its left edge aligns with the *y* in *your*.

12 Click outside of the arrow to deselect it. On the **INSERT tab**, in the **Illustrations group**, click **Rounded Rectangle** to insert a 1 × 1 rounded rectangle in the middle of your slide. Drag the rectangle so that so that its center sizing handle aligns with the arrow point and its left edge aligns with the *s* in *regulations*. On the **FORMAT tab**, in the **Shape Styles group**, click the small down arrow. In the last row, click the fifth style—**Intense Effect - Red, Accent 4**.

13 Click in the rectangle. Type **STOP** and then click in a blank area of the slide. Compare your screen with Figure B and make adjustments to the position of the shapes as necessary.

14 Submit your file as instructed. Sign out of your OneDrive and then close Internet Explorer.

FIGURE B

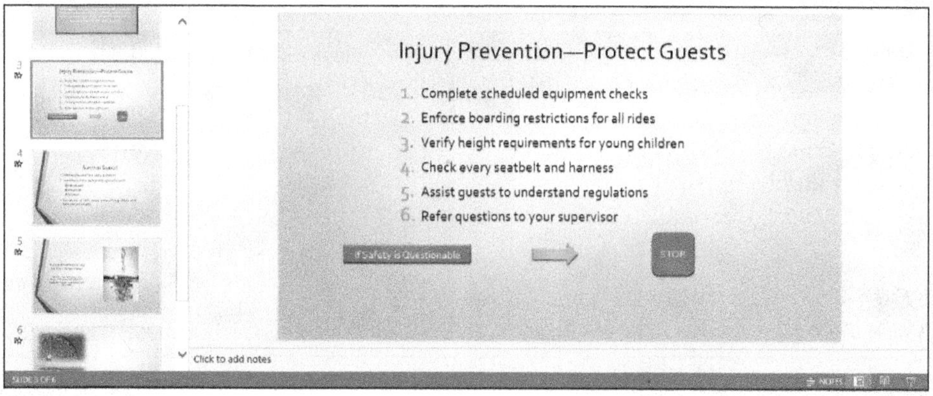

PROJECT 2B

Event Announcement

MyITLab®
Project 2B Training

PROJECT ACTIVITIES

In Activities 2.22 through 2.34, you will format slides in a presentation for the Sensation Park Entertainment Group's Marketing Director that informs employees about upcoming events at the company's amusement parks. You will enhance the presentation using SmartArt and WordArt graphics. Your completed presentation will look similar to Figure 2.36.

PROJECT FILES

For Project 2B, you will need the following files:

p02B_Celebrations
p02B_Canada_Contact
p02B_Mexico_Contact
p02B_US_Contact

You will save your presentation as:

Lastname_Firstname_2B_Celebrations

PROJECT RESULTS

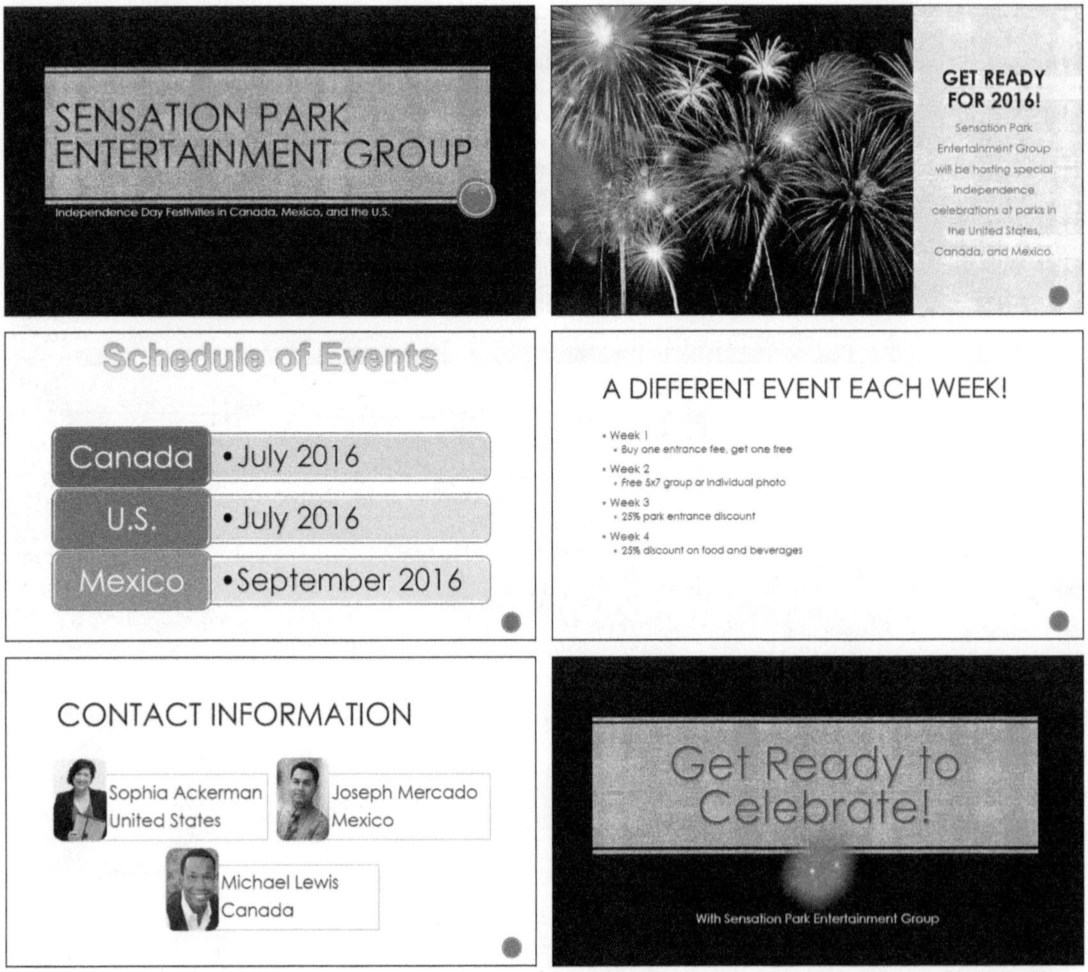

FIGURE 2.36 Project 2B Event Announcement

Objective 5 Remove Picture Backgrounds and Insert WordArt

Video P2-5

To avoid the boxy look that results when you insert an image into a presentation, use ***Background Removal*** to flow a picture into the content of the presentation. Background Removal removes unwanted portions of a picture so that the picture does not appear as a self-contained rectangle.

WordArt is a gallery of text styles with which you can create decorative effects, such as shadowed or mirrored text. You can choose from the gallery of WordArt styles to insert a new WordArt object or you can customize existing text by applying WordArt formatting.

Activity 2.22 | Removing the Background from a Picture and Applying Soft Edge Options

1. Start PowerPoint. From your student data files, open **p02B_Celebrations**. On the **VIEW tab**, in the **Show group**, if necessary, select the Ruler check box. In your **PowerPoint Chapter 2** folder, **Save** the file as **Lastname_Firstname_2B_Celebrations**

2. Display **Slide 6**. Click the picture to select it, and then on the **FORMAT tab**, in the **Adjust group**, click **Remove Background**. Compare your screen with Figure 2.37.

   PowerPoint determines what portion of the picture is the foreground—the portion to keep—and which portion is the background—the portion to remove. The background is overlaid in magenta, leaving the remaining portion of the picture as it will look when the background removal is complete. A rectangular selection area displays that you can move and size to select additional areas of the picture. The Background Removal options display in the Refine group on the ribbon.

FIGURE 2.37

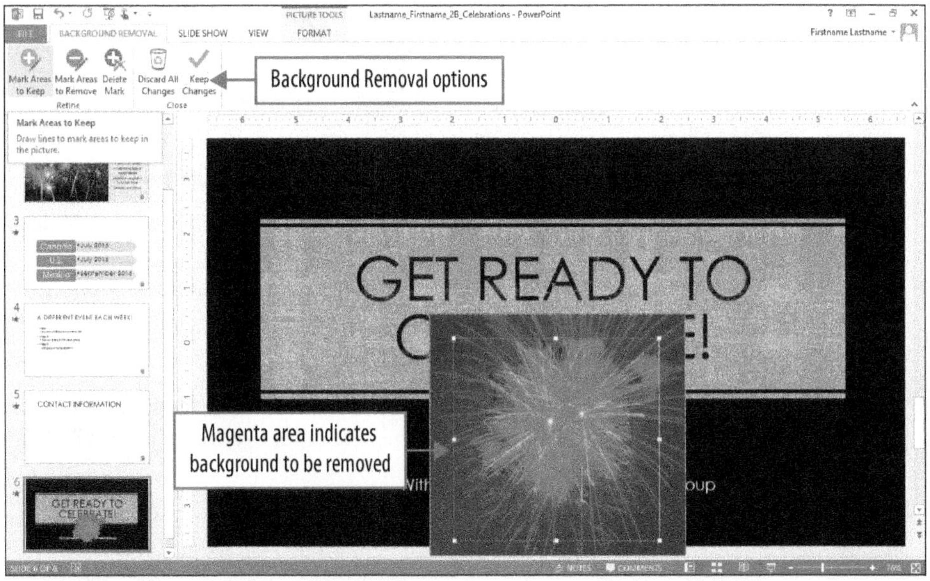

3. On the **Background Removal tab**, in the **Close group**, click **Keep Changes** to remove the background.

4. With the picture selected, on the **FORMAT tab**, in the **Picture Styles group**, click **Picture Effects**, point to **Soft Edges**, and then click **50 Point**. Compare your slide with Figure 2.38, and then **Save** your presentation.

FIGURE 2.38

Activity 2.23 | Applying WordArt Styles to Existing Text

1 On **Slide 6**, click anywhere in the word *Get* to activate the title placeholder, and then select the title—*Get Ready to Celebrate!* Click the **FORMAT tab**, and then in the **WordArt Styles group**, click **More** to display the WordArt gallery.

2 Point to several WordArt styles to view the change to the slide title. In the first row, click the first style—**Fill - White, Text 1, Shadow**. Click anywhere on the slide to cancel the selection.

3 Compare your screen with Figure 2.39, and then **Save** your presentation.

FIGURE 2.39

Activity 2.24 | Changing the Text Fill and Text Outline Colors of a WordArt Object

A WordArt object can be modified by changing the text fill and text outline colors.

1 On **Slide 6**, select the title. On the **FORMAT tab**, in the **WordArt Styles group**, click the **Text Fill button arrow**. Under **Theme Colors**, in the sixth column, click the fifth color—**Dark Red, Accent 2, Darker 25%.**

2 With the text still selected, in the **WordArt Styles group**, click the **Text Outline button arrow**. In the second column, click the first color—**White, Text 1**. Click anywhere on the slide to cancel the selection.

3 Compare your screen with Figure 2.40, and then **Save** your presentation.

FIGURE 2.40

Activity 2.25 | Inserting and Aligning a WordArt Object

In addition to formatting existing text using WordArt, you can insert a new WordArt object anywhere on a slide.

1 Display **Slide 3**. On the **INSERT tab**, in the **Text group**, click **WordArt**. In the gallery, in the second row, click the third WordArt style—**Gradient Fill - Brown, Accent 4, Outline - Accent 4**.

In the center of your slide, a WordArt placeholder displays *Your text here*. Text that you type will replace this text and the placeholder will expand to accommodate the text. The WordArt is surrounded by sizing handles with which you can adjust its size.

2 Type **Schedule of Events** to replace the WordArt placeholder text. Compare your screen with Figure 2.41.

FIGURE 2.41

3 With the WordArt selected, on the **FORMAT tab**, in the **Arrange group**, click **Align**, and then click **Align Top** to move the WordArt to the top of the slide.

4 Click in a blank area of the slide, and then compare your screen with Figure 2.42.

FIGURE 2.42

5 **Save** your presentation.

Activity 2.26 | Adding Text Effects to a WordArt

Text effects are formats applied to text that include shadows, reflections, glows, bevels, and 3-D rotations.

1 With **Slide 3** displayed, select the **WordArt** text. On the mini toolbar, change the **Font** to **Arial** and the **Font Size** to **66**.

2 On the **FORMAT tab**, in the **WordArt Styles group**, click **Text Effects**. Point to **Shadow**, and then compare your screen with Figure 2.43.

FIGURE 2.43

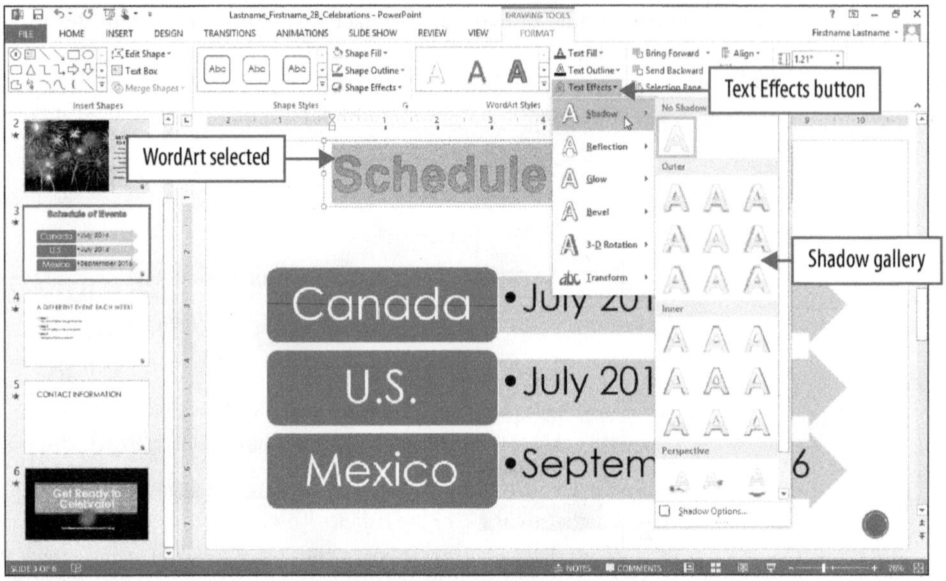

3 Under **Outer**, in the third row, click the third style—**Offset Diagonal Top Left**. Click in a blank area of the slide, and then compare your screen with Figure 2.44.

FIGURE 2.44

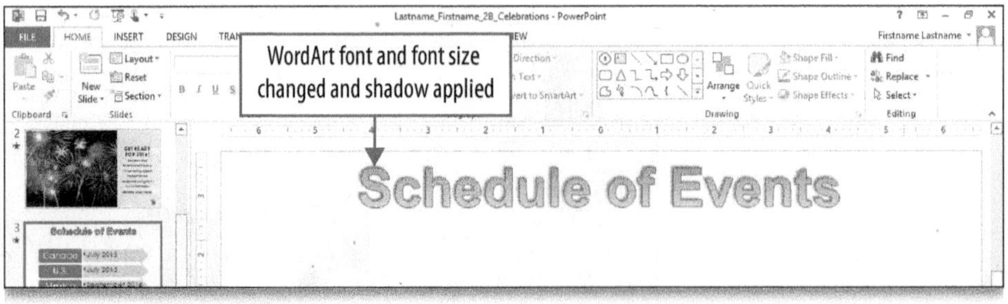

4 **Save** your presentation.

Objective 6 Create and Format a SmartArt Graphic

Video P2-6

A ***SmartArt graphic*** is a visual representation of information that you create by choosing from among various layouts to communicate your message or ideas effectively. SmartArt graphics can illustrate processes, hierarchies, cycles, lists, and relationships. You can include text and pictures in a SmartArt graphic, and you can apply colors, effects, and styles that coordinate with the presentation theme.

Activity 2.27 | Creating a SmartArt Graphic from Bulleted Points

You can convert an existing bulleted list into a SmartArt graphic. When you create a SmartArt graphic, consider the message that you are trying to convey, and then choose an appropriate layout. The table in Figure 2.45 describes types of SmartArt layouts and suggested purposes.

FIGURE 2.45

MICROSOFT POWERPOINT SMARTART GRAPHIC TYPES	
GRAPHIC TYPE	**PURPOSE OF GRAPHIC**
List	Shows non-sequential information
Process	Shows steps in a process or timeline
Cycle	Shows a continual process
Hierarchy	Shows a decision tree or displays an organization chart
Relationship	Illustrates connections
Matrix	Shows how parts relate to a whole
Pyramid	Shows proportional relationships with the largest component on the top or bottom
Picture	Includes pictures in the layout to communicate messages and ideas
Office.com	Additional layouts available from Office.com

1 Display **Slide 4**, and then click anywhere in the bulleted list placeholder. On the **HOME tab**, in the **Paragraph group**, click **Convert to SmartArt**. Below the gallery, click **More SmartArt Graphics**.

Three sections comprise the Choose a SmartArt Graphic dialog box. The left section lists the SmartArt graphic types. The center section displays the SmartArt layouts according to type. The third section displays the selected SmartArt graphic, its name, and a description of its purpose.

ANOTHER WAY Right-click in a bulleted list to display the shortcut menu, point to Convert to SmartArt, and then click More SmartArt Graphics.

2 On the left side of the **Choose a SmartArt Graphic** dialog box, click **List**. Use the ScreenTips to locate and then click **Vertical Box List**. Compare your screen with Figure 2.46.

FIGURE 2.46

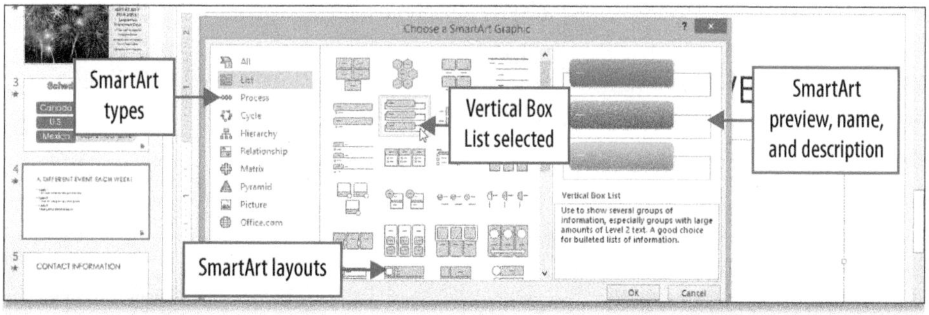

3 In the **Choose a SmartArt Graphic** dialog box, click **OK**. Compare your screen with Figure 2.47, and then **Save** your presentation.

It is not necessary to select all of the text in the list. By clicking in the list, PowerPoint converts all of the bullet points to the selected SmartArt graphic. On the ribbon, the SmartArt contextual tools display two tabs—Design and Format. The thick border surrounding the SmartArt graphic indicates that the SmartArt graphic is selected and displays the area that the object will cover on the slide.

FIGURE 2.47

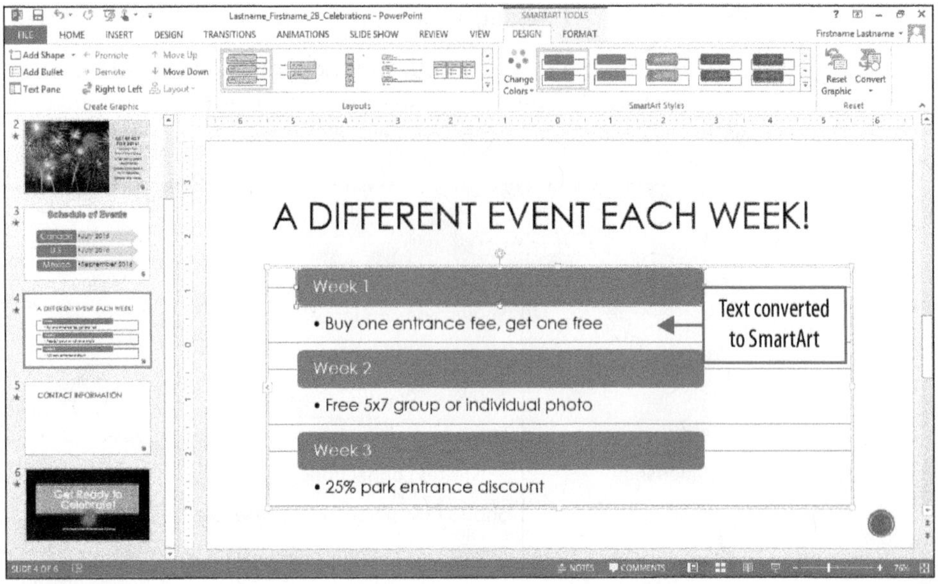

4 **Save** your presentation.

Activity 2.28 | Adding Shapes in a SmartArt Graphic

If a SmartArt graphic does not have enough shapes to illustrate a concept or display the relationships, you can add more shapes.

1 Click in the shape that contains the text *Week 3*. In the **SMARTART TOOLS**, click the **DESIGN tab**. In the **Create Graphic group**, click the **Add Shape arrow**, and then click **Add Shape After** to insert a shape at the same level. Type **Week 4**

The text in each of the SmartArt shapes resizes to accommodate the added shape.

ANOTHER WAY Right-click the shape, point to Add Shape, and then click Add Shape After.

2 On the **DESIGN tab**, in the **Create Graphic group**, click **Add Bullet** to add a bullet below the *Week 4* shape.

3 Type **25% discount on food and beverages** Compare your slide with Figure 2.48, and then **Save** your presentation.

FIGURE 2.48

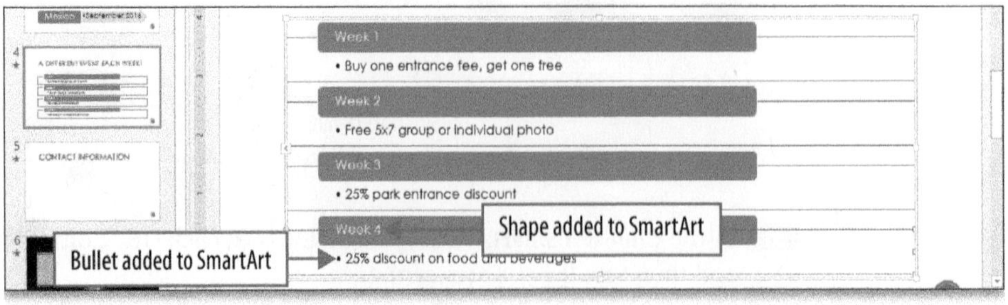

Activity 2.29 | Inserting a SmartArt Graphic Using a Content Layout

1 Display **Slide 5**. In the center of the content placeholder, click **Insert a SmartArt Graphic** to open the **Choose a SmartArt Graphic** dialog box.

2 On the left, click **Picture**, and then scroll as necessary and use the ScreenTips to locate **Picture Strips**. Click **Picture Strips** and then compare your screen with Figure 2.49.

FIGURE 2.49

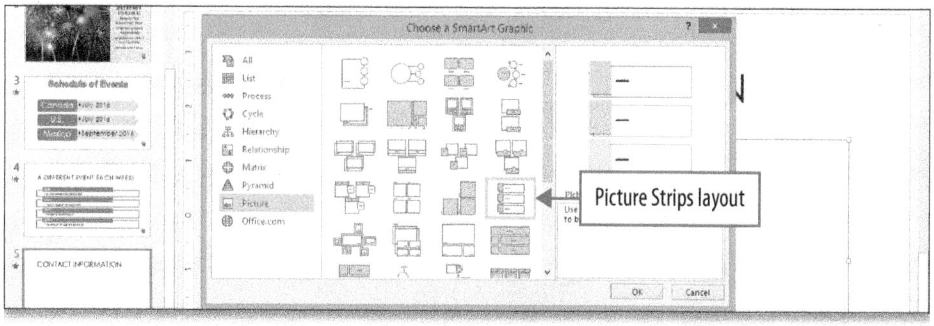

3 Click **OK** to insert the SmartArt graphic.

You can type text directly into the shapes or you can type text in the Text Pane, which may display to the left of your SmartArt graphic. You can display the Text Pane by clicking the Text Pane tab on the left side of the SmartArt graphic border, or by clicking the Text Pane button in the Create Graphic group. Depending on your software settings, the Text Pane may display.

Activity 2.30 | Inserting Pictures and Text in a SmartArt Graphic

1 In the SmartArt graphic, in the upper left text rectangle shape, type **Sophia Ackerman** and then press Enter. Type **United States** and then click in the text rectangle on the right. Type **Joseph Mercado** and then press Enter. Type **Mexico** and then click in the lower text rectangle. Type **Michael Lewis** and then press Enter. Type **Canada**

2 In the top left picture placeholder, click **Insert Picture**. In the **Insert Pictures** dialog box, to the right of **From a file**, click **Browse**. Navigate to your student data files, click **p02B_US_Contact**, and then click **Insert** to insert the picture.

3 Using the technique you just practiced, in the right picture placeholder, insert **p02B_Mexico_Contact**. In the lower picture placeholder, insert **p02B_Canada_Contact.**

4 Compare your screen with Figure 2.50, and then **Save** your presentation.

FIGURE 2.50

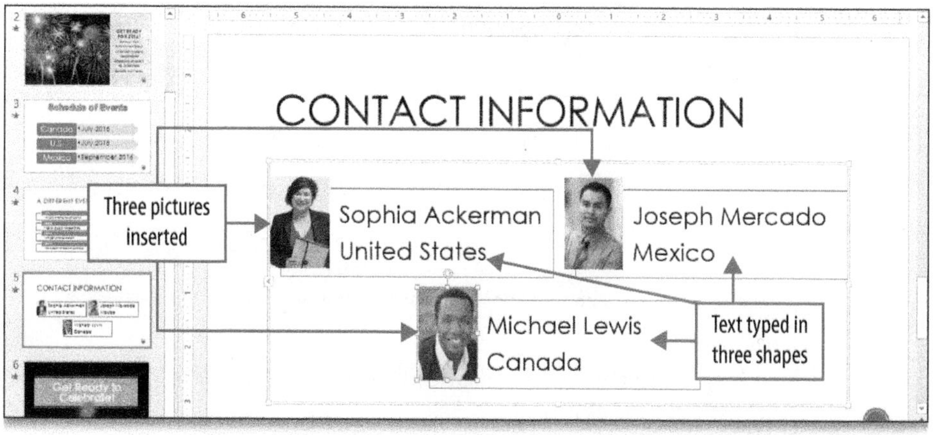

Activity 2.31 | Changing the Size and Shape of SmartArt Elements

You can select individual or groups of shapes in a SmartArt graphic and make them larger or smaller, and you can change selected shapes to another type of shape.

1 With **Slide 5** displayed, click the picture of *Sophia Ackerman*. Hold down Shift, and then click the pictures of *Joseph Mercado* and *Michael Lewis* so that all three pictures are selected.

2 On the **SMARTART TOOLS FORMAT tab**, in the **Shapes group**, click **Larger** two times to increase the size of the three pictures.

3 With the three pictures selected, on the **SMARTART TOOLS FORMAT tab**, in the **Shapes group**, click **Change Shape**. Under **Rectangles**, click the second shape—**Rounded Rectangle**.

4 Click anywhere on the slide to cancel the selection, and then compare your screen with Figure 2.51.

FIGURE 2.51

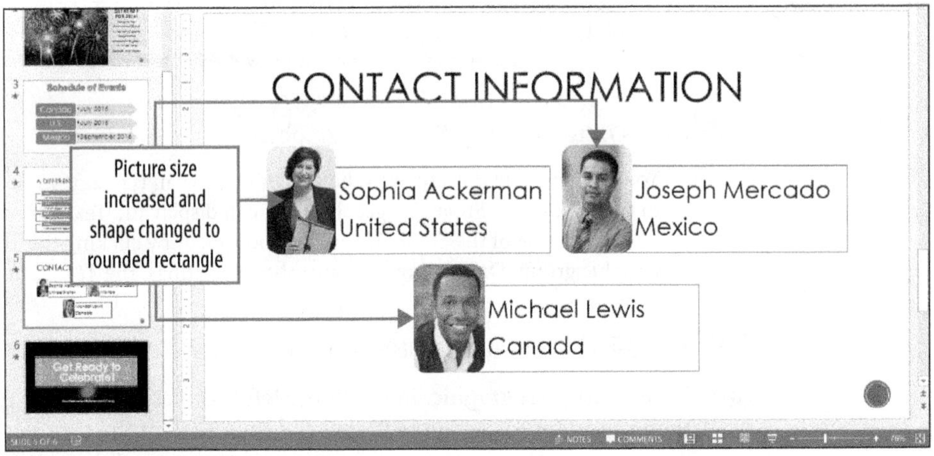

5 **Save** your presentation.

Activity 2.32 | Changing the SmartArt Layout

1 Display **Slide 3**, and then click anywhere in the SmartArt graphic. On the **SMARTART TOOLS DESIGN tab**, in the **Layouts group**, click **More**, and then click **More Layouts**. In the **Choose a SmartArt Graphic** dialog box, click **List**. Scroll up or down as necessary to locate and then click **Vertical Block List**. Compare your screen with Figure 2.52.

FIGURE 2.52

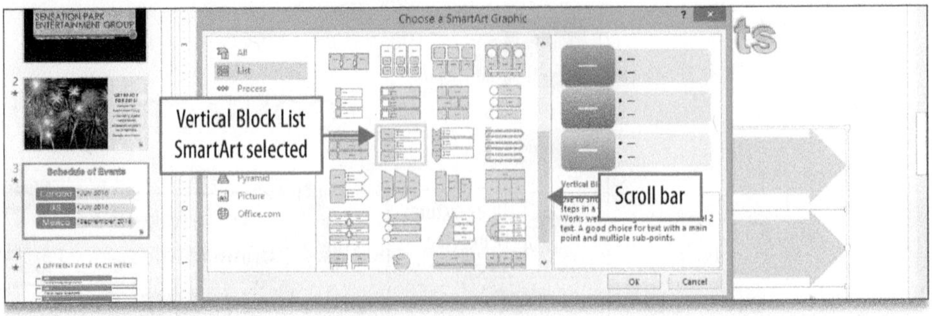

2 Click **OK**, and then **Save** the presentation.

Activity 2.33 | Changing the Color and Style of a SmartArt Graphic

SmartArt Styles are combinations of formatting effects that you can apply to SmartArt graphics.

1 With **Slide 3** displayed, if necessary, select the SmartArt. On the **SMARTART TOOLS DESIGN tab**, in the **SmartArt Styles group**, click **Change Colors**. In the color gallery, under **Colorful**, click the second style—**Colorful Range - Accent Colors 2 to 3**—to change the colors.

2 On the **DESIGN tab**, in the **SmartArt Styles group**, click **More** to display the **SmartArt Styles gallery**. Under **3-D**, click the third style, **Cartoon**. Compare your slide with Figure 2.53.

FIGURE 2.53

3 **Save** the presentation.

Activity 2.34 | Converting a SmartArt to Text

1 Display **Slide 4**, and then click anywhere in the SmartArt graphic. On the **SMARTART TOOLS DESIGN tab**, in the **Reset group**, click **Convert**, and then click **Convert to Text** to convert the SmartArt graphic back to a bulleted list. Compare your screen with Figure 2.54.

FIGURE 2.54

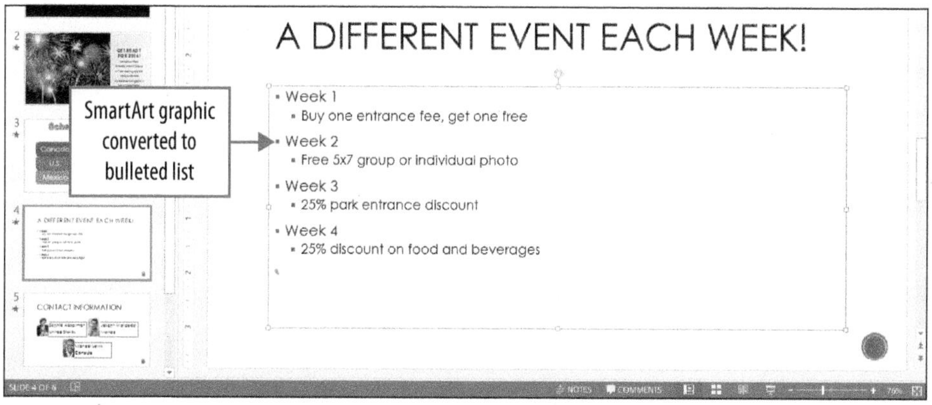

2 Insert a **Header & Footer** on the **Notes and Handouts**. Include the **Date and time updated automatically**, the **Page number**, and a **Footer** with the text **Lastname_Firstname_2B_Celebrations**

3 Display the document properties. As the **Tags** type **independence day, celebrations** and as the **Subject** type your course and section number. Be sure your name displays as the author, and then **Save** your file.

4 View the slide show from the beginning, and then make any necessary adjustments. **Save** your presentation. Print **Handouts 6 Slides Horizontal**, or submit your presentation electronically as directed by your instructor.

5 **Close** PowerPoint.

END | You have completed Project 2B

GO! with Office Online (formerly Web Apps)

Objective Create an Advertisement Presentation in PowerPoint Online

ALERT! Working with Web-Based Applications and Services

Computer programs and services on the web receive continuous updates and improvements, so the steps to complete this web-based activity may differ from the ones shown. You can often look at the screens and the information presented to determine how to complete the activity.

Activity | Creating an Advertisement Presentation in PowerPoint Online

In this activity, you will use PowerPoint Online to format a presentation similar to the one you created in Project 2B.

1 From the desktop, start Internet Explorer. Navigate to **http://onedrive.com**, and then sign in to your Microsoft account. Open your **GO! Web Projects** folder—or create and then open this folder if necessary.

2 On the OneDrive menu bar, click **Upload**, and then navigate to your student data files and select **p02_2B_Web**. Click **Open**. When the upload is complete, right click **p02_2B_Web**, and then click **Rename**. Using your own name, as the file name type **Lastname_Firstname_PPT_2B_Web** and then press Enter. Click your file, and then click **EDIT PRESENTATION**. Click **Edit in PowerPoint Online**.

3 Display **Slide 3**. In the content placeholder, click the first button—**Insert a SmartArt Graphic**. On the **SMARTART TOOLS DESIGN tab**, in the **Layouts group**, click the second layout—**Horizontal Bullet List** to change the SmartArt style.

4 Click in the upper left orange rectangle and notice that the content placeholder displays a bulleted list. Click the first bullet point—it may align with the left edge of the placeholder. Type **Canada** and then click in the indented bullet point below the text you typed. Type **July 2016** and then press Delete to remove the second bullet point.

5 Click the second solid bullet, and then type **U.S.** Click the indented bullet point below the text you typed. Type **July 2016** and then press Delete. Using the technique you practiced, in the third set of bullet points, type **Mexico** and **September 2016**

6 Compare your screen with Figure A.

7 Click outside the content placeholder to display the SmartArt graphic.

8 Select the SmartArt graphic, and then on the **SMARTART TOOLS DESIGN tab**, in the **SmartArt Styles group**, click **Change Colors**. Under **Colorful**, click the first style— **Colorful - Accent Colors**. In the **SmartArt Styles group**, click the small down arrow to display more styles, and then in the second row, click the third style—**Cartoon**.

FIGURE A

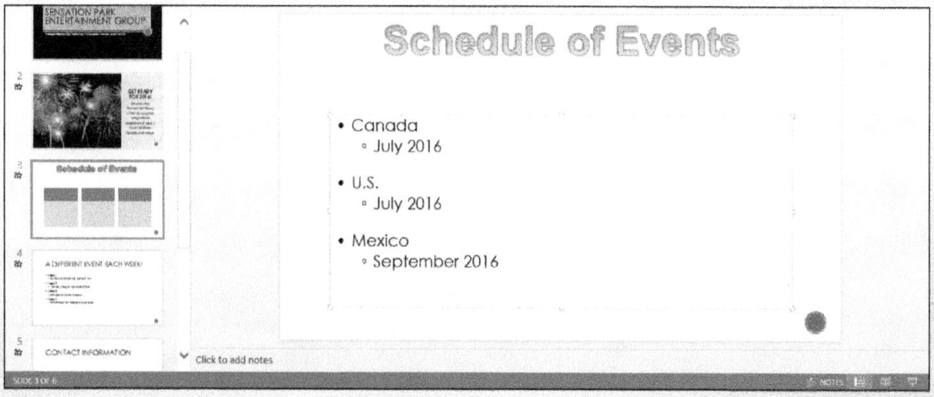

(GO! with Office Online (formerly Web Apps) continues on the next page)

9 Display **Slide 5**. In the content placeholder, click the first button—**Insert a SmartArt Graphic** . On the **SMARTART TOOLS DESIGN tab**, in the **Layouts group**, click the **More Layouts arrow**, and then in the third row, click the eighth layout—**Grouped List** to change the SmartArt style.

10 Click in the upper left shape. To the right of the first solid bullet, type **Sophia Ackerman** and then click in the indented bullet point below the text you typed. Type **United States** and then press Delete to remove the second bullet point.

11 Click to the right of the second solid bullet, and then type **Joseph Mercado** Click in the indented bullet point below the text you typed. Type **Mexico** and then press Delete. Using the technique you practiced, in the third set of bullet points, type **Michael Lewis** and **Canada**

12 Click outside the content placeholder to display the SmartArt graphic.

13 Select the SmartArt graphic, and then on the **SMARTART TOOLS DESIGN tab**, in the **SmartArt Styles group**, click **Change Colors**. Under **Colorful**, click the first style— **Colorful - Accent Colors**. In the **SmartArt Styles group**, click the **More Styles arrow**, and then in the second row, click the third style—**Cartoon**.

14 Click in a blank area of the slide and then compare your screen with Figure B.

15 Submit your file as instructed. Sign out of your OneDrive and then close Internet Explorer.

FIGURE B

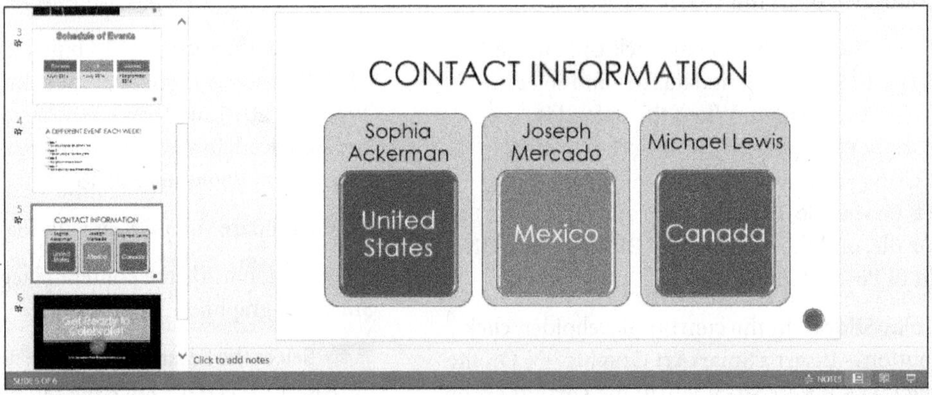

GO! with Microsoft Office 365

Andrew Rodriguez / Fotolia; FotolEdhar/ Fotolia; apops/ Fotolia; Yuri Arcurs/ Fotolia

Office 365 combines tools for collaboration and productivity and delivers them to multiple users in an organization by using *cloud computing*—applications and services that are accessed over the Internet with multiple devices. For example, one cloud service with which you might be familiar is *OneDrive*, a free web-based application with which you can save, store, organize, and share files online. This cloud service is available for anyone who has a free Microsoft account.

Another cloud service from Microsoft is *Office Web Apps*. These are the online companions to the desktop versions of Microsoft Office Word, Excel, PowerPoint, and OneNote that enable you to create, access, share, and perform light editing on Microsoft Office documents from any device that connects to the Internet and uses a supported *web browser*. A web browser is software, such as Internet Explorer, Firefox, Safari, or Chrome, that displays web pages.

For an organization, cloud computing enables the addition of services without investing in additional hardware and software. For you as a team member, you can use your web browser to access, edit, store, and share files. You do not need to have a full version of Office installed on your computer to do this. You have all the tools and security that large organizations have!

When you use Office 365, your email and storage servers are hosted by Microsoft. Your organization gets business-class security from Microsoft—a large, well-established company. Sophisticated security and data management features are built into Office 365 so that you can control *permissions*—access rights that define the ability of an individual or group to view or make changes to documents—and provide secure email and communications.

Activity | Using Lync to Collaborate by Using a Video Call

This group project relates to the **Bell Orchid Hotels**. If your instructor assigns this project to your class, you can expect to use **Lync** in **Office 365** to collaborate on the following tasks for this chapter:

- If you are in the **Accounting Group**, you and your teammates will conduct a video call to discuss and agree on the format of the drawing objects, slide transitions, comments, and graphics in your Loan Presentation.
- If you are in the **Engineering Group**, you and your teammates will conduct a video call to discuss and agree on the format of the drawing objects, slide transitions, comments, and graphics in your Safety Presentation.
- If you are in the **Food and Beverage Group**, you and your teammates will conduct a video call to discuss and agree on the format of the drawing objects, slide transitions, comments, and graphics in your New Menu Item Presentation.
- If you are in the **Human Resources Group**, you and your teammates will conduct a video call to discuss and agree on the format of the drawing objects, slide transitions, comments, and graphics in your New Employees Presentation.
- If you are in the **Operations Group**, you and your teammates will conduct a video call to discuss and agree on the format of the drawing objects, slide transitions, comments, and graphics in your Front Desk Clerk Training Presentation.
- If you are in the **Sales and Marketing Group**, you and your teammates will conduct a video call to discuss and agree on the format of the drawing objects, slide transitions, comments, and graphics in your Marketing Plan Presentation.

FIGURE A

END OF CHAPTER

SUMMARY

Use numbered and bulleted lists in a presentation to focus attention on specific items. The theme that you select includes default styles for bullets, but you can change the shape and color of the symbols.

Use pictures to illustrate an idea. The Online Pictures feature enables you to search Office.com for images that emphasize important points. Using good keywords is critical to a successful search to find a great picture!

Objects are easily modified in PowerPoint. Removing the picture background and cropping eliminate unnecessary picture parts. Smart guides and alignment options are used to position pictures and shapes.

Use SmartArt graphics to present information and to illustrate processes, hierarchies, cycles, lists, and relationships. SmartArt graphics may include text and pictures, and can be formatted with styles and color combinations for maximum impact.

GO! LEARN IT ONLINE

Review the concepts and key terms in this chapter by completing these online challenges, which you can find at **www.pearsonhighered.com/go**.

Matching and Multiple Choice: Answer matching and multiple choice questions to test what you learned in this chapter. MyITLab®

Crossword Puzzle: Spell out the words that match the numbered clues, and put them in the puzzle squares.

Flipboard: Flip through the definitions of the key terms in this chapter and match them with the correct term.

GO! FOR JOB SUCCESS

Video: Business Lunch Interpersonal Communications

Your instructor may assign this video to your class, and then ask you to think about, or discuss with your classmates, these questions:

FotolEdhar / Fotolia

In what specific ways did Sara and Jordan demonstrate improper interpersonal communication during their lunch with Karen?

As a manager, did Chris follow the rules of interpersonal communication with his client? Explain your answer.

In what ways did Sara, Jordan, and Theo demonstrate proper or improper *nonverbal* communication skills?

END OF CHAPTER

REVIEW AND ASSESSMENT GUIDE FOR POWERPOINT CHAPTER 2

Your instructor may assign one or more of these projects to help you review the chapter and assess your mastery and understanding of the chapter.

Review and Assessment Guide for PowerPoint Chapter 2

Project	Apply Skills from These Chapter Objectives	Project Type	Project Location
2C	Objectives 1-4 from Project 2A	**2C Skills Review** A guided review of the skills from Project 2A.	On the following pages
2D	Objectives 5-6 from Project 2B	**2D Skills Review** A guided review of the skills from Project 2B.	On the following pages
2E	Objectives 1-4 from Project 2A	**2E Mastery (Grader Project)** A demonstration of your mastery of the skills in Project 2A with extensive decision making.	In MyITLab and on the following pages
2F	Objectives 5-6 from Project 2B	**2F Mastery (Grader Project)** A demonstration of your mastery of the skills in Project 2B with extensive decision making.	In MyITLab and on the following pages
2G	Objectives 1-6 from Projects 2A and 2B	**2G Mastery (Grader Project)** A demonstration of your mastery of the skills in Projects 2A and 2B with extensive decision making.	In MyITLab and on the following pages
2H	Combination of Objectives from Projects 2A and 2B	**2H GO! Fix It** A demonstration of your mastery of the skills in Projects 2A and 2B by creating a correct result from a document that contains errors you must find.	Online
2I	Combination of Objectives from Projects 2A and 2B	**2I GO! Make It** A demonstration of your mastery of the skills in Projects 2A and 2B by creating a result from a supplied picture.	Online
2J	Combination of Objectives from Projects 2A and 2B	**2J GO! Solve It** A demonstration of your mastery of the skills in Projects 2A and 2B, your decision-making skills, and your critical thinking skills. A task-specific rubric helps you self-assess your result.	Online
2K	Combination of Objectives from Projects 2A and 2B	**2K GO! Solve It** A demonstration of your mastery of the skills in Projects 2A and 2B, your decision-making skills, and your critical thinking skills. A task-specific rubric helps you self-assess your result.	On the following pages
2L	Combination of Objectives from Projects 2A and 2B	**2L GO! Think** A demonstration of your understanding of the Chapter concepts applied in a manner that you would outside of college. An analytic rubric helps you and your instructor grade the quality of your work by comparing it to the work an expert in the discipline would create.	On the following pages
2M	Combination of Objectives from Projects 2A and 2B	**2M GO! Think** A demonstration of your understanding of the Chapter concepts applied in a manner that you would outside of college. An analytic rubric helps you and your instructor grade the quality of your work by comparing it to the work an expert in the discipline would create.	Online
2N	Combination of Objectives from Projects 2A and 2B	**2N You and GO!** A demonstration of your understanding of the Chapter concepts applied in a manner that you would in a personal situation. An analytic rubric helps you and your instructor grade the quality of your work.	Online
2O	Combination of Objectives from Projects 2A and 2B	**2O Cumulative Group Project for PowerPoint Chapter 2** A demonstration of your understanding of concepts and your ability to work collaboratively in a group role-playing assessment, requiring both collaboration and self-management.	Online

GLOSSARY

GLOSSARY OF CHAPTER KEY TERMS

Background Removal A feature that removes unwanted portions of a picture so that the picture does not appear as a self-contained rectangle.

Clip A single media file, such as art, sound, animation, or a movie.

Crop A command that removes unwanted or unnecessary areas of a picture.

Crop handles Handles used to remove unwanted areas of a picture.

Crop pointer The pointer used to crop areas of a picture.

Crosshair pointer The pointer used to draw a shape.

Eyedropper A tool that captures the exact color from an object on your screen and then applies the color to any shape, picture, or text.

Fill color The inside color of text or of an object.

RGB A color model in which the colors red, green, and blue are added together to form another color.

Ruler guides Dotted red vertical and horizontal lines that display in the rulers indicating the pointer's position.

Shape A slide object such as a line, arrow, box, callout, or banner.

Smart Guides Dashed lines that display on your slide when you are moving an object to assist you with alignment.

SmartArt graphic A visual representation of information that you create by choosing from among various layouts to communicate your message or ideas effectively.

SmartArt Styles Combinations of formatting effects that you can apply to SmartArt graphics.

Text Box An object with which you can position text anywhere on a slide.

Text effects Formats applied to text that include shadows, reflections, glows, bevels, and 3-D rotations.

WordArt A gallery of text styles with which you can create decorative effects, such as shadowed or mirrored text.

CHAPTER REVIEW

Apply 2A skills from these Objectives:

1 Format Numbered and Bulleted Lists
2 Insert Online Pictures
3 Insert Text Boxes and Shapes
4 Format Objects

Skills Review Project 2C Concerts

In the following Skills Review, you will format a presentation that describes annual Concerts in the Park events at several Sensation Park Entertainment Group amusement parks. Your completed presentation will look similar to Figure 2.55.

PROJECT FILES

For Project 2C, you will need the following file:

p02C_Concerts

You will save your presentation as:

Lastname_Firstname_2C_Concerts

PROJECT RESULTS

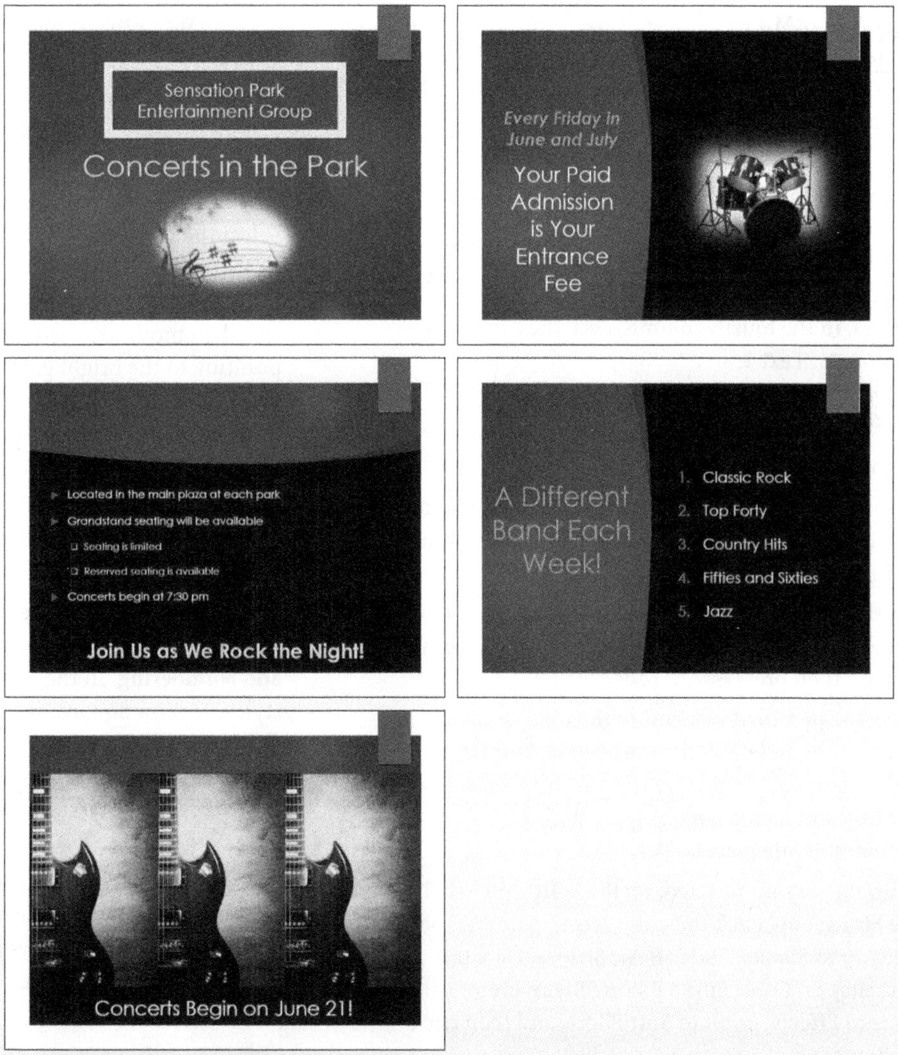

FIGURE 2.55

(Project 2C Concerts continues on the next page)

CHAPTER REVIEW

Skills Review Project 2C Concerts (continued)

1 Start PowerPoint. From the student data files that accompany this textbook, locate and open **p02C_Concerts**. On the **FILE tab**, click **Save As**, navigate to your **PowerPoint Chapter 2** folder, and then using your own name, save the file as **Lastname_Firstname_2C_Concerts**

a. If necessary, display the Rulers. With **Slide 1** displayed, on the **INSERT tab**, in the **Illustrations group**, click **Shapes**, and then under **Basic Shapes**, in the second row, click the fifth shape—**Frame**.

b. Move the pointer to align the ruler guides with the **left half of the horizontal ruler at 3 inches** and with the **upper half of the vertical ruler at 2.5 inches**, and then click to insert the Frame.

c. On the **FORMAT tab**, in the **Size group**, click in the **Shape Height** box to select the number, and then type **1.7** Click in the **Shape Width** box. Replace the selected number with **5.5** and then press Enter to resize the shape.

d. With the frame selected, type **Sensation Park Entertainment Group** and then change the **Font Size** to **28**. On the **FORMAT tab** in the **Shape Styles group**, click **Shape Fill**, and then under **Theme Colors**, in the fourth column, click the first color—**Gray-25%, Text 2**.

e. With the picture selected, hold down Shift, and then click the **frame shape** and the **title placeholder** so that all three objects are selected. Under **DRAWING TOOLS**, on the **FORMAT tab**, in the **Arrange group**, click **Align**, and then click **Align to Slide**. Click **Align** again, and then click **Align Center**. **Save** the presentation.

2 On the **INSERT tab**, in the **Images group**, click **Online Pictures**. In the **Office.com Search** box, type **sheet music close up** and then press Enter.

a. Click the picture of the two lines of music on a music sheet, and then click **Insert**. If you cannot find the image, choose another picture.

b. On the **FORMAT tab**, in the **Size group**, click in the **Shape Height** box. Replace the selected number with **2.5** and then press Enter to resize the image.

c. Drag the picture down and to the right until intersecting red dashed Smart Guides display, indicating that the picture is center aligned with the title and its top edge aligns with the bottom edge of the title placeholder.

d. With the picture selected, on the **FORMAT tab**, in the **Size group**, click the **Crop arrow**, and then point to **Crop to Shape**. Under **Basic Shapes**, click the first shape—**Oval**. In the **Picture Styles group**, click **Picture Effects**, point to **Soft Edges**, and then click **25 Point**.

3 Display **Slide 2**. On the right side of the slide, in the content placeholder, click **Online Pictures**. In the **Search Office.com** box, type **drum kit** and then press Enter. Insert the picture of the drum set on a white background. If the picture is not available, choose another image.

a. On the **FORMAT tab**, in the **Picture Styles group**, click **Picture Effects**, point to **Soft Edges**, and then click **50 Point**.

b. Click in the placeholder containing the text *Every Friday in June and July*. On the **HOME tab**, in the **Paragraph group**, click **Bullets** to remove the bullet symbol from the title.

c. Select the text *Every Friday in June and July*. On the **HOME tab**, in the **Font group**, click the **Font Color button arrow**. Below the gallery, click **Eyedropper**, and then move the eyedropper pointer so that it is pointing to the bright gold area of the drum on the right side of the picture. Click one time to apply the color to the selected text. Apply **Bold** and **Italic** and change the **Font Size** to **28**.

4 Display **Slide 3**, and then select the third and fourth bullet points—*Seating is limited* and *Reserved seating is available*.

a. On the **HOME tab**, in the **Paragraph group**, click the **Bullets button arrow**, and then click **Bullets and Numbering**. In the second row, click the first style—**Hollow Square Bullets**. Replace the number in the **Size** box with **90** and then click the **Color arrow**. Under **Recent Colors**, apply the color chosen using the eyedropper on Slide 2—**Tan**. Click **OK**.

b. Display **Slide 4**, and then click the bulleted list placeholder. Click the dashed border so that the border displays as a solid line, and then on the **HOME tab**, in the **Paragraph group**, click **Numbering** to change the bullet symbols to numbers.

(Project 2C Concerts continues on the next page)

Skills Review Project 2C Concerts (continued)

c. On the left side of the slide, select the title text, and then on the mini toolbar, click the **Font Color button arrow**. Under **Recent Colors**, click **Tan**.

5 Display **Slide 5**. On the **INSERT tab**, in the **Images group**, click **Online Pictures**. In the **Office.com search** box, type **electric guitar** and then press Enter. Insert the picture of the black electric guitar on the white, blue, and black background. If you cannot locate the picture, choose another image.

a. Change the picture **Height** to **4.75** and then drag the picture so that its upper left corner aligns with the upper left corner of the purple area on the slide. On the **FORMAT tab**, in the **Picture Styles group**, click **Picture Effects**, and then point to **Soft Edges**. Click **2.5 Point**.

b. Press Ctrl + D and then drag the duplicated picture to the right about 1 inch. Press Ctrl + D to insert a third picture.

c. Point to the third guitar picture that you inserted and then drag to the right so that its upper right corner aligns with the upper right corner of the purple area on the slide.

d. Hold down Shift and then click the first two guitar pictures so that all three pictures are selected. On the **FORMAT tab**, in the **Arrange group**, click **Align**, and then click **Align to Slide**. Click **Align** again, and then click **Align Middle**.

e. With the three pictures selected, click **Align**, and then click **Align Selected Objects**. Click **Align** again, and then click **Distribute Horizontally**.

6 With **Slide 5** displayed, on the **INSERT tab**, in the **Text group**, click **Text Box**. Move the pointer to align the ruler guides with the **left half of the horizontal ruler at 2 inches** and with the **lower half of the vertical ruler at 2.5 inches**, and then click to insert the text box.

a. Type **Concerts Begin on June 21!** Select the text and then change the **Font Size** to **32**. On the **FORMAT tab**, in the **Arrange group**, click **Align**, and then click **Align Center**.

b. Insert a **Header & Footer** on the **Notes and Handouts tab**. Include the **Date and time updated automatically**, the **Page number**, and a **Footer** with the text **Lastname_Firstname_2C_Concerts**

c. Display the document properties. As the **Tags**, type **concerts** and as the **Subject**, type your course and section number. Be sure your name displays as the author, and then **Save** your file.

d. View the slide show from the beginning. Print **Handouts 6 Slides Horizontal**, or submit your presentation electronically as directed by your instructor. **Close** the presentation.

END | You have completed Project 2C

CHAPTER REVIEW

Apply 2B skills from these Objectives:

5 Remove Picture Backgrounds and Insert WordArt
6 Create and Format a SmartArt Graphic

Skills Review Project 2D Corporate Events

In the following Skills Review, you will format a presentation by inserting and formatting WordArt and SmartArt graphics. Your completed presentation will look similar to Figure 2.56.

PROJECT FILES

For Project 2D, you will need the following file:

p02D_Corporate_Events

You will save your presentation as:

Lastname_Firstname_2D_Corporate_Events

PROJECT RESULTS

FIGURE 2.56

(Project 2D Corporate Events continues on the next page)

CHAPTER REVIEW

Skills Review Project 2D Corporate Events (continued)

1 Start PowerPoint. From the student data files that accompany this textbook, locate and open **p02D_Corporate_Events**. **Save** the presentation in your **PowerPoint Chapter 2** folder as **Lastname_Firstname_2D_Corporate_Events**

a. With **Slide 1** displayed, select the text **Corporate Event Planning**. On the **FORMAT tab**, in the **WordArt Styles group**, click **More**. In the second row, click the last style—**Fill – Brown, Accent 3, Sharp Bevel**. Click outside the placeholder.

b. On the **INSERT tab**, in the **Text group**, click **WordArt**. In the **WordArt gallery**, in the third row, click the last style—**Fill - Brown, Background 2, Inner Shadow**. With the text *Your text here* selected, type **Sensation Park**

c. With the WordArt selected, hold down Shift, and then click the subtitle. On the **FORMAT tab**, in the **Arrange group**, click **Align**, and then click **Align Selected Objects**. Click **Align** again, and then click **Align Left**.

2 Display **Slide 3**. In the center of the content placeholder, click **Insert a SmartArt Graphic** to open the **Choose a SmartArt Graphic** dialog box. On the left, click **List**, and then scroll as necessary and locate and click **Horizontal Bullet List**. Click **OK**.

a. In the SmartArt graphic, in the first gold rectangle, click *Text*. Type **Days and Times** and then click in the rectangle below the text you typed. Type **Weeknights** and then click in the second bullet point. Type **7 to 11 p.m.**

b. In the second gold rectangle, type **Packages** and then click in the rectangle below the text you typed. Type **Admission, parking, and dinner** and then delete the second text bullet point in the rectangle.

c. In the third gold rectangle, type **Capacity** and then click in the rectangle below the text you typed. Type **Maximum 750 guests** and then delete the second text bullet point in the rectangle.

d. On the **SMARTART TOOLS DESIGN tab**, in the **SmartArt Styles group**, click **Change Colors**, and then under **Colorful**, click the last style **Colorful Range - Accent Colors 5 to 6**. In the **SmartArt Styles group**, click **More**, and then under **3-D**, in the first row, click the fourth style—**Powder**.

e. Click in the **Days and Times** rectangle, hold down Shift, and then click the **Packages** and **Capacity** rectangles. On the **SMARTART TOOLS FORMAT** tab, in the **Shapes group**, click **Change Shape**. Under **Rectangles**, click the fourth shape—**Snip Same Side Corner Rectangle**.

3 Display **Slide 4**, and then click anywhere in the bulleted list. On the **HOME tab**, in the **Paragraph group**, click **Convert to SmartArt**. At the bottom of the gallery, click **More SmartArt Graphics**. On the left side of the **Choose a SmartArt Graphic** dialog box, click **List**. Locate and click **Grouped List**, and then click **OK** to convert the list to a SmartArt graphic.

a. Under **Family Evening**, click in the **Dinner and dessert** shape, and then on the **SMARTART TOOLS DESIGN tab**, in the **Create Graphic group**, click **Add Shape**. In the inserted shape, type **Special Children's Events**

b. With the *Special Children's Events* shape selected, add another shape, and then type **All ages**

c. On the **SMARTART TOOLS DESIGN tab**, in the **SmartArt Styles group**, click **Change Colors**. In the **Color** gallery, under **Colorful**, click the last style—**Colorful Range - Accent Colors 5 to 6**.

d. On the **DESIGN tab**, in the **SmartArt Styles group**, click **More** to display the **SmartArt Styles gallery**. Under **3-D**, in the first row, click the third style—**Cartoon**.

4 Display **Slide 5**. Select the picture of the admission tickets, and then on the **FORMAT tab**, in the **Adjust group**, click **Remove Background**. In the **Close group**, click **Keep Changes**.

a. With the picture selected, on the **FORMAT tab**, in the **Picture Styles group**, click **Picture Effects**. Point to **Soft Edges**, and then click **25 Point**.

b. Insert a **Header & Footer** on the **Notes and Handouts**. Include the **Date and time updated automatically**, a **Page number**, and a **Footer** with the text **Lastname_Firstname_2D_Corporate_Events**

c. Display the document properties. As the **Tags** type **corporate events** and as the **Subject** type your course and section number. Be sure your name displays as the author, and then **Save** your file.

d. View the slide show from the beginning. Print **Handouts 6 Slides Horizontal**, or submit your presentation electronically as directed by your instructor. **Close** the presentation.

END | You have completed Project 2D

CONTENT-BASED ASSESSMENTS

Mastering PowerPoint | Project 2E Coasters

MyITLab® grader

Apply 2A skills from these Objectives:

1. Format Numbered and Bulleted Lists
2. Insert Online Pictures
3. Insert Text Boxes and Shapes
4. Format Objects

In the following Mastering PowerPoint project, you will format a presentation describing new roller coasters under construction at several Sensation Park Entertainment Group amusement parks. Your completed presentation will look similar to Figure 2.57.

PROJECT FILES

For Project 2E, you will need the following file:

p02E_Coasters

You will save your presentation as:

Lastname_Firstname_2E_Coasters

PROJECT RESULTS

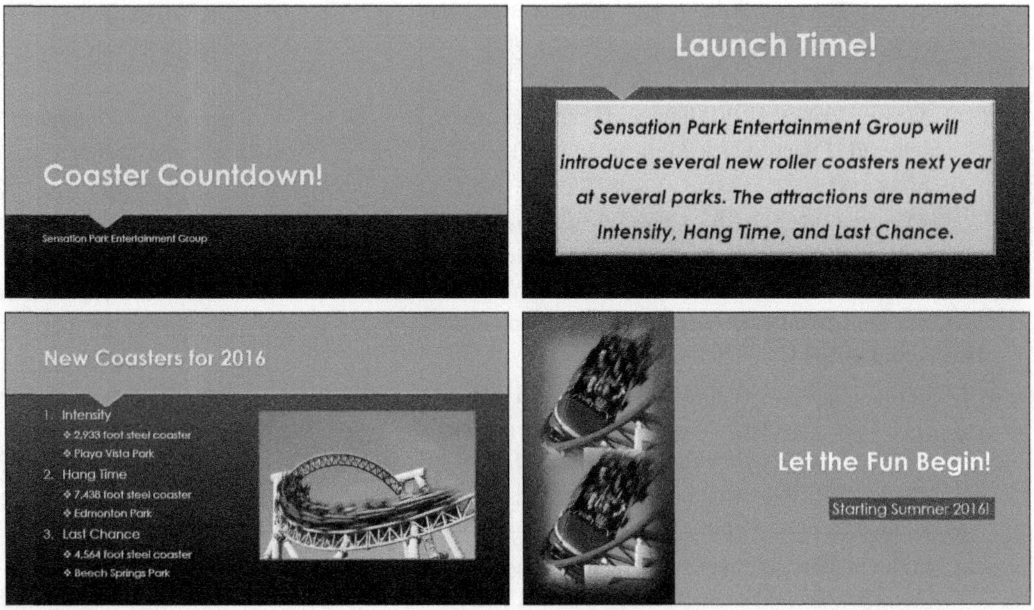

FIGURE 2.57

(Project 2E Coasters continues on the next page)

Mastering PowerPoint | Project 2E Coasters (continued)

1 Start PowerPoint. From the student data files that accompany this textbook, locate and open **p02E_Coasters**. In your **PowerPoint Chapter 2** folder, **Save** the file as **Lastname_Firstname_2E_Coasters**

2 On **Slide 2**, remove the bullet symbol from the paragraph, and then **Center** the paragraph. With the content placeholder selected, display the **Shape Styles** gallery, and then in the fourth row, apply the sixth style—**Subtle Effect - Blue-Gray, Accent 5**. Apply the **Art Deco** beveled shape effect to the placeholder.

3 On **Slide 3**, apply **Numbering** to the first-level bullet points—*Intensity, Hang Time,* and *Last Chance*. Under each of the numbered items, change all of the circle bullet symbols to **Star Bullets**, and then change the bullet color to **Aqua, Accent 1, Lighter 40%**—in the fifth column, the fourth color.

4 On **Slide 3**, select the title. Change the **Font Color** using the **Eyedropper**. With the eyedropper pointer, click anywhere in the thick, light yellow stripe on the roller coaster car at the right side of the picture to apply the light yellow color to the title. If necessary, use the Zoom slider to zoom in on the picture. On **Slides 1** and **2**, apply the same light yellow color to the slide title on each slide.

5 Display **Slide 3**, and then apply an **Aqua, 5 pt glow, Accent color 2** picture effect to the picture.

6 Display **Slide 4**. Insert an **Online Picture** by searching for **roller coaster** and then insert the close-up picture of the roller coaster with the red cars and the people raising their hands in the air. If you cannot locate the picture, choose another image. **Crop** the picture by dragging the bottom-center crop handle up so that the crop handle is positioned on the **lower half of the vertical ruler at 1 inch**.

7 Align the upper left corner of the picture with the top left corner of the slide, and then change the **Height** to **4.5** Modify the picture effect by applying a **50 Point Soft Edges** effect.

8 Duplicate the picture, and then use the **Align to Slide** option to align the pictures with the left edge of the slide and to distribute the pictures vertically.

9 Insert a **Text Box** aligned with the **horizontal ruler at 0 inches** and with the **lower half of the vertical ruler at 1 inch**. In the text box, type **Starting Summer 2016!** Change the **Font Size** to **28**. Change the **Shape Fill** to the last color in the last column—**Blue, Accent 6, Darker 50%**.

10 Select the title and the text box, and then, using the **Align Selected Objects** option, apply **Align Right** alignment. Apply the **Box** transition to all of the slides in the presentation, and then view the slide show from the beginning.

11 **Insert a Header & Footer** on the **Notes and Handouts**. Include the **Date and time updated automatically**, the **Page number**, and a **Footer** with the text **Lastname_Firstname_2E_Coasters**

12 Display the document properties. As the **Tags** type **coasters** and as the **Subject** type your course and section number. Be sure your name displays as the author, and then **Save** your file.

13 **Save** your presentation. Submit your presentation electronically or print **Handouts 4 Slides Horizontal** as directed by your instructor. **Close** PowerPoint.

END | You have completed Project 2E

CONTENT-BASED ASSESSMENTS

MyITLab® grader

Mastering PowerPoint | Project 2F Attractions

Apply 2B skills from these Objectives:

5 Remove Picture Backgrounds and Insert WordArt

6 Create and Format a SmartArt Graphic

In the following Mastering PowerPoint project, you will format a presentation describing new attractions at several of the Sensation Park Entertainment Group amusement parks. Your completed presentation will look similar to Figure 2.58.

PROJECT FILES

For Project 2F, you will need the following file:

p02F_Attractions

You will save your presentation as:

Lastname_Firstname_2F_Attractions

PROJECT RESULTS

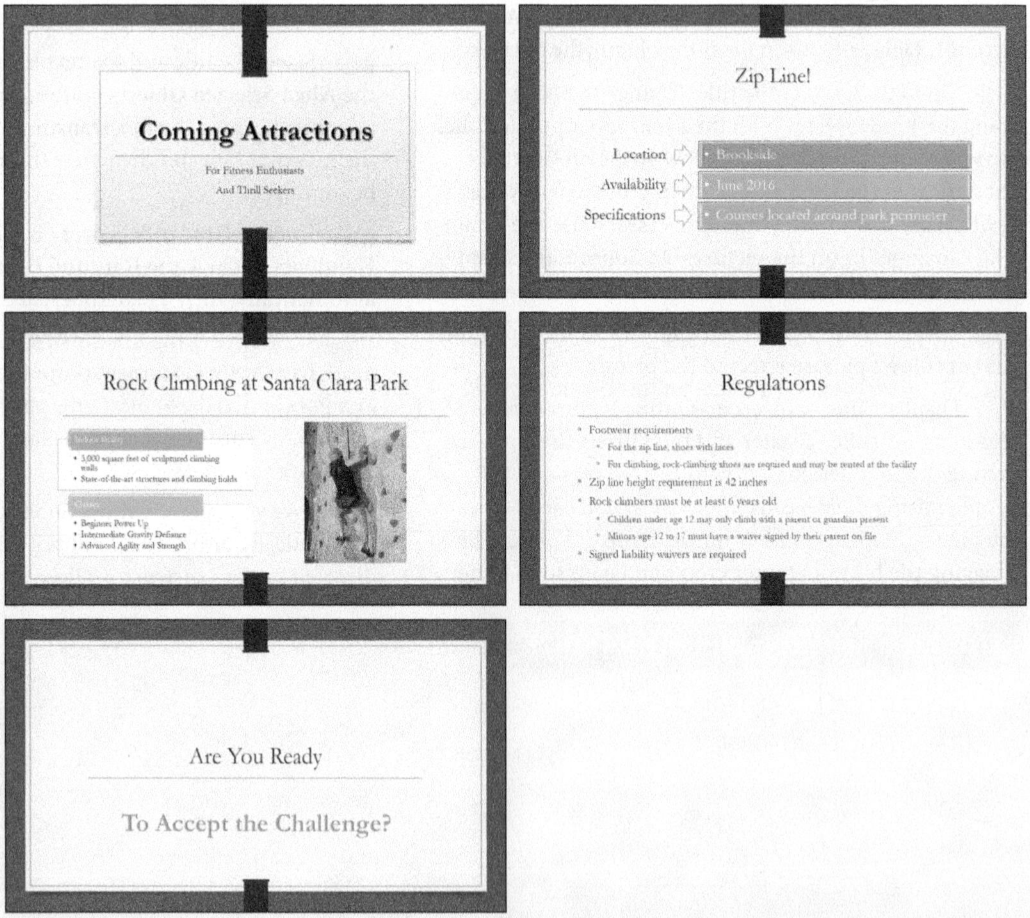

FIGURE 2.58

(Project 2F Attractions continues on the next page)

Mastering PowerPoint | Project 2F Attractions (continued)

1 Start PowerPoint. From the student data files that accompany this textbook, open **p02F_Attractions**, and then **Save** the file in your **PowerPoint Chapter 2** folder as **Lastname_Firstname_2F_Attractions**

2 On **Slide 1**, select the title and display the **WordArt Styles** gallery. In the third row, apply the first WordArt style—**Fill - Black, Text 1, Outline - Background 1, Hard Shadow - Background 1**. Change the **Text Outline** by applying, in the fourth column, the fourth color—**Dark Green, Text 2, Lighter 40%**.

3 On **Slide 2**, in the content placeholder, insert a **List** type **SmartArt** graphic using **Vertical Bracket List**. In the upper-left Text placeholder, type **Location** and then in the bullet point to the right of *Location*, type **Brookside** In the lower text placeholder, type **Availability** and then in the rectangle to the right of *Availability*, type **June 2016**

4 Click the *Availability* placeholder, and then add a shape after the placeholder. In the new placeholder, type **Specifications** and then add a bullet. Type **Courses located around park perimeter**

5 Change the SmartArt color to **Colorful Range - Accent Colors 4 to 5**, and then apply the **3-D Cartoon** style. Select the three bracket shapes, and then change the shapes to the **Right Arrow** shape. On the **FORMAT tab**, in the **Shapes group**, click the **Smaller** button two times to decrease the size of the arrows.

6 On **Slide 3**, convert the bulleted list to a **SmartArt** graphic by applying the **Vertical Box List** graphic. Change the SmartArt color to **Colorful Range - Accent Colors 4 to 5**, and then apply the **Polished 3-D** SmartArt style.

7 On **Slide 5**, insert a **WordArt**—in the first row, the last style—**Fill - Dark Teal, Accent 4, Soft Bevel**. Replace the WordArt text with **To Accept the Challenge?** Change the **Font Size** to **48**.

8 Hold down Shift and then drag the WordArt down so that its upper edge is positioned on the **lower half of the vertical ruler at 1**.

9 Apply the **Peel Off** transition to all the slides, and then view the slide show from the beginning.

10 **Insert** a **Header & Footer** on the **Notes and Handouts**. Include the **Date and time updated automatically**, the **Page number**, and a **Footer** with the text **Lastname_Firstname_2F_Attractions**

11 Display the document properties. As the **Tags** type **zip line, rock wall** and as the **Subject**, type your course and section number. Be sure your name displays as the author, and then **Save** your file.

12 **Save** your presentation. Submit your presentation electronically or print **Handouts 6 Slides Horizontal** as directed by your instructor. **Close** the presentation and exit PowerPoint.

END | You have completed Project 2F

CONTENT-BASED ASSESSMENTS

MyITLab® grader

Mastering PowerPoint | Project 2G Orientation

Apply 2A and 2B skills from these Objectives:

1. Format Numbered and Bulleted Lists
2. Insert Online Pictures
3. Insert Text Boxes and Shapes
4. Format Objects
5. Remove Picture Backgrounds and Insert WordArt
6. Create and Format a SmartArt Graphic

In the following Mastering PowerPoint project, you will edit an existing presentation that is shown to Sensation Park Entertainment Group employees on their first day of a three-day orientation. Your completed presentation will look similar to Figure 2.59.

PROJECT FILES

For Project 2G, you will need the following file:

p02G_Orientation

You will save your presentation as:

Lastname_Firstname_2G_Orientation

PROJECT RESULTS

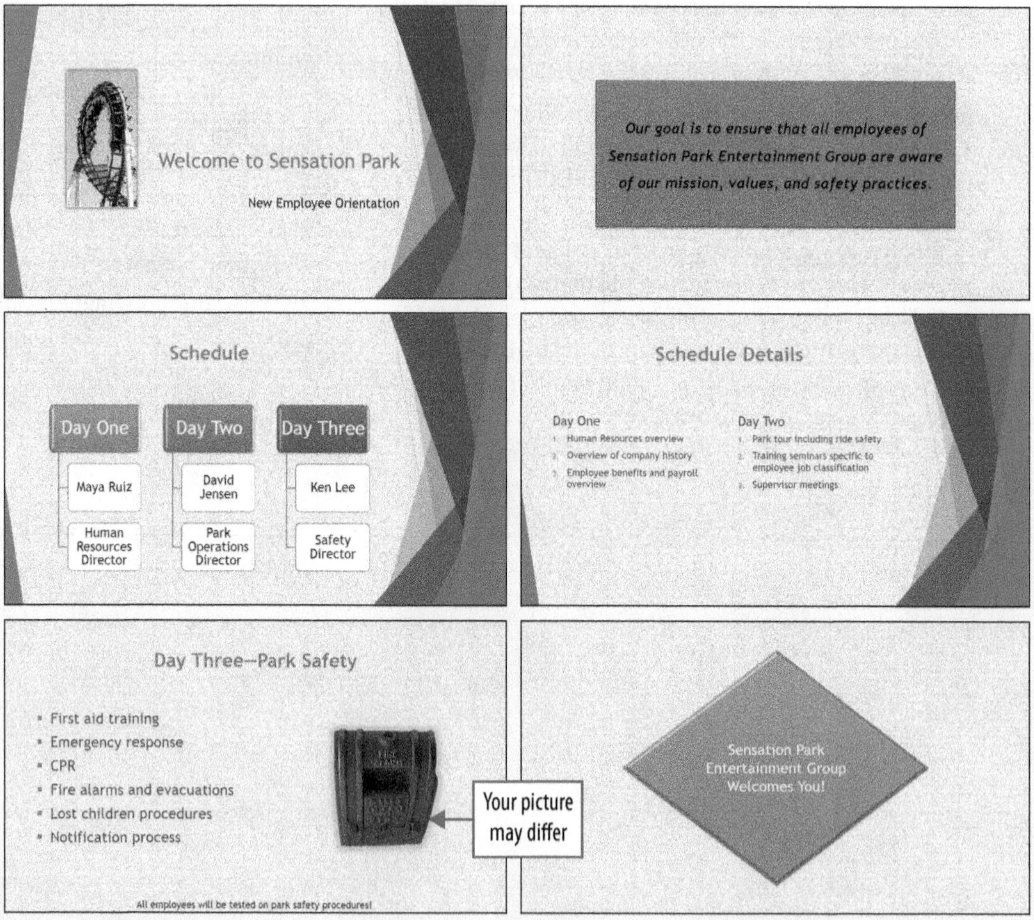

FIGURE 2.59

(Project 2G Orientation continues on the next page)

CONTENT-BASED ASSESSMENTS

Mastering PowerPoint Project 2G Orientation (continued)

1 Start PowerPoint, and then from your student data files, open the file **p02G_Orientation**. In your **PowerPoint Chapter 2** folder, **Save** the file as **Lastname_Firstname_2G_Orientation**

2 On **Slide 1**, format the subtitle—*New Employee Orientation*—with a **WordArt Style** using the second style in the first row—**Fill - Orange, Accent 1, Shadow**. Change the **Text Fill** to **Dark Red, Accent 2, Darker 50%**.

3 Select the picture and then **Crop** the image from the left side so that the center-left crop handle aligns with the **left half of the horizontal ruler at 5 inches**. Size the picture **Height** to **3.5** and then apply an **Orange, 8 pt glow, Accent color 1** picture effect to the image. Use the **Align Selected Objects** command to apply **Align Middle** to the title and the picture.

4 On **Slide 2**, remove the bullet symbol from the paragraph, and then change the **Shape Fill** to **Tan, Background 2, Darker 50%**, and the **Shape Outline** to **Black, Text 1**.

5 On **Slide 3**, convert the bulleted list to the **Hierarchy** type **SmartArt** graphic—**Hierarchy List**. Change the color to **Colorful Range - Accent Colors 3 to 4**, and then apply the **3-D Inset** style.

6 On **Slide 4**, change the two bulleted lists to **Numbering**. On **Slide 5**, change the bullet symbols to **Filled Square Bullets**, change the **Color** to **Tan, Background 2, Darker 50%**, and then change the **Size** to **100**

7 On **Slide 5**, in the placeholder on the right, insert an **Online Picture** by searching for **fire alarm** and then insert a picture of a fire alarm with a background. If the option is available, remove the background from the picture, and then apply the **Brown, 18 pt glow, Accent color 3** picture effect.

8 On **Slide 5**, insert a **Text Box** below the content placeholder on the left side of the slide. In the text box, type **All employees will be tested on park safety procedures!** Using the **Align to Slide** option **Align Center** the text box and apply **Align Bottom**.

9 On **Slide 6**, from the **Shapes** gallery, under **Basic Shapes**, insert a **Diamond** of any size anywhere on the slide. Resize the diamond so that its **Shape Height** is **6** and its **Shape Width** is **8**

10 Using the **Align to Slide** option, apply the **Align Center**, and **Align Middle** alignment commands to the diamond shape. Apply the **Moderate Effect - Brown, Accent 3** shape style, and then in the diamond, type **Sensation Park Entertainment Group Welcomes You!** Change the **Font Size** to **28**, and then apply the **Art Deco Bevel** shape effect to the diamond shape.

11 **Insert** a **Header & Footer** on the **Notes and Handouts**. Include the **Date and time updated automatically**, the **Page number**, and a **Footer** with the text **Lastname_Firstname_2G_Orientation** Apply to all.

12 Display the document properties. As the **Tags** type **orientation** and as the **Subject** type your course and section number. Be sure your name displays as the author, and then **Save** your file.

13 **Save** your presentation. Submit your presentation electronically or print **Handouts 6 Slides Horizontal** as directed by your instructor. **Close** PowerPoint.

END | You have completed Project 2G

CONTENT-BASED ASSESSMENTS

Apply a combination of the 2A and 2B skills.

GO! Fix It — Project 2H Summer Jobs — Online

GO! Make It — Project 2I Renovation Plans — Online

GO! Solve It — Project 2J Business Summary — Online

GO! Solve It — Project 2K Hotel

PROJECT FILES

For Project 2K, you will need the following file:

p02K_Hotel

You will save your presentation as:

Lastname_Firstname_2K_Hotel

Open the file p02K_Hotel and save it as **Lastname_Firstname_2K_Hotel** Complete the presentation by inserting an online picture on the first slide and applying appropriate picture effects. On Slide 2, format the bullet point as a single paragraph and apply a shape style, and then on Slide 3, convert the bulleted list to an appropriate SmartArt graphic. Change the SmartArt color and apply a style. On Slide 4, insert and attractively position a WordArt with the text Save the Date! Insert a header and footer that includes the date and time updated automatically, the file name in the footer, and the page number. Add your name, your course name and section number, and the tags **hotel, accommodations** to the Properties area. Save your presentation. Print or submit as directed by your instructor.

Performance Level

Performance Criteria	Exemplary	Proficient	Developing
Insert and format an appropriate online picture	An appropriate online picture was inserted and formatted in the presentation.	An online picture was inserted but was not appropriate for the presentation or was not formatted.	An online picture was not inserted.
Insert and format appropriate SmartArt graphic	Appropriate SmartArt graphic was inserted and formatted in the presentation.	SmartArt graphic was inserted but was not appropriate for the presentation or was not formatted.	SmartArt graphic was not inserted.
Insert and format appropriate WordArt	Appropriate WordArt was inserted and formatted in the presentation.	WordArt was inserted but was not appropriate for the presentation or was not formatted.	WordArt was not inserted.
Remove bullet point and apply appropriate shape style	Bullet point was removed and an appropriate shape style was applied.	Either the bullet point was not removed or the shape style was not applied.	Bullet point was not removed and a shape style was not applied.

END | You have completed Project 2K

OUTCOMES-BASED ASSESSMENTS

RUBRIC

The following outcomes-based assessments are open-ended assessments. That is, there is no specific correct result; your result will depend on your approach to the information provided. Make Professional Quality your goal. Use the following scoring rubric to guide you in how to approach the problem and then to evaluate how well your approach solves the problem.

The *criteria*—Software Mastery, Content, Format and Layout, and Process—represent the knowledge and skills you have gained that you can apply to solving the problem. The *levels of performance*—Professional Quality, Approaching Professional Quality, or Needs Quality Improvements—help you and your instructor evaluate your result.

	Your completed project is of Professional Quality if you:	Your completed project is Approaching Professional Quality if you:	Your completed project Needs Quality Improvements if you:
1-Software Mastery	Choose and apply the most appropriate skills, tools, and features and identify efficient methods to solve the problem.	Choose and apply some appropriate skills, tools, and features, but not in the most efficient manner.	Choose inappropriate skills, tools, or features, or are inefficient in solving the problem.
2-Content	Construct a solution that is clear and well organized, contains content that is accurate, appropriate to the audience and purpose, and is complete. Provide a solution that contains no errors in spelling, grammar, or style.	Construct a solution in which some components are unclear, poorly organized, inconsistent, or incomplete. Misjudge the needs of the audience. Have some errors in spelling, grammar, or style, but the errors do not detract from comprehension.	Construct a solution that is unclear, incomplete, or poorly organized; contains some inaccurate or inappropriate content; and contains many errors in spelling, grammar, or style. Do not solve the problem.
3-Format & Layout	Format and arrange all elements to communicate information and ideas, clarify function, illustrate relationships, and indicate relative importance.	Apply appropriate format and layout features to some elements, but not others. Overuse features, causing minor distraction.	Apply format and layout that does not communicate information or ideas clearly. Do not use format and layout features to clarify function, illustrate relationships, or indicate relative importance. Use available features excessively, causing distraction.
4-Process	Use an organized approach that integrates planning, development, self-assessment, revision, and reflection.	Demonstrate an organized approach in some areas, but not others; or, use an insufficient process of organization throughout.	Do not use an organized approach to solve the problem.

OUTCOMES-BASED ASSESSMENTS

Apply a combination of the 2A and 2B skills.

GO! Think Project 2L Interactive Ride

PROJECT FILES

Build from Scratch

For Project 2L, you will need the following file:

New blank PowerPoint presentation

You will save your presentation as:

Lastname_Firstname_2L_Interactive_Ride

As part of its mission to combine fun with the discovery of math and science, Sensation Park Entertainment Group is opening a new, interactive roller coaster at its South Lake Tahoe location. Sensation Park's newest coaster is designed for maximum thrill and minimum risk. In a special interactive exhibit located next to the coaster, riders can learn about the physics behind this powerful coaster and even try their hand at building a coaster.

Guests will begin by setting the height of the first hill, which determines the coaster's maximum potential energy to complete its journey. Next they will set the exit path, and build additional hills, loops, and corkscrews. When completed, riders can submit their coaster for a safety inspection to find out whether the ride passes or fails.

In either case, riders can also take a virtual tour of the ride they created to see the maximum speed achieved, the amount of negative G-forces applied, the length of the track, and the overall thrill factor. They can also see how their coaster compares with other Sensation Park coasters, and they can email the coaster simulation to their friends.

Using the preceding information, create a presentation that Marketing Director, Annette Chosek, will present at a travel fair describing the new attraction. The presentation should include four to six slides with at least one SmartArt graphic and one online picture. Apply an appropriate theme and use slide layouts that will effectively present the content, and use text boxes, shapes, and WordArt styles if appropriate. Apply font formatting and slide transitions, and modify text alignment and line spacing as necessary. Save the file as **Lastname_Firstname_2L_Interactive_Ride** and then insert a header and footer that includes the date and time updated automatically, the file name in the footer, and the page number. Add your name, your course name and section number, and the tags **roller coaster, new rides** to the Properties area. Print or submit as directed by your instructor.

END | You have completed Project 2L

Build from Scratch

GO! Think Project 2M Research — Online

Build from Scratch

You and GO! Project 2N Theme Park — Online

Build from Scratch

GO! Cumulative Group Project Project 2O Bell Orchid Hotels — Online

Enhancing a Presentation with Animation, Video, Tables, and Charts

GO! to Work Video P3

3

POWERPOINT 2013

PROJECT 3A

OUTCOMES
Customize a presentation with animation and video.

OBJECTIVES
1. Customize Slide Backgrounds and Themes
2. Animate a Slide Show
3. Insert a Video

PROJECT 3B

OUTCOMES
Create a presentation that includes data in tables and charts.

OBJECTIVES
4. Create and Modify Tables
5. Create and Modify Charts

In This Chapter

In this chapter, you will learn how to customize a presentation by modifying the theme, formatting the slide background, and applying animation to slide elements. Additionally, you will learn how to enhance your presentations by inserting tables and charts that help your audience understand numeric data and trends just as pictures and diagrams help illustrate a concept. The data that you present should determine whether a table or a chart would most appropriately display your information. Styles applied to your tables and charts unify these slide elements by complementing your presentation theme.

The projects in this chapter relate to the city of **Pacifica Bay**, a coastal city south of San Francisco. The city's access to major transportation provides both residents and businesses an opportunity to compete in the global marketplace. The city's mission is to create a more beautiful and more economically viable community for its residents. Each year the city welcomes a large number of tourists who enjoy exploring the rocky coastline and seeing the famous landmarks in San Francisco. The city encourages best environmental practices and partners with cities in other countries to promote sound government at the local level.

PROJECT 3A

Informational Presentation

MyITLab® Project 3A Training

PROJECT ACTIVITIES

In Activities 3.01 through 3.17, you will edit and format a presentation that Carol Lehman, Director of Pacifica Bay Parks and Recreation, is creating to inform residents about the benefits of using the city's parks and trails. Your completed presentation will look similar to Figure 3.1.

PROJECT FILES

For Project 3A, you will need the following files:

p03A_Hills
p03A_Trails
p03A_Video

You will save your presentation as:

Lastname_Firstname_3A_Trails

PROJECT RESULTS

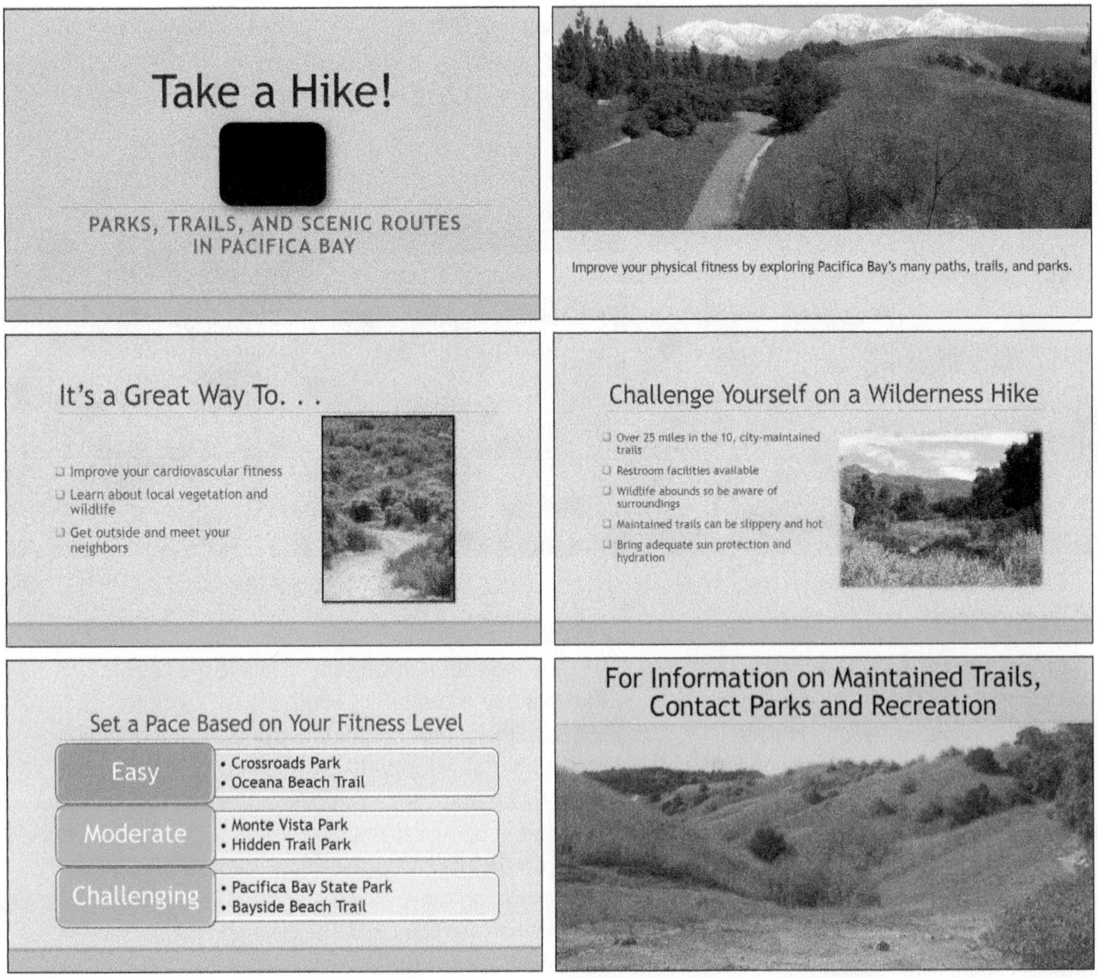

FIGURE 3.1 Project 3A Informational Presentation

Objective 1 Customize Slide Backgrounds and Themes

Video P3-1

You have practiced customizing presentations by applying themes with unified design elements, backgrounds, and colors that provide a consistent look in your presentation. Additional ways to customize a slide include changing theme fonts and colors, applying a background style, modifying the background color, or inserting a picture on the slide background.

NOTE **If You Are Using a Touchscreen**

- Tap an item to click it.
- Press and hold for a few seconds to right-click; release when the information or commands display.
- Touch the screen with two or more fingers and then pinch together to zoom in or stretch your fingers apart to zoom out.
- Slide your finger on the screen to scroll—slide left to scroll right and slide right to scroll left.
- Slide to rearrange—similar to dragging with a mouse.
- Swipe from edge: from right to display charms; from left to expose open apps, snap apps, or close apps; from top or bottom to show commands or close an app.
- Swipe to select—slide an item a short distance with a quick movement—to select an item and bring up commands, if any.

Activity 3.01 Changing Theme Colors

Recall that the presentation theme is a coordinated, predefined set of colors, fonts, lines, and fill effects. In this activity, you will open a presentation in which the Retrospect theme is applied, and then you will change the ***theme colors***—a set of coordinating colors that are applied to the backgrounds, objects, and text in a presentation.

1. From the student data files that accompany this textbook, locate and open **p03A_Trails**. Display the **Save As** dialog box, create a **New Folder** with the name **PowerPoint Chapter 3** and then using your own name, **Save** the file in the folder you created as **Lastname_Firstname_3A_Trails**

2. Click the **DESIGN tab**, and then in the **Variants group**, click **More**. Point to **Colors** to display the sets of theme colors. Point to several sets and notice the color changes on **Slide 1**.

3. Click **Green** to change the presentation colors, and then compare your screen with Figure 3.2.

   Changing the colors does not change the overall design of the presentation. In this presentation, the *Retrospect* presentation theme is still applied to the presentation. By modifying the theme colors, you retain the design of the *Retrospect* theme but apply colors that coordinate with the pictures in the presentation, and that are available as text, accent, and background colors.

FIGURE 3.2

4. **Save** your presentation.

Activity 3.02 | Changing Theme Fonts

In addition to theme colors, every presentation theme includes ***theme fonts*** that determine the font to apply to two types of slide text—headings and body. The ***Headings font*** is applied to slide titles and the ***Body font*** is applied to all other text. When you apply a new theme font to the presentation, the text on every slide is updated with the new heading and body fonts.

1. With **Slide 1** displayed, click anywhere in the title placeholder. Click the **HOME tab**, and then in the **Font group**, click the **Font button arrow**. Notice that at the top of the **Font** list, under **Theme Fonts**, Calibri Light (Headings) and Calibri (Body) display. Compare your screen with Figure 3.3.

FIGURE 3.3

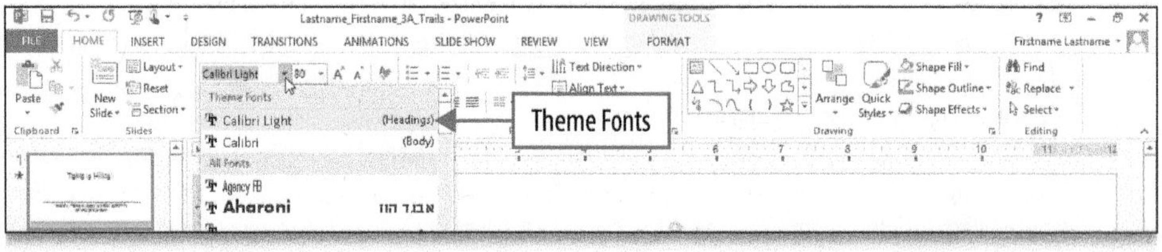

2. Click anywhere on the slide to close the Font list. Click the **DESIGN tab**, and then in the **Variants group**, click **More** . Point to **Fonts**.

   This list displays the name of each theme and the pair of fonts in the theme. The first and larger font in each pair is the Headings font and the second and smaller font in each pair is the Body font.

3. Point to several of the themes and watch as Live Preview changes the title and subtitle font. Scroll to the bottom of the **Fonts** list, and then click **Trebuchet MS**. Compare your screen with Figure 3.4, and then **Save** your presentation.

FIGURE 3.4

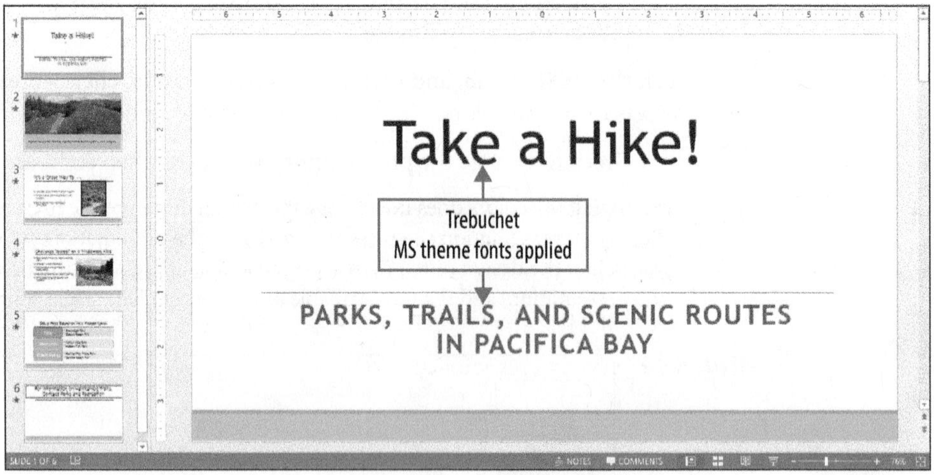

Activity 3.03 | Applying a Background Style

1. With **Slide 1** displayed, on the **DESIGN tab**, in the **Variants group**, click **More** . Point to **Background Styles**, and then compare your screen with Figure 3.5.

   A ***background style*** is a predefined slide background fill variation that combines theme colors in different intensities or patterns.

FIGURE 3.5

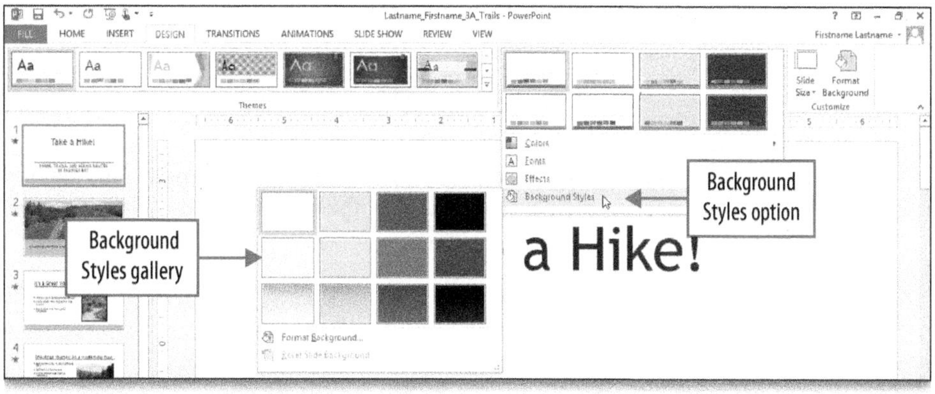

2 Point to each of the background styles to view the style on **Slide 1**. Then, in the first row, click **Style 2**. Compare your screen with Figure 3.6.

The background style is applied to all the slides in the presentation.

FIGURE 3.6

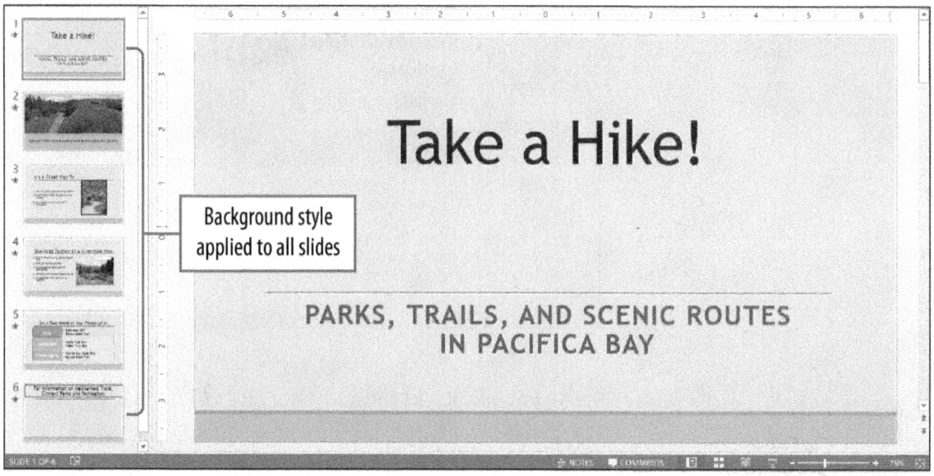

3 Display **Slide 5**. On the **DESIGN tab**, in the **Variants group**, click **More** . Point to **Background Styles**, and then in the third row, *right-click* the third style—**Style 11**—to display the shortcut menu. On the shortcut menu, click **Apply to Selected Slides** to apply the style to Slide 5.

Use this technique to apply a background style to individual slides.

4 **Save** your presentation.

Activity 3.04 | Hiding Background Graphics

Many of the PowerPoint 2013 themes contain graphic elements that display on the slide background. In the Retrospect theme applied to this presentation, the background includes a rectangle shape and line. Sometimes the background graphics interfere with or clash with the slide content. When this happens, you can hide the background graphics.

1 Display **Slide 2**, and notice the bright green rectangle and line at the bottom of the slide.

You cannot delete these objects because they are a part of the slide background; however, you can hide them.

2 On the **DESIGN tab**, in the **Customize group**, click **Format Background** to display the **Format Background** pane.

In the Format Background pane, you can customize a slide background by changing the formatting options.

3 In the **Format Background** pane, be sure that under **Fill**, the fill options display, and if necessary, click Fill to display the options. Under **Fill**, select the **Hide Background Graphics** check box. Compare your slide with Figure 3.7.

The background objects—the rectangle and line below the picture—no longer display.

FIGURE 3.7

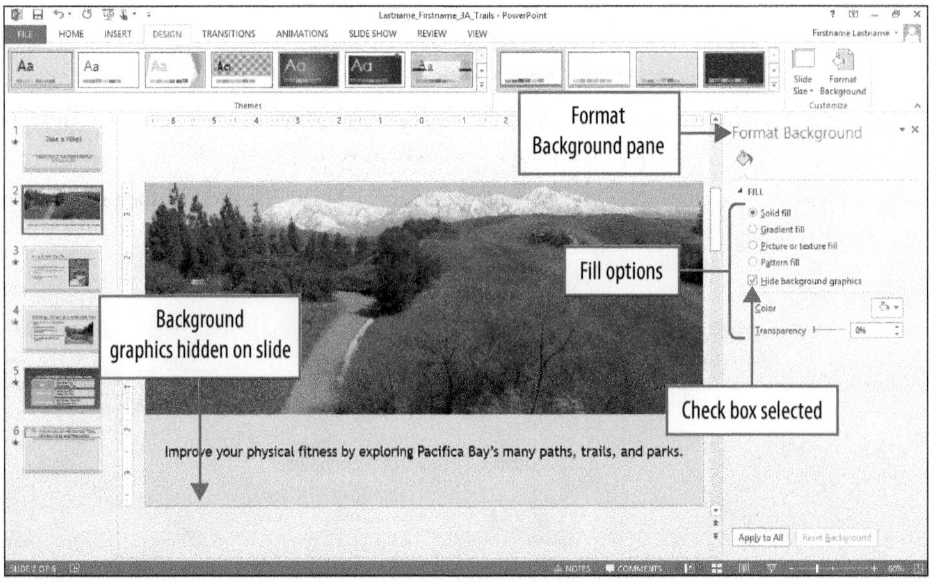

4 **Close** [X] the **Format Background** pane, and then **Save** [save] your presentation.

More Knowledge **Removing Background Objects from All Slides in a Presentation**

To remove the background objects from all of the slides in a presentation, in the Format Background pane, select the Hide background graphics check box, and then at the bottom of the Format Background pane, click Apply to All.

Activity 3.05 | Applying a Background Fill Color to a Slide

In addition to applying predefined background styles, you can apply a fill color to one or all of the slides in your presentation.

1 Display **Slide 1**. On the **DESIGN tab**, in the **Customize group**, click **Format Background**.

2 In the **Format Background** pane, under **Fill**, verify that **Solid fill** is selected, and select it if it is not. To the right of **Color**, click **Fill Color** [icon]. Under **Theme Colors**, in the third column, click the second color—**Tan, Background 2, Darker 10%**. Compare your screen with Figure 3.8.

The solid fill color is applied to the slide background.

FIGURE 3.8

3 Leave the **Format Background** pane open for the next Activity. **Save** your presentation.

***More* Knowledge** **Applying a Fill Color to All the Slides in a Presentation**

To apply a fill color to all of the slides in a presentation, in the Format Background pane, select the fill color that you want to apply, and then at the bottom of the Format Background pane, click Apply to All.

Activity 3.06 | Applying a Background Texture

1 Display **Slide 2**, and then in the slide thumbnails, hold down Shift and click **Slide 4** to select **Slides 2, 3,** and **4**.

Recall that you can select contiguous slides in this manner.

2 In the **Format Background** pane, under **Fill**, click **Picture or texture fill**.

A background picture or fill that is part of the Retrospect theme may display on the slide background of the three selected slides.

3 Under **Insert picture from,** to the right of **Texture**, click **Texture** . In the **Texture gallery,** in the third row, point to the fourth texture—**Recycled Paper**. Compare your screen with Figure 3.9.

FIGURE 3.9

4 Click **Recycled Paper** to apply the textured background to the three selected slides.

5 Leave the **Format Background** pane open for the next Activity, and then **Save** your presentation.

Activity 3.07 | Applying a Picture to the Slide Background and Adjusting Transparency

You can insert a picture on a slide background so that the image fills the entire slide.

1. Display **Slide 6**. In the **Format Background** pane, select the **Hide background graphics** check box.

2. Under **Fill**, click the **Picture or texture fill** option button. Under **Insert picture from**, click **File**. Navigate to your student data files, click **p03A_Hills**, and then click **Insert**. Compare your slide with Figure 3.10, and notice that the picture displays as the background of Slide 6.

   When a picture is applied to a slide background using the Format Background option, the picture is not treated as an object. The picture fills the entire background and you cannot move it or size it.

FIGURE 3.10

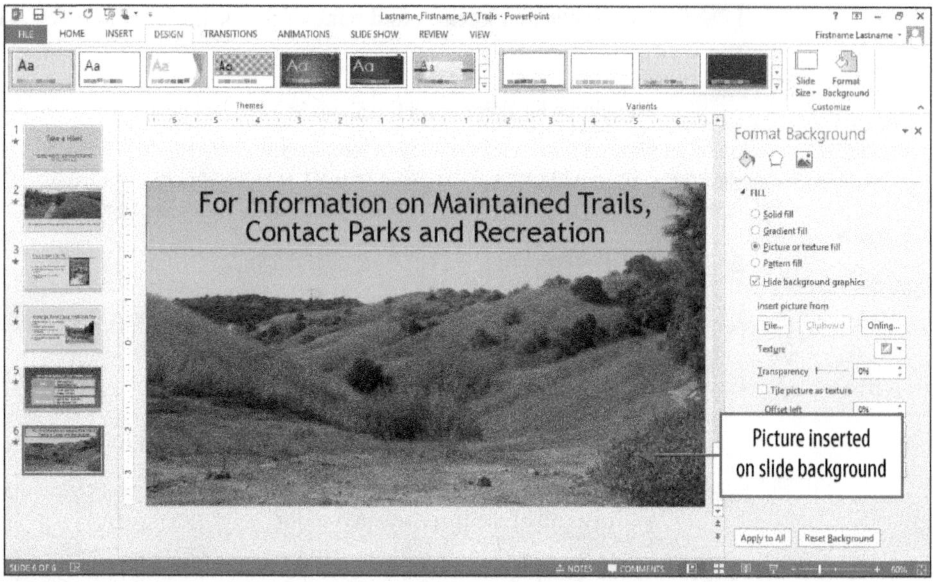

3. In the **Format Background** pane, to the right of **Transparency**, notice that *0%* displays, indicating that the picture is inserted in full color. Click in the **Transparency box**, and then replace the number with **50**

   The transparency setting lightens the picture on the slide background. You can use the transparency option when there are other objects on the slide that do not display well against the slide background.

BY TOUCH Drag the Transparency slider to the left or right with your finger to adjust the transparency of the figure.

4. Replace the number in the **Transparency box** with **10%**.

   The 10% transparency setting provides good contrast for the title while still displaying the picture in a vibrant color.

5. Click in the title placeholder. On the **FORMAT tab**, in the **Shape Styles group**, click **More** [▾]. In the fourth row, click the second style—**Subtle Effect - Green, Accent 1**. Click anywhere on the slide outside of the title placeholder. Compare your screen with Figure 3.11.

   Adequate contrast between the slide background and slide text is important because it improves slide readability. Use combinations of transparency and text placeholder styles and fills to improve contrast.

FIGURE 3.11

6 Leave the **Format Background** pane open for the next Activity, and then **Save** your presentation.

Activity 3.08 | Resetting a Slide Background

1 Display **Slide 5**. At the bottom of the **Format Background** pane, click **Reset Background**, and then compare your slide with Figure 3.12.

After making changes to a slide background, you may decide that the original formatting is the best choice for displaying the text and graphics on a slide. The Reset Background feature restores the theme and color theme formatting to a slide.

FIGURE 3.12

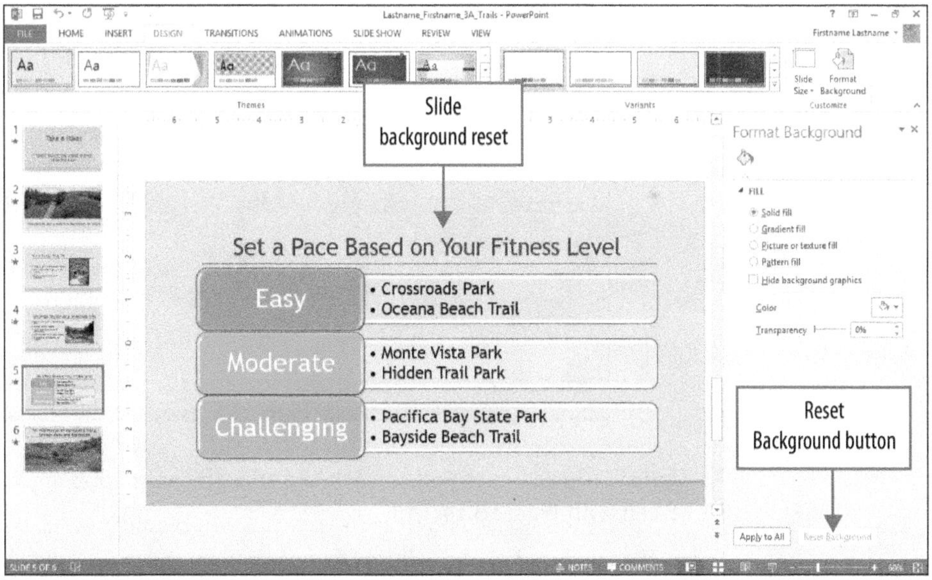

2 **Close** the **Format Background** pane, and then **Save** your presentation.

Objective 2 Animate a Slide Show

Video P3-2

Animation is a visual or sound effect added to an object or text on a slide. Animation can focus the audience's attention, providing the speaker with an opportunity to emphasize important points using the slide element as an effective visual aid.

Activity 3.09 | Applying Animation Entrance Effects and Effect Options

Entrance effects are animations that bring a slide element onto the screen. You can modify an entrance effect by using the animation Effect Options command.

1. Display **Slide 3**, and then click anywhere in the bulleted list placeholder. On the **ANIMATIONS tab**, in the **Animation group**, click **More** [▾], and then compare your screen with Figure 3.13.

   Recall that an entrance effect is animation that brings an object or text onto the screen. An ***emphasis effect*** is animation that emphasizes an object or text that is already displayed. An ***exit effect*** is animation that moves an object or text off the screen.

FIGURE 3.13

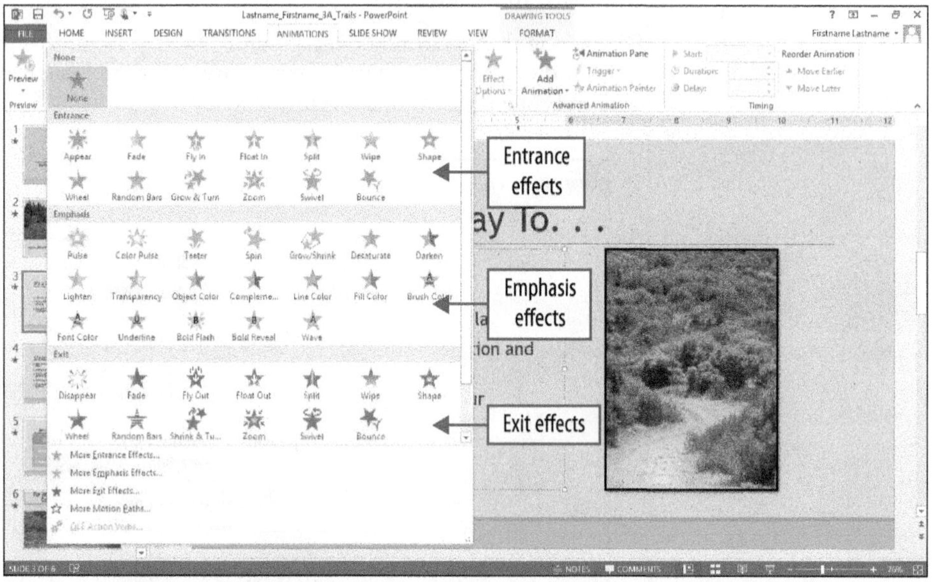

2. Under **Entrance**, click **Split**, and then notice the animation applied to the list. Compare your screen with Figure 3.14.

   The numbers *1*, *2*, and *3* display to the left of the bulleted list placeholder, indicating the order in which the bullet points will be animated during the slide show.

FIGURE 3.14

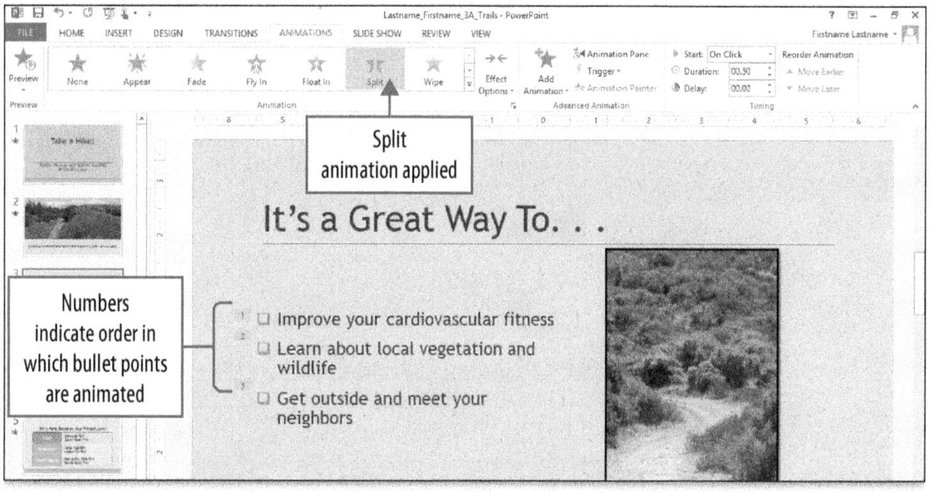

3 Select the bulleted list placeholder. In the **Animation group**, click **Effect Options**, and then compare your screen with Figure 3.15.

The Effect Options control the direction and sequence in which the animation displays. Additional options may be available with other entrance effects.

FIGURE 3.15

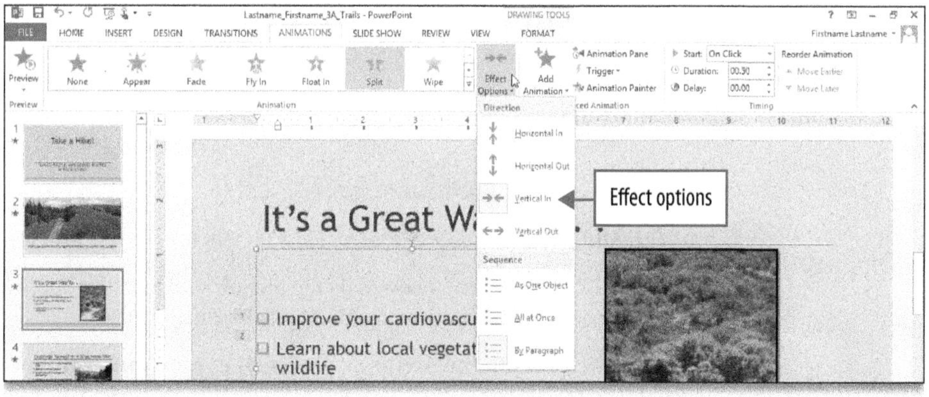

4 Click **Vertical Out** and notice the direction from which the animation is applied.

5 Select the picture. In the **Animation group**, click **More** [▾], and then below the gallery, click **More Entrance Effects**. In the lower left corner of the **Change Entrance Effect** dialog box, verify that the **Preview Effect** check box is selected. Compare your screen with Figure 3.16.

The Change Entrance Effect dialog box displays additional entrance effects grouped in four categories: Basic, Subtle, Moderate, and Exciting.

FIGURE 3.16

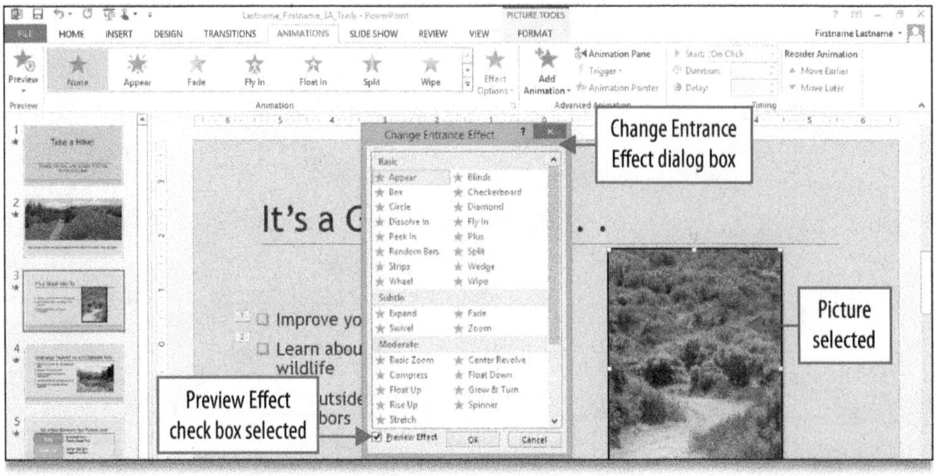

6 Under **Basic**, click **Dissolve In**, and then watch as Live Preview displays the picture with the selected entrance effect. Click **OK**.

The number *4* displays next to the picture, indicating that it is fourth in the slide animation sequence.

7 Select the title. On the **ANIMATIONS tab**, in the **Animation group**, click **More** ▾, and then under **Entrance**, click **Split** to apply the animation to the title.

The number *5* displays next to the title, indicating that it is fifth in the slide animation sequence.

8 **Save** the presentation.

Activity 3.10 | Reordering Animation

1 With **Slide 3** displayed, on the **ANIMATIONS tab**, in the **Preview group**, click **Preview**.

The list displays first, followed by the picture, and then the title. The order in which animation is applied is the order in which objects display during the slide show.

2 Select the title. On the **ANIMATIONS tab**, in the **Timing group**, under **Reorder Animation**, click the **Move Earlier** button two times, and then compare your screen with Figure 3.17.

To the left of the title placeholder, the number *1* displays. You can use the Reorder Animation buttons to change the order in which text and objects are animated during the slide show.

FIGURE 3.17

Activity 3.11 | Setting Animation Start Options

Timing options control when animated items display in the animation sequence.

1 With the title selected, on the **ANIMATIONS tab**, in the **Timing group**, click the **Start button arrow** to display three options—*On Click*, *With Previous*, and *After Previous*. Compare your screen with Figure 3.18.

The ***On Click*** option begins the animation sequence for the selected slide element when the mouse button is clicked or the Spacebar is pressed. The ***With Previous*** option begins the animation sequence at the same time as the previous animation or slide transition. The ***After Previous*** option begins the animation sequence for the selected slide element immediately after the completion of the previous animation or slide transition.

FIGURE 3.18

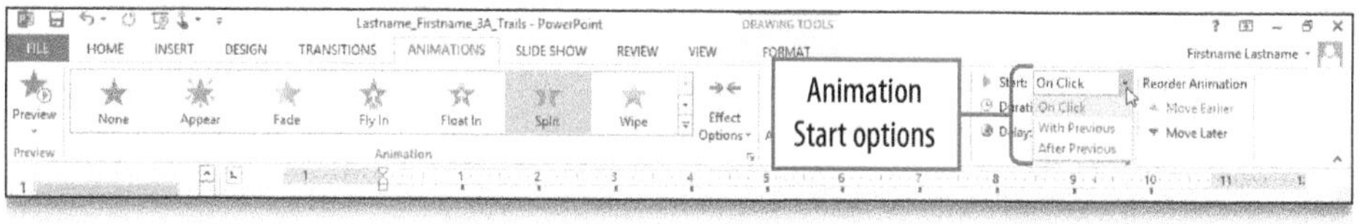

2 Click **After Previous**, and then notice that next to the title, the number *1* is changed to *0*, indicating that the animation will begin immediately after the slide transition; the presenter does not need to click the mouse button or press Spacebar to display the title.

3 Select the picture, and then in the **Timing group**, click the **Start arrow**. Click **With Previous** and notice that the number is changed to *3*, indicating that the animation will begin at the same time as the third bullet point in the bulleted list.

4 On the **ANIMATIONS tab**, in the **Preview group**, click **Preview** and notice that the title displays first, and that the picture displays at the same time as the third bullet point.

5 Display **Slide 1**, and then click in the title placeholder. On the **ANIMATIONS tab**, in the **Animation group**, click the **Entrance** effect **Fly In**, and then click the **Effect Options button**. Click **From Top**. In the **Timing group**, click the **Start arrow**, and then click **After Previous**.

The number *0* displays to the left of the title indicating that the animation will begin immediately after the slide transition.

6 **Save** your presentation.

Activity 3.12 | Setting Animation Duration and Delay Timing Options

1 On **Slide 1**, if necessary, select the title. In the **Timing group**, click the **Duration arrows** as necessary so that *00.75* displays in the **Duration** box. Compare your screen with Figure 3.19.

Duration controls the speed of the animation. You can set the duration of an animation by typing a value in the Duration box, or you can use the spin box arrows to increase and decrease the duration in 0.25-second increments. When you decrease the duration, the animation speed increases. When you increase the duration, the animation is slowed.

FIGURE 3.19

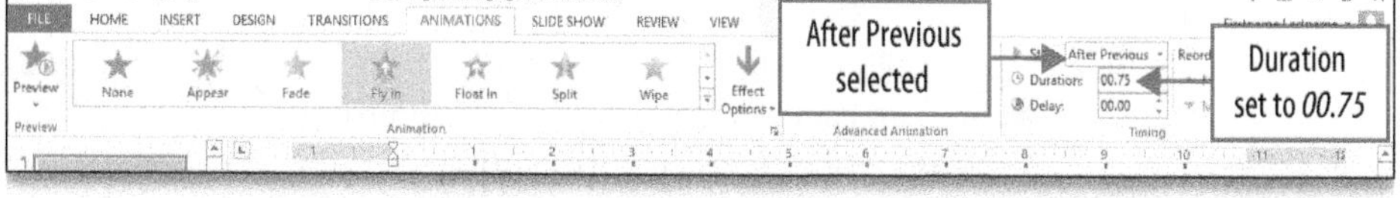

2 Select the subtitle, and then in the **Animation group**, apply the **Fly In** entrance effect. In the **Timing group**, click the **Start arrow**, and then click **After Previous**. In the **Timing group**, select the value in the **Delay** box, type **00.50** and then press Enter. Compare your screen with Figure 3.20.

You can use Delay to begin a selected animation after a specified amount of time has elapsed. Here, the animation is delayed by one-half of a second after the completion of the previous animation—the title animation. You can type a value in the Delay or Duration boxes, or you can use the up and down arrows to change the timing.

FIGURE 3.20

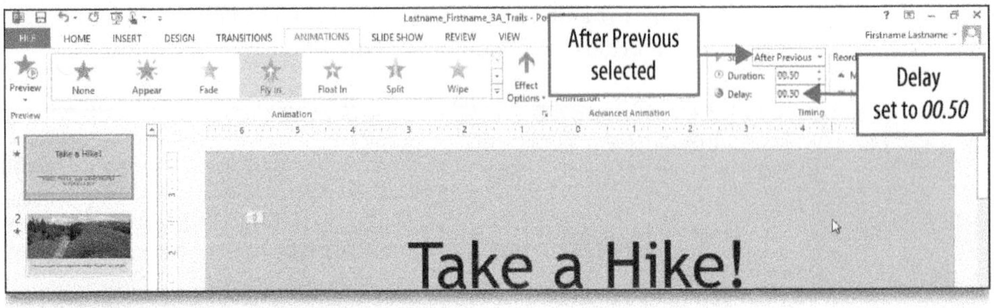

3 View the slide show from the beginning and notice the animation on Slides 1 and 3. When the black slide displays, press Esc to return to Normal view, and then **Save** your presentation.

Activity 3.13 | Using Animation Painter and Removing Animation

Animation Painter is a feature that copies animation settings from one object to another.

1 Display **Slide 3**, and then click anywhere in the bulleted list. On the **ANIMATIONS tab**, in the **Advanced Animation group**, click **Animation Painter**. Display **Slide 4**, and then point anywhere in the bulleted list placeholder to display the Animation Painter pointer. Compare your screen with Figure 3.21.

FIGURE 3.21

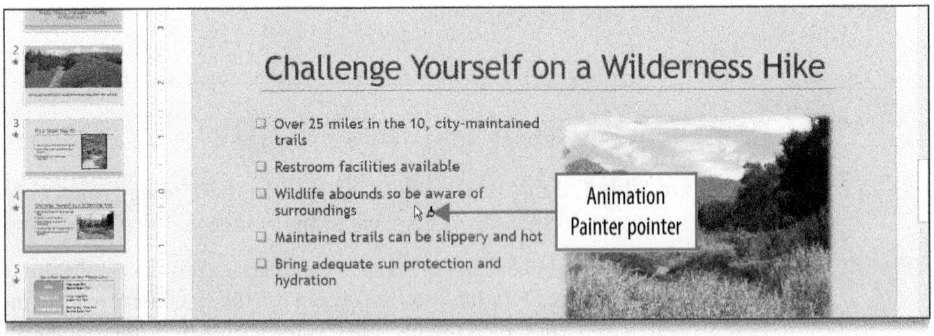

2 Click the bulleted list to copy the animation settings from the list on **Slide 3** to the list on **Slide 4**.

3 Display **Slide 3**, and then select the picture. Using the technique that you just practiced, use **Animation Painter** to copy the animation from the picture on **Slide 3** to the picture on **Slide 4**. With **Slide 4** displayed, compare your screen with Figure 3.22.

The numbers displayed to the left of the bulleted list and the picture indicate that animation is applied to the objects.

FIGURE 3.22

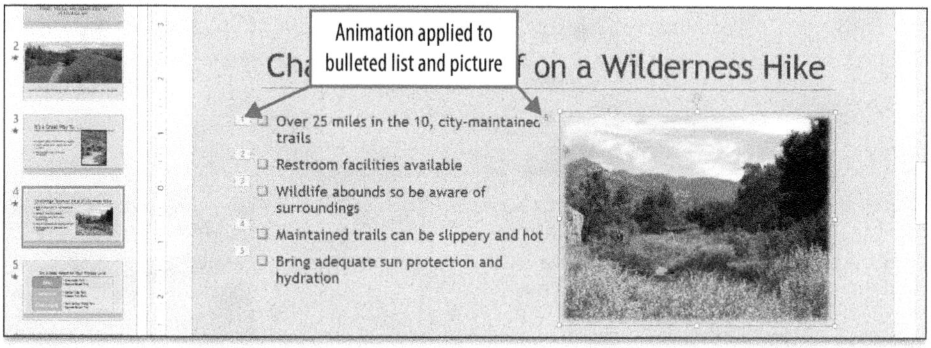

4 Display **Slide 3**, and then click in the title placeholder. On the **ANIMATIONS tab**, in the **Animation group**, click **More**. At the top of the gallery, click **None** to remove the animation from the title placeholder. Compare your screen with Figure 3.23, and then **Save** your presentation.

FIGURE 3.23

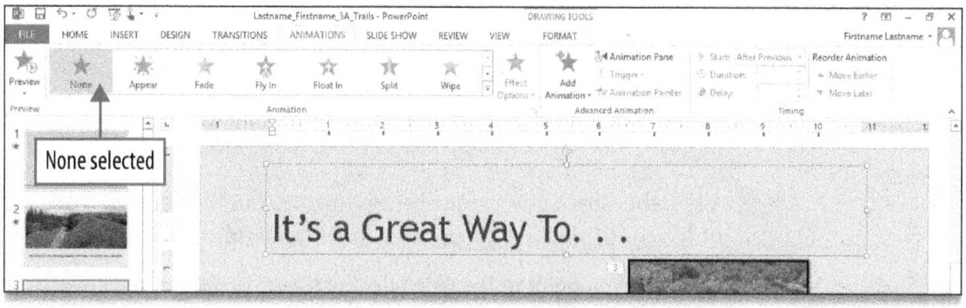

Objective 3 Insert a Video

Video P3-3

You can insert, size, and move videos in a PowerPoint presentation, and you can format videos by applying styles and effects. Video editing features in PowerPoint 2013 enable you to trim parts of a video and to compress the video to make the presentation easier to share.

Activity 3.14 Inserting a Video and Using Media Controls

1 Display **Slide 1**. On the **INSERT tab**, in the **Media group**, click **Video**, and then click **Video on My PC**. In the **Insert Video** dialog box, navigate to your student data files, and then click **p03A_Video**. Click **Insert**, and then compare your screen with Figure 3.24.

The video displays in the center of the slide, and media controls display in the control panel below the video. VIDEO TOOLS for FORMAT and PLAYBACK display on the Ribbon.

FIGURE 3.24

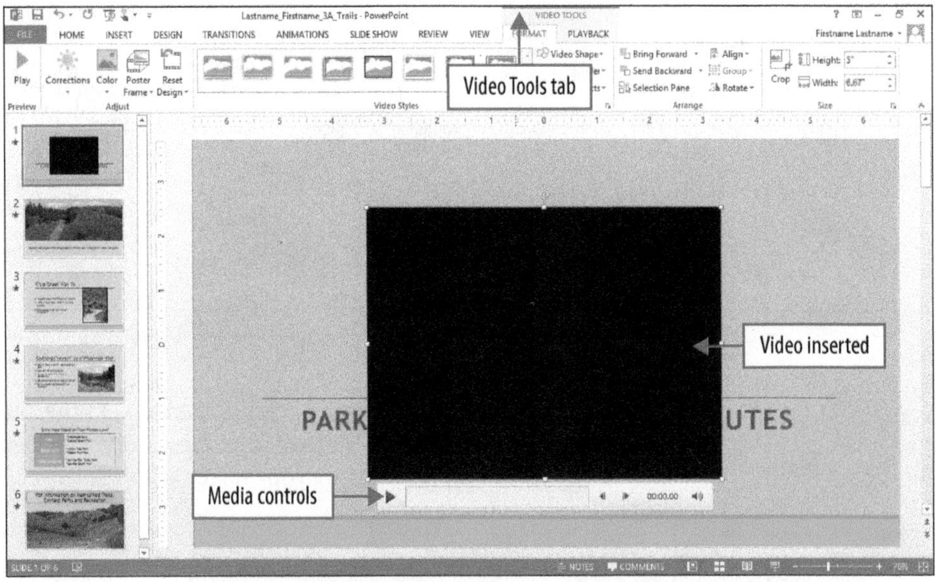

2 Below the video, in the media controls, click **Play/Pause** [▶] to view the video and notice that as the video plays, the media controls display the time that has elapsed since the start of the video.

3 View the slide show from the beginning. On **Slide 1**, after the subtitle displays, point to the video to display the [hand] pointer, and then compare your screen with Figure 3.25.

When you point to the video during the slide show, the media controls display.

FIGURE 3.25

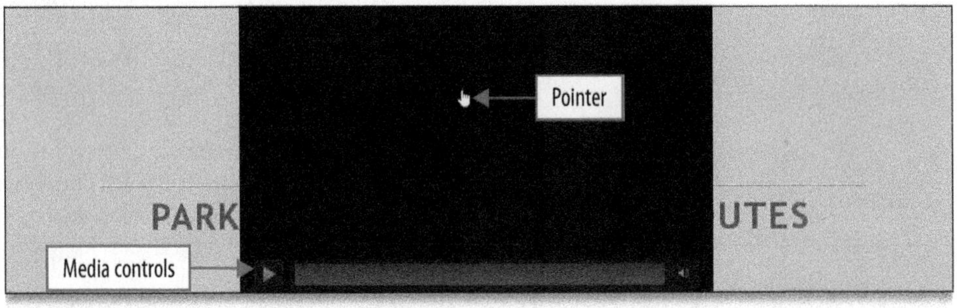

4 With the [hand] pointer displayed, click the mouse button to view the video. Move the pointer away from the video and notice that the media controls no longer display. When the video is finished, press Esc to exit the slide show.

5 **Save** [disk] your presentation.

Activity 3.15 | Sizing and Aligning a Video

1 With the video selected, on the **FORMAT tab**, in the **Size group**, click in the **Height** box. Type **2** and then press Enter. Notice that the video width adjusts proportionately.

2 On the **FORMAT tab**, in the **Arrange group**, click **Align**, and then click **Align Center**. Click **Align** again, and then click **Align Middle**. Compare your screen with Figure 3.26.

The video is centered horizontally and vertically on the slide.

FIGURE 3.26

3 **Save** your presentation.

Activity 3.16 | Changing the Style and Shape of a Video

You can apply styles and effects to a video and change the video shape and border. You can also recolor a video so that it coordinates with the presentation theme.

1 With **Slide 1** displayed, if necessary, select the video. On the **FORMAT tab**, in the **Video Styles group**, click **More** to display the **Video Styles** gallery.

2 Using the ScreenTips to view the style name, under **Subtle**, in the second row, click the last style—**Drop Shadow Rectangle**. Compare your screen with Figure 3.27.

FIGURE 3.27

3 In the **Video Styles group**, click **Video Shape**, and then under **Rectangles**, click the second shape—**Rounded Rectangle**. Compare your screen with Figure 3.28.

You can format a video with any combination of styles, shapes, and effects.

FIGURE 3.28

Activity 3.17 | Trimming and Compressing a Video and Setting Playback Options

You can ***trim***—delete parts of a video to make it shorter—and you can compress a video file to reduce the file size of your PowerPoint presentation.

1 If necessary, select the video. On the **PLAYBACK tab**, in the **Editing group**, click **Trim Video**, and then compare your screen with Figure 3.29.

At the top of the Trim Video dialog box, the file name and the video duration display. Below the video, a timeline displays with start and end markers indicating the video start and end time. Start Time and End Time boxes display the current start and end of the video. The Previous Frame and Next Frame buttons move the video forward and backward one frame at a time.

FIGURE 3.29

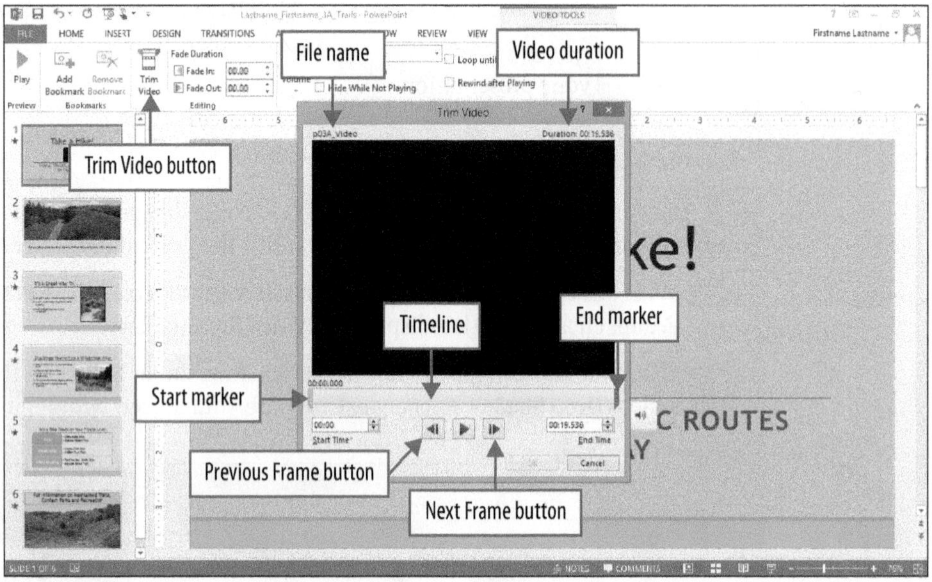

2 In the **End Time** box, replace the number with **00:16.865**. Compare your screen with Figure 3.30.

The blue section of the timeline indicates the portion of the video that will play during the slide show. The gray section indicates the portion of the video that is trimmed. The image in the Trim Video dialog box displays the last frame in the video based on the trim setting.

FIGURE 3.30

BY TOUCH

Drag the red ending marker with your finger until its ScreenTip displays the ending time that you want.

3 Click **OK** to apply the trim settings.

4 Click **FILE**, and then on the **Info tab**, click **Compress Media**. Read the description of each video quality option, and then click **Low Quality**. Compare your screen with Figure 3.31.

The Compress Media dialog box displays the slide number on which the selected video is inserted, the video file name, the original size of the video file, and when compression is complete, the amount that the file size was reduced.

FIGURE 3.31

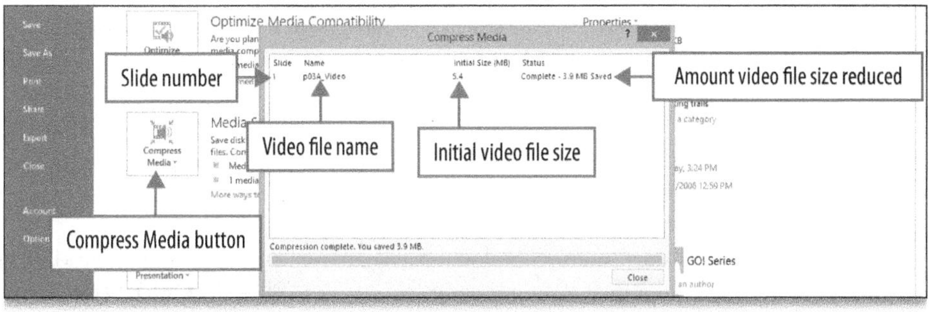

5 In the **Compress Media** dialog box, click **Close**, and then on the left, click **Save**.

6 If necessary, select the video. On the **PLAYBACK tab**, in the **Video Options group**, click the **Start arrow**, and then click **Automatically** so that during the slide show, the video will begin automatically. Compare your screen with Figure 3.32.

FIGURE 3.32

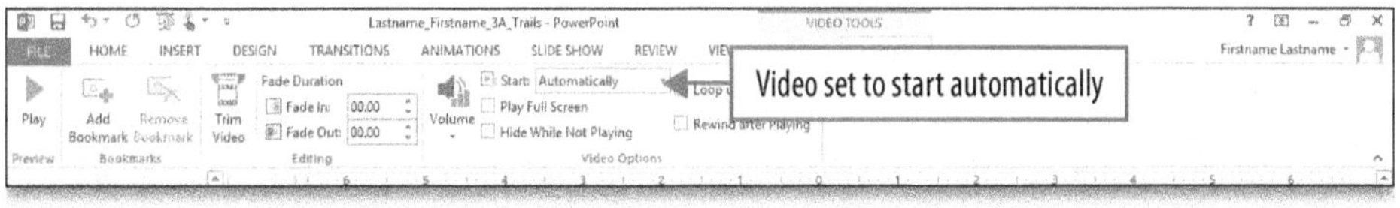

7 Click the **SLIDE SHOW tab**, in the **Start Slide Show group**, click the **From Beginning** button, and then view the slide show. Notice that on Slide 1, the video begins playing immediately after the subtitle displays. After you view the video, click the mouse button to advance to the next slide and then continue to view the presentation. Press Esc when the black slide displays.

8 Insert a **Header & Footer** on the **Notes and Handouts**. Include the **Date and time** updated automatically, the **Page Number**, and a **Footer**. In the **Footer** box, using your own name, type **Lastname_Firstname_3A_Trails** and then click **Apply to All**.

9 Display the document properties. As the **Tags**, type **walking trails** and as the **Subject**, type your course and section number. Be sure your name displays as the author, and then **Save** your file.

10 Print **Handouts 6 Slides Horizontal**, or submit your presentation electronically as directed by your instructor.

11 **Close** the presentation.

END | You have completed Project 3A

GO! with Office Online (formerly Web Apps)

Objective Create an Informational Presentation in PowerPoint Online

ALERT! **Working with Web-Based Applications and Services**

Computer programs and services on the web receive continuous updates and improvements, so the steps to complete this web-based activity may differ from the ones shown. You can often look at the screens and the information presented to determine how to complete the activity.

Activity | Creating an Informational Presentation in PowerPoint Online

In this activity, you will use PowerPoint Online to create a presentation similar to the one you created in Project 3A.

1. From the desktop, start Internet Explorer. Navigate to **http://onedrive.com**, and then sign in to your Microsoft account. Open your **GO! Web Projects** folder—or create and then open this folder if necessary.

2. On the OneDrive menu bar, click **Upload**, and then navigate to your student data files and select **p03_3A_Web**. Click **Open**. When the upload is complete, right-click **p03_3A_Web**, and then click **Rename**. Using your own name, as the file name, type **Lastname_Firstname_PPT_3A_Web** and then press Enter. Click your file, and then click **EDIT PRESENTATION**. Click **Edit in PowerPoint Online**.

3. On the **DESIGN tab**, in the **Variants group**, click **Variant 2** to apply the green variant to the entire presentation.

4. On **Slide 1**, double-click in the title placeholder, and then drag to select the title text—*Take a Hike!* On the **HOME tab**, in the **Font Group**, click the **Font arrow**, and then click **Candara**.

5. Display **Slide 2**, and then at the bottom of the slide, point to the text placeholder and then click its outside border. On the **FORMAT tab**, in the **Shape Styles group**, click the **Quick Styles arrow**, and then in the fourth row, click the second style—**Subtle Effect - Lime, Accent 1**. Change the **Font Size** to **48**.

6. With the placeholder selected, point to the center-left sizing handle, and then drag as far to the left as possible without exceeding the left edge of the slide. Repeat this process on the right side of the slide, and then click outside of the placeholder. Compare your screen with Figure A.

7. Display **Slide 3**, and then click the bulleted list. On the **ANIMATIONS tab**, in the **Animation group**, click **Fly In**. Click **Effect Options**, and then click **From Right**. Click the picture, and then in the **Animation group**, click **Appear**. Click the title, and then in the **Animation group**, click **Fly In**. Click **Effect Options**, and then click **From Top**.

8. With **Slide 3** displayed and the title selected, in the **Timing group**, under **Reorder Animation**, click **Move Earlier** several times until Move Earlier displays in gray, indicating that it will display first.

FIGURE A

(GO! with Office Online (formerly Web Apps) continues on the next page)

9 Display **Slide 4**, and then click the title. On the **ANIMATIONS tab**, in the **Animation group**, click **Fly In**. Click **Effect Options**, and then click **From Top**. Click the bulleted list, and then in the **Animation group**, click **Fly In**. Click **Effect Options**, and then click **From Right**. Click the **Picture**, and then in the **Animation group**, click **Appear**.

10 Display **Slide 6**, and then click in the title. On the **ANIMATIONS tab**, in the **Animation group**, click **Fly In**. Click **Effect Options**, and then click **From Top**.

11 On the **TRANSITIONS tab**, in the **Transition to This slide group**, click **Push**. Click **Effect Options**, and then click **From Left**. Click **Apply to All**.

12 On the **VIEW tab**, click **Slide Show**, and then view the presentation. If a security warning displays, click Allow once. Click the mouse button to advance through the slides.

13 Submit your file as instructed. Sign out of your OneDrive and then close Internet Explorer.

FIGURE B

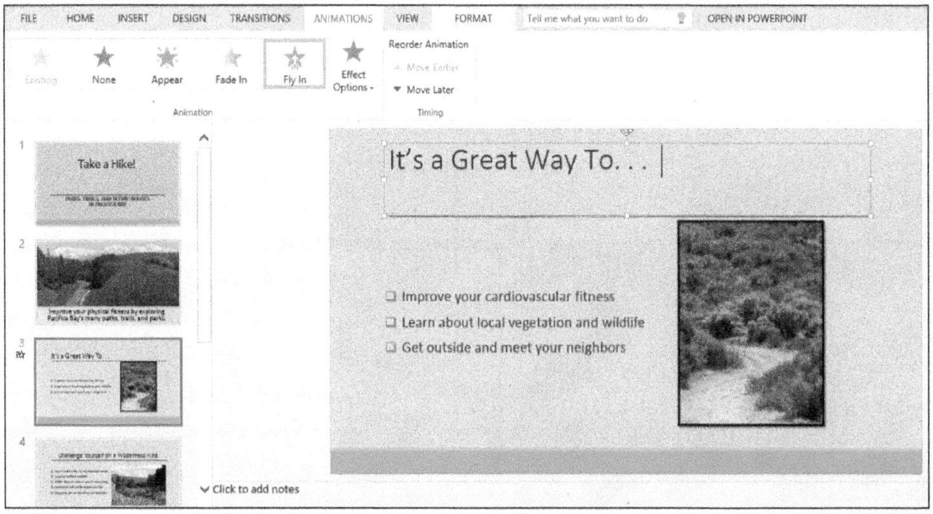

PROJECT 3B

Summary and Analysis Presentation

MyITLab®
Project 3B Training

PROJECT ACTIVITIES

In Activities 3.18 through 3.29, you will add a table and two charts to a presentation that Mindy Walker, Director of Parks and Recreation, is creating to inform the City Council about enrollment trends in Pacifica Bay recreation programs. Your completed presentation will look similar to Figure 3.33.

PROJECT FILES

For Project 3B, you will need the following file:
p03B_Enrollment

You will save your presentation as:
Lastname_Firstname_3B_Enrollment

PROJECT RESULTS

FIGURE 3.33 Project 3B Summary and Analysis Presentation

Objective 4 Create and Modify Tables

Video P3-4

A ***table*** is a format for information that organizes and presents text and data in columns and rows. The intersection of a column and row is referred to as a ***cell*** and is the location in which you type text in a table.

Activity 3.18 | Creating a Table

There are several ways to insert a table in a PowerPoint slide. For example, you can insert a slide with a Content Layout and then click the Insert Table button. Or, click the Insert tab and then click Table.

1 Start PowerPoint. From your student data files, open **p03B_Enrollment**, and then **Save** the presentation in your **PowerPoint Chapter 3** folder as **Lastname_Firstname_3B_Enrollment**

2 Display **Slide 2**. In the content placeholder, click **Insert Table** to display the **Insert Table** dialog box. In the **Number of columns** box, type **3** and then press Tab. In the **Number of rows** box, type **2** and then compare your screen with Figure 3.34.

Here you enter the number of columns and rows that you want the table to contain.

FIGURE 3.34

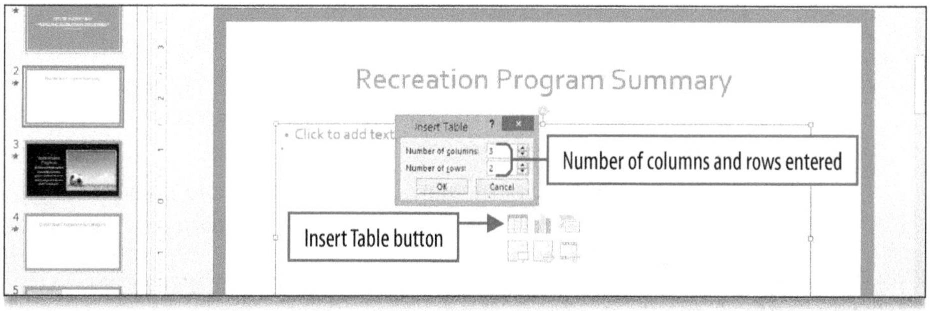

3 Click **OK** to create a table with three columns and two rows. Notice that the insertion point is blinking in the upper left cell of the table.

The table extends from the left side of the content placeholder to the right side, and the three columns are equal in width. By default, a style is applied to the table.

4 With the insertion point positioned in the first cell of the table, type **Athletics** and then press Tab.

Pressing Tab moves the insertion point to the next cell in the same row.

ALERT! **Did You Press Enter Instead of Tab?**

In a table, pressing Enter creates another line in the same cell. If you press Enter by mistake, you can remove the extra line by pressing Backspace.

5 With the insertion point positioned in the second cell of the first row, type **Leisure** and then press Tab. Type **Arts** and then press Tab to move the insertion point to the first cell in the second row. Compare your table with Figure 3.35.

FIGURE 3.35

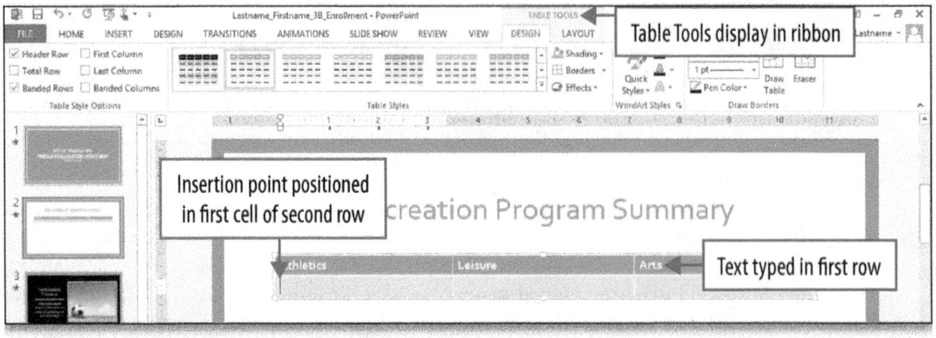

6 With the insertion point positioned in the first cell of the second row, type **Team sports** and then press Tab. Type **Personal development classes** and then press Tab. Type **Music and dance classes**

7 **Save** your presentation.

Activity 3.19 | Inserting Rows and Columns in a Table

You can modify the layout of a table by inserting or deleting rows and columns.

1 With the insertion point positioned in the last cell of the table, press Tab and notice that a new blank row is inserted.

When the insertion point is positioned in the last cell of a table, pressing Tab inserts a new blank row at the bottom of the table.

2 In the first cell of the third row, type **Youth** and then press Tab. Type **Older adults** and then press Tab. Type **Young adults** and then compare your table with Figure 3.36.

FIGURE 3.36

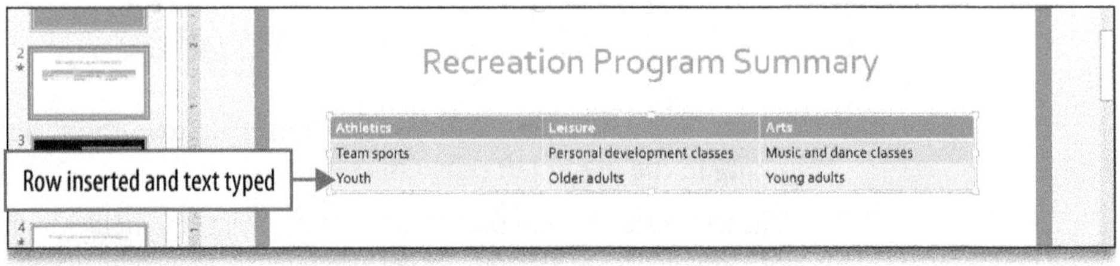

ALERT! **Did You Add an Extra Row to the Table?**

Recall that when the insertion point is positioned in the last cell of the table, pressing Tab inserts a new blank row. If you inadvertently inserted a blank row in the table, on the Quick Access Toolbar, click Undo.

3 Click in any cell in the first column, and then click the **LAYOUT tab**. In the **Rows & Columns group**, click **Insert Left.**

A new first column displays and the width of the columns adjust so that all four columns are the same width.

4 In the *second* row, click in the first cell, and then type **Largest Enrollments**

5 In the third row, click in the first cell, and then type **Primary Market** Compare your table with Figure 3.37.

FIGURE 3.37

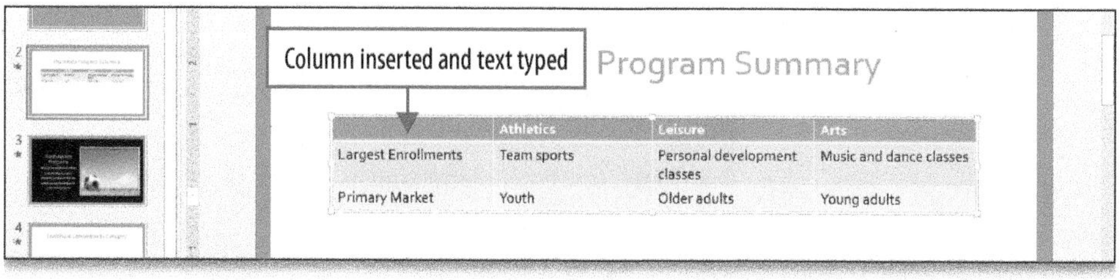

6 With the insertion point positioned in the third row, on the **LAYOUT tab**, in the **Rows & Columns group**, click **Insert Above** to insert a new third row. In the first cell of the new row, type **Average Enrollment** and then press Tab. Type the remaining three entries, pressing Tab to move from cell to cell: **85% of capacity** and **62% of capacity** and **78% of capacity**

> ***More* Knowledge** **Deleting Rows and Columns**
>
> To delete a row or column from a table, click in the row or column that you want to delete. Click the LAYOUT tab, and then in the Rows & Columns group, click Delete. In the displayed list, click Delete Columns or Delete Rows.

7 **Save** your presentation.

Activity 3.20 | Sizing a Table

A selected table is surrounded by sizing handles and can be resized in the same manner in which a shape or picture is resized.

1 Point to the bottom, center sizing handle to display the pointer. Compare your screen with Figure 3.38.

FIGURE 3.38

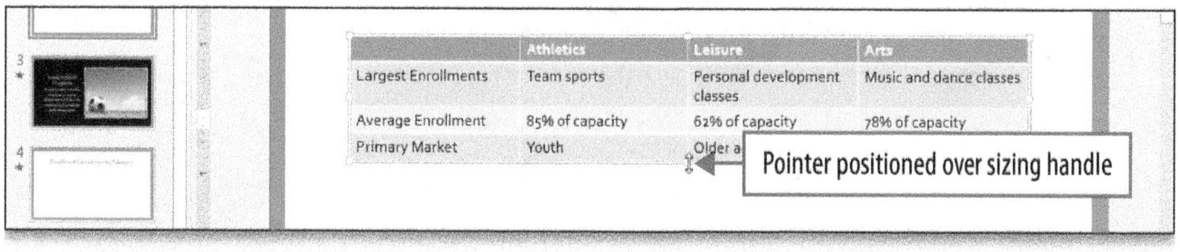

2 Drag down until the ruler guide is positioned on the **lower half of the vertical ruler at 2 inches**. Compare your screen with Figure 3.39.

A dim border and the red dotted ruler guides display, indicating the size of the table.

FIGURE 3.39

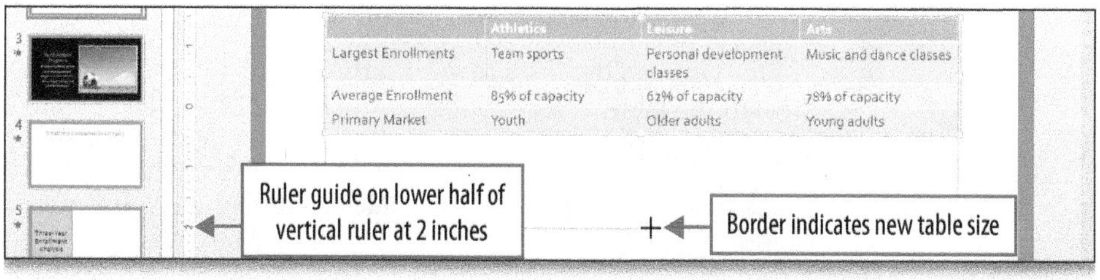

3 Release the mouse button to size the table, and then **Save** your presentation.

ANOTHER WAY On the LAYOUT tab, in the Table Size group, type an exact measurement in the Height or Width boxes.

Activity 3.21 | Distributing Rows and Aligning Table Text

1 Click in the first cell of the table. On the **LAYOUT tab**, in the **Cell Size group**, click **Distribute Rows.** Compare your table with Figure 3.40.

The Distribute Rows command adjusts the height of the rows in the table so that they are equal.

FIGURE 3.40

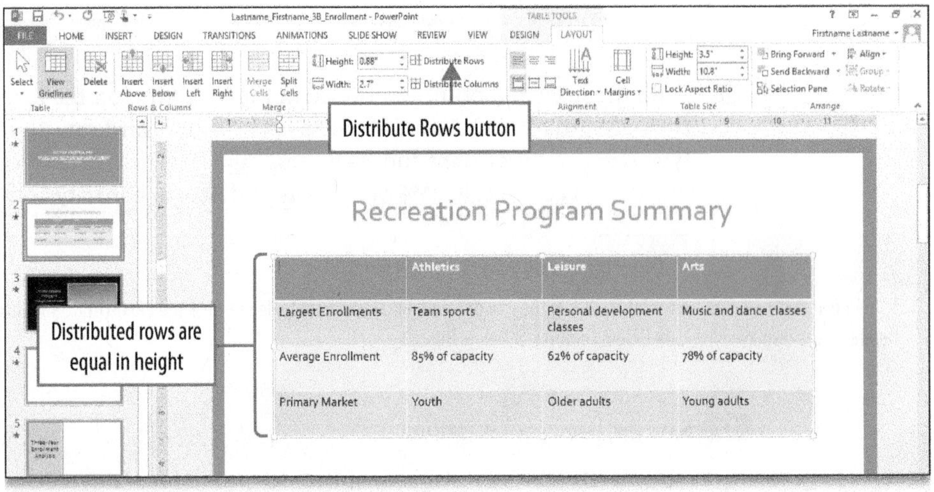

2 On the **LAYOUT tab**, in the **Table group**, click **Select**, and then click **Select Table**. In the **Alignment group**, click **Center**, and then click **Center Vertically**.

All of the table text is centered horizontally and vertically within the cells.

3 **Save** your presentation.

More Knowledge **Distributing Columns**

To distribute columns, click anywhere in the table, and then on the LAYOUT tab, in the Cell Size group, click Distribute Columns.

Activity 3.22 | Applying and Modifying a Table Style

You can modify the design of a table by applying a ***table style***. A table style formats the entire table so that it is consistent with the presentation theme. There are color categories within the table styles—Best Match for Document, Light, Medium, and Dark.

1 Click in any cell in the table. Under the **TABLE TOOLS**, click the **DESIGN tab**, and then in the **Table Styles group**, click **More**. In the displayed **Table Styles** gallery, point to several of the styles to view the Live Preview of the style.

2 Under **Light**, in the third row, click the fourth style—**Light Style 3 - Accent 3**—to apply the style to the table.

3 On the **TABLE TOOLS DESIGN tab**, in the **Table Style Options group**, clear the **Banded Rows** check box, and then select the **Banded Columns** check box. Compare your screen with Figure 3.41.

The check boxes in the Table Style Options group control where Table Style formatting is applied.

FIGURE 3.41

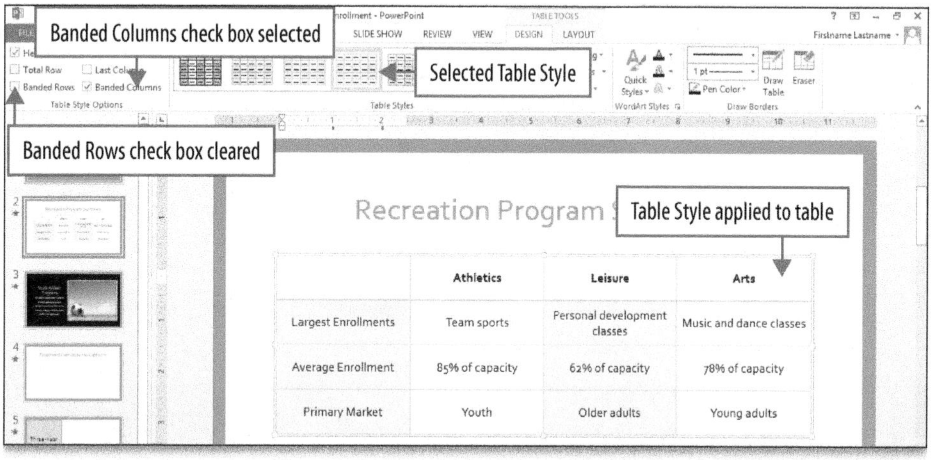

4 **Save** the presentation.

Activity 3.23 Applying Table Effects and Font Formatting

1 Move the pointer outside of the table so that it is positioned to the left of the first row in the table to display the pointer, as shown in Figure 3.42.

FIGURE 3.42

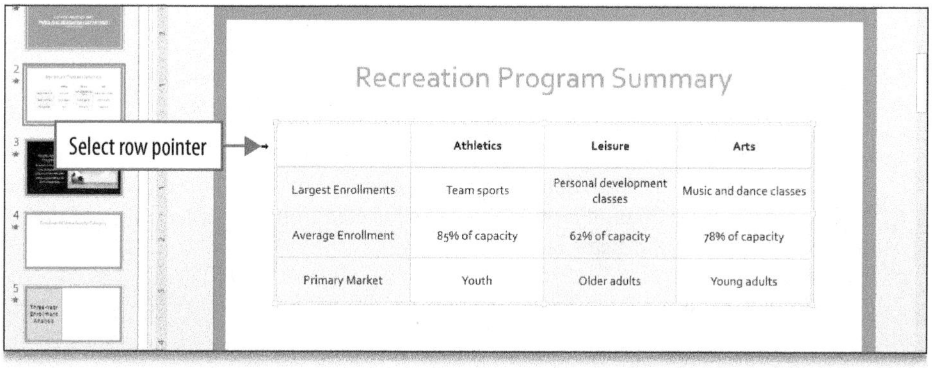

2 With the pointer pointing to the first row in the table, click the mouse button to select the entire row so that you can apply formatting to the selection. Move the pointer into the selected row, and then right-click to display the mini toolbar and shortcut menu. On the mini toolbar, change the **Font Size** to **28**.

3 With the first row still selected, on the **TABLE TOOLS DESIGN tab**, in the **Table Styles group**, click **Effects**. Point to **Cell Bevel**, and then under **Bevel**, click the first bevel—**Circle**.

4 Position the pointer above the first column to display the pointer, and then right-click to select the first column and display the mini toolbar and shortcut menu. Apply **Bold**.

5 Click in a blank area of the slide, and then compare your slide with Figure 3.43. **Save** the presentation.

FIGURE 3.43

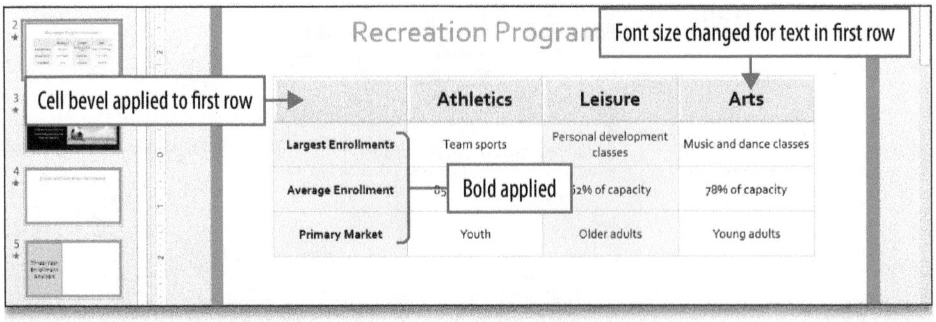

Objective 5 Create and Modify Charts

Video P3-5

A ***chart*** is a graphic representation of numeric data. Commonly used chart types include bar and column charts, pie charts, and line charts. A chart that you create in PowerPoint is stored in an Excel worksheet that is incorporated into the PowerPoint file.

Activity 3.24 | Inserting a Column Chart

A ***column chart*** is useful for illustrating comparisons among related numbers. In this activity, you will create a column chart that compares enrollment in each category of recreation activities by season.

1 Display **Slide 4**. In the content placeholder, click **Insert Chart** to display the **Insert Chart** dialog box. Compare your screen with Figure 3.44.

Along the left side of the dialog box, the types of charts that you can insert in your presentation display. Along the top of the dialog box, subtypes of the selected chart type display. By default, Column is selected and a Clustered Column chart displays in the preview area on the right side of the dialog box.

FIGURE 3.44

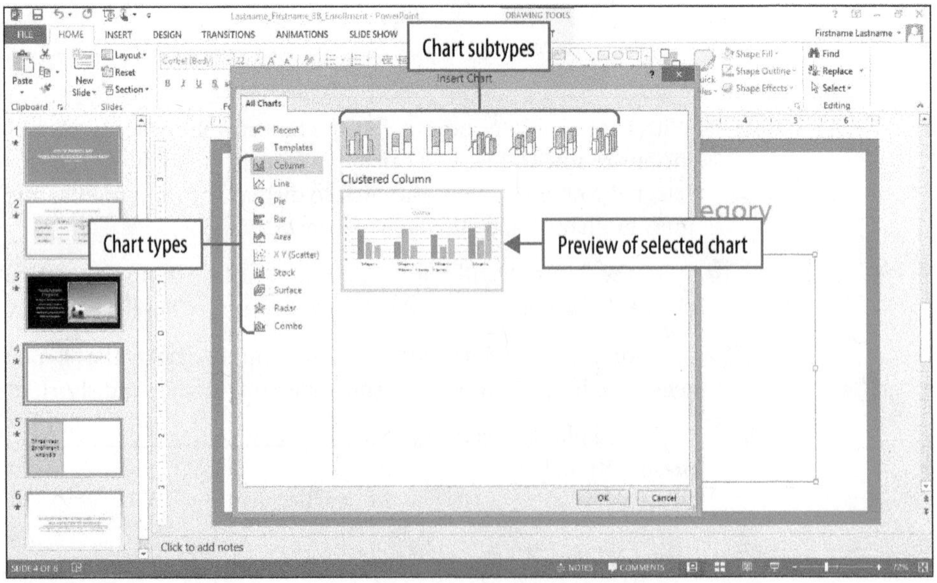

2 Along the top of the dialog box, point to each column chart to view the ScreenTip. Then, with the **Clustered Column** chart selected, click **OK**. Compare your screen with Figure 3.45.

The PowerPoint window displays a column chart in the content placeholder. Above the chart, a *Chart in Microsoft PowerPoint* worksheet window displays with cells, columns, and rows. A cell is identified by the intersecting column letter and row number, forming the ***cell reference***.

The worksheet contains sample data from which the chart on the PowerPoint slide is generated. The column headings—*Series 1*, *Series 2*, and *Series 3* display in the chart ***legend*** and the row headings—*Category 1*, *Category 2*, *Category 3*, and *Category 4*—display as ***category labels***. The legend identifies the patterns or colors that are assigned to the data series in the chart. The category labels display along the bottom of the chart to identify the categories of data.

FIGURE 3.45

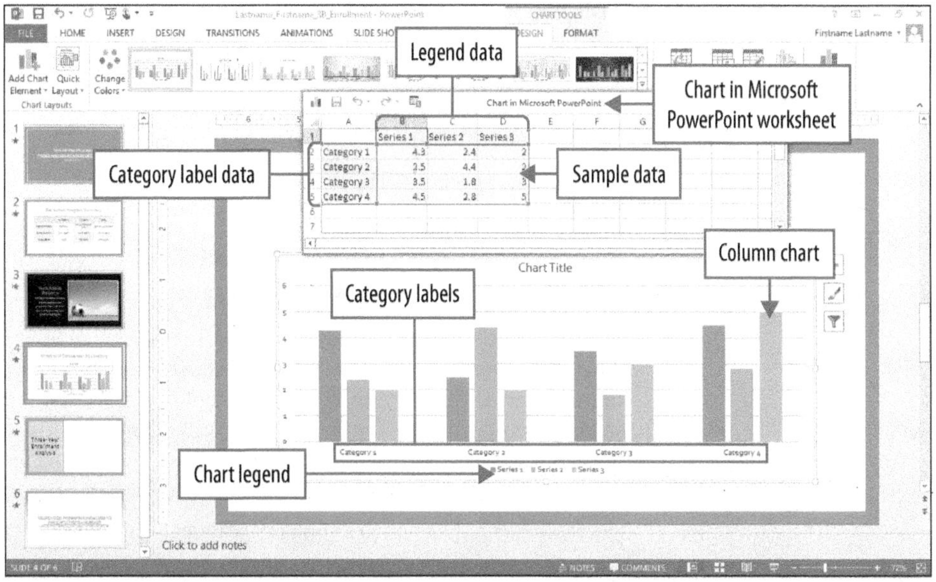

Activity 3.25 Entering Chart Data

1 In the *Chart in Microsoft PowerPoint* worksheet window, click in cell **B1**, which contains the text *Series 1*. Type **Athletics** and then press Tab to move to cell **C1**.

Below the chart, the chart legend is updated to reflect the change in the Excel worksheet.

2 In cell **C1**, which contains the text *Series 2*, type **Leisure** and then press Tab to move to cell **D1**. Type **Arts** and then press Tab. Notice that cell **A2**, which contains the text *Category 1*, is selected. Compare your screen with Figure 3.46.

The outlined cells define the area in which you are entering data. When you press Tab in the rightmost cell, the first cell in the next row becomes active.

FIGURE 3.46

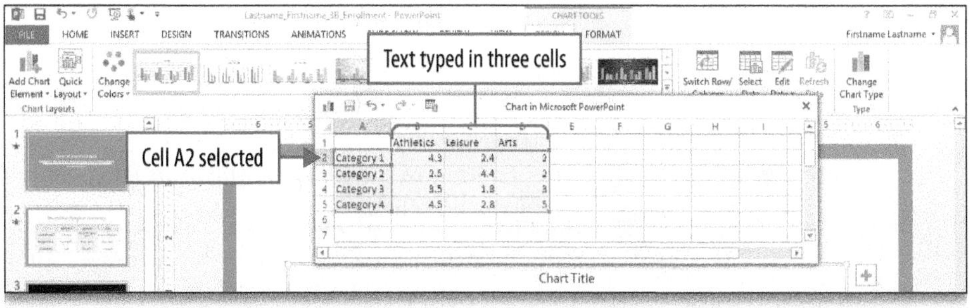

3 Beginning in cell **A2**, type the following data (starting with *Spring*), pressing Tab to move from cell to cell. Notice that as you enter the data, the chart columns resize to display the entered amounts.

	ATHLETICS	LEISURE	ARTS
Spring	895	630	720
Summer	1250	350	820
Fall	1490	585	690
Winter	1130	750	

4 In cell **D5**, which contains the value 5, type **710** and then press Enter.

Pressing Enter in the last cell of the outlined area maintains the existing data range.

ALERT! **Did You Press Tab After the Last Entry?**

If you pressed Tab after entering the data in cell D5, you expanded the chart range. In the Excel window, click Undo.

5 Compare your worksheet and your chart with Figure 3.47. Correct any typing errors by clicking in the cell that you want to change, and then retype the data.

Each of the 12 cells containing the numeric data that you entered is a ***data point***—a value that originates in a worksheet cell. Each data point is represented in the chart by a ***data marker***—a column, bar, area, dot, pie slice, or other symbol in a chart that represents a single data point. Related data points form a ***data series***; for example, there is a data series for *Athletics*, *Leisure*, and *Arts*. Each data series has a unique color or pattern represented in the chart legend. A placeholder for the chart title displays above the chart.

To the right of the chart, three buttons display. The ***Chart Elements button*** enables you to add, remove, or change chart elements such as the title, legend, gridlines, and data labels. The ***Chart Styles button*** enables you to set a style and color scheme for your chart. The ***Chart Filters button*** enables you to change which data displays in the chart.

FIGURE 3.47

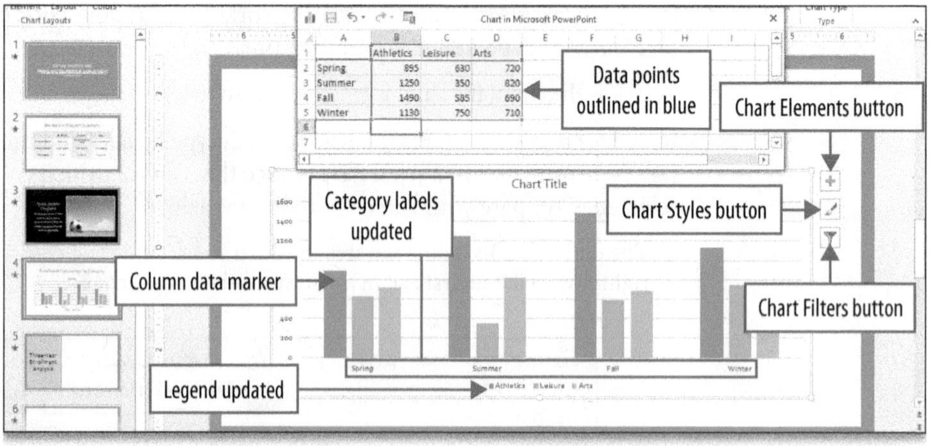

6 In the upper right corner of the *Chart in Microsoft PowerPoint* worksheet window, click **Close** ☒. **Save** the presentation.

When you save the presentation, the worksheet data is saved with it.

More Knowledge — Editing the Chart Data After Closing the Worksheet

You can redisplay the worksheet and make changes to the data after you have closed it. To do so, click the chart to select it, and then on the CHART TOOLS DESIGN tab in the Data group, click Edit Data.

Activity 3.26 | Applying a Chart Style and Modifying Chart Elements

A ***chart style*** is set of predefined formats applied to a chart, including colors, backgrounds, and effects. ***Chart elements*** are the various components of a chart, including the chart title, axis titles, data series, legend, chart area, and plot area.

1 Be sure the chart is selected; click the outer edge of the chart if necessary to select it. On the **CHART TOOLS DESIGN tab**, in the **Chart Styles group**, click **More** to display the **Chart Styles** gallery.

2 In the **Chart Styles** gallery, point to each style to Live Preview the style. Notice that as you point to a chart style, a ScreenTip indicates the chart style number. Click **Style 5**. Compare your screen with Figure 3.48.

This style includes lightly shaded column data markers. Horizontal gridlines display behind the columns.

FIGURE 3.48

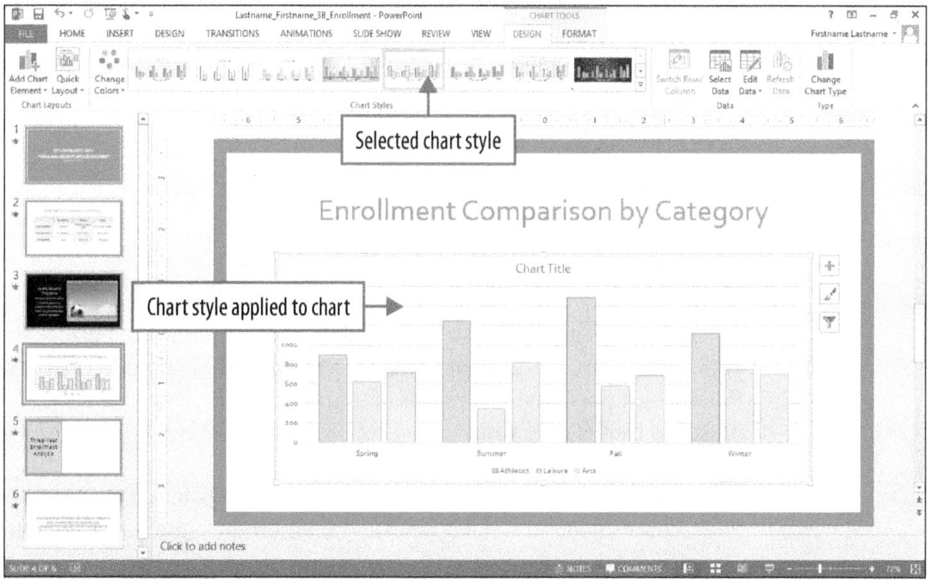

3 To the right of the chart, click **Chart Elements** [+], and then compare your screen with Figure 3.49.

A list of chart elements displays to the left of the chart. Here, you can select the chart elements that you wish to display in your chart. In this slide, the slide title describes the chart. Thus, chart title is not necessary.

FIGURE 3.49

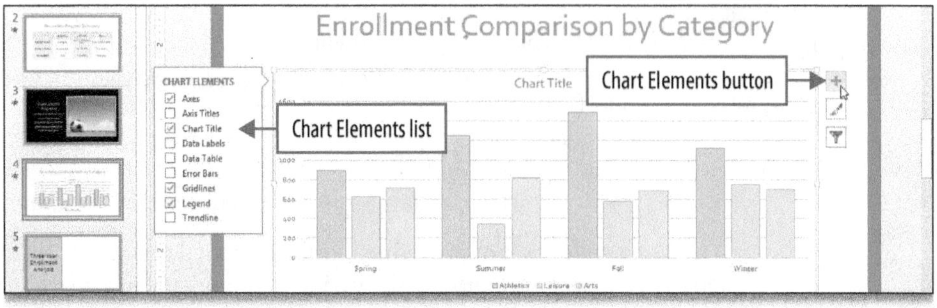

4 Under **Chart Elements**, click **Chart Title** to clear the check box and remove the chart title placeholder from the chart. Click **Chart Elements** [+] to close the Chart Elements list.

5 Click in a blank area of the slide, and then compare your screen with Figure 3.50. **Save** [Save] your presentation.

FIGURE 3.50

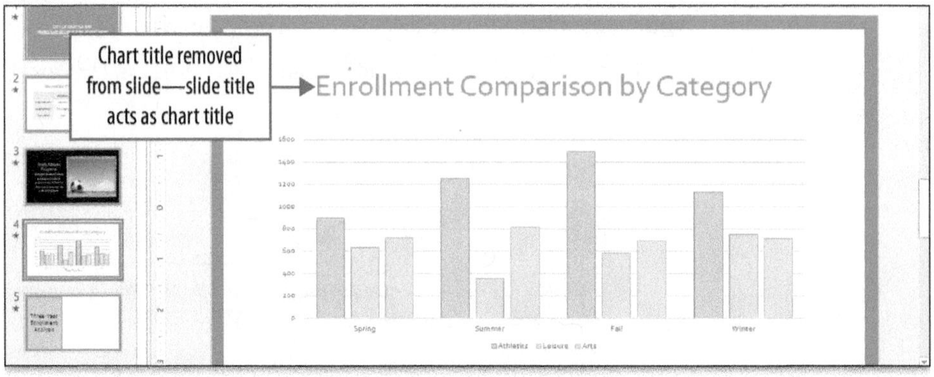

Activity 3.27 | Creating a Line Chart and Deleting Chart Data

To analyze and compare annual data over a three-year period, the presentation requires an additional chart. Recall that there are a number of different types of charts that you can insert in a PowerPoint presentation. In this activity, you will create a ***line chart***, which is commonly used to illustrate trends over time.

1 Display **Slide 5**. In the content placeholder, click **Insert Chart** [chart]. On the left side of the **Insert Chart** dialog box, click **Line**, and then on the right, click the fourth chart—**Line with Markers**. Click **OK**.

2 In the worksheet, click in cell **B1**, which contains the text *Series 1*. Type **Youth** and then press Tab. Type **Adult** and then press Tab. Type **Senior** and then press Tab.

3 Beginning in cell **A2**, type the following data, pressing Tab to move from cell to cell. If you make any typing errors, click in the cell that you want to change, and then retype the data.

	YOUTH	ADULT	SENIOR
2015	3822	1588	2240
2016	4675	1833	2534
2017	4535	1925	2897

4 In the worksheet, position the pointer over **row heading 5** so that the [→] pointer displays. Compare your screen with Figure 3.51.

FIGURE 3.51

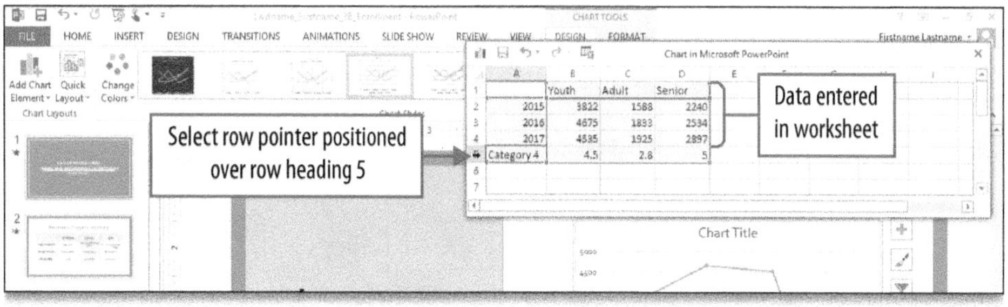

5 With the [→] pointer displayed, *right-click* to select the row and display the shortcut menu. On the shortcut menu, click **Delete** to delete the extra row from the worksheet, and then compare your screen with Figure 3.52.

The data in the worksheet contains four columns and four rows, and the outline area defining the chart data range is resized. You must delete columns and rows from the sample worksheet data that you do not want to include in the chart. You can add additional rows and columns by typing column and row headings and then entering additional data. When data is typed in cells adjacent to the chart range, the range is resized to include the new data.

FIGURE 3.52

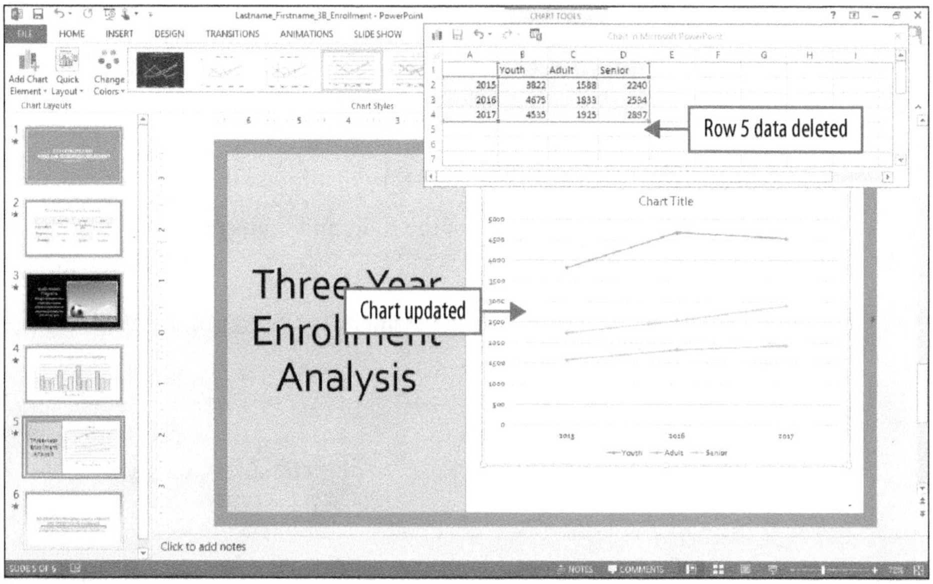

Activity 3.28 | Formatting a Line Chart

1 **Close** [X] the worksheet window. To the right of the chart, click **Chart Styles** [🖌]. Compare your screen with Figure 3.53.

The Chart Style gallery displays on the left side of the chart and the Style tab is active. The chart styles display in a vertical gallery.

FIGURE 3.53

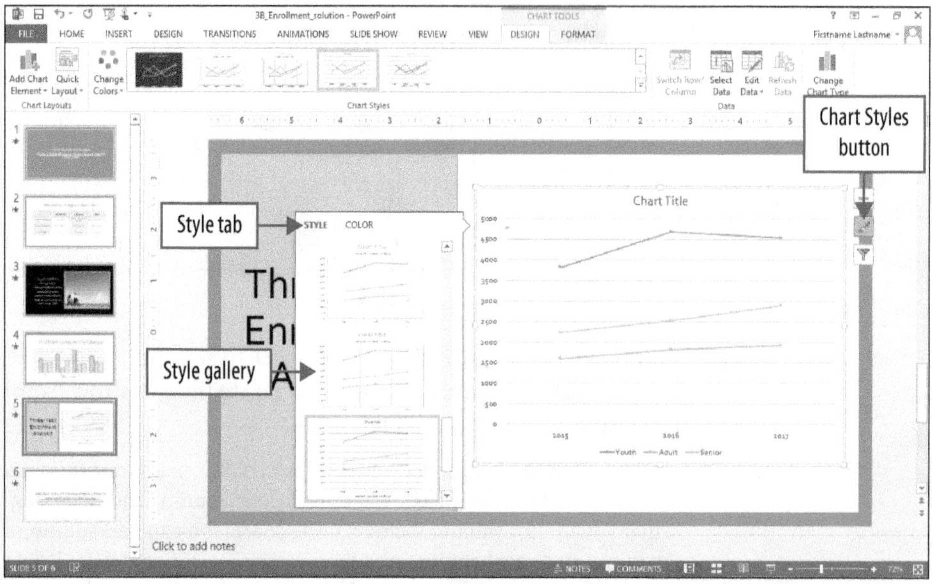

2 In the **Chart Style** gallery, be sure that **Style** is selected. Scroll the list, and point to various styles to view the ScreenTips and the effect of the style on the chart. Click **Style 6** and then click anywhere outside of the chart to close the Chart Style gallery.

The styles that display when you click the Chart Styles button are the same as those that display in the Chart Styles gallery on the ribbon. Apply chart styles using the technique that you prefer.

3 In the chart, click the text **Chart Title**, and then type **By Age Category**

4 Click in a blank area of the slide, and then compare your screen with Figure 3.54. **Save** your presentation.

FIGURE 3.54

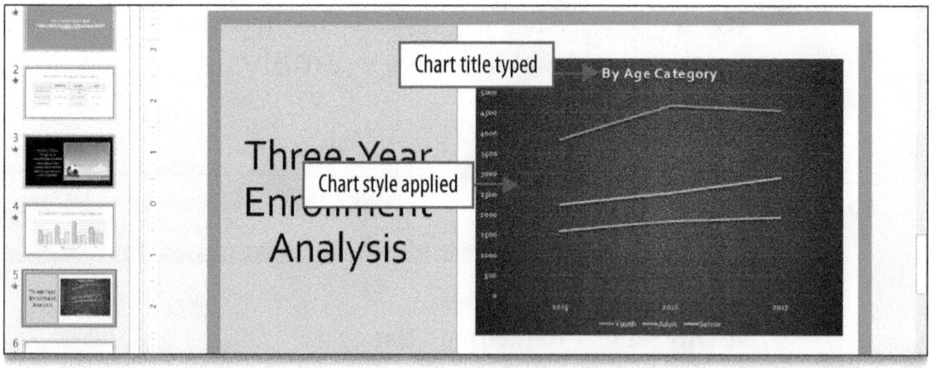

Activity 3.29 | Animating a Chart

1 Display **Slide 4**, and then click anywhere in the column chart to select it. On the **ANIMATIONS tab**, in the **Animation group**, click **More**, and then under **Entrance**, click **Split**.

2 In the **Animation group**, click **Effect Options**, and then under **Sequence**, click **By Series**. Compare your screen with Figure 3.55.

The By Series option displays the chart one data series at a time, and the numbers 1, 2, 3, and 4 to the left of the chart indicate the four parts of the chart animation sequence. The chart animation sequence includes the background, followed by the Athletics data series for each season, and then the Leisure series, and then the Arts series.

FIGURE 3.55

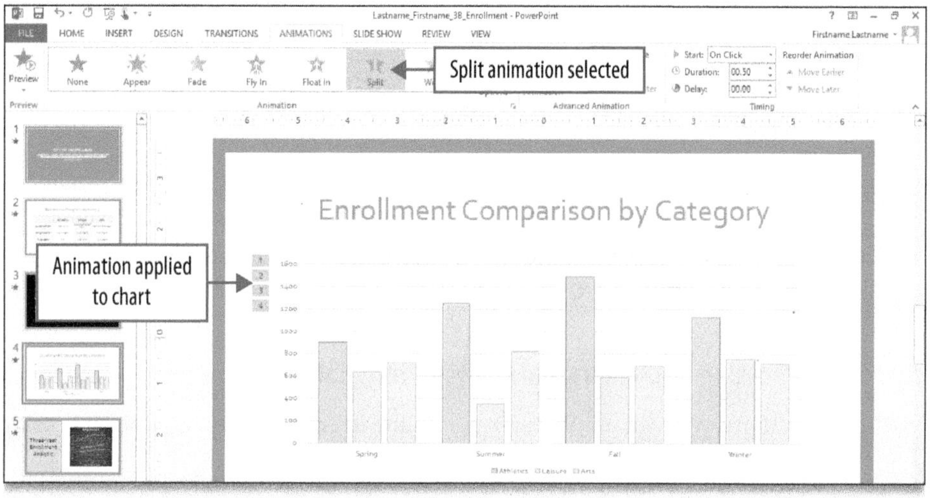

3 View the slide show from the beginning. On **Slide 4**, notice the chart animation sequence.

4 Insert a **Header & Footer** on the **Notes and Handouts**. Include the **Date and time** updated automatically, the **Page Number**, and a **Footer**. In the Footer box, using your own name, type **Lastname_Firstname_3B_Enrollment** and then click **Apply to All.**

5 Display the document properties. As the **Tags**, type **recreation enrollment** and as the **Subject,** type your course and section number. Be sure your name displays as the author, and then **Save** your file.

6 Print **Handouts 6 Slides Horizontal**, or submit your presentation electronically as directed by your instructor.

7 **Close** the presentation.

END | You have completed Project 3B

GO! with Office Online (formerly Web Apps)

Objective Create a Summary and Analysis Presentation in PowerPoint Online

ALERT! **Working with Web-Based Applications and Services**

Computer programs and services on the web receive continuous updates and improvements, so the steps to complete this web-based activity may differ from the ones shown. You can often look at the screens and the information presented to determine how to complete the activity.

Activity | Creating a Summary and Analysis Presentation in PowerPoint Online

In this activity, you will use PowerPoint Online to create a presentation similar to the one you created in Project 3B.

1 From the desktop, start Internet Explorer. Navigate to **http://onedrive.com**, and then sign in to your Microsoft account. Open your **GO! Web Projects** folder—or create and then open this folder if necessary.

2 On the OneDrive menu bar, click **Upload**, and then navigate to your student data files and select **p03_3B_Web**. Click **Open**. When the upload is complete, right-click **p03_3B_Web**, and then click **Rename**. Using your own name, as the file name, type **Lastname_Firstname_PPT_3B_Web** and then press Enter. Click your file, and then click **EDIT PRESENTATION**. Click **Edit in PowerPoint Online**.

3 Display **Slide 3**. In the text placeholder on the left side of the slide, type **The largest enrollment numbers in Pacifica Bay recreation programs continue to be in the athletic area, particularly in the youth soccer program.** Click outside of the placeholder to enter the text.

4 On the right side of the slide, click **Insert Picture**. From your student data files, insert **p03B_Web_Picture**.

5 With the picture selected, on the **FORMAT tab**, in the **Picture Styles group**, click the third style—**Metal Frame**.

6 Click in a blank area of the slide, and then compare your screen with Figure A.

7 Display **Slide 4**, and then select the title. On the **ANIMATIONS tab**, in the **Animation group**, click **Fly In**. Click **Effect Options**, and then click **From Top**. In the **Timing group**, click **Move Earlier** several times until the Move Earlier text displays in gray.

8 Display **Slide 5**, and then click in the title placeholder. Type **Three-Year Enrollment Analysis** and then click outside of the placeholder to enter the text.

FIGURE A

(GO! with Office Online (formerly Web Apps) continues on the next page)

9 On **Slide 5**, select the chart. On the **ANIMATIONS tab**, in the **Animation group**, click **Fade In**.

10 Compare your screen with Figure B.

11 Display **Slide 6**. In the title placeholder, type **Recreation Program Enrollments Are Expected to Increase** and then click outside of the placeholder to enter the text.

12 On the **VIEW tab**, click **Slide Show**, and then view the presentation. If a security warning displays, click Allow once. Click the mouse button to advance through the slides.

13 Submit your file as instructed. Sign out of your OneDrive and then close Internet Explorer.

FIGURE B

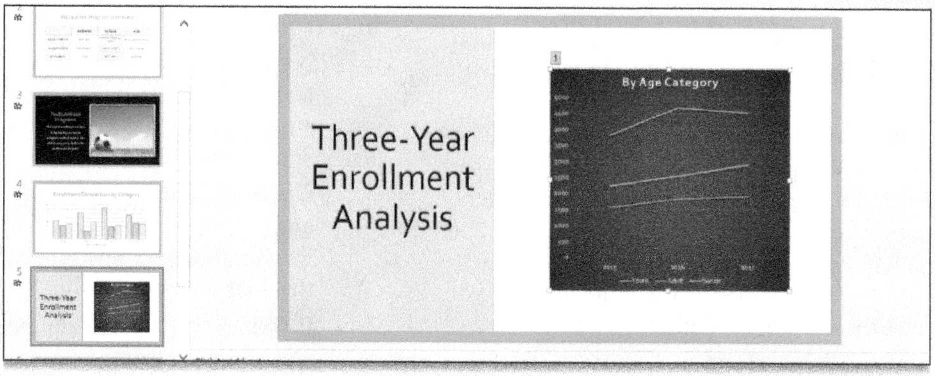

GO! with Microsoft Office 365

Andrew Rodriguez / Fotolia; FotolEdhar/ Fotolia; apops/ Fotolia; Yuri Arcurs/ Fotolia

The advantage of using Office 365 is that your organization does not have to purchase and install server hardware and software for sophisticated business applications and does not need a full-time IT person or staff just to manage the technology your teams need.

By using Office 365, you are able to have business-class services for your employees without investing in expensive hardware, software, and personnel. However, at least one person in an organization must be designated as the *Office 365 Administrator*—the person who creates and manages the account, adds new users, sets up the services your organization wants to use, sets permission levels, and manages the SharePoint team sites. You can have more than one Administrator if you want to share these tasks with others.

Microsoft provides easy-to-use instructions and videos to get you started, and you might also have contact with a Microsoft representative. You will probably find, however, that subscribing to and setting up the account, adding users, and activating services is a straightforward process that requires little or no assistance.

After purchasing the required number of licenses, you will add each team member as a user that includes his or her email address.

The Admin Overview page, as shown in the Figure below, assists the Office 365 Administrator. On the left there are links to manage the users and domains in your Office 365 account. This is where you can add new users, delete users, set permission levels, enter and change passwords, and update the user properties and the licenses.

In the center, you can see the various services available to you in Office 365. In the site shown in the Figure, Outlook, Lync, SharePoint (team sites), and a public-facing website are all part of the services.

Activity | Using a Team Site to Collaborate

This group project relates to the **Bell Orchid Hotels**. If your instructor assigns this project to your class, you can expect to use a SharePoint team site in **Office 365** to collaborate on the following tasks for this chapter:

- If you are in the **Accounting Group**, you and your teammates will finalize the Loan Presentation and post the final presentation on the SharePoint team site.
- If you are in the **Engineering Group**, you and your teammates will finalize the Safety Presentation and post the final presentation on the SharePoint team site.
- If you are in the **Food and Beverage Group**, you and your teammates will finalize the New Menu Item presentation and post the final presentation on the SharePoint team site.
- If you are in the **Human Resources Group**, you and your teammates will finalize the New Employees Orientation presentation and post the final presentation on the SharePoint team site.
- If you are in the **Operations Group**, you and your teammates will finalize the Front Desk Clerk Training Presentation presentation and post the final presentation on the SharePoint team site.
- If you are in the **Sales and Marketing Group**, you and your teammates will finalize the Marketing Plan Presentation presentation and post the final presentation on the SharePoint team site.

(GO! with Microsoft Office 365 continues on the next page)

Andrew Rodriguez / Fotolia; FotolEdhar/ Fotolia; apops/ Fotolia; Yuri Arcurs/ Fotolia

FIGURE A

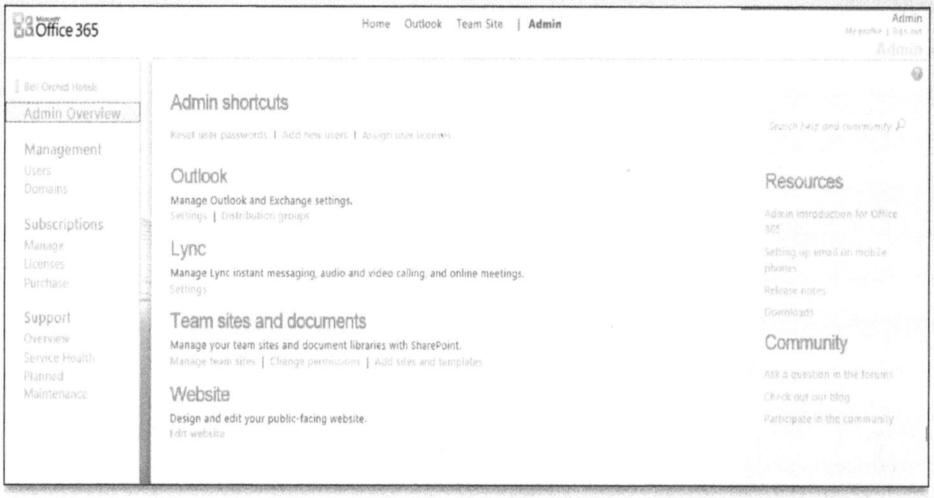

END OF CHAPTER

SUMMARY

There are many ways to modify a presentation theme and customize a presentation. You can apply background styles, insert pictures and textures on slide backgrounds, and change theme fonts and colors.

One way to enhance a presentation and engage an audience is by inserting interesting and informative video. Styles, shapes, and effects can be applied to videos. A video can be trimmed and compressed to make the file size smaller.

Use animation to focus audience attention on a particular slide element in order to draw attention to important points. Apply animation to slide elements in the order in which you want them to display.

Use tables to present information in an organized and attractive manner. Use charts to visually represent data. Apply styles to charts and tables to give your presentations a consistent and informative look.

GO! LEARN IT ONLINE

Review the concepts and key terms in this chapter by completing these online challenges, which you can find at **www.pearsonhighered.com/go.**

Matching and Multiple Choice: Answer matching and multiple choice questions to test what you learned in this chapter. MyITLab®

Crossword Puzzle: Spell out the words that match the numbered clues, and put them in the puzzle squares.

Flipboard: Flip through the definitions of the key terms in this chapter and match them with the correct term.

GO! FOR JOB SUCCESS

Video: Making Ethical Choices

Your instructor may assign this video to your class, and then ask you to think about, or discuss with your classmates, these questions:

FotolEdhar / Fotolia

Which behaviors in this video do you think were unethical?

Is it unethical to "borrow" things from your employer? Why? What would you do if you saw this behavior going on?

What do you think an employer could do to prevent unethical behavior?

END OF CHAPTER

REVIEW AND ASSESSMENT GUIDE FOR POWERPOINT CHAPTER 3

Your instructor may assign one or more of these projects to help you review the chapter and assess your mastery and understanding of the chapter.

Review and Assessment Guide for PowerPoint Chapter 3			
Project	**Apply Skills from These Chapter Objectives**	**Project Type**	**Project Location**
3C	Objectives 1-3 from Project 3A	**3C Skills Review** A guided review of the skills from Project 3A.	On the following pages
3D	Objectives 4-5 from Project 3B	**3D Skills Review** A guided review of the skills from Project 3B.	On the following pages
3E	Objectives 1-3 from Project 3A	**3E Mastery (Grader Project)** A demonstration of your mastery of the skills in Project 3A with extensive decision making.	In MyITLab and on the following pages
3F	Objectives 4-5 from Project 3B	**3F Mastery (Grader Project)** A demonstration of your mastery of the skills in Project 3B with extensive decision making.	In MyITLab and on the following pages
3G	Objectives 1-5 from Projects 3A and 3B	**3G Mastery (Grader Project)** A demonstration of your mastery of the skills in Projects 3A and 3B with extensive decision making.	In MyITLab and on the following pages
3H	Combination of Objectives from Projects 3A and 3B	**3H GO! Fix It** A demonstration of your mastery of the skills in Projects 3A and 3B by creating a correct result from a document that contains errors you must find.	Online
3I	Combination of Objectives from Projects 3A and 3B	**3I GO! Make It** A demonstration of your mastery of the skills in Projects 3A and 3B by creating a result from a supplied picture.	Online
3J	Combination of Objectives from Projects 3A and 3B	**3J GO! Solve It** A demonstration of your mastery of the skills in Projects 3A and 3B, your decision-making skills, and your critical thinking skills. A task-specific rubric helps you self-assess your result.	Online
3K	Combination of Objectives from Projects 3A and 3B	**3K GO! Solve It** A demonstration of your mastery of the skills in Projects 3A and 3B, your decision-making skills, and your critical thinking skills. A task-specific rubric helps you self-assess your result.	On the following pages
3L	Combination of Objectives from Projects 3A and 3B	**3L GO! Think** A demonstration of your understanding of the Chapter concepts applied in a manner that you would outside of college. An analytic rubric helps you and your instructor grade the quality of your work by comparing it to the work an expert in the discipline would create.	On the following pages
3M	Combination of Objectives from Projects 3A and 3B	**3M GO! Think** A demonstration of your understanding of the Chapter concepts applied in a manner that you would outside of college. An analytic rubric helps you and your instructor grade the quality of your work by comparing it to the work an expert in the discipline would create.	Online
3N	Combination of Objectives from Projects 3A and 3B	**3N You and GO!** A demonstration of your understanding of the Chapter concepts applied in a manner that you would in a personal situation. An analytic rubric helps you and your instructor grade the quality of your work.	Online
3O	Combination of Objectives from Projects 3A and 3B	**3O Cumulative Group Project for PowerPoint Chapter 3** A demonstration of your understanding of concepts and your ability to work collaboratively in a group role-playing assessment, requiring both collaboration and self-management.	Online
Capstone Project for PowerPoint Chapters 1-3	Combination of Objectives from Projects 1A, 1B, 2A, 2B, 3A, and 3B	A demonstration of your mastery of the skills in Chapters 1-3 with extensive decision making. **(Grader Project)**	In MyITLab and online

A comprehensive Book Capstone Project that covers all of the Word, Excel, Access, and PowerPoint chapters in this book is available online. Instructors can download the Book Capstone Project from the Instructor Resource Center.

GLOSSARY

GLOSSARY OF CHAPTER KEY TERMS

After Previous An animation option that begins the animation sequence for the selected slide element immediately after the completion of the previous animation or slide transition.

Animation A visual or sound effect added to an object or text on a slide.

Animation Painter A feature that copies animation settings from one object to another.

Background style A predefined slide background fill variation that combines theme colors in different intensities or patterns.

Body font A font that is applied to all slide text except slide titles.

Category labels Text that displays along the bottom of a chart to identify the categories of data.

Cell The intersection of a column and row in a table.

Cell reference The intersecting column letter and row number that identify a cell.

Chart A graphic representation of numeric data.

Chart elements The various components of a chart, including the chart title, axis titles, data series, legend, chart area, and plot area.

Chart Elements button A button that displays options for adding, removing, or changing chart elements.

Chart Filters button A button that displays options for changing the data displayed in a chart.

Chart style A set of predefined formats applied to a chart, including colors, backgrounds, and effects.

Chart Styles button A button that displays options for setting the style and color scheme for a chart.

Column chart A type of chart used for illustrating comparisons among related numbers.

Data marker A column, bar, area, dot, pie slice, or other symbol in a chart that represents a single data point.

Data point A chart value that originates in a worksheet cell.

Data series A group of related data points.

Emphasis effect Animation that emphasizes an object or text that is already displayed.

Entrance effect Animation that brings a slide element onto the screen.

Exit effect Animation that moves an object or text off the screen.

Headings font A font that is applied to all slide title text.

Legend A chart element that identifies the patterns or colors that are assigned to the data series in the chart.

Line chart A type of chart commonly used to illustrate trends over time.

On Click An animation option that begins the animation sequence for the selected slide element when the mouse button is clicked or the Spacebar is pressed.

Table A format for information that organizes and presents text and data in columns and rows.

Table style A format applied to a table that is consistent with the presentation theme.

Theme colors A set of coordinating colors that are applied to the backgrounds, objects, and text in a presentation.

Theme fonts The fonts applied to two types of slide text—headings and body.

Timing options Animation options that control when animated items display in the animation sequence.

Trim A command that deletes parts of a video to make it shorter.

With Previous An animation option that begins the animation sequence at the same time as the previous animation or slide transition.

CHAPTER REVIEW

Apply 3A skills from these Objectives:

1. Customize Slide Backgrounds and Themes
2. Animate a Slide Show
3. Insert a Video

Skills Review Project 3C Park

In the following Skills Review, you will format a presentation by applying slide background styles, colors, pictures, and animation. Your completed presentation will look similar to Figure 3.56.

PROJECT FILES

For Project 3C, you will need the following files:

p03C_Park
p03C_Park_Scenery
p03C_Park_Video

You will save your presentation as:

Lastname_Firstname_3C_Park

PROJECT RESULTS

FIGURE 3.56

(Project 3C Park continues on the next page)

CHAPTER REVIEW

Skills Review Project 3C Park (continued)

1 Start PowerPoint, from your student data files, open **p03C_Park**, and then **Save** the presentation in your **PowerPoint Chapter 3** folder as **Lastname_Firstname_3C_Park**

a. On the **DESIGN tab**, in the **Variants group**, click **More**, point to **Colors**, and then click **Orange Red** to change the theme colors.

b. On the **DESIGN tab**, in the **Variants group**, click **More**, point to **Fonts**, and then click **Candara** to change the theme fonts.

c. On the **DESIGN tab**, in the **Customize group**, click **Format Background**. In the **Format Background** pane, under **Fill**, click **Picture or texture fill**. Under **Insert picture from**, to the right of **Texture**, click the **Texture** button, and then in the third row, click the fourth texture—**Recycled Paper**.

d. **Close** the **Format Background** pane.

2 Display **Slide 2**. Hold down Ctrl and click **Slide 4** so that both **Slides 2** and **4** are selected. On the **DESIGN tab**, in the **Variants group**, click **More**, and then point to **Background Styles**. In the second row, *right-click* the third style—**Style 7**, and then on the shortcut menu, click **Apply to Selected Slides**.

a. Display **Slide 3**. On the **DESIGN tab**, in the **Customize group**, click **Format Background**. Select the **Hide Background Graphics** check box.

b. In the **Format Background** pane, under **Fill**, click the **Picture or texture fill** option button. Under **Insert picture from**, click **File**, and then navigate to your student data files. Click **p03C_Park_Scenery**, and then click **Insert**.

c. In the **Transparency** box, type **10%**

3 Display **Slide 5**. If necessary, display the **Format Background** pane.

a. In the **Format Background** pane, under **Fill**, verify that **Solid Fill** is selected.

b. To the right of **Color**, click **Fill Color**. In the third column, click the first color—**Tan, Background 2**.

c. **Close** the **Format Background** pane.

4 With **Slide 5** displayed, on the **INSERT tab**, in the **Media group**, click **Video**, and then click **Video on My PC**. Navigate to your student data files, and then click **p03C_Park_Video**. Click **Insert** to insert the video.

a. With the video selected, on the **FORMAT tab**, in the **Size group**, replace the value in the **Height** box with **2.5** and then press Enter.

b. On the **FORMAT tab**, in the **Arrange group**, click **Align**, and then click **Align Center**. Click **Align** again, and then click **Align Bottom** so that the video is centered and aligned with the lower edge of the slide.

c. With the video selected, on the **FORMAT tab**, in the **Video Styles** group, click **More**, and then under **Subtle**, click the third style—**Soft Edge Rectangle**.

d. In the **Video Styles group**, click **Video Shape**, and then under **Rectangles**, click the second shape—**Rounded Rectangle**.

e. With the video selected, on the **PLAYBACK tab**, in the **Video Options group**, click the **Start arrow**, and then click **Automatically**.

f. On the **PLAYBACK tab**, in the **Editing group**, click **Trim Video**. Select the number in the **End Time** box, and then type **00:14** and notice that the video ends with a picture of the park. Click **OK** to apply the trim settings.

5 Display **Slide 2**, and then select the text in the in the bulleted list placeholder. On the **HOME tab**, in the **Font group**, click the **Font Color button arrow**, and then in the second column, click the first color—**White, Text 1** so that the text displays with more contrast against the slide background.

a. With the bulleted list selected, on the **ANIMATIONS tab**, in the **Animation group**, click **More**, and then under **Entrance**, click **Split**.

b. In the **Animation group**, click **Effect Options**, and then click **Vertical Out**.

c. In the **Timing group**, click the **Start arrow**, and then click **After Previous** so that the list displays after the slide transition.

d. In the **Timing group**, click the **Duration up arrow** two times so that *01.00* displays in the **Duration** box. Click the **Delay up arrow** one time so that *00.25* displays in the **Delay** box.

(Project 3C Park continues on the next page)

Skills Review Project 3C Park (continued)

6 Display **Slide 3**, and then click in the title placeholder. On the **ANIMATIONS tab**, in the **Animation group**, click **More**, and then under **Entrance**, click **Wipe**. In the **Timing group**, click the **Start arrow**, and then click **After Previous** so that the title displays immediately after the slide transition.

a. With the title selected, in the **Advanced Animation group**, click **Animation Painter**. Click **Slide 1**, and then click the subtitle—*Remodel Update*—to apply the animation effect to the subtitle.

b. On **Slide 1**, select the title. Notice that in the Animation group, the Bounce animation is applied. On the **ANIMATIONS tab**, in the **Animation group**, click **More**, and then click **None** to remove the animation from the title.

c. Insert a **Header & Footer** for the **Notes and Handouts**. Include the **Date and time updated automatically**, the **Page number**, and a **Footer** with the file name **Lastname_Firstname_3C_Park**

d. On the **SLIDE SHOW tab**, in the **Start Slide Show group**, click **From Beginning**, and then view your presentation, clicking the mouse button to advance through the slides. When the video on Slide 5 finishes, press Esc to return to the presentation.

7 Click the **FILE tab**, and then on the **Info tab**, click **Compress Media**. Click **Low Quality** to make the presentation size smaller and easier to submit. When the compression is complete, in the **Compress Media** dialog box, click **Close**.

a. Display the document properties. As the **Tags** type **park remodel** and as the **Subject** type your course and section number. Be sure your name displays as the author, and then **Save** your file.

b. Print **Handouts 6 Slides Horizontal**, or submit your presentation electronically as directed by your instructor. **Close** the presentation.

END | You have completed Project 3C

CHAPTER REVIEW

Apply 3B skills from these Objectives:

4 Create and Modify Tables
5 Create and Modify Charts

Skills Review Project 3D Budget

In the following Skills Review, you will format a presentation by inserting and formatting a table, a column chart, and a line chart. Your completed presentation will look similar to Figure 3.57.

PROJECT FILES

For Project 3D, you will need the following file:

p03D_Budget

You will save your presentation as:

Lastname_Firstname_3D_Budget

PROJECT RESULTS

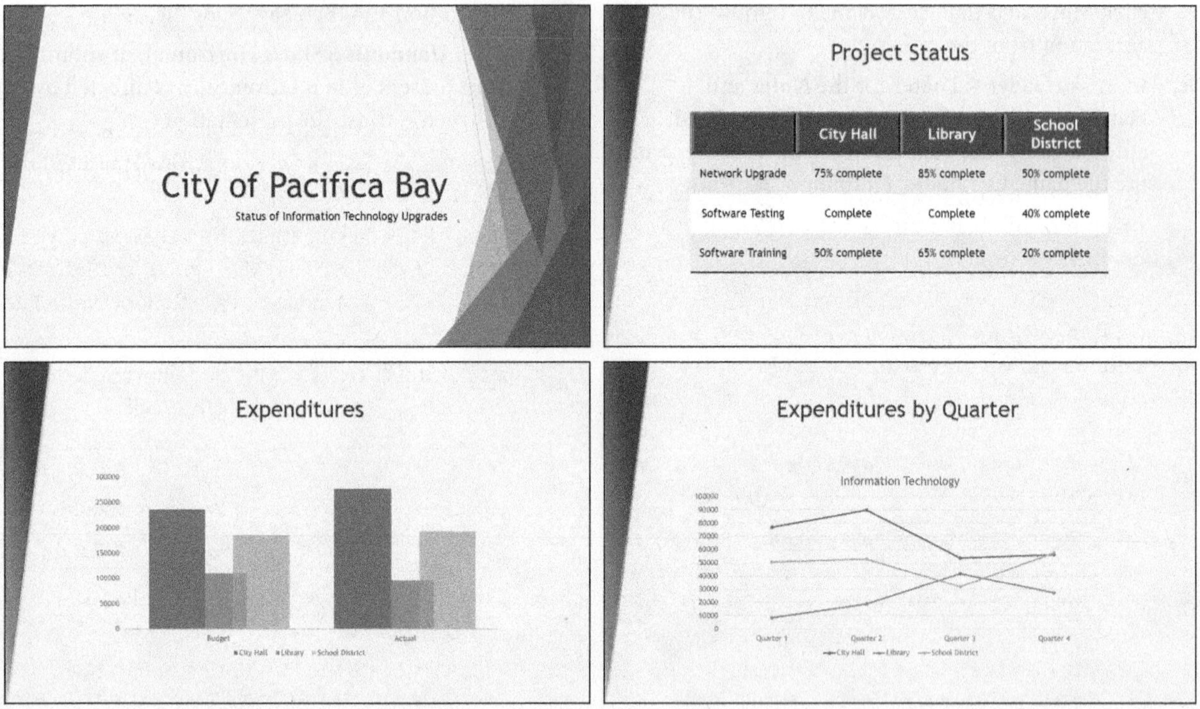

FIGURE 3.57

(Project 3D Budget continues on the next page)

Skills Review Project 3D Budget (continued)

1 Start PowerPoint, from your student data files, open **p03D_Budget**, and then **Save** the presentation in your **PowerPoint Chapter 3** folder as **Lastname_Firstname_3D_Budget**

a. Display **Slide 2**. In the content placeholder, click **Insert Table** to display the **Insert Table** dialog box. In the **Number of columns box**, type **3** and then press Tab. In the **Number of rows** box, type **2** and then click **OK** to create the table.

b. In the first row of the table, click in the second cell. Type **City Hall** and then press Tab. Type **School District** and then press Tab to move the insertion point to the first cell in the second row.

c. With the insertion point positioned in the first cell of the second row, type **Network Upgrade** and then press Tab. Type **75% complete** and then press Tab. Type **50% complete** and then press Tab to insert a new blank row. In the first cell of the third row, type **Software Training** and then press Tab. Type **50% complete** and then press Tab. Type **20% complete**

d. With the insertion point positioned in the last column, on the **LAYOUT tab**, in the **Rows & Columns group**, click **Insert Left** to insert a new column. Click in the top cell of the inserted column, and then type **Library** In the second and third rows of the inserted column, type **85% complete** and **65% complete**

e. With the insertion point positioned in the third row, on the **LAYOUT tab**, in the **Rows & Columns group**, click **Insert Above**. Click in the first cell of the row you inserted, type **Software Testing** and then press Tab. Type the remaining three entries in the row as follows: **Complete** and **Complete** and **40% complete**

2 At the center of the lower border surrounding the table, point to the sizing handle, and make the table larger by dragging down until the lower edge of the table aligns **on the lower half of the vertical ruler at 2 inches.**

a. Click in the first cell of the table. On the **LAYOUT tab**, in the **Cell Size group**, click **Distribute Rows.**

b. On the **LAYOUT tab**, in the **Table group**, click **Select**, and then click **Select Table.** In the **Alignment group**, click **Center**, and then click **Center Vertically.**

c. Click in any cell in the table. Under **TABLE TOOLS**, click the **DESIGN tab**, and then in the **Table Styles group**, click **More.** Under **Medium**, in the third row, click the second style—**Medium Style 3 - Accent 1**—to apply the style to the table.

d. Move the pointer outside of the table so that is positioned to the left of the first row in the table to display the ➡ pointer, and then click one time to select the entire row. On the **DESIGN tab**, in the **Table Styles group**, click **Effects.** Point to **Cell Bevel**, and then under **Bevel**, click the first bevel—**Circle.** Change the **Font Size** of the text in the first row to **24.**

3 Display **Slide 3.** In the content placeholder, click **Insert Chart** to display the **Insert Chart** dialog box. With the ***Clustered*** **Column** chart selected, click **OK.**

a. In the worksheet window, click in cell **B1**, which contains the text *Series 1*. Type **City Hall** and then press Tab to move to cell **C1.**

b. In cell **C1**, which contains the text *Series 2*, type **Library** and then press Tab to move to cell **D1**, which contains the text *Series 3*. Type **School District** and then press Tab.

c. Beginning in cell **A2**, type the following data, pressing Tab to move from cell to cell.

	City Hall	Library	School District
Budget	**235650**	**110500**	**185635**
Actual	**275895**	**95760**	**192570**

d. In the worksheet window, position the pointer over **row heading 4** so that the ➡ pointer displays. Then, drag down to select both **rows 4** and **5.** *Right-click* in one of the selected the rows to display the shortcut menu. On the shortcut menu, click **Delete. Close** the worksheet window.

e. With the chart selected, under **CHART TOOLS**, on the **DESIGN tab**, in the **Chart Styles group**, click **More.** In the **Chart Styles** gallery, in the second row, click **Style 13** to apply the style to the chart.

f. To the right of the chart, click **Chart Elements** [+], and then *clear* the **Chart Title** box to remove it from the chart.

(Project 3D Budget continues on the next page)

Skills Review Project 3D Budget (continued)

g. With the chart selected, click the **ANIMATIONS tab**, and then in the **Animation group**, click **More**. Under **Entrance**, click **Split**. In the **Animation group**, click **Effect Options**, and then under **Sequence**, click **By Series**.

4 Display **Slide 4**. In the content placeholder, click **Insert Chart**. On the left side of the **Insert Chart** dialog box, click **Line**, and then under **Line**, click the fourth chart—**Line with Markers**. Click **OK**.

a. In the worksheet, click in cell **B1**, which contains the text *Series 1*. Type **City Hall** and then press Tab. Type **Library** and then press Tab. Type **School District** and then press Tab.

b. Beginning in cell **A2**, type the following data, pressing Tab to move from cell to cell. After you finish entering the data, close the worksheet window.

	City Hall	Library	School District
Quarter 1	**76575**	**8265**	**50665**
Quarter 2	**89670**	**18675**	**52830**
Quarter 3	**53620**	**41730**	**31560**
Quarter 4	**56030**	**27090**	**57515**

c. Click in the **Chart Title**, and then type **Information Technology**

d. Insert a **Header & Footer** for the **Notes and Handouts**. Include the **Date and time updated automatically**, the **Page number**, and a **Footer** with the file name **Lastname_Firstname_3D_Budget**

e. Display the document properties. As the **Tags** type **technology budget** and as the **Subject** type your course and section number. Be sure your name displays as the author, and then **Save** your file.

f. Print **Handouts 4 Slides Horizontal**, or submit your presentation electronically as directed by your instructor. **Close** the presentation.

END | You have completed Project 3D

CONTENT-BASED ASSESSMENTS

Mastering PowerPoint | Project 3E Gardens

MyITLab® grader

Apply 3A skills from these Objectives:

1 Customize Slide Backgrounds and Themes
2 Animate a Slide Show
3 Insert a Video

In the following Mastering PowerPoint project, you will format a presentation created by the Pacifica Bay Public Relations department that describes the City of Pacifica Bay Botanical Gardens. Your completed presentation will look similar to Figure 3.58.

PROJECT FILES

For Project 3E, you will need the following files:

p03E_Garden
p03E_Flower
p03E_Video

You will save your presentation as:

Lastname_Firstname_3E_Garden

PROJECT RESULTS

FIGURE 3.58

(Project 3E Gardens continues on the next page)

CONTENT-BASED ASSESSMENTS

Mastering PowerPoint | Project 3E Gardens (continued)

1 Start PowerPoint. From the student data files that accompany this textbook, locate and open **p03E_ Garden**. Save the presentation in your **PowerPoint Chapter 3** folder as **Lastname_Firstname_3E_Garden**

2 Change the **Colors** for the presentation to **Violet**, and the **Fonts** to **Cambria**. On **Slide 1**, format the background by changing the **Color** of the Solid fill to **Gray - 25%, Text 2, Darker 90%**—in the fourth column, the last color.

3 Select **Slides 2** and **3**, and then format the background of the two selected slides with the **Green marble** texture.

4 On **Slide 2**, select the paragraph on the right side of the slide, and then apply the **Split** entrance effect. Change the **Effect Options** to **Horizontal Out**. Change the **Start** setting to **After Previous**, and then change the **Duration** to **01.00**.

5 Use **Animation Painter** to apply the same animation from the paragraph on **Slide 2** to the bulleted list on **Slide 3**. Then, on **Slide 3**, remove the animation from the title.

6 On **Slide 4**, hide the background graphics, and then format the background with a picture from your student data files—**p03E_Flower**. Change the **Transparency** to **50%**

7 Format the title placeholder with a **Shape Fill** color—in the fifth column, the last color—**Lavender, Accent 1, Darker 50%**.

8 From your student data files, insert the video **p03E_Video**. Change the **Video Height** to **6.25** and then using the **Align to Slide** option, apply the **Align Center** and **Align Bottom** options. Format the video by applying, from the **Video Styles** gallery, an **Intense** style—**Bevel Rectangle**.

9 Change the video **Start** setting to **Automatically**, and then trim the video to **00:14** Compress the video using the **Low Quality** setting.

10 **Insert** a **Header & Footer** on the **Notes and Handouts**. Include the **Date and time updated automatically**, the **Page number**, and a **Footer** with the text **Lastname_Firstname_3E_Garden**

11 Display the document properties. As the **Tags** type **botanical garden** and as the **Subject** type your course and section number. Be sure your name displays as the author, and then **Save** your file.

12 View the slide show from the beginning, and then print **Handouts 4 Slides Horizontal**, or submi t your presentation electronically as directed by your instructor. **Close** the presentation.

END | You have completed Project 3E

CONTENT-BASED ASSESSMENTS

Mastering PowerPoint | Project 3F Report

Apply 3B skills from these Objectives:

4 Create and Modify Tables
5 Create and Modify Charts

In the following Mastering PowerPoint project, you will format several of the slides in a presentation that the City Manager is developing for an upcoming City Council meeting. Your completed presentation will look similar to Figure 3.59.

PROJECT FILES

For Project 3F, you will need the following file:

p03F_Report

You will save your presentation as:

Lastname_Firstname_3F_Report

PROJECT RESULTS

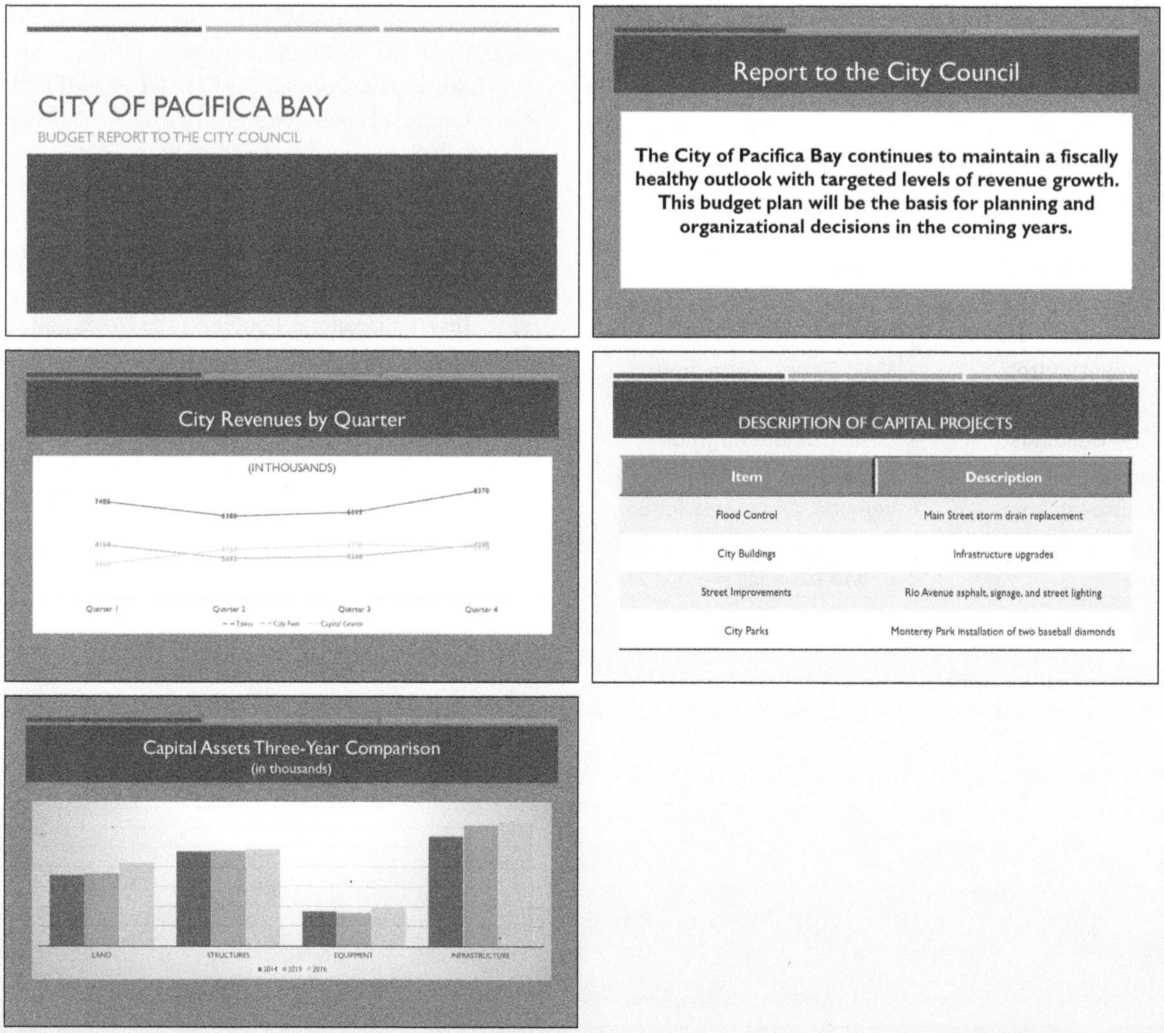

FIGURE 3.59

(Project 3F Report continues on the next page)

CONTENT-BASED ASSESSMENTS

Mastering PowerPoint | Project 3F Report (continued)

1 Start PowerPoint. From your student data files, open **p03F_Report**, and then **Save** the presentation in your **PowerPoint Chapter 3** folder as **Lastname_Firstname_3F_Report**

2 On **Slide 3**, in the content placeholder, insert a **Line with Markers** chart. In the worksheet, in cell **B1**, type **Taxes** and then enter the following data:

	Taxes	City Fees	Capital Grants
Quarter 1	7480	4154	2650
Quarter 2	6380	3092	3785
Quarter 3	6695	3260	4150
Quarter 4	8370	4190	3970

3 **Close** the worksheet window. Apply **Chart Style 7**, and then apply the **Wipe** entrance effect to the chart. Including the parentheses, change the **Chart Title** to **(In Thousands)**

4 On **Slide 4**, in the content placeholder, insert a **Table** with **2 columns** and **5 rows**, and then type the text in the table below

Item	Description
Flood Control	Main Street storm drain replacement
City Buildings	Infrastructure upgrades
Street Improvements	Rio Avenue asphalt, signage, and street lighting
City Parks	Monterey Park installation of two baseball diamonds

5 Resize the table so that its lower edge extends to **3 inches on the lower half of the vertical ruler**. Align the table text so that it is centered horizontally and vertically within the cells. Apply table style **Medium Style 3 - Accent 2**, and then to the first row, apply a **Cell Bevel** using the **Circle** effect. Change the **Font Size** of the text in the first row to **24**.

6 On **Slide 5**, in the content placeholder, insert a **Clustered Column** chart. In the worksheet, in cell **B1**, type **2014** and then enter the following data:

	2014	2015	2016
Land	71534	72823	83653
Structures	95746	95920	97812
Equipment	35042	33465	39767
Infrastructure	111586	121860	125873

7 **Close** the worksheet window. Apply **Chart Style 4** to the chart, and then display the **CHART ELEMENTS** list. Clear the **Data Labels** check box so that the data labels do not display at the top of each column. Apply the **Wipe** entrance effect to the chart. Change the **Effect Options** so that the animation is applied **By Series**. Change the **Timing** so that the animation starts **After Previous**. Remove the **Chart Title** element.

8 **Insert** a **Header & Footer** on the **Notes and Handouts**. Include the **Date and time updated automatically**, the **Page number**, and a **Footer** with the text **Lastname_Firstname_3F_Report**

9 Display the document properties. As the **Tags**, type **city council report** and as the **Subject**, type your course and section number. Be sure your name displays as the author, and then **Save** your file.

10 View the slide show from the beginning, and then print **Handouts 6 Slides Horizontal**, or submit your presentation electronically as directed by your instructor. **Close** the presentation.

END | You have completed Project 3F

CONTENT-BASED ASSESSMENTS

Mastering PowerPoint | Project 3G Travel

MyITLab® grader

Apply 3A and 3B skills from these Objectives:

1. Customize Slide Backgrounds and Themes
2. Animate a Slide Show
3. Insert a Video
4. Create and Modify Tables
5. Create and Modify Charts

In the following Mastering PowerPoint project, you will format a presentation that the Pacifica Bay Travel and Tourism Director will show at a conference for travel agents in California. Your completed presentation will look similar to Figure 3.60.

PROJECT FILES

For Project 3G, you will need the following files:

p03G_Travel
p03G_Video
p03G_Background

You will save your presentation as:

Lastname_Firstname_3G_Travel

PROJECT RESULTS

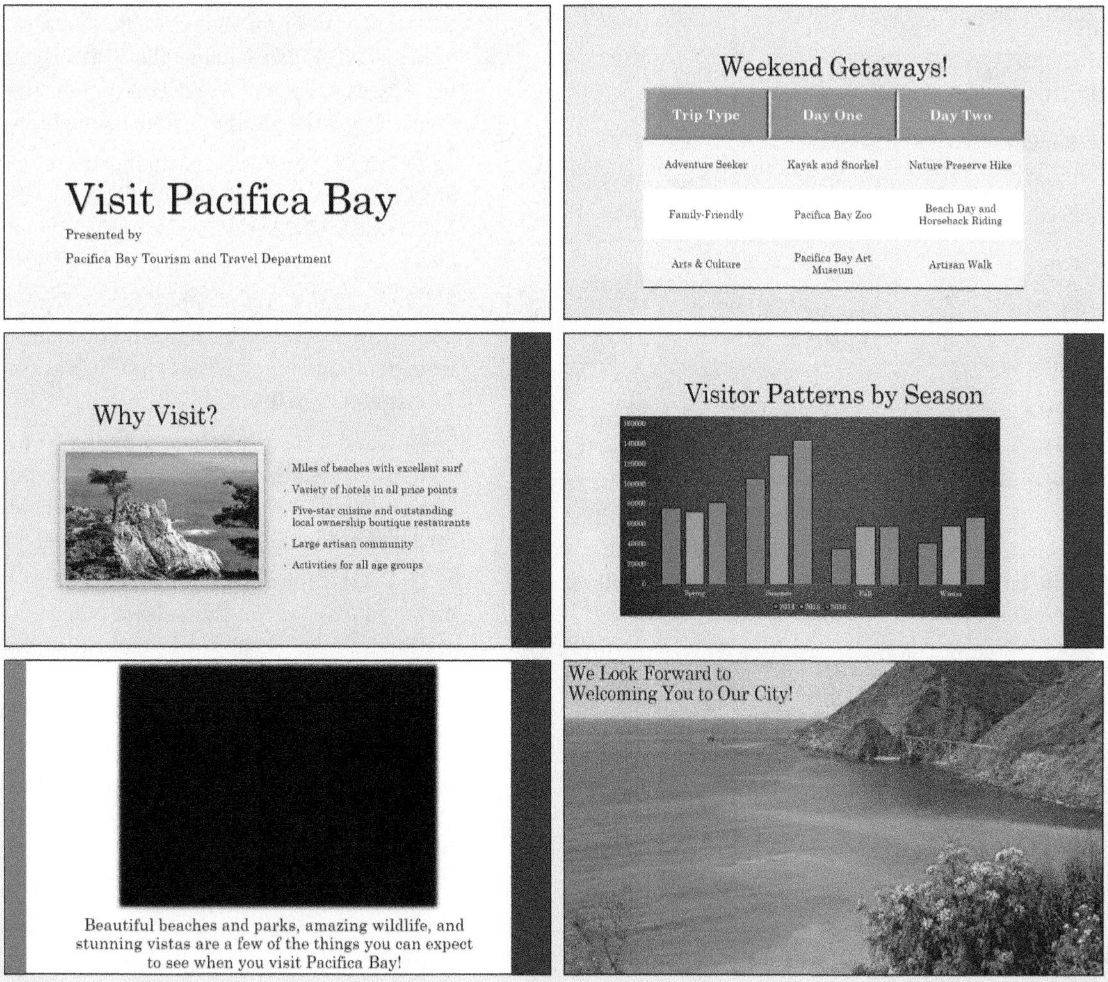

FIGURE 3.60

(Project 3G Travel continues on the next page)

Mastering PowerPoint Project 3G Travel (continued)

1 Start PowerPoint. From the student data files that accompany this textbook, locate and open **p03G_ Travel.** Save the presentation in your **PowerPoint Chapter 3** folder as **Lastname_Firstname_3G_Travel**

2 Change the **Colors** for the presentation to **Blue Warm.** On **Slide 1**, format the background with the **Water droplets Texture**, and then change the **Transparency** to **50%**

3 Select **Slides 2 through 4**, and then format the background of the selected slides with a **Solid fill** using the color **Teal, Accent 5, Lighter 60%**—in the second to last column, the third color.

4 On **Slide 2**, hide the background graphics, and then insert a **Table** with **3 columns** and **4 rows**. Apply table style **Medium Style 3 - Accent 3**, and then type the information in the table below.

Trip Type	Day One	Day Two
Adventure Seeker	Kayak and Snorkel	Nature Preserve Hike
Family-Friendly	Pacifica Bay Zoo	Beach Day and Horseback Riding
Arts & Culture	Pacifica Bay Art Museum	Artisan Walk

5 Resize the table so that its lower edge extends to **3 inches on the lower half of the vertical ruler**, and then distribute the table rows. Align the table text so that it is centered horizontally and vertically within the cells, and then change the **Font Size** of the first row of the table text to **24**. Apply a **Circle** style **Cell Bevel** to the first row.

6 On **Slide 3**, animate the picture using the **Wipe** entrance effect starting **After Previous**. Change the **Duration** to **01:00**. Apply the **Split** entrance effect to the bulleted list placeholder, and then change the **Effect Options** to **Vertical Out**.

7 On **Slide 4**, insert a **Clustered Column** chart. In the worksheet, in cell **B1** type **2014** and then enter the following data:

	2014	2015	2016
Spring	75600	72300	81460
Summer	105300	128730	143600
Fall	35900	58300	58320
Winter	41600	58430	67300

8 **Close** the worksheet window, apply **Chart Style 8** to the chart, and then remove the **Chart Title** element. Apply the **Wipe** entrance effect to the chart and change the **Effect Options** to **By Series.**

9 On **Slide 5**, apply the **Style 1** background style to this slide only. From your student data files, insert the video **p03G_Video.** Change the **Video Height** to **6** and use the **Align Center** and **Align Top** options to position the video. Apply the **Soft Edge Rectangle** video style.

10 On the **Playback tab**, change the **Video Options** to **Start** the video **Automatically. Trim** the video so that the **End Time** is **00:22** and then compress the media in **Low Quality.**

11 On **Slide 6**, hide the background graphics, and then format the slide background by inserting a picture from your student data files—**p03G_Background.** Set the **Transparency** to **0%**

12 **Insert** a **Header & Footer** on the **Notes and Handouts.** Include the **Date and time updated automatically**, the **Page number**, and a **Footer** with the text **Lastname_Firstname_3G_Travel**

13 Display the document properties. As the **Tags** type **travel, tourism** and as the **Subject** type your course and section number. Be sure your name displays as the author, and then **Save** your file.

14 View the slide show from the beginning, and then print **Handouts 6 Slides Horizontal**, or submit your presentation electronically as directed by your instructor. **Close** PowerPoint.

END | You have completed Project 3G

CONTENT-BASED ASSESSMENTS

Apply a combination of the 3A and 3B skills.

GO! Fix It Project 3H Housing Developments Online

GO! Make It Project 3I Water Usage Online

GO! Solve It Project 3J Aquatic Center Online

GO! Solve It Project 3K Power

PROJECT FILES

For Project 3K, you will need the following files:

p03K_Power
p03K_Tower

You will save your presentation as:

Lastname_Firstname_3K_Power

Open the file p03K_Power and save it as **Lastname_Firstname_3K_Power** Apply a theme and then format the slide background of the title slide with the picture found in your student data files—p03K_Tower. Format the title slide so that the title text displays attractively against the background. Format the background of at least one other slide using a background style, solid fill color, or texture. On Slide 3, insert a table with the following information:

Power Sources	Percent Used by City
Natural gas	32%
Hydroelectric	17%
Renewables	18%
Coal	23%
Nuclear	10%

On Slide 4, insert and format an appropriate chart to demonstrate the revenue collected from residential power sales over the past three years. Revenue in 2014 was 35.5 million dollars, in 2015 revenue was 42.6 million dollars, and in 2016 revenue was 48.2 million dollars. Apply appropriate animation and and insert an appropriate header and footer. Add your name, your course name and section number, and the tags **power sources, revenue** to the Properties. Save and then print or submit the presentation as directed by your instructor.

(Project 3K Power continues on the next page)

CONTENT-BASED ASSESSMENTS

GO! Solve It | Project 3K Power (continued)

Performance Level

Performance Elements	Exemplary	Proficient	Developing
	You consistently applied the relevant skills	You sometimes, but not always, applied the relevant skills.	You rarely or never applied the relevant skills.
Format two slide backgrounds with pictures and styles	Two slide backgrounds were formatted attractively and text displayed with good contrast against backgrounds.	Slide backgrounds were formatted but text did not display well, or only one slide background was formatted.	Slide backgrounds were not formatted with pictures or styles.
Insert and format appropriate table and chart	Appropriate table and chart were inserted and formatted and the entered data was accurate.	A table and a chart were inserted but were not appropriate for the presentation or either a table or a chart was omitted.	Table and chart were not inserted.
Apply appropriate animation	Appropriate animation was applied to the presentation.	Animation was applied but was not appropriate for the presentation.	Animation was not applied.

END | You have completed Project 3K

OUTCOMES-BASED ASSESSMENTS

RUBRIC

The following outcomes-based assessments are open-ended assessments. That is, there is no specific correct result; your result will depend on your approach to the information provided. Make Professional Quality your goal. Use the following scoring rubric to guide you in how to approach the problem and then to evaluate how well your approach solves the problem.

The *criteria*—Software Mastery, Content, Format and Layout, and Process—represent the knowledge and skills you have gained that you can apply to solving the problem. The *levels of performance*—Professional Quality, Approaching Professional Quality, or Needs Quality Improvements—help you and your instructor evaluate your result.

	Your completed project is of Professional Quality if you:	Your completed project is Approaching Professional Quality if you:	Your completed project Needs Quality Improvements if you:
1-Software Mastery	Choose and apply the most appropriate skills, tools, and features and identify efficient methods to solve the problem.	Choose and apply some appropriate skills, tools, and features, but not in the most efficient manner.	Choose inappropriate skills, tools, or features, or are inefficient in solving the problem.
2-Content	Construct a solution that is clear and well organized, contains content that is accurate, appropriate to the audience and purpose, and is complete. Provide a solution that contains no errors in spelling, grammar, or style.	Construct a solution in which some components are unclear, poorly organized, inconsistent, or incomplete. Misjudge the needs of the audience. Have some errors in spelling, grammar, or style, but the errors do not detract from comprehension.	Construct a solution that is unclear, incomplete, or poorly organized; contains some inaccurate or inappropriate content; and contains many errors in spelling, grammar, or style. Do not solve the problem.
3-Format & Layout	Format and arrange all elements to communicate information and ideas, clarify function, illustrate relationships, and indicate relative importance.	Apply appropriate format and layout features to some elements, but not others. Overuse features, causing minor distraction.	Apply format and layout that does not communicate information or ideas clearly. Do not use format and layout features to clarify function, illustrate relationships, or indicate relative importance. Use available features excessively, causing distraction.
4-Process	Use an organized approach that integrates planning, development, self-assessment, revision, and reflection.	Demonstrate an organized approach in some areas, but not others; or, use an insufficient process of organization throughout.	Do not use an organized approach to solve the problem.

OUTCOMES-BASED ASSESSMENTS

Apply a combination of the 3A and 3B skills.

GO! Think Project 3L Animal Sanctuary

Build from Scratch

PROJECT FILES

For Project 3L, you will need the following file:

New blank PowerPoint presentation

You will save your presentation as:

Lastname_Firstname_3L_Animal_Sanctuary

The Pacifica Bay Animal Sanctuary, a non-profit organization, provides shelter and care for animals in need, including dogs, cats, hamsters, and guinea pigs. The Sanctuary, which celebrates its tenth anniversary in July, has cared for more than 12,000 animals since it opened and is a state-of-the-art facility. Funding for the Sanctuary comes in the form of business sponsorships, individual donations, and pet adoption fees. The following table indicates revenue generated by the Sanctuary during the past three years.

	Fees	Donations	Sponsorships
2014	125,085	215,380	175,684
2015	110,680	256,785	156,842
2016	132,455	314,682	212,648

In addition to shelter services, the Sanctuary offers community service and training programs, veterinarian services, and vaccine clinics. Examples of these services include Canine Obedience classes, microchipping ($25 fee), and the Healthy Pet Hotline (free). Canine Obedience classes are for puppies and adult dogs to improve obedience, socialization, and behavior. Classes last two, three, or four months and cost $150 to $250.

Using the preceding information, create the first five slides of a presentation that the director of the Pacifica Bay Animal Sanctuary will show at an upcoming pet fair. Apply an appropriate theme and use slide layouts that will effectively present the content. Include a line chart with the revenue data, a table with the community service programs information, and at least one slide formatted with a dog or cat on the slide background. Apply styles to the table and chart, and apply animation and slide transitions to the slides. Use the techniques that you practiced in this chapter so that your presentation is professional and attractive. Save the file as **Lastname_Firstname_3L_Animal_Sanctuary** and then insert a header and footer that includes the date and time updated automatically, the file name in the footer, and the page number. Add your name, your course name and section number, and the keywords **animals, pets** to the properties. Save and then print or submit the presentation as directed by your instructor.

END | You have completed Project 3L

Build from Scratch

GO! Think Project 3M Water Sources — Online

Build from Scratch

You and GO! Project 3N Recreation Programs — Online

Build from Scratch

GO! Cumulative Group Project Project 3O Bell Orchid Hotels — Online

Glossary

.jpg An image file format, commonly pronounced *JPEG*, that stands for Joint Photographic Experts Group; this is a common file type used by digital cameras and computers to store digital pictures; JPEG is popular because it can store a high-quality picture in a relatively small file.

.png An image file format, commonly pronounced *PING*, that stands for Portable Network Graphic; this is an image file type that can be transferred over the Internet.

3-D The shortened term for *three-dimensional*, which refers to an image that appears to have all three spatial dimensions—length, width, and depth.

Absolute cell reference A cell reference that refers to cells by their fixed position in a worksheet; an absolute cell reference remains the same when the formula is copied.

Accounting Number Format The Excel number format that applies a thousand comma separator where appropriate, inserts a fixed U.S. dollar sign aligned at the left edge of the cell, applies two decimal places, and leaves a small amount of space at the right edge of the cell to accommodate a parenthesis for negative numbers.

Action Center Located in the notification area, a central place to view alerts and take actions related to things that need your attention.

Active cell The cell, surrounded by a black border, ready to receive data or be affected by the next Excel command.

Address bar (Internet Explorer) The area at the top of the Internet Explorer window that displays, and where you can type, a URL—Uniform Resource Locator—which is an address that uniquely identifies a location on the Internet.

Address bar (Windows File Explorer) The bar at the top of a folder window with which you can navigate to a different folder or library, or go back to a previous one; displays your current location in the folder structure as a series of links separated by arrows.

Administrator account A user account that lets you make changes that will affect other users of the computer; the most powerful of the three types of accounts because it permits the most control over the computer.

After Previous An animation option that begins the animation sequence for the selected slide element immediately after the completion of the previous animation or slide transition.

Aggregate functions Calculations such as Min, Max, Avg, and Sum that are performed on a group of records.

Alignment The placement of text or objects relative to the left and right margins.

Alignment guides Green vertical or horizontal lines that display when you are moving or sizing an object to assist you with object placement.

American Psychological Association (APA) One of two commonly used style guides for formatting research papers.

AND condition A compound criteria used to display records that match all parts of the specified criteria.

AND condition A condition in which records display only where all of the values are present in the selected fields.

Animation A visual or sound effect added to an object or text on a slide.

Animation Painter A feature that copies animation settings from one object to another.

App The term that commonly refers to computer programs that run from the device software on a smartphone or a tablet computer—for example, iOS, Android, or Windows Phone—or computer programs that run from the browser software on a desktop PC or laptop PC—for example Internet Explorer, Safari, Firefox, or Chrome. App is the shortened version of the word *application*.

App bar An area at the bottom of every Windows Store app containing various controls pertaining to the app.

App for Office A webpage that works within one of the Office applications, such as Excel, and that you download from the Office Store.

App switcher The thumbnail view of open apps that displays when you move your mouse down from the Back tip in the upper left corner; to switch to an app that is still open, you can click any of the thumbnails.

Append To add on to the end of an object; for example, to add records to the end of an existing table.

Application A set of instructions that a computer uses to accomplish a task; also called a program.

Apps for Office 2013 and SharePoint 2013 A collection of downloadable apps that enable you to create and view information within your familiar Office programs.

Arguments The values that an Excel function uses to perform calculations or operations.

Arithmetic operators The symbols +, −, *, /, %, and ^ used to denote addition, subtraction (or negation), multiplication, division, percentage, and exponentiation in an Excel formula.

Artistic effects Formats applied to images that make pictures resemble sketches or paintings.

Ascending order A sorting order that arranges text alphabetically (A to Z) and numbers from the lowest number to the highest number.

Aspect ratio The ratio of the width of a display to the height of the display.

Auto Fill An Excel feature that generates and extends values into adjacent cells based on the values of selected cells.

AutoCalculate A feature that displays three calculations in the status bar by default—Average, Count, and Sum—when you select a range of numerical data.

AutoComplete A feature that speeds your typing and lessens the likelihood of errors; if the first few characters you type in a cell match an existing entry in the column, Excel fills in the remaining characters for you.

AutoCorrect A feature that corrects common typing and spelling errors as you type, for example changing *teh* to *the*.

AutoFit An Excel feature that adjusts the width of a column to fit the cell content of the widest cell in the column.

AutoNumber data type A data type that describes a unique sequential or random number assigned by Access as each record is entered and that is useful for data that has no distinct field that can be considered unique.

AutoSum A button that provided quick access to the SUM function.

AVERAGE function An Excel function that adds a group of values, and then divides the result by the number of values in the group.

Axis A line that serves as a frame of reference for measurement and which borders the chart plot area.

Back tip The upper left corner of the screen that when pointed to displays a thumbnail image of the last screen you were on; you can use it to *go back* to your previous screen.

Background Removal A feature that removes unwanted portions of a picture so that the picture does not appear as a self-contained rectangle.

Background style A predefined slide background fill variation that combines theme colors in different intensities or patterns.

Backstage tabs The area along the left side of Backstage view with tabs to display screens with related groups of commands.

Backstage view A centralized space for file management tasks; for example, opening, saving, printing, publishing, or sharing a file. A navigation pane displays along the left side with tabs that group file-related tasks together.

Badge An icon that displays on the Lock screen, below the time, day, and date, that represents the status of your Internet connection, your battery if you are using a tablet or laptop, or any other Lock screen apps you might have selected.

Base The starting point when you divide the amount of increase by it to calculate the rate of increase.

Best Fit An Access command that adjusts the width of a column to accommodate the column's longest entry.

Between ... And operator A comparison operator that looks for values within a range.

Bevel A shape effect that uses shading and shadows to make the edges of a shape appear to be curved or angled.

Bibliography A list of cited works in a report or research paper; also referred to as Works Cited, Sources, or References, depending upon the report style.

Black slide A slide that displays after the last slide in a presentation indicating that the presentation is over.

Blank desktop database A database that has no data and has no database tools—you must create the data and tools as you need them; the database is stored on your computer or other storage device.

Body The text of a letter.

Body font A font that is applied to all slide text except slide titles.

Booting the computer The process of turning on a computer when the computer has been completely shut down.

Bound control A control that retrieves its data from an underlying table or query; a text box control is an example of a bound control.

Bound A term used to describe objects and controls that are based on data that is stored in tables.

Brightness The relative lightness of a picture.

Bulleted list A list of items with each item introduced by a symbol such as a small circle or check mark, and which is useful when the items in the list can be displayed in any order.

Bullets Text symbols such as small circles or check marks that precede each item in a bulleted list.

Calculated control A control that contains an expression, often a formula or function, that most often summarizes a field that contains numerical data.

Calculated field A field that stores the value of a mathematical operation.

Caption A property setting that displays a name for a field in a table, query, form, or report other than that listed as the field name.

Cascade Delete Related Records A cascade option that enables you to delete a record in a table on the *one* side of the relationship and also delete all of the related records in related tables.

Cascade options Relationship options that enable you to update records in related tables when referential integrity is enforced.

Cascade Update Related Fields A cascade option that enables you to change the data in the primary key field in the table on the *one* side of the relationship and update that change to any fields storing that same data in related tables.

Category axis The area along the bottom of a chart that identifies the categories of data; also referred to as the x-axis.

Category labels The labels that display along the bottom of a chart to identify the categories of data; Excel uses the row titles as the category names.

Cell The intersection of a column and a row.

Cell address Another name for a cell reference.

Cell content Anything typed into a cell.

Cell reference The identification of a specific cell by its intersecting column letter and row number.

Cell style A defined set of formatting characteristics, such as font, font size, font color, cell borders, and cell shading.

Center alignment The alignment of text or objects that is centered horizontally between the left and right margins.

Charms A set of buttons that display when you point or swipe in from the right side of the screen that you can use in every app—whether a Windows Store app or a desktop app—and that enable you to search, share, access devices, or adjust your PC settings.

Chart The graphic representation of data in a worksheet; data presented as a chart is usually easier to understand than a table of numbers.

Chart area The entire chart and all of its elements.

Chart elements The various components of a chart, including the chart title, axis titles, data series, legend, chart area, and plot area.

Chart Elements button A button that enables you to add, remove, or change chart elements such as the title, legend, gridlines, and data labels.

Chart Filters button A button that displays options for changing the data displayed in a chart.

Chart layout The combination of chart elements that can be displayed in a chart such as a title, legend, labels for the columns, and the table of charted cells.

Chart sheet A workbook sheet that contains only a chart.

Chart style The overall visual look of a chart in terms of its graphic effects, colors, and backgrounds; for example, you can have flat or beveled columns, colors that are solid or transparent, and backgrounds that are dark or light.

Chart Styles button A button that displays options for setting the style and color scheme for a chart.

Chart Styles gallery A group of predesigned chart styles that you can apply to an Excel chart.

Chart types Various chart formats used in a way that is meaningful to the reader; common examples are column charts, pie charts, and line charts.

Citation A note inserted into the text of a research paper that refers the reader to a source in the bibliography.

Click The action of pressing and releasing the left button on a mouse pointing device one time.

Clip A single media file such as art, sound, animation, or a movie.

Clip art Downloadable predefined graphics available online from Office.com and other sites.

Clipboard A temporary storage area that holds text or graphics that you select and then cut or copy.

Clipboard A temporary storage area for information that you have copied or moved from one place and plan to use somewhere else.

Cloud computing Refers to applications and services that are accessed over the Internet, rather than to applications that are installed on your local computer.

Cloud storage Online storage of data so that you can access your data from different places and devices.

Collaborate To work with others as a team in an intellectual endeavor to complete a shared task or to achieve a shared goal.

Collaboration The action of working together with others as a team in an intellectual endeavor to complete a shared task or achieve a shared goal.

Column A vertical group of cells in a worksheet.

Column break indicator A dotted line containing the words *Column Break* that displays at the bottom of the column.

Column chart A chart in which the data is arranged in columns and which is useful for showing data changes over a period of time or for illustrating comparisons among items.

Column heading The letter that displays at the top of a vertical group of cells in a worksheet; beginning with the first letter of the alphabet, a unique letter or combination of letters identifies each column.

Comma Style The Excel number format that inserts thousand comma separators where appropriate and applies two decimal places; Comma Style also leaves space at the right to accommodate a parenthesis when negative numbers are present.

Commands An instruction to a computer program that causes an action to be carried out.

Common dialog boxes The set of dialog boxes that includes Open, Save, and Save As, which are provided by the Windows programming interface, and which display and operate in all of the Office programs in the same manner.

Common field A field in two or more tables that stores the same data.

Comparison operators Symbols that are used to evaluate data in the field to determine whether it is the same (=), greater than (>), less than (<), or in between a range of values as specified by the criteria.

Complimentary closing A parting farewell in a business letter.

Compound criteria Multiple conditions in a query or filter.

Compressed file A file that has been reduced in size and that takes up less storage space and can be transferred to other computers faster than uncompressed files.

Compressed folder A folder that has been reduced in size and thus takes up less storage space and can be transferred to other computers quickly; also called a *zipped* folder.

Conditional format A format that changes the appearance of a cell—for example, by adding cell shading or font color—based on a condition; if the condition is true, the cell is formatted based on that condition, and if the condition is false, the cell is *not* formatted.

Constant value Numbers, text, dates, or times of day that you type into a cell.

Content control In a template, an area indicated by placeholder text that can be used to add text, pictures, dates, or lists.

Context menus Menus that display commands and options relevant to the selected text or object; also called *shortcut menus.*

Context sensitive A command associated with the currently selected or active object; often activated by right-clicking a screen item.

Context-sensitive commands Commands that display on a shortcut menu that relate to the object or text that you right-clicked.

Contextual tabs Tabs that are added to the ribbon automatically when a specific object, such as a picture, is selected, and that contain commands relevant to the selected object.

Contiguous slides Slides that are adjacent to each other in a presentation.

Contrast The difference between the darkest and lightest area of a picture.

Control An object on a form or report that displays data or text, performs actions, and lets you view and work with information.

Control layout The grouped arrangement of controls on a form or report; for example, the Stacked layout.

Copy A command that duplicates a selection and places it on the Clipboard.

COUNTIF function A statistical function that counts the number of cells within a range that meet the given condition and that has two arguments—the range of cells to check and the criteria.

Cover letter A document that you send with your resume to provide additional information about your skills and experience.

Criteria (Access) Conditions in a query that identify the specific records you are looking for.

Criteria (Excel) Conditions that you specify in a logical function.

Crop A command that removes unwanted or unnecessary areas of a picture.

Crop handles Handles used to remove unwanted areas of a picture.

Crop pointer The pointer used to crop areas of a picture.

Crosshair pointer The pointer used to draw a shape.

Crosstab query A query that uses an aggregate function for data that can be grouped by two types of information and displays the data in a compact, spreadsheet-like format with column headings and row headings.

Currency data type An Access data type that describes monetary values and numeric data that can be used in mathematical calculations involving values with one to four decimal places.

Custom web app A database that you can publish and share with others over the Internet.

Cut A command that removes a selection and places it on the Clipboard.

Dashboard A descriptive term for the Windows 8 Start screen that provides a one-screen view of links to information and programs that matter most to the signed-in user.

Data Facts about people, events, things, or ideas.

Data bar A cell format consisting of a shaded bar that provides a visual cue to the reader about the value of a cell relative to other cells; the length of the bar represents the value in the cell—a longer bar represents a higher value and a shorter bar represents s lower value.

Data entry The action of entering the data into a record in a database table or form.

Data management The process of managing your files and folders in an organized manner so that you can find information when you need it.

Data marker A column, bar, area, dot, pie slice, or other symbol in a chart that represents a single data point; related data points form a data series.

Data point A value that originates in a worksheet cell and that is represented in a chart by a data marker.

Data series Related data points represented by data markers; each data series has a unique color or pattern represented in the chart legend.

Data source (Access) The table or tables from which a form, query, or report retrieves its data.

Data source (Word) A document that contains a list of variable information, such as names and addresses, that is merged with a main document to create customized form letters or labels.

Data type The characteristic that defines the kind of data that can be stored in a field, such as numbers, text, or dates.

Data (Excel) Text or numbers in a cell.

Data (Windows) All the files—documents, workbooks, pictures, songs, and so on—that you create and store during the day-to-day use of your computer.

Database An organized collection of facts about people, events, things, or ideas related to a specific topic or purpose.

Database management system (DBMS) Database software that controls how related collections of data are stored, organized, retrieved, and secured; also known as a DBMS.

Database template A preformatted database that contains prebuilt tables, queries, forms, and reports that perform a specific task, such as tracking events.

Datasheet view The Access view that displays data organized in columns and rows similar to an Excel worksheet.

Date & Time A command with which you can automatically insert the current date and time into a document in a variety of formats.

Date control A control on a form or report that inserts the current date each time the form or report is opened.

Dateline The first line in a business letter that contains the current date and which is positioned just below the letterhead if a letterhead is used.

DBMS An acronym for database management system.

Default The term that refers to the current selection or setting that is automatically used by a computer program unless you specify otherwise.

Descending order A sorting order that arranges text in reverse alphabetical order (Z to A) and numbers from the highest number to the lowest number.

Deselect The action of canceling the selection of an object or block of text by clicking outside of the selection.

Design grid The lower area of the query window that displays the design of the query.

Design view An Access view that displays the detailed structure of a table, query, form, or report. For forms and reports, may be the view in which some tasks must be performed, and only the controls, and not the data, display in this view.

Desktop The area in Windows 8 where you use desktop apps and that serves as a surface for your work, like the top of an actual desk.

Desktop app The term that commonly refers to a computer program that is installed on your computer and requires a computer operating system like Microsoft Windows or Apple OS to run.

Desktop background Displays the colors and graphics of your desktop; you can change the desktop background to look the way you want it.

Desktop shortcuts Desktop icons that link to any item accessible on your computer or on a network, such as a program, file, folder, disk drive, printer, or another computer.

Destination table The table to which you import or append data.

Detail section The section of a form or report that displays the records from the underlying table or query.

Detail sheets The worksheets that contain the details of the information summarized on a summary sheet.

Details pane Displays the most common properties associated with the selected file.

Details view The file list view in File Explorer that displays a list of files or folders and their most common properties.

Dialog box A small window that displays options for completing a task.

Dialog Box Launcher A small icon that displays to the right of some group names on the ribbon, and which opens a related dialog box or pane providing additional options and commands related to that group.

Displayed value The data that displays in a cell.

Document properties Details about a file that describe or identify it, including the title, author name, subject, and keywords that identify the document's topic or contents; also known as *metadata*.

Dot leader A series of dots preceding a tab that guides the eye across the line.

Double-click The action of pressing the left mouse button twice in rapid succession while holding the mouse still.

Drag The action of moving something from one location on the screen to another while holding down the left mouse button; the action of dragging includes releasing the mouse button at the desired time or location.

Drag and drop The action of moving a selection by dragging it to a new location.

Drawing objects Graphic objects, such as shapes, diagrams, lines, or circles.

Drive An area of storage that is formatted with a file system compatible with your operating system and is identified by a drive letter.

Edit The process of making changes to text or graphics in an Office file.

Editing (PowerPoint) The process of modifying a presentation by adding and deleting slides or by changing the contents of individual slides.

Ellipsis A set of three dots indicating incompleteness; an ellipsis following a command name indicates that a dialog box will display if you click the command.

Em dash A punctuation symbol used to indicate an explanation or emphasis.

Embed code A code that creates a link to a video, picture, or other type of rich media content.

Emphasis effect Animation that emphasizes an object or text that is already displayed.

Enclosures Additional documents included with a business letter.

Endnote In a research paper, a note placed at the end of a document or chapter.

Enhanced ScreenTip A ScreenTip that displays more descriptive text than a normal ScreenTip.

Enterprise fund A municipal government fund that reports income and expenditures related to municipal services for which a fee is charged in exchange for goods or services.

Entrance effect Animation that brings a slide element onto the screen.

Excel pointer An Excel window element with which you can display the location of the pointer.

Excel table A series of rows and columns that contains related data that is managed independently from the data in other rows and columns in the worksheet.

Exit effect Animation that moves an object or text off the screen.

Expand Formula Bar button An Excel window element with which you can Increase the height of the Formula Bar to display lengthy cell content.

Expand horizontal scroll bar button An Excel window element with which you can increase the width of the horizontal scroll bar.

Explode The action of pulling out one or more pie slices from a pie chart for emphasis.

Export The process of copying data from one file into another file, such as an Access table into an Excel spreadsheet.

Expression A formula.

Extract The action of decompressing—pulling out—files from a compressed form.

Eyedropper A tool that captures the exact color from an object on your screen and then applies it to any shape, picture, or text.

Field (Access) A single piece of information that is stored in every record; represented by a column in a database table.

Field list A list of field names in a table.

Field properties Characteristics of a field that control how the field displays and how data can be entered in the field.

Fields (Word) In a mail merge, the column headings in the data source.

File A collection of information that is stored on a computer under a single name, for example a text document, a picture, or a program.

File Explorer The program within Windows 8 that displays the contents of libraries, folders, and files on your computer, and which also enables you to perform tasks related to your files and folders such as copying, moving, and renaming. File Explorer is at work anytime you are viewing the contents of a library, a folder, or a file.

File list Displays the contents of the current folder or library; if you type text into the Search box, only the folders and files that match your search will display here—including files in subfolders.

File properties Information about a file such as its author, the date the file was last changed, and any descriptive tags.

Fill color The inside color of text or of an object.

Fill handle The small black square in the lower right corner of a selected cell.

Fill The inside color of an object.

Filter The process of displaying only a portion of the data based on matching a specific value to show only the data that meets the criteria that you specify.

Filter by Form An Access command that filters the records in a form based on one or more fields, or based on more than one value in the field.

Filter by Selection An Access command that displays only the records that contain the value in the selected field and hides the records that do not contain the value.

Filtering The process of displaying only a portion of the total records (a subset) based on matching specific values to provide a quick answer to a question.

Find and replace A command that searches the cells in a worksheet—or in a selected range—for matches and then replaces each match with a replacement value of your choice.

First principle of good database design A principle of good database design stating that data is organized in tables so that there is no redundant data.

Flash Fill Recognizes a pattern in your data, and then automatically fills in values when you enter examples of the output that you want. Use it to split data from two or more cells or to combine data from two cells.

Flat database A simple database file that is not related or linked to any other collection of data.

Flip A command that creates a reverse image of a picture or object.

Floating object A graphic that can be moved independently of the surrounding text characters.

Folder A container in which you store files.

Folder structure The hierarchy of folders in Windows 8.

Folder window In Windows, a window that displays the contents of the current folder, library, or device, and contains helpful parts so that you can navigate the Windows file structure.

Font A set of characters with the same design and shape.

Font styles Formatting emphasis such as bold, italic, and underline.

Footer Text that displays at the bottom of every slide or that prints at the bottom of a sheet of slide handouts or notes pages.

Footnote In a research paper, a note placed at the bottom of the page.

Foreign key The field that is included in the related table so the field can be joined with the primary key in another table for the purpose of creating a relationship.

Form An Access object you can use to enter new records into a table, edit or delete existing records in a table, or display existing records.

Form Footer Information at the bottom of the screen in Form view or Layout view that is printed after the last detail section on the last page of a printout.

Form Header Information such as a form's title that displays at the top of the screen in Form view or Layout view and is printed at the top of the first page when records are printed as forms.

Form tool An Access tool that creates a form with a single mouse click, which includes all of the fields from the underlying data source (table or query).

Form view The Access view in which you can view, modify, delete, or add to the records in a table; but you cannot change the layout or design of the form.

Form Wizard An Access tool that walks you step by step through the creation of a form and that gives you more flexibility in the design, layout, and number of fields in a form.

Format Changing the appearance of cells and worksheet elements to make a worksheet attractive and easy to read.

Formatting The process of establishing the overall appearance of text, graphics, and pages in an Office file—for example, in a Word document.

Formatting marks Characters that display on the screen, but do not print, indicating where the Enter key, the Spacebar, and the Tab key were pressed; also called *nonprinting characters.*

Formula An equation that performs mathematical calculations on values in a worksheet.

Formula AutoComplete An Excel feature that, after typing an = (equal sign) and the beginning letter or letters of a function name, displays a list of function names that match the typed letter(s), and from which you can insert the function by pointing to its name and pressing the Tab key or double-clicking.

Formula Bar An element in the Excel window that displays the value or formula contained in the active cell; here you can also enter or edit values or formulas.

Free/Busy information In the Outlook calendar, one of four indicators—Busy, Free, Tentative, or Out of Office—associated with your availability for a specific date and time.

Free-form snip When using Snipping Tool, the type of snip that lets you draw an irregular line, such as a circle, around an area of the screen.

Freeze Panes A command that enables you to select one or more rows or columns and freeze (lock) them into place; the locked rows and columns become separate panes.

Full-screen snip When using Snipping Tool, the type of snip that captures the entire screen.

Function A predefined formula—a formula that Excel has already built for you—that performs calculations by using specific values in a particular order or structure.

Fund A sum of money set aside for a specific purpose.

Gallery An Office feature that displays a list of potential results instead of just the command name.

General format The default format that Excel applies to numbers; this format has no specific characteristics—whatever you type in the cell will display, with the exception that trailing zeros to the right of a decimal point will not display.

General fund The term used to describe money set aside for the normal operating activities of a government entity such as a city.

Goal Seek A what-if analysis tool that finds the input needed in one cell to arrive at the desired result in another cell.

Gradient fill A fill effect in which one color fades into another.

Graphical user interface The system by which you interact with your computer and which uses graphics such as an image of a file folder or wastebasket that you click to activate the item represented.

Graphics Pictures, charts, or drawing objects.

Group Footer Information printed at the end of each group of records; used to display summary information for the group.

Group Header Information printed at the beginning of each new group of records; for example, the group name.

Group, Sort, and Total pane A pane that displays at the bottom of the screen in which you can control how information is sorted and grouped in a report; provides the most flexibility for adding or modifying groups, sort orders, or totals options on a report.

Groups On the Office ribbon, the sets of related commands that you might need for a specific type of task.

GUI The acronym for a graphical user interface, pronounced *GOO-ee*.

Hanging indent An indent style in which the first line of a paragraph extends to the left of the remaining lines and that is commonly used for bibliographic entries.

Hard disk drive The primary storage device located inside your computer and where most of your files and programs are typically stored; usually labeled as drive C.

Header Text that prints at the top of each sheet of slide handouts or notes pages.

Headings font A font that is applied to all slide title text.

Hierarchy An arrangement where items are ranked and where each level is lower in rank than the item above it.

Icons Small images that represent commands, files, applications, or other windows.

IF function A function that uses a logical test to check whether a condition is met, and then returns one value if true, and another value if false.

Immersive The term that describes the Windows 8 style screens, meaning they have no borders, no menus, and they behave differently from traditional Windows desktop programs because there is no taskbar, an app cannot be minimized like a desktop program, nor can an app be dragged around as a smaller window; the idea is that you are immersed in the app with no screen distractions.

Import The process of copying data from another file, such as a Word table or an Excel workbook, into a separate file, such as an Access database.

Info tab The tab in Backstage view that displays information about the current file.

Information Data that is organized in a useful manner.

Inline Object An object or graphic inserted in a document that acts like a character in a sentence.

Innermost sort field When sorting on multiple fields in Datasheet view, the field that will be used for the second level of sorting.

Insertion point A blinking vertical line that indicates where text or graphics will be inserted.

Inside address The name and address of the person receiving the letter and positioned below the date line.

Interactive media Computer interaction that responds to your actions; for example by presenting text, graphics, animation, video, audio, or games. Also referred to as rich media.

Internet Explorer The web browser program developed by Microsoft that is included with Windows 8.

Is Not Null A criteria that searches for fields that are not empty.

Is Null A criteria that searches for fields that are empty.

Join line In the Relationships window, the line joining two tables that visually indicates the common fields and the type of relationship.

JPEG An acronym for Joint Photographic Experts Group, and which is a common file type used by digital cameras and computers to store digital pictures; JPEG is popular because it can store a high-quality picture in a relatively small file. A JPEG file has a .jpg file extension.

Jump List A list that displays when you right-click a button on the taskbar, and which displays locations (in the upper portion) and tasks (in the lower portion) from a program's taskbar button.

Justified alignment An arrangement of text in which the text aligns evenly on both the left and right margins.

Keyboard shortcut A combination of two or more keyboard keys, used to perform a task that would otherwise require a mouse.

KeyTip The letter that displays on a command in the ribbon and that indicates the key you can press to activate the command when keyboard control of the ribbon is activated.

Keywords Custom file properties in the form of words that you associate with a document to give an indication of the document's content; used to help find and organize files. Also called *tags*.

Label Another name for a text value, and which usually provides information about number values.

Label control A control on a form or report that contains descriptive information, usually a field name or title.

Landscape orientation A page orientation in which the paper is wider than it is tall.

Layout The arrangement of elements, such as title and subtitle text, lists, pictures, tables, charts, shapes, and movies, on a slide.

Layout Options Picture formatting options that control the manner in which text wraps around a picture or other object.

Layout Options button A button that displays when an object is selected and that has commands to choose how the object interacts with surrounding text.

Layout selector A small symbol that displays in the upper left corner of a selected control layout in a form or report that is displayed in Layout view or Design view; used to move or format an entire group of controls.

Layout view The Access view in which you can make changes to a form or report while the object is running—the data from the underlying data source displays.

Leader character Characters that form a solid, dotted, or dashed line that fills the space preceding a tab stop.

Left alignment The cell format in which characters align at the left edge of the cell; this is the default for text entries and is an example of formatting information stored in a cell.

Legend A chart element that identifies the patterns or colors that are assigned to the categories in the chart.

Lettered column headings The area along the top edge of a worksheet that identifies each column with a unique letter or combination of letters.

Letterhead The personal or company information that displays at the top of a letter.

Library A collection of items, such as files and folders, assembled from various locations.

Line break indicator A non-printing character in the shape of a bent arrow that indicates a manual line break.

Line chart A chart type that displays trends over time; time displays along the bottom axis and the data point values are connected with a line.

Line spacing The distance between lines of text in a paragraph.

Link A connection to data in another file.

List level An outline level in a presentation represented by a bullet symbol and identified in a slide by the indentation and the size of the text.

Live Layout A feature that reflows text as you move or size an object so that you can view the placement of surrounding text.

Live Preview A technology that shows the result of applying an editing or formatting change as you point to possible results—*before* you actually apply it.

Live tiles Tiles on the Windows 8 Start screen that are constantly updated with fresh information relevant to the signed-in user; for example, the number of new email messages, new sports scores of interest, or new updates to social networks such as Facebook or Twitter.

Local account A user account in which the information associated with each user is local to a single Windows 8 computer.

Location Any disk drive, folder, or other place in which you can store files and folders.

Lock screen The first screen that displays after turning on a Windows 8 device, which displays the time, day, and date, and one or more icons representing the status of the device's Internet connection, battery status on a tablet or laptop, and any Lock screen apps that are installed such as email notifications.

Lock screen apps Apps that display on a Windows 8 Lock screen and that show quick status and notifications, even if the screen is locked, and include Calendar, Mail, Messaging, and Weather.

Logical functions A group of functions that test for specific conditions and that typically use conditional tests to determine whether specified conditions are true or false.

Logical operators Operators that are used to evaluate data to determine if a condition is met (true) or not met (false). With two criteria, AND requires that both conditions be met and OR requires that either condition be met for a record to display in the query results.

Logical test Any value or expression that can be evaluated as being true or false.

Mail merge A feature that joins a main document and a data source to create customized letters or labels.

Main document In a mail merge, the document that contains the text or formatting that remains constant.

Major unit The value in a chart's value axis that determines the spacing between tick marks and between the gridlines in the plot area.

Manual column break An artificial end to a column to balance columns or to provide space for the insertion of other objects.

Manual line break A break that moves text to the right of the insertion point to a new line while keeping the text in the same paragraph.

Manual page break The action of forcing a page to end and placing subsequent text at the top of the next page.

Margins The space between the text and the top, bottom, left, and right edges of the paper.

MAX function An Excel function that determines the largest value in a selected range of values.

MEDIAN function An Excel function that finds the middle value that has as many values above it in the group as are below it; it differs from AVERAGE in that the result is not affected as much by a single value that is greatly different from the others.

Menu bar A group of menus.

Menu A list of commands within a category.

Merge & Center A command that joins selected cells in an Excel worksheet into one larger cell and centers the contents in the merged cell.

Message Bar The area directly below the ribbon that displays information such as security alerts when there is potentially unsafe, active content in an Office document that you open.

Metadata Details about a file that describe or identify it, including the title, author name, subject, and keywords that identify the document's topic or contents; also known as *document properties*.

Microsoft account A user account that allows you to set up one Windows 8 computer and then synchronize all the same settings from that computer to any other device you have that uses Windows 8.

Microsoft Design Language The design principles in Windows 8 that include tiles with white text on deeply colored backgrounds, consistent fonts, simpler navigation, and the use of the entire screen; the idea is that you are immersed in the app with no screen distractions.

Microsoft Office 365 A set of secure online services that enable people in an organization to communicate and collaborate by using any Internet-connected device—a computer, a tablet, or a mobile phone.

MIN function An Excel function that determines the smallest value in a selected range of values.

Mini toolbar A small toolbar containing frequently used formatting commands that displays as a result of selecting text or objects.

Modern Language Association (MLA) One of two commonly used style guides for formatting research papers.

Mouse pointer Any symbol that displays on your screen in response to moving your mouse.

MRU Acronym for *most recently used*, which refers to the state of some commands that retain the characteristic most recently applied; for example, the Font Color button retains the most recently used color until a new color is chosen.

Multiple-items form A form that enables you to display or enter multiple records in a table.

Name Box An element of the Excel window that displays the name of the selected cell, table, chart, or object.

Nameplate The banner on the front page of a newsletter that identifies the publication.

Navigate The process of exploring within the organizing structure of Windows.

Navigate (File Explorer): Explore within the file organizing structure of Windows 8.

Navigation area An area at the bottom of the Access window that indicates the number of records in the table and contains controls in the form of arrows that you click to navigate among the records.

Navigation pane In a folder window, the area on the left in which you can navigate to, open, and display favorites, libraries, folders, saved searches, and an expandable list of drives.

Newsletter A periodical that communicates news and information to a specific group.

No Paragraph Style The built-in paragraph style—available from the Paragraph Spacing command—that inserts *no* extra space before or after a paragraph and uses line spacing of 1.

Noncontiguous slides Slides that are not adjacent to each other in a presentation.

Nonprinting characters Characters that display on the screen, but do not print, indicating where the Enter key, the Spacebar, and the Tab key were pressed; also called *formatting marks*.

Normal template The template that serves as a basis for all Word documents.

Normal view A screen view that maximizes the number of cells visible on your screen and keeps the column letters and row numbers close to the columns and rows.

Normalization The process of applying design rules and principles to ensure that your database performs as expected.

Note In a research paper, information that expands on the topic, but that does not fit well in the document text.

Notes page A printout that contains the slide image on the top half of the page and notes that you have created on the Notes pane in the lower half of the page.

Notes pane An area of the Normal view window that displays below the Slide pane with space to type notes regarding the active slide.

Notification area Displays notification icons and the system clock; sometimes referred to as the *system tray*.

Notification bar In Internet Explorer 10, a bar at the bottom of your screen that displays information about pending downloads, security issues, add-ons, and other issues related to the operation of your computer.

NOW function An Excel function that retrieves the date and time from your computer's calendar and clock and inserts the information into the selected cell.

Number data type An Access data type that describes numbers that might be used in calculations.

Number format A specific way in which Excel displays numbers in a cell.

Number values Constant values consisting of only numbers.

Numbered list A list that uses consecutive numbers or letters to introduce each item in a list.

Numbered row headings The area along the left edge of a worksheet that identifies each row with a unique number.

Object A text box, picture, table, or shape that you can select and then move and resize.

Object anchor The symbol that indicates to which paragraph an object is attached.

Object tab In the object window, a tab that identifies the object and which enables you to make the open object active.

Object window An area of the Access window that displays open objects, such as tables, queries, forms, or reports; by default, each object displays on its own tab.

Objects (Access) The basic parts of a database that you create to store your data and to work with your data; for example, tables, queries, forms, and reports.

Office 365 Administrator In Office 365, the person who creates and manages the account, adds new users, sets up the services your organization wants to use, sets permission levels, and manages the SharePoint team sites.

Office Online (formerly Web Apps) The free online companions to Microsoft Word, Excel, PowerPoint, Access, and OneNote.

Office Presentation Service A Word feature to present your Word document to others who can watch in a web browser.

On Click An animation option that begins the animation sequence for the selected slide element when the mouse button is clicked or the Spacebar is pressed.

One-click Row/Column Insertion A Word table feature with which you can insert a new row or column by pointing to the desired location and then clicking.

One-to-many relationship A relationship between two tables where one record in the first table corresponds to many records in the second table—the most common type of relationship in Access.

OneDrive (formerly SkyDrive) A free file storage and file sharing service provided by Microsoft when you sign up for a Microsoft account.

Open dialog box A dialog box from which you can navigate to, and then open on your screen, an existing file that was created in that same program.

Operating system A specific type of computer program that manages the other programs on a computer—including computer devices such as desktop computers, laptop computers, smartphones, tablet computers, and game consoles.

Operators The symbols with which you can specify the type of calculation you want to perform in an Excel formula.

Option button In a dialog box, a round button that enables you to make one choice among two or more options.

Options dialog box A dialog box within each Office application where you can select program settings and other options and preferences.

OR condition A compound criteria used to display records that match at least one of the specified criteria.

Order of operations The mathematical rules for performing multiple calculations within a formula.

Outermost sort field When sorting on multiple fields in Datasheet view, the field that will be used for the first level of sorting.

Outline View A PowerPoint view that displays the presentation outline to the left of the Slide pane.

Page break indicator A dotted line with the text *Page Break* that indicates where a manual page break was inserted.

Page Footer Information printed at the bottom of every page in a report; most often includes the page number.

Page Header Information printed at the top of every page in a report.

Page Layout view A screen view in which you can use the rulers to measure the width and height of data, set margins for printing, hide or display the numbered row headings and the lettered column headings, and change the page orientation; this view is useful for preparing your worksheet for printing.

Page number control A control on a form or report that inserts the page numbers when displayed in Print Preview or when printed.

Paint A program that comes with Windows 8 with which you can create and edit drawings and display and edit stored photos.

Pane (Excel) A portion of a worksheet window bounded by and separated from other portions by vertical and horizontal bars.

Pane A separate area of a window.

Paragraph symbol The symbol ¶ that represents the end of a paragraph.

Parameter A value that can be changed.

Parameter query A query that prompts you for criteria before running the query.

Parent folder In the file organizing structure of File Explorer, the location where the folder you are viewing is saved—one level up in the hierarchy.

Parenthetical references References that include the last name of the author or authors, and the page number in the referenced source.

Paste area The target destination for data that has been cut or copied using the Office Clipboard.

Paste Options gallery A gallery of buttons that provides a Live Preview of all the Paste options available in the current context.

Paste The action of placing cell contents that have been copied or moved to the Clipboard into another location.

Path A sequence of folders (directories) that leads to a specific file or folder.

PC settings The area from which you can control almost everything about how Windows 8 looks and works; you can change colors and backgrounds, the picture on your Lock screen, or your account picture, manage other users (if you are the administrator), connect devices like printers, or set up a network.

PDF The acronym for Portable Document Format, which is a file format that creates an image that preserves the look of your file; this is a popular format for sending documents electronically because the document will display on most computers.

PDF Reflow The ability to import PDF files into Word so that you can transform a PDF back into a fully editable Word document.

Percent for new value = base percent + percent of increase The formula for calculating a percentage by which a value increases by adding the base percentage—usually 100%—to the percent increase.

Percentage rate of increase The percent by which one number increases over another number.

Personal folder A folder created for each user account on a Windows 8 computer, labeled with the account holder's name, and which contains the subfolders *Documents, Pictures, Music,* and *Videos.*

Picture element A point of light measured in dots per square inch on a screen; 64 pixels equals 8.43 characters, which is the average number of characters that will fit in a cell in an Excel worksheet using the default font.

Picture styles Frames, shapes, shadows, borders, and other special effects that can be added to an image to create an overall visual style for the image.

Pie chart A chart that shows the relationship of each part to a whole.

PING An acronym for Portable Network Graphic, and which is a common file type that can be transferred over the Internet. A PING file has a .png file extension.

Pixel The abbreviated name for a picture element.

Placeholder A box on a slide with dotted or dashed borders that holds title and body text or other content such as charts, tables, and pictures.

Placeholder text The text in a content control that indicates the type of information to be entered in a specific location.

Plot area The area bounded by the axes of a chart, including all the data series.

Point The action of moving your mouse pointer over something on your screen.

Point and click method The technique of constructing a formula by pointing to and then clicking cells; this method is convenient when the referenced cells are not adjacent to one another.

Point to The action of moving the mouse pointer over a specific area.

Pointer Any symbol that displays on your screen in response to moving your mouse and with which you can select objects and commands.

Pointing device A mouse, touchpad, or other device that controls the pointer position on the screen.

Points A measurement of the size of a font; there are 72 points in an inch.

Populate The action of filling a database table with records.

Portable Document Format A file format that creates an image that preserves the look of your file, but that cannot be easily changed; a popular format for sending documents electronically, because the document will display on most computers.

Portrait orientation A page orientation in which the paper is taller than it is wide.

Primary key The field in a table that uniquely identifies a record; for example, a Student ID number at a college.

Print Preview A view of a document as it will appear when you print it.

Print Titles An Excel command that enables you to specify rows and columns to repeat on each printed page.

Program A set of instructions that a computer uses to accomplish a task; also called an application.

Progress bar In a dialog box or taskbar button, a bar that indicates visually the progress of a task such as a download or file transfer.

Property Sheet A list of characteristics—properties—for fields or controls on a form or report in which you can make precise changes to each property associated with the field or control.

Protected View A security feature in Office 2013 that protects your computer from malicious files by opening them in a restricted environment until you enable them; you might encounter this feature if you open a file from an email or download files from the Internet.

pt The abbreviation for *point*; for example, when referring to a font size.

Query A database object that retrieves specific data from one or more database objects—either tables or other queries—and then, in a single datasheet, displays only the data you specify.

Quick Access Toolbar In an Office program window, the small row of buttons in the upper left corner of the screen from which you can perform frequently used commands.

Quick Analysis Tool A tool that displays in the lower right corner of a selected range with which you can analyze your data by using Excel tools such as charts, color-coding, and formulas.

Range Two or more selected cells on a worksheet that are adjacent or nonadjacent; because the range is treated as a single unit, you can make the same changes or combination of changes to more than one cell at a time.

Range finder An Excel feature that outlines cells in color to indicate which cells are used in a formula; useful for verifying which cells are referenced in a formula.

Rate = amount of increase/base The mathematical formula to calculate a rate of increase.

Read Mode A view in Word that optimizes the Word screen for the times when you are reading Word documents on the screen and not creating or editing them.

Read-Only A property assigned to a file that prevents the file from being modified or deleted; it indicates that you cannot save any changes to the displayed document unless you first save it with a new name.

Reading view A view in PowerPoint that displays a presentation in a manner similar to a slide show but in which the taskbar, title bar, and status bar remain available in the presentation window.

Recolor A feature that enables you to change all colors in the picture to shades of a single color.

Recommended Charts An Excel feature that displays a customized set of charts that, according to Excel's calculations, will best fit your data based on the range of data that you select.

Record All of the categories of data pertaining to one person, place, event, thing, or idea; represented by a row in a database table.

Record selector bar The vertical bar at the left edge of a record when it is displayed in a form that is used to select an entire record.

Record selector box The small box at the left of a record in Datasheet view that, when clicked, selects the entire record.

Record source The tables or queries that provide the underlying data for a form or report.

Rectangular snip When using Snipping Tool, the type of snip that lets you draw a precise box by dragging the mouse pointer around an area of the screen to form a rectangle.

Recycle Bin A folder that stores anything that you delete from your computer, and from which anything stored can be retrieved until the contents are permanently deleted by activating the Empty Recycle Bin command.

Redundant In a database, information that is duplicated in a manner that indicates poor database design.

Referential integrity A set of rules that Access uses to ensure that the data between related tables is valid.

Relational database A sophisticated type of database that has multiple collections of data within the file that are related to one another.

Relationship An association that you establish between two tables based on common fields.

Relative cell reference In a formula, the address of a cell based on the relative positions of the cell that contains the formula and the cell referred to in the formula.

Removable storage device A portable device on which you can store files, such as a USB flash drive, a flash memory card, or an external hard drive, commonly used to transfer information from one computer to another.

Report A database object that summarizes the fields and records from a query or table in an easy-to-read format suitable for printing.

Report Footer Information printed at the bottom of the last page of a report.

Report Header Information printed on the first page of a report; used for logos, titles, and dates.

Report tool An Access tool that creates a report with one mouse click and displays all of the fields and records from the record source that you select.

Report Wizard An Access tool that walks you step by step through the creation of a report and that gives you more flexibility in the design, layout, and number of fields in a report.

Resources A term used to refer collectively to the parts of your computer such as the central processing unit (CPU), memory, and any attached devices such as a printer.

RGB A color model in which the colors red, green, and blue are added together to form another color.

Ribbon The area at the top of a folder window in File Explorer that groups common tasks such as copying and moving, creating new folders, emailing and zipping items, and changing views on related tabs.

Rich media Computer interaction that responds to your actions; for example by presenting text, graphics, animation, video, audio, or games. Also referred to as interactive media.

Rich Text Format (RTF) A standard file format that contains text and some formatting such as underline, bold, italic, font sizes, and colors; RTF documents can be opened in many word processing programs and text editors.

Right alignment An arrangement of text in which the text aligns at the right margin, leaving the left margin uneven.

Right-click The action of clicking the right mouse button one time.

Roam The ability to set up one computer, for example a desktop computer, and then synchronize—roam—all the same settings to a laptop, to a tablet PC, to a Windows phone, or to any other device to which one signs in with the same Microsoft account.

Rotation handle A symbol with which you can rotate a graphic to any angle; displays above the top center sizing handle.

Rounding A procedure in which you determine which digit at the right of the number will be the last digit displayed and then increase it by one if the next digit to its right is 5, 6, 7, 8, or 9.

Row A horizontal group of cells in a worksheet.

Row heading The numbers along the left side of an Excel worksheet that designate the row numbers.

Ruler guides Dotted red vertical and horizontal lines that display in the rulers indicating the pointer's position.

Run The process in which Access looks at the records in the table(s) included in the query design, finds the records that match the specified criteria, and then displays the records in a datasheet; only the fields included in the query design display.

Salutation The greeting line of a business letter.

Sans serif font A font design with no lines or extensions on the ends of characters.

Scale A command that resizes a picture to a percentage of its size.

Scale to Fit Excel commands that enable you to stretch or shrink the width, height, or both, of printed output to fit a maximum number of pages.

Scaling The process of shrinking the width and/or height of printed output to fit a maximum number of pages.

Screen capture An image file that contains the contents of a computer screen.

Screenshot An image of an active window on your computer that you can paste into a document.

ScreenTip A small box that that displays useful information when you perform various mouse actions such as pointing to screen elements or dragging.

Scroll arrow An arrow at the top and bottom, or left and right, of a scroll bar that when clicked, moves the window in small increments.

Scroll bar A bar that displays on the bottom or right side of a window when the contents of a window are not completely visible; used to move the window up, down, left, or right to bring the contents into view.

Scroll box The box in the vertical and horizontal scroll bars that can be dragged to reposition the contents of a window or pane on the screen.

Second principle of good database design A principle stating that appropriate database techniques are used to ensure the accuracy and consistency of data as it is entered into the table.

Section A portion of a document that can be formatted differently from the rest of the document.

Section bar In Design view, a gray bar in a form or report that identifies and separates one section from another; used to select the section and to change the size of the section.

Section break A double dotted line that indicates the end of one section and the beginning of another section.

Section header A type of slide layout that changes the look and flow of a presentation by providing text placeholders that do not contain bullet points.

Secure environment A system that uses controlled servers to ensure the security and privacy of email, to control the storage and use of information and to protect against the loss of confidential data.

Select To specify, by highlighting, a block of data or text on the screen with the intent of performing some action on the selection.

Select All box A box in the upper left corner of the worksheet grid that, when clicked, selects all the cells in a worksheet.

Select query A type of Access query that retrieves (selects) data from one or more tables or queries, displaying the selected data in a datasheet; also known as a simple select query.

Selecting Highlighting, by dragging with your mouse, areas of text or data or graphics, so that the selection can be edited, formatted, copied, or moved.

Series A group of things that come one after another in succession; for example, January, February, March, and so on.

Serif font A font design that includes small line extensions on the ends of the letters to guide the eye in reading from left to right.

Server A computer that provides services on a network such as an email server or a file server.

Shape A slide object such as a line, arrow, box, callout, or banner.

Shapes Lines, arrows, stars, banners, ovals, rectangles, and other basic shapes with which you can illustrate an idea, a process, or a workflow.

SharePoint Collaboration software with which people in an organization can set up team sites to share information, manage documents, and publish reports for others to see.

Sheet tab scrolling buttons Buttons to the left of the sheet tabs used to display Excel sheet tabs that are not in view; used when there are more sheet tabs than will display in the space provided.

Sheet tabs The labels along the lower border of the Excel window that identify each worksheet.

Short Text data type An Access data type that describes text, a combination of text and numbers, or numbers that are not used in calculations, such as a Postal Code.

Shortcut menu A menu that displays commands and options relevant to the selected text or object; also called a *context menu*.

Show Formulas A command that displays the formula in each cell instead of the resulting value.

Shut down Turning off your computer in a manner that closes all open programs and files, closes your network connections, stops the hard disk, and discontinues the use of electrical power.

Simple select query Another name for a select query.

Single spacing The common name for line spacing in which there is *no* extra space before or after a paragraph and that uses line spacing of 1.

Single-record form A form that enables you to display or enter one record at a time in a table.

Sizing handles Small squares surrounding a picture that indicate that the picture is selected.

Sizing handles Small squares that indicate a picture or object is selected.

SkyDrive see OneDrive

Skype A Microsoft product with which you can make voice calls, make video calls, transfer files, or send messages—including instant message and text messages—over the Internet.

Sleep Turning off your computer in a manner that automatically saves your work, stops the fan, and uses a small amount of electrical power to maintain your work in memory.

Slide A presentation page that can contain text, pictures, tables, charts, and other multimedia or graphic objects.

Slide handout Printed images of slides on a sheet of paper.

Slide pane A PowerPoint screen element that displays a large image of the active slide.

Slide Sorter view A presentation view that displays thumbnails of all of the slides in a presentation.

Slide transitions Motion effects that occur in Slide Show view when you move from one slide to the next during a presentation.

Small caps A font effect that changes lowercase letters to uppercase letters, but with the height of lowercase letters.

Smart guides Dashed lines that display on your slide when you are moving an object to assist you with alignment.

SmartArt A designer-quality visual representation of your information that you can create by choosing from among many different layouts to effectively communicate your message or ideas.

SmartArt graphic A visual representation of information that you create by choosing from among various layouts to communicate your message or ideas effectively.

SmartArt Styles Combinations of formatting effects that you can apply to SmartArt graphics.

Snap (desktop apps): A Windows 8 desktop feature that automatically resizes windows when you move—*snap*—them to the edge of the screen.

Snip The image captured using Snipping Tool.

Snipping Tool A program included with Windows 8 with which you can capture an image of all or part of a computer screen, and then annotate, save, copy, or share the image via email.

Sort The process of arranging data in a specific order based on the value in each field.

Sorting The process of arranging data in a specific order based on the value in a field.

Source file When importing a file, refers to the file being imported.

Sparkline A tiny chart in the background of a cell that gives a visual trend summary alongside your data; makes a pattern more obvious.

Speakers icon Displays the status of the computer's speakers (if any).

Spin box A small box with an upward- and downward-pointing arrow that lets you move rapidly through a set of values by clicking.

Split Splits the window into multiple resizable panes that contain views of your worksheet. This is useful to view multiple distant parts of your worksheet at one time.

Split button A button divided into two parts and in which clicking the main part of the button performs a command and clicking the arrow opens a menu with choices.

Spreadsheet Another name for a worksheet.

Stacked layout A control layout format that is similar to a paper form, with label controls placed to the left of each text box control; the controls are grouped together for easy editing.

Start screen The first screen that displays after signing in to a Windows 8 device, which displays square and rectangular boxes—referred to as tiles—from which one can access apps, websites, programs, and tools for using the computer by clicking or tapping them.

Start search The search feature in Windows 8 in which, from the Start screen, you can begin to type and by default, Windows 8 searches for apps; you can adjust the search to search for files or settings.

Start tip The thumbnail that displays when you point to the lower left corner of your screen.

Statistical functions Excel functions, including the AVERAGE, MEDIAN, MIN, and MAX functions, which are useful to analyze a group of measurements.

Status bar The area along the lower edge of the Excel window that displays, on the left side, the current cell mode, page number, and worksheet information; on the right side, when numerical data is selected, common calculations such as Sum and Average display.

Structure In Access, the underlying design of a table, including field names, data types, descriptions, and field properties.

Style (PowerPoint) A collection of formatting options that you can apply to a picture, text, or an object.

Style (Word) A group of formatting commands, such as font, font size, font color, paragraph alignment, and line spacing that can be applied to a paragraph with one command.

Style guide A manual that contains standards for the design and writing of documents.

Subdatasheet A format for displaying related records when you click the plus sign (+) next to a record in a table on the *one* side of the relationship.

Subfolder A folder within a folder.

Subject line The optional line following the inside address in a business letter that states the purpose of the letter.

Subset A portion of the total records available.

SUM function A predefined formula that adds all the numbers in a selected range of cells.

Summary sheet A worksheet where totals from other worksheets are displayed and summarized.

Suppress A Word feature that hides header and footer information, including the page number, on the first page of a document.

Switch Row/Column A charting command to swap the data over the axis—data being charted on the vertical axis will move to the horizontal axis and vice versa

Switcher Another name for *app switcher*.

Synchronization The process of updating computer files that are in two or more locations according to specific rules—also called *syncing*.

Syncing The process of updating computer files that are in two or more locations according to specific rules—also called *synchronization*.

Synonyms Words with the same or similar meaning.

System tray Another name for the notification area on the taskbar.

Tab order The order in which the insertion point moves from one field to another in a form when you press the Tab key.

Tab stop A specific location on a line of text, marked on the Word ruler, to which you can move the insertion point by pressing the Tab key, and which is used to align and indent text.

Table A format for information that organizes and presents text and data in columns and rows.

Table area The upper area of the query window that displays field lists for the tables that are used in a query.

Table style A format applied to a table that is consistent with the presentation theme.

Tables and Related Views An arrangement in the Navigation Pane that groups objects by the table to which they are related.

Tabs (ribbon) On the Office ribbon, the name of each activity area.

Tags Custom file properties in the form of words that you associate with a document to give an indication of the document's content; used to help find and organize files. Also called *keywords*.

Taskbar The area of the desktop that contains program buttons, and buttons for all open programs; by default, it is located at the bottom of the desktop, but you can move it.

Team A group of workers tasked with working together to solve a problem, make a decision, or create a work product.

Template An existing document that you use as a starting point for a new document; it opens a copy of itself, unnamed, and then you use the structure—and possibly some content, such as headings—as the starting point for new a document.

Text alignment The horizontal placement of text within a placeholder.

Text box An object with which you can position text anywhere on a slide.

Text box control A bound control on a form or report that displays the data from the underlying table or query.

Text control A content control that accepts only a text entry.

Text effects Decorative formats, such as shadowed or mirrored text, text glow, 3-D effects, and colors that make text stand out.

Text string A sequence of characters.

Text values Constant values consisting of only text, and which usually provides information about number values; also referred to as labels.

Text wrapping The manner in which text displays around an object.

Theme A predesigned set of colors, fonts, lines, and fill effects that look good together and that can be applied to all of the objects in the database or to individual objects in the database.

Theme colors A set of coordinating colors that are applied to the backgrounds, objects, and text in a presentation.

Theme fonts The fonts to apply to two types of slide text—headings and body.

Thesaurus A research tool that provides a list of synonyms.

Thumbnail A reduced image of a graphic.

Tiles Square and rectangular boxes on the Windows 8 Start screen from which one can access apps, websites, programs, and tools for using the computer by simply clicking or tapping them.

Timing options Animation options that control when animated items display in the animation sequence.

Title bar The bar at the top edge of the program window that indicates the name of the current file and the program name.

Title slide A slide layout—most commonly the first slide in a presentation—that provides an introduction to the presentation topic.

Toggle button A button that can be turned on by clicking it once, and then turned off by clicking it again.

Toolbar In a folder window, a row of buttons with which you can perform common tasks, such as changing the view of your files and folders or burning files to a CD.

Trim A command that deletes parts of a video to make it shorter.

Triple-click The action of clicking the left mouse button three times in rapid succession.

Truncated Refers to data that is cut off or shortened because the field or column is not wide enough to display all of the data or the field size is too small to contain all of the data.

Trust Center An area of Access where you can view the security and privacy settings for your Access installation.

Trusted Documents A security feature in Office that remembers which files you have already enabled; you might encounter this feature if you open a file from an email or download files from the Internet.

Unbound control A control that does not have a source of data, such as the title in a form or report.

Underlying formula The formula entered in a cell and visible only on the Formula Bar.

Underlying value The data that displays in the Formula Bar.

Uniform Resource Locator An address that uniquely identifies a location on the Internet.

URL The acronym for Uniform Resource Locator, which is an address that uniquely identifies a location on the Internet.

USB flash drive A small data storage device that plugs into a computer USB port.

User account A collection of information that tells Windows 8 what files and folders the account holder can access, what changes the account holder can make to the computer system, and what the account holder's personal preferences are.

Value Another name for a constant value.

Value after increase = base x percent for new value The formula for calculating the value after an increase by multiplying the original value—the base—by the percent for new value (see the *Percent for new value* formula).

Value axis A numerical scale on the left side of a chart that shows the range of numbers for the data points; also referred to as the Y-axis.

Variant A variation on the presentation theme style and color.

Volatile A term used to describe an Excel function that is subject to change each time the workbook is reopened; for example the NOW function updates itself to the current date and time each time the workbook is opened.

Wallpaper Another term for the desktop background.

Web browser Software with which you display webpages and navigate the Internet.

What-if analysis The process of changing the values in cells to see how those changes affect the outcome of formulas in a worksheet.

Wildcard character In a query, a character that serves as a placeholder for one or more unknown characters in criteria; an asterisk (*) represents one or more unknown characters, and a question mark (?) represents a single unknown character.

Window A rectangular area on a computer screen in which programs and content appear, and which can be moved, resized, minimized, or closed.

Window snip When using Snipping Tool, the type of snip that captures the entire displayed window.

Windows 8 An operating system developed by Microsoft Corporation designed to work with mobile computing devices of all types and also with traditional PCs.

Windows Reader app A Windows Store app with which you can open a PDF or XPS file, zoom, find words or phrases, take notes, save changes, and then print or share the file.

Windows Store apps Apps built for specific purposes; for example, to view photos, read sports information, organize a list of contacts, or read updates to social networks like Facebook and Twitter.

With Previous An animation option that begins the animation sequence at the same time as the previous animation or slide transition

Wizard A feature in Microsoft Office that walks you step by step through a process.

WordArt A gallery of text styles with which you can create decorative effects, such as shadowed or mirrored text

Wordwrap The feature that moves text from the right edge of a paragraph to the beginning of the next line as necessary to fit within the margins.

Workbook An Excel file that contains one or more worksheets.

Workbook-level buttons Buttons at the far right of the Ribbon tabs that minimize or restore a displayed workbook.

Works Cited In the MLA style, a list of cited works placed at the end of a research paper or report.

Worksheet The primary document that you use in Excel to work with and store data, and which is formatted as a pattern of uniformly spaced horizontal and vertical lines.

Worksheet grid area A part of the Excel window that displays the columns and rows that intersect to form the worksheet's cells.

Writer's identification The name and title of the author of a letter, placed near the bottom of the letter under the complimentary closing—also referred to as the *writer's signature block*.

Writer's signature block The name and title of the author of a letter, placed near the bottom of the letter, under the complimentary closing—also referred to as the *writer's identification*.

X-axis Another name for the horizontal (category) axis.

XML Paper Specification A Microsoft file format that creates an image of your document and that opens in the XPS viewer.

XPS The acronym for XML Paper Specification—a Microsoft file format that creates an image of your document and that opens in the XPS viewer.

Y-axis Another name for the vertical (value) axis.

Zipped folder A folder that has been reduced in size and thus takes up less storage space and can be transferred to other computers quickly; also called a *compressed* folder.

Zoom The action of increasing or decreasing the size of the viewing area on the screen.

Index

H

I

J

K

L

Q

R

S

X

Y

Z